MANAGEMENT
Leading & Collaborating in a Competitive World

14e

Thomas S. Bateman
McIntire School of Commerce
University of Virginia

Robert Konopaske
McCoy College of Business
Texas State University

Mc
Graw
Hill

MANAGEMENT

Published by McGraw-Hill Education, 2 Penn Plaza, New York, NY 10121. Copyright © 2021 by McGraw-Hill
Education. All rights reserved. Printed in the United States of America. No part of this publication may be
reproduced or distributed in any form or by any means, or stored in a database or retrieval system, without the
prior written consent of McGraw-Hill Education, including, but not limited to, in any network or other electronic
storage or transmission, or broadcast for distance learning.

Some ancillaries, including electronic and print components, may not be available to customers outside the
United States.

This book is printed on acid-free paper.

1 2 3 4 5 6 7 8 9 LWI 24 23 22 21 20

ISBN 978-1-260-57097-7
MHID 1-260-57097-5

Cover Image: ©*Wang An Qi/Shutterstock*

All credits appearing on page or at the end of the book are considered to be an extension of the copyright page.

The Internet addresses listed in the text were accurate at the time of publication. The inclusion of a website does
not indicate an endorsement by the authors or McGraw-Hill Education, and McGraw-Hill Education does not
guarantee the accuracy of the information presented at these sites.

For my parents, Tom and Jeanine Bateman,
and Mary Jo, Lauren, T.J., and James

and

My parents, Art and Rose Konopaske,
and Vania, Nick, and Isabella

About the Authors

THOMAS S. BATEMAN

Thomas S. Bateman is professor emeritus (now living in Chicago) with the McIntire School of Commerce at the University of Virginia. For many years prior to his two decades at UVA teaching leadership and organizational behavior to students of every level, he taught at the University of North Carolina–Chapel Hill, the Institute for Management Development (IMD) in Lausanne, Switzerland,

Dan Addison/UVA University Communications

and Texas A&M University. Professor Bateman earned his doctorate in business administration at Indiana University, and his BA from Miami University.

Tom is an active management researcher, writer, and consultant. His editorial board memberships have included the *Academy of Management Review,* the *Academy of Management Journal,* and *Journal of Management.* His articles appear in journals such as the *Academy of Management Journal, Academy of Management Review, Journal of Applied Psychology, Organizational Behavior and Human Decision Processes, Journal of Organizational Behavior, Human Relations, Journal of Macromarketing,* and *Proceedings of the National Academy of Sciences.*

Tom's career-long research interests center on proactive behavior (including leadership) by employees at all levels, with a recent turn toward proaction targeting climate change and sustainability. Proaction—long-term-oriented behaviors intended to change current trajectories, avoid future problems, and create better futures—is a significant emphasis in this textbook.

Tom blogs for *Psychology Today,* and his recent work on psychological aspects of climate action appears in *Nature Climate Change, Global Environmental Change, GreenBiz,* and *The Conversation.* Tom's consulting work has included a variety of organizations, including Akima, Singapore Airlines, the Brookings Institution, Nokia, the U.S. Chamber of Commerce, the Nature Conservancy, LexisNexis, Weber Shandwick, the Association of Climate Change Officers, and Chicago's Field Museum of Natural History.

ROBERT KONOPASKE

Rob Konopaske is an associate professor of management and principles of management core course coordinator in the McCoy College of Business at Texas State University. At the College, he also serves as the director of the Institute for Global Business. A passionate educator who cares deeply about providing students with an exceptional learning experience, Rob has taught numerous undergraduate, graduate, and executive management courses, including Introduction to Management, Organizational Behavior, Human Resource Management, International Human Resources Management, and International Business. He has received numerous teaching honors while at Texas State University, most recently the 2016 Presidential Distinction Award, 2014 Gregg Master Teacher Award, and 2012–2013 Namesake for the PAWS Preview new student socialization program (an honor bestowed annually upon 8 out of approximately 2,000 faculty and staff). Rob earned his doctoral degree in business administration (management) at the University of Houston, a master's in international business studies (MIBS) degree from the University of South Carolina, and a bachelor of arts degree (Phi Beta Kappa) from Rutgers University. He has taught at the University of Houston, the University of North Carolina at Wilmington, and Florida Atlantic University.

Rob is co-author of several editions of popular textbooks: *Management: Leading & Collaborating in a Competitive World, M: Management, Organizational Behavior and Management, Human Resource Management,* and *Organizations: Behavior, Structure, Processes.* The eleventh edition of *Organizations* won a McGuffey Award (for longevity of textbooks and learning materials whose excellence has been demonstrated over time) from the national Text and Academic Authors' Association.

Rob's research has been published in such outlets as the *Journal of Applied Psychology, Academy of Management Executive, Management International Review, Business Horizons, Human Resource Management, Journal of Business*

Research, Journal of Management Education, Nonprofit Management and Leadership, Journal of Managerial Psychology, and *Human Resource Management Review.* Rob currently serves on the editorial board of the *International Journal of Human Resource Management.*

Rob has lived and worked internationally, speaks three languages, and has held management positions with a large nonprofit organization and a *Fortune* 500 multinational firm. He consults, trains, and conducts research projects for a wide range of companies and industries. Current or former clients include Credit Suisse, PricewaterhouseCoopers, Occidental Oil, and Johnson & Johnson.

Preface

Welcome to our 14th edition! Thanks to all for your recent and long-term support, plus our many new adopters. We are proud and exceptionally enthusiastic to offer you our collective best–ever learning experience.

Our Goals

Our threefold mission with this text is to inform, instruct, and inspire. We hope to *inform* readers by describing the important concepts, practices, and exemplars of modern management. We hope to *instruct* by helping readers identify their options, make good decisions, and take effective action. We hope to *inspire* not only by writing in an interesting way, but also by providing a real sense of the challenges and fascinating opportunities that lie ahead.

Inspiring is a word not often used to describe textbooks. But it's a long-standing goal for us. Whether your personal goals include teaching or learning or both, starting your own company, leading a team to greatness, building a strong organization, delighting your customers, or generally forging a positive and sustainable future, we want to inspire you to take meaningful action in pursuit of productive and fulfilling futures.

We hope to inspire you to be both a thinker and a doer. We want you to know the important issues, consider the consequences of your actions, and think before you act. But good thinking is not enough; management is a world of adaptive action.

Competitive Advantage

Students and future leaders need to understand certain realities. The world of management is competitive. It also is rich with important collaborative opportunities that can strengthen the performance of individuals, teams, and organizations.

Furthermore, managers have never faced so many tough challenges with so many potential risks and rewards. Never before has it been so imperative to your career that you learn the skills of management

You will compete with other people for jobs, resources, and promotions. Your employer will compete with others for contracts, clients, and customers. To survive the competition, and to thrive, you must perform in ways that give you an edge that makes others want to hire you, buy from you, and do repeat business with you. Now and over time, you will want them to choose you, not the competition.

By this standard, managers and organizations must *perform*. In this book we emphasize essential performance dimensions: *cost, quality, speed, innovation, service,* and *sustainability.* When managed well, these performance dimensions offer value to customers and competitive advantage to you and your organization.

Lacking performance on one or more of them puts you at a disadvantage. We elaborate on them all, throughout the book.

More than other management textbooks, we try to keep you focused on delivering important "bottom line" results. We want you to think continually about providing the goods (products and services) that make both you and your organization successful.

Good management processes and practices are the keys to producing what you and your employer want. This results-oriented focus is a unique highlight you will take away from this book.

Leading & Collaborating

Yes, business is competitive. But it's not that simple. In fact, to think strictly in terms of competition is overly cynical and often self-limiting, sometimes sabotaging performance.

Along with a realistic perspective on competitive realities, important action elements in managerial success are *collaboration* and *leadership*. To succeed, teams and organizations need people to work *with* rather than against one another. Put another way, you can't perform alone—the world is too complex, and business is too challenging.

You need to work with your teammates. Leaders and followers need to work as collaborators more than as adversaries. Work groups throughout your organization need to cooperate with one another. Business and government, often viewed as antagonists, can work productively together. And intense competitors sometimes collaborate on some things—for example, joint ventures—even as they compete in others.

How does an organization create competitive advantage through collaboration? It's all about the people, and it derives from good leadership.

Three stereotypes about leadership are that it comes from the top of the company, that it comes from one's immediate boss, and that it means being decisive and issuing commands. These stereotypes contain some truth, but realities are much more complex and challenging.

First, the person at the top may or may not provide effective leadership—in fact, truly good leadership is far too rare. Second, organizations need leaders at all levels, in every team and work unit. This includes you, beginning early in your career, and this is why leadership is a vital theme in this book. Third, leaders should be capable of being decisive and giving commands, but relying too much on this traditional approach isn't enough. Great leadership is far more inspirational than that, and helps people to both think differently and to work differently—including working collaboratively toward outstanding results.

True leadership—from your boss as well as from you—inspires collaboration, which in turn generates results that are good for you, your employer, and your customers.

As Always, Currency and Variety in the 14th Edition

It goes without saying that this textbook, in its 14th edition, remains on the cutting edge of topical coverage, updated throughout with both current business examples and recent management research. We continue to emphasize real results, diversity and inclusiveness, and sustainability—themes on which we were early and remain current leaders.

While still organizing the chapters around the classic management functions, we modernize those functions with a far more dynamic orientation. Looking constantly at change and the future, we describe the management functions as Delivering Strategic Value (for Planning), Building a Dynamic Organization (for Organizing), Mobilizing People (for Leading), and last but hardly least, Learning and Changing (for Controlling).

Special Features

We believe that the 14th edition provides our strongest-ever boxed features, representing three recurring themes. In addition to a concluding case, every chapter has a three-part unfolding story, plus stand-alone inserts offering contemporary management takes on social entrepreneurship, inclusiveness practices, and the digital world.

1. Management in Action, a hallmark feature, presents unfolding current three-part stories about today's business leaders and companies. The first part, "Manager's Brief," encourages students at the start of each chapter to begin thinking about one or more chapter themes in the context of the current business scene. For example, Chapter 1 introduces Facebook's Mark Zuckerberg and some of the challenges he and his company face. The second Management in Action element, "Progress Report," appears about halfway through each chapter and adds more chapter themes to the narrative. At each stage, we offer questions for class discussion, group work, or simply reflection. Closing out each unfolding story is "Onward," at the end of each chapter. This element also includes questions for further consideration and perhaps additional research.

2. Social Entrepreneurship boxes offer examples illustrating chapter themes from outside the private sector. Many students are deeply interested in social entrepreneurs and enterprises, inherently and for future employment possibilities. Examples include: Ashoka's Bill Drayton, "The Pioneer of Social Entrepreneurship" (Chapter 1); "Is Social Enterprise Becoming Big Business?" (Chapter 10); and "Providing Clean Water via 'Water ATMs'" (Chapter 17).

3. Inclusiveness Works are new boxes that discuss chapter themes from diverse and inclusive perspectives, based on data not stereotypes, with a goal of strengthening what too often are difficult workplace relationships. Examples include: "Women in Leadership Roles: A Strategy for Success" (Chapter 2); and "Reaping the Benefits through Empathy and Consideration" (Chapter 3).

4. The Digital World feature offers custom examples of how companies and other users employ digital/social media in ways that supplement and complement ideas in each chapter. Students of course will relate to the social media, but also learn of interesting examples and practices that most did not know before. Instructors will learn a lot as well!

That's the big picture. We believe the management stories in the boxed features light up the discussion and connect the major themes of the new edition with the many real worlds students will enter soon.

Up next is just a sampling of specific changes, updates, and new highlights in the 14th edition—enough to convey the wide variety of people, organizations, issues, and management challenges represented throughout the text.

Chapter 1

- New Inclusiveness Works feature about generational differences in the workplace.

- Updated Management in Action about Mark Zuckerberg of Facebook.

- New Digital World: "Chatbots: Good for Business?"

- Revised Social Entrepreneurship discussing Bill Drayton of Ashoka.

- New example of Uber's new CEO trying to make the company profitable again.

- Updated list of top five firms in *Fortune*'s 2018 Global 500 list.

- New example of PepsiCo offering KeVita probiotic non-soda and Bubly Sparkling Water.

- New example of Rocket Mortgage propelling Quicken Loans to the top of the mortgage provider market.

- New example in which Patagonia's Work Wear program makes over 50,000 repairs to customers' used clothing.

- New example of using Gallup's CliftonStrengths assessment to identify core strengths.

Chapter 2

- New Inclusiveness Works feature: "Women in Leadership Roles: A Strategy for Success."
- Updated Management in Action on Amazon thriving in any environment.
- Updated Social Entrepreneurship feature about combating climate change.
- New example of the U.S. congressional bill that could replace the Patient Protection and Affordable Care Act.
- New example in which zSpace's VR laptop allows users to see objects as if they were part of the real world.
- New example about Microsoft offering 12 weeks of full pay for employees who are new mothers and fathers.
- New example of Coca-Cola pledging to reduce the amount of sugar in its drinks by 2025.
- New example about the Eagle Flight game being a complement of the HTC Vive virtual reality headset.
- New example about Warby Parker, the fashion eyeglasses retailer, where employees learn the culture by keeping in mind four ground rules (which the company characterizes as "Nothing crazy").

Chapter 3

- New Inclusiveness Works feature about the benefits of a diverse workplace.
- Updated Management in Action about Uber trying to overcome its poor decisions.
- New Digital World about using predictive analytics to make better decisions.
- Revised Concluding Case: "Soaring Eagle Skate Company."
- New example exploring the uncertainty over Britain's departure from the European Union ("Brexit").
- New example of Netflix using data analytics to retain customers and inform the creation of original series.
- New examples of data breaches at companies, including Marriott Starwood Hotels, MyFitnessPal, Cambridge Analytica, and Facebook.

Chapter 4

- New Inclusiveness Works feature about incorporating diversity and inclusion into a company's brand.
- Revised Management in Action: "How Disney Scripts Its Own Success."
- Updated Social Entrepreneurship feature discussing Novo Nordisk's triple bottom line.
- New Digital World: "Managing Technology's Impact."
- New example of General Motors purchasing a $500 billion stake in Lyft.

- New example of Chipotle's zero-tolerance policy for food safety violations.
- New example of Salesforce's 1-1-1 philanthropic model of doing business.
- New example of AT&T's acquisition of AlienVault to help businesses respond to cybersecurity attacks.

Chapter 5

- New Inclusiveness Works feature discussing equitable pay for all employees.
- Revised Management in Action feature about Ginni Rometty's attempts to transform IBM and the world.
- New Digital World: "How Digital Monitoring Helps Ensure Ethics."
- Updated Concluding Case: "Oré Earth Skin Care Tries to Stay Natural."
- New example of Apple slowing down older iPhones to encourage upgrades.
- New example of Facebook employees writing 5-star reviews for the Portal video-chat device on Amazon.
- New example of Starbucks setting a goal of hire 10,000 refugees across 75 countries by 2023.
- New example of a fully sustainable model applying a circular borrow-use-return approach.

Chapter 6

- New Inclusiveness Works: "Bridging Cultural Divides: Beyond Words."
- Revised Management in Action: "How Alibaba Is Becoming a Global Brand."
- Updated Social Entrepreneurship box about student entrepreneurs competing for the $1 million Hult Prize.
- Revised Digital World: "Global Email Etiquette."
- Updated Social Entrepreneurship: "Empowering Latina Entrepreneurs."
- New example of Netflix expanding into 190 countries in just seven years.
- New example predicting that approximately 800 million jobs worldwide will be lost to automation over the next decade.
- New example describing China's growing economic and political influence.
- New example discussing NAFTA's replacement, the U.S.-Mexico-Canada Agreement (USMCA).

Chapter 7

- New Inclusiveness Works feature about start-ups and diversity.
- Revised Management in Action about Starbucks's entrepreneurial beginnings.

- Updated Concluding Case: "Rolling Out Soft Scroll."
- New example indicating that e-commerce sales of physical goods in the United States surpassed $500 billion.
- New example of companies engaged in B2B commerce, including Amazon, Alibaba, Otto, Flipkart, and SAP.
- New example of how most start-ups begin with $5,000 of less in capitalization.
- New example of peer-to-peer (P2P) loaning platforms like Credit or Prosper.

Chapter 8

- New Inclusiveness Works feature about hearing all voices in organizations.
- Revised Management in Action feature about Mary Barra's leadership of GM.
- Updated Concluding Case about moving to a cloud system to create efficiencies.
- Updated Digital World: "Will Online Networks Replace Traditional Hierarchies?"
- New example of PlumSlice Labs creating an advisory board with executives from Walmart, GlaxoSmithKline, Workforce Software, SAP, and Retail Consulting.
- New example of Johnson & Johnson's decentralized approach to managing its 260 operating companies in 60 countries.
- New example of companies like GoPro, Snap Inc., and H&M integrating their marketing and communications functions.
- New example of TTEC integrating more humanity into digital interactions with customers.

Chapter 9

- New Inclusiveness Works feature about engaging early career employees.
- Updated Management in Action: "Making Walmart Agile."
- New Digital World feature about engaging customers through social listening.
- Updated Social Entrepreneurship discussing how to scale social enterprises.
- New example of Coca-Cola, Dr Pepper Snapple Group, and PepsiCo coming together to cut 20 percent of the sugar-based calories in their soft drinks by 2025.
- New example of Walmart's CEO trying to reduce bureaucracy and revitalize company growth by encouraging employee initiative.
- New example of Banana Republic using predictive data to open a pop-up discount ad as an online shopper is about to close the window.
- New example of recent winners of the Malcolm Baldridge National Quality Award.

Chapter 10

- New Inclusiveness Works about providing feedback across cultures.
- Updated Management in Action: "How Google Lands Top Talent."
- Revised Concluding Case about HR planning at Invincibility Systems.
- New Social Entrepreneurship box discussing whether social enterprise is becoming big business.
- New Digital World feature: "Can Your Social Media Profile Keep You from Landing a Great Job?"
- New example of companies preferring internal to external recruitment including Gap Inc., Palo Alto Networks, and Blizzard Entertainment.
- New example of companies being fined for violating U.S. equal employment laws like UPS paying $4.9 million to settle a religious discrimination lawsuit.
- New example of why companies use 360-degree performance appraisals.

Chapter 11

- New Inclusiveness Works: "Avoiding Age Discrimination."
- Updated Management in Action exploring how Accenture innovates through inclusion.
- New Digital World: "Using AI to Hire a More Diverse Workforce."
- New example of companies that have strong commitment to inclusion, including Kaiser Permanente, AT&T, and New York Life.
- New example of diversity initiatives in companies like Northrup Grumman employing veterans and Comcast NBCUniversal using diverse suppliers.
- New example of National Industries for the Blind with 6,000 employees with visual impairments.
- New example of Deloitte and Honeywell monitoring career progress of women, minorities, and employees with disabilities.

Chapter 12

- New Inclusiveness Works: "Including the LGBTQ Community."
- Updated Management in Action about Merck's CEO, Kenneth Frazier, focusing on long-term results.
- New Digital World: "How AI Is Affecting Leadership."
- Revised Social Entrepreneurship feature about manufacturing disaster-resilient homes.
- New example of a vision in which Richard Branson, CEO of Virgin Group, foresees the entire world powered by renewable energy by 2050.

- New example discussing how advances in automated decision making could dramatically change managers' roles.
- New example of transformational leaders, including Mary Barra (CEO of General Motors), Reed Hastings (CEO of Netflix), Mark Bertolini (CEO of Aetna), and Shantanu Narayen (CEO of Adobe).

Chapter 13

- New Inclusiveness Works: "Improving D&I Initiatives with Intrinsic Motivation."
- Updated Management in Action about SAS being a great place to work.
- New Digital World about using technology to motivate employees.
- New example of Notejoy, an organizational collaboration platform, helping its employees set specific and measurable goals.
- New example of how Ryan LLC, a tax firm, rewards its employees with four-week paid sabbaticals and subsidies for health club memberships.
- New example of Blue Cross and Blue Shield of North Carolina hiring college graduates for its two-year Rotational Development Program.
- New example of how psychological contracts are changing.

Chapter 14

- New Inclusiveness Works: "Empathy in Teams Helps Cohesion and Inclusiveness."
- Revised Management in Action feature discussing teamwork at Whole Foods Market.
- New Concluding Case: "Un-Teamwork at Quadra."
- Updated Social Entrepreneurship box about social entrepreneurs using co-working spaces.
- New example of Nestlé's InGenius program encouraging employees and external partners to collaborate to develop new business ideas.
- New example of virtual teams functioning effectively.
- New example in which Spotify creates "squads" of agile, self-organized teams to create new products.
- New example of ways to resolve conflict among B2B commerce partners.

Chapter 15

- New Inclusiveness Works in which organizations use storytelling to become more inclusive.
- Updated Management in Action: "Communicating, SoundCloud Style."
- New Digital World: "Gmail Predicts What You Want to Say."
- Revised Concluding Case regarding communicating at Best Trust Bank.

- New example of companies like Adobe, Gap, and IBM shifting to frequent, informal employee performance check-ins.
- New example of the CEO of T-Mobile posting about company products to more than 5 million followers on his Twitter account.
- New example of companies like Unisys, Sprint, and Hewlett-Packard training employees to use social media productively.
- New example of Vynamic implementing a policy preventing work-related communication among employees after hours during the week and all weekend long.

Chapter 16

- New Inclusiveness Works: "Making a Measurable Impact with D&I Initiatives."
- New Management in Action: "Tracking Employees to Control Health Care Costs."
- Revised Social Entrepreneurship discussing better ways to measure social impact.
- New Digital World feature about technology enabling timely performance reviews.
- New example of Teco Energy assigning project teams to prevent problems.
- New example discussing how data-driven visual dashboards allow managers to monitor organizational performance indicators in real time.
- New example of Chipotle rolling out Zenput, a mobile food safety protocol platform, to prevent future food safety issues.

Chapter 17

- New Inclusiveness Works discussing how technology can help remove unconscious bias.
- Revised Management in Action about Elon Musk's ups and downs as he pursues technology's possibilities and challenges.
- New Concluding Case: "Innovating at Worldwide Games."
- Updated Digital World about BYOD and BYOA work policies.
- New example of product innovations like foldable phones, rollup TVs, and more nature fluid interactions with voice-activated digital assistants.
- New example discussing how innovative food producers like Impossible Foods and Beyond Meat are introducing new "meatless meats" to the market.
- New example describing blockchain's potential game-changing impact on the integrity of everything from online transactions to e-voting.
- New example of Neiman Marcus installing interactive touch screens in its fitting rooms, allowing customers to adjust lighting and request clothing sizes and colors.

Chapter 18

- New Inclusiveness Works: "Changing for Religious Inclusion."
- Revised Management in Action discussing how Shell Oil and other fossil-fuel companies are beginning to embrace renewable energies.
- New Social Entrepreneurship: "Leveraging AI to Build a Better Future."
- New Digital World: "Tech-Savvy Gen Z Enters the Workforce."
- New example discussing Kodak's decision not to pivot away from its lucrative film development business into the disruptive digital camera space.
- New example about using unfreezing to identify performance gaps at different organizational levels.
- New example of Bill Gates's list of technologies that will change the world for the better, including affordable ways to capture carbon dioxide from greenhouse-gas emissions and energy-efficient toilets functioning without a sewer system.

A Team Effort

This book is the product of a fantastic McGraw-Hill team. Moreover, we wrote this book believing that we are part of a team with the course instructor and with students. The entire team is responsible for the learning process.

For students our goal, like that of other instructors, is to create a positive learning environment. But in the end, the raw material of this course is just words. It is up to you to use them as a basis for further reflection, deep learning, and constructive action.

What you do with the things you learn from this course, and with the opportunities the future holds, *counts.* As a manager, you can make a dramatic difference for yourself and for other people. What managers do matters *tremendously.*

Acknowledgments

This book could not have been written and published without the valuable contributions of many individuals.

Our reviewers over the last 13 editions contributed time, expertise, and terrific ideas that significantly enhanced the quality of the text. The reviewers for the 14th edition are:

Laura Alderson, *University of Memphis*

Martha Andrews, *University of North Carolina-Wilmington*

Andrew Bennett, *Old Dominion University*

Alyncia Bowen, *Franklin University*

Guy B. Bradbury, *University of Mount Olive*

Summer Zwanziger Elsinger, *Upper Iowa University*

James P. Froh, *Capella University*

Jeffrey Gauthier, *State University of New York-Plattsburgh*

Anne Kelly Hoel, *University of Wisconsin-Stout*

Eileen Kearney, *Montgomery County Community College*

Dan Morrell, *Middle Tennessee State University*

Sherilyn Reynolds, *San Jacinto College*

Robert Waris, *University of Missouri-Kansas City*

Tiffany Woodward, *East Carolina University*

Many individuals contributed directly to our development as textbook authors. Dennis Organ provided one of the authors with an initial opportunity and guidance in textbook writing. Jack Ivancevich did the same for Rob Konopaske. John Weimeister has been a friend and adviser from the very beginning. Thanks also to Christine Scheid for so much good work on previous editions and for continued friendship.

Enthusiastic gratitude to the entire McGraw-Hill Education team, starting with director Mike Ablassmeir, who—and this is more than an aside—spontaneously and impressively knew *Rolling Stone*'s top three drummers of all time. Mike has long provided deep expertise and an informed perspective, not to mention friendship and managerial cool in everything we do. Not technically an author, Mike is most certainly an educator for us and for the instructors and students who learn from the products he leads.

Special thanks to teammates without whom the book would not exist, let alone be such a prideworthy product:

Our sincere appreciation to Kelsey Darin for her expert guidance and energetic help (not to mention enthusiasm for older musicians and bands we could relate to), as well as to Christine Vaughan for her being a tech-savvy, authoring platform guru.

Debbie Clare: so creative, energetic, always thinking of unique ideas, and encouraging us to engage in new ways of sharing how much the 14th edition means to us.

Claire Hunter: positive, patient, easily amused (thankfully), amazingly effective at keeping us on track and focused.

Thomas and Shannon Finn: thoughtful, creative, timely, and remarkably good at meeting deadlines.

Thanks to you all for getting some of our jokes, for being polite about the others, and for being fun as well as talented and dedicated throughout the project.

Finally, we thank our families. Our parents, Jeanine and Tom Bateman, and Rose and Art Konopaske, provided us with the foundation on which we have built our careers. They continue to be a source of great support. Our wives, Mary Jo and Vania, were encouraging, insightful, and understanding throughout the process. Our children, Lauren, T.J., and James Bateman; and Nick and Isabella Konopaske, provided an unending source of inspiration for our work and our nonwork. Thank you.

Thomas S. Bateman
Chicago, IL

Robert Konopaske
San Marcos, TX

Bottom Line

In this ever more competitive environment, there are six essential types of performance on which the organization beats, equals, or loses to the competition: cost, quality, speed, innovation, service, and sustainability. These six performance dimensions, when done well, deliver value to the customer and competitive advantage to you and your organization.

Throughout the text, Bateman and Konopaske remind students of these six dimensions and their impact on the bottom line with marginal icons. This results-oriented approach is a unique hallmark of this textbook. Questions that further emphasize the bottom line are answered in the Instructor's Manual.

Bottom Line
It's easy to become so focused on maximizing one goal that you lose sight of other important goals. You're optimizing if you make sure that no important result is ignored. *What could be the negative consequences of making decisions that maximize only quality?*

Bottom Line
"Costs" aren't exactly synonymous with "ethics." But by considering the potential costs to all parties, you can make high-quality ethical decisions that you can more effectively sell to others. *What are some costs of treating employees or customers unethically?*

Bottom Line
A diverse workforce can lead to greater responsiveness. *Why might a customer who wants something new get a faster response from a company that tolerates different styles?*

Bottom Line
Innovation can improve all bottom-line practices. *How can innovation support a differentiation strategy?*

Bottom Line
Make sure that you reward the right things, not the wrong things. Sound obvious? You'd be surprised how often this principle is violated! *What is rewarding, and not rewarding, about feedback from your manager?*

Bottom Line
Aspire to become world class at every one of your competitive goals. *What does it mean to be world class at a goal such as quality or sustainability?*

In CASE You Haven't Noticed . . .

Bateman and Konopaske have put together an outstanding selection of case studies of various lengths that highlight companies' ups and downs, stimulate learning and understanding, and challenge students to respond.

Instructors will find a wealth of relevant and updated cases in every chapter, using companies—big and small—that students will enjoy learning about.

CHAPTER-UNFOLDING CASES

Each chapter begins with a "Management in Action: Manager's Brief" section that describes an actual organizational situation, leader, or company. The "Manager's Brief" is referred to again within the chapter in the "Progress Report" section, showing the student how the chapter material relates back to the company, situation, or leader highlighted in the chapter opener. At the end of the chapter, the "Onward" section ties up loose ends and brings the material full circle for the student. Answers to Management in Action section questions can be found in the Instructor's Manual.

SOCIAL ENTREPRENEURSHIP

Social Entrepreneurship boxes have been updated in each chapter to familiarize students with this fast-growing sector. Answers to Social Entrepreneurship questions are included in the Instructor's Manual.

INCLUSIVENESS WORKS

In each chapter, an Inclusiveness Works box has been added to highlight some of the diversity and inclusion challenges faced by managers and employees today.

THE DIGITAL WORLD

The Digital World feature offers unique examples of how companies and other users employ digital/social media in ways that capitalize on various ideas in each chapter.

CONCLUDING CASES

Each chapter ends with a case based on disguised but real companies and people that reinforces key chapter elements and themes.

SUPPLEMENTARY CASES

At the end of each part, an additional case is provided for professors who want students to delve further into part topics.

Outstanding Pedagogy

Management: Leading & Collaborating in a Competitive World is pedagogically stimulating and is intended to maximize student learning. With this in mind, we used a wide array of pedagogical features—some tried and true, others new and novel:

END-OF-CHAPTER ELEMENTS

- **Key terms** are page-referenced to the text and are part of the vocabulary-building emphasis. These terms are defined again in the glossary at the end of the book.
- **Retaining What You Learned** provides clear, concise responses to the learning objectives, giving students a quick reference for reviewing the important concepts in the chapter.
- **Discussion Questions,** which follow, are thought-provoking questions on concepts covered in the chapter and ask for opinions on controversial issues.
- **Experiential Exercises** in each chapter bring key concepts to life so students can experience them firsthand.

Assurance of Learning

This 14th edition contains revised learning objectives, and learning objectives are called out within the chapter where the content begins. The Retaining What You Learned for each chapter ties the learning objectives back together as well. And, finally, our test bank provides tagging for the learning objective that the question covers, so instructors will be able to test material covering all learning objectives, thus ensuring that students have mastered the important topics.

Comprehensive Supplements

INSTRUCTOR'S MANUAL

The Instructor's Manual was revised and updated to include thorough coverage of each chapter as well as time-saving features such as an outline, key student questions, class prep work assignments, guidance for using the unfolding cases, video supplements, and, finally, PowerPoint slides.

TEST BANK

The Test Bank includes more than 100 questions per chapter in a variety of formats. It has been revised for accuracy and expanded to include a greater variety of comprehension and application (scenario-based) questions as well as tagged with Bloom's Taxonomy levels and AACSB requirements.

POWERPOINT PRESENTATION SLIDES

The PowerPoint presentation collection contains an easy-to-follow outline including figures downloaded from the text. In addition to providing lecture notes, the slides also include questions for class discussion as well as company examples not found in the textbook. This versatility allows you to create a custom presentation suitable for your own classroom experience.

You're in the driver's seat.

Want to build your own course? No problem. Prefer to use our turnkey, prebuilt course? Easy. Want to make changes throughout the semester? Sure. And you'll save time with Connect's auto-grading too.

65%
Less Time Grading

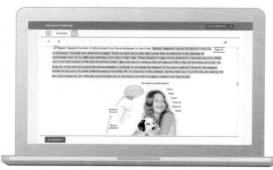

Laptop: McGraw-Hill; Woman/dog: George Doyle/Getty Images

They'll thank you for it.

Adaptive study resources like SmartBook® 2.0 help your students be better prepared in less time. You can transform your class time from dull definitions to dynamic debates. Find out more about the powerful personalized learning experience available in SmartBook 2.0 at **www.mheducation.com/highered/connect/smartbook**

Make it simple, make it affordable.

Connect makes it easy with seamless integration using any of the major Learning Management Systems— Blackboard®, Canvas, and D2L, among others—to let you organize your course in one convenient location. Give your students access to digital materials at a discount with our inclusive access program. Ask your McGraw-Hill representative for more information.

Padlock: Jobalou/Getty Images

Solutions for your challenges.

A product isn't a solution. Real solutions are affordable, reliable, and come with training and ongoing support when you need it and how you want it. Our Customer Experience Group can also help you troubleshoot tech problems— although Connect's 99% uptime means you might not need to call them. See for yourself at **status. mheducation.com**

Checkmark: Jobalou/Getty Images

Effective, efficient studying.

Connect helps you be more productive with your study time and get better grades using tools like SmartBook 2.0, which highlights key concepts and creates a personalized study plan. Connect sets you up for success, so you walk into class with confidence and walk out with better grades.

Study anytime, anywhere.

Download the free ReadAnywhere app and access your online eBook or SmartBook 2.0 assignments when it's convenient, even if you're offline. And since the app automatically syncs with your eBook and SmartBook 2.0 assignments in Connect, all of your work is available every time you open it. Find out more at **www.mheducation.com/readanywhere**

> *"I really liked this app—it made it easy to study when you don't have your text-book in front of you."*
>
> - Jordan Cunningham, Eastern Washington University

No surprises.

The Connect Calendar and Reports tools keep you on track with the work you need to get done and your assignment scores. Life gets busy; Connect tools help you keep learning through it all.

Calendar: owattaphotos/Getty Images

Learning for everyone.

McGraw-Hill works directly with Accessibility Services Departments and faculty to meet the learning needs of all students. Please contact your Accessibility Services office and ask them to email accessibility@mheducation.com, or visit **www.mheducation.com/about/accessibility** for more information.

Top: Jenner Images/Getty Images, Left: Hero Images/Getty Images, Right: Hero Images/Getty Images

Brief Contents

Contents

PART ONE FOUNDATIONS OF MANAGEMENT

CHAPTER 3

Managerial Decision Making   76

PART TWO PLANNING: DELIVERING STRATEGIC VALUE

CHAPTER 4

Planning and Strategic
Management   108

PART THREE ORGANIZING: BUILDING A DYNAMIC ORGANIZATION

PART FOUR LEADING: MOBILIZING PEOPLE

PART FIVE CONTROLLING: LEARNING AND CHANGING

CHAPTER 18

Creating and Leading Change   554

Photo on pages xxi, xxii, xxiv, xxv, and xxvii: Wang An Qi/Shutterstock

The Management Process

Foundations of Management

- Managing and Performing
- The External and Internal Environments
- Managerial Decision Making

**Planning:
Delivering Strategic Value**

- Planning and Strategic Management
- Ethics, Corporate Responsibility, and Sustainability
- International Management
- Entrepreneurship

Strategy Implementation

Organizing: Building a Dynamic Organization

- Organization Structure
- Organizational Agility
- Human Resources Management
- Managing the Diverse Workforce

**Leading:
Mobilizing People**

- Leadership
- Motivating for Performance
- Teamwork
- Communicating

**Controlling:
Learning and Changing**

- Managerial Control
- Managing Technology and Innovation
- Creating and Leading Change

CHAPTER 1
Managing and Performing

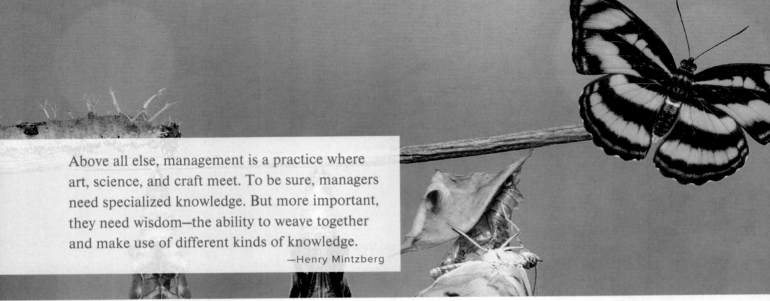

Above all else, management is a practice where art, science, and craft meet. To be sure, managers need specialized knowledge. But more important, they need wisdom—the ability to weave together and make use of different kinds of knowledge.
—Henry Mintzberg

Mathisa/Shutterstock

learning objectives

After studying Chapter 1, you will be able to:

LO 1-1 Summarize the major challenges of managing in the new competitive landscape.

LO 1-2 Describe the sources of competitive advantage for a company.

LO 1-3 Explain how the functions of management are evolving in today's business environment.

LO 1-4 Compare how the nature of management varies at different organizational levels.

LO 1-5 Define the skills you need to be an effective manager.

LO 1-6 Understand the principles that will help you manage your career.

chapter outline

Management in Action

FACEBOOK'S MARK ZUCKERBERG: MANAGING IN GOOD TIMES—AND BAD

MANAGER'S BRIEF

PROGRESS REPORT

ONWARD

What does a manager do? Dream up a bold new mission for the company? Build a corporate structure that ensures success? Lead and inspire others? Keep the company on track toward its goals?

Most managers perform all these functions to some degree, perhaps none more publicly than Mark Zuckerberg, founder and CEO of Facebook. He has seen his company grow into a worldwide phenomenon with more than 2 billion active users. Given that the company reported approximately $55 billion in revenue in 2018,[1] it seems Zuckerberg's passion for connecting people has paid off. With Facebook's swift and unparalleled success, it's tempting to overlook the management challenges Zuckerberg confronted when first starting out, as well as the challenges he now confronts as the head of a global media giant.

Tom Williams/CQ Roll Call/Getty Images

Zuckerberg's past hurdles included the need for capital to fund the company's rapid growth. In 2012, he announced an initial public offering (IPO) of stock to attract cash and then saw the company experience a damaging initial drop in its stock price. Next came the soaring popularity of smartphones, which encouraged Facebook users to go mobile. To adapt, the firm developed its mobile app to carry advertising. Those mobile ads now earn more than 80 percent of the company's revenue.

More recent challenges relate not only to Facebook as a company but to Zuckerberg's personal character. Facebook was accused of aiding the spread of fake news during the 2016 presidential campaign, and Zuckerberg was alleged to be personally negligent in

foreseeing these dangers. Under severe public scrutiny, Zuckerberg agreed to testify before Congress, where he faced 10 hours of questioning over two days.[2] But the problems didn't end there. Just a few months later, Facebook's stock plummeted, losing $119 billion in market value, marking the biggest one-day loss in U.S. history. Fears of slowing growth, increasing costs, and more severe government regulation all fueled the dramatic loss.

Zuckerberg began his congressional testimony by saying, "It was my mistake, and I'm sorry. I started Facebook, I run it, and I'm responsible for what happens here."[3] In effect, he did what successful managers must do: take ownership of their mistakes.

Ultimately, Facebook's future will come down to the decisions its founder makes to navigate many coming headwinds, such as an increased interest in privacy.[4] We'll take a closer look at how he's addressing these challenges in our progress report later in the chapter.

Facebook's CEO Mark Zuckerberg is an innovator who combines technological know-how with a vision for the future. Together, those qualities have helped him build a business idea into a major corporation that continues to transform how people connect with one another.[5] So far, Zuckerberg has been able to navigate the media company through challenging times, such as recent criticism involving its role in spreading fake news.

Consider the pioneering ride-hailing service Uber as a contrasting example. Since its founding in 2009, the company was seen as a golden tech start-up that disrupted the traditional taxi transportation industry. Unfortunately, the good times did not last. In 2017, Travis Kalanick, the CEO and co-founder of the company, resigned under a cloud of controversy.[6] Issues contributing to his departure included complaints of a work culture that allowed sexual harassment and discrimination, a lawsuit alleging the company stole a trade secret, and disagreements with major investors.[7] At the end of 2017, Uber reported a net loss of $4.5 billion.[8] The new CEO, Dara Khosrowshahi, hopes to erase the loss and make the company profitable by expanding internationally and growing its food delivery service (Uber Eats) prior to an initial public stock offering.[9]

In business, there is no alternative to managing well. Companies may fly high for a while, but they cannot do well for very long without good management. It's the same for individuals: the best performers succeed by focusing on fundamentals, knowing what's important, and managing well. The aim of this book is to help you succeed in those pursuits.

Managing in a Competitive World

LO 1-1 Summarize the major challenges of managing in the new competitive landscape.

When the economy is soaring, business seems easy. Investing in the stock market seems like a sure bet when the bulls are carrying the market higher and higher. But the reality is, things change.

The great economic recession of 2008 eradicated the real estate boom and ushered in an era of falling stock prices and company profits, and widescale employee layoffs. More recently, a trade war with China, the renegotiation of the North American Free Trade Agreement (NAFTA), higher tariffs levied on steel and aluminum imports, and interest rate hikes to control inflation have contributed to uncertainty in the U.S. economy.[10] In 2018, the stock market experienced "extreme volatility," ending with the worst year for stocks since the great recession a decade earlier.[11]

At such times, it becomes clear that managing is a challenge requiring knowledge and skills to adapt to new circumstances.

Effective managers must continually acquire knowledge and skills to adapt to new circumstances.

What defines the competitive landscape of business? You will be reading about many relevant issues in the coming chapters, but we begin here by highlighting four ongoing challenges that characterize the business landscape: globalization, technological change, the importance of knowledge and ideas, and collaboration across organizational boundaries.

Globalization

Far more than in the past, today's enterprises are global, with offices and production facilities in countries all over the world. Corporations operate worldwide, transcending national borders. Companies that want to grow often need to tap international markets. The change from a local to a global marketplace presents big opportunities for small companies too.[12]

Fortune magazine annually publishes a list of the world's most admired companies. Whereas U.S. companies used to dominate, Switzerland-based Nestlé was the most admired maker of consumer food products in 2018, Japan's Toyota Motor was the most admired producer of motor vehicles, and Britain's Diagio was the most admired provider of beverages.[13] According to *Fortune*'s 2018 Global 500 list, the five largest firms are Walmart (United States), State Grid (China), Sinopec Group (China), China National Petroleum (China), and Royal Dutch Shell (United Kingdom–the Netherlands).[14]

Globalization also means that a company's talent and competition can come from anywhere. IBM operates in over 175 countries in order to develop deep relationships with local clients.[15] Even though IBM's headquarters are located in the United States, more than one-third of its employees are based in India.[16] Kentucky-based Yum! Brands (KFC, Pizza Hut, and Taco Bell) has more than 45,000 restaurants in more than 140 countries. On average, Yum! Brands opens seven stores per day in international locations.[17]

PepsiCo's former chief executive, Indra Nooyi, brought a much-needed global viewpoint to a company whose international business was growing three times faster than sales in the United States. Nooyi, who was raised in India and educated there and in the United States, helped steer the company toward more "better for you" and "good for you" snacks (Naturally Bare Chips) and drinks (KeVita probiotic non-soda and Bubly Sparkling Water) to offset declining sales of sugary soda.[18]

Globalization affects small companies as well as large. Many small companies export their goods. Many domestic firms assemble their products in other countries. And companies are under pressure to improve and lower the price of their products in the face of intense competition from foreign manufacturers. Managers today must ask themselves, "How can we be the best in the world?"

For students, it's not too early to think globally. Participating in the Global Business Institute program at Indiana University, one hundred students from North Africa, South Asia, and the Middle East came to the United States to pitch entrepreneurial business ideas to a panel of experts. The panel consisted of officials from Coca-Cola and the U.S. Department of State. The most recent winner was Team Morocco, who proposed a business for a medical device that can repair skull damage.[19]

Globalization has changed the face of the workforce. Managers in this competitive environment need to attract and effectively manage a talent pool from all over the globe.

Pitju/Getty Images

Technological Change

Online customer engagement, artificial intelligence and machine learning, data protection and privacy, and cloud computing are only some of the ways that technology is vitally important in the business world.[20] Technology both complicates things and creates new opportunities. The challenges come from the rapid rate at which communication, commerce, transportation, information, and other technologies change.[21] For example, after just a couple of decades of widespread desktop use, customers switched to laptop models, which required different accessories. Then, users turned to mini-laptops, tablets, smartphones, and smartwatches to meet their mobility technology needs.[22] Good managers anticipate and respond to changing customers' wants and needs.

Later chapters discuss technology in more detail, but here we highlight the Internet and its effects. How are these forces impacting business?[23] It is a global and digital marketplace, a means for manufacturing goods and services, a distribution channel, a platform for connecting customers, an information service, an arena for social activism,[24] and more. It drives down costs and accelerates globalization. It improves efficiency of decision making. Managers can use it to learn what companies around the world are doing in real time.

Although these advantages create business opportunities, they also create threats from hackers and computer viruses, competitors as they capitalize sooner on new developments than you do, and groups that use Internet activism maliciously to unfairly hurt a public image. Internet activism also can give people a powerful way to expose corrupt or harmful practices and motivate organizations to change their ways for the better.[25]

Things continue to change at breakneck speed. Nearly two decades ago, tech guru Tim O'Reilly coined the term "Web 2.0" to describe the exciting new wave of social networking start-ups that allow users to publish and share information. But most failed or stalled; very few, other than Facebook, made a profit.[26] Web 2.0 redefined the ways in which customers and sellers, employees and employers, interact and share knowledge.

Next came Web 3.0, described as a "read-write-execute" web where applications, search results, and online services are more tailored, integrated, and relevant to users.[27] Think about the last time you searched for a product on Amazon and a list of related products appeared on the screen as alternatives. Web 3.0 is giving way to the Internet of Things and 24/7 mobile accessibility, where smartphones, wearable fitness trackers, smart homes, and so forth interpret human activities and communicate this information wirelessly through networks to be used in myriad ways (tally miles walked, send reminders, and regulate home temperature).[28]

What's next for the digital frontier? It's hard to predict with precision, but as billions of people and businesses worldwide demand more personalized and connected experiences, artificial intelligence will simplify the interfaces between humans and technology. Instead of people adapting to new technologies as in the past, technology will adapt to people's preferences.[29] For example, AI-powered chatbots that answer your questions on company websites could be supplemented by AI virtual agents with faces and voices that converse with customers.[30]

In 2019, projections suggest that tens of millions of Americans will be using Amazon's Alexa or other AI-powered speech recognition tools to search the Internet.[31] Homeowners can use Alexa to control any smart device, including washers and dryers, light bulbs, door locks, and thermostats.[32]

Knowledge Management

Companies and managers need good new ideas. Because companies in advanced economies have become so efficient at producing physical goods, most workers have been freed up to provide services or "abstract goods" such as software, entertainment, data, and advertising. These workers, whose primary contributions are ideas and problem-solving expertise, are

The Digital World

Chatbots: Good for Business?

If you've ever interacted with a company online, you've probably encountered a chatbot. These AI programs are designed to simulate human conversation, using either text or voice prompts and responses. Today, companies use chatbots in a variety of ways. Often, you may not even know you're interacting with one. Have a customer service issue you want addressed? "Chatting with an assistant" often means chatting with a chatbot. Want to check your account balance? A chatbot can help you with that, too.

The benefits of using chatbots for businesses are many. Research suggests that by 2022, chatbots will have saved companies $8 billion. The majority of companies adopting AI to enhance the user's online experience are employing chatbots to improve customer service.[33] For example, Amtrak's "Julie" helps customers find information, book a reservation, and plan a vacation.[34] Yet savvy organizations are also using bots to recruit and train employees and to help current employees book travel and fill out expense reports.[35]

However, managers also need to use caution when applying this new technology. Although chatbots are often adept at mimicking human speech, they have one major shortcoming: they are not humans. They may not understand the nuances of human conversation like sarcasm or humor. You might have heard "I'm sorry, I don't know that one" when talking to Alexa or Siri. Such responses can be frustrating for customers—and risky for companies. Firms also need to consider security issues relating to chatbots, such as where and how to store the data they use and acquire.[36]

Despite these risks, chatbots appear to be here to stay, with companies continuing to invest money into creating ever-more lifelike and helpful bots.

1. As a manager, what issues would you want to consider before employing a chatbot at your organization?
2. Many businesses are relying on chatbots to enhance customer service. Do you think this is an effective strategy? Why or why not?

often referred to as *knowledge workers.* Managing these workers poses some particular challenges,[37] which we examine throughout this book.

Because the success of modern businesses so often depends on the knowledge used for innovation and the delivery of services, organizations need to manage that knowledge.[38] **Knowledge management** is the set of practices aimed at discovering and harnessing an organization's intellectual resources—fully using the intellects of the organization's people. Knowledge management is about finding, unlocking, sharing, and capitalizing on the most precious resources of an organization: people's expertise, skills, wisdom, and relationships. The nearby "Inclusiveness Works" box explores how important knowledge transfer is to organizational survival.

Knowledge managers find these human assets, help people collaborate and learn, generate new ideas, and harness those ideas into successful innovations.

knowledge management

Practices aimed at discovering and harnessing an organization's intellectual resources.

Collaboration across Boundaries

Leveraging knowledge for maximum impact requires people in different departments, divisions, or subunits of the organization to collaborate and communicate effectively. For example, "T-shaped" managers break out of the traditional corporate hierarchy to share knowledge freely across the organization (the horizontal part of the T) while remaining committed to the bottom-line performance of their individual business units (the vertical part).[39]

Inclusiveness Works

Move Over Boomers, Here Comes the Next Generation of Leaders

Rawpixel.com/Shutterstock

The workforce is changing rapidly. A large number of Baby Boomers (born 1946–1964) will be exiting the workforce over the next 15 years. In fact, according to the Pew Research Center, approximately 10,000 Boomers turn 65 each day in the United States.[40]

This talent exodus will translate into career opportunities for younger generations. Gen Xers (born 1965–1979) occupy many middle-level jobs, but there are not enough of them to fill all of the soon-to-be-vacant positions. Enter the Millennial generation (born 1980–1996), who make up the largest generational demographic on record.[41] These early 30- and 20-somethings are flooding the job market and will need to move quickly from team leader and frontline managerial positions into higher responsibilities.

Senior managers possess "know-how" and "know-who" that are critical to the long-term success of their organizations. Thus, before Gen Xers and Millennials can assume higher-level positions, senior managers need to transfer organizational knowledge to the less experienced newcomers.

Complicating this need is the fact that individuals within the same generation differ in their attitudes, personalities, and behaviors. This can affect everything from communication, customer service, teamwork, job satisfaction, morale, and retention to overall organizational performance.

And very soon managers will have to account for and integrate the attitudes and personalities of yet another generation: Gen Z (born in or after 1997), the oldest members of which are now entering the workforce.[42]

1. How can organizations most effectively transfer organizational knowledge from one generation to another?
2. Have you seen examples of how people of different ages have interacted ineffectively because of inaccurate stereotypes? Examples of different generations working effectively together?

Consulting firm McKinsey originally developed this T-shaped concept as a way for its employees to view clients' problems from both broad and deep perspectives.[43]

Toyota keeps its product development process efficient by bringing together design engineers and manufacturing employees from the very beginning. Often, manufacturing employees can help simplify a design so that it is easier to make without defects or unnecessary costs. Toyota employees listen to input from all areas of the organization, so this type of collaboration is a natural part of the organization's culture: using software to share their knowledge—best practices they have developed for design and manufacturing.[44]

Collaboration can occur beyond the boundaries of the organization itself. Companies today sometimes work with rather than against their competitors—you'll read some examples later—in a dynamic sometimes called **coopetition**.[45] Companies also collaborate with their customers—some better than others—by actively and continuously listening and responding. Amazon is starting to open "4-star" brick-and-mortar stores. Only the products that customers love and that have received at least a 4-star rating on the website will be for sale at these shops.[46] Because 90 percent of consumers read online reviews before visiting a business, most companies pay attention to customer comments on Yelp, TripAdvisor, Amazon, Google, Twitter, and many more sites.[47] Customer feedback management software can search these and other sites and generate statistics and reports. Companies can respond to negative online reviews with the goal of winning over their critics.[48]

coopetition

Simultaneous competition and cooperation among companies with the intent of creating value.

Managing for Competitive Advantage

LO 1-2 Describe the sources of competitive advantage for a company.

Bottom Line

Because it's easy for managers to be so busy that they lose sight of what really drives performance, you will periodically see icons as bottom-line reminders of the need for innovation, quality, service, speed, cost competitiveness, and sustainability. *Which two or more of these advantages do you think would be hardest to deliver at the same time—and most importantly, why?*

innovation

The introduction of new goods and services; a change in method or technology; a positive, useful departure from previous ways of doing things.

The early Internet years turned careers (and lives) upside down. Students dropped out of school to join Internet start-ups or start their own. Managers in big corporations quit their jobs to do the same. Investors pounced, and invested heavily. The risks were often ignored or downplayed—sometimes tragically as the boom went bust in 2000.

And consider an earlier industry with similar transforming power: automobiles. There have been at least 2,000 carmakers—how many remain?

What is the lesson to be learned from the failures in these important transformational industries? A key to understanding the success of a company is the competitive advantage it holds and how well it can sustain that advantage.

To survive and win over time, you have to gain and sustain advantages over your competitors. You do this by being better than your competitors at doing valuable things for your customers. But what does this mean, specifically? To succeed, managers must deliver performance. The fundamental drivers of competitive advantage and bottom-line performance are innovation, quality, service, speed, cost competitiveness, and sustainability.

Innovation

Companies must continually innovate. **Innovation** is the introduction of new goods and services. Your firm must adapt to changes in consumer demands and to new competitors.

Products don't sell forever; in fact, they don't sell for nearly as long as they used to because competitors are continuously introducing new products. Your firm must continually innovate, or it will die. In 2018, once successful retailer Toys R Us announced it was closing all 800 of its remaining U.S. stores, resulting in 33,000 lost jobs.[49] A reason for the company's demise was its inability to overcome intense competition from Amazon, Target, and Walmart.[50]

Nearly 20 years ago, Blockbuster was the market leader of the video rental industry. It didn't see the need to offer customers an alternative to driving to their retail stores to rent a movie, nor did the company eliminate late charges because they were a major source of revenue. Reed Hastings, founder of Netflix, displaced Blockbuster by allowing customers to order videos that would be delivered by mail. Customers could watch a video for as long as they wanted, then mail it back to Netflix. In 2010, Blockbuster filed for bankruptcy.[51] Netflix has become a successful $11.6 billion company.[52]

The need for innovation is driven in part by globalization. One important reason is that facilities in other countries can manufacture appliances or write software code at a lower cost than those in the United States; U.S. facilities thus operate at a disadvantage. Therefore, they must provide something their foreign competitors can't—and often that requires delivering something new.

Nevertheless, as labor and other costs rise in overseas markets, and as U.S. companies find ways to improve efficiency at home, the future for North American facilities may brighten. Nissan decided to invest $170 million to expand production in Smyrna, Tennessee, for the assembly of its all-new Nissan Altima.[53] Also, Fiat-Chrysler Automobiles (FCA) has announced plans to expand manufacturing operations in the United States. In 2018, FCA reported that it is reviving a manufacturing plant located in Detroit, Michigan, to build the Jeep Grand Cherokee.[54]

Innovation is today's holy grail. For example, Apple was named the 2018 number-one most-admired company in *Fortune*'s innovativeness category.[55] Like the other sources of competitive advantage, innovation comes from people, it must be a strategic goal, and it must be managed properly. Later chapters show you how great companies innovate.

Quality

Most companies claim that they are committed to quality. In general, **quality** is the excellence of your product. Customers expect high-quality goods and services, and often they will accept nothing less.

quality
The excellence of your product (goods or services).

Historically, quality pertained primarily to the physical goods that customers bought; it referred to attractiveness, lack of defects, and dependability. The traditional approach to quality was to check work after it was completed and then eliminate defects, using inspection and statistical data to determine whether products were up to standards. But then W. Edwards Deming, J. M. Juran, Phil Crosby, and other quality gurus convinced managers to take a more complete approach to achieving *total* quality. This includes *preventing* defects before they occur, *achieving zero defects* in manufacturing, and *designing* products for quality. The goal is to solve and eradicate from the beginning all quality-related problems and to live a philosophy of *continuous improvement* in the way the company operates.[56]

Trevor Lush/Purestock/SuperStock

Quality is further provided when companies customize goods and services to the wishes of the individual consumer. Choices at Starbucks give consumers thousands of variations on the drinks they can order. Gatorade GX allows customers to create customized bottles. Nike's 90/10 pack sneakers give customers the opportunity to participate in designing their own shoes, and Icon Meals permits customers to create custom meal plans online.[57]

Providing world-class quality requires a thorough understanding of what quality really is.[58] Quality can be measured in terms of product performance, customer service, reliability (avoidance of failure or breakdowns), conformance to standards, durability, and aesthetics. Only when you move beyond broad, generic concepts such as "quality" and identify specific quality requirements can you identify problems, target needs, set precise performance standards, and deliver world-class value.

By the way, *Fortune* magazine's 2018 number-one company for quality of products and services also was Apple.

> When you're out of quality, you're out of business.
>
> *—Phil Crosby*

Service

Important quality measures often pertain to the service customers receive. This dimension of quality is particularly important because the service sector has come to dominate the U.S. economy. In recent years, the fastest-growing job categories have been almost entirely health care services, and the jobs with the greatest declines are primarily in manufacturing and farming, fishing, and forestry occupations.[59] Services include intangible products such as insurance, hotel accommodations, medical care, and haircuts.

Service means giving customers what they want or need, when they want it. So, service is focused on continually meeting the needs of customers to establish mutually beneficial long-term relationships.[60] Thus cloud computing companies, in addition to providing online access to software, applications, and other computer services, also help their customers store and analyze large amounts of customer and employee data.

An important dimension of service quality is making it easy and enjoyable for customers to experience a service or to buy and use products. At all its parks and resorts, Disney's employees treat every customer as a VIP (Very Individual Person) by personalizing guest experiences to make them feel special. Disney Institute teaches business professionals "exceptional service, though carefully architected backstage, should look spontaneous and personalized on stage." Spontaneous interactions with customers can create long-lasting memories and affirm the company's brand promise.[61]

service

The speed and dependability with which an organization delivers what customers want.

Speed

Google constantly improves its search product at a rapid rate. In fact, its entire culture is based on rapid innovation. Sheryl Sandberg, chief operating officer of Facebook, made a mistake early in her previous position as vice president of Google because she was moving too fast to plan carefully. Although the mistake cost the company a few million dollars, Google co-founder Larry Page responded to her explanation and apology by saying he was actually glad she had made the mistake. It showed that she appreciated the company's values. Page told Sandberg, "I want to run a company where we are moving too quickly and doing too much, not being too cautious and doing too little. If we don't have any of these mistakes, we're just not taking enough risks."[62]

Although it's unlikely that Google actually favors mistakes over moneymaking ideas, Page's statement expressed an appreciation that in the modern business environment, **speed**—rapid execution, response, and delivery—often separates the winners from the losers.

speed

Fast and timely execution, response, and delivery of products.

How fast can you develop and get a new product to market? How quickly can you respond to customer requests? You are far better off if you are faster than the competition—and if you can respond quickly to your competitors' actions. In *The Lean Startup,* Eric Ries captures this idea of moving quickly: "The only way to win is to learn faster than anyone else."[63]

Speed isn't everything—you can't get sloppy in your quest to be first. But other things being equal, faster companies are more likely to be the winners, slow ones the losers. Even pre-Internet, companies were getting products to market and in the hands of customers faster than ever. Now the speed requirement has increased exponentially. Everything, it seems, is on fast-forward.

Speed is no longer just a goal of some companies; it is a strategic imperative. In 2018, Quicken Loans (owned by

Quicken Loans became quicker than before and quicker than many others when it introduced Rocket Mortgage.

dpa picture alliance/Alamy Stock Photo

Rock Holdings Inc.) supplanted Wells Fargo as the largest provider of mortgage loans in the United States.[64] Two years ago, Quicken announced its new mortgage service, Rocket Mortgage.[65] The self-service mortgage application is marketed as fast, secure, and completely online.[66]

Cost Competitiveness

Walmart keeps driving hard to find new ways to cut billions of dollars from its already very low distribution costs. It leads the industry in efficient distribution, but competitors are copying Walmart's methods, so the efficiency no longer gives it as much of an advantage.[67]

Walmart's efforts are aimed at **cost competitiveness**, which means keeping costs low enough so that the company can realize profits and price its products (goods or services) at levels that are attractive to consumers. Needless to say, if you can offer a desirable product at a lower price, it is more likely to sell.

JetBlue Airlines, in an effort to compete against discounting rivals like Spirit Airlines, announced that it would begin offering a basic economy airfare in 2019.[68] Joanna Geraghty, President of JetBlue, told employees that the new no frills fare option is in reaction to customer preferences and not offering it would put the airline's success at risk.[69]

One reason every company must worry about cost is that consumers can use the Internet to easily compare prices from thousands of competitors. Consumers looking to buy popular items, such as cameras, printers, and plane fares, can go online to research the best models and the best deals. If you can't cut costs and offer attractive prices, you can't compete.

cost competitiveness
Keeping costs low to achieve profits and be able to offer prices that are attractive to consumers.

Sustainability

Avoiding wasteful use of energy can bolster a company's financial performance while being kind to the environment. Efforts to cut energy waste are just one way to achieve an important form of competitive advantage: **sustainability**, which at its most basic is the effort to minimize the use and loss of resources, especially those that are polluting and nonrenewable.

Although sustainability means different things to different people,[70] in this text we emphasize a long-term perspective on sustaining the natural environment and building tomorrow's business opportunities while effectively managing today's business.[71]

In the United States, corporate efforts aimed at sustainability have fluctuated as environmental laws are strengthened or loosened; overall, the worldwide trend has been in the direction of greater concern for sustainability. Many companies have discovered that addressing sustainability issues often produces bottom-line benefits. Companies with strong sustainability performance that have also become financial winners include Danish bioscience company Corporate Knights, financial services provider Banco do Brasil, French luxury-goods maker Kering, and U.S. food spice firm McCormick.[72]

Patagonia does not want customers to discard their outdoor gear that has a broken zipper, tear in the sleeve, or chewed up Velcro closure. Known as the Worn Wear program, the company hopes to keep its products out of landfills by offering free repairs with no questions asked. The program is working. In 2017, 14 employees from its Reno, Nevada, service center made more than 50,000 clothing repairs.[73]

Sustainability is about protecting our options.[74] Done properly, sustainability allows people to live and work in ways that can be maintained over the long term (generations) without depleting or harming our environmental, social, and economic resources.

sustainability
Minimizing the use of resources, especially those that are polluting and nonrenewable.

Delivering All Types of Performance

Don't assume that you can settle for delivering just one of the six competitive advantages: low cost alone, or quality alone, for example. As illustrated in Exhibit 1.1, the best managers and companies deliver on all of these performance dimensions.

Staying Ahead of the
Competition

Bottom Line

Don't focus on one aspect
of performance and neglect
the others. You might be
better at or more interested
in one than the others, but
every one is important and
you—more broadly, your
employer—should strive
for all six. *Imagine you're
in your first management
job, supervising a team.
What would be your
natural tendency? Which
performance measures
would you focus on, and
why? How can you be sure to
pay attention to the others?*

Some trade-offs will occur among the six sources of competitive advantage, but this doesn't need to be a zero-sum game in which improving one requires weakening another. The best managers try to optimize among multiple performance dimensions over time.

The Functions of Management

LO 1-3 Explain how the functions of management are evolving in today's business environment.

management

The process of working with people and resources to accomplish organizational goals.

planning

The management function of systematically making decisions about the goals and activities that an individual, a group, a work unit, or the overall organization will pursue; see also *strategic planning*.

Management is the process of working with people and resources to accomplish organizational goals. Good managers do those things both effectively and efficiently. To be *effective* is to achieve organizational goals. To be *efficient* is to achieve goals with minimal waste of resources—that is, to make the best possible use of money, time, materials, and people. Some managers fail on both criteria, or focus on one at the expense of another. The best managers achieve high performance by focusing on both effectiveness *and* efficiency.

These definitions have been around for a long time. But as you know, business is changing radically. The real issue is how to *do* these things.[75]

Although the specifics of doing business are changing, there are still plenty of timeless principles that make managers, and companies, great. While fresh thinking and new approaches are required now more than ever, tried and true management practices remain relevant, useful, and adaptable, with fresh thinking, to the 21st-century business environment.

In the business world today, great executives not only adapt to changing conditions but also apply—rigorously, consistently, and with discipline—the fundamental management principles.

These fundamentals include the four traditional functions of management: *planning, organizing, leading,* and *controlling.* These are used in organizations of every type. They remain as relevant as ever, and they are needed in start-ups as much as in established corporations. But their form has evolved.

Planning: Delivering Strategic Value

Planning is specifying the goals to be achieved and deciding in advance the appropriate actions needed to achieve those goals. Planning activities include analyzing current situations, anticipating futures, determining objectives, deciding the types of activities in which the company will engage, choosing corporate and business strategies, and determining the

Social Entrepreneurship

The Pioneer of Social Entrepreneurship

Can a company do well and do good at the same time? The idea that business success and positive social change can and indeed should happen together is the driving force behind social enterprise, or social entrepreneurship. Think of social entrepreneurs as change agents, managers who commit themselves and their organizations to creating not only private value in the form of profit, but also social value in various forms, including innovation, sustainability, and accountability. In fact, social entrepreneurs use the same basic management functions to achieve business excellence and to advance positive social goals.

A leading force behind the growing strength of social entrepreneurship is Ashoka, founded by Bill Drayton in 1980. Since its founding, the group has expanded its operations to over 90 countries and has grown to include more than 3,500 social entrepreneurs.[76] Ashoka works worldwide to enable everyone to be a "changemaker" by identifying and supporting "Fellows," creating communities for them, and helping build business, social, and financial systems to encourage even more social innovation.

Fellows around the world work on problems in education, women's health, the environment, justice, obesity, mental health, and human trafficking, among many others. In addition, Ashoka has implemented "changemaker" curriculum in over 500 college and university campuses across 50 countries with social innovation and problem solving as core values.[77] (Check out https://www.ashoka.org/en/our-network to see whether your college or university is among them.)

In Drayton's view, anyone can be a social entrepreneur. All it takes, he says, is the ability to see a problem, put others' skepticism aside, and allow yourself the time to inch your way first toward a vision and then to a solution that works. You'll read about social entrepreneurs in every chapter of this book.[78]

1. Do you think every manager should have the responsibility to do good and do well? Why or why not?
2. What other means to create social innovation besides efforts like Ashoka's do you think can be effective?

resources needed to achieve the organization's goals. Plans set the stage for action and for major achievements.

The planning function for the new business environment, as discussed in Part 2 of this book, is more dynamically described as *delivering strategic value.* **Value** is an important concept.[79] Fundamentally, it describes the monetary amount associated with how well a job, task, good, or service meets users' needs. Those users might be business owners, customers, employees, society, and even nations.[80] The better you meet those needs (in terms of quality, speed, efficiency, and so on), the more value you deliver.

That value is strategic when it contributes to meeting the organization's goals. On a more personal level, you will do well to periodically ask yourself and your boss, "How can I add value?" Answering that question will enhance your contributions, your job performance, and your career.

Delivering strategic value is a continual process of identifying opportunities to create, seize, strengthen, and sustain competitive advantage. Effectively creating value requires fully considering a new and changing set of stakeholders and issues, including the government, the natural environment, globalization, and the dynamic economy in which ideas are king and entrepreneurs are both formidable competitors and potential collaborators. You learn about these and related topics in Chapter 4 (planning and strategic management), Chapter 5 (ethics, corporate responsibility, and sustainability), Chapter 6 (international management), and Chapter 7 (entrepreneurship).

> You will do well to periodically ask yourself and your boss, "How can I add value?"

value

The monetary amount associated with how well a job, task, good, or service meets users' needs.

Organizing: Building a Dynamic Organization

Organizing is assembling and coordinating the human, financial, physical, informational, and other resources needed to achieve goals. Organizing activities include attracting people

organizing

The management function of assembling and coordinating human, financial, physical, informational, and other resources needed to achieve goals.

Rosalind Brewer, former president and CEO of Sam's Club, focused on building a dynamic organization. She recently was appointed COO and group president of Starbucks.

Sarah Bentham/AP Images

leading

The management function that involves the manager's efforts to stimulate high performance by employees.

controlling

The management function of monitoring performance and making needed changes.

to the organization, specifying job responsibilities, grouping jobs into work units, marshaling and allocating resources, and creating conditions so that people and things work together to achieve maximum success.

Part 3 of the book describes the organizing function as *building a dynamic organization.* Historically, organizing involved creating an organization chart by identifying business functions, establishing reporting relationships, and having a human resources department that administered plans, programs, and paperwork. Now and in the future, effective managers will be using new forms of organizing and viewing their people as their most valuable resources. They will build organizations that are flexible and adaptive, particularly in response to changing competitive threats and customer needs. Progressive human resource practices that attract, reward, and retain the very best diverse workforce will help ensure company success. You will learn about these topics in Chapter 8 (organization structure), Chapter 9 (organizational agility), Chapter 10 (human resources management), and Chapter 11 (managing the diverse workforce).

Leading: Mobilizing People

Leading is stimulating people to be high performers. It includes motivating and communicating with employees, individually and in groups. Leading involves connecting directly with people, helping to guide and inspire them toward achieving team and organizational goals. Leading takes place in teams, departments, and divisions as well as at the top of all types of organizations.

In earlier textbooks, the leading function described how managers motivate workers to come to work and execute top management's plans by doing their jobs. Today and in the future, managers must be good at mobilizing people to contribute their ideas—to use their brains in ways never needed or dreamed of in the past.

As described in Part 4, managers must rely on a very different kind of leadership (Chapter 12) that empowers and motivates people (Chapter 13). More now than ever, great work must be done via great teamwork (Chapter 14), both within work groups and across group boundaries. Ideally, underlying these processes will be effective interpersonal and organizational communication (Chapter 15).

Controlling: Learning and Changing

Planning, organizing, and leading do not guarantee success. The fourth function, **controlling**, monitors performance and implements necessary changes. By controlling, managers make sure the organization's resources are being used properly and that the organization is meeting its goals such as quality and worker safety.

When managers implement their plans, they often find that things are not working out as planned. The controlling function makes sure that goals are met. It addresses the question, "Are our actual outcomes consistent with our established goals?" It then makes adjustments as needed.

Successful organizations pay close attention to the controlling function. But Part 5 of the book makes it clear that today and for the future, key managerial challenges are far more dynamic than in the past; they involve continually *learning and changing.* Controls must still be in place, as described in Chapter 16. But new technologies and other innovations (Chapter 17) make it possible to control more effectively and to help people use their brains, learn, make creative contributions, and help the organization change in ways that forge a successful future (Chapter 18).

The four management functions apply to you personally as well. You must find ways to create value; organize for your own personal effectiveness; mobilize your talents and skills as well as those of others; monitor performance; and constantly learn, develop, and change for the

Management in Action

NAVIGATING FACEBOOK THROUGH TURBULENT TIMES

MANAGER'S BRIEF

PROGRESS REPORT

ONWARD

As discussed in the opening of this chapter, Facebook is facing challenges from multiple fronts. Much of the company's success will depend upon how well Mark Zuckerberg is able to perform the basic functions of management during turbulent times.

Good managers plan how to deliver strategic value, not just for the present but for the future. Seeing the success of competitors like Snapchat and Instagram, Zuckerberg began planning ways to integrate into Facebook a similar time-limited video platform, called Stories, that could serve as another way for people to connect and also generate revenue for the company. Facebook rolled out Stories slowly; it first launched on a limited basis in 2017 and has expanded since then, eventually launching Stories Ads in 2018.[81]

At the same time, Zuckerberg is organizing the company to best achieve goals and prepare it for opportunities. For example, Zuckerberg has been organizing the company to stay at the forefront of artificial intelligence (AI) innovation by investing heavily in AI research and buying start-ups to consolidate a pool of top talent.[82] As he once said, "We buy companies to get excellent people."[83]

Of course, it's never enough for a manager to organize the efforts of good people; effective managers must lead them as well. Admitting to the mistakes he has made with regard to election meddling and privacy breaches is part of that leadership, but so is earning the trust and loyalty of employees. Despite criticism to do otherwise, Zuckerberg has stood by his COO Sheryl Sandberg, who oversaw

tremendous growth of Facebook since 2008. He's also been an advocate of giving employees the freedom to create. As he once said, "[employees] need the ability to fully exercise all their creativity and all their capacity, or else they're not going to be having the biggest impact that they can have on the world."[84] Such leadership breeds trust, which is what Zuckerberg needs to earn from his team to overcome recent problems.

Finally, Zuckerberg must control performance and implement change. For example, during the backlash about Facebook's role in the 2016 election, Zuckerberg changed the mission of the company: "Make the world more open and connected" became "Bring the world closer together." The investment in AI is one way of achieving this goal, as algorithms attempt to identify hate speech and fake news. Facebook also set up a "War Room" preceding the 2018 midterm elections to combat election meddling and has agreed to work with governments to come up with regulations to better ensure individual privacy.[85]

1. To what extent was Zuckerberg's decision to change Facebook's mission statement a good one?

2. Every facet of a manager's performance is under scrutiny. Based on what you've read and what you know of Facebook's challenges, which function of management do you think Zuckerberg is performing most effectively? Which do you think he's performing least effectively? Explain your answers.

future. As you proceed through this book and course, we encourage you not merely to read as if management were an impersonal course subject but to reflect on it from a personal perspective as well, integrating ideas for your own personal and professional development.

Performing All Four Management Functions

As a manager, your typical day will not be neatly divided into the four functions. You will be doing many things more or less simultaneously.[86] Your days will be busy and fractionated, spent dealing with interruptions, meetings, and firefighting. There will be plenty to do that you wish you could be doing but can't seem to get to. These activities will include all four management functions. Some managers are particularly skilled in one or two of the four functions but not in the others. But you should devote adequate attention and resources to *all four* functions. You can be a skilled planner and controller, but if you organize your people improperly or fail to inspire them to perform at high levels, you will not be realizing your potential as a manager. Likewise, it does no good to be the kind of manager who loves to organize and lead, but who doesn't really understand where to go or how to determine whether you are on the right track. Good managers practice all four management functions. Knowing what they are, you can periodically ask yourself (and your manager) whether you are devoting adequate attention to *all* of them.

Management Levels and Skills

LO 1-4 Compare how the nature of management varies at different organizational levels.

Organizations—particularly large organizations—have many levels. In this section, you learn about the types of managers found at three broad organizational levels: top level, middle level, and frontline.

Top-Level Managers

top-level managers

Senior executives responsible for the overall management and effectiveness of the organization.

Top-level managers are the senior executives of an organization and are responsible for its overall management. Top-level managers, often referred to as *strategic managers,* focus on long-term issues and emphasize the survival, growth, and overall effectiveness of the organization.

Top managers are concerned not only with the organization as a whole but also with the interaction between the organization and its external environment. This interaction often requires managers to work extensively with outside stakeholders and organizations.

The chief executive officer (CEO) is the top-level manager in most companies. This individual is the primary strategic manager of the firm and has authority over everyone within it. Others include the chief operating officer (COO), chief finance officer (CFO), chief information (or technology, or knowledge) officer, and other chiefs in the C-suite, including ethics, strategy (or corporate development), human resources, and marketing (or branding). Functional chiefs sometimes have the title of senior vice president (SVP).[87] A likely role for the modern C-suite could well be chief sustainability officer or even chief media officer.[88]

Traditionally, the role of top-level managers has been to set overall direction by formulating strategy and controlling resources. But now top managers are increasingly called upon to be not only strategic architects but also true organizational leaders. As leaders, they must create and articulate a broader corporate purpose with which people can identify—and one to which people will enthusiastically commit.

> Top managers are increasingly called upon to be not only strategic architects but also effective organizational leaders.

Middle-Level Managers

middle-level managers

Managers located in the middle layers of the organizational hierarchy, reporting to top-level executives.

Middle-level managers are located in the organizational hierarchy below top-level management and above frontline managers. They are responsible for translating the general goals and plans developed by strategic managers into more specific objectives and activities.

Middle-level managers break down company objectives into business unit targets; aggregate separate business unit plans for higher-level corporate; and serve as translators of internal communication, interpreting and relaying top management's priorities downward, and translating information from the front lines upward.

Not long ago the stereotype of the middle manager connoted mediocre, unimaginative bureaucrats who defended the status quo. But middle managers are closer than top managers to day-to-day operations, customers, frontline managers, suppliers, and employees—so they have a working knowledge of problems and opportunities.[89] They also have many creative ideas—often better than their bosses. Middle managers can play crucial roles in determining which entrepreneurial ideas are blocked and which are supported,[90] and how well they integrate with top management's strategic initiatives.[91] Good middle managers provide the operating skills and practical problem solving that keep the company working.[92]

Frontline Managers

frontline managers

Lower-level managers who supervise the operational activities of the organization.

Frontline managers, or *operational managers,* are lower-level managers who supervise the operations of the organization. These managers often have titles such as *supervisor, team leader,* or *assistant manager.* They are directly involved with nonmanagement employees, implementing the specific plans developed with middle managers. This organizational role is critical because operational managers are the link between management and nonmanagement human resources. Your first management position probably will fit into this category.

Traditionally, frontline managers have been directed and controlled from above to make sure that they successfully implement operations in support of company strategy. But in leading companies, their roles have expanded. Whereas the operational execution aspect of the role remains vital, in leading companies frontline managers are increasingly called on to be innovative and entrepreneurial, managing for growth and new business development.

Managers on the front line are crucial to creating and sustaining quality, innovation, and other drivers of financial performance.[93] In outstanding organizations, talented frontline managers are not only *allowed* to initiate new activities but are *expected* to by their top- and middle-level managers. And they are given freedom, incentives, and support to find ways to do so.[94] Frontline managers at ADP, a human resource solutions provider, help with major organizational change efforts by providing feedback to senior managers about the potential impact of the change and communicating why the change is needed to nonmanagement employees.[95]

Working Leaders with Broad Responsibilities

In small firms—and in those large companies that have adapted to the times—managers have strategic, tactical, *and* operational responsibilities. They are *complete* business people; they have knowledge of all business functions, are accountable for results, and focus on serving customers both inside and outside their firms. This requires the ability to think strategically, translate strategies into specific objectives, coordinate resources, and do real work with all types of stakeholders.

In short, today's best managers are adept at drawing from a variety of skills, behaviors, and knowledge to be successful.[96] They focus on relationships with other people and on achieving results. They don't just make decisions, give orders, wait for others to produce, and then evaluate results. They get their hands dirty, work hard, solve problems, and produce value.

What does all of this mean in practice? How do managers spend their time—what do they actually do? A classic study of top executives found that they spend their time engaging in 10 key activities or roles, falling into three categories: interpersonal, informational, and decisional.[97] Exhibit 1.2 summarizes these roles. Even though the study was done decades

Decisional Roles	Informational Roles	Interpersonal Roles
Entrepreneur: Searching for new business opportunities and initiating new projects to create change.	*Monitor:* Seeking information to understand the organization and its environment; serving as the center of communication.	*Leader:* Staffing, developing, and motivating people.
Disturbance handler: Taking corrective action during crises and other conflicts.	*Disseminator:* Transmitting information from source to source, sometimes interpreting and integrating diverse perspectives.	*Liaison:* Maintaining a network of outside contacts that provide information and favors.
Resource allocator: Providing funding and other resources to units or people; includes making significant organizational decisions.	*Spokesperson:* Speaking on behalf of the organization about plans, policies, actions, and results.	*Figurehead:* Performing symbolic duties (for example, ceremonies) and serving other social and legal demands.
Negotiator: Engaging in negotiations with parties outside the organization as well as inside (for example, resource exchanges).	n/a	n/a

EXHIBIT 1.2
Managerial Roles: What Managers Do

SOURCE: Adapted from Mintzberg, H., *The Nature of Managerial Work.* New York: Harper & Row, 1973, pp. 92–93.

ago, it remains highly relevant as a description of what executives do. And even though the study focused on top executives, managers at all levels engage in all these activities. As you review the table, you might ask yourself, "Which of these activities do I enjoy most? Where do I excel? Which would I like to improve?" Whatever your answers, you will be learning more about these activities throughout this course.

Must-Have Management Skills

LO 1-5 Define the skills you need to be an effective manager.

Performing management functions and roles, and achieving competitive advantage, are the cornerstones of a manager's job. However, understanding this does not ensure success. Managers need a variety of skills to do these things well. Skills are specific abilities that result from knowledge, information, practice, and aptitude. Although managers need many individual skills, which you will learn about throughout this textbook, there are three broad, essential categories: technical skills, conceptual and decision skills, and interpersonal and communication skills.[98]

Newly promoted supervisors and managers can underestimate the challenges of management and the many skills required.[99] But when managers apply these three critical management skills to the four management functions, the result is high performance.

technical skill

The ability to perform a specialized task involving a particular method or process.

Technical   A **technical skill** is the ability to perform a specialized task that involves a certain method or process. The technical skills you learn in school will provide you with the opportunity to get an entry-level position; they will also help you as a manager. For example, your accounting and finance courses will develop the technical skills you need to understand and manage the financial resources of an organization.

conceptual and decision skills

Skills pertaining to abilities that help to identify and resolve problems for the benefit of the organization and its members.

Conceptual and Decision   **Conceptual and decision skills** involve the ability to identify and resolve problems for the benefit of the organization and everyone concerned. Managers use these skills when they consider the organization's overall strategy, the interactions among its different parts, and the role of the business in its external environment. As you acquire greater responsibility, you will use your conceptual and decision skills with increasing frequency. Much of this book is devoted to enhancing your conceptual and decision skills, but experience also plays an important part in their development.

interpersonal and communication skills

People skills; the ability to lead, motivate, and communicate effectively with others.

Interpersonal and Communication   **Interpersonal and communication skills** influence the managers ability to work well with people. These skills are often called *people skills.* Managers spend the great majority of their time interacting with people,[100] and they must develop their abilities to lead, motivate, and communicate effectively with those around them.

The importance of these skills varies by managerial level. Technical skills are most important early in your career. Conceptual and decision skills become more important than technical skills as you rise higher in the company. But interpersonal skills such as communicating effectively with customers and being a good team player are important throughout your career, at every level of management.

An example of a manager with these skills is Mark Bertolini, former chief executive and chair of Aetna, which provides health insurance and related services. As a young employee doing assembly work for Ford Motor Company, Bertolini became interested in union management, so he decided to study business and earned a degree in accounting and then a master's degree in finance. Those two specialties involve valuable technical skills, but Bertolini rose through the management ranks at a series of insurance companies because he also has a passion for people. He was constantly engaged in learning about people and forging networks with them. He saw tapping into networks and learning about how to lead people as the key skills that allow managers to get results. At Aetna, Bertolini was not only an expert at insurance matters, but also a promoter of employee health, yoga, and meditation. Furthermore, challenges in his personal life—he survived a spinal cord injury and donated a kidney to his son—helped him to empathize with others, including clients.[101]

You and Your Career

At the beginning of your career, your contribution to your employer depends on your own performance; often that's all you're responsible for. But on becoming a manager, you are responsible for a group. To use an orchestra analogy, instead of playing an instrument, you're a conductor, coordinating others' efforts.[102] The challenge is much greater than most first-time managers expect it to be.

LO 1-6 Understand the principles that will help you manage your career.

Throughout your career, you'll need to lead teams effectively as well as influence people over whom you have no authority; thus the human skills are especially important. Business people often talk about **emotional intelligence**,[103] or EQ—the skills of understanding yourself (including strengths and limitations), managing yourself (dealing with emotions, making good decisions, seeking and using feedback, exercising self-control), and dealing effectively with others (listening, showing empathy, motivating, leading, and so on).

Bakhtiar Zein/123RF

Executives who score low on EQ are less likely to be rated as excellent on their performance reviews, and their divisions tend not to perform as well.[104] But please take note: The common phrase "emotional intelligence" is controversial.[105] You should *not* consider EQ to be a type of intelligence but as a set of skills that you can learn and develop. The issue is not lack of ability to change (you can), but the lack of motivation to learn and apply such skills.[106]

A common complaint about leaders, especially newly promoted ones who had been outstanding individual performers, is that they lack what is perhaps the most fundamental of EQ skills: empathy with other people. Chris Myers, co-founder and CEO of BodeTree, sees EQ as one of the most important characteristics of successful business leaders because they need to be able to connect, understand, and inspire their employees.[107]

emotional intelligence

Skills of understanding yourself, managing yourself, and dealing effectively with others.

What should you do to forge a successful, gratifying career? You may want to consider being both a specialist and a generalist, to be self-reliant and connected, to actively manage your relationship within your organization, to keep current with technology trends that could help you improve your performance, and to know what is required not only to survive but also to thrive in today's world.

Be Both a Specialist and a Generalist

If you think your career will be as a specialist, think again. Chances are, you will not want to stay forever in strictly technical jobs with no managerial responsibilities. Accountants are promoted to team leaders and accounting department heads, sales representatives become sales managers, writers become editors, and nurses become nursing directors. As your responsibilities increase, you must deal with more people, understand more about other aspects of the organization, and make bigger and more complex decisions. Beginning to learn now about these managerial challenges will yield benefits sooner than you think.

So, it will help if you can become both a specialist and a generalist.[108] Seek to become a *specialist:* You should be an expert in something useful. This will give you specific skills that help you provide concrete, identifiable value to your organization and to customers. And over time, you should learn to be a *generalist,* knowing enough about a variety of subject matters so that you can think strategically and work with different perspectives. Exhibit 1.3 gives you more career advice from experts.

Putting this another way, exploit (use, apply, take advantage of) what you know, and explore (search) for new experiences, ideas, knowledge, and perspectives. To both exploit and explore is to be ambidextrous;[109] organizations should do this, and so should we all.[110]

Career Advice from the Experts

Escape the industry-specific silo.	*Develop a skill set that transcends a single function, industry, or career path.*
Know what you know.	*And find ways to apply it.*
Be a lifelong learner.	*No one can rest on what they already know.*
Manage your online presence.	*Expand your network, and post about your industry and functional expertise.*
Never compromise your integrity.	*Do the right thing and remember that perception and reality matter.*
Take a long view.	*Look at your career as a journey, and stay true to yourself.*
Prevent obsolescence.	*Job security comes from current and transportable skills.*
Zig-zag strategically.	*Job changing can be high-risk but not if you have measurable accomplishments.*
Be willing to take on tough projects.	*Continually challenge yourself.*

SOURCES: "Need a New Year's Resolution? 10 Ideas for a Stronger Career in 2017," *American Recruiters*, January 2, 2017, www.americanrecruiters.com; Kennedy, Joyce Lain, "Best Career Advice for 2013," *Chicago Tribune*, December 23, 2012, http://www.chicagotribune.com; Sanders, Lorraine, "Hilary Novelle Hahn's Zig-Zag Career Guide," *Fast Company*, November 13, 2012, http://www.fastcompany.com; Kadlec, Dan, "Graduation Day Advice: 5 Steps to a Great Career," *Time*, May 9, 2012, http://business.time.com.

Be Self-Reliant

To be self-reliant means to take full responsibility for yourself and your actions.[111] You cannot count on your manager or your company to take care of you. A useful metaphor is to think of yourself as a business, with you as president and sole employee.

To be self-reliant, find new ways to make your overall performance better. Take responsibility for change; be an innovator.[112] Don't just do your work and wait for new projects; look for opportunities to contribute in new ways, to develop new products and processes, and to generate constructive change that strengthens the company and benefits customers and colleagues.

Success requires more than talent; you also have to be willing to work hard. The elite, world-class performers in many fields (including managers and leaders) reach the top tier only after 10 years or more of hard work and skillful coaching.[113] The key is to engage in consistent practice, looking at the results and identifying where to improve.

It's easy to see how this works for violinists or football players, but what about business managers? The answer is to focus on getting better results each time you try any business task, whether it's writing a report, making a presentation, or interpreting a financial statement. To know whether you're getting better, make a point of asking for feedback from customers, colleagues, managers, and mentors.

> Don't just do your work and wait for new projects; look for opportunities to contribute in new ways.

To develop your full potential, assess yourself, including your interests, aptitudes, and personal character strengths. Reflect on it, ask others who know you well, conduct a formal exercise in which you learn what others consider to be your "best self,"[114] and use advances in psychology to identify your signature strengths such as Gallup's CliftonStrengths assessment.[115] Consider the professional image and reputation you would like to develop,[116] and continue building your capabilities. Consider the suggestions found throughout this book, and your other coursework, as you pursue these objectives.

Connect with People

Being connected means having many good working relationships and interpersonal contacts. For example, those who want to become partners in professional service organizations, such as social media marketing, accounting, advertising, and consulting firms, strive constantly to build a network of contacts. Their connectedness goal is to work not only with multiple clients but also with a half dozen or more senior partners, including several from outside their home offices and some from outside their country. Social relationships improve newcomers' knowledge of the organization and their jobs, their social integration into the firm, and their commitment to the organization.[117] Networks of diverse individuals can make huge contributions to your professional development no matter what your career—even if you hope to be inducted into the Major League Baseball Hall of Fame on the first ballot.[118]

Social capital is the goodwill stemming from your social relationships, and you can mobilize it on your behalf. It aids career success, compensation, employment, team effectiveness, the success of new ventures, entrepreneurship, and relationships with suppliers and other outsiders.[119] Today much of that social capital can be tapped online at social networking websites. Besides the social sites such as Instagram, some of these sites are aimed at helping people tap business networks. For example, LinkedIn has more than 590 million registered members worldwide, with total revenue from premium subscriptions, marketing, and talent solutions of $5.3 billion.[120]

All business is a function of human relationships.[121] Building competitive advantage depends not only on you but on other people. Management is personal. Commercial dealings are personal. Purchase decisions, repurchase decisions, and contracts all hinge on relationships. Even the biggest business deals—takeovers—are intensely personal and emotional. Without healthy and productive work relationships, you will not achieve your potential as a manager and leader.

Actively Manage Your Relationship with Your Organization

We have noted the importance of taking responsibility for your own actions and your own career. Unless you are self-employed and your own boss, one way to do this is to think about the nature of the relationship between you and your employer. Exhibit 1.4 shows two possible relationships—and you have some control over which relationship develops.

Relationship #1 is one in which you view yourself as an employee and passively expect your employer to tell you what to do and give you pay and benefits. Your employer is in charge, and you are a passive recipient of its actions. Your contributions are likely to be adequate but minimal—you won't make contributions that strengthen your organization, and if all organizational members take this perspective, the organization is not likely to prosper in the long run. Personally, you may lose your job or keep your job in a declining organization, or unengaged in your work.

In contrast, relationship #2 is a two-way relationship in which you and your organization both benefit from one another. The mind-set is different: Instead of doing what you are told, you think about how you can contribute and add value—and you act accordingly. To the extent that your organization values your contributions, you are likely to benefit in return by receiving full rewards, support for further personal development, and a more gratifying job and work environment. If you think in broad terms about how you can help your company, and if others think like this as well, there is likely to be continuous improvement in the company's ability to innovate, cut costs, and deliver quality products quickly to an expanding

social capital

Goodwill stemming from your social relationships; a competitive advantage in the form of relationships with other people and the image other people have of you.

Bottom Line

To encourage visitors to your LinkedIn profile to think of you as a future manager, be sure to include skills and experiences that suggest you have good interpersonal and team leadership skills.

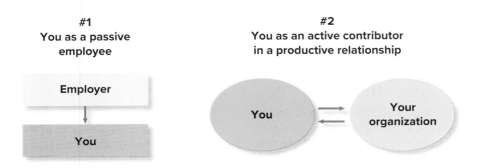

#1
You as a passive employee

Employer

You

#2
You as an active contributor in a productive relationship

You

Your organization

EXHIBIT 1.4
Two Relationships: Which Will You Choose?

Management in Action

WORKING FOR FACEBOOK'S MARK ZUCKERBERG

Despite the troubles Facebook has encountered recently, it still rates as one of the best places to work in the United States. And for all the criticism Mark Zuckerberg has received for his management of the company, he still received a 96 percent approval rating from his employees in 2018.[122] Will the managerial decisions he makes moving forward be enough to overcome the political and market challenges confronting Facebook? Only time will tell. But it's clear that Zuckerberg has been able to create an organization that people still believe in, and that's due in part to his ability to implement skills essential to managers and employees alike.

Clearly his technical, communication, and interpersonal skills have earned him the trust and respect of those who work for him. Matt Cohler, an early employee and now a venture capitalist, describes Zuckerberg as "a learn-it-all person. . . . He maintains a relentless focus on innovation, but at the same time he's an applied-science and engineering guy."[123] And he possesses the ability to conceptualize a vision of the future that people are eager to follow. Mike Vernal, a former engineering employee, says of Zuckerberg, "Most people think day

to day or week to week. Mark thinks century to century." Zuckerberg, for example, feels that AI can be used as a positive force in society: "In the next five to 10 years, AI is going to deliver so many improvements in the quality of our lives."[124] You will be learning more about AI in future chapters.[125]

Despite accusations that Zuckerberg is driven by profit at the expense of his users' privacy, the optimism he is known for by many of his employees has carried over into his personal life. He and Priscilla Chan, his wife, founded the ChanZuckerberg Initiative in 2015. One of its initiatives is to cure, prevent, or manage all disease in our children's lifetime, for which Zuckerberg donated $5.3 billion in 2018.[126] However, May 2019 brought this *Washington Post* opinion piece: "Mark Zuckerberg claims that, at Facebook, 'The Future Is Private'. Don't Believe Him." So, the challenges continue . . .[127]

1. Based on what you know about Zuckerberg, what's your assessment of his overall management style?
2. Based on what you know about Zuckerberg, would you be inclined to work for him? Why or why not?

customer base. As the company's bottom line strengthens, benefits accrue to many stakeholders as well as to you and other employees.

What contributions can you make? You can do your basic work. But you can, and should, go further. You can figure out new ways to add value—by thinking of and implementing new ideas that improve processes and results. You can do this by using your technical knowledge and skills, as in developing a better information system, accounting technique, or sales strategy.

You also can contribute with your conceptual and human skills and your managerial actions (see Exhibit 1.5). You can execute the essential management functions and deliver competitive advantage. You can deliver strategic value (Part 2 of this book). You can take actions that help build a more dynamic organization (Part 3). You can mobilize people to contribute to their fullest potential (Part 4). And you can learn and change—and help your colleagues and company learn and change—to adapt to changing realities and forge a successful future (Part 5).

Survive and Thrive

You will be accountable for your actions and for results. In the past, people at many companies could show up, do an OK job, get a decent evaluation, and get a raise equal to the cost of living and maybe higher. Today, managers must do a lot more, better. Management

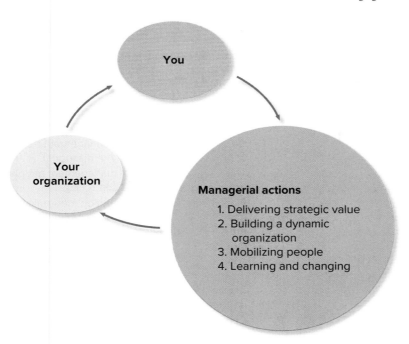

You

Your organization

Managerial actions
1. Delivering strategic value
2. Building a dynamic organization
3. Mobilizing people
4. Learning and changing

EXHIBIT 1.5
Managerial Action Is Your Opportunity to Contribute

scholar Peter Drucker, in considering what makes managers effective, noted that some are charismatic whereas some are not, and some are visionary whereas others are more numbers-oriented.[128] But successful executives do share some common practices:

- They convey to others "Why we do what we do."
- They ask "What needs to be done?" not just "What do I want to do?"
- They write an action plan. They don't just think, they do, based on a sound, ethical plan.
- They take responsibility for decisions. This requires checking up, revisiting, and changing if necessary.
- They focus on opportunities, not just problems. Problems have to be solved, and problem solving prevents more damage. But capturing opportunities is what creates great results.

Career success is most likely if you are flexible, creative, and motivated. You need to learn how to think strategically, make decisions, and work in teams. You will learn more about these and other topics, essential to your successful career, in the upcoming chapters.

KEY TERMS

conceptual and decision skills, p. 18

controlling, p. 14

coopetition, p. 8

cost competitiveness, p. 11

emotional intelligence, p. 19

frontline managers, p. 16

innovation, p. 8

interpersonal and communication skills, p. 18

knowledge management, p. 7

leading, p. 14

management, p. 12

middle-level managers, p. 16

organizing, p. 13

planning, p. 12

quality, p. 9

service, p. 10

social capital, p. 21

speed, p. 10

sustainability, p. 11

technical skill, p. 18

top-level managers, p. 16

value, p. 13

RETAINING WHAT YOU LEARNED

You learned that change is the only constant for managers in today's business world. You also learned that high-performance managers seek to deliver superior value to customers by providing high-quality, innovative services or products in a timely, cost-effective, and sustainable manner.

The fundamental functions and activities of management are just as important as they were "back in the day." However, their forms have evolved greatly and their strategies and tactics continue to change. Depending on your organizational level, you'll be expected to engage in certain roles and master a variety of managerial skills. Your career, and your professional and personal development along the way, are in your hands.

LO 1-1   Summarize the major challenges of managing in the new competitive landscape.

- In business, there is no alternative to managing well. The best managers succeed by focusing on the fundamentals and knowing what's important.
- The goal of this book is to help you become an effective, high-performance manager.
- Managers today must deal with dynamic forces that create greater change than ever before, including globalization, technological change (including the continuing development and new applications of the Internet), knowledge management, and collaboration across organizational boundaries.

LO 1-2   Describe the sources of competitive advantage for a company.

- Because business is a competitive arena, you need to deliver value to customers in ways that are superior to what your competitors provide.

- Competitive advantages result from innovation, quality, service, speed, cost competitiveness, and sustainability.

LO 1-3   Explain how the functions of management are evolving in today's business environment.

- Despite massive change, management retains certain functions that will not disappear.
- The primary functions of management are planning, organizing, leading, and controlling.
- Planning is analyzing a situation, determining the goals that will be pursued, and deciding in advance the actions needed to pursue these goals.
- Organizing is assembling the resources needed to complete the job and coordinating employees and tasks for maximum success.
- Leading is motivating people and stimulating high performance.
- Controlling is monitoring the progress of the organization or the work unit toward goals and then taking corrective action as needed.
- In the modern business environment, these functions require creating strategic value, building a dynamic organization, mobilizing people, and learning and changing.

LO 1-4   Compare how the nature of management varies at different organizational levels.

- Top-level, strategic managers are the senior executives responsible for the organization's overall management.
- Middle-level, tactical managers translate general goals and plans into more specific objectives and activities.

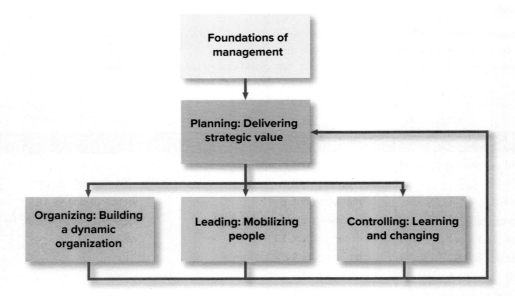

The Management Process

- Frontline, operational managers are lower-level managers who supervise operations.
- Managers at all levels must perform a variety of interpersonal, informational, and decision roles.
- Even at the operational level, the best managers think strategically and operate like complete business people.

LO 1-5   Define the skills you need to be an effective manager.

- To execute management functions successfully, managers need technical skills, conceptual and decision skills, and interpersonal and communication skills.
- A technical skill is the ability to perform a specialized task involving certain methods or processes.
- Conceptual and decision skills help the manager recognize complex and dynamic issues, analyze the factors that influence those issues or problems, and make appropriate decisions.

- Interpersonal and communication skills enable the manager to interact and work well with people.
- As you rise to higher organizational levels, technical skills tend to become less important and conceptual skills become more important, whereas interpersonal and communication skills remain extremely important at every level.

LO 1-6   Understand the principles that will help you manage your career.

- You are more likely to succeed in your career if you become both a specialist and a generalist. You should be self-reliant but also connected.
- You should actively manage your relationship with your organization and continuously improve your skills so you can perform as needed in the changing work environment.

DISCUSSION QUESTIONS

1. Identify and describe a great manager. What makes him or her stand out from average managers?
2. Have you ever seen or worked for an ineffective manager? Describe the behaviors that contributed to the manager's ineffectiveness.
3. Describe in as much detail as possible how the Internet and globalization affect your daily life.
4. Identify some examples of how different organizations collaborate across boundaries.
5. Name a great organization. How do you think management contributes to making it great?
6. Name an ineffective organization. What can management do to improve it?
7. Give examples you have seen of firms that are outstanding and weak on each of the six pillars of competitive advantage. Why do you choose the firms you do?

8. Describe your use of the four management functions in the management of your daily life.
9. Discuss the importance of technical, conceptual, and interpersonal skills at school and in jobs you have held.
10. What are your strengths and weaknesses as you contemplate your career? How do they relate with the skills and behaviors identified in the chapter?
11. Devise a plan for developing yourself and making yourself attractive to potential employers. How would you go about improving your managerial skills?
12. Consider the managers and companies discussed in the chapter. Have they been in the news lately, and what is the latest? If their image, performance, or fortunes have gone up or down, what has changed to affect how they have fared?

EXPERIENTIAL EXERCISES

1.1   Your Personal Network

1. See the nearby figure showing primary and secondary connections. Working on your own, write down all of your primary contacts—individuals you know personally who can support you in attaining your professional goals. Then begin to explore their secondary connections. Make assumptions about possible secondary connections that can be made for you by contacting your primary connections. For example, through one of your teachers (primary), you might be able to obtain some names of potential employers (secondary). (10–15 min.)

2. Then meet with your partner or small group to exchange information about your primary and secondary networks and to exchange advice and information on how best to use these connections as well as how you could be helpful to them. (about 5 min. per person; 10–30 min. total, depending on group size)

3. Add names or types of names to your list based on ideas you get by talking with others in your group. (2–5 min.)

4. Discuss with your large group or class, using the following discussion questions. (10 min.)

QUESTIONS

1. What were some of the best primary sources identified by your group?

2. What were some of the best sources for secondary contacts identified by your group?

3. What are some suggestions for approaching primary contacts?

4. What are some suggestions for approaching secondary contacts, and how is contacting secondary sources different from contacting primary contacts?

5. What did you learn about yourself and others from this exercise?

SOURCE: de Janasz, Suzanne C., Dowd, Karen O. and Schneider, Beth Z., *Interpersonal Skills in Organizations.* New York: McGraw-Hill, 2002, p. 211.

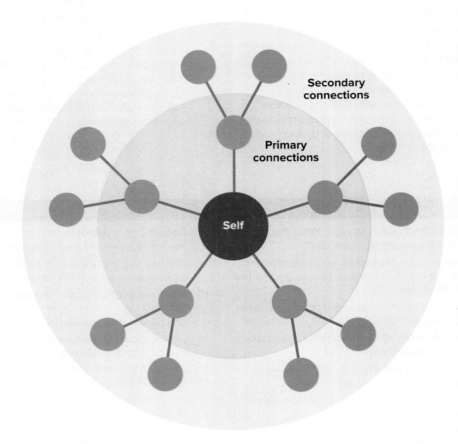

Primary and Secondary Connections

SOURCE: Excerpted from Jauch, Lawrence R., Bedeian, Arthur G., Coltrin, Sally A. and Glueck, William F., *The Managerial Experience: Cases, Exercises, and Readings,* 5th ed. Chicago: South-Western, 1989.

1.2   Are You An Effective Manager?

OBJECTIVES

1. To recognize what behaviors contribute to being a successful manager.

2. To develop a ranking of critical behaviors that you personally believe are important for becoming an effective manager.

INSTRUCTIONS

1. Following is a partial list of behaviors in which managers may engage. Rank these items in terms of their importance for effective performance as a manager. Put a 1 next to the item that you think is most important, 2 for the next most important, down to 10 for the least important.

2. Bring your rankings to class. Be prepared to justify your results and rationale. If you can add any behaviors to this list that might lead to success or greater management effectiveness, write them in.

Managerial Behaviors Worksheet

_____ Collaborates with people from different parts of the organization.

_____ Looks for ways to incorporate technology into the operation.

_____ Ensures that services/products are of a high quality and delivered on time.

_____ Keeps costs down and looks for ways to be more efficient.

_____ Makes decisions to help achieve the goals of the organization.

_____ Is organized and effectively allocates resources.

_____ Motivates others to perform at a high level.

_____ Makes sure goals are met and implements changes when necessary.

_____ Exhibits good interpersonal and communication skills.

_____ Is skilled at identifying and resolving problems.

SOURCE: Adapted from Jauch, Lawrence R., Bedeian, Arthur G., Coltrin, Sally A. and Glueck, William F., *The Managerial Experience: Cases, Exercises, and Readings,* 5th ed. Chicago: South-Western, 1989.

1.3   Career Skills Development

OBJECTIVES

1. To develop an understanding of your career-related strengths.
2. To identify career-related skills and behaviors requiring development.
3. To increase confidence in your marketability.

INSTRUCTIONS

Read the instructions for each activity, think about them, and then provide your response.

Career Development Worksheet

Think about a part- or full-time job, or a volunteer role that you've held.

1. Describe <u>activities</u> and <u>skills</u> at which you excelled and which helped you succeed:
   a. _____
   b. _____
   c. _____

   d. _____
   e. _____

2. Identify <u>activities</u> and <u>skills</u> that you wanted to master but were unable to do so due to lack of training or time:
   a. _____
   b. _____
   c. _____
   d. _____
   e. _____

3. Referring to #2, identify steps you could take now to develop these important <u>activities</u> and <u>skills:</u>
   a. _____
   b. _____
   c. _____
   d. _____
   e. _____

SOURCE: Adapted from Gordon, Judith R., *Diagnostic Approach to Organizational Behavior.* Upper Saddle River, NJ: Pearson Education, 1983.

Concluding Case

A NEW MANAGER AT USA HOSPITAL SUPPLY

As Matt Greer drove to work, he smiled, recalling the meeting at the end of the previous day. Inez Rodriguez, the founder and owner of the company where he worked, USA Hospital Supply, had summoned him to her office where she shook his hand and exclaimed, "Congratulations!"

As they settled into chairs, Inez reviewed the conversation she'd had with the company's board of directors that morning: USA Hospital had been growing steadily for the past 10 years despite the economy's ups and downs. Although Inez had always been an insightful and enthusiastic leader of her five-person sales team, the increased sales activity was becoming too difficult to manage along with her other obligations. She needed a leader who could focus exclusively on sales.

She had interviewed several candidates outside the firm as well as members of her current sales team, which included Matt and two other reps. In the end, Inez told Matt, the choice was obvious: He was far and away the best sales rep on the team, he had extensive knowledge of the company's product mix, and if anyone could help the sales team achieve its goals, it was Matt. She offered him the job as the company's first sales manager. He eagerly accepted. When he left work that evening, he was bursting with ideas, full of confidence.

Now Matt pulled into the office park where USA Hospital was located and found a parking space in the lot outside the one-story office and warehouse facility. As usual, he was one of the first employees to arrive. By habit, he strode toward his cubicle, but after a second, he recalled that Inez had arranged for the small firm's accountant and computer systems manager to share an office so Matt could have an office of his own. He entered his new space and settled into the chair behind his desk.

At that instant, his confidence began to give way to nervousness. Matt realized that although he knew a lot about selling supplies to hospitals and doctor's offices, he had never given much thought to managing. Obviously, he mused, his job was to see that his department met or exceeded its sales targets. But how?

Matt needed to write down some ideas. He typed out a list of the four sales reps: Usha, Kyle, Tyreke, and Emma. Emma handled the large corporate accounts, Usha covered the East Coast, Tyreke called on accounts in the South, and Kyle handled the Midwest. Until today, Matt had been building a fast-growing territory west of the Mississippi. Now who was going to do that? Matt was tempted to keep that work for himself; he knew he could build a base of loyal clients better than anyone. Still, he wondered whether he could excel as a manager and as a sales rep at the same time.

While he was pondering that challenge, Emma walked past the door and, without stopping, politely called, "Congratulations!" through the doorway. Matt's heart sank as he realized that Emma had also wanted this job. They had always enjoyed a friendly rivalry as talented salespeople; now what would happen to their relationship? Matt glanced at his inbox and saw status reports from Tyreke and Kyle, both of whom were out with clients. What about Usha? Matt wasn't sure he remembered her plans for this week.

Obviously, he needed to catch up on what everyone was doing, and that gave him a new idea. He could build on his strengths by traveling with each of the sales reps and coaching them. That way, he could show them all his proven methods for closing a sale, and they could learn to sell as well as he did. Matt thought, "That's what a good manager does: Shows employees how to do the job right." He was starting to feel less nervous as he began to write an email to his team.

DISCUSSION QUESTIONS

1. How will Matt's approach to quality and service affect his company's performance?

2. Which of the basic functions of management has Matt considered? How well is he preparing to carry out these functions?

3. Which management skills does Matt have? In what areas do you think he has the greatest need to develop skills? How can he actively manage his development as a manager?

ENDNOTES

1. Macrotrends, https://www.macrotrends.net/stocks/charts/FB/facebook/revenue.
2. Tony Romm, "Facebook's Zuckerberg Just Survived 10 Hours of Questioning by Congress," *The Washington Post,* April 11, 2018, https://www.washingtonpost.com/news/the-switch/wp/2018/04/11/zuckerberg-facebook-hearing-congress-house-testimony/?utm_term=.40390de10e1d.
3. Tony Romm, "Facebook's Zuckerberg Just Survived 10 Hours of Questioning by Congress," *The Washington Post,* April 11, 2018, https://www.washingtonpost.com/news/the-switch/wp/2018/04/11/zuckerberg-facebook-hearing-congress-house-testimony/?utm_term=.40390de10e1d.
4. Tedra DeSue, "Zuckerberg Is Finally Discovering Privacy but Advertisers Are Quitting Facebook," *CCN.com,* March 11, 2019, https://www.ccn.com/zuckerberg-facebook-privacy-advertisers-quit.
5. J. McGregor, "Why Mark Zuckerberg's New Year's Challenge to Himself Just Might Work," *The Washington Post,* January 4, 2016, www.washingtonpost.com.
6. M. Isaac, "Uber Founder Travis Kalanik Resigns as C.E.O.," *The New York Times,* June 21, 2017, www.nytimes.com.
7. T. Taulli, "Uber IPO: What Can We Expect?" *Forbes,* December 29, 2018, www.forbes.com; E. Newcomer and B. Stone, "The Fall of Travis Kalanick Was a Lot Weirder and Darker Than You Thought," *Bloomberg Businessweek,* January 18, 2018, www.bloomberg.com.
8. "Uber Lost $4.5 Billion in 2017, but Its Revenue Jumped," *Los Angeles Times,* February 14, 2018, www.latimes.com.
9. E. Newcomer, "Uber Revenue Slows as Quarterly Loss Surges to $1.1 Billion," *Bloomberg,* November 14, 2018, www.bloomberg.com; L. Feiner, "These Are the Tech Start-ups Worth Billions That Are Expected to Go Public Next Year," *CNBC,* October 18, 2018, www.cnbc.com.
10. "Top 8 Business Stories of 2018," CNN Business Video, https://www.cnn.com/videos/business/2018/12/21/top-business-stories-2018.cnn-business, accessed February 4, 2019.
11. C. Isidore, "2018 Was the Worst for Stocks in 10 Years," *CNN Business,* December 31, 2018, www.cnn.com.
12. "3 Reasons U.S. Companies Succeed on the Global Market," *Inc. Europe,* November 20, 2017, www.inc.com; S. Green, F. Hassan, J. Immelt, M. Marks, and D. Meiland, "In Search of Global Leaders," *Harvard Business Review,* August 2003, pp. 38–45.
13. "World's Most Admired Companies," *Fortune,* http://fortune.com/worlds-most-admired-companies, accessed December 12, 2018.
14. "Global 500," *Fortune,* http://fortune.com/global500, accessed December 12, 2018.
15. IBM's 2017 Annual Report, https://www.ibm.com/annualreport/2017/assets/downloads/IBM_Annual_Report_2017.pdf, accessed December 15, 2018.
16. V. Goel, "IBM Now Has More Employees in India Than in the U.S.," *The New York Times,* September 28, 2017, https://www.nytimes.com.
17. See company website, http://www.yum.com/company/, accessed December 15, 2018.
18. D. Kline, "PepsiCo Continues Its Push into Healthy Snacks," *The Motley Fool,* June 1, 2018, www.fool.com; J. Creswell, "Pepsi Dips Its Toes into the Sparking Water Market," *The New York Times,* February 8, 2018, www.nytimes.com.
19. See program website, https://kelley.iu.edu/faculty-research/centers-institutes/international-business/programs-initiatives/global-business-institute.cshtml, accessed December 12, 2018.
20. D. Weldon, "Top Analytics and Business Intelligence Trends for 2019," *Information Management,* December 4, 2018, www.information-management.com.
21. D. Hinchcliffe, "How Can Businesses Keep Up with Tech Change Today?" *ZDNet,* May 31, 2016, www.zdnet.com.
22. A. Scroxton, "Deloitte Predicts Major Advances in Mobile Technology in 2017," *Computer Weekly,* January 11, 2017, www.computerweekly.com.
23. A. Meola, "The Critical Role of Infrastructure in the Internet of Things," *Business Insider,* December 21, 2016, www.businessinsider.com; "Industry 4.0: Top 10 Critical Trends for 2017," *Information Age,* December 28, 2016, www.information-age.com.
24. X. Lao, J. Zhang, and C. Marquis, "Mobilization in the Internet Age: Internet Activism and Corporate Response," *Academy of Management Journal* 59 (2016), pp. 2045–68.

25. X. R. Luo, J. Zhang, and C. Marquis, "Mobilization in the Internet Age: Internet Activism and Corporate Response," *Academy of Management Journal* 59 (2016), pp. 2045–68.

26. "The Party's Over," *Fortune,* June 1, 2010, http://tech.fortune.cnn.com.

27. "Web 1.0 vs. Web 2.0 vs. Web 3.0 vs. Web 4.0 vs. Web 5.0; A Bird's Eye on the Evolution and Definition," *Flatworld,* www.business.com, accessed January 17, 2015.

28. A. Greenfield, "Rise of the Machines: Who Is the 'Internet of Things' Good For?" *The Guardian,* June 6, 2017, https://www.theguardian.com.

29. "Tech Vision 2017: Technology for People, The Era of the Intelligent Enterprise," *Accenture,* www.accenture.com, accessed February 26, 2017.

30. J. Atchinson, "5 Artificial Intelligence Trends to Watch in 2019," *Inc.,* November 28, 2018, www.inc.com.

31. C. Heine, "Here's What You Need to Know about Voice AI, the Next Frontier of Brand Marketing," *Advertising Week,* August 6, 2017, www.adweek.com.

32. A. Villas-Boas, "14 Ways You Can Control Your Home with Your Voice Using Amazon's Echo and Alexa," *Business Insider,* January 10, 2017, www.businessinsider.com.

33. Juniper Research, "Chatbot Conversations to Deliver $8 Billion in Cost Savings by 2022," July 24, 2017, https://www.juniperresearch.com/analystxpress/july-2017/chatbot-conversations-to-deliver-8bn-cost-saving.

34. Amtrak.com, "Meet Julie: Your Virtual Assistant," https://www.amtrak.com/about-julie-amtrak-virtual-travel-assistant, accessed March 20, 2019.

35. Mya, https://mya.com, accessed March 20, 2019.

36. Kieran Alger, "To Bot or Not? The Rise of AI Chatbots in Business," December 11, 2018, https://www.forbes.com/sites/delltechnologies/2018/12/13/to-bot-or-not-the-rise-of-ai-chatbots-in-business/#1c8442b1375d.

37. Robert Austin, "Managing Knowledge Workers," *Science,* July 21, 2006, accessed at ScienceCareers.org, http://sciencecareers.sciencemag.org.

38. D. McIver, C. Lengnick-Hall, and M. Lengnick-Hall, "Understanding Work and Knowledge Management from a Knowledge-in-Practice Perspective," *Academy of Management Review* 38 (2013), pp. 597–620; K. Dekas, T. Bauer, and B. Well, et al., "Organizational Citizenship Behavior, Version 2.0: A Review and Qualitative Investigation of OCBs for Knowledge Workers at Google and Beyond," *Academy of Management Perspectives* 27 (2013), pp. 219–37.

39. I. Wladawasky-Berger, "The Rise of the T-Shaped Organization," *The Wall Street Journal,* December 18, 2015, www.wsj.com; Morten T. Hansen and Bolko von Oetinger, "Introducing T-Shaped Managers: Knowledge Management's Next Generation," *Harvard Business Review,* March 2001, www.hbr.org.

40. R. Fry, "Millennials Overtake Baby Boomers as America's Largest Generation," Pew Research Center, April 25, 2016, www.pewresearch.org.

41. R. Fry, "Millennials Overtake Baby Boomers as America's Largest Generation," Pew Research Center, April 25, 2016, www.pewresearch.org.

42. M. Dimock, "Defining Generations: Where Millennials End and Generation Z Begins," Pew Research Center, March 17, 2019, http://www.pewresearch.org/fact-tank/2019/01/17/where-millennials-end-and-generation-z-begins.

43. "Working with McKinsey," *Blog,* January 12, 2013, www.workingwithmckinsey.blogspot.com.

44. D. Sturdevant, "(Still) Learning from Toyota," *McKinsey Quarterly,* February 2014, www.mckinsey.com.

45. D. R. Gnyawali and T. R. Charleton, "Nuances in the Interplay of Competition and Cooperation: Towards a Theory of Coopetition," *Journal of Management* 44 (2018), pp. 2511–34.

46. E. Price, "Amazon Just Opened a New Store in California That Only Sells Highly-Rated Products," *Fortune,* November 5, 2018, http://fortune.com/2018/11/05/amazon-4-star-california/.

47. H. Ripley, "Who's Managing Your Online Reviews?" *Entrepreneur,* January 26, 2017, www.entrepreneur.com.

48. M. Assouline, "The Ultimate Guide to Responding to Positive and Negative Google Reviews," October 29, 2018, www.blog.hubspot.com; S. Vozza, "How to Turn a Bad Review into a Great Opportunity," *Fast Company,* accessed January 17, 2015, http://www.fastcompany.com.

49. R. Siegel, "Toys R Us Workers Are Training Sears Workers to Fight for Severance," *The Washington Post,* February 4, 2019, www.washingtonpost.com.

50. "Toys R Us Comeback in Works as Bankruptcy Auction Canceled," *CBS News,* October 3, 2018, www.cbsnews.com.

51. G. Satell, "A Look Back at Why Blockbuster Really Failed and Why It Didn't Have To," *Forbes,* September 5, 2014, http://www.forbes.com.

52. NFLX Company Financials, NASDAQ, www.nasdaq.com, accessed December 15, 2018.

53. "Nissan Invests $170 Million in U.S. Assembly Plants to Build All-New Altima," https://nissannews.com/en-US/nissan/usa/releases/nissan-invests-170-million-in-u-s-assembly-plants-to-build-all-new-altima, accessed December 16, 2018.

54. D. Kiley, "Detroit Retools: GM Closing Plants, FCA Opening One, Ford Standing Pat," *Forbes,* December 7, 2018, https://www.forbes.com.

55. "Fortune's Most Admired Companies (Innovation)," http://fortune.com/worlds-mostadmired-companies/, accessed February 26, 2017.

56. O. Port, "The Kings of Quality," *BusinessWeek,* August 30, 2004, p. 20.

57. J. Scipioni, "Gatorade Chief Says New 'Customized' Sports Drink Is a Game-Changer," *Fox Business,* July 19, 2018, https://www.foxbusiness.com; D. Green and J. Avella, "Nike Lets Customers Add Glitter, Paint, and Wacky Laces to Their Sneakers," *Business Insider,* March 23, 2018, https://www.businessinsider.com; B. Ladd, "The Next Big Trends in Food Are Being Driven by Amazon, Icon Meals, and Mercatus," *Forbes,* December 3, 2018, https://www.forbes.com.

58. W. E. Deming, *Out of the Crisis* (Cambridge, MA: MIT Press, 2000); D. A. Garvin, "Manufacturing Strategic Planning," *California Management Review,* Summer 1993, pp. 85–106.

59. Bureau of Labor Statistics, "Employment Projections by Major Occupational Group," Table 1.1, April 2018, www.bls.gov.

60. D. E. Bowen, "The Changing Role of Employees in Service Theory and Practice: An Interdisciplinary View," *Human Resource Management Review* 26 (2016), pp. 4–13.

61. B. Jones, "How Disney Uses Spontaneity to Make Customers Feel Like True VIPs," *Forbes,* April 24, 2018, https://www.forbes.com.

62. Adam Lashinsky, "Chaos by Design," *Fortune,* October 2, 2006, http://money.cnn.com.

63. E. Ries, *The Lean Startup: How Today's Entrepreneurs Use Continuous Innovation to Create Radically Successful Businesses* (New York: Crown Business, 2011).

64. See company website, https://www.quickenloans.com/, accessed December 16, 2018; S. Sharf, "Quicken Loans Overtakes Wells Fargo as America's Largest Mortgage Lender," *Forbes,* February 5, 2018, https://www.forbes.com.

65. A. Mason, "Is the Rocket Mortgage a Fast Ride to Trouble?" *CBS News,* February 9, 2016, www.cbsnews.com.

66. See Quicken Loans website, "Our Mortgage Process," www.quickenloans.com, accessed February 4, 2019.

67. K. Gustafson, "This Wal-Mart Tactic Should Send Shivers across Retail," *CNBC,* May 19, 2016, www.cnbc.com; P. Wahba, "Who's Eating Walmart's Lunch? Lots of Companies," *Fortune,* May 19, 2015, www.walmart.com.

68. M. Schlangenstein, "JetBlue Mimics Larger U.S. Rivals by Adding No-Frills Fare Class," *Bloomberg,* September 28, 2018, www.bloomberg.com.

69. M. Schlangenstein, "JetBlue Mimics Larger U.S. Rivals by Adding No-Frills Fare Class," *Bloomberg,* September 28, 2018, www.bloomberg.com.

70. J. Pfeffer, "Building Sustainable Organizations: The Human Factor," *Academy of Management Perspectives* 24 (2010), pp. 34–45.

71. S. L. Hart, *Capitalism at the Crossroads,* 3rd ed. (Upper Saddle River, NJ: Wharton School Publishing, 2010).

72. Morten T. Hansen, Herminia Ibarra, and Urs Peyer, "The Best-Performing CEOs in the World," *Harvard Business Review,* November 2014, http://hbr.org, p. 90.

73. A. Engel, "The Most Sustainable Companies in 2019," *The Washington Post,* August 31, 2018, www.washingtonpost.com.

74. B. Doppelt, *Leading Change toward Sustainability* (Sheffield, UK: Greenleaf, 2010).

75. J. W. Cortada, *21st Century Business* (London: Financial Times/Prentice Hall, 2001).

76. Ashoka, "Ashoka's History," https://www.ashoka.org/en-US/ashoka%27s-history, accessed February 21, 2019.

77. Ashoka, "About Ashoka," https://www.ashoka.org/en/about-ashoka, accessed February 21, 2019; "Bill Drayton," bteam.org, http://bteam.org/team/bill-drayton/, accessed February 21, 2019; Mee-Hyoe Koo, "Interview with Bill Drayton, Pioneer of Social Entrepreneurship," *Forbes,* September 30, 2013, https://www.forbes.com/sites/meehyoekoo/2013/09/30/interview-with-bill-drayton-pioneer-of-social-entrepreneurship/#79d31973bed4.

78. Ashoka, "About Ashoka," https://www.ashoka.org/en/about-ashoka, accessed February 21, 2019; "Bill Drayton," bteam.org, http://bteam.org/team/bill-drayton/, accessed February 21, 2019; Mee-Hyoe Koo, "Interview with Bill Drayton, Pioneer of Social Entrepreneurship," *Forbes,* September 30, 2013, https://www.forbes.com/sites/meehyoekoo/2013/09/30/interview-with-bill-drayton-pioneer-of-social-entrepreneurship/#79d31973bed4.

79. D. Lepak, K. Smith, and M. S. Taylor, "Value Creation and Value Capture: A Multilevel Perspective," *Academy of Management Review 23* (2007), pp. 180–94.

80. A. Kroeger and C. Weber, "Developing a Conceptual Framework for Comparing Social Value Creation," *Academy of Management Review 39* (2014), pp. 513–40.

81. Sonenshine, "Why 'Stories' Took over Your Smartphone" *Atlantic,* May 3, 2018, https://www.theatlantic.com/technology/archive/2018/05/smartphone-stories-snapchat-instagram-facebook/559517/.

82. Drew Harwell, "Facebook, Boosting Artificial Intelligence Research, Says It's 'Not Going Fast Enough,'" *The Washington Post,* July 17, 2018, https://www.washingtonpost.com/technology/2018/07/17/facebook-boosting-artificial-intelligence-research-says-its-not-going-fast-enough/?utm_term=.1e575c850997.

83. Geoff Weiss, "Mark Zuckerberg: I Would Only Hire Someone to Work for Me If I Would Work for Them," *Business Insider,* March 10, 2015, https://www.businessinsider.com/mark-zuckerberg-on-hiring-2015-3.

84. Geoff Weiss, "Mark Zuckerberg: I Would Only Hire Someone to Work for Me If I Would Work for Them," *Business Insider,* March 10, 2015, https://www.businessinsider.com/mark-zuckerberg-on-hiring-2015-3.

85. Sheera Frenkel and Mike Isaac, "Inside Facebook's Election 'War Room,'" *The New York Times,* September 19, 2018, https://www.nytimes.com/2018/09/19/technology/facebook-election-war-room.html.

86. R. Webber, "General Management Past and Future," *Financial Times Mastering Management,* 1997.

87. M. Menz, "Functional Top Management Team Members: A Review, Synthesis, and Research Agenda," *Journal of Management 38* (2012), pp. 45–80.

88. "Chase Hires Andrew Knott as Chief Media Officer," *Adweek,* July 23, 2018, www.adweek.com; D. Gerdeman, "What Do Chief Sustainability Officers Do?" *Forbes,* October 8, 2014, www.forbes.com.

89. C. Wolf and S. Floyd, "Strategic Planning Research: Toward a Theory-Driven Agenda," *Journal of Management 43* (2017), pp. 1754–88.

90. C. Ren and C. Guo, "Middle Managers' Strategic Role in the Corporate Entrepreneurial Process: Attention-Based Effects," *Journal of Management 37* (2011), pp. 1586–1610.

91. A. Raes, M. Heijltjes, U. Glunk, et al., "The Interface of the Top Management Team and Middle Managers: A Process Model," *Academy of Management Review 36* (2011), pp. 102–26.

92. Q. N. Huy, "In Praise of Middle Managers," *Harvard Business Review,* September 2001, pp. 72–79.

93. L. A. Hill, "New Manager Development for the 21st Century," *Academy of Management Executive,* August 2004, pp. 121–26.

94. C. Bartlett and S. Goshal, "The Myth of the Generic Manager: New Personal Competencies for New Management Roles," *California Management Review 40,* no. 1 (1997), pp. 92–116.

95. K. Soteres, "4 Ways to Empower Frontline Managers to Become Change Management Champions," ADP website, June 27, 2018, www.adp.com.

96. "16 Essential Leadership Skills for the Workplace of Tomorrow," *Forbes,* December 27, 2017, www.forbes.com.

97. H. Mintzberg, *The Nature of Managerial Work* (New York: Harper & Row, 1973).

98. R. Katz, "Skills of an Effective Administrator," *Harvard Business Review 52* (September–October), pp. 90–102.

99. L. A. Hill, "New Manager Development for the 21st Century," *Academy of Management Executive,* August 2004, pp. 121–26.

100. H. Mintzberg, "The Manager's Job: Folklore and Fact," *Harvard Business Review 53* (July–August 1975), pp. 49–61.

101. D. Gelles, "At Aetna, a C.E.O.'s Management by Mantra," *The New York Times,* February 27, 2015, www.nytimes.com; "Nontraditional Path: From

Pre-Med Dropout to Next Aetna CEO," *DiversityInc,* October 28, 2010, http://diversityinc.com; Aetna, "Executive Biographies: Mark T. Bertolini," About Us: Corporate Profile, http://www.aetna.com, accessed February 25, 2011.

102. L. A. Hill, "New Manager Development for the 21st Century," *Academy of Management Executive,* August 2004, pp. 121–26.

103. D. Goleman, R. Boyatzis, and A. McKee, *Primal Leadership: Realizing the Power of Emotional Intelligence* (Boston: Harvard Business School Press, 2002); O. Ybarra, E. Kross, and J. Sanchez-Burks, "The 'Big Idea' That Is Yet to Be: Toward a More Motivated, Contextual, and Dynamic Model of Emotional Intelligence," *Academy of Management Perspectives 28* (2014), pp. 93–107.

104. O. Ybarra, E. Kross, and J. Sanchez-Burks, "The "Big Idea" That Is Yet to Be: Toward a More Motivated, Contextual, and Dynamic Model of Emotional Intelligence," *Academy of Management Perspectives,* 28 (2014), pp. 93–107; Stephen Xavier, "Control Yourself: What Role Does Emotional Intelligence Play in Executive Leadership?" *US Business Review,* March 2006, Business & Company Resource Center, http://galenet.galegroup.com.

105. J. McClesky, "Emotional Intelligence and Leadership: A Review of the Progress, Controversy, and Criticism," *International Journal of Organizational Analysis 22,* no. 1 (2014), pp. 76–93; J. Antonakis, N. Ashkanasy, and M. Dasborough, "Does Leadership Need Emotional Intelligence?" *Leadership Quarterly 20* (2009), pp. 247–61; E. A. Locke, "Why Emotional Intelligence Is an Invalid Concept," *Journal of Organizational Behavior 26* (2005), pp. 425–31.

106. R. Boyatzis, "Get Motivated," *Harvard Business Review,* January 2004, p. 30.

107. C. Myers, "When It Comes to Success in Business, EQ Eats IQ for Breakfast," *Forbes,* June 18, 2018, https://www.forbes.com.

108. C. Cenize-Levine, "To Advance in Your Career, Is It Better to Be a Specialist or Generalist?" *Forbes,* January 30, 2018, www.forbes.com.

109. M. Benner and M. Tushman, "Reflections on the 2013 Decade Award 'Exploitation, Exploration, and Process Management: The Productivity Dilemma Revisited' Ten Years Later," *Academy of Management Review 40* (2015), pp. 497–514; P. Junni, R. Sarala, and T. Vas, et al., "Organizational Ambidexterity and Performance: A Meta-analysis," *Academy of Management Perspectives,* 27 (2013), pp. 299–312; C. A. O'Reilly III and M. Tushman, "Organizational Ambidexterity: Past, Present, and Future," *Academy of Management Perspectives 27* (2013), pp. 324–38; J. Birkinshaw and K. Gupta, "Clarifying the Distinctive Contribution of Ambidexterity to the Field of Organization Studies," *Academy of Management Perspectives 27* (2013).

110. T. Bateman and A. Hess, "Different Personal Propensities among Scientists Predict Deeper vs. Broader Knowledge Contributions," *Proceedings of the National Academy of Sciences,* March 2, 2015.

111. D. T. Hall, J. Yip, and K. Doiron, "Protean Careers at Work: Self-Direction and Values Orientation in Psychological Success," *Annual Review of Organizational Psychology and Organizational Behavior 5* (2018), pp. 129–56.

112. K. Inkson and M. B. Arther, "How to Be a Successful Career Capitalist," *Organizational Dynamics,* Summer 2001, pp. 48–60.

113. A. Ericsson, M. Prietula, and E. Cokely, "The Making of an Expert," *Harvard Business Review,* July–August, 2007, http://www.hbr.org; Geoffrey Colvin, "What It Takes to Be Great," *Fortune,* October 19, 2006, http://money.cnn.com.

114. L. M. Roberts, J. Dutton, G. Spreitzer, E. Heaphy, and R. Quinn, "Composing the Reflected Best-Self Portrait: Building Pathways for Becoming Extraordinary in Work Organizations," *Academy of Management Review 30* (2005), pp. 712–36.

115. Company website, https://www.gallupstrengthscenter.com/home/en-us, accessed February 8, 2019.

116. M. E. P. Seligman, *Authentic Happiness: Using the New Positive Psychology to Realize Your Potential for Lasting Fulfillment* (New York: Free Press, 2002).

117. E. W. Morrison, "Newcomers' Relationships: The Role of Social Network Ties during Socialization," *Academy of Management Journal 45* (2002), pp. 1149–60.

118. R. Cotton, Y. Shen, and R. Llvne-Tarandach, "On Becoming Extraordinary: The Content and Structure of the Developmental Networks of Major League Baseball Hall of Famers," *Academy of Management Journal 54* (2011), pp. 15–46.

119. C. Galunic, G. Ertug, and M. Gargiulo, "The Positive Externalities of Social Capital: Benefiting from Senior Brokers," *Academy of*

Management Journal 55 (2012), pp. 1213–31; P. Adler and S. Kwon, "Social Capital: Prospects for a New Concept," *Academy of Management Review* 27 (2002), pp. 17–40.

120. See company website, https://www.linkedin.com/company/linkedin/about/, accessed December 16, 2018; Microsoft's 2018 Annual Report, https://www.linkedin.com/company/linkedin/about/, accessed December 16, 2018.

121. T. Peters, *Liberation Management* (New York: Alfred A. Knopf, 1992).

122. Glassdoor, https://www.glassdoor.com/Award/Top-CEOs-LST_KQ0,8.htm.

123. Amarendra Bhushan Dhiraj, "Fortune's 50 Top Business Leaders of 2016, Mark Zuckerberg and Jeff Bezos Tops," *CEO World,* November 23, 2016, http://ceoworld. biz/2016/11/23/fortunes-50-top-business-leaders-2016-mark-zuckerberg-jeff-bezos-tops./

124. Catherine Clifford, "Facebook CEO Mark Zuckerberg: Elon Musk's Doomsday AI Predictions Are 'Pretty Irresponsible'," *"CNBC,* July 24, 2017, https://www.cnbc.com/2017/07/24/mark-zuckerberg-elon-musks-doomsday-ai-predictions-are-irresponsible.html.

125. Karen Hao, "Why AI Is a Threat to Democracy—And What We Can Do to Stop It," *MIT Technology Review,* February 26, 2019, www.technologyreview.com.

126. Christina Farr, "Mark Zuckerberg Is Selling up to $13 billion of Facebook Stock to Fund an Ambitious Project to End Disease: Here's an Early Look Inside," *CNBC,* September 15, 2018, https://www.cnbc.com/2018/09/14/chan-zuckerberg-initiative-what-is-it-doing-so-far.html.

127. https://www.washingtonpost.com/lifestyle/style/mark-zuckerberg-claims-that-at-facebook-the-future-is-private-dont-believe-him/2019/05/03/b42f7564-6cf4-11e9-a66d-a82d3f3d96d5_story.html?utm_term=.095dfb7cb6ce&wpisrc=nl_most&wpmm=1.

128. P. Drucker, "What Makes an Effective Executive?" *Harvard Business Review,* June 2004, pp. 58–63.

The Evolution of Management

For thousands of years, managers have wrestled with the same issues and problems confronting executives today. Around 1100 BC, the Chinese practiced the four management functions—planning, organizing, leading, and controlling—discussed in Chapter 1. Between 400 BC and 350 BC, the Greeks recognized management as a separate art and advocated a scientific approach to work. The Romans decentralized the management of their vast empire before the birth of Christ. During medieval times, the Venetians standardized production through the use of an assembly line, building warehouses and using an inventory system to monitor the contents.[1]

But throughout history, most managers operated strictly on a trial-and-error basis. The challenges of the Industrial Revolution changed that. Management emerged as a formal discipline at the turn of the century. The first university programs to offer management and business education, the Wharton School at the University of Pennsylvania and the Amos Tuck School at Dartmouth, were founded in the late 19th century. By 1914, 25 business schools existed.[2]

Thus, the management profession as we know it today is relatively new. This appendix explores the roots of modern management theory. Understanding the origins of management thought will help you grasp the underlying contexts of the ideas and concepts presented in the chapters ahead.

Although this appendix is titled "The Evolution of Management," it might be more appropriately called "The Revolutions of Management" because it documents the wide swings in management approaches over the past 100+ years. Out of the great variety of ideas about how to improve management, parts of each approach have survived and been incorporated into modern perspectives on management. Thus, the legacy of past efforts, triumphs, and failures has become our guide to future management practice.[3]

EARLY MANAGEMENT CONCEPTS AND INFLUENCES

Communication and transportation constraints hindered the growth of earlier businesses. Therefore, improvements in management techniques did not substantially improve performance. However, the Industrial Revolution changed that. As companies grew and became more complex, minor improvements in management tactics produced impressive increases in production quantity and quality.[4]

The emergence of **economies of scale**—reductions in the average cost of a unit of production as the total volume produced increases—drove managers to strive for further growth. The opportunities for mass production created by the Industrial Revolution spawned intense and systematic thought about management problems and issues—particularly efficiency, production processes, and cost savings.[5]

Exhibit A.1 provides a time line depicting the evolution of management thought through the decades. This historical perspective is divided into two major sections: classical approaches and contemporary approaches. Many of these approaches overlapped as they developed, and they often had a significant impact on one another. Some approaches were a direct reaction to the perceived deficiencies of previous approaches. Others developed as the needs and issues confronting managers changed over the years. All the approaches attempted to explain the real issues facing managers and provide them with tools to solve future problems.

Exhibit A.1 will reinforce your understanding of the key relationships among the approaches and place each perspective in its historical context.

CLASSICAL APPROACHES

The classical period extended from the mid-19th century through the early 1950s. The major approaches that emerged during this period were systematic management,

EXHIBIT A.1
The Evolution of Management Thought

Classical approaches				Contemporary approaches			
1900	1920	1940	1960	1980	2000	2020	2040

Systematic management	Bureaucracy	Quantitative management	Systems theory	Corporate social responsibility	Sustainability	Current and future revolutions
Scientific management	Administrative management	Human relations	Organizational behavior	Contingency theory	Leveraging digital technologies	

scientific management, administrative management, human relations, and bureaucracy.

Systematic Management During the 19th century, growth in U.S. business centered on manufacturing.[6] Early writers such as Adam Smith believed the management of these firms was chaotic, and their ideas helped to systematize it. Most organizational tasks were subdivided and performed by specialized labor. However, poor coordination caused frequent problems and breakdowns of the manufacturing process.

The **systematic management** approach attempted to build specific procedures and processes into operations to ensure coordination of effort. Systematic management emphasized economical operations, adequate staffing, maintenance of inventories to meet consumer demand, and organizational control. These goals were achieved through

- Careful definition of duties and responsibilities.
- Standardized techniques for performing these duties.
- Specific means of gathering, handling, transmitting, and analyzing information.
- Cost accounting, wage, and production control systems to facilitate internal coordination and communications.

An Early Labor Contract

The following rules, taken from the records of Cocheco Company, were typical of labor contract provisions in the 1850s.

1. The hours of work shall be from sunrise to sunset, from the 21st of March to the 20th of September inclusively; and from sunrise until eight oclock, p.m., during the remainder of the year. One hour shall be allowed for dinner, and half an hour for breakfast during the first mentioned six months; and one hour for dinner during the other half of the year; on Saturdays, the mill shall be stopped one hour before sunset, for the purpose of cleaning the machinery.

2. Every hand coming to work a quarter of an hour after the mill has been started shall be docked a quarter of a day; and every hand absenting him or herself, without absolute necessity, shall be docked in a sum double the amount of the wages such hand shall have earned during the time of such absence. No more than one hand is allowed to leave any one of the rooms at the same time—a quarter of a day shall be deducted for every breach of this rule.

3. No smoking or spiritous liquors shall be allowed in the factory under any pretense whatsoever. It is also forbidden to carry into the factory, nuts, fruits, etc. books, or papers during the hours of work.

SOURCE: Sullivan, W., "The Industrial Revolution and the Factory Operative in Pennsylvania," *The Pennsylvania Magazine of History and Biography* 78 (1954), pp. 478–79.

Systematic management emphasized internal operations because managers were concerned primarily with meeting the explosive growth in demand brought about by the Industrial Revolution. In addition, managers were free to focus on internal issues of efficiency, in part because the government did not constrain business practices significantly. Finally, labor was poorly organized. As a result, many managers were oriented more toward things than toward people.

Systematic management did not address all the issues 19th-century managers faced, but it tried to raise managers awareness about the most pressing concerns of their job.

Scientific Management Systematic management failed to lead to widespread production efficiency. This shortcoming became apparent to a young engineer named Frederick Taylor, who was hired by Midvale Steel Company in 1878. Taylor discovered that production and pay were poor, inefficiency and waste were prevalent, and most companies had tremendous unused potential. He concluded that management decisions were unsystematic and that no research to determine the best means of production existed.

In response, Taylor introduced a second approach to management, known as **scientific management**.[7] This approach advocated the application of scientific methods to analyze work and to determine how to complete production tasks efficiently. For example, U.S. Steels contract with the United Steel Workers of America specified that sand shovelers should move 12.5 shovelfuls per minute; shovelfuls should average 15 pounds of river sand composed of 5.5 percent moisture.[8]

Taylor identified four principles of scientific management:

1. Management should develop a precise, scientific approach for each element of ones work to replace general guidelines.

2. Management should scientifically select, train, teach, and develop each worker so that the right person has the right job

3. Management should cooperate with workers to ensure that jobs match plans and principles.

4. Management should ensure an appropriate division of work and responsibility between managers and workers.

To implement this approach, Taylor used techniques such as time-and-motion studies. With this technique, a task was divided into its basic movements, and different motions were timed to determine the most efficient way to complete the task.

After the "one best way" to perform the job was identified, Taylor stressed the importance of hiring and training the proper worker to do that job. Taylor advocated the standardization of tools, the use of instruction cards to help workers, and breaks to eliminate fatigue.

Another key element of Taylors approach was the use of the differential piecerate system. Taylor assumed workers were motivated by receiving money. Therefore, he implemented a pay system in which workers were paid additional wages when they exceeded a standard level of output for

Frederick Taylor (left) and Dr. Lillian Gilbreth (right) were early experts in management efficiency.

Bettmann/Getty Images

George Rinhart/Corbis/Getty Images

Scientific Management and the Model T

At the turn of the century, automobiles were a luxury that only the wealthy could afford. They were assembled by craftspeople who put an entire car together at one spot on the factory floor. These workers were not specialized, and Henry Ford believed they wasted time and energy bringing the needed parts to the car. Ford took a revolutionary approach to automobile manufacturing by using scientific management principles.

After much study, machines and workers in Ford's new factory were placed in sequence so that an automobile could be assembled without interruption along a moving production line. Mechanical energy and a conveyor belt were used to take the work to the workers.

The manufacture of parts likewise was revolutionized. For example, formerly it had taken one worker 20 minutes to assemble a flywheel magneto. By splitting the job into 29 operations, putting the product on a mechanical conveyor, and changing the height of the conveyor, Ford cut production time to 5 minutes.

By 1914, chassis assembly time had been trimmed from almost 13 hours to 1½ hours. The new methods of production required complete standardization, new machines, and an adaptable labor force. Costs dropped significantly, the Model T became the first car accessible to the majority of Americans, and Ford dominated the industry for many years.

SOURCE: Kroos, H. and Gilbert, C., *The Principles of Scientific Management.* New York: Harper & Row, 1911.

each job. Taylor concluded that both workers and management would benefit from such an approach.

Scientific management principles were widely embraced. Other proponents, including Henry Gantt and Frank and Lillian Gilbreth, introduced many refinements and techniques for applying scientific management on the factory floor. One of the most famous examples of the application of scientific management is the factory Henry Ford built to produce the Model T.[9] The legacy of Taylor's scientific management approach is broad and pervasive. Most important, productivity and efficiency in manufacturing improved dramatically. The concepts of scientific methods and research were introduced to manufacturing. The piecerate system gained wide acceptance because it more closely aligned effort and reward. Taylor also emphasized the need for cooperation between management and workers. And the concept of a management specialist gained prominence.

Despite these gains, not everyone was convinced that scientific management was the best solution to all business problems. First, critics claimed that Taylor ignored many job-related social and psychological factors by emphasizing only money as a worker incentive. Second, production tasks were reduced to a set of routine, machinelike procedures that led to boredom, apathy, and quality control problems. Third, unions strongly opposed scientific management techniques because they believed management might abuse its power to set the standards and the piecerates, thus exploiting workers and diminishing their importance. Finally, although scientific management resulted in intense scrutiny of the internal efficiency of organizations, it did not help managers deal with broader external issues such as competitors and government regulations, especially at the senior management level.

Administrative Management The **administrative management** approach emphasized the perspective of senior managers within the organization and argued that management was a profession and could be taught.

An explicit and broad framework for administrative management emerged in 1916, when Henri Fayol, a French mining engineer and executive, published a book summarizing his management experiences. Fayol identified five functions and 14 principles of management. The five functions, which are very similar to the four functions discussed in Chapter 1, are planning, organizing, commanding, coordinating, and controlling. Exhibit A.2 lists and defines the 14 principles. Although some critics claim Fayol treated the principles as universal truths for management, he actually wanted them applied flexibly.[10]

A host of other executives contributed to the administrative management literature. These writers discussed a broad spectrum of management topics, including the social responsibilities of management, the philosophy of management, clarification of business terms and concepts, and organizational principles. Chester Barnard's and Mary Parker Follet's contributions have become classic works in this area.[11]

Barnard, former president of New Jersey Bell Telephone Company, published his landmark book *The Functions of the Executive* in 1938. He outlined the role of the senior executive: formulating the purpose of the organization, hiring key individuals, and maintaining organizational communications.[12] Mary Parker Follet's 1942 book *Dynamic Organization* extended Barnard's work by emphasizing the continually changing situations that managers face.[13] Two of her key contributions—the notion that managers desire flexibility and the differences between motivating groups and individuals—laid the groundwork for the modern contingency approach discussed later in this appendix.

All the writings in the administrative management area emphasize management as a profession along with fields such as law and medicine. In addition, these authors offered many recommendations based on their personal experiences, which often included managing large corporations. Although these perspectives and recommendations were considered sound, critics noted that they might not work in all settings. Different types of personnel, industry conditions, and technologies may affect the appropriateness of these principles.

Human Relations A fourth approach to management, **human relations**, developed during the 1930s. This approach aimed at understanding how psychological and social processes interact with the work situation to influence performance. Human relations was the first major approach to emphasize informal work relationships and worker satisfaction.

This approach owes much to other major schools of thought. For example, many of the ideas of the Gilbreths (scientific management) and Barnard and Follet (administrative management) influenced the development of human relations from 1930 to 1955. In fact, human relations emerged from a research project that began as a scientific management study.

Western Electric Company, a manufacturer of communications equipment, hired a team of Harvard researchers led by Elton Mayo and Fritz Roethlisberger. They were to investigate the influence of physical working conditions on workers' productivity and efficiency in one of the company's factories outside Chicago. This research project, known as the *Hawthorne Studies,* provided some of the most interesting and controversial results in the history of management.[14]

The Hawthorne Studies were a series of experiments conducted from 1924 to 1932. During the first stage of the project (the illumination experiments), various working conditions, particularly the lighting in the factory, were altered to determine the effects of those changes on productivity. The researchers found no systematic relationship between the factory lighting and production levels. In some cases, productivity continued to increase even when the illumination was reduced to the level of moonlight. The researchers concluded that the workers performed and reacted differently because the researchers were observing them. This reaction is known as the **Hawthorne Effect**.

This conclusion led the researchers to believe productivity may be affected more by psychological and social factors

---

EXHIBIT A.2

Fayol's 14 Principles of Management

1. *Division of work*—divide work into specialized tasks and assign responsibilities to specific individuals.

2. *Authority*—delegate authority along with responsibility.

3. *Discipline*—make expectations clear and punish violations.

4. *Unity of command*—each employee should be assigned to only one supervisor.

5. *Unity of direction*—employees efforts should be focused on achieving organizational objectives.

6. *Subordination of individual interest to the general interest*—the general interest must predominate.

7. *Remuneration*—systematically reward efforts that support the organizations direction.

8. *Centralization*—determine the relative importance of superior and subordinate roles.

9. *Scalar chain*—keep communications within the chain of command.

10. *Order*—order jobs and material so they support the organizations direction.

11. *Equity*—fair discipline and order enhance employee commitment.

12. *Stability and tenure of personnel*—promote employee loyalty and longevity.

13. *Initiative*—encourage employees to act on their own in support of the organizations direction.

14. *Esprit de corps*—promote a unity of interests between employees and management.

than by physical or objective influences. With this thought in mind, they initiated the other four stages of the project. During these stages, the researchers performed various work group experiments and had extensive interviews with employees. Mayo and his team eventually concluded that productivity and employee behavior were influenced by the informal work group.

Human relations proponents argued that managers should stress primarily employee welfare, motivation, and communication. They believed social needs had precedence over economic needs. Therefore, management must gain the cooperation of the group and promote job satisfaction and group norms consistent with the goals of the organization.

Another noted contributor to the field of human relations was Abraham Maslow.[15] In 1943, Maslow suggested that humans have five levels of needs. The most basic needs are the physical needs for food, water, and shelter; the most advanced need is for self-actualization, or personal fulfillment. Maslow argued that people try to satisfy their lower-level needs and then progress upward to the higher-level needs. Managers can facilitate this process and achieve organizational goals by removing obstacles and encouraging behaviors that satisfy peoples needs and organizational goals simultaneously.

Although the human relations approach generated research into leadership, job attitudes, and group dynamics, it drew heavy criticism.[16] Critics believed that one result of human relations—a belief that a happy worker was a productive worker—was too simplistic. Whereas scientific management overemphasized the economic and formal aspects of the workplace, human relations ignored the more rational side of the worker and the important characteristics of the formal organization. However, human relations was a significant step in the development of management thought because it prompted managers and researchers to consider the psychological and social factors that influence performance.

Bureaucracy Max Weber, a German sociologist, lawyer, and social historian, showed how management itself could be more efficient and consistent in his book *The Theory of Social and Economic Organizations*.[17] The ideal model for management, according to Weber, is the **bureaucracy** approach.

Weber believed bureaucratic structures can eliminate the variability that results when managers in the same organization have different skills, experiences, and goals. Weber advocated that the jobs themselves be standardized so that personnel changes would not disrupt the organization. He emphasized a structured, formal network of relationships among specialized positions in an organization. Rules and regulations standardize behavior, and authority resides in positions rather than in individuals. As a result, the organization need not rely on a particular individual but will realize efficiency and success by following the rules in a routine and unbiased manner.

According to Weber, bureaucracies are especially important because they allow large organizations to perform the many routine activities necessary for their survival. Also,

A Human Relations Pioneer

In 1837, William Procter, a ruined English retailer, and James Gamble, son of a Methodist minister, formed a partnership in Cincinnati to make soap and candles. Both were known for their integrity, and soon their business was thriving.

By 1883, the business had grown substantially. When William Cooper Procter, grandson of the founder, left Princeton University to work for the firm, he wanted to learn the business from the ground up. He started working on the factory floor. "He did every menial job from shoveling rosin and soap to pouring fatty mixtures into crutchers. He brought his lunch in a paper bag . . . and sat on the floor [with the other workers] and ate with them, learning their feelings about work."

By 1884, Cooper Procter believed, from his own experience, that increasing workers psychological commitment to the company would lead to higher productivity. His passion to increase employee commitment to the firm led him to propose a scandalous plan: share profits with workers to increase their sense of responsibility and job satisfaction. The surprise was audible on the first dividend day, when workers held checks equivalent to seven weeks pay.

Still, the plan was not complete. Workers saw the profit sharing as extra pay rather than as an incentive to improve. In addition, Cooper Procter recognized that a fundamental issue for the workers, some of whom continued to be his good friends, was the insecurity of old age. Public incorporation in 1890 gave Procter a new idea. After trying several versions, by 1903 he had discovered a way to meet all his goals for labor: a stock purchase plan. For every dollar a worker invested in P&G stock, the company would contribute four dollars worth of stock.

Finally, Cooper Procter had resolved some key issues for labor that paid off in worker loyalty, improved productivity, and an increasing corporate reputation for caring and integrity. He went on to become CEO of the firm, and P&G today remains one of the most admired corporations in the United States.

SOURCES: Schisgall, O., *Eyes on Tomorrow*. Chicago: Ferguson, J.G., 1981; Welsh, T., "Best and Worst Corporate Reputations," *Fortune*, February 7, 1994, pp. 58–66.

bureaucratic positions foster specialized skills, eliminating many subjective judgments by managers. In addition, if the rules and controls are established properly, bureaucracies should be unbiased in their treatment of people—both customers and employees.

Many organizations today are bureaucratic. Bureaucracy can be efficient and productive. However, bureaucracy is not the appropriate model for every organization. Organizations or departments that need rapid decision making and flexibility may suffer under a bureaucratic approach. Some people may not perform their best with excessive bureaucratic rules and procedures.

Other shortcomings stem from a faulty execution of bureaucratic principles rather than from the approach itself. Too much authority may be vested in too few people; the procedures may become the ends rather than the means; or managers may ignore appropriate rules and regulations. Finally, one advantage of a bureaucracy—its permanence—can also be a problem. Once a bureaucracy is established, dismantling it is difficult.

CONTEMPORARY APPROACHES

The contemporary approaches to management include quantitative management, organizational behavior, systems theory, and the contingency perspective. The contemporary approaches have developed at various times since World War II, and they continue to represent the cornerstones of modern management thought.

Quantitative Management Although Taylor introduced the use of science as a management tool early in the 20th century, most organizations did not adopt the use of quantitative techniques for management problems until the 1940s and 1950s.[18] During World War II, military planners began to apply mathematical techniques to defense and logistics problems. After the war, private corporations began assembling teams of quantitative experts to tackle many of the complex issues confronting large organizations. This approach, referred to as **quantitative management**, emphasizes the application of quantitative analysis to management decisions and problems.

Quantitative management helps a manager make a decision by developing formal mathematical models of the problem. Computers facilitated the development of specific quantitative methods. These include such techniques as statistical decision theory, linear programming, queuing theory, simulation, forecasting, inventory modeling, network modeling, and break-even analysis. Organizations apply these techniques in many areas, including production, quality control, marketing, human resources, finance, distribution, planning, and research and development.

Despite the promise quantitative management holds, managers do not rely on these methods as the primary approach to decision making. Typically, they use these techniques as a supplement or tool in the decision process. Many managers will use results that are consistent with their experience, intuition, and judgment, but they often reject results that contradict their beliefs. Also, managers may use the process to compare alternatives and eliminate weaker options.

Several explanations account for the limited use of quantitative management. Many managers have not been trained in using these techniques. Also, many aspects of a management decision cannot be expressed through mathematical symbols and formulas. Finally, many of the decisions managers face are nonroutine and unpredictable.

Organizational Behavior During the 1950s, a transition took place in the human relations approach. Scholars began to recognize that worker productivity and organizational success are based on more than the satisfaction of economic or social needs. The revised perspective, known as **organizational behavior**, studies and identifies management activities that promote employee effectiveness through an understanding of the complex nature of individual, group, and organizational processes. Organizational behavior draws from a variety of disciplines, including psychology and sociology, to explain the behavior of people on the job.

During the 1960s, organizational behaviorists heavily influenced the field of management. Douglas McGregor's Theory X and Theory Y marked the transition from human relations.[19] According to McGregor, Theory X managers assume workers are lazy and irresponsible and require constant supervision and external motivation to achieve organizational goals. Theory Y managers assume employees *want* to work and can direct and control themselves. McGregor advocated a Theory Y perspective, suggesting that managers who encourage participation and allow opportunities for individual challenge and initiative would achieve superior performance.

Other major organizational behaviorists include Chris Argyris, who recommended greater autonomy and better jobs for workers,[20] and Rensis Likert, who stressed the value of participative management.[21] Through the years, organizational behavior has consistently emphasized development of the organizations human resources to achieve individual and organizational goals. Like other approaches, it has been criticized for its limited perspective, although more recent contributions have a broader and more situational viewpoint. In the past few years, many of the primary issues addressed by organizational behavior have experienced a rebirth with a greater interest in leadership, employee involvement, and self-management.

Systems Theory The classical approaches as a whole were criticized because they (1) ignored the relationship between the organization and its external environment and (2) usually stressed one aspect of the organization or its employees at the expense of other considerations. In response to these criticisms, management scholars during the 1950s stepped back from the details of the organization to attempt to understand it as a whole system. These efforts were based on a general scientific approach called **systems theory**.[22] Organizations are open systems, dependent on inputs from the outside world, such as raw materials, human resources, and capital. They transform these inputs into outputs that (ideally) meet the markets needs for goods and services. The environment reacts to the outputs through a feedback loop; this feedback provides input for the next cycle of the system. The process repeats itself for the life of the system, as illustrated in Exhibit A.3.

Systems theory also emphasizes that an organization is one system in a series of subsystems. For instance, Southwest Airlines is a subsystem of the airline industry, and the flight crews are a subsystem of Southwest. Systems theory points out that each subsystem is a component of the whole and is interdependent with other subsystems.

Contingency Perspective Building on systems theory ideas, the **contingency perspective** refutes universal

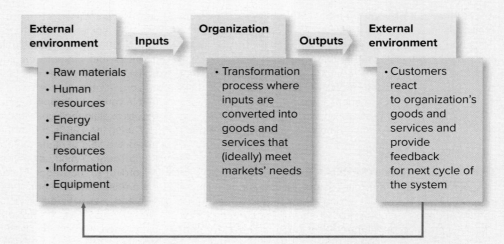

Open-System
Perspective of an
Organization

principles of management by stating that a variety of factors, both internal and external to the firm, may affect the organization's performance.[23] Therefore, there is no one best way to manage and organize because circumstances vary.

Situational characteristics are called **contingencies**. Understanding contingencies helps a manager know which sets of circumstances dictate which management actions. You will learn recommendations for the major contingencies throughout this text. The contingencies include

1. Circumstances in the organizations external environment.
2. The internal strengths and weaknesses of the organization.
3. The values, goals, skills, and attitudes of managers and workers in the organization.
4. The types of tasks, resources, and technologies the organization uses.

With an eye to these contingencies, a manager may categorize the situation and then choose the proper competitive strategy, organization structure, or management process for the circumstances.

Researchers continue to identify key contingency variables and their effects on management issues. As you read the topics covered in each chapter, you will notice similarities and differences among management situations and the appropriate responses. This perspective should represent a cornerstone of your own approach to management. Many of the things you will learn about throughout this course apply a contingency perspective.

CURRENT EVENTS AND AN EYE ON THE FUTURE

The end of the 20th century brought pressures on corporations to care about things beyond shareholder value, and to take more responsibility for their impact on broader social issues. You will learn more about ethics, corporate social responsibility, sustainability, and climate change in other chapters. The 1990s ushered in a digital revolution that transformed business, followed by a succession of ever-changing technological developments that continue to create new

competitive challenges and opportunities. These too will be recurring themes in future chapters. Meanwhile and forever after, managers will need to attend to and deal with an infinite array of current events—domestic and international economic developments, political trends and disruptions, market trends, and more. Today's news stories become history, but the most important ones will continue to affect business and society in the future. What are the most important current events unfolding as you read this? What can you learn from them, and how might they affect the future?

This appendix has summarized the major schools of management thought. Some institutions offer more general courses in business history, and the subject is well worth knowing. What goes on today derives from what went on yesterday, which stemmed from what began years, decades, even centuries ago. Regardless of era and whether economies are rising or falling, it helps to examine the past for help in making good decisions today and in the future.

Knowledge of history could help with economic recoveries and mitigate or prevent future fiascos. Knowing history *could*—if used properly—have a positive impact on *the* future, and on *your* future.[24]

KEY TERMS

administrative management   A classical management approach that attempted to identify major principles and functions that managers could use to achieve superior organizational performance, p. 35

bureaucracy   A classical management approach emphasizing a structured, formal network of relationships among specialized positions in the organization, p. 36

contingencies   Factors that determine the appropriateness of managerial actions, p. 38

contingency perspective   An approach to the study of management proposing that the managerial strategies, structures, and processes that result in high performance depend on the characteristics, or important contingencies, of the situation in which they are applied, p. 37

economies of scale Reductions in the average cost of a unit of production as the total volume produced increases, p. 32

Hawthorne Effect People's reactions to being observed or studied resulting in superficial rather than meaningful changes in behavior, p. 35

human relations A classical management approach that attempted to understand and explain how human psychological and social processes interact with the formal aspects of the work situation to influence performance, p. 35

organizational behavior A contemporary management approach that studies and identifies management activities that promote employee effectiveness by examining the complex and dynamic nature of individual, group, and organizational processes, p. 37

quantitative management A contemporary management approach that emphasizes the application of quantitative analysis to managerial decisions and problems, p. 37

scientific management A classical management approach that applied scientific methods to analyze and determine the one best way to complete production tasks, p. 33

systematic management A classical management approach that attempted to build into operations the specific procedures and processes that would ensure coordination of effort to achieve established goals and plans, p. 33

systems theory A theory stating that an organization is a managed system that changes inputs into outputs, p. 37

DISCUSSION QUESTIONS

1. How does today's business world compare with the one of 40 years ago? What is different about today, and what is not so different?

2. What is scientific management? How might today's organizations use it?

3. Exhibit A.2 lists Fayol's 14 principles of management, first published in 1916. Are they as useful today as they were then? Why or why not? *When* are they most, and least, useful?

4. What are the advantages and disadvantages of a bureaucratic organization?

5. In what situations are quantitative management concepts and tools applicable?

6. Choose any organization and describe its system of inputs and outputs.

7. Why did the contingency perspective become such an important approach to management? Generate a list of contingencies that might affect the decisions you make in your life or as a manager.

8. For each of the management approaches discussed in the appendix, give examples you have seen. How effective or ineffective were they?

Experiential Exercises

A.1 APPROACHES TO MANAGEMENT

OBJECTIVES

1. To help you conceive a wide variety of management approaches.

2. To clarify the appropriateness of different management approaches in different situations.

INSTRUCTIONS

Your instructor will divide your class randomly into groups of four to six people. Acting as a team, with everyone offering ideas and one person serving as official recorder, each group will be responsible for writing a one-page memo to your present class. The subject matter of your group's memo will be "My advice for managing people today is . . ." The fun part of this exercise (and its creative element) involves writing the memo from the viewpoint of the person assigned to your group by your instructor.

Among the memo viewpoints your instructor may assign are

- An ancient Egyptian slave master (building the great pyramids).
- Henri Fayol.
- Frederick Taylor.
- Mary Parker Follet.
- Douglas McGregor.
- A contingency management theorist.
- A Japanese auto company executive.
- The chief executive officer of IBM in the year 2030.
- Commander of the Starship *Enterprise* II in the year 3001.
- Others as assigned by your instructor.

Use your imagination, make sure everyone participates, and try to be true to any historical facts you've encountered. Attempt to be as specific and realistic as possible. Remember, the idea is to provide advice about managing people from another point in time (or from a particular point of view at the present time).

Make sure you manage your 20-minute time limit carefully. A recommended approach is to spend 2 to 3 minutes putting the exercise into proper perspective. Next, take about 10 to 12 minutes brainstorming ideas for your memo, with your recorder jotting down key ideas and phrases. Have your recorder use the remaining time to write your group's one-page memo, with constructive comments and help from the others. Pick a spokesperson to read your group's memo to the class.

SOURCE: Krietner, R. and Kinicki, A., *Organization Behavior*, 3rd ed. New York: Richard D. Irwin, 1994, pp. 30–31.

OBJECTIVES

1. To learn to identify the components of a complex system.
2. To understand better how organizations function as systems.

INSTRUCTIONS

1. Think about your university from the perspective of being an open system.
2. Answer the questions on the University System Analysis Worksheet individually, or in small groups, as directed by your instructor.

University System Analysis Worksheet

1. Referring back to Exhibit A.3, what subsystems compose your university system? Diagram the system.

_____

_____

_____

2. Identify the following in your university system: inputs, transformations, outputs, and goods or services.

_____

_____

_____

3. What are the strengths of the current system? What are the weaknesses? (Is it a system failure when a student fails to graduate?)

_____

_____

_____

4. What changes (if any) would you make to the transformation process?

_____

_____

_____

SOURCE: Adapted from Gordon, J., *A Diagnostic Approach to Organizational Behavior.* Englewood Cliffs, NJ: Prentice Hall, 1983, p. 38.

ENDNOTES

1. C. George, *The History of Management Thought* (Englewood Cliffs, NJ: Prentice-Hall, 1972).
2. C. George, *The History of Management Thought* (Englewood Cliffs, NJ: Prentice-Hall, 1972).
3. P. Godfrey, J. Hassard, E. O'Connor, et al., "What Is Organizational History? Toward a Creative Synthesis of History and Organization Studies," *Academy of Management Review* 41 (2016), pp. 590–608.
4. A. D. Chandler, *Scale and Scope: The Dynamic of Industrial Capitalism* (Cambridge, MA: Belknap Press of Harvard University Press, 1990).
5. A. D. Chandler, *Scale and Scope: The Dynamic of Industrial Capitalism* (Cambridge, MA: Belknap Press of Harvard University Press, 1990).
6. J. Baughman, *The History of American Management* (Englewood Cliffs, NJ: Prentice Hall, 1969), chap. 1.
7. C. George, *The History of Management Thought* (Englewood Cliffs, NJ: Prentice-Hall, 1972), chaps. 5–7; F. Taylor, *The Principles of Scientific Management* (New York: Harper & Row, 1911).
8. J. Case, "A Company of Business People," *Inc.*, April 1993, pp. 70–93.
9. J. Schlosser and E. Florian, "Fortune 500 Amazing Facts!" *Fortune*, April 2004.
10. H. Fayol, *General and Industrial Management*, trans. C. Storrs (Marshfield, MA: Pitman Publishing, 1949).
11. C. George, *The History of Management Thought* (Englewood Cliffs, NJ: Prentice-Hall, 1972), chap. 9; J. Massie, "Management Theory," in *Handbook of Organizations*, ed. J. March (Chicago: Rand McNally, 1965), pp. 387–422.
12. C. Barnard, *The Functions of the Executive* (Cambridge, MA: Harvard University Press, 1938).
13. C. George, *The History of Management Thought* (Englewood Cliffs, NJ: Prentice-Hall, 1972); J. Massie, "Management Theory," in *Handbook of Organizations*, ed. J. March (Chicago: Rand McNally, 1965), pp. 387–422.
14. E. Mayo, *The Human Problems of Industrial Civilization* (New York: Macmillan, 1933); F. Roethlisberger and W. Dickson, *Management and the Worker* (Cambridge, MA: Harvard University Press, 1939).
15. A. Maslow, "A Theory of Human Motivation," *Psychological Review* 50 (July 1943), pp. 370–96.
16. A. Carey, "The Hawthorne Studies: A Radical Criticism," *American Sociological Review* 32, no. 3 (1967), pp. 403–16.
17. M. Weber, *The Theory of Social and Economic Organizations*, trans. T. Parsons and A. Henderson (New York: Free Press, 1947).
18. C. George, *The History of Management Thought* (Englewood Cliffs, NJ: Prentice-Hall, 1972), chap. 11.
19. D. McGregor, *The Human Side of Enterprise* (New York: McGraw-Hill, 1960).
20. C. Argyris, *Personality and Organization* (New York: Harper & Row, 1957).
21. R. Likert, *The Human Organization* (New York: McGraw-Hill, 1967).
22. L. von Bertalanffy, "The History and Status of General Systems Theory," *Academy of Management Journal* 15 (1972), pp. 407–26; D. Katz and R. Kahn, *The Social Psychology of Organizations*, 2nd ed. (New York: Wiley, 1978).
23. J. Thompson, *Organizations in Action* (New York: McGraw-Hill, 1967); J. Galbraith, *Organization Design* (Reading, MA: Addison-Wesley, 1977); D. Miller and P. Friesen, *Organizations: A Quantum View* (Englewood Cliffs, NJ: Prentice-Hall, 1984).
24. S. Cummings and T. Bridgman, "The Relevant Past: Why the History of Management Should Be Critical for Our Future," *Academy of Learning & Education* 10 (2011), pp. 77–93.

CHAPTER 2
The External and Internal Environments

> The essence of a business is outside itself.
> —Peter Drucker

kay/Getty Images

learning objectives

After studying Chapter 2, you will be able to:

LO 2-1 Describe how environmental forces influence organizations and how organizations can influence their environments.

LO 2-2 Distinguish between the macroenvironment and the competitive environment.

LO 2-3 Identify elements of the competitive environment.

LO 2-4 Summarize how organizations respond to environmental uncertainty.

LO 2-5 Define elements of an organization's culture.

LO 2-6 Discuss how an organization's culture and climate affect its response to its external environment.

chapter outline

The Macroenvironment
The Economy
Technology
Laws and Regulations
Demographics
Social Issues
Sustainability and the Natural Environment

The Competitive Environment
Competitors
New Entrants
Substitutes and Complements
Suppliers
Customers

Environmental Analysis
Environmental Scanning
Scenario Development
Forecasting
Benchmarking

Actively Managing the External Environment
Changing the Environment You Are In
Influencing Your Environment
Adapting to the Environment: Changing the Organization
Choosing an Approach

The Internal Environment of Organizations: Culture and Climate
Organization Culture
Organizational Climate

Management in Action

AMAZON: SURVIVING AND THRIVING IN ANY ENVIRONMENT

Most companies strive to succeed in a specific environment. That goal doesn't seem to be enough for Amazon, however. Under founder and CEO Jeff Bezos, Amazon strives to succeed in *every* environment.

Bezos founded the company in 1994 as an online discount bookseller during the early days of the Internet. Amazon's success was hard-won. There were thousands of online retail start-ups at the time, and just as many failed. Amazon hung on, despite taking almost a decade to become profitable. When it finally posted a profit in 2003, the *Wall Street Journal* called it "one of the most powerful survivors on the Internet."

Today the company has grown from selling books to selling virtually everything. It has developed an e-reader, introduced the Echo as an AI voice service, patented its 1-Click ordering technology, is exploring using drones to facilitate same-day-delivery, and is posing a threat to Netflix as the number one streaming service provider.[1] Far from that scrappy start-up in the 1990s, Amazon is now the fourth most valuable firm in the United States and the largest e-commerce company in the world.[2]

As if virtual domination wasn't enough, Amazon is expanding in the brick-and-mortar physical environment. There's more than a touch of irony in the fact that national brick-and-mortar bookstore chains have gone bankrupt (e.g., Border's Books) or have been damaged (e.g., Barnes & Noble) during Amazon's rise to the top, but now Amazon is opening its own brick-and-mortar bookstores in this now depleted environment. Called Amazon Books, the first store opened in Seattle in 2015, and Amazon has since opened stores nationwide, with plans to expand.[3]

In 2017, Amazon also acquired the largest organic grocery store chain, Whole Foods, and its 460 locations across North America. Patrons of Whole Foods now receive discounts if they are also Amazon Prime members, and the Amazon logo can be seen throughout the

Morgan Lieberman/FilmMagic/Getty Images

stores. Venturing further into the food industry, Amazon has launched its own grocery store brand—Amazon Go. It's the first completely cashierless store of its kind. The first stores opened in 2018, with plans to open more in the future.[4]

What does all this add up to? In 2018, Amazon's revenue was a whopping $233 billion, up from $178 billion in 2017. Bezos seems to possess an ability to not only thrive in multiple environments, but also transform them.

To push the boundaries in the ways that Amazon has, its managers must scrutinize and analyze environmental forces. Technology and global competition are two of the forces shaping the environment in which Amazon operates. As you study this chapter, consider what other forces Amazon's managers should monitor.

Organization as an Open System

open systems

Organizations that are affected by, and that affect, their environment.

inputs

Goods and services organizations take in and use to create products or services.

outputs

The products and services organizations create.

external environment

All relevant forces outside a firm's boundaries, such as competitors, customers, the government, and the economy.

competitive environment

The immediate environment surrounding a firm; includes suppliers, customers, rivals, and the like.

LO 2-1 Describe how environmental forces influence organizations and how organizations can influence their environments.

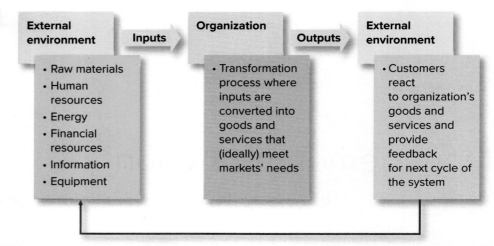

In this chapter, we discuss how pressures from outside the organization help create the context in which managers and their companies must operate.

Organizations are **open systems**—that is, they are affected by and in turn affect their external environments. For example, they take in **inputs** such as human resources and investment capital from their environment and use them to create products and services that are **outputs** to their environment, as shown in Exhibit 2.1. But when we use the term **external environment** here, we mean more than an organization's clients or customers; the external environment includes *all* relevant forces outside the organization's boundaries.

Many of these factors are uncontrollable. Companies large and small are affected by recessions, government regulations, new laws, competitors' actions, and other factors. But their lack of control does not mean that managers can ignore such forces, use them as excuses for poor performance, and try to just get by. Managers must monitor external developments and respond effectively. Moreover, sometimes managers can influence components of the external environment. Later in the chapter, we will examine ways in which organizations can do just that.

Exhibit 2.2 shows the external and internal environments of a business organization. The organization exists in its **competitive environment**, which is composed of the firm and its rivals, suppliers, customers (buyers), new entrants, and substitute or complementary

The External and Internal Environments of Organizations

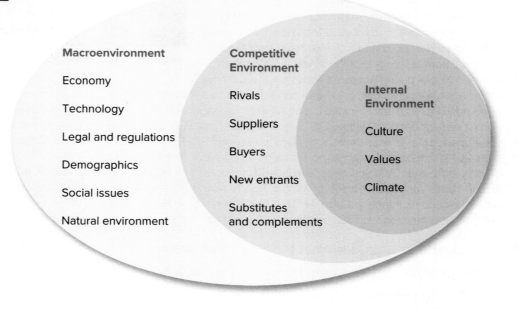

products. At the more general level is the **macroenvironment**, which includes legal, political, economic, technological, demographic, and social and natural factors that generally affect all organizations.

This chapter discusses the basic characteristics of an organization's external environment and the importance of those environments for strategic management. We also examine the *internal environment,* or *culture,* of the organization and the ways that culture may influence the organization's response to its external environment.

Later chapters delve more deeply into many of the basic environmental forces introduced here. For example, technology receives deeper treatment in Chapter 17. The global environment gets a thorough treatment in Chapter 6. Other chapters focus on ethics, social responsibility, and the natural environment. Chapter 18 reiterates the theme that recurs throughout this text: Organizations must change continually because environments change continually.

macroenvironment

The general environment; includes governments, economic conditions, and other fundamental factors that generally affect all organizations.

The Macroenvironment

All organizations operate in a macroenvironment, which is defined by the most general elements in the external environment that can influence strategic decisions. Top management teams must consider external factors before taking action.

LO 2-2 Distinguish between the macroenvironment and the competitive environment.

The Economy

Although most Americans think in terms of the U.S. economy, the economic environment for organizations is much larger—created by complex interconnections among the economies of different countries. Growth and recessions occur worldwide as well as domestically.

The economic environment affects managers' ability to function effectively and influences their strategic choices. Interest and inflation rates affect the availability and cost of capital, growth opportunities, prices, costs, and consumer demand for products. Changes in the value of the dollar on world exchanges make American products cheaper (or more expensive) than their foreign competitors. Unemployment rates affect labor availability, the wages the firm must pay, and product demand.

Extended periods of low unemployment pose difficult challenges for businesses. In the beginning of 2019, the U.S. unemployment rate was 4.0 percent which was close to full employment.[5] At this low unemployment rate, businesses find it challenging to find workers; open positions lead to missed sales or lower-quality customer service. Another challenge is the risk of higher interest rates. Higher demand for workers fuels wage inflation. To control this inflation, the Federal Reserve raises interest rates which make it more costly for businesses to borrow capital for investment.[6]

Making the hiring situation worse is the participation rate, or percentage of eligible individuals who could be working, dropped from 66 percent in 2008 to just below 63 percent during the fourth quarter of 2018.[7] The participation rate is projected to decline further to 61 percent by 2026.[8]

Governments exert influence over the economy. In several countries, the federal government is a major employer and customer for business and military goods and services. Some governments spend more money than they receive, making them major borrowers in the financial markets (adding to the national debt). These government activities can increase or decrease a nation's economic activity.

The stock market is another important economic influence. When investors bid up stock prices, companies have more capital to implement their strategies. Stock market observers watch trends in major indexes such as the Dow Jones Industrial Average, Standard and Poor's 500, and NASDAQ Composite, which combine many companies' performance into a single measure. Stock indexes tell managers about overall expectations for business value.

Bottom Line

With increased competition from foreign and domestic companies, managers must look for ways to reduce costs. *Does low cost mean low quality? Why or why not?*

> *Economic conditions change over time and are difficult to predict.*

In publicly held companies, managers throughout the organization feel required to meet Wall Street's earnings expectations. Such external pressures usually have a positive effect—they help make many firms more efficient and profitable. But failure to meet expectations can cause a company's stock price to drop, making it more difficult for the firm to raise additional capital for investment. Managers' compensation also may be affected, particularly if they have been issued stock options. The net effect of these pressures often is that managers focus on short-term results at the expense of the long-term health of their organizations. Even worse, a few managers may be tempted to engage in unethical or unlawful behavior that misleads investors.[9] We will discuss managerial ethics in Chapter 5 and stock options in Chapter 10.

Economic conditions change over time and are difficult to predict. Bull and bear markets come and go. Periods of dramatic growth may be followed by recessions. Every trend undoubtedly will end—but when? Even when times seem good, budget deficits or other considerations create concern about the future.

Technology

Today a company cannot succeed without incorporating into its strategy the myriad technologies that continually evolve. Technological advances create new products and services, more efficient production and delivery techniques, and better ways of managing and communicating. As technologies evolve, new industries, markets, and competitive niches develop.

The 3D printing process has revolutionized design.

Maciej Frolow/Getty Images

For example, early entrants in autonomous vehicle technology or artificial intelligence–powered digital aids (e.g., Alexa and Siri) tried to establish dominant positions, and later entrants worked on technological advances that would give them a competitive niche. Advances in technology also permit companies to enter markets that otherwise would be unavailable to them. Advances in augmented reality led to the creation of zSpace's VR laptop, which allows users to wear head-tracking 3D glasses to see objects as if they were part of the real world.[10]

Augmented reality, popularized when millions of people played Pokémon Go in the summer of 2016, now is used for more serious purposes. Microsoft recently signed a $480 million contract with the U.S. Army to allow the Army to purchase over 100,000 military-grade HoloLens headsets to aid in live combat.[11]

New technologies also provide new production techniques. A new manufacturing technique called rotary friction welding can weld two metal components together by rotating one part at a high speed against a stationary part. The aerospace, automotive, electrical, and oil and gas industries are utilizing this welding method because of its quick speed, high integrity, and high energy efficiency.[12]

In addition, new technologies provide new ways to manage and communicate. Cloud computing enables businesses to host their websites, build Internet applications, track invoices, and protect applications from data loss or disruption among many other uses.[13] Videoconference platforms like Skype, Zoom, and Cisco's WebEx allow managers and employees to collaborate easily and efficiently. Strategies developed around new technological advances create a competitive advantage; strategies that ignore or lag behind competitors' technologies lead to obsolescence and extinction. This issue is so important that we devote an entire chapter (Chapter 17) to it.

Bottom Line

Managers with access to timely and relevant information gain a significant competitive edge. *What are some technologies that have given managers fast access to information?*

Laws and Regulations

U.S. government policies impose strategic constraints on organizations but may also provide opportunities.[14] Some managers view the U.S. Patient Protection and Affordable Care Act (PPACA), which requires businesses with 50 or more full-time employees to offer health insurance, primarily as a compliance-related cost; whereas others see it as an opportunity for their companies.[15] This requirement increases an employers' labor costs, but it also can be used more strategically than competitors when recruiting and retaining talent.[16]

Giving employees more generous benefits could add to the cost of compensating them. At this writing, Congress is debating and revising a bill titled the American Health Care Act that, if passed, would replace the PPACA.[17]

The government can affect business opportunities through tax laws, economic policies, and international trade rulings. For example, in some countries bribes and kickbacks are common and expected ways of doing business, but for U.S. firms, they are illegal practices. Some U.S. businesses like Legg Mason and United Technologies have been fined for using bribery when competing internationally.[18] But laws can also assist organizations. U.S. federal and state governments protect property rights, including copyrights, trademarks, and patents, making it more attractive economically to start businesses in the United States than in countries where laws and law enforcement offer less protection.

As described in Exhibit 2.3, *regulators* are government agencies that have the power to investigate company practices and take legal action to ensure compliance with laws.

Often, the business community sees government as an adversary. However, many organizations realize that government can be a source of competitive advantages for an individual company or an entire industry. Public policy may prevent or limit new foreign or domestic competitors from entering an industry. Government may subsidize failing companies or provide tax breaks to some. Federal patents protect innovative products or production process technologies. Legislation may be passed to support industry prices, thereby guaranteeing profits or survival. The government may even intervene to ensure the survival of certain key industries or companies, as it has done to help auto companies, airlines, and agricultural businesses.

Demographics

Demographics are measures of various characteristics of the people who make up groups or other social units. Proactive managers consider workforce demographics in formulating their human resource strategies. Population changes influence the size and composition of the labor force. The number of young workers will decline while the fastest-growing age group will be workers who are 55 and older, who are expected to represent over one-fourth of the labor force in 2026.[19]

demographics

Measures of various characteristics of the people who make up groups or other social units.

Agency Name	Purpose
Securities and Exchange Commission (SEC)	Protects investors and maintains fair, honest, and efficient markets.
Occupational Safety and Health Administration (OSHA)	Enforces workplace safety and health standards.
Equal Employment Opportunity Commission (EEOC)	Enforces federal laws that prohibit discrimination in the workplace.
National Labor Relations Board (NLRB)	Safeguards employees' rights to organize and to determine whether to have unions as their bargaining representative.
Office of Federal Contract Compliance Programs (OFCCP)	Monitors federal contractors to make sure they take affirmative action to ensure equal employment opportunities.

EXHIBIT 2.3
Some Governmental Agencies That Regulate Businesses

Inclusiveness Works

Women in Leadership Roles: A Strategy for Success

Too often companies treat diversity and inclusion as a task to be checked off rather than as an opportunity to gain a competitive advantage. Yet research has shown that diverse workforces don't just satisfy legal requirements, they make companies more profitable.

According to research by McKinsey & Company, organizations with the most ethnically diverse workforces were 33 percent more likely to be leaders in profitability. Organizations with the least diverse workforces were 29 percent less likely to attain above-average profitability. As stated in the research report, "not only were [these firms] not leading, they were lagging."[20]

The benefits aren't restricted to ethnic diversity; gender diversity is also a boon for bottom lines, particularly when women are in leadership positions. According to the report, organizations that ranked the highest for gender diversity in executive teams were "21% more likely to outperform on profitability and 27% more likely to have superior value creation."[21] Research from the Peterson Institute for International Economics confirms this finding.

According to the Peterson report, a firm increasing its executive leadership team to 30 percent women translates on average to a 15 percent increase in profitability.[22]

The reasons for such benefits are multifaceted, but some researchers contend that a diversified management team increases the effectiveness of monitoring staff performance. A larger percentage of the talent pool also perceives firms with diverse workforces as more desirable, thereby bolstering recruitment, promotion, and retention of top talent. This same perception also works *against* firms: Those perceived as lacking diversity lose out on top talent, so overall productivity suffers.[23]

Bottom line? Smart managers understand that diversity isn't a challenge; it's a strategy for success.

1. Why do you think that firms that are more diverse are often more profitable? What may explain these findings?
2. As a potential job seeker, would the diversity of a firm matter to you in your choice of workplace? Why or why not?

The education and skill levels of the workforce are another crucial demographic factor that managers must consider. The share of the U.S. labor force with at least some college education has been increasing steadily over the past several decades.[24] Even so, many companies find that they must invest in training their entry-level workers, who may not possess adequate levels of teamwork, writing, or problem-solving skills required by today's workplace.[25]

As the number of people in the workforce with a college education changes, managers must consider how this affects work and careers.

Rawpixel.com/Shutterstock

Employers are finding it difficult to recruit employees for jobs that require knowledge of a skilled trade, such as machinists, ironworkers, and electricians.[26] However, as education levels increase around the globe, managers can send even technical tasks to lower-priced but highly trained workers overseas. We discuss this further in Chapter 6.

Immigration is another important factor affecting the U.S. population and labor force.[27] Immigrants of working age frequently have different educational and occupational backgrounds from the rest of the labor force. Immigration is one reason the labor force continues to become more ethnically diverse. In 2017, more than 27 million workers (or 17 percent) of the total U.S. labor force was foreign-born.[28]

A more diverse workforce has many advantages, but managers are legally required to be inclusive regarding women, minorities, and others with respect to employment, advancement opportunities, and compensation. They must make strategic plans to recruit, retain, train, motivate, and effectively use people of diverse demographic backgrounds who have the skills to achieve the company's mission. We discuss the issue of managing the diverse workforce in greater depth in Chapters 10 and 11.

Social Issues

Societal trends have major implications for management of the labor force, corporate social actions, and strategic decisions about products and markets. For example, society's view toward working parents who want time off to spend quality time with their newborn is changing. While U.S. law requires companies to provide 12 weeks of unpaid leave for new parents, that won't be enough to meet the expectations of today's top talent. Microsoft offers 12 weeks of full pay for new mothers and fathers. Netflix provides unlimited paid parental leave during the year following the adoption or birth of a child.[29]

Many firms extend such benefits to all employees or allow them to design their own benefits packages, where they can choose from a menu of available benefits. Domestic partners, whether they are in a marital relationship or not, are covered by many employee benefit programs. Firms provide these benefits as a source of competitive advantage: attracting and retaining an experienced workforce.

How companies respond to social issues can affect their brand reputations, which in turn can help or hinder their competitiveness. For companies in the soft-drink industry, one issue demanding a response is the epidemic of obesity and associated health problems such as diabetes. Coca-Cola has pledged to reduce the amount of sugar in its drinks by 2025 in Asia and Australia to aid in the fight against these epidemics. The company has also expanded into sparkling water to appeal to health-conscious consumers. PepsiCo is also offering healthier beverage alternatives. In 2018, PepsiCo bought SodaStream, a carbonated water maker that allows consumers to transform tap water into unflavored or flavored sparkling water at home.[30]

Social Entrepreneurship

Combating Climate Change

Despite its far-reaching impact, the problem of climate change has struggled to gain center stage in the United States. The Paris Agreement is a landmark multination pact that took effect around the world in November 2016, calling on all participating countries, including the United States, to curb their emissions of the greenhouse gases that contribute to planet-wide warming temperatures.

Arguing that controlling climate change is good for business, hundreds of U.S. companies petitioned President Trump's White House to hold to former president Obama's commitment to the Paris Agreement. The companies included Dannon, eBay, Gap, General Mills, Intel, Kellogg, Mars, Monsanto, Nike, Patagonia, Staples, Starbucks, and many smaller firms. Their open letter to the president said, in part, "Failure to build a low-carbon economy puts American prosperity at risk. But the right action now will create jobs and boost US competitiveness. Implementing the Paris Agreement will enable and encourage businesses and investors to turn the billions of dollars in existing low-carbon investments into the trillions of dollars the world needs to bring clean energy and prosperity to all."[31] Their petition, however, went unheeded, as President Trump announced on June 1, 2017, that the United States would withdraw from the pact, effective at the end of 2020.

Despite the government's intent to withdraw from the pact, many businesses have begun their own initiatives to combat climate change. Firms are reexamining everything from their standard supply chains to the types of energy they consume to the materials they use to make products.[32] LEGO, for example, recently introduced new blocks made of plant-based, sustainable materials. It has set a goal to have the majority of its production processes be sustainable by 2030.[33] In 2018, Starbucks launched its "Greener Stores" initiative, aiming to have 10,000 environmentally friendly stores by 2025. Accomplishing this goal would involve being able to generate enough of its operating energy through wind and solar to offset all the electricity it uses in the United States and Canada.[34]

Combating climate change will require efforts from individuals, governments, and businesses alike. The impact of any one person, just as with one company, will be minimal. Collectively, however, positive change is possible.

1. What do you think the role of business should be in relation to the environment?
2. Do you patronize businesses based on their sustainability efforts? Why or why not?

Sustainability and the Natural Environment

Organizations depend on the natural environment to provide them with resources. Depending on their products and processes, they may need trees for paper, steel for manufacturing goods, petroleum to fuel transportation or make plastics, and adequate air and water quality to maintain a healthy workforce. In addition, the ways in which organizations operate will have some impact on the quantity and quality of natural resources available. When the quantity is depleted or the quality is damaged, costs for resources skyrocket. Furthermore, the impact on natural resources—whether negatively by poisoning wells or positively by restoring forests—affects the quality of life for citizens in the areas where companies operate. Decisions that affect the natural environment therefore shape the climate of social issues and the political and legal environments.

Less than a decade ago, the explosion of BP's Deepwater Horizon drilling rig in the Gulf of Mexico killed 11 workers and caused more than 200 million barrels of oil to gush into the Gulf and spread toward the coastlands of Mississippi and Louisiana. After BP took 87 days to cap the underwater well, over 1,100 miles of marshes and beaches in four Gulf states were contaminated.[35] BP had to set aside tens of billions of dollars to cover all costs of the spill and its cleanup. In addition, the U.S. government fined the company billions of dollars. To prevent similar accidents in the future, it imposed more regulations on oil companies that want to drill in the Gulf.[36]

The Competitive Environment

LO 2-3 Identify elements of the competitive environment.

All managers are affected by the components of the macroenvironment we've just discussed. But each organization also interacts directly with others in a closer, more immediate competitive environment. As shown in Exhibit 2.4, the competitive environment includes rivalries among current competitors and the impact of new entrants, substitute and complementary products, suppliers, and customers.

The model shown in the exhibit originally was developed by Harvard professor Michael Porter, a noted authority on strategic management. According to Porter, successful managers do more than simply react to the environment; they act in ways that actually shape or change the organization's environment. In strategic decision making, Porter's model is an

EXHIBIT 2.4
The Competitive Environment

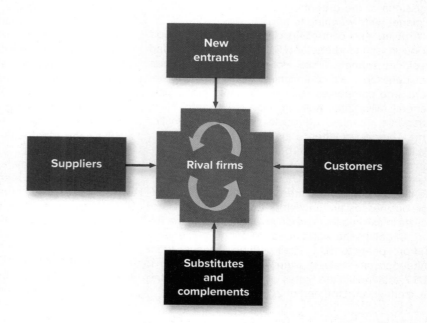

excellent method to help managers analyze the competitive environment and adapt to or influence the nature of their competition.

Competitors

Competitors within an industry must deal with one another. When organizations compete for the same customers and try to win market share at the others' expense, all must react to and anticipate their competitors' actions.

The competition between Coke and Pepsi products is intense.

Alpha and Omega Collection/Alamy Stock Photo

The first question to consider is this: Who is the competition? Sometimes the answer is obvious. The major competitors in the market for soft drinks are Coca-Cola and PepsiCo. But consumer tastes have shifted away from soda to bottled water and other beverages. Young people, who in the past were the main consumers of soft drinks, increasingly prefer to buy water, coffee, or energy drinks, so sales of soda have declined for years. Adding to this decline, a number of cities have applied new taxes to soda purchases. Therefore, Coca-Cola and PepsiCo now compete in introducing new, less sugary products, not just in winning consumers over to their brand of cola.[37]

Thus, as a first step in understanding their competitive environment, organizations must identify their competitors. Competitors may include (1) small domestic firms, especially in tiny, premium markets; (2) strong regional competitors; (3) big new domestic companies exploring new markets; (4) overseas firms, especially those that try to solidify their position in small niches (a traditional Japanese tactic) or draw on an inexpensive labor force on a large scale (as in China); and (5) newer entries, such as firms offering their products on the web.

The growth in competition from other countries has been especially significant with the worldwide reduction in international trade barriers. For example, the Asia-Pacific Economic Cooperation (APEC) promotes free trade and sustainable growth among its 21 member nations (including the United States). Managers today confront a particular challenge from low-cost producers abroad (see Chapter 6).

After identifying competitors, the next step is to analyze *how* they compete. Competitors use tactics such as price reductions, new-product introductions, and traditional and social media advertising campaigns to gain advantage over their rivals. In its competition against PepsiCo, Coca-Cola outdoes its rival with much heavier spending on advertising.[38] The emphasis on promotion helps the company win a larger share of not only the cola market but also juices (its Minute Maid outsells PepsiCo's Tropicana) and sports drinks (its Powerade is beating PepsiCo's Gatorade).

PepsiCo is competing in other ways. It launched a global Pepsi Generations campaign designed to celebrate the brand's history within the music industry. Limited edition cans featured stars such as Michael Jackson, Ray Charles, and Britney Spears.[39]

It's essential to understand what competitors are doing when you are honing your own strategy. If soft-drink consumption continues to fall, Coke cannot be complacent about its leadership over Pepsi. Most of Coke's sales are beverages. PepsiCo, in contrast, has expanded into a broader range of products, hoping to grow sales whether consumers are looking for a fun treat or a healthful snack. Besides reducing salt and sugar in traditional snacks such as chips, the company is expanding healthful options under its Quaker brand (e.g., Gluten Free oatmeal), Bare Snacks, and Health Warrior.[40] Coke lacks a presence in these areas but is expanding its investments in healthier drinks like sparkling water products and beverage start-ups, including Suja Life, which makes high-pressure processed juices.[41]

Competition is most intense when there are many direct competitors (including foreign contenders), when industry growth is slow, and when the product or service cannot be differentiated in some way. New, high-growth industries offer enormous opportunities

Bottom Line

Companies often compete through innovation, quality, service, and cost. *In which of these areas would you say PepsiCo tried to create a competitive advantage? We will discuss competitive strategy further in Chapter 4.*

It's essential to understand what competitors are doing when you are refining your own strategy.

for profits. When an industry matures and growth slows, profits drop. Then intense competition causes an industry shakeout: weaker companies are eliminated, and the strong companies survive.[42]

New Entrants

New entrants into an industry compete with established companies. New entrants in the market for entertainment come from unexpected quarters as increasing broadband speeds and more powerful microprocessors enable many different ways to enjoy movies, TV shows, sports, concerts, videos, and games online. Cable and satellite television saw viewers flock to Hulu, Blockbuster lost movie sales to Netflix, and the makers of video game consoles have watched sales dry up as consumers switched to playing games on apps for their smartphones.

When there are many factors that prevent new companies from entering an industry, the threat to established firms is less serious. But if there are few such **barriers to entry**, the threat of new entrants is more serious. Some major barriers to entry are government policy, capital requirements, brand identification, cost disadvantages, and distribution channels.

The government can limit or prevent entry, as occurs when the Food and Drug Administration (FDA) forbids a new drug to enter the market. On the other hand, when a firm's patent expires, other companies can enter the market and threaten once-dominant pharmaceutical companies—for example, when Johnson & Johnson lost patent protection for the prostate-cancer drug Zytiga. Zytiga had earned the company $1.4 billion in just nine months in 2018. In the face of new stiff competition from generic drug makers, Johnson & Johnson is continuing to fight for a new patent.[43]

Other barriers are less formal but can have the same effect. Capital requirements may be so high that companies won't risk such large amounts of money. Brand identification forces new entrants to spend heavily to overcome customer loyalty. Imagine the costs involved in trying to launch a new cola against Coke or Pepsi. The cost advantages that established companies hold—due to large size, favorable locations, existing assets, and so forth—can be formidable entry barriers.

Finally, existing competitors may have such tight distribution channels that new entrants have difficulty getting their goods or services to customers. For example, established food products already have supermarket shelf space. New entrants must displace existing products with promotions, price breaks, intensive selling, and other tactics.

Substitutes and Complements

Besides products that directly compete, other products can affect a company's performance by being substitutes for or complements of the company's offerings. A *substitute* is a potential threat; customers use it as an alternative, buying less of one kind of product but more of another. A *complement* is a potential opportunity because customers buy more of a given product if they also demand more of the complementary product. Exhibit 2.5 lists a dozen products and their potential substitutes and complements.

Technological advances and economic efficiencies enable firms to develop substitutes for existing products. After Amazon introduced the Kindle e-reader and Barnes & Noble introduced the competing Nook—and even more so as the companies were able to lower the price of these devices—consumers began treating e-books as an attractive substitute for printed books. But even as consumers were still gravitating toward e-readers, Apple launched the iPad tablet computer. Because it is lightweight and versatile, consumers treated it as a substitute not only for e-readers, but also, in some cases, as a substitute for a basic laptop computer.

Companies don't have to be at the mercy of customers switching to a substitute. To avoid losing out when others create a new substitute, some companies try to create their own substitute products. PepsiCo's investment in development of new sweeteners for drinks and a line of more healthful snacks offers substitutes for consumers avoiding the calories, fat, and sugar of its "fun for you" products. Anticipating that a growing share of consumers will care

barriers to entry

Conditions that prevent new companies from entering an industry.

Bottom Line

Cost is often a major barrier to entry. *Would cost be a bigger barrier for someone who opens a new tattoo shop or a developer of mobile game apps? Why?*

If the Product Is . . .	The Substitute Might Be . . .
Chipotle Burrito Bowl	Chick-fil-A meal
Apple Watch	Samsung Galaxy Watch
Ford F-150 truck	Chevy Silverado truck
Evernote	Dropbox

If the Product Is . . .	The Complement Might Be . . .
HTC Vive virtual reality headset	Eagle Flight game
Amazon streaming video	Strawberry Twizzlers
Healthclub membership	Workout clothes
Apartment rental	IKEA furniture

EXHIBIT 2.5

Potential Substitutes and Complements

about healthful snacking, PepsiCo's former CEO Nooyi believed the company's products should include many choices that can aid health and well-being.[44]

Besides identifying and planning for substitutes, companies must consider taking advantage of complements for their products. When people are buying new homes, they are also buying appliances and landscaping products. When customers purchase new smartphones, they may also buy new cases, screen protectors, car kits, battery chargers, and insurance. And when consumers munch on Lay's, Doritos, or Cheetos snacks, they are bound to get thirsty and need a complementary product—say, an ice-cold Pepsi or Sierra Mist. PepsiCo owns all these food and drink brands; thus the company sells products that are complements as well as substitutes. If PepsiCo meets its goal to shift more of its product line to healthier fare, it may become known for its complementary products, too—say, some Tropicana juice with your Quaker oatmeal.[45]

As with substitutes, a company needs to watch for new complements that can change the competitive landscape. Publishers that originally saw e-readers and tablet computers as a threat—as substitutes for their print publications—worked on complements for their print products such as electronic books and magazines plus apps for reading content online. Textbook and cookbook publishers teamed up with software company Inkling to prepare e-book versions that support the use of multimedia and interactive features. These books offer capabilities that would be impossible in the print versions and therefore sell at higher prices.[46]

Suppliers

Recall from our discussion at the start of the chapter that organizations are open systems that acquire resources (inputs) from their environments and convert those resources into products or services (outputs) that they sell. Suppliers provide the resources needed for production. Those resources include people (supplied by trade schools and universities), raw materials (from producers, wholesalers, and distributors), information (supplied by researchers and consulting firms), and financial capital (from banks, crowdfunding, and other sources).

> Organizations are at a disadvantage if they become overly dependent on a single powerful supplier.

Suppliers are important beyond the mere provision of resources. The resources they supply may be outstanding or defective. They can provide excellent or poor-quality service. Suppliers can raise their prices. Powerful suppliers' price increases can reduce an organization's profits, particularly if the organization cannot pass them on to its customers.

Organizations are at a disadvantage if they become overly dependent on a powerful supplier. A supplier accrues power if the buyer has few other sources of supply or if the supplier has many other buyers. Dependence also results from high **switching costs**—the fixed costs buyers face if they change suppliers. For example, once a buyer learns how to use a

switching costs

Fixed costs buyers face when they change suppliers.

supply chain management

The managing of the network of facilities and people that obtain materials from outside the organization, transform them into products, and distribute them to customers.

final consumer

A customer who purchases products in their finished form.

intermediate consumer

A customer who purchases raw materials or wholesale products before selling them to final customers.

supplier's equipment, such as a data analytics application, the buyer faces both economic and psychological costs in changing to a new supplier.

Of course, close supplier relationships can be an advantage. Food and beverage companies work closely with the makers of the flavorings and additives that make their products appealing to consumers. With companies such as PepsiCo and Coca-Cola looking to offer more healthful and natural soft drinks, suppliers such as Archer Daniels Midland answered the call. ADM bought food-ingredients maker Wild Flavors for $3 billion to supply unique blends of vitamins and minerals, sweeteners based on the stevia plant, energy boosters extracted from coffee beans, and new flavors such as ginger and chili.[47]

Supply chain management is a vital contributor to a company's competitiveness and profitability. By **supply chain management**, also known as the *extended enterprise,* we mean the managing of the entire network of facilities and people that obtain raw materials from outside the organization, transform them into products, and distribute them to customers.[48]

Increasing competition requires managers to pay ever-closer attention to their costs. They can no longer afford to hold large and costly inventories, waiting for orders to come in; once orders do come in, some products still sitting in inventory might be outdated. Customers today look for products built to their specific needs and preferences—and they want them delivered quickly at the lowest available price. This requires the supply chain to be not only efficient but also *flexible,* so that the organization's output can quickly respond to changes in demand.

Choosing the right supplier is an important strategic decision. Suppliers can affect manufacturing time, product quality, and inventory levels. The relationship between suppliers and the organization is changing in many companies. The close supplier relationship has become a preferred model for organizations using a just-in-time manufacturing approach (discussed in Chapters 16 and 17). And in some companies, innovative managers form strategic partnerships with their key suppliers in developing new products or new production techniques. We describe this kind of strategic partnership in more detail in Chapter 9.

Customers

Without customers to purchase its goods or services, a company won't survive. Customers can be intermediate (wholesalers and retailers) or final (end users), depending on where they are in the value chain. You are a **final consumer** when you upgrade to new iPhone or eat lunch at Panera Bread. **Intermediate consumers** buy raw materials or wholesale products and then sell to final consumers, as when Lenovo, Dell, and Hewlett-Packard buy processors from Intel to use in their laptop computers.

Intermediate customers make more purchases than individual final consumers do. Types of intermediate customers include retailers, who buy clothes from wholesalers and manufacturers' representatives before selling them to their customers, and industrial buyers, who buy raw materials (such as chemicals) before converting them into final products. Selling to intermediate customers is often called *business-to-business (B2B)* selling. Notice in these B2B examples that the intermediate customer eventually goes on to become a seller.

Like suppliers, customers are important to organizations for reasons other than the money they provide for goods and services. Customers can demand lower prices, higher quality, unique product specifications, or better service. They also can play competitors against one another, as occurs when a car buyer (or a purchasing agent) collects offers from different dealerships and negotiates for the best price. Customers want to be actively involved with their products, as when the buyer of an iPhone customizes it with ring tones, wallpaper, and a variety of apps.

LEGO has taken customer input to another level by inviting the company's online community to submit and vote on new product ideas. LEGO employees review submissions

FedEx partners with many health care companies to provide logistics of all types from factory floor to a patient's front door.
oleschwander/Shutterstock

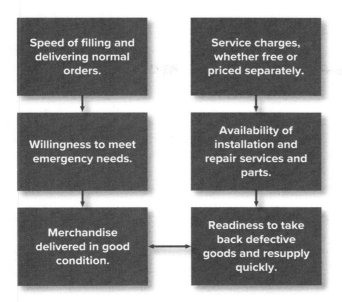

SOURCE: Adapted from Kotler, P., *Marketing Management: Analysis, Planning, Implementation and Control,* 9th ed. Englewood Cliffs, NJ: Prentice Hall, 1990.

EXHIBIT 2.6

Actions and Attitudes Affect Customer Service

that receive 10,000 votes and choose a winner. LEGO gives final approval and recognizes the design creator on all packaging and marketing materials. The designer then receives 1 percent of worldwide sales.[49]

The Internet empowers customers. It provides easy information about product features and pricing. In addition, Internet users informally create and share messages about a product, providing flattering free "advertising" at best or embarrassing and even erroneous bad publicity at worst. Companies try to use this to their advantage by creating opportunities for consumers and the brand to interact.

Another way companies connect with customers is through social media sites like LinkedIn *Company Pages,* which allows companies to invite individuals to join company-related groups. Recently, Netflix used LinkedIn to host a Q&A session that garnered over 1,000 responses from its followers.[50]

As we discussed in Chapter 1, customer service means giving customers what they want or need, the way they want it, the first time. This usually depends on the speed and dependability with which an organization can deliver its products. Exhibit 2.6 shows several actions and attitudes that contribute to excellent customer service.

A company is at a disadvantage if it depends too heavily on powerful customers. Customers are powerful if they make large purchases or if they can easily find alternative places to buy. If you are the largest customer of a firm and you can buy from others, you have power over that firm, and you likely can negotiate with it successfully. Your firm's biggest customers—especially if they can buy from other sources—will have the greatest negotiating power over you.

Customer relationship management is discussed more fully in Chapter 9. As you read "Management in Action: Progress Report," consider how Amazon distinguishes itself with customers by seeking advantages in its relationships with other parties in the competitive environment.

Bottom Line

In all businesses—services and manufacturing—strategies that emphasize good customer service provide a critical competitive advantage. *Identify some excellent and poor customer service that you have received.*

Environmental Analysis

Failing to understand key environmental influences, or to identify important opportunities and threats, severely undermines managers' ability to make decisions and execute plans. For example, if managers know little about customer likes and dislikes, they cannot effectively design new products, hire more employees, schedule production, or develop

LO 2-4 Summarize how organizations respond to environmental uncertainty.

Management in Action

AMAZON REINVENTS THE COMPETITIVE ENVIRONMENT

Amazon is known for its focus on customers, and it's easy to see that focus in its online retail operations. Its 1-Click ordering system, its Prime memberships (offering two-day delivery of unlimited purchases plus unlimited music and video streaming services for a one-time annual fee), its enormous product range, and its frequently discounted prices all attest to its commitment to make online shopping as rewarding and easy as possible.

But Amazon's view of its "customer set" is broader than just consumers who buy things. It also includes more than 2 million individuals and small companies that sell a huge array of products in Amazon's third-party Marketplace. Rather than compete with these sellers, Amazon has made them part of the family. In exchange for a cut of their proceeds, the online giant provides selling space on its site, handles warehousing and logistics for many sellers, and offers business coaching for some. With the help of this business, Amazon, already the largest online retailer in the world, is now the world's second-largest retailer of any kind, trailing only Walmart.[51]

Jeff Bezos credits Amazon's success in large part to the contribution these third-party sellers make to the number and variety of products it can offer. With hundreds of millions of separate stock-keeping units (SKUs), Amazon's inventory with these third-party sellers far surpasses Walmart's 8 million and is a big reason more online shoppers go to Amazon's site than any other.[52] The company has also designed Amazon Web Services (AWS), cloud-computing software that powers the site, to supply unbeatable speed and capacity even during peak shopping seasons.

1. No individual member of Amazon's Marketplace could pose a serious competitive threat to Amazon's business today. But Amazon wasn't always the giant it is now. Why do you think Bezos thought it was important to absorb potential competitors into his business?
2. Identify as many of Amazon's external competitors as you can in the market for retail consumer goods. What effect do you think the Marketplace has on these competitors?

marketing plans. Timely and accurate environmental information is crucial for running a successful business.

But information about the environment is not always readily available. Managers find it difficult to forecast how well their own products will sell, let alone how a competitor might respond. In other words, managers often operate under conditions of uncertainty. **Environmental uncertainty** means that managers do not have enough information about the environment to understand it or predict the future.

Uncertainty arises from two related factors: complexity and dynamism. Environmental *complexity* is the number of issues to which a manager must attend and their interconnectedness. For example, industries with many firms competing in vastly different ways are more complex—and uncertain—than industries with only a few key firms competing in fewer ways. Environmental *dynamism* is the degree of discontinuous change occurring within the industry. High-growth industries with products and technologies that change rapidly are more uncertain than stable industries where changes are less dramatic and more predictable.[53]

By analyzing environmental forces—in both the macroenvironment and the competitive environment—managers can identify opportunities and threats that might affect the organization. As environmental uncertainty increases, managers must develop methods like the following for collecting and interpreting information.

environmental uncertainty

When managers do not have enough information about the environment to understand or predict the future.

> Managers continually make important decisions under conditions of uncertainty.

Environmental Scanning

Managers cope with environmental uncertainty by trying to identify what might be important. Frequently, organizations and individuals act out of ignorance, only to regret those actions later. IBM had an opportunity to purchase the technology behind xerography, but turned it down. Xerox saw the potential, and the rest is history. On the other hand, Xerox researchers later developed the technology for the original computer mouse, but executives did not see the potential and the company missed a huge opportunity.

To understand and predict environmental changes, opportunities, and threats, companies such as Hyatt Hotels, Capital One Financial, and VMware spend time and money monitoring events. **Environmental scanning** means both searching for useful information and interpreting what is important and what is not. Managers can ask questions such as these:

Who are our current competitors?
Are there few or many entry barriers to our industry?
What substitutes exist for our product or service?
Is the company too dependent on powerful suppliers?
Is the company too dependent on powerful customers?[54]

Answers to these questions help managers develop **competitive intelligence**, the information necessary to decide how best to manage in their competitive environments. You can see how Porter's competitive analysis, discussed earlier, can guide environmental scanning. Exhibit 2.7 describes two environments: an attractive environment, which provides competitive advantage and high potential, and an unattractive environment, which puts a firm at a competitive disadvantage and offers low potential.[55]

environmental scanning
Searching for and sorting through information about the environment.

competitive intelligence
Information that helps managers determine how to compete better.

Caiaimage/Paul Bradbury/Getty Images

Scenario Development

As managers attempt to determine the effects of environmental forces on their organizations, they can develop **scenarios** depicting possible futures. Deciphering trends and predicting how events might unfold is a valuable activity, helping managers to plan ahead to deal with problems and envision a positive future to strive for.[56] Scenarios combine different factors into alternative pictures of future environments and the firm itself.

For example, when Congress and the president forecast the size of the federal budget deficit, they develop several scenarios about what the economy is likely to do in the coming years. Managers often develop a *best-case scenario* (the occurrence of events favorable to the firm), a *worst-case scenario* (the occurrence of unfavorable events), and at least one middle-ground alternative. The formal practice of scenario development was pioneered by Royal Dutch Shell.

Scenario development helps managers develop contingency plans for what they should do given different future situations.[57] For example, as a manager you will be involved in budgeting for your area. You likely will be asked to list initiatives that you would eliminate in case of an economic downturn, and new investments you would make if your firm does better than expected.

Effective managers regard the scenarios they develop as living documents: rather than preparing them once and forgetting them, they update them with relevant new factors as things change over time.

scenario
A narrative that describes a particular set of future conditions.

Environmental Factor	Unattractive	Attractive
Competitors	Many; low industry growth; equal size; commodity	Few; high industry growth; unequal size; differentiated
Threat of entry	High threat; few entry barriers	Low threat; many entry barriers
Substitutes	Many	Few
Suppliers	Few; high bargaining power	Many; low bargaining power
Customers	Few; high bargaining power	Many; low bargaining power

EXHIBIT 2.7
Attractive and Unattractive Environments

Forecasting

forecasting

Method for predicting how variables will change the future.

Whereas environmental scanning identifies important influences, and scenario development generates alternative pictures of the future, a **forecast** is a single prediction about the future. For example, in making capital investments, firms make forecasts about future interest rates. In deciding to expand or downsize a business, firms predict the demand for goods and services or the supply and demand of required labor. Publications such as the *Economist*'s *Global Forecasting Service,* PricewaterhouseCoopers's *Trendsetter Barometer Business Outlook,* Kiplinger's *Economic Outlook,* and the Conference Board's economic reports provide forecasts to businesses.

Although forecasts are designed to help executives predict the future, their accuracies vary greatly. Because they extrapolate from the past to project the future, forecasts are most accurate when the future proves to look a lot like the past. Forecasts are *potentially* most useful when the future will look radically different from the past, but unfortunately that is when forecasts tend to be less accurate.

The more things might change, the less confidence we have in our forecasts. The best advice for using forecasts includes the following:

Use multiple forecasts, and perhaps average their predictions.
Remember that accuracy decreases the farther into the future you are trying to predict.
Forecasts are no better than the assumptions made and the data used to construct them.
Use simple forecasts (rather than complicated ones) when possible.
Keep in mind that important events often are surprises and represent a departure from predictions.[58]

Benchmarking

benchmarking

The process of comparing an organization's practices and technologies with those of other companies.

In addition to trying to predict environment changes, firms can undertake intensive study of other firms' best practices to understand their sources of competitive advantage. **Benchmarking** means identifying the best-in-class performance by a company in a given area, say, product development or customer service, and then comparing your processes to theirs. To accomplish this, a benchmarking team collects information on its own company's operations and those of the other firm to determine gaps. These gaps serve as a point of entry to learn the underlying causes of performance differences. Ultimately, the team maps out a set of best practices that lead to world-class performance. We will discuss benchmarking further in Chapter 4.

Actively Managing the External Environment

It is essential to manage the external environment effectively. Clothing retailers who pay no attention to changes in the public's style preferences, or manufacturers who don't make sure they have reliable supply sources, are soon out of business. In managing their environments, managers and companies have several primary options: (1) selecting a new environment, (2) influencing the environment, and (3) adapting to the environment. This section describes the options briefly; we will elaborate on them in Chapter 4.

strategic maneuvering

An organization's conscious efforts to change the boundaries of its task environment.

domain selection

Entering a new market or industry using an existing expertise.

Changing the Environment You Are In

Organizations need not be stuck within a particular environment; they have options for determining where they operate. We refer to this as **strategic maneuvering**. By making a conscious effort to change the boundaries of its competitive environment, a firm can maneuver around potential threats and capitalize on arising opportunities.[59] Managers can use several strategic maneuvers, including domain selection, diversification, merger and acquisition, and divestiture.[60]

Domain selection is the entrance by a company into another suitable market or industry. For example, a market may have limited competition or regulation, ample suppliers and customers, or high growth. PepsiCo's decision to buy Stacy's Pita Chips and Smartfood Popcorn was based on the company's goal of selling more healthful snacks.[61]

Diversification occurs when a firm invests in different types of businesses or products or when it expands geographically to reduce its dependence on a single technology or market. Apple successfully diversified its product line when it added the iPod, iTouch, iPad, and iPhone to its offerings of personal and laptop computers. As the popularity of the devices spread, Apple identified an opportunity to further diversify in order to tap the fast-growing mobile app market. In 2017, Apple's App Store revenues jumped 35 percent from the previous year fueled by AR apps such as Pokémon Go. The store offered over 2.2 million apps and reported about 28 billion downloads worldwide. This part of Apple's empire generated over $26 billion for app developers, of which Apple retained 30 percent of the revenues.[62]

A **merger** or **acquisition** takes place when two or more firms combine, or one firm buys another, to form a single company. Mergers and acquisitions can offer greater efficiency from combined operations or can give companies relatively quick access to new markets or industries. Acquisitions also can quickly give a company access to a business, technology, or existing customer bases in different geographic markets.[63] The largest deal in 2018 was Cigna Group's acquisition of Express Scripts Holding Co., both of which are in the health care industry, for over $54 billion.[64]

Divestiture occurs when a company sells one or more businesses. A 2018 study found that 87 percent of large companies plan to sell one or more of their businesses within the next two years.[65] For example, General Motors announced that it would close five plants in North America, which could result in the layoffs of 15,000 employees. Part of the $2.5 billion savings will likely be allocated to emerging high-potential businesses like electric vehicle production. Cadillac is expected to be GM's lead brand in this growing category.[66] Mary Barra, CEO of General Motors, stated, "We will continue to strengthen our core business and invest in the technologies that will transform the future of mobility," She added, "Managing both well is critical to position General Motors for success for generations to come."[67]

Some companies, called **defenders**, stay within a limited, stable product domain. In contrast, **prospectors** are more likely to engage in strategic maneuvering.[68] Aggressive companies like Alphabet and Amazon continuously change the boundaries of their competitive environments by seeking new products and markets, diversifying, and merging or acquiring new enterprises. In these and other ways, corporations put their competitors on the defensive and force them to react.

Influencing Your Environment

In addition to redefining the boundaries of their environment, managers and organizations can develop proactive responses aimed at changing the environment. Two general types of proactive responses are independent action and cooperative action.

Independent Action   A company uses **independent strategies** when it acts on its own to change some aspect of its current environment.[69] Exhibit 2.8 shows the definitions and uses of these strategies. For example, Southwest Airlines demonstrates competitive aggression by cutting fares when it enters a new market, and Amazon uses competitive aggression whenever it launches a new product such as the Amazon Alexa or Echo to establish its dominance as a technological leader.

When Kellogg Company promotes the cereal industry as a whole, it demonstrates competitive pacification. Procter & Gamble's Always brand advertises the empowering "Always #LikeAGirl" (public relations).[70] Bank of America, Salesforce, Beats, and other companies have signed on to Product Red, a program in which they market special Red-themed products and donate a percentage of the profits to the Global Fund, a project to help end AIDS in Africa (voluntary action).[71] Shoe company Vans sued Target for allegedly copying Van's trademark Old Skool sneakers (legal action).[72] Over the past decade, the pharmaceutical industry spent approximately $2.5 billion to lobby and fund members of Congress (political action).[73] Each of these examples shows how single organizations can have an impact on their environments.

diversification

A firm's investment in a different product, business, or geographic area.

merger

One or more companies combining with another.

acquisition

One firm buying another.

divestiture

A firm selling one or more businesses.

defenders

Companies that stay within a stable product domain as a strategic maneuver.

prospectors

Companies that continuously change the boundaries for their task environments by seeking new products and markets, diversifying and merging, or acquiring new enterprises.

independent strategies

Strategies that an organization acting on its own uses to change some aspect of its current environment.

EXHIBIT 2.8   Independent Action

Strategy	Definition	Examples
Competitive aggression	Exploiting a distinctive competence or improving internal efficiency for competitive advantage	Aggressive pricing, comparative advertising (Taco Bell)
Competitive pacification	Independent action to improve relations with competitors	A food truck parking farther away from an established truck
Public relations	Establishing and maintaining favorable images in the minds of those making up the environment	Adidas sponsoring the World Cup or Olympics
Voluntary action	Voluntary commitment to various interest groups, causes, and social problems	Walmart donating supplies to wildfire victims
Legal action	Engaging a company in a private legal battle	Apple and Qualcomm engaging in multibillion-dollar legal dispute
Political action	Efforts to influence elected representatives to create a more favorable business environment or limit competition	Issue advertising; lobbying at state and national levels

corporate diplomacy

An umbrella term for attempting to influence external stakeholders through a variety of strategic activities

cooperative strategies

Strategies used by firms who want to reach their objectives in cooperation with other firms through alliances and partnerships rather than by competing with them.

Corporate diplomacy[74] is an umbrella term for attempting to influence external stakeholders through a variety of strategic activities. Corporate diplomacy is an emerging concept attempted by some businesses operating in challenging international political and social environments. Managers negotiate stakeholder relationships as they strive to achieve a firm's profit-oriented goals. As examples, multinational enterprises can play political roles in addressing social issues in less developed and even conflict-prone host countries where they operate. Powerful multinationals, especially, can sometimes influence governmental policies and local circumstances to help resolve social or political conflicts, thus generating societal benefits beyond their own profits.

Cooperative Action   In some situations, two or more organizations—companies in different industries, private- and public-sector partners, and even competitors, as mentioned in Chapter 1[75]—work together using **cooperative strategies** to influence the environment.[76] Exhibit 2.9 shows several examples. Contracting occurs when suppliers and customers, or managers and labor unions, sign formal agreements about the terms and conditions of their future relationships. Contracts are explicit attempts to make a future relationship

EXHIBIT 2.9
Cooperative Action

Strategy	Definition	Examples
Contraction	Negotiating an agreement between the organization and another group to exchange goods, services, information, patents, and so on.	Starbucks and Keurig Green Mountain enter into a contract to offer more Starbucks K-Cup pack offerings.
Cooptation	Absorbing new elements into the organization's leadership structure to avert threats to its stability or existence.	Consumer and labor representatives are added to a large retailer's board of directors.
Coalition	Two or more group coalescing and acting jointly with respect to some set of issues for some period of time.	The Business Roundtable and the U.S. Chamber of Commerce lobby Congress on behalf of businesses.

SOURCE: Adapted from Zeithami, C. and Zeithami, V., "Environmental Management: Revising the Marketing Perspective," *Journal of Marketing*, Spring 1984.

predictable. An example of cooptation might occur when universities invite wealthy alumni to join their boards of directors.

Finally, examples of coalition formation are when businesses band together to curb the rise of employee health care costs and when organizations in the same industry form industry associations and special interest groups. You may have seen cooperative advertising strategies, such as when dairy producers, beef producers, orange growers, and the like jointly pay for television commercials or online advertising.

A vital element of the external environment, inviting both independent and cooperative actions, is the question of what to do about climate change.[77] Scientists are certain and unified in the knowledge that global warming and severe weather events are worsening, and that carbon emissions are the overwhelming cause.[78] Climate change harms not just the iconic polar bear and other wildlife, but just about every aspect of human existence, from food and water to human migration, conflict, and local economies.[79]

Even managers who don't believe or care about climate change must consider more sustainable practices and products due to pressure from customers, competitors, and investors. Organizations in every sector, and the people working within them, are relevant actors and decision makers who cannot avoid dealing with dramatically escalating physical, social, and political changes. Whatever their opinions, managers have to deal with such issues.

As just one example, Richard Branson (CEO of Virgin Group) and Jochen Zeitz (founder of his namesake foundation) co-founded The B Team, a not-for-profit group of global leaders working collaboratively to drive a "better way of doing business for the well-being of people and planet."[80] The B Team's Net-Zero by 2050 initiative enlists several CEOs and their companies who are working together to phase out all greenhouse gas emissions by the middle of the 21st century.[81]

Chapter 5 asks you to think about ethics and corporate social responsibility, broad domains that include managerial response to climate change. Other questions include: What is happening currently in the political and business worlds around climate action, and what is your personal perspective?

Adapting to the Environment: Changing the Organization

To cope with environmental uncertainty and change, organizations frequently make adjustments in their structures and work processes. A common way to adapt is by decentralizing decision making. For example, if a company faces a growing number of competitors in various markets, if different customers want different things, and if production facilities are being built in different regions of the world, it becomes impossible for the chief executive (or a small group of top executives) to keep abreast of all developments and understand all operating details. The top management team then gives authority to lower-level managers to make decisions that will benefit the firm. Johnson & Johnson, a health care company with 134,000 employees working in 260 operating companies around the world, uses a decentralized approach.[82] The term **empowerment** is used frequently today to talk about this type of decentralized authority. We will address decision making and empowerment in more detail in Chapters 3 and 9.

To cope with changing circumstances, organizations can establish more flexible structures. In today's business world, the term *bureaucracy* generally has a bad connotation. Most of us recognize that bureaucratic organizations tend to be formal and stable; frequently they are unable to adjust to changes or exceptional circumstances that don't "fit the rules." Although bureaucratic organizations can be efficient if the environment is stable, they tend to be slow-moving and plodding. When products, technologies, customers, or competitors are changing, *organic* structures give organizations the flexibility to adjust to change. We will discuss organic structures in more detail in Chapter 9.

Adapting at the Boundaries   Because they are open systems, organizations are exposed to uncertainties regarding both their inputs and outputs. To compete, they can create buffers on both the input and output boundaries with the environment. **Buffering** creates supplies of excess resources to meet unpredictable needs.

empowerment

The process of sharing power with employees, thereby enhancing their confidence in their ability to perform their jobs and their belief that they are influential contributors to the organization.

buffering

Creating supplies of excess resources in case of unpredictable needs.

On the input side, organizations establish relationships with employment agencies to hire part-time and temporary help during rush periods when labor demand is difficult to predict. In the United States, these workers, known as *contingent workers,* buffer labor input uncertainties.[83]

In 2017, there were 5.9 million contingent workers in the United States,[84] and contingent opportunities are growing. Adecco, a temporary staffing firm, believes the demand for temporary staff will continue to be strong in 2019 despite fears of a global trade war and evidence of a slowdown in economic growth. "Temporary staffing is an excellent way to cope with this geopolitical climate," Chief Executive Alain Dehaze said.[85]

> In today's business world, the term *bureaucracy* generally has a bad connotation.

On the output side of the system, most organizations use inventories that allow them to keep merchandise on hand in case a rush of customers decide to buy their products. Auto dealers are a common example of this use of buffers, but we see buffer inventories in fast-food restaurants, bookstores, clothing stores, and even real estate agencies.[86]

Organizations also may try **smoothing**, or leveling normal fluctuations at environmental boundaries. For example, during winter months in the north, when automobile sales drop off, dealers cut the price of their in-stock vehicles to increase demand. At the end of each clothing season, retailers discount their merchandise to make room for incoming inventories. Such smoothing helps to level off fluctuations in demand.

smoothing

Leveling normal fluctuations at the boundaries of the environment.

flexible processes

Methods for adapting the technical core to changes in the environment.

Bottom Line

Online shopping lets customers quickly find products at the cost and quality levels they want. *What might "flexible processes" mean for a groceries home delivery company?*

Adapting at the Core   Buffering and smoothing manage uncertainties at system boundaries, firms also can establish **flexible processes** that allow for adaptation in their technical core. For example, firms customize their goods and services to meet the varied and changing demands of customers. Even in manufacturing, where it is difficult to change basic core processes, firms adopt techniques of mass customization that help them create flexible factories. Instead of mass-producing large quantities of a "one-size-fits-all" product, organizations use mass customization to produce individually customized products at low cost.

Whereas Henry Ford used to claim that "you could have a Model T in any color you wanted, as long as it was black," auto companies now offer a wide array of colors, trim lines, accessories, and navigation and onboard entertainment options. Mass customization uses a network of independent operating units to perform a specific process or task such as making a dashboard assembly on an automobile. When an order comes in, different modules join forces to deliver the product or service as specified by the customer.[87] We will discuss mass customization and flexible factories in more depth in Chapter 9.

Choosing an Approach

In choosing your approach to managing the external environment, three general considerations provide guidance. First, environmental actions are most useful when aimed at elements of the environment that (1) cause the company problems, (2) provide it with opportunities, and (3) allow the company to change successfully. Thus, public concern about the obesity epidemic and its impact on health could be a problem for the sales and reputation of a company that makes snacks and soft drinks. PepsiCo's former CEO Nooyi believed it would be irresponsible to try to change that concern, so she focused on what the company could do to address it: change its product mix to include more healthful alternatives without abandoning the idea that it's fine to enjoy an occasional fun snack.

Second, organizations should choose responses that fit the environmental component of interest. Competitive actions help manage the competitive environment, political action influences the legal environment,[88] and contracting helps manage customers and suppliers.

Third, companies should choose actions that offer the most benefit at the lowest cost. Return-on-investment calculations should incorporate short-term financial considerations as well as long-term impact. Strategic managers who consider these factors carefully will more effectively guide their organizations to competitive advantage.

The Internal Environment of Organizations: Culture and Climate

We have discussed the external environment, both the macroenvironment and the competitive environment. Managers' actions are shaped also by forces inside the organization. These forces, creating an internal culture and climate, are conditions, routines, and beliefs that influence the decisions and behavior of employees at all organizational levels.

At Warby Parker, the fashion eyeglasses retailer, employees learn the culture by keeping in mind four ground rules (see Exhibit 2.10), which the company characterizes as "Nothing crazy."[89]

LO 2-5 Define elements of an organization's culture.

Organization Culture

An organization's culture is like an individual's personality. **Organization culture** is the set of important assumptions about the organization and its goals and practices that members of the company share. It is a system of shared values about what is important and beliefs about how the world works.

A company's culture provides a framework that guides people's behavior on the job.[90] For example, the way people dress and behave, the way they interact with each other and with customers, and the work habits that managers value are usually quite different at a bank than they are at a rock music company, and different again at a law firm or an advertising agency.

Cultures can be strong or weak. Strong cultures can have great influence on how people think and behave. A strong culture is one in which people understand and strongly believe in the firm's goals, priorities, and practices. A strong culture can be a real advantage to the organization if the behaviors it encourages and facilitates are appropriate and effective ones. As examples, the Walt Disney Company's culture encourages extraordinary devotion to customer service, and the culture at design firm IDEO encourages world-class innovation.

But a strong culture can be counterproductive when changes become necessary. Ideas and practices that have "worked" for years can become ineffective or when the external environment changes, as new technologies become available or new customer demands arise. Strong cultures can breed overconfidence and thoughtlessly inspire wrong-headed efforts, as recently at Wells Fargo when strong productivity incentives prompted hard-striving employees to create new accounts that customers never requested, and charging customers unfair mortgage fees and for unneeded car insurance.[91]

When a merger or acquisition brings together organizations with strong cultures, long-standing habits and ingrained beliefs are likely to clash. In 2018, several high-profile deals were announced, including CVS purchasing Aetna and Dr Pepper Snapple merging with Keurig Green Mountain.[92] Time will tell whether the expected value creation is realized.

organization culture
The set of important assumptions about the organization and its goals and practices that members of the company share.

LO 2-6 Discuss how an organization's culture and climate affect its response to its external environment.

Ground Rules at Warby Parker	Treat customers the way we'd like to be treated.
	Create an environment where employees can think big, have fun, and do good.
	Get out there.
	Green is good.

EXHIBIT 2.10
Culture Ground Rules at Warby Parker

The Digital World

Communicating with Employees to Build Organization Culture

Part of what makes up an organization's culture is how employees communicate with each other.[93] As technology provides new ways to manage and communicate, some organizations are providing internal communication applications (apps) to help employees work together.

One popular app that fosters team-building among employees is Slack.[94] This cloud-based application was originally designed for internal use at a company developing an online game. Today it allows teams to create group sites in which team members can communicate through "channels" and threads on certain topics they can choose to join or leave. It also allows members to message each other directly. Slack thereby helps companies retain their institutional knowledge by serving as a repository of information related to a project, all of which employees can easily search.

Other popular team-building apps include Hipchat, Campfire, and Basecamp.[95] Like Slack, these apps help people communicate within their organizations as teams, subteams, and project-specific groups. In doing so, they allow managers to build an organization culture that supports efficient, fluid, and productive communication.

1. What potential advantages are there to enabling employees to communicate in team-building apps like Slack?
2. What potential drawbacks are there to such applications?

If cultures collide, like in the case of Amazon's recent acquisition of Whole Foods, then value is likely to be destroyed.[96]

In contrast, weak organization cultures lack strong shared values and breed confusion about corporate goals. It is not clear what principles should or really do guide decisions. Some managers may pay lip service to an important behavior ("we would never cheat a customer") but behave very differently ("don't tell him about the bug in the software, we'll take care of it later"). Weak and confused cultures foster poor performance and sometimes worse.

Most managers would agree that they want to create and maintain a strong culture that will make their company more effective. They encourage high values, laudable goals, and useful behaviors. They want to create a culture that is appropriate in every sense for the organization's competitive environment.[97]

Diagnosing Culture   You will find it helpful to understand organization culture. Perhaps you are thinking about working there and you want a good fit, or maybe you are working there now and want to deepen your understanding of how your employer operates and what it expects of you. How would you go about making the diagnosis? A variety of things will give you useful insights:

Corporate mission statements and official goals are a starting point because they communicate the firm's desired public image. Most companies have a mission statement. Your school has one, and you can probably find it online. But are these statements a true expression of culture? Many employees are not aware of their companies' mission.[98] So, even after reading mission statements or reviewing official company goals, you need to figure out whether these reflect reality and how the firm actually conducts business.

Its important business practices—how a company responds to problems and challenges, makes strategic decisions, and actually treats employees and customers say a lot about what top management really values. Target announced a new strategy to invest $5 million by 2022 in "green chemistry innovation." Working with multiple stakeholders, the retailer wants to identify and reduce the number and types of potentially harmful chemicals in the products it sells.[99] You can use such decisions to assess corporate values and desired actions.

Symbols, rites, and ceremonies give further clues about culture. Status symbols, from reserved parking spaces to large corner offices, can tell you about the hierarchy and how power operates. Who is hired and fired and why, and the activities that are most rewarded, indicate the firm's real values.

The stories people tell carry a lot of information about the company's culture. Every company has its myths, legends, and true stories about important past decisions and actions that convey what managers respect, admire, and don't tolerate. The stories often feature the company's heroes, once or still active, who brought to life what the organization especially wants and depends on. A famous business hero and icon, Herb Kelleher, co-founder of Southwest Airlines, was known for his astute business acumen and great sense of humor. He told jokes and sang to flight attendants and passengers, sometimes helped baggage handlers load luggage, and famously wore an Elvis Presley jumpsuit.[100]

Cultural assessments can make the difference between business and personal successes and failures. As noted earlier, when two companies are considering a merger, acquisition, or joint venture, failing to consider cultural differences can sink the new arrangements.[101] You are likely to be better off in a culture that (1) suits your preferences and (2) you understand well rather than poorly.

Managing Culture   The best managers manage culture actively. First, they articulate clearly the ideals to pursue and values to exhibit. They repeat these often until they become well known and accepted throughout the organization.

Second, the best managers communicate with employees regularly, are actively involved and visible, and set the right examples. They not only talk about the vision, but embody it. This makes executive pronouncements credible, provides personal examples others can emulate, and builds trust that progress will continue over time.

Moments of truth are decision dilemmas in which hard choices must be made. Imagine top management trumpeting a culture that emphasizes quality products, but in a moment of truth a manager makes a decision that harms quality. Perhaps a part used in a batch of assembled products is found to be defective. Whether the manager decides to replace the costly part or to ship it in order to save time and money will go a long way toward reinforcing or destroying a quality-oriented culture.

To reinforce a desired culture, managers should celebrate and reward those who exemplify it. By hiring judiciously, teaching newcomers, and rewarding and promoting people on the basis of desired actions, management can ensure that the culture will strengthen and persist.

Managing culture requires time and effort, but the best managers understand its importance. The potential payoffs include the performance benefits of a strong and appropriate culture, plus the avoidance of the many costs of a weak or inappropriate one.

Organizational Climate

An organization's *climate* is the practical, day-to-day aspect of its culture. **Organizational climate** consists of the patterns of attitudes and behaviors that shape people's perceptions of an organization.[102] Like the weather, is it sunny or dark, stormy or calm? Many tests and surveys measure organizational climate in terms of morale, employees' relationships with managers and co-workers, handling of conflicts, openness and effectiveness of communication, methods for measuring and rewarding performance, and how clearly people understand their work roles.

Both climate and deeper culture influence the internal work environment, how people experience their work, and organizational effectiveness. Because organizational climate is easier to measure, managers often find that dimensions of organizational climate are more manageable levers to pull. Later chapters explore a variety of management responsibilities that shape organizational climate, including maintaining ethical conduct (Chapter 5),

Bottom Line
A culture aligned with its external environment helps the organization succeed. *To be aligned with its environment, what values should a meal kit delivery company have?*

organizational climate

The patterns of attitudes and behavior that shape people's experience of an organization.

appraising and rewarding performance (Chapter 10), valuing diversity (Chapter 11), leading (Chapter 12), motivating employees (Chapter 13), fostering teamwork (Chapter 14), communicating (Chapter 15), and leading change (Chapter 18).

Capably and continually addressing key aspects of an organization's climate enables managers to strengthen competitive advantages and develop new ones as needed. What is required is a climate that motivates and enables workers to achieve the organization's strategy. As you read "Management in Action: Onward," consider what the climate at Amazon is like under the leadership of Jeff Bezos.

Management in Action

MANAGER'S BRIEF

PROGRESS REPORT

ONWARD

THE INTERNAL CULTURE AT AMAZON

In his 2016 annual letter to shareholders, Amazon CEO Jeff Bezos noted that corporate cultures are "enduring, stable, hard to change."[103] A recent *New York Times* investigation had publicly revealed Amazon's culture to be ruthlessly competitive and intensely stressful, often bringing white-collar employees at its Seattle headquarters to tears at their desks. Distribution-center workers had grievances too, as evidenced by a 2014 Supreme Court ruling that they did not have to be paid for the time it took to screen them for stolen goods every day.

Bezos launched his own investigation into the company culture, and publicly refuted the newspaper's report. In a further response, his shareholder letter went on to say, "We never claim that our approach is the right one—just that it's ours."[104]

It's hard to argue with a related observation in Bezos's letter about culture and performance: that people work best in a culture that suits them. Clearly, some people thrive on internal competition, others prefer teamwork, and still others do best when they pursue their goals alone. Bezos believes people "self-select," choosing to leave employers whose climates don't suit them.

There is a fine line between being competitive and being cut-throat, and clearly Bezos is OK with walking that line. Many companies overlook the effect internal culture can have on productivity, and neglect to closely monitor that culture as a result. The recent struggles Uber has faced due to its chaotic and discriminatory internal culture

are evidence of this. But Bezos has always focused on developing a high-intensity culture that spurs productivity and growth. As if in response to media criticism, Bezos, in Amazon's 2017 annual report, wrote, "Building a culture of high standards is well worth the effort, and there are many benefits. Naturally and most obviously, you're going to build better products and services for customers."[105]

Still, it seems as if Amazon has tried to address criticisms of its high-standard, high-intensity culture. The company eased some policies that rewarded competitive behavior and launched a retraining program to provide coaching and support to poor performers. Those employees can appeal the assignment, accept and try to improve, or resign with severance.[106] Amazon is also raising its minimum wage to $15 an hour.[107]

Such changes appear to be working, at least in part. At the end of 2018, current and former employees ranked Amazon's work environment a 3.8 out of 5. Clearly there's room for improvement, but this rating is up from 3.4 in 2015.[108]

1. A shareholder letter from Bezos called Amazon a good place to fail, since "failure and invention are inseparable twins." What do you think is the relationship between failure and invention?
2. Is it possible for a company to be as innovative and successful as Amazon without having a culture of "high standards"? Why or why not?

KEY TERMS

acquisition, p. 59

barriers to entry, p. 52

benchmarking, p. 58

buffering, p. 61

competitive environment, p. 44

competitive intelligence, p. 57

cooperative strategies, p. 60

corporate diplomacy, p. 60

defenders, p. 59

demographics, p. 47

diversification, p. 59

divestiture, p. 59

domain selection, p. 58

empowerment, p. 61

environmental scanning, p. 57

environmental uncertainty, p. 56

external environment, p. 44

final consumer, p. 54

flexible processes, p. 62

forecasting, p. 58

independent strategies, p. 59

inputs, p. 44

intermediate consumer, p. 54

macroenvironment, p. 45

merger, p. 59

open systems, p. 44

organization culture, p. 63

organizational climate, p. 65

outputs, p. 44

prospectors, p. 59

scenario, p. 57

smoothing, p. 62

strategic maneuvering, p. 58

supply chain management, p. 54

switching costs, p. 53

RETAINING WHAT YOU LEARNED

You learned how pressures from outside the organization create the context in which managers must function. The macroenvironment includes broad forces like the economy, laws, and technology. The competitive environment is closer to the organization and includes forces like competitors, suppliers, and customers. Effective managers need to stay aware of labor force and other trends that can affect their businesses. An organization's competitive environment can range from favorable to unfavorable. Proactive managers attempt to manage environmental uncertainty through a variety of strategies. Organization culture provides an internal values framework that guides people's behavior at work. Organizational climate is people's day-to-day experience of a company's business practices.

LO 2-1   Describe how environmental forces influence organizations and how organizations can influence their environments.

- Organizations are open systems that are affected by, and in turn affect, their external environments.
- Organizations receive financial, human, material, and information resources from the environment; transform those resources into finished goods and services; and then send those outputs back into the environment to meet market needs.

LO 2-2   Distinguish between the macroenviroment and the competitive environment.

- The macroenvironment is the economic, legal and political, technological, demographic, social, and natural environment forces that influence strategic decisions.
- The competitive environment is composed of forces closer to the organization, such as current competitors, new entrants, substitute and complementary products, suppliers, and customers.
- A key distinction between the macroenvironment and the competitive environment is the amount of control a firm can exert on external forces.

- Macroenvironmental forces such as the economy and social trends are much less controllable than are forces in the competitive environment such as suppliers and customers.

LO 2-3   Identify elements of the competitive environment.

- Elements in the competitive environment can be favorable or unfavorable. To determine how favorable a competitive environment is, managers should consider the nature of the competitors, potential new entrants, threat of substitutes, opportunities from complements, and relationships with suppliers and customers.
- Analyzing how these forces influence the organization provides an indication of potential threats and opportunities.
- Effective management of the firm's supply chain is one way to achieve a competitive advantage.
- Attractive environments tend to be those with high industry growth, few competitors, products that can be differentiated, few potential entrants, many barriers to entry, few substitutes, many suppliers (none with much power), and many customers.
- After identifying and analyzing competitive forces, managers formulate strategies that minimize the power external forces have over the organization.

LO 2-4   Summarize how organizations respond to environmental uncertainty.

- Responding effectively to the environment often requires devising proactive strategies to change the environment.
- Strategic maneuvering involves changing the boundaries of the competitive environment through domain selection, diversification, mergers, and the like.
- Independent strategies require not moving into a new environment but rather changing some aspect

Macroenvironment

Economy

Technology

Legal and regulations

Demographics

Social issues

Natural environment

Competitive
Environment

Rivals

Suppliers

Buyers

New entrants

Substitutes
and complements

Internal
Environment

Culture

Values

Climate

EXHIBIT 2.2 (revisited)

The External and
Internal Environments of
Organizations

of the current environment through competitive aggression, public relations, legal action, and others.

- Cooperative strategies, such as contracting, cooptation, and coalition building, are those in which two or more organizations work together.
- Organizations can become better able to handle environmental change by decentralizing authority, buffering or smoothing, and establishing flexible processes.

LO 2-5   Define elements of an organization's culture.

- An organization's culture is its set of shared values and practices related to what is most important and how the world works.
- The culture provides a framework that guides people's behavior at work.
- Elements of the culture may be expressed in corporate mission statements and official goals, assuming these reflect how the organization actually operates.

- Business practices are a basic cultural indicator. Symbols, rites, ceremonies, and the stories people tell express and reinforce cultural values.

LO 2-6   Discuss how an organization's culture and climate affect its response to its external environment.

- A culture can be strong or weak. A strong culture with appropriate values and best practices is an obvious advantage. Weak cultures lack shared values and breed confusion about goals and decisions.
- Managing and changing the culture to align it with the organization's environment requires strong, long-term commitment by the CEO and other managers.
- Managers should articulate high ideals and convey values by communicating and modeling them, making decisions that are consistent with them, and rewarding those who demonstrate them.
- An organization's climate shapes the day-to-day attitudes and behaviors of its people. When the climate is positive and predictable, employees want to and are best able to carry out the organization's strategy.

DISCUSSION QUESTIONS

1. This chapter's opening quote by Peter Drucker said, "The essence of a business is outside itself." What do you think this means? Do you agree?

2. What are the most important forces in the macroenvironment facing companies today?

3. What are the main differences between the macroenvironment and the competitive environment?

4. What kinds of changes do companies make in response to environmental uncertainty?

5. We outlined several proactive responses that organizations can make to the environment. What examples have you seen recently of an organization's responding effectively to its environment? Did the effectiveness of

the response depend on whether the organization was facing a threat or an opportunity?

6. Select two organizations that interest you. Do some research and talk with an employee or two, if possible. How would you characterize the cultures they have? Write a paragraph that describes each culture.

7. When you visited colleges to select one to attend, were there cultural differences in the campuses that made a difference in your choice? Did these differences help you decide which college to attend?

EXPERIENTIAL EXERCISES

2.1   External Environment Analysis

OBJECTIVE

To give you the experience of performing an analysis of a company's external environment.

INSTRUCTIONS

Select a company you want to learn more about. Using online and/or library resources, including websites on the company's industry and its website and annual report, fill out the following External Environment Worksheet for that company.

External Environment Worksheet

Laws and regulations

What are some key laws and regulations under which this company and industry must operate?

_____

_____

The economy

How does the state of the economy influence the sales of this company's products?

_____

Technology

What new technologies strongly affect the company you have selected?

_____

_____

Demographics

What changes in the population might affect the company's customer base?

_____

_____

Social issues

What changes in society affect the market for your company's products?

_____

_____

Suppliers

How does your company's relationship with suppliers affect its profitability?

_____

_____

Competitors

What companies compete with the firm you have selected? Do they compete on price, on quality, or on other factors?

_____

_____

New entrants

Are new competitors to the company likely? Possible?

_____

_____

Substitutes and complements

Is there a threat of substitutes for the industry's existing products? Are there complementary products that suggest an opportunity for collaboration?

_____

_____

Customers

What characteristics of the company's customer base influence the company's competitiveness?

_____

_____

DISCUSSION QUESTIONS

1. What has the company done to adapt to its environment?

2. How does the company attempt to influence its environment?

SOURCE: McShane, Steven L. and Von Glinow, Mary Ann, *Organizational Behavior,* 3rd ed. New York: McGraw-Hill, 2005, p. 499.

2.2   Corporate Culture Preference Scale

OBJECTIVE

This self-assessment is designed to help you identify a corporate culture that fits most closely with your personal values and assumptions.

INSTRUCTIONS

Read each pair of the statements in the Corporate Culture Preference Scale and circle the statement that describes the organization you would prefer to work in. This exercise is completed alone so students assess themselves honestly without concerns of social comparison. However, class discussion will focus on the importance of matching job applicants to the organization's dominant values.

Corporate Culture Preference Scale

I would prefer to work in an organization:

1a. Where employees work well together in teams.	OR	1b. That produces highly respected products or services.
2a. Where top management maintains a sense of order in the workplace.	OR	2b. Where the organization listens to customers and responds quickly to their needs.
3a. Where employees are treated fairly.	OR	3b. Where employees continuously search for ways to work more efficiently.
4a. Where employees adapt quickly to new work requirements.	OR	4b. Where corporate leaders work hard to keep employees happy.
5a. Where senior executives receive special benefits not available to other employees.	OR	5b. Where employees are proud when the organization achieves its performance goals.
6a. Where employees who perform the best get paid the most.	OR	6b. Where senior executives are respected.
7a. Where everyone gets his or her job done like clockwork.	OR	7b. That is on top of new innovations in the industry.
8a. Where employees receive assistance to overcome any personal problems.	OR	8b. Where employees abide by company rules.
9a. That is always experimenting with new ideas in the marketplace.	OR	9b. That expects everyone to put in 110 percent for peak performance.
10a. That quickly benefits from market opportunities.	OR	10b. Where employees are always kept informed of what's happening in the organization.
11a. That can quickly respond to competitive threats.	OR	11b. Where most decisions are made by the top executives.
12a. Where management keeps everything under control.	OR	12b. Where employees care for each other.

SOURCE: McShane, Steven L. and Von Glinow, Mary Ann, *Organizational Behavior,* 3rd ed. New York: McGraw-Hill, 2005, p. 499. Copyright ©2005 McGraw-Hill Global Education Holdings LLC. All rights reserved. Used with permission.

Scoring Key for the Corporate Culture Preference Scale

Scoring instructions: In each space, write in a "1" if you circled the statement and "0" if you did not. Then add up the scores for each subscale.

Control culture $\qquad \dfrac{}{(2a)} + \dfrac{}{(5a)} + \dfrac{}{(6b)} + \dfrac{}{(8b)} + \dfrac{}{(11b)} + \dfrac{}{(12a)} = \underline{\quad}$

Performance culture $\qquad \dfrac{}{(1b)} + \dfrac{}{(3b)} + \dfrac{}{(5b)} + \dfrac{}{(6a)} + \dfrac{}{(7a)} + \dfrac{}{(9a)} = \underline{\quad}$

Relationship culture $\qquad \dfrac{}{(1a)} + \dfrac{}{(3a)} + \dfrac{}{(4b)} + \dfrac{}{(8a)} + \dfrac{}{(10b)} + \dfrac{}{(12b)} = \underline{\quad}$

Responsive culture $\qquad \dfrac{}{(2b)} + \dfrac{}{(4a)} + \dfrac{}{(7b)} + \dfrac{}{(9a)} + \dfrac{}{(10a)} + \dfrac{}{(11a)} = \underline{\quad}$

Interpreting your score: These corporate cultures may be found in many organizations, but they represent only four of many possible organization cultures. Also, keep in mind none of these subscales is inherently good or bad. Each is effective in different situations. The four corporate cultures are defined here, along with the range of scores for high, medium, and low levels of each dimension based on a sample of MBA students:

Corporate Culture Dimension and Definition	Score Interpretation
Control culture: This culture values the role of senior executives to lead the organization. Its goal is to keep everyone aligned and under control.	High: 3 to 6 Medium: 1 to 2 Low: 0
Performance culture: This culture values individual and organizational performance and strives for effectiveness and efficiency.	High: 5 to 6 Medium: 3 to 4 Low: 0 to 2
Relationship culture: This culture values nurturing and well-being. It considers open communication, fairness, teamwork, and sharing a vital part of organizational life.	High: 6 Medium: 4 to 5 Low: 0 to 3
Responsive culture: This culture values its ability to keep in tune with the external environment, including being competitive and realizing new opportunities.	High: 6 Medium: 4 to 5 Low: 0 to 3

Concluding Case

TATA MOTORS: FROM CHEAP TO AWESOME?

The barriers to entry are so high in the automotive industry that it is rare to see a new entrant. A notable exception has been Malaysia's PRGA Motors, the country's largest maker of commercial vehicles, which about five years ago promised to become a leading carmaker in the fast-growing economies of the developing world. Comparing its ambitious plan to the iconic Volkswagen Beetle and Ford Model T, PRGA launched the Synapse in 2017. Branded a "people's car," the Synapse was priced at $2,000 to $2,500. PRGA Motors marketed the stripped-down minicar to first-time automobile customers in rural areas. The goal was to make the Synapse the standard transportation for Malaysian families working their way up to the middle class.

The promised launch was so ambitious that PRGA could not realistically meet expectations. Production was postponed for about a year and a half, and then the company determined it couldn't afford to sell the Synapse profitably at the promised price. The first Synapses to roll off assembly lines were priced just $800 below PRGA's closest competitor's line, which offered more storage space and a more powerful engine. The Synapse's safety performance also ran into embarrassing problems; some reportedly caught fire.

Sales of the Synapse have been disappointing. After reaching its maximum sales of 10,000 in April 2018, recent reports of the "people's car" indicate 2,500 units are sold each month. Some have suggested that the low sales were a result of the unacceptably low level of quality and features built into the vehicle, including an underpowered and noisy motor, no stereo or air conditioning, and wires visible in the driver's compartment. Another reason for the Synapse's decline was a missed target market, namely young urban drivers. The Synapse's cheap and unsafe image turned off many of these would-be buyers.

The Synapse's failure was frustrating to PRGA Motors, which had invested $400 million to develop the car and hundreds of millions more building a factory capable of creating a high volume of automobiles. If it were to be successful in the long run, PRGA Motors would need to adjust its strategy to overcome the myriad barriers to success in the automotive industry.

PRGA Motors has changed both its marketing and manufacturing strategies. Shifting its focus from first-time rural buyers to young urban customers, the company recently launched the Synapse Snap and Synapse LX. It is trying to rebrand the Synapse from "cheapest car in the world" to an "awesome" car that is also affordable. Priced as high as $3,600, these improved Synapse models can include several upgrades like power steering, music systems with Bluetooth connectivity, and enhanced interior and exterior features.

Also, PRGA has responded with maintenance contracts, test drives, and safety improvements. It has revenues from

its commercial vehicles to stay afloat. Perhaps the Synapse will still become the people's car. Start-ups often make mistakes, and some of them recover brilliantly. What made PRGA's stumble remarkable was its grand scale.

DISCUSSION QUESTIONS

1. Which barriers to entry contributed most to PRGA Motors's lack of success with the original Synapse?

2. Which macroenvironmental factors did PRGA Motors consider when adjusting the marketing and manufacturing strategies to achieve success with the more recent Snap and LX models?

3. To what degree do you believe PRGA Motors will succeed in delivering a successful low-cost vehicle to consumers?

ENDNOTES

1. Tim Goodman, "A Redefined Amazon Studios Is Primed to Disrupt Its Rivals' Plans," *Hollywood Reporter,* August 8, 2018, https://www.hollywoodreporter.com/bastard-machine/tv-critics-notebook-amazon-studios-1133242.

2. Stefan Pajović, "8 Largest E-Commerce Companies in the World and No, Alibaba Is Not the Largest Chinese E-Commerce," *Axiom,* February 18, 2018, https://axiomq.com/blog/8-largest-e-commerce-companies-in-the-world/.

3. Michael Schaub, "Amazon Will Open 3 More Bookstores, Including One in Pacific Palisades," *Los Angeles Times,* June 4, 2018, https://www.latimes.com/books/la-et-jc-amazon-stores-20180604-story.html.

4. Matt McFarland, "I Spent 53 Minutes in Amazon Go and Saw the Future of Retail," *CNN Business,* October 3, 2018, https://www.cnn.com/2018/10/03/tech/amazon-go/index.html.

5. "The Employment Situation—January 2019," news release, Bureau of Labor Statistics, U.S. Department of Labor, February 1, 2019, www.bls.gov.

6. P. Davidson, "The Pros and Cons of U.S. Unemployment Rate Falling Below 4%," *USA Today,* May 7, 2018, www.usatoday.com.

7. "The Employment Situation—November 2018," December 7, 2018, U.S. Bureau of Labor Statistics, www.bls.gov.

8. "Labor Force Participation Rates Projected to Decline over the Next Decade," Bureau of Labor Statistics, U.S. Department of Labor, November 1, 2017, www.bls.gov.

9. P. Henning, "When Money Gets in the Way of Corporate Ethics," *The New York Times,* April 17, 2017, www.nytimes.com.

10. C. Fink, "This Week in XR: Blippar Closes, AR Laptop Wins CES, Immersal Launches, Magic Leap Flooded, and More," *Forbes,* December 21, 2018, www.forbes.com.

11. J. Brustein, "Microsoft Wins $480 Million Army Battlefield Contract," *Bloomberg,* November 28, 2018, www.bloomberg.com.

12. "UK Researchers Hope to Bring Rotary Friction Welding to the Manufacturing Mainstream," *The Engineer,* December 13, 2018, https://www.theengineer.co.uk/rotary-friction-welding-manufacturing/; "AFRC Rotary Friction Welding Effort Set to Offer New Ways to Reduce Waste and Save Time for UK Industry," *Machinery,* December 20, 2018, www.machinery.co.uk.

13. S. Freeman, "Cloud Computing for Small Businesses: What You Need to Know," *Forbes,* December 18, 2018, www.forbes.com.

14. Marc Levinson, "Job Creation in the Manufacturing Revival," Congressional Research Service Report for Congress R41898, June 20, 2012, available at http://www.fas.org/sqp/crs/misc/R41898.pdf.

15. U.S. Department of Health and Human Services (DHHS), "Small Employers: Top Five Things to Know," *HealthCare.gov,* http://

www.healthcare.gov; Internal Revenue Service (IRS), "Small Business Health Care Tax Credit for Small Employers," http://www.irs.gov; DHHS, "Large Employers: Insurance and Tax Information," *HealthCare.gov,* http://www.healthcare.gov; IRS, "Affordable Care Act Tax Provisions," http://www.irs.gov; DHHS, "About the Law: Provisions of the Affordable Care Act, by Year," *HealthCare.gov,* http://www.healthcare.gov; Jen Wieczner, "Why Your Boss Is Dumping Your Wife," *MarketWatch,* February 22, 2013, http://www.marketwatch.com.

16. "Communicating with Employees about Health Care Benefits under the Affordable Care Act," Society for Human Resource Management, July 25, 2016, www.shrm.org.

17. "H.R. 1628—American Health Care Act of 2017," U.S. Congress, www.congress.gov, accessed December 21, 2018.

18. "SEC Enforcement Actions: FCPA Cases 2018," U.S. Securities and Exchange Commission, www.sec.gov, accessed February 11, 2019.

19. "Employment Projections—2016–26," October 24, 2017, U.S. Bureau of Labor Statistics, www.bls.gov, accessed December 21, 2018.

20. Vivian Hunt et al., "Delivering through Diversity," McKinsey & Company, January 2018, https://www.mckinsey.com/~/media/mckinsey/business%20functions/organization/our%20insights/delivering%20through%20diversity/delivering-through-diversity_full-report.ashx.

21. Vivian Hunt et al., "Delivering through Diversity," McKinsey & Company, January 2018, https://www.mckinsey.com/~/media/mckinsey/business%20functions/organization/our%20insights/delivering%20through%20diversity/delivering-through-diversity_full-report.ashx.

22. Marcus Noland and Tyler Moran, "Study: Firms with More Women in the C-Suite Are More Profitable," Peterson Institute for International Economics, February 8, 2016, https://piie.com/commentary/op-eds/study-firms-more-women-c-suite-are-more-profitable?ResearchID=2915.

23. Tim Worstall, "Business Gender Diversity Solved: More Women Means More Profits," *Forbes,* February 10, 2016, https://www.forbes.com/sites/timworstall/2016/02/10/business-gender-diversity-solved-more-women-means-more-profits/#7b6de18f170f.

24. Bureau of Labor Statistics, "Profile of the Labor Force by Educational Attainment," August 2017, https://www.bls.gov/spotlight/2017/educational-attainment-of-the-labor-force/home.htm.

25. D. Bortz, "Skills Employers Look for in College Graduates," *Monster,* www.monster.com, accessed February 16, 2019.

26. See, for example, A. Gross and J. Marcus, "High-Paying Trade Jobs Sit Empty, While High School Grads Line Up for University," NPR, April 25, 2018, www.npr.org; J. Wright, "America's Skilled Trades

Dilemma: Shortages Loom as Most-in-Demand Group of Workers Ages," *Forbes,* March 7, 2013, http://www.forbes.com.

27. Bureau of Labor Statistics, news release, "Labor Force Characteristics of Foreign-Born Workers Summary," May 17, 2018, http://www.bls.gov.

28. Bureau of Labor Statistics, news release, "Labor Force Characteristics of Foreign-Born Workers Summary," May 17, 2018, www.bls.gov.

29. C. Gorman, "And Equal Leave for All: Parental Leave Policies Are Changing," *Inc.,* January 29, 2019, www.inc.com.

30. E. Mandel, "Coca-Cola Makes Another Pledge to Reduce Sugar High," *Atlanta Business Chronicle,* June 25, 2018, www.bizjournals.com; A. H. Mahmud, "Coca-Cola Singapore Ready to Fight Diabetes, but Says Sugary Drink Tax Not Very Effective," *Channel NewsAsia,* December 4, 2018, www.channelnewsasia.com; A. Lucas, "Coca-Cola's Chairman Thinks We Should Change How We Talk about Soda Sales," *CNBC,* December 7, 2018, www.cnbc.com; S. Scheer and M. Geller, "PepsiCo Puts Fizz into Healthy Drinks with $3.2 Billion SodaStream Deal," Reuters, August 20, 2018, www.reuters.com.

31. Fortune Media IP Limited.

32. Simon Mainwaring, "Why and How Business Must Tackle Climate Change Now," *Forbes,* October 25, 2018, https://www.forbes.com/sites/simonmainwaring/2018/10/25/why-and-how-business-must-tackle-climate-change-now/#77a15fd4712b.

33. Adrian Woloszyk, "LEGO Goes Sustainable with Blocks Made from Sugarcane," *Business Insider, Nordic,* August 3, 2018, https://nordic.businessinsider.com/danish-lego-goes-sustainable-with-sugary-green-plants-/

34. Mike Snider, "Starbucks Brews a Greener Plan for 10,000 Environmentally Friendly Stores," *USA Today,* September 13, 2018, https://www.usatoday.com/story/money/business/2018/09/13/starbucks-greener-stores-eco-friendly/1291573002/.

35. P. Howell, "BP Oil Spill Haunts Off-Shore Drilling Industry 8 Years Later," *CNBC,* April 20, 2018, www.cnbc.com.

36. C. Robertson, J. Schwartz, and R. Perez-Pena, "BP to Pay $18.7 Billion for Deepwater Horizon Oil Spill," *The New York Times,* July 2, 2015, www.nytimes.com.

37. K. Taylor, "Pepsi Is Laying Off Up to 100 Workers in Philadelphia and Blaming a 2-Month-Old Soda Tax," *Business Insider,* March 1, 2017, www.businessinsider.com; J. Kaplan, "Coca-Cola, PepsiCo Hit with Wave of Soda Taxes," *Bloomberg,* November 9, 2016, www.bloomberg.com; A. Petroff, "Pepsi Gets Aggressive on Cutting Sugar," *CNNMoney,* October 17, 2016, www.money.cnn.com.

38. T. Team, "Coca-Cola's Advertising and Marketing Efforts Are Helping It to Stay on Top," *Forbes,* September 26, 2016, www.forbes.com.

39. See company website, www.pepsico.com, accessed December 22, 2018.

40. J. Forgrieve, "PepsiCo Continues Health Kick, Reveals First Startups for Its Accelerator Program," *Forbes,* November 13, 2018, www.forbes.com; "PepsiCo Expands Better-for-You Snack Portfolio with Bare Snacks Pact," *Convenience Store News,* June 1, 2018, www.csnews.com; M. Watrous, "Inside PepsiCo's Innovation Agenda," *Food Business News,* April 18, 2016, www.foodbusinessnews.net.

41. J. Kaplan, "Coca-Cola's Focus on Healthier Drinks Pays Off," *Bloomberg,* April 24, 2018, www.bloomberg.com.

42. D. J. Collis and C. A. Montgomery, *Corporate Strategy: Resources and Scope of the Firm* (New York: McGraw-Hill/Irwin, 1997).

43. C. Yasiejko, "J&J Loses Ruling over Patent for Prostate Cancer Drug Zytiga," *Bloomberg,* October 26, 2018, www.bloomberg.com.

44. R. Safian, "How PepsiCo CEO Indra Nooyi Is Steering the Company toward a Purpose-Driven Future," *Fast Company,* January 9, 2017, www.fastcompany.com.

45. PepsiCo website, http://www.pepsico.com.

46. Danielle Kucera, "Inkling Builds a Better (and Pricier) E-Book," *Bloomberg Businessweek,* February 12, 2013, http://www.businessweek.com.

47. J. Bunge and P. Evans, "ADM to Buy Wild Flavors for $3 Billion," *The Wall Street Journal,* July 7, 2014, www.wsj.com.

48. Adapted from H. L. Lee and C. Billington, "The Evolution of Supply-Chain-Management Models and Practice at Hewlett-Packard," *Interfaces* 25, no. 5 (September–October 1995), pp. 42–63. See also Edward W. Davis and Robert E. Spekman, *The Extended Enterprise: Gaining Competitive Advantage through Collaborative Supply Chains* (Upper Saddle River, NJ: Prentice Hall, 2004).

49. See company website, www.lego.com, accessed February 11, 2019.

50. K. Warren, "Netflix Held a Q&A on LinkedIn and Everyone Seemed to Have the Same 2 Burning Questions," *Business Insider,* September 14, 2018, www.businessinsider.com.

51. Peter Carbonara, "Walmart, Amazon Top World's Largest Retail Companies," *Forbes*, June 6, 2018, https://www.forbes.com/sites/petercarbonara/2018/06/06/worlds-largest-retail-companies-2018/#2a46958213e6.

52. Ovidijus Jurevicius, "Amazon SWOT Analysis 2017," *Strategic Management Insight,* January 8, 2017, https://www.strategicmanagementinsight.com/swot-analyses/amazon-swot-analysis.html; Ángel González, "Third-Party Sellers Giving Amazon a Huge Boost," *Seattle Times*, May 31, 2016, http://www.seattletimes.com/business/amazon/amazon-to-host-forum-for-its-marketplace-merchants/

53. A. A. Buchko, "Conceptualization and Measurement of Environmental Uncertainty: An Assessment of the Miles and Snow Perceived Environmental Uncertainty Scale," *Academy of Management Journal* 37, no. 2 (April 1994), pp. 410–25.

54. A. F. Hagen, "Corporate Executives and Environmental Scanning Activities: An Empirical Investigation," *SAM Advanced Management Journal* 60, no. 2 (Spring 1995), pp. 41–47; R. L. Daft, "Chief Executive Scanning, Environmental Characteristics, and Company Performance: An Empirical Study," *Strategic Management Journal* 9, no. 2 (March–April 1988), pp. 123–39; M. Yasai-Ardekani, "Designs for Environmental Scanning Systems: Tests of a Contingency Theory," *Management Science* 42, no. 2 (February 1996), pp. 187–204.

55. S. Ghoshal, "Building Effective Intelligence Systems for Competitive Advantage," *Sloan Management Review* 28, no. 1 (Fall 1986), pp. 49–58; K. D. Cory, "Can Competitive Intelligence Lead to a Sustainable Competitive Advantage?" *Competitive Intelligence Review* 7, no. 3 (Fall 1996), pp. 45–55.

56. P. S. Adler, "Alternative Economic Futures: A Research Agenda for Progressive Management Scholarship," *Academy of Management Perspectives* 30 (2016), pp. 123–28.

57. P. J. H. Schoemaker, "Multiple Scenario Development: Its Conceptual and Behavioral Foundation," *Strategic Management Journal* 14, no. 3 (March 1993), pp. 193–213.

58. R. R. Peterson, "An Analysis of Contemporary Forecasting in Small Business," *Journal of Business Forecasting Methods & Systems* 15, no. 2 (Summer 1996), pp. 10–12; S. Makridakis, "Business Forecasting for Management: Strategic Business Forecasting," *International Journal of Forecasting* 12, no. 3 (September 1996), pp. 435–37.

59. R. A. D'Aveni, *Hypercompetition—Managing the Dynamics of Strategic Maneuvering* (New York: Free Press, 1994); M. A. Cusumano, "Strategic Maneuvering and Mass-Market Dynamics: The Triumph of VHS over Beta," *Business History Review* 66, no. 1 (Spring 1992), pp. 51–94.

60. Model adapted from C. Zeithaml and V. Zeithaml, "Environmental Management: Revising the Marketing Perspective," *Journal of Marketing* 48 (Spring 1984), pp. 46–53.

61. D. Kline, "PepsiCo Continues Its Push into Healthy Snacks," *The Motley Fool,* June 1, 2018, www.fool.com.

62. C. Jones, "Apple's App Store Generated over $11 Billion in Revenue for the Company Last Year," *Forbes,* January 6, 2018, www.forbes.com; S. Costello, "How Many Apps Are in the App Store?" *Lifewire,* April 7, 2018, www.lifewire.com; "Global App Revenue Grew 35% in 2017 to Nearly $60 Billion," *Sensor Tower,* January 5, 2018, https://sensortower.com.

63. R. Thomson, R. Thomas, and M. Garay, "Deloitte M&A Trends: Year End Report 2016," www2.deloitte.com, accessed March 5, 2017.

64. S. Stebbins, "The 10 Biggest Mergers and Acquisitions of 2018," *USA Today,* December 10, 2018, www.usatoday.com; A. Jeffery, "Cigna Closes $54 Billion Purchase of Express Scripts," *CNBC,* December 20, 2018, www.cnbc.com.

65. P. Hammes, "How Can Divesting Fuel Your Future Growth?" EY Global Corporate Divestment Study 2018, https://www.ey.com, February 18, 2019.

66. Company press release, "Sysco Reaches Agreement to Sell 11 US Foods Distribution Centers to Performance Food Group Contingent on Consummation of Sysco–US Foods Merger," February 2, 2015, http://investors.sysco.com, accessed February 20, 2015.

67. M. Henney, "GM Lifts Outlook after Plans to Cut 15,000 North American Workers, Stock Jumps," *Fox Business,* January 11, 2019, www.foxbusiness.com.

68. R. Miles and C. Snow, *Organizational Strategy, Structure, and Process* (New York: McGraw-Hill, 1978).

69. C. Zeithaml and V. Zeithaml, "Environmental Management: Revising the Marketing Perspective," *Journal of Marketing* 48 (Spring 1984), pp. 46–53.

70. "The 20 Best PR Campaigns of the Past Two Decades," *PR Week,* September 25, 2018, www.prweek.com.

71. Organization website (RED), http://www.red.org, accessed March 5, 2017.

72. K. Wynne, "Vans Is Suing Target, Alleging That the Retailer Copied Their Old Skool Sneaker," *Newsweek,* December 23, 2018, www.newsweek.com.

73. C. McGreal, "How Big Pharma's Money—and Its Politicians—Feed the Opioid Crisis," *The Guardian,* October 19, 2017, www.theguardian.com.

74. D. R. Gnyawali and T. R. Charleton, "Nuances in the Interplay of Competition and Cooperation: Towards a Theory of Coopetition," *Journal of Management* 44 (2018), pp. 2511–34.

75. D. R. Gnyawali and T. R. Charleton, "Nuances in the Interplay of Competition and Cooperation: Towards a Theory of Coopetition," *Journal of Management* 44 (2018), pp. 2511–34.

76. W. P. Burgers, "Cooperative Strategy in High Technology Industries," *International Journal of Management* 13, no. 2 (June 1996), pp. 127–34; J. E. McGee, "Cooperative Strategy and New Venture Performance: The Role of Business Strategy and Management Experience," *Strategic Management Journal* 16, no. 7 (October 1995), pp. 565–80.

77. D. Titley, "Climate Wars: The End of the Beginning?" *The Washington Post,* February 15, 2019.

78. A. Dessler, "Why the Green New Deal Makes Me Hopeful about Climate Change," *Houston Chronicle,* February 15, 2019.

79. M. Shephard, "6 Compelling Reasons Climate Change Might Be a National Emergency," *Fortune,* February 15, 2019.

80. See company website, "The B Team and Ceres Introduce New Primer for Building Climate Competent Boards," The B Team, May 16, 2018, www.bteam.org.

81. See company website, "The B Team and Ceres Introduce New Primer for Building Climate Competent Boards," The B Team, May 16, 2018, www.bteam.org.

82. See company website, "Company Annual Report 2017," www.investor.jnj.com, accessed February 11, 2019.

83. C. Vandlen, "Making 'Cents' of Temps: The Costs and Benefits of Contingent Workers," *Cornell HR Review,* May 16, 2011, www.cornellreview.org.

84. Bureau of Labor Statistics, "Contingent and Alternative Employment Arrangements Summary," news release, June 7, 2018, www.bls.gov.

85. "Adecco Says Global Uncertainty Not Hitting Temporary Staff Demand," *Reuters,* August 9, 2018, www.reuters.com.

86. M. B. Meznar, "Buffer or Bridge? Environmental and Organizational Determinants of Public Affairs Activities in American Firms," *Academy of Management Journal* 38, no. 4 (August 1995), pp. 975–96.

87. D. Lei, "Advanced Manufacturing Technology: Organizational Design and Strategic Flexibility," *Organization Studies* 17, no. 3 (1996), pp. 501–23; J. W. Dean Jr. and S. A. Snell, "The Strategic Use of Integrated Manufacturing: An Empirical Examination," *Strategic Management Journal* 17, no. 6 (June 1996), pp. 459–80.

88. P. Sun, K. Mellahi, and M. Wright, "The Contingent Value of Corporate Political Ties," *Academy of Management Perspectives* 26 (2012), pp. 68–82.

89. See company website, "We Have a Couple of Ground Rules at Warby Parker," Warby Parker, www.warbyparker.com, accessed February 18, 2018.

90. E. H. Schein, "Organizational Psychology Then and Now: Some Observations," *Annual Review of Organizational Psychology and Organizational Behavior* 2 (2015), pp. 1–19; S. Giorgi, C. Lockwood, and M. Glynn, "The Many Faces of Culture: Making Sense of 30 Years of Research on Culture in Organization Studies," *Academy of Management Annals* 9 (2015), pp. 1–54; H. Kilmann, M. J. Saxton,

and R. Serpa, *Gaining Control of the Corporate Culture* (San Francisco: Jossey-Bass, 1985); K. S. Cameron and R. E. Quinn, *Diagnosing and Changing Organizational Culture: Based on the Competing Values Framework* (Englewood Cliffs, NJ: Addison-Wesley, 1998).

91. J. Wattles, B. Geier, M. Egan, and D. Wiener-Bronner, "Wells Fargo's 20-Month Nightmare," *CNN Business,* April 24, 2018, www.money.cnn.com.

92. D. Wiener-Bronner, "Amazon and Whole Foods, CVS and Aetna: A Scorecard of the Biggest Deals," *CNN Business,* March 8, 2018, www.money.cnn.com.

93. Alex Malouf, "Why Organizational Culture (and Employee Communications) Should Matter to You," May 25, 2017, https://www.entrepreneur.com/article/294820.

94. https://slack.com/, accessed March 20, 2019.

95. Scott Gerber, "9 Most Effective Apps for Internal Communication, February 22, 2017, https://www.business.com/articles/9-most-effective-apps-for-internal-communication

96. M. Gelfand, S. Gordon, C. Li, V. Choi, and P. Prokopowicz, "One Reason Mergers Fail: The Two Cultures Aren't Compatible," *Harvard Business Review,* October 2, 2018, www.hbr.org.

97. K. S. Cameron and R. E. Quinn, *Diagnosing and Changing Organizational Culture: Based on the Competing Values Framework* (Englewood Cliffs, NJ: Addison-Wesley, 1998).

98. C. Groscurth, "Why Your Company Must Be Mission-Driven," *Gallup Business Journal,* March 6, 2014, http://www.gallup.com.

99. Company press release, "Target Recently Announced a New Strategy to Invest $5 Million by 2022 in Green Chemistry Innovation," January 25, 2017, www.corporate.target.com.

100. M. Schlangenstein, "Discount Airline Pioneer Herb Kelleher Dies," *Bloomberg,* January 3, 2019, www.bloomberg.com.

101. J. Koob, "Early Warnings on Culture Clash," *Mergers & Acquisitions,* July 1, 2006, Business & Company Resource Center, http://galenet.galegroup.com.

102. D. R. Denison, "What Is the Difference between Organizational Culture and Organizational Climate? A Native's Point of View on a Decade of Paradigm Wars," *Academy of Management Review* 21, no. 3 (1996), pp. 619–54.

103. 2016 Shareholder Letter, Amazon.com, https://www.sec.gov/Archives/edgar/data/1018724/000119312516530910/d168744dex991.htm.

104. Jacob Kastrenakes, "Jeff Bezos on Amazon's Culture: 'We Never Claim That Our Approach Is the Right One,'" *The Verge.com,* April 5, 2016, http://www.theverge.com/2016/4/5/11373438/amazon-corporate-culture-comment-jeff-bezos.

105. Sonia Thompson, "Why Jeff Bezos Puts Relentless Focus on Amazon's Company Culture," *Inc.,* June 25, 2018, https://www.inc.com/sonia-thompson/how-jeff-bezos-cultivates-a-culture-of-high-standards-at-amazon.html.

106. Daphne Howland, "Amazon Revamps HR Strategies to Aid Underperforming Employees," *Retail Dive.com,* January 23, 2017, http://www.retaildive.com/news/amazon-revamps-hr-strategies-to-aid-underperforming-employees/434526/.

107. Isobel Asher Hamilton, "Amazon Is Raising Its Minimum Wage to $15 Following Pressure from Bernie Sanders," *Business Insider,* October 2, 2018, https://www.businessinsider.com/amazon-raises-minimum-wage-to-15-dollars-2018-10.

108. Áine Cain, "Amazon Will Raise Its Minimum Wage to $15 an Hour—Here's What It's Really Like to Work There, According to Employees," *Business Insider,* October 2, 2018, https://www.businessinsider.com/what-its-like-to-work-at-amazon-2018-2.

CHAPTER 3
Managerial Decision Making

> No sensible decision can be made any longer without taking into account not only the world as it is, but the world as it will be.
>
> —Isaac Asimov

Monty Rakusen/Image Source

learning objectives

After studying Chapter 3, you will be able to:

LO 3-1 Describe the kinds of decisions you will face as a manager.

LO 3-2 Summarize the steps in making "rational" decisions.

LO 3-3 Recognize the pitfalls you should avoid when making decisions.

LO 3-4 Evaluate the pros and cons of using a group to make decisions.

LO 3-5 Identify procedures to use in leading a decision-making group.

LO 3-6 Explain how to encourage creative decisions.

LO 3-7 Discuss the processes by which decisions are made in organizations.

LO 3-8 Describe how to make decisions in a crisis.

chapter outline

Characteristics of Managerial Decisions
Lack of Structure   Conflict
Uncertainty and Risk

The Phases of Decision Making
Identifying and Diag-   Making the Choice
nosing the Problem   Implementing the
Generating Alternative   Decision
Solutions   Evaluating the Decision
Evaluating Alternatives

The Best Decision

Barriers to Effective Decision Making
Psychological Biases   Social Realities
Time Pressures

Decision Making in Groups
Potential Advantages of Using a Group
Potential Problems of Using a Group

Managing Group Decision Making
Leadership Style   Encouraging Creativity
Constructive Conflict   Brainstorming

Organizational Decision Making
Constraints on Decision Makers
Organizational Decision Processes
Decision Making in a Crisis

Management in Action

CAN UBER OVERCOME ITS POOR DECISIONS?

Uber Technologies, the app-based ride-hailing service launched in San Francisco in 2010, claimed to be "changing the logistical fabric of cities around the world" by allowing users to hail a ride via their smartphone. Since going global in 2013, the company now has over 3 million drivers who have provided over 10 billion rides for passengers in more than 600 cities and 65 countries around the world.[1]

Valued in early 2019 as high as $120 billion, Uber appears to have made some smart decisions.[2] Its aggressive strategy put some competitors like Sidecar out of business and put pressure on others like Lyft. The company took market share from many cities' public transportation and taxi services and introduced ride-sharing options, started a delivery service, and began exploring self-driving cars.

However, Uber has also made decisions that damaged its reputation—and may threaten its future growth. By insisting its drivers are independent contractors rather than employees, the company adopted a business model whose legality was questioned. It came under scrutiny in some countries for conducting flawed background checks on drivers, and protests by taxi drivers forced it from some markets.

In the United States, the company was charged with "fraudulent and arguably criminal conduct" for investigating a lawyer and plaintiff suing the company. When local taxi drivers protested President Trump's first immigration order and Uber appeared to capitalize by keeping its airport service rolling, the backlash forced Travis Kalanick, the company's founder and CEO, to resign from the president's Economic Advisory Council.[3]

Anton Gvozdikov/Shutterstock

Meanwhile, allegations by a female software engineer at Uber about a company culture rife with sexism and harassment forced the company to investigate, an issue we explore later in the chapter. A report also surfaced alleging that the company misused a data-collecting tool to engage in systematic deception intended to evade authorities in multiple cities.[4] And a video of Kalanick dealing angrily with an Uber driver went viral, forcing Kalanick to apologize publicly. A few months later, he resigned as CEO.

It appears that these issues have damaged not only Uber's reputation but also its market share. By the start of 2019, Lyft, Uber's main competitor, had increased its market share to approximately 35 percent, more than triple what it was three years ago.[5] Add to that Uber's largest market, New York City, recently passed a ride-sharing minimum wage law that will bite into Uber's margins and will set a regulatory precedent that might be adopted by other cities in which Uber operates.[6]

Uber has transformed the ride-hailing industry and perhaps is not done innovating yet, but the company clearly needs to reexamine its management decision-making processes. As you read this chapter, consider what makes decision making difficult, and how managers can overcome those difficulties and make the right choices.

Bottom Line

You'll be making many decisions, often under time pressure and without all the facts. By learning how to make good decisions under these conditions, you'll be more successful. *What makes a management decision a "good" decision?*

The best managers continually make decisions. Some are small and minor, while others are strategic decisions that influence an organization's direction and performance. When Satya Nadella replaced Steve Ballmer as CEO of Microsoft in 2014, he encouraged employees to "build stuff that people like." It was a small but important shift in the Windows-centric culture.[7] Soon after, Nadella made a bigger decision to pivot Microsoft away from selling operating systems to providing cloud computing services and subscription products that generate regularly recurring revenue.[8] Microsoft's Azure now competes with Amazon Web Services in the rapidly expanding cloud infrastructure space.[9]

If you can't make good decisions, you won't be an effective manager. This chapter discusses what kinds of decisions managers face, how they often make them, and how they *should* make them.

Characteristics of Managerial Decisions

LO 3-1 Describe the kinds of decisions you will face as a manager.

Managers make decisions frequently about challenges and opportunities.[10] Some situations that require a decision are relatively simple; others seem overwhelming. Some require immediate action; others take months or even years to unfold.

Actually, managers often ignore challenges.[11] For several reasons, they avoid taking action.[12] First, managers can't be sure how much time, energy, and trouble lie ahead once they start working on an issue. Second, getting involved is risky; tackling a problem but failing to solve it successfully can hurt a manager's image and personal brand. Third, because problems can be so complex, it is easier to procrastinate or to focus on less demanding activities. Managers may lack the insight, courage, or will to decide.

It is important to understand why decision making can be so challenging. Exhibit 3.1 illustrates several characteristics of managerial decisions that contribute to their difficulty and pressure. Most managerial decisions lack structure and entail risk, uncertainty, lack of structure, and conflict.

programmed decisions

Decisions encountered and made before, having objectively correct answers, and solvable by using simple rules, policies, or numerical computations.

nonprogrammed decisions

New, novel, complex decisions having no proven answers.

certainty

The state that exists when decision makers have accurate and comprehensive information.

Lack of Structure

Lack of structure is common in managerial decision making.[13] Although some decisions are routine and clear-cut, for most there is no automatic procedure to follow. Problems are often novel and unstructured, leaving the decision maker uncertain about how to proceed.

An important distinction illustrating this point is between programmed and nonprogrammed decisions. **Programmed decisions** have been encountered and made in the past. They have objectively correct answers and can be solved by using simple rules, policies, or numerical computations. If you face a programmed decision, a clear procedure or structure exists for arriving at the right decision. For example, if you are a small-business owner and must decide how to update your strategic plan. You can refer back to the process used the last time the plan was updated. Exhibit 3.2 gives some other examples.

If most important decisions were programmed, managerial life would be much easier. But managers typically face **nonprogrammed decisions**: new, novel, complex decisions having no certain outcomes. They have a variety of possible solutions, all of which have merits and drawbacks. The decision maker must create and use a method for making the decision; there is no predetermined structure on which to rely. As Exhibit 3.1 suggests, important, difficult decisions tend to be nonprogrammed, and they require creative approaches.

EXHIBIT 3.1

Characteristics of Managerial Decisions

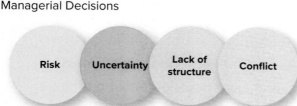

Uncertainty and Risk

If you have all the information you need and can predict precisely the consequences of your actions, you are operating under a condition of **certainty**.[14] When your manager asks you to predict what will happen or explain something

EXHIBIT 3.2
Comparing Programmed versus Nonprogrammed Decisions

	Programmed Decisions	Nonprogrammed Decisions
Problem	Frequent, repetitive, routine. Certainty regarding cause-and-effect relationships.	Novel, unstructured. Uncertainty regarding cause-and-effect relationships.
Procedure	Dependence on policies, rules, and established procedures.	Need for creativity, intuition, and creative problem solving.
Examples		
Company	Policies to follow when posting an open position on job boards.	Changing from proprietary server to cloud storage.
University	Income formulas to determine amount of student financial aid.	Create a design for a new engineering building.
Health care	Procedure for discharging patients.	Purchase of advanced imaging equipment.
Government	Merit system for promoting federal employees.	Response to an unexpected state budget shortfall.

SOURCE: Adapted from Gibson, J., Ivancevich, J., Donnelly, J., Jr., and Konopaske, R., *Organizations: Behavior, Structure, Processes,* 14th ed. New York: McGraw-Hill, 2011.

that did happen, he or she might get frustrated if you don't offer a single, confident answer. This is because people usually prefer *feeling* certain—even if their "certainty" is mistaken or misleading.[15]

But perfect certainty as we define it here is rare. For important, nonprogrammed managerial decisions, uncertainty is the fact of life.

Uncertainty means the manager has insufficient information to know the consequences of different actions. Business people do not like uncertainty; it can prevent them from taking action. For example, uncertainty over Great Britain's decision to exit the 28-member European Union (Brexit) has led to slower than average economic growth as British companies scale back investments and hiring plans.[16] But economies don't strengthen until consumer confidence increases, which doesn't happen until employment rises.

When you can estimate the likelihood of various outcomes of a decision but still do not know with certainty what will happen, you are facing **risk**. Risk exists when the probability of an action being successful is less than 100 percent and losses may occur. If the decision is the wrong one, you may lose money, time, momentum, or other important resources.

Risk, like uncertainty, is a fact of life in managerial decision making.[17] But this is not the same as taking a risk. While some risk takers are admired and entrepreneurs and investors thrive on taking risks, the reality is that good decision makers prefer to *manage* risk. They accept the fact that decisions entail risk, but they do everything they can to anticipate the risk, minimize it, and control it.

The stories detailed in "The Greatest Business Decisions of All Time" are creative approaches to managing risk. A classic example is how Henry Ford, when facing high levels of employee turnover and discontent, doubled workers' pay and switched from two 9-hour shifts to three 8-hour shifts per day. These improvements cost Ford $10 million, but his gamble paid off with higher retention rates and productivity levels.[18] Ford could not have known with certainty that his changes would work, but he assessed his options and took a calculated risk.

A more recent example is how GoPro launched a contest on social media to gather user-generated content. Using the GoPro Hero7, over 25,000 people submitted video clips to GoPro's Million Dollar Challenge. In exchange for this content, GoPro offered to divide $1 million to those whose clips were chosen to be featured in the official highlight reel. By involving users in this contest, the organization reduced risk by gathering authentic content from current users. This will likely help GoPro expand its customer base by demonstrating how its camera can be used in a variety of ways.[19]

uncertainty

The state that exists when decision makers have insufficient information.

risk

The state that exists when the probability of success is less than 100 percent and losses may occur.

Social Entrepreneurship

Saul Garlick's Social Enterprise: Nonprofit or For-Profit?

When visiting Mpumalanga, South Africa, as a boy, Saul Garlick was shocked at the village's lack of resources: "The small rural village had nothing—no classrooms, no electricity, no water."[20] He decided he wanted to help. While in high school, Garlick founded Student Movement for Real Change (SMRC), a nonprofit whose mission was to fight poverty by encouraging entrepreneurship in Africa. The organization recruited students to "live with local families, hunt for water sources, farm alongside villages and absorb day-to-day nuances of life in a developing country with the goal of building social businesses along with the local residents."[21]

As a nonprofit, the organization was funded through donations, and SMRC started to grow. As a 23-year-old working full time for the organization, Garlick began to draw a salary and hired someone to run the daily operations. Even with the help, Garlick was under constant pressure to raise funds to keep the operation functioning when instead he wanted to spend more time doing the core work of the organization.

If he wanted to have a high-impact social enterprise, Garlick needed a business model that could sustain itself. He believed that a market-based solution was his best hope to help him reduce poverty in Africa, resulting in his decision to buy out his nonprofit, SMRC, and launch a for-profit social enterprise, ThinkImpact.[22]

By borrowing $450,000 from friends, family, and angel investors, Garlick developed a strategy to set ThinkImpact on a profitable course. The for-profit social enterprise developed an eight-week program bringing students and entrepreneurs together from universities and communities around the globe to work with locals in Rwanda, Panama, South Africa, Kenya, Ghana, and Mexico. The curriculum is designed to spark the creative talents of individuals while developing their problem-solving skills.

ThinkImpact has expanded into funding, supporting, and launching new social enterprises. Its mission is to "start and grow cross-cultural social enterprises built on an asset-based approach and immersive collaboration."[23] ThinkImpact's entrepreneurs have started social enterprises in such areas as agriculture, health, and engineering and tech businesses. The belief that inspires those involved in ThinkImpact is that social enterprises and the experience of building them can change lives.

1. Why do you think Garlick thought a for-profit, market-based solution was best for his organization?
2. How might uncertainty and risk played a role in Garlick's decision to become a for-profit organization?

Conflict

conflict

Opposing pressures from different sources, occurring on the level of psychological conflict or conflict between individuals or groups.

Important decisions are even more difficult because of the conflicts managers face. **Conflict**, which exists when a manager must consider opposing pressures from different sources, occurs at two levels.

First, individual decision makers experience psychological conflict when several options are attractive or when none of the options is attractive. For instance, a manager may have to decide whom to lay off when she doesn't want to lay off anyone. Or she may have three promising job applicants for one position—but choosing one means she has to reject the other two.

Second, conflict arises between people. A chief financial officer argues in favor of increasing long-term debt to finance an acquisition. The chief executive officer, however, prefers minimal debt and finds the funds elsewhere. A marketing department wants more product lines to sell, and the engineers want higher-quality products. But the production people want to lower costs by having longer production runs of fewer products with minimal changes. Few decisions are without conflict.

In the "Social Entrepreneurship" feature, how much "structure" and how many programmed decisions do you see? Try to identify and describe the uncertainties, risks, and potential conflicts in the major unprogrammed decisions.

The Phases of Decision Making

Faced with these challenges, how can you make good decisions? The ideal, most rational and analytical decision-making process includes six steps. As Exhibit 3.3 illustrates, decision makers should (1) identify and diagnose the problem, (2) generate alternative solutions, (3) evaluate alternatives, (4) make the choice, (5) implement the decision, and (6) evaluate the decision.

LO 3-2 Summarize the steps in making "rational" decisions.

Identifying and Diagnosing the Problem

The first phase in the decision-making process is to recognize that a problem exists and must be solved. Typically, a manager realizes some discrepancy between the current state (the way things are) and a desired state (the way things ought to be). Such discrepancies—say, in organizational or unit performance—may be detected by comparing current performance against (1) *past* performance, (2) the *current* performance of *other* organizations or units, or (3) *future* expected performance as determined by plans and forecasts.[24]

The "problem" may be an opportunity that can be exploited with appropriate action. In that case, decisions involve deciding whether and how to seize the opportunity.[25] To recognize important opportunities as a manager, you will need to understand your company's macro- and competitive environments (described in Chapter 2).

Recognizing that a problem (or opportunity) exists is only the beginning of this phase. The decision maker must dig in deeper and attempt to analyze its possible causes. For example, a sales manager knows that sales have dropped drastically. If he is leaving the company soon or believes the decreased sales volume is due to the economy (which he can't do anything about), he won't take action. But if he does try to solve the problem, he should not automatically reprimand his sales staff, add new people, or increase the advertising budget. He must analyze *why* sales are down and then develop a solution appropriate to his analysis. Asking why, of yourself and others, is essential to understanding the real problem.

Michael Ortner and Rakesh Chilakapati co-founded a company called Capterra, which created an online directory of companies that sell business software. Their problem was that they wanted to bring more traffic to their website; more listings would make the site more valuable to buyers, and more buyers would make the site more attractive to vendors.[26]

The company asked *why* traffic was low by surveying the directory's users. Buyers wanted to see reviews of vendors; the underlying problem was that the website lacked a key feature that buyers would find helpful.[27]

Exhibit 3.4 lists some useful questions to ask and answer in this phase.[28]

Generating Alternative Solutions

The second phase of decision making links problem diagnosis to the development of alternative courses of action aimed at solving the problem. Managers generate at least some alternative solutions based on past experiences.[29]

Solutions range from ready-made to custom-made.[30] Decision makers who employ **ready-made solutions** use ideas they have tried before or follow the advice of others who have faced similar problems. **Custom-made solutions**, by contrast, must be designed for specific problems. This technique often combines ideas into new, creative solutions.

ready-made solutions
Ideas that have been seen or tried before.

custom-made solutions
New, creative solutions designed specifically for the problem.

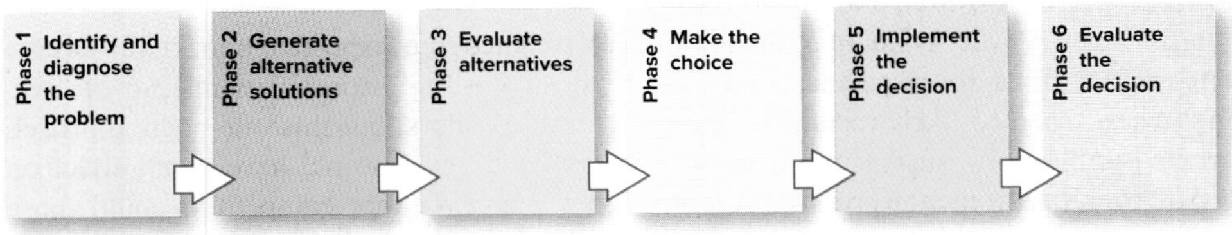

Phase 1 Identify and diagnose the problem → Phase 2 Generate alternative solutions → Phase 3 Evaluate alternatives → Phase 4 Make the choice → Phase 5 Implement the decision → Phase 6 Evaluate the decision

EXHIBIT 3.3
The Phases of Decision Making

EXHIBIT 3.4

EXHIBIT 3.4
Questions for Identifying
and Diagnosing Problems

How can you best describe the difference between what is actually happening and what should be happening?
What is/are the cause(s) of the deviation?
What short- and long-term goals need to be met?
Which goals are absolutely critical to the success of the decision?

For example, IDEO, a design and innovation firm, helped its start-up-in-residence, Pill-Pack, to change how customers of advanced age, of limited mobility, or with serious illnesses interact with their pharmacy. PillPack launched a simple, fast home-delivery service that sorts patients' multiple prescriptions and over-the-counter medicines into packets that are organized by the date and time they should be taken. Pills arrive in an organized, recyclable dispenser with a label that includes an image of the pill. Customers can coordinate refills with or ask questions of PillPack's pharmacists via phone or email on a 24/7 basis. There is no charge for the packaging and delivery service.[31] Recently, Amazon purchased PillPack for $1 billion as part of Amazon's focus on acquiring "technologies and know-how to enable Amazon to serve customers more effectively."[32]

Potentially, custom-made solutions can be devised for any challenge. Later in the chapter, we will discuss how to generate creative ideas.

Often, many more alternatives are available than managers realize. For example, what would you do if one of your competitors reduced prices? Managers sometimes assume that cutting prices in response to a competitor's price cuts is their only option, but it is not. Alternatives include conveying consumer risks of low-priced products, building awareness of your products' features and overall quality, and communicating your cost advantage to your competitors so they realize that they can't win a price war. If you do decide to cut your price as a last resort, do it fast; if you do it slowly, your competitors will gain sales in the meantime, which may embolden them to employ the same tactic again in the future.[33]

Returning to the example of Capterra, Michael Ortner was eager to launch the product reviews, but Rakesh Chilakapati, the company's technology manager at the time, wanted to proceed cautiously because of the time and expense required to add the feature, along with fear that some vendors would get bad reviews and leave the directory. So to generate alternatives, the two partners studied existing websites with product reviews (for example, Amazon, eBay, and Edmunds.com). They identified a variety of ways to offer reviewing features. They could simply post testimonials from satisfied customers. They could allow or forbid anonymous comments. They could require reviewers to list both positive and negative points. The big question that remained was whether the features attractive to buyers would repel sellers.[34]

> When generating alternatives, the first one that comes to mind may not be the best one.

Evaluating Alternatives

The third phase of decision making involves determining the value or adequacy of the alternatives that were generated. Which solution will be the best?

Especially when decisions are important, alternatives should be evaluated with careful thought and logic. Fundamental to this process is to predict the consequences that will occur if the different options are put into effect. Managers should consider several types of consequences, including quantifiable measures of success such as lower costs, higher sales, lower employee turnover, and higher profits.

At Capterra, the evaluation of alternatives weighed the expected impact of reviews on buyers against the expected impact on vendors. Posting testimonials instead of inviting reviews seemed likely to protect the goodwill of vendors, but this one-sided approach seemed unlikely to satisfy buyers, so the founders doubted it would have much effect on traffic overall. Anonymous reviews seemed risky because vendors' competitors could abuse

Which goals does each alternative meet and fail to meet?
Which alternatives are most acceptable to you and to other important stakeholders?
If several alternatives might solve the problem, which can be implemented at the lowest cost or greatest profit?
If no alternative achieves all your goals, can two or more of the best ones be combined?

EXHIBIT 3.5
Questions for Evaluating Alternatives

the system, so they dropped that alternative. Requiring both pros and cons in the reviews would encourage balanced information about vendors, an apparent plus. But Ortner knew that many vendors still worried about the risk of negative reviews.[35]

An important technology affecting the analysis of alternatives is the ability to collect and analyze big data. The term refers to massive amounts of structured and unstructured data that exceed the capabilities of a traditional computer database. Businesses today can gather details about Internet usage, consumer behavior, and employee skills and activities, among many other things. Organizations can store the data, search them for patterns or trends, and analyze them to identify alternatives that previously would have gone unnoticed.

Evaluation that would have relied heavily on intuition or experience now can be data-driven. For example, companies are using big data to make more effective decisions about pay. Netflix uses data analytics to configure its recommendation algorithm for its users. By using customer data, Netflix saves an estimated $1 billion a year from customer retention and can create original series that are guaranteed to be hits.[36]

To evaluate alternatives, refer to your original goals, defined in the first phase. Next, you should consider the questions in Exhibit 3.5.

Several additional questions help:[37]

Is our information about alternatives complete and current? If not, can we get more and better information?

Does the alternative meet our primary objectives?

What problems could we have if we implement the alternative?

Of course, results cannot be forecast with perfect accuracy. But sometimes decision makers can build in safeguards against an uncertain future by considering the potential consequences of several scenarios. Then they generate **contingency plans**—alternative courses of action that can be implemented depending on how the future unfolds.

For example, during an economic crisis when it is unclear when a recovery might begin and how strong it will be or what shape it will take, the range of potential outcomes is wide, and many companies will not survive. Firms could consider at least four future economic scenarios:[38]

1. A most optimistic scenario in which trade and capital flows resume, further recession is averted, globalization stays on course, and developed and emerging economies continue to integrate as confidence rebounds quickly.
2. A battered-but-resilient scenario in which the recession continues for a long period, recovery is slow, confidence is shaken but does rebound, and globalization slowly gets back on course.
3. Stalled globalization, in which the global recession is significant, the intensity varies greatly from nation to nation, but overall growth is slow.
4. A long freeze, in which the recession lasts more than five years, economies everywhere stagnate, and globalization goes into reverse.

As you read this, what economic scenario is unfolding? What are the important current events and trends? What scenarios could evolve six or eight years from now? How will *you* prepare?

contingency plans

Alternative courses of action that can be implemented based on how the future unfolds.

Some decisions do not work out. Although this can surprise and frustrate, you should have contingency plans that will help you still achieve your desired goals.

ESB Professional/Shutterstock

Making the Choice

Once you have considered the possible consequences of your options, it is time to make your decision. The temptation to overanalyze can lead to paralysis by analysis—that is, indecisiveness caused by too much analysis. When it comes time to decide, assertive decision making can help an organization seize new opportunities or thwart challenges.

Indecisiveness became a risk at Capterra because Ortner and Chilakapati had conflicting worries. Ortner continued to see the lack of reviews as a missed opportunity, whereas Chilakapati remained focused on the risks of adding this feature. Ortner further researched the situation by calling vendors who had expressed concerns about reviews; he became convinced that they, too, were simply not seeing the opportunities of this additional feature and would come around when experience showed them the value. Finally, after three months of debate, Ortner was enjoying his regular five-mile run when he concluded that the analysis had to end, and he must make a decision. As president, he made the final call, respecting Chilakapati's concerns but announcing that it was time to try the reviews.[39]

> The process of considering multiple scenarios raises important "what if" questions for decision makers and highlights the need for contingency plans.

As you make your decision, important guiding concepts include maximizing, satisficing, and optimizing.[40]

maximizing

A decision realizing the best possible outcome.

Maximizing is achieving the best possible outcome. The maximizing decision realizes the greatest positive consequences and the fewest negative consequences. In other words, maximizing results in the greatest benefit at the lowest cost, with the largest expected total return. Maximizing requires searching thoroughly for a complete range of alternatives, carefully assessing each alternative, comparing one to another, and then choosing or creating the very best.

satisficing

Choosing an option that is acceptable, although not necessarily the best or perfect.

Satisficing is choosing the first option that is minimally acceptable or adequate. When you satisfice, you compare your choice against your goal, not against other options. Satisficing means that a search for alternatives stops after you find one that is OK. You do not expend the time or energy to gather more information. Instead you make the expedient decision based on readily available information.

Let's say you are purchasing new equipment, and your goal is to avoid spending too much money. You would be maximizing if you checked out all your options and their prices and then bought the cheapest one that met your performance requirements. But you would be satisficing if you bought the first adequate option that was within your budget and failed to look for less expensive options.

Satisficing is sometimes a result of laziness; other times, there is no other known option because time is short, information is unavailable, or other constraints make maximizing impossible. When the consequences are not huge, satisficing can even be the ideal approach. But in other situations, when managers satisfice, they fail to consider options that might be better.

optimizing

Achieving the best possible balance among several goals.

Optimizing means that you achieve the best possible balance among several goals. Perhaps, in purchasing equipment, you are interested in quality and durability as well as price. So instead of buying the cheapest piece of equipment that works, you buy the one with the best combination of attributes, even though there may be options that are better on the price criterion and others that are better on the quality and durability criteria. The same idea applies to achieving business goals: One marketing strategy could maximize sales, whereas a different strategy might maximize profit. An optimizing strategy is the one that achieves the best balance among multiple goals.

Implementing the Decision

The decision-making process does not end once you make a choice. The chosen alternative must be implemented. Sometimes the people involved in making the choice are the same people who put it into effect. At other times, they delegate the responsibility for implementation to others, such as when a top management team changes a policy or operating procedure and has operational managers carry out the change.

At Capterra, implementation of the decision to add customer reviews included 10 months of software development, followed by invitations to vendors to encourage their customers to submit reviews. Notice that the implementation took into account the concerns about negative reviews by giving the vendors some control over who submitted the initial reviews.[41]

Unfortunately, sometimes managers make decisions but don't take action. Implementing may fail to occur when *talking* a lot is mistaken for *doing* a lot; when people forget that merely making a decision changes nothing; when meetings, plans, and reports are seen as actions, even if they have no effect on what people actually do; and if managers don't check to ensure that what was decided was actually done.[42]

Managers should plan implementation carefully. Adequate planning requires several steps:[43]

1. Determine how things will look when the decision is fully operational.
2. Chronologically order, perhaps with a flow diagram, the steps necessary to achieve a fully operational decision.
3. List the resources and activities required to implement each step.
4. Estimate the time needed for each step.
5. Assign responsibility for each step to specific individuals.

Decision makers should assume that things will *not* go smoothly during implementation. It is useful to take a little extra time to identify *potential problems* and *potential opportunities* associated with implementation. Then you can take actions to prevent problems and be ready to seize unexpected opportunities. Exhibit 3.6 lists several useful questions that should be asked in the implementation stage of decision making.

Many of the chapters in this book are concerned with implementation issues: how to implement strategy, allocate resources, organize for results, lead and motivate people, manage change, and so on. View the chapters from this perspective and learn as much as you can about how to implement properly.

> Decision makers should assume that things will *not* go smoothly during implementation.

Evaluating the Decision

The final phase in the decision-making process is evaluating the decision. It involves collecting information on how well the decision is working. Quantifiable goals—a 20 percent increase in sales, a 95 percent reduction in accidents, 100 percent on-time deliveries—can be set before implementing the solution. Then objective data can be gathered to determine their success or failure accurately.

Decision evaluation is useful whether the conclusion is positive or negative. Feedback that suggests the solution is working implies that the decision should be continued and perhaps applied elsewhere in the organization. Negative feedback means that either (1) implementation will require more time, resources, effort, or thought; or (2) the solution wasn't good enough.

The feedback for Capterra was positive. In the first year of offering customer reviews, the site gathered about 500 reviews. A year after that, the site had 2,000 reviews, with about 40 percent of them unsolicited. Most reviews were positive. Even though some are less than glowing, traffic to the site grew to 25,000 reviews; vendors see the review feature as a benefit because they are getting more business. Revenues jumped, and the executives concluded that customer reviews were a great idea.[44]

If the decision appears inadequate, it's time to adjust. The process cycles back to the first phase: (re)defining the problem. The decision-making process begins anew, preferably with more information, new suggestions, and an approach that attempts to eliminate the mistakes made the first time around.

Bottom Line
It's easy to become so focused on maximizing one goal that you lose sight of other important goals. You're optimizing if you make sure that no important result is ignored. *What could be the negative consequences of making decisions that maximize only quality?*

EXHIBIT 3.6
Questions for Implementing Decisions

What problems could this action cause?
What can we do to prevent the problems?
What unintended benefits or opportunities could arise?
How can we make sure they happen?
How can we be ready to act when the opportunities come?

The Best Decision

System 1 information processing

A type of decision-making process that is reflexive and done quickly without careful thought.

System 2 information processing

A type of decision-making process that is reflective and done slowly with deliberative thought.

vigilance

A process in which a decision maker carefully executes all stages of decision making.

How can managers tell whether they have made the best decision? Most think they are pretty good decision makers. Some of us wish we could be more decisive, and it does seem that the business world values decisiveness. But making fast decisions is not the same as as making *good* decisions.

But being a perfectly and consistently rational decision maker is impossible. We are not as objective as we think we are, and it's only human to make mistakes, especially for complex, conflict-ridden managerial decisions that must be made in uncertain and risky circumstances. Fact is, people use two types of decision-making processes, what Nobel laureate Daniel Kahneman calls **System 1** and **System 2 information processing**.[45] The first (also called Type 1) is reflexive: emotional, intuitive, instinctive, and done quickly and automatically without careful thought. The second (Type 2) is reflective: analytic, calculating, slow and deliberative, and tries to attain the best possible outcomes.[46]

That's a well-researched and simply-stated bottom line. But how those processes work, and the effects they have, is complicated—a subject of infinite research possibilities and full-semester courses for students who want deep dives into this fascinating and important domain.

Although nothing can guarantee a "best" decision, managers should at least be confident that they followed proper *procedures* that will yield the best possible decision under the circumstances. This means that the decision makers were appropriately vigilant in making the decision. **Vigilance** occurs when the decision makers carefully and conscientiously execute all six phases of decision making, including effective implementation and evaluation.[47]

Even if managers reflect on their decision-making activities and conclude that they executed each step conscientiously, they still will not know whether the decision will work; after all, nothing guarantees a good outcome. But they *will* know that they did their best to make the best possible decision.

Barriers to Effective Decision Making

Full, vigilant execution of the six-phase decision-making process are the exception rather than the rule. But when managers use such rational processes, better decisions result.[48] Managers who make sure they engage in these processes are more effective.

But it is easy to neglect or improperly execute these processes. The problem may be improperly defined goals. Not enough solutions may be generated, or they may be evaluated incompletely. A *satisficing* rather than *maximizing* choice may be made. Implementation may be poorly planned or executed, or evaluation may be inadequate or nonexistent.

And as discussed next, decisions are influenced by subjective psychological biases, time pressures, and social realities.

Psychological Biases

Recalling reflexive System 1 (or Type 1) vs. reflective System 2 (Type 2) decision-making processes, people are far from objective in the way they gather, evaluate, and apply information in making their choices. People have biases that interfere with objective rationality. The examples that follow represent only a few of the many documented subjective biases.[49]

illusion of control

People's belief that they can influence events even when they have no control over what will happen.

The **illusion of control** is a belief that one can influence events even when one has no control over what will happen. Gambling is one example: Some people believe they have the skill to beat the odds, even though most of the time they cannot. In business, such overconfidence can lead to failure because decision makers ignore risks and fail to objectively evaluate the odds of success.

Managers may believe they can do no wrong or maintain a general optimism about the future that can lead to believing they are immune to risk and failure.[50] They may overrate the value of their experience. They may believe that a previous project met its goals because of their decisions alone, so they can succeed on the next project by doing everything the same way.

Framing effects refer to how problems or decision alternatives are phrased or presented and how these subjective influences can override objective facts. In one example, managers indicated a desire to invest more money in a course of action that was reported to have a 70 percent chance of profit than in one said to have a 30 percent chance of loss.[51] The choices were equivalent in their chances of success; it was the way the options were framed that determined the managers' choices.

Managers may be quick to frame a problem as being similar to problems they have already handled, so they don't search for new alternatives. Soon after taking over as CEO of Yahoo!, people expected Marissa Mayer to turn around the failing Internet pioneer by making major strategy changes. Mayer had risen through the ranks at her previous employer, Google, to eventually lead the company's all-important search business. Unfortunately, her product expertise wasn't enough to fix Yahoo![52] Critics said that she made only minor tactical changes, such as changing Yahoo!'s home page layout, to an "outdated success formula."[53] Her actions were not enough to keep the famous company from being sold to Verizon for $4.8 billion in 2017. Mayer resigned from the board of directors and the company was renamed Altaba.[54]

Often, decision makers **discount the future**. That is, in their evaluation of alternatives, they weigh short-term costs and benefits more heavily than longer-term costs and benefits. Consider your own decision about whether to go for a dental checkup. The choice to go poses short-term financial costs, anxiety, and perhaps physical pain. The choice not to go will inflict even greater costs and more severe pain if dental problems worsen. How do you choose? Many people decide to avoid the short-term costs by not going for regular checkups, but end up facing greater pain in the long run.

The same bias applies to students who don't keep up with assignments, dieters who sneak dessert or skip an exercise routine, and people who take the afternoon off to play golf when they really need to work. It can also affect managers who hesitate to invest funds in research and development programs that may not pay off until far into the future. In all these cases, avoiding short-term costs or seeking short-term rewards results in negative long-term consequences.

Asian managers tend to think with a longer-term outlook than do American managers, and many believe that this provides competitive advantage for long-term success.[55] Western myopia is driven in part by Wall Street's focus on quarterly earnings, causing managers to make decisions based primarily on short-run considerations and to neglect long-term problems and opportunities. Why is it so hard to make decisions with the long term in mind?

In contrast, when U.S. companies sacrifice present value to invest for the future—such as when Weyerhaeuser incurs enormous costs for its reforestation efforts that won't lead to harvest until 60 years in the future—it seems the exception rather than the rule. Discounting the future partly explains governmental budget deficits, environmental destruction, decaying infrastructure, and failure to act strongly enough on climate change. Fortunately, people can override this bias with effort.[56]

Time Pressures

In today's rapidly changing business environment, the premium is on acting quickly and keeping pace. The most conscientiously made business decisions can become irrelevant or disastrous if managers take too long to make them.

How can managers make decisions quickly? Some natural tendencies, at least for North Americans, might be to skimp on analysis (not be too vigilant),

framing effects

A decision bias influenced by the way in which a problem or decision alternative is phrased or presented.

discounting the future

A bias weighting short-term costs and benefits more heavily than longer-term costs and benefits.

Bottom Line

When you want to pursue sustainability, think in terms of the long-term consequences of your decisions. *As a manager, what might be the long-term consequences of not investing in renewable energy?*

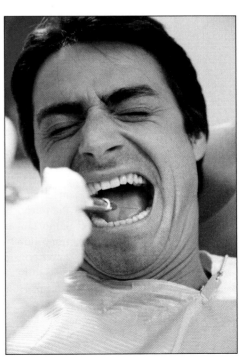

Delaying dental checkups can have a negative impact on the future. It may save money today but lead to larger costs (and more pain) later.

Ingram Publishing

Management in Action

A HUGE PROBLEM AT UBER

Susan Fowler kept meticulous records of the year she worked for Uber as a software engineer. During that time, she was an exemplary employee but reportedly faced repeated instances of sexism and sexual harassment, only to see the offending managers let off with a reprimand at best. Sometimes her complaints to human resources were denied; sometimes they were belittled and minimized as a "first offense"; and at other times, according to the blog post she wrote later, Fowler was told she herself was the problem. She resigned in December 2016 from what she called "an organization in complete, unrelenting chaos"[57] after a transfer she requested was blocked and she was told she could be fired for reporting a manager who discriminated against her. Such actions on the part of Uber are clearly illegal.

Fowler's blog post also included allegations that brutally competitive behavior originated with the company's top managers: "It seemed like every manager was fighting their peers and attempting to undermine their direct supervisor so that they could have their direct supervisor's job. . . . They boasted about it in meetings, told their direct reports about it, and the like."[58] During Fowler's time at the company, she says the percentage of women employees dwindled from 25 percent to about 6 percent.

Her accusations sparked an immediate reaction from the company's founder and then CEO Travis Kalanick. At a meeting of all employees, Kalanick announced an investigation into the company culture, to be led by former U.S. attorney general Eric Holder and board member Ariana Huffington (founder of *Huffington Post*). "I am authentically and fully dedicated to getting to the bottom of this," Kalanick said.[59]

In response to Fowler's accusations and the subsequent investigation, many top executives at Uber resigned, including Kalanick himself, and over 20 employees were fired over incidents of discrimination, harassment, and bullying. Many more employees were disciplined. In addition, Holder's report contained a list of recommendations, ranging from the handling of internal complaints to a greater emphasis on diversity training and recruitment, to ensure such discrimination and behavior would not be repeated.[60]

1. Why do you think it took so long for Uber to recognize that it had a problematic corporate culture? Consider the psychological biases, time pressures, and social realities discussed in this section when formulating your answer.
2. The Holder investigation provided recommendations to resolve the culture at Uber. If you were an executive at Uber, what would you do to solve these problems? Again, consider barriers to effective decision making and ways to overcome them.

suppress conflict, and make decisions on one's own without consulting others.[61] These strategies may speed up decision making, but they reduce decision quality.

The speed trap can be as dangerous as moving too slowly.[62] In an Internet start-up that went bankrupt, fast decisions initially helped the firm achieve its growth objectives. Early on, the founders did everything they could to create a sense of urgency: They planned a meeting to "light a fire under the company," calling it a "state-of-emergency address" with the purpose of creating "the idea of panic with an emerging deadline." Speed became more important than content. They failed to consider multiple alternatives, used little information, didn't fully acknowledge competing views, and didn't consult outside advisers. They never considered slowing down to be an option.

Can managers under time pressure make decisions that are both timely and high quality? An important study of effective decision-making processes in a fast-paced, high-tech industry revealed the tactics that such companies use.[63] First, instead of relying on old data, long-range planning, and futuristic forecasts, they focus on real-time information: current information obtained with little or no time delay.

> The speed trap can be as dangerous as moving too slowly.

For example, they constantly monitor daily operating measures such as work in process rather than checking periodically the traditional accounting-based indicators such as profitability.

Second, they involve people more effectively and efficiently in the decision-making process. They rely heavily on trusted experts, and this yields both good advice and the

The Digital World

Predictive Analytics: Helping Businesses Make Faster, Better Decisions

As you just read, in today's business environment, managers face extreme pressure to make fast, effective decisions. However, the large volume of data they receive can complicate the decision-making process.

Enter predictive analytics, which uses AI technologies to analyze and mine large amounts of data to help make predictions about future trends and events.[64] Using predictive analytics, managers are better able to make decisions based on not just how the company is performing today, but how it can adapt to better perform tomorrow.

Large companies, such as Amazon, Netflix, and Airbnb, are integrating predictive analytics as a core part of their business planning. With the aid of this technology, Amazon can change the price of its products based on customer purchasing and searching activity.[65] Smaller operations are also jumping in. For example, Apex Parks, which runs 16 amusement and water parks in the United States, has begun using AI to better target its marketing and make more effective decisions.[66] Some universities are also utilizing predictive analytics to better retain students.[67]

1. What do you think of companies turning to predictive analytics to guide their strategic planning?
2. In what industries do you see predictive analytics being most useful? Why?

---

confidence to act quickly despite uncertainty. They also take a realistic view of conflict: they value differing opinions, but they know that if disagreements are not resolved, the top executive must make the final choice in the end. Slow-moving firms, in contrast, are stymied by conflict. Like the fast-moving firms, they seek consensus; but when disagreements persist, they fail to decide.

Social Realities

Many decisions are made by a group rather than by an individual manager. In slow-moving firms, interpersonal factors decrease decision-making effectiveness. Even the manager acting alone is accountable to the boss and to others and must consider the preferences and reactions of many people. Therefore, many decisions are the result of intensive social interactions, bargaining, and politicking.

The remainder of this chapter focuses on the social context of decisions, including decision making in groups and the realities of decision making in organizations.

Bottom Line

You'll feel pressure to make quick decisions, but rushing can lead to mistakes. Fortunately, you can be vigilant while moving quickly, avoiding the speed trap. *When you are under time pressure, what can you do to avoid making poor decisions?*

Decision Making in Groups

Sometimes managers convene groups of people in order to make important decisions. Some advise that in today's complex business environment, significant problems should *always* be tackled by groups.[68] As a result, managers must understand how groups operate and how to use them to improve decision making.

The basic philosophy behind using a group to make decisions is captured by the adage, "two heads are better than one." But is this statement really valid? Yes, it is—but only potentially, not necessarily.

Size of team matters. Too few members may not yield additional creative thinking or problem solving. Too many members are hard to coordinate and manage. When in doubt, five or six is probably optimal.[69]

If enough time is available, groups usually make higher-quality decisions than most individuals acting alone. However, groups often are inferior to the *best* individual.[70]

LO 3-4 Evaluate the pros and cons of using a group to make decisions.

EXHIBIT 3.7
Pros and Cons of Using
Groups to Make Decisions

Potential Advantages	Potential Disadvantages
Larger pool of information.	One person dominates.
More perspectives and approaches.	Satisficing.
Intellectual stimulation.	Groupthink.
People understand the decision.	Goal displacement.
People are committed to the decision.	Social loafing.

Bottom Line

If one person dominates a group discussion, it may feel like you're speeding up the decision making. But one dominant person reduces decision quality, and most of you will have wasted your time. *When you're meeting with a group, what can you do to encourage everyone to participate?*

How well the group performs depends on how effectively it capitalizes on the potential advantages and minimizes the potential problems of using a group. Exhibit 3.7 summarizes these issues.

Potential Advantages of Using a Group

If other people have something to contribute, using groups to make a decision offers at least five potential advantages:[71]

1. More information is available when several people are making the decision. If one member doesn't have all the facts or needed expertise, another member might.
2. A greater number of perspectives on the issues, or different approaches to solving the problem, are available. The problem may be new to one group member but familiar to another. Or the group may need to consider other viewpoints—financial, legal, marketing, human resources, and so on—to achieve an optimal solution.
3. Group discussion provides an opportunity for intellectual stimulation. It can get people thinking and unleash their creativity to a far greater extent than would be possible with individual decision making.

Those three potential advantages of using a group improve the odds that a more fully informed, higher-quality decision will result. Thus managers should involve people with different backgrounds, experiences, perspectives, and access to information. They should not involve only their colleagues who think the same way they do.

4. People who participate in a group discussion are more likely to understand why the decision was made. They will have heard the relevant arguments both for the chosen alternative and against the rejected alternatives.
5. Group discussion typically leads to a higher level of commitment to the decision. Buying into the proposed solution translates into high motivation to ensure that it is executed well.

The last two advantages improve the chances that the decision will be implemented successfully. Therefore, managers should involve the people who will be responsible for implementing the decision as early in the deliberations as possible.

Potential Problems of Using a Group

Things can go wrong when groups make decisions. Most of the potential problems concern the processes through which group members interact with one another:[72]

1. Sometimes one group member dominates the discussion. When this occurs—such as when a strong leader makes his or her preferences clear—the result is the same as it would be if the dominant individual made the decision alone. Individual dominance has two disadvantages. First, the dominant person does not necessarily have the most valid opinions—and may even have the most unsound ideas. Second, even if that person's preference leads to a good decision, convening as a group will have been a waste of everyone else's time.

2. Satisficing is more likely with groups. Most people don't like meetings and will do what they can to end them. This may include criticizing members who want to keep exploring new and better alternatives. The result is a satisficing rather than an optimizing or maximizing decision.

3. Pressure to avoid disagreement can lead to a phenomenon called **groupthink**. This occurs when people choose not to disagree or raise objections. Some groups want to think as one, tolerate no dissension, and strive to remain cordial. They can be overconfident, complacent, and perhaps too willing to take risks. Pressure to go along with the group's preferred solution stifles creativity and other positive behaviors characteristic of vigilant decision making.

Heated arguments can arise when team members have differing opinions and are more concerned with winning the dispute than resolving the initial problem.

laflor/Getty Images

4. Goal displacement often occurs in groups. The goal of group members should be to come up with the best possible solution to the problem. But when **goal displacement** occurs, new goals emerge to replace the original ones. It is common for two or more group members to have different opinions and present their conflicting cases. Attempts at rational persuasion become heated disagreement. Winning the argument becomes the new goal. Saving face and defeating the other person's idea become more important than solving the problem.

5. When members of a group do not feel their contribution is important, they may engage in social loafing by working less hard when in a group.[73] This tendency to not pull one's own weight while working in groups poses many problems. Social loafing reduces cohesiveness between group members, resulting in lower group performance and higher absenteeism.[74] Chapter 14 discusses how managers can address social loafing and other barriers to building effective teams.

groupthink

A phenomenon that occurs in decision making when group members avoid disagreement as they strive for consensus.

goal displacement

A decision-making group loses sight of its original goal and a new, less important goal emerges.

Effective managers pay close attention to the group process; they manage it carefully. You have just read about the pros and cons of using a group to make decisions, and you are about to read how to manage the group's decision-making process. Chapter 12, on leadership, helps you decide *when* to use groups to make decisions.

Managing Group Decision Making

As Exhibit 3.8 illustrates, effectively managing group decision making has three major requirements: (1) an appropriate leadership style, (2) the constructive use of disagreement and conflict, and (3) the enhancement of creativity.

LO 3-5 Identify procedures to use in leading a decision-making group.

Leadership Style

The leader of a decision-making group must attempt to minimize process-related problems. The leader should avoid dominating the discussion or allowing another individual to dominate. Less vocal group members should be encouraged to air their opinions and suggestions, and all members should be asked for dissenting viewpoints.

At the same time, the leader should not allow the group to pressure people into conforming. The leader should be alert to the dangers of groupthink and satisficing. Also, she should

Inclusiveness Works

Diverse Teams: Reaping the Benefits through Empathy and Consideration

The benefits of a diverse workplace have been well documented. Diversity has been found to drive innovation and is critical to cultural understanding in a global marketplace. An inclusive workforce also helps companies recruit and retain top talent.[75] But diverse teams also face challenges. For example, a poorly managed team with diverse members might lack cohesion, inhibiting open communication, creative thinking, and, ultimately, productivity. Effective management in such environments is therefore critical.

To start, a team leader who displays cross-cultural competence is essential. Cross-cultural competence includes the ability to adapt to and empathize with a variety of cultural perspectives.[76] Research has also found that consideration plays a role in managing diverse teams, as highly considerate leaders improve team cohesion and functioning.[77]

Leaders of diverse teams who are empathetic and considerate of the backgrounds and perspectives of team members can foster cohesion and trust by making sure all team members feel heard and understood. With diverse teams, it's not just about the perception of difference and sameness in relation to the team; it's about each individual's perception of his or her place on the team.[78]

In the early stages of team formation, therefore, it's wise for leaders to create opportunities for team members to share stories and experiences beyond the task at hand. This could be through team-building exercises, shared meals, or special events. The more each team member gets to know the other members as individuals, the more likely trust and cohesion is to develop. Similarly, during early phases of team formation, effective leaders should have one-on-one check-ins with team members to allow each member's voice to be heard.[79]

The more that perceived differences among team members diminish through increased communication, the more each member is apt to trust the team. Trust builds cohesion and fosters willingness to share ideas and think creatively to achieve team goals.

1. What are some benefits of diverse teams? What are some potential drawbacks?
2. How have you or those you have worked with demonstrated cultural competence in the workplace?

EXHIBIT 3.8

Managing Group Decision Making

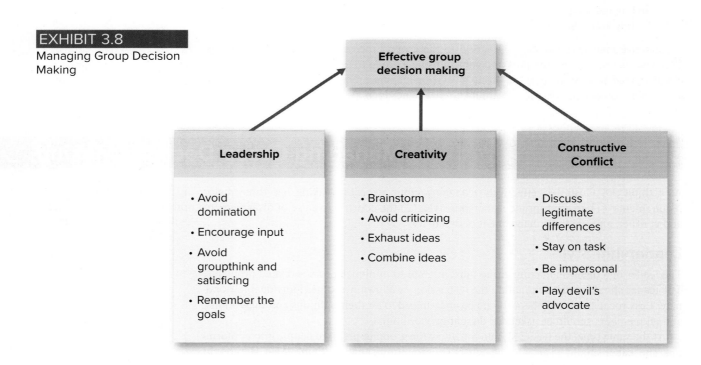

be attuned to indications that group members are losing sight of the primary objective: to come up with the best possible solution to the problem.

These suggestions have two implications. First, don't lose sight of the problem and your goals. Second, make a decision! Slow-moving organizations whose group members can't come to an agreement will be standing still while their competitors move ahead.

> First, don't lose sight of the problem and your goals. Second, make a decision! Don't fall prey to analysis paralysis.

Constructive Conflict

Total and consistent agreement among group members can be destructive. It can lead to groupthink, uncreative solutions, and a waste of the knowledge and diverse viewpoints that people bring to a group. Therefore, a certain amount of constructive conflict should exist.[80] Pixar, which depends on creativity to make its animated films great, encourages constructive conflict with a standard for production meetings: Whenever someone wants to criticize an idea, the critic must attach an idea for improvement. In this way, good ideas can become great, and great ideas can become amazing. The practice is so much a part of Pixar's culture, it even has a name, "plussing."[81]

The most constructive type of conflict is **cognitive conflict**, or differences in perspectives or judgments about issues. In contrast, **affective conflict** is emotional and directed at other people. Affective conflict is likely to be destructive to the group because it can lead to anger, bitterness, goal displacement, and lower-quality decisions. Cognitive conflict can air legitimate differences of opinion and develop better ideas and problem solutions. Conflict, then, should be task-related rather than personal.[82] But even task-related conflict is good only when managed properly.[83]

Managers can generate constructive conflict through structured processes like **devil's advocacy**, in which a group member identifies and states the problems with an idea being considered. The group leader can formally assign people to play this role. Requiring people to point out problems can reduce inhibitions about disagreeing and make the conflict less personal and emotional.

An alternative to devil's advocacy is the dialectic. The **dialectic** goes a step beyond devil's advocacy by requiring a structured debate about two conflicting courses of action.[84] The philosophy of the dialectic stems from Plato and Aristotle, who advocated synthesizing the conflicting views of a thesis and an antithesis. Structured debates between plans and counterplans can be useful prior to making a strategic decision. For example, one team might present the case for acquiring a firm while another team advocates not making the acquisition.

Constructive conflict does not need to be generated on such a formal basis, and is not solely the leader's responsibility. Any team member can introduce cognitive conflict by being honest with opinions, by being unafraid to disagree with others, by pushing the group to action if it is taking too long or making the group slow down if necessary, and by advocating long-term considerations if the group is too focused on short-term results. Introducing constructive conflict is a legitimate and necessary responsibility of all group members interested in improving the group's decision-making effectiveness.

cognitive conflict
Issue-based differences in perspectives or judgments.

affective conflict
Emotional disagreement directed toward other people.

devil's advocate
A person who has the job of criticizing ideas to ensure that their downsides are fully explored.

dialectic
A structured debate comparing two conflicting courses of action.

Encouraging Creativity

As you've already learned, ready-made solutions to a problem can be inadequate or unavailable. In such cases, custom-made solutions are necessary, so the group must be creative in generating ideas.

Some say that the most fundamental unit of value is ideas. Creativity is more than just an option; it is essential to survival. Allowing people to be creative may be one of the manager's most important and challenging responsibilities.

You might be saying to yourself, "I'm not creative." But even if you are not an artist or a musician, you do have potential to be creative in countless other ways. You don't need to be

LO 3-6 Explain how to encourage creative decisions.

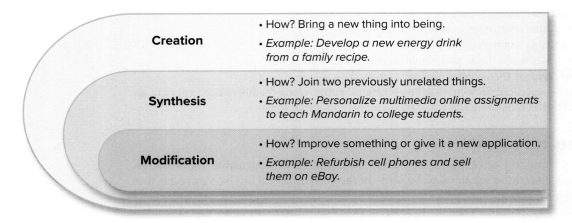

EXHIBIT 3.9   Creative Actions

a genius in school either—Thomas Edison and Albert Einstein were not particularly good students. Nor does something need to change the world to be creative; the little things can always be done in new, creative ways that add value to the product and for the customer. Exhibit 3.9 describes three ways to be creative along with some ideas of college student entrepreneurs who turned their creativity into businesses.[85]

How do you become more creative?[86] Recognize the almost infinite little opportunities to be creative. Assume you can be creative if you give it a try. Escape from work once in a while. Read widely and try new experiences. Take a course or find a good book about creative thought processes; plenty are available. Exchange ideas and seek and give feedback.[87] And be aware that creativity is social;[88] your creativity will be affected by your social relationships at work, including your connections with other people outside your immediate close network.[89] Talk to people, often, about the issues and ideas with which you are wrestling.

How do you get creativity out of other people?[90] Give creative efforts the credit they are due and don't punish creative failures. Avoid extreme time pressure if possible.[91] Stimulate and challenge people intellectually, and keep them busy. Listen to employees' ideas and allow enough time to explore different ideas. Put together groups of people with different styles of thinking and behaving. Get your people in touch with customers. Experiment with ways to stimulate fresh modes of thinking. Design company IDEO tells clients to install long communal tables or other spaces for employees to gather. Providing mobile chairs and desks encourages employees to get out of their silos to find new people to collaborate with.[92] And strive to be creative yourself—you'll set a good example.

People are likely to be more creative if they believe they are capable, if they know that their co-workers expect creativity, and if they believe that their employer values creativity.[93] As a manager, you can do much to help employees develop these beliefs by how you listen, what you allow, and what you reward and punish. At Westin Hotels, management signals that it values creativity by inviting employees to submit ideas to improve the hotel's performance. The employee with the best idea is awarded an all-expenses-paid vacation.[94]

Brainstorming

A common technique used to elicit creative ideas is brainstorming. In **brainstorming**, group members generate as many ideas about a problem as they can. As the ideas are presented, they are posted so that everyone can read them, and people can use the ideas as building blocks. The group is encouraged to say anything that comes to mind, with one exception: no criticism of other people or their ideas is allowed.

In the proper brainstorming environment—free of criticism—people are less inhibited and more likely to voice their unusual, creative, or even wild ideas. By the time people have

Bottom Line

Most creative ideas do not come from the lone genius in the basement laboratory, but from people talking and working together. *Why is listening to team members, customers, and others useful in stimulating creativity?*

brainstorming

A process in which group members generate as many ideas about a problem as they can; criticism is withheld until all ideas have been proposed.

exhausted their ideas, a long list of alternatives has been generated. Only then does the group turn to the evaluation stage. At that point, many ideas can be considered, modified, or combined into a creative, custom-made solution to the problem.

Brainstorming isn't necessarily as effective as some people think. Sometimes in a brainstorming session, people are inhibited and anxious, they conform to others' ideas, they set low standards, and they engage in noncreative behaviors including cocktail party-type conversations—complimenting one another, repeating ideas, telling stories—that are nice but don't promote creativity. Exhibit 3.10 shows how McKinsey creates effective brainstorming sessions.[95]

Brainstorming is a technique used to generate as many ideas as possible to solve a problem. You have probably engaged in brainstorming sessions for various class or work projects.
REDPIXEL.PL/Shutterstock

Other techniques that help include *brainwriting* (taking time to write down ideas silently), using trained facilitators, setting high performance goals, brainstorming electronically so that people aren't competing for air time, and even building a playground with fun elements that can foster creativity.[96] Some facilitators use brainwriting apps like Stormboard, Tecmark 635, and Stormz to capture output from participants.[97]

Organizational Decision Making

Individuals and groups make decisions constantly throughout every organization. To understand decision making in organizations, a manager should consider (1) the constraints decision makers face, (2) organizational decision processes, and (3) decision making during a crisis.

Constraints on Decision Makers

Organizations—or, more accurately, the people who make important decisions—cannot do whatever they wish. Resources are scarce,[98] and various constraints—financial, legal, market, human, and organizational—inhibit certain actions. Laws may constrain the kinds of business activities in which a firm can participate. Labor unions may defeat a contract proposed by management, and managers and investors may block a takeover attempt. A tight labor market may delay a company's expansion due to lack of qualified job applicants. In strategic alliances, the allies should pursue rational decisions collaboratively, not separately.[99] Even brilliant ideas must take into account the practical matters of implementation.[100]

LO 3-7 Discuss the processes by which decisions are made in organizations.

Bottom Line
You may be an innovator if you come up with a creative idea. But you still need to implement it. *Assuming you are a frontline manager, what should you do next? With whom should you share this new idea?*

EXHIBIT 3.10
Improving Brainstorming Effectiveness

1. Choose participants based on their expertise and knowledge of the challenge.
2. Use well-thought-out questions as a platform to spark new ideas.
3. Break up large groups into subgroups of 3–5 people.
4. Ask subgroups to think deeply to generate 2–3 solutions for each key question explored.
5. Do not have the full group evaluate the winning ideas, but rather ask subgroups to identify their top 2 or 3 ideas. Describe next steps (e.g., top management team will evaluate ideas).
6. Act quickly on key ideas and provide feedback to all participants.

Suppose you have a great idea that will provide a revolutionary service for your bank's customers. You won't be able to put your idea into action immediately. You will have to sell it to the people who can give you the go-ahead and to those whose help you will need to carry out the project. You might start by convincing your manager of your idea's value. Next, the two of you may have to discuss it with a vice president. Then maybe the president has to be sold. At each stage, you must listen to these individuals' opinions and suggestions and often incorporate them into your original concept. Ultimately, you will have to craft a proposal acceptable to others.

In addition, you should carefully think through ethical and legal considerations. Decision makers must consider ethics and the preferences of many constituent groups—the realities of life in organizations. You will have plenty of opportunity to think more about ethical issues in Chapter 5.

Organizational Decision Processes

bounded rationality

A less-than-perfect form of rationality in which decision makers cannot be perfectly rational because decisions are complex and complete information is unavailable or cannot be fully processed.

Just as with individuals and groups, organizational decision making historically was described with rational models like the one depicted earlier, in Exhibit 3.3. But Nobel laureate Herbert Simon challenged the rational model and proposed an important alternative. Due to **bounded rationality**, decision makers cannot be truly rational because (1) they have imperfect, incomplete information about alternatives and consequences; (2) the problems they face are so complex; (3) human beings simply cannot process all the information to which they are exposed; (4) there is not enough time to process all relevant information fully; and (5) people, including managers within the same firm, have conflicting goals.

When these conditions hold—and they do for most consequential managerial decisions—perfect rationality will give way to more biased, subjective, messier decision processes. For example, the **incremental model** of decision making occurs when managers make small decisions, take baby steps, and move cautiously toward a bigger solution. The classic example is the budgeting process, which traditionally begins with the budget from the previous period and makes incremental decisions from that starting point.

incremental model

Model of organizational decision making in which major solutions arise through a series of smaller decisions.

The **coalition model** of decision making arises when people disagree on goals or compete with one another for resources. The decision process becomes political as groups of individuals band together and try collectively to influence the decision. Two or more coalitions form, each representing a different preference, and each tries to use power and negotiations to sway the decision.

coalition model

Model of organizational decision making in which groups with differing preferences use power and negotiation to influence decisions.

Organizational politics, in which people try to influence decisions so that their own interests will be served, can reduce decision-making effectiveness.[101] One of the best ways to reduce such politics is to create common goals for members of the team—that is, make the decision-making process a collaborative, rather than a competitive, exercise by establishing a goal around which the group can rally. In one study, top management teams with stated goals such as "build the biggest financial war chest" for an upcoming competitive battle or "build the best damn machine on the market" were less likely to have dysfunctional conflict and politics between members.[102] On a personal level, if you find yourself in a conflict, you and your adversary may be focused on the wrong goals. Work to find common ground in the form of an important goal that you both want to achieve.

garbage can model

Model of organizational decision making depicting a chaotic process and seemingly random decisions.

The **garbage can model** of decision making occurs when people aren't sure of their goals, or disagree about the goals, and likewise are unsure of or in disagreement about what to do. This situation occurs because some problems are so complex that they are not well understood, and because decision makers move in and out of the decision process due to having so many other things to attend to as well. This model implies that some decisions are chaotic and almost random. You can see that this is a dramatic departure from rationality in decision making.

crisis management (CM)

Process of identifying, preparing for, and dealing with potentially catastrophic threats to an organization.

Decision Making in a Crisis

LO 3-8 Describe how to make decisions in a crisis.

In crises, managers must make decisions under a great deal of pressure.[103] **Crisis management (CM)** is the process of identifying, preparing for, and dealing with potentially catastrophic events or damage to an organization.[104]

You know some of the most famous recent crises: wildfires, flooding, and other severe weather devastation, ongoing political crises that have shaken many governments around the world, and the lasting effects of the great recession from a decade ago.

Information technology is a crucial arena highly vulnerable to crises. Businesses, homes, government agencies, hospitals, and other organizations continually send critical information through public and private networks, and any technical failure—sometimes accidental, sometimes maliciously intentional—could be magnified by the speed and reach of information technology. In 2018, massive account data breaches were all too common. Companies reporting hacked accounts include Marriott Starwood Hotels (500 million accounts), MyFitnessPal (150 million accounts), Cambridge Analytica (87 million accounts), and Facebook (29 million accounts).[105]

Superstorm Sandy hit the East Coast with fierce devastation. Managers had to make critical decisions to keep people safe.

Roschetzky Photography/ Shutterstock

One crucial area is the electrical grid, which links utilities and carries power to each user. Hackers can access the U.S. electrical grid and interfere with its operations.[106] It almost feels routine how often hackers gain unethical, illegal, and dangerous access to databases and systems of companies and government agencies.

Managing crises effectively requires dealing with both internal organizational dynamics and the outside world.[107] The response to IT-related crises must involve senior executives in online communication, both to protect the firm's reputation and to communicate with outside experts, news sources, and key external and internal stakeholders. Managers rely on IT tools to help monitor and respond immediately to problems, including scandals, boycotts, rumors, cyberattacks, and other crises.[108]

Artificial intelligence, data analytics, and machine learning are emerging and potentially powerful tools that are expected to enhance cybersecurity.[109] Managers would be well-advised to keep up with these trends.

Although many companies still don't concern themselves with crisis management, this is a recipe for compounding disaster; it is imperative that management prepare for possible crises. As illustrated in Exhibit 3.11, an effective plan for crisis management (CM) includes several elements.[110]

Ultimately, management should be able to answer the following questions:[111]

What kinds of crises could affect your company?
Can your company detect a crisis in its early stages?
How will it manage a crisis if one occurs?
What team inside the company would lead the response effort?
What can it learn from a crisis to improve its response next time?

EXHIBIT 3.11
Elements in an Effective Crisis Plan

Strategic actions such as integrating crisis management (CM) into strategic planning and official policies.

Evaluation and diagnostic actions such as conducting audits of threats, and establishing tracking systems for early warning signals.

Technical and structural actions such as creating a CM team and dedicating a budget to CM.

Communication actions such as providing training for dealing with the media, local communities, and police and government officials.

Psychological and cultural actions such as providing training and psychological support services regarding the human and emotional impacts of crises.

SOURCES: Meyers, G. with Holusha, J., *When It Hits the Fan: Managing the Nine Crises of Business.* Boston: Houghton Mifflin, 1986; Bacharach, S. and Bamberger, P., "9/11 and New York City Firefighters' Post Hoc Unit Support and Control Climates: A Context Theory of the Consequences of Involvement in Traumatic Work-Related Events," *Academy of Management Journal* 50 (2007), pp. 849–68.

Crises can harm personal and work relationships and long-term performance. But with effective crisis management—which must include learning from the event and its aftermath[112]—old as well as new problems can be resolved, new strategies and competitive advantages may appear, and positive change can emerge. And if someone steps in and manages the crisis well, a hero is born.

> When people step in and manage the crisis well, heroes are born.

As a leader during a crisis, don't pretend that nothing happened (as did managers at one firm after a visitor died in the hallway despite employees' efforts to save him).[113] Communicate and reinforce the organization's values. Try to find ways for people to support one another and remember that others will take cues from your behavior. You should be optimistic but brutally honest. Show emotion, but not fear. "You have to be cooler than cool," says Gene Kranz of *Apollo 13* ground control fame.

But don't ignore the problems or downplay them and reassure too much; don't create false hopes. Give people the bad news straight—you'll gain credibility, and when the good news comes, it will really mean something.

Management in Action

UBER IN CRISIS?

There is little doubt that Uber's innovative concept and technology have revolutionized transportation. There is also little doubt that Uber's scandals have hurt its business. When companies reach such crisis points, change often must start at the top, which is what Uber did when its board selected Dara Khosrowshahi to replace Travis Kalanick as CEO.

Khosrowshahi is charged with transforming the aggressive, free-wheeling culture that was at least partly responsible for Uber's initial success into a more grounded and ethical one that can endure for the long term. As CEO, Khosrowshahi must understand the source of Uber's problems while also inspiring change for the future. Just months after taking over, he summed up Uber's situation as follows: "We were probably trading off doing the right thing for growth, and thinking about competition maybe a bit too aggressively, and some of those things were mistakes. . . . The question is, do you learn from those mistakes? 2017 [was] a really tough year, but this is going to result in us being a better company."[114]

What changes will make Uber a stronger company? Of course, a big part of Khosrowshahi's job is to repair Uber's image, but that can't be done with public relations alone. Uber's policies with regard to its full-time employees, driver partners, and customers need to reflect a more inclusive and ethical ethos as well.

In an effort to change its corrosive corporate culture, Uber hired Bo Young Lee to be its first chief diversity and inclusion officer, and the percentage of women in Uber's operations is slowly rising.[115] At the end of 2018, Uber announced a change to its rate structure that would value its drivers' time at a higher rate so they would earn more on shorter trips.[116] Uber also introduced a loyalty program for drivers and riders.[117] Finally, Uber incorporated into its mobile app safety features, such as Ride Check, which allows for swifter detection and notification of emergencies, as well as two-factor authentication, which helps keep riders' exact addresses anonymous.[118]

Still, it hasn't been all positive news for Uber. In early 2018, not long after Khosrowshahi took over, a woman in Arizona was killed by a self-driving car in the Uber pilot program, which had some critics claiming Uber was again putting profit over safety.[119] And claims of gender discrimination haven't completely gone away, as the U.S. Equal Employment Opportunity Commission opened an investigation into Uber's hiring practices in 2018. Whether that investigation was looking into past practices or ongoing ones is unclear as of this writing.

What is clear is that Uber is trying to learn from its mistakes, and Khosrowshahi is trying to change the image of the company. "We believe we can be a force for good," he said. "We've changed our actions but the cultural change continues."[120] Time will tell how successful they will be.

1. Based on what you've read, what organizational decision-making process best describes Khosrowshahi's approach to transforming Uber?
2. What actions has Uber taken that align with effective crisis planning? What additional steps can it take?

KEY TERMS

affective conflict, p. 93

bounded rationality, p. 96

brainstorming, p. 94

certainty, p. 78

coalition model, p. 96

cognitive conflict, p. 93

conflict, p. 80

contingency plans, p. 83

crisis management (CM), p. 96

custom-made solutions, p. 81

devil's advocate, p. 93

dialectic, p. 93

discounting the future, p. 87

framing effects, p. 87

garbage can model, p. 96

goal displacement, p. 91

groupthink, p. 91

illusion of control, p. 86

incremental model, p. 96

maximizing, p. 84

nonprogrammed decisions, p. 78

optimizing, p. 84

programmed decisions, p. 78

ready-made solutions, p. 81

risk, p. 79

satisficing, p. 84

System 1 information processing, p. 86

System 2 information processing, p. 86

uncertainty, p. 79

vigilance, p. 86

RETAINING WHAT YOU LEARNED

In Chapter 3, you learned that most managers make less than perfectly rational decisions because they lack the necessary information, time, or structure. The ideal decision-making process includes six steps (see Exhibit 3.3 recreated below). The best decision hinges on the manager's ability to be vigilant at all stages of the decision-making process. Various barriers can diminish the effectiveness of the decision-making process. While there are advantages and disadvantages of making decisions in groups, a good leader can manage the challenges by using the right leadership style, allowing constructive conflict, encouraging creativity, and brainstorming.

Decision making in organizations is complex and individuals are often bounded by multiple constraints. Decisions can be made incrementally, through coalitions, or in a chaotic garbage can manner. Decision making during organizational crises is particularly challenging; managers should anticipate and plan for it.

LO 3-1   Describe the kinds of decisions you will face as a manager.

- Most important managerial decisions lack structure and are characterized by uncertainty, risk, and conflict.
- Despite these challenges, managers are expected to make rational decisions in a timely manner.

LO 3-2   Summarize the steps in making "rational" decisions.

- The ideal decision-making process involves six phases. The first, identifying and diagnosing the problem (or opportunity), requires recognizing a discrepancy between the current state and a desired state and then delving below surface symptoms to identifying underlying causes of the problem.
- The second phase, generating alternative solutions, involves applying ready-made or designing custom-made solutions.
- The third, evaluating alternatives, means predicting the consequences of different alternatives, sometimes through building scenarios of the future.
- Fourth, choosing a solution; the solution might maximize, satisfice, or optimize.
- Fifth, implementing the decision; this phase requires more careful planning than it often receives.
- Finally, evaluating how well the decision is working. This means managers gather objective, valid information about the impact the decision is having. If the evidence suggests the problem is not getting solved, either a better decision or a better implementation plan must be developed.

LO 3-3   Recognize the pitfalls you should avoid when making decisions.

- Situational and human limitations lead most decision makers to satisfice rather than maximize or optimize.

EXHIBIT 3.3 (revisited)   The Phases of Decision Making

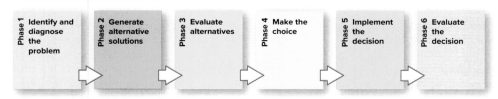

Phase 1 Identify and diagnose the problem → Phase 2 Generate alternative solutions → Phase 3 Evaluate alternatives → Phase 4 Make the choice → Phase 5 Implement the decision → Phase 6 Evaluate the decision

- Psychological biases, time pressures, and the social realities of organizational life may prevent rational execution of the six phases.
- Vigilance and an understanding of how to manage decision-making groups and organizational constraints will improve the process and result in better decisions.

LO 3-4   Evaluate the pros and cons of using a group to make decisions.

- Advantages of using groups include more information, perspectives, and approaches brought to bear on problem solving; intellectual stimulation; greater understanding of the final decision; and higher commitment to the decision once it is made.
- Potential dangers or disadvantages of using groups include individual domination of discussions, satisficing, groupthink, goal displacement, and social loafing.

LO 3-5   Identify procedures to use in leading a decision-making group.

- Effective leaders in decision-making teams avoid dominating the discussion; encourage people's input; avoid groupthink and satisficing; and stay focused on the group's goals.
- They encourage constructive conflict via devil's advocacy and the dialectic, posing opposite sides of an issue or solutions to a problem.

LO 3-6   Explain how to encourage creative decisions.

- When creative ideas are needed, leaders should set a good example by being creative themselves. They should recognize the almost infinite little opportunities for creativity and have confidence in their own creative abilities.
- They can inspire creativity in others by providing creative freedom, rewarding creativity, and not punishing creative failures.
- Leaders should encourage interaction with customers, stimulate discussion, and protect people from managers who might squelch the creative process.
- Brainstorming is one of the most popular techniques for generating creative ideas.

LO 3-7   Discuss the processes by which decisions are made in organizations.

- Decision making in organizations can be a highly complex process. Individuals and groups are constrained by a variety of factors and constituencies. In practice, decision makers are boundedly rational rather than purely rational.
- Some decisions are made on an incremental basis. Coalitions form to represent different preferences. The process is often chaotic, as depicted in the garbage can model.
- Politics can also enter the process, decisions are negotiated, and crises come and go.

LO 3-8   Describe how to make decisions in a crisis.

- Crisis conditions make sound, effective decision making more difficult. However, it is possible for crises to be managed well.
- A strategy for crisis management can be developed beforehand, and the mechanisms readied, so that if crises do arise, decision makers are prepared.

DISCUSSION QUESTIONS

1. Discuss Uber's success and crises in terms of risk, uncertainty, and how its managers are handling the company's challenges. What is the current news on this company?
2. Identify some risky decisions you have made. Why did you take the risks? How did they work out? Looking back, what did you learn?
3. Identify a decision you made that had important unexpected consequences. Were the consequences good, bad, or both? Should you, and could you, have done anything differently in making the decision?
4. What effects does time pressure have on your decision making? In what ways do you handle it well and not so well?
5. Recall a recent decision that you had difficulty making. Describe it in terms of the phases of decision making in Exhibit 3.3.
6. What do you think are some advantages and disadvantages to using computer technologies in decision making?
7. Do you think that when managers make decisions they follow the decision-making steps as presented in this chapter? Which steps are apt to be overlooked or given inadequate attention? What can people do to make sure they do a more thorough job?
8. Discuss the potential advantages and disadvantages of using a group to make decisions. Give examples from your experience.
9. Suppose you are the CEO of a major corporation and one of your company's oil tanks has ruptured, spilling thousands of gallons of oil into a river that empties into the ocean. What do you need to do to handle the crisis?
10. Identify some problems you want to solve. Brainstorm with others a variety of creative solutions.

EXPERIENTIAL EXERCISES

3.1   Decision Making In Action

OBJECTIVE

Learn how to improve your ability to make higher-quality decisions.

INSTRUCTIONS

Refer again to Exhibit 3.3. Think back to a recent expensive purchase you made. It could have been a bike, phone, suit for interviews, and so forth. In order to evaluate the quality of your decision, please think about your purchase when answering each of the questions below.

Decision Making Worksheet

1. What problem did you hope to solve by making this purchase?
   _____

2. What alternative (or competing) products did you consider?
   _____

3. How did you evaluate the different alternative (or competing) products? Did you identify each product's strengths and weaknesses? How much of a role did cost play in your decision?
   _____

4. When you made the final choice, was it a maximizing, satisficing, or optimizing outcome?
   _____

5. Before purchasing the product, did you test it out? If so, how many times?
   _____

6. Was your decision to make the purchase a positive or negative one? Did it satisfy your original need(s)?
   _____

3.2   Group Problem Solving at a Social Enterprise

OBJECTIVE

To understand the dynamics of group decision making through role-playing a meeting between a president and her employees.

INSTRUCTIONS

1. Identify 5 students to play the roles of the employees. Ask these 5 individuals to read their roles below.

2. Identify 1 student to play the role of the president of the social enterprise (Taylor Johnson). Ask this individual to read his/her role below.

3. Set up a table with 6 chairs at the front of the classroom.

4. Ask the remaining students in the audience to observe how the 6 individuals behave and then answer the discussion questions below.

5. When everyone is ready, Taylor Johnson joins the others at the table in her office, and the scene commences.

6. The meeting continues until there is a successful close unless an argument develops and no progress is made after 10–15 minutes.

DISCUSSION QUESTIONS

1. How did each member frame the problem? What did each member discuss?

2. How effectively did the group generate and evaluate alternatives?

3. What was its final decision?

4. Evaluate the effectiveness of the group's decision making.

5. How could the group's effectiveness be enhanced?

OVERVIEW

The role-play exercise is based on a meeting between a manager of a social enterprise and her 5 employees. Each character's role is designed to re-create a realistic business meeting. Each character brings to the meeting a unique perspective on a major problem confronting the social enterprise as well as some personal views of the other characters developed over several years of knowing them in business and social contexts.

CAST OF CHARACTERS

Taylor Johnson, the president, founded the enterprise 10 years ago as a way to connect outstanding teachers who have recently earned their teaching degrees with students in schools located in economically disadvantaged areas. The new teachers agree to serve in the disadvantaged schools for a 3-year period in exchange for a reasonably good salary and forgiveness of up to $30,000 of their student loans. Taylor is well known for her hard-driving, selfless style of leadership. A charismatic leader, she is highly skilled at bringing diverse stakeholders together. However, Taylor admits that she lacks knowledge related to online classroom and teaching technologies. In the old days, this wouldn't be an issue. However, Taylor's competitors are beginning to overtake the social enterprise by offering new teachers training, mobile devices, and online learning tools (e.g., online homework, interactive videos, eBooks, and so forth) to help them create high-performance classrooms. She doesn't know whether the enterprise should continue doing what it does best (placing new teachers into traditional face-to-face teaching environments) or begin preparing its recruits to teach online and hybrid (combining face-to-face with online modules) classes.

Amit Patel, head of information technology, has worked for the enterprise for 6 months. A recent college graduate, Amit reports directly to Taylor. She is on a mission to modernize the way the enterprise does its work. She feels strongly that the enterprise should be shifting more of its IT operations to the cloud. Also, Amit feels that a great deal of insight could be mined from 10 years of data currently stored in antiquated servers at the enterprise. Amit believes she could make these changes without spending a lot of funds. Unfortunately, Amit's zeal for rapid change has been a cause of concern for Felipe and Taylor who prefer a more methodical approach to change.

Felipe Rodriguez, director of fund-raising, reports directly to Johnson. He has held this position for 8 years and is a very close friend of Taylor's. Donations and grants for the most recent year are down by 10 percent. Prior to joining the enterprise, he worked as a fund-raiser for a major university in the region. The university offered a wide variety of online and hybrid courses. Felipe would often refer to these innovations when seeking donations from alumni. He was widely viewed as successful at his work.

Mike Clarke, manager in charge of recruiting new teachers, works for Felipe. After working for the enterprise as an entry-level recruiter for two years, Mike was recently promoted to this position. Though a persuasive recruiter of new teachers, he has noticed a recent decline in the number of recruits willing to teach in traditional face-to-face learning environments. He is progressive in his thinking and believes that the enterprise needs to change how it does business in order to keep up with the competitors. Mike and Amit feel they are agents of change and want to modernize the enterprise.

TODAY'S MEETING

Taylor has called the meeting with these three managers to decide whether the social enterprise should begin preparing its new recruits to teach not only traditional face-to-face classes, but also hybrid and online classes. This decision has to be made within 15 minutes because the enterprise's largest client just called and asked to meet with Taylor immediately. Taylor is concerned that the school may be on the verge of discontinuing the contract with the enterprise. If that's the case, Taylor wants the managers to help her decide on a counteroffer to win back the client school. Losing this client school is not an option given that it makes up 40 percent of the enterprise's revenue.

SOURCE: Adapted from Gordon, Judith R., *A Diagnostic Approach to Organizational Behavior* (Upper Saddle River, NJ: Pearson Education, Inc., 1983).

Concluding Case

SOARING EAGLE SKATE COMPANY

As a child, Mikala Eagle loved riding her skateboard and doing tricks. By the time she was a teenager, she was so good that she began entering and winning professional contests. By her twenties, Eagle was so successful and popular that she could make skateboarding her career. A skateboard maker sponsored her in competitions around the world.

The sponsorship and prize money paid enough to support her for several years, but she was barely getting by. Eagle knew she would have to take her business in new directions so she decided to launch her own brand of skateboard. She called it Soaring Eagle Skate Company. To finance her venture, she pooled her personal savings with money from her friend Pete Williams, who wanted to invest in the company. Together they came up with $75,000. It didn't take long for young skaters to snap up Soaring Eagle skateboards. The launch was an instant success.

As the company prospered, Eagle considered ideas for expansion. Another of Eagle's friends designed a line of clothing she thought would appeal to Eagle's skateboarding fans, and Eagle's name on the product would lend it credibility. However, Eagle discovered that the business of shorts and shirts is far different from the business of sports equipment. The price markups were tiny, and the sales channels were different. Three years into the expansion, Soaring Eagle had invested millions of dollars in the line but was losing money. Eagle decided to sell off that part of the business to a clothing company and cut her losses.

Soon after that experiment, co-founder Williams proposed another idea: They should begin selling other types of sports equipment—inline roller skates and ice skates. Selling equipment for other kinds of sports would produce more growth than the company could obtain by focusing on just one sport. Eagle was doubtful. She was considered one of the most knowledgeable people in the world about skateboarding, but she knew nothing about inline and ice skating. Eagle argued that the company would be better off focusing on the sport in which it offered the most expertise. Surely there were ways to seek growth within that sport— or at least to avoid the losses that came from investing in industries in which the company lacked experience.

Williams continued to press Eagle to try his idea. He pointed out that unless the company took some risks and expanded into new areas, there was little hope that they could continue to earn much of a return on their investment. Eagle was conflicted. Her takeaway from their failed attempt to sell clothing was that they needed to be careful about expansion. But Williams was adamant that they needed to generate new revenue streams. She could go along with Williams and take the chance of losing more money, or she could take her savings and try to buy Williams's share of the company and run Soaring Eagle on her own.

DISCUSSION QUESTIONS

1. How do the characteristics of management decisions—uncertainty, risk, conflict, and lack of structure—affect the decision facing Mikala Eagle?

2. What steps can Eagle take to increase the likelihood of making the best decision in this situation?

ENDNOTES

1. Uber Newsroom, https://www.uber.com/newsroom/company-info/, accessed February 22, 2019.
2. "How Uber Could Justify a $120 Billion Valuation," *Forbes,* December 3, 2018, https://www.forbes.com/sites/greatspeculations/2018/12/03/how-uber-could-justify-a-120-billion-valuation/#2d06b9c17f9b.
3. Kara Swisher, "Uber CEO Travis Kalanick Is Leaving Donald Trump's Advisory Council," Recode.net, February 2, 2017, http://www.recode.net/2017/2/2/14490950/travis-kalanick-uber-ceo-leaves-donald-trump-advisory-council.
4. Mike Isaac, "Uber Uses Tech to Deceive Authorities Worldwide," *The New York Times,* March 4, 2017, p. 1, https://www.nytimes.com/2017/03/03/technology/uber-greyball-program-evade-authorities.html.
5. Brandy Betz, "Lyft Gains Market Share from Uber," *Seeking Alpha,* December 12, 2018, https://seekingalpha.com/news/3416492-lyft-gains-market-share-uber.
6. Joshua Brustein, "New York Sets Nation's First Minimum Wage for Uber, Lyft Drivers," *Bloomberg,* December 4, 2018, https://www.bloomberg.com/news/articles/2018-12-04/new-york-sets-nation-s-first-minimum-wage-for-uber-lyft-drivers.
7. "Opening Windows, Microsoft at Middle Age," *The Economist,* April 4, 2015, www.economist.com.
8. "The Best-Performing CEOs in the World 2018," *Harvard Business Review,* November–December 2018, www.hbr.org.
9. J. Novet, "How Satya Nadella Tripled Microsoft's Stock Price in Just over Four Years," *CNBC,* July 18, 2018, www.cnbc.com.
10. E. Larson, "A Checklist for Making Faster, Better Decisions," *Harvard Business Review,* March 7, 2016, www.hbr.org.
11. M. Magasin and F. L. Gehlen, "Unwise Decisions and Unanticipated Consequences," *Sloan Management Review* 41 (1999), pp. 47–60.
12. G. Llopis, "Four Reasons Leaders Are Too Afraid of Making the Wrong Decisions," *Forbes,* July 16, 2015, www.forbes.com.
13. B. Bass, *Organizational Decision Making* (Homewood, IL: Richard D. Irwin, 1983).
14. J. March, "Bounded Rationality, Ambiguity, and the Engineering of Choice," *Bell Journal of Economics* 9 (1978), pp. 587–608.
15. D. Messick and M. Bazerman, "Ethical Leadership and the Psychology of Decision Making," *Sloan Management Review* (Winter 1996), pp. 9–22.
16. D. Milliken, "Brexit Uncertainty Is 'Starting to Bite' for UK Firms," Reuters, October 7, 2018, www.reuters.com.
17. A. F. Hoskisson, R. E. Chirico, F. Zyung, and J. Y. Gambeta, "Managerial Risk Taking: A Multitheoretical Review and Future Research Agenda," *Journal of Management* 43 (2017), pp. 137–69.
18. Alex Taylor III, "The Greatest Business Decisions of All Time: Ford," *Fortune,* October 1, 2012, http://money.cnn.com/gallery/news/companies/2012/10/01/greatest-business-decisions.fortune/index.html.
19. D. Mathies, "User-Generated GoPro Hero7 Black Highlight Reel Has All the Feels," *Digital Trends,* December 17, 2018, www.digitaltrends.com; P. Boachie, "User-Generated Content Brings Authenticity to Brands," *Adweek,* April 13, 2018, www.adweek.com.
20. E. Chhabra, "A Social Entrepreneur's Quandary: Nonprofit or For-Profit?" *The New York Times,* July 10, 2013, http://www.nytimes.com.
21. E. Chhabra, "A Social Entrepreneur's Quandary: Nonprofit or For-Profit?" *The New York Times,* July 10, 2013, http://www.nytimes.com.
22. N. Richardson, "Transformative Thinking for Sale," *Inc.,* May 28, 2013, http://www.inc.com.
23. ThinkImpact, www.thinkimpact.com/about, accessed February 22, 2019.
24. M. McCall and R. Kaplan, *Whatever It Takes: Decision Makers at Work* (Englewood Cliffs, NJ: Prentice-Hall, 1985).
25. D. W. Williams and M.S. Wood, "Rule-Based Reasoning for Understanding Opportunity Evaluation," *Academy of Management Perspectives* 29 (2015), pp. 218–36.
26. Amy Barrett, "The Case for User Reviews," *Inc.,* September 1, 2010, http://www.inc.com.
27. Amy Barrett, "The Case for User Reviews," *Inc.,* September 1, 2010, http://www.inc.com.
28. Q. Spitzer and R. Evans, *Heads, You Win! How the Best Companies Think* (New York: Simon & Schuster, 1997).
29. C. Gettys and S. Fisher, "Hypothesis Plausibility and Hypotheses Generation," *Organizational Behavior and Human Performance* 24 (1979), pp. 93–110.
30. E. R. Alexander, "The Design of Alternatives in Organizational Contexts: A Pilot Study," *Administrative Science Quarterly* 24 (1979), pp. 382–404.
31. K. Finley, "Want to Learn to Code? Google Says You Should Play with Blocks," *Wired,* June 28, 2016, www.wired.com.
32. D. Primack, "PillPack Is Raising More Money to Take on Pharmacies," *Fortune,* September 6, 2016, www.fortune.com; Company website, https://www.pillpack.com; Company website, http://www.ideo.com/work/disrupting-the-drugstore; S. Terlep and L. Stevens, "Amazon Buys Online Pharmacy PillPack for $1 Billion," *The Wall Street Journal,* June 28, 2018, www.wsj.com; S. Perez, "Amazon's 2018 Acquisitions Totaled $1.65B, Led by PillPack and Ring," *TechCrunch,* February 4, 2019, https://techcrunch.com.
33. A. R. Rao, M. E. Bergen, and S. Davis, "How to Fight a Price War," *Harvard Business Review,* March–April 2000, pp. 107–16.
34. Amy Barrett, "The Case for User Reviews," *Inc.,* September 1, 2010, http://www.inc.com.
35. Amy Barrett, "The Case for User Reviews," *Inc.,* September 1, 2010, http://www.inc.com.
36. "How Netflix Uses Big Data to Drive Success," *Inside Big Data,* January 20, 2018, https://insidebigdata.com; E. Dans, "How Analytics Has Given Netflix the Edge over Hollywood," *Forbes,* May 27, 2018, www.forbes.com.
37. Q. Spitzer and R. Evans, *Heads, You Win! How the Best Companies Think* (New York: Simon & Schuster, 1997).
38. L. Bryan and D. Farrell, "Leading through Uncertainty," *McKinsey Quarterly,* December 2008, http://www.mckinsey.com.
39. Amy Barrett, "The Case for User Reviews," *Inc.,* September 1, 2010, http://www.inc.com.
40. M. McCall and R. Kaplan, *Whatever It Takes: Decision Makers at Work* (Englewood Cliffs, NJ: Prentice-Hall, 1985).
41. Amy Barrett, "The Case for User Reviews," *Inc.,* September 1, 2010, http://www.inc.com.
42. J. Pfeffer and R. Sutton, *The Knowing-Doing Gap* (Boston: Harvard Business School Press, 2000).

43. D. Siebold, "Making Meetings More Successful," *Journal of Business Communication* 16 (Summer 1979), pp. 3–20.

44. Amy Barrett, "The Case for User Reviews," *Inc.,* September 1, 2010, http://www.inc.com; Company website, "Capterra Surpasses 25,000 Software Reviews," press release on September 26, 2015.

45. D. Kahneman, *Thinking, Fast and Slow* (New York: Farrar, Straus and Giroux, 2011).

46. G. P. Hodgkinson and E. Sadler-Smith, "The Dynamics of Intuition and Analysis in Managerial and Organizational Decision Making," *Academy of Management Perspectives,* 32 (2018), pp. 473–92.

47. I. Janis and L. Mann, *Decision Making* (New York: Free Press, 1977); B. Bass, *Organizational Decision Making* (Homewood, IL: Richard D. Irwin, 1983).

48. Daniel Michaels, "Innovation Is Messy Business," *The Wall Street Journal,* January 24, 2013, http://online.wsj.com; Jon Ostrower and Joann S. Lublin, "The Two Men behind the 787," *The Wall Street Journal,* January 24, 2013, http://online.wsj.com.

49. J. W. Dean Jr. and M. Sharfman, "Does Decision Process Matter? A Study of Strategic Decision-Making Effectiveness," *Academy of Management Journal* 39 (1996), pp. 368–96; R. Nisbett and L. Ross, *Human Inference: Strategies and Shortcomings* (Englewood Cliffs, NJ: Prentice-Hall, 1980).

50. D. Messick and M. Bazerman, "Ethical Leadership and the Psychology of Decision Making," *Sloan Management Review* (Winter 1996), pp. 9–22.

51. T. Bateman and C. Zeithaml, "The Psychological Context of Strategic Decisions: A Model and Convergent Experimental Findings," *Strategic Management Journal* 10 (1989), pp. 59–74.

52. E. Kim, "The Rise and Fall of Marissa Mayer, the Once Beloved CEO of Yahoo," *Business Insider,* January 14, 2016, www.businessinsider.com.

53. A. Hartung, "How Bad Leadership Doomed Yahoo: CEO Mistakes Are Costly," *Forbes,* December 6, 2015, www.forbes.com.

54. A. Ha, "Verizon Reportedly Closes In on a Yahoo Acquisition with a $250M Discount," *TechCrunch,* February 15, 2007, www.techcrunch.com; J. Swartz and E. Weise, "Big Yahoo Changes: Marissa Mayer to Depart; Company to Be Renamed Altaba," *USA Today,* January 9, 2017, www.usatoday.com.

55. D. Barton, "Capitalism for the Long Term," *Harvard Business Review,* March 2011, pp. 84–91.

56. Y. Bayer and Y. Osher, "Time Preference, Executive Functions, and Ego-depletion: An Exploratory Study," *Journal of Neuroscience, Psychology, and Economics* 11 (2018), pp. 127–34.

57. Susan J. Fowler, "Reflecting on One Very Strange Year at Uber," February 9, 2017, https://www.susanjfowler.com/blog/2017/2/19/reflecting-on-one-very-strange-year-at-uber.

58. Susan J. Fowler, "Reflecting on One Very Strange Year at Uber," February 9, 2017, https://www.susanjfowler.com/blog/2017/2/19/reflecting-on-one-very-strange-year-at-uber.

59. Mike Isaac, "Inside Uber's Aggressive, Unrestrained Workplace Culture," *The New York Times,* February 22, 2017, https://www.nytimes.com/2017/02/22/technology/uber-workplace-culture.html.

60. Julia Carrie Wong, "Uber CEO Travis Kalanick Resigns Following Months of Chaos," *The Guardian,* June 21, 2017, https://www.theguardian.com/technology/2017/jun/20/uber-ceo-travis-kalanick-resigns.

61. E. Meyer, *The Culture Map: Breaking through the Invisible Boundaries of Global Business* (New York, Public Affairs, 2014); N. Adler, *International Dimensions of Organizational Behavior* (Boston: Kent, 1990).

62. L. Perlow, G. Okhuysen, and N. Repenning, "The Speed Trap: Exploring the Relationship between Decision Making and Temporal Context," *Academy of Management Journal* 45 (2002), pp. 931–55.

63. K. M. Esenhardt, "Speed and Strategic Choice: How Managers Accelerate Decision Making," *California Management Review* 32 (Spring 1990), pp. 39–54.

64. Jacky Chou, "Artificial Intelligence Can Help Leaders Make Better Decisions Faster," *Entrepreneur,* August 15, 2018, https://www.entrepreneur.com/article/317748, accessed March 20, 2019.

65. Richard Williams, "Making Faster Decisions with AI," *Financial Management,* February 1, 2019, https://www.fm-magazine.com/issues/2019/feb/make-faster-decisions-with-ai.html, accessed March 20, 2019.

66. Richard Williams, "Making Faster Decisions with AI," *Financial Management,* February 1, 2019, https://www.fm-magazine.com/issues/2019/feb/make-faster-decisions-with-ai.html, accessed March 20, 2019.

67. Dorian Thomas, "The Future of Predictive Analytics in Higher Education," Cloud for Good, September 18, 2018, https://cloud4good.com/announcements/future-predictive-analytics-higher-education/, accessed March 20, 2019.

68. Q. Spitzer and R. Evans, "New Problems in Problem Solving," *Across the Board,* April 1997, pp. 36–40.

69. E. Larson, "3 Best Practices For High Performance Decision-Making Teams," *Forbes,* March 23, 2017, www.forbes.com.

70. G. W. Hill, "Group versus Individual Performance: Are N + 1 Heads Better than 1?" *Psychological Bulletin* 91 (1982), pp. 517–39.

71. N. R. F. Maier, "Assets and Liabilities in Group Problem Solving: The Need for an Integrative Function," *Psychological Review* 74 (1967), pp. 239–49.

72. N. R. F. Maier, "Assets and Liabilities in Group Problem Solving: The Need for an Integrative Function," *Psychological Review* 74 (1967), pp. 239–49.

73. B. Latane, K. Williams, and S. Harkins, "Many Hands Make Light the Work: The Causes and Consequences of Social Loafing," *Journal of Personality and Social Psychology* 37 (1979), pp. 822–32; J. George, "Extrinsic and Intrinsic Origins of Perceived Social Loafing in Organizations," *Academy of Management Journal* 35 (1992), pp. 191–206.

74. S. Murphy, S. Wayne, R. Liden, and B. Erdogan, "Understanding Social Loafing: The Role of Justice Perceptions and Exchange Relationships," *Human Relations* 56 (2003), pp. 61–84.

75. Forbes Insights, "Global Diversity and Inclusion: Fostering Innovation through a Diverse Workforce," 2011, https://www.americanbar.org/content/dam/aba/administrative/intellectual_property_law/ipw17-forbes-insights.pdf.

76. Claude Koehl, "Managing Diversity: 10 Steps to Multicultural Team Success," *Training: The Source for Professional Development,* October 14, 2016, https://trainingmag.com/managing-diversity-10-steps-multicultural-team-success/.

77. Astrid Homan and Lindred Greer, "Considering Diversity: The Positive Effects of Considerate Leadership in Diverse Teams," *Group Processes and Intergroup Relations* 16, no. 1 (January 10, 2013), pp. 105–25, https://journals-sagepub-com.ezp.bentley.edu/doi/pdf/10.1177/1368430212437798.

78. Meir Shemla and Jurgen Wegge, "Managing Diverse Teams by Enhancing Team Identification: The Mediating Role of Perceived Diversity," *Human Relations,* July 18, 2018, pp. 1–23, https://journals-sagepub-com.ezp.bentley.edu/doi/pdf/10.1177/0018726718778101.

79. Kat Boogaard, "How to Be a Better Manager (When Your Team Members Are All Different)," *The Muse,* https://www.themuse.com/advice/how-to-be-a-better-manager-when-your-team-members-are-all-different.

80. D. A. Garvin and M. A. Roberto, "What You Don't Know about Making Decisions," *Harvard Business Review,* September 2001, pp. 108–16.

81. Christopher Borrelli, "'Brave' Co-Director, Producer Take Up Arms to Promote Pixar's Latest," *Chicago Tribune,* June 21, 2012, http://www.chicagotribune.com.

82. A. Amason, "Distinguishing the Effects of Functional and Dysfunctional Conflict on Strategic Decision Making: Resolving a Paradox for Top Management Teams," *Academy of Management Journal* 39 (1996), pp. 123–48; R. Dooley and G. Fyxell, "Attaining Decision Quality and Commitment from Dissent: The Moderating Effects of Loyalty and Competence in Strategic Decision-Making Teams," *Academy of Management Journal,* August 1999, pp. 389–402.

83. C. De Dreu and L. Weingart, "Task versus Relationship Conflict, Team Performance, and Team Member Satisfaction: A Meta-Analysis," *Journal of Applied Psychology* 88 (2003), pp. 741–49.

84. R. Cosier and C. Schwenk, "Agreement and Thinking Alike," *Academy of Management Executive* 4, no. 1 (1990), pp. 69–74.

85. G. Ruhe, "9 Cool College Start-ups," *Inc.,* http://www.inc.com, accessed March 1, 2015.

86. S. Harvey, "Creative Synthesis: Exploring the Process of Extraordinary Group Creativity," *Academy of Management Review* 39 (2014), pp. 324–43; J. Perry-Smith and P. Vittorio, "From Creativity to Innovation: The Social Network Drivers of the Four Phases of the Idea Journey," *Academy of Management Review* 42 (2017), pp. 53–79.

87. K. DeStobbeleir, S. Ashford, and D. Buyens, "Self-Regulation of Creativity at Work: The Role of Feedback-Seeking Behavior in Creative Performance," *Academy of Management Journal* 54 (2011), pp. 811–31; Y. Gong, S. Cheung, M. Wang, and J. Huang, "Unfolding the Proactive Process for Creativity: Integration of the Employee Proactivity, Information Exchange, and Psychological Safety Perspectives," *Journal of Management* 38 (2010), pp. 1611–33.

88. S. Harvey, "Creative Synthesis: Exploring the Process of Extraordinary Group Creativity," *Academy of Management Review* 39 (2014), pp. 324–43; J. Perry-Smith and P. Vittorio, "From Creativity to Innovation: The Social Network Drivers of the Four Phases of the Idea Journey," *Academy of Management Review* 42 (2017), pp. 53–79.

89. J. E. Perry-Smith and P. V. Mannucci, "From Creativity to Innovation: The Social Network Drivers of the Four Phases of the Idea Journey," *Academy of Management Review* 42 (2017), pp. 53–79; M. Bear, "Putting Creativity to Work: The Implementation of Creative Ideas in Organizations," *Academy of Management Journal* 55 (2012), pp. 1102–19; J. Perry-Smith and C. Shalley, "The Social Side of Creativity: A Static and Dynamic Social Network Perspective," *Academy of Management Review* 28 (2003), pp. 89–106; J. Perry-Smith, "Social yet Creative: The Role of Social Relationships in Facilitating Individual Creativity," *Academy of Management Journal* 49 (2006), pp. 85–101.

90. S. Finkelstein, "What Stan Lee Knew about Managing Creative People," *Harvard Business Review*, November 13, 2018, www.hbr.org; "Innovation from the Ground Up," *Industry Week*, March 7, 2007, http://www.industryweek.com(interview of Erika Andersen); T. M. Amabile, "A Model of Creativity and Innovation in Organizations," in *Research in Organizational Behavior*, ed. B. Straw and L. Cummings, vol. 10 (Greenwich, CT: JAI Press, 1988), pp. 123–68.

91. T. Amabile, C. Hadley, and S. Kramer, "Creativity under the Gun," *Harvard Business Review*, August 2002, pp. 52–61.

92. N. Stevenson, "13 Ways to Make Your Workspace More Creative," *IDEO blog*, March 6, 2017, www.ideo.com.

93. S. Farmer, P. Tierney, and K. Kung McIntyre, "Employee Creativity in Taiwan: An Application of Role Identity Theory," *Academy of Management Journal* 46 (2003), pp. 618–30.

94. W. Craig, "10 Ways to Encourage Company Innovation in Your Employees," *Forbes*, November 13, 2018, www.forbes.com.

95. K. Coyne and S. Coyne, "Seven Steps to Better Brainstorming," *McKinsey Quarterly*, March 2011, http://www.mckinsey.com.

96. R. Greenfield, "Brainstorming Doesn't Work; Try This Technique Instead," *Fast Company*, July 29, 2014, www.fastcompany.com.

97. J. Brandon, "Forget Brainstorming, Try These 'Brainwriting' Apps," *Inc.*, July 6, 2016, www.inc.com.

98. S. Sonenshein, "How Organizations Foster the Creative Use of Resources," *Academy of Management Journal* 57 (2014), pp. 814–48; P. Puranam, N. Stieglitz, M. Osman, et al., "Modeling Bounded Rationality in Organizations: Progress and Prospects," *Academy of Management Annals* 9 (2015), pp. 337–92.

99. J. Walter, F. Fellermanns, and C. Lechner, "Decision Making within and between Organizations: Rationality, Politics, and Alliance Performance," *Journal of Management* 38 (2012), pp. 1582–1610.

100. M. de Jong, N. Marston, and E. Roth, "The Eight Essentials of Innovation," McKinsey & Company, April 2015, www.mckinsey.com; T. Levitt, "Creativity Is Not Enough," *Harvard Business Review*, August 2002, pp. 137–44.

101. J. O. Cheong and C. Kim, "Determinants of Performance in Government: Focusing on the Effect of Organizational Politics and Conflicts in Organizations," *International Journal of Public Administration* 41 (2018), pp. 535–47; M. Garbuio and D. Lovallo, "Does Organizational Politics Kill Company Growth?" *Review of International Business and Strategy* 27, no. 4 (2017), pp. 410–33; J. W. Dean Jr. and M. Sharfman, "Does Decision Process Matter? A Study of Strategic Decision-Making Effectiveness," *Academy of Management Journal* 39 (1996), pp. 368–96.

102. K. Eisenhardt, J. Kahwajy, and L. J. Bourgeois III, "How Management Teams Can Have a Good Fight," *Harvard Management Review*, July–August 1997, pp. 77–85.

103. W. Kahn, M. Barton, and S. Fellows, "Organizational Crises and the Disturbance of Relational Systems," *Academy of Management Review* 38 (2013), pp. 377–96; C. M. Pearson and I. I. Mitroff, "From Crisis Prone to Crisis Prepared: A Framework for Crisis Management," *Academy of Management Executive*, February 1993, pp. 48–59.

104. C. M. Pearson and I. I. Mitroff, "From Crisis Prone to Crisis Prepared: A Framework for Crisis Management," *Academy of Management Executive* 7, no. 1 (1993), pp. 48–59; I. I. Mitroff, "Crisis Management: Cutting through the Confusion," *Sloan Management Review* 29, no. 2 (1988), pp. 15–20.

105. P. Leskin, "The 21 Scariest Data Breaches of 2018," *Business Insider*, December 30, 2018, www.businessinsider.com.

106. J. Dlouhy and M. Riley, "Russian Hackers Attacking U.S. Power Grid and Aviation, FBI Warns," *Bloomberg*, March 15, 2018, www.bloomberg.com.

107. J. Bundy, M. Pfarrer, C. Short, and W. T. Coombs, "Crises and Crisis Management: Integration, Interpretation, and Research Development," *Journal of Management* 43 (2017), pp. 1661–92.

108. S. Moore, "Disaster's Future: The Prospects for Corporate Crisis Management and Communication," *Business Horizons*, January–February 2004, pp. 29–36.

109. B. Thomas, "Why AI Is Crucial to Cyber Security," *CIO*, June 16, 2017, www.cio.com.

110. G. Meyers with J. Holusha, *When It Hits the Fan: Managing the Nine Crises of Business* (Boston: Houghton Mifflin, 1986); S. Bacharach and P. Bamberger, "9/11 and New York City Firefighters' Post Hoc Unit Support and Control Climates: A Context Theory of the Consequences of Involvement in Traumatic Work-Related Events," *Academy of Management Journal* 50 (2007), pp. 849–68.

111. M. McCall and R. Kaplan, *Whatever It Takes: Decision Makers at Work* (Englewood Cliffs, NJ: Prentice-Hall, 1985).

112. D. C. Kayes, *Organizational Resilience: How Learning Sustains Organizations in Crisis, Disaster, and Breakdowns* (New York: Oxford University Press, 2015); J. Bundy, M. Pfarrer, C. Short, and W. T. Coombs, "Crises and Crisis Management: Integration, Interpretation, and Research Development," *Journal of Management* 43 (2017), pp. 1661–92.

113. J. Dutton, P. Frost, M. Worline, J. Lilius, and J. Kanov, "Leading in Times of Trauma," *Harvard Business Review*, January 2002, pp. 54–61.

114. Sheelah Kolhatkar, "At Uber, a New CEO Shifts Gears," *The New Yorker*, April 9, 2018, https://www.newyorker.com/magazine/2018/04/09/at-uber-a-new-ceo-shifts-gears.

115. Barbara Booth, "A Year Later, What Uber Has Done to Revamp Its Troubled Image," *CNBC*, June 20, 2018, https://www.cnbc.com/2018/06/20/a-year-later-what-uber-has-done-to-revamp-its-troubled-image.html.

116. Jefferson Graham, "Uber Adjusts Rate Structure for Drivers," *USA Today*, November 30, 2018, https://www.usatoday.com/story/tech/talkingtech/2018/11/30/uber-adjusts-rate-structure-drivers/2155793002/.

117. Jefferson Graham, "Uber Adjusts Rate Structure for Drivers," *USA Today*, November 30, 2018, https://www.usatoday.com/story/tech/talkingtech/2018/11/30/uber-adjusts-rate-structure-drivers/2155793002/.

118. Taylor Dunn, "Uber CEO Talks Safety, Company Culture, Future IPO and Flying Ubers," *ABC News*, September 5, 2018, https://abcnews.go.com/Business/uber-ceo-talks-safety-company-culture-future-ipo/story?id=57634888.

119. Madison McGaw, "Has Uber's Cutthroat Culture Actually Changed?" *Vanity Fair*, December 12, 2018, https://www.vanityfair.com/news/2018/12/has-ubers-cutthroat-culture-actually-changed.

120. Madison McGaw, "Has Uber's Cutthroat Culture Actually Changed?" *Vanity Fair*, December 12, 2018, https://www.vanityfair.com/news/2018/12/has-ubers-cutthroat-culture-actually-changed.

Zappos Eliminates All Managers and Titles

In 2014, Zappos's CEO Tony Hsieh surprised many observers in the business world by announcing to his 1,500 or so employees that the e-retailer famous for its shoes was doing away with job titles, managers, and other artifacts associated with traditional top-down management and replacing it with a system where employees are expected to act like entrepreneurs. This new approach or holacracy encourages employees to self-manage and self-organize, thus eliminating the need for bosses. One of the management system's overarching goals is to "create a dynamic workforce where everyone has a voice and bureaucracy doesn't stifle innovation."

Why did Zappos adopt this new way to organize itself? As the company grew in size, it became more difficult to provide customers with a "WOW" or exceptional customer experience. Responding to customer feedback slowed as layers of employees and managers increased. Holacracy empowers employees to quickly surface and act on customer feedback.

How does a holacracy works? According to advocate Brian Robertson, a holacracy functions when employees know what they are responsible for and have the freedom to deliver those results as they see fit. This approach works best when the organization encourages changes and improvements to be made beyond what is required.

Holacracy organizes employees into circles of responsibility—similar to functional areas (like marketing and customer service) and employee special interest areas (like career development and so forth). Though democratic and self-governing, the circles do not operate in a vacuum because they are arranged in a hierarchy (circles report to higher-level circles) and follow detailed procedures for running meetings and making decisions. Employees are free to choose which circles to which they want to belong and on what projects they would like to work. The circles are responsible for achieving a specific set of responsibilities. At meetings, employees are encouraged to address and resolve in a proactive manner "tensions" or problems related to internal (e.g., unfair workloads) or external (e.g., a way to enhance the customer experience) issues. Rather than reporting to a manager with the power to hire or fire, as is the case in hierarchically organized companies, a "lead link" helps employees accomplish the circle's responsibilities and communicates between circles.

Zappos is not the first company in history to experiment with employee self-management. For example, Gore & Associates (maker of Gore-Tex) has no formal chain of command and provides its associates with freedom to self-select work projects and choose associates with relevant expertise to assist in the development of those projects. Semco Partners, a Brazilian industrial machinery manufacturer, engages its 3,000-plus employees through participative management, where employees set their own work hours and pay levels, hire and review their supervisors, and decide which new businesses to enter. Johnsonville Sausage Company eliminated its hierarchy and introduced "self-managed, self-organizing teams throughout the company." Ralph Styer, the CEO who championed this radical change, believed that "helping human beings fulfill their potential is of course a moral responsibility, but it's also good business practice." He believed in the connection between employee happiness and organizational performance: "Learning, striving people are happy people and good workers."

Were the employees at Zappos happy about their expanded responsibilities and freedom to self-govern? How did the managers accept this change? It was mixed. In an email to all staff at the company, Hsieh said that everyone had a choice to make: either embrace the new holacratic system or accept a three-month severance package and resign. Two hundred and ten (or 14 percent) of the staff resigned. Of those who left the company, 20 (or 7 percent) were managers. Does that mean that the 86 percent of staff who decided to stay did so because they believe in the new holacratic approach? Time will tell. One may speculate that the individuals who chose to remain at Zappos did so because they are either "believers" or lack the interest or motivation to switch jobs at the moment.

Of the employees who stayed, some shared concerns about the new management approach like using the complicated new lingo, adjusting to the rapidly changing work roles and expectations, and the "ever-expanding number of circles and the endless meetings" that take employees away from achieving their work goals. On the upside, holacracy promotes employees' ownership and encourages even the lowest-paid employees to add items to meeting agendas that are subsequently discussed and acted upon.

What became of the 267 ex-managers at Zappos? The company created a new circle titled "Reinventing Yourself" that helped many of these individuals find new roles. Some eventually moved on.

There may be an irony in the way that Zappos shifted from a hierarchical management structure to one that is based on democratic, self-organizing circles. The mandate for this change came from Tony Hsieh, the CEO. Those employees and managers who did not agree with the "top-down" change were asked to leave the company. This irony suggests that even for visionary business leaders like Hsieh, radical change may not be easy to accomplish in a consensus-driven manner.

Five years later, Zappos and its employees continue to adapt to the new holacratic system of management. John Bunch, an employee who helped the company make the transition, is patient and is taking the long view: "We believe that, over time, the ability for people to be empowered and entrepreneurial will make people happy."

DISCUSSION QUESTIONS

1. To what degree do you think that Zappos's new holacratic approach to organizing will enhance its competitive advantage in innovation, quality, service, speed, and cost competitiveness? Explain.

2. Think about how a current or former employer is organized. To what degree would a holacracy approach work in that setting? What would be the benefits of switching to the new system? What objections would likely be offered to resist the change?

SOURCES: Adapted from company website, Zappos Insights, https://www.zapposinsights.com/about/holacracy, accessed February 24, 2019; Scudamore, B., "Zappos CEO Tony Hsieh Sums Up His Secret Superpower in a Single Word," *Inc.*, January 24, 2018, www.inc.com; Noguchi, Y., "Zappos: A Workplace Where No One and Everyone Is the Boss," *NPR*, July 21, 2015, http://www.npr.org; Gelles, D., "At Zappos, Pushing Shoes and a Vision," *The New York Times*, July 17, 2015, http://www.nytimes.com; Silverman, R., "At Zappos, Banishing Bosses Brings Confusion," *The Wall Street Journal*, May 20, 2015, http://www.wsj.com; Petriglieri, G., "Making Sense of Zappos' War on Manager," *Harvard Business Review*, May 19, 2015, http://www.hbr.org; Denning, S., "Zappos Says Goodbye to Bosses," *Forbes*, January 15, 2015, http://www.forbes.com; Fisher, L., "Ricardo Semler Won't Take Control," *Strategy + Business*, November 29, 2005, http://www.strategy-business.com.

CHAPTER 4
Planning and Strategic Management

> For tomorrow belongs to the people who plan for it today.
>
> —African Proverb

Robert Churchill/Getty Images

learning objectives

After studying Chapter 4, you will be able to:

LO 4-1 Summarize the basic steps in any planning process.

LO 4-2 Describe how to integrate strategic planning with tactical and operational planning.

LO 4-3 Identify elements of the external environment and internal resources of the firm to analyze before formulating a strategy.

LO 4-4 Define core capabilities and explain how they provide the foundation for business strategy.

LO 4-5 Summarize the types of choices available for corporate strategy.

LO 4-6 Discuss how companies can achieve competitive advantage through business strategy.

LO 4-7 Describe the keys to effective strategy implementation.

chapter outline

An Overview of Planning Fundamentals
  The Basic Planning Process

Levels of Planning
  Strategic Planning
  Tactical and Operational Planning
  Aligning Tactical, Operational, and Strategic Planning

Strategic Planning
  Step 1: Establishing Mission, Vision, and Goals
  Step 2: Analyzing External Opportunities and Threats
  Step 3: Analyzing Internal Strengths and Weaknesses
  Step 4: SWOT Analysis and Strategy Formulation
  Step 5: Strategy Implementation
  Step 6: Strategic Control

Management in Action

HOW DISNEY SCRIPTS ITS OWN SUCCESS

MANAGER'S BRIEF

PROGRESS REPORT

ONWARD

TCD/Prod.DB/Alamy Stock Photo

Walt Disney, the founder of the Disney company, once described his intended audience as "children from 6 to 60." That's an ambitious target for any business, in any time period, yet, founded in 1923, the Disney company has been touching the hearts and minds of children and adults alike for almost a hundred years now. In fact, Disney's reach may be more powerful now than ever before: Disney has ranked as the most valuable media brand in the world for four consecutive years,[1] and in 2018 Disney's revenue was $59 billion, more than double what it was just 10 years earlier. Far from resting on its laurels, Disney is still growing. The billion dollar question is, what's the secret to the company's success?

According to Sean Bailey, president of Walt Disney Studios motion picture production, the secret is actually quite simple, and it originated with Walt Disney himself: take "beautiful, timeless stories" with lasting relevance and apply a modern sensibility to them that audiences will find relatable.[2]

Take *Beauty and the Beast,* for example. Disney's first iteration of this "tale as old as time" was back in 1991 as an animated feature. It was the highest-grossing film of the year. Fast-forward to 2017. Disney released a live-action version of *Beauty and the Beast,* starring Emma Watson, best known for playing the brave, precocious, and headstrong Hermione Granger in the Harry Potter movies. Famously donning combat boots instead of silk slippers, Watson embodied the "tale as old as time," but with the modern twist that young audiences could relate to. The film came in third at the box office that year, grossing over $500 million worldwide.

Audiences can now see live-action versions of Disney's animated classics *Dumbo, The Lion King,* and *Aladdin.* With more live-action remakes coming including *Mulan* and *Pinocchio,* Disney's secret to success will continue to be refined and retested.

As you read this chapter, think about the challenges of drawing new revenue from remakes of old properties. What environmental factors would you be tracking to help determine whether this strategy will be financially successful?

To imagine Disney—or any organization—navigating into the future without a plan is almost impossible. Planning describes what managers decide to do and how they intend to do it. It provides the framework, focus, and direction for meaningful action. This chapter examines the most important concepts and processes involved in planning and strategic management. By learning these concepts and reviewing the steps outlined, you will be on your way to understanding current approaches to strategic management in today's organizations.

An Overview of Planning Fundamentals

Although management pioneers such as Alfred Sloan of General Motors instituted formal planning processes, planning became a widespread management function only during the past few decades. Initially, larger organizations adopted formal planning, but now even small firms operated by aggressive, opportunistic entrepreneurs engage in planning activities.[3]

As discussed in Chapter 1, planning is the intentional, systematic process of deciding what goals and activities a person, group, work unit, or organization will pursue in the future. Planning is not haphazard response to a crisis; it is a purposeful effort that is directed and controlled by managers and often draws on the knowledge and experience of employees throughout the organization. Planning provides individuals and work units with a clear map to follow; at the same time, this map should be flexible enough to allow for unique circumstances and changing conditions.

Planning is one of the most common management practices but typically is not done very well; most firms do not come close to realizing its potential benefits.[4] Thoughtful execution of the ideas in this chapter will strengthen your employers' chances of success.

LO 4-1 Summarize the basic steps in any planning process.

The Basic Planning Process

Because planning is a decision process—you're deciding what to do and how to go about doing it—the important steps followed during formal planning are similar to the basic decision-making steps we discussed in Chapter 3. Exhibit 4.1 summarizes the similarities between decision making and planning—including the fact that both move not just in one direction but in a cycle. The outcomes of decisions and plans are evaluated, and if necessary, they are revised.

We now describe the basic planning process in more detail. Later in this chapter, we will discuss how managerial decisions and plans fit into the larger purposes of the organization—its strategy, mission, vision, and goals.

situational analysis

A process planners use to gather, interpret, and summarize all information relevant to the planning issue under consideration.

Step 1: Situational Analysis   Planning begins with a **situational analysis**. Within their time and resource constraints, planners should gather, interpret, and summarize all information relevant to the planning issue in question. A thorough situational analysis analyzes past events, examines current conditions, and attempts to forecast future trends. It focuses on the internal forces at work in the organization or work unit and, consistent with the open-systems approach (see Chapter 2), examines influences from the external environment. The outcomes of this step are the identification and diagnosis of planning assumptions, issues, and problems.

A thorough situational analysis will help you make important planning decisions. For example, if you are a manager in a magazine company considering the launch of an online sports publication for the teen market, you should analyze the number of teens who subscribe to online magazines, the appeal of the teen market to advertisers, your firm's ability to serve this market effectively, current economic conditions, the level of teen interest in sports, and any online sports magazines already serving this market and their current sales. Such a detailed analysis will help you decide whether to proceed with the next step in your magazine launch.

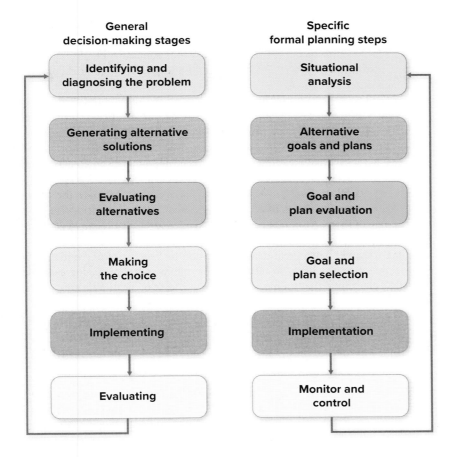

General decision-making stages	Specific formal planning steps
Identifying and diagnosing the problem	Situational analysis
Generating alternative solutions	Alternative goals and plans
Evaluating alternatives	Goal and plan evaluation
Making the choice	Goal and plan selection
Implementing	Implementation
Evaluating	Monitor and control

EXHIBIT 4.1
Decision-Making Stages (Chapter 3) and Formal Planning Steps (Chapter 4)

goal

A target or end that management desires to reach.

plans

The actions or means managers intend to use to achieve organizational goals.

Bottom Line

Contingency plans that keep service levels high during a major storm can seal a utility company's reputation for caring about customers. Managers must decide how crucial service is to their strategy—and how willing customers will be to forgive them for temporary service interruptions during power outages. *During a major storm, what utility services—water, wastewater, or electricity—do you expect to receive with minimal interruption? Would you pay more to make these services more reliable?*

Step 2: Alternative Goals and Plans   Based on the situational analysis, the planning process should generate alternative goals that could be pursued and the alternative plans that could be used to achieve those goals. This step should stress creativity and encourage managers and employees to think broadly about their work.

Once a range of alternatives has been developed, the merits of these different plans and goals will be evaluated. Continuing with our online sports magazine example, the alternatives you might want to consider include whether the magazine should be targeted at young men, young women, or both, and whether it should be sold only online, or also through subscriptions and newsstands.

Goals are the targets or ends the manager wants to reach. **Plans** are the actions or means the manager intends to use to achieve goals. At a minimum, plans should outline alternative actions for attaining each goal, the resources required to reach the goal through those means, and the obstacles that may develop.

After General Motors declared bankruptcy and borrowed billions from the U.S. government in 2009, management made plans for a return to profitability. The plans included reducing costs by producing fewer trucks, eliminating several brands, introducing smaller vehicles, keeping fewer vehicles in inventory, and closing hundreds of dealerships. GM also introduced cars it hoped would be more popular, including the Cruze compact and the Sonic subcompact. Despite difficulties such as meeting demand with a reduced workforce and the lower profitability of smaller vehicles, the company moved back into the black a year after the bankruptcy, and in two years it reported its strongest financial performance in over a decade.[5]

Contingency plans are "what if" plans. They include actions to be taken if initial plans do not work well or if events demand a sudden change.

Recent natural disasters have reminded many businesses how important contingency planning can be. Walmart in the United States has an Emergency Operations Center that tracks natural disaster impacts and keeps store operations running even after a disaster.[6] In such moments, customers are grateful to have access to water, food, batteries, pharmaceuticals supplies, and other necessities.

Most major corporations have contingency plans in place to respond to major disasters—to make sure vital data are backed up and can be recovered, for instance, and that employees know what to do when a crisis occurs. But contingency plans are important for more common situations as well. For example, many businesses are affected by snowstorms, increases in energy prices, network breakdowns, new competitors, and changes in consumer tastes.

Step 3: Goal and Plan Evaluation   Next, managers will evaluate the advantages, disadvantages, and potential effects of each goal and plan. They must prioritize their goals and eliminate some of them. Also, managers will consider carefully the implications of alternative plans for meeting high-priority goals.

In particular, they will pay a great deal of attention to the cost of any initiative and the return on investment that is likely to result. In our online sports magazine example, your evaluation might determine that online sales alone wouldn't be profitable enough to justify the launch. It may need to be supplemented by podcasts and promoted via social media. Also, maybe you could improve profits by printing a hardcopy edition for newsstands and mail subscriptions. To decide, you would estimate the costs and expected returns of such alternatives, trying to follow the decision steps advised in Chapter 3.

Step 4: Goal and Plan Selection   Once managers have assessed goals and plans, they try to select the best. The evaluation process helps to identify trade-offs and decide what to do. For example, if your plan is to launch a number of new online publications, and you're trying to choose among them, you might weigh the different up-front investment each requires, the size of each market, which one fits best with your existing product line or company image, and so on. Experienced judgment always plays an important role in this process. However, as you will discover later in the chapter, relying on judgment alone may not be the best way to proceed.

Typically, the planning process leads to a written set of goals and plans that are appropriate and feasible for a particular set of circumstances. In some organizations, the alternative generation, evaluation, and selection steps generate planning **scenarios**, as discussed in Chapter 2. A different contingency plan is attached to each scenario. The manager pursues the goals and implements the plans associated with the most likely and desirable scenario. However, the manager will also be prepared to switch to another set of plans if the situation changes and another scenario becomes relevant. This approach helps the firm anticipate and manage problems and allows greater flexibility and responsiveness.

scenario

A narrative that describes a particular set of future conditions.

Panera Bread officially opened the fifth "Panera Cares Community Cafe" in Boston.

Ken Crane/ZUMAPRESS.com/Alamy Stock Photo

Step 5: Implementation   Once managers have selected the goals and plans, they must implement the plans designed to achieve the goals. Even the best plans are useless if they are not implemented properly. Managers and employees must understand the plan, have the resources to implement it, and be motivated to do so. As we mentioned earlier, employees usually are better informed, more committed, and more

highly motivated when a goal or plan is one they helped develop.

Successful implementation requires a plan to be linked to other systems in the organization, particularly the budget and reward systems. If the manager does not have a budget with financial resources to execute the plan, the plan is probably doomed. Similarly, goal achievement must be linked to the organization's reward system. Many organizations use incentive programs to encourage employees to achieve goals and to implement plans properly. Commissions, salaries, promotions, bonuses, and other rewards are based on successful performance.

Lyft, the ride-sharing company, recently entered into a long-term strategic alliance with General Motors to build an "integrated network of on-demand autonomous vehicles in the U.S."[7] As part of the deal, GM bought a $500 million stake in Lyft, currently the second-largest ride-sharing service in the United States.[8]

The ultimate success of this alliance will hinge on the plan's successful implementation. So far, it has been slower than expected given the seemingly complicated relationship between GM and Lyft. The ride-sharing company has created partnerships with several other companies, including GM's rival Ford, and the large automaker has been focusing on its own autonomous vehicle, the Chevy Cruise.[9]

Step 6: Monitor and Control   The sixth step in the formal planning process—monitoring and controlling—is essential. Without it, you will never know whether your plan is succeeding. Remember, planning works in a cycle; it is an ongoing, repetitive process. Managers must continually monitor the actual performance of their work units against the units' goals and plans. They also need to develop control systems to measure that performance and allow them to take corrective action when needed.

The nearby "Social Entrepreneurship" box discusses how Novo Nordisk monitors progress toward achieving important organizational goals. We will discuss the important issue of control systems later in this chapter and in Chapter 16.

> Even the best strategy won't be effective without a strong focus on implementation.

Bottom Line
Aligning plans and goals with a firm's financials is a key element of success. *How might a plan to improve employee retention be tied to a company's financial measures?*

Social Entrepreneurship

Novo Nordisk Monitors Progress with Its Triple Bottom Line

While some companies simply talk about operating in a more socially and environmentally conscious manner, others put this philosophy into action. Headquartered in Denmark, Novo Nordisk is a leading global provider of diabetes care solutions. The firm follows a triple bottom line (TBL: economic, societal, and environmental) strategy, meaning decisions are based on the belief that "a healthy economy, environment, and society are fundamental to long-term business success." Novo Nordisk's goal is to operate its business so that diabetes solutions benefit both the business and patients, while meeting societal expectations in the process. To ensure that the TBL philosophy would stick, Novo Nordisk took the uncommon step of incorporating it into its company bylaws.[10]

In addition to standard financial performance measures, Novo Nordisk monitors multiple short- and long-term goals within the social and environmental areas. The 2018 Annual Report highlights not just the company's economic performance, but its social and environmental performance as well.[11] Novo Nordisk is therefore breaking with traditional profit-only business models by setting and monitoring meaningful social and environmental goals.

The TBL model seems to be working. Over 29 million diabetes patients received treatment using Novo Nordisk's diabetes drugs and products in 2018, which generated $5.8 billion in net profits. The company is positioned to perform well financially while continuing to make a significant, multilevel impact in social and environmental spheres as well.[12]

1. Why do you think more companies don't incorporate a TBL philosophy into their bylaws?
2. Assume you want your employer to consider adopting a TBL philosophy. How would you pitch the idea? With whom would you speak?

Management in Action

PLANNING FOR A MEDIA GIANT

Disney is not only one of the most successful media companies in the world, it's also one of the largest. Disney has four business divisions, engaged in nearly every kind of commercial entertainment. Walt Disney Studios division produces movies, music, and stage shows under the banners of Disney, Pixar, Marvel Studios, Lucasfilm, Touchstone Pictures, and most recently 21st Century Fox. The Media Networks group covers publishing, radio, and broadcast and cable television, including Disney/ABC Television and ESPN. The Parks and Resorts group encompasses 11 theme parks and scores of resorts around the world, as well as its own cruise line. Disney's Consumer Products and Interactive Media division offers entertainment on digital platforms, including console games and the Internet, and extends the business value of characters and story lines by operating Disney Stores and licensing its creations for use on toys, clothing, art objects, and a wide variety of other consumer goods.

Keeping this media giant running effectively and efficiently requires planning—lots of it. The man in charge of keeping the magic alive through activities carried out by more than 200,000 employees is Disney's CEO, Robert Iger. Iger and his executive team must define an overall direction and goal for the company and keep an eye on how well each business group is contributing to achievement of that goal. Iger does this by spotting opportunities for growth in the industry—hence the expansion into cable

television and, more recently, into interactive entertainment, the revitalization of past movie hits, and streaming services. He also looks for characters and brands Disney can make more valuable because of its access to more channels. For example, Disney could afford to pay generously for Pixar and Marvel because those companies' characters generate sales in products as diverse as theme parks, video games, and sweatshirts.

Iger meets weekly with the heads of the business units. Although he keeps an eye on the company's overall direction, he gives each unit's head wide latitude. As the Walt Disney Studios division embarks on a years-long effort to revitalize some of its classic animated features, Iger and the company's management team will be watching closely to see whether this strategy is as effective abroad as it may be at home or whether new environmental analyses suggest other avenues for the film company to explore.[13]

1. Examine the organization and acquisitions of Disney through the framework of the basic planning process. How does Disney's operations align with each step of the process?
2. Conduct your own situational analysis for Disney. Based on your assessment of the current media landscape, where would you suggest Igor focus more attention and resources?

Levels of Planning

LO 4-2 Describe how to integrate strategic planning with tactical and operational planning.

strategic planning

A set of procedures for making decisions about the organization's long-term goals and strategies; see also *planning*.

In Chapter 1, you learned about the three major types of managers: top-level (strategic managers), middle-level (tactical managers), and frontline (operational managers). Because planning is an important management function, managers at all three levels engage in it.[14] However, the scope and activities of the planning process often differ at different levels.

Strategic Planning

Strategic planning involves making decisions about the organization's long-term goals and strategies. Strategic plans have a strong external orientation and cover major portions of the organization. Senior executives are responsible for the development and execution of the strategic plan, although they usually do not implement the entire plan personally.

Strategic goals are major targets or results that relate to the long-term survival, value, and growth of the organization. Strategic managers—top-level managers—usually establish goals that reflect both effectiveness (providing appropriate outputs) and efficiency (a high ratio of outputs to inputs). Typical strategic goals include achieving growth, increasing

1. Where will we be active?
2. How will we get there (e.g., by increasing sales or acquiring another company)?
3. How will we win in the market (e.g., by keeping prices low or offering the best service)?
4. How fast will we move and in what sequence will we make changes?
5. How will we obtain financial returns (low costs or premium prices)?

EXHIBIT 4.2
Effective Strategies Answer Five Questions

market share, improving profitability, boosting return on investment, fostering both quantity and quality of outputs, increasing productivity, improving customer service, and contributing to society.

Organizations usually have a number of mutually reinforcing strategic goals. For example, a computer manufacturer may have as its strategic goals the launch of a specified number of new products in a particular time frame, of higher quality, with a targeted increase in market share. Each of these goals supports and contributes to the others.

A **strategy** is a pattern of actions and resource allocations designed to achieve the goals of the organization. As Exhibit 4.2 illustrates, an effective strategy provides a basis for answering five broad questions about how the organization will meet its objectives.[15] Former Procter & Gamble CEO A. G. Lafley and consultant Roger Martin emphasize that the answers to the "where" and "how" questions should be aimed at winning (question 3), which requires offering a better "value proposition" than the competition. Merely matching the competition, they say, is neither strategic nor a path to success.

For example, P&G gave new life to its Oil of Olay skin care brand by addressing the concerns of middle-aged women and by improving the active ingredients in its product. In addition, the global consumer company used its strength in selling to mass-market retailers to persuade them to set up attractive displays for the beauty product. With the value proposition of an affordable, attractive, widely available product serving a previously ignored market segment, P&G's strategic goal is to achieve leadership in the skin care market.[16]

Though still trailing its rivals Dove, Neutrogena, and Nivea, the Olay brand is sold in about 100 countries and its value doubled to just over $4 billion in the past 10 years.[17]

In setting a strategy, managers try to match the organization's skills and resources to the opportunities in the external environment. Every organization has certain strengths and weaknesses; strategies should capitalize and help build on strengths that satisfy consumers and other key factors in the organization's external environment. Organizations also can implement strategies that change or influence the external environment, as discussed in Chapter 2.

strategic goals

Major targets or end results relating to the organization's long-term survival, value, and growth.

strategy

A pattern of actions and resource allocations designed to achieve the organization's goals.

Tactical and Operational Planning

Once the organization's strategic goals and plans are identified, they serve as the foundation for planning done by middle-level and frontline managers. As you can see in Exhibit 4.3, goals and plans become more specific and involve shorter periods of time as they move from the strategic level to the tactical level and then to the operational level. A strategic plan will typically have a time horizon from three to seven years—but sometimes even decades, as with the audacious plan to establish a human colony on Mars. Tactical plans may have a time horizon of a year or two, and operational plans may cover a period of months.

	Managerial Level	Level of Detail	Time Horizon
Strategic	Top	Low	Long (3–7 years)
Tactical	Middle	Medium	Medium (1–2 years)
Operational	Frontline	High	Short (<1 year)

EXHIBIT 4.3
Hierarchy of Goals and Plans

tactical planning

A set of procedures for translating broad strategic goals and plans into specific goals and plans that are relevant to a distinct portion of the organization, such as a functional area like marketing.

operational planning

The process of identifying the specific procedures and processes required at lower levels of the organization.

Bottom Line

Ideally, strategic plans integrate all the bottom-line practices of the firm. *What might happen if a company's innovation practices were not aligned with its strategy?*

Whole Foods has operational goals that focus on high quality, freshness, taste, nutritional value, safety, and appearance.

Mike Kemp/Rubberball/Getty Images

Tactical planning translates broad strategic goals and plans into specific goals and plans that are relevant to a particular unit in the organization—often a functional area like customer service or human resources. Tactical plans focus on the major actions a unit must take to fulfill its part of the strategic plan. For example, if the strategy calls for the rollout of a new product line, the tactical plan for the manufacturing unit might involve the design, testing, and installation of the equipment needed to produce the new line.

Operational planning identifies the specific procedures and processes required at lower levels of the organization. Frontline managers usually focus on routine tasks such as production runs, customer service product updates, delivery schedules, and the human resources requirements described in later chapters.

The planning model we have been describing is a hierarchical one, with top-level strategies flowing down through the levels of the organization into more specific goals and plans and ever-shorter time frames. But the planning sequence is not as rigid as it sounds so far. As we will see later, managers at all levels may be involved in developing and contributing to the strategic plan.

Furthermore, lower-level managers may be making decisions that shape strategy, whether or not top executives realize it. Managers at all levels may be involved in developing and contributing to the strategic plan. Furthermore, lower-level managers may be making decisions that shape strategy, whether or not top executives realize it. Realized strategies—the actual pattern of decisions and actions over time—come from deliberate planning but also from the many decisions and actions arising throughout the organization and not anticipated in the plan. Top managers make intentional plans, while middle- and operating-level managers influence how strategies unfold.[18]

The fast-casual food chain, Chipotle Mexican Grill, has experienced significant growth since its founding in Denver in 1993.[19] In 2016, however, its strategy of "Food With Integrity" was negatively affected by food-related health outbreaks that sickened hundreds of customers.[20] At the store level, inconsistent employee management and food preparation practices contributed to its problems.[21] Steve Ells, former CEO of Chipotle, focused on restoring customer and investor confidence in the restaurant chain by correcting several of these operational-level issues.[22]

However, in July 2018, Chipotle faced another major outbreak of food poisoning at one of its Ohio restaurants due to employees leaving food at unsafe temperatures. CEO Brian Niccol announced that Chipotle would retrain staff to emphasize its zero-tolerance policy for food safety violations.[23]

The lesson for top managers is to make sure they communicate some of the strategy to all organizational levels *and* pay attention to what is *actually happening* throughout.

Aligning Tactical, Operational, and Strategic Planning

To be fully effective, the organization's strategic, tactical, and operational goals and plans must be aligned—that is, ideally they will be consistent, mutually supportive, and focused on achieving the common purpose and direction. Whole Foods Market, for example, links its tactical and operational planning directly to its strategic planning. The firm describes itself on its website as a mission-driven company that aims to set the standards for excellence for food retailers. The firm measures its success in fulfilling its vision by "customer satisfaction, team member excellence and happiness, return on capital investment, improvement in the state of the environment, and local and larger community support."[24]

Whole Foods's strategic goal is "to sell the highest-quality products that also offer high value for our customers." Its operational goals focus on ingredients, freshness, taste, nutritional value, safety, and appearance that meet or exceed its customers' expectations, including guaranteeing product satisfaction. Tactical goals include store environments that are

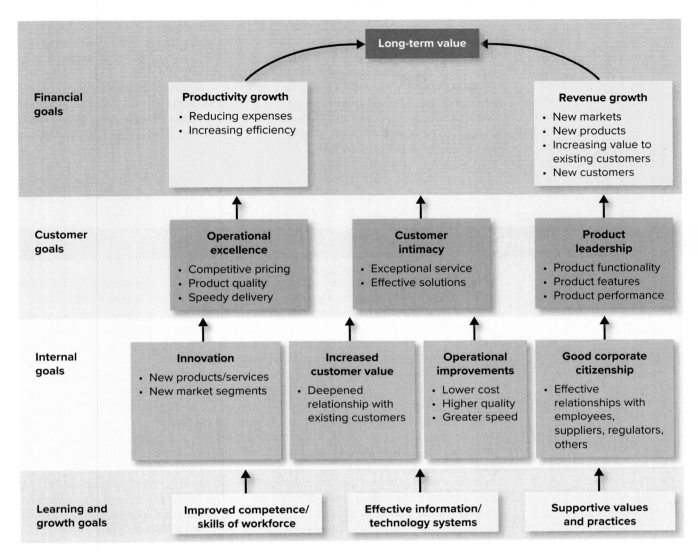

SOURCES: Adapted from Kaplan, R. and Norton, D., "Plotting Success with Strategy Maps," *Optimize*, February 2004, online; and Kaplan, R. and Norton, D., "Having Trouble with Your Strategy? Then Map It," *Harvard Business Review*, September–October 2000.

EXHIBIT 4.4

The Strategy Map: Creating Value by Aligning Goals

"inviting, fun, unique, informal, comfortable, attractive, nurturing, and educational" and are safe and inviting for employees.

One method for aligning the organization's strategic and operational goals is a *strategy map*. A strategy map is a tool for communicating strategic goals and helping employees to understand the parts they will play in helping to achieve them. The map illustrates the four key drivers (or "balanced scorecard") of a firm's long-term success: the skills of its people and their ability to grow and learn; the effectiveness of its internal processes; its ability to deliver value to customers; and ultimately its ability to grow its financial assets. The map shows how specific plans and goals in each area link to the others, and can generate real improvements in an organization's performance.

Exhibit 4.4 shows a strategy map and how the various goals of the organization relate to each other to create long-term value. As an example, let's assume that a company's primary financial goal is "to increase revenues by enhancing the value we offer to existing customers by making our prices the lowest available." (Walmart and Costco might be good examples.) The company will have corresponding goals and plans to support that strategy. Learning

and growth goals might include bringing in the most efficient production technologies and training the staff to use them. These in turn will lead to the internal goals of improved production speed and lower cost, which in turn lead to the customer goal of competitive pricing, making the original financial goal feasible.

As a contrasting example, a financial strategy of revenue growth through new products might lead to people and technology goals that speed up product design, internal processes that lead to innovation, and a customer goal of perceived product leadership. Whatever the strategy, the strategy map can be used to develop the appropriate measures and standards in each operational area and to show how they all are linked.[25]

Strategic Planning

Strategic decision making is one of the most exciting topics in management today. Many organizations are changing the ways they develop and execute their strategic plans.

Traditionally, strategic planning emphasized a top-down approach. Senior executives and specialized planning units developed goals and plans for the entire organization. Tactical and operational managers received those goals and plans, and their own planning activities were limited to specific procedures and budgets for their units.

Over the years, new planning techniques and approaches have emerged, many of which have become essential for analyzing complex business challenges and competitive issues. In many instances, however, senior executives spent too much time with their planning specialists to the exclusion of managers in the rest of the organization. A gap often developed between strategic managers and tactical and operational managers, and employees throughout the organization became alienated and uncommitted to the organization's success.[26]

Today, however, senior executives increasingly are involving managers throughout the organization in the strategy formation process.[27] This more participative approach can improve planning effectiveness and organizational performance.[28] The problems described earlier and the rapidly changing environment of the past few decades years forced executives to look to all levels of the organization for ideas and innovations to make their firms more competitive. Although the CEO and other top managers continue to set the strategic direction, or "vision," for the organization, tactical and operational managers can provide valuable input to the organization's strategic plan. In some cases, these managers also have substantial autonomy to formulate or change their own plans. This authority increases flexibility and responsiveness, critical requirements for success today.

Because of these trends, firms often use the term *strategic management* to describe the process. **Strategic management** involves managers from all parts of the organization in the formulation and implementation of strategic goals and strategies. It integrates strategic planning and management into a single process. Strategic planning becomes an ongoing activity in which all managers are encouraged to think strategically and focus on long-term, externally oriented issues as well as short-term tactical and operational issues.

strategic management

A process that involves
managers from all parts
of the organization in
the formulation and
implementation of strategic
goals and strategies.

As shown in Exhibit 4.5, the strategic management process has six major components:

1. Establishing mission, vision, and goals.
2. Analyzing external opportunities and threats.
3. Analyzing internal strengths and weaknesses.
4. SWOT (strengths, weaknesses, opportunities, and threats) analysis and strategy formulation.
5. Strategy implementation.
6. Strategic control.

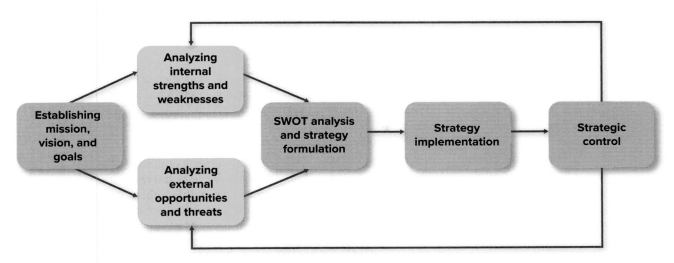

EXHIBIT 4.5
The Strategic Management Process

Because this process is a planning and decision process, it is similar to the planning framework discussed earlier. Although organizations may use different terms or emphasize different parts of the process, the components and concepts described in this section are found—explicitly or implicitly—in every organization. Even a small entrepreneurial firm can benefit from the kind of planning framework we describe here.

Step 1: Establishing Mission, Vision, and Goals

The first step in strategic planning is establishing a mission, a vision, and goals for the organization. The **mission** is a clear and concise expression of the basic purpose of the organization. It describes what the organization does, for whom it does it, and its basic good or service. Here are some mission statements of firms that you will recognize:[29]

> *TED:* "Spread ideas."
> *Google:* "Organize the world's information and make it universally accessible and useful."
> *Starbucks:* "Our mission is to inspire and nurture the human spirit – one person, one cup, and one neighborhood at a time."

Smaller organizations, of course, may have missions that aren't as broad as these. For example, the local bar close to most campuses has this implicit mission: "to sell large quantities of inexpensive beer to college students in a noisy, enjoyable environment."

While the mission describes the organization's ongoing purpose, the **strategic vision** points to the future—it provides a perspective on where the organization is headed and what it can become. It is typically aspirational. Ideally, the vision statement clarifies the long-term direction of the company and its strategic intent.

The most effective vision statements inspire organization members. They offer a worthwhile target for the entire organization to work together to achieve. Often these statements are not strictly financial because financial targets alone may not motivate all organization members. For example, NASA's Armstrong Flight Research Center focuses on the future of flight and exploration. Similarly, Habitat for Humanity envisions "a world where everyone has a decent place to live."

The chief executive officer of the organization, with the input and approval of the board of directors, establishes the mission, vision, and major strategic goals. These should be communicated or at least accessible to everyone who has contact with the organization. Large

mission

An organization's basic purpose and scope of operations.

strategic vision

The long-term direction and strategic intent of a company.

The strategic vision points to the future— where the organization is headed and what it can become.

firms and organizations provide public formal statements of their missions, visions, goals, and even values. For example, in support of its vision that "Austin is prosperous," the city established goals such as these:[30]

- Promote and measure business entrepreneurship, innovation, and a culture of creativity.
- Implement policies that create, nurture, and retain small and local businesses and minority- and women-owned businesses.
- Build on the Austin metropolitan area's position as a leader in global trade.
- Invest in the region's people through long-term job training for living wage jobs.

Different city departments contribute to various aspects of this vision as they carry out their operational plans in collaboration with local businesses and residents.

Lofty words in a vision and mission statement mean little without strong support from leadership. Elon Musk, CEO of SpaceX, is committed to its mission of revolutionizing space technology to enable individuals to inhabit other planets. Musk, despite significant setbacks (e.g., a rocket exploded on the launchpad) and a widely publicized missed deadline, continues to support this goal. Musk wants to help humans become a "spacefaring civilization." He believes that humans will be traveling to Mars with the goal of establishing a colony on the Red planet within the next decade.[31]

Where leadership is strong, statements of visions and goals clarify the organization's purpose to key constituencies outside the organization. They also help employees focus their talent, energy, and commitment in pursuit of organizational goals. When you consider employment with a firm, reviewing its statements of mission, vision, and goals is a good first step in determining whether the firm's purposes and values will be compatible with your own.

LO 4-3 Identify elements of the external environment and internal resources of the firm to analyze before formulating a strategy.

stakeholders

Groups and individuals who affect and are affected by the achievement of the organization's mission, goals, and strategies.

Some view renewable resources as a threat; others as an opportunity.

Gabriel Murad/123RF

Step 2: Analyzing External Opportunities and Threats

The mission and vision drive the second component of the strategic management process: analyzing external environment. Effective strategic management depends on an accurate and thorough evaluation of the competitive environment and macroenvironment (Chapter 2).

The important activities in an environmental analysis include the ones shown in Exhibit 4.6. The analysis begins with an examination of the industry. Next, organizational stakeholders are examined. **Stakeholders** are groups and individuals who affect and are affected by the achievement of the organization's mission, goals, and strategies. These include buyers, suppliers, competitors, government and regulatory agencies, unions and employee groups, the financial community, owners and shareholders, and trade associations. The environmental analysis assesses these stakeholders and the ways they influence the organization.[32]

The environmental analysis also should examine other forces in the environment, such as economic conditions and technological factors. One critical task in environmental analysis is forecasting future trends. As noted in Chapter 2, forecasting techniques range from simple judgment to complex mathematical models that examine systematic relationships among many variables. Even simple quantitative techniques outperform the intuitive assessments of experts. Judgment is susceptible to bias, and managers have a limited ability to process information. Managers should use subjective judgments as inputs to quantitative models or when they confront new situations.

The difference between an opportunity and a threat depends in part on how a company positions itself strategically. For example, some states have required electric utilities to get a certain share of their power from renewable sources such as wind and solar energy rather than from

EXHIBIT 4.6
Environmental Analysis

Industry and Market Analysis

- **Industry profile:** major product lines and significant market segments in the industry.
- **Industry growth:** growth rates for the entire industry, growth rates for key market segments, projected changes in patterns of growth, and the determinants of growth.
- **Industry forces:** threat of new industry entrants, threat of substitutes, economic power of buyers, economic power of suppliers, and internal industry rivalry (recall Chapter 2).

Competitor Analysis

- **Competitor profile:** major competitors and their market shares.
- **Competitor analysis:** goals, strategies, strengths, and weaknesses of each major competitor.
- **Competitor advantages:** the degree to which industry competitors have differentiated their products or services or achieved cost leadership.

Political and Regulatory Analysis

- **Legislation and regulatory activities** and their effects on the industry.
- **Political activity:** the level of political activity that organizations and associations within the industry undertake (see Chapter 5).

Social Analysis

- **Social issues:** current and potential social issues and their effects on the industry.
- **Social interest groups:** consumer, environmental, and similar activist groups that attempt to influence the industry (see Chapters 5 and 6).

Human Resources Analysis

- **Labor issues:** key labor needs, shortages, opportunities, and problems confronting the industry (see Chapters 10 and 11).

Macroeconomic Analysis

- **Macroeconomic conditions:** economic factors that affect supply, demand, growth, competition, and profitability within the industry.

Technological Analysis

- **Technological factors:** scientific or technical methods that affect the industry, particularly recent and potential innovations (see Chapter 17).

fossil fuels, including coal, oil, and natural gas. This requirement poses a threat to utilities because the costs of fossil fuel energy are less, and customers demand low prices.

However, some companies see strategic opportunities in renewable power. CropEnergies AG is a leading manufacturer of bioethanol in Europe, producing 1.3 million cubic meters per year. Bioethanol, the world's number-one biofuel, replaces fossil fuels and reduces CO_2 by up to 70 percent. The company will likely continue to grow as the demand for renewable energy increases worldwide, particularly in the transportation sector.[33]

Similarly, overflowing landfills are an expensive challenge for many municipalities, but a growing number are seeing an opportunity in the form of energy generation. As garbage decomposes, it produces methane gas, which is used as a fuel to power plants and manufacturing facilities. The U.S. Environmental Protection Agency (EPA) formed an outreach program that partners with stakeholders—communities, landfill owners, and utilities—that, by early 2019, had more than 600 methane-to-energy conversion projects.[34]

The Digital World

Managing Technology's Impact

Corporations must plan their strategies and analyze external opportunities and threats. Yet technological advancements have in some ways complicated this process. Few in their respective industries realized what Netflix would do to Blockbuster, what Amazon would do to bookstores, what Uber would do to taxi services, or what Airbnb would do to the hotel industry. Managers must always be looking out for new technologies that may disrupt or perhaps even revolutionize their industries.[35]

For example, today many companies are closely watching developments in 3D printing to determine how this technology may affect them both now and in the future.[36] In the automotive field, diagnosing an engine problem, sending the digital diagnosis to the technician, and printing the needed part by the time the car has been towed will be made possible through the use of 3D printing.[37] This technology will surely have a profound impact on the industry in the years to come. The question is, how will companies adapt?

Managers must plan for a dynamic digital future in which their inventory, supply chain, vendors, timing, and infrastructure issues will evolve quickly. For those able to see the strategic value of new business models, there will be many new opportunities.

1. How might managers analyze the technological environment for products that do not yet exist?
2. What other industries do you think 3D printing will affect?

Step 3: Analyzing Internal Strengths and Weaknesses

As managers conduct an external analysis, they also assess the strengths and weaknesses of major functional areas inside their organization. Exhibit 4.7 lists some of the major components of this internal resource analysis. For example, is your firm strong enough financially to handle the lengthy and costly investment new projects often require? Can your existing staff execute its part of the plan, or do you need to provide new training or hire new people? Internal analysis gives strategic decision makers an inventory of the organization's existing

EXHIBIT 4.7

Internal Resource Analysis

Financial Analysis

Examines financial strengths and weaknesses through financial statements such as a balance sheet and an income statement, and compares trends to historical and industry figures (see Chapter 18).

Marketing Audit

Examines strengths and weaknesses of major marketing activities and identifies markets, key market segments, and the competitive position (market share) within key markets.

Operations Analysis

Examines the strengths and weaknesses of the manufacturing, production, or service delivery activities of the organization (see Chapters 9, 16, and 17).

Other Internal Resource Analyses

Examines, as necessary and appropriate, the strengths and weaknesses of other organizational activities, such as research and development (product and process), management information systems, engineering, and purchasing.

Human Resources Assessment

Examines strengths and weaknesses of all levels of management and employees and focuses on key human resources activities, including recruitment, selection, placement, training, labor (union) relationships, compensation, promotion, appraisal, quality of work life, and human resources planning (see Chapters 10 and 11).

functions, skills, and resources as well as its overall performance level. Many of your other business courses will prepare you to conduct a detailed internal analysis.

Resources and Core Capabilities   Strategic planning has been strongly influenced in recent years by a focus on internal resources. **Resources** are inputs to production (recall systems theory) that can be accumulated over time to enhance the performance of a firm.

Resources can take many forms, but they tend to fall into two broad categories: (1) tangible assets such as real estate, production facilities, raw materials, and so on; and (2) intangible assets such as company reputation, culture, technical knowledge, and patents as well as accumulated learning and experience. The Walt Disney Company, for example, has based its strategic plan on combinations of tangible assets (e.g., hotels and theme parks) and intangible assets (brand recognition, talented craftspeople, and culture focused on customer service).[38]

Internal analysis provides a clearer understanding of how a company can compete through its resources. Resources provide competitive advantage only under certain circumstances. First, the resource provides advantage if it is instrumental in creating customer value—increasing the benefits customers derive from a good or service relative to the costs they incur.[39] For example, Amazon's AI-powered search technology, its ability to track customer preferences, its ability to offer personalized recommendations each time its site is accessed, and its quick product delivery system are valuable resources that enhance Amazon's competitiveness.

Second, resources are a source of advantage if they are rare and not equally available to all competitors. Even for extremely valuable resources, if all competitors have equal access, the resource cannot provide competitive advantage. For companies such as IBM, AT&T, Toshiba, Boeing, 3M, and others, patented formulas are both rare and valuable.

Third, resources provide competitive advantage if they are difficult to imitate. Since its founding in 1999, Salesforce has helped 150,000 companies—like RED, T-Mobile, Carlo's Bake Shop, and Unilever—manage customer relationships in a more effective and efficient manner.[40] Marc Benioff, chair and CEO, has a unique vision: "The business of business is improving the state of the world." In line with this direction, employees are encouraged to be "trailblazers" who help customers find their own paths to success. The culture is also unique as it values trust, customer service, innovation, and equality.

The company also encourages philanthropy as it invites all entrepreneurs and companies to "Pledge 1%" of product, time, and resources to support communities and the social sector. Since starting this 1-1-1 philanthropic model 18 years ago, Salesforce has donated more than $240 million in grants, 3.5 million in hours of community service, and product donations for nearly 40,000 nonprofits and education institutions.[41] It comes as little surprise that its been listed several times on *Fortune's* Great Companies to Work For list, including #2 in 2019.[42]

As shown in Exhibit 4.8, when resources are valuable, rare, inimitable, and organized, they comprise a company's core capabilities. A **core capability** (also referred to as "competence") is something a company does especially well relative to its competitors. Mercedes-Benz has a core competence in high-performance engine design and manufacturing, Chick-fil-A provides a consistently pleasant dining experience for its customers, and Instagram has a core competency of creating photo-filters with a simplistic app. As in these examples, a core competence typically refers to a set of skills or expertise in some activity rather than physical or financial assets.

Benchmarking   To assess and improve performance, some companies use benchmarking, the process of assessing how well one company's basic functions and skills compare with those of another company or set of companies. As introduced in Chapter 2, the goal of benchmarking is to understand the "best practices" of other firms thoroughly and to undertake actions to achieve lower costs and better performance.

LO 4-4 Define core capabilities and explain how they provide the foundation for business strategy.

resources

Inputs to a system that can enhance performance.

Bottom Line

Amazon provides value via speed, low cost, and excellent customer service. *What are some resources Amazon needs to deliver these benefits?*

core capability

A unique skill and/or knowledge an organization possesses that gives it an edge over competitors.

wildpixel/Getty Images

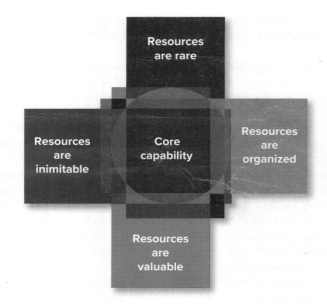

EXHIBIT 4.8
Resources and Core Capability

According to consulting firm Accenture, benchmarking has four elements:[43]

1. Decide what needs to be measured and which metrics will be used.
2. Collect and validate the data; compile initial findings.
3. Assess initial findings to see if additional data need to be collected.
4. Analyze results and make final recommendations to key stakeholders.

Not Invented Here syndrome (NIH)

A negative attitude toward knowledge (ideas, technologies) derived from an external source.

Adding to the Chapter 3 discussion of psychological biases, an important bias that inhibits benchmarking is the **Not Invented Here syndrome (NIH)**: a negative attitude toward knowledge (ideas, technologies) derived from an external source.[44] Managers tend to favor what their own company does and are hesitant to adapt methods from elsewhere, even when they are potential useful. But companies that use benchmarking programs strategically—applying good ideas no matter where they come from and adapting them in customized fashion to their own situations—can make great strides in eliminating operational inefficiencies and improving competitiveness. Examples include Toyota, Berkshire Hathaway Energy, Corning, Wipro, and Shopify.

Benchmarking may be of limited use when it helps a company perform only as well as its competitors; strategic management ultimately is about surpassing those companies. Companies can gain additional advantage via *internal* benchmarking: comparing different internal units against one another to disseminate the company's best practices throughout the organization.

Bottom Line

Benchmarking can identify best practices both outside and inside your company. *In some famous benchmarking examples, businesses learned from pit crews for race car teams. What kinds of bottom-line practices could that industry demonstrate?*

Opel, a car manufacturer formerly owned by General Motors (GM), used benchmarking to compare best practices from other GM brands. However, that was unable to help Opel close performance gaps. PSA Group bought Opel from GM, and everything changed. Opel was able to benchmark much more effectively by gathering performance data among other vehicle brands. The company cut fixed costs by 28 percent by having "compressed" assembly plants and attained a 5 percent profit margin.[45]

Step 4: SWOT Analysis and Strategy Formulation

Once managers have analyzed the external environment and internal organizational resources, they have the information they need to assess the organization's strengths, weaknesses, opportunities, and threats. Such an assessment is called a **SWOT analysis**.

SWOT analysis

A comparison of strengths, weaknesses, opportunities, and threats that helps executives formulate strategy.

Strengths and weaknesses refer to internal resources. For example, an organization's strengths might include skilled management, positive cash flow, and well-known and highly regarded brands. Weaknesses might be lack of spare production capacity and the absence of reliable suppliers.

Opportunities and threats arise in the macroenvironment and competitive environment. Examples of opportunities are a new technology that could make the supply chain more efficient, and an underserved market niche. Threats could include the possibility that competitors will enter the underserved niche if it is shown to be profitable.

SWOT analysis helps managers summarize the relevant, important facts from their external and internal analyses. Based on this summary, they can identify the primary and secondary strategic issues their organization faces. The managers then formulate a strategy that will use the SWOT analysis to pursue opportunities by capitalizing on the organization's strengths, neutralizing its weaknesses, and countering potential threats.

For example, David Handmaker enjoyed several years of unfettered growth since opening his printing company, Next Day Flyers, in Los Angeles. However, over time he noticed that his competitors were more adept at finding and serving online customers. Handmaker needed a plan to restore healthy business growth by migrating parts of his marketing and printing services online before it was too late. But Next Day Flyers originally aimed at local customers, which raised questions about whether the company could serve the needs of geographically dispersed customers.

Handmaker and his team needed to analyze what the firm did well and how it needed to improve relative to the competitive printing marketplace. Exhibit 4.9 summarizes this example in a format commonly used for a basic SWOT analysis. The company developed a strategy calling for it to hire talent with the skills, knowledge, and experience to help Next Day Flyers establish a professional presence on the web, including simple online ordering; free online design services; free printing templates; blog with design and marketing tips; and customer support by phone, email, and live chat.[46]

As a company is formulating strategy, its competitors are, too. Therefore the strategy management process must keep evolving. The more uncertainty that exists in the external environment, the more the strategy needs to focus on strengthening internal capabilities through practices such as seeking new company expertise, opportunistic knowledge sharing, and continuous process improvement.[47] To keep it competitive, Next Day Flyers identified

EXHIBIT 4.9

Sample SWOT Analysis:
Next Day Flyers

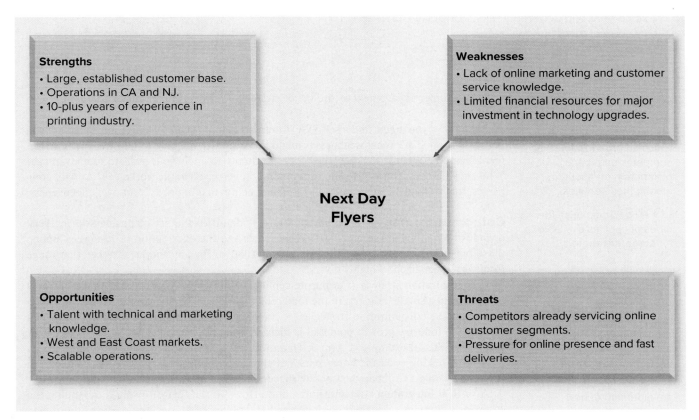

Strengths
- Large, established customer base.
- Operations in CA and NJ.
- 10-plus years of experience in printing industry.

Weaknesses
- Lack of online marketing and customer service knowledge.
- Limited financial resources for major investment in technology upgrades.

Next Day Flyers

Opportunities
- Talent with technical and marketing knowledge.
- West and East Coast markets.
- Scalable operations.

Threats
- Competitors already servicing online customer segments.
- Pressure for online presence and fast deliveries.

SOURCES: Based on information from Myers, R., "That Sounds Like a Plan," *Inc.* 36 (2014), pp. 90–92; and Next Day Flyers company website, "About Next Day Flyers," http://www.nextdayflyers.com.

Inclusiveness Works

Making Diversity and Inclusion the Brand

Everyone has heard stories of companies blundering marketing campaigns in foreign markets. Mercedes-Benz entered the Chinese market with the brand name "Bensi," which means "rush to die" in Chinese. Cosmetics giant Clairol launched a curling iron in Germany under the brand "Mist Stick"; unfortunately for Clairol, "mist" is slang for manure in German. Nike had to recall thousands of sneakers when a design pattern meant to resemble fire also resembled the Arabic word for Allah.[48] Such oversights speak to a lack of cultural consideration when doing business.

Taking into account the cultures and perspectives of others isn't just an option for businesses any longer; it's essential. In fact, some businesses are making diversity and inclusion the brand itself. Companies in the hospitality industry are at the forefront of this movement.

Following accusations of discrimination on its platform a few years ago, Airbnb has been working to foster diversity and inclusion within its organization and make diversity the face of its company. CEO Bryan Chesky said during a recent interview, "Our mission and inclusion are the same thing. You can't really separate these two issues."[49] That same year, Airbnb hired its first "Diversity Chief" to accelerate the hiring of women and underrepresented minorities.[50]

In 2017, Airbnb launched its "We Accept" ad during the Superbowl, featuring a montage of diverse faces with the text, "We believe no matter who you are, where you're from, who you love, or who you worship, we all belong. The world is more beautiful, the more you accept. #weaccept" The ad garnered more social media attention than any other ad during the Superbowl and was viewed over 19 million times.[51]

Airbnb has also made changes to its service, such as requiring all hosts to agree to a nondiscrimination policy. It has also added an "Open Door" policy for travelers to lodge reports of discrimination, with the guarantee of rebooking the guest in similar accommodations while it investigates such claims.[52]

Airbnb has recorded profits in the last two years and is expected to hold an IPO in the near future. Clearly, its embrace of diversity and inclusion is paying off.

1. Why might companies want to consider diversity and inclusion a core capability?
2. How might companies incorporate diversity and inclusion into their strategic planning?

---

corporate strategy

The set of businesses, markets, or industries in which an organization competes and the distribution of resources among those entities.

LO 4-5 Summarize the types of choices available for corporate strategy.

concentration

A strategy an organization uses to operate a single business and compete in a single industry.

vertical integration

The acquisition or development of new businesses that produce parts or components of the organization's product.

online customer engagement as the major strategy it needed to commit to and continue to develop.

By the way, you might find a self-SWOT analysis helpful when seeking a job. What are you particularly good at? What weaknesses might you need to overcome to improve your employment chances? What firms offer the best opportunity to apply your skills to full advantage? Who are your competitors? How is your generation perceived in the workplace? As with companies, this kind of analysis can lead to a plan of action that improves your own effectiveness.

Corporate Strategy   A **corporate strategy** identifies the set of businesses, markets, or industries in which the organization competes and the distribution of resources among those businesses. Exhibit 4.10 shows basic alternatives for a corporate strategy that range from very specialized to highly diverse.

A **concentration** strategy (the purple center of the figure) focuses on a single business competing in a single industry. In the food retailing industry, Trader Joe's, Kroger, and Safeway all pursue concentration strategies. A company pursues concentration strategies when (perceived) industry growth potential is high or when the company has a narrow range of competencies. An example is Arm & Hammer™, which pursues a concentration strategy by making baking soda for home personal care application; the strategy has enabled the Church & Dwight Company to operate successfully for nearly 175 years.

A **vertical integration** strategy (horizontal arrows in the figure) involves expanding the company's domain to include supplier and distributors. At one time, Henry Ford had fully integrated his company from the ore mines needed to make steel all the way to the showrooms where his cars were sold. Vertical integration generally is used to reduce costs

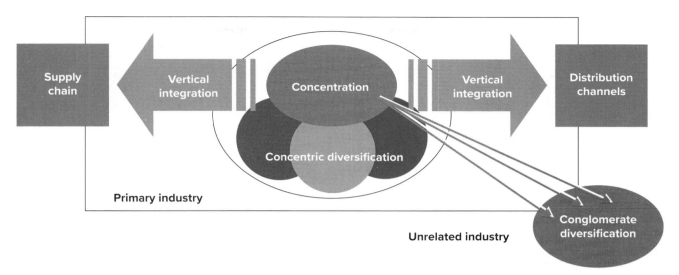

EXHIBIT 4.10
Summary of Corporate Strategies

associated with suppliers or distributors and to reduce the uncertainties created by unpredictable business relationships.

A strategy of **concentric diversification** (expanded center of the figure) moves into new but related businesses. William Marriott expanded his original restaurant business outside Washington, DC, by moving into airline catering, hotels, and fast food. Each of these businesses within the hospitality industry is related in terms of the services it provides, the skills necessary for success, and the customers it attracts. Often companies such as Marriott pursue a strategy of concentric diversification to take advantage of their strengths in one business to gain advantage in another.

Success in a concentric diversification strategy requires adequate management and other resources for operating more than one business. Guitar maker C. F. Martin once tried expanding through purchases of other instrument companies, but management was stretched too thin to run them well. The company divested the acquisitions and returned to its concentration strategy.[53]

In contrast to concentric diversification, **conglomerate diversification** (multiple arrows pointing outside the primary industry) is a corporate strategy of expansion into unrelated businesses. For example, General Electric Corporation diversified from its original base in electrical and home appliance products into health, finance, aviation, renewable energy, and transportation. Typically, companies pursue a conglomerate diversification strategy to minimize risks due to market fluctuations in one industry.

The diversified businesses of an organization are sometimes called its business *portfolio*. One of the most popular techniques for analyzing a corporation's strategy for managing its portfolio is the BCG matrix, developed by the Boston Consulting Group. Exhibit 4.11 shows the BCG matrix. Each business in the corporation is plotted on the matrix based on the growth rate of its market and the relative strength of its competitive position in that market (market share). To convey additional information visually, each business can be represented by a circle whose size indicates its contribution to corporate revenues.

In the BCG matrix, high-growth, weak-competitive-position businesses are called *question marks*. They require substantial investment to improve their position; otherwise divestiture is recommended. High-growth, strong-competitive-position businesses are the *stars*. These businesses require heavy investment, but their strong position allows them to generate the needed revenues.

Low-growth, strong-competitive-position businesses are called *cash cows*. These businesses generate revenues in excess of their investment needs and therefore fund other businesses. Finally, low-growth, weak-competitive-position businesses are the *dogs*. Once any remaining revenues from these businesses are realized, the businesses are divested.

concentric diversification

A strategy used to add new businesses that produce related products or are involved in related markets and activities.

conglomerate diversification

A strategy used to add new businesses that produce unrelated products or are involved in unrelated markets and activities.

Bottom Line

Companies that integrate vertically often do so to reduce their costs. *Why might buying from a division of your company be less costly than buying on the open market?*

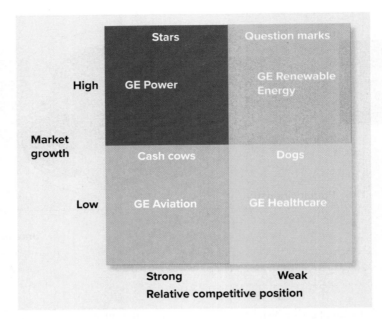

EXHIBIT 4.11

Mapping GE's Business Units and Product Lines to the BCG Matrix

The BCG matrix alone is not a substitute for management judgment, creativity, insight, or leadership. But it is a well-known tool that, along with others, can help top corporate executives and the individual business managers understand their business portfolios and strategic options.[54] This approach helps companies like General Electric that need to weigh the relative merits of many business units and product lines.

When GE struggled in some of its widely diversified businesses, the company refocused on its strength as a manufacturer, targeting three industries: energy, health care, and transportation. Not only do these industries offer significant growth potential, but GE already dominates the markets for electric turbines and jet engines. Therefore, besides selling off NBC Universal and GE Capital, GE acquired wind farms and blade manufacturers, and 3D printing companies to manufacture aircraft components.[55]

Trends in Corporate Strategy   Corporate America periodically is swept by waves of mergers and acquisitions (M&As). The targets chosen for mergers and acquisitions depend on the corporate strategy of either concentrating or diversifying the business portfolio.

Many recent deals were aimed at helping companies expand their market share and product offerings within related industries. For example, AT&T acquired the cybersecurity firm Alien-Vault in order to help small- and medium-sized businesses respond to cybersecurity attacks.[56]

The value of implementing a more diversified corporate strategy depends on circumstances. Many argue that unrelated diversification hurts a company more often than it helps. Many diversified companies have sold their peripheral businesses so they could concentrate on a more focused portfolio. In contrast, the diversification efforts of an organization competing in a slow-growth, mature, or threatened industry often are applauded.

Business Strategy   Once corporate strategies are determined, managers must determine how they will compete in each business area. **Business strategy** defines the major actions by which an organization builds and strengthens its competitive position. A business can gain competitive advantage using one of two generic business strategies: low cost and differentiation.[57]

Businesses using a **low-cost strategy** attempt to be efficient and to offer standard, no-frills products. Walmart Stores uses the power of its giant size to negotiate favorable prices from suppliers, enabling it to sell at prices below those of most competing retailers. Its size allows it to provide goods and services more efficiently (at lower cost), which leads to higher sales. market share, and profits.

business strategy

The major actions by which a business competes in a particular industry or market.

LO 4-6 Discuss how companies can achieve competitive advantage through business strategy.

low-cost strategy

A strategy an organization uses to build competitive advantage by being efficient and offering a standard no-frills project.

Companies that succeed with a low-cost strategy often are large and take advantage of economies of scale in production or distribution. An organization using this strategy generally must be the cost leader in its industry or market segment. However, even a cost leader must offer a product that is acceptable to customers compared with competitors' products.

Alternatively, an organization may pursue a **differentiation strategy**. With a differentiation strategy, a company attempts to be unique in its industry or market segment along some dimensions (other than cost) that customers value. This unique or differentiated position within the industry often is based on high product quality, excellent marketing and distribution, or superior service. Nordstrom's well-known commitment to outstanding, personalized customer service in the retail apparel industry is an excellent example of a differentiation strategy.

Whatever strategy managers adopt, the most effective strategy is one that competitors are unwilling or unable to imitate. If the organization's strategic plan is one that can easily be adopted by industry competitors, it will yield only short-term advantage. For example, a strategy to gain market share by being the first to offer an innovative product may or may not succeed, depending in part on competitive responses. In some industries, technologies advance so fast that the first company to provide a new product is quickly challenged by later entrants offering superior products.[58]

differentiation strategy

A strategy an organization uses to build competitive advantage by being unique in its industry or market segment along one or more dimensions.

> **Bottom Line**
> A high-quality strategy is often more difficult for competitors to imitate. *What would be hard about imitating Nordstrom's strategy for top-quality service?*

Functional Strategy   The final step in strategy formulation is to establish the major functional strategies. **Functional strategies** are implemented by each functional area of the organization to support the business strategy. The typical functional areas include production, human resources, marketing and sales, research and development, finance, and distribution.

For example, Bloomin' Brands, the parent company of restaurant chains Outback Steakhouse, Bonefish Grill, Carrabba's Italian Grill, and Fleming's Prime Steakhouse, set a business strategy with targets for aggressive growth and greater efficiency built on the chains' reputation for offering good food at affordable prices. To achieve this, functional strategies included improving employee retention through enhanced training and development, adding innovative items to menus, and launching a multi-brand loyalty program.[59]

Functional strategies typically are developed by functional managers with input and approval from the executives responsible for business strategy. Senior strategic decision makers review the functional strategies to ensure that each major department is operating consistently with the business strategies. For example, even if they saved money, automated production techniques would not be appropriate for a piano company like Steinway, whose products are strategically positioned (and priced) as high-quality and handcrafted.

At companies that compete based on product innovation, strategies for the research and development functions are especially critical. Microsoft creates most of its products and services internally, so it is committed to investing heavily in R&D. The company spends 13 percent of its revenue in R&D, which was equivalent to $14.7 billion in 2018.[60]

functional strategies

Strategies implemented by each functional area of the organization to support the organization's business strategy.

Carrabba's Italian Grill wants its employees to behave in ways that meet the company's strategy to provide good food at reasonable cost.

Jonathan Weiss/Shutterstock

Step 5: Strategy Implementation

As with any plan, simply formulating a good strategy is not enough. Strategic managers also must ensure that the new strategies are implemented effectively and efficiently. The best executives and strategy consultants realize that clever planning techniques and a good strategy do not guarantee success.

Many organizations are extending more participative strategic management process to implementation. Managers at all levels are involved with formulating strategy and identifying and executing ways to implement it. Senior executives still may oversee the implementation process, but they are placing responsibility and authority in the hands of others.

LO 4-7   Describe the keys to effective strategy implementation.

In general, strategy implementation involves these steps:

Step 1: Define strategic tasks. Articulate in simple language what a particular unit must do to create or sustain a competitive advantage. Define strategic tasks to help employees understand how they contribute.

Step 2: Assess organization capabilities. Evaluate the organization's ability to implement the strategic tasks. A task force might interview employees and managers to identify issues that help or hinder implementation. Then the results are summarized for top management.

Step 3: Develop an implementation agenda. Management decides how it will change its own activities and procedures; what skills and individuals are needed in key roles; and what structures, measures, information, and rewards can best support the needed actions.

Step 4: Implement. The top management team, the employee task force, and others develop the implementation plan. The top management team monitors progress. The task force continues its work by providing feedback about how others in the organization are responding to the changes.

This process, though straightforward, does not always go smoothly. Exhibit 4.12 shows six barriers to strategy implementation and provides some key principles for overcoming these silent killers. By paying closer attention to the processes by which strategies are implemented, executives, managers, and employees can make sure that strategic plans are actually carried out.[61]

strategic control system

A system designed to support managers in evaluating the organization's progress regarding its strategy and, when discrepancies exist, taking corrective action.

Step 6: Strategic Control

The final component of the strategic management process is strategic control. A **strategic control system** helps managers evaluate the organization's progress with its strategy and, when discrepancies exist, identify needed corrective actions. The system must encourage efficient operations that are consistent with the plan while allowing flexibility to adapt to changing conditions.

EXHIBIT 4.12   Attacking the Six Barriers to Strategy Implementation

Change starts with the leader	
The Silent Killers	**Beating the Silent Killers**
Top-down or laissez-faire senior management style	The CEO creates a partnership with the top team and lower levels to develop a compelling business direction, create an enabling organizational context, and delegate authority to clearly accountable individuals and teams.
Unclear strategy and conflicting priorities	The top team, as a group, develops a statement of strategy and priorities that members are willing to stand behind.
An ineffective senior management team	Involve the top team in all steps in the change process so that its effectiveness is challenged and developed.
Poor vertical communication	Establish an honest, fact-based dialog with lower levels about the new strategy and the barriers to implementing it.
Poor coordination across functions, businesses, or borders	Define a set of businesswide initiatives and new organizational roles and responsibilities that require "the right people to work together on the right things in the right way to implement the strategy."
Inadequate down-the-line leadership skills and development	Lower-level managers develop skills through newly created opportunities to lead change and drive key business initiatives. They are supported with just-in-time coaching, training, and targeted recruitment. Those who still are not able to make the grade must be replaced.

SOURCE: Beer, M. and Eisenstat, R. A., "The Silent Killers of Strategy Implementation and Learning Barriers," *MIT Sloan Management Review* 4, no. 4 (Summer 2000), pp. 29–40.

Most strategic control systems include a budget to monitor and control major financial expenditures. As a first-time manager, you are likely to work with your work unit's budget—a key aspect of your organization's strategic plan. Your executive team may give you budget assumptions and targets for your area, reflecting your part in the overall plan, and you may be asked to revise your budget once all the budgets in your organization have been consolidated and reviewed.

The dual responsibilities of a control system—efficiency and flexibility—often seem contradictory with respect to budgets. The budget usually establishes spending limits, but changing conditions or the need for innovation may require different financial commitments during the period. To solve this dilemma, some companies use two budgets: strategic and operational. For example, managers at Texas Instruments control two budgets under the OST (objectives–strategies–tactics) system. The strategic budget creates and maintains long-term effectiveness, and the operational budget is tightly monitored to achieve short-term efficiencies.

The broader topic of control, including budgets in particular, is discussed in more detail in Chapter 16. In "Management in Action: Onward," consider the significance of controls to Disney's decisions about its portfolio of businesses.

> ## Bottom Line
> Firms that follow low-cost strategies exert downward pressure on competitors' prices. *How can managers compete against a low-cost strategy so that their firm can continue to charge higher prices for its goods or services?*

Management in Action

DISNEY'S STRATEGY UNDER ROBERT IGER: STREAMING TALES AS OLD AS TIME

Walt Disney Company's mission, as reported on its corporate website, is "to be one of the world's leading producers and providers of entertainment and information, using its portfolio of brands to differentiate its content, services and consumer products." The statement adds, "The company's primary financial goals are to maximize earnings and cash flow, and to allocate capital toward growth initiatives that will drive long-term shareholder value." In pursuit of this two-part objective, Disney is always thinking about ways to evolve and grow. Solidifying its place atop the global marketplace requires CEO Robert Iger to continually make strategic decisions about where to invest and what to divest.

Disney's largest sources of revenues are cable networks and theme parks, with cable providing, by far, the greatest profits. Recently, Disney entered into a media rights contract with the NFL and a deal to air NBA games on ESPN and ABC. In the theme park arena, profitability during a sluggish economy let Disney build when construction costs were low, so it renovated Disney California Adventure, expanded Hong Kong Disneyland, and added a cruise ship to its fleet. In June 2016, Disney opened a theme park in Shanghai, China, and is currently seeking locations to build additional parks in China, which offers billions of new consumers, and around the world.[62]

Disney's movie studios are of course also a core part of Disney's operations. To increase the brand's appeal with teenage boys, this unit purchased Lucasfilm, producer of *Star Wars*. In keeping with its strategy to tell "tales as old as time" with a modern sensibility, Disney has been pursuing

studios that can feed into this pipeline of timeless tales. Its purchase of Marvel gave Disney rights to the timeless heroes of *Ironman, Hulk, Captain America,* and, most recently, *Black Panther* movies, which was the highest-grossing film of 2018 (with Marvel's *Avengers* the second highest). Disney also just completed the purchase of Fox movie and television studios, which will give it rights to more beloved characters, such as those from the *X-Men* series and the *Fantastic Four*.

The next phase in Igor's strategic vision is for Disney to start its own streaming service, to be called Disney Plus. The service will compete with the likes of Netflix, Hulu, and Amazon. In addition to the classic content Disney already can provide on this platform, it intends to create original live-action content derived from these well-established stories. For example, it will create a live-action *Star Wars* series as well as live-action series based on Marvel characters.[63]

With the recent purchase of Fox studios, it wouldn't be a surprise for a live-action *X-Men* series to appear on Disney Plus as well. With Disney's new venture into streaming services, it seems as if Disney will continue scripting its own success.

- How clear is Walt Disney Company's mission? How well does its strategy support the mission?
- In the BCG matrix (see again Exhibit 4.11), where would you place Disney's main businesses? How well is Disney matching its strategic moves to the businesses' positions in the matrix?

MANAGER'S BRIEF

PROGRESS REPORT

ONWARD

KEY TERMS

RETAINING WHAT YOU LEARNED

In Chapter 4, you learned that managerial planning is a conscious, systematic process of deciding which goals and activities the organization will pursue in the future. Directed and controlled by managers, this purposeful effort should draw on the experience and knowledge of employees throughout the organization. As shown in Exhibit 4.1, the Chapter 3 decision-making model links closely to the formal planning process. Strategic planning should be integrated with tactical and operational planning. Before formulating a strategy, managers should analyze the external environment and internal resources, including core capabilities. A firm can concentrate narrowly or broaden its strategy via related or unrelated diversification. Companies can achieve competitive advantage by being unique and differentiated, or by focusing on cost via efficiency and lower prices. Effective implementation is critical to the success of any strategy.

EXHIBIT 4.1 (revisited)

Decision-Making Stages (Chapter 3) and
Formal Planning Steps (Chapter 4)

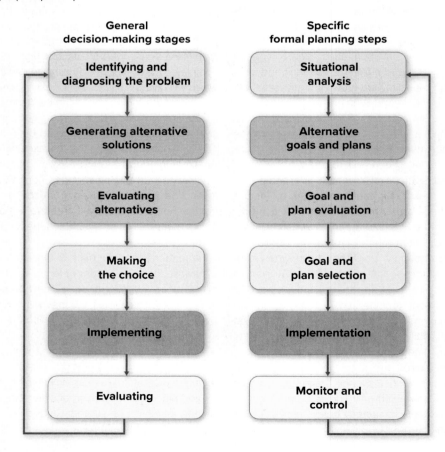

LO 4-1   Summarize the basic steps in any planning process.

- The planning process begins with a situation analysis of the external and internal forces affecting the organization. This examination helps identify and diagnose issues and problems and can bring to the surface alternative goals and plans for the firm.
- The advantages and disadvantages of these goals and plans should be evaluated and compared against one another.
- Implementing goals and plans involves communicating the plan to employees, allocating resources, and making certain that other systems such as rewards and budgets support the plan.
- Control systems to monitor how implementation is faring: progress toward the goals.

LO 4-2   Describe how to integrate strategic planning with tactical and operational planning.

- Strategic planning is different from operational planning in that it involves making long-term decisions about the entire organization.
- Tactical planning translates broad goals and strategies into specific actions to be taken within the organization's subunits.
- Operational planning identifies the specific short-term procedures and processes required at lower levels of the organization.

LO 4-3   Identify elements of the external environment and internal resources of the firm to analyze before formulating a strategy.

- Strategic planning is designed to leverage the strengths of a firm while minimizing the effects of its weaknesses.
- It is difficult to know a firm's potential advantages without a proper internal analysis. Close examine might indicate, for instance, a particularly talented marketing department or a uniquely efficient production system.
- However, managers cannot determine whether internal characteristics are sources of competitive advantage until they learn from external analyses how well competitors compare.

LO 4-4   Define core capabilities and explain how they provide the foundation for business strategy.

- A core competence is something a company does especially well relative to its competitors.
- When this competence is significantly important to market success, it can be a competitive advantage.
- It can provide a sustainable advantage if it is valuable, rare, difficult to imitate, and well organized.

LO 4-5   Summarize the types of choices available for corporate strategy.

- Corporate strategy identifies the breadth of a firm's competitive domain.
- Corporate strategy can be kept narrow, as in a concentration strategy, or can move to suppliers and buyers via vertical integration.
- Corporate strategy also can broaden a firm's domain via concentric (related) diversification or conglomerate (unrelated) diversification.

LO 4-6   Discuss how companies can achieve competitive advantage through business strategy.

- Companies gain competitive advantage in two primary ways. They can attempt to be unique in some way by pursuing a differentiation strategy, or they can focus on efficiency and price by pursuing a low-cost strategy.

LO 4-7   Describe the keys to effective strategy implementation.

- Many good plans fail due to poor implementation.
- Strategy must be actively supported, for example, by structure, technology, human resources, rewards, information systems, culture, and leadership.
- Ultimately, the success of a plan depends on how well employees at low levels are able and willing to implement it.
- Participative management is one important approach to gaining employees' input and commitment to strategy implementation.

DISCUSSION QUESTIONS

1. This chapter opened with a quote stating: "For tomorrow belongs to the people who plan for it today." What does this mean for strategic management?
2. List the six steps in the formal planning process. Suppose you manage a local business and you want to launch a new website. What activities would you carry out during each step to create the site?
3. Your friend is frustrated because he's having trouble selecting a career. He says, "I can't plan because the future is too complicated. Anything can happen, and there are too many choices." What would you say to him to change his mind?
4. How do strategic, operational, and tactical planning differ? How might the three levels complement one another in an organization?
5. How might an organization such as Urban Outfitters use a strategy map? With your classmates and using Exhibit 4.4 as a guide, develop a possible strategy map for the company.

6. What accounts for the shift from strategic planning to strategic management? In which industries or companies is this essential? Why?

7. Review Exhibit 4.6, which lists the components of an environmental analysis. Why is this so vitally important to a company's strategic planning process?

8. What are the core capabilities of Harley-Davidson Motor Company motorcycles? How do these capabilities help Harley-Davidson compete against foreign competitors such as Yamaha and Suzuki?

9. How could SWOT analysis help newspaper companies remain competitive in the new media environment?

10. What are the key challenges in strategy implementation? What are some barriers to success, and what can you do about them?

EXPERIENTIAL EXERCISES

4.1   Business Strategies Need Adjusting

OBJECTIVE

To study why and how a company adjusts its business strategy to adapt to changing external environments.

INSTRUCTIONS

Using an Internet browser or a college's library research portal, identify a recent article from such business news outlets as *The Wall Street Journal, Bloomberg Business, Forbes,* or *Fast Company* that describes a company that is changing its short- and long-term business strategies. Please read the article and provide answers to the following questions:

1. How would you describe the company's former business strategy?

_____

_____

_____

_____

_____

_____

2. Why is the company changing its strategy? What external forces are encouraging it to change?

_____

_____

_____

_____

_____

_____

3. How would you describe the new business strategy?

_____

_____

_____

_____

_____

_____

_____

_____

4. What strategic goals or major targets does the company hope to achieve?

_____

_____

_____

_____

_____

_____

_____

_____

5. How does the company intend to translate its new strategic goals into tactical or operational plans? Which levels of management will carry out these plans?

_____

_____

_____

_____

6. To what extent do you think the new strategy will be successful in addressing or adapting to the external forces? Explain.

SOURCE: Adapted from McGrath, R. R. Jr., *Exercises in Management Fundamentals,* 1st ed. (Upper Saddle River, NJ: Pearson Education, 1985), p. 15.

Concluding Case

WISH YOU WOOD TOY STORE

Wish You Wood is a toy boutique located in the main shopping strip of a resort town near Piney Lake. People who own cabins near the lake or come to visit the local state park enjoy browsing through the town's stores, where they pick up pottery, paintings, and Wish You Wood's beautifully crafted wooden toys. For these shoppers, Wish You Wood is more than a store; it is a destination they associate with family and fun.

The store's owners, Russell and Vanessa Harris, personally select the toys from craftspeople around the world. They enjoy their regular customers but believe selling mostly to vacationers has limited the company's growth. They decided that the lowest-cost way to expand would be to sell toys online. However, after several years of trying, traffic to the store's website was still unimpressive. They were able to drive some business to their site using social media, but the site never took off in the way they had hoped.

Russell and Vanessa concluded that the next-best way to sell online would be to partner with Amazon. Amazon lets other retailers sell products on its site. The Harrises signed an agreement with Amazon to list the store's most popular items. Customers could then purchase Wish You Wood toys right from Amazon's site. Under Amazon's participation agreement, the listings must be honest and may not link to Wish You Wood's own website or invite phone calls from customers. In exchange for giving the products exposure on the site, Amazon charges a monthly fee plus a commission on each sale.

Initially, Russell and Vanessa were thrilled about their decision to partner with Amazon. They tracked each month's sales and compared them with in-store sales. In the first five months, sales jumped 45 percent, mainly because of sales on Amazon. Then, suddenly, sales of its popular toy train sets stopped altogether. Puzzled, Vanessa visited Amazon to make sure the train sets were still listed. To her surprise, she found that the train set was there, at the usual price of $149, listed right after the same set available directly from Amazon at $129. She and Russell concluded that shoppers were now buying the product directly from Amazon. It appeared that their store had helped Amazon identify a product consumers value.

The Harrises worried that they needed a new strategy. If they matched Amazon's price, they would lose most of the profit on their most popular items. Wish You Wood was too small of a business to negotiate better prices from its suppliers. If the store didn't match Amazon's price, it would continue to lose sales to Amazon. Russell and Vanessa wondered whether they should pull out of Amazon altogether or find a way to continue working with the partner that had become a competitor. They also considered rethinking which toys to offer on Amazon.

DISCUSSION QUESTIONS

1. Prepare a SWOT analysis for Wish You Wood, based on the information given. Using the SWOT analysis, what general corporate strategy would you recommend for Wish You Wood?

2. Should the store continue or change its current approach?

ENDNOTES

1. "Disney Sparkles as Most Valuable Media Brand of the Year," *Brand Finance,* https://brandfinance.com/news/press-releases/disney-sparkles-as-most-valuable-media-brand-of-the-year/, accessed February 12, 2019.

2. Frank Pallotta, "Disney's Formula for Rebooting Tales as Old as Time," Clickondetroit.com, March 17, 2017, http://www.clickondetroit.com/entertainment/disneys-formula-for-rebooting-tales-as-old-as-time.

3. J. Bracker and J. Pearson, "Planning and Financial Performance of Small Mature Firms," *Strategic Management Journal* 7 (1986), pp. 503–22; P. Waalewijn and P. Segaar, "Strategic Management: The Key to Profitability in Small Companies," *Long Range Planning* 26, no. 2 (April 1993), pp. 24–30.

4. C. Wolf and S. W. Floyd, "Strategic Planning Research: Toward a Theory-Driven Agenda," *Journal of Management* 43 (2017), pp. 1754–88.

5. D. Welch, "GM Doubles Profit in North America to Record on Truck Surge," *Bloomberg Business,* July 23, 2015, http://www.bloomberg. com; S. Terlep, "GM Caps Profitable Year," *The Wall Street Journal,* February 24, 2011, http://online.wsj.com; B. Cox, "For Big Three Automakers, an Unlikely Time for a Turnaround," *Fort Worth Star-Telegram,* April 15, 2011, http://www.star-telegram.com; D. Barkholz, "Dealers: We Want More Cars!" *Automotive News,* August 23, 2010, Business & Company Resource Center, http://galenet.galegroup.com.

6. See company website, "2018 Global Responsibility Report," https:// corporate.walmart.com, accessed February 25, 2019.

7. Company press release, "GM and Lyft to Shape the Future of Mobility," January 4, 2016, www.media.gm.com.

8. "GM and Lyft Plan to Deploy Thousands of Self-Driving Chevy Bolts," *Fortune,* February 17, 2017, www.fortune.com.

9. A. Ohnsman, "Honeymoon's Over? GM Cruise Said to Turn to Uber as Lyft Alliance Cools," *Forbes,* October 18, 2017, www.forbes.com; M. Wayland, "GM–Lyft Relationship? It's Complicated," *Automotive News,* December 11, 2017, www.autonews.com; B. Clerkin, "After $500M Investment, GM Cools on Lyft," DMV.org, June 25, 2018, www.dmv.org.

10. https://www.sec.gov/cgi-bin/viewer?action=view&cik= 353278&accession_number= 0001628280-19-000870&xbrl_type=v#, accessed March 11, 2019.

11. Company website, "Triple Bottom Line," http://www.novonordisk-us.com, accessed March 11, 2019.

12. Company website, "2018 Annual Report," http://www.novonordisk-us.com, accessed March 11, 2019.

13. "Disney Sparkles as Most Valuable Media Brand of the Year," *Brand Finance,* https://brandfinance.com/news/press-releases/disney-sparkles-as-most-valuable-media-brand-of-the-year/, accessed February 12, 2019.

14. C. Wolf and S. W. Floyd, "Strategic Planning Research: Toward a Theory-Driven Agenda," *Journal of Management* 43, no. 6 (2017), pp. 1754–88.

15. D. C. Hambrick and J. W. Fredrickson, "Are You Sure You Have a Strategy?" *Academy of Management Executive* 19, no. 4 (2005), pp. 51–62.

16. Brendan Byrnes, "Playing to Win: How Procter & Gamble Inc. Eased Its Market Cap by $100 Billion," *The Motley Fool,* February 27, 2013, http://www.fool.com(interview with Roger Martin); unsigned review of *Playing to Win: How Strategy Really Works,* by A. G. Lafley and Roger Martin, *The Economist,* January 12, 2013, http://www.economist.com; Dan Schawbel, "A. G. Lafley: Develop a Strategy to Win at Business," *Forbes,* February 5, 2013, http://www.forbes.com (interview with A. G. Lafley).

17. "Olay: Advertising and Marketing Assignments," *Adbrands,* January 19, 2019, www.adbrands.net.

18. C. Wolf and S. W. Floyd, "Strategic Planning Research: Toward a Theory-Driven Agenda," *Journal of Management* 43, no. 6 (2017), pp. 1754–88.

19. K. Hardy, "How to Prevent Another Chipotle," *QSR Magazine,* May 2016, www.qsrmagazine.com.

20. A. Carr, "Recovery Efforts Stalled, Chipotle Faces Challenges That Go Well beyond Food Safety," *Fast Company,* December 14, 2016, www.fastcompany.com.

21. K. Hardy, "How to Prevent Another Chipotle," *QSR Magazine,* May 2016, www.qsrmagazine.com.

22. A. Carr, "Recovery Efforts Stalled, Chipotle Faces Challenges That Go Well Beyond Food Safety," *Fast Company,* December 14, 2016, www.fastcompany.com.

23. Neuman, "Chipotle to Retrain Employees after Latest Outbreak of Food Poisoning," NPR, August 17, 2018, www.npr.org.

24. Whole Foods Market.

25. R. Kaplan and D. Norton, "Plotting Success with 'Strategy Maps,'" *Optimize,* February 2004, http://www.optimizemag.com; R. S. Kaplan and D. P. Norton, "Having Trouble with Your Strategy? Then Map It," *Harvard Business Review,* September–October 2000.

26. M. Randall, "Employees Can't Carry Out a Strategy If They Didn't Help Plan It," *Business Insider,* July 1, 2013, www.businessinsider.com; J. L. Bower and C. G. Gilbert, "How Managers' Everyday Decisions Create or Destroy Your Company's Strategy," *Harvard Business Review,* February 2007, pp. 72–79; "Business: Fading Fads," *The Economist,* April 22, 2000, pp. 60–61.

27. S. W. Floyd and P. J. Lane, "Strategizing throughout the Organization: Management Role Conflict in Strategic Renewal," *Academy of Management Review* 25, no. 1 (January 2000), pp. 154–77.

28. B. Wooldridge, T. Schmid, and S. Floyd, "The Middle Management Perspective on Strategy Process: Contributions, Synthesis, and Future Research," *Journal of Management* 34 (2008), pp. 1190–1221.

29. Mission statements quoted from the organizations' websites: TED, "About," www.ted.com; Google, "Our Mission," www.google.com; Starbucks, "Our Company," www.starbucks.com.

30. See city website, "A Vision for Austin's Future," www.austintexas.gov.

31. J. O'Callaghan, "Will SpaceX Really Be Flying People to Mars in 10 Years?" *Forbes,* December 14, 2018, www.forbes.com; A. Yuhas, "SpaceX to Send Two People around the Moon Who Paid for a 2018 Private Mission," *The Guardian,* February 28, 2017, www.theguardian. com; Company website, "About SpaceX," www.spacex.com/about/; N. Drake, "Elon Musk: A Million Humans Could Live on Mars by the 2060s," *National Geographic,* September 27, 2016, www.nationalgeographic.com.

32. A. A. Thompson and A. J. Strickland III, *Strategic Management: Concepts and Cases,* 8th ed. (New York: Richard D. Irwin, 1995), p. 23; R. Edward Freeman, J. S. Harrison, and A. C. Wicks, *Managing for Stakeholders* (New Haven, CT: Yale University Press, 2007).

33. See company website, "About Us," CropEnergies AG, www.cropenergies.com, accessed February 25, 2019.

34. Organizational website, "Landfill Gas Energy Project Data," U.S. Environmental Protection Agency, www.epa.gov, accessed February 25, 2019.

35. "Meet the 2018 CNBC Disruptor 50 Companies," *CNBC,* May 22, 2018, https://www.cnbc.com/2018/05/22/meet-the-2018-cnbc-disruptor-50-companies.html.

36. Elisabeth Briar, "Next Billion-Dollar Startups News: 3-D Printing Startup Markforged Raises $82 Million," *Forbes,* March 20, 2019, https://www.forbes.com/sites/elisabethbrier/2019/03/20/next-billion-dollar-startups-news-3-d-printing-startup-markforged-raises-82-million/#3101b4165fca.

37. Jeff Kerns, "How 3D Printing Is Changing Auto Manufacturing," November 4, 2016, https://www.machinedesign.com/3d-printing/how-3d-printing-changing-auto-manufacturing.

38. D. J. Collis and C. A. Montgomery, *Corporate Strategy: A Resource-Based Approach,* 2nd ed. (New York: McGraw-Hill/Irwin, 2005).

39. R. L. Priem, "A Consumer Perspective on Value Creation," *Academy of Management Review* 32, no. 1 (2007), pp. 219–35.

40. See company website, Salesforce, https://www.salesforce.com, accessed February 26, 2019.

41. See company website, Salesforce, https://www.salesforce.com, accessed February 26, 2019.

42. Fortune's 2019 Best Companies to Work For, *Fortune,* http://fortune. com/best-companies/salesforce/, accessed February 26, 2019.

43. Accenture company report, "Achieving High Performance: The Value of Benchmarking," http://www.accenture.com, accessed March 8, 2015.

44. D. Antons and F. T. Piller, "Opening the Black Box of 'Not Invented Here': Attitudes, Decision Biases, and Behavioral Consequences," *Academy of Management Perspectives* 29 (2015), pp. 195–217.

45. "How Benchmarking Helped Opel Rebound," *Automotive News,* August 1, 2018, www.autonews.com; "As Part of PSA, Opel Discovers the Joy of Collaboration," *Automotive News,* August 6, 2018, www.autonews.com.

46. Company website, "About Next Day Flyers," http://www. nextdayflyers.com, accessed March 8, 2015; R. Myers, "That Sounds Like a Plan," *Inc.* 36 (2014), pp. 90–92.

47. L. Rainee and A. Perrin, "Technology Adoption by Baby Boomers (and Everybody Else)," Pew Research, March 22, 2016, www. pewinternet.org; Company website, "Ernst & Young: Younger Managers Rise in the Ranks: Managing the Generational Mix and Preferred Workplace Perks," http://www.ey.com, accessed March 10, 2015; V. Giang, "Here Are the Strengths and Weaknesses of Millennials, Gen X, and Boomers," *Business Insider,* September 9, 2013, http://www.businessinsider.com.

48. Geoffrey James, "20 Epic Fails in Global Branding," *Inc.,* October 29, 2014, https://www.inc.com/geoffrey-james/the-20-worst-brand-translations-of-all-time.html.

49. Jessi Hempel, "Airbnb's Slow-Moving Mission to Win Over African Americans," *Wired,* July 7, 2018, https://www.wired.com/story/airbnbs-slow-moving-mission-to-win-over-african-americans/.

50. Jessica Guynn, "Airbnb Diversity Chief: Tech Should Reflect 'Diverse Tapestry of America,'" *USA Today,* March 4, 2016, https://www.usatoday.com/story/tech/news/2016/03/04/airbnb-hires-first-chief-diversity-officer-from-peace-corps/81242224/.

51. Shorty Awards, https://shortyawards.com/2nd-socialgood/weaccept, accessed February 24, 2019.

52. Jessi Hempel, "Airbnb's Slow-Moving Mission to Win Over African Americans," *Wired,* July 7, 2018, https://www.wired.com/story/airbnbs-slow-moving-mission-to-win-over-african-americans/.

53. A. Bluestein, "The Success Gene," *Inc.,* April 2008, pp. 83–94.

54. P. Haspeslagh, "Portfolio Planning: Uses and Limits," *Harvard Business Review* 60, no. 1 (1982), pp. 58–67; R. Hamermesh, *Making Strategy Work* (New York: Wiley, 1986); R. A. Proctor, "Toward a New Model for Product Portfolio Analysis," *Management Decision* 28, no. 3 (1990), pp. 14–17.

55. T. Mann and E. Henning, "GE Doubles Down on 3-D Printing with European Deals," *The Wall Street Journal,* September 6, 2016, www.wsj.com; D. Weston, "GE Acquires LM Wind Power," *Wind Power Monthly,* October 11, 2016, www.windpowermonthly.com; J. Wieczner, "Last Big Chunk of GE Capital Sold to Wells Fargo," *Fortune,* October 13, 2015, www.fortune.com; Associated Press, "GE Energy and Other Firms Buy Wind Farms in France," *Bloomberg Businessweek,* January 2, 2013, http://www.businessweek.com.

56. R. Reints, "AT&T to Acquire Company AlienVault," *Fortune,* July 10, 2018, www.fortune.com.

57. M. Porter, *Competitive Advantage* (New York: Free Press, 1985), pp. 11–14.

58. F. F. Suarez and G. Lanzolla, "The Role of Environmental Dynamics in Building a First Mover Advantage Theory," *Academy of Management Review* 32, no. 2 (2007), pp. 377–92.

59. Company website, Investor Presentation Q3, January 3, 2016, www.investors.bloominbrands.com.

60. See company website, "Microsoft AnnualReport 2018," www.microsoft.com, accessed February 26, 2019.

61. R. A. Eisenstat, "Implementing Strategy: Developing a Partnership for Change," *Planning Review,* September–October 1993, pp. 33–36.

62. Robert Niles, "Disney CEO Calls Construction of New Theme Parks 'Inevitable,'" *Theme Park Insider,* May 8, 2018, https://www.themeparkinsider.com/flume/201805/6092/.

63. Brooks Barnes, "Disney's Profit Soars, but Focus Remains on Its Coming Streaming Service," *The New York Times,* November 8, 2018, https://www.nytimes.com/2018/11/08/business/media/disney-earnings-streaming-service.html.

CHAPTER 5
Ethics, Corporate Responsibility, and Sustainability

Trust and integrity are precious resources, easily squandered, hard to regain.

—Sissela Bok

xtock/Shutterstock

learning objectives

After studying Chapter 5, you will be able to:

LO 5-1   Describe how different ethical perspectives guide decision making.

LO 5-2   Explain how companies influence their ethics environment.

LO 5-3   Outline a process for making ethical decisions.

LO 5-4   Summarize the important issues surrounding corporate social responsibility.

LO 5-5   Discuss reasons for businesses' growing interest in the natural environment.

LO 5-6   Identify actions managers can take to manage with the environment in mind.

chapter outline

Ethics
   Ethical Systems
   Business Ethics
   The Ethics Environment
   Ethical Decision Making
   Courage

Corporate Social Responsibility
   Contrasting Views
   Reconciliation

The Natural Environment and Sustainability
   A Risk Society
   Sustainable Growth
   Environmental Agendas for the Future

Management in Action

GINNI ROMETTY: TRYING TO TRANSFORM IBM AND THE WORLD

The standard for principled leadership is set high for IBM's chief executive, Ginni Rometty. Rometty took charge of IBM upon the 2012 retirement of the widely admired Sam Palmisano, who, in the wake of the economic collapse that triggered the Great Recession, saw an opportunity for the company to distinguish itself by committing to helping clients and building relationships based on trust and personal responsibility.

In an expression of Palmisano's values-based vision, IBM began to use the tagline "Smarter Planet." IBM would help companies, cities, and communities around the world make better decisions aimed at improving business results, living conditions, and the health of the planet. Palmisano's vision set IBM on course for years of growth, as businesses, city governments, and non-governmental organizations saw how the company could help them meet their goals.

When Rometty took over in 2012, she saw the Smarter Planet strategy as positioning IBM for a future in which (1) data will drive more decisions, (2) cloud computing will transform how industries operate, and (3) mobile and social media will facilitate personalized user engagement.[1] In a world of big data, billions of social media users worldwide, and businesses turning to cloud computing services, clearly Rometty's vision was on target.

Rometty has led IBM, a company founded in 1911 in the era of the Model-T Ford, through an unprecedented shift away from legacy hardware and services to business initiatives that can harness new technologies and transform the planet for the better. To do so, Rometty

Feature Photo Service for IBM/AP Images

recently made a $34 billion investment with the purchase of Red Hat, a firm that specializes in distributing open-source cloud technology.[2]

Rometty believes that together with Red Hat, IBM can become a leader in what's being called a hybrid cloud—a cloud computing system that will allow businesses to share and use data across public and private platforms. While it's a complex and risky undertaking, a refined, fully functioning hybrid cloud is expected to enable data and resource sharing and accessibility in a way that has never been possible—making for a Smarter Planet.

At the 2019 Consumer Electronics Show, Rometty said that to be trusted means that "you have to prepare society for whatever set of technologies it is that are coming along."[3] IBM's perfecting of the hybrid cloud would do just that.

IBM has shown that business success can grow out of values that emphasize focusing on the needs of others. As you read this chapter, think about how well IBM's values-driven approach positions the company to be ethical and successful.

How would you measure the success of a company such as IBM? By this quarter's profits and its value in the stock market? By the degree of trust people place in its managers and consultants? By the good it does in improving quality of life by helping people make better decisions? Although a company might enjoy high profits in one quarter without these virtues, many argue that in the long run, all these measures of success are interdependent and essential.

This chapter addresses the values and manner of doing business adopted by managers as they carry out their corporate and business strategies. In particular, we will explore ways of applying **ethics**, the system of rules that governs the ordering of values. We do so based on the premise that managers, their organizations, and their communities thrive over the long term when they apply ethical standards that direct them to act with integrity.

We also consider the idea that organizations and their managers have a responsibility[4] to meet social obligations beyond earning profits within legal and ethical constraints. As you study this chapter, consider what kind of manager you want to be. What reputation do you hope to have? Would you prefer that others mention you as a notably ethical manager? It's your call as to whether and how to make that a priority.

ethics

The system of rules that governs the ordering of values; see also *corporate social responsibility*.

It's a Big Issue

Scandals periodically engulf company executives, independent auditors, politicians and regulators, and shareholders and employees.[5] In some, executives at public companies make misleading statements to inflate stock prices, undermining the public's trust in the integrity of the financial markets. Often the scandals are perpetrated by a number of people cooperating with one another, and many of the guilty parties had been otherwise upstanding individuals. Lobbyists have been accused—and some convicted—of buying influence with lavish gifts to politicians. Executives have admitted to bribing representatives of foreign governments in order to secure large sales contracts.

What recent news disturbs you about managers' behavior? Tainted products in the food supply . . . actions that harm the environment . . . Internet hacks and scams . . . scandals in sports . . . employees pressured to meet sales or production targets by any means? The list goes on, and the public becomes cynical. In a 2018 survey by public relations firm Edelman, only about 44 percent of respondents trusted business leaders to be good stewards of their organizations.[6]

> Temptations exist in every organization and at every level.

When corporations behave badly, it's often not the top executives but the rank-and-file employees who suffer most. For example, Wells Fargo's leaders created a sales incentive system that strongly encouraged cross-selling (example: the bank's employees were expected to convince a customer with only a savings account to open a checking account). Cross-selling is a common practice, but this program was particularly aggressive. The pressure to reach sales quotas was so high that many employees committed fraud by opening over 3.5 million phony customer accounts—unbeknownst to the customers.[7]

The scandal came to light after some customers complained of being forced to pay fees on accounts they didn't know existed. Wells Fargo paid over $185 million in government fines, and, of course, its reputation as a trusted bank was damaged.[8] After yet another scandal where employees altered documents for mortgage loans, Wells Fargo agreed to pay a $2 billion fine to the Department of Justice.[9]

Other recent corporate scandals include the Facebook–Cambridge Analytica data breach and Apple's slowing down of older iPhones.[10]

Simply talking about famous cases as examples of lax company ethics doesn't get at the heart of the problem. Clearly, these cases have culprits, and their ethical lapses are obvious. But this makes it too easy to simply say "Of course I would never do things like that."

The fact is that temptations exist in every type of work and every organization. Many of the decisions you will face will pose ethical dilemmas, and the right thing to do is not always evident or easy.

It's a Personal Issue

"Answer true or false: 'I am an ethical manager.' If you answered 'true,' here's an uncomfortable fact: You're probably not."[11] These sentences are the first in a *Harvard Business Review* article called "How (Un)Ethical Are You?" The point is that most of us think we are good decision makers, ethical, and unbiased. But the fact is, most people have unconscious biases that favor themselves and their own group. For example, managers often hire people who are like them, think they are immune to conflicts of interest, take more credit than they deserve, and blame others when they deserve some blame themselves.

Knowing that you have biases may help you try to overcome them, but usually that's not enough. Consider the act of telling a lie.[12] Many people lie—some more than others, and in part depending on the situation, usually presuming that they will benefit somehow. At a basic level, we all can make ethical arguments against lying and in favor of honesty. Yet it is useful to think thoroughly about the real consequences of lying.[13] Exhibit 5.1 summarizes the possible outcomes of telling the truth or lying in different situations. People often lie or commit other ethical transgressions somewhat mindlessly, without realizing the full array of negative personal consequences.

Ethics issues are not easy, and not just for newsworthy corporate CEOs. For example, if your employer pays for a laptop computer and the time you spend sitting in front of it, is it ethical for you to use it for tasks unrelated to your work?

What if you stream games for your own and your co-workers' enjoyment, or take a two-hour lunch to locate the best deal on a flat-panel TV? Besides lost productivity, employers are most concerned about computer users spreading viruses, leaking confidential information, and creating a hostile work environment by downloading inappropriate web content.

EXHIBIT 5.1
Possible Outcomes of Lying and Telling the Truth

Reason for the Lie	Results of Lying	Results of Telling the Truth
Negotiation	• Short-term gain and economically positive. • Harms long-term relationship. • Must rationalize to oneself.	• Supports high-quality, long-term relationship. • Develops reputation of integrity. • Models behavior to others.
Conflicting expectations	• Easier to lie than to address the underlying conflict. • Does not solve underlying problem. • Liar must rationalize the lie to preserve positive self-concept.	• Emotionally more difficult than lying. • May correct underlying problem. • Develops one's reputation as an honest person.
To keep a confidence (that may require at least a lie of omission)	• Maintains relationship with the party for whom confidence is kept. • May project deceitfulness to the deceived party.	• Violates a trust to the confiding party. • Makes one appear deceitful to all parties in the long run.
To report your own performance (within an organization)	• Might advance oneself or one's cause. • Develops dishonest reputation over time.	• Creates a reputation of honesty and integrity. • Performance report may not always be positive.

SOURCE: Adapted from Gover, S. L., "The Truth, the Whole Truth, and Nothing but the Truth: The Causes and Management of Workplace Lying," in *The Academy of Management Executive: The Thinking Manager's Source* (Mississippi State, MS: Academy of Management, 2005).

Sometimes employees write blogs or post comments online about their company and its products. Obviously, companies do not want their employees to say bad things about them, but some companies are concerned about employees who are overly enthusiastic. When employees plug their companies and products on comments or review pages, the practice is spamming at best and deceptive if the employees don't disclose their relationship with their company.

It also is deceptive when companies create fictional blogs as a marketing tactic without disclosing their sponsorship, and when they pay bloggers to write positive comments about them–a practice known as "astroturfing" because the "grassroots" interest it builds is fake. Examples include cosmetic company Sunday Riley encouraging employees to post positive reviews and ratings of their beauty products on Sephora's website,[14] and Facebook employees writing 5-star reviews for the Portal video-chat device on Amazon.[15] Managers at the social networking behemoth asked employees to remove the reviews.

Are these examples too small to worry about? No, minor ethical lapses may lead to major problems. This chapter will help you think through decisions with ethical ramifications.

Ethics

ethical issue

Situation, problem, or opportunity in which an individual must choose among several actions that must be evaluated as morally right or wrong.

The aim of ethics is to identify both the rules that should govern people's behavior and the values or "goods" worth pursuing. Ethical decisions are guided by the underlying values of the individual. Values are principles of conduct such as caring, being honest, keeping promises, pursuing excellence, showing loyalty, being fair, acting with integrity, respecting others, and being a responsible citizen.[16]

Most people would agree that all of these values are admirable guidelines for behavior. However, ethics becomes a more complicated issue when a situation dictates that you must chooses one value over others. An **ethical issue** is a situation, problem, or opportunity in which an individual must choose among several actions that must be evaluated as morally right or wrong.[17]

> Ethics becomes a more complicated issue when a situation dictates that you must choose one value over others—for instance, when other people's values differ from yours.

Ethical issues arise in every facet of life; we concern ourselves here with business ethics in particular. **Business ethics** comprise the moral principles and standards that guide behavior in the world of business.[18]

LO 5-1 Describe how different ethical perspectives guide decision making.

Ethical Systems

Moral philosophy refers to the principles, rules, and values people use in deciding what is right or wrong. This is a simple definition in the abstract but often terribly complex and difficult when facing real choices. How do you decide what is right and wrong? Do you know what criteria you apply and how you apply them?

Ethics scholars point to several major ethical systems as potential guides (see Exhibit 5.2).[19] The first, **universalism**, states that all people should uphold certain values, such as honesty, that society needs to function. Universal values are principles so fundamental to human existence that they are important in all societies—for example, rules against murder, deceit, torture, and oppression.

Some efforts have been made to establish global, universal ethical principles for business. The Caux Roundtable, a group of international executives based in Caux,

business ethics

The moral principles and standards that guide behavior in the world of business. See also *ethics*.

moral philosophy

Principles, rules, and values people use in deciding what is right or wrong.

universalism

The ethical system stating that all people should uphold certain values that society needs to function.

EXHIBIT 5.2

Examples of Decisions
Made under Different
Ethical Systems

Universalism	A nonprofit organization treats all of its employees who work in different countries with fairness and dignity.
Egoism	An entrepreneur builds a successful company for personal growth and financial gain; and ultimately, employs thousands of employees.
Utilitarianism	Employees of a mid-sized company, after losing two major customers, accept a 10 percent reduction in salary so no one has to be laid off.
Relativism	A college student refuses to share answers with a fellow student during an exam because her friends would engage in such behavior.
Virtue ethics	A manager believes that it is critical to stand up for what is right and not be unduly influenced by her manager or other organizational pressure.

Switzerland, worked with business leaders from Japan, Europe, and the United States to create the **Caux Principles**. Two basic ethical ideals underpin the Caux Principles: *kyosei* and human dignity. *Kyosei* means living and working together for the common good, allowing cooperation and mutual prosperity to coexist with healthy and fair competition. Human dignity concerns the value of each person as an end, not a means to the fulfillment of others' purposes.

Universal principles can be powerful and useful, but what people say, hope, or think they would do is often different from what they *really* do, faced with conflicting demands in real situations. Different individuals in different circumstances apply different moral philosophies. Consider each of the following moral philosophies and the actions to which they might lead.[20]

Egoism and Utilitarianism   According to **egoism**, acceptable behavior is that which maximizes benefits for the individual. "Doing the right thing," the focus of moral philosophy, is defined by egoism as "do the act that promotes the greatest good for oneself." If everyone follows this system, according to its proponents, the well-being of society as a whole should increase. This notion is similar to Adam Smith's concept of the invisible hand in business. Smith argued that if every organization follows its own economic self-interest, the total wealth of society will be maximized.

Unlike egoism, **utilitarianism** directly seeks the greatest good for the greatest number of people. Consider how utilitarianism might justify laying off about half of the 1,200 workers from the Nabisco plant (maker of Oreos, Chips Ahoy, and Ritz Crackers) in Chicago. The

Employees sometimes feel that "borrowing" a few office supplies from their company helps compensate for any perceived unfairness in pay or other benefits.

allesalltag/Alamy Stock Photo

Caux Principles

A regenerative, collaborative economic system that contrasts with the linear economy described earlier by minimizing input, waste, emissions, and energy leakage.

egoism

An ethical system defining acceptable behavior as that which maximizes consequences for the individual.

utilitarianism

An ethical system stating that the greatest good for the greatest number should be the overriding concern of decision makers.

company moved production to more modern facilities in Mexico. According to Irene Rosenfeld, former CEO of Mondelez International (which owns Nabisco), the move increased efficiency and productivity, two essential ingredients that help Nabisco compete successfully in 165 countries around the world.[21] Maintaining global competitiveness will help ensure that thousands of other Nabisco employees who were not laid off will continue to have jobs and careers with the company.

relativism

Philosophy that bases ethical behavior on the opinions and behaviors of relevant other people.

Relativism   **Relativism** defines ethical behavior based on the opinions and behaviors of relevant other people. In the Nabisco Oreo layoff example, leaders of other U.S. manufacturers (especially bakers) who are operating aging, less efficient facilities are likely to understand and even support the layoffs. However, city officials in Chicago and the plant's laid-off employees would disagree.

Relativism acknowledges the existence of different ethical viewpoints. For example, *norms,* or standards of expected and acceptable behavior, vary from one culture to another. A study of Russian versus U.S. managers found that all followed norms of informed consent about chemical hazards in work situations and paying wages on time. But in Russia more than in the United States, business people were likely to consider the interests of a broader set of stakeholders (in this study, keeping factories open for the sake of local employment), to keep double books to hide information from tax inspectors and criminal organizations, and to make personal payments to government officials in charge of awarding contracts.[22] Relativism defines ethical behavior according to how others behave.

virtue ethics

Perspective that what is moral comes from what a mature person with "good" moral character would deem right.

Virtue Ethics   The moral philosophies just described apply different types of rules and reasoning. **Virtue ethics** is a perspective that goes beyond the conventional rules of society by suggesting that what is moral must come also from what a mature person with good "moral character" would deem right. Society's rules provide a moral minimum, and then moral individuals can transcend rules by applying their personal virtues such as faith, honesty, and integrity.

Kohlberg's model of cognitive moral development

Classification of people based on their level of moral judgment.

Individuals differ in this regard. **Kohlberg's model of cognitive moral development** classifies people into categories based on their level of moral judgment.[23] People in the *preconventional* stage make decisions based on rewards and punishments and immediate self-interest. People in the *conventional* stage conform to the expectations of ethical behavior held by groups or institutions such as society, family, or peers. People in the *principled* stage see beyond authority, laws, and norms and follow their self-chosen ethical principles.[24]

Some people reside forever in the preconventional stage, some move into the conventional stage, and some develop further yet into the principled stage. Over time, and through education and experience, people may change their values and ethical behavior.[25]

These major ethical systems underlie personal moral choices and ethical decisions in business.

LO 5-2 Explain how companies influence their ethics environment.

Business Ethics

Insider trading, sweatshops, and modern slavery;[26] bribery and kickbacks; and other scandals create negative perceptions of business and business leaders. People use illegal and unethical means to beat their rivals,[27] increase profits, or improve their personal positions. Neither young managers nor consumers believe top executives are doing a good job of establishing high ethical standards.[28] Some joke that *business ethics* is a contradiction in terms.

A recent survey found that about half of the employees in large companies have observed misconduct in the workplace.[29] Many people feel ethically conflicted, stressed, and exhausted as companies sometimes encourage them to behave in ways that differ from their own sense of right and wrong.[30] Many managers must deal frequently with ethical dilemmas, and the issues are becoming increasingly complex. For example, many people seek spiritual renewal in the workplace, in part reflecting a broader religious awakening in the United States, whereas others argue that this trend violates religious freedom and the separation of church and boardroom.[31]

Exhibit 5.3 shows some other important examples of ethical dilemmas in business. Think about how you would address each of these issues as a manager. What ethical principles are you applying?

The Ethics Environment

Responding to a series of corporate scandals—particularly the high-profile cases of Enron and WorldCom—Congress passed the **Sarbanes-Oxley Act** in 2002 to improve and maintain investor confidence. The law requires companies to have more independent board directors (not just company insiders), to adhere strictly to accounting rules, and to have senior managers personally sign off on financial results. Violations can result in heavy fines and criminal prosecution. One of the biggest impacts of the law was the requirement for companies and their auditors to provide reports to financial statement users about the effectiveness of internal controls over the financial reporting process.

Companies that make the effort to meet or exceed these requirements can reduce their risks, by lowering the likelihood of misdeeds and the consequences if an employee does break the law.[32] But some executives said Sarbanes-Oxley distracted from their real work and made them more risk-averse. Some complained about the time and money needed to comply with the internal control reporting—millions of dollars at big businesses. But some discovered that the effort helped them avoid mistakes and improve efficiency.

Should pharmaceutical companies be allowed to advertise directly to the consumer if the medicine can be obtained only with a prescription from a doctor? When patients request a particular product, doctors are more likely to prescribe it—even if the patients haven't reported the corresponding symptoms.

John Flournoy/McGraw-Hill Education

Sarbanes-Oxley Act

An act passed into law by Congress to establish strict accounting and reporting rules in order to make senior managers more accountable and to improve and maintain investor confidence.

EXHIBIT 5.3
Some Ethical Issues in Business

CEO pay	What is a fair level of pay for a top executive? Twenty times, or hundreds of times, what the average company worker earns? Whatever other companies want to pay their top executives?
Climate	What is a company's responsibility for its impact on the climate? For example, if operations in one country contribute to rising global temperatures that lead to greater floods in another country, how should the company respond?
Globalization	When a company operates in countries with lower costs, what are its obligations, if any, to the workers in those countries? What standards should it meet for pay rates?
Health care	With health care costs outpacing inflation, employers struggle to cover the cost of health insurance for workers. Are they ethically obligated to provide this benefit?
Obesity	As an obesity epidemic threatens health and adds to health care costs, what role, if any, should employers play in encouraging healthy employee lifestyles?
Online privacy	What obligations do employers have in protecting the privacy of employee information and information about customers?
Social media	What ethical obligations do employees have in commenting about their employer on social media? What ethical obligations do employers have concerning their employees' privacy on social media?
Wages	When adjusted for inflation, the median wage in the United States has fallen over the past decades. What should employers do to promote a sense that their compensation is fair?

Sarbanes-Oxley created legal requirements intended to improve ethical behavior. After his inauguration, President Donald Trump announced that he wanted to ease legal constraints on business, including Wall Street. In 2018, the Federal Reserve Board (led by the president's appointees) signaled its willingness to consider easing rules that are designed to prevent huge losses by banks that make bets with their own capital. Known as the Volcker Rule, the restrictions were implemented in the aftermath of the 2008 financial crisis.[33] This decision to ease constraints will likely have the effect of putting customers' assets at risk.

Maintaining a positive ethical climate is always challenging, but it is especially complex for organizations with international activities.[34] Different cultures and countries may have different standards of behavior, and managers have to decide when relativism is more appropriate than adherence to firm standards. Exchange of courtesies is one thing, but a danger is posed for the unwary business person in areas of the world where bribery and graft are commonplace, which is why Congress passed the Foreign Corrupt Practices Act.

(Un)ethical actions are influenced not only by laws and by individual virtue, but also by the company's work environment. Unethical corporate behavior may be the responsibility of an unethical individual, but it often also reveals a company culture that is ethically lax.[35]

ethical climate

In an organization, the processes by which decisions are evaluated and made on the basis of right and wrong.

The **ethical climate** of an organization refers to the processes by which decisions are evaluated and made on the basis of right and wrong.[36] For employees, the right ethical climate can be a source of ethical personal actions plus pride, satisfaction, and commitment to the employer, while the wrong climate will cause unethical behavior or dissatisfaction and quitting.[37]

Whether or not you want to do much volunteer work, it could be of interest to learn about employers' volunteerism climates. Most volunteer work stems from individuals' personal commitment to and passion for a cause, but some companies create policies that encourage and support volunteer activities off or on company time.[38] And, whereas you might want to make your own choices regardless of what your boss and other people think, you might consider also how much they will appreciate or stigmatize the volunteer work that you do.[39]

Several years ago at California-based Nvidia, the IT firm decided to forgo holiday parties to spend the money and time giving facelifts to schools in the community. Employees have made untold donations of new lawn and upkeep equipment and logged thousands of hours applying new paint, adding sod, and creating murals. In an annual event called "Project Inspire" employee teams volunteer to improve local high school classrooms and playgrounds. It's not surprising Nvidia ranked in the top five in *Fortune*'s "The 50 Best Workplaces for Giving Back" in 2018.[40]

Danger Signs   Maintaining consistent ethical behavior by all employees is an ongoing challenge. What are some danger signs that an organization may be allowing or even encouraging unethical behavior? Exhibit 5.4 lists many factors that could create a climate conducive to unethical behavior.[41]

Regardless of your employer's ethical climate, you are responsible for the decisions you make. It's said that your reputation is your most precious asset. Here's a suggestion: When making decisions, explicitly consider their impact on your personal reputation.

You can have strong personal character, but if you "manage" ethics only by benign neglect, you won't develop a reputation as an ethical leader. Here's another suggestion

EXHIBIT 5.4

Danger Signs of Unethical Behavior in Your Organization

1. Excessive emphasis on **short-term revenues** over longer-term considerations.
2. Failure to establish a **written code of ethics.**
3. A desire for simple, **quick-fix solutions** to ethical problems.
4. An **unwillingness** to take an ethical stand that imposes financial costs.
5. Consideration of ethics solely as a **legal issue** or a public relations tool.
6. **Lack of clear procedures** for handling ethical problems.
7. Responding to the **demands of shareholders** at the expense of other constituencies.

if you want to take ethics to the next level: Set a goal for yourself to be seen by others as both a moral person and as a moral manager—someone who influences others to behave ethically. When you are both personally moral and a moral manager, you will truly be an **ethical leader**.[42]

ethical leader

One who is both a moral person and a moral manager influencing others to behave ethically.

Corporate Ethical Standards   To create a culture that encourages ethical behavior, managers must be more than ethical people. They also should lead others to behave ethically.[43] Ethics is an integral part of the culture at 3M. Kristen Ludgate, Associate General Counsel and Chief Compliance Officer, commented: "At 3M, it's not enough to just win in business—it matters how you do it."[44] Employees are expected to follow the 3M Code of Conduct when making decisions and to ask questions when unsure about something. The $30 billion science-based company has been recognized numerous times on *Ethisphere*'s list of World's Most Ethical Companies.[45]

> Fear of exposure compels people more strongly in some cultures than in others.

OshKosh provides questions for employees to ask themselves when facing ethical decisions: "Are my actions legal?" "Am I being fair, honest and ethical?" "Will I sleep soundly tonight?" and "What would I tell my child to do?" The implication: If you wouldn't want a decision highlighted in the media, then don't do it.[46] This "light of day" or "sunshine" ethical framework can be a powerful influence.

Such fear of exposure compels people more strongly in some cultures than in others. In some Asian countries, anxiety about losing face often makes executives resign immediately if they are caught in ethical transgressions or if their companies are embarrassed by revelations in the media. By contrast, in the United States, exposed executives might respond with indignation, intransigence, pleading the Fifth Amendment, stonewalling, and mounting an everyone-else-does-it self-defense, or by not admitting wrongdoing and giving no sign that resignation ever crossed their minds. Partly because of legal tradition, the attitude often is never explain, never apologize, don't admit the mistake, and do not resign, even if the entire world knows exactly what happened.[47]

Ethics Codes   The Sarbanes-Oxley Act required public companies periodically to disclose whether they have adopted a code of ethics for senior financial officers—and if not, why not. Often such statements are just for show, but when implemented well, they can

The Digital World

How Digital Monitoring Helps Ensure Ethics

While corporate HR programs work hard to ensure that employees are behaving ethically, some companies use technology to enforce compliance and limit their liability if a violation occurs.[48] For example, most companies have a policy stating that they can monitor content on company-provided computers, phones, tablets, email, and other Internet-based activities.

Goldman Sachs's compliance department takes digital monitoring a step further by examining all employee email and social media with an algorithm that looks for key words, which, when flagged, receive additional scrutiny to determine if there is an issue. Employees sign a release stating that they are aware emails are reviewed. Examples of words and phrases monitored are "worst investment," "I trusted you," and various types of profanity.[49]

Although employees may not like such monitoring, companies indeed have the right to monitor devices that use the organization's accounts, provided they inform employees. Experts suggest that to stay out of trouble, you should treat every message you send from a company account as if it may be monitored by others.[50]

1. How would you feel knowing your messages are being monitored at work?
2. What ethical implications for the employee–employer relationship does such surveillance pose?

change a company's ethical climate for the better and truly encourage ethical behavior. Executives say they pay most attention to their company's code of ethics when they feel that stakeholders (customers, investors, lenders, and suppliers) try to influence them to do so, to promote a positive image.[51]

Most ethics codes address subjects such as employee conduct, community and environment, shareholders, customers, suppliers and contractors, political activity, and technology. The nonprofit Ethics Resource Center conducts research and assists companies interested in establishing a corporate code of ethics.[52]

Ethics codes must be carefully written and tailored to individual companies' philosophies. Exhibit 5.5 reprints the Commitments section of The Hershey Company's code of ethics.

To make an ethics code effective, do the following: (1) Involve those who have to live with it in writing the statement; (2) focus on real-life situations that employees can relate to; (3) keep it short and simple, so it is easy to understand and remember; (4) write about values and shared beliefs that are important and that people can really believe in; and (5) set the tone at the top, having executives talk about and live up to the statement.[53]

When reality differs from the statement—as when a motto says people are our most precious asset or a product is the finest in the world, but in fact people are treated poorly or product quality is weak—the statement becomes a joke to employees rather than a guiding light.

Ethics Programs   Corporate ethics programs commonly include formal ethics codes that articulate the company's expectations: ethics committees that develop policies, evaluate actions, and investigate violations; ethics communication systems that give employees a means of reporting problems or getting guidance; ethics officers or ombudspersons who investigate allegations and provide education; ethics training programs; and disciplinary processes for addressing unethical behavior.[54]

EXHIBIT 5.5

The Hershey Company's Ethical Commitments

> We have each made a commitment to operate ethically and to lead with integrity. This commitment is embedded in the Hershey values. Our Code of Ethical Business Conduct ("Code") shows us how to uphold this commitment as we interact with the various groups that have a stake in our Company's success.

OUR COMMITMENT TO FELLOW EMPLOYEES

We treat one another fairly and with respect, valuing the talents, experiences and strengths of our diverse workforce.

OUR COMMITMENT TO CONSUMERS

We maintain the trust consumers place in our brands, providing the best products on the market and adhering to honest marketing practices.

OUR COMMITMENT TO THE MARKETPLACE

We deal fairly with our business partners, competitors and suppliers, acting ethically and upholding the law in everything we do.

OUR COMMITMENT TO STOCKHOLDERS

We act honestly and transparently at all times, maintaining the trust our stockholders have placed in us.

OUR COMMITMENT TO THE GLOBAL COMMUNITY

We comply with all global trade laws, protecting our natural resources and supporting the communities where we live, work and do business.

SOURCE: The Hershey Company, "Code of Ethical Business Conduct." Accessed March 20, 2015. http://www.thehersheycompany.com. All rights reserved. Used with permission.

Ethics programs can range from compliance-based to integrity-based.[55] **Compliance-based ethics programs** are designed by corporate counsel to prevent, detect, and punish legal violations. Program elements include establishing and communicating legal standards and procedures, assigning high-level managers to oversee compliance, auditing and monitoring compliance, reporting criminal misconduct, punishing wrongdoers, and taking steps to prevent offenses in the future.

Such programs can reduce illegal behavior and help a company stay out of court. But as a former chair of the Securities and Exchange Commission said, "It is not an adequate ethical standard to aspire to get through the day without being indicted."

Integrity-based ethics programs go beyond the mere avoidance of illegality; they are concerned with the law but also with instilling in people a personal responsibility for ethical behavior. With such a program, companies and people govern themselves through a set of guiding principles that they embrace.

For example, the Americans with Disabilities Act (amended in 2008) required companies to change the physical work environment so it will allow people with disabilities to function on the job. Mere compliance would involve making the changes necessary to avoid legal problems. Integrity-based programs would go further by training people to understand and perhaps change attitudes toward people with disabilities, and sending clear signals that people with disabilities also have valued abilities. This effort goes far beyond taking action to stay out of trouble with the law.[56]

compliance-based ethics programs

Company mechanisms typically designed by corporate counsel to prevent, detect, and punish legal violations.

integrity-based ethics programs

Company mechanisms designed to instill in people a personal responsibility for ethical behavior.

Ethical Decision Making

LO 5-3 Outline a process for making ethical decisions.

We've said it's not easy to make ethical choices. Such decisions are complex.[57] For starters, you may face pressures that are difficult to resist. Furthermore, it's not always clear that a problem has ethical dimensions; they don't hold up signs that say "Hey, I'm an ethical issue, so think about me in moral terms!"[58]

Making ethical decisions takes moral *awareness* (realizing the issue has ethical implications), moral *judgment* (knowing what actions are morally defensible), and moral *character* (the strength and persistence to act in accordance with your ethics despite the challenges).[59]

The philosopher John Rawls created a thought experiment based on the "veil of ignorance."[60] Imagine that you are making a decision about a policy that will benefit or disadvantage some groups more than others. For example, a policy might provide extra vacation time for all employees but eliminate flextime, which allows parents of young children to balance their work and family responsibilities. Or you're a university president considering raising tuition or cutting financial support for study abroad.

Now pretend that you belong to one of the affected groups, but you don't know which one—for instance, those who can afford to study abroad or those who can't, or a young parent or a young single person. You won't find out until after the decision is made. How would you decide? Would you be willing to risk being in the disadvantaged group? Would your decision be different if you were in a group other than your own? Rawls maintained that only a person ignorant of his own identity can make a truly ethical decision. A decision maker can apply the veil of ignorance to help minimize personal bias.

Thinking before deciding, and having an ethics-oriented conversation with others, can help you and others make more ethical decisions.[61] You can use the process illustrated in Exhibit 5.6. Understand the various moral standards (universalism, relativism, etc.), as described earlier in the chapter. Go through the problem-solving model from Chapter 3 and recognize the impacts of your alternatives: Which people do they benefit and harm, which are able to exercise their rights, and whose rights are denied? You now know the full scope of the moral problem.

Excuses for unethical behavior often are bogus.[62] "I was told to do it" implies a person has no personal thoughts and blindly obeys. "Everybody's doing it"

Excuses are often bogus.

EXHIBIT 5.6   A Process for Ethical Decision Making

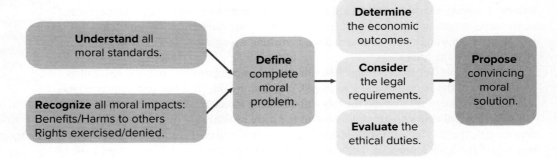

SOURCE: Hosmer, L. T., *The Ethics of Management,* 4th ed. (New York: McGraw-Hill/Irwin, 2003), p. 32. Fig. 5.1A.

Bottom Line

"Costs" aren't exactly synonymous with "ethics." But by considering the potential costs to all parties, you can make high-quality ethical decisions that you can more effectively sell to others. *What are some costs of treating employees or customers unethically?*

often really means that someone is doing it, but it's rarely everybody; regardless, following convention doesn't mean correctness. "Might equals right" is just a rationalization. "It's not my problem" is sometimes a wise perspective, if it's a battle you can't win, but sometimes it's a cop-out. "I didn't mean for that to happen, it just felt right at the time" can be prevented with more forethought and analysis.

You must also consider legal requirements to ensure full compliance, and the economic outcomes of your options, including costs and potential profits.[63] Some are obvious: fines and penalties. Others, such as corrective actions and lower morale, are less obvious. Ultimately, the effects on customers, employees, and others can be huge. Being fully aware of the potential costs can help prevent people from straying into unethical terrain.

Courage

As stated earlier, behaving ethically requires not just moral awareness and moral judgment, but also moral character. It sometimes requires courage to take actions consistent with your ethics when others don't want you to.[64]

Think about how hard it can be to do the right thing.[65] On the job, how hard would it be to walk away from lots of money just to stick to your ethics? To tell colleagues or your boss that you believe they've crossed an ethical line? To disobey a boss's order? To go over your boss's head to someone in senior management with your suspicions about accounting practices? To go outside the company to alert authorities if someone is being hurt and management refuses to correct the problem?

Courage plays a role in the moral awareness involved in identifying an act as unethical, the moral judgment to consider the repercussions fully, and the moral character to take the ethical action. Consider, for example, how difficult it is to deliver unpleasant news, even if you believe that honesty is important and is the way you would want to be treated.

Immediately after being named CEO of General Motors in 2014, Mary Barra was grilled by a Senate investigating committee over the company's handling of a flawed ignition switch linked to 12 deaths. The automaker came under scrutiny after admitting that some employees knew of the problem for a decade. The new CEO took responsibility: "something went wrong with our process in this instance and terrible things happened."[66] Barra went on to attribute the unethical actions to GM's cultural problems and has since devoted herself to transforming it into an organization focused on accountability.[67]

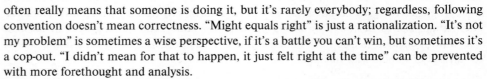

Even more courage is necessary when you decide that the only ethical course of action is *whistleblowing*[68]—telling others, inside or outside the organization, of wrongdoing. The road for whistleblowers is rocky. When whistleblowers

Management in Action

THE STATE OF ETHICS AT IBM

It wasn't long ago that the technology industry was one of the most trusted. Recent concerns about transparency, the handling of personal data, and individual privacy, however, have substantially eroded public trust.[69] In light of these recent trends, IBM CEO Ginni Rometty has some work to do to prevent IBM from being engulfed in this firestorm of controversy.

IBM is trying to tackle this challenge. It has a set of policies aimed at building trust, including a policy for business conduct and ethics and one for protecting data privacy. The ethics policy states, "It is IBM's policy to conduct itself ethically and lawfully in all matters and to maintain IBM's high standards of business integrity."[70] It puts employees on notice that there are consequences for unethical conduct.

IBM's policies also explicitly call for fairness, equity, a commitment to quality, and compliance with laws, including employment and anti-corruption laws. Its data privacy laws call for employees to collect only relevant personal information, keep it as accurate as possible, and take measures to keep it secure, among other requirements.

Compliance with ethical standards is most likely when managers and employees at all levels are committed to the standards. IBM is committed to three stated values:

1. Dedication to every client's success.
2. Innovation that matters, for our company and the world.
3. Trust and personal responsibility in all relationships.[71]

These statements appear on the company's website, where any employee or concerned citizen can be reminded of what IBM is striving to achieve.

Even with formal statements and consequences for behavior, maintaining ethical conduct is a challenge, especially for a global company, because employees encounter differences in standards and practices in other countries. Through the early 2000s and as it began transitioning to a Smarter Planet focus, IBM and some of its employees were involved in a number of bribery and corruption scandals.[72]

In recent years, IBM has seemingly been able to clean up its act. No allegations of ethics violations have emerged in the headlines. Living up to its own code of ethics, however, will require continued vigilance throughout all levels at the company.

- Besides the measures described, how else can IBM promote ethical conduct by its employees?
- In a technology industry that increasingly not only has access to people's personal data but also requires such data in order to innovate and be profitable, how can IBM maintain its ethical responsibility to the planet it's trying to improve?

go public, others often see them as acting against the company's interests. Many, perhaps most, whistleblowers suffer consequences such as being ostracized, treated rudely, or given undesirable assignments.

Some organizations offer channels for employees to report ethics problems so they can deal with them internally. Ideally, the reporting method should keep the whistleblower's identity secret, management should investigate and respond quickly, and there should be no retaliation against whistleblowers who use proper channels.

For ethical managers, the goal is to lead employees to maintain high ethical standards, which creates an environment in which whistleblowing is unnecessary. After reading "Management in Action: Progress Report," consider how IBM promotes ethical conduct and how this might reinforce employees' moral courage.

By the way, you might find a self-SWOT analysis helpful when seeking a job. What are you particularly good at? What weaknesses might you need to overcome to improve your employment chances? What firms offer the best opportunity to apply your skills to full advantage? Who are your competitors? How is your generation perceived in the workplace? As with companies, this kind of analysis can lead to a plan of action that improves your own effectiveness.

Inclusiveness Works

Treating All Employees Equally also Means Paying Them Fairly, without Discrimination

As part of their ethical code of conduct, most firms pledge to treat all employees fairly, yet few incorporate a pledge to *pay* all employees fairly. Currently, on average, women in the United States earn about 80 percent of every dollar men earn. This pay gap persists across almost all occupations and industries, with finance, marketing and sales, and physicians showing the largest disparity.[73] A diversity and inclusion program, therefore, must account for pay inequities.

Although progress has been far from swift, the problem is starting to be addressed. In 2016, the Obama administration enacted the White House Equal Pay Pledge. Companies who signed agreed to "Commit to conducting an annual company-wide gender pay analysis across occupations; reviewing hiring and promotion processes and procedures to reduce unconscious bias and structural barriers; and embedding equal pay efforts into broader enterprise-wide equity initiatives."[74]

Over 100 companies signed on, including Target, MasterCard, International Hotel Group, AT&T, and Adobe. Others, though not signing the pledge, committed to addressing the pay gap.

Adobe, one of the first signatories to the White House pledge, is among a number of companies to issue pay reports about its U.S. workforce. Others include Starbucks, Apple, Intel, and Salesforce.[75] Some best practices for achieving pay equity are emerging.

First and foremost, achieving pay equity has to start at the top. Senior leadership should set the goal and make it a companywide commitment. Implementation and monitoring of the plan must be unbiased and rigorous, with audits using outside experts.[76]

In addition, reporting of the results needs to be clear and transparent. Despite some progress, the pay gap still exists. Citibank, for example, recently reported a median gender pay gap of 29 percent.[77] But if there's a silver lining it's that Citibank reported the disparity itself—and, by doing so, acknowledged the problem. One more small but necessary step to righting this systematic wrong.

1. Why do you think it's rare that companies achieve pay parity? Is it implicit bias, organizational impediments, or something else?
2. What role, if any, do you think government should play in influencing the pay structure of privately owned companies?

Corporate Social Responsibility

LO 5-4 Summarize the important issues surrounding corporate social responsibility.

stewardship

Contributing to the long-term welfare of others.

Stewardship means contributing to the long-term welfare of others.[78] Does business ever operate this way? Consider the following examples:

- IKEA's "War Child" initiative gives children a safe place to play in Middle Eastern conflict zones.
- Starbucks has a goal to hire 10,000 refugees across 75 countries by 2023 and 25,000 veterans by 2025.
- Coca-Cola has donated over $820 million to causes that support women's empowerment, access to clean drinking water, and the development of disadvantaged youth.
- Adidas hosts various events that raise awareness of plastic pollution in the oceans.
- Walt Disney Company's "VoluntEARS" program has a goal of reaching five million hours of employee community service by 2020.[79]

Should business be responsible for social concerns beyond its own economic well-being? Do social concerns affect a corporation's financial performance? In the 1960s and 1970s, the political and social environment became more important to U.S. corporations as society turned its attention to issues such as equal opportunity, pollution control, energy and natural resource conservation, and consumer and worker protection.[80] Public debate addressed these issues and the ways business should respond to them. This controversy focused on the concept of corporate social responsibility.

Corporate social responsibility (CSR) is the obligation toward society assumed by business.[81] Corporate social responsibility reflects the social imperatives and the social consequences of business practices; it consists broadly of policies and practices that reflect business responsibility for some wider societal good.[82] This can range from local or small-scale problems to issues of politics, diplomacy, international relations, and peace through commerce.[83] Interesting questions to contemplate include why past corporate irresponsibilities are easily forgotten, and whether and how current managers of an organization should be held responsible for the irresponsible actions of the managers who came before them.[84]

CSR actions and policies take into account stakeholders' expectations and often consider the **triple bottom line** of economic, social, and environmental performance.[85] The precise policies and practices underlying CSR lie at the discretion of the corporation. Some companies refer to their CSR practices in terms of sustainability, on the grounds that these efforts maintain positive long-term relationships with communities, employees, customers, governments, and the natural environment.[86]

Social responsibilities can be categorized[87] as shown in Exhibit 5.7. The **economic responsibilities** of business are to produce goods and services that society wants at a price that perpetuates the business and satisfies its obligations to investors. For Smithfield Foods, the largest pork producer in the United States, this means selling bacon, ham, and other products to customers at prices that maximize Smithfield's profits and keep the company growing over the long term. Economic responsibility may also extend to offering certain products to needy consumers at a reduced price.

Legal responsibilities are to obey local, state, federal, and relevant international laws. Laws affecting Smithfield cover a wide range of requirements, from filing tax returns to meeting worker safety standards. **Ethical responsibilities** include meeting other societal expectations, not written as law. Smithfield took on this level of responsibility when it responded to requests by major customers, including McDonald's, Walmart, and Safeway, that it discontinue the practice of using gestation crates to house its sows. The customers

corporate social responsibility (CSR)

Obligation toward society assumed by business. See also *ethics*.

triple bottom line

Economic, social, and environmental performance.

economic responsibilities

To produce goods and services that society wants at a price that perpetuates the business and satisfies its obligations to investors.

legal responsibilities

To obey local, state, federal, and relevant international laws.

ethical responsibilities

Meeting other social expectations, not written as law.

EXHIBIT 5.7

Pyramid of Global Corporate Social Responsibility and Performance

Be a good global corporate citizen.   Do what is *desired* by global stakeholders.

Philanthropic responsibility

Be ethical.   Do what is *expected* by global stakeholders.

Ethical responsibility

Obey the law.   Do what is *required* by global stakeholders.

Legal responsibility

Be profitable.   Do what is *required* by global capitalism.

Economic responsibility

SOURCE: Carroll, A., "Management Ethically with Global Stakeholders: A Present and Future Challenge," *Academy of Management Executive: The Thinking Manager's Source* (Mississippi State, MS: Academy of Management, 2004).

were reacting to pressure from animal rights advocates who consider it cruel for sows to live in the two-foot by seven-foot crates during their entire gestation period, which means they cannot walk, turn around, or stretch their legs for months at a time.[88] Smithfield was not legally required to make the change (except in two states), and the arrangement was costly, but the company's decision helped its public image—that is, until it backed out of the plan, citing economic woes.

philanthropic responsibilities

Additional behaviors and activities that society finds desirable and that the values of the business support.

transcendent education

An education with five higher goals that balance self-interest with responsibility to others.

Finally, **philanthropic responsibilities** are additional behaviors and activities that society finds desirable and that the values of the business support. Examples include supporting community projects and making charitable contributions. Philanthropic activities can be more than mere altruism; managed properly, strategic philanthropy can become not an oxymoron but a way to build goodwill in a variety of stakeholders and even add to shareholder wealth.[89]

Many believe that a 21st-century education must help students think about responsibilities beyond self-interest and profitability. Such an education teaches students to leave a legacy that extends beyond the bottom line—a transcendent education.[90] A **transcendent education** has five higher goals that balance self-interest with responsibility to others: *empathy* (feeling your decisions as potential victims might feel them, to gain wisdom), *generativity* (learning how to give as well as take, to others in the present as well as to future generations), *mutuality* (viewing success not merely as personal gain, but a common victory), *civil aspiration* (thinking not just in terms of don'ts [lie, cheat, steal, kill], but also in terms of positive contributions), and *intolerance of inhumanity* (speaking out against unethical actions).

> A transcendent education teaches students to leave a legacy that extends beyond the financial bottom line.

Contrasting Views

Two basic and contrasting views describe principles that guide managerial responsibility. The first holds that managers act as agents for shareholders and, as such, are obligated to maximize the present value of the firm. This tenet of capitalism is widely associated with the early writings of Adam Smith in *The Wealth of Nations* and later with Milton Friedman, the Nobel Prize–winning economist of the University of Chicago. With his now-famous dictum, "The social responsibility of business is to increase profits," Friedman contended that organizations may help improve the quality of life as long as such actions are directed at increasing profits.

Some considered Friedman to be "the enemy of business ethics," but his position was ethical: he believed that it was unethical for unelected business leaders to decide what was best for society and unethical for them to spend shareholders' money on projects unconnected to key business interests.[91] Furthermore, the context of Friedman's famous statement includes the qualifier that business should increase its profits while conforming to society's laws and ethical customs.

The second perspective, different from the profit maximization perspective, is that managers should be motivated by principled moral reasoning. Adam Smith wrote about a world different from the one we are in now, driven in the 18th century by the self-interest of small owner-operated farms and craft shops trying to generate a living income for themselves and their families. This self-interest was quite different from that of top executives of modern corporations.[92]

It is noteworthy that Adam Smith also wrote *A Theory of Moral Sentiments,* in which he argued that "sympathy," defined as a proper regard for others, is the basis of a civilized society.[93] Smith argued further that "the wise and virtuous man is at all times willing that this own private interest should be sacrificed to public interest" if circumstances require it.[94]

Advocates of corporate social responsibility argue that organizations have a wider range of responsibilities that extend beyond the production of goods and services at a profit. As members of society, organizations should actively and responsibly participate in the community and in the larger environment.

Many people were shocked to hear that Equifax, one of three major consumer credit reporting agencies, didn't prevent hackers from breaching its servers and accessing the personal records of over 145 million Americans. The records contained names, addresses, Social Security numbers, driver's license numbers, and birthdays.[95] A government report into the massive information breach found that out-of-date software was to blame and that the hack went undetected for 76 days.[96] The report also stated that Equifax waited six weeks to tell the public about the breach.[97] By all accounts, the agency should have taken more effective steps to protect the sensitive customer data with which it was entrusted and to promptly alert the public after becoming aware of the breach.

Reconciliation

Profit maximization and corporate social responsibility used to be regarded as antagonistic, leading to opposing policies. The two views seem paradoxical, but they can converge.[98] The Coca-Cola Company set a goal to improve its water efficiency in manufacturing operations by 25 percent over a 10-year period (ending in 2020).[99] The company is improving water efficiency in the production process and treating its wastewater.[100] From a practical perspective, Coca-Cola's planners have identified water shortages as a strategic risk and water stewardship as a major priority. For over 10 years, it has partnered with the World Wildlife Fund to conserve and sustain water resources, especially in water-stressed regions like the Middle East and North Africa. According to Kathryn Casson, Director of Public Affairs, Communications, and Sustainability, "We need business to act as catalysts for change in local watersheds, so that we can create the conditions for collaborative, sustainable management of freshwater resources."[101]

The U.S. Department of Agriculture and Coca-Cola North America are partnering to restore and protect damaged watersheds in national forests.

John Konstantaras/AP Images for Coca-Cola

Earlier attention to corporate social responsibility focused on alleged wrongdoing and how to control it. More recently, attention has also centered on the possible competitive advantage of socially responsible actions.

The relationship between corporate social performance and corporate financial performance is complex;[102] socially responsible organizations are sometimes but not necessarily more or less successful in financial terms.[103] But on net, the accumulated evidence indicates that social responsibility is associated with better financial performance.[104] Companies can avoid unnecessary and costly regulation if they are socially responsible. Such actions also can pay dividends to the conscience, public image, and market response, although engaging in highly controversial activities can have mixed effects on employees and market reactions.[105] Society's problems also can offer business opportunities via vigorous efforts to solve them.

Firms can perform cost–benefit analyses to identify actions that will maximize profits while satisfying the demand for corporate social responsibility from multiple stakeholders.[106] In other words, managers can treat corporate social responsibility as they would treat all investment decisions. This has been the case as firms attempt to reconcile their business practices with their effect on the natural environment.

The Natural Environment and Sustainability

Most large corporations developed in an era of abundant raw materials, cheap energy, and unconstrained waste disposal.[107] But many of the technologies developed during this era have contributed to the destruction of ecosystems. Industrial-age systems follow a linear flow of extract, produce, sell, use, and discard—what some call a take–make–waste approach.[108]

At the same time, perhaps no time in history has offered greater possibilities for a change in business thinking than the 21st century. Some maintain that ecological sustainability

LO 5-5 Discuss reasons for businesses' growing interest in the natural environment.

> Business used to look at environmental issues as a no-win situation, but now a paradigm shift is taking place.

is now the key driver of innovation.[109] And, whereas some are pessimistic about the planet's future, many are both resolute about creating a healthier planet, and more optimistic now than in recent years. One such optimist is Sanjit Bunker Roy, creator of India's Barefoot College (featured in the nearby "Social Entrepreneurship" box).

Business used to look at environmental issues as a no-win situation; you either help the environment and hurt your business or help your business at a cost to the environment. But now a paradigm shift is taking place in corporate environmental management: the deliberate incorporation of environmental values into competitive strategies and into the design and manufacturing of products.[110] In addition to philosophical reasons, companies go green to satisfy consumer demand, to react to a competitor's actions, to meet requests from customers or suppliers, to comply with legal requirements, and to create competitive advantage.

GE used to view environmental rules as a burden and a cost; now it sees environmentally friendly technologies as one of the global economy's most significant business opportunities.

Social Entrepreneurship

A College Built by and for the Poor

India's Barefoot College is an educational organization working in 1,300 villages across nearly 96 of the world's least developed countries in Asia, Africa, the Pacific islands, and South America. Its mission is to improve rural lives and communities through learning-by-doing training programs in health care, women's empowerment, solar energy, water, and land development that are designed and built by and for the poor.[111]

Barefoot College is based on the guiding principles of service and sustainability espoused by Mahatma Gandhi, along with a commitment to equality, shared decision making, and self-reliance. Its projects have brought artificial light to more than a million people and provide clean water and solar energy for cooking and heating to thousands of communities. Its Enriche program is dedicated to using simple methods to empower rural women of all ages, even if illiterate, with the scientific and engineering skills they need to undertake environmental stewardship, manage solar energy, and protect women's reproductive health.

Each woman in the program is trained to teach others in turn. Those trained in the six-month solar energy program in Tilonia, India, come from around the world. They receive fellowship grants from the Indian government while enrolled and leave with a stipend for starting their own business.

Founder Sanjit Bunker Roy, educated in Delhi, was from a wealthy background, but in his 20s he decided to try living on $1 a day. Based on that experience, as a young social worker in 1972 he was inspired to create Barefoot College, which he calls "the only College where the teacher is the learner and the learner the teacher."[112] He has been honored by *Time* magazine

Ashley Cooper pics/Alamy Stock Photo

for his "grass roots social entrepreneurship" and was *Business Standard*'s 2016 Social Entrepreneur of the Year. Says Roy, "People find something in themselves that they never thought they had. And then go back to the communities they are from and show what they learned—that's how leaders are born."[113]

By educating more than 7,000 children from impoverished rural villages each year, Barefoot College is doing its part to give birth to a new generation of leaders.

1. In what ways do you think Barefoot College's mission and goals demonstrate a utilitarian philosophy of ethics?
2. Which of Barefoot College's guiding principles have you observed where you have worked or volunteered?

Since launching its Ecomagination program in 2004, GE has invested over $20 billion in clean tech R&D that is helping address environmental challenges. Its solutions include wind turbines, materials for solar energy cells, and energy-efficient home appliances. These have delivered $270 billion in revenue, a green image for the GE brand, and a leadership position in many rapidly growing markets including high-efficiency jet engines and locomotives.[114]

A Risk Society

We live in a risk society. That is, the creation and distribution of wealth generate by-products that can cause injury, loss, or danger to people and the environment.[115] The fundamental sources of risk in modern society are the excessive production of hazards and ecologically unsustainable consumption of natural resources.[116] Risk has proliferated through population explosion, industrial pollution, and environmental degradation.[117]

Industrial pollution risks include air pollution, smog, global warming, ozone depletion, acid rain, toxic waste sites, nuclear hazards, obsolete weapons arsenals, industrial accidents, and hazardous products. Tens of thousands of uncontrolled toxic waste sites have been documented in the United States alone. The situation is far worse in some other parts of the world. The pattern, for toxic waste and many other risks, is one of accumulating risks and inadequate remedies.

The institutions that create environmental and technological risk (corporations and government agencies) are responsible for controlling and managing the risks.[118] Patagonia admits openly that its business activities (its factories use water and release carbon into the air) contribute to climate change. The company uses this factual acknowledgment to do whatever is within its control to "reduce, neutralize, or even reverse the root causes of climate change."[119]

Some of the world's worst environmental problems are in China because of its rapid industrialization and its huge population and size. The smog in Beijing is so unhealthy on certain days that the government closes factories and schools and bans half the vehicles until the pollution level drops.[120] One study by the Health Effects Institute (HEI) found that China has about 1.6 million premature deaths per year due to its air pollution.[121] The country's environmental problems affect more than large cities. Hundreds of millions of China's rural population drink unclean water. At least the problem is recognized; the central government is pressuring local authorities to clean up or shut down dirty factories.[122] Still, most cleanup efforts focus on big cities while rural areas worsen.

Developing countries are often seen as sustainability laggards, focused solely on raising people out of poverty. Regulatory agencies can be weak and hesitant to impose restrictions, but visionary individuals the world over can pioneer successful sustainability efforts.[123]

Sustainable Growth

Sustainable growth is economic growth and development that meet the organization's present needs without harming the ability of future generations to meet their needs.[124] Sustainability is fully compatible with the natural ecosystems that generate and preserve life.[125]

Businesses are both a cause of and a solution to environmental degradation, and clearly have a major role to play in sustainability debates and strategies.[126]

Increasingly, firms are paying attention to their total environmental impact throughout the life cycle of their products.[127] **Life-cycle analysis (LCA)** is a process of analyzing all inputs and outputs, through the entire cradle-to-grave life of a product, to determine the total environmental impact of the production and use of a product. LCA quantifies the total use of resources and the releases into the air, water, and land. Reporting worldwide **carbon footprints** is a big step in environmental reporting in that industry. Previously mentioned apparel maker Patagonia uses LCA to analyze the carbon footprint at each stage of its supply chain from farm to factory.[128]

LCA considers the extraction of raw materials, product packaging, transportation, and disposal. Consider packaging alone. Goods make the journey from manufacturer to wholesaler to retailer to customer; then they are recycled back to the manufacturer. They may be packaged and repackaged several times, from bulk transport, to large crates, to cardboard boxes, to individual consumer sizes. Repackaging not only creates waste but also costs time. The design of initial packaging in sizes and formats adaptable to the final customer can minimize the need for repackaging, cut waste, and realize financial benefits.

LO 5-6 Identify actions managers can take to manage with the environment in mind.

sustainable growth

Economic growth and development that meets present needs without harming the needs of future generations.

life-cycle analysis (LCA)

A process of analyzing all inputs and outputs, through the entire "cradle-to-grave" life of a product, to determine total environmental impact.

carbon footprint

The output of carbon dioxide and other greenhouse gases.

Timberland pays particular attention to life-cycle analysis, as implied by this question on its recycled material shoe boxes.

Jill Braaten/McGraw-Hill Education

Bottom Line

Packaging isn't the most glamorous of business topics, but it holds great potential for reducing costs and increasing speed while helping the environment. You can always find opportunities to improve results in unexpected places where others haven't tried. *Think of a product you recently purchased that seemed to have excess packaging. How could its packaging be made more environmentally friendly?*

Rather than the linear take–make–waste production model described earlier, a fully sustainable model applies a circular borrow–use–return approach.[129] Whereas the former model engages in harmful extraction, generates huge quantities of waste and pollution, and depletes natural resources (a process in which resources move from cradle to grave), the cradle-to-cradle approach is ecologically benign and restorative. In its ideal form, this sustainable approach extracts energy and raw materials without harm, phases out the use of nonrenewable resources, designs processes and products that recirculate so they don't cause environmental or socioeconomic harm, keeps toxic substances in closed-loop industrial cycles, and recirculates biological materials back.

Companies can integrate such green practices with strategy in a variety of ways. Certainly they develop and market green products; Toyota's bold move to develop the Prius paid off handsomely with early market dominance.[130] Companies also can emphasize green attributes in their marketing but need to avoid misleading claims (greenwashing) and public backlash. For instance, Warren Buffett's MidAmerican Energy Co. stated that it would soon be the first U.S. utility with 100 percent renewable energy. However, management left out the fact that this claim relied on a wind farm that would provide power only while the wind was blowing. The company would still need to operate coal plants to deliver fossil fuel-based power as needed.[131]

Companies also can acquire other firms with sustainability (and image) in mind. L'Oréal bought The Body Shop, Colgate-Palmolive bought Tom's of Maine, and Group Danone bought Stonyfield's.[132] To expand its product line into healthier, plant-based foods that have a lower impact on the environment, Unilever is acquiring The Vegetarian Butcher. The meat-substitute company markets "nochicken" nuggets and "chickburgers" mostly through health food stores.[133] Burt's Bees was a firm with decades of leadership and experience with sustainability. Clorox purchased it for growth and to convince environmental stakeholders that the company's strategic change was genuine, but also to acquire knowledge about the green product space.[134]

If you are interested in learning more, you can check out the Global Reporting Initiative (GRI) list of sustainability performance indicators. This useful resource, at www.globalreporting.org, aims to help companies improve their sustainability practices, including transparent reporting.

Environmental Agendas for the Future

In the past, most companies were oblivious to their negative environmental impact. More recently, many began striving for low impact. Now some strive for positive impact, eager to sell solutions to the world's problems.[135]

Consider climate change and the world's shortage of clean water. By 2050, approximately 5.0 billion people (about half of the projected global population) may be living in areas of the world with scarce water resources.[136] When Dow Chemical's Freeport, Texas, site had trouble getting enough water to run its processes during droughts, it installed technology to monitor the water system 24/7 and reduced water consumption by a billion gallons a year.[137] Marriott is pursuing a goal to reduce energy and water consumption by 20 percent per occupied hotel room.[138] Levi Strauss & Co. saved over 2 billion liters of water by reducing up to 96 percent of the water usually used in denim finishing through its Water<Less® initiative.[139]

You don't have to be a manufacturer or a utility to jump on the green bandwagon. Tech giant Microsoft intends to reduce its carbon emissions by 75 percent by 2030, equivalent to 10 million metric tons of carbon emissions.[140]

Collaborative efforts will be essential—for example, the energy industry and environmentalists working with rather than against one another.[141] Networks of companies with a common ecological vision can combine their efforts into highly impactful action.[142] Over two dozen plastic-producing companies formed the Alliance to End Plastic Waste and agreed to spend $1 billion to clean up ocean debris, to improve recycling, and to create new technologies to reduce pollution.[143]

An important development is the **circular economy**: a regenerative, collaborative economic system that contrasts with the linear economy described earlier by minimizing input, waste, emissions, and energy leakage. In Kalundborg, Denmark, such a collaborative alliance exists among an electric power generating plant, an oil refiner, a biotech production plant, a plasterboard factory, cement producers, heating utilities, a sulfuric acid producer, and local agriculture and horticulture. Chemicals, energy (for both heating and cooling), water, and organic materials flow among companies. Resources are conserved, waste materials generate revenues, and water, air, and ground pollution all are reduced.[144]

In addition to how the world can benefit from sustainable practices, many now believe that preparing for and adapting to climate change is a major and fast-growing challenge. The United Nations set the Sustainable Development Goals (SDGs) that are important to everyone including the business world.[145] Nonprofit organizations and accounting firms offer methodologies that value ecosystems. The for-profit Global Environment Fund currently has invested about $1 billion in firms focused on environmental and natural resources.[146] Solving environmental problems is one of the biggest financial opportunities in the history of commerce, while also a huge opportunity to do both well and good.[147]

circular economy

A regenerative, collaborative economic system that contrasts with the linear economy described earlier by minimizing input, waste, emissions, and energy leakage.

Management in Action

IBM TAKES RESPONSIBILITY

Because openness builds the kind of trust IBM wants as the basis for its relationships, the company publishes its values and policies online along with an annual Corporate Responsibility Report. IBM's understanding of its role in corporate citizenship is to commit its knowledge and resources to solve some of the world's most difficult social and environmental challenges.

Recently, IBM launched its Science of Social Good initiative. The initiative is built on the premise that "applied science and technology can solve the world's toughest problems; accelerating the rate and pace of solutions through the scientific method."[148] IBM scientists and engineers have partnered with experts across businesses, universities, and nongovernmental agencies to help curb online hate speech, conserve energy, mitigate the opioid crisis, and help find cures to infectious disease.

In sub-Saharan Africa, for example, the electric grid is often inadequate and unstable, with approximately 80 percent of Africans living without electricity. Instead of trying to build a vast, costly, and energy-inefficient grid to reliably supply energy, scientists are hoping they can shape South Africa's future by going straight to renewable green energy. In 2018, IBM scientists in Johannesburg, South Africa,

created the Research Empower Solar app that South Africans can access for free to help them do just that.

As one IBM scientist explains, it is due to frequent blackouts in African cities that battery-based solar systems have grown in popularity. However, because there are so many solar options, consumers often feel overwhelmed by their choices. Says the IBM scientist, "With our app, we eliminate these barriers to entry by enabling users to design a system for themselves."[149]

In 2018, IBM earned the Catalyst Award for the fourth time; the award recognizes corporate initiatives that help accelerate progress for women. It also received the Climate Achievement award for meeting its greenhouse gas management goals. In fact, over the past 15 years, IBM reduced its greenhouse gas emissions by 43 percent, exceeding its target of 35 percent by 2020. *Forbes* ranked IBM fifth in its annual "America's 100 Best Corporate Citizens."[150]

1. How is IBM's commitment to corporate social responsibility good for IBM as a business? Explain.
2. Do you see corporate social responsibility as being purely philanthropic or a way to increase a firm's long-term profitability? Explain.

MANAGER'S BRIEF

PROGRESS REPORT

ONWARD

KEY TERMS

business ethics, p. 142

carbon footprint, p. 157

Caux Principles, p. 143

circular economy, p. 159

compliance-based ethics programs, p. 149

corporate social responsibility (CSR), p. 153

economic responsibilities, p. 153

egoism, p. 143

ethical climate, p. 146

ethical issue, p. 142

ethical leader, p. 147

ethical responsibilities, p. 153

ethics, p. 140

integrity-based ethics programs, p. 149

Kohlberg's model of cognitive moral development, p. 144

legal responsibilities, p. 153

life-cycle analysis (LCA), p. 157

moral philosophy, p. 142

philanthropic responsibilities, p. 154

relativism, p. 144

Sarbanes-Oxley Act, p. 145

stewardship, p. 152

sustainable growth, p. 157

transcendent education, p. 154

triple bottom line, p. 153

universalism, p. 142

utilitarianism, p. 143

virtue ethics, p. 144

RETAINING WHAT YOU LEARNED

In Chapter 5, you learned that ethics is an important and personal issue that affects employee and organizational behavior. Ethical decisions are influenced by personal values and which ethical system people use to frame a given problem. Companies attempt to influence their ethics environment by establishing ethical programs or codes. Codes prescribe guidelines for behavior. Making ethical decisions requires moral awareness, moral judgment, and moral character. A model of ethical decision making is repeated below. Corporate social responsibility suggests that corporations have not only economic but also legal, ethical, and philanthropic responsibilities. While most companies used to view the natural environment as a source of raw materials and profit, now more companies are adopting a greener agenda for business reasons as well as personal commitment to sustainable development.

EXHIBIT 5.6 (revisited)
A Process for Ethical Decision Making

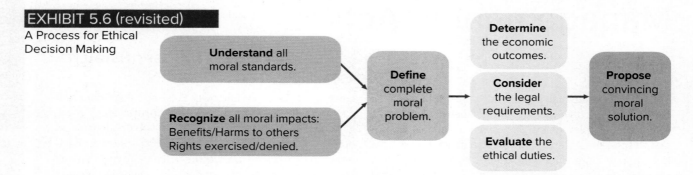

SOURCE: Hosmer, L. T., *The Ethics of Management*, 4th ed. (New York: McGraw-Hill/Irwin, 2003), p. 32. Fig. 5.1A.

LO 5-1 Describe how different ethical perspectives guide decision making.

- The purpose of ethics is to identify the rules that govern human behavior and the "goods" that are worth seeking.
- Ethical decisions are guided by the individual's values or principles of conduct such as honesty, fairness, integrity, respect for others, and responsible citizenship.
- Different ethical systems include universalism, egoism and utilitarianism, relativism, and virtue ethics.
- These philosophical systems, as practiced by different individuals according to their level of cognitive moral development and other factors, underpin the ethical stances of individuals and organizations.

LO 5-2 Explain how companies influence their ethics environment.

- Different organizations apply different ethical perspectives and standards.
- Ethics codes sometimes are helpful, although they must be implemented properly.
- Ethics programs can range from compliance-based to integrity-based.
- Ethics codes address employee conduct, community and environment, shareholders, customers, suppliers and contractors, political activity, and technology.

LO 5-3   Outline a process for making ethical decisions.

- Making ethical decisions requires moral awareness, moral judgment, and moral character.
- When faced with ethical dilemmas, the veil of ignorance is a useful metaphor and provides a useful tactic for ethical decision making.
- You can know various moral standards (universalism, relativism, and so on), use the problem-solving model described in Chapter 3, identify the positive and negative effects of your alternatives on different parties, consider legal requirements and the costs of unethical actions, and then evaluate your ethical duties.

LO 5-4   Summarize the important issues surrounding corporate social responsibility.

- Corporate social responsibility is the extension of the corporate role beyond economic pursuits. It includes not only economic but also legal, ethical, and philanthropic responsibilities.
- Advocates believe managers should consider societal and human needs in their business decisions because corporations are members of society and carry a wide range of responsibilities.
- Critics of corporate responsibility believe managers' first responsibility is to increase profits for the shareholders who own the corporation.
- The two perspectives are potentially reconcilable, especially if managers choose to address areas of social responsibility that contribute to the organization's strategy.

LO 5-5   Discuss reasons for businesses' growing interest in the natural environment.

- In the past, most companies viewed the natural environment as a resource to be used for raw materials and profit. But consumer, regulatory, competitive, and other pressures arose. Executives often viewed these pressures as burdens, constraints, and costs to be borne.
- Now more companies view the interface between business and the natural environment as a potential win–win opportunity.
- Some are adopting a greener agenda for philosophical reasons and personal commitment to sustainable development.
- Many also are recognizing the potential financial benefits of managing with the environment in mind and are integrating environmental issues into corporate and business strategy.
- Some see entering businesses that help rather than harm the natural environment as one of the great commercial opportunities in history.

LO 5-6   Identify actions managers can take to manage with the environment in mind.

- Organizations have contributed risk to society and bear some responsibility for reducing it.
- They also are capable of helping to solve environmental problems.
- Relevant actions are described in the chapter, including strategic initiatives, life-cycle analysis, and interorganizational alliances.

DISCUSSION QUESTIONS

1. Consider the various ethical systems described early in the chapter. Identify concrete examples from your own past decisions or the decisions of others you have seen or read about.
2. Choose one or more topics from Exhibit 5.3 and discuss their current status and the ethical issues surrounding them.
3. Identify and discuss illegal, unethical, and socially responsible business actions in the current news.
4. Does your school have a code of ethics? If so, what does it say? Is it effective? Why or why not?
5. You have a job you like at which you work 40 to 45 hours per week. How much and what types of off-the-job volunteer work do you engage in? How will you react if your boss makes it clear he or she wants you to cut back on the outside activities and devote more hours to your job?
6. What are the arguments for and against the concept of corporate social responsibility? Where do you stand and why? Give your opinions about some of the in-text examples.
7. What do you think of the concept of a transcendent education as described in the chapter? What can be done to implement such a vision for education?
8. What is the current status of the Sarbanes-Oxley Act? What do executives think of it now? What impact has it had?
9. A company in England slaughtered 70,000 baby ostrich chicks each year for their meat. It told a teen magazine that it would stop if it received enough complaints. Analyze this policy, practice, and public statement using the concepts discussed in the chapter.
10. A Nike ad years ago in the U.S. magazine *Seventeen* showed a picture of a girl, aged perhaps 8 or 9. The ad read,

   If you let me play . . .

   I will like myself more.

   I will have more self-confidence.

   I will suffer less depression.

   I will be 60 percent less likely to get breast cancer.

I will be more likely to leave a man who beats me.

I will be less likely to get pregnant before I want to.

I will learn what it means to be strong.

If you let me play sports.

Assess this ad in terms of chapter concepts surrounding ethics and social responsibility. What questions would you ask in doing this analysis?

11. Should companies be held accountable for actions of decades past, then legal but since made illegal, as their harmful effects become known? Why or why not?

12. Discuss courage as a requirement for ethical behavior. What personal examples can you offer, either as an actor or as an observer? What examples are in the news?

EXPERIENTIAL EXERCISES

5.1   Measuring Your Ethical Work Behavior

OBJECTIVES

1. To explore a range of ethically perplexing situations.
2. To understand your own ethical attitudes.

INSTRUCTIONS

Make decisions in the situations described in the Ethical Behavior Worksheet. You will not have all the background information on each situation; instead, you should make whatever assumptions you feel you would make if you were actually confronted with the decision choices described. Select the decision choice that most closely represents the decision you feel you would make personally. You should choose decision options even though you can envision other creative solutions that were not included in the exercise.

Ethical Behavior Worksheet

SITUATION 1

You are taking a very difficult chemistry course, which you must pass to maintain your scholarship and to avoid damaging your application for graduate school. Chemistry is not your strong suit, and, because of a just-below-failing average in the course so far, you will have to earn a grade of 90 or better on the final exam, which is two days away. A school custodian, who is aware of your plight, informs you that he found the master for the chemistry final in a trash barrel and has saved it. He will make it available to you for a price, which is high but which you could afford. What would you do?

_____ (a) I would tell the custodian thanks, but no thanks.

_____ (b) I would report the custodian to the proper officials.

_____ (c) I would buy the exam and keep it to myself.

_____ (d) I would not buy the exam myself, but I would let some of my friends, who are also flunking the course, know that it is available.

SITUATION 2

You have been working on some financial projections manually for two days now. It seems that each time you think you have them completed, your manager shows up with a new assumption or another what-if question. If you only had a copy of a spreadsheet software program for your personal computer, you could plug in the new assumptions and revise the estimates with ease. Then a colleague offers to

let you make a copy of some software that is copyrighted. What would you do?

_____ (a) I would accept my friend's generous offer and make a copy of the software.

_____ (b) I would decline to copy it and plug away manually on the numbers.

_____ (c) I would decide to go buy a copy of the software myself, for $300, and hope I would be reimbursed by the company in a month or two.

_____ (d) I would request another extension on an already overdue project date.

SITUATION 3

Your small manufacturing company is in serious financial difficulty. A large order of your products is ready to be delivered to a key customer when you discover that the product is simply not right. It will not meet all performance specifications, will cause problems for your customer, and will require rework in the field; however, this, you know, will not become evident until after the customer has received and paid for the order. If you do not ship the order and receive the payment as expected, your business may be forced into bankruptcy. And if you delay the shipment or inform the customer of these problems, you may lose the order and go bankrupt. What would you do?

_____ (a) I would not ship the order and place my firm in voluntary bankruptcy.

_____ (b) I would inform the customer and declare voluntary bankruptcy.

_____ (c) I would ship the order and inform the customer after I received payment.

_____ (d) I would ship the order and not inform the customer.

SITUATION 4

You are the co-founder and president of a new venture, manufacturing products for the recreational market. Five months after launching the business, one of your suppliers informs you it can no longer supply you with a critical raw material because you are not a large-quantity user. Without the raw material, the business cannot continue. What would you do?

_____ (a) I would grossly overstate my requirements to another supplier to make the supplier think I am a much larger potential customer to secure the raw material from that supplier, even though this would mean the supplier will no longer be able to service another, noncompeting small manufacturer who may thus be forced out of business.

_____ (b) I would promise the supplier that several large orders will be placed within the next 6 months.

_____ (c) I would pay off the supplier because I have reason to believe that the supplier could be persuaded to meet my needs with a sizable under-the-table payoff that my company could afford.

_____ (d) I would declare voluntary bankruptcy.

SITUATION 5

You are on a marketing trip for your new venture for the purpose of calling on the purchasing manager of a major prospective client. Your company is manufacturing an electronic system that you hope the purchasing manager will buy. During your conversation, you notice on the cluttered desk of the purchasing manager several copies of a cost proposal for a system from one of your direct competitors. This purchasing manager has previously reported misfiling several of your own company's proposals and has asked for additional copies. The purchasing manager leaves the room momentarily to get you a cup of coffee, leaving you alone with your competitor's proposals less than an arm's length away. What would you do?

_____ (a) I would do nothing but await the manager's return.

_____ (b) I would sneak a quick peek at the proposal, looking for bottom-line numbers.

_____ (c) I would put the copy of the proposal in my briefcase.

_____ (d) I would wait until the man returns and ask his permission to see the copy.

5.2   Ethical Stance

Are the following actions ethical or unethical in your opinion? Why? Consider the actions individually and discuss them in small groups.

- Calling in sick when you really are not.
- Taking office supplies home for personal use.
- Cheating on a test.
- Turning in someone for cheating on a test or paper.
- Overcharging on your company expense report.
- Trying to flirt your way out of a speeding ticket.
- Splicing cable from your neighbor.
- Surfing the net on company time.
- Cheating on income tax.
- Lying (exaggerating) about yourself to influence someone of the opposite sex.
- Looking at pornographic sites on the web through the company network
- Lying about your education on a job application.
- Lying about experience in a job interview.

Concluding Case

ORÉ EARTH SKIN CARE TRIES TO STAY NATURAL

Alyssia Franklin is a marketing manager for Oré Earth Skin Care. Four years ago, when she was hired to help with promotional campaigns, she was thrilled because she loved Oré Earth's products. Above all else, Oré Earth products spoke to Alyssia's values: promising all natural ingredients, using only sustainable, environmentally friendly practices. For Alyssia, going to work was like carrying out a mission, promoting both beauty and concern for the planet's well-being. No doubt, her commitment and enthusiasm helped pave the way for her promotion to marketing manager.

Currently, Alyssia and her team are preparing a promotional campaign for a new product line, Oré Essentials, which includes lipsticks, foundation, and eye shadows tinted with a plant extract called orellana. The exciting feature of Oré Essentials is that orellana is harvested deep in the Amazon rain forest, and because of its sustainable practices, Oré Earth will obtain this special ingredient in a socially responsible manner.

The company set up a contract with a tribe living in a remote village. The people of the tribe are supposed to grow and harvest the orellana, which is part of the area's ecosystem, and Oré Earth has promised to pay a fair price to the whole tribe so the people can maintain their village and their way of life. Consumers will get a beautiful product and the pleasure of knowing that they are helping preserve an endangered rain forest ecology and its people.

But when Alyssia sat down for a meeting with the photography crew that traveled to the village, some concerns began to surface. She was looking at stunning photos of tribe members arrayed in grass skirts as they stood behind a pile of fruit from the orellana tree. As she was selecting her favorite shots, one of the photographers commented that the translator had made some surprising remarks on the return trip from the village. Apparently the pile of orellana fruit had been gathered just for the photo shoot. The tribe doesn't really bother with growing and harvesting orellana;

the people of this area aren't primarily farmers, and there aren't actually many orellana trees within a day's walk of the village. The first year the tribe had tried selling orellana to Oré Earth, it grew only enough to earn a few hundred dollars. Confused, Alyssia decided to take a closer look at the financials for this product line.

She found purchasing transactions for "orellana/annatto," and after a little research learned that under either name, the product is just an inexpensive dye. In fact, under the latter name, it is used as a common food coloring. It turns out that Oré Earth made most of its purchases from a mainstream supplier, which is far cheaper than persuading remote villagers to provide orellana. Alyssia felt betrayed and upset.

The next day she asked her boss, the divisional vice president, why the company pretended to care about a remote village if it was just a front for a brand. Her boss replied, "But we *do* care! We send them tens of thousands of dollars every year. Sure, they don't actually grow that stuff for us, but they could, and we'll buy it if they do. Anyway, our aid has provided a school and a health clinic, not to mention food and clothing. We've helped the tribe members stay healthy and preserve their language and culture."[151]

Alyssia considered what her boss said. She thought about the traditional designs the marketing department had copied from the tribe as decorations for the Oré Essentials packaging. "So," Alyssia asked, "does this mean we're using their culture to build an image for our brand, and, in exchange, they get money to keep their culture alive?"

Her boss nodded encouragingly. "That's exactly what I'm saying. It's a win–win situation." Alyssia felt somewhat better, but she left the office unsure still of what to make of this revelation.

DISCUSSION QUESTIONS

1. What ethical issues is Alyssia facing in this situation? What possible marketing claims about the company's relationship with the Amazonian tribe would cross a line into unethical territory? What claims could it make ethically?

2. How could Oré Earth create an ethical climate that would help managers such as Alyssia ensure that they are behaving ethically?

3. How effectively do you think Oré Earth is practicing corporate social responsibility in this situation? Explain the reasoning behind your evaluation.

ENDNOTES

1. Steve Lohr, "IBM's Rometty on the Data Challenge to the Culture of Management," *The New York Times,* March 7, 2013, http://bits.blogs.nytimes.com.

2. Alex Sherman and Lora Kolodny, "IBM to Acquire Red Hat in Deal Valued at $34 Billion," *CNBC,* October 28, 2018, https://www.cnbc.com/2018/10/28/ibm-to-acquire-red-hat-in-deal-valued-at-34-billion.html.

3. Ahiza Garcia, "Ginni Rometty Is Shaping IBM's Future with a $34 Billion Acquisition," *CNN Business,* March 10, 2019, https://www.cnn.com/2019/03/10/tech/ibm-ceo-ginni-rometty-profile/index.html.

4. D. A. Waldman and R. M. Balven, "Responsible Leadership: Theoretical Issues and Research Directions," *Academy of Management Perspectives* 28 (2014), pp. 224–34.

5. A. Piazza and J. Jourdan, "When the Dust Settles: The Consequences of Scandals for Organizational Competition," *Academy of Management Journal* 61 (2018), pp. 165–90; K. Schnatterly, K. Gangloff, and A. Tuschke, "CEO Wrongdoing: A Review of Pressure, Opportunity, and Rationalization," *Journal of Management* 44 (2018), pp. 2405–32.

6. Edelman Berland, "2018 Edelman Trust Barometer: Executive Summary," www.edelman.com.

7. M. Egan, "Wells Fargo Uncovers Up to 1.4 Million More Fake Accounts," *CNN Business,* August 31, 2017, https://money.cnn.com; U. Berliner, "Wells Fargo Admits to Nearly Twice as Many Possible Fake Accounts—3.5 Million," *NPR,* August 31, 2017, www.npr.org.

8. M. Corkery, "Wells Fargo Struggling in Aftermath of Fraud Scandal," *The New York Times,* January 13, 2017, www.nytimes.com.

9. "Wells Fargo Agrees to Pay $2.09 Billion Penalty for Allegedly Misrepresenting Quality of Loans Used in Residential Mortgage-Backed Securities," U.S. Department of Justice, August 1, 2018, www.justice.gov.

10. A. Newcomb, "Facebook Data Harvesting Scandal Widens to 87 Million People," *NBC News,* April 4, 2018, www.nbcnews.com; K. Leswing, "Apple Responds to Report That the US Government Is Investigating the iPhone Slowdown," *Business Insider,* January 31, 2018, www.businessinsider.com.

11. M. Banaji, M. Bazerman, and D. Chugh, "How (Un)Ethical Are You?" *Harvard Business Review,* December 2003, pp. 56–64.

12. K. Leavitt and D. Sluss, "Lying for Who We Are: An Identity-Based Model of Workplace Dishonesty," *Academy of Management Review* 40 (2015), pp. 587–610.

13. S. L. Grover, "The Truth, the Whole Truth, and Nothing but the Truth: The Causes and Management of Workplace Lying," *Academy of Management Executive* 19 (May 2005), pp. 148–57.

14. R. Murray, "Can You Really Trust Online Reviews? Here's How to Spot the Fake Ones," *Today Show,* November 21, 2018, www.today.com.

15. A. Hamilton, "Facebook Employees Were Caught Writing 5-Star Reviews for Its Portal Device on Amazon, and Now They Must Take Them Down," *Business Insider,* January 18, 2019, www.businessinsider.com.

16. M. E. Guy, *Ethical Decision Making in Everyday Work Situations* (New York: Quorum Books, 1990).

17. O. C. Ferrell and J. Fraedrich, *Business Ethics: Ethical Decision Making and Cases,* 3rd ed. (Boston: Houghton Mifflin, 1997).

18. O. C. Ferrell and J. Fraedrich, *Business Ethics: Ethical Decision Making and Cases,* 3rd ed. (Boston: Houghton Mifflin, 1997).

19. M. E. Guy, *Ethical Decision Making in Everyday Work Situations* (New York: Quorum Books, 1990).

20. O. C. Ferrell and J. Fraedrich, *Business Ethics: Ethical Decision Making and Cases,* 3rd ed. (Boston: Houghton Mifflin, 1997).

21. G. Trotter, "Nearly a Year after Layoffs, Former Oreo Plant Workers Struggle to Find Their Way," *Chicago Tribune,* February 17, 2017, www.chicagotribune.com; T. James, "Nabisco Plant," *Chicago Tribune,* November 2, 2016, www.chicagotribune.com; G. Trotter, "Laid Off Oreo Bakery Workers Question Mondelez CEO on Job Cuts," *Chicago Tribune,* May 19, 2016, www.chicagotribune.com.

22. A. Spicer, T. Dunfee, and W. Biley, "Does National Context Matter in Ethical Decision Making? An Empirical Test of Integrative Social Contracts Theory," *Academy of Management Journal* 47 (2004), pp. 610–20; W. Bailey and A. Spicer, "When Does National Identity Matter? Convergence and Divergence in International Business Ethics," *Academy of Management Journal,* 2007, pp. 1462–80; K. Martin, J. Cullen, J. Johnson, and K. Parboteeah, "Deciding to Bribe: A Cross-Level Analysis of Firm and Home Country Influences on

Bribery Activity," *Academy of Management Journal*, 2007, pp. 1401–22.

23. L. Kohlberg and D. Candee, "The Relationship of Moral Judgment to Moral Action," in *Morality, Moral Behavior, and Moral Development*, ed. W. M. Kurtines and J. L. Gerwitz (New York: Wiley, 1984); J. O. Y. Chung and S. H. Hsu, "The Effect of Cognitive Moral Development on Honesty in Managerial Reporting," *Journal of Business Ethics* 145 (2017), pp. 563–75.

24. L. K. Trevino, "Ethical Decision Making in Organizations: A Person-Situation Interactionist Model," *Academy of Management Review*, 1992, pp. 601–17.

25. S. Hannah, B. Avolio, and D. May, "Moral Maturation and Moral Conation: A Capacity Approach to Explaining Moral Thought and Action," *Academy of Management Review* 36 (2011), pp. 663–85.

26. A. Crane, "Modern Slavery as a Management Practice: Exploring the Conditions and Capabilities for Human Exploitation," *Academy of Management Review* 38 (2013), pp. 49–69.

27. G. Kilduff, A. Galinsky, A. Gallo, et al., "Whatever It Takes to Win: Rivalry Increases Unethical Behavior," *Academy of Management Journal* 59 (2016), pp. 1508–34.

28. J. Badarocco Jr. and A. Webb, "Business Ethics: A View from the Trenches," *California Management Review*, Winter 1995, pp. 8–28; G. Laczniak, M. Berkowitz, R. Brookes, and J. Hale, "The Business of Ethics: Improving or Deteriorating?" *Business Horizons*, January–February 1995, pp. 39–47.

29. "State of Ethics in Large Companies," Ethics & Compliance Initiative, www.ethics.org, accessed March 14, 2017.

30. J. Kammeyer-Mueller, L. Simon, and B. Rich, "The Psychic Cost of Doing Wrong: Ethical Conflict, Divestiture Socialization, and Emotional Exhaustion," *Journal of Management* 38 (2012), pp. 784–808.

31. V. Anand, B. Ashforth, and M. Joshi, "Business as Usual: The Acceptance and Perpetuation of Corruption in Organizations," *Academy of Management Executive*, May 2004, pp. 39–53.

32. S. Glover, "SOX Compliance Proves Beneficial to Organizations, Fuels Risk Consciousness," *National Underwriter Property & Casualty*, November 15, 2010, pp. 34, 36; P. Sweeney, "Will New Regulations Deter Corporate Fraud?" *Financial Executive*, January–February 2011, pp. 54–57.

33. J. Hamilton, "Goldman Urges Do-Over by Trump Regulators in Easing Volcker Rule," *Bloomberg*, October 22, 2018, www.bloomberg.com; B. Bain and R. Schmidt, "Wall Street Gets Win as Fed Set to Ease Volcker Trade Limits," *Bloomberg*, May 30, 2018, www.bloomberg.com.

34. J. A. Aragon-Correa, A. Marcus, and N. Hurtado-Torres, "The Natural Environmental Strategies of International Firms: Old Controversies and New Evidence on Performance and Disclosure," *Academy of Management Perspectives* 30 (2016), pp. 24–39.

35. R. E. Allinson, "A Call for Ethically Centered Management," *Academy of Management Executive*, February 1995, pp. 73–76.

36. R. T. De George, *Business Ethics*, 3rd ed. (New York: Macmillan, 1990).

37. A. Simha and J. Cullen, "Ethical Climates and Their Effects on Organizational Outcomes: Implications from the Past and Prophecies for the Future," *Academy of Management Perspectives*, 2012, p. 146.

38. J. Rodell, J. Booth, J. Lynch, and K. Ziipay, "Corporate Volunteering Climate: Mobilizing Employee Passion for Societal Causes and Inspiring Charitable Action," *Academy of Management Journal* 60 (2017), pp. 1662–81.

39. J. Rodell and J. Lynch, "Perceptions of Employee Volunteering: Is It 'Credited' or 'Stigmatized' by Colleagues?" *Academy of Management Journal* 59 (2016), pp. 611–35.

40. "The 50 Best Workplaces for Giving Back in 2018," *Fortune*, February 9, 2018, www.fortune.com.

41. R. A. Cooke, "Danger Signs of Unethical Behavior: How to Determine If Your Firm Is at Ethical Risk," *Journal of Business Ethics*, April 1991, pp. 249–53.

42. L. K. Trevino and M. Brown, "Managing to Be Ethical: Debunking Five Business Ethics Myths," *Academy of Management Executive*, May 2004, pp. 69–81.

43. L. K. Trevino and M. Brown, "Managing to Be Ethical: Debunking Five Business Ethics Myths," *Academy of Management Executive*, May 2004, pp. 69–81.

44. See company website, "3M Named a 2017 World's Most Ethical Company," www.news.3m.com, accessed March 1, 2019.

45. See organization website, "World's Most Ethical Companies," *Ethisphere*, http://www.worldsmostethicalcompanies.com/honorees/, accessed March 1, 2019.

46. Company website, "The OshKosh Way: A Corporate Code of Ethics & Standards of Conduct," www.oshkoshcorp.com, accessed March 14, 2017.

47. C. Handy, *Beyond Uncertainty: The Changing Worlds of Organizations* (Boston: Harvard Business School Press, 1996).

48. Michael S. Fischer, "How Technology Facilitates Compliance Programs: PwC," May 24, 2018, https://www.thinkadvisor.com/2018/05/24/how-technology-facilitates-compliance-programs-pwc/?slreturn=20190221093853.

49. Eamon Javers, "You Won't Believe What Gets an Email Flagged at Goldman: CNBC Has the List," June 16, 2006, https://www.cnbc.com/2016/06/15/you-wont-believe-what-gets-an-email-flagged-at-goldman-cnbc-has-the-list.html.

50. Maurie Beckman, "Is Your Boss Secretly Reading Your Emails?" November 29, 2018, https://www.fool.com/careers/2018/11/29/is-your-boss-secretly-reading-your-emails.aspx.

51. J. Stevens, H. Steensma, D. Harrison, and P. Cochran, "Symbolic or Substantive Document? The Influence of Ethics Codes on Financial Executives' Decisions," *Strategic Management Journal* 26 (2005), pp. 181–95; J. Weber, "Does It Take an Economic Village to Raise an Ethical Company?" *Academy of Management Executive* 19 (May 2005), pp. 158–59.

52. Ethics Resource Center website, http://www.ethics.org, accessed March 14, 2017.

53. R. J. Zablow, "Creating and Sustaining an Ethical Workplace: Ethics Resource Center (ERC)," "Code Construction and Content," *The Ethics Resource Center Toolkit*, http://www.ethics.org; J. Brown, "Ten Writing Tips for Creating an Effective Code of Conduct," Ethics Resource Center, http://www.ethics.org.

54. G. R. Weaver, L. K. Trevino, and P. L. Cochran, "Corporate Ethics Programs as Control Systems: Influences of Executive Commitment and Environmental Factors," *Academy of Management Journal* 42 (1999), pp. 41–57.

55. L. S. Paine, "Managing for Organizational Integrity," *Harvard Business Review*, March–April 1994, pp. 106–17.

56. Government website, "ADA Amendments Act of 2008," http://www.eeoc.govaccessed March 20, 2015; F. Hall and E. Hall, "The ADA: Going beyond the Law," *Academy of Management Executive*, February 1994, pp. 7–13; A. Farnham, "Brushing Up Your Vision Thing," *Fortune*, May 1, 1995, p. 129.

57. C. Moore and F. Gino, "Approach, Ability, Aftermath: A Psychological Process Framework of Unethical Behavior at Work," *Academy of Management Annals* 9 (2015), pp. 235–89.

58. L. K. Trevino and M. Brown, "Managing to Be Ethical: Debunking Five Business Ethics Myths," *Academy of Management Executive*, May 2004, pp. 69–81.

59. L. K. Trevino and M. Brown, "Managing to Be Ethical: Debunking Five Business Ethics Myths," *Academy of Management Executive*, May 2004, pp. 69–81.

60. M. Banaji, M. Bazerman, and D. Chugh, "How (Un)Ethical Are You?" *Harvard Business Review*, December 2003, pp. 56–64.

61. C. Moore and F. Gino, "Approach, Ability, Aftermath: A Psychological Process Framework of Unethical Behavior at Work," *Academy of Management Annals* 9 (2015), pp. 235–89; B. Gunia, L. Wang, L. Huang, J. Wang, and K. Murnighan, "Contemplation and Conversation: Subtle Influences on Moral Decision Making," *Academy of Management Journal* 55 (2012), pp. 13–33.

62. V. Anand, B. Ashforth, and M. Joshi, "Business as Usual: The Acceptance and Perpetuation of Corruption in Organizations," *Academy of Management Executive* (May 2004), pp. 39–53; Remi Trudel and June Cotte, "Does Being Ethical Pay?" *The Wall Street Journal*, May 12, 2008, http://online.wsj.com.

63. T. Thomas, J. Schermerhorn Jr., and J. Dienhart, "Strategic Leadership of Ethical Behavior in Business," *Academy of Management Executive*, May 2004, pp. 56–66.

64. D. Comer and L. Sekerka, "Keep Calm and Carry On (Ethically): Durable Moral Courage in the Workplace," *Human Resource Management Review* 28 (2018), pp. 116–30.

65. L. K. Trevino and M. Brown, "Managing to Be Ethical: Debunking Five Business Ethics Myths," *Academy of Management Executive,* May 2004, pp. 69–81.

66. C. Riley, "GM CEO Mary Barra to Testify before Congress," *CNN Business,* March 20, 2014, www.money.cnn.com.

67. B. George, "Courage: The Defining Characteristic of Great Leaders," HBS Working Knowledge, *Forbes,* April 24, 2017.

68. L. L. Watts and M. R. Buckley, "A Dual-Processing Model of Moral Whistleblowing in Organizations," *Journal of Business Ethics* 146 (2017), pp. 669–83.

69. Sanjay Nair, "2018 Trust in Technology," Edelman Trust Barometer, March 21, 2018, https://www.edelman.com/post/trust-in-technology-2018.

70. IBM, "IBM Principles and Policies," Explore IBM, https://www.ibm.com/ibm/responsibility/ibm_policies.html#bce, accessed March 15, 2019.

71. https://www.ibm.com/ibm/values/us/.

72. Arne Alsin, "The IBM Hall of Shame: A (Semi)Complete List of Bribes, Blunders and Fraud," *Medium.com,* November 26, 2016, https://medium.com/worm-capital/the-ibm-hall-of-shame-a-semi-complete-list-of-bribes-blunders-and-fraud-19e674a5b986#.wg23ud43p; "IBM, Revenue Quebec Employees Arrested in UPACRaid," *CBC News,* March 11, 2015, http://www.cbc.ca/news/canada/montreal/ibm-revenue-quebec-employees-arrested-in-upac-raid-1.2990211.

73. AAUW, "The Simple Truth about the Gender Pay Gap," *Economic Security,* https://www.aauw.org/research/the-simple-truth-about-the-gender-pay-gap/, accessed March 15, 2019.

74. Obama White House, "White House Equal Pay Pledge," https://obamawhitehouse.archives.gov/webform/white-house-equal-pay-pledge, accessed March 15, 2019.

75. Courtney Connley, "Starbucks Has Closed Its Pay Gap in the US—Here Are 4 Other Companies That Have Done the Same," *CNBC,* March 23, 2018, https://www.cnbc.com/2018/03/23/5-companies-that-have-reached-100-percent-pay-equity-in-the-u-s.html.

76. Barbara Frankel, "How Companies Are Achieving Pay Equity," *Diversity Best Practices,* April 9, 2018, https://www.diversitybestpractices.com/how-companies-are-achieving-pay-equity.

77. Jena McGregor, "Citigroup Is Revealing Pay Gap Data Most Companies Don't Want to Share," *The Washington Post,* January 16, 2019, https://www.washingtonpost.com/business/2019/01/16/citigroup-is-revealing-pay-gap-data-most-companies-dont-want-share/?utm_term=.3609a1699a58.

78. M. Hernandez, "Toward an Understanding of the Psychology of Stewardship," *Academy of Management Review* 37 (2012), pp. 172–93.

79. K. Payseno, "Top 20 Corporate Social Responsibility Initiatives of 2018," SmartRecruiters, June 28, 2018, www.smartrecruiters.com.

80. L. Preston and J. Post, eds., *Private Management and Public Policy* (Englewood Cliffs, NJ: Prentice-Hall, 1975).

81. O. C. Ferrell and J. Fraedrich, *Business Ethics: Ethical Decision Making and Cases,* 3rd ed. (Boston: Houghton Mifflin, 1997).

82. M. Nalick, M. Josefy, A. Zardkoohi, et al., "Corporate Sociopolitical Involvement: A Reflection of Whose Preferences?" *Academy of Management Perspectives* 30 (2016), pp. 384–403.

83. M. Westermann-Behaylo, K. Rehbein, and T. Fort, "Enhancing the Concept of Corporate Diplomacy: Encompassing Political Corporate Social Responsibility, International Relations, and Peace through Commerce," *Academy of Management Perspectives* 29 (2015), pp. 387–404; A. Simha and J. Cullen, "Ethical Climates and Their Effects on Organizational Outcomes: Implications from the Past and Prophecies for the Future," *Academy of Management Perspectives* 26 (2012), pp. 20–34.

84. S. Mena, J. Rintamaki, P. Fleming, et al., "On the Forgetting of Corporate Irresponsibility," *Academy of Management Review* 41 (2016), pp. 720–38; J. Schrempf-Stirling, G. Palazzo, and R. Phillips, "Historic Corporate Social Responsibility," *Academy of Management Review* 41 (2016), pp. 700–19.

85. C. Flammer, "Corporate Social Responsibility and Shareholder Reaction: The Environmental Awareness of Investors," *Academy of Management Journal* 56 (2013), pp. 758–81; H. Aguinis and A. Glavas, "What We Know and Don't Know about Corporate Social Responsibility: A Review and Research Agenda," *Journal of Management,* 2012, pp. 932–68.

86. D. Matten and J. Moon, "'Implicit' and 'Explicit' CSR: A Conceptual Framework for a Comparative Understanding of Corporate Social Responsibility," *Academy of Management Review,* 2008, pp. 404–24.

87. A. Carroll, "Managing Ethically with Global Stakeholders: A Present and Future Challenge," *Academy of Management Executive,* May 2004, pp. 114–20.

88. D. Jackson and G. Marx, "Pork Producers Defend Gestation Crates, but Consumers Demand Change," *Chicago Tribune,* August 3, 2016, www.chicagotribune.com.

89. P. Godfrey, "The Relationship between Corporate Philanthropy and Shareholder Wealth," *Academy of Management Review* 30 (2005), pp. 777–98; H. Wang and C. Qian, "Corporate Philanthropy and Corporate Financial Performance: The Roles of Stakeholder Response and Political Access," *Academy of Management Journal* 54 (2011), pp. 1159–81.

90. R. Giacalone, "A Transcendent Business Education for the 21st Century," *Academy of Management Learning & Education,* 2004, pp. 415–20.

91. M. Witzel, "Not for Wealth Alone: The Rise of Business Ethics," *Financial Times Mastering Management Review,* November 1999, pp. 14–19.

92. D. C. Korten, *When Corporations Ruled the World* (San Francisco: Berrett-Koehler, 1995).

93. C. Handy, *Beyond Uncertainty: The Changing Worlds of Organizations* (Boston: Harvard Business School Press, 1996).

94. D. Barton, "Capitalism for the Long Term," *Harvard Business Review,* March 2011, pp. 84–91.

95. B. Fung, "145 Million Social Security Numbers, 99 Million Addresses and More: Every Type of Personal Data Equifax Lost to Hackers, by the Numbers," *The Washington Post,* May 8, 2018, www.washingtonpost.com.

96. G. Fleishman, "Equifax Data Breach, One Year Later: Obvious Errors and No Real Changes, New Report Says," *Fortune,* September 8, 2018, www.fortune.com.

97. G. Fleishman, "Equifax Data Breach, One Year Later: Obvious Errors and No Real Changes, New Report Says," *Fortune,* September 8, 2018, www.fortune.com.

98. D. Quinn and T. Jones, "An Agent Morality View of Business Policy," *Academy of Management Review* 20 (1995), pp. 22–42; D. A. Waldman and D. E. Bowen, "Learning to Be a Paradox-Savvy Leader," *Academy of Management Perspectives* 30 (2016), pp. 316–27.

99. Company website, "Improving Our Water Efficiency," www.coca-cola.com, accessed March 14, 2017.

100. Coca-Cola Company, "About Water Stewardship," http://www.coca-colacompany.com; Coca-Cola Company, "Setting a New Goal for Water Efficiency," http://www.coca-colacompany.com; Coca-Cola Company, "RAIN: The Replenish Africa Initiative," http://www.coca-colacompany.com.

101. K. Casson and S. Orr, "Coca-Cola Intensifies Water Stewardship Partnerships in Middle East and North Africa," press release, March 22, 2018, www.coca-colacompany.com.

102. M. Delmas, D. Etzion, and N. Nairn-Birch, "Triangulating Environmental Performance: What Do Corporate Social Responsibility Ratings Really Capture?" *Academy of Management Perspectives* 27 (2013), pp. 255–67; J. A. Aragon-Correa, A. Marcus, and N. Hurtado-Torres, "The Natural Environmental Strategies of International Firms: Old Controversies and New Evidence on Performance and Disclosure," *Academy of Management Perspectives* 30 (2016), pp. 24–39.

103. D. Schuler and M. Cording, "A Corporate Social Performance-Corporate Financial Performance Behavioral Model for Consumers," *Academy of Management Review* 31 (2006), pp. 540–58; K. Kim, M. Kim, and C. Qian, "Effects of Corporate Social Responsibility on Corporate Financial Performance: A Competitive-Action Perspective," *Journal of Management* 44 (2018), pp. 1097–1118.

104. M. Orlitzky, F. Schmidt, and S. Rynes, "Corporate Social and Financial Performance: A Meta-Analysis," *Organization Studies* 24 (2003), pp. 403–41; J. Peloza, "The Challenge of Measuring Financial Impacts from Investments in Corporate Social Performance," *Journal of Management* 35 (2009), pp. 1518–41.

105. D. Turban and D. Greening, "Corporate Social Performance and Organizational Attractiveness to Prospective Employees," *Academy of Management Journal* 40 (1997), pp. 658–72; M. Turner, T. McIntosh, and S. Reid, "Corporate Implementation of Socially Controversial CSR Initiatives: Implications for Human Resource Management," *Human Resource Management Review* 19 (2019), pp. 125–36.

106. A. McWilliams and D. Siegel, "Corporate Social Responsibility: A Theory of the Firm Perspective," *Academy of Management Review* 26 (2001), pp. 117–27.

107. S. L. Hart and M. B. Milstein, "Global Sustainability and the Creative Destructions of Industries," *Sloan Management Review,* Fall 1999, pp. 23–33.

108. P. M. Senge and G. Carstedt, "Innovating Our Way to the Next Industrial Revolution," *Sloan Management Review,* Winter 2001, pp. 24–38.

109. C. K. Prahalad and M. R. Rangaswami, "Why Sustainability Is Now the Key Driver of Innovation," *Harvard Business Review,* September 2009, pp. 56–64.

110. C. Holliday, "Sustainable Growth, the DuPont Way," *Harvard Business Review,* September 2001, pp. 129–34; P. Bansal and K. Roth, "Why Companies Go Green: A Model of Ecological Responsiveness," *Academy of Management Journal* 43 (2000), pp. 717–36.

111. Barefoot College website, https://www.barefootcollege.org, accessed March 15, 2019.

112. Sudipto Day, "Social Entrepreneur of the Year: A Place for Learning and Unlearning," *Business Standard,* March 8, 2017, http://www.business-standard.com/article/companies/social-entrepreneur-of-the-year-a-place-for-learning-unlearning-117030800010_1.html.

113. Sudipto Day, "Social Entrepreneur of the Year: A Place for Learning and Unlearning," *Business Standard,* March 8, 2017, http://www.business-standard.com/article/companies/social-entrepreneur-of-the-year-a-place-for-learning-unlearning-117030800010_1.html.

114. Company website, "5 Ways Companies Can Weave Sustainability into Their DNA," www.ge.com, accessed March 1, 2019; K. Anderson, "Profit by Tackling Massive Social and Environmental Problems," *Forbes,* February 19, 2017, www.forbes.com; D. Lubin and D. Esty, "The Sustainability Imperative," *Harvard Business Review,* May 2010, pp. 42–50.

115. G. George, S. Schillebeeckx, and T. Liak, "The Management of Natural Resources: An Overview and Research Agenda," *Academy of Management Review* 58 (2015), pp. 1595–1613.

116. P. Shrivastava, "Ecocentric Management for a Risk Society," *Academy of Management Review* 20 (1995), pp. 118–37.

117. P. Shrivastava, "Ecocentric Management for a Risk Society," *Academy of Management Review* 20 (1995), pp. 118–37.

118. P. Shrivastava, "Ecocentric Management for a Risk Society," *Academy of Management Review* 20 (1995), pp. 118–37.

119. Company website, "Our Business and Climate Change," www.patagonia.com, accessed March 14, 2017.

120. "China Pollution: Factories Closed by Beijing Smog," *BBC News,* December 19, 2015, www.bbc.com.

121. D. Stanway, "China Cuts Smog but Health Damage Already Done: Study," Reuters, April 16, 2018, www.reuters.com.

122. "Four-fifths of China's Water from Wells 'Unsafe Because of Pollution,'" *The Guardian,* April 12, 2016, www.theguardian.com; E. Albert, "China's Environmental Crisis," Council on Foreign Relations, January 18, 2016, www.cfr.org.

123. K. Haanaes, D. Michael, J. Jurgens, and S. Rangan, "Making Sustainability Profitable," *Harvard Business Review,* March 2013, pp. 110–14.

124. Organization website, "Sustainable Development," International Institute for Sustainable Development (IISD), www.iisd.org, accessed March 1, 2019; M. Gunther, "Green Is Good," *Fortune,* March 22, 2007, http://money.cnn.com.

125. S. Waddock, "Leadership Integrity in a Fractured Knowledge World," *Academy of Management Learning & Education,* 2007, pp. 543–57.

126. R. Martin and A. Kemper, "Saving the Planet: A Tale of Two Strategies," *Harvard Business Review,* April 2012, pp. 48–56.

127. J. O'Toole, "Do Good, Do Well: The Business Enterprise Trust Awards," *California Management Review,* Spring 1991, pp. 9–24;

P. Shrivastava, "Ecocentric Management for a Risk Society," *Academy of Management Review* 20 (1995), pp. 118–37.

128. Patagonia, "The Footprint Chronicles," http://www.patagonia.com, accessed March 17, 2017.

129. B. Doppelt, *Leading Change toward Sustainability* (Sheffield, UK: Greenleaf, 2010).

130. P. Eisenstein, "Toyota Struggles to Save Breakthrough Prius Hybrid," *CNBC,* December 16, 2018, www.cnbc.com; G. Unruh and R. Etternson, "Growing Green," *Harvard Business Review,* June 2010, pp. 94–100.

131. C. Martin and E. Chasan, "Investors Are Increasingly Calling Out Corporate Greenwashing," *Bloomberg,* August 20, 2018, www.bloomberg.com.

132. G. Unruh and R. Etternson, "Growing Green," *Harvard Business Review,* June 2010, pp. 94–100.

133. "Unilever Buys Meat-Free Food Company The Vegetarian Butcher," *The Guardian,* December 19, 2018, www.theguardian.com.

134. J. Moyer, "Burt Shavitz, Cantankerous Hippie Co-founder of Burt's Bees, Dead at 80," *The Washington Post,* July 6, 2015, www.washingtonpost.com; G. Unruh and R. Etternson, "Growing Green," *Harvard Business Review,* June 2010, pp. 94–100.

135. J. Howard-Grenville et al., "Sustainable Development for a Better World: Contributions of Leadership, Management and Organizations," *Academy of Management Discoveries* 3 (2017), pp. 107–10.

136. Organization website, "World Water Development Report 2018," March 19, 2018, www.unwater.org; "World Population Projected to Reach 9.8 Billion in 2050, and 11.2 Billion in 2100," United Nations Department of Economic and Social Affairs, June 21, 2017.

137. G. Colvin, "The King of Water," *Fortune,* July 5, 2010, pp. 52–59.

138. Marriott, "Reducing Our Footprint," http://www.marriott.com, accessed March 21, 2015.

139. Company website, "Water<Less® Innovations," Levi Strauss & Co., www.levi.com, accessed January 21, 2019.

140. Microsoft, "Microsoft Pledges to Cut Carbon Emissions by 75 Percent by 2030," news release, November 14, 2017, https://blogs.microsoft.com.

141. D. VanderHart, "Environmentalists and Power Companies Reached an Important—and Surprising—Agreement," *Portland Mercury,* January 13, 2016, www.portlandmercury.com.

142. G. Pinchot and E. Pinchot, *The Intelligent Organization* (San Francisco: Berrett-Koehler, 1996); S. L. Hart, *Capitalism as the Crossroads,* 3rd ed. (Upper Saddle River, NJ: Wharton School Publishing, 2010).

143. J. Kaskey, "Big Plastic Trash Plan Is Just a Drop in the Polluted Ocean," *Bloomberg,* January 16, 2019, www.bloomberg.com.

144. http://www.symbiosis.dk/en.

145. J. Howard-Grenville et al., "Sustainable Development for a Better World: Contributions of Leadership, Management and Organizations," *Academy of Management Discoveries* 3 (2017), pp. 107–10.

146. Company website, "About GEF," Global Environment Fund, www.globalenvironmentfund.com, accessed March 17, 2017.

147. S. L. Hart, "Beyond Greening: Strategies for a Sustainable World," *Harvard Business Review,* January–February 1997, pp. 66–76.

148. IBM, "Responsibility at IBM," https://www.research.ibm.com/science-for-social-good/, accessed March 15, 2019.

149. IBM Research Editorial Staff, "New IBM ResearchApp Shines a Light on Solar Energy for Africa," IBM Research Blog, https://www.ibm.com/blogs/research/2018/04/app-solar-energy-africa/, accessed March 15, 2019.

150. IBM, "2017 Corporate Responsibility Report," https://www.ibm.com/ibm/responsibility/2017/, accessed March 15, 2019.

151. Megan McDonough.

CHAPTER 6
International Management

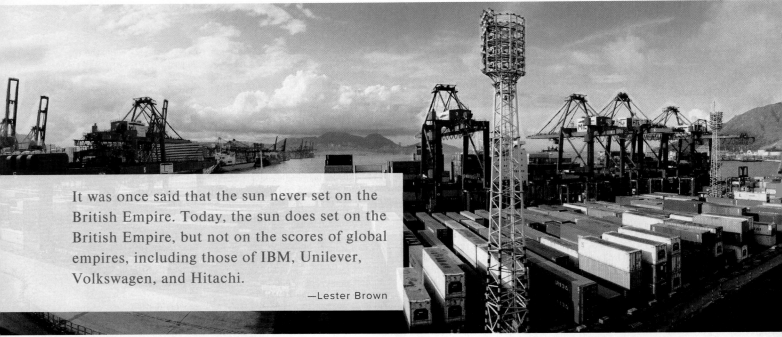

It was once said that the sun never set on the British Empire. Today, the sun does set on the British Empire, but not on the scores of global empires, including those of IBM, Unilever, Volkswagen, and Hitachi.

—Lester Brown

James Hardy/PhotoAlto sas/Alamy Images

learning objectives

After studying Chapter 6, you will be able to:

LO 6-1 Discuss what integration of the global economy means for companies and their managers.

LO 6-2 Describe how the world economy is becoming more integrated than ever before.

LO 6-3 Define the strategies organizations use to compete in the global marketplace.

LO 6-4 Compare the various entry modes organizations use to enter overseas markets.

LO 6-5 Explain how companies can staff overseas operations.

LO 6-6 Summarize the skills and knowledge managers need to manage globally.

LO 6-7 Identify ways in which cultural differences between countries influence management.

chapter outline

Managing in Today's (Global) Economy
International Challenges and Opportunities
Outsourcing and Jobs

The Geography of Business
Western Europe
Asia: China and India
The Americas
Africa and the Middle East

Global Strategy
Pressures for Global Integration
Pressures for Local Responsiveness
Choosing a Global Strategy

Entry Mode
Exporting
Licensing
Franchising
Joint Ventures
Wholly Owned Subsidiaries

Working Overseas
Skills of the Global Manager
Understanding Cultural Issues
Ethical Issues in International Management

Management in Action

HOW ALIBABA IS BECOMING A GLOBAL BRAND

Online shoppers around the world recently spent an astounding $30.8 billion in a record-shattering 24-hour buying spree.[1] While some of the more than 40,000 participating brands that day included familiar U.S. retailers like Macy's, Target, Starbucks, Costco, and the Gap, the website where this frenzy occurred is one that many U.S. shoppers have yet to hear of—China's e-commerce giant Alibaba, led by co-founder Jack Ma.

The occasion was the annual anti–Valentine's Day holiday known as Singles' Day, which unattached Chinese consumers have been celebrating every November 11, mostly quietly, for about 20 years. But since 2009, when Alibaba decided to join the handful of companies then offering shopping discounts on Singles' Day, it has grown into the biggest one-day shopping blitz in the world. Celebrities like Scarlet Johannsen and David Beckham host live events leading up to the midnight opening, and online events run for the entire 24 hours.

Alibaba has been growing by leaps and bounds, helped by a new generation of young and sophisticated tech-savvy shoppers in China with middle-class tastes and money to spend. They are an attractive market for brands from around the world, including the United States, and for smaller vendors as well, who can sell their wares on Alibaba's third-party market in much the same way they do on Amazon.

To fund the growth it seeks at home and abroad, Alibaba raised $25 billion (another record-breaking number) from its IPO, listing itself in the United States. It employs about 100,000 people (far fewer than its nearest rival, Amazon), and posted revenues of over $37 billion in 2018,[2] with over 600 million users annually (more than double the annual users of Amazon).[3]

VCG/Visual China Group/Getty Images

Alibaba reports approximately $550 billion in annual sales on its sites, which is more than all the online sales combined in the United States.[4]

In addition to its e-commerce site, Alibaba is in the digital media, entertainment, and cloud computing businesses, and co-founder Ma has promised to expand his company's toehold in the United States. He stresses that his company will remain true to its stated principles, which put customers first, employees second, and shareholders third.

"Our philosophy is that we want to be an ecosystem," he says. "Our philosophy is to empower others to sell, empower others to service, making sure the other people are more powerful than us. With our technology, our innovation, our partners—10 million small business sellers—they can compete with Microsoft and IBM. Our philosophy is, using Internet technology we can make every company become Amazon."[5]

How well can Alibaba translate its dedication to elevating the thrill of online shopping to consumers in the United States? As you read this chapter, consider what qualities of the international business environment present threats and opportunities for this company.

The direction of Alibaba's growth resembles that of many successful businesses in recent decades. The company started out by satisfying customers in a local market. As sales increased, the company began serving a larger region. Eventually, it began selling goods to and running operations in other countries. Now it boasts sales and develops managers around the globe.

Today's corporate giants—and many ambitious, creative small businesses—need employees and sales in other countries to meet their growth objectives. U.S. multinational corporations now employ almost one-third of their workers outside the United States, and the overseas share is growing. Sales of some product categories are growing faster outside the United States. Popular with older riders in the United States, Harley-Davidson is marketing its motorcycles to first-time, younger riders in international markets. In a recent year, the firm sold approximately 45,000 motorcycles in Europe, the Middle East, and Africa.[6]

Or consider how Netflix expanded into 190 countries in just seven years, attracting over 70 million international subscribers. In 2018, the company earned for the first time higher international streaming revenues than it did from the U.S. market.[7]

Because of such trends, today's managers need to be able to plan how their company will enter markets around the world. That planning begins with understanding the importance of the global economy and the opportunities and threats of the fast-changing global environment.

Managing in Today's (Global) Economy

The global economy matters because our economy *is* global—because your customers, competitors, employees, and suppliers could be located anywhere in the world. For managers, this makes the business environment more complex and exciting than ever: a global economy with threats and opportunities around the world, accompanied by a need to know their customers' specific needs and values, which may vary considerably from place to place.

We will describe how managers can select strategies for this world. But first, let's see how the ever-greater interconnection, or integration, of the world economy is shaping business today.

LO 6-1 Discuss what integration of the global economy means for companies and their managers.

International Challenges and Opportunities

Increasing prosperity and lower trade barriers helped many nations integrate into a now-global economy. This integration has had many important consequences. First, even as the world's economic output grew, the volume of exports grew even (and much) faster. Second, foreign direct investment (FDI) plays an ever-increasing role in the global economy as companies of all sizes invest overseas. Third, imports penetrate more deeply into the world's largest economies. The growth of imports is a natural by-product of the growth of world trade and the trend toward manufacturing component parts, or even entire products, overseas before shipping them back home for final sale.

Finally, the growth of world trade, FDI, and imports means that companies around the globe are finding their home markets under attack from foreign competitors. This is true in the United States, where Chinese companies are purchasing once iconic firms like AMC, Legendary Entertainment Group, and Motorola Mobility.[8]

What does all this mean for today's managers? Opportunities are greater because many formerly protected national markets are open for business. The potential for export and for making direct investments overseas is greater today than ever before. The environment is more complex due to the challenges of working in radically different cultures and coordinating globally dispersed operations. And the environment is more competitive because of cost-efficient overseas competitors.

Companies both large and small view the world as their marketplace.

Companies both large and small view the world, not just their own country, as their marketplace. As Exhibit 6.1 shows, the United States has no monopoly on international business. Of the top 10 corporations

EXHIBIT 6.1   Top 10 Global Firms

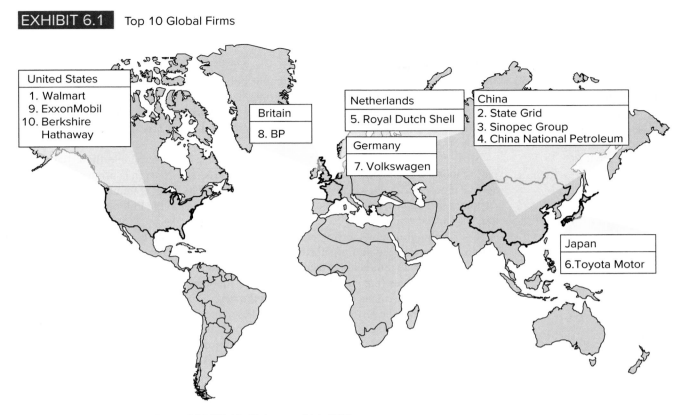

United States
1. Walmart
9. ExxonMobil
10. Berkshire Hathaway

Britain
8. BP

Netherlands
5. Royal Dutch Shell

Germany
7. Volkswagen

China
2. State Grid
3. Sinopec Group
4. China National Petroleum

Japan
6. Toyota Motor

SOURCE: "Global 500," *Fortune,* January 26, 2019, http://fortune.com/global500/.

in the world, 7 are based in countries outside the United States. Companies have dispersed their manufacturing, marketing, and research facilities to locations around the globe where cost and skill conditions are most favorable. This trend is so pervasive in industries such as automobiles, aerospace, and electronics that it is increasingly irrelevant to talk about "American products" or "Chinese products" or "German products."

For example, the headquarters of an automaker no longer says much about where a particular car is made. The American-Made Index ranks vehicles based on where they were assembled, whether they have a high percentage of domestic parts, and how popular they are among U.S. consumers. Surprisingly, the "most American" models in 2018 were Jeep Cherokee, Honda Odyssey, and Honda Ridgeline.[9] A country headquarters doesn't limit a car company either. In 2018, Toyota sold over 1 million Corollas to claim the title of best-selling car in the world.[10]

This is not just for the largest corporations. Many small companies limit their international involvement to exporting, or sourcing from or setting up production facilities overseas. Others acquire existing small businesses to gain talent and access to new markets. Based in Denver, AppIt Ventures develops custom software apps for client companies. It wasn't long before the company expanded internationally by purchasing a software development company in India. Two years later, AppIt acquired an app development firm in Great Britain. Both acquisitions gave AppIt access to skilled talent and additional markets.[11]

There are other, perhaps less obvious, benefits to collaborating with other countries on trade. Because trade allows each country to obtain more efficiently what it cannot as easily produce on its own, it lowers prices overall and makes more goods more widely available. This in turn raises living standards—and may broaden the market for a manager's own products, both locally and abroad. Trade makes new technologies and methods more widely available, again raising the standard of living. Finally, collaborating with others on trade creates links between people and cultures that, particularly over the long run, can lead to cooperation in other areas.

Outsourcing and Jobs

outsourcing

Contracting with an outside provider to produce one or more of an organization's goods or services.

offshoring

Moving work to other countries.

In recent years, the issues of offshoring and outsourcing became important sources of controversy. **Outsourcing** occurs when an organization contracts with an outside provider to produce one or more of its goods or services. **Offshoring** is a specific type of outsourcing whereby companies move jobs to providers in another country, typically where wages are lower.

Most concerns about offshoring refer to outsourcing because people think that high-paying jobs are being lost to low-cost countries overseas. The concern is prompted by widespread reports of major corporations relocating assembly lines, computer programming, customer service centers, and other parts of their operations to the Philippines, India, Mexico, China, and elsewhere.

The decline in manufacturing employment in the United States is evident, and many blame corporate greed and offshoring. However, considerable evidence suggests that the cause of this job decline is not offshoring but innovation. One important trend is how automation technologies (e.g., machine learning and robotics) are replacing human beings in some jobs.[12] One estimate suggests that over the next 12 years, approximately 800 million jobs worldwide will be lost to automation.[13] These innovations mean that companies need fewer workers to produce the same quantity of goods or services. The important question, then, is how to prepare the workforce for the types of jobs most needed in the United States of the future—jobs requiring creativity like marketers and designers, and personal interaction with employees and other stakeholders. Also needed is the use of judgment in physical work (e.g., general contractors), and tailored approaches to particular situations like teachers responding to individual student needs rather than following a predetermined routine.[14]

inshoring

Moving work from other countries back to the headquarters country. Work may be done by a domestic provider or in-house.

Job transfers from offshoring are a small fraction of the 150 million jobs in the United States.[15] Most jobs require workers to be close to their markets; people still shop at their local supermarkets and automobile dealers, visit their doctors, and attend community schools. Importantly, as offshoring increases efficiency, it frees funds for expansion and additional employment. Offshoring is also offset somewhat when foreign companies hire workers in the United States—for example, Toyota, Accenture, Samsung, and Sony are all large employers.

But people (employees, families) are deeply affected when their jobs are lost. Some organizations decide that they have a social responsibility to retrain their displaced workers to help prepare them for jobs that are less likely to move overseas. Others are less helpful. In this and so many other ways, managers have some latitude, multiple options, and a variety of ways to make decisions that have both positive and negative business and human consequences.

Many American companies are outsourcing and offshoring to save money. This photo is from a call center in Hyderabad, India.

Rolex Dela Pena/EPA/Shutterstock

Automation reduces labor costs, making it less necessary to move jobs overseas. Also, managers who offshore to save on wages are often surprised by increasing wage rates and the added costs of travel, training, supply chain disruption, quality control, language barriers, and the resistance of some customers who prefer to deal with local personnel.

These drawbacks, along with political pressure, have led some companies to engage in **inshoring**, or moving work back to the United States. For example, a large domestic insurer may stop using a call center in Bangalore in favor of one based in the United States. Deloitte Consulting found that 34 percent of companies that outsourced to international locations soon after inshored the operations due to quality and cost concerns.[16]

Using the same example, if the domestic insurer were to create an internal (or in-house) call center staffed with its own employees and managers, that would be an example of **insourcing**.[17]

In deciding whether to offshore, managers should not start out with the assumption that it will be cheaper for them to do so. Instead, here are some factors to take into account:

What competitive advantage do the products offer? If, say, fast delivery, reliability, and customer contact are paramount, then offshoring is a less attractive option. But if the product is widely available and standardized, like a calculator, and the only competitive advantage is price, the lowest possible production cost is essential and offshoring is beneficial.

Is the business in its early stages of life? If so, offshoring may well be inappropriate because managers need to stay close to the business and its customers to solve problems and make sure everything is going according to plan. When the business is more mature, managers can afford to consider moving some operations overseas.

Can production savings be achieved locally? Automation can often achieve significant labor cost savings and eliminate the advantage of moving production abroad. Where automation is not feasible, as with computer call centers, then offshoring becomes more attractive.

Can the entire supply chain be improved? As we discussed in Chapter 2, enormous productivity savings are possible when managers develop an efficient supply chain, from suppliers to manufacturing to customers. These improvements permit both lower cost and faster customer service. If the supply chain is already highly efficient or routine, and more savings are needed, then offshoring can achieve efficiencies.[18]

insourcing

Producing in-house one or more of an organization's goods or services.

The Geography of Business

As we saw in Chapter 2, an organization's external environment includes its economic, technological, legal/regulatory, demographic, social, and natural environments. When today's managers think about the economic potential of a market, the laws that protect their property, and the resources they need for making products, they should be thinking about where the best opportunities lie anywhere in the world. Exhibit 6.2 provides examples of current issues we will consider in each area of this international environment.

LO 6-2 Describe how the world economy is becoming more integrated than ever before.

The global economy is more integrated than ever before. For example, the World Trade Organization (WTO), formed in 1995, now has 164 member countries responsible for most of the world's trade. The WTO provides a forum for nations to increase their trade capacity, negotiate trade agreements, and procedures for administering the agreements and resolving disputes. Issues that are currently under negotiation include complaints about U.S. tariffs on steel and aluminum imports on the grounds that they conflict with free trade. To follow how these and other issues are playing out, you can explore the "Trade Topics—Disputes" section of the WTO website, http://www.wto.org.

> The global economy is a major force for integration.

The global economy is dominated by countries in three regions: North America, western Europe, and Asia. Meanwhile, developing regions and specific countries represent important areas for economic development and growth.

Western Europe

In 1992, twelve European nations signed the Maastricht Treaty, which formally established the European Union (EU) and paved the way for the creation of a single currency, the euro.[19] The EU allows most goods, services, capital, and human resources to flow freely across its national borders. These efforts helped the region emerge as an economic

EXHIBIT 6.2
Key Aspects of the Global Environment

Economic environment	Foreign investment; growth of developing nations; rising wages in developing nations
Technological environment	Internet, artificial intelligence, augmented reality, and cloud computing
Legal/regulatory environment	Free trade agreements; anticorruption laws
Demographics	Aging population in developed nations; growing population worldwide, especially in the developing world
Social issues	Cultural differences; bribery concerns
Natural environment	Intensifying demand for resources, including oil, water, and food; growing desire for sustainable products and operations; increasingly endangered species; climate change

superpower. Currently, its 28 members boast a population of more than 513 million and a GDP (gross domestic product) of US$17.3 trillion, about US$2 trillion less than that of the United States.[20]

Maintaining European unification has not always been easy. In 2016, British voters surprised many observers during a national referendum by opting to leave the European Union (dubbed "Brexit" or British Exit).[21]

What would a British exit from the EU mean for the future of the European Union? Some speculate that that it could pave the way for voters in other member nations to consider a similar decision.[22]

Despite these difficulties, unification has created a globally more competitive Europe, one that U.S. managers must take into account. In 2018, Apple purchased Shazam, the London-based audio-recognition platform.[23] PayPal bought iZettle, which is an online payment platform that operates in 12 European markets.[24]

Despite these political, economic, and regulatory challenges, Europe will continue to be a hugely important force in global business. At the time of writing, some political developments (e.g., Brexit) suggest uncertainty for the short term, but undoubtedly, less eventful periods will return.

Bottom Line

Globalization requires continuous improvements in all bottom-line practices. *Why might constant innovation be important for a U.S. company in a global market?*

Asia: China and India

China has the world's largest population and a fast-growing middle class. It has industrialized rapidly and, until recently, experienced several years of unbridled economic expansion.[25] In 2018, annual economic growth has slowed to about 6.5 percent, the slowest in 28 years, partly due to strained relations with the United States over trade.[26] The United States imposed higher tariffs on several Chinese imports, which led to reciprocal tariffs on American exports to China.[27]

China is the world's largest consumer of basic raw materials, such as steel and cement, as well as the world's largest cell phone market. It is the largest exporter of goods into the United States, a cause of political concern in the United States because of the U.S. trade imbalance with China. In 2018, China exported nearly $380 billion more to than it imported from the United States.[28]

As a consuming nation, China's appeal to managers lies in its huge population of 1.39 billion people and its economic growth. Chinese companies have moved into more complex manufacturing operations such as auto parts, optical devices, and advanced electronics.

Rising incomes in China create a paradox for business expansion: New middle-class consumers in China are purchasing more products, both foreign and domestic; at the same time, low-cost manufacturers are moving out of China to set up operations in lower-wage countries.[29] Other companies are staying in China, like General Motors, which produces a local car brand, Baojun, aimed at satisfying the demands of middle-class Chinese consumers by focusing on reliability and affordability.[30] Other companies are expanding in China to serve the huge market there, including American Express, Boeing, and Starbucks.[31]

More and more, China's growing consumption makes it a highly attractive market. But China continues to have an even greater global impact as an exporting nation. The enormous size of its labor force, combined with relatively low labor costs, has given it a competitive advantage in manufacturing. This has led many U.S. and European managers to relocate operations to China and to import an increasing number and variety of Chinese products, instead of continuing to do business with local manufacturers.

The Baojun E100, an affordable and nonpolluting electric car built in China.

SHUANG LI/Alamy Stock Photo

India too is a vital player in the global marketplace. The nation is still developing, and its poverty is severe, but its 1.3 billion people (the world's second-largest population), many of them entering the working and professional classes, make India an essential market. For many U.S. companies, India provides online support for computer software, software development, call centers, and other services. In fact, so many companies have set up shop in India that the demand for Indian workers with strong technical and English language skills is exceeding the supply. Companies such as Wipro, Infosys, and Tata Group are responding with expanded training programs.[32]

South Korea, Taiwan, and Singapore are important trading partners of the United States not merely because of their wage rates, but because many of their companies have competitive advantages in areas such as engineering and technological know-how. South Korea's Samsung has the largest share of the world's market for flat-screen televisions and second-largest share (after Apple) in smartphones.[33] Taiwan's Hon Hai is the leader in contract manufacturing of electronics. You may not have heard of Hon Hai (also known as Foxconn) because it specializes in making components for brand-name products of other companies, including Apple iPhones and Sony PlayStation and Nintendo Wii video game consoles.[34]

These Asian countries and others have joined with the United States, Australia, and Russia to form the 21-member Asia-Pacific Economic Cooperation (APEC) trade group. Combined, APEC members' economies account for more than half of world output (GDP) and 54 percent of world trade.[35]

Another international organization, the Association of Southeast Asian Nations (ASEAN), brings together 10 developing nations, including Indonesia, Malaysia, and Thailand. Economic growth in Vietnam and the Philippines is predicted to remain high at about 6 percent per annum.[36] Along with economic development, ASEAN aims to promote cultural development and political security.

The Americas

North and South America constitute a mix of industrialized countries, such as Canada and the United States, and growing economies such as Argentina, Brazil, Chile, and Mexico. The winter fruit you eat may come from Chile, the coffee you drink from Colombia, and the shirt you wear from Honduras.

Ratified in 1993, the **North American Free Trade Agreement (NAFTA)** effectively combined the economies of the United States, Canada, and Mexico into the world's largest trading bloc, currently with just over 490 million U.S., Canadian, and Mexican consumers and

North American Free Trade Agreement (NAFTA)

An economic pact that combined the economies of the United States, Canada, and Mexico into one of the world's largest trading blocs.

total trade reaching $1.1 trillion.[37] Although the United States has a long-standing agreement with Canada, after NAFTA Mexico quickly became the United States' third-largest trading partner. U.S. industries that have benefited include capital goods suppliers, manufacturers of consumer durables, grain producers and distributors, construction equipment manufacturers, the auto industry, and the financial industry, which gained privileged access into a previously protected market.

In 2018, the Trump administration renegotiated the trade agreement with the leadership of Canada and Mexico, resulting in the new U.S.–Mexico–Canada Agreement (USMCA).[38] A major goal of the renegotiation was to more evenly distribute the benefits of the trade agreement among the three members.[39] This new agreement is far from becoming law and replacing NAFTA because it has to be passed by a divided U.S. Congress, which has signaled its intent to make major changes.

After a protracted recession and several political scandals, Brazil's economy still has hurdles to overcome before it may begin growing again.[40] Brazil is the largest economy in South America, and all eyes are on Jair Bolsonaro, the newly elected president, who has pledged to implement economic reforms.[41]

As in Asia, South American companies rely on innovation and technology, rather than simply cost advantages, to compete in the global marketplace. "Start-Up Chile," an accelerator for immigrants funded by the Chilean government, helps high-potential entrepreneurs launch their start-up companies. Since its inception in 2010, it fueled the growth of 1,600 companies in 85 countries, and reports a portfolio valuation of US$1.4 billion.[42]

Other agreements have been established to promote U.S. trade with Central and South America. The Central America–Dominican Republic Free Trade Agreement (CAFTA-DR) includes Costa Rica, El Salvador, Guatemala, Honduras, Nicaragua, and the Dominican Republic.[43] Additional trade agreements have been negotiated on a country-by-country basis with Chile, Peru, Colombia, and Panama. The countries of South America have formed their own trading bloc, called Mercosur, to promote trade within the continent.

Africa and the Middle East

The economy of the Middle East is best known for its export of oil. Although oil exploration and drilling take place in many parts of the world, the oil-rich countries of the Middle East supply by far the most oil to the world's buyers, most of it going to buyers in Asia. The main Middle Eastern supplier of U.S. oil imports is Saudi Arabia,[44] with other major suppliers being Canada, Mexico, and Venezuela.

The United States' dependence on foreign oil has decreased since the shale oil boom in Texas, New Mexico, North Dakota, and Alaska.[45] Nevertheless, U.S. businesses remain concerned about the Middle East because activities there can shape the price of oil, which is important not only for transportation but also for the manufacture of many products including fertilizer and plastic.

Africa was long seen by managers only as a continent afflicted by dire poverty. The continent is still plagued by epidemics, draught, political instability, and ongoing wars. But areas of progress and growth in the middle class in some countries have provided opportunities for businesses willing to learn the needs of the population and make the effort to navigate a challenging environment. For example, the mobile phone industry has leapfrogged the landline phase of communications in Africa.

The nearby "Social Entrepreneurship" box discusses how student social entrepreneurs are tackling some of the world's toughest challenges. As part of its Smarter Planet initiative (described in the "Management in Action" for Chapter 5), IBM learns about Africa's huge potential by sending in teams to help local governments solve problems. As it came to know the region, IBM began selling services, setting up partnerships with local companies, and opening research facilities in Kenya and South Africa, and other countries.[46]

Social Entrepreneurship

Student Social Entrepreneurs Compete for $1 Million

The Hult Prize Foundation is a student business competition and start-up accelerator that awards $1 million to talented social entrepreneurs from universities around the world. The annual competition identifies and provides seed funding to promising "start-up social enterprises that tackle grave issues faced by billions of people."[47]

Each year, about 1,500 students from 150 countries around the world participate in the Hult Prize and spend over 2.5 million hours on solving the world's most pressing issues. Since its founding in 2009, students from more than 600 schools have competed for the Hult Prize. Former president Bill Clinton, now of the Clinton Global Initiative, presents the prize money to the student winners.

Here are some recent start-ups that were awarded the Hult Prize:

- *Rice Inc.* is a start-up operating in Myanmar. It provides a standardized service that supplies farmers with equipment to keep their rice dry, which minimizes harvest losses and waste. The increased quality and supply then increases farmer profitability.[48]

- *Roshni Rides* provides a private shuttle service of motorized rickshaws in south Asia for refugees who need transportation to get to school, work, medical facilities, or local markets for a fixed discounted fee.[49]

- *Magic Bus* came up with a way for bus riders in Nairobi to pre-book their tickets using a text messaging system and a popular mobile pay app, making transportation easier and more reliable.[50]

Stephanie Keith/Getty Images News/Getty Images

- *NanoHealth* won for its work in providing affordable, holistic medical services for impoverished "slum-dwellers" who suffer from chronic diseases.[51]

Are student social entrepreneurs who compete for the Hult Prize making a difference? Yes. According to Muhammad Yunus, Nobel Peace Prize winner for his pioneering work in microlending: "If you can create a real business, the beginning of a prototype, you can change the world."

1. Of the four recent award-winning start-ups mentioned, which do you find most likely to succeed? Why?
2. The Hult Prize has been awarded to new social enterprises from all over the world. Why do you think the competition has a global focus?

Global Strategy

A crucial task for an international manager is to determine the best strategy for competing in a global marketplace. To determine the most appropriate global strategy—from among global, international, transnational, multinational—managers can plot a company's position on an integration–responsiveness grid (Exhibit 6.3). The vertical axis measures pressures for global integration, and the horizontal axis measures pressures for local responsiveness.

LO 6-3 Define the strategies organizations use to compete in the global marketplace.

Pressures for Global Integration

Several reasons can cause managers to want or need a common global strategy (high pressures for global integration on the vertical axis of Exhibit 6.3) rather than one tailored to individual markets (low pressures such as universal customer needs, necessity to reduce costs, or the presence of competitors with a global strategy).

Universal needs exist when consumer tastes and product preferences in different countries are similar. Products that serve universal needs require little adaptation across national markets; thus global strategic integration is facilitated. This is the case in many markets:

Pressures for global integration

	Low Pressures for local responsiveness High

High

GLOBAL
Views the world as a single market. Operations are controlled centrally from the corporate office.

TRANSNATIONAL
Specialized facilities permit local responsiveness. Complex coordination mechanisms provide global integration.

Low

INTERNATIONAL
Uses existing capabilities to expand into foreign markets.

MULTINATIONAL
Several subsidiaries operating as stand-alone business units in multiple countries.

EXHIBIT 6.3
Cross-National Organizational Models

SOURCES: Bartlett, C. A. and Ghoshal, S., *Managing across Borders: The Transnational Solution. Boston*, MA: Harvard Business School Press, 1991; Harzing, A. W., "An Empirical Analysis and Extension of the Bartlett and Ghoshal Typology of Multinational Companies," *Journal of International Business Studies* 31, no. 1 (2000), pp. 101–20.

> Universal needs encourage managers to develop a global strategy.

Bottom Line

Lowering costs is a goal of many companies' strategic plans. *What is one way in which a global strategy can help reduce costs?*

electronic products such as virtual reality headsets, certain basic foodstuffs (rice and bananas), and medical equipment (scalpels and bandages).

Competitive pressures to reduce costs may cause managers to integrate manufacturing globally. Costs are particularly important when price is the main competitive weapon and competition is intense (as with smartphones). It is important also if key competitors are based in countries where labor and other operating costs are low. In these cases, products are more likely to be standardized and perhaps produced in few locations to capture economies of scale.

When competitors engage in global strategic coordination, this too creates pressures to integrate globally. A competitor that centrally coordinates the purchase of raw materials worldwide (i.e., buys high-volume quantities) may achieve significant price reductions compared with firms that allow subsidiaries to handle purchases locally. Global competition can create pressures to centralize in corporate headquarters certain decisions being made by different national subsidiaries. Once one multinational company adopts global strategic coordination, its competitors may follow suit to remain competitive.

Pressures for Local Responsiveness

The second dimension of the grid, on the horizontal axis of Exhibit 6.3, is the need for responsiveness to local tastes and conditions. In some circumstances, managers must help their companies adapt to different needs or demands in different host locations. Strong pressures for local responsiveness emerge when consumer tastes and preferences differ significantly among countries. Compared with consumers in Europe and Japan, many Americans look for strength and safety features when choosing a vehicle, thus the popularity of trucks and SUVs. Europeans tend toward automobiles that excel in performance and quality, whereas Japanese prefer vehicles that are reliable, affordable, and long-lasting.[52] Automakers must tailor their marketing messages to these differences in consumer demand.

Pressures for local responsiveness also emerge when there are differences in traditional practices among countries. For example, in Great Britain people drive on the left side of the road, creating a demand for right-hand-drive cars, whereas in neighboring France and elsewhere, people drive on the right side of the road. Obviously, automobiles must be customized to accommodate this difference in traditional practices.

For restaurant and fast-food chains, what people like to eat locally creates pressures for local responsiveness. Recently, Yum! announced that it opened its first Taco Bell restaurant in Thailand.[53] To make the menu more appealing to Thai customers, the company offers an extra-spicy sauce and local beer brands.[54] KFC, with more than 5,000 restaurants in China, has adapted its menu to appeal to Chinese palates by serving local favorites like egg tarts, shrimp and chicken sandwiches, and lavender and green tea ice cream.[55]

Finally, economic and political demands of host-country governments require local responsiveness. Most important, threats of protectionism, economic nationalism, and local content rules (rules requiring that a certain percentage of a product be manufactured locally) dictate that international companies manufacture locally. Countries may impose tariffs (taxes on imports) or quotas (restrictions on the number of imports allowed into a country) to protect domestic industries from foreign competition perceived to be unfair or not in the nation's interests.

In 2018, the United States imposed high tariffs on billions of dollars' worth of imported goods from China, Canada, Mexico, and the European Union.[56] These countries all retaliated by slapping tariffs on thousands of U.S. goods.[57] The U.S. government justified the tariffs as a response to complaints that these countries had been taking advantage of U.S. trade policies.[58] Others interpret this and other protectionist actions as being motivated primarily by political objectives.[59] Whatever the reasons for them, tariffs and quotas influence managers' decisions about whether it is economically advantageous, or even possible, to operate locally or rely on exporting.

Choosing a Global Strategy

As Exhibit 6.3 shows, managers can use four approaches to international competition: the international model, the multinational model, the global model, and the transnational model. Organizations using each model compete globally, but they differ in the strategy they use and in the structures and systems that drive their operations.

Kulnisha Studio/Shutterstock

The International Model   In the **international model**, managers use their firm's core capabilities to expand into foreign markets. As the Exhibit 6.3 grid indicates, it is most appropriate when there are few pressures for economies of scale *or* local responsiveness. Caterpillar is an example of a company operating with the international model. Its industry doesn't compete on cost, and its earth moving equipment doesn't need to be tailored to local tastes.

The international model uses subsidiaries in each country in which the company does business, under the control exercised by the parent company. Although subsidiaries may have some latitude to adapt products to local conditions, core functions such as research and development (R&D) are centralized in the parent company. Consequently, subsidiaries' dependence on the parent company for new products, processes, and ideas requires a great deal of coordination and control by the parent company.

The advantage of this model is that it facilitates the transfer of skills and know-how from the parent company to subsidiaries around the globe. IBM and Xerox, among many others, profited from the transfer of their core skills in technology and R&D overseas. The overseas successes of Airbnb, Domino's, and Nike are based more on marketing know-how than on technological expertise. Toyota and Honda successfully penetrated U.S. markets from their base in Japan with their core competencies in manufacturing relative to local competitors. General management skills provided advantages that explain the growth of international hotel chains such as Marriott International, Hyatt Hotels, and Hilton Worldwide.

One disadvantage of the international model is that it does not provide much latitude for responding to local conditions. Another is that it does not provide opportunity to achieve a low-cost position via scale economies.

The Multinational Model   Where global efficiency is not required but adapting to local conditions offers advantages, the multinational model is appropriate. The **multinational model**, sometimes referred to as *multidomestic,* uses subsidiaries in each country in which the company does business and allows those offices to respond to local conditions. Each local subsidiary is a self-contained unit with all operating functions in the host market. Thus each has its own manufacturing, marketing, research, and human resources functions. Because of this autonomy, each multinational subsidiary can customize its products and strategies according to the tastes and preferences of local consumers, competitive conditions, and political, legal, and social structures.

international model

An organizational model that is composed of a company's overseas subsidiaries and characterized by greater control by the parent company over local product and marketing strategies than is the case in the multinational model.

Bottom Line

The international model helps spread quality and service standards globally. *Give examples of products for which quality standards apply globally.*

multinational model

An organizational model that consists of the subsidiaries in each country in which a company does business, and provides a great deal of discretion to those subsidiaries to respond to local conditions.

global model

An organizational model consisting of a company's overseas subsidiaries and characterized by centralized decision making and tight control by the parent company over most aspects of worldwide operations; typically adopted by organizations that base their global competitive strategy on cost considerations.

transnational model

An organizational model characterized by centralizing certain functions in locations that best achieve cost economies; basing other functions in the company's national subsidiaries to facilitate greater local responsiveness; and fostering communication among subsidiaries to permit transfer of technological expertise and skills.

A good example of a multinational firm is Heineken, a Netherlands-based brewing company. Heineken has three major global brands—Heineken, Amstel, and Affligem—but it also offers regional and local brands. The company attempts to adapt its products to local attitudes and tastes while maintaining its high quality. The company produces more than 300 brands around the world, from its international brands to local and specialty brews. The localized portfolio includes Red Stripe in Jamaica, Tiger in Asia, and Tecate in Mexico. Countries have considerable autonomy in the beers that they brew locally.[60]

Major disadvantages of the multinational form include higher manufacturing costs and duplication of effort. Although a multinational can transfer core skills among its international operations, it cannot realize scale economies from centralizing manufacturing facilities and offering a standardized product to the global marketplace. Moreover, because a multinational approach tends to decentralize strategic decisions (discussed further in Chapters 8 and 9), launching coordinated global moves against competitors is difficult. This can be a significant disadvantage when competitors have this ability.

The Global Model   The **global model** is designed to market a standardized product in the global marketplace and to manufacture that product in a limited number of locations having favorable mixes of costs and skills. The global model is adopted by companies that view the world as one market and assume no tangible differences among countries in consumer tastes and preferences.

As part of its effort to improve efficiency while broadening its global appeal, Toyota shifted the platform of its top-selling Corolla to the Toyota New Global Architecture (TNGA) platform.[61] The new design reduces weight, boosts fuel economy, and increases safety, all while providing better handling and a quieter ride.[62] Toyota is betting that this change will help the Corolla maintain its enviable position as the top-selling car in the world.[63]

Companies adopting the global model construct global-scale manufacturing facilities in a few selected locations. They realize scale economies by spreading the fixed costs of investments in new-product development, plants and equipment, and the like over worldwide sales. By using centralized manufacturing facilities and global marketing strategies, Sony was able to push down its unit costs to the point where it became the low-cost player in the global television market. This enabled Sony to take market share away from Philips, RCA, and Zenith, all of which used traditional manufacturing operations based in each major national market (a multinational approach). Because operations are centralized, subsidiaries usually are limited to marketing and service functions.

On the downside, the global model requires a great deal of coordination, with significant management and paperwork costs. Moreover, because a company pursuing a purely global approach tries to standardize its goods and services, it may be less responsive to consumer tastes and demands in different countries. Attempts to lower costs through global product standardization may result in a product that fails to satisfy anyone.

For example, although Procter & Gamble has been quite successful using a global approach, the company experienced problems when it tried to market Cheer laundry detergent in Japan. The product did not suds up as promoted in Japan because the Japanese use a great deal of fabric softener, which suppresses suds. Moreover, the claim that Cheer worked in all water temperatures was irrelevant in Japan, where most washing is done in cold water.

The Transnational Model   Achieving competitive advantage often requires managers to pursue local responsiveness, transfer of know-how, and cost economies simultaneously.[64] The transnational model is designed to help them do just that. It is an approach that enables managers to "think globally but act locally."

In companies that adopt the **transnational model**, functions are centralized where it makes sense to do so, but a great deal of decision making also takes place at the local level. In addition, the experiences of local subsidiaries are shared worldwide to improve the firm's overall knowledge and capabilities. For example, research, training, international human resources management, and the overall development of the corporate strategy and global brand image tend to be centralized at home. Other functions may be centralized as well, but not necessarily in the home country.

To achieve cost economies, companies base global-scale production plants for labor-intensive products in low-wage countries such as Bangladesh, Mexico, or Philippines, and locate production plants that require a skilled workforce in high-skill countries such as the Netherlands and Singapore. Companies can find locations with an optimal balance of needed skills and relatively low costs.[65]

Marketing, service, and final assembly functions tend to be based in the national subsidiaries for greater local responsiveness. Thus major components are manufactured in centralized production plants to realize scale economies and then shipped to local plants, where the final product is assembled and customized to fit local needs.

Panasonic's experience in China has made it more of a transnational company.[66] Panasonic, a Japanese company, initially saw China primarily as a low-cost site for manufacturing its home appliances. In the early years, it served the Chinese market by removing features to make low-cost versions of its appliances. But as China's economy developed, consumers began buying new products from local Chinese producers. Panasonic's management realized it needed to view China as more than a source of cheap labor. As a first step, it set up a unit called Panasonic Corporation of China to provide research and development and marketing support, as well as back-office services, to the manufacturing facilities in China. Recently, Panasonic announced it will open headquarters in China. The Chinese headquarters will be geared toward generating demand for its housing equipment and appliances.[67]

Bottom Line

The transnational model tries to deliver on all bottom-line practices. *Does that mean the transnational model is always best? Why or why not?*

Management in Action

ALIBABA'S GLOBAL STRATEGY

Alibaba's websites—Taobao and Tmall Global—are not well known in the United States. Alibaba co-founder Jack Ma wants to change that. He is pursuing a major expansion in the United States, which he hopes will not only bring more U.S. shoppers to Alibaba's sites, but also attract more U.S. vendors, large and small. Some large companies, including Target, made their first appearance in China via Tmall Global.[68] If Ma succeeds in expanding his company's presence in the United States, thousands and possibly millions of other vendors, including the kinds of small operations that thrive in Amazon's third-party marketplace, could follow.

The attraction of China's huge and increasingly profitable market is substantial. Some estimates suggest the new Chinese middle class alone is as big a market as the entire U.S. population.[69] These shoppers are sophisticated and tech-savvy, and despite the risk of counterfeits (a problem Alibaba routinely contends with), they covet—and are willing to pay for—the international brands that make up a fast-growing proportion of the site's Western vendors. There may be no better way for U.S. vendors to reach them than through sites such as those owned by Alibaba.

Ma has indicated he wants to capitalize on the opportunity to serve U.S. small vendors, and customers, too. In fact, Ma's plans for Alibaba in the United States are so aggressive that he anticipates that within the next 15 years, the annual Singles' Day online sales event will be as popular in the United States as it already is in China.[70]

But while Alibaba is the dominant online force in Asia, its expansion plans in the United States will likely prove more challenging. Ma recently decided to slow down Alibaba's U.S. cloud expansion due to problems recruiting top talent in Silicon Valley. Notably, the challenge, as reported by Alibaba, had less to do with money and more to do with cultural differences:

> The cloud division also has struggled to recruit top talent in Silicon Valley, in part because the sales department emphasized team performance over individual achievements.... Alibaba salespeople aren't compensated with commissions but via a bonus pool shared among multiple employees. That stood in contrast with many Silicon Valley companies.[71]

Surely this is a temporary impediment to Alibaba's long-term plans, yet it's a reminder that any expansion strategy a firm chooses must account for cultural divides—and how to bridge them.

- In what ways do you think Alibaba's Jack Ma is responding to the need for global integration? How does his strategy exemplify local responsiveness?
- Which global strategy (international, multinational, global, or transnational) do you think is most appropriate for Alibaba? Why?

MANAGER'S BRIEF

PROGRESS REPORT

ONWARD

Panasonic also set up a global marketing organization to share knowledge about its best practices. Such efforts are critical for Panasonic, whose performance had suffered from efforts to remain profitable in the highly competitive market for electronics such as televisions.

Perhaps the most important distinguishing characteristic of the transnational organization is the fostering of communications among subsidiaries and the ability to integrate the efforts of subsidiaries (when doing so makes sense). Communicating effectively across subsidiaries requires the head office to play an active role, creating formal mechanisms such as transnational committees staffed by people from the various subsidiaries. Equally important is to transfer managers among subsidiaries on a regular basis. This creates a global network of personal contacts in different subsidiaries with whom they can share information as the need arises.

Now that you have seen examples of the need to balance global integration and local responsiveness, consider how those pressures apply to Alibaba's situation as described in "Management in Action: Progress Report."

Entry Mode

LO 6-4 Compare the various entry modes organizations use to enter overseas markets.

Bottom Line

Exporting offers scale economies and increases sales. *Can services be exported? Why or why not?*

When considering global expansion, international managers must decide on the best means of entering an overseas market. The five basic ways to expand overseas are exporting, licensing, franchising, entering into a joint venture with a host-country company, and setting up a wholly owned subsidiary in the host country.[72] Exhibit 6.4 compares the entry modes.

Exporting

Most manufacturing companies begin global expansion as exporters and later switch to one of the other modes for serving an overseas market. The advantages of exporting are that it (1) provides scale economies by avoiding the costs of manufacturing in other countries and (2) is consistent with a pure global strategy. By manufacturing the product in a centralized location and then exporting it to other national markets, the company can realize substantial scale economies from its global sales volume.

However, exporting has a number of drawbacks. First, other countries might offer lower-cost locations for manufacturing the product. An alternative is manufacturing in a location where the mix of costs and skills is most favorable and then export from that location to other markets.

EXHIBIT 6.4
Comparison of Entry Modes

	Exporting	Licensing	Franchising	Joint Venture	Wholly Owned Subsidiary
Advantages					
	Scale economies	Lower development costs	Lower development costs	Access to local knowledge	Maintains control over technology
	Consistent with pure global strategy	Lower political risk	Lower political risk	Shared costs and risk may be the only option	Maintains control over operations
Disadvantages					
	No low-cost sites	Loss of control over technology	Loss of control over quality	Loss of control over technology and conflict between partners	High cost
	High transportation costs				High risk
	Tariff barriers				

A second drawback of exporting is that high transportation costs can make it uneconomical, particularly for bulk products. Chemical companies get around this by manufacturing their products on a regional basis, serving several countries in a region from one facility.

A third drawback is that host countries can impose (or threaten to impose) tariff barriers. Trade arrangements described earlier, including the World Trade Organization and APEC, work to minimize this risk. However, tariffs continue to affect trade between particular countries in various industries.

Licensing

International licensing is an arrangement by which a licensee in another country buys the rights to manufacture a company's product in its own country for a negotiated fee (typically royalty payments on the number of units sold). The licensee then puts up most of the capital necessary to get the overseas operation going. The advantage of licensing is that the company need not bear the costs and risks of opening up an overseas market.

In nine years, Cold Stone Creamery expanded its franchises into 24 countries outside the United States, including Brazil, shown here.

walterericsy/Shutterstock

However, a problem arises when a company licenses its technological expertise to overseas companies. Technological know-how is the basis of the competitive advantage of many multinational companies. But RCA Corporation lost control over its color TV technology by licensing it to a number of Japanese companies. The Japanese companies quickly assimilated RCA's technology and then used it to enter the U.S. market, eventually gaining a bigger share of the U.S. market than RCA held.

Sometimes, licensing is a reasonable alternative when it is not feasible for a firm to operate on its own. Due to a "challenging regulatory, legal and competitive environment," Netflix recently decided to pursue a licensing strategy in China. In lieu of operating on its own, the company will license content to existing online service providers.[73]

Franchising

In many respects, franchising is similar to licensing. However, whereas licensing is a strategy pursued primarily by manufacturing companies, franchising is used primarily by service companies. Baskin-Robbins, H&R Block, The Little Gym, and many others have expanded overseas by franchising.[74] 7-Eleven has expanded through franchising to the point where it has over 63,000 stores in 17 countries.[75]

In franchising, the company sells limited rights to use its brand name in return for a lump-sum payment and a share of the franchisee's profits. Unlike most licensing agreements, the franchisee has to agree to abide by strict rules regarding how it does business. Thus, McDonald's expects the franchisee to run its restaurants in a manner identical to that used under the McDonald's name elsewhere in the world.

The advantages of franchising as an entry mode are similar to those of licensing. The franchisees put up capital and assume most of the risk. However, local laws can limit this advantage.

The most significant disadvantage of franchising concerns quality control. The company's brand name guarantees consistency in the company's product. Thus a business traveler booking into a Hilton International hotel in Dubai can reasonably expect the same quality of room, food, and service that he or she would receive in Chicago. But if overseas franchisees are less concerned about quality than they should be, the impact can go beyond lost sales in the local market to a decline in the company's reputation worldwide. If a business traveler has an unpleasant experience at the Hilton in Dubai, she or he may decide never to go to another Hilton hotel—and urge colleagues to do likewise.

Bottom Line

Franchising is one way to maintain standards globally. *Why does quality control pose a risk in franchising?*

Joint Ventures

Establishing a joint venture (a formal business agreement discussed in more detail in Chapter 17) with a company in another country has long been a popular means of entering a new market. Joint ventures benefit a company through (1) the local partner's knowledge of the host country's competitive conditions, culture, language, political systems, and business systems; and (2) the sharing of development costs and/or risks with the local partner.

In many countries, political considerations make joint ventures the *only* feasible entry mode. Before China opened its borders to trade, many U.S. companies, including Eastman Kodak, AT&T, Ford, and GM, did business in the country via joint ventures.

In 2017, Moscow State University and Beijing Institute of Technology opened a joint venture in China, Shenzhen MSU-BIT University. The university offers programs in international economy and trade, Russian language, mathematics, and materials science and engineering. Approved by Shenzhen Municipal People's Government, Shenzhen MSU-BIT University is the first partnership between Russian and Chinese institutions of higher education. It "aims to build a world-class comprehensive university . . . and is committed to developing elite education and high-level research activities."[76]

Fueling this trend in cross-border ventures is China's goal to become a major education hub and the fact that several state-owned enterprises (SOEs) in China want to modernize the way they do business. One way to accomplish both of these goals is by attracting students and scholars from premier learning institutions.[77]

As attractive as they sound, joint ventures have their problems. First, as in the case of licensing, a company runs the risk of losing control over its technology to its venture partner. American Superconductor (AMSC) and China's Sinovel Wind Group Co. entered into a joint venture to work on wind power projects, but Sinovel admitted it stole source code from AMSC to use in its own wind turbines.[78]

Second, companies may find themselves at odds with one another. For example, one joint venture partner may want to move production to a country where demand is growing, but the other would prefer to keep its factories at home running at full capacity. Conflict over who controls what within a joint venture is a primary reason many fail.[79]

In fact, many of the early joint ventures American and European companies entered into with companies in China lost money or failed precisely because of conflicts over control. To offset these disadvantages, experienced managers strive to iron out technology, control, and other potential conflicts up front, when they first negotiate the joint venture agreement.

Wholly Owned Subsidiaries

Establishing a wholly owned subsidiary—that is, an independent company owned by the parent corporation—is the most costly method of serving an overseas market. Companies that use this approach must bear the full costs and risks (as opposed to joint ventures, in which the costs and risks are shared, or licensing, in which the licensee bears most of the costs and risks).

Nevertheless, setting up a wholly owned subsidiary offers two clear advantages. First, when a company's competitive advantage is based on technology, a wholly owned subsidiary reduces the risk of losing control over the technology. Wholly owned subsidiaries are thus the preferred mode of entry in the semiconductor, electronics, and pharmaceutical industries.

> Setting up a wholly owned subsidiary offers two clear advantages.

However, this advantage is limited by the extent to which the government of the country where the subsidiary is located will protect intellectual property such as patents and trademarks. Obviously this is a vital consideration.

Second, a wholly owned subsidiary gives a company tight control over operations in other countries, which is necessary if the company chooses to pursue a global strategy. Establishing a global manufacturing system requires world headquarters to have a high degree of control over the operations of national affiliates. Unlike licensees or joint venture partners, wholly owned subsidiaries usually accept centrally determined decisions about how to produce, how much to produce, and how to price output for transfer among operations.

Working Overseas

When establishing operations overseas, headquarters executives can choose to send **expatriates** (individuals from the parent country), use **host-country nationals** (natives of the host country), and deploy **third-country nationals** (citizens of a country other than the home country or the host country). Most corporations use all three types of employees, as each has distinctive advantages and disadvantages.

Sending expatriates can cost three to four times as much as employing host-country nationals. Moreover, in many countries—particularly developing countries in which firms are trying to get an economic foothold—the personal security of expatriates is a big issue. Firms therefore may send their expatriates on shorter assignments, or avoid the problem by not sending people to some countries and instead use chat, email, online collaboration platforms, conference calls, videoconferences and other means to communicate between international divisions.

Working internationally can be highly stressful, even for experienced globetrotters. Exhibit 6.5 shows some of the primary stressors for expatriates at different stages of their assignments. It also shows how managers can cope with the stress, plus some things companies can do to help with the adjustments.

Expatriate assignments are valuable for professional and personal development, and having a pool of experienced expatriates is useful. On the other hand, local employees tend to be more available, are familiar with the culture and language, and usually cost less. In addition, local governments often provide incentives to companies that create good jobs for their citizens, or they may place restrictions on the use of expatriates.

Such advantages, coupled with the often-inadequate educational systems of developing nations, create stiff competition for local management talent. The result is that China, India, and many countries in Latin America do not have enough qualified talent to fill the demand for local executives. In China, there is currently a shortage of job candidates with the right soft skills, namely leadership, people management, and interpersonal, verbal, and written communication. Companies are expected to invest heavily in training and development to build these critical skills areas.[80]

LO 6-5 Explain how companies can staff overseas operations.

expatriates
Parent-company nationals who are sent to work at a foreign subsidiary.

host-country nationals
Natives of the country where an overseas subsidiary is located.

third-country nationals
Natives of a country other than the home country or the host country of an overseas subsidiary.

Estimates are that nearly 15 percent of all employee transfers are to an international location.

EXHIBIT 6.5   Expatriate Stressors and Coping Responses

Stage	Primary Stressors	Executive Coping Response	Employer Coping Response
Assignment acceptance	Unrealistic evaluation of stressors to come. Hurried time frame.	Think of assignment as a growth opportunity rather than an instrument to vertical promotion.	Do not make hard-to-keep promises. Clarify expectations.
Pre- and post-arrival	Ignorance of cultural differences.	Do not make unwarranted assumptions of cultural competence and cultural rules.	Provide pre-, during-, and post-assignment training. Encourage support-seeking behavior.
Novice	Cultural blunders or inadequacy of coping responses. Ambiguity owing to inability to decipher meaning of situations.	Observe and study functional value of coping responses among locals. Do not simply replicate responses that worked at home.	Provide follow-up training. Seek advice from locals and expatriate network.
Mastery	Frustration with inability to perform boundary-spanning role. Bothered by living with a cultural paradox.	Internalize and enjoy identification with both cultures and walking between two cultures.	Reinforce rather than punish dual identification by defining common goals.
Repatriation	Disappointment with unfulfilled expectations. Sense of isolation. Loss of autonomy.	Realistically reevaluate assignment as a personal and professional growth opportunity.	Arrange pre-repatriation briefings and interviews. Schedule post-repatriation support meetings.

SOURCE: Adapted from Sanchez, J., Spector, P., and Cooper, C., *Academy of Management Executive*, May 2000, pp. 96–106.

LO 6-6 Summarize the skills and knowledge managers need to manage globally.

failure rate

The number of expatriate managers of an overseas operation who come home early.

Skills of the Global Manager

Estimates are that nearly 15 percent of all employee transfers are to an international location. However, the **failure rate** among expatriates (defined as those who come home early) is higher for American expatriates compared to those international assignees from Europe and Asia.[81] The cost of each of these failed assignments can be higher than three times the expatriate's total annual compensation.[82]

The causes of failure overseas go beyond technical capability and include personal and social issues. Hosts' attitudes and behaviors toward expatriates can be more or less welcoming both at the beginning and over time.[83] In a recent survey of human resource managers around the globe, two-thirds said the main reason for the failures is family issues, especially dissatisfaction of the employee's spouse or partner.[84] The problem may be compounded for dual-career couples, in which one spouse may have to give up his or her job to join the expatriate manager in the new location. For both the expatriate and the spouse, adjustment requires flexibility, emotional stability, empathy for the culture, communication skills, resourcefulness, initiative, diplomatic skills, and coping strategies.[85]

Companies such as Colgate, Johnson & Johnson, Bechtel, Monsanto, and Dow Chemical have worked to identify the skills that predict expatriate success (Exhibit 6.6). Importantly,

EXHIBIT 6.6

Identifying International Executives

End-State Dimensions	Description
1. Sensitivity to cultural differences.	When working with people from other cultures, works hard to understand their perspective.
2. Business knowledge.	Has a solid understanding of the company's products and services.
3. Courage to take a stand.	Is willing to take a stand on issues.
4. Brings out the best in people.	Has a special talent for dealing with people.
5. Acts with integrity.	Can be depended on to tell the truth regardless of circumstances.
6. Is insightful.	Is good at identifying the most important part of a complex problem.
7. Is committed to success.	Clearly demonstrates commitment to seeing the organization succeed.
8. Takes risks.	Takes personal as well as business risks.
Learning-Oriented Dimensions	**Survey Items**
1. Uses feedback.	Has changed as a result of feedback.
2. Is culturally adventurous.	Enjoys the challenge of working in countries other than his or her own.
3. Seeks opportunities to learn.	Takes advantage of opportunities to do new things.
4. Is open to criticism.	Does not appear brittle—as if criticism might cause him or her to break.
5. Seeks feedback.	Pursues feedback even when others are reluctant to give it.
6. Is flexible.	Doesn't get so invested in things that he or she cannot change when something doesn't work.

SOURCE: Spreitzer, G. M., McCall, M. W. and Mahoney, J. D., "Early Identification of International Executive Potential," *Journal of Applied Psychology* 82, no. 1 (1997), pp. 6–29. ©1997 by American Psychological Association.

- Structure assignments clearly: Develop clear reporting relationships and job responsibilities.
- Create clear job objectives.
- Develop performance measurements based on objectives.
- Use effective, validated selection and screening criteria (both personal and technical attributes).
- Prepare expatriates and families for assignments (briefings, training, support).
- Create a vehicle for ongoing communication with expatriates.
- Anticipate repatriation to facilitate reentry when they come back home.
- Consider developing a mentor program that will help monitor and intervene in case of trouble.

EXHIBIT 6.7
How to Prevent Failed Global Assignments

in addition to such things as cultural sensitivity, technical expertise, and business knowledge, an individual's success abroad may depend greatly on his or her ability to learn from experience.[86]

Boeing, SAP, Iberdrola, Hyundai, AT&T, Siemens, and others with large international staffs have extensive training programs to prepare employees for international assignments. Exhibit 6.7 suggests ways to improve their likelihood of success. Other companies, such as Coca-Cola, Motorola, Chevron, and Mattel, extend this training to include employees who may be located in the United States but who also deal in international markets. These programs focus on areas such as language,[87] culture, and career development.

Going on overseas assignments affects careers. A manager selected for a post overseas usually is being groomed to become a more effective manager in an era of globalization. In addition, she often will have more responsibility, challenge, and operating leeway than at home. Yet expatriates often worry about being out of the loop on decisions and key developments back home. Good companies and managers address this issue with effective communication between subsidiaries and headquarters and visitations to and from the home office.

Understanding Cultural Issues

In many ways, cultural issues represent the most elusive aspect of international business. In the era of the "global village," it is easy to forget how deep and enduring cultural differences can be. The fact that people everywhere drink Coke, wear blue jeans, use smartphones, and drive Toyotas doesn't mean we are all becoming alike. Each country is unique for reasons rooted in history, culture, language, geography, social conditions, race, and religion.[88] These differences complicate any international activity and represent the fundamental issues that inform and guide how a company should conduct business across borders.

Ironically, although most of us would guess that the trick to working abroad is learning about a foreign culture, our problems often stem from being oblivious to our own cultural conditioning. Most of us are unaware of how our own culture influences our everyday behavior. Because of this, we adapt poorly to situations that are unique or foreign to us.

Without realizing it, some managers may act out of **ethnocentrism**—a tendency to judge foreign people or groups by the standards of one's own culture or group and to see one's own standards as superior. This tendency may

ethnocentrism

The tendency to judge others by the standards of one's own group or culture, which are seen as superior.

LO 6-7 Identify ways in which cultural differences between countries influence management.

In this era, when people from all over the globe are collaborating on business issues, it is vital to learn about and respect different cultures.

Rawpixel.com/Shutterstock

Inclusiveness Works

Bridging Cultural Divides: Beyond Words

As markets become more globalized, so too does the workplace. Multinational teams are more common than ever, and managers need to account for nuances of cultural difference to ensure inclusive and productive work environments. Of course, effective communication depends on the language we use and how we use it. But to truly bridge cultural differences, it's important to go beyond language and consider differences in cultural values and beliefs.

Organizational structure, for example, is understood differently among cultures.[89] Some cultures adhere to strict hierarchies, whereas others emphasize a more horizontal approach. Managers from a hierarchy are accustomed to a higher degree of deference than those from a more collaborative structure. Similarly, employees, sensing an air of condescension from a superior, might shut down entirely, thinking their ideas don't matter.

Managers must also account for attitudes about work and the workplace so that all team members are in sync.[90] Differences in attitudes regarding workplace attire, punctuality, and deadlines—to name just a few—can affect a team's cohesion and productivity.[91]

Being aware of these cultural differences isn't enough, however. Managers must address these issues proactively and in ways that are culturally sensitive. Fostering an inclusive and productive work environment isn't merely about acknowledging that cultural differences exist; it's about trying to understand and bridge those differences in a way that leverages everyone's talents.

1. What other cultural attitudes about work might be helpful to address when managing a multinational team?
2. Can you provide a culturally sensitive way of addressing punctuality for a team comprised of members who have different beliefs about what that means?

be unconscious: "in Brazil, people seem so emotional" or "Germans want everything done a certain way" or "Japanese people are hard to read; they never tell you what they're really thinking." Or people may not recognize the values underlying a local culture—for example, assuming that the culture is backward because it does not air American or European TV shows or movies, when actually it is trying to maintain its traditional values and norms.

Such assumptions are one reason people traveling abroad frequently experience **culture shock**—the disorientation and stress associated with being in a foreign environment. Managers are better able to navigate this transition if they are sensitive to their surroundings, including social norms and customs, and adjust their behavior to the new circumstances.[92] Employers can help by conveying cultural norms and suggesting behaviors that contribute to success in the host country.

A wealth of cross-cultural research has been conducted on the differences and similarities among various countries.[93] Perhaps best known is the work of Geert Hofstede, who identified four types of differences between country cultures within multinational corporations:[94]

culture shock

The disorientation and stress associated with being in a foreign environment.

> *Power distance:* the extent to which a society accepts the fact that power in organizations is distributed unequally.
>
> *Individualism/collectivism:* the extent to which people act on their own or as a part of a group.
>
> *Uncertainty avoidance:* the extent to which people in a society feel threatened by uncertain and ambiguous situations.
>
> *Masculinity/femininity:* the extent to which a society values quantity of life (e.g., accomplishment, money) over quality of life (e.g., compassion, beauty).

Of course, it is easy to stereotype, exaggerate, and overgeneralize differences among countries. Colombians often prefer to act as part of a group, just as many Australians enjoy acting individualistically. Globalization by now may have blurred some of Hofstede's distinctions. Still, to suggest that no cultural differences exist is equally simplistic. Clearly, cultures such as the United States that emphasize individualism differ significantly from collectivist cultures such as those of Pakistan, Taiwan, and Venezuela.

Instructors differ regarding how much detail they want you to know from this material. The Hofstede data are used widely in cross-cultural scholarship, but they are old. In fact, recent analyses indicate more differences *within* countries than *between* countries, indicating that culture and country are not the same.[95]

How much do you think cultural differences have changed in the past several decades? You and classmates can view the exhibit, consider familiar countries, and discuss what among the old data has changed versus stayed the same. Whatever you decide about similarities versus differences, it remains useful to think about Hofstede's dimensions as possible regional and corporate cultural descriptors—while perhaps identifying additional possibilities.

Cross-cultural management extends beyond U.S. employees going abroad. It includes effective management of **inpatriates**—foreign nationals who are transferred to work at the parent company. These employees bring extensive knowledge about how to operate effectively in their home countries. They also will be better prepared to communicate their organization's products and values when they return. But they often have the same types of problems as American expatriates and may be even more neglected because parent-company managers see the home country as normal—requiring no period of adjustment. Yet the language, customs, expense, geography, and lack of local community support in the United States are at least as daunting to inpatriates as the experience of American nationals abroad.

inpatriate

A foreign national brought in to work at the parent company.

Thus, culture shock works both ways. Effective managers are sensitive to these issues and consider them when dealing with foreign-national employees. In contrast to American-born employees, co-workers or customers from other countries might tend to communicate less directly, place more emphasis on hierarchy and authority, or make consensus-based decisions. In general, managers of international groups can manage misunderstandings by acknowledging cultural differences and establishing behavioral norms to correct and prevent problems that upset group members, or by removing group members who demonstrate they cannot work effectively with others.[96]

Good managers help their employees adjust. Basic issues include the following:

Meetings: Americans tend to have specific views about the purpose of meetings and how much time should be spent. International workers may have different preconceptions about the nature and length of meetings, and managers should make sure foreign nationals are comfortable with the American approach.

Work(aholic) schedules: Workers from other countries can work long hours, but in countries with strong labor organizations they often get (and take) many more weeks of vacation than American workers. Europeans in particular may balk at working on weekends. Matters such as these should be addressed at the beginning of the work assignment.

Email: Not everyone loves email and texting; whether a cultural or an individual preference, many prefer to communicate in person. Particularly when potential language difficulties exist, managers should avoid relying on email for important matters at least at the outset.

Fast-trackers: Although U.S. companies may put a young MBA graduate on the fast track to upper management, most other cultures still see no substitute for the wisdom gained through experience. This is something U.S. managers working abroad should bear in mind.

Feedback: Everyone likes praise, but excessive positive feedback is more prevalent in the United States than in other cultures—a useful fact for American expats receiving performance reviews overseas, and U.S. managers when they give reviews to foreign nationals.[97]

The Digital World

Global Email Etiquette

International management in the digital age means connecting with people across the globe who often have different cultural norms and expectations. It's important to be aware of these potential differences, especially through email where the only way to convey an idea is through the words we choose. For example, a brief, straightforward email may be interpreted as rushed or abrupt.[98]

The degree of formality in email varies from culture to culture. In many cultures, it is expected (and polite) to begin with a personal question about one's family, but in other cultures, this would be considered prying or rude.[99]

How should managers handle these issues? Rules of thumb include avoiding idioms or slang, steering clear of jargon that may be easily misunderstood, being careful with humor, and above all else, researching the cultures of the people with whom you are interacting.[100]

When engaging directly with customers, experts say the key is to use technology to engage in "hyperlocal" communication, accounting for aspects of a person's local community, or microculture.[101]

1. What other potential challenges must managers consider to be effective with email communication?
2. What benefits do you see to engaging your international clients "hyperlocally"?

Ethical Issues in International Management

If managers are to function effectively overseas, they must understand how culture affects both how they are perceived and how others behave. One of the most sensitive issues in this regard is how culture plays out in terms of ethics.[102] Assessments of right and wrong get blurred as we move from one culture to another, as actions that are normal and customary in one setting may be unethical—even illegal—in another. Bribes are a classic example, as they can be an accepted part of commercial transactions in many Asian, African, Latin American, and Middle Eastern cultures. Even companies from cultures that view bribery as a form of corruption sometimes feel they must offer bribes when they think that this is part of the culture they are dealing with.[103]

Consequently, companies with global operations should be at least as active as domestic corporations in identifying, establishing, and enforcing standards for ethical behavior. For example, global supply chains (Chapter 2) can reduce costs, but also make it difficult to monitor and control critical processes such as labor practices and supply sourcing. Legally, U.S. companies must determine and report on whether their products contain "conflict minerals" from the Democratic Republic of Congo region. Analysis of every conflict minerals report submitted to the Securities and Exchange Commission found that almost 80 percent admitted they were unable to determine such materials' country of origin, and only 1 percent could honestly certify themselves conflict-free.[104]

In Chapter 5, we identified a number of steps organizations can take to clarify and encourage ethical behavior. The primary difference in the international context is that this must be done with not just domestic employees, but also overseas colleagues and partners, who may have their own expectations.

Research has identified five core values that most people embrace regardless of their nationality or religion: compassion, fairness, honesty, responsibility, and respect for others. These values lie at the heart of human experience and human rights and seem to transcend more superficial differences between countries and regions. Knowing these shared values can help to build more effective partnerships, across as well as within cultures. Perhaps as long as people understand that they share some core values, they can collaborate effectively despite their differences.[105]

To a large extent, the challenge of managing across borders comes down to the practical philosophies and everyday systems developed for working with people. International

Management in Action

CONTROLLING ALIBABA'S PROBLEM WITH COUNTERFEITS

China's rising middle class has increasingly sophisticated tastes and the money to spend on gratifying them. Willing to pay for high-quality brands, these consumers are growing more savvy about rejecting the counterfeit goods that have long plagued Alibaba's retail platforms, especially Taobao. Black-market sites where counterfeits are rampant are actually experiencing a decline as China's newly wealthy young consumers flex their spending muscle and choose to shop where they can place their trust.

Problems with counterfeits at Alibaba caused U.S. trade officials to place Taobao on its watchlist of "notorious markets" starting in 2012. Alibaba responded with efforts to combat fakes—hiring a staff of 2,000 and enlisting 5,000 volunteers to help identify counterfeit goods, setting aside 150 million yuan (almost US$22 million) to buy and test suspected fakes and designing algorithms that help spot fakes by monitoring data such as price. The company invested in a $2.4 million lobbying effort in Washington to seek removal from the list, and a reprieve was finally granted.

In 2016, however, the United States Trade Representative returned Taobao to its blacklist, and again in 2018.[106]

The designation itself carries no official consequences and hasn't shown any significant signs of impeding Alibaba's growth. But for a company that aims to aggressively expand into U.S. markets, the counterfeiting problem is something that Alibaba must resolve.

Alibaba has become more aggressive in addressing the issue: It has been taking to Chinese courts to sue vendors for selling fake goods.[107] It has also been using data analytics and working more closely with brands and law enforcement to weed out the problem.

In its annual intellectual property protection report to begin 2019, Alibaba has claimed success, reporting that only 1 out of every 10,000 transactions is now suspected of being counterfeit goods. Their claim is not without skeptics, however. In its most recent report, the World Trademark Review still found Taobao to be the platform where fake goods could be most easily found.[108]

- What is Alibaba's ethical responsibility for controlling the sale of counterfeit goods on its websites?
- What cultural issues can you identify in this example?

managers need to develop a portfolio of behaviors and methods adapted to different cultural situations. These adjustments, however, should not compromise the values, integrity, and strengths of their home- country cultures.

When managers understand and work effectively across cultures, they can capitalize on the opportunities that our global economy offers. The implications of globalization are evident with Alibaba's emergence as a world player. People around the world are becoming more educated, launching businesses, and enjoying a higher standard of living. The opportunities to responsibly serve their needs are enormous, and even small, local business managers can learn about people's needs and meet them globally. Probably many more will start participating in Alibaba's e-markets.

KEY TERMS

culture shock, p. 188

ethnocentrism, p. 187

expatriates, p. 185

failure rate, p. 186

global model, p. 180

host-country nationals, p. 185

inpatriate, p. 189

inshoring, p. 172

insourcing, p. 173

international model, p. 179

multinational model, p. 179

North American Free Trade Agreement (NAFTA), p. 175

offshoring, p. 172

outsourcing, p. 172

third-country nationals, p. 185

transnational model, p. 180

RETAINING WHAT YOU LEARNED

In Chapter 6, you learned how globalization is changing the competitive landscape and influencing the behavior of managers and companies. The lowering of trade barriers is fueling the movement toward increased globalization. Companies use different strategies to compete, including international, multinational, global, and transnational. Each strategy emphasizes a different mix of global integration and local responsiveness. The five methods of entering an overseas market are exporting, licensing, franchising, entering into a joint venture, and setting up a wholly owned subsidiary. When staffing an overseas operation, companies can deploy expatriates from the headquarters' country, host-country nationals, and third-country nationals. To decrease the risk of failure, expatriates should possess not only technical capability but also personal and social skills. By recognizing cultural differences, people can find it easier to work together collaboratively and benefit from the exchange.

LO 6-1   Discuss what integration of the global economy means for companies and their managers.

- In recent years, rapid growth has occurred in world trade, foreign direct investment, and imports.
- One consequence is that companies around the globe are now finding their home markets under attack from international competitors.
- The global competitive environment is becoming a much tougher place in which to do business. However, companies now have access to markets that previously were denied to them.

LO 6-2   Describe how the world economy is becoming more integrated than ever before.

- The gradual lowering of barriers to free trade is making the world economy more integrated.
- This means that the modern manager operates in an environment that offers more opportunities but is also more complex and competitive than that faced by the manager of a generation ago.

LO 6-3   Define the strategies organizations use to compete in the global marketplace.

- The international corporation builds on its existing core capabilities in R&D, marketing, manufacturing, and so on to penetrate overseas markets.
- A multinational is a more complex form that usually has fully autonomous units operating in multiple countries. Subsidiaries have latitude to address local issues such as consumer preferences, political pressures, and economic trends in their own regions of the world.
- The global organization pulls control of overseas operations back into the headquarters and approaches the world market as a unified whole to maximize efficiency on a global scale.

- A transnational attempts to achieve both local responsiveness and global integration by coordinating specialized facilities positioned around the world.

LO 6-4   Compare the various entry modes organizations use to enter overseas markets.

- Companies can enter overseas markets by exporting, licensing, franchising, entering into a joint venture, and setting up a wholly owned subsidiary.
- Each mode has advantages and disadvantages.

LO 6-5   Explain how companies can staff overseas operations.

- Most executives use a combination of expatriates, host-country nationals, and third-country nationals.
- Expatriates can establish new country operations quickly, transfer the company's culture, and bring in specific technical skills.
- Host-country nationals have the advantages of being familiar with local customs and culture, costing less, and being viewed more favorably by local governments.
- Third-country nationals often are used as a compromise in politically touchy situations or when home-country expatriates are not available.

LO 6-6   Summarize the skills and knowledge managers need to manage globally.

- The causes of failure overseas extend beyond technical capability and include personal and social issues.
- Important knowledge permeates the chapter, but in particular see Exhibit 6.6.

LO 6-7   Identify ways in which cultural differences between countries influence management.

- Culture influences our actions and perceptions as well as the actions and perceptions of others. Unfortunately, we often are unaware of how culture influences us, and this can cause problems.
- Managers must be able to change their behavior to match the needs and customs of people they work with. Hofstede's classic research identified four dimensions of cultural differences; some say those differences are disappearing but this should not be assumed. It is important not to stereotype or overgeneralize, but potential differences deserve attention and mutual accommodation.
- By recognizing cultural differences and discussing behavioral norms for dealing with them, people can find it easier to work together collaboratively and benefit from the exchange.
- Legal and ethical issues create particularly important challenges.

DISCUSSION QUESTIONS

1. Why is the world economy becoming more integrated? What are the implications of this integration for international managers?

2. Imagine you are the CEO of a major company; choose your favorite products or industry. What approach to global competition would you choose for your firm: international, multinational, global, or transnational? Why?

3. Why have franchises been so popular as a method of international expansion in the fast-food industry? Contrast this with high-tech manufacturing, where joint ventures and partnerships have been more popular. What accounts for the differences across industries?

4. What are the pros and cons of using expatriates, host-country nationals, and third-country nationals to run overseas operations? If you were expanding your business, what approach would you prefer to use?

5. If you had entered into a joint venture with a foreign company but knew that women were not treated fairly in that culture, would you consider sending a female expatriate to handle the start-up? Why or why not?

6. Consider Hofstede's four cultural dimensions. He identified them in a huge global corporation several decades ago. Do you think cultural differences since then have decreased due to globalization? What evidence do you draw from?

7. What are the biggest cultural obstacles that we must overcome if we are to work effectively in Mexico? Are there different obstacles in France? Japan? China?

EXPERIENTIAL EXERCISES

6.1 Global Integration—Local Responsiveness Worksheet

OBJECTIVE

To understand how companies compete in the global marketplace.

INSTRUCTIONS

An effective way to learn how companies respond to the competing pressures to be globally integrated and locally responsive is to study them in action. Referring back to Exhibit 6.3, search online for examples of companies that are currently using a global, transnational, international, or multinational organizational model. Please provide answers to the following questions:

PART I: GLOBAL MODEL

Name of company using a *global* organizational model:

_____

URL of website/article describing the company's *global* strategy:

_____

Explain why the company uses a *global* strategy to compete:

_____

_____

_____

PART II: TRANSNATIONAL MODEL

Name of company using a *transnational* organizational model:

_____

URL of website/article describing the company's *transnational* strategy:

_____

Explain why the company uses a *transnational* strategy to compete:

_____

_____

_____

PART III: INTERNATIONAL MODEL

Name of company using an *international* organizational model:

_____

URL of website/article describing the company's *international* strategy:

_____

Explain why the company uses an *international* strategy to compete:

PART IV: MULTINATIONAL MODEL

Name of company using a *multinational* organizational model:

_____

URL of website/article describing the company's *multinational* strategy:

_____

Explain why the company uses a *multinational* strategy to compete:

_____

_____

_____

SOURCE: Adapted from McGrath, R. R. Jr., *Exercises in Management Fundamentals,* 1st ed. Upper Saddle River, NJ: Pearson Education, 1985, p. 177.

6.2   Cross-Cultural Anthropologist

Assume you are a cross-cultural anthropologist. In this role, please visit multiple public places that are frequented by one or more ethnic or cultural groups. Observe four to five behaviors that strike you as unique or different compared to what you consider to be "normal." After you make your observations, walk to a quiet location and record what you observed in a notebook or mobile device. Think about why these behaviors caught your attention in the first place and then analyze them from the perspective of Hofstede's cultural dimensions (individualism/collectivism, power distance, uncertainty avoidance, and masculinity/femininity).

LEARNING OBJECTIVES

1. To help students interpret nonverbal communication in a more culturally neutral manner.

2. To encourage students to understand their own reactions to different cultural behaviors.

3. To reinforce the importance of observation skills in cross-cultural encounters.

STEPS

1. Visit multiple public places where you can observe the behaviors of one or more ethnic or cultural groups. Examples include major airports, ethnic associations, foreign consulates, religious entities, cultural centers, museums, and cultural or affinity groups at universities.

2. Bring a notebook or mobile device and:
   a. On the *left* side of the page, make a column titled: ***"Observation/description."***
      i. In this section, describe what you saw. Any behavior that strikes you as different, frustrating, funny, or confusing is appropriate. Stick to the facts when describing these behaviors. Write down 5–10 observed behaviors.
   b. On the *right* side of the page, make a column titled: ***"How This Observation Relates to Hofstede's Dimensions."***
      i. In this section, interpret the behaviors by using Hofstede's dimensions (individualism/collectivism, uncertainty avoidance, power distance, and masculinity/femininity). How can these dimensions help explain what you observed? Explain.

3. Type and hand in your anthropologist's analysis. This should include:
   a. Your name, date, and the name of each public place you visited.
   b. 5–10 observed behaviors (left side of notebook) that you made while visiting the place(s) and a description of how these observations relate to Hofstede's cultural dimensions (right side of notebook).

SOURCE: Adapted from Kohls, L. R. and Knight, J. M., *Cross-Cultural Journal in Developing Intercultural Awareness: A Cross-Cultural Training Handbook*. Yarmouth, ME: Intercultural Press, 1994, p. 67.

Concluding Case

A GLOBAL LAUNCH FOR TREASURE CUP?

Nina Lopez and Matt O'Rourke have been trying to raise capital to expand their growing chain of cupcake shops, Treasure Cup. They make a full range of traditional cupcakes, but they found immediate success with their signature cupcakes, those that have a range of fillings, from ice cream to candy to exotic fruits. They opened their first store 10 years ago and quickly expanded throughout their state. They now own 15 stores in four states in the Northeast and are looking toward further expansion.

Initially, Nina and Matt were thinking they would try to branch out nationally, but with the swift success they've had, and the fact that they both were born in countries outside of the United States, they decided to set their sights even bigger and expand overseas. Their Treasure Cups have broad appeal, and their fillings can be easily tailored to local taste. Nina and Matt therefore concluded not to limit themselves by looking at just the U.S. market. They had already proven that they could scale; now was the time to capitalize on their experience and success.

The plan is now to launch Treasure Cup as a global company, serving clients in multiple countries. However, some potential investors have expressed doubts about their ability to operate globally before the company has built out beyond one region in the United States. One investor asked Matt and Nina whether they really were prepared to respond to the needs of business clients located hundreds or thousands of miles away.

DISCUSSION QUESTIONS

1. What aspects of global integration do Nina and Matt need to consider in order to be successful?

2. Which entry mode strategy—franchising or wholly owned stores—should they pursue to help Treasure Cup succeed as an international brand?

3. If you were Nina or Matt, what would you do? Explain your response.

ENDNOTES

1. Arjun Kharpal, "Alibaba Sets New Singles Day Record with More Than $30.8 Billion in Sales in 24 Hours," *CNBC,* November 11, 2018, https://www.cnbc.com/2018/11/11/alibaba-singles-day-2018-record-sales-on-largest-shopping-event-day.html.

2. Statista, "Annual Revenue of Alibaba Group from 2010 to 2018," https://www.statista.com/statistics/225614/net-revenue-of-alibaba/, accessed March 21, 2019.

3. Alibabagroup.com, "Alibaba Group Announces December Quarter 2018 Results," https://www.alibabagroup.com/en/news/press_pdf/p190130.pdf.

4. Erika Kinetz, "U.S. Brands Suffer Collateral Damage in Chinese Corporate War," *Chicago Tribune,* March 16, 2019, https://www.chicagotribune.com/business/ct-biz-alibaba-tmall-jd-com-20180423-story.html.

5. Anita Balakrishnan, "Jack Ma Explains the Difference between Alibaba and Amazon: 'Amazon Is More Like an Empire,'" *CNBC News,* January 18, 2017, http://www.cnbc.com/2017/01/18/jack-ma-difference-between-alibaba-and-amazon.html.

6. C. Isidore, "These Are the Top U.S. Exports," *CNN Business,* March 7, 2018, www.money.cnn.com.

7. L. Brennan, "How Netflix Expanded to 190 Countries in 7 Years," *Harvard Business Review,* October 12, 2018, www.hbr.com.

8. C. Morris, "10 Iconic American Companies Owned by Chinese Investors," *CNBC,* May 11, 2017, www.cnbc.com.

9. K. Mays, "The 2018 Cars.com American-Made Index," June 21, 2018, www.cars.com.

10. "2018 Best Selling Cars in the World," *Fortune,* www.fortune.com, accessed March 3, 2019.

11. "Colorado Software Company Applt Ventures Acquires London Software Shop," news release, January 25, 2017, www.businessnewswire.com.

12. L. Dormehl, "Replaced by Robots: 10 Jobs That Could Be Hit Hard by the A.I. Revolution," *Digital Trends,* November 4, 2018, www.digitaltrends.com; M. Chui, J. Manyika, and M. Miremadi, "Where Machines Could Replace Humans–and Where They Can't (Yet)," *McKinsey Quarterly,* July 2016, www.mckinsey.com.

13. M. Grothaus, "These Are the Few Jobs That Robots Won't Take from Us," *Fast Company,* August 30, 2018, www.fastcompany.com.

14. M. Grothaus, "These Are the Few Jobs That Robots Won't Take from Us," *Fast Company,* August 30, 2018, www.fastcompany.com; M. Chui, J. Manyika, and M. Miremadi, "Where Machines Could Replace Humans–and Where They Can't (Yet)," *McKinsey Quarterly,* July 2016, www.mckinsey.com.

15. "Labor Force Statistics from the Current Population Survey," *Bureau of Labor Statistics,* January 18, 2019, www.bls.gov.

16. "From Bangalore to Boston: The Trend of Bringing IT Back In-House," Deloitte, www.deloitte.com, accessed January 30, 2019.

17. N. McLernon and J. Walters, "Insourcing Survey 2014," PricewaterhouseCoopers, March 2014, http://www.pwc.com; "From Bangalore to Boston: The Trend of Bringing IT Back In-House," Deloitte, www.deloitte.com, accessed January 30, 2019.

18. D. Eriksson, P. Helletofth, L. Ellram, and C. Sansone, "To Offshore or Reshore? The Battle of Data Points," *Supply Chain Management Review,* May 2, 2018, www.scmr.com.

19. "Five Things You Need to Know about the Maastricht Treaty," European Central Bank, February 15, 2017, www.ecb.europa.eu.

20. World Bank, "European Union," data.worldbank.org, accessed March 3, 2018; World Bank, "GDP (Current US$)," data.worldbank.org, accessed March 3, 2018.

21. S. Erlanger, "Britain Votes to Leave E.U.; Cameron Plans to Step Down," *The New York Times,* June 23, 2016, www.nytimes.com.

22. R. Noack, "These Countries Could Be Next Now That Britain Has Left the E.U.," *The Washington Post,* June 24, 2016.

23. P. Sawers, "13 European Companies Acquired by U.S. Tech Giants in 2018," *Venture Beat,* December 24, 2018, www.venturebeat.com.

24. R. Iyengar, "PayPal Buys Swedish Startup iZettle for $2.2 Billion," *CNN Business,* May 18, 2018, www.money.cnn.com.

25. G. Orr, "What Can We Expect in China in 2019?" *McKinsey Quarterly,* December 2018, www.mckinsey.com.

26. K. Bradsher, "China's Economy, by the Numbers, Is Worse Than It Looks," *The New York Times,* January 20, 2019, www.nytimes.com; H. Tan, "China's Economy Grew 6.6% in 2018, the Lowest Pace in 28 Years," *CNBC,* January 20, 2019, www.cnbc.com; J. McDonald, "China's 2018 Economic Growth Sunk to a Three-Decade Low," *Time,* January 21, 2019, www.time.com.

27. K. Bradsher, "China's Economy, by the Numbers, Is Worse Than It Looks," *The New York Times,* January 20, 2019, www.nytimes.com; H. Tan, "China's Economy Grew 6.6% in 2018, the Lowest Pace in 28 Years," *CNBC,* January 20, 2019, www.cnbc.com; J. McDonald, "China's 2018 Economic Growth Sunk to a Three-Decade Low," *Time,* January 21, 2019, www.time.com.

28. "The People's Republic of China, U.S.-China Trade Facts," Office of the United States Trade Representative, https://ustr.gov/countries-regions/china-mongolia-taiwan/peoples-republic-china, accessed September 4, 2019.

29. K. Rapoza, "Trade War Casualties: Factories Shifting Out of China," *Forbes,* July 30, 2018, www.forbes.com.

30. D. Welch, "GM Is Building Cheap Cars for China's Masses," *Bloomberg Businessweek,* May 24, 2018, www.bloomberg.com.

31. B. De Lea, "Boeing, American Express among Companies Expanding in China Despite Trade Conflict," *Fox Business,* May 4, 2018, www.foxbusiness.com.

32. J. Mendoca and N. Alawadhi, "IT Firms Are Spending Millions to Train Workforce to Meet Increasing Demand for Digital Services," *Economic Times,* October 21, 2015, www.tech.economictimes.indiatimes.com.

33. C. Miller, "Latest Gartner Data Shows Apple Edge Out Samsung in Market Share during Q4 2016," *9to5Mac,* February 15, 2017, www.9to5mac.com.

34. "How Taiwan's Hon Hai Exemplified a Historic Turn in Asian Tiger Manufacturing," *Forbes Asia,* March 2017, www.forbes.com.

35. Office of the United States Trade Representative, "U.S.–APEC Trade Facts," http://www.ustr.gov, accessed March 20, 2017.

36. "Economic Outlook for Southeast Asia, China, and India 2017," OECD, January 23, 2017, www.oecd.org.

37. *CIA Factbook,* www.cia.gov; accessed March 4, 2019, R. Mathieson and J. Wingrove, "Trillion Dollar Nafta Deal Gets New Life: Balance of Power," *Bloomberg,* August 27, 2018, www.bloomberg.com.

38. J. Tankersley, "Trump Loves the New NAFTA, Congress Doesn't," *The New York Times,* February 6, 2019, www.nytimes.com; G. Gertz, "5 Things to Know about USMCA, the New NAFTA," Brookings Institute, October 2, 2018, www.brookings.edu.

39. R. Mathieson and J. Wingrove, "Trillion Dollar Nafta Deal Gets New Life: Balance of Power," *Bloomberg,* August 27, 2018, www.bloomberg.com.

40. J. McGeever, "Brazil's Economy Almost Ground to a Halt in Fourth Quarter: Reuters Poll," *U.S. News & World Report,* February 25, 2019, www.money.usnews.com.

41. J. McGeever, "Brazil's Economy Almost Ground to a Halt in Fourth Quarter: Reuters Poll," *U.S. News & World Report,* February 25, 2019, www.money.usnews.com.

42. J. Moed, "Start-Up Chile's Impact 2010-2018: Inside the Revolutionary Startup Accelerator," *Forbes,* November 19, 2018, www.forbes.com.

43. Office of the United States Trade Representative, "Free Trade Agreements," http://www.ustr.gov, accessed March 4, 2019.

44. R. Rapier, "Where America Gets Its Oil: The Top 10 Foreign Suppliers of Crude to the U.S.," *Forbes,* April 11, 2016, www.forbes.com.

45. M. Egan, "Here Comes the Next Wave of the U.S. Oil Boom," *CNNMoney,* February 17, 2017, www.money.cnn.com; M. Philips, "U.S. Oil Imports from Africa Are Down 90 Percent," *Bloomberg Business,* May 22, 2014, http://www.bloomberg.com; K. Dhillon, "Why Are U.S. Oil Imports Falling?" *Time,* April 17, 2014, http://www.time.com.

46. Company website, "IBM Research Africa," http://research.ibm.com/labs/africa/, accessed March 4, 2019.

47. Hultprize.org, http://www.hultprize.org/, accessed March 16, 2019.

48. Phyo Thura Htay, "The Nobel Prize for Students: Rice Startup Operating in Myanmar Wins 1 Million Dollars," *Prospects,* January 8, 2019, https://www.prospectsasean.com/the-nobel-prize-for-students-rice-startup-from-myanmar-wins-1-million-dollars/.

49. Angus Chen, "How 3 Rickshaws Won a Million Dollar Prize," *NPR,* September 20, 2017, https://www.npr.org/sections/goatsandsoda/2017/09/20/551888066/how-3-rickshaws-won-a-million-dollar-prize.

50. Angus Chen, "$1 Million Goes to an App That Leads to a Better Bus Commute," September 26, 2016, https://www.npr.org/sections/goatsandsoda/2016/09/26/495466938/a-million-dollars-goes-to-an-app-that-leads-to-a-better-bus-commute.

51. Eleanor Klibanoff, "'And the Million Dollar Hult Prize Goes to a Doc in a Box,'" September 26, 2014, https://www.npr.org/sections/goatsandsoda/2014/09/26/351515298/and-the-million-dollar-hult-prize-goes-to-a-doc-in-a-box.

52. Company website, "Comparison between Japanese, European and American Vehicles," www.info.japanesecartrade.com, accessed March 4, 2019.

53. E. Goldberg, "Yum Brands Opens Its First Taco Bell Location in Thailand," *Franchising,* March 13, 2019, www.franchising.com.

54. "Taco Bell Is Launching in Thailand with a Special Menu That Offers Extra Spicy Food and Local Beer," *Business Insider,* January 22, 2019, www.businessinsider.com.

55. A. Bhatia, "20 Bizarre KFC Food Items Thankfully Not Served in the USA," *The Travel,* September 22, 2018, www.thetravel.com; H. Jacobs, "KFC Is by Far the Most Popular Fast Food Chain in China and It's Nothing Like the U.S. Brand—Here's What It's Like," *Business Insider,* April 15, 2018, www.businessinsider.com.

56. "Trade Wars, Trump Tariffs and Protectionism Explained," *BBC News,* July 26, 2018, www.bbc.com.

57. "China Hits Back after U.S. Imposes Tariffs Worth $34bn," *BBC,* July 6, 2018, www.bbc.com.

58. "China Hits Back after U.S. Imposes Tariffs Worth $34bn," *BBC,* July 6, 2018, www.bbc.com.

59. J. Perlez and C. Buckley, "Trump Injects High Risk into Relations with China," *The New York Times,* January 24, 2017, www.nytimes.com.

60. Heineken website, www.thehenekencompany.com, accessed March 4, 2019.

61. S. Loveday, "Redesigned 2020 Toyota Corolla Sedan: All You Need to Know," *U.S. News & World Report,* January 18, 2019, www.cars.usnews.com.

62. S. Loveday, "Redesigned 2020 Toyota Corolla Sedan: All You Need to Know," *U.S. News & World Report,* January 18, 2019, www.cars.usnews.com.

63. E. Falkenberg-Hull, "Redesigned 2020 Toyota Coralla Gives First New Car Buyers More to Appreciate," *Biz Journals,* February 26, 2019, www.bizjournals.com.

64. A.-W. Harzing, "An Empirical Analysis and Extension of the Bartlett and Ghoshal Typology of Multinational Companies," *Journal of International Business Studies* 31, no. 1 (2000), pp. 101–20; Sucheta Nadkarni, Pol Herrmann, and Pedro David Perez, "Domestic Mindsets and Early International Performance: The Moderating Effect of Global Industry Conditions," *Strategic Management Journal* 32, no. 5 (May 2011), pp. 510–31; S. M. Morris and S. A. Snell, "Intellectual Capital Configurations and Organizational Capability: An Empirical Examination of Human Resource Subunits in the Multinational Enterprise," *Journal of International Business Studies* 42, no. 6 (2011), pp. 805–27; Elaine Ferndale, Jaap Paauwe, Shad S. Morris, Günther K. Stahl, Philip Stiles, Jonathan Trevor, and Patrick M. Wright, "Context-Bound Configurations of Corporate HR Functions in Multinational Corporations," *Human Resource Management* 49, no. 1 (January–February 2010), pp. 45–66.

65. J. Sandberg, "How Long Can India Keep Office Politics Out of Outsourcing?" *The Wall Street Journal,* February 27, 2007, http://online.wsj.com.

66. Toshiro Wakayama, Junjiro Shintaku, and Tomofumi Amano, "What Panasonic Learned in China," *Harvard Business Review,* December 2012, pp. 109–113; Daisuke Wakabayashi, "Panasonic to Pare Unprofitable Units," *The Wall Street Journal,* March 28, 2013, http://online.wsj.com.

67. D. Chiba, "Panasonic Plans Country Headquarters in China and US," *Nikkei Asian Review,* September 29, 2018, https://asia.nikkei.com.

68. "Target Has Partnered with Alibaba's Tmall to Sell in China," *Business Insider Intelligence,* September 16, 2016, https://www.businessinsider.com/target-has-partnered-with-alibabas-tmall-to-sell-in-china-2016-9.

69. Zhou Xin, "The Question Mark Hanging over China's 400 Million-Strong Middle Class," *South China Morning Post,* October 12, 2018, https://www.scmp.com/economy/china-economy/article/2168177/question-mark-hanging-over-chinas-400-million-strong-middle.

70. Daniel Geiger, "Chinese E-Commerce Giant Alibaba Expands Downtown Manhattan Headquarters," *Crain's,* December 27, 2016, http://www.crainsnewyork.com/article/20161227/REAL_ESTATE/161229944/chinese-online-retail-giant-alibaba-expands-lower-manhattan-headquarters-as-it-plans-new-york-expansion-known-as-an-alternative-to-amazon-the-hangzhou-based-company-founded-by-billionaire-jack-ma-is-valued-at-200-billion.

71. Jennifer Elias, "Alibaba Halts U.S. Cloud Expansion because of Silicon Valley Recruiting Woes," *Silicon Valley Business Journal,* September 4, 2018, https://www.bizjournals.com/sanjose/news/2018/09/04/alibaba-us-cloud-expansion-hiring-issues-aws.html.

72. C. H. Moon, "The Choice of Entry Modes and Theories of Foreign Direct Investment," *Journal of Global Marketing* 11, no. 2 (1997), pp. 43–64; I. Maignan and B. A. Lukas, "Entry Mode Decisions: The Role of Managers' Mental Models," *Journal of Global Marketing* 10, no. 4 (1997), pp. 7–22.

73. V. Sharma, "Eros Elbows Way into China through Content Licensing Deal with iQiyi," Reuters, September 10, 2018, www.reuters.com; "Netflix Joins Ranks of U.S. Tech Companies Admitting They Can't Conquer China," *MarketWatch,* October 24, 2016, www.marketwatch.com.

74. "2018 Top Global Franchises," *Entrepreneur,* www.entrepreneur.com, accessed February 1, 2019.

75. "7-Eleven® Tops Entrepreneur's 2017 Franchise 500," company press release, January 10, 2017, www.prnewswire.com.

76. University website, "About the University," http://en.szmsubit.edu.cn, accessed February 1, 2019; Media Report, "Shenzhen MSU-BIT University Welcomes Undergraduate Students for the Second Year," August 6, 2018, http://en.szmsubit.edu.cn.

77. Company website, "About Kunshan University—Overview," www.dukekunshan.edu.cn, accessed March 20, 2017; "Western Universities Expanding Joint Ventures in China," *ICEF Monitor,* September 30, 2014, http://monitor.icef.com.

78. C. Smythe, "Sinovel Must Pay $59 Million as Punishment in Trade Secrets Case," *Bloomberg,* July 6, 2018, www.bloomberg.com.

79. R. C. Beasley, "Reducing the Risk of Failure in the Formation of Commercial Partnerships," *Licensing Journal* 24, no. 4 (April 2004), p. 71; Elie Chrysostome, Roli Nigam, and Chaire Stephen Jarilowski, "Revisiting Strategic Learning in International Joint Ventures: A Knowledge Creation Perspective," *International Journal of Management* 30, no. 1 (March 2013), pp. 88–98.

80. K. Hille, "Western Faces Are Vital to China," *Financial Times,* December 9, 2010, Business & Company Resource Center, http://galenet.galegroup.com; J. S. Lublin, "Finding Top Talent in China, India, Brazil," *The Wall Street Journal,* April 11, 2011, http://online.wsj.com.

81. R. Tung, "Selection and Training of Personnel for Overseas Assignments," *Columbia Journal of World Business* 15 (1981), pp. 68–78; R. Tung, "Selection and Training Procedures of U.S., European, and Japanese Multinationals," *California Management Review* 25 (1981), pp. 57–71.

82. B. Veltkamp, "How to Manage the Cost of Expatriate Assignments," *CFO,* June 8, 2015, www.cfo.com.

83. H. Y. Kang and J. Shen, "Antecedents and Consequences of Host-Country Nationals' Attitudes and Behaviors toward Expatriates: What We Do and Do Not Know," *Human Resource Management Review* 28 (2018), pp. 164–75.

84. P. Capell, "Know before You Go: Expats' Advice to Couples," *Career Journal Europe,* May 2, 2006, http://www.careerjournaleurope.com; Mila Lazarova, Mina Westman, and Margaret A. Shaffer, "Elucidating the Positive Side of the Work-Family Interface on International Assignments: A Model of Expatriate Work and Family Performance," *Academy of Management Review* 35, no. 1 (January 2010), pp. 93–117.

85. C. Yu-Ping and M. Shaffer, "The Influence of Expatriate Spouses' Coping Strategies on Expatriate and Spouse Adjustment," *Journal of Global Mobility* 6, no. 1 (2018), pp. 20–39; R. A. Swaak, "Expatriate Failures: Too Many, Too Much Cost, Too Little Planning," *Compensation & Benefits Review,* November–December 1995, pp. 50–52.

86. G. M. Sprietzer, M. W. McCall, and J. D. Mahoney, "Early Identification of International Executive Potential," *Journal of Applied Psychology* 82, no. 1 (1997), pp. 6–29; R. Mortensen, "Beyond the Fence Line," *HRMagazine,* November 1997, pp. 100–9; "Expatriate Games," *Journal of Business Strategy,* July–August 1997, pp. 4–5;

"Building a Global Workforce Starts with Recruitment," *Personnel Journal* (special supplement), March 1996, pp. 9–11; Ming Li, William H. Mobley, and Aidan Kelly, "When Do Global Leaders Learn Best to Develop Cultural Intelligence? An Investigation of the Moderating Role of Experiential Learning Style," *Academy of Management Learning & Education* 12, no. 1 (March 2013), pp. 32–50; Nicola M. Pless, Thomas Maak, and Günther K. Stahl, "Developing Responsible Global Leaders through International Service-Learning Programs: The Ulysses Experience," *Academy of Management Learning & Education* 10, no. 2 (June 2011), pp. 237–60.

87. D. Welch and L. Welch, "Developing Multilingual Capacity: A Challenge for the Multinational Enterprise," *Journal of Management* 44 (2018), pp. 854–59.

88. H. Barkema, X. Chen, G. George, Y. Luo, and A. Tsui, "West Meets East: New Concepts and Theories," *Academy of Management Review* 58 (2015), pp. 460–79.

89. Katie Reynolds, "How Cultural Differences Impact International Business in 2017," Hult International Business School, https://www.hult.edu/blog/cultural-differences-impact-international-business/, accessed March 16, 2019.

90. Ellen Sheng, "How to Manage Cultural Differences in Global Teams," *Fast Company,* January 12, 2016, https://www.fastcompany.com/3054879/how-to-manage-cultural-differences-in-global-teams.

91. Karen Farnen, "Cultural Differences and Communication Problems with International Business," *Small Business Chronicle,* March 6, 2019, https://smallbusiness.chron.com/cultural-differences-communication-problems-international-business-81982.html.

92. John Slocum, "Coming to America," *Human Resource Executive,* October 2, 2008, http://www.hrexecutive.com; K. Oberg, "Cultural Shock: Adjustment to New Cultural Environments," *Practical Anthropology* 7 (1960), pp. 177–82.

93. H. Barkema, X. Chen, G. George, Y. Luo, and A. Tsui, "West Meets East: New Concepts and Theories," *Academy of Management Review* 58 (2015), pp. 460–79.

94. G. Hofstede, "Motivation, Leadership, and Organization: Do American Theories Apply Abroad?" *Organizational Dynamics* 9, (Summer 1980), pp. 42–63.

95. B. Kirkman, K. Lowe, and C. Gibson, "A Retrospective on Culture's Consequences: The 35-Year Journey," *Journal of International Business Studies* 48 (2017), pp. 12–29; V. Taras, P. Steels, and B. Kirkman, "Does Country Equate with Culture? Beyond Geography in the Search for Cultural Boundaries," *Management International Review* 56 (2016), pp. 455–87.

96. E. Meyer, *The Culture Map* (New York: Public Affairs, 2014); J. Brett, K. Behfar, and M. C. Kern, "Managing Multicultural Teams," *Harvard Business Review,* November 2006, pp. 84–91.

97. E. Meyer, *The Culture Map* (New York: Public Affairs, 2014); D. Stamps, "Welcome to America," *Training,* November 1996, pp. 23–30.

98. Keith Ferrazzi, "How to Avoid Virtual Miscommunication," April 12, 2013, https://hbr.org/2013/04/how-to-avoid-virtual-miscommun.

99. Eric Barton, "Master the Art of Global Email Etiquette," November 7, 2013, http://www.bbc.com/capital/story/20131106-lost-in-translation.

100. Raul Sanchez and Daniel H. Bullock, "Bridging the Cross-Cultural Gap through Global Business Email Etiquette," February 22, 2017, https://www.business.com/articles/bridging-the-cross-cultural-gap-through-global-business-email-etiquette/.

101. Len Shneyder, "Think Global but Send Hyperlocal Email Communications," March 18, 2019, https://marketingland.com/think-global-but-send-hyperlocal-email-communications-258537.

102. L. K. Trevino and K. A. Nelson, *Managing Business Ethics: Straight Talk about How to Do It Right* (New York: Wiley, 1995).

103. Transparency International, "Leading Exporters Undermine Development with Dirty Business Overseas," news release, October 4, 2006, http://www.transparency.org.

104. Y. H. Kim and G. Davis, "Challenges for Global Supply Chain Sustainability: Evidence from Conflict Minerals Reports," *Academy of Management Journal* 59 (2016), pp. 1896–1916.

105. A. B. Desai and T. Rittenburg, "Global Ethics: An Integrative Framework for MNEs," *Journal of Business Ethics* 16 (1997), pp. 791–800; P. Buller, J. Kohls, and K. Anderson, "A Model for Addressing Cross-Cultural Ethical Conflicts," *Business & Society* 36, no. 2 (June 1997), pp. 169–93.

106. "U.S. Puts Alibaba's Taobao on Blacklist for Counterfeit Products—Again," Reuters, January 12, 2018, http://fortune.com/2018/01/12/alibaba-taobao-blacklist-counterfeit-products/.

107. Arjun Kharpal, "Alibaba Sues Sellers of Counterfeit Goods for the First Time after It Was Blacklisted by the U.S.," *CNBC.com,* January 4, 2017, http://www.cnbc.com/2017/01/04/alibaba-sues-sellers-of-counterfeit-goods-for-the-first-time-after-it-was-blacklisted-by-the-us.html.

108. Lim Yan Liang, "Fake Goods Weeded Out Successfully on Taobao: Alibaba," *The Straits Times-Asia,* January 16, 2019, https://www.straitstimes.com/asia/fake-goods-weeded-out-successfully-on-taobao-alibaba.

CHAPTER 7
Entrepreneurship

Don't sit down and wait for the opportunities to come.
Get up and make them

—Madam C.J. Walker

IgorGolovniov/Shutterstock

learning objectives

After studying Chapter 7, you will be able to:

LO 7-1   Describe why people become entrepreneurs and what it takes, personally.

LO 7-2   Summarize how to assess opportunities to start new businesses.

LO 7-3   Identify common causes of success and failure.

LO 7-4   Discuss common management challenges.

LO 7-5   Explain how to increase your chances of success, including good business planning.

LO 7-6   Describe how managers of large companies can foster entrepreneurship.

chapter outline

Entrepreneurship
  Why Become an Entrepreneur?
  What Does It Take to Succeed?
  What Business Should You Start?
  What Does It Take, Personally?
  Success and Failure
  Common Management Challenges
  Increasing Your Chances of Success

Corporate Entrepreneurship
  Building Support for Your Idea
  Building Intrapreneurship
  Management Challenges
  Entrepreneurial Orientation

Management in Action

STARBUCKS'S ENTREPRENEURIAL BEGINNINGS

MANAGER'S BRIEF

PROGRESS REPORT

ONWARD

Shortly after joining Starbucks, a four-store Seattle retailer and wholesaler of fresh-roasted coffee beans, a young employee named Howard Schultz traveled to Italy. He was then the company's director of retail operations and marketing. Deeply impressed by the laid-back culture and popularity of the neighborhood espresso bars and coffeehouses he visited in Italy, Schultz noted how much people enjoyed gathering there, in "a place between work and home," to socialize and enjoy long, leisurely conversations. He returned to Seattle determined to persuade the owners of Starbucks to let him try the coffeehouse concept in the United States.

The experiment was so successful that, within a few short years, Schultz had left Starbucks to found his own coffeehouse chain, called Il Giornale, and then purchased Starbucks himself, with capital from local investors. Almost immediately he began expanding. When the company held its IPO in 1992, there were 160 stores; the company now operates thousands of stores around the world.

Schultz, who stepped down as Starbucks's CEO in 2017, grew up in Brooklyn, New York. He was one of three children in a family living on a marginal income with, as he says, "nothing to fall back on."[1] A football scholarship took him to Northern Michigan University, where he became the first in his family to earn a college degree. Later he went on to executive-level jobs at Xerox and the U.S. division of a Swedish housewares company before moving to Seattle to join Starbucks.

Sorbis/Shutterstock

What drove him to take the inspiration found in his visit to Italy and turn it into a multibillion-dollar company? Schultz credits luck with a fair part of his success, claiming, "I've gotten more credit than I deserve" for the company's many years of success. But he does describe his entrepreneurial ambitions this way: "I willed it to happen," he says. "I took my life in my hands, learned from anyone I could, grabbed what opportunity I could, and molded my success step by step."[2]

That spirit still informs his thinking and seems to be guiding his ambitions. Schultz has left Starbucks only to set his sights on other big business and political aspirations.[3]

Schultz founded a company on the realization that he could market a familiar product in a coffeehouse environment that was new to U.S. consumers. As you read about the qualities of successful entrepreneurs and the challenges they must overcome, think about which qualities and challenges you see in Schultz and his vision for Starbucks.

As Howard Schultz and countless others have demonstrated, great opportunity is available to skilled entrepreneurs who are willing to work hard to achieve their dreams.

Entrepreneurs are people who create new social entities.[4] To be an entrepreneur is to initiate and build an organization rather than being only a passive part of one.[5] The entrepreneurial process involves discovering, evaluating, and capitalizing on opportunities to create new and future goods and services.[6]

Entrepreneurship occurs when an enterprising individual pursues a lucrative opportunity. *Creating value* is a central objective of entrepreneurship, just as it is in strategic management. Wealth may be an entrepreneur's ultimate goal, but it won't come without providing value for other individuals, organizations, and/or society.[7]

Managers in established organizations generally follow or modify the routines that others established. Entrepreneurs begin with a relatively blank slate. They must create and initiate ideas for new products, services, and procedures and experiment with them until they find the most appropriate ones for their new businesses. Ideally you will learn by doing, and anticipate and cope with changes in the macro- and competitive environments.[8]

How does entrepreneurship differ from managing a small business?[9] A **small business** is often defined as having fewer than 500 employees, being independently owned and operated, not dominant in its field, and not characterized by many innovative practices.[10]

Entrepreneurship rarely means starting a business with a lot of funding from outside investors, growing rapidly, and then taking the venture public. Few start-ups follow this path, even in Silicon Valley.[11] Most start-ups, nationwide and worldwide, are "lifestyle" or traditional businesses, founded by people who tend not to manage particularly aggressively and expect normal, moderate sales, profits, and growth.

In contrast, an **entrepreneurial venture** has growth and high profitability as primary objectives. Entrepreneurs manage aggressively and develop innovative strategies, practices, and products. They and their financial backers usually seek rapid growth, immediate and high profits, and sometimes a quick sellout with large capital gains. This is the path of the glamorous, newsworthy firms that you hear about on CNBC, but not the path of the huge majority of start-ups and small businesses.[12]

The Excitement of Entrepreneurship   Consider these words from Jeffry Timmons, a leading entrepreneurship scholar and author: "[The] new generation of entrepreneurs has altered permanently the economic and social structure of this nation and the world. . . . It will determine more than any other single impetus how the nation and the world will live, work, learn, and lead in this century and beyond."[13]

Overhype? Well, partly, because the rate of new business formation is slowing down.[14] Given that 99 percent of companies in the United States are small businesses, another economic slowdown could reduce employment rates.[15] The Small Business Administration reports that there are over 30 million small businesses in the United States accounting for over half of all jobs.[16]

Entrepreneurship often contributes to economic growth, but it's not automatic.[17] It aids growth especially in higher-income countries, and the amount of growth depends on the nature of the entrepreneurial activities. Productive entrepreneurial activities—innovation, and particularly high-technology start-ups in contrast to necessity-based entrepreneurship—drive country wealth and growth.

Myths about Entrepreneurship   Simply put, entrepreneurs generate new ideas and turn them into business ventures.[18] But entrepreneurship is not simple, and is frequently misunderstood; we need more research and theory,[19] although we do have a lot of useful knowledge. Review Exhibit 7.1 to start thinking about the myths and realities of this important career option.

Another myth, not in the exhibit, is that being an entrepreneur is great because you can get rich quick and enjoy a lot of leisure time while your employees run the company. But the reality is much more difficult. During the start-up period, you are likely to have a lot of bad days. It's stressful (sometimes[20]) and exhausting. Even if you don't have employees,

---

entrepreneurship

The pursuit of lucrative opportunities by enterprising individuals.

Bottom Line

Entrepreneurship is inherently about innovation—creating a new venture where one didn't exist before. *How is entrepreneurship different from inventing a new product?*

small business

A business having fewer than 500 employees, independently owned and operated, not dominant in its field, and not characterized by many innovative practices.

entrepreneurial venture

A new business having growth and high profitability as primary objectives.

Myth 1—Entrepreneurs are gamblers.
Reality—Successful entrepreneurs take very careful, calculated risks. They try to influence the odds, often by getting others to share risk with them and by avoiding or minimizing risks if they have the choice. Often they slice up the risk into smaller, digestible pieces; only then do they commit the time or resources to determine whether [each] piece will work.
Myth 2—Entrepreneurs experience a great deal of stress and pay a high price.
Reality—Being an entrepreneur is stressful. But there is no evidence that it is more so than other highly demanding professional roles, and entrepreneurs find their jobs very satisfying. They have a high sense of accomplishment, are healthier, and are much less likely to retire than those who work for others.
Myth 3—If an entrepreneur is talented, success will happen in a year or two.
Reality—An old maxim among venture capitalists says a lot: The lemons ripen in two and a half years, but the pearls take seven or eight. Rarely is a new business established solidly in less than three or four years.
Myth 4—Entrepreneurs are lone wolves and cannot work with others.
Reality—The most successful entrepreneurs are leaders who build great teams and effective relationships working with peers, directors, investors, key customers, key suppliers, and the like.

EXHIBIT 7.1
Some Myths about Entrepreneurs

SOURCE: Spinelli, S. Jr. and Adams, R. J., *New Venture Creation: Entrepreneurship for the 21st Century,* 9th ed., 2012, pp. 46–47. Copyright ©2012 McGraw-Hill Global Education Holdings LLC. All rights reserved. Used with permission.

you should expect communications breakdowns and other people problems with customers, agents, vendors, distributors, family, subcontractors, lenders, and whomever. Legendary software entrepreneur Dan Bricklin advised that the most important thing to remember is this: "You are not your business. On those darkest days when things aren't going so well—and trust me, you will have them—try to remember that your company's failures don't make you an awful person. Likewise, your company's successes don't make you a genius or superhuman."[21]

As you read this chapter, you will learn about two primary sources of new venture creation: independent entrepreneurship and intrapreneurship. **Entrepreneurs** are individuals who establish a new organization without the benefit of corporate support. **Intrapreneurs** are new venture creators working inside big companies; they are corporate entrepreneurs, using their company's resources to build a profitable line of business based on a fresh new idea.[22] Thus, entrepreneurship is an activity that can and should contribute greatly to mature organizations. Entrepreneurship is vitally important across the entire life cycle of an organization.[23]

entrepreneur

Individual who establishes a new organization without the benefit of corporate sponsorship.

intrapreneurs

New venture creators working inside big companies.

Entrepreneurship

Exhibit 7.2 lists some extraordinary entrepreneurs. The companies they founded are famously successful—and all of the founders started in their 20s. Two young entrepreneurs who started a highly successful business are Tony Hsieh and Nick Swinmurn. About 20 years ago, Swinmurn had the then-new idea to sell shoes online, but he needed money to get started. Hsieh, who at age 24 had already just sold his first start-up, agreed to take a chance on the new venture. It was a smart decision. Ten years later, Amazon purchased Zappos for $1.2 billion.[24]

The real, more complete story of entrepreneurship is not about the famous people in Exhibit 7.2—it's mostly about people you've probably never heard of. Often it's about young people, and definitely it's about people of all demographic groups.[25]

LO 7-1 Describe why people become entrepreneurs and what it takes, personally.

EXHIBIT 7.2
Successful Entrepreneurs
Who Started in Their 20s

Entrepreneurial Company	Founder(s)
Snapchat	Evan Spiegel
Kitchens for Good	Aviva Paley
Instagram	Kevin Systrom
Green Gas	David Cooch and Kyle Kornack
PartPic	Jewel Burks
Spotify	Daniel Ek
Zero Waste Solutions	Shavila Singh

SOURCES: Wilson, A. and Toma, G., "Forbes 30 Under 30," *Forbes*, www.forbes.com, accessed February 4, 2019; Heath, A. and Stone, M., "The Fabulous Life of Snap CEO Evan Spiegel," *Business Insider*, March 3, 2017, www.businessinsider.com; Howard, C. and Inverso, E., "Forbes 30 Under 30," *Forbes*, www.forbes.com, accessed March 25, 2017.

Bottom Line

Today's concern for sustainability presents a tremendous variety of opportunities to entrepreneurs who care about the environment. *What are some environmentally friendly start-ups you've heard about? What do you think of their profit potential?*

jvmodel.com/Shutterstock

They have built companies, thrived personally, created jobs, and made positive contributions to their communities through their businesses. Or they're just starting out.

Why Become an Entrepreneur?

Jessica Mah was an entrepreneur before she even finished school. At the age of 13, she went into business selling computer parts and templates on eBay. While in college at the University of California–Berkeley, she and another student, Andy Su, founded InternshipIN, which provided information about internship opportunities.

When she graduated, Mah was ready to launch another venture. Mah again partnered with Su, this time founding inDinero, a company that helps small-business owners manage their money and taxes. Basically, inDinero keeps track of transactions, analyzes where their money is going, and provides financial reports. The idea for inDinero came from Mah's own experience: For some people excited about starting a new business, working with customers and products is more exciting and easier to learn than handling money.[26] In addition to running inDinero, Mah is now an investor in XFactor Ventures, a venture capital firm designed to help women-owned start-up companies.[27]

Entrepreneurs start their own firms because of the challenge, the profit potential, and the satisfaction they hope lie ahead. Others launch their own businesses to achieve a better quality of life than they might have at big companies. They seek independence and a feeling of being part of the action. They feel tremendous satisfaction in building something from nothing, seeing it succeed, and watching the market embrace their ideas and products.

People also start their own companies when they see their progress or ideas blocked at big corporations. Or, they may quit to become entrepreneurs after not receiving a promotion or being frustrated by corporate life. Well worth considering is the hybrid path: starting a business while retaining your "day job."[28]

When people find conventional paths to economic success closed to them, they may migrate to another location and turn to entrepreneurship.[29] Migration is to move within or across meaningful social or political boundaries, both intra- and internationally.[30] In the late 19th century, mining entrepreneurs moved to the western United States. The Cuban community in Miami has produced many successful entrepreneurs, as has the Vietnamese community throughout the United States. Sometimes the immigrant's experience gives him or her useful knowledge about foreign suppliers or markets that present an attractive business opportunity.

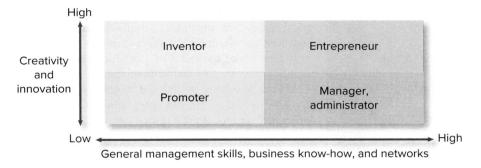

High

Creativity
and
innovation

| Inventor | Entrepreneur |
| Promoter | Manager, administrator |

Low ←———————————————————→ High
General management skills, business know-how, and networks

SOURCE: Timmons, J. A. and Spinelli, S. Jr., *New Venture Creation: Entrepreneurship for the 21st Century,* 7th ed., 2007, pp. 67–68. Copyright ©2007 McGraw-Hill Global Education Holdings LLC.

EXHIBIT 7.3
Who Is the Entrepreneur?

What Does It Take to Succeed?

What can we learn from the people who start their own companies and succeed? What enables entrepreneurs to succeed? In general terms, Exhibit 7.3 shows that successful entrepreneurs are innovators who also have good knowledge and skills in management, business, and networking.[31] In contrast, inventors may be highly creative but may lack the skills to turn their ideas into a successful business. Manager–administrators may be great at ensuring efficient operations but aren't necessarily innovators. Promoters have a different set of marketing and selling skills—useful for entrepreneurs, but those skills can be hired, whereas innovativeness and business management skills remain the essential combination for successful entrepreneurship.

What Business Should You Start?

You need a good idea, and you need to find or create the right opportunity. The following discussion offers some general considerations for choosing a type of business.

The Idea   Many entrepreneurs and observers say that in contemplating your business, you must start with a great idea. A great product, a viable market, and good timing are essential ingredients.

LO 7-2 Summarize how to assess opportunities to start new businesses.

Many great organizations have been built on a different kind of idea: the founder's desire to build a great organization rather than to offer a particular product.[32] Examples abound. After trying unsuccessfully to get into law school, Sara Blakely went on to found shapewear company Spanx, which made her into a billionaire. J. Willard Marriott knew he wanted to be in business for himself but didn't have a product in mind until he opened an A&W root beer stand. Masaru Ibuka had no specific product idea when he founded Sony in 1945. Sony's first product attempt, a rice cooker, didn't work, and its first product (a tape recorder) didn't sell. The company stayed alive by making and selling crude heating pads.

Many now-great companies had early failures. But the founders persisted; they believed in themselves and in their dreams of building great organizations. Be prepared to kill or revise an idea, but never give up on your company—this has been a prescription for success for many great entrepreneurs and business leaders. Think about Sony, Disney, Hewlett-Packard, Procter & Gamble, IBM, and Walmart: Their founders' greatest achievements—their greatest ideas—are their organizations.[33]

The Opportunity   Opportunity is at the core of entrepreneurship[34]; entrepreneurs find ways to spot, create, and capture opportunities.[35] Entrepreneurial companies can explore domains that big companies miss or avoid, and introduce goods or services that

Limor Fried, Adafruit Industries, combined her academic knowledge and personal interests to prove her capabilities as an entrepreneur.

Brian Ach/Getty Images

capture the market because they are simpler, cheaper, more accessible, or more convenient. Limor Fried spotted her opportunity when she got involved with a hobby that flew under the radar of most traditional businesses: building clever do-it-yourself electronic gadgets. When Fried was in school, she relaxed by ordering parts to build homemade MP3 players, programmable jewelry, and other fun gadgets. As she posted her creations on her personal website, she began attracting requests from people wanting her to sell them kits so they could make the same items themselves. Fried took some personal funds and started Adafruit Industries, now a 100-employee business racking up $40 million in sales annually.[36]

To spot opportunities, think carefully about events and trends as they unfold. Consider, for example, the following possibilities:[37]

Technological discoveries. Start-ups in biotechnology, microcomputers, artificial intelligence, robotics, and nanotechnology followed technological advances. Freenome is a company that is using machine learning techniques with breakthroughs in genomic science to help people detect, treat, and prevent diseases such as cancer.[38]

Demographic changes. Health care organizations of all kinds have sprung up to serve an aging population, from exercise studios to assisted-living facilities. One business that targets the aging American population is fitness program SilverSneakers by Tivity Health, which offers a variety of classes with low-impact choreography and can be taken while seated. Classes can be modified for fitness levels or for those who have difficulty getting around.[39]

Lifestyle and taste changes. Start-ups have capitalized on new technology, music and clothes trends, desire for new convenience foods, and ever-growing interest in sports. In recent years, more consumers want to help take care of the environment, and more businesses are concerned about showing consumers that they care, too.

Economic dislocations, such as booms or failures. Rising oil prices and fears over climate change spurred a variety of developments related to renewable energy or energy efficiency.

Calamities such as wars and natural disasters. Online cyberattacks have led to the creation of a multibillion industry to help businesses and government agencies prevent future attacks. Destructive hurricanes, floods, and tornadoes raised awareness of the importance of emergency preparedness.

Government initiatives and rule changes. Deregulation spawned new airlines and trucking companies. Whenever the government changes regulations, tightens energy efficiency requirements, and so forth, opportunities arise for entrepreneurs to think of new ideas for products and processes

franchising

An entrepreneurial alliance between a franchisor (an innovator who has created at least one successful store and wants to grow) and a franchisee (a partner who manages a new store of the same type in a new location).

Franchises   One important type of opportunity is the franchise. You may know intuitively what franchising is, or you can at least name some prominent franchises: Great Clips, Subway, Taco Bell, and Anytime Fitness. **Franchising** is an entrepreneurial alliance between two organizations, the franchisor and the franchisee.[40] The franchisor is the innovator who has created at least one successful store and seeks partners to operate the same concept in other local markets. For the franchisee, the opportunity is wealth creation via a proven (but not failureproof!) business concept, with the added advantage of the franchisor's expertise. For example, the Panera Bread chain of bakery-cafés has expanded rapidly in recent years. In 2019, you could find over 2,000 Panera stores across 48 states.[41]

People often assume that buying a franchise is less risky than starting a business from scratch, but the evidence is mixed.

If you are contemplating a franchise, consider its market presence (local, regional, or national); market share and profit margins; national programs for marketing and purchasing; the nature of the business, including required training and degree of field support; terms of the license agreement (e.g., 20 years with automatic renewal versus less than 10 years or no renewal); capital required; and franchise fees and royalties.[42]

Although some people think success with a franchise is a no-brainer, would-be franchisees have a lot to consider. Luckily, plenty of useful sources exist for learning more, including the International Franchise Association (http://www.franchise.org), the Small Business Administration (http://www.sba.gov), Franchise Chat (http://www.franchise-chat.com), and *Entrepreneur* magazine's online Franchises page

Jonathan Weiss/Shutterstock

(http://www.entrepreneur.com), which includes rankings as well as articles profiling franchisors and franchisees. In addition, take your time investigating business opportunities, consulting with an accountant or lawyer who has experience.

The Next Frontiers   The next frontiers for entrepreneurship—where do they lie? The powerful potential of big data to improve decision making is opening up tremendous opportunities for businesses that can help their clients collect, store, manage, and analyze data. Sectors and product categories that have recently enjoyed huge growth are health care, education, and, of course, mobile apps.[43]

One fascinating opportunity for entrepreneurs is space travel. With increasing demand for satellite launches and interest in space tourism, smaller entrepreneurs are entering the field. SpaceX has been transporting cargo to the International Space Station for NASA and is developing the capability to transport astronaut crews. NASA also has granted a cargo-shuttling contract to Orbital Sciences Corporation.

More futuristic still is the concept of entrepreneur Robert Bigelow. His company, Bigelow Aerospace, has created a residence module for living in space. Bigelow signed a $17.8 million contract with NASA and launched a module into space in 2016. The module is attached to the International Space Station and will be used for long-term storage until at least 2020.[44]

Changes have been coming fast in the health care sector in the United States. Health care providers have been digitizing their data for patient care, medication management, and treatment outcomes—a trend that yields opportunities for hardware and software businesses that understand the needs of these clients. In addition, rising costs for health care and health insurance create opportunities for entrepreneurs with ideas for restraining those costs. For example, apps that promote fitness or help patients manage chronic conditions can appeal to consumers, insurance companies, and employers. Google Ventures invests about one-third of the money it receives from Alphabet to fund health care and life science start-ups.[45]

E-commerce   Conducting business online is a trend that continues to expand. With e-commerce, as with any start-up, entrepreneurs need sound business models and practices. The potential payoff can be significant in this burdening industry. E-commerce sales of physical goods in the United States reached nearly $505 billion in 2018 and

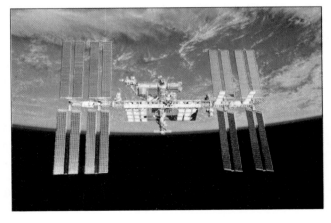

The International Space Station is a habitable artificial satellite. Currently the largest artificial body in orbit, it is sometimes visible with the naked eye from Earth.

Source: National Aeronautics and Space Administration (NASA)

are projected to grow to over \$735 billion by 2023.[46] Growing comfort with online shopping, increasing popularity of digital voice assistants to make purchases, and overall convenience and speed of online transactions are driving this rapid growth.[47]

Tomas Slimas, co-founder and chief marketing officer of drop-shipping firm Oberlo, agrees: "It's never been easier to launch your own online store, find a product to sell, or start an advertising campaign. In the near-future we'll see even more aspiring entrepreneurs breaking through into the world of e-commerce, who may not have had the means to do so previously."[48]

For individuals planning to start a new e-commerce business, it's important to understand that digital commerce is more than mobile-based shopping and social media–based influence; it's also about integrating technologies like artificial intelligence, digital wallet payments, and customization.[49]

Once a digital entrepreneur decides on what type of business to launch, she needs to make a decision regarding which business model to adopt. Perhaps this is easier said than done as there are myriad models. Some of the more common e-commerce models include storefront, subscription, and business-to-business (B2B).[50]

A storefront website is designed to sell products that are made from the seller or third parties and once purchased, drop shipped to customers. There are hundreds of thousands of such sites, including large enterprises like Amazon, Alibaba, Otto, Flipkart, and Walmart. Subscription websites like *The New York Times* and *Harvard Business Review* allow individuals to read or access information similar to subscribing to a newspaper or magazine. Firms that specialize in selling products or services online to other companies engage in a business-to-business (B2B) model. For example, HubSpot provides inbound marketing software that helps client companies attract new customers. Other well-known examples of B2B companies include Microsoft, UPS, Intel, SAP, Adobe, and Salesforce.

What about businesses whose primary focus is not e-commerce? Start-ups and established small companies can create attractive websites that add to their professionalism, give them access to more customers, and bring them closer to suppliers, investors, and service providers. Companies can move much more quickly than in the past and save money on activities including customer service/support, technical support, data retrieval, public relations, investor relations, selling, requests for product literature, and purchasing. Setting up shop online costs less than ever.

social entrepreneurship

Leveraging resources to address social problems.

social enterprise

Organization that applies business models and leverages resources in ways that address social problems.

Social Entrepreneurship   Social entrepreneurship has been around for decades, but is surging in popularity and impact and as a focus for research.[51] **Social entrepreneurship** has been defined in many ways, but most fundamentally it refers to leveraging resources to address social problems.[52]

It does so by using market-based methods.[53] Organizations that do this are **social enterprises**.[54] Social entrepreneurship creates social value by stimulating social change or meeting social needs.[55]

Such enterprises can advance societal well-being in one or more broad domains, including: (1) the environment—for example, energy conservation, responsible consumption, and habitat conservation; (2) social and economic inclusion—for example, empowering marginalized groups, revitalized neighborhoods, improving educational attainment, and reducing community violence; (3) health and well-being—for example, preventing and reducing health risk behaviors and improving access to health care; and (4) civic engagement, such as community volunteering, charitable giving, and responsible investing.[56]

One of the best-known examples of social entrepreneurship is the Nobel Prize–winning work of Dr. Muhammad Yunus of the Grameen Foundation, which has helped provide over \$6.5 billion in microloans to millions of impoverished women in south Asia.[57] Another is Scott Harrison's "charity: water," which funds over 35,000 water projects to provide clean water to more than 9.5 million people in 27 countries.[58] Additional examples include Moringa School, which teaches software development skills to unemployed youth in Kenya, Rwanda, Ghana, and Pakistan who aspire to be programmers,[59] and Sustainable Ocean Alliance, a network of young leaders in 60 countries working to protect the world's waters.[60]

Social Entrepreneurship

Empowering Latina Entrepreneurs

When she was 5 years old, Nely Galan and her family left their native Cuba to begin a new life in the United States. As a child, Galan admired Sherry Lansing, the first female president of Paramount Pictures. Today, Galan is following in Lansing's footsteps, becoming the first Latina president of the Miami-based TV network Telemundo. The "Tropical Tycoon" also went on to found her own business, Galan Entertainment, which launched TV channels in Latin America and produced original programming from sitcoms to *telenovelas* (soap operas).

Being an entertainment mogul was not enough though. Galan founded Adelante (http://theadelantemovement.com), a movement "designed to empower Latinas in the U.S. economically through inspiration, training, and resources on entrepreneurship." Galan believes that helping Latinas become more financially successful has a positive impact on their communities and families. The potential ripple effect is significant when considering that the Latina population in the United States is expected to grow to about 13 percent of the U.S. population by 2050.

Galan has also joined forces with Coca-Cola's effort to empower 5 million women entrepreneurs by 2020.[61] Citing a personal goal to train 30,000 Latinas in the United States to become entrepreneurs, Galan sums up her passion this way: "I am a woman that believes in ownership and entrepreneurship as the way for most women to have financial freedom and become actualized."[62]

In 2016, she published her manifesto for doing just that. Her book *Self Made: Becoming Empowered, Self-Reliant, and Rich in Every Way* hit #1 on *The New York Times* bestseller list. In it, she shares her knowledge and experience as an entrepreneur.[63] Seeing

Imeh Akpanudosen/Getty Images

that Latina-owned businesses have increased at more than twice the national average in recent years and contribute almost $700 billion to the U.S. economy is a sign that Galan's message is getting through.[64]

- What do you think motivates Galan to help Latinas become successful entrepreneurs?

- Why do you think Coca-Cola is collaborating with Galan to empower female entrepreneurs?

Social entrepreneurship is not charity, and it is different from corporate social responsibility (CSR),[65] which you read about in Chapter 5. CSR is not necessarily practiced with profit as a guiding principle, and corporations often relegate it to a side activity. As described in the nearby "Social Entrepreneurship" box, social entrepreneurship fully incorporates social as well as economic value into mainstream thinking and decision making. It provides dual, shared value: creating economic value plus social or societal benefit simultaneously.[66] See Exhibit 7.4 for more examples.

Combining social and commercial goals isn't new; consider hospitals, universities, and arts organizations.[67] And not all social problems can be solved by entrepreneurial solutions. But pursuing the dual goal of both economic and social value may be developing as a new norm, with positive social outcomes as key to long-term success.

Pierre Omidyar, founder of eBay, states: "You really can make the world better in any sector—in nonprofits, in business, or in government. It's not a question of one sector's struggling against another, or of 'giving back' versus 'taking away.' That's old thinking. A true

EXHIBIT 7.4

More Examples of Social Enterprises

Company Name	Description
40K Plus Education	Sets learning "pods" in rural villages that offer tablet-based after-school tutoring to students of government and low-cost private schools.
Barrier Break	Employs deaf people to provide online services for those who are hearing impaired, utilizing an innovative "Sign-and-Talk" business over video-enabled web connections.
Edom Nutritional Solutions	Manufactures organically fortified staple flours cost-effectively and sells them at affordable prices to the malnourished in East Africa.
Jack and Jake's	Has developed a local/organic wholesale company, sourcing food from within a 100-mile radius of New Orleans to provide healthy food for hospitals and schools.
Not Mass Produced	Is an online marketplace for local, independent businesses in the UK; its flagship site sources local food for UK restaurants, wholesale purchasers, and retail consumers.
Solidarium	Partners with Walmart and JCPenney to sell ethically produced, fair trade consumer products, selling over 100,000 units and paying its producers 50 percent more than competitors.

SOURCE: Courtesy of Village Capital.

philanthropist will use every tool he can to make an impact. Today business is a key part of the equation, and the sectors are learning to work together."[68]

Opportunities exist to make substantial positive impact on virtually every societal need and to make a profit doing so. Profit is likely to make societal value creation more sustainable over the long run.

What Does It Take, Personally?

Many people assume that there is an entrepreneurial personality. No single personality type predicts entrepreneurial success, but you are more likely to succeed as an entrepreneur if you apply certain perspectives and behaviors:[69]

1. *Commitment and determination:* Successful entrepreneurs are decisive, tenacious, disciplined, willing to sacrifice, and able to immerse themselves in their enterprises. Entrepreneurial passion[70] can play an important role in all of these things.
2. *Leadership:* They are self-starters, team builders, superior learners, and teachers. Communicating a vision for the future of the company—an essential component of leadership that you'll learn more about in Chapter 12—clearly has an impact on venture growth.[71]
3. *Opportunity obsession:* They have an intimate knowledge of customers' needs, are market driven, and are obsessed with value creation and enhancement.
4. *Tolerance of risk, ambiguity, and uncertainty:* They are calculated risk takers and risk managers, tolerant of stress, and able to resolve problems.
5. *Creativity, self-reliance, and ability to adapt:* They are open-minded, restless with the status quo, able to learn quickly, highly adaptable, creative, skilled at conceptualizing, and attentive to details.
6. *Motivation to excel:* They have a strong results orientation, set high but realistic goals, have a strong drive to achieve, know their own weaknesses and strengths, and focus on what can be done rather than on the reasons things can't be done.

Perhaps more than personality trait, your effectiveness will be driven by your interest in the nature of the work itself and the consequences that it generates. This might be a good time to think about your own interests and aspirations.[72] To do so, you could consider the personal appeal of working in a big corporation, plus these potential entrepreneurial identities[73]— Darwinian (focused on the firm's financial success), Communitarian (focused on contributing to customer communities), or Missionary (focused on the firm as an agent for change).

Making Good Choices   Success is a function not just of knowledge and luck but of making good decisions.[74] Choosing well is difficult in the entrepreneurial context of high uncertainty and risk (recall Chapter 3). Being human, and like other managers, entrepreneurs have biases, and these can be made worse by time pressures and intense emotions. For instance, biases related to illusion of control (Chapter 3), optimism, and overconfidence can increase motivation (including oneself, employees, investors, and customers) but cause other problems. Entrepreneurs tend to be overconfident about the success of their ideas (and themselves), self-generated financial projections, and ability to salvage their projects when they probably should move on to other thing, potentially undermining success.

How can you make good choices about which business to start? Exhibit 7.5 presents a model for conceptualizing entrepreneurial ventures and making the best possible choices. It depicts ventures along two dimensions: innovation and risk. The new venture may involve high or low levels of innovation or the creation of something new and different. It can also be characterized by low or high risk. Risk refers primarily to the probability of major financial loss. But it also is more than that; it includes psychological risk as perceived by the entrepreneur, including risks to reputation and ego.[75]

The upper-left quadrant, high innovation/low risk, depicts ventures of truly novel ideas with little risk. As examples, the inventors of LEGO building blocks and Velcro fasteners could build their products by hand at little expense. A pioneering product idea from Google might fit here if there are no current competitors and because, for a company of that size, the financial risks of new product investments can seem relatively small.

In the upper-right quadrant, high innovation/high risk, novel product ideas are accompanied by high risk because the financial investments are high and the competition is great. A new heart transplant surgical process or a new driverless car technology would likely fall into this category.

Most small business ventures are in the low innovation/high risk cell (lower right). They are fairly conventional entries in well-established fields. New restaurants, retail shops, and commercial firms involve high investment for the small-business entrepreneur and face direct competition from similar businesses. Finally, the low innovation/low risk category includes ventures that require minimal investment and/or face minimal competition for strong market demand. Examples are some service businesses having low start-up costs and those involving entry into small towns if there is no competitor and demand is adequate. An example is a car detailing service run out of someone's home garage.

How is this matrix useful? It helps entrepreneurs think about their ventures and decide whether they suit their particular objectives. It also helps identify effective and ineffective strategies. You might find one cell more appealing than others. The lower-left cell is likely to have relatively low payoffs but to provide more security. The higher risk/return trade-offs

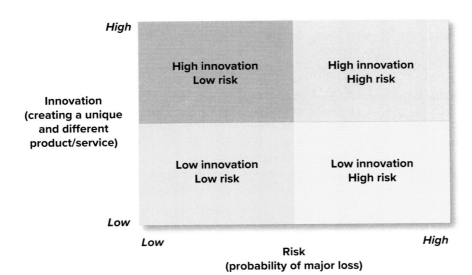

EXHIBIT 7.5
Entrepreneurial Strategy Matrix

SOURCE: Sonfield, M. and Lussier, R., "The Entrepreneurial Strategy Matrix: A Model for New and Ongoing Ventures," *Business Horizons,* May–June 1997.

are in other cells, especially the upper right. So you might place your new venture idea in the appropriate cell and determine whether that cell is the one in which you would prefer to operate. If it is, the venture is one that perhaps should be pursued, pending fuller analysis. If it is not, you can reject the idea or take steps to move it toward a different cell.

The matrix also can help entrepreneurs remember a useful point: successful companies do not always require a cutting-edge technology or an exciting new product. Even companies offering the most mundane products—the type that might reside in the lower-left cell—can gain competitive advantage by doing basic things differently from and better than competitors.

LO 7-3 Identify common causes of success and failure.

Success and Failure

Success or failure lies ahead for entrepreneurs starting their own companies as well as for those starting new businesses within bigger corporations. Entrepreneurs succeed or fail in private, public, and not-for-profit sectors; in nations at all stages of development; and in all nations, regardless of their politics.[76]

Start-ups have at least two major liabilities: newness and smallness.[77] New companies are relatively unknown and need to learn how to be better than established competitors at something that customers value. There are factors that can increase your firm's odds of survival, such as reaching a critical mass of at least 10 or 20 people, has revenues of $2 million or $3 million, and is pursuing opportunities with growth potential.[78]

Management in Action

MANAGER'S BRIEF

PROGRESS REPORT

ONWARD

STARBUCKS RISKS SUCCESS AND FAILURE

Part of being an entrepreneur is experiencing occasional failures. Despite Starbucks's worldwide success, the company has not always succeeded in its attempts to be innovative.

Some of Schultz's bold moves have, of course, been famously successful, including in the areas of social responsibility and sustainability. His company was the first to offer full employment benefits to part-timers and health care coverage to employees' domestic partners, was a pioneer in the use of ethically sourced coffee, and was the first in the industry to use post-consumer recycled fiber in its beverage cups. More recently, it committed to stop using plastic straws by 2020.[79]

Of course, highly individualized orders for exotic specialty coffee drinks once unknown to U.S. consumers are now iconic staples in the company's thousands of stores. Digital payment and mobile ordering are other innovations for which Starbucks can take credit.

But some product ideas have missed the mark. A product called "drinking chocolate," essentially a liquid dessert popular in Europe, was an almost immediate failure. A partnership between Starbucks and PepsiCo yielded a bottled blend of coffee and soda that failed, though it did make way for bottled Frappuccino. Another dessert, called "sorbetto," failed. Efforts to build a new line of low-calorie fruit smoothies failed as well. Smoothies are still offered, but the brand-building effort was abandoned.[80] More recently,

the Fizzio line of carbonated drinks, with three flavors rolled out in 16 states, has fizzled.[81]

In addition to product failures, Starbucks also has dealt with failure in some of its expansion efforts. The company's products failed to catch on in some countries, such as Israel, and even some continents. After decades of trying, Starbucks still hasn't made a dent in the Australian market.[82]

Yet failure can never deter the entrepreneurial spirit. In fact, Starbucks is finally trying to expand into the market that served as the inspiration for its very existence. In 2018, Starbucks opened its first store in Milan, Italy, perhaps the toughest coffee market in the world. The event was so momentous that Howard Schultz came for the launch. "Everything we have experienced, since that first moment of inspiration 35 years ago, to now being a daily part of millions of people's lives around the world, we bring with great respect to Italy," he said.[83]

It will be a few years before we can register it here as an entrepreneurial success or a failure. Either way, Starbucks is sure to keep taking chances.

- How would you categorize Starbucks's decisions to test new products in terms of high or low innovation and risk? Why?
- How is Starbucks's decision making about testing new products and markets different from that of a start-up company, and how is it similar?

To understand further the factors that influence success and failure, we'll consider the economic environment, various management-related hazards, and initial public stock offerings (IPOs).

The Role of the Economic Environment   Entrepreneurial activity stems from the economic environment[84] as well as the behavior of individuals. Money is a critical resource for all new businesses. Increases in the money supply and the supply of bank loans, real economic growth, and improved stock market performance lead to both improved prospects and increased sources of capital. In turn, the prospects and the capital increase the rate of business formation. Under favorable conditions, many aspiring entrepreneurs find early success. But economic cycles can quickly change favorable conditions into downturns. To succeed, entrepreneurs must have the foresight and talent to survive when the environment becomes more hostile.

> Economic cycles can quickly change favorable conditions into downturns, and vice versa.

Although good economic times may make it easier to start a company and to survive, bad times can offer an opportunity to expand. Ken Hendricks of ABC Supply found a business opportunity in a grim economic situation: A serious downturn in the manufacturing economy of the Midwest contributed to the shutdown of his town's largest employer, the Beloit Corporation. Hendricks purchased the company's buildings and lured a diverse group of new employers to town despite the economic challenges. In fact, Hendricks turned around struggling suppliers that ABC acquired.[85] Another silver lining in difficult economic times is that it's easier to recruit talent.

Business Incubators and Accelerators

The need to provide a nurturing environment for fledgling enterprises led to the creation of business incubators. **Business incubators**, often located in industrial parks or abandoned factories, are protected environments for new, small businesses. Incubators offer benefits such as low rents and shared costs for up to a 5-year period.[86] Shared staff costs, such as for receptionists and secretaries, avoid the expense of a full-time employee but still provide convenient access to services. The staff manager is usually an experienced businessperson or consultant who advises the new business owners. Incubators often are associated with universities, which provide technical and business services for the new companies.

business incubators
Protected environments for new, small businesses.

Whereas a business incubator hatches new businesses in a gradual way in a noncompetitive environment, a **business accelerator** is a 3- to 6-month intensive process designed to help budding entrepreneurs build and launch rapidly successful ventures. There are at least 2,000 accelerator programs in the world, including Y Combinator, 500 Startups, and TechStars.[87] Accelerators pay participants to attend structured learning sessions, and receive in return an equity stake (e.g., 6 or 7 percent). Industry experts, venture capitalists, and fellow cohort members serve as sounding boards and mentors.[88]

business accelerator
Organization that provides support and advice to help young businesses grow.

Common Management Challenges

As an entrepreneur, you are likely to face several common challenges that you should be aware of and then manage effectively when the time comes.

LO 7-4 Discuss common management challenges.

You Might Not Enjoy It

Some managers and employees can specialize in what they love, whether it's selling or accounting. But entrepreneurs usually have to do it all, at least in the beginning. If you love product design, you also have to sell what you create. If you love marketing, get ready to manage the money too. This last challenge can be stressful on many founders of start-ups.[89] Serial entrepreneur, Judge Graham, sums it up: "Whether it's their own money they have invested or investors' money, needing to generate revenue and soon is a priority."[90]

The Digital World

Crowdfunding New Ideas

One of the main challenges for entrepreneurs is securing funding. Many go the traditional route of bank loans, personal or family savings, or lines of credit. Other sources for funding include venture capitalists, angel investors, or small-business grants.[91]

In addition to these conventional methods, entrepreneurs increasingly turn to the Internet. Crowdfunding sites like Kickstarter, GoFundMe, and Indiegogo raise billions to fund new business ideas. Entrepreneurs post short pitches about their idea to garner funding pledges, often in exchange for some type of reward, such as early access to a product.

In addition to this donation-based form of crowdfunding, two other forms exist: debt crowdfunding (in which peer-to-peer lending occurs) and equity crowdfunding (in which stock is traded for equity).[92]

Crowdfunding sites can be beneficial because they cut down on many of the hassles of finding funding, including payment processing and certain legal hurdles.[93]

The same idea applies for social entrepreneurs. Sites like Fundly, Kiva, and CrowdRise provide funding all over the world for microloans and socially beneficial projects.[94]

While online sites won't replace traditional funding sources like banks and venture capital groups, they do increase opportunities for entrepreneurs to realize their visions.

1. In comparison to more traditional methods, how effective do you think crowdfunding is?
2. Have you ever pledged money on a crowdfunding site? Why or why not?

Survival Is Difficult

Companies without a track record tend to have more trouble lining up lenders, investors, and customers. When economic conditions cool or competition heats up, a small start-up serving a niche market may have limited options for survival. Failure can be devastating.

Founders of a start-up must make key decisions in so many areas of business that mistakes are potentially a devastating risk. Jawbone, former maker of headsets, fitness trackers, and wireless speakers, failed after a 17-year run despite receiving $930 million in funding. Contributing to the company's demise was intense competition from Fitbit devices and Apple Watch, successfully aligning products with changing consumer tastes, and inconsistent product quality.[95]

Growth Creates New Challenges

In the beginning, entrepreneurs keep their business afloat with dogged determination to win customers and keep them happy. They work long hours at low pay, deliver great service, get good word-of-mouth advertising, and their business grows. When keeping up with all the work becomes physically impossible, entrepreneurs feel they need to bring in help.

Julie Ladd, founder of CopyShark.net, says she got ready to contract for help after she spent six months doing everything alone: "I was working 70-plus hours a week and wasn't able to get the turnaround time that my clients needed."[96] The challenge, of course, is that you not only have to come up with the money to keep paying people for the long haul, but also have to figure out who will bring enough skills, motivation, and commitment to the company.

Growth seems to be a consuming goal for most entrepreneurs. But some company founders reach the size where they're happy and don't want to grow any further. Other founders pursue slow growth. Jason Fried, co-founder of Basecamp (formerly known as 37signals), refuses to grow so fast that the workload and stress would push employees to the point of quitting: "I like the people who work here too much. I don't want them to burn out." With a relatively small staff of 54 people, Basecamp is successful with nearly 2.9 million individual and 100,000 company subscribers.[97]

Bottom Line

Entrepreneurs can increase their companies' size, but they still have to keep a high-value business model and provide great customer service. *What might be a sign that a small company is growing too fast?*

It's Hard to Delegate

As the business grows, entrepreneurs often hesitate to delegate to other people work that they are used to doing themselves. Leadership deteriorates into micromanagement, in which managers monitor too strictly, to the minutest detail. During the early Internet craze, many company founders with great technical knowledge but little experience became instant experts in every phase of business, including branding and advertising.[98] Turns out, they didn't know as much as they thought, and their companies crashed.

Fortunately, many entrepreneurs observe the consequences of their behavior and figure out how to manage more effectively. Kit Hickey and her business partners had a good problem on their hands. Within a month of launching Ministry of Supply, they sold 6,000 shirts and acquired 4,000 customers. The leadership team had to scale production from 300 to 6,000 shirts per month. Their solution was to divide responsibilities and then empower each other to make customers as happy as possible. For example, one partner was in charge of product development and technology, another was the head of customer advocacy, and so forth. These decisions, combined with agile problem solving and transparent communication, helped Ministry of Supply grow rapidly to meet surging customer demand.[99]

Misuse of Funds

Many unsuccessful entrepreneurs blame their failure on inadequate financial resources. Yet failure due to a lack of financial resources doesn't necessarily indicate a real lack of money; it could mean a failure to use the available money properly. A lot of start-up capital may be wasted—on expensive locations, great furniture, and fancy stationery.

Entrepreneurs who fail to use their resources wisely usually make one of two mistakes: They apply financial resources to the wrong uses, or they maintain inadequate control over their resources.

This can be a problem when a lucky entrepreneur gets a big infusion of cash from a venture capital firm or an initial offering of stock. For start-ups, where the money on the line comes from the entrepreneur's own assets, he or she has more incentive to be careful.

Poor Controls

Entrepreneurs, in part because they are very busy, often fail to use formal control systems. One common entrepreneurial malady is an aversion to record keeping. Expenses mount, but records do not keep pace. Pricing decisions are based on intuition without adequate reference to costs. As a result, the company does not earn profit margins adequate to support growth.

Blinded by the light of growing sales, many entrepreneurs fail to maintain vigilance over other aspects of the business. Experts agree that to build and run a successful company, business owners need to control operational costs.[100] In many instances, small changes can yield big savings. Canadian North, an airline company, turned to technology to reduce employees' workload and increase efficiency. By switching to an automated accounts payable system, the airline saved approximately $300 million annually.[101] Tom Bowman, founder of a small creative services firm, cut electricity costs by 40 percent by installing a new air conditioner for the office and emissions by 65 percent by trading the company's SUV for a Prius.[102]

Even in high-growth companies, great numbers can mask brewing problems. In the absence of controls, the business veers out of control. So, don't get overconfident; keep asking critical questions. Is our success based on just one big customer? Is our product just a fad that can fade away? Can other companies easily enter our domain and hurt our business? Are we losing a technology lead? Do we really understand the numbers, know where they come from, and have any hidden causes for concern?

Mortality and Succession

One long-term measure of an entrepreneur's success is the eventual fate of the venture after the founder's retirement or death. Founding entrepreneurs have trouble disengaging,[103] and

---

Bottom Line

You probably will pay close attention to costs at the beginning, but success sometimes brings neglect. Don't fall into that trap. *An entrepreneur who loves selling delegates bookkeeping to an accountant. What potential risks and rewards does this pose to the business?*

often fail to plan for succession. When death occurs, estate tax problems or the lack of a skilled replacement for the founder can lead to business failure. In the United States and around the world, only one-third of family-owned businesses survive after the second generation takes over.[104]

Family members who are mediocre performers are resented by others. Outsiders can be more objective and contribute expertise the family might not have. Issues of management succession are often the most difficult of all, causing serious conflict and possible breakup of the firm.

Management guru Peter Drucker offered the following advice to help family-managed businesses survive and prosper.[105] Family members working in the business must be at least as capable and hard-working as other employees, at least one key position should be filled by a nonfamily member, and someone outside the family and the business should help plan succession.

Going Public   Contrary to myth, liquidity constraints are not the major barrier to entry for most start-ups.[106] Most start-up efforts begin with $5,000 or less in capitalization. But some companies—not nearly as many[107] as you might assume from reading the *Wall Street Journal*—reach a point at which the owners want to go public. **Initial public stock offerings (IPOs)** offer a way to raise capital through federally registered and underwritten sales of shares in the company.[108] You need lawyers and accountants who know current regulations.

The reasons for going public include raising more capital, reducing debt or improving the balance sheet and enhancing net worth, pursuing otherwise unaffordable opportunities, and improving credibility with customers and other stakeholders—you're in the big leagues now. Disadvantages include the expense, time, and effort involved; the tendency to become more interested in the stock price and capital gains than in running the company properly; and the creation of a long-term relationship with an investment banking firm that won't necessarily always be a good one.[109]

Executing IPOs and other approaches to acquiring capital are complex, legalistic, and beyond the scope of this chapter. Sources for more information include the National Venture Capital Association (www.nvca.org) and the Small Business Association's Small Business Learning Center (http://www.sba.gov/learning-center).

Increasing Your Chances of Success

Entrepreneurs need to think through their business idea carefully to help ensure its success. We discuss here the importance of good planning and different types of resources.

Planning   So you think you have identified a business opportunity. And you have the personal drive to make it a success. Now what? Where should you begin?

The Business Plan
Your excitement and intuition may convince you that you are on to something. But they might not convince anyone else. You need more thorough planning and analysis. This effort will help convince other people to get on board and help you avoid costly mistakes.

The first formal planning step is to do an opportunity analysis. An **opportunity analysis** includes a description of the good or service, an assessment of the opportunity, an assessment of the entrepreneur (you), a specification of activities and resources needed to translate your idea into a viable business, and your source(s) of capital.[110] Exhibit 7.6 shows the questions you should answer in an opportunity analysis.

The opportunity analysis, or opportunity assessment plan, focuses on the opportunity, not the entire venture. It provides the basis for making a decision on whether to act. Then the **business plan** describes all the elements involved in starting the new venture.[111] The business plan describes the venture and its market, strategies, and future directions. It often has functional plans for marketing, finance, manufacturing, and human resources.

---

initial public offering (IPO)

Sale to the public, for the first time, of federally registered and underwritten shares of stock in the company.

LO 7-5 Explain how to increase your chances of success, including good business planning.

---

opportunity analysis

A description of the good or service, an assessment of the opportunity, an assessment of the entrepreneur, specification of activities and resources needed to translate your idea into a viable business, and your source(s) of capital.

---

business plan

A formal planning step that focuses on the entire venture and describes all the elements involved in starting it.

What market need does my idea fill?
What personal observations have I experienced or recorded with regard to that market need?
What social condition underlies this market need?
What market research data can be marshaled to describe this market need?
What patents might be available to fulfill this need?
What competition exists in this market? How would I describe the behavior of this competition?
What does the international market look like?
What does the international competition look like?
Where is the money to be made in this activity?

EXHIBIT 7.6
Opportunity Analysis

SOURCE: Hisrich, R. and Peters, M., *Entrepreneurship: Starting, Developing, and Managing a New Enterprise,* p. 41. Copyright ©1998 McGraw-Hill Global Education Holdings LLC. All rights reserved. Used with permission.

Exhibit 7.7 shows an outline for a typical business plan. The business plan (1) helps determine the viability of your enterprise, (2) guides you as you plan and organize, and (3) helps you obtain financing. It is read by potential investors, suppliers, customers, and others. Get help in writing a sound plan!

Key Planning Elements

The business needs enough cash to cover start-up expenses and keep the company running during slow periods. The initial budget should cover one-time costs, such as the fee to form a corporation, and ongoing expenses such as supplies and rent for the first few months. The company's founders may start the business with their own money, or they may seek financing in the form of debt (taking out a loan from family, friends, or a bank) or equity (taking money in exchange for an ownership share in the company). Typically, start-ups get most of their money from the owners, their families, and loans and credit lines from banks. Other kinds of investors, such as venture capital firms, generate a lot of publicity for splashy deals but provide a very small share of start-up funds.[112]

Raising money to start a business can be one of the entrepreneur's greatest challenges. Peer-to-peer loans are an alternative to using a bank. Using online platforms like P2P Credit or Prosper, individual investors loan up to $40,000 to small businesses.[113] For example, Hannah Attwood wanted to raise money to open a cloth diaper supply and cleaning service. After four banks rejected her, Attwood secured from investors a three-year loan to help launch her new business. Combining the loan with her own savings, Attwood was able to purchase industrial washers and dryers.[114]

Just as the Internet has transformed every other aspect of business, it is poised to remake the challenge of raising start-up money. This trend started with the use of social media tools to link would-be entrepreneurs with people who want to make great ideas happen. At crowdfunding websites, such as AngelList, FundersClub, Indiegogo, and Kickstarter, the entrepreneurs post their ideas and anyone can donate to the cause.

Until recently, crowdfunding was mostly limited to small contributions from people who gave in exchange for a company-provided experience, discount, or product sample; the funders don't receive equity in the business. The main reason is that the Securities and Exchange Commission, which regulates investing, needs to ensure that investors on these sites have the same protections available to traditional investors. In 2012, however, Congress passed the Jumpstart Our Business Startups Act (JOBS Act), which makes it easier for start-ups to receive funding from online investors (crowdfunding) and to go public. Results are mixed. Two years after the act was passed, the number of IPOs reached a 14-year high. In 2016, the number of IPOs reached the lowest the market has seen since 2009, but the number has been growing since.[115]

EXHIBIT 7.7   Outline of a Business Plan

I.   EXECUTIVE SUMMARY

Description of the Business Concept and the Business

Opportunity and Strategy

Target Market and Projections

Competitive Advantages

Costs

Sustainability

The Team

The Offering

II.   THE INDUSTRY AND THE COMPANY AND ITS PRODUCT(S) OR SERVICE(S)

The Industry

The Company and the Concept

The Product(s) or Service(s)

Entry and Growth Strategy

III.   MARKET RESEARCH AND ANALYSIS

Customers

Market Size and Trends

Competition and Competitive Edges

Estimated Market Share and Sales

Ongoing Market Evaluation

IV.   THE ECONOMICS OF THE BUSINESS

Gross and Operating Margins

Profit Potential and Durability

Fixed, Variable, and Semivariable Costs

Months to Breakeven

Months to Reach Positive Cash Flow

V.   MARKETING PLAN

Overall Marketing Strategy

Pricing

Sales Tactics

Service and Warranty Policies

Advertising and Promotion Distribution

VI.   DESIGN AND DEVELOPMENT PLANS

Development Status and Tasks

Difficulties and Risks

Product Improvement and New Products

Costs

Proprietary Issues

VII.   MANUFACTURING AND OPERATIONS PLAN

Operating Cycle

Geographical Location

Facilities and Improvements

Strategy and Plans

Regulatory and Legal Issues

VIII.   MANAGEMENT TEAM

Organization

Key Management Personnel

Management Compensation and Ownership

Other Investors

Employment and Other Agreements and Stock Option and Bonus Plans

Board of Directors

Other Shareholders, Rights, and Restrictions

Supporting Professional Advisers and Services

IX.   OVERALL SCHEDULE

X.   CRITICAL RISKS, PROBLEMS, AND ASSUMPTIONS

XI.   THE FINANCIAL PLAN

Actual Income Statements and Balance Sheets

Pro Forma Income Statements

Pro Forma Balance Sheets

Pro Forma Cash Flow Analysis

Breakeven Chart and Calculation

Cost Control

Highlights

XII.   PROPOSED COMPANY OFFERING

Desired Financing

Offering

Capitalization

Use of Funds

Investor's Return

XIII.   APPENDIXES

Inclusiveness Works

Start-Ups and Diversity

For all its merits, the technology sector has been infamously poor at diversifying its workforce. Despite years of being under the microscope, the industry as a whole isn't making much progress. Major technology companies started publishing diversity reports in 2014. In one example, Google's female representation that year was 30 percent. In its latest 2018 report it was . . . 30 percent. Essentially no progress has been made by the tech giant.[116]

Unfortunately, it's not looking much better for tech start-ups. A 2018 survey of tech start-up founders reported approximately 78 percent of organizations had no formal plan or policies to promote diversity. When asked when the tech industry will be representative of the general population when it comes to race and ethnicity, more than 20 percent said at least two decades; 18 percent said never. Notably, among the start-up founders taking part in the survey, only 17 percent identified as female.[117]

When it comes to access in the tech start-up ecosystem, women and minority entrepreneurs are at a distinct disadvantage, both in funding and in representation. All hope is not lost, however. There are ways of remedying this situation. Improving access to venture capital funding is a must. The venture capital funding rate for all-female tech start-ups aligns with the rate for female founders across all industries: approximately 2 percent.[118] Beyond funding, cultivating an inclusive community of mentors for underrepresented populations is also critical. Mentors serve not only as role models, but also can provide insight into how to articulate a vision that will attract more funding.[119]

1. What's your perspective on changing the face of the tech industry? Are you pessimistic about a turnaround, or are you hopeful? Why?
2. What do you think is the root cause for the lack of diversity and inclusion in the tech sector? Funding, representation, implicit bias? Explain your rationale.

Most business plans devote so much attention to financial projections that they neglect other important information—information that matters greatly to astute investors. In fact, financial projections tend to be overly optimistic. Investors know this and discount the figures. In addition to the numbers, the best plans convey—and make certain that the entrepreneurs have carefully thought through—five key factors: the people, the opportunity, the competition, the context, and risk and reward.[120]

The *people* should be energetic and have skills and expertise directly relevant to the venture. For many astute investors, the people are the most important variable, more important even than the idea. Arthur Rock, a legendary venture capitalist who helped start Intel, Teledyne, and Apple, stated, "I invest in people, not ideas. If you can find good people, if they're wrong about the product, they'll make a switch."[121]

The *opportunity* should provide a competitive advantage that can be defended. Customers are the focus here: Who is the customer? How does the customer make decisions? How will the product be priced? How will the venture reach all customer segments? How much does it cost to acquire and support a customer and to produce and deliver the product? How easy or difficult is it to retain a customer?

It is also essential to fully consider the *competition*. The plan must identify current competitors and their strengths and weaknesses, predict how they will respond to the new venture, indicate how the new venture will respond to the competitors' responses, identify future potential competitors, and consider how to collaborate with or face off against actual or potential competitors.

> The opportunity should provide a competitive advantage that can be sustained.

The original plan for Zappos was for its website to compete with other online shoe retailers by offering a wider selection than they did. However, most people buy shoes in stores, so Zappos co-founders Nick Swinmurn and Tony Hsieh soon realized that they needed a broader view of the competition. They began focusing more on service and planning a distribution method that would make online shopping as successful as visiting a store.[122]

The *environmental context* should be a favorable one from regulatory and economic perspectives. Such factors as tax policies, rules about raising capital, interest rates, inflation, and exchange rates will affect the viability of the new venture. Importantly, the plan should make clear that you know that the context inevitably will change, should forecast how the changes will affect the business, and should describe how you will deal with the changes.

The *risk* must be understood and addressed as fully as possible. Although you cannot predict the future, you must contemplate head-on the possibilities of key people leaving, interest rates changing, a key customer leaving, or a powerful competitor responding ferociously. Then describe what you will do to prevent, avoid, or cope with such possibilities.

You should also speak to the end of the process: how to get money out of the business eventually. Will you go public? Will you sell or liquidate? What are the various possibilities for investors to realize their ultimate gains?[123]

Entrepreneurs should carefully consider the five key factors when developing a business plan: the people, the opportunity, the competition, the context, and risk and reward. Commonly, financial projections dominate the plan while these other important factors are overlooked or undervalued.

John Lund/Marc Romanelli/Blend Images/Getty Images RF

Selling the Plan

Your goal is to get the right investors to support the plan. You want more than just financial support; you want high-quality partners so that your relationships will continue to be productive.[124] Thus an important decision is whom you try to convince to back your plan.

Many entrepreneurs want passive investors who will give them money and let them do what they want. Doctors and dentists generally fit this image. Professional venture capitalists do not—they demand more control and more of the returns.

But when a business goes wrong—and chances are, it will—nonprofessional investors are less helpful and less likely to advance more (needed) money. Sophisticated investors have seen sinking ships before and know how to help. They are more likely to solve problems, provide more money, and navigate financial and legal waters.[125]

View the plan as a way for you to figure out how to reduce risk, maximize reward, and convince others that you understand the entire new venture process. Don't put together a plan built on naïveté or overconfidence, or one that cleverly hides major flaws. You might not fool others, and you certainly would be fooling yourself.

Nonfinancial Resources　Also crucial to the success of a new business are nonfinancial resources, including legitimacy in the minds of the public and the various ways in which other people can help.

Legitimacy

legitimacy

People's judgment of a company's acceptance, appropriateness, and desirability, generally stemming from company goals and methods that are consistent with societal values.

An important resource for the new venture is **legitimacy**—people's judgment of a company's acceptance, appropriateness, and desirability.[126] When the market confers legitimacy, it helps overcome the liability of newness that creates a high percentage of new venture failure.[127]

Legitimacy helps a firm acquire other resources such as top managers, good employees, financial resources, and government support. In a three-year study of start-ups, the likelihood a company would succeed at selling products, hiring employees, and attracting investors depended most on how skillfully entrepreneurs demonstrated that their business was legitimate.[128]

A business is legitimate if its goals and methods are consistent with societal values. You can generate legitimacy by visibly conforming to rules and expectations created by governments, credentialing associations, and professional organizations; by visibly endorsing widely held values; and by visibly practicing widely held beliefs.[129]

Networks

The entrepreneur is aided greatly by having a strong network of people. **Social capital**—being part of a social network and having a good reputation—helps entrepreneurs gain access to useful information, gain trust and cooperation from others, recruit employees, form successful business alliances, receive funding from venture capitalists, and become more successful.[130] Social capital provides a lasting source of competitive advantage.[131]

social capital

Goodwill stemming from your social relationships; a competitive advantage in the form of relationships with other people and the image other people have of you.

Top Management Teams

The top management team is another crucial resource. Gordon Logan is CEO and founder of Sport Clips, a hair salon franchise specially designed to appeal to male customers of all ages. After experiencing an early setback as an entrepreneur, Logan brought together a top management team to design a plan to help Sport Clips grow at a rapid yet manageable pace. In 2018, Sport Clips had more than 1,800 franchises operating in every state of the union.[132]

Advisory Boards

Whether or not the company has a formal board of directors, entrepreneurs can assemble a group of people willing to serve as an advisory board. Board members with business experience can help an entrepreneur learn basics such as how to do cash flow analysis, identify needed strategic changes, and build relationships with bankers, accountants, and attorneys.

Partners

Often two people go into business together as partners. Partners can help one another access capital, spread the workload, share the risk, and share expertise.

But despite the potential advantages of having a compatible partner, partnerships are not always marriages made in heaven. "Mark" talked three of his friends into joining him in starting his own telecommunications company because he didn't want to try it alone. He learned quickly that while he wanted to put money into growing the business, his three partners wanted the company to pay for their cars and meetings in the Bahamas. The company collapsed. "I never thought a business relationship could overpower friendship, but this one did. Where money's involved, people change."

To be successful, partners need to acknowledge one another's talents, let each other do what they do best, communicate honestly, and listen to one another. Partners also must learn to trust each other by making and keeping agreements. If they must break an agreement, it is crucial that they give early notice and clean up after their mistakes.

Corporate Entrepreneurship

Large corporations are more than passive bystanders watching independent entrepreneurs create new businesses. Even established companies try to find and pursue new and profitable ideas—and they need in-house entrepreneurs (sometimes called intrapreneurs)[133] to do so.

LO 7-6 Describe how managers of large companies can foster entrepreneurship.

Building Support for Your Idea

A manager who has a new idea to capitalize on a market opportunity will need to get others in the organization to buy in or sign on. In other words, you need to build a network of allies who support and will help implement the idea.

Bottom Line

Recall from Chapter 3 that creativity spawns new ideas, but innovation requires actually implementing those ideas so they become realities. If you work in an organization and have a good idea, you must convince other people to get on board. *How would you convince people to get behind your new idea?*

If you need to build support for a project idea, the first step involves *clearing the investment* with your immediate boss or bosses.[134] At this stage, you explain the idea and seek approval to look for wider support.

Higher executives often want evidence that the project is backed by your peers before committing to it. This involves *making cheerleaders*—people who will support the manager before formal approval from higher levels.

Next, *horse trading* begins. You can offer promises of payoffs from the project in return for support, time, money, and other resources that peers and others contribute.

Finally, you should *get the blessing* of relevant higher-level officials. This usually involves a formal presentation. You will need to guarantee the project's technical and political feasibility. Higher management's endorsement of the project and promises of resources help convert potential supporters into an enthusiastic team. At this point, you can go back to your boss and make specific plans for going ahead with the project. Along the way, expect some resistance and frustration—and use passion and perseverance, as well as business logic, to persuade others to get on board.

Building Intrapreneurship

Success in fostering a culture in which intrapreneurs flourish comes from making an intentional decision to foster entrepreneurial thinking and behavior, creating new venture teams, and changing the compensation system so that it encourages, supports, and rewards creative and innovative behaviors. In other words, building intrapreneurship derives from careful and deliberate strategy.

Two well-known approaches used to stimulate internal entrepreneurial activity are skunkworks and bootlegging. **Skunkworks** are project teams designated to develop a new product. A team is formed with a specific goal within a specified time frame. A respected person is chosen to manage the skunkworks. In this approach to corporate innovation, risk takers are not punished for taking risks and failing—their former jobs are held for them. The risk takers also have the opportunity to earn large rewards.

skunkworks

A project team designated to produce a new, innovative product.

bootlegging

Informal work on projects, other than those officially assigned, of employees' own choosing and initiative.

Bootlegging refers to informal efforts—as opposed to official job assignments—in which employees work to create new products and processes of their own choosing and initiative. Informal can mean secretive, such as when a bootlegger believes the company or the boss will frown on those activities. But companies should tolerate some bootlegging, and some even encourage it. To a limited extent, they allow people freedom to pursue pet projects without asking what they are or monitoring progress. Bootlegging likely will lead to some lost time but also to learning and some profitable innovations.

Google encourages all employees to be intrapreneurs. Employees can spend 20 percent of their workweek (known as the 20 Percent Rule) developing new product or service ideas. One group of engineers thought that Google could beat any other service doing email, so they created Gmail. The idea was a success, and the service now has over a billion users.[135] At Google, as elsewhere, intrapreneurship derives from deliberate strategic thinking and execution.

Management Challenges

Organizations that encourage intrapreneurship face an obvious risk: the effort can fail. One author noted, "There is considerable history of internal venture development by large firms, and it does not encourage optimism."[136] However, failing to foster intrapreneurship may represent a subtler but greater risk than encouraging it. The organization that resists entrepreneurial initiative may lose its ability to adapt and be creative when needed.

The most dangerous risk in corporate entrepreneurship is overreliance on a single project. Many companies fail while awaiting the completion of one large, innovative project.[137] The successful entrepreneurial organization avoids overcommitment to a single project and relies on its entrepreneurial spirit to produce at least one winner from among several projects.

Organizations also court failure when they spread their entrepreneurial efforts over too many projects.[138] If there are many projects, each effort may be too small in scale. Managers will consider the projects unattractive because of their small size. Or those recruited to manage the projects may have difficulty building power and status within the organization.

The hazards in intrapreneurship, then, are related to scale. One large project is a threat, as are too many underresourced projects. But a carefully managed approach to this strategically important process will upgrade an organization's chances for long-term survival and success.

Entrepreneurial Orientation

Earlier in this chapter, we described the characteristics of individual entrepreneurs. To conclude the chapter, we do the same for companies: We describe how highly entrepreneurial companies differ from those that are not. CEOs play a crucial role in promoting entrepreneurship within large corporations.[139]

Entrepreneurial orientation is an organization's tendency to engage in activities designed to identify and capitalize successfully on opportunities to launch new ventures by entering new or established markets with new or existing goods or services.[140] Entrepreneurial orientation is determined by five tendencies: to allow independent action, innovate, take risks, be proactive, and be competitively aggressive. Entrepreneurial orientation should enhance the likelihood of success and may be particularly important for conducting business internationally.[141]

To allow *independent action* is to grant to individuals and teams the freedom to exercise their creativity, champion promising ideas, and carry them through to completion. *Innovativeness* requires the firm to support new ideas, experimentation, and creative processes; it requires a willingness to depart from existing practices and venture beyond the status quo. *Risk taking* comes from a willingness to commit significant resources, and perhaps borrow heavily, to venture into the unknown.

To be *proactive* is to act in anticipation of future problems and opportunities. A proactive firm changes the competitive landscape; other firms merely react. Proactive firms are forward thinking and fast to act and are leaders rather than followers. Similarly, some individuals are more likely to be proactive, to shape and create their own environments, than others who more passively cope with the situations in which they find themselves.[142] Proactive firms encourage and allow individuals and teams to be proactive.

Finally, *competitive aggressiveness* is the firm's tendency to challenge competitors directly and intensely to achieve entry or improve its position. In other words, it is a competitive tendency to outperform one's rivals in the marketplace. This might take the form of striking fast to beat competitors to the punch, to take them on head-to-head, and to analyze and target their weaknesses.

Thus, what makes a firm entrepreneurial is its engagement in an effective combination of independent action, innovativeness, risk taking, proactiveness, and competitive aggressiveness.[143] The relationship between these factors and the performance of the firm is a complicated one that depends on many things.[144] Still, you can imagine how the opposite profile—too many constraints on action, business as usual, extreme caution, passivity, and a lack of competitive fire—will inhibit entrepreneurial activity.

Without entrepreneurship, how would firms survive and thrive in a constantly changing environment? If your bosses don't create environments that foster entrepreneurship, consider trying your own experiments.[145] Find and talk with others who share your entrepreneurial bent. What can you learn from them, and teach them?

Sometime it takes individuals and teams of experimenters to show the possibilities to those at the top. Ask yourself and others: Between the bureaucrats and the entrepreneurs, who have a more positive impact? And who have more fun?

entrepreneurial orientation

The tendency of an organization to identify and capitalize successfully on opportunities to launch new ventures by entering new or established markets with new or existing goods or services.

Management in Action

STARBUCKS IS RETAINING ITS ENTREPRENEURIAL SPIRIT

Howard Schultz has stepped down as CEO of Starbucks, but the entrepreneurial spirit he instilled in the company lives on. Even as it has become a worldwide corporate brand in more than 60 countries, the company has its own "entrepreneur in residence."

The company hired Richard Tait, not because he is a coffee expert but because he has a creative mind and has been successful at bringing new products to market. Tait is the co-founder of the board game "Cranium" and launched a series of new businesses at Microsoft. In his current position, he is responsible for "helping the company foster a culture of innovation" and lending an "entrepreneurial lens" to its planning and decision making, with a focus on speed and agility. Tait, who also is on the steering committee for Starbucks's Innovation Lab, says his role is to maintain the "energy and passion of a start-up inside the rhythm of a large corporation."[146]

That passion has led Starbucks to begin launching a new high-end "Reserve" line that will take three different forms: the Reserve Roastery, Reserve Store, and the Reserve Bar.[147] Starbucks's Reserve Roasteries are expansive, immersive spaces where customers can watch the process of roasting while sipping on anything from select coffees to select cocktails. They have opened in just a few major cities around the world, including Milan, Tokyo, and New York.[148] The Reserve Stores and Reserve Bars are scaled-down versions of the Roastery concept.

Meanwhile, Starbucks continues to innovate as a socially conscious company, with a promise to open stores

Eyesonmilan/Shutterstock

in low- and middle-income communities in the United States to provide jobs in these communities. In a new expansion strategy, drive-thrus and express stores will help the company expand in the United States without risking the oversaturation it faced some years ago when some stores were forced to close.[149]

- What evidence do you see that Starbucks supports intrapreneurial behavior? What are some of the risks a large company takes in doing so?
- How would you like to work for a big company (Starbucks, or choose your favorite) and hold the title "entrepreneur in residence"? What would your job entail?

KEY TERMS

bootlegging, p. 220

business accelerator, p. 211

business incubators, p. 211

business plan, p. 214

entrepreneur, p. 201

entrepreneurial orientation, p. 221

entrepreneurial venture, p. 200

entrepreneurship, p. 200

franchising, p. 204

initial public offering (IPO), p. 214

intrapreneurs, p. 201

legitimacy, p. 218

opportunity analysis, p. 214

skunkworks, p. 220

small business, p. 200

social capital, p. 219

social enterprise, p. 206

social entrepreneurship, p. 206

RETAINING WHAT YOU LEARNED

In Chapter 7, you learned that people become entrepreneurs for a variety of reasons. Successful entrepreneurs are innovators, but also possess management, business, and networking skills. While there is no single entrepreneurial personality, certain characteristics contribute to their success. To start a new business, it is important to monitor the current business environment and other indicators. Choosing a business idea to pursue should be based on planning and trial and error, and fit with risk preferences and personal interests. Effective planning and getting advice from experienced experts are helpful in preventing failure. Common challenges include getting started, warding off competitors, managing growth, and controlling finances. Developing and executing a comprehensive business plan will increase the chances of success. Successful entrepreneurs develop social capital and a network of customers, partners, boards, and other talented people. Managers of large companies can encourage intrapreneurship by using skunkworks and allowing bootlegging. A portfolio of projects should be chosen carefully and funded appropriately. An entrepreneurial orientation in a company comes from encouraging independent action, innovativeness, risk taking, proactive behavior, and competitive aggressiveness.

LO 7-1 **Describe why people become entrepreneurs and what it takes, personally.**

- People become entrepreneurs because of the profit potential, the challenge, and the satisfaction they anticipate (and often receive) from participating in the process, and sometimes because they are blocked from more traditional avenues of career advancement.
- As shown in Exhibit 7.3, successful entrepreneurs are innovators, and they have good knowledge and skills in management, business, and networking.
- Although there is no single entrepreneurial personality, certain characteristics are helpful: commitment and determination; leadership skills; opportunity obsession; tolerance of risk, ambiguity, and uncertainty; creativity; self-reliance; the ability to adapt; and motivation to excel.

LO 7-2 **Summarize how to assess opportunities to start new businesses.**

- You should always be on the lookout for new ideas, monitoring the current business environment and other indicators of opportunity.
- Trial and error and preparation play important roles. Assessing the business concept on the basis of how innovative and risky it is, combined with your personal interests and tendencies, also will help you make good choices.
- Ideas should be carefully assessed via opportunity analysis and a thorough business plan.

LO 7-3 **Identify common causes of success and failure.**

- New ventures are inherently risky. The economic environment plays an important role in the success or failure of the business, and the entrepreneur should anticipate and be prepared to adapt in the face of changing economic conditions.
- How you handle a variety of common management challenges also can mean the difference between success and failure, as can the effectiveness of your planning and your ability to mobilize nonfinancial resources, including other people who can help.

LO 7-4 **Discuss common management challenges.**

- When new businesses fail, the causes often can be traced to some common challenges that entrepreneurs must manage well. You might not enjoy the entrepreneurial process.
- Survival—including getting started and fending off competitors—is difficult.

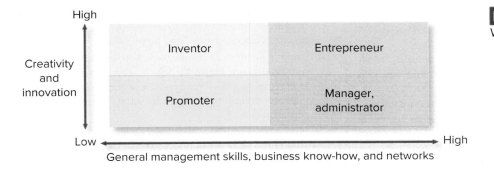

EXHIBIT 7.3 (revisited)
Who Is the Entrepreneur?

SOURCE: Timmons, T. A. and Spinelli, S. Jr., *New Venture Creation: Entrepreneurship for the 21st Century,* 7th ed., 2007, pp. 67–68. Copyright 2007 The McGraw-Hill Companies, Inc. Reprinted with permission.

- Growth creates new challenges, including reluctance to delegate work to others. Funds may be put to improper use, and financial controls may be inadequate.
- Many entrepreneurs fail to plan well for succession.
- When needing or wanting new funds, initial public offerings provide an option, but they represent an important and difficult decision that must be considered carefully.

LO 7-5   Explain how to increase your chances of success, including good business planning.

- The business plan helps you think through your idea thoroughly and determine its viability. It also convinces (or fails to convince) others to participate.
- The plan describes the venture and its future, provides financial projections, and includes plans for marketing, manufacturing, and other business functions.
- The plan should describe the people involved in the venture, a full assessment of the opportunity (including customers and competitors), the environmental context (including regulatory and economic issues), and the risk (including future risks and how you intend to deal with them).
- Successful entrepreneurs also understand how to develop social capital, which enhances legitimacy and helps develop a network of others including customers, talented people, partners, and boards.

LO 7-6   Describe how managers of large companies can foster entrepreneurship.

- Intrapreneurs work within established companies to develop new goods or services that allow the corporation to reap the benefits of innovation.
- To facilitate intrapreneurship, organizations use skunkworks—special project teams designated to develop a new product—and allow bootlegging—informal efforts beyond formal job assignments in which employees pursue their own pet projects.
- Organizations should select projects carefully, have an ongoing portfolio of projects, and fund them appropriately.
- Ultimately, a true entrepreneurial orientation in a company comes from encouraging independent action, innovativeness, risk taking, proactive behavior, and competitive aggressiveness.

DISCUSSION QUESTIONS

1. On a 1 to 10 scale, what is your level of personal interest in becoming an entrepreneur? Why did you rate yourself as you did?

2. How would you assess your capability of being a successful entrepreneur? What are your strengths and weaknesses? How would you increase your capability?

3. Most entrepreneurs use their own savings or borrow from family and friends to launch a start-up. How much capital could you possibly raise?

4. Identify and discuss new ventures that fit each of the four cells in the entrepreneurial strategy matrix.

5. Brainstorm a list of ideas for new business ventures. Where did you get the ideas? Which ones are most and least viable, and why?

6. Identify some businesses that recently opened in your area. What are their chances of survival, and why? How would you advise the owners or managers of those businesses to ensure their success?

7. Assume you are writing a story about what it's really like to be an entrepreneur. To whom would you talk, and what questions would you ask?

8. Conduct interviews with two entrepreneurs, asking whatever questions most interest you. Share your findings with the class. How do the interviews differ from one another, and what do they have in common?

9. Review Exhibit 7.1. Which myths did you believe? Do you still? Why or why not? Interview two entrepreneurs by asking each myth as a true-or-false question. Then ask them to elaborate on their answers. What did they say? What do you conclude?

10. With your classmates, form small teams of skunkworks. Your charge is to identify an innovation that you think would benefit your school and to outline an action plan for bringing your idea to reality.

11. Identify a business that recently folded. What were the causes of the failure? What could have been done differently to prevent the failure?

12. Does franchising appeal to you? What franchises would most and least interest you, and why?

13. The chapter specified some of the changes in the external environment that can provide business opportunity (technological discoveries, lifestyle and taste changes, and so on). Identify some important recent changes or current trends in the external environment and the business opportunities they might offer.

14. Choose an Internet company with which you are familiar and brainstorm ideas for how its services or approach to business can be improved. How about starting a new Internet company altogether—what would be some possibilities?

15. Find some inspiring examples of social entrepreneurship and describe them to your class.

16. Brainstorm some new ideas for a social enterprise. What challenges do you foresee, and how would you proceed?

EXPERIENTIAL EXERCISES

7.1   Take an Entrepreneur to Dinner

OBJECTIVES

1. To get to know what an entrepreneur does, how she or he got started, and what it took to succeed.

2. To interview a particular entrepreneur in depth about his or her career and experiences.

3. To acquire a feeling for whether you might find an entrepreneurial career rewarding.

INSTRUCTIONS

1. Identify an entrepreneur in your area you would like to interview.

2. Contact the person you have selected and make an appointment. Be sure to explain why you want the appointment and to give a realistic estimate of how much time you will need.

3. Identify specific questions you would like to have answered and the general areas about which you would like information. (See the following suggested interview questions, although there probably won't be time for all of them.) Using a combination of open-ended questions—such as general questions about how the entrepreneur got started, what happened next, and so forth—and closed-ended questions—such as specific questions about what his or her goals were, if he or she had to find partners, and so forth—will help keep the interview focused yet allow for unexpected comments and insights.

4. Conduct the interview. If both you and the person you are interviewing are comfortable, using a small voice recorder during the interview can be of great help to you later. Remember, too, that you most likely will learn more if you are an interested listener.

5. Evaluate what you have learned. Write down the information you have gathered in some form that will be helpful to you later on. Be as specific as you can. Jotting down direct quotes is more effective than statements such as "highly motivated individual." Also be sure to make a note of what you did not find out.

6. Write a thank-you note. This is more than a courtesy; it will also help the entrepreneur remember you favorably should you want to follow up on the interview.

Suggested Interview

QUESTIONS FOR GATHERING INFORMATION

- *Would you tell me about yourself before you started your first venture?*

  Were your parents, relatives, or close friends entrepreneurial? How so?

  Did you have any other role models?

  What was your education/military experience? In hindsight, was it helpful? In what specific ways?

What was your previous work experience? Was it helpful? What particular chunks of experience were especially valuable or relevant?

In particular, did you have any sales or marketing experience? How important was this in starting your company?

- *How did you start your venture?*

  How did you spot the opportunity? How did it surface?

  What were your goals? What were your lifestyle or other personal requirements? How did you fit these factors together?

  How did you evaluate the opportunity in terms of the critical elements for success? The competition? The market?

  Did you find or have partners? What kind of planning did you do? What kind of financing did you have?

  Did you have a start-up business plan of any kind? Please tell me about it.

  How much time did it take from conception to the first day of business? How many hours a day did you spend working on it?

  How much capital did it take? How long did it take to reach a positive cash flow and break-even sales volume?

  If you did not have enough money at the time, what were some ways in which you "bootstrapped" the venture (i.e., bartering, borrowing, and the like)? Tell me about the pressures and crises during that early survival period.

  What outside help did you get? Did you have experienced advisers? Lawyers? Accountants? Tax experts? Patent experts? How did you develop these networks and how long did it take?

  What was your family situation at the time?

  What did you perceive to be your own strengths? Weaknesses?

  What did you perceive to be the strengths of your venture? Weaknesses?

  What was your most triumphant moment? Your worst moment?

  Did you want to have partners or do it solo? Why?

- *Once you got going . . .*

  What were the most difficult gaps to fill and problems to solve as you began to grow rapidly?

  When you looked for key people as partners, advisers, or managers, were there any personal attributes or attitudes you were especially seeking because you knew they would fit with you and were important to success? How did you find them?

  Are there any attributes among partners and advisers that you would definitely try to avoid?

  Have things become more predictable? Or less?

  Do you spend more/same/less time with your business now than in the early years?

  Do you feel more managerial and less entrepreneurial now? In terms of the future, do you plan to harvest? To maintain? To expand?

  Do you plan ever to retire? Would you explain?

  Have your goals changed? Have you met them?

QUESTIONS FOR CONCLUDING
(CHOOSE ONE)

- What do you consider your most valuable asset—the thing that enabled you to make it?
- If you had it to do over again would you do it again in the same way?
- Looking back, what do you feel are the most critical concepts, skills, attitudes, and know-how you needed to get your company started and grown to where it is today? What will be needed for the next five years? To what extent can any of these be learned?
- Some people say there is a lot of stress being an entrepreneur. What have you experienced? How would you say it compares with other hot-seat jobs, such as the head of a big company or a partner in a large law, consulting, or accounting firm?
- What are the things that you find personally rewarding and satisfying as an entrepreneur? What have been the rewards, risks, and trade-offs?
- Who should try to be an entrepreneur? Can you give me any ideas there?
- What advice would you give an aspiring entrepreneur? Could you suggest the three most important lessons you have learned? How can I learn them while minimizing the tuition?

SOURCE: Timmons, T. A., *New Venture Creation,* 3rd ed. 1994. Copyright ©1994 McGraw-Hill Global Education Holdings LLC. All rights reserved. Used with permission.

7.2   Starting a New Business

OBJECTIVES

1. To introduce you to the complexities of going into business for yourself.
2. To provide hands-on experience in making new business decisions.

INSTRUCTIONS

1. Your instructor will divide the class into teams and assign each team the task of investigating the start-up of one of the following businesses:
   a. Submarine sandwich shop
   b. Day care service
   c. Bookstore
   d. Gasoline service station
   e. Other

2. Each team should research the information necessary to complete the New Business Start-Up Worksheet. The following agencies or organizations might be of assistance:
   a. Small Business Administration
   b. Local county/city administration agencies
   c. Local chamber of commerce
   d. Local small-business development corporation
   e. U.S. Department of Commerce
   f. Farmer's Home Administration
   g. Local realtors
   h. Local business people in the same or a similar business
   i. Banks and S&Ls

3. Each team presents its findings to the class.

New Business Start-Up Worksheet

1. *Product*

   What customer need will we satisfy? _____

   How can our product be unique? _____

2. *Customer*

   Who are our customers? What are their profiles? _____

   Where do they live/work/play? _____

   What are their buying habits? _____

   What are their needs? _____

3. *Competition*

   Who/where is the competition? _____

   What are their strengths and weaknesses? _____

   How might they respond to us? _____

4. *Suppliers*

   Who/where are our suppliers? _____

   What are their business practices? _____

   What relationships can we expect? _____

5. *Location*

   Where are our customers/competitors/suppliers?   _____

   What are the location costs?   _____

   What are the legal limitations to location?   _____

6. *Physical Facilities/Equipment*   _____

   Rent/own/build/refurbish facilities?   _____

   Rent/lease/purchase equipment?   _____

   Maintenance?   _____

7. *Human Resources*   _____

   Availability?   _____

   Training?   _____

   Costs?   _____

8. *Legal/Regulatory Environment*   _____

   Licenses/permits/certifications?   _____

   Government agencies?   _____

   Liability?   _____

9. *Cultural/Social Environment*   _____

   Cultural issues?   _____

   Social issues?   _____

10. *International Environment*   _____

    International issues?   _____

11. *Other*   _____

Concluding Case

ROLLING OUT SOFT SCROLL

Hannah Toberman had enjoyed her engineering job at Allstar Electronics, but she was beginning to grow restless. Most of her work for the past 5 years had involved designing minor adjustments to existing products. She worried she would lose her edge in a fast-changing industry, and work just didn't engage her imagination or problem-solving skills the way it once did.

In her spare time, she found herself pursuing new ideas, researching some of the latest technology, and testing out some possible inventions. Hannah became increasingly interested in one idea: an e-reader made with flexible materials that could be rolled up and stuffed into a backpack, briefcase, or purse. At first she doubted it could be made, but with some investigation, Hannah began to develop a design for the device. She called it the Soft Scroll.

The more Hannah considered the Soft Scroll, the more she thought it would be an exciting new product for Allstar to offer. It would open up a whole new area of sales for the company, which was experiencing slower growth in recent years. Hannah collected a few of the drawings she had created, estimated the manufacturing costs, and prepared a proposal. She invited her supervisor and two of her colleagues to a meeting, saying only that she had an idea she wanted to share.

As Hannah began her presentation, she could see the other engineers' excitement to explore the concept. However, her manager sighed. "Hannah, you know our situation, right? In the present economy, we can't get financing for risky new projects. We have to focus on enhancements to current products that will increase our profit margins." Disappointed, Hannah could tell the discussion was over.

That weekend, Hannah spent hours at her desk at home, beginning to plan her escape from Allstar Electronics. She perused the Small Business Administration website, looking for advice on writing a new business plan, and explored her LinkedIn network, looking for contacts who might give her advice—and possibly funding—for her start-up, Soft Scroll. By the end of the weekend, nervous but also more excited than she had been in years, Hannah had completed the outline of her business plan.

DISCUSSION QUESTIONS

1. What actions could Allstar Electronics take to foster intrapreneurship? What consequences does it suffer from failing to do so?

2. What information should Hannah include in her business plan?

3. Describe three nonfinancial resources likely to be important for the future of Soft Scroll. How can Hannah ensure that her business has those resources?

ENDNOTES

1. Catherine Clifford, "How Starbucks' Howard Schultz Went from the Projects to Creating 300,000 Jobs and a $3 Billion Fortune," *CNBC.com*, December 2, 2016, http://www.cnbc.com/2016/12/02/how-starbucks-howard-schultz-went-from-the-projects-to-creating-300000-jobs-and-a-3-billion-fortune.html.

2. Catherine Clifford, "How Starbucks' Howard Schultz Went from the Projects to Creating 300,000 Jobs and a $3 Billion Fortune," *CNBC.com*, December 2, 2016, http://www.cnbc.com/2016/12/02/how-starbucks-howard-schultz-went-from-the-projects-to-creating-300000-jobs-and-a-3-billion-fortune.html.

3. Kate Sullivan and Poppy Harlow, "Former Starbucks CEO Howard Schultz: I Am Seriously Thinking of Running for President," *CNN*, January 28, 2019, https://www.cnn.com/2019/01/27/politics/howard-schultz-starbucks-2020-president/index.html.

4. H. Aldrich and M. Ruef, "Unicorns, Gazelles, and Other Distractions on the Way to Understanding Real Entrepreneurship in the United States," *Academy of Management Perspectives* 32 (2018), pp. 458-72.

5. J. A. Timmons, *New Venture Creation* (Burr Ridge, IL: Richard D. Irwin, 1994).

6. S. Shane and S. Venkataraman, "The Promise of Entrepreneurship as a Field of Research," *Academy of Management Review* 25 (2000), pp. 217-26.

7. M. A. Hitt, R. D. Ireland, D. Sirmon, and C. Trahms, "Strategic Entrepreneurship: Creating Value for Individuals, Organizations, and Society," *Academy of Management Perspectives*, May 2011, pp. 57-75.

8. H. Aldrich and M. Ruef, "Unicorns, Gazelles, and Other Distractions on the Way to Understanding Real Entrepreneurship in the United States," *Academy of Management Perspectives* 32 (2018), pp. 458-72.

9. W. Megginson, M. J. Byrd, S. R. Scott Jr., and L. Megginson, *Small Business Management: An Entrepreneur's Guide to Success,* 2nd ed. (Boston: Irwin McGraw-Hill, 1997).

10. "Summary of Size Standards by Industry Sector," U.S. Small Business Administration, February 26, 2016, www.sba.gov.

11. T. Soper, "How This Ex-Amazon Manager Turned $300 into a Fast-Growing Startup without Outside Invesestment," *Geekwire,* December 13, 2018, www.geekwire.com; J. Dey Rey, "The Rise of Giant Consumer Companies That Said No to Investor Money," *Recode,* August 29, 2018, www.recode.net.

12. H. Aldrich and M. Ruef, "Unicorns, Gazelles, and Other Distractions on the Way to Understanding Real Entrepreneurship in the United States," *Academy of Management Perspectives* 32 (2018), pp. 458-72.

13. J. Timmons and S. Spinelli, *New Venture Creation: Entrepreneurship for the 21st Century,* 6th ed. (New York: McGraw-Hill/Irwin, 2004), p. 3.

14. E. Dinlersoz, "Business Formation Statistics: A New Census Bureau Product That Takes the Pulse of Early-Stage U.S. Business Activity," U.S. Census Bureau, February 8, 2018, www.census.gov.

15. "2018 Small Business Profile," U.S. Small Business Administration Office of Advocacy, www.sba.gov, accessed March 7, 2019; J. Hecht, "Are Small Businesses Really the Backbone of the Economy?" *Inc.,* December 17, 2014, http://www.inc.com.

16. "How Big of an Impact Do Small Businesses Make? Recent Publication Has the Answers," U.S. Small Business Administration, www.sba.gov, accessed February 4, 2019.

17. S. Terjesen, J. Hessels, and D. Li, "Comparative International Entrepreneurship: A Review and Research Agenda," *Journal of Management* 42 (2016), pp. 299-344.

18. J. Timmons and S. Spinelli, *New Venture Creation: Entrepreneurship for the 21st Century,* 6th ed. (New York: McGraw-Hill/Irwin, 2004).

19. R. Arend, H. Sarooghi, and A. Burkemper, "Effectuation as Ineffectual? Applying the 3E Theory-Assessment Framework to a Proposed New Theory of Entrepreneurship," *Academy of Management Review* 40 (2015), pp. 630-51.

20. R. Baron, R. Franklin, and K. Hmieleski, "Why Entrepreneurs Often Experience Low, Not High, Levels of Stress: The Joint Effects of Selection and Psychological Capital," *Journal of Management* 42 (2016), pp. 742-68.

21. D. Bricklin, "Natural-Born Entrepreneur," *Harvard Business Review,* September 2001, pp. 53-59, 58.

22. S. Ramoglou and E. W. K. Tsang, "A Realist Perspective of Entrepreneurship: Opportunities as Propensities," *Academy of Management Review* 41 (2016), p. 410; D. Williams, "The 4 Essential Traits of 'Intrapreneurs,'" *Forbes*, October 30, 2013, http://www.forbes.com; Alexandra Levit, "'Insider' Entrepreneurs," *The Wall Street Journal,* April 6, 2009, http://online.wsj.com.

23. M. A. Hitt, R. D. Ireland, D. Sirmon, and C. Trahms, "Strategic Entrepreneurship: Creating Value for Individuals, Organizations, and Society," *Academy of Management Perspectives,* May 2011, pp. 57-75.

24. T. Hsieh, "Why I Sold Zappos," *Inc.*, June 1, 2010, http://www.inc.com.

25. R. Fairlie, "Kaufman Index of Entrepreneurial Activity," Ewing Marion Kauffman Foundation, April 2014, http://www.kaufmann.org; C. Conner, "Who's Starting America's New Businesses? And Why?" *Forbes,* July 22, 2012.

26. J. Jennings and C. Brush, "Research on Women Entrepreneurs: Challenges to (and from) the Broader Entrepreneurship Literature?" *Academy of Management Annals* 7 (2013), pp. 663-715; inDinero, "About inDinero," http://www.indinero.com, accessed March 25, 2017; "Coolest College Start-Ups: Where Are They Now?" *Inc.,* March 2011, http://www.inc.com; E. Lee, "The Small-Business Numbers Cruncher," *San Francisco Chronicle,* January 3, 2011, Business & Company Resource Center, http://galenet.galegroup.com.

27. A. Konrad, "Led by Female Founder for Female Founders, VC Fund XFactor Ventures Has Big Plans to Triple in Size," *Forbes,* June 7, 2018, www.forbes.com.

28. J. Raffiee and J. Feng, "Should I Quit My Day Job?" *Academy of Management Journal* 57 (2014), pp. 936-63.

29. H. Aldrich, *Ethnic Entrepreneurs: Immigrant Business in Industrial Societies* (Newbury Park, CA: Sage, 1990).

30. R. Waldinger, "A Cross-Border Perspective on Migration: Beyond the Assimilation/Transnationalism Debate," *Journal of Ethnic and Migration Studies* 43, no. 1 (2016), pp. 3-17.

31. J. Jennings and C. Brush, "Research on Woman Entrepreneurs: Challenges to (and from) the Broader Entrepreneurship Literature?" *Academy of Management Annals* 7 (2013), pp. 663-715; J. Timmons and S. Spinelli, *New Venture Creation: Entrepreneurship for the 21st Century,* 6th ed. (New York: McGraw- Hill/Irwin, 2004).

32. J. Collins and J. Porras, *Built to Last* (London: Century, 1996).

33. J. Collins and J. Porras, *Built to Last* (London: Century, 1996).

34. D. Shepherd, T. Williams, and H. Patzelt, "Thinking about Entrepreneurial Decision Making: Review and Research Agenda," *Journal of Management* 41 (2015), pp. 11-46; D. Williams and M. Wood, "Rule-Based Reasoning for Understanding Opportunity Evaluation," *Academy of Management Perspectives* 29 (2015), pp. 218-36; B. Mathias and B. Williams, "The Impact of Role Identities on Entrepreneurs' Evaluation and Selection of Opportunities," *Journal of Management* 43 (2017), pp. 892-918.

35. J. Jennings and C. Brush, "Research on Women Entrepreneurs: Challenges to (and from) the Broader Entrepreneurship Literature?" *Academy of Management Annals* 7 (2013), pp. 663-715; C. Navis and O. V. Ozbek, "The Right People in the Wrong Places: The Paradox of Entrepreneurial Entry and Successful Opportunity Realization," *Academy of Management Review* 41 (2016), pp. 109-29; K. H. Vesper, *New Venture Mechanics* (Englewood Cliffs, NJ: Prentice Hall, 1993).

36. Forbes profile, "Limor Fried," www.forbes.com, accessed February 4, 2019.

37. K. H. Vesper, *New Venture Mechanics* (Englewood Cliffs, NJ: Prentice Hall, 1993).

38. L. Columbus, "25 Machine Learning Startups to Watch in 2018," *Forbes,* August 26, 2018, www.forbes.com.

39. Company website, "Classes," www.silversneakers.com, accessed February 4, 2019.

40. P. J. Sauer, "Serving Up Success," *Inc.,* January 2007, http://www.inc.com.

41. Panera, "Our History," www.panerabread.com, accessed February 4, 2019.

42. J. Timmons and S. Spinelli, *New Venture Creation: Entrepreneurship for the 21st Century,* 6th ed. (New York: McGraw-Hill/Irwin, 2004).

43. D. Fenn, "30 Under 30," *Inc.,* July 2, 2012.

44. Press release, "NASA May Extend BEAM's Time on the International Space Station," NASA, October 2, 2017, www.nasa.gov; Bigelow Aerospace, "The First Private Space Habitat Is Here," http://www.bigelowaerospace.com, accessed March 29, 2015.

45. S. Shead, "The VC Arm of Google's Parent Company Is Betting Its Billions on Life-Enhancing Healthcare Startups," *Business Insider,* September 10, 2017, www.businessinsider.com.

46. "Retail E-Commerce Sales in the United States from 2017 to 2023 (in million U.S. dollars)," *Statistica,* www.statistic.com, accessed March 10, 2019.

47. G. Popomaronis, "E-commerce in 2018: Here's What the Experts Are Predicting," *Forbes,* December 15, 2017, www.forbes.com.

48. G. Popomaronis, "E-commerce in 2018: Here's What the Experts Are Predicting," *Forbes,* December 15, 2017, www.forbes.com.

49. B. Carmody, "Top Seven E-Commerce Platforms in 2018," *Inc.,* January 14, 2018, www.inc.com.

50. C. Joseph, "Types of eCommerce Business Models," *Chron,* www.smallbusiness.chron.com, accessed March 10, 2019.

51. J. E. Vascellaro, "Selling Your Designs Online," *The Wall Street Journal,* April 5, 2007, http://online.wsj.com.

52. J. Short, T. Moss, and G. Lumpkin, "Research in Social Entrepreneurship: Past, Contributions and Future Opportunities," *Strategic Entrepreneurship Journal* 3 (2009), pp. 161–94; S. Zahra and M. Wright, "Entrepreneur's Next Act," *Academy of Management Perspectives,* 2011, pp. 67–83.

53. P. Dacin, M. T. Dacin, and M. Matear, "Social Entrepreneurship: Why We Don't Need a New Theory and How We Move Forward from Here," *Academy of Management Perspectives* 24 (2010), pp. 37–57.

54. J. Battilan, M. Sengul, A. C. Pache, and J. Model, "Harnessing Productive Tensions in Hybrid Organizations: The Case of Work Integration Social Enterprises," *Academy of Management Journal* 58 (2015), pp. 1658–85.

55. T. Miller, M. Grimes, J. McMullen, and T. Vogus, "Venturing for Others with Heart and Head: How Compassion Encourages Social Entrepreneurship," *Academy of Management Review* 37 (2012), pp. 616–40.

56. U. Stephan, M. Patterson, C. Kelly, and J. Mair, "Organizations Driving Positive Social Change: A Review and an Integrative Framework of Change Processes," *Journal of Management* 42 (2016), pp. 1250–81.

57. J. Mair and I. Marti, "Social Entrepreneurship Research: A Source of Explanation, Prediction, and Delight," *Journal of World Business* 41 (2006), pp. 36–44.

58. Organization website, "Meet the Founder," https://my.charitywater.org/about/scott-harrison-story, accessed March 10, 2019.

59. Organization website, "About Moringa School," https://www.moringaschool.com/about, accessed March 10, 2019.

60. A. Wilson and G. Toma, "The 2019 30 Under 30 Social Entrepreneurs," *Forbes,* www.forbes.com, accessed March 10, 2019.

61. "Coca-Cola and Nely Galan Honor Latinas on International Women's Day and Beyond," *Yahoo Finance,* March 29, 2015, http://finance.yahoo.com

62. S. Cole, "Meet the Woman Inspiring Thousands of American Latina Entrepreneurs," *Fast Company,* March 16, 2015, http://www.fastcompany.com; D. Parnell, "Media Mogul Nely Galan, on Succeeding through Diversity," *Forbes,* March 13, 2015, http://www.forbes.com.

63. Joan Caplin, "Entrepreneur's Journey to Becoming 'Self-Made,'" *Time,* January 31, 2017, http://time.com/collection-post/4609186/nely-galan-american-voices.

64. Rohit Arora, "The Stunning Success of Latino-Owned Businesses Spurs Entrepreneurship," *Forbes,* September 26, 2018, https://www.forbes.com/sites/rohitarora/2018/09/26/the-stunning-success-of-latino-owned-businesses-spurs-entrepreneurship/#80a356 31d077.

65. M. Driver, "An Interview with Michael Porter: Social Entrepreneurship and the Transformation of Capitalism," *Academy of Management Learning & Education* 11 (2012), pp. 421–31.

66. M. Porter and M. Kramer, "Creating Shared Value," *Harvard Business Review,* January–February 2011, pp. 62–77.

67. H. Sabeti, "The For-Benefit Enterprise," *Harvard Business Review,* November 2011, pp. 98–194.

68. P. Omidyar, "eBay's Founder on Innovating the Business Model of Social Change," *Harvard Business Review,* September 2011, pp. 41–44.

69. J. A. Timmons, *New Venture Creation* (Burr Ridge, IL: Richard D. Irwin, 1994).

70. M. Cardon, J. Wincent, J. Singh, and M. Drnovsek, "The Nature and Experience of Entrepreneurial Passion," *Academy of Management Review* 34 (2009), pp. 511–32.

71. J. R. Baum and E. A. Locke, "The Relationship of Entrepreneurial Traits, Skill, and Motivation to Subsequent Venture Growth," *Journal of Applied Psychology* 89 (2004), pp. 587–98.

72. C. Murnieks, E. Mosakowski, and M. Cardon, "Pathways of Passion: Identity Centrality, Passion, and Behavior among Entrepreneurs," *Journal of Management* 40 (2014), pp. 1583–1606.

73. E. Fauchart and M. Gruber, "Darwinians, Communitarians, and Missionaries: The Role of Founder Identity in Entrepreneurship," *Academy of Management Journal* 54 (2011), pp. 935–57.

74. D. Shepherd, T. Williams, and H. Patzelt, "Thinking about Entrepreneurial Decision Making: Review and Research Agenda," Journal of Management, 41 (2015), pp. 11-46.

75. M. Sonfield and R. Lussier, "The Entrepreneurial Strategy Matrix: A Model for New and Ongoing Ventures," *Business Horizons,* May–June 1997, pp. 73–77.

76. J. E. Lange, "Entrepreneurs and the Continuing Internet: The Expanding Frontier," in J. Timmons and S. Spinelli, *New Venture Creation: Entrepreneurship for the 21st Century,* 6th ed. (New York: McGraw-Hill/Irwin, 2004).

77. J. Raffiee and J. Feng, "Should I Quit My Day Job? A Hybrid Path to Entrepreneurship," *Academy of Management Journal* 57 (2014), pp. 936–63; S. Venkataraman and M. Low, "On the Nature of Critical Relationships: A Test of the Liabilities and Size Hypothesis," in *Frontiers of Entrepreneurship Research* (Babson Park, MA: Babson College, 1991), p. 97.

78. "Sink or Swim: Why Some Startups Succeed and Others Don't," *The Guardian,* July 23, 2015, www.theguardian.com; J. Timmons and S. Spinelli, *New Venture Creation: Entrepreneurship for the 21st Century,* 6th ed. (New York: McGraw-Hill/Irwin, 2004).

79. Abha Bhattarai, "Starbucks Will Stop Handing Out Plastic Straws by 2020," *Washington Post,* July 9, 2018, https://www.washingtonpost.com/news/business/wp/2018/07/09/starbucks-will-stop-handing-out-plastic-straws-by-2020/?utm_term=.d8634d0f0351.

80. Daniel B. Kline, "Starbucks' 4 Biggest Product Flops and Failures," *The Motley Fool,* January 23, 2016, https://www.fool.com/investing/general/2016/01/23/starbucks-x-biggest-product-flops-and-failures.aspx.

81. Daniel B. Kline, "Starbucks' Fizzio Soda Line Has Gone Flat," *The Motley Fool,* October 7, 2016, https://www.fool.com/investing/2016/10/07/starbucks-fizzio-soda-line-has-gone-flat.aspx.

82. Ashley Turner, "Why There Are Almost No Starbucks in Australia," *CNBC,* July 25, 2018, https://www.cnbc.com/2018/07/20/starbucks-australia-coffee-failure.html.

83. "Starbucks Opens First Outlet in Italy," *BBC,* September, 6, 2018, https://www.bbc.com/news/business-45430915

84. K. P. Arin, V. Z. Huang, M. Minniti, and A. M. Nandialath, "Revisiting the Determinants of Entrepreneurship: A Bayesian Approach," *Journal of Management* 41 (2105), pp. 607–31.

85. L. Buchanan, "Create Jobs, Eliminate Waste, Preserve Value," *Inc.,* December 2006, pp. 94–106.

86. I. Hathaway, "What Startup Accelerators Really Do," *Harvard Business Review,* March 1, 2016, www.hbr.org.

87. Company website, www.ycombinator.com; Company website, https://500.co; Company website, www.techstars.com; "Getting Up to Speed," *The Economist,* January 16, 2014, www.theeconomist.com; A. Cremades, "10 Startup Accelerators Based on Successful Exits," *Forbes,* August 7, 2018, www.forbes.com.

88. I. Hathaway, "What Startup Accelerators Really Do," *Harvard Business Review,* March 1, 2016, www.hbr.org.

89. Norm Brodsky, "Street Smarts: Our Irrational Fear of Numbers," *Inc.,* January 2009, http://www.inc.com.

90. Norm Brodsky, "Street Smarts: Our Irrational Fear of Numbers," *Inc.,* January 2009, http://www.inc.com.

91. Martin Zwilling, "The 10 Most Reliable Ways to Fund a Startup," February 20, 2019, https://www.entrepreneur.com/slideshow/299773.

92. Alejandro Cremades, "How Crowdfunding Works for Entrepreneurs," *Forbes,* January 12, 2019, https://www.forbes.com/sites/alejandrocremades/2019/01/12/how-crowdfunding-works-for-entrepreneurs/#45d625e2c531.

93. Alejandro Cremades, "How Crowdfunding Works for Entrepreneurs," *Forbes,* January 12, 2019, https://www.forbes.com/sites/alejandrocremades/2019/01/12/how-crowdfunding-works-for-entrepreneurs/#45d625e2c531.

94. Angelique Moss, "Top 5 Crowdfunding Platforms That Nonprofits, Social Causes Can Use," September 5, 2018, https://medium.com/swlh/top-5-crowdfunding-platforms-that-nonprofits-social-causes-can-use-8e3dad9c29c7.

95. M. Juetten, "Failed Startups: Jawbone," *Forbes,* February 5, 2019, www.forbes.com; I. Jafrey, "5 Infamous Startup Failures in 2017: Pick Your Lessons," *CIO,* February 5, 2018, www.cio.com.

96. S. E. Needleman, "When It's Time to Take on Help," *The Wall Street Journal,* January 16, 2011, http://online.wsj.com.

97. Company website, www.basecamp.com, accessed March 10, 2019; J. Stillman, "Slow Business: The Case against Fast Growth," *Inc.,* September 18, 2012, http://www.inc.com.

98. S. Finkelstein, "The Myth of Managerial Superiority in Internet Startups: An Autopsy," *Organizational Dynamics,* Fall 2001, pp. 172–85.

99. K. Hickey, "5 Lessons from Managing Our Startup's Rapid Growth," *Forbes,* April 9, 2013, http://www.forbes.com.

100. A. Cordeiro, "Sweet Returns," *The Wall Street Journal,* April 23, 2009, http://www.wsj.com.

101. T. Smale, "How to Reduce Operational Costs," *Entrepreneur,* April 19, 2017, www.entrepreneur.com.

102. T. Smale, "How to Reduce Operational Costs," *Entrepreneur,* April 19, 2017, www.entrepreneur.com.

103. E. D. Rouse, "Beginning's End: How Founders Psychologically Disengage from Their Organizations," *Academy of Management Journal* 59 (2016), pp. 1605–29.

104. L. Bolelovic, "Most Companies Don't Last 50 Years, but These Pittsburgh Businesses Have," *Pittsburgh Post-Gazette,* December 19, 2016, www.post-gazette.com; G. Stalk and H. Foley, "Avoid the Traps That Can Destroy Family Businesses," *Harvard Business Review,* January–February 2012, pp. 25–27.

105. P. F. Drucker, "How to Save the Family Business," *The Wall Street Journal,* August 19, 1994, p. A10.

106. H. Aldrich and M. Ruef, Unicorns, Gazelles, and Other Distractions on the Way to Understanding Real Entrepreneurship in the United States. *Academy of Management Perspectives* 32 (2018), 458–72.

107. H. Aldrich and M. Ruef. Unicorns, Gazelles, and Other Distractions on the Way to Understanding Real Entrepreneurship in the United States. *Academy of Management Perspectives* 32 (2018), 458–72.

108. D. Gamer, R. Owen, and R. Conway, *The Ernst & Young Guide to Raising Capital* (New York: Wiley, 1991).

109. D. Gamer, R. Owen, and R. Conway, *The Ernst & Young Guide to Raising Capital* (New York: Wiley, 1991).

110. R. D. Hisrich and M. P. Peters, *Entrepreneurship: Starting, Developing, and Managing a New Enterprise* (Burr Ridge, IL: Irwin, 1994).

111. R. D. Hisrich and M. P. Peters, *Entrepreneurship: Starting, Developing, and Managing a New Enterprise* (Burr Ridge, IL: Irwin, 1994).

112. J. Wiens and J. Bell-Masterson, "How Entrepreneurs Access Capital and Get Funded," Kaufmann Foundation, June 2, 2015, http://www.kauffman.org.

113. P2P Credit, "Small Business Loans," www.p2p-credit.com, accessed February 6, 2019; Prosper, "Get a Small Business Loan," www.prosper.com, accessed February 6, 2019.

114. Lending Club, "Business Loans," http://www.lendingclub.com, accessed March 31, 2015; Prosper, "Company Overview," http://www.prosper.com, accessed March 31, 2015; I. Mount, "When Banks Won't Lend, There Are Alternatives, though Often Expensive," *The New York Times,* August 1, 2012, http://www.nytimes.com.

115. T. Poletti, "The Government Tried to Encourage IPOs, but It Helped Create the Age of the Unicorn," *MarketWatch,* December 31, 2017, www.marketwatch.com; M. Zeidel, "The JOBS Act: Did It Accomplish Its Goals?" *Corporate Governance and Financial Regulation,* Harvard Law School, July 18, 2016, bwww.corporate.law.harvard.edu; "JOBS Act, One Year Later: Hang Tight, Equity Crowdfunding Is Coming," *Entrepreneur,* April 5, 2013, http://www.entrepreneur.com; "Crowdfunding Industry on Fire: Trends to Watch," *Entrepreneur,* April 8, 2013, http://www.entrepreneur.com; Becky Yerak, "Is Promise Worth Peril?" *Chicago Tribune,* February 24, 2013, sec. 2, pp. 1, 3; Sarah E. Needleman and Lora Kolodny, "Site Unseen: More 'Angels' Invest via Internet," *The Wall Street Journal,* January 23, 2013, http://online.wsj.com.

116. Zac Laval, "It's Up to Startups to Solve Tech's Diversity Issue," *The Sociable,* December 14, 2018, https://sociable.co/business/startups-solve-tech-diversity-issue/.

117. Paris Martineau, "Startup Founders Think Real Progress on Diversity Is Years Away," *Wired,* December 13, 2018, https://www.wired.com/story/startup-founders-think-real-progress-diversity-years-away/.

118. Emma Hinchliffe, "Funding for Female Founders Stalled at 2.2% of VC Dollars in 2018," *Fortune,* January 28, 2019, http://fortune.com/2019/01/28/funding-female-founders-2018/.

119. Deepak Krishnamurthy, "Here's How to Improve Diversity in Startups," World Economic Forum, January 22, 2019, https://www.weforum.org/agenda/2019/01/here-s-how-to-improve-diversity-in-startups/.

120. W. A. Sahlman, "How to Write a Great Business Plan," *Harvard Business Review,* July–August 1997, pp. 98–108.

121. W. A. Sahlman, "How to Write a Great Business Plan," *Harvard Business Review,* July–August 1997, pp. 98–108.

122. M. Copeland, "Start Last, Finish First," *Business 2.0 Magazine,* February 2, 2006, http://www.money.cnn.com.

123. W. A. Sahlman, "How to Write a Great Business Plan," *Harvard Business Review,* July–August 1997, pp. 98–108.

124. B. Hallen and E. C. Pahnke, 'When Do Entrepreneurs Accurately Evaluate Venture Capital Firms' Track Records? A Bounded Rationality Perspective," *Academy of Management Journal* 59 (2016), pp. 1535–60; L. Huang and A. Knight, "The Development and Effects of the Entrepreneur-Investor Relationship," *Academy of Management Review* 42 (2017), pp. 80–102.

125. M. Zimmerman and G. Zeitz, "Beyond Survival: Achieving New Venture Growth by Building Legitimacy," *Academy of Management Review* 27 (2002), pp. 414–21.

126. A. L. Stinchcombe, "Social Structure and Organizations," in J. G. March, ed., *Handbook of Organizations* (Chicago: Rand McNally, 1965), pp. 142–93.

127. A. L. Stinchcombe, "Social Structure and Organizations," in J. G. March, ed., *Handbook of Organizations* (Chicago: Rand McNally, 1965), pp. 142–93.

128. L. Taylor, "Want Your Start-Up to Be Successful? Appearance Is Everything," *Inc.,* February 23, 2007, http://www.inc.com.

129. L. Taylor, "Want Your Start-Up to Be Successful? Appearance Is Everything," *Inc.,* February 23, 2007, http://www.inc.com.

130. R. A. Baron and G. D. Markman, "Beyond Social Capital: How Social Skills Can Enhance Entrepreneurs' Success," *Academy of Management Executive,* February 2000, pp. 106–16.

131. J. Florin, M. Lubatkin, and W. Schulze, "A Social Capital Model of High-Growth Ventures," *Academy of Management Journal* 46 (2003), pp. 374–84.

132. Press release, "Sport Clips Haircuts Tops Category in Forbes 2018 'Best Franchises to Buy,'" Sport Clips, June 5, 2018, https://sportclips.com.

133. A. J. Kacperczyk, "Opportunity Structures in Established Firms: Entrepreneurship versus Intrapreneurship in Mutual Funds," *Administrative Science Quarterly* 57 (2012), pp. 484–521; S. C. Parker, "Intrapreneurship or Entrepreneurship?" *Journal of Business Venturing* 26 (2011), pp. 19–34.

134. R. M. Kanter, *The Change Masters* (New York: Simon & Schuster, 1983).

135. A. Huspeni, "Google's 20 Percent Rule Actually Helps Employees Fight Back against Unreasonable Managers," *Entrepreneur,* June 7, 2017, www.entrepreneur.com; B. Adams, "How Google's 20

Percent Rule Can Make You More Productive and Energetic," *Inc.,* December 28, 2016, www.inc.com.

136. R. M. Kanter, C. Ingols, E. Morgan, and T. K. Seggerman, "Driving Corporate Entrepreneurship," *Management Review* 76 (April 1987), pp. 14–16.

137. J. Argenti, *Corporate Collapse: The Causes and Symptoms* (New York: Wiley, 1979).

138. R. M. Kanter, C. Ingols, E. Morgan, and T. K. Seggerman, "Driving Corporate Entrepreneurship," *Management Review* 76 (April 1987), pp. 14–16.

139. Y. Ling, Z. Simsek, M. Lubatkin, and J. Veiga, "Transformational Leadership's Role in Promoting Corporate Entrepreneurship: Examining the CEO–TMT Interface," *Academy of Management Journal,* 2008, pp. 557–76; A. A. Engelen, V. Gupta, L. Strenger, and M. Brettel, "Entrepreneurial Orientation, Firm Performance, and the Moderating Role of Transformational Leadership Behaviors," *Journal of Management* 41 (2015), pp. 1069–97.

140. G. T. Lumpkin and G. G. Dess, "Clarifying the Entrepreneurial Orientation Construct and Linking It to Performance," *Academy of Management Review* 21 (1996), pp. 135–72; G. G. Dess and G. T. Lumpkin, "The Role of Entrepreneurial Orientation in Stimulating Effective Corporate Entrepreneurship," *The Academy of Management Executive* 19 (February 2005), pp. 147–56; A. A. Engelen, V. Gupta, L. Strenger, and M. Brettel, "Entrepreneurial Orientation, Firm Performance, and the Moderating Role of Transformational Leadership Behaviors," *Journal of Management* 41 (2015), pp. 1069–97.

141. H. J. Sapienza, E. Autio, G. George, and S. A. Zahra, "A Capabilities Perspective on the Effects of Early Internationalization on Firm Survival and Growth," *Academy of Management Review* 31 (2006), pp. 914–33.

142. T. Bateman and J. M. Crant, "The Proactive Dimension of Organizational Behavior," *Journal of Organizational Behavior,* 1993, pp. 103–18.

143. G. T. Lumpkin and G. G. Dess, "Clarifying the Entrepreneurial Orientation Construct and Linking It to Performance," *Academy of Management Review* 21 (1996), pp. 135–72.

144. M. Gabrielsson, P. Gabrielsson, and P. Dimitratos, "International Entrepreneurial Culture and Growth of International New Ventures," *Management International Review* 54 (2014), pp. 445–71.

145. C. Pinchot and E. Pinchot, *The Intelligent Organization* (San Francisco: Barrett-Koehler, 1996).

146. Daniel B. Kline, "Wal-Mart and Starbucks Are Trying to Think Like Start-Ups," *The Motley Fool,* March 16, 2017, https://www.fool.com/investing/2017/03/16/wal-mart-and-starbucks-are-trying-to-think-like-st.aspx.

147. Adam Campbell-Schmitt, "Roastery, Reserve Bar, Regular Starbucks: What's the Difference?" *Food and Wine,* December 20, 2018, https://www.foodandwine.com/news/starbucks-roastery-reserve-bar-store-difference.

148. Gary Stern, "Starbucks' Reserve Roastery Is Spacious and Trendy, So Why Is It Slowing Down Expansion?" *Forbes,* January 22, 2019, https://www.forbes.com/sites/garystern/2019/01/22/starbucks-reserve-roastery-its-spacious-and-trendy-but-why-is-starbucks-slowing-down-expansion/#57b668161bc6.

149. Trefis Team, "Starbucks Is Maintaining Its Competitive Edge," *Forbes,* October 13, 2016, https://www.forbes.com/sites/greatspeculations/2016/10/13/how-is-starbucks-maintaining-its-competitive-edge/#41a3ab1a759c.

Will Foxconn Remain Apple's Top Supplier of iGadgets?

Apple is famous for its attractive and highly prized electronics, including iPhones, Mac computers and laptops, and iPad tablets. However, Apple doesn't actually make any of its products. Rather, it develops ideas, designs devices, and promotes the products and its brand. To put the devices together, Apple relies on a set of contractors.

One key contractor is an electronics firm called Foxconn, based in Taiwan. With factories located in China, Foxconn has combined manufacturing expertise with low-cost labor to win deals to make computers and key components such as motherboards. As consumers have slowed their spending on laptop computers in favor of smaller devices such as the iPad tablet computer and smartphones, Foxconn has benefited. Until recently, it was the only company making Apple's iPad and one of just two makers of Apple's iPhone. Workers at Foxconn facilities also produce the Sony PlayStation 3, the Nintendo Wii, and Amazon's Kindle Fire. It also produces TVs for Sony, Sharp, and Toshiba. In China alone, Foxconn employs almost 1.2 million workers, making it one of the largest employers in the world. Many of those workers live in on-site dormitories, eat in company-run dining halls, and relax in bookstores and gyms located right at their workplace.

Foxconn has experienced some tragic problems. In 2010, the company drew international media attention when it came to light that several workers at Foxconn's plant in Shenzhen (a city in southern China) had committed suicide. Questions arose about whether working conditions were so horrible as to drive workers to kill themselves. Apple sent executives accompanied by suicide prevention experts to the plant to investigate. Although Apple requires its contract partners to meet specific standards in its code of conduct, and it visits over 100 facilities a year to ensure compliance, it had failed to uncover any problems at Foxconn before the suicides came to light.

In the following year, Foxconn was again in the news about a tragedy when an explosion in its Chengdu, China, plant killed 3 workers and injured 15. Initial investigations suggested that the explosion was the result of a fairly basic manufacturing safety problem: because of improper ventilation, dust collected in the air of a metal-polishing shop, and the dust ignited. If such a problem occurred in the United States, regulators would quickly shut down the facility for violating safety requirements.

Embarrassed by the media and pressured by important customers such as Apple, Foxconn acted to improve working conditions. At the Shenzhen plant, it brought in counselors, improved training of managers and the staff answering calls on the employee hotline, and launched a morale-boosting program called Care–Love, which sponsors employee outings. In the factories in Chengdu and elsewhere, the company took measures to improve ventilation. Along with these changes, Foxconn began giving out raises. In Shenzhen, workers' wages more than doubled.

Since Foxconn launched the effort to improve morale, employee turnover has fallen, and the suicides seem to have ended. Unfortunately, the payoff for the company is difficult to measure. Higher costs have erased profits, and Foxconn's stock price has tumbled. So now the company is looking for lower-cost locations. It opened facilities in China's interior cities, where wage rates are about one-third below those of Shenzhen. Making matters more challenging for Foxconn is the fact that it intends to cut nearly $3 billion from its operating costs, which will likely result in layoffs. The news comes on the heels of reports that Apple's iPhone XS, XS Max, and XR didn't sell as well as expected in 2018.

Also, Apple CEO Tim Cook has shifted some of the production of iPhones and iPad minis to Pegatron, another Taiwan-based electronics manufacturer. Pegatron also makes products for Microsoft, Dell, and Hewlett-Packard.

DISCUSSION QUESTIONS

1. What threats, opportunities, strengths, and weaknesses can you identify at Foxconn? How is it addressing these with its strategy?

2. If Foxconn's management hired you to offer advice on improving its ethical decision making and corporate social responsibility, what measures would you suggest? Why?

3. Why do you think Tim Cook, after years of using Foxconn for most of Apple's production needs, shifted some production to Pegatron?

SOURCES: Keane, S., "Foxconn, Apple's Main iPhone Supplier, to Reportedly Slash $2.9B in Costs," CNET, November 21, 2018, www.cnet.com; Dou, E., "Apple Shifts Supply Chain away from Foxconn to Pegatron," The Wall Street Journal, May 29, 2013, http://www.wsj.com; Kan, M., "Foxconn Builds Products for Many Vendors, but Its Mud Sticks to Apple," MacWorld, October 24, 2012, http://www.macworld.com; Culpan, T., Lifei, Z. and Einhorn, B., "Foxconn: How to Beat the High Cost of Happy Workers," Bloomberg Businessweek, May 5, 2011, http://www.businessweek.com; Nystedt, D., "Apple: Foxconn 'Saved Lives' with Suicide Prevention Efforts," PC World, February 15, 2011, http://www.pcworld.com; Bussey, J., "Measuring the Human Cost of an iPad Made in China," The Wall Street Journal, June 3, 2011, http://online.wsj.com; "Apple Report Details Response to Foxconn Suicides," eWeek, February 15, 2011, Business & Company Resource Center, http://galenet.galegroup.com; Dalrymple, J., "Apple Reports on Foxconn, Supplier Workplace Standards," CNET News, February 14, 2011, http://news.cnet.com.

Information for Entrepreneurs

If you are interested in starting or managing a small business, you have access to many sources of useful information.

PUBLISHED SOURCES

The first step is a complete search of materials in libraries and on the Internet. You can find a huge amount of published information, databases, and other sources about industries, markets, competitors, and personnel. Some of this information will have been uncovered when you searched for ideas. Listed here are additional sources that should help get you started.

Guides and Company Information

Valuable information is available in special issues and on the websites of *Bloomberg Business, Forbes, Inc., The Economist, Fast Company,* and *Fortune,* as well as online in the following:

- Hoovers.com
- ProQuest.com

Valuable Sites on the Internet

- Entrepreneurship (http://www.kauffman.org/what-we-do/entrepreneurship), the website of the Kauffman Center for Entrepreneurial Leadership, Ewing Marion Kauffman Foundation
- *Fast Company* (http://www.fastcompany.com)
- EY (Ernst & Young) (http://www.ey.com)
- *Inc.* magazine (http://www.inc.com)
- Entrepreneur.com and magazine (http://www.entrepreneur.com)
- EDGAR database (http://www.sec.gov)—subscription sources, such as ThomsonResearch (http://www.thomsonfinancial.com), provide images of other filings as well
- Thomson Venture Economics (https://vx.thomsonib.com/VxComponent/vxhelp/VentureXpert_Fact_Sheet.pdf)

Journal Articles via Computerized Indexes

- Factiva with Dow Jones, Reuters *, The Wall Street Journal*
- EBSCOhost
- FirstSearch
- Ethnic News Watch
- LEXIS/NEXIS
- *The New York Times* (http://www.nytimes.com)
- InfoTrac from Gale Group
- ABI/Inform and other ProQuest databases
- RDS Business Reference Suite
- *The Wall Street Journal* (http://www.wsj.com)

Statistics

- Stat-USA (https://www.usa.gov/statistics)—U.S. government subscription site for economic, trade, and business data and market research
- U.S. Bureau of the Census (http://www.census.gov)—the source of many statistical data, including
  - *Statistical Abstract of the United States*
  - *American FactFinder*—population data
  - Economic programs (http://www.census.gov/econ/www/index.html)—data by sector
  - County business patterns
  - Zip code business patterns
- Knight Ridder . . . *CRB Commodity Yearbook*
- Manufacturing USA, Service Industries USA, and other sector compilations from Gale Group
- *Federal Reserve Bulletin*
- Survey of Current Business
- Bureau of Labor Statistics (http://www.bls.gov)
- Global Insight, formerly DRI-WEFA
- International Financial Statistics—International Monetary Fund
- World Development Indicators—World Bank
- Bloomberg Database

Consumer Expenditures

- New Strategist Publications

Projections and Forecasts

- ProQuest
- InfoTech Trends
- Guide to Special Issues and Indexes to Periodicals *(Grey House Directory of Special Issues)*
- RDS Business Reference Suite
- Value Line Investment Survey

Market Studies

- LifeStyle Market Analyst
- MarketResearch.com
- Scarborough Research
- Simmons Market Research Bureau

Consumer Expenditures

- New Strategist Publications
- Consumer Expenditure Survey
- Euromonitor

Other Sources

- Wall Street transcript
- Brokerage house reports from Investext, Multex, and so on
- Company annual reports and websites

OTHER INTELLIGENCE

Everything entrepreneurs need to know will not be found in libraries because this information needs to be highly specific and current. This information is most likely available from people—industry experts, suppliers, and the like. Summarized here are some useful sources of intelligence.

Trade Associations

Trade associations, especially the editors of their publications and information officers, are good sources of information. Trade shows and conferences are prime places to discover the latest activities of competitors.

Employees

Employees who have left a competitor's company often can provide information about the competitor, especially if the employee departed on bad terms. Also, a firm can hire people away from a competitor. Although consideration of ethics in this situation is important, the number of experienced people in any industry is limited, and competitors must prove that a company hired a person intentionally to get specific trade secrets to challenge any hiring legally. Students who have worked for competitors are another source of information.

Consulting Firms

Consulting firms frequently conduct industry studies and then make this information available. Frequently, in such fields as computers or software, competitors use the same design consultants, and these consultants can be sources of information.

Market Research Firms

Firms doing market studies, such as those listed under the previously mentioned published sources, can be sources of intelligence.

Key Customers, Manufacturers, Suppliers, Distributors, and Buyers

These groups are often a prime source of information.

Public Filings

Federal, state, and local filings, such as filings with the Securities and Exchange Commission (SEC), Patent and Trademark Office, or Freedom of Information Act filings, can reveal a surprising amount of information. There are companies that process inquiries of this type.

Reverse Engineering

Reverse engineering can be used to determine costs of production and sometimes even manufacturing methods. An example of this practice is the experience of Advanced Energy Technology Inc. of Boulder, Colorado, which learned firsthand about such tactics. No sooner had it announced a new product, which was patented, than it received 50 orders, half of which were from competitors asking for only one or two of the items.

Networks

The networks mentioned in this chapter can be sources of new venture ideas and strategies.

Other

Classified ads, buyers' guides, labor unions, real estate agents, courts, local reporters, and so on can all provide clues.

The U.S. government is engaging in new and more extensive outreach efforts so that small-business owners will use government resources more and understand them more easily. In 2009, the U.S. Small Business Administration launched a community forum, the first government-sponsored online community built specifically for small-business owners, on the Business Gateway site of Business.gov. The forum combines discussion threads, blogs, and resource articles. The goals for the SBA and 21 other federal agencies that cosponsor the site are to engage in dialogue with the public, leverage the expertise that exists in both the public and private sectors, and help government serve entrepreneurs better.

SOURCES: Timmons, J. A. and Spinelli, S. Jr., *New Venture Creation,* 7th ed. Burr Ridge, IL: McGraw-Hill/Irwin, 2007, pp. 103–4; K. Klein, "Government Resources for Entrepreneurs," *BusinessWeek,* March 3, 2009.

CHAPTER 8
Organization Structure

An organization, no matter how well designed, is only as good as the people who live and work in it.

—Dee Hock

Chi Ian Chao/Getty Images

learning objectives

After studying Chapter 8, you will be able to:

LO 8-1 Explain how differentiation and integration influence an organization's structure.

LO 8-2 Summarize how authority operates.

LO 8-3 Define the roles of the board of directors and the chief executive officer.

LO 8-4 Discuss how span of control affects structure and managerial effectiveness.

LO 8-5 Explain how to delegate effectively.

LO 8-6 Distinguish between centralized and decentralized organizations.

LO 8-7 Summarize ways organizations can be structured.

LO 8-8 Identify the unique challenges of the matrix organization.

LO 8-9 Describe important integrative mechanisms.

chapter outline

Fundamentals of Organizing
Differentiation
Integration

The Vertical Structure
Authority in Organizations
Hierarchical Levels
Span of Control
Delegation
Decentralization

The Horizontal Structure
The Functional Organization
The Divisional Organization
The Matrix Organization
The Network Organization

Organizational Integration
Coordination by Standardization
Coordination by Plan
Coordination by Mutual Adjustment
Coordination and Communication

Looking Ahead

Management in Action

LEADERSHIP AND STRUCTURAL CHANGE AT GENERAL MOTORS

The history of General Motors (GM) shows that size and longevity do not guarantee success. GM once dominated the U.S. auto industry with a "price ladder" strategy in which Chevrolet, Pontiac, GMC, Oldsmobile, Buick, and Cadillac catered to specific slices of the consumer market. But after GM's U.S. market share peaked in 1962 at 51 percent, the company steadily began losing share to smaller, more nimble, and more innovative competition. By 2008, GM's U.S. market share was less than half what it was in 1962, and when customer demand and bank lending dried up in the 2008 financial crisis, GM nearly collapsed.

The federal government stepped in with money to keep GM alive through a Chapter 11 managed bankruptcy. The company survived, and in July 2009, the old General Motors Corporation reemerged as General Motors Company. GM has spent the last decade trying to regain its footing as a leader in the automotive industry.

No one understands all the change that GM has gone through more than Mary Barra. She began working with GM as a co-op student in 1980 and is now the company's CEO. After getting her bachelor of science degree in electrical engineering in 1985 and her MBA from Stanford in 1990, Barra went on to hold a number of administrative and executive positions at GM. She was named as the company's CEO in 2014, the first female CEO in the company's history.[1]

Barra's challenges revitalizing GM have been many. In the years leading up to the bankruptcy, GM had become known for a culture in which managers were slow to act, reluctant to speak up, and averse to change. Barra set out to change that, trying to teach a storied multinational car company to be more nimble,

Gregory Bull/AP/Shutterstock

more innovative, and more customer-centric, and she is succeeding.

After years of precipitous decline, GM's market share in the United States has steadied, leveling off at around 17 percent since 2015. In 2014, the year Barra took over, the company earned just under $4 billion in profit. In 2018, GM saw profits north of $8 billion. GM's ability to increase profitability has stemmed in large part to Barra's fearlessness in restructuring the company's organization and vision. She has sold off older legacy car lines that were no longer profitable, while acquiring firms working on self-driving technology. Under Barra, GM has also invested heavily in ride-sharing initiatives and electric vehicles.

All of this restructuring and investment is in service to a new vision Barra has articulated in three goals: "Zero crashes, zero emissions and zero congestion."[2] For now, it seems GM is on the right path.

Mary Barra believes that the structure of a company plays a critical role in how fast and effectively it can seize new opportunities. As you read this chapter, notice the options available for an organization's structure, and consider whether GM's management has made the right choices to enable continued growth and a more responsive culture.

Since its emergence from bankruptcy, General Motors has been running neck and neck with Toyota and Volkswagen to keep its spot as the world's biggest auto company, even as its U.S. market share slips and it struggles with investor doubts about its ability to operate efficiently. How could the company respond to this situation? The way in which a company organizes itself to address an issue such as declining market share may determine whether its strategy will succeed. GM, like many companies, is working hard to make certain that its strategy and structure are aligned.

This chapter describes the most important components of organization structure. We begin by covering basic principles of differentiation and integration. Next we discuss the vertical structure, which includes issues of authority, hierarchy, delegation, and decentralization. We then describe the horizontal structure, which includes functional, divisional, and matrix forms. Finally, we show how organizations can integrate across multiple units: coordination by standardization, coordination by plan, and coordination by mutual adjustment.

In the chapter following this, we continue with the topic of organization structure but take a different perspective. In that chapter, we focus on the flexibility and responsiveness of an organization—that is, how capable it is of changing its form and adapting to strategy, technology, the environment, and other challenges it confronts.

Fundamentals of Organizing

LO 8-1 Explain how differentiation and integration influence an organization's structure.

_____

organization chart

The reporting structure and division of labor in an organization.

_____

differentiation

An aspect of the organization's internal environment created by job specialization and the division of labor.

_____

integration

The degree to which differentiated work units work together and coordinate their efforts.

_____

division of labor

The assignment of different tasks to different people or groups.

_____

specialization

A process in which different individuals and units perform different tasks.

People often learn about a firm's structure first by looking at its organization chart. The **organization chart** depicts the positions in the firm and the way they are arranged. The chart provides a picture of the reporting structure (who reports to whom) and the various activities that people perform. Most companies have official organization charts that present this information.

Exhibit 8.1 shows a traditional organization chart. It conveys several types of information.

1. The boxes represent different clusters of jobs.
2. The titles in the boxes show the work that each unit performs.
3. The solid lines show reporting and authority relationships: superior–subordinate connections.
4. Each horizontal layer indicates one level of management. A level indicates all persons of the same rank or units of the same rank reporting to someone in the level above.

Not shown in the chart, but just as important in describing an organization's structure, are two additional concepts: differentiation and integration. **Differentiation** means that the organization is composed of many units that work on different kinds of tasks, using different skills and work methods. **Integration** means that the work of these differentiated units is coordinated into an overall product.[3]

Differentiation

Carrying out the many tasks within an organization requires specialization and division of labor. Without these, the totality of work would be too complex—not to mention too much load—for any individual.[4]

Differentiation is created through division of labor and job specialization. **Division of labor** means that the work of the organization is subdivided into smaller tasks. **Specialization** refers to the fact that different people or groups perform those smaller parts of the organization's overall work. As you can see, the two concepts are closely related. Work is divided, and people specialize in certain work tasks.

Differentiation is high when an organization has many subunits and many kinds of specialists. Renowned Harvard professors Lawrence and Lorsch found that organizations in complex, dynamic environments (plastics firms, in their study) developed a high degree of differentiation to cope with the complex challenges. Companies in simple, stable

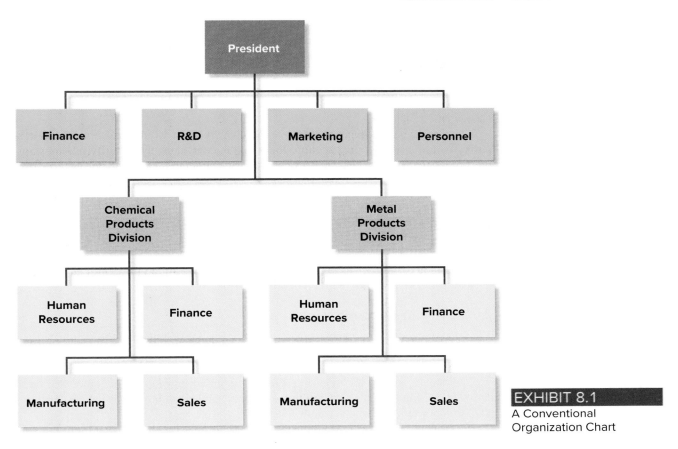

EXHIBIT 8.1
A Conventional
Organization Chart

environments (container companies) had low levels of differentiation. Companies in intermediate environments (food companies) showed intermediate differentiation.[5] Exhibit 8.2 shows some examples.

As organizations differentiate their structures, managers must simultaneously consider issues of integration.

Integration

As organizations differentiate their structures, managers must consider how best to integrate their different activities. The different units are part of the same organization, and at least some degree of communication and cooperation must occur among them. Integration and its related concept, **coordination**, refer to the procedures that link the parts of the organization to achieve the organization's overall mission.

coordination
The procedures that link the various parts of an organization for the purpose of achieving the organization's overall mission.

EXHIBIT 8.2
Examples of
Differentiation

Automotive Firms	Fast-Food Companies	Cement Companies
• Operate in complex and dynamic environments. • Require high degree of differentiation.	• Operate in intermediate environments. • Require intermediate levels of differentiation.	• Operate in simple, stable environments. • Require low levels of differentiation.

SOURCE: Adapted from Lawrence, P. and Lorsch, J., *Organization and Environment*. Homewood, IL: Richard D. Irwin, 1969.

Integration is achieved through structural mechanisms that enhance collaboration and coordination. Any job activity that links different work units performs an integrative function. Remember, the more highly differentiated your firm, the greater the need for integration among the different units. Lawrence and Lorsch found that highly differentiated firms were successful if they also had high levels of integration. Organizations are more likely to fail if they exist in complex environments and are highly differentiated but fail to integrate adequately.[6]

These concepts underpin the rest of the chapter. First we discuss vertical differentiation within organization structure. Relevant concepts include authority relationships, the board of directors, the chief executive officer, hierarchical levels, delegation, and decentralization.

The Vertical Structure

LO 8-2 Summarize how authority operates.

LO 8-3 Define the roles of the board of directors and the chief executive officer.

---

authority

The legitimate right to make decisions and to tell other people what to do.

To understand issues such as reporting relationships, authority, and responsibility, we need to begin with the vertical dimension of a firm's structure.

Authority in Organizations

The functioning of every organization depends on the use of **authority**, the legitimate right to make decisions and to tell other people what to do. For example, a boss has the authority to tell subordinates what to do.

Traditionally, authority resides in positions more than in people. The job of vice president of a division has authority over that division, regardless of how many people come and go in that position and who currently holds it.

The owners of a firm have ultimate authority. In most small, simply structured companies, the owner also acts as manager. Sometimes the owner hires another person to manage the business and its employees. The owner gives this manager some authority to oversee the operations, but the manager is accountable to—that is, reports and defers to—the owner.

Formal position authority is generally the primary means of running an organization. An order that a boss gives to a lower-level employee is usually carried out. As this occurs throughout the organization day after day, the organization can move forward and achieve its goals.[7]

However, power in an organization is not always position-dependent. People with particular expertise, experience, or personal qualities may have considerable *informal* authority—for example, when people carry themselves with confidence, can provide valuable information, or work closely with those who have high positions.[8] We will say more about informal sources of power in the next chapter and Chapter 12. For now, we discuss the formal authority structure of the organization from the top down, beginning with the board of directors.

Board of Directors   In corporations, the owners are the stockholders. But because there are many stockholders, most of whom are busy doing other things and lacking timely information, few are directly involved in managing the company. Instead, stockholders elect a board of directors to oversee the organization.

The board, led by the chair, makes major decisions affecting the organization, subject to corporate charter and bylaw provisions. Boards perform at least three major sets of duties: (1) selecting, evaluating, rewarding, and perhaps replacing the CEO; (2) determining the firm's strategic direction and reviewing financial performance; and (3) ensuring ethical, socially responsible, and legal conduct.[9]

The board's membership usually includes some of the company's top executives—called *inside directors*. Outside members of the board tend to be executives at other companies. The trend in recent years has been toward reducing the number of insiders and increasing the number of outsiders. Today, most boards have more outside than inside directors. Boards made up of strong, independent outsiders are more likely to provide different information and perspectives and to prevent big mistakes.

The best boards tend to be those who are active, critical participants in determining company strategies. Even so, in the wake of stricter legislation and lawsuits, many boards have shifted their focus to compliance issues, such as audits, financial reporting, and laws against discrimination. These issues are critically important, but a board staffed mainly with legal and regulatory experts cannot always give management the necessary direction on strategy.[10]

The job of CEO typically consists of leading the board of directors, motivating employees, and promoting positive change while being accountable for the overall success of the company.

Tom Merton/AGE Fotostock

The owner and managers of a small business or start-up may need the expertise of a board of directors as much as or more than a large company does. Some owners set up a board of advisers, such as owners of noncompeting companies, retired executives, strategists, technology experts, and perhaps their banker or accountant. PlumSlice Labs, a tech company that provides web and mobile applications for the retail industry, recently created an advisory board with current and former executives of GlaxoSmithKline, Walmart, WorkForce Software, SAP, and Retail Consulting.[11]

Other small-business owners join organizations that facilitate regular meetings of business owners with different areas of expertise. Members of peer advisory groups, like The Alternative Board, can share problems and exchange solutions with fellow members in confidential, facilitated monthly meetings.[12]

Generally speaking, companies benefit from having a board of directors. Board members bring credibility and networks that expand business opportunities, hold executives accountable for their actions, and leadership make difficult or unpopular strategic decisions.[13]

Also, inclusive boards help companies succeed. Companies benefit even more when the board is diverse in terms of gender, race, and ethnicity. Diverse (gender, race, and ethnicity) boards helped their companies achieve higher financial returns compared with those with less diverse boards.[14]

Chief Executive Officer   The authority officially vested in the board of directors is assigned to a chief executive officer (CEO), who occupies the top of the organizational pyramid. The CEO is personally accountable to the board and to the owners for the organization's performance.

In some corporations, one person holds all three positions of CEO, chair of the board of directors, and president.[15] More commonly, however, one person holds two of those positions, with the CEO serving also as either the board chair or the president of the organization. When the CEO is president, the chair may be honorary and may do little more than conduct meetings. In other cases, the chair may be the CEO, and the president is second in command.

In recent years, the trend has been to separate the position of CEO and board chair. Sometimes this change is related to improved corporate governance; board oversight is easier when the CEO is not so dominant. In other cases, the board acts to reduce an unpopular CEO's power or to help prepare for a successor to the CEO.

Top Management Team   Increasingly, CEOs share their authority with other key members of the top management team or C-suite (the "C" stands for "chief"). Top management teams typically are composed of the CEO, president, chief operating officer, chief financial officer, chief information officer, chief human resources officer, and other key executives. Rather than make critical decisions on their own, CEOs at companies such as Netflix, Facebook, and Salesforce regularly meet with their top management teams to make decisions as a unit.[16]

Hierarchical Levels

In Chapter 1, we introduced the organizational pyramid, comprised of multiple levels and commonly called the **hierarchy**. The authority structure is the glue that holds vertical levels together.

The key responsibilities at the top management level include **corporate governance**—a term describing the oversight of the firm by its executive staff and board of directors. The Sarbanes-Oxley Act (Chapter 5), along with requirements of the Securities and Exchange Commission, imposed new, tighter corporate governance rules. For example, company CEOs and CFOs (chief financial officers) now have to personally certify the accuracy of their firm's financial statements.

A powerful trend for U.S. businesses over the past few decades has been to reduce the number of hierarchical levels. Most executives today believe that fewer layers create a more efficient, fast-acting, and cost-effective organization. This also holds true for the **subunits** of major corporations. A study in a financial services company found that branches with fewer levels tended to have higher operating efficiency than did branches with more.[17]

This trend and research might seem to suggest that hierarchy is a bad thing, but it offers benefits as well. A hierarchy provides management career paths that help organizations retain and develop ambitious, talented people, giving them gradually more challenging experiences as they prepare for executive positions. Where there is little hierarchy, employees who see little chance of promotion may leave to find better opportunities elsewhere. A well-designed hierarchy also can ensure that managers have a reasonable number of people to monitor, as described next.[18]

Span of Control

The number of subordinates who report directly to an executive or supervisor is called the **span of control**. The implications of span of control for the shape of an organization are straightforward. Holding size constant, narrow spans build a tall organization that has many reporting levels. Wide spans create a flat organization with fewer reporting levels.

A span of control can be too narrow or too wide. The optimal span of control maximizes effectiveness because it is (1) narrow enough to permit managers to maintain control over direct reports, but (2) not so narrow that it leads to overcontrol and an excessive number of managers who oversee a small number of people.

Companies that employ the right level of control can realize cost savings through reduced levels of management, better customer experiences as decisions are made closer to the frontline, and more reliable communication between people at different levels within the organization.[19]

What is the optimal number of direct reports? Five, according to Napoleon Bonaparte.[20] A Deloitte study found average span of control at large companies to be about 11 direct reports.[21] Another study found that managers in an internal audit department would average 4 to 6 direct reports; auditors' jobs tend to be complex, varied, and require frequent communication with their manager.[22]

The optimal span of control depends on a number of factors,[23] as shown in Exhibit 8.3.

Delegation

As work is spread out over various levels and spans of control, delegating work becomes paramount. A manager **delegates** when she assigns a task to someone at a lower level. It often requires the subordinate to report back to his or her boss about how effectively the assignment was carried out.

Delegation is perhaps the most fundamental process of management because it entails getting work done through others. It is important at all hierarchical levels. The process can occur between any two individuals in any type of structure with regard to any task.

---

hierarchy

The authority levels of the organizational pyramid.

corporate governance

The role of a corporation's executive staff and board of directors in ensuring that the firm's activities meet the goals of the firm's stakeholders.

Bottom Line

A "flat" structure with fewer horizontal layers saves time and money. *Why not eliminate all middle layers to save the most time and money?*

LO 8-4 Discuss how span of control affects structure and managerial effectiveness.

subunits

Subdivisions of an organization.

span of control

The number of subordinates who report directly to an executive or supervisor.

delegation

The assignment of new or additional responsibilities to a subordinate.

Factors	Use a Wide Span of Control When . . .
The nature of the work	Work is clearly defined and unambiguous.
Subordinates' preparation	Subordinates are highly trained and have access to information.
Managers' capabilities	Managers are capable and supportive of subordinates.
Comparability of subordinates' jobs	Subordinates have similar jobs and are rated on comparable performance measures.
Subordinates' supervisory preferences	Subordinates prefer autonomy and independence.
Organizational size	The organization is small.

EXHIBIT 8.3
When Is a Wide Span of Control Better?

Note: If the opposite conditions exist, a narrow span of control may be more appropriate.
SOURCES: Adapted from "Span of Control: What Factors Should Determine How Many Direct Reports a Manager Has?" Society for Human Resource Management, April 25, 2013, http://www.shrm.org; Jehiel, P., "Information Aggregation and Communication in Organizations," *Management Science* 45, no. 5 (May 1999), pp. 659–69; Altaffer, A., "First-Line Managers: Measuring Their Span of Control," *Nursing Management* 29, no. 7 (July 1998), pp. 36–40.

Some managers are comfortable fully delegating an assignment to subordinates; others are not.[24] Consider how the two office managers in the following example gave out the same assignment. Are both of these statements examples of delegation? How are they similar, and how different?

> **Manager A:** "Call Mike Johnson at WorkRite Computer. Ask him to give you the price list on an upgrade for our desktop computers. I want to move up to an Intel Core i9 processor with 16 gigs of memory and at least a 2-terabyte hard drive. Ask them to give you a demonstration of the Windows 10 operating system and Microsoft Office 365. I want to be able to establish collaboration capability for the entire group. Invite Cochran and Rodriguez to the demonstration and let them try it out. Have them write up a summary of their needs and the potential applications they see for the new systems. Then prepare me a report with the costs and specifications of the upgrade for the entire department. Oh, yes, be sure to ask for information on service costs."

> **Manager B:** "I'd like to do something about our desktop computers. I've been getting some complaints that the current computers are too slow, can't run the most recent software, and freeze periodically. Could you evaluate our options and give me a recommendation on what we should do? Our budget is around $2,000 per person, but I'd like to stay under that if we can. Feel free to talk to some of the managers to get their input, but we need to have this done as soon as possible."

Responsibility, Authority, and Accountability

When delegating work, it helps to keep in mind the important distinctions among authority, responsibility, and accountability. **Responsibility** means that a person is supposed to carry out an assigned task. When delegating work responsibilities, the manager also can delegate to the subordinate enough authority to get the job done. Authority, recall, means that the person has the power and the right to make decisions, give orders, draw on resources, and do whatever else is necessary to fulfill the responsibility.

Ironically, it is quite common for people to have more responsibility than authority; they must perform as well as they can through informal influence tactics instead of relying purely on authority. More about informal power and how to use it appears in Chapter 12.

As the manager delegates responsibilities, subordinates are accountable for achieving results. **Accountability** means that the subordinate's manager has the right to expect the subordinate to perform the job and the right to take corrective action if the subordinate fails to do so. The subordinate must report upward on the status and quality of his or her task performance.

responsibility
The assignment of a task that an employee is supposed to carry out.

accountability
The expectation that employees will perform a job, take corrective action when necessary, and report upward on the status and quality of their performance.

However, the ultimate responsibility—accountability to higher-ups—lies with the manager doing the delegating. Managers remain responsible and accountable not only for their own actions but also for the actions of their subordinates. Managers should not resort to delegation to others as a means of escaping their own responsibilities.

LO 8-5 Explain how to delegate effectively.

Bottom Line

Effective delegation helps develop direct reports while raising the quality of service they provide to customers or co-workers. *How might an effort at delegation backfire?*

Advantages of Delegation   Delegating work offers important advantages when done right. Not delegating, or delegating ineffectively, sharply reduces what a manager can achieve, and hurts morale.

Effective delegation leverages the manager's energy and talent and those of his or her subordinates. It allows you to accomplish much more than you would be able to do on your own. You also save one of your most valuable assets—time—by giving some of your responsibilities to other people. You then are free to devote energy to important, higher-level activities such as planning, setting objectives, and monitoring performance.

A big advantage of delegation is that it helps managers develop effective subordinates. Delegation essentially gives the subordinate a more important job. The subordinate now has an opportunity to develop new skills and to demonstrate potential for additional responsibilities and perhaps promotion. The subordinate receives a vital form of on-the-job training that could pay off in the future. In addition, for at least some employees, delegation promotes a sense of being an important, contributing member of the organization, so these employees tend to feel a stronger commitment, perform their tasks better, and engage in more innovation.[25]

Look again at the different ways the two office managers gave out the same assignment. The approach that is more likely to empower subordinates and help them develop will be obvious to you. (You might also quickly conclude which of the two managers you would prefer to work for.)

Delegation done well benefits the organization as well as the people.[26] Allowing managers to devote more time to important managerial functions while lower-level employees carry out assignments means that jobs are done more efficiently and cost-effectively. As subordinates develop and grow in their own jobs, their contributions to the organization grow as well.

It is worth noting that not all managers like to delegate. For example, Steve Jobs preferred to micromanage and get involved deeply with each product Apple designed.[27] This approach worked for a guru like Jobs, but many organizations can and do rely heavily on effective delegation.

How Should Managers Delegate?   To reach its potential, delegation must be done properly. As Exhibit 8.4 shows, effective delegation proceeds through several steps.[28]

The first step in the delegation process, defining the goal, requires the manager to have a clear understanding of the outcome he or she wants. Then the manager should select a person who is capable of performing the task. Delegation is especially useful when an employee can benefit from developing new skills through the experience.

The person who gets the assignment should be given authority, time, and resources to carry out the task successfully. Required resources often include people, money, and equipment, plus important information that puts the assignment in context. The manager and the subordinate should work together and communicate periodically about the assignment: progress, problems, and ideas. While the subordinate performs the assignment, the manager is available and stays aware of its current status. These checkups also provide an important opportunity to offer encouragement and praise.

Some tasks, such as disciplining subordinates and conducting performance reviews, should not be delegated. But when managers err, it usually is because they delegated too little rather than too much. The manager who wants to learn how to delegate more effectively should remember this distinction: If you are not delegating, you are merely doing things; but the more you delegate, the more you are truly managing and building an organization.[29]

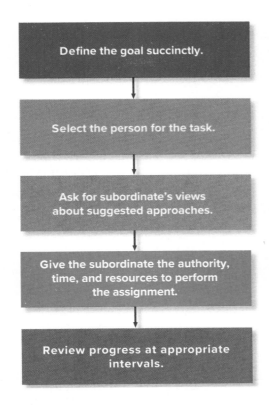

EXHIBIT 8.4
The Steps in Effective
Delegation

LO 8-6 Distinguish between centralized and decentralized organizations.

Decentralization

Delegating responsibility and authority *decentralizes* decision making.[30] In a **centralized organization**, important decisions usually are made at the top. In **decentralized organizations**, more decisions are made at lower levels. Ideally, decision making occurs at the level of the people who are most directly affected and have the most relevant knowledge about the work. This is particularly important when the business environment is fast-changing and decisions must be made quickly and well.

Sometimes organizations change their degree of centralization, depending on the particular challenges they face. Tougher times often cause senior management to take charge of decisions, whereas in times of rapid growth, decisions are pushed further down the chain of command.

Johnson & Johnson has practiced decentralization for over 130 years. The $70 billion consumer and health care behemoth has hundreds of operating companies around the world. After purchasing a firm, Johnson & Johnson expects it to remain decentralized and autonomous. This strategy encourages each operating company to provide value to their unique customer base.[31]

Most American executives today understand the advantages of pushing decision-making authority down to the point of the action. The level that deals directly with problems and opportunities has the most relevant information and can best foresee the consequences of decisions. Executives also know that the decentralized approach allows people to take faster action.[32]

Global food giant Nestlé decentralizes decision-making power to employees in over 100 countries so they can be responsive to local consumers. The company believes that allowing local employees to make decisions is key to growing the company's global market share. The role of the company's headquarters in Switzerland is to do strategic planning and distribute information.[33]

> Delegating responsibility and authority *decentralizes* decision making.

centralized organization

An organization in which high-level executives make most decisions and pass them down to lower levels for implementation.

decentralized organization

An organization in which lower-level managers make important decisions.

Bottom Line

Decentralization often speeds decision making. *What makes centralized decision making slower?*

At times, decentralizing decision making—allowing decisions to be made by people working at lower hierarchical levels—can be an advantage. These are the managers who deal directly with the problem and are most likely to know the best solutions.

GaudiLab/Shutterstock

The Horizontal Structure

LO 8-7 Summarize ways organizations can be structured.

line departments

Units that deal directly with the organization's primary goods and services.

staff departments

Units that support line departments.

Up to this point, we've described structure along the vertical dimension, giving perspective on how managers and employees at different levels relate to one another. But structures are differentiated horizontally as well, and the two structural elements relate to one another in important ways.

As the work of organizations becomes ever more complex, tasks must subdivide—that is, *departmentalize*—into smaller units or departments. One important distinction is between line and staff departments. **Line departments** are those that have responsibility for the principal activities of the firm. Line units deal directly with the organization's primary goods or services; they make things, sell things, or provide customer service. At General Motors, line departments include product design, fabrication, assembly, distribution, and the like.

Line managers typically have much authority and power in the organization. They are responsible for making major operating decisions. They are accountable for the bottom-line results of their units.

Staff departments are those that provide specialized or professional expertise that supports line departments. They include research, legal, accounting, public relations, and human resources departments. Usually, each of these specialized units often has its own vice president. Some are vested with a great deal of authority, as when accounting or finance groups approve and monitor budgetary activities.

In traditionally structured organizations, conflicts often arise between line and staff departments. Career paths and success in many staff functions depend on having a particular functional expertise, whereas success in line functions is based more on knowing the organization's industry. Thus, although line managers might be eager to pursue new products and customers, staff managers might seem to constrain these efforts with a focus on functional requirements and procedures. Line managers might be more willing to take risks for the sake of growth, whereas staff managers might focus more on protecting the company from risks.

But in today's organizations, staff units tend to be focused less on monitoring and controlling performance and more on moving toward new roles providing strategic support and expert advice.[34] For example, managers in human resources—considered back in the day to

EXHIBIT 8.5   The Functional Organization

be a not-very-powerful staff function—have expanded from merely creating procedures that meet legal requirements to helping organizations plan for, recruit, develop, and keep the kinds of employee talent who will provide long-term competitive advantage.[35] Such strategic thinking not only makes staff managers more valuable to their organizations, but also can reduce conflict between line and staff.

As organizations divide work into different units, some common patterns develop in the way departments become clustered and arranged. The three basic approaches to **departmentalization** are functional, divisional, and matrix. We will talk about each and point out some similarities and differences.

The Functional Organization

In a **functional organization**, jobs (and departments) are specialized and grouped according to business functions and the skills they require: production, marketing, human resources, research and development, finance, accounting, and so forth. Exhibit 8.5 illustrates a basic functional organization chart.

Functional departmentalization is common in both large and small organizations. Large companies may organize along several functional units, including groupings unique to their businesses. For example, AMC Theatres, which operates over 7,600 screens in 636 theaters across eight countries, has vice presidents of finance, content and programming, U.S. operations, global development, marketing, accounting, human resources, and general counsel.[36] Kiva, a nonprofit organization, also uses a functional grouping (see the nearby "Social Entrepreneurship" box).

As shown in Exhibit 8.6, the traditional functional approach to departmentalization has a number of potential advantages.

The functional form does have disadvantages. People may care more about their own function than about the company as a whole, and their attention to functional tasks may

departmentalization

Subdividing an organization into smaller subunits.

functional organization

Departmentalization around specialized activities such as production, marketing, and human resources.

Bottom Line

When similar functions are grouped, savings often result. *Why might a company centralize its human resources department?*

Economies of scale can be realized. When people with similar skills are grouped, the unit can purchase more efficient equipment and make larger, discounted purchases.

People have greater opportunity for specialized training and in-depth skill development.

Performance standards are better maintained. People with similar training and interests may develop a shared concern for high performance.

Technical specialists are relatively free of administrative work.

Environmental monitoring is more effective. Each functional group is more closely attuned to developments in its own field and therefore can adapt more readily.

Decision making and lines of communication are simple and clearly understood.

EXHIBIT 8.6

Advantages of Functional Departmentalization

SOURCES: Adapted from Cross, R. and Baird, L., "Technology Is Not Enough: Improving Performance by Building Organizational Memory," *Sloan Management Review* 41, no. 3 (Spring 2000), pp. 69–78; Duncan, R., "What Is the Right Organizational Structure?" *Organizational Dynamics* 7 (Winter 1979), pp. 59–80.

Social Entrepreneurship

Kiva Organizes by Function

Imagine having an idea to start a food stand or car cleaning business. Also imagine that you and your family live in poverty and don't have an extra $50 to buy initial supplies to launch the business. Where can you turn? To the local bank? It is unlikely a bank will provide a small, unsecured loan to you.

Kiva, a nonprofit organization, is trying to meet this need. Kiva connects via the Internet a global network of lenders with entrepreneurs in impoverished communities. Individuals can lend as little as $25 to help empower a budding entrepreneur start a business to feed his or her family. In just 15 years, 1.8 million lenders have made it possible for Kiva to make nearly $1.3 billion in loans to individuals in 81 different countries, including the United States.[37] With an average repayment rate of 97 percent, this social enterprise is making an impact on the lives of countless individuals, their families, and their communities.[38]

While some nonprofits may choose to organize around the clients they serve or the regions they operate in, Kiva takes a different approach. Kiva's organization structure is unique in how it contributes to the enterprise's efficiency and effectiveness. Given the global complexity of Kiva's operations, the organization hopes to achieve economies of scale by grouping employees and volunteers with similar training and skills into eight functional areas. Exhibit 8.6 lists other benefits of functional departmentalization.

- Why do you think Kiva is using a functional approach to structuring its organization?

- Referring to the eight areas illustrated, which are considered line activities? Staff activities?

make them lose focus on overall product quality and customer satisfaction. Managers develop functional expertise but do not acquire knowledge of the other areas of the business; they become specialists but not generalists. Between functions, conflicts arise, and communication and coordination fall off. In short, although functional differentiation might exist, functional integration might not.

For these reasons, the functional structure is most appropriate in simple, stable environments. If the organization becomes fragmented (or *dis*integrated), it will have difficulty developing and bringing new products to market and responding quickly to customer demands. Particularly when companies are growing and facing changing environments, they need to integrate more effectively. Other forms of departmentalization are more flexible and responsive than the functional structure.

Companies like GoPro, Snap Inc., H&M, and Volkswagen have taken steps to integrate their marketing and communications functions.[39] Both functions have experience in capturing, analyzing, and making decisions based on data from interacting with customers on social media. The goal of combining the two functions is to become more customer-centric and efficient. Leaders of these companies want a data-driven approach to business strategy.

Managers facing tough demands for total quality, customer service, innovation, and speed have learned the shortcomings of the functional form: it is highly differentiated and creates barriers to coordination across functions. Cross-functional coordination is essential for delivering every performance dimension. The functional organization will not disappear, in part because functional specialists will always be needed, but functional managers will make fewer decisions. The more important units will be cross-functional teams that have integrative responsibilities for products, processes, or customers.[40]

EXHIBIT 8.7   The Divisional Organization

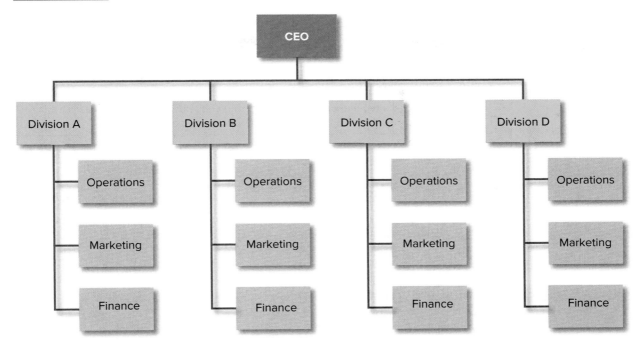

The Divisional Organization

The functional structure's weaknesses bring us to an alternative form, the **divisional organization**. As organizations grow and functional departments struggle managing diverse arrays of products, customers, and geographic regions, they can restructure such that *every* division houses *all* functions. Division A in Exhibit 8.7 has its own operations, marketing, and finance departments, Division B also has its own operations, marketing, and finance departments, and so on.

In this structure, separate divisions act almost as separate businesses or profit centers, working autonomously to accomplish the goals of the entire enterprise. Exhibit 8.8 presents examples of how the same work would be organized under functional and divisional structures.

divisional organization

Departmentalization that groups units around products, customers, or geographic regions.

Functional Organization	Divisional Organization
Chain of restaurants with departments for purchasing, food safety, transportation, human resources, operations, and finance, responsible for all locations.	Chain of restaurants with one division for each region (e.g., Northeast, Midwest, and Southeast) of the country managing all functions in that region.
Automotive manufacturer with departments for research and development, engineering, purchasing, production, and sales, managing all automotive products.	Automotive manufacturer with product groups (e.g., SUV or truck), each staffed with employees to manage that automobile's development, engineering, purchasing, production, and sales.
One legal department serving the needs of all the domestic and international subsidiaries of a multinational company, reporting to corporate leadership.	A legal department at the offices of each subsidiary in which the multinational firm operates, reporting to the leadership in charge of that subsidiary's operations.

EXHIBIT 8.8

Examples of Functional and Divisional Organization

SOURCE: Adapted from Strauss, George and Sayles, Leonard R., *Behavioral Strategies for Managers*. Upper Saddle River, NJ: Prentice Hall, 1980, p. 221.

EXHIBIT 8.9

Product Departmentaliza-
tion: Some Advantages

Product managers focus on a particular product line. They have clear bottom-line responsibility with measurable impact on the larger organization. Also, managers can compare and contrast the performance of different divisions.

Product managers have significant autonomy and control. They are more empowered to make decisions and often control needed resources.

Product managers are strategic. They develop long-term design, forecasting, and marketing strategies for their product line.

Product managers receive broader training. They develop a broad set of skills, which they need because they will be assessed on bottom-line performance.

SOURCE: Adapted from Boehm, R. and Phipps, C., "Flatness Forays," *McKinsey Quarterly* 3 (1996), pp. 128–43.

Organizations can create divisions around products, customers, or geographic regions, as described in the following sections.

Product Divisions   In the product organization, all functions that contribute to a product are organized under one product manager. Johnson & Johnson uses this form, organizing into three broad product categories: consumer health care, medical devices, and pharmaceuticals. Within these categories are over 250 independent company divisions in 60 countries, many of which are responsible for particular product lines. Ethicon develops and sells surgical equipment, whereas Consumer Products includes Johnson's baby shampoo and Aveeno hair and skin products.[41]

The product approach to departmentalization offers a number of advantages, described in Exhibit 8.9. Because the product structure is more flexible than the functional structure, it is better for unstable environments in which firms must be able adapt and change rapidly.

But the product structure also has disadvantages. It is difficult to coordinate across product lines. And although managers learn to become generalists, they may not acquire the depth of functional expertise that comes from working in the functional structure. Furthermore, duplicating functions in every product division, compared with centralizing each function at headquarters, is expensive.

Decision making is decentralized in this structure, so top management can lose some control over decisions made in the divisions. Delegating and decentralizing properly, as discussed earlier, are essential.[42]

Bottom Line

Customer and geographic divisions often serve customers faster. *Suppose your international company sells scientific equipment to high schools, universities, and businesses. Would you set up customer divisions or geographic divisions? Why?*

Customer and Geographic Divisions   Some companies build divisions around groups of customers or around different geographic areas. A hospital can organize its services around child, adult, intensive, psychiatric, and emergency cases. Banks have different units handling customers with banking (checking and savings) and mortgage needs. The Internal Revenue Service is organized around customer groups such as large business and international, small business and self-employed, and tax-exempt and government agencies.[43]

Divisions also can be structured around geographic regions. Geographic distinctions include district, territory, region, and country. Macy's Group has geographic divisions for its operations including Macy's North Central, Northeast, Northwest, South, and Southwest as well as Macys.com for online shoppers.

The primary advantage of both the product and customer/regional approaches to departmentalization is the ability to focus on customer needs and provide faster, better service. But again, duplication of activities across many customer groups and geographic areas is expensive. As you read "Management in Action: Progress Report," consider how well the advantages and drawbacks of these divisional structures might apply to General Motors.

Management in Action

GENERAL MOTORS EXPERIENCES A CRISIS AND LEADERSHIP CHANGE

Shortly after Mary Barra took over at GM, the company had to recall over 30 million cars and trucks at a cost of $5.9 billion. Nearly 3 million of the recalls were attributed to a faulty ignition switch that has been linked to 124 deaths as of this writing. Evidence suggests that GM managers knew about this problem for more than 10 years but waited until 2014 to address it.[44]

This tragic series of events, along with GM's near collapse in 2008, have profoundly shaped Barra's strategy and managing style. She attributes these low points in GM's history to a rigid bureaucracy that had become slow, inefficient, and ultimately ineffective. "Having gone through bankruptcy and then the ignition switch crisis has fundamentally made me more impatient," Barra said in an interview. "Time is not our friend."[45]

Barra has since wasted no time in shaking things up at GM. She has set out to create a culture that's more flexible, informal, and open. Barra wants everyone at GM to have a voice. She is also relentlessly streamlining operations.

What is different is that Barra is doing this while GM is posting strong earnings. To justify the announcement of a postponement of renovation projects, in a letter to all GM employees, Barra said, "Today, our structural costs are not aligned with the market realities nor the transformational priorities ahead. . . . We must take significant actions now to address this while our company and the economy are strong."[46]

In effect, Barra is taking aggressive restructuring steps now so that the company is more agile and fiscally sound to contend with any future downturns or bumps in the road. Barra knows firsthand the pain GM experienced by waiting too long to implement change. She is determined to not let it happen again.

- What do you think of downsizing during profitable times? What are the risks? What are the benefits?
- What do you think will be the impact of GM's effort to create a more open and agile organization?

The Matrix Organization

Many structures are more complex than the basic forms that you just read about; often they are hybrids of multiple forms.[47] A **matrix organization** is a hybrid form of organization in which functional and divisional forms overlap. Managers and staff personnel report to two bosses—a functional manager and a divisional manager. Thus matrix organizations have a dual rather than a single line of command.[48]

A large majority of U.S. employees spend at least some of their work time operating in a matrix.[49] In Exhibit 8.10, each project manager draws employees from each functional area to form a group for the project. The employees working on those projects report to the individual project manager as well as to the manager of their functional area.

Starbucks uses a matrix with four features: The functional hierarchy helps develop and implement corporate strategies; two geographic divisions, global and United States, help the company adapt to local markets; product divisions develop and manage specific product lines; and, teams at each coffee store provide customer service that directly affects sales.[50]

The matrix form originated in the aerospace industry, first with TRW in 1959 and then with NASA. Applications now occur in hospitals and health care agencies, entrepreneurial organizations, government laboratories, financial institutions, and multinational corporations.[51] Other companies that have used or currently use the matrix form include Caterpillar, Hughes Aircraft, General Motors, and Texas Instruments.[52]

LO 8-8 Identify the unique challenges of the matrix organization.

matrix organization

An organization composed of dual reporting relationships in which some employees report to two superiors—a functional manager and a divisional manager.

EXHIBIT 8.10　　Matrix Organization Structure

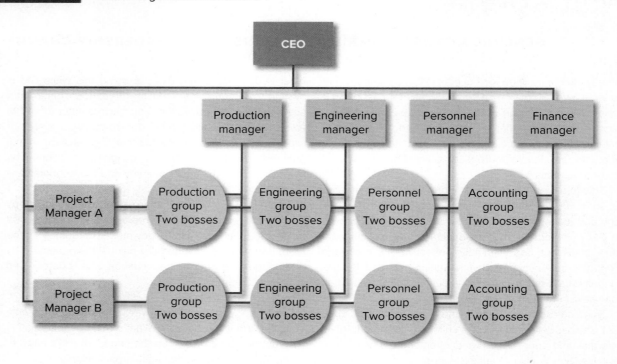

Pros and Cons of the Matrix Form　Like other structures, the matrix has both strengths and weaknesses. Exhibit 8.11 summarizes the advantages and disadvantages of the matrix. Its major potential advantage is a higher degree of flexibility and adaptability.

The same exhibit summarizes the potential shortcomings of the matrix form. Many of the disadvantages stem from the matrix's inherent violation of the **unity-of-command principle**,

EXHIBIT 8.11

Strengths and Weaknesses of the Matrix Design

Advantages

- Linkage of employees at all levels and in all functions to the company's goals and strategy.
- More information shared across functions.
- Communication fostered—especially valuable for complex assignments where different groups depend on each other.
- Greater responsiveness to customers from bringing together information about customer needs and organizational capabilities.
- Creative ideas from cross-functional work.
- Loyalty to the organization as a whole rather than to a function or division.

Disadvantages

- Unclear responsibilities and competing priorities.
- Violation of the unity-of-command principle.
- Accountability difficult to define.
- Lower employee engagement.
- Possible conflict and stress for employees who must manage a dual reporting role.
- Additional time required for meetings and other communications to coordinate work.
- Extensive collaboration needed but not always easy to reward.

SOURCES: Based on Bazigos, M. and Harter, J., "Revisiting the Matrix Organization," *McKinsey Quarterly,* January 2016, www.mckinsey.com; Krell, E., "Managing the Matrix," *HR Magazine,* April 2011, 69–71; Lash, R., "Cracking the Matrix Code," *Canadian HR Reporter,* March 28, 2011, pp. 16–18.

which states that a person should have only one boss. Reporting to two superiors can create confusion and a difficult interpersonal situation unless steps are taken to prevent these problems.

Matrix Survival Skills   The need to collaborate effectively is particularly high in the matrix, and this can be difficult because people often rotate teams, teammates, and bosses. To a large degree, problems can be avoided if the key managers in the matrix learn the behavioral skills needed in this structure.[53] These skills vary depending on the job in the four-person diamond structure shown in Exhibit 8.12.

The top executive, who heads the matrix, must learn to balance power and emphasis between the product and functional requirements. Product or division managers and functional managers must learn to collaborate and manage their conflicts constructively. Finally, the two-boss managers or employees at the bottom of the diamond must learn how to be responsible to two superiors. This means prioritizing multiple demands and sometimes even reconciling conflicting orders.

Some people function poorly under these ambiguous, conflictual circumstances; sometimes this signals the end of their careers with the company. Ideally people in the matrix learn to communicate effectively with one another, rise above the difficulties, and manage these work relationships constructively.

> The key to managing in the matrix is to realize that the matrix is a process.

The Matrix Form Today   The popularity of the matrix form waned during the late 1980s, when many companies had difficulty implementing it. But recently it has come back strong. Reasons for this resurgence include pressures to consolidate costs and be faster to market, creating needs for better coordination across functions or across countries for firms with global business strategies. Many of the challenges created by the matrix are particularly acute in an international context, mainly because of the distances involved and the differences in local markets.[54]

The key to managing today's matrix is to realize that the matrix is a process. Managers who have appropriately adopted the matrix structure because of the complexity of the challenges they confront, but have trouble implementing it, often haven't strengthened the interpersonal relationships in ways that make the matrix effective.

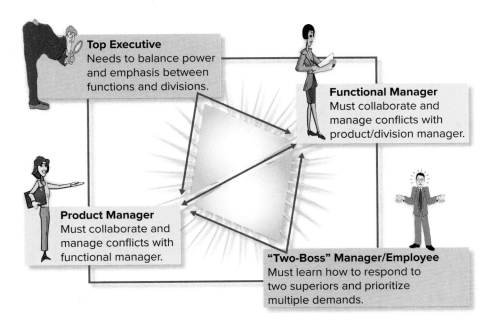

Top Executive
Needs to balance power and emphasis between functions and divisions.

Functional Manager
Must collaborate and manage conflicts with product/division manager.

Product Manager
Must collaborate and manage conflicts with functional manager.

"Two-Boss" Manager/Employee
Must learn how to respond to two superiors and prioritize multiple demands.

It is not enough to create a flexible organization merely by changing its structure. Managers must also attend to the norms, values, and attitudes that shape how people within their organizations behave.[55] We will address these issues in the next chapter and in Part 4 of the book, which focuses on how to lead and manage people.

The Network Organization

network organization

A collection of independent, mostly single-function firms that collaborate on a good or service.

Functional, divisional, and matrix structures are variations of the traditional hierarchical organization. In contrast, the **network organization** is a collection of independent, mostly single-function firms that collaborate to produce a good or service. As depicted in Exhibit 8.13, the network organization describes not one organization but the web of relationships among many firms. Network organizations are flexible arrangements among designers, suppliers, producers, distributors, and customers where each firm is able to pursue its own distinctive competence plus work effectively with other members of the network.

Often, members of the network communicate electronically and share information to be able to respond quickly to customer demands. In effect, the normal boundary of a firm becomes blurred or porous as managers within it interact closely with network members outside it. The network as a whole, then, can display the technical specialization of the functional structure, the market responsiveness of the product structure, and the balance and flexibility of the matrix.[56]

dynamic network

Temporary arrangements among partners that can be assembled and reassembled to adapt to the environment.

A very flexible version of the network organization is the **dynamic network**—also called the *modular* or *virtual* corporation. It is composed of temporary arrangements that can be assembled and reassembled to meet a changing competitive environment. The members of the network are held together by contracts that stipulate results expected—market mechanisms—rather than by hierarchy and authority. Poorly performing firms can be removed and replaced. Such arrangements are common in the electronics, toy, and apparel industries, each of which creates and sells trendy products at a fast pace.

Dynamic networks are suitable when much of the work can be done independently by experts. For example, TTEC is an Englewood, Colorado–based business process outsourcing company dedicated to integrating more humanity into digital interactions with customers. When a customer asks a question (via chat) about how to protect her camera when hiking, an expert suggests hiking-friendly camera cases. The company's expert network covers 24 countries.[57]

In another example, Amanda Abella was writing a book called *Make Your Money Honey.* She reached out to 100 freelance bloggers and writers to ask if they would help her market the book. Abella received many responses, and she collaborated with them

Bottom Line

Networks can improve cost, quality, service, speed, sustainability, and innovation. *Which functions would you include in a network to improve sustainability?*

EXHIBIT 8.13
A Network Organization

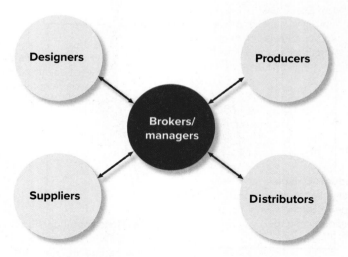

SOURCE: Miles, Raymond E. and Snow, Charles C., "Organizations: New Concepts for New Forms," *California Management Review* 28, no. 3 (Spring 1986), pp. 62–73.

via joint webinars and interviews. Their work paid off, and the book became an Amazon bestseller.[58]

Networks are flexible, innovative, and quick to respond to threats and opportunities. They reduce costs and risk. But for these arrangements to be successful, several things must happen:

The firm must choose the right specialty. It must be something (good or service) that the market needs and that the firm is better at providing than other firms.

The firm must choose collaborators who are excellent at what they do and that provide complementary strengths.

The firm must make certain that all parties fully understand the strategic goals of the partnership.

Each party must be able to trust all the others with strategic information and trust that each collaborator will deliver quality products even if the business grows quickly and makes heavy demands.

The role of managers changes in a network from supervising direct reports to more like that of a **broker**. Broker/managers serve several important boundary roles that aid network integration and coordination:

Designer role: a network architect who envisions a set of groups or firms whose collective expertise can focus on a particular good or service.

Process engineering role: a network co-operator who lays out the flow of resources and relationships and makes certain that everyone shares common goals, standards, payments, and the like.

Nurturing role: a network developer who nurtures and enhances the network (maintains and strengthens the team) to make certain the relationships are healthy and mutually beneficial.[59]

broker

A person who assembles and coordinates participants in a network.

Inclusiveness Works

Creating a Structure to Hear All Voices

Part of the problem that almost led to the collapse of GM was its rigid hierarchical structure. Layers of bureaucracy and a stiff, formal culture made it such that employees were afraid to voice their opinions. As a result, the company became slow, stale, and inefficient.[60]

It's not an uncommon problem in large organizations, even smaller ones, especially those that are established with protocols and policies that have been in place for years, sometimes decades. So how does a firm create a more open, inclusive environment in which everyone has an opportunity to speak and actually be heard?[61] Not surprisingly, it has a lot to do with structure.

Yes, cultivating a culture where employees feel free to share ideas and opinions is a critical part of ensuring everyone feels empowered and valued. But that culture is often created by the structures the organization sets up. Structure can foster a diversity of voices in a number of ways.

Giving workers a seat on executive boards not only sends a signal of proactive inclusion, it also empowers workers, as they will be privy to the higher-level agenda of the firm as a whole. Including them at the top increases the possibility of a stronger voice at lower levels. Of course, flatter organization structures can foster a more informal, collaborative environment in which the sharing of opinions and ideas becomes more organic, a natural functioning of the organization itself. Firms can also implement more formal processes, such as periodic employee surveys, "suggestion and idea" boxes where employees can submit their thoughts, and systematic meetings in which teams gather to voice ideas, suggestions, and complaints.[62]

- How important do you think structure is in fostering an inclusive atmosphere for sharing ideas and opinions?
- Which of the methods discussed here do you think would be most beneficial for this end? Why?

Organizational Integration

LO 8-9 Describe important integrative mechanisms.

At the beginning of this chapter, we said organizations are structured around differentiation and integration. So far, we have focused on *differentiation*. As organizations differentiate their structures, they also need to *integrate* and *coordinate* the work of different parts of the organization. Typically, the more differentiated the organization, the more difficult integration is.

Due to specialization and the division of labor, different groups of managers and employees develop different perspectives. Depending on whether people are in a functional department or a divisional group, or are line or staff, they will think and act in ways that are geared toward their own work units. In short, people working in separate functions, divisions, and business units tend to forget and misunderstand one another's perspectives. When this happens, it is difficult for managers to combine their activities into an integrated whole.

Managers have several options for making sure that units doing different work that needs to be coordinated will work together to achieve a common purpose. If employees need to work closely to achieve joint objectives, managers can reward team performance, thus motivating teamwork. In other situations, they might rely more on individuals with unique talents and ideas, so they set up flexible work arrangements and reward individual performance. This inspires strong individual contributions while encouraging people to share knowledge and develop respect for one another's contributions.[63]

> Typically, the more differentiated the organization, the more difficult and important the integration.

You will learn more about how rewards motivate in a later chapter. Additional coordination methods include standardization, plans, and mutual adjustment.[64]

Coordination by Standardization

standardization

Establishing common routines and procedures that apply uniformly to everyone.

Work is standardized when organizations coordinate activities by establishing routines and standard operating procedures that remain in place over time. **Standardization** constrains actions and integrates various units by regulating what people do. People often know how to act, and how to interact, because standard operating procedures determine what they should do. For example, managers may establish standards for which types of computer equipment the organization will use. This simplifies the purchasing and computer-training process—everyone will be on a common platform—and makes it easier for the different parts of the organization to communicate with each other.

formalization

The presence of rules and regulations governing how people in the organization interact.

To improve coordination, organizations also can rely on **formalization**—rules and regulations governing how people interact. Simple, often written, policies regarding attendance, dress, and decorum, for example, may help eliminate a good deal of uncertainty at work.

An important assumption underlying both standardization and formalization is that the rules and procedures should apply to most (if not all) situations. These approaches, therefore, are most appropriate in situations that are relatively stable and unchanging.

When the situation requires flexibility, standardization may not work well. Who hasn't complained about red tape, when rules and procedures—common features of slow bureaucracies—prevented timely action and problem resolution?[65]

Coordination by Plan

coordination by plan

Interdependent units are required to meet deadlines and objectives that contribute to a common goal.

Managers also can establish goals and schedules for interdependent units. **Coordination by plan** does not require the same high degree of stability that standardization does. Units can have some freedom in how they work as long as they meet the deadlines and targets needed by other units as specified in agreed-upon plans.

In writing this textbook, we (the authors) sat down with a publication team that included the editors, the marketing staff, the production group, and support staff. Together, we developed a plan that included dates and deliverables: what was to be accomplished and when it would be forwarded to others in the work flow. The plan allowed flexibility for each subunit as long as each delivered as planned. The agreed-upon plan allowed us to work together smoothly and productively.

The Digital World

Will Online Networks Replace Traditional Hierarchies?

According to journalist and author Malcolm Gladwell, the United States is reaching a "generational tipping point" in which Millennials are bringing dramatic changes in the structure and function of organizations. Gladwell states that Baby Boomers and other older generations prefer to organize in hierarchies with strong leadership, respect for expertise, a clear strategy, and a guiding ideology.[66]

In comparison, Gladwell points out that Millennials have a different worldview: "[Millennials] take a profoundly different attitude toward authority and toward expertise."[67] As the first generation to grow up with unfettered access to social networking sites, online gaming, and smartphones, these "digital natives" prefer to organize around and seek information from their peers via online social networks.

Because Millennials as children became accustomed to such "open, leaderless platforms," they gravitate naturally toward organizations that are collaborative in nature.[68] In comparison to Boomers,

Millennials tend to bristle when working for bosses who exert their authority by micromanaging and imposing too much structure and too many rules on employees. Perhaps this mismatch helps explain why as many as 43 percent of Millennial employees plan to quit their jobs within two years.[69]

What does this generational shift mean for organizations that use hierarchical structures? Managers may want to begin shifting their cultures and designing jobs and teams in a way that encourages collaborative, network-driven engagement. Such adjustments are arriving, as Millennials became the largest generation in the U.S. workforce in 2016.[70]

1. Based on your experience, do you think Millennials have a different worldview than people from earlier generations? If so, in what way?
2. As a manager, how would your understanding of Millennials affect the structure of your organization?

Coordination by Mutual Adjustment

The simplest and most flexible approach to coordination may be just to have interdependent parties talk to one another. **Coordination by mutual adjustment** involves discussions to figure out jointly how to approach problems and devise solutions that are agreeable to everyone. Work teams are common in part because they allow flexible coordination; teams can operate under the principle of mutual adjustment.

coordination by mutual adjustment

Units interact with one another to make accommodations to achieve flexible coordination.

Secure information sharing is vital at the National Counterterrorism Center, shown here. Technology enables efficient and safe sharing, but new external developments require unceasing adaptation and better coordination.

nd3000/Shutterstock

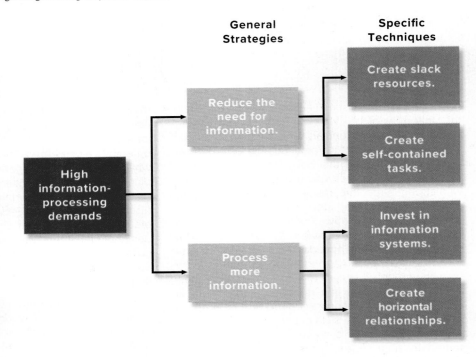

EXHIBIT 8.14
Managing High Information-Processing Demands

The flexibility of mutual adjustment as a coordination device does not come without some cost. Hashing out every issue takes time, and may or may not result in clear mutual understanding. Imagine how long it would take to accomplish our work if people had to talk through every task and situation. But mutual adjustment can work when problems are novel and cannot be programmed in advance with rules, procedures, or plans. During crises, in which daily operating procedures don't apply, mutual adjustment is essential.

Coordination and Communication

Business environments tend to be complex, dynamic, and therefore uncertain. Huge amounts of information flow from the external environment to the organization and back to the environment. To cope, organizations must acquire, process, and respond to that information. Doing so has direct implications for how firms organize. Organizations need to develop structures for processing a lot of information, effectively.

To cope with high uncertainty and heavy information demands, managers can use the two general strategies shown in Exhibit 8.14. First, management can act to reduce the need for information. Second, it can increase its capacity to handle more information.[71]

Option 1: Reducing the Need for Information   Managers can reduce the need for information in two ways: (1) creating slack resources and (2) creating self-contained tasks. Slack resources are extra resources on which organizations can rely in a pinch so that if they get caught off guard, they can still adjust. Inventory, for example, is a type of slack resource that provides extra stock on hand in case it is needed. With extra inventory, an organization does not need as much information about sales demand, lead times, and so on.

Like slack resources, creating self-contained tasks allows organizations to reduce the need for some information. Creating self-contained tasks refers to changing from a functional organization to a product or project organization and giving each unit the resources it needs to perform its task. Information-processing problems are reduced because each unit has its own full complement of specialties, rather than needing to share functional expertise

Bottom Line

Cross-unit coordination can lead to effective problem solving. *Why does more shared information tend to improve solutions?*

among a number of different product teams. Communications then flow within each team rather than among a complex array of interdependent groups.

Option 2: Increasing Information-Processing Capability Instead of or in addition to reducing the need for information, managers can attempt to increase the firm's information-processing capability. They can invest in information systems, which usually means employing or expanding computer systems. But increasing an organization's information-processing capability can also mean engaging in better knowledge management (Chapter 1)—capitalizing on the intellect and experience of the organization's human assets to increase collaboration and effectiveness.

One way to do that is by creating horizontal relationships between units to foster coordination and thus integration. The following horizontal processes range from the simplest to the most complex:[72]

1. *Direct contact (mutual adjustment)* among managers who share a problem. In a university, for example, a residence hall adviser might call a meeting to resolve differences between feuding students.
2. *Liaison roles,* or specialized jobs to handle communications between two departments. A fraternity representative is a liaison between the fraternity and the interfraternity council, the university, or the local community.
3. *Task forces,* or groups of representatives from different departments, brought together temporarily to solve a common problem. For example, students, faculty, and administrators may be members of a task force charged with bringing distinguished speakers to campus.
4. *Permanent interdepartmental decision-making groups.* An executive council made up of department heads might meet regularly to make decisions affecting a college of engineering or liberal arts.
5. *Product, program, or project managers* who direct interdisciplinary groups with a common task to perform. In a college of business administration, a faculty administrator might head an executive education program of professors from several disciplines.
6. *Matrix organizations,* composed of dual relationships in which some managers report to two bosses. Your instructors, for example, may report to department heads in their respective disciplines and to a director of undergraduate or graduate programs.

You will learn more about some of these in later chapters covering teams, intergroup relations, and communicating.

Looking Ahead

The organization chart, differentiation, integration, authority, delegation, and coordination convey fundamental information about an organization's structure. However, the information so far provides only a snapshot. The real organization is more like a motion picture—it moves! More flexible and innovative, even virtual, new forms of organizations are evolving continually.

Even if you know departments and authority relationships, you still have much to understand. How do things really get done? Who influences whom, and how? Which managers are the most powerful? How effective is the top leadership? Which groups are most and which are least effective? How do communications flow throughout the organization? The rest of the book discusses these dynamics.

As you read "Management in Action: Onward," consider how the organizing concepts from this chapter help you evaluate the challenges facing General Motors, but also notice where personal relationships and other human factors come into play.

Management in Action

TRANSFORMING GM FOR THE FUTURE

Since taking over at GM, Mary Barra has been focused on swift, decisive, forward-looking action. Her mantra has been "Innovate now." Barra's passion for change and innovation is so strong that she wants GM to one day be thought of as a tech company, not a car company.[73]

Barra has been moving the company toward a focus on electric cars, self-driving technology, and ride-sharing services. In 2017, GM unveiled the Chevy Bolt, a car Barra long championed, as an "affordable all-electric vehicle with over 200 miles per charge." It was immediately named *Motor Trend's* 2017 Car of the Year, suggesting the once staid and slow company is now able to maneuver quickly and to successfully push into uncharted markets. GM recently announced that it is moving away from hybrid lines to invest more heavily in all-electric cars.[74]

GM is also planning to launch in 2020 self-driving technology in its signature line, Cadillac, and to all its car lines by 2023.[75] To achieve these goals, GM is partnering with tech firms. Ultimately, GM is going all in on its vision for the future: that cars will be electric and self-driving, operating more on digital technology than the mechanical hardware that launched the company more than 100 years ago.

Such a long and storied history hasn't inhibited Barra from trying to transform for the future. As she said in a recent interview, "We don't have a right to exist. . . . We have to earn our right to be General Motors."[76]

- What do you think of Barra's vision for GM's future? Do you think the focus and investment on self-driving, electric vehicles is a wise one?
- What structural challenges will GM face in trying to reconceive itself as a tech company?

KEY TERMS

RETAINING WHAT YOU LEARNED

In Chapter 8, you learned that the structure of organizations is determined fundamentally by their degrees of differentiation and integration. People and groups are assigned specialized tasks, and these tasks are coordinated to achieve the organizations' overall mission. Bosses exercise authority throughout organizations' hierarchies, even though owners or stockholders have ultimate authority. Boards of directors report to stockholders, advise management, consider the firm's legal interests, and protect stockholders' rights. Span of control refers to the number of people who report directly to a manager. Delegation, the assignment of tasks and responsibilities, offers a variety of benefits but must be managed carefully. In centralized organizations, top managers make the most important decisions whereas in decentralized organizations, many decisions are delegated to lower levels. Organizations can be structured in a variety of forms, including function, division (product, customers, or geographic), matrix, and network. Matrix structures allow a company to adapt to changing conditions, but present unique challenges to people working within them. Managers can coordinate interdependent units through standardization, plans, and mutual adjustment.

LO 8-1 Explain how differentiation and integration influence an organization's structure.

- Differentiation means that organizations have many parts. Specialization means that various individuals and units throughout the organization perform different tasks. The assignment of tasks to different people or groups often is the division of labor. But the specialized tasks in an organization cannot all be performed independently of one another.
- Coordination links the various tasks to achieve the organization's overall mission.
- An organization with many specialized tasks and work units is highly differentiated; the more differentiated the organization is, the more integration or coordination is required.

LO 8-2 Summarize how authority operates.

- Authority is the legitimate right to make decisions and tell other people what to do. It is exercised throughout the hierarchy because bosses have the authority to give orders to subordinates.
- Through the day-to-day operation of authority, the organization proceeds toward achieving its goals. Owners or stockholders have ultimate authority.

LO 8-3 Define the roles of the board of directors and the chief executive officer.

- Boards of directors report to stockholders. The board of directors controls or advises management, considers the firm's legal and other interests, and protects stockholders' rights.
- The chief executive officer reports to the board and is accountable for the organization's performance.

LO 8-4 Discuss how span of control affects structure and managerial effectiveness.

- Span of control is the number of people who report directly to a manager. Narrow spans create tall organizations, and wide spans create flat ones.
- No single span of control is always appropriate; the optimal span is determined by characteristics of the work, the subordinates, the manager, and the organization.

LO 8-5 Explain how to delegate effectively.

- Delegation—the assignment of tasks and responsibilities—has many potential advantages for the manager, the subordinate, and the organization.
- But to be effective, the process must be managed carefully. The manager should define the goal, select the person, solicit opinions, provide resources, schedule checkpoints, and discuss progress periodically.

LO 8-6 Distinguish between centralized and decentralized organizations.

- In centralized organizations, top managers make the most important decisions.
- In decentralized organizations, many decisions are delegated to lower levels.

LO 8-7 Summarize ways organizations can be structured.

- Organizations can be structured on the basis of function, division (product, customers, or geographic), matrix, and network.
- Each form has advantages and disadvantages.

LO 8-8 Identify the unique challenges of the matrix organization.

- The matrix is a complex structure with dual authority relationships. A well-managed matrix enables organizations to adapt to change.
- But it can also create confusion and interpersonal difficulties. People in all positions in the matrix—top executives, product and function managers, and two-boss employees—must acquire unique survival skills.

LO 8-9 Describe important integrative mechanisms.

- Managers can coordinate interdependent units through standardization, plans, and mutual adjustment.
- Standardization stems from work routines and standard operating procedures. They typically are accompanied by formalized rules.
- Coordination by plan is more flexible and allows more freedom in how tasks are carried out but keeps interdependent units focused on joint goals and schedules.
- Mutual adjustment involves feedback and discussions among related parties to accommodate each other's needs. It is the most flexible and simplest to administer, but it is time-consuming.
- Two general ways to deal with high information loads are to reduce the need for information (e.g., through creating slack resources and self-contained units) and processing more information (e.g., through investing in information systems and creating horizontal relationships).

DISCUSSION QUESTIONS

1. Based on the description of General Motors in this chapter, give some examples of differentiation in that organization. In other words, what specialized tasks have to be performed, and how is labor divided at General Motors? Also, how does General Motors integrate the work of these different units? Based on what you have learned in this chapter, would you say General Motors has an effective structure? Why or why not?

2. What are some advantages and disadvantages of being in the CEO position?

3. Would you like to sit on a board of directors? Why or why not? If you did serve on a board, what kind of organization would you prefer? As a board member, in what kinds of activities do you think you would most actively engage?

4. Interview a member of a board of directors, and discuss that member's perspectives on his or her role.

5. Pick a job you have held and describe it in terms of span of control, delegation, responsibility, authority, and accountability.

6. Why do you think managers have difficulty delegating? What can be done to overcome these difficulties?

7. Consider an organization in which you have worked, draw its organization chart, and describe it by using terms in this chapter. How did you like working there, and why?

8. Would you rather work in a functional or divisional organization? Why?

9. If you learned that a company has a matrix structure, would you be more or less interested in working there? Explain your answer. How would you prepare yourself to work effectively in a matrix?

10. Brainstorm a list of specific ways to integrate interdependent work units. Discuss the activities required and the pros and cons of each approach.

EXPERIENTIAL EXERCISES

8.1   The Business School Organization Chart

OBJECTIVES

1. To clarify the factors that determine organization structure.

2. To provide insight into the workings of an organization.

3. To examine the working relationships within an organization.

INSTRUCTIONS

1. Draw an organization chart for your business school. Be sure to identify all the staff and line positions in the school. Specify the chain of command and the levels of administration. Note the different spans of control. Are there any advisory groups, task forces, or committees to consider?

2. Review the chapter material on organization structure to help identify both strong and weak points in your school's organization. Now draw another organization chart for the school, incorporating any changes you believe would improve the quality of the school. Support the second chart with a list of recommended changes and reasons for their inclusion.

DISCUSSION QUESTIONS

1. Is your business school well organized? Why or why not?

2. In what ways is the school's structure designed to suit the needs of students, faculty, staff, the administration, and the business community?

8.2   Designing a Student-Run Organization That Provides Consulting Services

OBJECTIVES

1. To appreciate the importance of the total organization on group and individual behavior.

2. To provide a beginning organization design experience that will be familiar to students.

BACKGROUND

The Industry Advisory Council for your school has decided to sponsor a student-run organization that will provide business consulting services to nonprofit groups in your community. The council has donated $20,000 toward start-up costs and has agreed to provide office space, computer equipment, and other materials as needed. The council hopes that the organization will establish its own source of funding after the first year of operation.

TASK 1

The dean of the school wants you to develop alternative designs for the new organization. Your task is to identify the main design dimensions or factors to be dealt with in establishing such an organization and to describe the issues that must be resolved for each factor. For example, you might provide an organization chart to help describe the structural issues involved. Before jumping ahead with your design, you may also have to think about (1) groups in the community that could use your help and (2) problems they face. Remember, though, your task is to create the organization that will provide services, not to provide an in-depth look at the types of services provided.

You and your team are to brainstorm design dimensions to be dealt with and to develop a one- or two-page outline that can be shared with the entire class. You have one hour to develop the outline. Select two people to present your design. Assume that you will all be involved in the new organization, filling specific positions.

TASK 2

After the brainstorming period, the spokespersons will present the group designs or preferred design and answer questions from the audience.

TASK 3

The instructor will comment on the designs and discuss additional factors that might be important for the success of this organization.

8.3   When Should a Company Decentralize?

OBJECTIVE

To explore the conditions under which a company should decentralize its structure and decision making.

INSTRUCTIONS

The following scenarios describe situations faced by hypothetical companies that currently have a *centralized* organization structure. As you review each of the scenarios, provide your opinion as to whether the company should move to a more *decentralized* organization structure.

1. Company X produces one specialized product line for heart surgeons in the United States.
   - Maintain current centralized organization structure

   or

   - Move to a more decentralized organization structure

   Defend your choice:

---

2. Company Y makes over 100 electronic products and has to respond rapidly to the moves of its competitors.
   - Maintain current centralized organization structure

   or

   - Move to a more decentralized organization structure

   Defend your choice:

---

3. Company Z's managers are becoming increasingly comfortable with delegating tasks and responsibilities to subordinates in order to develop their decision-making skills.
   - Maintain current centralized organization structure

   or

   - Move to a more decentralized organization structure

   Defend your choice:

SOURCE: Adapted from McGrath, R. R. Jr., *Exercises in Management Fundamentals.* Englewood Cliffs, NJ: Prentice Hall, 1985, pp. 59–60.

Concluding Case

STANLEY LYNCH INVESTMENT GROUP

The Stanley Lynch Investment Group is a large investment firm headquartered in New York. The firm has 12 major investment funds, each with analysts operating in a separate department. Along with knowledge of the financial markets and the businesses it analyzes, Stanley Lynch's competitive advantage comes from its advanced and reliable computer systems. Thus an effective information technology (IT) division is a strategic necessity, and the company's chief information officer (CIO) holds a key role at the firm.

When the company hired J. T. Kundra as a manager of technology, he learned that the IT division at Stanley Lynch consisted of 68 employees, most of whom specialized in serving the needs of a particular fund. The IT employees serving a fund operated as a distinct group, each of them led by a manager who supervised several employees. (Five employees reported to J. T.)

He also learned that each group set up its own computer system to store information about its projects. The problems with that arrangement quickly became evident. As J. T. tried to direct his group's work, he would ask for documentation of one program or another. Sometimes, no one was sure where to find the documentation; often he would get three different responses from three different people with three versions of the documentation. And if he was interested in another group's project or a software program used in another department, getting information was next to impossible. He lacked the authority to ask employees in another group to drop what they were doing to hunt down information he needed.

J. T. concluded that the entire IT division could serve the firm much better if all authorized people had easy access to the work that had already been done and the software that was available. The logical place to store that information was online. He wanted to get all IT projects set up in a cloud so that file sharing, and therefore knowledge sharing, would be more efficient and reliable. A challenge would be to get the other IT groups to buy in to the new system given that he had authority over so few of the IT workers.

J. T. started by working with his group to blueprint how the system would work. Then he met with two higher-level managers who report to the CIO. He showed them the plan and explained that fast access to information would improve the IT group's quality and efficiency, thus increasing the productivity of the entire firm. He suggested that the managers require all IT employees to use the cloud system. He even persuaded them that their use of the system should be measured for performance appraisals, which directly impacts annual bonuses.

The various IT groups quickly came to appreciate that the system would enhance performance. Adoption was swift, and before long, the IT employees came to think of it as one of their most important software systems.

DISCUSSION QUESTIONS

1. Give an example of differentiation in Stanley Lynch's organization structure and an example of integration in this structure.

2. What role did authority play in the adoption of the cloud system by the IT division at Stanley Lynch?

3. How did the IT division use coordination to achieve greater integration?

ENDNOTES

1. Peter Valdes-Dapena, "Mary Barra's Impatience Could Save GM: 'Time Is Not Our Friend,'" *CNN Business,* March 10, 2019, https://www.cnn.com/2019/03/10/business/gm-ceo-mary-barra-profile/index.html.

2. Peter Valdes-Dapena, "Mary Barra's Impatience Could Save GM: 'Time Is Not Our Friend,'" *CNN Business,* March 10, 2019, https://www.cnn.com/2019/03/10/business/gm-ceo-mary-barra-profile/index.html.

3. R. N. Ashkenas and S. C. Francis, "Integration Managers: Special Leaders for Special Times," *Harvard Business Review* 78, no. 6 (November–December 2000), pp. 108–16.

4. T. Malone, R. Laubacher, and T. Johns, "The Big Idea: The Age of Hyperspecialization," *Harvard Business Review*, July 1, 2011, http://www.hbr.org; A. West, "The Flute Factory: An Empirical Measurement of the Effect of the Division of Labor on Productivity and Production Cost," *American Economist* 43, no. 1 (Spring 1999), pp. 82–87.

5. P. Lawrence and J. Lorsch, *Organization and Environment* (Homewood, IL: Richard D. Irwin, 1969).

6. P. Lawrence and J. Lorsch, *Organization and Environment* (Homewood, IL: Richard D. Irwin, 1969); B. L. Thompson, *The New Manager's Handbook* (New York: McGraw-Hill, 1994). See also S. Sharifi and K. S. Pawar, "Product Design as a Means of Integrating Differentiation," *Technovation* 16, no. 5 (May 1996), pp. 255–64; W. B. Stevenson and J. M. Bartunek, "Power, Interaction, Position, and the Generation of Cultural Agreement in Organizations," *Human Relations* 49, no. 1 (January 1996), pp. 75–104.

7. A. J. Ali, R. C. Camp, and M. Gibbs, "The Ten Commandments Perspective on Power and Authority in Organizations," *Journal of Business Ethics* 26, no. 4 (August 2000), pp. 351–61; R. F. Pearse, "Understanding Organizational Power and Influence Systems," *Compensation & Benefits Management* 16, no. 4 (Autumn 2000), pp. 28–38.

8. J. Pfeffer, *Power: Why Some People Have It—and Others Don't* (New York: HarperCollins, 2010).

9. S. F. Shultz, *Board Book: Making Your Corporate Board a Strategic Force in Your Company's Success* (New York: AMACOM 2000); R. D. Ward, *Improving Corporate Boards: The Boardroom Insider Guidebook* (New York: Wiley 2000).

10. O. Faleye, R. Hoitash, and U. Hoitash, "The Trouble with Too Much Board Oversight," *MIT Sloan Management Review*, March 19, 2013, http://www.sloanreview.mit.edu; T. Perkins, "The 'Compliance Board,'" *The Wall Street Journal*, March 2, 2007, http://online.wsj.com.

11. J. Goldman, "How to Build the Best Advisory Board for Your Tech Company," *Inc.,* July 28, 2017, www.inc.com.

12. The Alternative Board, "About," http://www.thealternativeboard.com, accessed March 14, 2019; Profile, "The Alternative Board (TAB)," *Entrepreneur,* October 1, 2018, www.entrepreneur.com.

13. B. Tenenbaum, "Is It Worth Having a Board of Directors?" *Forbes,* July 23, 2016, www.forbes.com.

14. S. H. Jeong and D. A. Harrison, "Glass Breaking, Strategy Making, and Value Creating: Meta-Analytic Outcomes of Women as CEOs and TMT Members," *Academy of Management Journal* 60 (2017), pp. 1219-62;V. Hunt, D. Layton, and S. Prince, "Why Diversity Matters," McKinsey & Company, January 2015, www.mckinsey.com.

15. C. M. Daily and D. R. Dalton, "CEO and Board Chair Roles Held Jointly or Separately: Much Ado about Nothing?" *Academy of Management Executive* 11, no. 3 (August 1997), pp. 11-20.

16. D. Larcker and B. Tayan, "How Netflix Redesigned Board Meetings," *Harvard Business Review,* May 8, 2018, https://hbr.org; K. Sterling, "Why Mark Zuckerberg Thinks One-on-One Meetings Are the Best Way to Lead," *Inc.,* September 28, 2017, www.inc.com; J. Bort, "How Salesforce CEO Marc Benioff Uses Artificial Intelligence to End Internal Politics at Meetings," *Business Insider,* May 18, 2017, www.businessinsider.com.

17. S. Vickery, C. Droge, and R. Germain, "The Relationship between Product Customization and Organizational Structure," *Journal of Operations Management* 17, no. 4 (June 1999), pp. 377-91. See also N. Nohria, W. Joyce, and B. Roberson, "What Really Works," *Harvard Business Review,* July 2003.

18. A. Acharya, R. Lieber, L. Seem, and T. Welchman, "Understanding Five Managerial Archetypes Can Help," McKinsey & Company, www. mckinsey.com, accessed March 14, 2019.

19. M. Sweeney, "Organization De-Layering: Do You Have the Agility to Compete?" Accenture, www.accenture.com, accessed March 14, 2019.

20. D. Van Fleet and A. Bedeian, "A History of the Span of Management," *Academy of Management Review* 2 (1977), pp. 356-72. Results of Corporate Executive Board survey reported in McIlvaine, "Flat, Fast and . . . Risky?"

21. "Global Human Capital Trends 2016 Report," Deloitte Insights, www2.deloitte.com, accessed February 10, 2019.

22. D. Miller and M. Puleo, "Relieving the Overwhelmed Organization: How Measuring Supervisory Burden in Your Organization Structure Can Boost Performance," Deloitte Consulting LLP, 2015, www2. deloitte.com.

23. C. Wong, P. Elliott-Miller, H. Laschinger, et al., "Examining the Relationships between Span of Control and Manager Job and Unit Performance Outcomes," *Journal of Nursing Management* 23 (2015), pp. 156-68.

24. M. Akinola, A. Martin, and K. Phillips, "To Delegate or Not to Delegate: Gender Differences in Affective Associations and Behavioral Responses to Delegation," *Academy of Management Journal* 61 (2018), pp. 1467-91.

25. S. Lloyd, "Managers Must Delegate Effectively to Develop Employees," Society for Human Resource Management, February 2, 2012, http://www.shrm.org; Z. X. Chen and S. Aryee, "Delegation and Employee Work Outcomes: An Examination of the Cultural Context of Mediating Processes in China," *Academy of Management Journal* 50, no. 1 (2007), pp. 226-38.

26. M. Akinola, A. Martin, and K. Phillips, "To Delegate or Not to Delegate: Gender Differences in Affective Associations and Behavioral Responses to Delegation," *Academy of Management Journal* 61 (2018), pp. 1467-91.

27. I. Kalb, "3 Ways Micromanagers Can Destroy a Company," *Business Insider* (online), July 7, 2014, http://www.businessinsider.com; S. Finkelstein, "In Praise of Micromanagement," *BBC,* October 3, 2013, http://www.bbc.com.

28. "How to Delegate More Effectively," *Community Banker,* February 2009, p. 14; B. Nefer, "Don't Be Delegation-Phobic," *Supervision,* December 2008, Business & Company Resource Center, http:// galenet.galegroup.com; J. Mahoney, "Delegating Effectively," *Nursing Management* 28, no. 6 (June 1997), p. 62; J. Lagges, "The Role of Delegation in Improving Productivity," *Personnel Journal,* November 1979, pp. 776-79.

29. G. Matthews, "Run Your Business or Build an Organization?" *Harvard Management Review,* March-April 1984, pp. 34-44.

30. A. Arya, H. Frimor, and B. Mittendorf, "Decentralized Procurement in Light of Strategic Inventories," *Management Science* 61 (2015), pp. 578-85.

31. Company website, "About Johnson & Johnson," www.jnj.com, accessed March 15, 2019; E. Fry, "Can Big Still Be Beautiful," *Fortune,* July 22, 2016, www.fortune.com; K. King, "Johnson & Johnson: Company Overview," Technology and Operations Management, Harvard Business School Course, December 8, 2015, www.rectom.hby.org.

32. R. Forrester, "Empowerment: Rejuvenating a Potent Idea," *Academy of Management Executive* 14, no. 3 (August 2000), pp. 67-80; M. L. Perry, C. L. Pearce, and H. P. Sims Jr., "Empowered Selling Teams: How Shared Leadership Can Contribute to Selling Team Outcomes," *Journal of Personal Selling & Sales Management* 19, no. 3 (Summer 1999), pp. 35-51.

33. T. McDowell, D. Agarwal, D. Miller, T. Okamoto, and T. Page, "Organizational Design: The Rise of Teams," Deloitte University Press, February 29, 2016, www.dupress.deloitte.com; K. Hara, "Nestlé's CEO Sees Decentralization as Key," *Nikkei Asian Review,* June 26, 2014 , http://www.asia.nikkei.com.

34. E. E. Lawler III, "New Roles for the Staff Function: Strategic Support and Services," in *Organizing for the Future,* J. Galbraith, E. E. Lawler III, & Associates (San Francisco: Jossey-Bass, 1993).

35. L. Barratt-Pugh and S. Bahn, "HR Strategy during Culture Change: Building Change Agency," *Journal of Management & Organization,* February 10, 2015, pp. 1-14; A. Adams, "Changing Role of HR," *Human Resources,* June 2010, pp. 45-48.

36. E. Perlman, "These Are Some of the Biggest Cinema Chains in the World," *Verdict,* December 5, 2017, www.verdict.co.uk; Company website, "Executive Officers & Board of Directors," AMC Theatres, http://investor.amctheatres.com, accessed February 9, 2019.

37. Devin Thorpe, "Kiva Is Really a Crowdfunded Bank for Refugees and Other 'Unbankables,'" *Forbes,* September 24, 2018, https:// www.forbes.com/sites/devinthorpe/2018/09/24/kiva-is-really-a-crowdfunded-bank-for-refugees-and-other-unbankables/#a74ca71220aa.

38. Kiva, "About Us," https://www.kiva.org/about, accessed March 18, 2019.

39. R. Starr, "10 Examples of Great Integrated Marketing Campaigns," *Small Business Trends,* December 31, 2018, https://smallbiz trends.com.

40. G. S. Day, "Creating a Market-Driven Organization," *Sloan Management Review* 41, no. 1 (Fall 1999), pp. 11-22.

41. Johnson & Johnson, "Our Products," http://www.jnj.com, accessed March 31, 2017.

42. B. T. Lamont, V. Sambamurthy, K. M. Ellis, and P. G. Simmonds, "The Influence of Organizational Structure on the Information Received by Corporate Strategists of Multinational Enterprises," *Management International Review* 40, no. 3 (2000), pp. 231-52.

43. Organization website, "At-a-Glance: IRS Divisions and Principal Offices," www.irs.gov, accessed March 31, 2017.

44. Chris Isidore, "Death Toll for GM Ignition Switch: 124," *CNNMoney. com,* December 10, 2015, http://money.cnn.com/2015/12/10/news/ companies/gm-recall-ignition-switch-death-toll/.

45. Peter Valdes-Dapena, "Mary Barra's Impatience Could Save GM: 'Time Is Not Our Friend,'" *CNN Business,* March 10, 2019, https:// www.cnn.com/2019/03/10/business/gm-ceo-mary-barra-profile/ index.html.

46. Michael Wayland, "GM Halts Renovation Projects as Barra Makes Case for Cost Cuts," *Automotive News,* November 1, 2018, https://www.autonews.com/article/20181101/OEM/181109961/ gm-halts-renovation-projects-as-barra-makes-case-for-cost-cuts.

47. J. Battilana and M. Lee, "Advancing Research on Hybrid Organizing: Insights from the Study of Social Enterprises," *Academy of Management Annals* 8 (2014), pp. 397-441.

48. D. Levinthal and M. Workiewicz, "When Two Bosses Are Better Than One: Nearly Decomposable Systems and Organizational Adaptation," *Organization Science* 29 (2018), pp. 207-24.

49. B. Rigoni and B. Nelson, "The Matrix: Teams Are Gaining Greater Power in Companies," *Gallup Business Journal,* May 17, 2016, www.gallup.com.

50. P. Meyer, "Starbucks Coffee's Organizational Structure & Its Characteristics," Panmore Institute, September 8, 2018, http:// panmore.com.

51. J. Galbraith, "Matrix Is the Ladder to Success," *Bloomberg Business,* http://www.businessweek.com, accessed April 5, 2015; W. Bernasco, P. C. de Weerd Nederhof, H. Tillema, and H. Boer, "Balanced Matrix Structure and New Product Development Process at Texas Instruments Materials and Controls Division," *R&D Management* 29, no. 2 (April 1999), pp. 121–31; J. K. McCollum, "The Matrix Structure: Bane or Benefit to High Tech Organizations?" *Project Management Journal* 24, no. 2 (June 1993), pp. 23–26; R. C. Ford, "Cross-Functional Structures: A Review and Integration of Matrix," *Journal of Management* 18, no. 2 (June 1992), pp. 267–94; H. Kolodny, "Managing in a Matrix," *Business Horizons,* March– April 1981, pp. 17–24.

52. "What Is a Matrix Organization? Definition and Example," Market Business News, https://marketbusinessnews.com, accessed February 10, 2019.

53. D. Cackowski, M. K. Najdawi, and Q. B. Chung, "Object Analysis in Organizational Design: A Solution or Matrix Organizations," *Project Management Journal* 31, no. 3 (September 2000), pp. 44–51; J. Barker, "Conflict Approaches of Effective and Ineffective Project Managers: A Field Study in a Matrix Organization," *Journal of Management Studies* 25, no. 2 (March 1988), pp. 167–78; G. J. Chambers, "The Individual in a Matrix Organization," *Project Management Journal* 20, no. 4 (December 1989), pp. 37–42, 50; S. Davis and P. Lawrence, "Problems of Matrix Organizations," *Harvard Business Review,* May–June 1978, pp. 131–42.

54. M. Staples, "Perspectives on Global Organizations," McKinsey & Company (2012), http://www.mckinsey.com; A. Ferner, "Being Local Worldwide: ABB and the Challenge of Global Management Relations," *Industrielles* 55, no. 3 (Summer 2000), pp. 527–29; C. Bartlett and S. Ghoshal, "Matrix Management: Not a Structure, a Frame of Mind," *Harvard Business Review* 68 (July–August 1990), pp. 138–45.

55. J. Tata, S. Prasad, and R. Thorn, "The Influence of Organizational Structure on the Effectiveness of TQM Programs," *Journal of Managerial Issues* 11, no. 4 (Winter 1999), pp. 440–53; S. Davis and P. Lawrence, "Problems of Matrix Organizations," *Harvard Business Review,* May–June 1978, pp. 131–42.

56. R. E. Miles and C. C. Snow, *Fit, Failure, and the Hall of Fame* (New York: Free Press, 1994); G. Symon, "Information and Communication Technologies and Network Organization: A Critical Analysis," *Journal of Occupational and Organizational Psychology* 73, no. 4 (December 2000), pp. 389–95.

57. Company website, "About Us," TTEC, www.ttec.com, accessed March 15, 2019.

58. A. Abella, "5 Ways to Collaborate with Freelancers So Everyone Wins," *Due,* October 18, 2017, www.due.com.

59. R. E. Miles and C. C. Snow, *Fit, Failure, and the Hall of Fame* (New York: Free Press, 1994).

60. Peter Valdes-Dapena, "Mary Barra's Impatience Could Save GM: 'Time Is Not Our Friend,'" *CNN Business,* March 10, 2019, https://www.cnn.com/2019/03/10/business/gm-ceo-mary-barra-profile/index.html.

61. Cat Graham, "Five Strategies to Create a Culture of Inclusion," *Forbes,* June 20, 2018, https://www.forbes.com/sites/forbes humanresourcescouncil/2018/06/20/five-strategies-to-create-a-culture-of-inclusion/#274cbedc1c96.

62. Rachel Sharp, "Breaking the Silence: Employee Voice," *HR Magazine,* July 9, 2018, https://www.hrmagazine.co.uk/article-details/breaking-the-silence-employee-voice.

63. S. C. Kang, S. S. Morris, and S. A. Snell, "Relational Archetypes, Organizational Learning, and Value Creation: Extending the Human Resource Architecture," *Academy of Management Review* 32, no. 1 (2007), pp. 236–56.

64. J. G. March and H. A. Simon, *Organizations* (New York: Wiley, 1958); J. D. Thompson, *Organizations in Action* (New York: McGraw-Hill, 1967).

65. deloitte.com; P. S. Adler, "Building Better Bureaucracies," *Academy of Management Executive* 13, no. 4 (November 1999), pp. 36–49.

66. Justin Menza, "Malcolm Gladwell: A Generational Tipping Point Is Coming," *CNBC,* January 31, 2013, https://www.cnbc.com/id/100425294.

67. Justin Menza, "Malcolm Gladwell: A Generational Tipping Point Is Coming," *CNBC,* January 31, 2013, https://www.cnbc.com/id/100425294.

68. "Five Ways Work Will Change in the Future," *The Guardian,* November 29, 2015, https://www.theguardian.com/society/2015/nov/29/five-ways-work-will-change-future-of-workplace-ai-cloud-retirement-remote.

69. Zack Friedman, "43% of Millennials Plan to Quit Their Job within 2 Years," *Forbes,* May 22, 2018, https://www.forbes.com/sites/zackfriedman/2018/05/22/millennials-quit-job/#2dcf3b2957f1.

70. Richard Fry, "Millennials Are the Largest Generation in the U.S. Labor Force," April 11, 2018, https://www.pewresearch.org/fact-tank/2018/04/11/millennials-largest-generation-us-labor-force/.

71. J. Galbraith, "Organization Design: An Information Processing View," *Interfaces* 4 (Fall 1974), pp. 28–36. See also S. A. Mohrman, "Integrating Roles and Structure in the Lateral Organization," in *Organizing for the Future,* ed. J. Galbraith, E. E. Lawler III, & Associates (San Francisco: Jossey-Bass, 1993); B. B. Flynn and F. J. Flynn, "Information-Processing Alternatives for Coping with Manufacturing Environment Complexity," *Decision Sciences* 30, no. 4 (Fall 1999), pp. 1021–52.

72. J. Galbraith, "Organization Design: An Information Processing View," *Interfaces* 4 (Fall 1974), pp. 28–36; S. A. Mohrman, "Integrating Roles and Structure in the Lateral Organization," in *Organizing for the Future,* ed. J. Galbraith, E. E. Lawler III, & Associates (San Francisco: Jossey-Bass, 1993).

73. Hannah Genig, "Mary Barra Hopes GM Will Be Considered a Tech Company in the Near Future," *Benzinga,* October 29, 2018, https://www.benzinga.com/news/18/10/12584384/mary-barra-hopes-gm-will-be-considered-a-tech-company-in-the-near-future.

74. Fred Lambert, "GM Confirms It's Moving Away from Hybrids to Focus on All-Electric," *Elektrek,* January 15, 2019, https://electrek.co/2019/01/15/gm-moving-away-hybrids-focus-all-electric/.

75. Oscar Gonzalez, "GM Plans to Roll Out Self-Driving Technology to All Cadillacs in 2020," *The Street,* June 6, 2018, https://www.thestreet.com/technology/gm-to-rollout-self-driving-tech-to-vehicles-in-2020-14613871.

76. Peter Valdes-Dapena, "Mary Barra's Impatience Could Save GM: 'Time Is Not Our Friend,'" *CNN Business,* March 10, 2019, https://www.cnn.com/2019/03/10/business/gm-ceo-mary-barra-profile/index.html.

CHAPTER 9
Organizational Agility

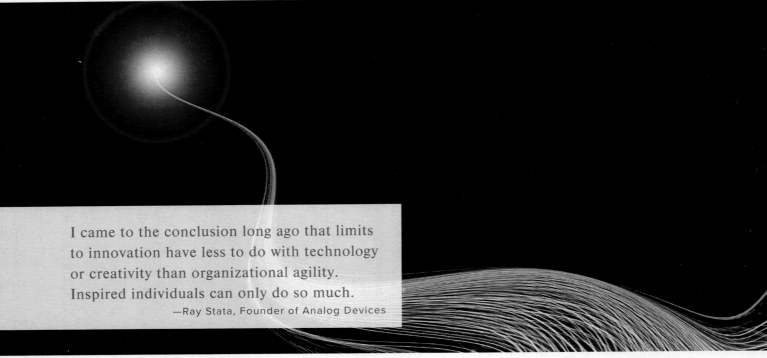

> I came to the conclusion long ago that limits to innovation have less to do with technology or creativity than organizational agility. Inspired individuals can only do so much.
> —Ray Stata, Founder of Analog Devices

John Lund/Blend Images LLC

learning objectives

After studying Chapter 9, you will be able to:

LO 9-1   Discuss why it is critical for organizations to be responsive.

LO 9-2   Describe the qualities of an organic organization structure.

LO 9-3   Identify strategies and dynamic organizational concepts that can improve an organization's responsiveness.

LO 9-4   Explain how a firm can be both big and small.

LO 9-5   Summarize how firms organize to meet customer requirements.

LO 9-6   Identify ways that firms organize around different types of technology.

chapter outline

The Responsive Organization

Strategy and Organizational Agility
Organizing around Core Capabilities
Strategic Alliances
The High-Involvement Organization

Organizational Size and Agility
The Case for Big
The Case for Small
Being Big and Small

Customers and the Responsive Organization
Customer Relationship Management
Quality Initiatives

Technology and Organizational Agility
Types of Technology Configurations
Organizing for Flexible Manufacturing
Organizing for Speed: Time-Based Competition

Final Thoughts on Organizational Agility

Management in Action

MAKING WALMART AGILE

In 1962, in the small town of Rogers, Arkansas, Sam Walton opened the first Walmart. The concept was simple: offer low prices and great customer service. Clearly the concept was a good one. By 1990, Walmart had become the largest retailer in the United States. Today, Walmart is the largest retailer in the world.[1]

As we've seen with Sears, Toys 'R' Us, and other once dominant retailers, past success doesn't ensure future success. To stay competitive and remain on top, Walmart has had to evolve with the times, which means responding to both internal and external forces. For example, in the 1980s, Walmart was one of the first retailers to implement digital point-of-sale systems for faster and more accurate checkout experiences. In the 1990s, Walmart decided to expand to compete on a global level. And in the 21st century, the retail giant has continued to adapt and change, creating its online store in 2000 and expanding its products and services such as grocery delivery ever since.

That forward-thinking spirit of adaptability and innovation is needed now more than ever. The emergence of Amazon has threatened Walmart's retail primacy like no competitor has in decades. In less than 10 years, Amazon's annual revenues have increased by more than $200 billion, an increase of 700 percent.[2] Walmart's revenues have been flat in comparison. With $500 billion in annual revenue, Walmart is still the current leader in retail, but Amazon is closing the gap. And Walmart knows it.

In response, Walmart managers have begun to reorganize and reinvest, with a focus on e-commerce and re-creating the company's online services. It began acquiring successful and trendy online retailers to gain knowledge and also expand its customer base. Walmart's hope is that these online retailers—such as Jet, Shoes.com, and Bonobos—will be attractive

kevinbrine/123RF

to younger segments of the population that wouldn't ordinarily shop at a Walmart brick-and-mortar store. It purchased India's largest online retailer, Flipkart, to become more competitive in global markets.[3]

Managers at the firm are also working to expand on its already successful online grocery service, partnering with online delivery services for faster and more efficient service.[4] In 2018, Walmart launched its redesigned website and brand new mobile app.[5]

Of course, all of these changes are implemented in pursuit of the same simple concept that served as the opening of the very first Walmart store: the promise to deliver great service and lower prices. The early returns have been looking favorable, as 2018 was Walmart's strongest in nearly a decade. Continued agility will be key to sustained success in the years to come.

Walmart is trying to maintain its position as one of the world's most powerful retail firms, with an organization that enables innovation and demands high performance. As you read this chapter, consider whether Walmart can remain competitive in a profoundly changing business world.

Like Walmart, today's successful companies can't afford to rest on their previous accomplishments. If they do, they easily become vulnerable—to an economic collapse, new competing products, sudden shifts in customer preferences, or countless other environmental shocks and changes. That is, they need to make sure that their structures and systems—and the people within—remain *adaptable*. When structures and systems are designed well, and people can deliver as needed, the organization is flexible and agile enough to succeed in a changing world.[6]

Such an organization is ambidextrous. As some people have the gift of writing with either hand, an **ambidextrous organization** is simultaneously good at *exploitation* (using what it knows to efficiently and quickly perform as needed) and *exploration* (seeking and creating new ways to meet future needs).[7] In this chapter, you will see ways to organize people, information, and work that have helped organizations excel at both exploitation and exploration.

The Responsive Organization

LO 9-1 Discuss why it is critical for organizations to be responsive.

Bottom Line

Speed is vital to an organization's survival. *How can lack of speed kill an organization?*

The formal structure is put in place to control people, decisions, and actions. But in today's fast-changing business environment, responsiveness—quickness, agility, the ability to adapt to changing demands—is vital to a firm's survival.[8]

Many decades after Max Weber wrote about bureaucracy as a rational way to run large modern organizations, two British management scholars (Burns and Stalker) described what they called the **mechanistic organization**.[9] The mechanistic structure they described was similar to Weber's bureaucracy, but they stated further that the modern corporation has a new option. The **organic structure** is much less rigid and, in fact, emphasizes flexibility.

Compared with the mechanistic structure, in the organic structure:

1. Jobholders have broader responsibilities, and they change as needs arise.
2. Communication occurs through advice and information rather than through orders and instructions.
3. Decision making and influence are more decentralized and informal.
4. Expertise is highly valued.
5. Jobholders rely more heavily on judgment than on rules.
6. Commitment to the organization's goals is more important than obedience to authority.
7. Employees depend more on one another and relate more informally and personally.

Exhibit 9.1 contrasts the formal structure of an organization—epitomized by the organization chart—to the informal structure, which is more organic. As you compare these two charts, what do you notice that should concern this company's managers? Astute managers are keenly aware of the network of interactions among the organization's members, and they work within this network to increase agility. Employees who engage actively in formal and informal networks are likely to perform at higher levels.[10] They find and use diverse and valuable information from different parts of the organization to do their jobs better.[11]

The ideas underlying the organic structure and networks are the foundation for the newer, faster-moving forms of organization described in this chapter. To prepare for and adapt to an uncertain future, managers need to be able to respond to fast-appearing threats and opportunities.

---

ambidextrous organization

An organization that is simultaneously good at exploitation and exploration.

mechanistic organization

A form of organization that seeks to maximize internal efficiency.

organic structure

An organizational form that emphasizes flexibility.

EXHIBIT 9.1
Formal and Informal
Organization Structures

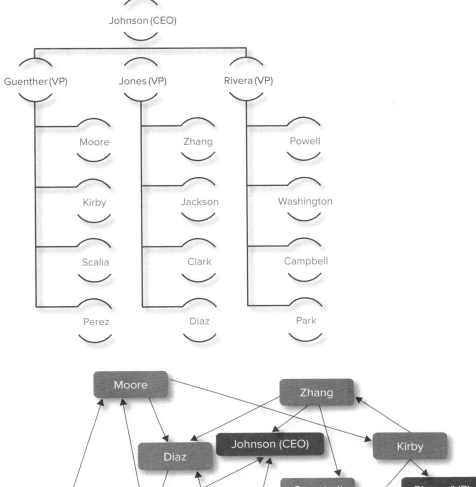

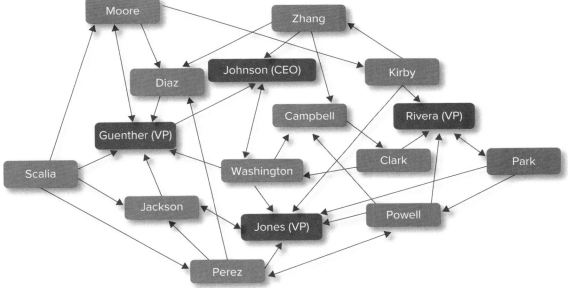

SOURCE: Adapted from Soda, G. and Zaheer, A., "A Network Perspective on Organizational Architecture: Performance Effects of the Interplay of Formal and Informal Organization," *Strategic Management Journal* 33 (2012), pp. 751–71.

Strategy and Organizational Agility

The U.S. military introduced the acronym VUCA—volatility, uncertainty, complexity, and ambiguity—that has become a general shorthand indicating the difficult circumstances leaders must face.[12] Certain strategies, and the structures, processes, and relationships that accompany them, can help an organization respond quickly and effectively to those

LO 9-2 Describe the qualities of an organic organization structure.

challenges. Managers can leverage their people and assets to make the firm more agile and competitive. As described next, these decisions and actions are based on the firm's core capabilities, its strategic alliances, its ability to learn, and its ability to engage all the people in the organization in achieving its objectives.

Organizing around Core Capabilities

A different, new, and important perspective on strategy and organization builds on the concept of core capabilities.[13] As you learned in Chapter 4, a core capability is the knowledge, expertise, or skill that underlies a company's ability to be a leader in providing a range of goods or services.[14] Here we add a useful distinction between two types of capabilities—ordinary and dynamic.[15]

Ordinary capabilities pertain to basic administrative and operational functions needed to produce and sell current products (goods and services). They involve capable people, facilities and equipment, procedures and routines, and administrative coordination. Organizations must have access to such ordinary capabilities, either owning and doing them directly or hiring them out to other providers.

But in a VUCA world, ordinary capabilities alone rarely provide long-term competitive advantage. They can provide temporary advantage in quality, speed, and efficiency, but are easy to imitate as companies hire consultants and implement well-known "best practices."

Dynamic capabilities are "higher-level" strategic activities involving adapting rapidly to (or even proactively shaping; see Chapter 18) the ever-changing business environment. Whereas ordinary capabilities are about doing basic things right, dynamic capabilities are about doing the right things at the right time, based on new product and process development, unique managerial actions, and a change-oriented organizational culture that spots and seizes opportunities.

Dynamic capabilities—sensing change, seizing opportunities, and changing practices faster than competitors do—overarch the organization's structure and can provide the foundations of sustainable competitive advantage.[16]

Dynamic capabilities focus less on efficiency and more on innovation. Developing world-class dynamic capabilities opens the door to a variety of future opportunities. Strategically, this means that companies should commit to excellence and leadership in dynamic capabilities. Organizationally, this means that the corporation should be viewed as a portfolio of capabilities, not just a portfolio of specific businesses.

It's not enough to have valuable resources that provide capabilities; those resources have to be managed in a way that provides an advantage over competitors.[17] Managers must do three things. First, they must accumulate the right resources (such as talented people) by determining what resources they need, acquiring and developing those resources, and eliminating resources that don't provide value. Next, they must combine the resources in ways that give the organization capabilities, such as researching new products or resolving customers' problems. These combinations may involve knowledge sharing and alliances between departments or with other organizations.

Third, managers need to leverage or exploit their resources. They do this by identifying opportunities where their competencies deliver value to customers—say, by creating new products or by delivering existing products better than competitors—and then by coordinating and deploying the resources properly. The nearby "Inclusiveness Works" box discusses further how modifying internal structures can boost the ROI from human capital.

Strategic Alliances

As we discussed in previous chapters, the modern organization has a variety of links with other organizations.[18] Sometimes even competing companies form temporary partnerships that, because of the tensions created by competing and cooperating simultaneously,[19] are more complex than the standard relationships with traditional stakeholders such as suppliers and clients. Today even fierce competitors are working *together* at unprecedented levels to achieve their strategic goals.

---

ordinary capabilities

Capabilities pertaining to basic administrative and operational functions.

---

dynamic capabilities

Higher-level strategic capabilities (compared with ordinary capabilities) that aid rapid adaptation.

Bottom Line

Core capabilities can be a source of quality and innovation. *Does your school have a core capability? If so, what is it, and why do you identify it as such?*

LO 9-3 Identify strategies and dynamic organizational concepts that can improve an organization's responsiveness.

Inclusiveness Works

Engaging Younger Generations

Bridging generational differences is typically not easy, yet it's essential for a thriving and productive workplace. Early career employees tend to have a different perspective on what work means as well as what they find motivating. In addition, approximately 75 percent of workers under the age of 34 believe that job-hopping is beneficial to their career.[20]

From a business standpoint, employee turnover is expensive. A recent study estimated that the cost of employee turnover totaled more than $600 million in 2018 and is likely to increase to $680 million by 2020.[21]

Of course, anyone is more likely to leave a job (or boss) if they don't feel included or if the practices of the business simply don't align with their values. It's important, then, that managers understand the life experiences and perspectives of those new to the workforce. What are some workplace strategies that can help attract and retain young employees?

1. *Flexible work arrangements.* While many older workers are comfortable with more conventional 9-to-5 work hours, many younger workers find this approach stifling and rigid. Having grown up in a mobile and connected world, they want some flexibility with regard to where and when they do their work. Managers need to reassess traditional work models to partially meet

these expectations to attract and retain younger employees.
2. *Involvement in decision making.* Raised by parents who encouraged and valued their opinions, younger employees are likely wanting to be heard even without the benefit of having relevant experience. Managers should look for ways to engage them in projects that build their knowledge of the organization and customers.
3. *Different types of feedback.* Many younger employees prefer more frequent feedback, positive reinforcement, and encouragement to keep them motivated and on track.[22]

Of course, creating an inclusive environment for early career employees can't be done at the expense of more seasoned workers. A pressing challenge for managers is how to modify internal organization structures so they are inclusive of the needs and wants of all generations.

1. How much do you think the generational differences in workplace perspectives and behaviors is overstated? What aspects ring true to you? Which ones seem less relevant?
2. If you were the manager of a workforce that was diverse in age, what strategies would you do to create an inclusive environment?

For example, Coca-Cola, Dr Pepper Snapple Group, and PepsiCo have come together to cut by 20 percent the amount of sugar-based calories in their soft drinks by 2025.[23] Atos, a European IT services company, is joining forces with Google to create artificial intelligence solutions for large companies.[24] In these and other examples, strategic alliances allow participants to respond to customer demands or environmental threats far faster and less expensively than each would be able to do on its own.

A **strategic alliance** is a formal relationship created with the purpose of joint pursuit of mutual goals. Different organizations share administrative authority, form social links, and accept joint ownership. Alliances occur between companies and their competitors, governments, and universities. As with the two previous examples, collaboration often crosses national and cultural boundaries. And for an example of a company that has made downsizing part of its effort to enjoy the advantages of being both big and small, see "Management in Action: Progress Report."

Companies form strategic alliances to develop new technologies, enter new markets, and reduce manufacturing costs. Alliances enable companies to move faster and more efficiently; they also can be the only practical way to bring

strategic alliance

A formal relationship created among independent organizations with the purpose of joint pursuit of mutual goals.

Arne Beruldsen/Shutterstock

Management in Action

WALMART FORGES STRATEGIC ALLIANCES

There was a time not too long ago that Walmart was reluctant to form strategic alliances, preferring instead to go it alone. With the emergence of Amazon as the e-commerce retail leader, those times have changed.

As Walmart continues to focus on and invest in the e-commerce sector, the retail giant has made an about-face when it comes to strategic alliances, partnering with some of the biggest names in the tech industry across not only the United States but the world. As Walmart CEO Doug McMillon put it, "We're learning to partner with others in new ways."[25] Those "others" include such heavy hitters as Google, Microsoft, and Waymo.

Though the partnerships are designed to strengthen Walmart's position in the more unfamiliar territory of e-commerce, its strategy in doing so remains the same: to deliver great service and lower prices. According to Greg Foran, Walmart's U.S. CEO, "For today's customer, the experience we create has to be easy, fast, friendly, and fun."[26]

Walmart's alliance with Google will allow Walmart customers to use Google home devices to shop for most any retail product. In partnering with companies like Waymo, the self-driving vehicle unit of Alphabet, Walmart is testing out different ways of shuttling Walmart customers to stores to pick up orders.

The alliances aren't restricted to U.S. firms by any stretch. Walmart recently formed a partnership with Rakuten, Japan's largest online retailer.[27] This adds to the alliance it had already formed with China's largest online retailer, JD.com. And if it's not partnering with the world's tech giants, Walmart is acquiring them, as it did with its recent acquisition of Flipkart, India's largest online retailer.[28]

Although these partnerships are a relatively new business strategy for Walmart to achieve its goals, they're helping to make the firm more agile and competitive in a retail market space that is more fluid and dynamic than ever.

- What's your assessment of Walmart's focus on forming strategic alliances with tech firms to become more competitive in the digital market space? What are the benefits? What are the potential problems?
- Which alliances will prove most important to Walmart—its domestic alliances with firms such as Google or its overseas alliances with firms such as Rakuten?

Faster Wi-Fi and coffee—a wonderful strategic alliance. Starbucks switched from AT&T to Google to provide free wireless Internet in its 7,000 U.S. stores. This move allows customers to surf the Internet up to 10 times faster.

Phichat Phruksarojanakun/ Shutterstock

together a wide variety of needed specialists. Rather than hiring experts who understand the technology and market segments for each new product, companies can form alliances with partners that already have those experts on board.[29]

Managers typically devote plenty of time to screening potential partners in financial terms. For the alliance to work, the partners also must consider one another's areas of expertise and the incentives involved in the structure of the alliance. A comparison of research and development alliances found that the most innovation occurred when the partners were experts in moderately different types of research. If the partners were very different, they shared ideas and innovated more when the alliance was set up through equity (stock) ownership; for similar partners, more innovation came via research contracts rather than equity.[30]

Managers must foster and develop the human relationships in the partnership that facilitate interpersonal cooperation and coordination of activities.[31] Thus U.S. companies may need to pay extra attention to the human side of alliances. Exhibit 9.2 shows some recommendations for how to do this. In fact, most of the ideas apply not only to strategic alliances but to any type of relationship.[32]

The best alliances are true partnerships that meet these criteria:
1. *Relationship:* Both partners work hard on developing a positive working relationship.
2. *Metrics:* The partners measure how they're going to succeed, not just the end result.
3. *Differences:* The partners embrace differences in one another.
4. *Control:* Both partners encourage collaborative behavior with less emphasis on formal systems and structures.
5. *Management:* The partners manage their internal stakeholders who are involved in the alliance.

SOURCE: Adapted from Hughes, J. and Weiss, J., "Simple Rules for Making Alliances Work," *Harvard Business Review,* November 2007, www.hbr.org.

EXHIBIT 9.2
How I's Can Become We's

Bottom Line
Alliances can increase speed and innovation while lowering costs. *How might an alliance increase innovation?*

The High-Involvement Organization

Participative management—involving employees in decision making—can be a good way to create a competitive advantage. In a **high-involvement organization**, top leaders ensure consensus about the direction in which the business is heading by seeking input from their team and middle managers and sometimes from lower levels, depending on the issue. Task forces, study groups, and other techniques foster participation in important decisions. Also fundamental to the high-involvement organization is continual feedback to participants regarding how they are doing compared with the competition and how effectively they are meeting the strategic agenda.

> Participative management is a good way to create competitive advantage.

high-involvement organization

A type of organization in which top management ensures that there is consensus about the direction in which the business is heading.

The organizational form is relatively flat and decentralized, built around a customer or product (good or service). Employee involvement is particularly powerful when the environment changes rapidly, work is creative, complex activities require coordination and commitment, and firms need major breakthroughs in innovation and speed. A perfect example is high-technology companies facing stiff international competition.[33]

Organizational Size and Agility

One of the most important characteristics of an organization is its size.[34] Large organizations are typically less organic and more bureaucratic. Consider Walmart, which has more than 2 million employees. CEO Doug McMillon is trying to reduce bureaucracy (and revitalize company growth) by encouraging employees to take more initiative. He removed one layer of management from Walmart stores in order to give employees a larger say in how the stores are run.[35]

As firms (and government agencies, nongovernmental organizations (NGOs), and social enterprises) grow, they become more complex structurally. Managers deal with this by introducing more rules, procedures, and paperwork—in short, with bureaucratic controls that increase efficiency but often weaken the ability to innovate.[36]

Let's consider whether and how large companies can be agile, adaptive, and responsive to competitive and consumer demands?

LO 9-4 Explain how a firm can be both big and small.

Bottom Line
Large size often leads to scale economies. *How has General Electric's large size affected its ability to compete?*

The Case for Big

Big was best after World War II, when foreign competition was limited and growth seemed limitless. To meet high demand for its products, U.S. industry embraced high-volume, low-cost manufacturing methods. IBM, General Motors (GM), and Alcoa all grew into global companies during those decades.

Alfred Chandler, a pioneer in strategic management, noted that big companies were the engine of economic growth throughout the 20th century.[37] Size creates scale economies—that is, lower costs per unit of production. Size can offer specific advantages such as lower operating costs, greater purchasing power, and easier access to capital.

Walmart's size gives it the purchasing power to buy merchandise in larger volumes and sell it at lower prices than its competitors can. Size also creates **economies of scope**; materials and processes employed in one product can be used to make related products. With such advantages, huge companies with lots of money may be the best at taking on large foreign rivals in huge global markets.

The Case for Small

But a huge, complex organization can find it hard to manage relationships with customers and among its own units. Too much success can breed complacency, and the resulting inertia hinders change. This is a surefire formula for being left in the dust by hungry competitors.

Giant companies have stumbled as consumers demand a greater diversity of high-quality, customized products supported by excellent service. Some evidence shows that as firms get larger and their market share grows, customers begin to view their products as having lower quality. Also, once a company has captured a big share of the market, future growth is hard because gaining more new customers takes costlier efforts or a fresh approach.

Walmart's low-price strategy helped it become the largest U.S. corporation in terms of sales, but sales growth flattened out. The company's response—cutting labor costs—helped profits in the short term but drove away some shoppers frustrated with unstocked shelves and difficulty finding help. Walmart recently placed last in the American Customer Satisfaction Index for department and discount stores.[38]

Larger companies also are more difficult to coordinate and control. Although size can enhance efficiency by spreading fixed costs over more units, it also may create bureaucratic hassles that constrain performance. General Motors (GM) has operations around the world. Its European operations caused financial losses for nearly two decades because of all of its various activities from designing new models to building cleaner engines. In order to stop losing more money, GM sold its European operations to France's PSA Group.[39] To describe this problem, a new term has entered the business vocabulary: *diseconomies of scale,* or the costs of being too big. "Small is beautiful" has become a favorite phrase of entrepreneurial business managers.[40]

Nimble small firms frequently outmaneuver big bureaucracies. Smaller companies can move fast, provide quality goods and services to targeted market niches, and inspire greater involvement from their people. They introduce new and better products, and they steal market share. The premium now is on flexibility and responsiveness—the unique potential strengths of the small firm.

An extreme example is Kobold Watch, staffed by founder Michael Kobold and three employees. The small company makes and sells premium mechanical wristwatches priced at thousands of dollars each. Kobold advertises online and through word of mouth generated by sales to celebrities, including former president Bill Clinton, Kiefer Sutherland, and Bruce Springsteen. When sales surge, Kobold calls on two other watchmakers to help out as needed. Kobold intentionally limits production to 2,500 watches a year—not just to maintain the prestige of the brand, but also to keep the company small and fast-moving.[41]

Being Big and Small

Small *is* beautiful for unleashing energy and speed. But in buying and selling, size offers market power. The challenge, then, is to be both big and small to capitalize on the advantages of each.

When Intuit grew from a software start-up to an established company selling popular accounting software, it brought in a leader recruited from General Electric, Steve Bennett, to mesh big-company skills with Intuit's entrepreneurial energy. While CEO, Bennett helped the company reevaluate its strategy to find areas of new growth. By focusing on QuickBooks and TurboTax, Intuit captured most of the market for accounting and tax preparation software. The company is also popular among employees as it was named to *Fortune*'s 2018 "100 Best Companies to Work For" list.[42]

economies of scope

Economies in which materials and processes employed in one product can be used to make other, related products.

Bottom Line

Small size may improve speed. *A salesperson learns about a customer's new challenge. Why might a small company be able to react to this information faster?*

The challenge is to be big and act small to capitalize on the advantages of each.

Social Entrepreneurship

Increasing Impact: Scaling Social Enterprises

Social enterprises are organizations that act as businesses but pursue social or environmental goals. They typically begin as small, grassroots efforts whose goal is to create a sustainable organization that helps solve important social problems. For example, Living Goods, a U.S.-based nonprofit, sells essential products such as high-efficiency stoves, fortified foods, and pharmaceuticals "through an Avon-like network of microfranchises in Uganda" that is reducing child deaths by more than 25 percent.[43]

What happens when social enterprises want to scale their operations to help more people? How can they expand globally? Here are some unique issues social enterprises face when planning for growth:

1. *Consider alliances with governments.* Governments are the largest consumers of social investment. If a social enterprise's mission aligns with a government's social investment priorities, the two can form a productive alliance. For example, the G8 governments view social enterprises as a way of "tackling social problems, driving innovation and helping economic growth."[44]
2. *Partner with big businesses.* Big businesses can bring considerable resources to bear on social problems. For this to happen, social enterprises need to develop a viable business model that big businesses are willing to support. Network for Good, an online giving and fundraising platform, was founded in 2001 with the help of such companies as the Cisco Foundation and Yahoo! As of 2019, the social enterprise has processed over $2.5 billion for more than 125,000 nonprofits.[45]
3. *Do not lose sight of what matters.* As a social enterprise grows in size and complexity, it risks

Roberts Publishing Services/McGraw-Hill Education

becoming unresponsive to those whom it originally intended to serve. Selco Solar, a provider of sustainable energy solutions, manages this risk of becoming too big by "incubating others who can replicate their model in other geographic areas, rather than scaling themselves." Selco now has over 500 employees who have helped impact the lives of over 1 million impoverished people.[46] Like for-profit companies, social enterprises need to strike the right balance between big and small.

- As social enterprises try to get larger, what unique challenges do they face?
- What are some of the drawbacks associated with partnering with governments or big businesses?

Here's an alternative perspective: companies such as Starbucks and Amazon are very large companies that work hard to act small and maintain a sense of intimacy with employees and customers. Both are considered among the best-managed companies in the world. To avoid problems of growth and size, they decentralize decision making and organize around small, adaptive, team-based work units.

Like many businesses, many social enterprises want to grow, in order to expand their impact. The nearby "Social Enterprise" box discusses some unique issues related to scaling SEs.

Downsizing   As large companies attempt to gain or regain responsiveness, they sometimes consider downsizing.

Trong Nguyen/Shutterstock

downsizing

The planned elimination of positions or jobs.

Downsizing is the planned elimination of positions or jobs. Common approaches to downsizing include eliminating functions, hierarchical levels, or even whole units.[47] Another option is to replace full-time employees with less expensive part-time or temporary workers. Some companies manage their downsizing better than others by attempting to make the process fair and helpful to all affected.[48]

Recognizing that people will be unemployed, anxious, and perhaps unable to pay their bills, managers usually opt for downsizing only in response to some kind of pressure. Traditionally, companies have downsized when product demand falls and seems unlikely to rebound in the short run. Laying off workers is a way to avoid paying people who aren't needed to produce goods or services, and reduce costs so that the company remains profitable—or at least viable—until the next upturn in business.

Manufacturing in the United States had been hit hard by layoffs and closings in recent years. The last recession forced widespread downsizing across many industries, not just manufacturing. Although companies rehired workers during the recovery, tough competition still dictates that they stay as lean as possible.

You might refer back to our discussion in Chapter 1 about some of the things you can do to manage your own career successfully in an era where downsizing is a normal occurrence.

Customers and the Responsive Organization

LO 9-5 Summarize how firms organize to meet customer requirements.

Bottom Line

Today's customers demand excellent service and new high-quality, low-cost products—fast. *How does a rigid bureaucracy make it difficult to meet all these challenges at once?*

customer relationship management (CRM)

A multifaceted process focusing on creating two-way exchanges with customers to foster intimate knowledge of their needs, wants, and buying patterns.

An organization's strategy and size influence its agility, adaptability, and structure. The point of designing and structuring a responsive, agile organization is to enable it to meet and exceed the expectations of its customers—the people who purchase its good or services and whose continued patronage helps drive sustained success.

Any business unit must take into account at least three core players in the *strategic triangle:* the company itself, the competition, and the customer. Successful organizations use their strengths to create value by meeting customer requirements better than competitors do. In this section, we discuss how organizations maintain and extend a competitive advantage with their customers.

Customer Relationship Management

Customer relationship management (CRM) is a multifaceted process, typically using information technologies, that fosters two-way exchanges with customers so that firms know "intimately" their needs, wants, and buying patterns.[49] Firms acquire this knowledge by applying predictive analytical techniques to the voluminous data (aka, big data) collected from customers. The goal of this analysis is to identify patterns from current and historical data sets in order to make the best possible business decisions.

Ideally, a company can use predictive analysis to figure out how to deliver exactly what customers want.[50] Banana Republic uses big data to predict when someone viewing its website is about to close the window, so the company places a pop-up ad offering a discount to entice the customer to stay.[51] Companies that use CRM effectively learn to both understand and anticipate the needs of current and potential customers. In that way, CRM is part of a business strategy for managing customers to maximize their long-term value to the enterprise.[52]

As you know, customers want quality goods and services, low cost, innovative products, and speed. Traditional thinking is that trade-offs must be made among these basic customer wants. For instance, customers wanted high quality or low costs passed along in the form of low prices. But world-class companies know that the trade-off mentality no longer applies. Customers want it *all*, and they know that somewhere an organization exists that will provide it all.

World-class companies know that they must improve upon the traditional trade-off mentality.

If all companies try to satisfy customers, how can one firm realize a competitive advantage? World-class companies know that almost any advantage is temporary because competitors will strive to catch up. Simply stated—although obviously not easily done—a company attains and retains competitive advantage by continuing to improve. This concept—in Japan famously called *kaizen,* or continuous improvement—is a vital part of operations strategy.

The traditional meaning of "customer" has grown to include internal customers. The word *customer* now refers to any recipient of work—the next person or unit in the production process or wherever the work goes next in the sequence.[53] This highlights the interdependence among units, and means that all functions—not just marketing people—have to be concerned with customer satisfaction. Any recipient of a person's work, whether co-worker, boss, subordinate, or external party, should be viewed as the customer.

OpturaDesign/Shutterstock

Professor Michael Porter offered a deeper and now very popular way to understand how organizations can add customer value to their products. A **value chain** is the sequence of activities that flow from raw materials to the delivery of a good or service, with additional value created at each step. The value chain offers great opportunity to implement socially and environmentally business practices.[54]

You can see a generic value chain in Exhibit 9.3. Each step in the chain adds value to the good or service:

value chain

The sequence of activities that flow from raw materials to the delivery of a good or service, with additional value created at each step.

> *Research and development* focus on innovation and new products.
> *Inbound logistics* receive and store raw materials and distribute them to operations.
> *Operations* transform the raw materials into final product.
> *Outbound logistics* warehouse the product and handle its distribution.
> *Marketing and sales* identify customer requirements and get customers to purchase the product.
> *Service* offers customer support, such as repair, after the item has been bought.

When the total value created—that is, what customers are willing to pay—exceeds the cost of providing the good or service, the result is the profit margin.[55]

EXHIBIT 9.3   Generic Value Chain

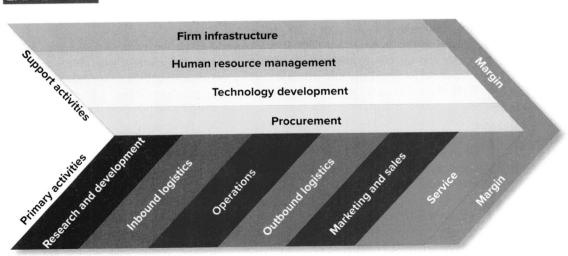

SOURCE: Porter, M., *Competitive Advantage: Creating and Sustaining Superior Performance.* New York: Free Press, 1985.

The Digital World

Managing Customers Today: Engaging in "Social Listening"

Part of engaging in customer relationship management (CRM) for companies in today's social media landscape is knowing that company and employee mistakes can go viral at the speed of light. Tweets about employees treating customers poorly, photos of unhygienic facilities, and recordings of ineffective customer service calls can be posted easily, reaching thousands (even millions) of social media users in minutes. Being able to directly address customer complaints, or quickly realize and then address an issue, is critical to effective "social CRM."[56]

Salesforce's Service Cloud, for example, is used by companies such as Adidas, The Container Store, and Athena Health.[57] Service Cloud software scans for and locates messages about clients' products on social media platforms. When the software detects a problem, Service Cloud agents then step in and offer to help, potentially saving a client's customer relationship.[58]

1. Given how frequently things go viral, how consequential do you think any single negative viral thread is for an organization today?
2. Do you think CRM offers a solution that is agile enough to keep up with the speed of e-commerce and social media?

Managers can add customer value and build competitive advantage by paying close attention to the value chain—each step in it, plus the ways in which each step interacts with the others. For example, Walmart adds customer value via economies of scale, reducing its materials and operations costs, and Amazon adds customer value by developing innovative distribution channels.

An excellent way to leverage the value chain is for different elements of the chain to collaborate in finding and creating new sources of value. Nike shares its business plans and strategies with its suppliers—what it calls its strategic partners—to encourage collaborative thinking. Sales staff communicate with operations staff, before the manufacturing process even starts, to develop new products jointly. Service managers constantly report back to operations about defects and work with operations and suppliers to reduce and eliminate them. Creating productive collaborations can dramatically improve a company's agility and responsiveness.

Quality Initiatives

The effort to be more responsive brings managers face to face with the need to ensure consistently high quality. Systematic ways of meeting that need include total quality management, six sigma, and ISO 9001 standards.

Total quality management (TQM) is a comprehensive approach to improving product quality and thereby customer satisfaction.[59] TQM is characterized by a strong customer orientation (external and internal) and has become an umbrella theme for organizing work. TQM requires integrative mechanisms that aid group problem solving, information sharing, and cooperation across business functions. As a consequence, the walls that separate stages and functions fade, and the organization operates in a more team-oriented manner.[60]

One of the founders of the quality management movement was W. Edwards Deming. When he started, his work was largely ignored by American companies, but it was adopted eagerly by Japanese firms that wanted to shed their products of their post–World War II reputation for shoddiness. The quality emphasis of Japanese car manufacturing was one direct result of Deming's work, which has since been adopted by many American and other companies worldwide. As listed in Exhibit 9.4, Deming's "14 points" of quality emphasized a holistic approach to management that demands intimate understanding of the process—the delicate interaction of materials, machines, and people that determines productivity, quality, and competitive advantage.

---

total quality management (TQM)

An integrative approach to management that supports the attainment of customer satisfaction through a wide variety of tools and techniques that result in high-quality goods and services.

Bottom Line

High quality requires organizationwide commitment. *What happens when the commitment to quality at the top of the company is weaker than the commitment to saving money?*

At six sigma, a product or process is defect-free 99.99966 percent of the time.

1. Create constancy of purpose—strive for long-term improvement rather than short-term profit.

2. Adopt the new philosophy—don't tolerate delays and mistakes.

3. Cease dependence on mass inspection—build quality into the process on the front end.

4. End the practice of awarding business on price tag alone—build long-term relationships.

5. Improve constantly and forever the system of production and service—at each stage.

6. Institute training and retraining—continually update methods and thinking.

7. Institute leadership—provide the resources needed for effectiveness.

8. Drive out fear—people must believe it is safe to report problems or ask for help.

9. Break down barriers among departments—promote teamwork.

10. Eliminate slogans, exhortations, and arbitrary targets—supply methods, not buzzwords.

11. Eliminate numerical quotas—they are contrary to the idea of continuous improvement.

12. Remove barriers to pride in workmanship—allow autonomy and spontaneity.

13. Institute a vigorous program of education and retraining—people are assets, not commodities.

14. Take action to accomplish the transformation—provide a structure that enables quality.

Six Sigma   An approach called **six sigma quality** is one of the most important contributors to total quality management: a set of statistical tools to analyze the causes of product defects. Sigma is the Greek letter used to designate the estimated standard deviation or variation in a process. (The higher the sigma level, the lower the amount of variation and the higher the quality.) The product defects analyzed can include anything that results in customer dissatisfaction—for example, late delivery, wrong shipment, or poor customer service as well as problems with the product itself.

Once the defect is identified, managers then engage the organization in a determined, comprehensive effort to eliminate its causes and reduce it to the lowest practicable level. At six sigma, a product or process is defect-free 99.99966 percent of the time—fewer than 3.4 defects or mistakes per million. Reaching that goal almost always requires a fundamental restructuring of internal processes and relationships with suppliers and customers.

Managers may create teams from all parts of the organization to implement the process improvements that will prevent defects from arising. Motorola, where six sigma was developed, and General Electric, whose success with six sigma helped to make the technique famous, credit the method with helping them improve efficiency and quality. Today many companies are combining six sigma's drive to improve quality with a method of improving efficiency known as lean manufacturing, described later in this chapter. This hybrid effort, often called *lean six sigma*, is a powerful driver of responsiveness and agility.

Commitment to total quality requires a thorough, extensive, integrated approach to organizing. To encourage American companies to make that commitment and achieve excellence, the Malcolm Baldrige National Quality Award was established in 1987. Recent winners include Donor Alliance in Denver, Colorado; Integrated Project Management Company Inc. in Burr Ridge, Illinois; and Memorial Hospital and Health Care Center in Jasper, Indiana.[61]

six sigma quality

A method of systematically analyzing work processes to identify and eliminate virtually all causes of defects, standardizing the processes to reach the lowest practicable level of any cause of customer dissatisfaction.

A company can improve its responsiveness to customers and convey to them clearly that it has done so via certifications from the International Organization for Standardization (known globally as ISO), which sets a wide variety of exacting standards for parts, materials, products, and organizational processes and practices.

ISO 9001

A series of quality standards developed by a committee working under the International Organization for Standardization to improve total quality in all businesses for the benefit of producers and consumers.

ISO 9001   The requirements for a quality management system that will ensure such best practices are spelled out in **ISO 9001**. Any type or size of organization can improve its total quality by successfully meeting specific standards set out in seven principles:[62]

1. *Customer focus*—meeting customer requirements and trying to exceed customer expectations.
2. *Leadership*—establishing unity of purpose and direction, and creating conditions for people to achieve the organization's quality objectives.
3. *Engagement of people*—empowering and engaging people to enhance their capability to create and deliver value.
4. *Process approach*—creating interrelated, coherent processes that are understood and predictable result in consistent and predictable results.
5. *Improvement*—focusing on continuous improvement to maintain performance, react to changes in internal or external conditions, and create new opportunities.
6. *Evidence-based decision making*—making decisions based on the analysis and evaluation of data and information will likely result in desired outcomes.
7. *Relationship management*—managing relationships with all interested parties who may influence organizational performance contributes to sustained success.

U.S. companies first became interested in ISO 9001 because overseas customers, particularly those in the European Union, embraced it. Companies that comply with the quality guidelines of ISO 9001 can apply for official certification. Some countries and companies demand certification as an acknowledgment of compliance before they will do business. Some U.S. customers are making the same demand.

Pursuing certification is not the end of the quality effort, but an initial step. Rather than defining how to operate perfectly, ISO 9001 standards establish practices that enable the organization to keep improving—assuming that it continues to follow these best practices.

Technology and Organizational Agility

LO 9-6 Identify ways that firms organize around different types of technology.

technology

The systematic application of scientific knowledge to a new product, process, or service.

We have discussed strategy, size, and customers as influences on organizational design and agility. We now turn to one more critical factor affecting an organization's structure and responsiveness: its technology.

Broadly, **technology** is the methods, processes, systems, and skills used to transform resources (inputs) into products (outputs). We will discuss technology and innovation more fully in Chapter 17, but here we highlight how technology affects organizational design.

Types of Technology Configurations

Research by Joan Woodward laid the foundation for understanding technology and structure. According to Woodward, three basic technologies characterize how work is done: small batch, large batch, and continuous process. These classifications are equally useful for describing either service or manufacturing technologies. Each differs in terms of volume produced and variety of goods/services offered. Each also has a different influence on how managers organize and structure the work of their organizations.[63]

small batch

Technologies that produce goods and services in low volume.

Small Batch Technologies   When a company provides goods or services in very low volume or **small batches**, it is called a *job shop*. A typical example of a job shop is B & B Tool Company in Bristol, Connecticut. Founded over 50 years ago, the firm manufacturers high precision machine components for such industries as medical, semiconductor, telecommunications, packaging, and aircraft.[64] In the service industry, local restaurants or doctors' offices are job shops because they provide a high variety of low-volume, customized services.

In a small batch organization, structure tends to be organic: not a lot of rules and formal procedures, and (often) decentralized decision making. People engage heavily in mutual adjustment.

Large Batch Technologies   As volume increases, product variety usually decreases. Companies with higher volumes and lower varieties than a job shop use **large batch**, or mass production, technologies. Examples include the auto assembly operations of General Motors, Ford, and Toyota. In the service sector, Panera and Chipotle are good examples. Their production runs are highly standardized, and all customers receive similar (if not identical) products. Machines and robotics tend to replace people in the physical execution of work. People run the machines.

With large batch technology, structure tends to be more mechanistic: more rules and formal procedures, more centralized decision making, and higher spans of control.

Continuous Process Technologies   Companies at the very-high-volume end of the scale use **continuous process** technologies—normally they do not stop and start. International Paper and Occidental Chemicals use continuous process technologies to produce a very limited number of products. People are removed from the physical work itself, which is done entirely by machines and/or computers. In some cases, people run the computers that run the machines.

Continuous process technology requires less monitoring and supervision, so structure can be more organic: fewer rules and regulations and more informal communication.

Organizing for Flexible Manufacturing

Although volume and variety traditionally required trade-offs, companies today try to produce both high-volume and high-variety products at the same time. This is **mass customization**.[65] Automobiles, clothes, computers, and other products are manufactured to match each customer's taste, specifications, and budget. Although this seemed only a fantasy a few years ago, mass customization quickly became prevalent among leading firms. You now can buy clothes cut to your proportions, supplements with the exact blend of the vitamins and minerals you like, and textbooks with chapters chosen by your professor.

Companies want to deliver mass customization at low cost. They organize (see Exhibit 9.5) around a dynamic network of relatively independent operating units.[66] Each unit performs a specific process or task—called a *module*—such as making a component, performing a credit check, or using a particular welding method. Outside suppliers or vendors may perform some modules.

Different modules join forces to make the good or provide a service. The unique requests of each customer determine when and how the various modules interact with one another. The manager's responsibility is to make it easier and less costly for modules to come together, complete their tasks, and then recombine to meet the next customer demand.

Mass customization is a never-ending campaign to expand the number of ways a company can satisfy customers.

Dell revolutionized the concept of mass customization. The production process from order to delivery is managed electronically, which allows Dell to build servers efficiently and its customers to know where their server is during each step of the process.

Paul Sakuma/AP Images

large batch	continuous process	mass customization
Technologies that produce goods and services in high volume.	A process that is highly automated and has a continuous production flow.	The production of varied, individually customized products at the low cost of standardized, mass-produced products.

EXHIBIT 9.5
Key Features in Mass Customization

Area	High Variety and Customization
Product design	Collaborative design; significant input from customers.
	Short product development cycles.
	Constant innovation.
Operations and processes	Flexible processes.
	Business process reengineering (BPR).
	Use of modules.
	Continuous improvement (CI).
	Reduced setup and changeover times.
	Reduced lead times.
	JIT delivery and processing of materials and components.
	Production to order.
	Shorter cycle times.
Quality management	Quality measured in customer delight.
	Defects treated as capability failures.
Organizational structure	Dynamic network of relatively autonomous operating units.
	Learning relationships.
	Integration of the value chain.
	Team-based structure.
Workforce management	Empowerment of employees.
	High value on knowledge, information, and diversity of employee capabilities.
	New product teams.
	Broad job descriptions.
Emphasis	Low-cost production of high-quality, customized products.

SOURCE: Reprinted with permission of APICS—The Educational Society for Resource Management, *Production and Inventory Management* 41, no. 1 (2000), pp. 56–65.

computer-integrated manufacturing (CIM)

The use of computer-aided design and computer-aided manufacturing to sequence and optimize multiple production processes.

Computer-Integrated Manufacturing   Mass customization is made possible by **computer-integrated manufacturing (CIM)**, which links computerized production efforts. Two major elements of CIM, computer-aided design and computer-aided manufacturing, share data for product design, testing, manufacturing, and quality control.

These systems can produce high-variety and high-volume products at the same time.[67] They may also offer greater control and predictability of production processes, reduced waste, faster throughput times, and higher quality. Suuchi, Inc., based in Bergen, New Jersey, uses technology and automation to design and manufacture women's clothing, bags, and home goods like cushion covers. Supplier to several American fashion brands, Suuchi can replenish inventory in as quickly as 5 days.[68]

But managers cannot buy their way out of competitive trouble simply by investing in superior technology alone. They also must ensure that their organization has the necessary strategic and people strengths.

flexible factories

Manufacturing plants that have short production runs, are organized around products, and use decentralized scheduling.

Flexible Factories   CIM enables **flexible factories**, which serve customers needing fast turnaround on relatively small orders. In contrast to traditional factories, flexible factories have short production runs, organize work flow around products, and use decentralized scheduling.[69] Instead of moving large orders of standard products through assembly lines, flexible factories have work cells or teams focus on one product at a time. The people on the shop floor doing the work make scheduling decisions, so they can adapt schedules as needed.

Lean Manufacturing Another organizing approach, **lean manufacturing**, strives for the highest possible productivity and total quality, cost-effectively, by eliminating unnecessary steps in the production process and continually striving for improvement. Rejects are unacceptable, and underused staff, overhead, and inventory are considered wasteful. Well-managed lean production allows a company to develop, produce, and distribute products with half or less of the human effort, space, tools, time, and overall cost.[70]

The emphasis is on quality, speed, and flexibility more than on cost, efficiency, and hierarchy. A well-known example is small in detail but large in symbolism: Line workers sometimes have authority to immediately halt the operation and signal for help if they spot a problem. That's a lot of delegated power and discretion, given up by management to operative-level workers in the interest of flexibility, quality, and speedy problem solving.

The lean approach is used for services as well as manufacturing. Banks use lean principles to support their growth strategies, energy companies to lower costs, and retailers to improve customer service.[71] Dana White, CEO of Detroit-based beauty salon Paralee Boyd, hired engineers from car manufacturers to help her implement lean methods in designing her salon.[72]

Many companies have tried to become leaner by cutting overhead costs, laying off operative-level workers, eliminating layers of management, and using capital equipment more efficiently. But if the move to lean manufacturing is simply a harsh, haphazard cost-cutting approach, the result will be chaos, overworked people, and low morale.

Meeting the conditions specified in Exhibit 9.6 helps to ensure that the lean approach works well.

lean manufacturing

An operation that strives to achieve the highest possible productivity and total quality, cost-effectively, by eliminating unnecessary steps in the production process and continually striving for improvement.

Bottom Line
Lean manufacturing strives for high quality, speed, sustainability, and low cost. *Which of the quality improvement approaches could be combined with lean manufacturing?*

Some hospitals use lean principles to reduce costs and patient waiting times while improving safety.

Ariel Skelley/Getty Images

People are broadly trained rather than specialized.
Communication is informal and horizontal among line workers.
Equipment is general-purpose.
Work is organized in teams, or cells, that produce a group of similar products.
Supplier relationships are long-term and cooperative.
Product development is concurrent, not sequential, and is done by cross-functional teams.

EXHIBIT 9.6
Conditions That Support Lean Manufacturing

SOURCES: Sahin, F., "Manufacturing Competitiveness: Different Systems to Achieve the Same Results," *Production and Inventory Management Journal* 41, no. 1 (First Quarter 2000), pp. 56–65; Vasilash, G. S., "Flexible Thinking: How Need, Innovation, Teamwork a Whole Bunch of Machining Centers Have Transformed TRW Tillsonburg into a Model of Lean Manufacturing," *Automotive Manufacturing & Production* 111, no. 10 (October 1999), pp. 64–65.

Organizing for Speed: Time-Based Competition

Companies worldwide have devoted so much energy to improving product quality that high quality is now the prevailing standard in many industries. Competition has driven quality to such heights—although less lofty when firms operate primarily on a low-cost basis—that quality alone is no longer enough to differentiate one competitor from another. Time is an additional advantage that can separate market leaders from also-rans.[73]

> Time is a key competitive advantage that can separate market leaders from also-rans.

Companies must learn what the customer needs and meet those needs as quickly as possible. **Time-based competition (TBC)** refers to strategies that reduce the total time needed to deliver the good or service. TBC has several key organizational elements: logistics, just-in-time (JIT), and concurrent engineering.

time-based competition (TBC)

Strategies aimed at reducing the total time needed to deliver a good or service.

logistics

The movement of the right goods in the right amount to the right place at the right time.

Logistics   The movement of resources into the organization (inbound) and products from the organization to its customers (outbound) is called **logistics**. Like the supply chain (Chapter 2), logistics can become a vital advantage when managed well.

The world of logistics includes the great mass of parts, materials, and products moving via trucks, trains, planes, and ships from and to every region of the globe. Depending on the product, duplication and inefficiency in distribution can cost far more than making the product itself, and slowdowns can cause products to go out of stock so that consumers choose alternatives.

One technology that helps some companies improve logistics efficiency and speed is radio frequency identification (RFID) tags. When manufacturers label their products with RFID tags, automated readers track where each product is in the distribution system, including which items are selling in each store. Macy's and Dillard's use RFID tags on apparel and shoes for inventory tracking; this ensures that items are replenished and in front of customers during peak selling periods.[74]

Walmart is trying to keep its well-known leadership role in distribution by asking suppliers to use RFID. However, many of them cannot afford to institute the new system while also meeting Walmart's demands to keep prices at a minimum.[75]

just-in-time (JIT)

A system that calls for subassemblies and components to be manufactured in very small lots and delivered to the next stage of the production process just as they are needed.

Just-in-Time Operations   An additional element of TBC is **just-in-time (JIT)** operations. JIT manufactures subassemblies and components in very small lots and delivers them to the next stage in the process precisely at the time needed (just in time). A customer order triggers a factory order and the production process. The supplying work centers do not produce the next lot of product until the consuming work center requires it. Even external suppliers deliver to the company just in time.

Just-in-time is a companywide philosophy oriented toward eliminating waste and improving materials throughout all operations. It reduces excess inventory and costs. The ultimate goal of JIT is to serve the customer better by providing higher levels of quality and service.

Dell was an early and effective just-in-time operation. Production of a customized computer begins upon receiving a consumer's order with specifications. Contrast this approach with traditional production methods, which require extremely costly warehousing of inventory and parts, uncertain production runs, considerable waste, no customizing capability, and lengthy delivery times.

JIT represents a number of key production and organizational concepts, including:

Elimination of waste. Eliminate all waste of time, people, machinery, space, and materials.

Perfect quality. Produce perfect parts and produce products exactly when needed in the exact quantities needed.

Reduced cycle times. Reduce setup times for equipment, move parts only short distances (machinery is placed in closer proximity), and eliminate all delays.

Employee involvement. The workers make production decisions. Managers and supervisors are coaches. Top management pledges that there will never be layoffs due to employees finding new efficiencies.

Value-added manufacturing. Do only those things that add value to the finished product. If it doesn't add value, don't do it. For example, inspection does not add value to the finished product, so make the product correctly the first time so inspection is no longer necessary.

Discovery of problems and prevention of recurrence. Foolproofing, or fail-safing, is a key component of JIT. People try to find the weak link in the chain by forcing problem areas to the surface in order to take preventive measures.

JIT has limits. It's not the most efficient choice when the costs of delivery exceed the costs of storage. And if suppliers have trouble fulfilling orders, the whole system breaks down. JIT requires close ties with suppliers, so finding ready replacements can be difficult.

Concurrent Engineering   JIT is a vital component of TBC, but JIT traditionally concentrates on reducing time in only one function: manufacturing. TBC attempts to deliver speed in *all* functions—product development, manufacturing, logistics, and services. Customers will not be impressed if you manufacture quickly but it takes weeks for them to receive their products or get a problem solved.

Many companies use concurrent (sometimes called simultaneous) engineering as a cornerstone of their TBC strategy. **Concurrent engineering**—also an important component of total quality management—is a major departure from the old development process that did various functional tasks sequentially. When R&D completed its part of the project, the work was passed over the wall to engineering, which completed its task and passed it over the wall to manufacturing, and so on. This process was highly inefficient, and errors took a long time to correct.

In contrast, concurrent engineering uses a team-based approach to incorporate the perspectives of all functions—and customers and suppliers—from the beginning of the process. This results in a higher-quality product that is designed for efficient manufacturing *and* meeting customer needs.[76] ADDA, a UK company that builds steel reinforcements, has its engineers work with designers and constructors as part of its fully integrated building information model (BIM). With more communication during the design process, they coordinate and perform far more effectively.[77]

Some managers resist the idea of concurrent engineering. Why should marketing, product planning and design, and R&D allow manufacturing to get involved in their work? First, decisions made during the early, product concept stage determine most of the manufacturing cost and quality. Second, manufacturing can offer ideas about the product because of its experience with the prior generation of the product and with direct customer feedback. Third, the other functions can learn early on what manufacturing can and cannot do. Fourth, when manufacturing is involved from the start, it is a full and true partner and will be more committed to decisions it helped make.

Relevant functions communicating with each other regularly creates more opportunity to improve processes, maximize efficiency, and reduce cost.

Glow Images

Final Thoughts on Organizational Agility

You know now that each major approach to organizing has strengths and limitations. Know also that the advantages of even innovative, leading-edge structures and systems are likely to be short-lived if they become fixed rather than remain flexible. Smart managers and smart competitors soon catch up.

Today's advantages are tomorrow's table stakes: the minimum requirements that need to be met if an organization expects to be a major player. To retain or gain a competitive edge, managers should remember the principle with which we opened this chapter: The best organizations—and this includes the best managers within them—do not sit still. They keep thinking strategically, and continually improve their operations.

concurrent engineering

A design approach in which all relevant functions cooperate jointly and continually in a maximum effort aimed at producing high-quality products that meet customers' needs.

Management in Action

TRYING TO BECOME THE WORLD'S MOST AGILE RETAIL GIANT

Although Walmart's focus has been on strengthening its position in the digital retail space, its ultimate goal goes beyond that. With nearly 12,000 brick-and-mortar retail locations worldwide, Walmart is trying to configure itself to be able to sell as many products as possible across as many platforms as possible.[78] To be successful in its promise to deliver great service and lower prices, heavy focus and investment in technology was, of course, essential. But Walmart isn't stopping there.

Recently, Walmart has been reducing its overall workforce, laying off in-store personnel as well as those in the corporate headquarters.[79] Part of that downsizing is a result of Walmart continuing to streamline its in-store services. For years, it's been testing different cashierless payment methods with varying degrees of success.[80]

But its past challenges won't deter it from continuing to innovate. It opened a new store in Dallas called Sam's Club Now, which is a response to Amazon's new brick-and-mortar stores Amazon Go. The company newsletter described it as "putting Sam's Club on the cutting edge of innovation . . . using all available technologies—including computer vision, AR, machine learning, artificial intelligence, robotics."[81]

Walmart is also trying to streamline its supply chain. In 2018, it announced it would be closing approximately 10 percent of its Sam's Club locations. Walmart's announcement said, "Transforming our business means managing our real estate portfolio—we need a strong fleet of clubs that are fit for the future. . . . We've decided to right-size our fleet and better align our locations with our strategy."[82] Not only would the cuts reduce workforce and overhead costs, but many warehouses would be converted to e-commerce hubs for more effective online orders and deliveries.

Of course, becoming more streamlined and agile doesn't guarantee success, and it doesn't automatically result in consistent results. Walmart experienced higher than expected growth in 2018, but it also cut its earnings forecast for 2019.[83] In trying to maintain its status as the world's retail giant, Walmart will continue its strategy to become more agile. The question will be how well it's able to transform itself to execute that strategy.

- What do you think of Walmart's decision to close warehouses and reduce its workforce? Do you think it will prove effective? Why or why not?
- Walmart is often in the news. Does it seem like its strategy to become more agile is working today? Why or why not?

KEY TERMS

ambidextrous organization, p. 270

computer-integrated manufacturing (CIM), p. 284

concurrent engineering, p. 287

continuous process, p. 283

customer relationship management, (CRM), p. 278

downsizing, p. 278

dynamic capabilities, p. 272

economies of scope, p. 276

flexible factories, p. 284

high-involvement organization, p. 275

ISO 9001, p. 282

just-in-time (JIT), p. 286

large batch, p. 283

lean manufacturing, p. 285

logistics, p. 286

mass customization, p. 283

mechanistic organization, p. 270

ordinary capabilities, p. 272

organic structure, p. 270

six sigma quality, p. 281

small batch, p. 282

strategic alliance, p. 273

technology, p. 282

time-based competition (TBC), p. 286

total quality management (TQM), p. 280

value chain, p. 279

RETAINING WHAT YOU LEARNED

In Chapter 9, you learned that organizations exert control internally through formal structures and must respond to fast-changing demands in their environments. Organic structures, which are flexible in nature, are decentralized, informal, and guided by the actions of people with broad responsibilities. Certain strategies and organizational forms improve responsiveness, including core capabilities, strategic alliances, learning organizations, and high-involvement organizations. Small firms have certain advantages over their larger counterparts, including the ability to act quickly, respond to customer demands, and serve small niches. The ideal organization today harnesses the power of large firms while staying flexible. Driven to meet customer needs, firms adopt the principles of continuous improvement, total quality management, and six sigma quality (often combined with lean manufacturing). Reengineering efforts completely overhaul processes with the goal of providing world-class customer service. To organize for flexible manufacturing, organizations pursue mass customization via computer-integrated manufacturing and lean manufacturing. To organize for time-based competition, firms strengthen their logistics operations, consider just-in-time operations, and use concurrent engineering.

LO 9-1 Discuss why it is critical for organizations to be responsive.

- Organizations have a formal structure to help control what goes on within them.
- But to survive today, firms need more than control—they need responsiveness. They must act quickly and adapt to fast-changing demands.

LO 9-2 Describe the qualities of an organic organization structure.

- The organic form emphasizes flexibility. Organic organizations are decentralized, informal, and dependent on the judgment and expertise of people with broad responsibilities.
- The organic form is not a single formal structure but a concept that underlies all the new forms discussed in this chapter.

LO 9-3 Identify strategies and dynamic organizational concepts that can improve an organization's responsiveness.

- New and emerging organizational concepts and forms include core capabilities, strategic alliances, learning organizations, and high-involvement organizations.

LO 9-4 Explain how a firm can be both big and small.

- Historically, large organizations have had important advantages over small organizations. Today small size has advantages, including the ability to act quickly, respond to customer demands, and serve small niches.
- The ideal firm today combines the advantages of both large and small. It creates many small, flexible units, while corporate levels add value by taking advantage of size and power.

LO 9-5 Summarize how firms organize to meet customer requirements.

- Firms have embraced principles of continuous improvement, total quality management, and six sigma quality (often combined with lean manufacturing) to respond to customer needs.
- Baldrige criteria and ISO 9001 standards help firms organize to meet high quality specifications.
- Extending these, reengineering efforts are directed at completely overhauling processes to provide world-class customer service.

LO 9-6 Identify ways that firms organize around different types of technology.

- Organizations tend to move from organic structures to mechanistic structures and back to organic structures as they transition from small batch to large batch and continuous process technologies.
- For flexible manufacturing, organizations pursue mass customization via computer-integrated manufacturing and lean manufacturing.
- To organize for time-based competition, firms strengthen their logistics operations, consider just-in-time operations, and use concurrent engineering.

DISCUSSION QUESTIONS

1. Discuss evidence you have seen of the imperatives for change, flexibility, and responsiveness faced by today's firms.
2. Describe large, bureaucratic organizations with which you have had contact that have not responded flexibly to customer demands. Also describe examples of satisfactory responsiveness. What do you think accounts for the differences between the responsive and non-responsive organizations?
3. Considering the potential advantages of large and small size, would you describe the feel of your college or university as big, small, or small within big? Why? What might make it feel different?
4. What is a core capability? What would you say are the core capabilities of Toyota, Walmart, and Apple? Brainstorm some creative new products and markets to which these capabilities could be applied.
5. If you were going into business for yourself, what would be your personal core capabilities? What capabilities do you have now, and what capabilities will you develop? Describe what your role would be in a

network organization and the capabilities and roles of other firms you would want in your network.

6. Using an Internet search engine, search for "strategic alliance" and identify three recently formed alliances. For each alliance, identify whether the companies' other products are generally competitors or complementary products. What are the goals of each alliance? What brought them together? Discuss how you think a strategic alliance is or is not an effective way for these organizations to meet their goals.

7. What skills will you need to work effectively in (a) a learning organization, and (b) a high-involvement organization? Be specific, generating long lists. Would you enjoy working in these environments? Why or why not? What can you do to prepare yourself for these eventualities?

EXPERIENTIAL EXERCISES

9.1   Mechanistic and Organic Structures

OBJECTIVES

1. To think about your own preferences when it comes to working in a particular organization structure.

2. To examine aspects of organizations by using as an example this class you are a member of.

INSTRUCTIONS

1. Complete the Mechanistic and Organic Worksheet here.

2. Meet in groups of four to six persons. Share your data from the worksheet. Discuss the reasons for your responses and analyze the factors that probably encouraged your instructor to choose the type of structure that now exists.

Mechanistic and Organic Worksheet

1. Indicate your general preference for working in one of these two organization structures by circling the appropriate response:

| Mechanistic | 1 | 2 | 3 | 4 | 5 | 6 | 7 | 8 | 9 | 10 | Organic |

2. Indicate your perception of the form of organization that is used in this class by circling the appropriate response for each item:

A. **Task role definition**

| Rigid | 1 | 2 | 3 | 4 | 5 | 6 | 7 | 8 | 9 | 10 | Flexible |

B. **Communication**

| Vertical | 1 | 2 | 3 | 4 | 5 | 6 | 7 | 8 | 9 | 10 | Multidirectional |

C. **Decision making**

| Centralized | 1 | 2 | 3 | 4 | 5 | 6 | 7 | 8 | 9 | 10 | Decentralized |

D. **Sensitivity to the environment**

| Closed | 1 | 2 | 3 | 4 | 5 | 6 | 7 | 8 | 9 | 10 | Open |

SOURCE: From Davis, Keith and Newstrom, John W., *Human Behavior at Work*, p. 346. Copyright ©1993 McGraw-Hill Global Education Holdings LLC. All rights reserved. Used with permission.

9.2   The Woody Manufacturing Company

OBJECTIVE

To apply the concepts learned about structure and agility at the individual, group, and organizational levels in designing the Woody Manufacturing Company.

TASK 1 (INDIVIDUAL ASSIGNMENT)

a. Read the following case study of the Woody Manufacturing Company.

b. Review the chapter carefully and choose the organizational design orientation that you feel can best guide you in developing the design for Mr. Woody.

c. Write down your thoughts on alternative management structures, pay systems, and allocation of work to individuals and groups.

TASK 2 (TEAM ASSIGNMENT)

a. Get together with your team and develop a proposal for Mr. Woody that, if followed, would help him fulfill his vision.

b. Prepare a five-minute presentation. Your typewritten team proposal is due prior to your team presentation in Mr. Woody's conference room.

Designing a New Furniture Company

Mr. Woody, the owner/operator of a small furniture company specializing in the manufacture of high-quality bar stools, has experienced a tremendous growth in demand for his products. He has standing orders for $750,000. Consequently, Mr. Woody has decided to expand his organization and attack the market aggressively. His stated mission is "to manufacture world-class products that are competitive in the world market in quality, reliability, performance, and profitability." He would like to create a culture where "pride, ownership, employment security, and trust" are a way of life. He just finished a set of interviews, and he has hired 32 new workers with the following skills:

Four skilled craftspeople.

Ten people with some woodworking experience.

Twelve people with no previous woodworking experience or other skills.

One nurse.

One schoolteacher.

One bookkeeper.

Three people with some managerial experience in nonmanufacturing settings.

Mr. Woody (with your help) must now decide how to design his new organization. This design will include the management structure, pay system, and the allocation of work to individuals and groups. The bar stool–making process has 15 steps:

1. Wood is selected.
2. Wood is cut to size.
3. Defects are removed.
4. Wood is planed to exact specifications.
5. Joints are cut.
6. Tops are glued and assembled.
7. Legs/bases are prepared.
8. Legs/bases are attached to tops.
9. Bar stools are sanded.
10. Stain is applied.
11. Varnish is applied.
12. Bar stools are sanded.
13. Varnish is reapplied.
14. Bar stools are packaged.
15. Bar stools are delivered to the customer.

Mr. Woody currently manufactures three kinds of bar stools (pedestal, four-legged corner, and four-legged recessed). There is no difference in the difficulty of making the three types of bar stools. Major cost variations have been associated with defective wood, imprecise cuts, and late deliveries to customers. Mr. Woody must decide how to organize his company to maintain high quality and profits.

He has thought about several options. He could have some individuals perform the first step for all types of bar stools; he could have an individual perform several steps for one type of bar stool; or he could have a team perform some combination of steps for one or more bar stools. He wonders whether how he organized would affect quality or costs. He's also aware that although the demand for all types of bar stools has been roughly equal over the long run, there were short periods where one type of bar stool was in greater demand than the others. Because Mr. Woody wants to use his people effectively, he has committed an expert in work design to help him set up an optimal organization.

Concluding Case

DIY STORES

DIY Stores is a nationwide chain that offers every tool and supply for repairing and maintaining a home. Besides the wide variety of products, tools, and services, what sets DIY apart is its sales associates. The company hires experienced do-it-yourselfers and retired trade workers, assigns them to work in departments where their know-how is relevant, provides training in new products and creative methods, and pays them a little more than they could earn by working for another retailer. Together these efforts make DIY Stores a place where shoppers can go to get all the ingredients and advice they need for their project to succeed.

Over the past couple of decades, however, consumers have found an alternative to getting advice from workers in a store: Many prefer to do their research online. If consumers can find online a "how to" article or view an instructional YouTube video to figure out the best way to fix a leaky toilet

or make a small bedroom look airy and bright, why trek into a store to ask? Essentially, the Internet put DIY's competitive advantage at risk. The retailer needed to change with the times.

DIY's solution was to go where the consumers were: online. Management decided the company needed to supplement its in-store experts with online experts, employees who shared the same kinds of information on the Internet as they did in the stores. The company's corporate communications department was charged with developing a plan for this effort.

The corporate communications department initially thought the most efficient approach would be to hire a team of writers to work in offices at headquarters, blogging about new products and maintenance tips. But when they presented this plan to top management, one of the vice presidents raised a question: The company's salespeople were its base of knowledge. Why bring in new people? Why not figure out a way to use the human assets the company already had?

The communications people went back to work and arrived at an unusual plan. The company would identify Internet-savvy sales associates and create a new position for them. The associates who accepted the new position would work three days a week in a store and two days a week in an office, with their schedules staggered so that the online response team would be active seven days a week. The company's executives were enthusiastic about this plan.

After a lengthy recruitment process, 2,000 associates were hired for this new hybrid position. Meanwhile, the company built an online "Do It with Us" web page where customers could submit questions, read tips, share ideas, and find links to information about new products available at DIY's stores.

After a three-day training program, the sales associates started the online conversation with DIY. Within months, they and the site's visitors had started thousands of conversation threads. And in an unexpected development, the sales associates also became a valued source of knowledge for DIY's other employees. In stores, at headquarters, and in the regional offices, if someone wants product or project information, they often start their search at the "Do It with Us" web page.

DISCUSSION QUESTIONS

1. How would you assess DIY's agility in adapting to the challenges presented by online access to repair and renovation information?

2. What else can DIY do to address customer needs and remain competitive in the digital space?

3. If you were an employee, would you appreciate a hybrid position like the ones established at DIY? Why or why not?

ENDNOTES

1. Peter Carbonara, "Walmart, Amazon Top World's Largest Retail Companies," *Fortune,* June 6, 2018, https://www.forbes.com/sites/petercarbonara/2018/06/06/worlds-largest-retail-companies-2018/#67c5f7fe13e6.

2. "Net Sales Revenue of Amazon from 2004 to 2018 (in billion U.S. dollars)," *Statista,* https://www.statista.com/statistics/266282/annual-net-revenue-of-amazoncom/ accessed March 24, 2019.

3. Monique Claiborne, "2 Things You Can Learn from Walmart's Reinvention," *Inc.,* https://www.inc.com/monique-claiborne/2-lessons-on-walmarts-reinvention-that-every-entre.html accessed March 24, 2019.

4. "Walmart 'Delivers' on New Partnerships," *Store Brands,* https://storebrands.com/walmart-delivers-new-partnerships accessed March 24, 2019.

5. Greg Swan, "Why Walmart's Ecommerce Strategy Makes Them a Contender against Amazon," *CP Strategy,* January 21, 2019, https://www.cpcstrategy.com/blog/2019/01/walmart-ecommerce/.

6. C. Helfat and J. Martin, "Dynamic Managerial Capabilities: Review and Assessment of Managerial Impact on Strategic Change," *Journal of Management* 41 (2015), pp. 1281–1312.

7. C. O'Reilly and M. Tushman, "Ambidexterity as a Dynamic Capability: Resolving the Innovator's Dilemma," Research Paper no. 1963, Stanford Graduate School of Business, March 2007, http://ssrn.com/abstract 5978493; C. A. O'Reilly III and M. Tushman, "Organizational Ambidexterity: Past, Present, and Future," *Academy of Management Perspectives* 27 (2013), pp. 324–38.

8. P. Sebastian, J. Fourne, J. Jansen, and T. Mom, "Strategic Agility in MNEs," *California Management Review* 56 (2014), pp. 13–38; P. M. Wright, L. Dyer, and M. G. Takla, "What's Next? Key Findings from the 1999 State-of-the-Art and Practice Study," *Human Resource Planning* 22, no. 4 (1999), pp. 12–20; Donald Sull, "How to Thrive in Turbulent Markets," *Harvard Business Review,* February 2009, pp. 78–88.

9. T. Burns and G. Stalker, *The Management of Innovation* (London: Tavistock, 1961); W. Sine, H. Mitsuhashi, and D. Kirsch, "Revisiting Burns and Stalker: Formal Structure and New Venture Performance in Emerging Economic Sectors," *Academy of Management Journal* 49 (2006), pp. 121–32.

10. G. Soda and A. Zaheer, "A Network Perspective on Organizational Architecture: Performance Effects of the Interplay of Formal and Informal Organization," *Strategic Management Journal* 33 (2012), pp. 751–71.

11. G. Soda and A. Zaheer, "A Network Perspective on Organizational Architecture: Performance Effects of the Interplay of Formal and Informal Organization," *Strategic Management Journal* 33 (2012), pp. 751–71.

12. P. Schoemaker, S. Heaton, and D. Teece, "Innovation, Dynamic Capabilities, and Leadership," *California Management Review* 61 (2018), pp. 15–42.

13. G. Hamel and C. K. Prahalad, "Competing for the Future," *Harvard Business Review,* July–August 1994, pp. 122–28.

14. G. Hamel and C. K. Prahalad, "Competing for the Future," *Harvard Business Review,* July–August 1994, pp. 122–28; C. Helfat and J. Martin, "Dynamic Managerial Capabilities: Review and Assessment of Managerial Impact on Strategic Change," *Journal of Management* 41 (2015), pp. 1281–1312.

15. D. J. Teece, "The Foundations of Enterprise Performance: Dynamic and Ordinary Capabilities in an (Economic) Theory of Firms," *Academy of Management Perspectives* 28 (2014), pp. 328–52.

16. P. Schoemaker, S. Heaton, and D. Teece, "Innovation, Dynamic Capabilities, and Leadership," *California Management Review* 61 (2018), pp. 15–42.

17. D. G. Sirmon, M. A. Hitt, and R. D. Ireland, "Managing Firm Resources in Dynamic Environments to Create Value: Looking inside the Black Box," *Academy of Management Review* 32, no. 1 (2007), pp. 273–92.

18. S. Albers, F. Wohlgezogen, and E. Zajac, "Strategic Alliance Structures: An Organization Design Perspective," *Journal of Management* 42 (2016), pp. 582–614.

19. D. R. Gnyawali and T. R. Charleton, "Nuances in the Interplay of Competition and Cooperation: Towards a Theory of Coopetition," *Journal of Management* 44 (2018), pp. 2511–34.

20. Jean Chatzky, "Job-Hopping Is on the Rise. Should You Consider Switching Roles to Make More Money?" *CNBC,* April 24, 2018, https://www.nbcnews.com/better/business/job-hopping-rise-should-you-consider-switching-roles-make-more-ncna868641.

21. Chastity Fox, "Work Institute Releases National Employee Retention Report," Work Institute, May 1, 2018, https://workinstitute.com/about-us/news-events/articleid/2259/2018%20retention%20report.

22. David Villa, "All You Need to Know to Motivate Millennials," *Forbes,* March 30, 2018, https://www.

forbes.com/sites/forbesagencycouncil/2018/03/30/
all-you-need-to-know-to-motivate-millennials/#7d17bda960ae.

23. "How Coca-Cola Is Helping to Reduce Sugar and Bring the Industry's Balance Calories Initiative to Life in East Los Angeles," Coca-Cola Company, December 21, 2017, https://www.coca-colacompany.com.

24. "Atos and Google Cloud Form a Global Partnership to Deliver Secure Hybrid Cloud, Machine Learning and Collaboration Solutions to the Enterprise," news release, Atos, April 24, 2018, https://atos.net.

25. Matthew Boyle, "A Guide to Walmart's Ragtag Alliance against Amazon," *Bloomberg,* August 7, 2018, https://www.bloomberg.com/news/features/2018-08-07/walmart-s-built-a-ragtag-alliance-of-tech-firms-to-battle-amazon.

26. Matthew Boyle, "A Guide to Walmart's Ragtag Alliance against Amazon," *Bloomberg,* August 7, 2018, https://www.bloomberg.com/news/features/2018-08-07/walmart-s-built-a-ragtag-alliance-of-tech-firms-to-battle-amazon.

27. Daphne Howland, "Walmart, Rakuten Announce 'Strategic Alliance,'" *Retail Dive,* January 26, 2018, https://www.retaildive.com/news/walmart-rakuten-announce-strategic-alliance/515666/.

28. Monique Claiborne, "2 Things You Can Learn from Walmart's Reinvention," *Inc.,* https://www.inc.com/monique-claiborne/2-lessons-on-walmarts-reinvention-that-every-entre.html accessed March 24, 2019.

29. G. Slowinski, E. Hummel, A. Gupta, and E. R. Gilmont, "Effective Practices for Sourcing Innovation," *Research-Technology Management,* January–February 2009, pp. 27–34.

30. R. C. Sampson, "R&D Alliances and Firm Performance: The Impact of Technological Diversity and Alliance Organization on Innovation," *Academy of Management Journal* 50, no. 2 (2007), pp. 364–86.

31. R. Gulati, F. Wohlgezogen, and P. Zhelyazkov, "The Two Facets of Collaboration: Cooperation and Coordination in Strategic Alliances," *Academy of Management Annals* 6 (2012), pp. 531–83.

32. R. M. Kanter, "Collaborative Advantage: The Art of Alliances," *Harvard Business Review,* July–August 1999, pp. 96–108; J. B. Cullen, J. L. Johnson, and T. Sakano, "Success through Commitment and Trust: The Soft Side of Strategic Alliance Management," *Journal of World Business* 35, no. 3 (Fall 2000), pp. 223–40; P. Kale, H. Singh, and H. Perlmutter, "Learning and Protection of Proprietary Assets in Strategic Alliances: Building Relational Capital," *Strategic Management Journal* 21, no. 3 (March 2000),pp. 217–37.

33. M. Marchington and A. Kynighou, "The Dynamics of Employee Involvement and Participation during Turbulent Times," *International Journal of Human Resource Management* 23 (2012), pp. 3336–54; R. J. Vandenberg, H. A. Richardson, and L. J. Eastman, "The Impact of High Involvement Work Process on Organizational Effectiveness: A Second-Order Latent Variable Approach," *Group & Organization Management* 24, no. 3 (September 1999), pp. 300–39; G. M. Spreitzer and A. K. Mishra, "Giving Up Control without Losing Control: Trust and Its Substitutes Effects on Managers Involving Employees in Decision Making," *Group & Organization Management* 24, no. 2 (June 1999), pp. 155–87; S. Albers Mohrman, G. E. Ledford, and E. E. Lawler III, *Strategies for High Performance Organizations The CEO Report: Employee Involvement, TQM, and Reengineering Programs in Fortune 1000 Corporations* (San Francisco: Jossey-Bass, 1998).

34. M. Josefy, S. Kuban, R. D. Ireland, et al., "All Things Great and Small: Organizational Size, Boundaries of the Firm, and a Changing Environment," *Academy of Management Annals* 8 (2015), pp. 715–802.

35. H. Peterson, "Walmart Is Cutting Management Roles at Some Stores," *Business Insider,* February 13, 2018, www.businessinsider.com; P. Wahba, "Walmart's CEO Calls on Staff to Be Like Han Solo, Other Star Wars Rebels," *Fortune,* June 5, 2015, www.fortune.com.

36. J. Mote, G. Jordan, J. Hage, et al., "Too Big to Innovate? Exploring Organizational Size and Innovation Processes in Scientific Research," *Science and Public Policy* 43 (2016), pp. 332–37.

37. J. Smothers, M. Novicevic, M. Buckley, S. Carraher, L. Bynum, M. Hayek, and Alfred D. Chandler Jr., "Historical Impact and Historical Scope of His Works," *Journal of Management History* 16 (2010), pp. 521–26; Alfred Chandler, *The Economist,* May 17, 2007, http://www.economist.com; C. Farrell and Alfred Chandler, "Big

Business Big Loss," *Bloomberg Businessweek,* May 14, 2007, http://www.businessweek.com.

38. D. Kline, "Customer Satisfaction: These Are America's Best-Liked Retailers," *USA Today,* March 12, 2018, www.usatoday.com; The American Customer Satisfaction Index, "ACSI: Retail Customer Satisfaction Drops Despite Improvements for Online Shopping," press release, February 18, 2015, http://www.theacsi.org.

39. J. White, "GM Shifts from Bigger Is Better to Less Global, More Profitable," Reuters, March 6, 2017, www.reuters.com.

40. L. L. Hellofs and R. Jacobson, "Market Share and Customers' Perceptions of Quality: When Can Firms Grow Their Way to Higher versus Lower Quality?" *Journal of Marketing* 63, no. 1 (January 1999), pp. 16–25.

41. E. Doerr, "Kobolds Spirit of America: Navy Seals, Made in America, and Pandemonium," *Forbes,* July 4, 2014, http://www.forbes.com; J. Dean, "The Greatly Improbable, Highly Enjoyable, Increasingly Profitable Life of Michael Kobold," *Inc.,* May 2007, pp. 126–34.

42. "2018 100 Best Companies to Work For," *Fortune,* http://fortune.com/best-companies/, accessed March 16, 2019; "Company Fast Facts," http://www.intuit.com, accessed April 11, 2015.

43. Living Goods, "Who We Are," https://livinggoods.org/, accessed March 24, 2019.

44. E. Howard, "10 Things We Learned about Scaling Global Social Enterprise," *The Guardian,* November 20, 2014, http://www.theguardian.com.

45. Network for Good, "About Us," www.networkforgood.org, accessed March 24, 2019.

46. Selco, "Who We Are," www.selco-india.com, accessed March 24, 2019.

47. D. DeRue, J. Hollenbeck, M. Johnson, D. Ilgen, and D. Jundt, "How Different Team Downsizing Approaches Influence Team-Level Adaptation and Performance," *Academy of Management Journal* 51 (2008), pp. 182–96; W. F. Cascio, "Downsizing: What Do We Know? What Have We Learned?" *Academy of Management Executive* 7 (February 1993), pp. 95–104; S. J. Freeman, "The Gestalt of Organizational Downsizing: Downsizing Strategies as Package of Change," *Human Relations* 52, no. 12 (December 1999), pp. 1505–41.

48. C. Trevor and A. Nyberg, "Keeping Your Headcount When All about You Are Losing Theirs: Downsizing, Voluntary Turnover Rates, and the Moderating Role of HR Practices," *Academy of Management Journal* 51 (2008), pp. 259–76.

49. S. Dewnarain, H. Ramkissoon, and F. Mavondo, "Social Customer Relationship Management: An Integrated Conceptual Framework," *Journal of Hospitality Marketing and Management* 28 (2019), pp. 172–88.

50. B. Kerschberg, "Five Steps to Master Big Data and Predictive Analytics in 2014," *Forbes,* January 3, 2014, http://www.forbes.com; "Predictive Analytics 101: Next-Generation Big Data Intelligence," Intel IT Center, March 2013, http://www.intel.com; "Predicting the Future, Part 1: What Is Predictive Analytics?" IBM Developer Works, http://www.ibm.com, accessed May 27, 2015.

51. S. Balkhi, "How Companies Are Using Big Data to Boost Sales, and How You Can Do the Same," *Entrepreneur,* January 18, 2019, www.entrepreneur.com.

52. S. Sluis, "Mobile Sales to Represent Half of E-Commerce by 2018," *Customer Relationship Management* 18 (2014), pp. 15–18; T. Wailgum, "CRM Definition and Solutions," *CIO,* March 6, 2007, http://www.cio.com; M. Burns, "CRM Survey 2011," *CA Magazine,* May 2011, http://www.camagazine.com; M. Burns, "CRM Survey 2010," *CA Magazine,* April 2010, http://www.camagazine.com.

53. K. Ishikawa, *What Is Total Quality Control? The Japanese Way,* trans. D. J. Lu (Englewood Cliffs, NJ: Prentice-Hall, 1985); J. Seibert and J. Lingle, "Internal Customer Service: Has It Improved?" *Quality Progress* 40, no. 3 (March 2007), OCLC First Search, http://firstsearch.oclc.org.

54. H. L. Lee and C. S. Tang, "Socially and Environmentally Responsible Value Chain Innovations: New Operations Management Research Opportunities," *Management Science* 64 (2018), pp. 983–96.

55. M. Porter, *Competitive Advantage: Creating and Sustaining Superior Performance* (New York: Free Press, 1985); Internet Center for

Management and Business Administration, "The Value Chain," Strategy pages, *NetMBA,* http://www.netmba.com.

56. Anthony Carranza, "Leveraging the Power and Benefits of Social CRM," February 22, 2017, https://www.business.com/articles/leveraging-the-power-and-benefits-of-social-crm.

57. Salesforce company website, https://www.salesforce.com/products/service-cloud/customer-stories/#!page=1, accessed March 24, 2019.

58. Salesforce company website, https://www.salesforce.com/products/service-cloud/overview/#, accessed March 24, 2019.

59. Organization website, "Learn about Quality," https://asq.org/quality-resources/total-quality-management, accessed March 18, 2019.

60. B. Creech, *The Five Pillars of TQM: How to Make Total Quality Management Work for You* (New York: Plume Publishing, 1995); J. R. Evans and W. M. Lindsay, *Management and Control of Quality* (Mason, OH: South-Western College Publishing, 1998).

61. National Institute of Standards and Technology, "Five Role-Model Organizations Win 2018 Baldrige National Quality Award," news release, November 15, 2018, http://www.nist.gov.

62. International Organization for Standardization, "ISO 9000 Quality Management," www.iso.org, accessed March 18, 2019.

63. J. Woodward, *Industrial Organization: Theory and Practice* (London: Oxford University Press, 1965).

64. Company website, "Welcome to B&B Tool Company," www.bbtoolco.com, accessed March 18, 2019.

65. J. H. Gilmore and B. J. Pine, eds., *Markets of One: Creating Customer-Unique Value through Mass Customization* (Cambridge, MA: Harvard Business Review Press, 2000); B. J. Pine, *Mass Customization: The New Frontier in Business Competition* (Cambridge, MA: Harvard Business School Press, 1992).

66. M. Zhang, X. Zhao, and Y. Qi, "The Effects of Organizational Flatness, Coordination, and Product Modularity on Mass Customization Capability," *International Journal of Production Economics* 158 (2014), pp. 145–55; F. Sahin, "Manufacturing Competitiveness: Different Systems to Achieve the Same Results," *Production and Inventory Management Journal* 41, no. 1 (First Quarter 2000), pp. 56–65.

67. S. Wadhwa and K. S. Rao, "Flexibility: An Emerging Meta-Competence for Managing High Technology," *International Journal of Technology Management* 19, no. 7–8 (2000), pp. 820–45.

68. Company website, "Suuchi Services," www.suuchi.com, accessed March 18, 2019; P. Kavilanz, "An Indian Technologist Creating Factory Jobs in America," *CNN Business,* April 6, 2017, www.money.cnn.com.

69. A. Bozek and M. Wysocki, "Flexible Job Shop with Continuous Material Flow," *International Journal of Production Research* 53 (2015), pp. 1273–90; B. A. Peters and L. F. McGinnis, "Strategic Configuration of Flexible Assembly Systems: A Single Period Approximation," *IIE Transaction* 31, no. 4 (April 1999), pp. 379–90.

70. J. K. Liker and J. M. Morgan, "The Toyota Way in Services: The Case of Lean Product Development," *Academy of Management Perspectives* 20, no. 2 (May 2006), pp. 5–20; "Strategic Reconfiguration: Manufacturing's Key Role in Innovation," *Production and Inventory Management Journal,* Summer–Fall 2001, pp. 9–17; J. Jusko, "Lean Confusion," *Industry Week,* September 2010, pp. 32–34; F. Sahin, "Manufacturing Competitiveness: Different Systems to Achieve the Same Results," *Production and Inventory Management Journal* 41, no. 1 (First Quarter 2000), pp. 56–65.

71. P. Guarraia, G. Carey, A. Corbett, and K. Neuhaus, "Lean Six Sigma for the Services Industry," Bain & Company, May 20, 2008, http://www.bain.com.

72. T. Klich, "A Detroit Entrepreneur Applies Lean Auto Manufacturing Principles to Build a Beauty Salon," *Forbes,* December 14, 2018, www.forbes.com.

73. W. Yang and K. Meyer, "Competitive Dynamics in an Emerging Economy: Competitive Pressures, Resources, and the Speed of Action," *Journal of Business Research* 68 (2015), pp. 1176–85; C. H. Chung, "Balancing the Two Dimensions of Time for Time-Based Competition," *Journal of Managerial Issues* 11, no. 3 (Fall 1999), pp. 299–314; D. R. Towill and P. McCullen, "The Impact of Agile Manufacturing on Supply Chain Dynamics," *International Journal of Logistics Management* 10, no. 1 (1999), pp. 83–96. See also G. Stalk and T. M. Hout, *Competing against Time: How Time-Based Competition Is Reshaping Global Markets* (New York: Free Press, 1990).

74. B. Thau, "Is The 'RFID Retail Revolution' Finally Here? A Macy's Case Study," *Forbes,* May 15, 2017, www.forbes.com.

75. D. Kaplan, "The Rise, Fall, and Return of RFID," *Supply Chain Dive,* August 21, 2018, www.supplychaindive.com.

76. J. E. Ettlie, "Product Development beyond Simultaneous Engineering," *Automative Manufacturing & Production* 112, no. 7 (July 2000), p. 18; U. Roy, J. M. Usher, and H. R. Parsaei, eds.,*Simultaneous Engineering: Methodologies and Applications* (Newark, NJ: Gordon and Breach, 1999); M. M. Helms and L. P. Ettkin, "Time-Based Competitiveness: A Strategic Perspective," *Competitiveness Review* 10, no. 2 (2000), pp. 1–14.

77. Company website, "ADDA BIM Process," ADDA, https://adda-bim.com, accessed March 18, 2019.

78. Nick Statt, "How Walmart Is Trying to Reinvent In-Store Shopping to Win Black Friday," *The Verge,* November 22, 2018, https://www.theverge.com/2018/11/22/18106711/walmart-black-friday-cyber-monday-in-store-shopping-amazon-competition.

79. Tonya Garcia, "Wal-Mart Has Announced Thousands of Layoffs since Publicizing Bonuses and Benefits Expansion," *MarketWatch,* February 1, 2018, https://www.marketwatch.com/story/wal-mart-has-announced-thousands-of-layoffs-since-publicizing-bonuses-and-benefits-expansion-2018-01-30.

80. Suman Bhattacharyya, "Inside Walmart's Journey to Cashierless Retail," *Digiday,* July 9, 2018, https://digiday.com/retail/inside-walmarts-journey-cashierless-retail/.

81. Jamie Iannone, "Sam's Club Now—Reimagining the Future of Retail," Sam's Club website, October 29, 2018, https://corporate.samsclub.com/blog/2018/10/29/sams-club-now-reimagining-the-future-of-retail.

82. Lauren Thomas and Nick Wells, "Here's a List of Where Walmart Is Closing More Than 60 Sam's Club Stores," *CNBC,* January 12, 2018, https://www.cnbc.com/2018/01/12/heres-a-map-of-where-walmart-is-closing-more-than-60-sams-club-stores.html.

83. Waverly Colville and Lauren Thomas, "Walmart Cuts Earnings Outlook for 2019," *CNBC,* October 16, 2018, https://www.cnbc.com/2018/10/16/walmart-cuts-its-2019-earnings-forecast.html.

CHAPTER 10
Human Resource Management

You can get capital and erect buildings, but it takes people to build a business.

—Thomas J. Watson, Founder, IBM

iStockphoto/Getty Images

learning objectives

After studying Chapter 10, you will be able to:

LO 10-1   Discuss how companies use human resource management to gain competitive advantage.

LO 10-2   Give reasons companies recruit both internally and externally for new hires.

LO 10-3   Identify various methods for selecting new employees.

LO 10-4   Evaluate the importance of spending on training and development.

LO 10-5   Discuss options for who appraises an employee's performance.

LO 10-6   Describe the fundamental aspects of reward systems.

LO 10-7   Summarize how unions and labor laws influence human resource management.

chapter outline

Strategic Human Resource Management
The HR Planning Process

Staffing
Recruitment   Workforce Reductions
Selection

Developing the Workforce
Training and Development

Performance Appraisal
What Do You Appraise?
Who Should Do the Appraisal?
How Do You Give Employees Feedback?

Designing Reward Systems
Pay Decisions   Employee Benefits
Incentive Systems and   Legal Issues in Compen-
Variable Pay   sation and Benefits
Executive Pay and Stock   Health and Safety
Options

Labor Relations
Labor Laws   Collective Bargaining
Unionization   What Does the Future
                             Hold?

Management in Action

HOW GOOGLE LANDS TOP TALENT

Year after year, we hear that U.S. schools are not graduating enough engineers and software developers to meet employers' demand for skilled technology workers. Yet Google gets about 2 million job applicants a year and hires only the best of the best. Essentially, getting a job at Google is approximately 10 times harder than getting accepted into Harvard.[1] How does Google win the competition for talent?

An obvious place to find answers is in the way the company treats its nearly 100,000 workers. First, it pays its employees well. And second, though perhaps just as importantly, it works hard to create a workplace that is now famous for its perks and employee accommodations. Benefits include onsite exercise facilities, permission to bring pets to work, a popular stress-reducing mindfulness training program, and free food in all company cafeterias. In addition, Google also takes into account the personal needs and work–life balance of its employees. It offers onsite child care, arrangements for job sharing and telecommuting, and extended time off to pursue personal passions and interests.

Perhaps most significant is the excitement of being part of something meaningful. Those with a passion for technology have considered the company a desirable place to work because it's always developing cutting-edge software that can potentially change the world.

Because Google is an attractive employer, it can be picky about whom it hires. The company selects people who are passionate and who value intellectual excellence. As Laszlo Bock, the company's former human resources guru, put it, "A good rule of thumb is to hire only people who are better than you."[2]

Anton Gvozdikov/Shutterstock

Google applies its prowess in analyzing data to figure out how to acquire, develop, and keep talented people. Every year, Google conducts its Googlegeist employee survey to measure employee attitudes about work, and the company carefully tracks all kinds of people-related measures such as managers' effectiveness. It gives all employees an active voice and helps the company track the trajectory of the organization's morale.

Even popular companies like Google can't rest on their laurels. Recently, Google has come under scrutiny for lack of diversity, mishandling of sexual harassment claims, and dissatisfaction with pay and benefits. These tensions were reflected in the 2019 Googlegeist, which showed confidence in leadership had dropped to a six-year low.[3] Seventy-four percent of Googlers still felt "positive" about the current management's ability to effectively lead Google in the future, but clearly there is work to be done. It's up to management to listen more closely to the voice of its employees and take proactive measures to resolve these simmering issues. That's what good human resource management is all about.

In receiving roughly 2 million job applications each year, Google has a huge challenge as well as an opportunity. It has to decide which people to hire; how to bring out the best in them; and how to keep them positive, passionate, and productive. As you read this chapter, think about how the strategic use of people drives Google's and every company's strengths and weaknesses.

Google's practice of wooing bright people with exciting challenges and generous perks has distinguished the company in important ways. The opening quote by Thomas Watson, founder of IBM, summarizes our view of the importance of people to any organization.

Human resource management (HRM)

Formal systems for the management of people within an organization.

Human resource management (HRM) deals with formal systems for managing people at work. Historically known as personnel management and serving primarily fairly routine administrative tasks, human resources executives now make vital contributions to high-level decision making and strategic efforts to deal with ever-changing circumstances and challenges.[4] HR also is a pervasive aspect of organizational and managerial life: Your first contacts with employers likely will be with their HR recruiters, and you will continue interacting closely with HR managers and programs throughout your career.

Practices vary greatly from company to company, depending on top executives' preferences, organizational size,[5] and the extent and type of international activities.[6] This chapter describes many of the topics and techniques that most students will experience.

We begin this chapter by describing HRM as it relates to strategic management and then discuss its nuts and bolts: legal issues, staffing, training, performance appraisal, rewards, and labor relations. In the chapter following this one, we describe in depth the unique importance, challenges, and opportunities of the diverse modern workforce.[7]

Strategic Human Resource Management

LO 10-1 Discuss how companies use human resource management to gain competitive advantage.

HRM plays a vital strategic role as organizations attempt to compete through people.[8] Recall (Chapter 4) that firms hold a competitive advantage when they possess or develop resources that are valuable, rare, inimitable, and organized. We can use the same criteria to talk about the strategic impact of human resources when it:

1. *Creates value.* People can increase value through their efforts to decrease costs or provide something unique to customers. Companies such as Corning and Xerox use empowerment programs, total quality initiatives, and continuous improvement efforts designed to increase the value that employees bring to the bottom line.
2. *Is rare.* People provide competitive advantage when their skills, knowledge, and abilities are better than competitors' and hard to find. Top companies invest a great deal to hire talented people and train them well. Google and top consulting firms hire top students in a wide variety of majors, and the recruits develop new skills with training, work assignments, and other methods.
3. *Is difficult to imitate.* People provide advantage when their capabilities and contributions cannot be copied by others. Netflix, SolarCity, and Rackspace are known for creating unique cultures that get the most from employees (through teamwork and motivation) and are difficult to imitate.

4. *Is organized.* People provide advantage when organizations know how to deploy them as needed based on their experience, skills, and potential. Johnson & Johnson, Colgate, and other companies have formal systems for developing high-potential employees so they fill openings with people who are well acquainted with the company's culture, customers, and industry.

> People can provide competitive advantage when their skills, knowledge, and abilities are better than competitors'. Potentially, that is, unless they are managed poorly.

These four criteria highlight the importance of people and show how integral HRM is to strategic management.[9] At a growing number of companies, HR managers participate in high-level strategy meetings to identify key issues and propose new methods of acquiring, training, and keeping talent will help the company meet its goals.[10]

This strategic focus for HRM, implemented well,[11] brings positive business results.[12] Effective human resources practices relate to higher corporate valuations in the stock market.[13] Innovation—useful new ideas that emerge from the focused creativity of the organization's people—is ever more critical to gaining and maintaining competitive advantage. Employee skills, knowledge, and abilities are among the most distinctive and renewable resources on which a company can draw.

Thus, firms recognize that success depends on what people know. The term **human capital** is used today to describe the strategic value of employee knowledge and abilities.[14]

HR managers must know their company's business and help line managers hire well and motivate their people. They also must deal with tough ethical challenges. Ideally HR managers serve their employer's bottom line and the people who work there at all levels as well as external stakeholder. Dealing ethically and effectively with so many priorities is far more easily said than done.[15]

In the long run, organizations are best served when HR leaders are strong advocates for at least four sets of values: strategic, ethical, legal, and financial.[16] But on a day-to-day basis, HR managers have many other specific concerns regarding people and the overall personnel puzzle. Which HR activities require the most attention depends in part on whether the organization is growing, declining, or standing still. This leads to the practical issues involved in HR planning.

human capital

The knowledge, skills, and abilities of employees that have economic value.

Etsy is known for creating a unique culture that gets the most from employees.

Chris Goodney/Bloomberg/Getty Images

The HR Planning Process

"Get me the right kind and the right number of people at the right time." It sounds simple enough, but it requires HR planning based on knowing your firm's strategic purpose, what's going on in the external environment, and how best to satisfy stakeholders both inside the company (top executives, line managers, and employees throughout) and outside (customers, the government, investors, communities, and so on).[17]

The HR planning process occurs in three stages: planning, programming, and evaluating. First, to ensure that the right number and types of people are available, HR managers need to know the organization's business plans: where the company is headed, the mix of businesses and the industries they will compete in, expected future growth, and so forth.

Few actions are more damaging to morale than laying off recently hired college graduates because of inadequate planning. Hiring enough employees to scale an organization can be challenging, too.

Social Entrepreneurship

Is Social Enterprise Becoming Big Business?

Growth is an important goal for many social enterprises. A larger organization with more resources and employees generally makes more progress toward fulfilling the enterprise's mission. More social enterprises than ever are being created and brought to scale. Forty-two percent of existing social enterprises were created in the past 10 years.[18] In fact, what was once known as a collection of small, philanthropic start-ups on the periphery of mainstream business is now becoming the new paradigm for what mainstream business should be.

In a recent survey, 65 percent of CEOs listed "inclusive growth" as a top-three strategic concern.[19] There are a number of factors driving this trend. Today, businesses are expected to be not only providers of services and products, but also ethical stewards and socially responsible entities. These expectations are the new normal. This shift is forcing businesses to rethink conventional paradigms of the past. Consumers now have more of a voice through social media and other platforms, forcing businesses to be more responsive. In a broader political context, faith in government is falling, and people are increasingly coming to expect business to fill the void.[20]

The World Social Enterprise Forum was held last year in Scotland. It's an annual event meant for social enterprise leaders to collaborate and strategize about ways to make the movement stronger. This year, 1,400 delegates from 47 countries attended. In describing the convergence of social enterprise and big business, one CEO said, "Partnerships between social and private enterprises have come a long way. . . . But over the last few years we've really reached a tipping point—the corporate sector is recognizing that it can make a significant difference in communities through social enterprise partnerships."[21] Time will tell whether this trend continues.

- Assume you're the manager of a social enterprise. How would you go about growing your business?

- To what degree do you see commercial businesses adopting the social enterprise model? Do you think it's a passing trend or a revolution in the business world?

The second element of the HR planning process is to choose and implement specific human resources activities, such as recruitment, training, and performance appraisals. In this stage, the company's plans are implemented. Third, human resources activities are evaluated to determine whether they are producing the results needed to contribute to the organization's business plans.

Exhibit 10.1 illustrates the components of the human resources planning process. In this chapter, we focus on human resources planning and programming. You will learn much more about these processes in later chapters.

Demand Forecasts   Perhaps the most difficult part of human resources planning is conducting demand forecasts—that is, determining how many and what types of people are needed.

Demand forecasts for people needs stem from organizational plans. Companies consider current sales and projected future sales growth as they estimate production capacity needed to meet future demand, the sales force required, the support staff needed, and so forth. They calculate the number of labor-hours required to operate a plant, sell the product, distribute it, serve customers, and so forth. These estimates determine the demand for different types of workers.

Labor Supply Forecasts   Managers also forecast the supply of labor by estimating the number and quality of current employees as well as the available external supply of workers. To estimate internal supply, managers typically rely on past experiences and data regarding turnover, terminations, retirements, promotions, and transfers.

Externally, organizations look at workforce trends to make projections. In the United States, demographic trends have contributed to a shortage of workers with appropriate skills and education level. Jobs in technical, financial, and health care industries often

 **EXHIBIT 10.1**   An Overview of the HR Planning Process

Planning	Programming	Evaluating
HR Environmental Scanning • Labor markets • Technology • Legislation • Competition • Economy **HR Planning** • Demand forecast • Internal labor supply • External labor supply • Job analysis	**HR Activities** • Recruitment • Selection • Diversity and inclusion • Training and development • Performance appraisal • Reward systems • Labor relations	**Results** • Productivity • Quality • Innovation • Satisfaction • Turnover • Absenteeism • Health

require much more training and schooling than the traditional labor-intensive jobs that they replaced. Demand for highly qualified employees continues to outpace supply; this is one reason some jobs are being transferred overseas. A recent survey of IT managers revealed that 82 percent lack employees with adequate cybersecurity skills to protect their organizations from cyberattacks.[22]

Some demographic trends we discussed in Chapter 2 may worsen this situation. Though some Baby Boomers (born 1946–1964) are continuing to work past retirement age, their retirements are removing large numbers of educated and trained employees from the workforce.[23] And in math, science, and engineering graduate schools, fewer than half of the students receiving graduate degrees are American-born. To fill U.S. jobs, companies must hire U.S. citizens or immigrants with permission to work in the United States.

One response to a skills shortage is to automate routine and repetitive tasks.[24] However, technology advances cannot fill the jobs gap in low- and middle-skilled jobs. So, many companies partner with community colleges to provide students with academic and hands-on training. Infosys partnered with a community college in Rhode Island to help students learn new ways to work with new technology, develop marketable skills, and form a professional network. The company hopes to form similar partnerships with community colleges across the United States.[25] Siemens Energy, in order to staff its high-tech production plant in Charlotte, North Carolina, launched an apprenticeship program for high school seniors. Selected graduating seniors enter into a four-year on-the-job training program while completing an associate's degree at Central Piedmont Community College.[26]

Companies also increase the labor supply by recruiting workers from other countries. For example, each year the U.S. government awards H-1B (temporary) visas to college-educated people in such high-skilled, highly demanded areas as engineering and teaching. Managers at high-tech companies (Microsoft and Alphabet) and consulting firms (Deloitte and EY [formerly Ernst & Young]) rely on H-1B employees to fill key positions.[27]

Earlier forecasts of a diverse workforce have become fact, adding greatly to the pool of available talent. The next chapter is devoted entirely to this topic.

Reconciling Supply and Demand   Once managers have a good idea of the supply of and the demand for various types of employees, they can start developing ways to reconcile the two. In some cases, they need more people than they currently have (a labor deficit). Then, organizations can hire new employees, promote current employees to new positions, or outsource work to contractors. In other cases, organizations have more people

andreypopov/123RF

than they need (a labor surplus). If this is known far enough in advance, attrition—the normal turnover of employees—can reduce the surplus. In other instances, the organization may lay off employees or transfer them to other areas.

When managers do need to hire, one tool they can use is their organization's compensation policy. HR departments spend a lot of time gathering information about pay scales for the various jobs they have available and making sure their compensation system is fair and competitive. We discuss pay issues later in this chapter.

Job Analysis   Issues of supply and demand are fairly "macro" activities—conducted at an organizational level. HR planning also has a more detailed micro side called **job analysis** that does two things.[28] First, it tells the HR manager about each job's specific and essential tasks, duties, and responsibilities. This information is the *job description*. The job description for an accounting manager might specify that the position will be responsible for preparing monthly, quarterly, and annual financial reports; issuing and paying bills; preparing budgets; ensuring the company's compliance with laws and regulations; working closely with line managers on financial issues; and supervising an accounting department.

job analysis

A tool for determining what is done on a given job and what should be done on that job.

Second, job analysis describes the knowledge, skills, abilities, and other characteristics (KSAOs) needed to perform the job. This is called the *job specification*. For our accounting manager, the job requirements might include a degree in accounting or business, knowledge of computerized accounting systems, prior managerial experience, and excellent communication skills.

Job analysis provides the information needed for virtually every human resources activity: recruitment, training, selection, appraisal, and reward systems. It can help organizations defend themselves in lawsuits over employment practices—for example, by clearly specifying what a job requires if someone claims unfair dismissal.[29] Ultimately, job analysis helps increase the value that employees add because it clarifies what is really required to perform effectively.

> Job analysis provides the information needed for virtually every HR activity.

Staffing

LO 10-2 Give reasons companies recruit both internally and externally for new hires.

Once HR planning is completed, managers can focus on staffing the organization. The staffing function consists of three related activities: recruitment, selection, and outplacement.

Recruitment

recruitment

The development of a pool of applicants for jobs in an organization.

Recruitment activities increase the pool of candidates who can be hired. Recruitment may be internal to the organization (considering current employees for promotions and transfers) or external. Each approach has advantages and disadvantages.[30]

Internal Recruiting   The advantages of internal recruiting are that companies know their employees, and employees know their organization; external candidates may find they don't like working there. A big advantage is that opportunities for promotions can encourage employees to remain with the company, work hard, and perform well. Recruiting from outside the company can be demoralizing to employees. Many companies, such as Gap Inc., Palo Alto Networks, and Blizzard Entertainment, prefer internal to external recruiting for these reasons.

Internal staffing has some drawbacks. If employees lack needed skills, internal recruitment yields a limited applicant pool, leading to suboptimal choices. An internal recruitment policy can inhibit or delay needed changes at a company if current employees resist it. In changing from a rapidly growing, entrepreneurial organization to a mature business with more stable growth, Dell went outside the organization to hire managers who better fit those requirements.

Internal recruiters often posts open positions on the company's intranet. The posted job description includes a list of responsibilities and the minimum skills and experience required. Employees are encouraged to apply online for the internal position.

External Recruiting   External recruiting brings in new blood and can inspire innovation. Among the most frequently used sources of outside applicants are online job boards, company websites, employee referrals, and college campus recruiting. For specialized positions, more companies use networking sites such as LinkedIn, Facebook, and Twitter because the job boards generate many unqualified leads that are overwhelming to process.

Employers prefer referrals by current employees and online job boards.[31] Some companies encourage employees to refer their friends by offering cash rewards. In fact, word-of-mouth recommendations are the way most job positions get filled. Not only is this recruitment method relatively inexpensive, but employees tend to know who will be a good fit with the company. Web job boards such as Snagajob, Indeed, SimplyHired, CareerBuilder, Monster, Glassdoor, and ZipRecruiter easily reach a large pool of job seekers.

littleny/Shutterstock

Selection

Selection builds on recruiting and is a decision about whom to hire. As important as these decisions are, they sometimes are made in careless or cavalier ways. Here we describe a number of selection practices to which you may soon be exposed, if you haven't been already.

Applications and Résumés   As a first step, employers review the profiles and backgrounds of many job applicants. Applications and résumés provide basic information including the applicant's name, educational background, citizenship, work experiences, certifications, and the like. Their appearance and accuracy say something about the applicant; spelling mistakes, for example, typically lead to immediate disqualification (something to keep in mind when preparing your own). Although a useful starting point, applications and résumés tend not to be extremely useful for making final selection decisions.

Interviews   The most popular selection tool is interviewing, and nearly every company does this. Interviewers must be careful about what they ask and how they ask it. Federal law requires employers to avoid discriminating against people based on criteria such as gender and race; questions that distinguish candidates according to protected categories can be evidence of discrimination.

In a **structured interview**, the interviewer conducts the same interview with each applicant. One type—the *situational interview*—uses hypothetical situations. Here is a sample question used by a restaurant hiring manager to assess applicants for a server position: "Assume a customer became upset because you accidentally overcharged him for his meal. How would you handle the situation?" An answer that said "I would refer the customer to my supervisor" has some logic to it, but might suggest that the applicant felt incapable of handling the situation on his or her own, or unwilling to try.

The second type of structured interview—the *behavioral description interview*—explores what candidates have actually done in the past. Applicants for a position at Microsoft might be asked: "Tell me about a time when your performance let a team member down. Why do you think that happened? What would you do differently now, knowing what you

LO 10-3 Identify various methods for selecting new employees.

selection

Choosing from among qualified applicants to hire.

structured interview

Selection technique that involves asking all applicants the same questions and comparing their responses to a standardized set of answers.

The Digital World

Can Your Social Media Profile Keep You from Landing a Great Job?

Organizations have made it a practice to check the references of prospective employees as well as paying for background checks. Today, 70 percent of employers also review the social media profiles of people they are considering for a job or internship. Another 7 percent say they plan to start doing so in the near future. Of those who review candidates' social media profiles, 57 percent say they have seen something online that has kept them from hiring a candidate. And once you get the job, don't think your social media profile no longer matters: 48 percent of employers check the social media accounts of their current employees.[32]

Employers can legally search for anything a prospective or current employee has posted to a public profile. Whereas some states have banned employers from requesting password access to applicants' or employees' social media posts, others have not.[33]

Experts suggest that to keep yourself from missing out on potential employment opportunities, avoid posting suggestive photos, using profanity, or showing or discussing alcohol or drug use.[34] Yet deleting your profile isn't a smart idea either: Almost half (47 percent) of all employers say they would not hire someone they can't find online (perhaps fearing they have something to hide).[35] The bottom line: Use your social media profiles carefully, and consider what you post and what you make public.

1. Do you consider current or future employers when you post things to social media? Why or why not?
2. Do you think employers should be allowed to request your social media passwords to gain access to posts you have not shared publicly? Why or why not?

Interviewers can use different types of questions during the same interview.

know?"[36] Because behavioral questions are based on real events, they can provide useful information about how the candidate will actually perform in the future.

Employers can conduct unstructured interviews, where they ask each potential employee different questions, or structured interviews in which the employer asks everyone the same questions.

Chris Ryan/Age Fotostock

Reference Checks Résumés, applications, and interviews rely on the honesty of the applicant. To make an accurate selection decision, employers have to be able to trust candidates' words. Unfortunately, some candidates exaggerate their qualifications or hide criminal backgrounds. Ramesh Tainwala resigned as CEO of Samsonite after it was discovered he falsely listed a doctorate degree in business on his résumé.[37] Once lost, a reputation is hard to regain.

Because of these and more ambiguous ethical gray areas, employers supplement candidate-provided information with reference checks. Virtually all organizations contact listed references or former employers and educational institutions. Although checking references makes sense, complete information can be difficult to obtain because applicants have won costly lawsuits against former employers who spoke negatively about them.

Nevertheless, employers should make a practice of checking references.[38] Occasionally they raise a red flag: Past employers usually just verify basic employment facts, but sometimes they will advise caution.

Background Checks A higher level of scrutiny comes from background investigations. Checks include Social Security verification, prior employment and education verification, and criminal history. Additional checks can be conducted if they relate to the job in question, including a motor vehicle records (for jobs involving driving) and a credit history (for money-handling jobs).[39]

Basic background checks are fast and easy to perform. Roughly 70 percent of hiring managers visit social networking sites, especially Facebook, Twitter, and LinkedIn, to learn about job candidates.[40] Many companies do not make offers to candidates based on unprofessional content they find online.[41] Using Facebook information can uncover potentially useful information, but (1) is *not* likely to aid in selecting higher performers and (2) *is* likely to be unfairly discriminatory.[42]

Personality Tests   Using tests to measure candidates' personalities is popular among companies.[43] Companies that use personality tests include JPMorgan Chase, ExxonMobil, and Hewlett-Packard.[44] Some personality types have been associated with greater job satisfaction and performance when the organization builds groups of people with similar positive traits.[45] However, personality tests can be discriminatory and often do not accurately predict job performance.

A number of well-known assessments measure personality traits such as conscientiousness, extraversion, stress tolerance, emotional control, and honesty. Typical questions are "Do you like to socialize with people?" and "Do you enjoy working hard?" Some personality tests try to determine the types of working conditions that the candidate prefers, to see whether he would be motivated and productive in the particular job. For example, if a candidate prefers making decisions on her own but the job requires gaining the cooperation of others, another candidate might be a better fit.

Drug Testing   Many companies use drug testing as a pre-hire screening instrument. The Drug-Free Workplace Act of 1988 legalized testing of applicants and employees of federal and Department of Defense contractors, among others. Currently, about half of U.S. employers screen for drugs.[46] Quest Diagnostics, a leading drug testing laboratory, found that 4.2 percent of workers tested positive for illegal drugs in 2018, the highest level in a decade.[47] To avoid discrimination against individuals with disabilities, companies wait to conduct drug testing until after they have made a conditional job offer.

In recent years, some firms have relaxed their drug policies, especially with regard to marijuana use.[48] This shift is partly due to several states legalizing the use of medical and recreational marijuana, and a growing labor shortage in certain industries.[49] Companies that fire a worker for failing a drug test because of medical marijuana could be found guilty of discriminating. For many jobs, however, it is critical that workers not be under the influence of any substance, legal or illegal.

Cognitive Ability Tests   Among the oldest employment selection devices are cognitive ability tests. These tests measure a range of intellectual abilities, including verbal comprehension (vocabulary, reading) and numerical aptitude (mathematical calculations). These tests have right and wrong answers. Cognitive ability is a good predictor of employees' ability to learn on the job, which helps them perform well.[50]

Performance Tests   In a performance test, the test taker performs a sample of the job. Most companies use some type of performance test, typically for administrative assistant and clerical positions. The most widely used performance test is the typing test. However, performance tests have been developed for almost every occupation, including managerial positions.

Assessment centers are the most notable offshoot of the managerial performance test.[51] Originating in World War II, a typical **assessment center** consists of 10 to 12 candidates participating in a variety of exercises or situations. Some involve group interactions, and others are performed individually. The exercises allow displays of managerial behaviors and skills such as leadership, decision making, and communicating. Assessors, generally line managers, observe and record information about the candidates' performance.

assessment center

A managerial performance test in which candidates participate in a variety of exercises and situations.

Integrity Tests   Sometimes employers, like AT&T and Hospitality Management Corp., administer integrity tests to assess candidates' honesty. The Employee Polygraph Protection Act (EPPA) bans the use of polygraphs, or lie detector tests, for most employment purposes.[52] Paper-and-pencil tests include questions such as whether a person has ever thought about stealing and whether he or she believes other people steal ("What percentage of people take more than $1 from their employer?"). However, the accuracy of these tests is debatable.[53]

reliability

The consistency of test scores over time and across alternative measurements.

Reliability and Validity   For all selection methods, two crucial issues need to be addressed: reliability and validity. **Reliability** is the consistency of test scores over time and across alternative measurements. If three interviewers talked to the same job candidate but drew very different conclusions about his abilities, the interview procedures have questionable reliability.

Validity is the accuracy of the selection test. The most common form of validity, *criterion-related validity,* refers to the degree to which a test actually predicts or correlates with job performance. *Content validity* concerns the degree to which selection tests measure a representative sample of the knowledge, skills, and abilities required for the job. Both types of validity are useful and important, particularly when defending employment decisions in court.

validity

The degree to which a selection test predicts or correlates with job performance.

Workforce Reductions

Hiring is not the only type of staffing decision. Unfortunately, managers sometimes must make difficult decisions to terminate people's employment.

Layoffs   In 2018, several companies laid off employees, including Tesla, McDonald's, Hewlett-Packard, and Citigroup.[54] Dismissing anyone is tough, but laying off a substantial portion of the workforce is devastating.[55] The victims of restructuring face all the difficulties of being fired—loss of self-esteem, demoralizing job searches, and the stigma of being out of work.

Even under the best circumstances, downsizing can be traumatic for an organization and its employees. What can be done to manage downsizing as well as possible?

First, firms should avoid excessive hiring to avoid needing major or multiple downsizings. Other common mistakes are making slow, small, frequent layoffs; implementing voluntary early retirement programs that entice the best people to leave; and laying off so many people that the company's work can no longer be performed. Instead, firms can engage in a number of positive practices to ease the pain and increase the effectiveness of downsizing (see Exhibit 10.2).

outplacement

The process of helping people who have been dismissed from the company regain employment elsewhere.

Employers can offer **outplacement**: helping dismissed people regain employment elsewhere. Even then, the impact of layoffs goes further than the employees who leave. For many of the employees who remain with the company, fear and distrust may overshadow the relief of still having a job. In many respects, how management deals with dismissals will affect the productivity and satisfaction of those who remain.

A thoughtful and fair dismissal process can ease tensions somewhat and help remaining employees adjust to the new work situation. It helps if care is taken during the actual layoff process—if workers receive fair notice, severance pay, and help in finding a new job.

EXHIBIT 10.2
Best Practices When Downsizing

Use downsizing only as a last resort, when other methods of improving performance by innovating or changing procedures have been exhausted.

Give special attention and help to those who have lost their jobs.

Identify and protect talented people.

Choose positions to be eliminated by engaging in analysis and strategic thinking.

Train people to cope with the new situation.

Communicate constantly with people about the process and invite ideas for alternative ways to operate more efficiently.

Identify how the organization will operate more effectively in the future; emphasize this positive future and remaining employees' new roles in attaining it.

SOURCES: Adapted from Cascio, W. F., "Strategies for Responsible Restructuring," *Academy of Management Executive* 19, no. 4 (2005), pp. 39–50; Cascio, W. F., "Downsizing: What Do We Know? What Have We Learned?" *Academy of Management Executive* 7 (February 1993); Freeman, S. J., "The Gestalt of Organizational Downsizing: Downsizing Strategies as Package of Change," *Human Relations* 52, no. 12 (December 1999); Hitt, M. B. et al., "Rightsizing: Building and Maintaining Strategic Leadership and Long-Term Competitiveness," *Organizational Dynamics,* Fall 1994, pp. 18–31.

Termination   People sometimes get fired for poor performance. **Employment-at-will** or *termination-at-will* means that an employee may be fired for *any* reason. A Tennessee court established this in 1884 and the Supreme Court upheld it in 1908.[56] The logic is that if an employee can quit at any time, the employer can dismiss at any time.

employment-at-will

The legal concept that an employer can terminate an employee for any reason.

Courts in most states have made exceptions to this doctrine. Employees cannot be fired for refusing to break the law, taking time off for jury duty, or whistleblowing to report illegal company behavior. For example, if a worker reports an environmental violation to a regulatory agency and the company fires her, the courts may argue that the firing was unfair because the employee acted for the good of the community. Union contracts that limit an employer's ability to fire without cause are another major exception to the employment-at-will doctrine.

> How management deals with terminations will affect the productivity and morale of those who remain.

Employers can avoid the pitfalls of dismissals by developing progressive and positive disciplinary procedures.[57] In this context, *progressive* means that a manager takes graduated steps in attempting to correct unwanted behaviors. For example, an employee who has been absent receives a verbal reprimand for the first offense. A second offense invokes a written reprimand. A third offense results in employee counseling and probation, and a fourth results in a paid leave day to think over the consequences of future rule infractions.

The **termination interview**, in which the manager discusses the dismissal with the employee, is stressful for both parties. The immediate superior should be the one to deliver the bad news to employee. However, it is wise to have a third party, such as an HR manager, present to provide guidance and take notes on the meeting. Terminations can lead to lawsuits, so the manager should prepare carefully by knowing all the facts of the situation and reviewing any documents to make sure they justify the termination.

termination interview

A discussion between a manager and an employee about the employee's dismissal.

Ethics and common sense dictate that the manager should be truthful but respectful, and state the facts.[58] Exhibit 10.3 provides some other guidelines for conducting a termination interview.

Do's	Don'ts
• Make termination the last step in a clear and fair process, being certain you have the facts.	• Don't spring a termination on an employee as a total surprise.
• Be sure the person terminating the employee is the employee's direct supervisor.	• Don't start a meeting unprepared, causing the terminated employee to wait awkwardly while you find answers or call in an HR representative.
• Be prepared with answers to basic questions such as the official end date and any severance benefits.	• Don't beat around the bush; state the termination simply and briefly.
• Consult with the human resources department to identify any benefits available; give the employee a written list of information about benefits and policies.	• Don't get caught up in responding to the employee's emotions or views about fairness; focus on practical realities including the need to move on.
• Invite a trained HR representative to attend the meeting.	• Don't argue with the employee or apologize.
• Listen respectfully.	• Don't offer to help the employee find another job, if you cannot honestly give a good reference.

EXHIBIT 10.3
Advice on Termination

SOURCES: Ashkenas, Ron, "If You Have to Fire an Employee—Here's How to Do It Right," *Forbes,* March 11, 2013, http://www.forbes.com; Haden, Jeff, "The Best Way to Fire an Employee," *Inc.,* March 19, 2012, http://www.inc.com; Korn, Melissa, "The Best Ways to Fire Somebody," *The Wall Street Journal,* October 26, 2012, http://online.wsj.com.

EXHIBIT 10.4   U.S. Equal Employment Laws

Act	Major Provisions	Enforcement and Remedies
Fair Labor Standards Act (1938)	Creates exempt (salaried) and nonexempt (hourly) employee categories, governing overtime and other rules; sets minimum wage, child labor laws.	Enforced by Department of Labor, private action to recover lost wages; civil and criminal penalties also possible.
Equal Pay Act (1963)	Prohibits gender-based pay discrimination between two jobs substantially similar in skill, effort, responsibility, and working conditions.	Fines up to $10,000, imprisonment up to 6 months, or both; enforced by Equal Employment Opportunity Commission (EEOC); private actions for double damages up to 3 years' wages, liquidated damages, reinstatement, or promotion.
Title VII of Civil Rights Act (1964)	Prohibits discrimination based on race, sex, color, religion, or national origin in employment decisions: hiring, pay, working conditions, promotion, discipline, or discharge.	Enforced by EEOC; private actions, back pay, front pay, reinstatement, restoration of seniority and pension benefits, attorneys' fees and costs.
Executive Orders 11246 and 11375 (1965)	Requires equal opportunity clauses in federal contracts; prohibits employment discrimination by federal contractors based on race, color, religion, sex, or national origin.	Established Office of Federal Contract Compliance Programs (OFCCP) to investigate violations; empowered to terminate violator's federal contracts.
Age Discrimination in Employment Act (1967)	Prohibits employment discrimination based on age for persons over 40 years; restricts mandatory retirement.	EEOC enforcement; private actions for reinstatement, back pay, front pay, restoration of seniority and pension benefits; double unpaid wages for willful violations; attorneys' fees and costs.
Vocational Rehabilitation Act (1973)	Requires affirmative action by all federal contractors for persons with disabilities; defines disabilities as physical or mental impairments that substantially limit life activities.	Federal contractors must consider hiring persons with disabilities capable of performance after reasonable accommodations.
Americans with Disabilities Act Amendments Act (2008)	Extends affirmative action provisions of Vocational Rehabilitation Act to private employers; requires workplace modifications to facilitate employees with disabilities; prohibits discrimination against persons with disabilities.	EEOC enforcement; private actions for Title VII remedies.
Civil Rights Act (1991)	Clarifies Title VII requirements: disparate treatment impact suits, business necessity, job relatedness; shifts burden of proof to employer; permits punitive damages and jury trials.	Punitive damages limited to sliding scale only in intentional discrimination based on sex, religion, and disabilities.
Family and Medical Leave Act (1991)	Requires 12 weeks' unpaid leave for medical or family needs: paternity, family member illness.	Private actions for lost wages and other expenses, reinstatement.

Legal Issues and Equal Employment Opportunity   Many laws govern employment decisions and practices. They will directly affect your day-to-day work as a manager as well as your employer's HR function. Exhibit 10.4 shows many of the most important U.S. employment laws.

Failure to comply with these laws exposes the organization to charges of unfair practices, expensive lawsuits, and civil and even criminal penalties. UPS had to pay a $4.9 million settlement in a religious discrimination lawsuit. The company has a policy stating that male employees cannot have beards or grow their hair below the collar. The lawsuit accused UPS of discriminating against men whose religion conflicted with this policy.[59] IHOP in Nevada and New York agreed to pay $700,000 to settle a sexual harassment and retaliation lawsuit after numerous female employees came forward to report misconduct by owners, supervisors, managers, and co-workers.[60]

One common reason employers are sued is **adverse impact**—when an employment practice has a disproportionately negative effect on a group protected by the Civil Rights Act.[61] For example, if equal numbers of qualified men and women apply for jobs but a particular employment test results in far fewer women being hired, the test had an adverse impact and can be challenged legally on that basis.

Most companies have procedures to ensure compliance with labor and equal opportunity laws. They monitor and compare salaries by race, gender, length of service, and other categories. Smart and effective management practices treat employees as fairly as possible to motivate employees to do their best work and provide legal protection as well.

adverse impact

When a seemingly neutral employment practice has a disproportionately negative effect on a protected group.

Developing the Workforce

Competitive environments require managers to upgrade continually the skills and performance of employees—as well as their own. Continuous growth increases both personal and organizational effectiveness. It makes organization members more useful in their current jobs and prepares them to take on new responsibilities. It helps the organization meet new challenges and take advantage of new methods and technologies. It also requires appraising employees' performance and giving them effective and timely feedback so they will be motivated to perform at high levels. We will discuss each of these activities in turn.

LO 10-4 Evaluate the importance of spending on training and development.

Bottom Line
Training improves employee skills. *How might you measure the costs and benefits of training people?*

Ⓠ

Training and Development

U.S. businesses spend more than $85 billion annually on employee training.[62] The greatest share goes to training that the organization itself delivers to its employees. The remainder goes to external training companies and technologies.[63]

The average amount spent per employee on training is under $1000, a slight increase over several years.[64] This lack of investment is a great concern because today's jobs require more education while the education level of U.S. workers has not kept pace.

Although we use the general term *training* here, training sometimes is distinguished from development. **Training** usually refers to teaching lower-level employees how to perform their current jobs, whereas **development** involves teaching managers and professional employees broader skills needed for their current and future jobs.

Cold Stone Creamery spends a portion of its training budget to develop computerized simulations that show how employee actions affect store performance. The company uses computer games because they are familiar and appealing to its young employees.

Sorbis/Shutterstock

Overview of the Training Process   Training usually starts with a **needs assessment**. Managers conduct an analysis to identify who needs what types of training. Job analysis and performance and developmental measurements are useful for this purpose. Then it's time to design the training content and delivery methods and decide whether a program will be provided on or off the job. Common methods include instructor-led classroom training, online or computer-based technologies, webinars, conferences, and on-the-job training.[65]

training	**development**	**needs assessment**
Teaching lower-level employees how to perform their present jobs.	Helping managers and professional employees learn the broad skills needed for their present and future jobs.	An analysis identifying the jobs, people, and departments for which training is necessary.

Inclusiveness Works

When Feedback Crosses Cultures

Providing constructive feedback to employees is not an easy task—for the simple reason that people prefer to be praised rather than criticized. How a manager delivers the feedback is of course critical in any appraisal meeting, but it becomes even more so when accounting for cultural differences.

A precursor to any effective feedback strategy is to understand that our natural style for conveying information isn't universal.[66] What we think is a perfectly normal way to coach others on their performance may be perceived differently than intended. Just as much as personality, culture shapes how we give and receive information, so it is important to account for differences in cultural backgrounds when trying to effectively communicate feedback.

Attentiveness to language cues can help in understanding these cultural differences. For example, some cultures, like the United States and Germany, tend to prefer direct, straightforward feedback, whereas others, like China and Mexico, tend to prefer more indirect channels. Individuals who speak in more absolute terms—"totally," "completely," "definitely"—are more likely accustomed to direct means of communication. Those who tend to use qualifying terms such as "kind of," "possibly," or "a bit" are likely to come from cultures that rely on indirect methods of feedback.[67] It's important to understand that neither is "better" than the other, which brings us to the final point.

Managers can benefit greatly in all communications by exhibiting humility and patience.[68] When it comes to cross-cultural relations, there is no "right" way. The trick is to find the way that is most right for employees you're trying to empower.

1. Have you ever had to provide critical feedback to someone from a different culture? Have you ever received critical feedback from someone from a different culture? What made it a successful or an unsuccessful experience?
2. Which strategy discussed here do you think is most critical for effective cross-cultural communication, and why?

Finally, managers should evaluate program effectiveness. Measures of effectiveness include employee reactions (evaluation survey), learning (tests), improved performance on the job, and bottom-line results such as an increase in sales or reduction in defect rates following the training.

orientation training

Training designed to introduce new employees to the company and familiarize them with policies, procedures, culture, and the like.

Types of Training   Orientation training is used to familiarize new employees with their new jobs, work units, and the organization in general. Done well, orientation training has a number of benefits, including lower employee turnover, increased morale, better productivity, and lower recruiting and training costs.

team training

Training that provides employees with the skills and perspectives they need to collaborate with others.

Team training teaches people the skills they need to work together and stimulates interaction among team members. Before the start of the 2018 holiday season, Gap Inc. set out to hire 65,000 seasonal associates. Because some new hires would be new to retailing, Gap Inc. offered them plenty of training with its experienced teams. The new seasonal hires learned key retail skills plus how to work productively with full-time team members.[69]

diversity training

Programs that focus on identifying and reducing biases against people with differences and developing the skills needed to manage a diversified workforce.

Diversity training builds awareness of diversity's advantages and challenges, and teaches skills for strengthening work relationships—the kinds of things you will learn in the next chapter.

Management training programs often seek to improve managers' people skills—their ability to delegate effectively, motivate their subordinates or direct reports, and communicate and inspire high performance. Coaching—receiving customized personal training from a boss or consultant—can be one of the most effective management development tools.

Managers also can learn a lot in programs used for all employees such as job rotation, or by attending special seminars. As you read "Management in Action: Progress Report," consider how Google's management training and coaching complement its hiring methods.

Management in Action

GOOGLE'S HIRING AND TRAINING PROCESSES

Google's hiring strategy is to position the company as a highly attractive place to work, receive a flood of applications, and make collaborative decisions about which applicants will fit best with Google's demanding and creative culture.

Now streamlined to take about six weeks, the selection process is demanding and occasionally quirky. Candidates generally undergo four to five structured interviews and meet with several Google employees, including potential future peers and direct reports, and may complete work sample tests as well. The interviewers compile an extensive file of information to use in making a group decision.

Google generally looks for the following attributes: (1) ability to learn and apply knowledge to solve problems; (2) willingness to lead and follow others; (3) humility when faced with new or opposing information; (4) desire to take ownership and defend ideas; and (5) "Googlyness," or the type of personality and values that will fit into Google's overall culture. But what that "culture" means is continuing to evolve.[70]

In recent years, Google, along with the tech industry as a whole, has come under increased scrutiny for lacking a diverse workforce. Men still make up approximately 70 percent of its workforce; more than half of all employees are white, and Asian Americans account for about a third. Only 4 percent are Latino; less than 3 percent are African American. The one positive development in the latest report shows women in leadership positions has increased from 4 percent in 2014 to 25 percent in 2018.[71]

A companywide diversity effort includes anti-bias training, new hiring practices, the formation of identity groups within the company, benchmarking of other companies' diversity initiatives, and efforts to cast a much wider net when recruiting. Google expects the changes to show results over time. "Google is in this for the long haul," says VP of engineering Anna Patterson. "Diversity makes all tech better, and our products better."[72]

With regard to training, data-driven decisions match topics to particular employees for whom the training will deliver meaningful results. Google has also implemented what they call "g2g," or one Google employee teaching another Google employee. These g2g's can be within the same field or in a different one. The idea, according to Google, is to create a culture of learning. Another program Google has implemented is called the "Whisper Course," which is a takeoff on microlearning. The whisper course is a series of emails that offer tips and suggestions for improving some aspect of employees' work-related skills. The key to this form of training is that it doesn't occur outside of work in a classroom, but rather within the context of daily work life, thus allowing employees to apply and internalize the lesson more readily.[73]

- Which of the five attributes listed above do you feel would be most important for employees to have?
- Which of the two strategies that Google uses as part of its training program do you think would be more effective? Explain your answer.

Performance Appraisal

As earlier chapters have shown, managers have a wide range of responsibilities. A core responsibility is to manage employee performance.[74] This will be an ongoing focus—along with managing team and organizational performance—for the rest of this book.

A core component of performance management, and one you will experience throughout your career as both receiver and giver, is **performance appraisal (PA)**: the assessment of job performance. Done well, it can help employees improve their performance, pay, and chances for promotion; foster communication between managers and employees; and increase individual, team, and organization effectiveness. Done poorly, it can lead to resentment, a drop in motivation, lower performance, and sometimes lawsuits.

Performance appraisal serves two basic purposes. First, it generates information managers need to evaluate past performance. They use those judgments to make salary, promotion, and termination decisions; help employees understand and accept the basis of those decisions; and create documentation that can support their decisions in court.

LO 10-5 Discuss options for who appraises an employee's performance.

performance appraisal (PA)

Assessment of an employee's job performance.

Second, performance appraisal serves a developmental purpose. The information can be used to identify and plan the additional training, learning, and experience employees need to grow. The feedback and coaching people receive help them improve their performance and prepare them for greater future responsibilities.

What Do You Appraise?

Performance appraisals assess three basic categories of employee performance: traits, behaviors, and results. Trait appraisals involve subjective judgments about employee characteristics related to performance. They include dimensions such as initiative, leadership, and attitude. Usually the manager will use a numerical scale to indicate the extent to which an employee "possesses" each trait. For example, if the measured trait is attitude, the employee might be rated anywhere from 1 (very negative attitude) to 5 (very positive attitude).

Trait scales are common because they are simple to use and provide a standard measure for all employees. But often they are not valid as performance measures. Because they tend to be ambiguous as well as highly subjective—does the employee really have a bad attitude, or is he or she just shy?—they tend to have low validity and can be unsuitable for feedback purposes.

Behavioral appraisals, although still subjective, focus on more observable aspects of performance. They were developed in response to the problems of trait appraisals. These scales focus on specific, prescribed behaviors that can help ensure that all parties understand what the ratings are really measuring. Because they are less ambiguous, they can provide useful feedback–for instance, with peer evaluations in student groups.[75] Exhibit 10.5 contains an example of a behaviorally anchored rating scale (BARS) for evaluating quality.

Results appraisals are more objective, focusing on production data such as sales volume (for a salesperson), units produced (for a line worker), or profits (for a manager). One approach to results appraisals—**management by objectives (MBO)**—involves a subordinate and a supervisor agreeing in advance on specific performance goals (objectives). They then develop a plan that describes the time frame and criteria for determining whether the objectives have been reached. The aim is to agree on a set of objectives that are clear, specific, and reachable. For example, an objective for a salesperson might be "Add three big new customers during the following year."

management by objectives (MBO)

A process in which objectives set by a subordinate and a supervisor must be reached within a given time period.

EXHIBIT 10.5

Example of BARS for Evaluating Team Member Effectiveness

Team member effectiveness includes several areas, including how much each member contributes to the team's work.		
Outstanding	5	Made critical contributions to the team's final product. Came to all team meetings prepared. Completed work in a timely and high-quality manner. Offered to help teammates. Took on extra work.
	4	Made important contributions to the team's final product. Came to all team meetings prepared. Completed work in a timely and high-quality manner.
Average	3	Made a solid contribution to the team's final product. Came to all team meetings prepared. Completed work in a generally timely and acceptable-quality manner.
	2	Made a moderate contribution to the team's final product. Missed some team meetings and was inadequately prepared for many. Completed work sporadically and it lacked quality.
Poor	1	Made no meaningful contribution to the team's final product. Missed most team meetings and deadlines. Did low-quality work.

SOURCE: Adapted from Ohland, M., Loughry, M. and Woehr, D., et al., "The Comprehensive Assessment of Team Member Effectiveness: Development of a Behaviorally Anchored Rating Scale for Self- and Peer Evaluation," *Academy of Management Learning & Education* 11 (2012), pp. 609–30.

MBO has several important advantages. First, it avoids the biases and measurement difficulties of trait and behavioral appraisals. At the end of the review period, employees are judged on actual job performance as compared against objectives. Second, because the employee and manager have agreed on objectives, the employee is likely to understand and be more committed to reaching them. Third, MBO allows employees to adapt their approach as needed (within limits, for instance legal and ethical), to achieve the desired results.

But the approach has disadvantages as well. It can result in unrealistic objectives being set, frustrating the employee and the manager. The objectives can be too rigid, leaving the employee with insufficient flexibility should circumstances change. Finally, MBO often focuses too much on short-term achievement at the expense of longer-term goals.

None of these systems is easy to do properly, and all have drawbacks that must be guarded against. In choosing an appraisal method, the following guidelines can help:

1. Base performance standards on job analysis.
2. Communicate performance standards to employees.
3. Evaluate employees on specific performance-related behaviors rather than on a single global or overall measure.
4. Document the PA process carefully.
5. If possible, use more than one rater (discussed in the next section).
6. Have a formal and fair appeal process.
7. Always take legal considerations into account.[76]

Who Should Do the Appraisal?

Just as multiple methods can gather performance appraisal information, multiple people can provide it. Managers and supervisors are the traditional sources, because they often are in the best position to observe an employee's performance. However, companies also can use peers, team members, and customers to provide input. These sources often have different perspectives and often are best at identifying leadership potential and interpersonal skills.

One increasingly popular source of appraisal is a manager's subordinates. Managers then receive feedback on how their employees view them. Often this information is given in confidence to the manager and not shared with superiors. Even so, this approach can make managers (and their direct reports) uncomfortable, but the feedback they get can be extremely useful and help them improve their management style. Because this process gives employees power over their bosses, usually it is used for development purposes only, not for salary or promotion decisions.

Internal and external customers also can provide performance appraisal information, particularly for companies like Ford and Honda that emphasize total quality management. Internal customers can be anyone inside the organization who depends on an employee's work output.

Usually it's a good idea to ask employees to evaluate their own performance. Although self-appraisals may be biased upward, self-evaluation increases employees' involvement in the review process and is a good starting point for establishing performance and developmental goals.

Because each source of PA information has limitations, and because different people see different aspects of performance, Tesco, Philips, Penguin Random House, and many other companies ask more than one source for appraisal information. In **360-degree appraisal**, people obtain feedback from every direction: subordinates, peers, outsiders (customers, vendors), and superiors.[77] Often the person being rated can select the appraisers, subject to a manager's

360-degree appraisal

Process of using multiple sources of appraisal to gain a comprehensive perspective on one's performance.

imtmphoto/Shutterstock

approval, with the understanding that the individual appraisals are kept confidential; results are consolidated for each group of appraisers.

The 360-degree appraisal offers many advantages. It provides a much fuller picture of a person's strengths and weaknesses, and it often captures information that other methods miss. For example, an employee may have a difficult relationship with his or her supervisor yet be highly regarded by peers and subordinates. The approach can lead to significant improvement, as people often are very motivated to improve their ratings. The 360-degree method has improved managers' performance in many countries, but cultural differences can affect its impact.[78]

On the downside, employees are not always willing to rate their colleagues harshly, so a certain uniformity of ratings may result. Importantly, the 360-degree appraisal does not measure actual job performance, so objective criteria such as sales and cost targets should be used as well. Therefore the objective of this method usually is personal development rather than a basis for administrative decisions such as raises. For those, appraisal methods like MBO are more appropriate.[79]

How Do You Give Employees Feedback?

Appraisals are most effective when they stem from a familiar work relationship rather than being just a top-down formal judgment issued only once a year. Managers of sports teams do not wait until the season is over to appraise their players; they work together throughout the season to improve individual and team performance. In high-functioning companies, informal appraisal and feedback are always taking place. Managers communicate with their employees frequently, praising or coaching as appropriate and together assessing progress toward goals. When managers and employees have good relationships and open communication, the annual formal feedback should rarely be a surprise.

> In high-functioning organizations, informal appraisal and feedback are happening constantly.

Giving and receiving PA feedback are stressful tasks for both managers and subordinates. The purposes of PA conflict to some degree. Providing developmental feedback requires understanding and support, but the manager must also be objective and be able to make tough decisions. Employees want to know how they are doing, but typically they are uncomfortable about getting feedback. And the organization's need to make HR decisions conflicts with the individual employee's need to maintain a positive image.[80] These conflicts often make PA interviews difficult.

There is no one best way to do a PA interview. Appraisal feedback generally works best when it is specific and constructive—related to clear goals or behaviors and clearly intended to help the employee rather than simply criticize. Managers have an interest not just in rating performance but in raising it, and effective appraisals take that into account. In addition, the appraisal is likely to be more meaningful and satisfying when the manager gives the employee an opportunity to discuss and respond to the appraisal.

One of the most difficult conversations comes when an employee is performing poorly. Exhibit 10.6 contains a PA interview format to use when an employee is performing below acceptable levels.

Here are some guidelines for giving feedback to employees performing at average levels:

1. Summarize the employee's performance and be specific.
2. Explain why the employee's work is important to the organization.
3. Thank the employee for doing the job.
4. Raise any relevant issues, such as areas for improvement.
5. Express confidence in the employee's future good performance.

Performance appraisal is a core component of the much broader, continuous process of performance management (PM). Whereas PA is a discrete (often, once a year) event, PM (done well) is an ongoing process requiring many activities. Performance management includes a variety of strategically chosen managerial processes,[81] including more giving feedback more frequently, leading, motivating, teaming, and communicating (all elaborated in later chapters).

Bottom Line
Effective feedback raises employee performance. *What kind of feedback is most likely to be effective?*

1. **Summarize** the employee's performance as specifically as possible. Describe the performance in behavioral or outcome terms, such as sales or absenteeism. Don't say the employee has a poor attitude; rather, explain which employee behaviors indicate a poor attitude.

2. **Describe** the expectations and standards, again being specific.

3. **Determine** the causes for the low performance; get the employee's input.

4. **Discuss** solutions to the problem with the employee playing a major role.

5. **Agree** to a solution. As a supervisor, you have input into the solution. Raise issues and questions but also provide support.

6. **Agree** to a timetable for improvement.

7. **Document** the meeting.

8. **Follow up** with meetings if needed.

EXHIBIT 10.6
A PA Interview Format for Underperforming Employees

Designing Reward Systems

Giving people appropriate rewards—most obviously, pay and benefits—is a vital HR activity. Traditionally pay has been the primary monetary reward, but benefits receive a great deal of attention today.[82] The typical employer now pays about 31 percent of payroll costs in benefits.[83] Benefits costs have risen faster than wages and salaries, fueled by the rapidly rising cost of medical care. Accordingly, employers attempt to reduce benefits costs, even as their value to employees is rising.

LO 10-6 Describe the fundamental aspects of reward systems.

Benefits are more complex than they used to be. Many new types are available, and tax laws affect myriad benefits such as health insurance and pension plans.

> The typical employer today pays about 31 percent of payroll costs in benefits.

Pay Decisions

Reward systems serve the strategic purposes of attracting, motivating, and retaining people. Wages are based on a complex set of forces. Exhibit 10.7 shows some of the factors that influence the wage mix.

Three types of decisions are crucial for designing an effective pay plan: pay level, pay structure, and individual pay.

Pay level refers to the choice of whether to be a high-, average-, or low-paying employer. Compensation is a major cost for any organization, so low wages can be justified on a short-term financial basis. But being the high-wage employer—the highest-paying company in the region—ensures that the company will attract many applicants. Being a wage leader may be important during times of low unemployment or intense competition.

The *pay structure* decision is how to price different jobs within the organization. Jobs similar in worth usually are grouped into job families. Each job family has a pay grade with a floor and a ceiling. Exhibit 10.8 illustrates a hypothetical pay structure.

Finally, *individual pay decisions* determine different pay rates for different people holding jobs of similar worth within the same job family. These pay differences are decided in

Internal Factors	External Factors
Compensation policy of organization	Conditions of labor market
Worth of job	Cost of living
Employee's relative worth	Collective bargaining
Employer's ability to pay	Legal requirements

EXHIBIT 10.7
Factors Affecting the Wage Mix

SOURCE: Snell, S. A. and Bohlander, G. W., *Managing Human Resources,* 16th ed. Boston, MA: Cengage Learning, 2012.

EXHIBIT 10.8
Pay Structure

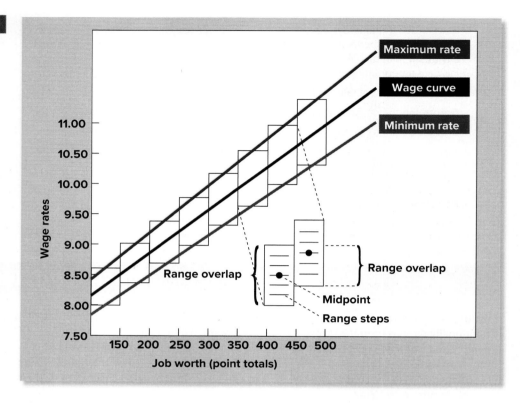

SOURCE: Sherman, A., Bohlander, G. and Snell, S., *Managing Human Resources,* 11th ed. Boston, MA: South-Western, 1998.

two ways. First, some individuals in the same job family have more seniority than others. Second, some are better performers than others and therefore deserve higher pay. These decisions may become more difficult as more employees use online resources such as Glassdoor.com and Salary.com to check whether their pay is above or below the average for similar job titles.[84]

Incentive Systems and Variable Pay

Various incentive systems have been devised to encourage and motivate employees to be more productive.[85] The most common type of incentive system is the individual incentive plan. An individual incentive system uses an objective standard against which a worker's performance is compared. Pay for each person is determined accordingly. Sales jobs commonly use such plans—for example, a salesperson will receive extra compensation for exceeding a sales target. Another widely used individual incentive is management bonuses.

When designed effectively, individual incentive plans can be highly motivating. Some companies, including Walmart, use them for nonmanagers. In the first quarter of 2018, the retailer paid $560 million in bonuses to almost 900,000 employees. Walmart hopes that using bonuses to reward hourly employees for meeting sales, profit, and inventory targets each quarter will improve job satisfaction and reduce turnover.[86]

Group incentive plans base pay on group performance. These plans can give employees a sense of shared participation and even ownership in the performance of the team or unit.

Profit-sharing plans usually apply to a division or organization as a whole, although some incentives may still be tailored to subunit performance. In most companies, the profit-sharing plan uses a formula that allocates an annual amount to each employee if the company exceeds a profit target. For example, New Belgium Brewing Company offers profit sharing as a benefit, and the amount of money given to employees depends on the company meeting performance goals.[87]

Bottom Line

Incentives can influence any aspect of performance. *Think about the duties and responsibilities of a typical Walmart store employee. What should the company provide bonuses for?*

One disadvantage of profit-sharing plans is that they do not reward individual performance. However, they do give all employees a stake in the company's success, and thereby motivate efforts to improve the company's profitability.

When objective performance measures are not available but the company still wants to base pay on performance, it uses a merit pay system. Individuals' pay raises and bonuses are based on the merit rating they receive from their manager.

Executive Pay and Stock Options

Executive pay and stock options, particularly for CEOs, are major sources of controversy. One reason is that the gap between the pay of top executives and the average pay of employees has widened considerably. In the mid-1960s in the United States, the average company paid its CEO roughly 20 times as much as it paid its average nonmanagement worker. More recently, the ratio of CEO pay to average-worker pay soared to around 360-to-1.[88] People differ as to whether or not they approve of such high management-to-worker pay dispersion, but recent research shows an important bottom line: Bigger differences relate to stronger firm performance in the short term but worse performance in the long run.[89]

The fastest-growing part of executive compensation comes from stock options and grants. Stock options give the holder the right to purchase shares of stock at a specified price. If the company's stock price is $8 a share, the company may award a manager the right to purchase a specific number of shares of company stock at that price. If the price of the stock rises to $10 a share after a specified holding period—usually three years or more—the manager can exercise the option. She pays $8 per share, sells the shares on the stock market at $10, and keeps the difference. (Of course, if the stock price never rises above $8, the options will be worthless.) For many top managers, large option grants have become a major source of additional compensation.

Companies issue options to managers to align their interests with those of the company's owners, the shareholders. The assumption is that managers will become even more focused on making the company successful, delivering stock price increases. Assuming that the executives continue to own stock year after year, the amount of their wealth tied to the company's performance—and their incentive to work hard for the company—should continually increase.[90]

Many critics say that excessive use of options encourages executives to focus on short-term results to drive up the price of their stock at the expense of their firm's long-run competitiveness. Others say that lucrative options have motivated questionable or even unethical behavior. A plunging stock market highlights another problem with stock options: Many options become essentially worthless, so they provide no reward.[91]

Employee Benefits

Like pay systems, employee benefit plans are subject to regulation. Some benefits are required by law, and some are optional for employers.

The three basic required benefits are workers' compensation, Social Security, and unemployment insurance. *Workers' compensation* provides financial support to employees suffering a work-related injury or illness. *Social Security,* as established in the Social Security Act of 1935, provides financial support to retirees; in subsequent amendments, the act was expanded to cover employees with disabilities. The funds come from payments made by employers, employees, and self-employed workers. *Unemployment insurance* provides financial support to employees who are laid off for reasons they cannot control. Companies that terminate fewer employees pay less into the unemployment insurance fund; thus organizations have an incentive to keep terminations at a minimum.

Many benefits are not required to be employer-provided. The most common are pension plans and medical and hospital insurance, and they are undergoing major changes. For decades, most Americans under the retirement age were covered by health insurance plans provided by their employers. But as the cost of providing this benefit has soared far faster than other compensation costs, employers started dropping it or providing very limited policies.

Bottom Line
Many organizations continually seek ways to reduce benefits costs. *What benefits have you received from an employer? Did you ever consider the cost of those benefits?*

Employee benefits include those required by law, such as workers' compensation, Social Security, and unemployment insurance, and those chosen by the employer. Retirement plans and paid vacation time are examples of employer-provided, nonrequired benefits.

Triangle Images/Getty Images

cafeteria benefit program

An employee benefit program in which employees choose from a menu of options to create a benefit package tailored to their needs.

flexible benefit programs

Benefit programs in which employees are given credits to spend on benefits that fit their unique needs.

comparable worth

Principle of equal pay for different jobs of equal worth.

In 2010 the federal government responded to concern about the rising number of uninsured people and the high cost of care by passing the Patient Protection and Affordable Care Act. At this writing, Congress is debating alternative health care laws such as the American Health Care Act. Congress introduced the bill in 2017, but members are still revising it.[92]

At the same time, retirement benefits have shifted away from guaranteed pension payments. Whereas a promised monthly payout used to be the norm, now only about 7 percent of companies offer this to new employees.[93] Instead, employers, and perhaps their employees, may contribute to an individual retirement account or 401(k) plan, which is invested. When the employee retires, he gets the total amount accumulated in the account.

Because of the wide variety of possible benefits and considerable differences in employee preferences and needs, companies often use **cafeteria** or **flexible benefit programs**. Employees receive credits that they spend on benefits they most desire. They use their credits toward customized packages of benefits—medical and dental insurance, dependent care, life insurance, and so on.

Legal Issues in Compensation and Benefits

Several laws affect employee compensation and benefits. The Fair Labor Standards Act sets minimum wage, maximum hour, and child labor provisions.[94] The Equal Pay Act (EPA) of 1963 prohibits unequal pay for men and women who perform equal work. Equal work means jobs that require equal skill, effort, and responsibility and are performed under similar working conditions. Although equal pay for equal work may sound like common sense, many employers have fallen victim to this law by rationalizing that men, traditionally the breadwinners, deserve more pay than women or by giving equal jobs different titles (senior assistant versus office manager) as the sole basis for pay differences.

The **comparable worth** doctrine implies that women who perform *different* jobs of *equal* worth as those performed by men in the same company should be paid the same wage.[95] In contrast to equal-pay-for-equal-work, comparable worth means that the jobs need *not* be the same to require the same pay. For example, nurses (predominantly female) were paid considerably less than skilled craftworkers (predominantly male), even though the two jobs were found to be of equal value or worth.[96] Under the Equal Pay Act, this would not constitute pay discrimination because the jobs are very different. But under the comparable worth concept, these findings indicate discrimination because the jobs are of equal worth.

To date, no federal law requires comparable worth, and the Supreme Court has made no decisive rulings about it. However, some states—including Arkansas, Idaho, Iowa, Kentucky, Maine, Massachusetts, North and South Dakota, Oklahoma, and Tennessee—have comparable worth laws for public sector employees.[97]

Some laws pertain mostly to benefit practices. The Pregnancy Discrimination Act of 1978 states that pregnancy is a disability and qualifies a woman to receive the same benefits that she would with any other disability. The Employee Retirement Income Security Act (ERISA) of 1974 protects private pension programs from mismanagement. ERISA requires that retirement benefits be paid to those who vest or earn a right to draw benefits. It ensures retirement benefits for employees whose companies go bankrupt or who otherwise cannot meet their pension obligations.

Health and Safety

The Occupational Safety and Health Act (OSHA) of 1970 requires employers to pursue workplace safety. Employers must maintain records of injuries and deaths caused by workplace accidents and submit to on-site inspections. Large-scale industrial accidents and nuclear power plant disasters worldwide have focused attention on the importance of workplace safety.

Coal mining is one of many industries that benefit from safety laws. Mining is one of the five most dangerous jobs to perform, according to the U.S. Bureau of Labor Statistics. Mine safety tragically returned to American consciousness in April 2010, when a coal mine explosion at the Massey Energy Company's Upper Big Branch Mine killed 29 workers. An independent investigation found that the accident could have been prevented and was attributable to safety system failures. Don Blankenship, the former CEO, was convicted of conspiracy to willfully violate mine health and safety standards.[98]

Yet, according to the Mine Safety and Health Administration, mines have become safer. In the 1980s, hundreds of coal miners died in mine accidents every year. Since the Massey disaster, the number of annual fatalities was less than 50.[99]

Another area of concern is the safety of young immigrant workers. A recent study found that Latino immigrants have the highest workplace fatality rate (3.7 per 100,000 workers) than all other workers. Reasons include lack of safety training and language and cultural barriers.[100]

Labor Relations

Labor relations is the system of relations between workers and management. When workers organize for the purpose of negotiating with management to improve their wages, hours, or working conditions, two processes are involved: unionization and collective bargaining. Labor unions recruit members, collect dues, and negotiate to ensure that employees are treated fairly regarding pay, safety, and other issues. Although fewer people than before belong to labor unions, these processes have evolved since the 1930s in the United States to provide important employee rights.[101]

LO 10-7 Summarize how unions and labor laws influence human resource management.

labor relations

The system of relations between workers and management.

Labor Laws

Try to imagine what life would be like with unemployment at 25 percent. Pretty grim, you would say. Legislators in 1935 felt that way too. Therefore, organized labor received its Magna Carta with the passage of the National Labor Relations Act.

The National Labor Relations Act (also called the Wagner Act after its legislative sponsor) ushered in an era of rapid unionization by (1) declaring labor organizations legal, (2) establishing five unfair employer labor practices, and (3) creating the National Labor Relations Board (NLRB). Prior to the act, employers could fire workers who favored unions, and federal troops often put down strikes. Today the NLRB conducts unionization elections, hears complaints of unfair labor practices, and issues injunctions against offending employers.

The Wagner Act boosted union growth by enabling workers to use the law and the courts to organize and collectively bargain for better wages, hours, and working conditions. Many workplace improvements that now are taken for granted, including minimum wages, health benefits, maternity leave, the 35-hour workweek, and worker protections in general were largely the result of collective bargaining over many years by unions.

For years, the Service Employees International Union has aggressively tried to organize workers at McDonald's, the largest fast-food chain in the world. So far, the company remains union-free. For a manager, what would be the pros and cons of a union?

Dan Holm/Shutterstock

Public policy began on the side of organized labor in 1935, but over the next 25 years the pendulum swung toward management's side. The Labor-Management Relations Act, or Taft-Hartley Act (1947), protected employers' free speech rights, defined unfair labor practices by unions, and permitted workers to decertify (reject) a union as their representative.

Finally, the Labor-Management Reporting and Disclosure Act, or Landrum-Griffin Act (1959), swung the public policy pendulum midway between organized labor and management. By declaring a bill of rights for union members, establishing control over union dues increases, and imposing reporting requirements for unions, Landrum-Griffin focused on curbing abuses by union leadership and ridding unions of corruption.

Unionization

How do workers join unions? Through a union organizer or local union representative, workers learn what benefits they receive by joining.[102] The National Labor Relations Board will conduct a certification election if at least 30 percent of the employees sign authorization cards. Management has several choices at this stage: to recognize the union without an election, to consent to an election, or to contest the number of cards signed and resist an election.

If an election is warranted, an NLRB representative will conduct one by secret ballot. A simple majority of those voting determines the winner. If the union wins the election, it is certified as the bargaining unit representative.

During the campaign preceding the election, management and the union each try to convince the workers how to vote. Most workers, though, are somewhat resistant to campaign efforts, having made up their minds well before the NLRB appears on the scene. If the union wins the election, management and the union are legally required to bargain in good faith to obtain a collective bargaining agreement or contract.

Deciding whether or not to join a union can be a complicated choice with conflicting considerations.[103] Exhibit 10.9 shows the major influences on union votes.[104] First, economic factors: Unions attempt to raise the average wage rate for their members. Second, job dissatisfaction: Specific triggers include poor supervisory practices, favoritism, and perceived unfair or arbitrary discipline and discharge. Third is the belief that the union can obtain desired benefits. Finally, the image of the union: For instance, stories of union corruption and dishonesty can discourage workers from unionizing.

Collective Bargaining

In the United States, management and unions engage in a periodic ritual (typically every three years) of negotiating an agreement over wages, benefits, hours, and working conditions. Two types of disputes can arise during this process. First, before an agreement is

EXHIBIT 10.9
Determinants of Union
Voting Behavior

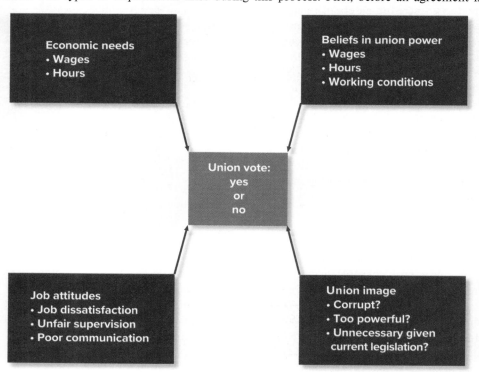

reached, the workers may go on strike to compel agreement on their terms. This is an *economic strike* and is permitted by law.

Strikes today are not common, although they sometimes occur as a last resort. Strikers are not paid if they are on strike, and few workers want to undertake this hardship unnecessarily. In addition, managers may legally hire replacement workers during a strike, offsetting some of the strike's effect. Finally, workers are as aware as managers of the tough competition companies face today, and if treated fairly they usually will share management's interest in reaching an agreement.

Once an agreement is signed, management and the union sometimes disagree over interpretation of the agreement. Usually they settle their disputes through arbitration. **Arbitration** is the use of a neutral third party, typically jointly selected, to resolve the dispute. U.S. companies use arbitration while an agreement is in effect to avoid *wildcat strikes* (in which workers walk off the job in violation of the contract) or unannounced work stoppages.

What does a collective bargaining agreement contain? In a **union shop**, a union security clause specifies that workers after a while must join the union. **Right-to-work** states, through restrictive legislation, do not permit union shops; that is, workers have the right to work without being forced to join a union. The southern United States has many right-to-work states.

The wage component of the contract spells out pay rates, including premium pay for overtime and paid holidays. Individual rights usually specify how seniority is considered in decisions such as pay, job bidding, and layoffs.

The grievance procedure is a feature of any contract. Through the grievance procedure, unions perform a vital service for their members by giving them a voice in what goes on during contract negotiations and contract administration.[105] In about 50 percent of discharge cases that go to arbitration, the arbitrator overturns management's decision and reinstates the worker.[106]

Unions have a legal duty to provide fair representation, which means they must represent and protect the rights of all workers in the bargaining unit.

arbitration

The use of a neutral third party to resolve a labor dispute.

union shop

An organization with a union and a union security clause specifying that workers must join the union after a set period of time.

right-to-work

Legislation that allows employees to work without having to join a union.

What Does the Future Hold?

In recent years, union membership has declined to about 10.5 percent of the U.S. labor force—down from a peak of more than 33 percent at the end of World War II (see Exhibit 10.10). Automation eliminated many of the manufacturing jobs that used to be union strongholds. Employees in most office jobs are less interested in joining unions and are more difficult to organize. Tough global competition has made managers less willing to give in to union demands, and therefore the benefits of unionization are less apparent to many workers—particularly to young, skilled workers who no longer expect to stay with one company all their lives.

EXHIBIT 10.10

Decline in Union Membership, 1983–2018

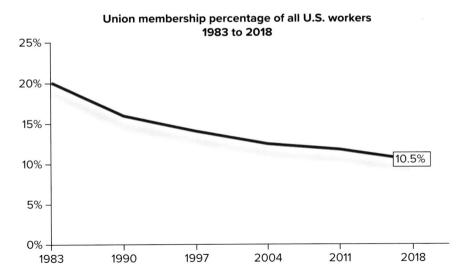

SOURCE: Data adapted from the Bureau of Labor Statistics, "Union Membership Rate 10.5 Percent in 2018, Down from 21.1 Percent in 1983," press release, January 25, 2019, https://www.bls.gov/opub/ted/2019/union-membership-rate-10-point-5-percent-in-2018-down-from-20-point-1-percent-in-1983.htm?view_full.

Management in Action

GOOGLE: HIRING FOR CHANGE

No industry moves and evolves faster than tech. Therefore, organizations that do not actively manage for change are likely to become obsolete in short order. Managing for change at Google begins with its hiring process.

Google is focused on creation and innovation. Projects and roles at Google are fluid and dynamic, which requires a workforce that is able to adapt and change according to ever-evolving demands. So when the HR specialists at Google are looking at new candidates, they're seeking traits that don't necessarily indicate that of a specialist, but rather a generalist—someone who's passionate and equipped to jump into any project and be an immediate asset. One of the most important traits that a candidate can have, then, is curiosity.[107]

Curious individuals are interested not just in one thing, as a specialist might be, but in everything. Curious individuals continually seek to learn and explore, which is the foundation for everything Google does. Former CEO of Google, Eric Schmidt, says, "'learning animals' have the smarts to handle massive change and the character to love it."[108]

Part of ensuring that Google is hiring curious generalists is implementing a rather unorthodox element to its hiring practice. In most organizations, one person ultimately decides who gets hired or not. At Google, however, all hiring is done by committee. Each prospective candidate who makes it through the initial round of interviews with the hiring manager is passed along to an independent hiring committee, which then further assesses the candidate. To be hired, all committee members must agree.[109]

Of course, this committee process slows down the hiring process substantially. The hope at Google is that a delay in weeks will pay off for many more years of productivity in work environments that are constantly changing.

1. What are your thoughts about the preference of generalists over specialists? What benefits and drawbacks do you see in this approach?
2. Do you think Google's HR strategy will enable it to maintain a competitive advantage? Why or why not? What will it have to do to sustain advantage?

In recent years, union membership has declined to about 10.5 percent of the U.S. labor force.

Some people applaud unions' decline. Others hope for a reemergence. Unions are adapting to changing workforce demographics; they are paying more attention to women, older workers, government employees, and people who work at home.

When companies recognize that their success depends on the talents and energies of employees, the interests of unions and managers can converge. Rather than one side exploiting or fighting the other, unions and managers can find common ground in developing, valuing, and involving employees. Whether or not employees belong to a union, they, not companies, own their own human capital. And these employees are free to leave the organization, taking their human capital with them.

This leaves organizations in a particularly vulnerable position if HR performs poorly, for instance by treating employees as their least important stakeholder. To establish a strong competitive capability, organizations need ways to obtain, retain, and engage their people properly, as addressed in the coming chapters..

"Management in Action: Onward" explores why and how this is a critical issue for Google.

KEY TERMS

adverse impact, p. 309

arbitration, p. 321

assessment center, p. 305

cafeteria benefit program, p. 318

comparable worth, p. 318

development, p. 309

diversity training, p. 310

employment-at-will, p. 307

flexible benefit programs, p. 318

RETAINING WHAT YOU LEARNED

In Chapter 10, you learned that by aligning their human resources and strategies, organizations can achieve a competitive advantage. Hiring the right number and types of employees requires effective planning. Organizations should design their HR systems to reinforce key employee behaviors. Internal and external recruitment each has advantages and disadvantages. Companies use a variety of selection methods when choosing whom to hire, including interviews and cognitive ability tests. It is important that organizations use methods that are valid and reliable. In order to maintain a competitive edge, companies need talented, flexible workers who engage in continuous training and development. While supervisors typically provide performance appraisals for their subordinates, organizations may seek this information from multiple sources. An organization's reward system consists of pay and benefits. Labor relations involve the interactions between workers and management. In addition to negotiating agreements with management, unions develop grievance procedures to protect member rights. Labor laws seek to protect the rights of operative-level employees and managers.

LO 10-1 Discuss how companies use human resource management to gain competitive advantage.

- To succeed, companies must align their human resources to their strategies. Effective planning is necessary to make certain that the right number and types of employees are available to implement a company's strategic plan.

- Companies that compete on cost, quality, service, and so on also should use their staffing, training, appraisal, and reward systems to elicit and reinforce the kinds of behaviors that underlie their strategies.

LO 10-2 Give reasons companies recruit both internally and externally for new hires.

- Sometimes companies prefer to recruit internally to make certain that employees are familiar with organizational policies and values.

- In other instances, companies prefer to recruit externally, such as through employee referrals, job boards, newspaper advertising, and campus visits, to find people with new ideas and fresh perspectives.

- External recruiting is also necessary to fill positions when the organization is growing or needs skills that do not exist among its current employees.

LO 10-3 Identify various methods for selecting new employees.

- There are myriad selection techniques from which to choose. Interviews and reference checks are the most common. Personality tests and cognitive ability tests measure an individual's aptitude and potential to do well on the job. Other selection techniques include assessment centers and integrity tests.

Planning	Programming	Evaluating
HR Environmental Scanning • Labor markets • Technology • Legislation • Competition • Economy **HR Planning** • Demand forecast • Internal labor supply • External labor supply • Job analysis	**HR Activities** • Recruitment • Selection • Diversity and inclusion • Training and development • Performance appraisal • Reward systems • Labor relations	**Results** • Productivity • Quality • Innovation • Satisfaction • Turnover • Absenteeism • Health

EXHIBIT 10.1 (revisited)

An Overview of the HR Planning Process

Background and reference checks verify that the information supplied by employees is accurate.

- Regardless of the approach used, any test should be able to demonstrate reliability (consistency across time and different interview situations) and validity (accuracy in predicting job performance).
- In addition, selection methods must comply with equal opportunity laws, which are intended to ensure that companies do not discriminate in any employment practices.

LO 10-4   Evaluate the importance of spending on training and development.

- People cannot depend on a single set of skills for all of their working lives. In today's changing, highly competitive world, old skills quickly become obsolete, and new ones become essential for success.
- Refreshing or updating an individual's skills requires continuous training, designed with measurable goals and methods that will achieve those goals.
- Gaining a competitive edge depends on having the most talented, flexible workers in the industry.

LO 10-5   Discuss options for who appraises an employee's performance.

- Many companies use multiple sources for appraisals because different people see different sides of an employee's performance. Typically, a superior evaluates an employee, but peers and team members are often well positioned to see aspects of performance that a superior misses. Even a manager's subordinates can provide input to get yet another perspective on the evaluation.
- Particularly in companies concerned about quality, internal and external customers can be surveyed.
- Employees should evaluate their own performance, to engage them in the process and get them thinking about future goals.

LO 10-6   Describe the fundamental aspects of reward systems.

- Rewards systems include pay and benefits.
- Pay systems have three basic components: pay level, pay structure, and individual pay determination. To achieve an advantage over competitors, executives can pay generally higher wages, but this decision must be weighed against the need to control costs.
- To achieve internal equity (paying people what they are worth relative to their peers within the company), managers must look at the pay structure, making certain that pay differentials are based on valid and fair criteria.
- Individual pay determination is often based on merit and contributions. Importantly, men and women should receive equal pay for equal work, and managers may wish to base pay decisions on the idea of comparable worth (equal pay for an equal contribution).

LO 10-7   Summarize how unions and labor laws influence human resource management.

- Labor relations involve the interactions between workers and management. Unions provide one mechanism by which this relationship is conducted.
- Unions seek to present a collective voice for workers, to make their needs and wishes known to management. Also, they negotiate agreements with management regarding a range of issues such as wages, hours, working conditions, job security, and health care.
- One important tool that unions can use is the grievance procedure, established through collective bargaining. This mechanism gives employees a way to seek redress for wrongful action by management. In this way, unions protect the rights of all employees.
- Labor laws seek to protect the rights of both employees and managers so that their relationship can be productive and agreeable.

DISCUSSION QUESTIONS

1. How will changes in the labor force affect HRM practices for the next decade?
2. Describe the major regulations governing HRM practices. Which, if any, have benefited you? Which ones could have benefited you but were not applied?
3. How could job analysis be relevant to each of the six key HRM activities discussed in the chapter (i.e., planning, staffing, training, performance appraisal, reward systems, labor relations)?
4. What are the various methods for recruiting employees? Why are some better than others? In what sense are they better? Describe some of your personal experiences.
5. What is a test? Give some examples of tests used by employers that you have seen or heard about.

6. What purposes do performance appraisals serve? Why are there so many appraisal methods? Which have you experienced, and what do you think of how they were used?
7. What are some key ideas to remember when conducting a performance appraisal? What mistakes and best practices have you seen?
8. How would you define an effective reward system? What role do benefits serve in a reward system?
9. Why do workers join unions? What implications would this have for an organization that wishes to remain nonunion?
10. Discuss the advantages and disadvantages of collective bargaining for the employer and the employee.

EXPERIENTIAL EXERCISES

10.1   The Legal Interview

OBJECTIVES

1. To introduce you to the complexities of employment law.
2. To identify interview practices that might lead to discrimination in employment.

INSTRUCTIONS

1. Working alone, review the text material on interviewing and discrimination in employment.
2. In small groups, complete the Legal Interview Worksheet.

3. After the class reconvenes, group spokespersons present group findings.

Legal Interview Worksheet

The employment interview is one of the most critical steps in the employment selection process. It also may be an occasion for discriminating against individual employment candidates. The following represents questions that interviewers often ask job applicants. Identify the legality of each question by circling L (legal) or I (illegal) and briefly explain your decision.

Interview Question	Legality	Explanation
1. Could you provide us with a photo for our files?	L I	_____
2. Have you ever used another name (previous married name or alias)?	L I	_____
3. What was your maiden name?	L I	_____
4. What was your wife's maiden name?	L I	_____
5. What was your mother's maiden name?	L I	_____
6. What is your current address?	L I	_____
7. What was your previous address?	L I	_____
8. What is your Social Security number?	L I	_____
9. Where was your place of birth?	L I	_____
10. Where were your parents born?	L I	_____
11. What is your national origin?	L I	_____
12. Are you a naturalized citizen?	L I	_____
13. What languages do you speak?	L I	_____
14. What is your religious/church affiliation?	L I	_____
15. What is your racial classification?	L I	_____
16. How many dependents do you have?	L I	_____
17. What are the ages of your dependent children?	L I	_____
18. What is your marital status?	L I	_____
19. How old are you?	L I	_____
20. Do you have proof of your age (birth certificate or baptismal record)?	L I	_____
21. Whom do we notify in case of an emergency?	L I	_____
22. What are your height and weight?	L I	_____
23. Have you ever been arrested?	L I	_____
24. Do you own your own car?	L I	_____
25. Do you own your own house?	L I	_____
26. Do you have any charge accounts?	L I	_____
27. Have you ever had your salary garnished?	L I	_____
28. To what organizations do you belong?	L I	_____
29. Are you available to work on Saturdays and Sundays?	L I	_____
30. Do you have any form of disability?	L I	_____

10.2   The Pay Raise

OBJECTIVES

1. To further your understanding of salary administration.
2. To examine the many facets of performance criteria, performance criteria weighting, performance evaluation, and rewards.

INSTRUCTIONS

1. Working in small groups, complete the Pay Raise Worksheet.
2. After the class reconvenes, group spokespersons present group findings.

Pay Raise Worksheet

April Knepper is the new supervisor of an assembly team. It is time for her to make pay raise allocations for her subordinates. She has been budgeted $30,000 to allocate among her seven subordinates as pay raises. There have been some ugly grievances in other work teams over past allocations, so Knepper has been advised to base the allocations on objective criteria that can be quantified, weighted, and computed in numerical terms. After she makes her allocations, Knepper must be prepared to justify her decisions. All of the evaluative criteria available to Knepper are summarized as follows:

| Employee | Seniority | Output Rating* | Absent Rate | Supervisory Ratings | | | |
				Skills	Initiative	Attitude	Personal
David Bruce	15 yrs.	0.58	0.5%	Good	Poor	Poor	Nearing retirement. Wife just passed away. Having adjustment problems.
Eric Cattalini	12 yrs.	0.86	2.0	Excellent	Good	Excellent	Going to night school to finish his BA degree.
Chua Li	7 yrs.	0.80	3.5	Good	Excellent	Excellent	Legally deaf.
Marilee Miller	1 yr.	0.50	10.0	Poor	Poor	Poor	Single parent with three children.
Victor Munoz	3 yrs.	0.62	2.5	Poor	Average	Good	Has six dependents. Speaks little English.
Derek Thompson	11 yrs.	0.64	8.0	Excellent	Average	Average	Married to rich wife. Personal problems.
Sarah Vickers	8 yrs.	0.76	7.0	Good	Poor	Poor	Women's activist. Wants to create a union.

* Output rating determined by production rate less errors and quality problems.

Concluding Case

INVINCIBILITY SYSTEMS

The 17,000 employees of Invincibility Systems design and make aerospace and defense equipment, such as spacecraft and missile propulsion systems. Along with cutting-edge engineering, the company stands out for its cutting-edge human resource management. Invincibility has hired quantitative experts to analyze HR data with the same care it uses to analyze rocket trajectories.

A few years ago, HR team members began collecting and analyzing data that would better address human resources challenges. They first wanted to improve recruiting. They collected data on the various sources of past applicants and the candidates actually selected. Then they used statistical analysis to identify which sources of applicants generated the most hires, as well as the sources that generated hires who went on to perform well.

The results of the analysis enabled Invincibility to make its recruiting process more efficient. Focusing on the most productive sources of top employees saved time and money that formerly had gone toward recruiting through channels that were less fruitful.

Next the HR team turned its efforts toward workforce planning. Each department of Invincibility collects data describing its personnel—for example, job categories, skill sets, career goals, years with the company, and performance reviews. It runs statistical analyses to predict the likelihood that employees will leave the company in the coming year. The results, coupled with sales forecasts, enable the company to predict how many new employees will need to be hired in each department.

The variety of factors that the HR team considers is key to making informed decisions that will benefit the company. For example, regressions are used to determine whether turnover is related to changes in employee benefits and even the month of the year. If the analysis shows that a factor has been significant in the past, the HR team accounts for it in the forecasts. In one situation, the team found that retirements in a department rose after the company announced that it would be phasing out health insurance benefits for retirees. More experienced workers left before the phase-out took effect. When the company prepared to phase out similar benefits in another division, the planners knew they would need to step up recruiting efforts in preparation for an uptick in retirements.

Some of the data Invincibility uses for planning are unsuitable for other kinds of HR decisions. For example, the company has found that employees' ages and marital status are relevant for predicting whether they are likely to leave the company. Turnover rates are higher among unmarried employees and recently hired employees (who tend to be younger). Thus the company plans greater recruiting efforts in departments where it has higher levels of young and unmarried employees. It also may consider stepping up its efforts to mentor and train employees in these departments for greater retention. However, it does not make employment decisions such as hiring and promotion based on these factors.

DISCUSSION QUESTIONS

1. Besides those identified, what other factors should Invincibility Systems take into account in its HR planning?

2. What legal concerns does the data analysis at Invincibility raise? How should the company address those issues?

3. Besides its use for HR planning and recruiting, how might Invincibility's data analysis be applied to improving the company's training programs?

ENDNOTES

1. Michael Schneider, "Google Gets 2 Million Applications a Year. To Have a Shot, Your Resume Must Pass the '6-Second Test,'" *Inc.,* https://www.inc.com/michael-schneider/its-harder-to-get-into-google-than-harvard.html accessed March 25, 2019.

2. Richard Feloni, "Google's Former HR Boss Shared the Company's 4 Rules for Hiring the Best Employees," *Business Insider,* March 8, 2018, https://www.businessinsider.com/how-google-hires-exceptional-employees-2016-2.

3. Nick Bastone, "Employee Confidence in Google CEO Sundar Pichai and His Leadership Team Is Reportedly at a Six-Year Low," *Business Insider,* February 1, 2019, https://www.businessinsider.com/google-ceo-sundar-pichai-employee-confidence-2019-2.

4. D. Ulrich and J. Dulebohn, "Are We There Yet? What's Next for HR?" *Human Resource Management Review* 25 (2015), pp. 188–204; D. Stone and D. Deadrick, "Challenges and Opportunities Affecting the Future of Human Resource Management," *Human Resource Management Review* 25 (2015), pp. 139–45.

5. T. T. Krishnan and H. Scullion, "Talent Management and Dynamic View of Talent in Small and Medium Enterprises," *Human Resource Management Review* 27 (2017), pp. 431–41.

6. G. Wood, M. Wang, and A. Veen, "How Far Has International HRM Travelled? A Systematic Review of Literature on Multinational Corporations (2000–2014)," *Human Resource Management Review* 29 (2019), pp. 59–75; C. Brewster, W. Mayrhofer, and A. Smale, "Crossing the Streams: HRM in Multinational Enterprises and Comparative HRM," *Human Resource Management Review* 26 (2016), pp. 285–97; A. Ariss and Y. Sidani, "Comparative International Human Resource Management: Future Research Directions," *Human Resource Management Review* 26 (2016), pp. 352–58; S. Khilji, I. Tarique, and R. Schuler, "Incorporating the Macro View in Global Talent Management," *Human Resource Management Review* 25 (2015), pp. 236–48.

7. L. Shore, J. Cleveland, and D. Sanchez, "Inclusive Workplaces: A Review and Model," *Human Resource Management Review* 28 (2018), pp. 176–89.

8. R. E. Ployhart, "Strategic Organizational Behavior (STROBE): The Missing Voice in the Strategic Human Capital Conversation," *Academy of Management Perspectives* 29 (2015), pp. 342–56.

9. R. E. Ployhart, (2015). "Strategic Organizational Behavior (STROBE): The Missing Voice in the Strategic Human Capital Conversation," *Academy of Management Perspectives* 29 (2015), pp. 342–56; J. Marler, "Strategic Human Resource in Context: A Historical and Global Perspective," *Academy of Management Perspectives* 26 (2012), pp. 6–11.

10. N. Gardner, D. McGranahan, and W. Wolf, "Question for Your HR Chief: Are We Using Our 'People Data' to Create Value?" *McKinsey Quarterly,* March 2011, https://www.mckinseyquarterly.com; D. Ulrich and J. Dulebohn, "Are We There Yet? What's Next for HR?" *Human Resource Management Review* 25 (2015), pp. 188–204.

11. C. Ostroff and D. Bowen, "Reflections on the 2014 Decade Award: Is There Strength in the Construct of HR System Strength?" *Academy of Management Review* 41 (2016), pp. 196–214.

12. A. Denisi and C. Smith, "Performance Appraisal, Performance Management, and Firm-Level Performance: A Review, a Proposed Model, and New Directions for Future Research," *Academy of Management Annals* 8 (2014), pp. 127–79; G. Saridakis, Y. Lai, and C. Cooper, "Exploring the Relationship between HRM and Firm Performance: A Meta-analysis of Longitudinal Studies," *Human Resource Management Review* 27 (2017), pp. 87–96; D. D. Shin and A. Konrad, "Causality between High-Performance Work Systems and Organizational Performance," *Journal of Management* 43 (2017), pp. 973–97.

13. A. Cardenal, "Costco vs. Wal-Mart: Higher Wages Mean Superior Returns for Investors," *The Motley Fool,* March 12, 2014, www.fool.com.

14. J. Hollenbeck and B. Jamieson, "Human Capital, Social Capital, and Social Network Analysis: Implications for Strategic Human Resource Management," *Academy of Management Perspectives* 29 (2015), pp. 370–85; D. Kryscynski and D. Ulrich, "Making Strategic Human Capital Relevant: A Time-Sensitive Opportunity," *Academy of Management Perspectives* 29 (2015), pp. 357–69; A. Nyberg and

P. Wright, "50 Years of Human Capital Research: Assessing What We Know, Exploring Where We Go," *Academy of Management Perspectives* 29 (2015), pp. 287–95.

15. M. Marchington and M. Marchington, "Human Resource Management (HRM): Too Busy Looking Up to See Where It Is Going Longer Term?" *Human Resource Management Review* 25 (2015), pp. 176–87.

16. P. M. Wright and S. A. Snell, "Partner or Guardian? HR's Challenge in Balancing Value and Values," *Human Resource Management* 44, no. 2 (2005), pp. 177–82.

17. M. Marchington and M. Marchington, "Human Resource Management (HRM): Too Busy Looking Up to See Where It Is Going Longer Term?" *Human Resource Management Review* 25 (2015), pp. 176–87; D. Ulrich and J. Dulebohn, "Are We There Yet? What's Next for HR?" *Human Resource Management Review* 25 (2015), pp. 188–204.

18. Robin Meyerhoff, "Why Social Entrepreneurs and Big Business Need Each Other More Than Ever," *Forbes,* November 1, 2018, https://www.forbes.com/sites/sap/2018/11/01/why-social-entrepreneurs-and-big-business-need-each-other-more-than-ever/#7bd0367245b4.

19. Josh Bersin, "The Rise of the Social Enterprise: A New Paradigm for Business," *Forbes,* April 3, 2018, https://www.forbes.com/sites/joshbersin/2018/04/03/the-rise-of-the-social-enterprise-a-new-paradigm-for-business/#552f68e571f0.

20. Deloitte Insights, "The Rise of the Social Enterprise," 2018 Deloitte Global Human Capital Trends, https://www2.deloitte.com/content/dam/insights/us/articles/HCTrends2018/2018-HCtrends_Rise-of-the-social-enterprise.pdf.

21. Robin Meyerhoff, "Why Social Entrepreneurs and Big Business Need Each Other More Than Ever," *Forbes,* November 1, 2018, https://www.forbes.com/sites/sap/2018/11/01/why-social-entrepreneurs-and-big-business-need-each-other-more-than-ever/#7bd0367245b4.

22. K. Sheridan, "Cyber-Security Skills Shortage Leaves Companies Vulnerable," *InformationWeek,* August 1, 2016, www.information week.com.

23. "What Does the Coming Labor Shortage from Retiring Baby Boomers Mean for Your Company?" The Conference Board, www.conference-board.org, accessed March 19, 2019; A. Mathur, "The Baby Boomers Are Doing Just That, Booming," *Forbes,* February 8, 2019, www.forbes.com.

24. R. Dobbs, J. Manyika, and J. Woetzel, "How U.S. Can Fill the Skills Gap," *Fortune,* May 12, 2015, www.fortune.com.

25. "Infosys Forms Community College Partnership in Rhode Island," WPRI, February 12, 2019, https://www.wpri.com.

26. J. Selingo, "Wanted: Factory Workers, Degree Required," *The New York Times,* January 30, 2017, www.nytimes.com.

27. A. Elahi, "What Is an H-1B Visa, and Why Are Tech Companies Worried about Them?" *Chicago Tribune,* February 1, 2017, www.chicagotribune.com.

28. D. E. Hartley, *Job Analysis at the Speed of Reality* (Amherst, MA: HRD Press, 1999); F. P. Morgeson and M. A. Campion, "Accuracy in Job Analysis: Toward an Inference-Based Model," *Journal of Organizational Behavior* 21, no. 7 (November 2000), pp. 819–27; J. S. Shippmann, R. A. Ash, L. Carr, and B. Hesketh, "The Practice of Competency Modeling," *Personnel Psychology* 53, no. 3 (Autumn 2000), pp. 703–40.

29. J. S. Shippmann, *Strategic Job Modeling: Working at the Core of Integrated Human Resources* (Mahwah, NJ: Erlbaum, 1999).

30. M. Applegate, "Difference between the Internal & External Recruitment Strategies," *Houston Chronicle,* http://www.chron.com, accessed April 14, 2015; D. E. Terpstra, "The Search for Effective Methods," *HR Focus,* May 1996, pp. 16–17; H. G. Heneman III and R. A. Berkley, "Applicant Attraction Practices and Outcomes among Small Businesses," *Journal of Small Business Management* 37, no. 1 (January 1999), pp. 53–74; J.-M. Hiltrop, "The Quest for the Best: Human Resource Practices to Attract and Retain Talent," *European Management Journal* 17, no. 4 (August 1999), pp. 422–30.

31. G. Crispin and M. Mehler, "10th Annual CareerXroads Source of Hire Report: by the Numbers," CareerXroads, March 2011, http://www.careerxroads.com; J. Light, "Recruiters Rethink Online Playbook," *The Wall Street Journal,* January 18, 2011, http://online.wsj.com.

32. "More Than Half of Employers Have Found Content on Social Media That Caused Them NOT to Hire a Candidate, According to Recent CareerBuilder Survey," *PR Newswire,* August 9, 2018, https://www.prnewswire.com/news-releases/more-than-half-of-employers-have-found-content-on-social-media-that-caused-them-not-to-hire-a-candidate-according-to-recent-careerbuilder-survey-300694437.html.

33. Sachi Barreiro, "State Laws on Social Media Password Requests by Employers," https://www.nolo.com/legal-encyclopedia/state-laws-on-social-media-password-requests-by-employers.html, accessed March 29, 2019.

34. Jillian Kramer, "What Recruiters Look at When Stalking Your Social Media," March 14, 2018, https://www.glassdoor.com/blog/what-recruiters-look-at-social-media/.

35. Saige Driver, "Keep It Clean: Social Media Screenings Gain in Popularity," October 7, 2018, https://www.businessnewsdaily.com/2377-social-media-hiring.html.

36. J. Scott, "Five Interview Questions That Reveal Top Talent," May 2013, www.online.citi.com..

37. D. Shane, "Samsonite CEO Quits after Doctorate Drama," *CNNMoney,* June 2, 2018, https://money.cnn.com.

38. "Conducting Background Investigations and Reference Checks," Society for Human Resource Management, September 20, 2018, www.shrm.org.

39. "Conducting Background Investigations and Reference Checks," Society for Human Resource Management, September 20, 2018, www.shrm.org.

40. CareerBuilder, "70% of Employers Are Snooping Candidates' Social Media Profiles," June 15, 2017, www.careerbuilder.com.

41. CareerBuilder, "More Than Half of Employers Have Found Content on Social Media That Caused Them Not to Hire a Candidate, According to Recent CareerBuilder Survey," August 9, 2018, www.careerbuilder.com.

42. C. C. Van Iddekinge, S. Lanivich, P. Roth, and E. Junco, "Social Media for Selection? Validity and Adverse Impact Potential of a Facebook-Based Assessment," *Journal of Management* 42 (2016), pp. 1811–35.

43. "Can Personality Tests Really Tell You If an Employee Will Succeed?" *Forbes,* January 7, 2019, www.forbes.com; L. Weber, "Today's Personality Tests Raise the Bar for Job Seekers," *The Wall Street Journal,* April 14, 2015, www.wsj.com.

44. Company profiles, "JP Morgan," "ExxonMobil," "Hewlett Packard," *Assessment Training,* https://www.assessment-training.com, accessed March 2, 2019.

45. R. E. Ployhart, J. A. Weekley, and K. Baughman, "The Structure and Function of Human Capital Emergence: A Multilevel Examination of the Attraction-Selection-Attrition Model," *Academy of Management Journal* 49, no. 4 (2006), pp. 661–77.

46. M. White, "Weed the People? Companies Relax Drug-Testing Policies in Bid to Attract More Workers," *NBC News,* May 7, 2018, https://www.nbcnews.com; R. Greenfield and J. Kaplan, "Why More Employers Are Skipping Drug Tests," *Money,* March 7, 2018, www.money.com.

47. S. Mukherjee, "Far More U.S. Workers Had Positive Drug Tests for Cocaine, Meth, and Marijuana in 2017 Than the Year Before," *Fortune,* May 9, 2018, http://fortune.com.

48. J. Reidy and D. Hewick, "Are Employer Drug-Testing Programs Obsolete?" Society for Human Resource Management, May 23, 2018, www.shrm.org; C. Rugaber, "Labor Shortage: More Businesses Are Mellowing Out over Hiring Marijuana Smokers," *USA Today,* May 3, 2018, www.usatoday.com; R. Greenfield and J. Kaplan, "The Coming Decline of the Employment Drug Test," *Bloomberg,* March 5, 2018, www.bloomberg.com.

49. K. Steinmetz, "Report Predicts 18 States Will Legalize Pot by 2020," *Fortune,* January 26, 2015, http://www.fortune.com; C. Rubin, "Medical Marijuana Laws Leave Employers Dazed and Confused," *Inc.,* February 12, 2010, http://www.inc.com.

50. H. Heneman III, T. Judge, and J. Kammeyer-Mueller, *Staffing Organizations,* 8th ed. (New York: McGraw-Hill, 2015).

51. W. Arthur Jr., D. J. Woehr, and R. Maldegen, "Convergent and Discriminant Validity of Assessment Center Dimensions: A Conceptual and Empirical Reexamination of the Assessment Center Construct-Related Validity Paradox," *Journal of Management* 26, no. 4 (2000), pp. 813–35; R. Randall, E. Ferguson, and F. Patterson,

"Self-Assessment Accuracy and Assessment Center Decisions," *Journal of Occupational and Organizational Psychology* 73, no. 4 (December 2000), p. 443.

52. "Employee Polygraph Protection Act (EPPA)," United States Department of Labor, Wage and Hour Division, www.dol.gov, accessed March 19, 2019.

53. American Psychological Association, "The Truth about Lie Detectors (aka Polygraph Tests)," http://www.apa.org, accessed April 14, 2015; D. S. Ones, C. Viswesvaran, and F. L. Schmidt, "Comprehensive Meta-analysis of Integrity Test Validities: Findings and Implications for Personnel Selection and Theories of Job Performance," *Journal of Applied Psychology* 78 (August 1993), pp. 679-703.

54. J. Scipioni, "Major Companies Have Announced Big Layoffs This Month," *Fox Business,* June 14, 2018, www.foxbusiness.com; R. Ferris and L. Kolodny, "Tesla to Cut 9% of Jobs in 'Difficult but Necessary' Reorganization," *CNBC,* June 12, 2018, www.cnbc.com.

55. S. Adams, "What to Do as Soon as You Get Laid Off," *Forbes,* February 18, 2015, http://www.forbes.com; R.-L. DeWitt, "The Structural Consequences of Downsizing," *Organization Science* 4, no. 1 (February 1993), pp. 30-40; P. P. Shah, "Network Destruction: The Structural Implications of Downsizing," *Academy of Management Journal* 43, no. 1 (February 2000), pp. 101-12.

56. See *Adair v. United States,* 2078 U.S. 161 (1908); D. A. Ballam, "Employment-at-Will: The Impending Death of a Doctrine," *American Business Law Journal* 37, no. 4 (Summer 2000), pp. 653-87.

57. L. Petersen, "Is It Less Risky to Terminate an Employee within the First 90 Days of Employment?" *HR Magazine,* September 2014, pp. 20-21, http://www.shrm.org; J. A. Segal, "A Warning about Warnings," *HR Magazine,* February 2009, pp. 67-70; International Public Management Association for Human Resources (IPMA-HR), "Progressive Discipline," IPMA-HR website, http://www.ipma-hr. org; U.S. Chamber of Commerce, "Progressive Discipline," http:// business.uschamber.com; D. Grote, "Positive Approach to Employee Discipline," *ManagerNewz,* March 12, 2007, http://archive. managernewz.com.

58. "How to Discipline and Fire Employees," *Entrepreneur,* http://www .entrepreneur.com, accessed April 14, 2015; J. W. Bucking, "Employee Terminations: Ten Must-Do Steps When Letting Someone Go," *Supervision,* May 2008, Business & Company Resource Center, http:// galenet.galegroup.com; M. Price, "Employee Termination Process Is Tough for Those on Both Sides," *Journal Record* (Oklahoma City, OK),October 23, 2008, Business & Company Resource Center, http://galenet.galegroup.com.

59. "UPS to Pay $4.9 Million to Settle EEOC Religious Discrimination Suit," EEOC press release, December 21, 2018, www.eeoc.gov.

60. "Pancake Chain IHOP to Pay $700,000 to Settle Sexual Harassment and Retaliation Lawsuit," EEOC press release, February 20, 2019, www.eeoc.gov.

61. R. Gatewood and H. Field, *Human Resource Selection,* 3rd ed. (Chicago: Dryden Press, 1994), pp. 36-49; R. A. Baysinger, "Disparate Treatment and Disparate Impact Theories of Discrimination: The Continuing Evolution of Title VII of the 1964 Civil Rights Act," in *Readings in Personnel and Human Resource Management,* ed. R. S. Schuler, S. A. Youngblood, and V. L. Huber (St. Paul, MN: West Publishing, 1987).

62. "2018 Training Industry Report," *Training Magazine,* www.trainingmag .com, accessed March 20, 2019.

63. "2018 Training Industry Report," *Training Magazine,* www.trainingmag .com, accessed March 20, 2019.

64. "2018 Training Industry Report," *Training Magazine,* www.trainingmag .com, accessed March 20, 2019.

65. "2018 Training Industry Report," *Training Magazine,* www.trainingmag .com, accessed March 20, 2019.

66. Andy Molinski, "Giving Feedback across Cultures," *Harvard Business Review,* February 15, 2013, https://hbr.org/2013/02/ giving-feedback-across-cultures.

67. Erin Meyer, "How to Give and Receive Feedback across Cultures," *Fast Company,* February 8, 2016, https://www.fastcompany. com/3056385/how-to-give-and-receive-feedback-across-cultures.

68. Venkatesan Swaminathan, "Leadership in Multicultural Environment," *Strategic Finance* 98, no. 11 (November 2016), pp. 21-22.

69. Gap Inc., "Gap Inc. to Hire 65,000 Seasonal Associates for the Holidays," September 17, 2018, https://corporate.gapinc.com.

70. Nick Bastone, "Former CEO Eric Schmidt Says Google Had to Revamp Its Whole Hiring Process because They Were Interviewing Candidates 16 Times," *Business Insider,* November 7, 2018, https:// www.businessinsider.com/eric-schmidt-google-hiring-process-2018-11.

71. Nitasha Tiku, "Google's Diversity Stats Are Still Very Dismal," *Wired,* June 14, 2018, https://www.wired.com/story/ googles-employee-diversity-numbers-havent-really-improved/.

72. Ellen McGirt, "Google Searches Its Soul," *Fortune,* February 1, 2017, http://fortune.com/google-diversity/.

73. "Learning & Development Best Practices from the Top Silicon Valley Companies," *Medium,* May 21, 2018, https://medium.com/@vibons_ video/learning-development-best-practices-from-the-top-silicon-valley-companies-792a615220aa.

74. A. Schleicher et al., "Putting the System into Performance Management Systems: A Review and Agenda for Performance Management Research," *Journal of Management* 44 (2018), pp. 2209-45.

75. M. Ohland, M. Loughry, D. Woehr, et al., "The Comprehensive Assessment of Team Member Effectiveness: Development of a Behaviorally Anchored Rating Scale for Self- and Peer Evaluation," *Academy of Management Learning & Education* 11 (2012), pp. 609-30.

76. For more information, see K. Wexley and G. Latham, *Increasing Productivity through Performance Appraisal* (Reading, MA: Addison-Wesley, 1994).

77. H. Bernardin, R. Konopaske, and C. Hagan, "A Comparison of Adverse Impact Levels Based on Top-down, Multisource, and Assessment Center Data: Promoting Diversity and Reducing Legal Challenges," *Human Resource Management* 51 (2012), pp. 313-41; I. O'Boyle, "Traditional Performance Appraisal versus 360-Degree Feedback," *Training & Management Development Methods* 27 (2013), pp. 201-07.

78. F. Shipper, R. C. Hoffman, and D. M. Rotondo, "Does the 360 Feedback Process Create Actionable Knowledge Equally across Cultures?" *Academy of Management Learning & Education* 6, no. 1 (2007), pp. 33-50.

79. G. Toegel and J. Conger, "360 Degree Assessment: Time for Reinvention," *Academy of Management Learning and Education* 2, no. 3 (September 2003), p. 297; L. K. Johnson, "Retooling 360s for Better Performance," *Harvard Business School Working Knowledge,* February 23, 2004, https://hbswk.hbs.edu/archive/ retooling-360s-for-better-performance.

80. M. Edwards and A. J. Ewen, "How to Manage Performance and Pay with 360-Degree Feedback," *Compensation and Benefits Review* 28, no. 3 (May-June 1996), pp. 41-46. See also S. Crabtree, "What Your Employees Need to Know," *Gallup Management Journal,* April 13, 2011, Business & Company Resource Center, http://galenet. galegroup.com; R. S. Schuler, *Personnel and Human Resource Management* (St. Paul, MN: West Publishing, 1984).

81. R. E. Ployhart, "Strategic Organizational Behavior (STROBE): The Missing Voice in the Strategic Human Capital Conversation," *Academy of Management Perspectives* 29 (2015), pp. 342-56.

82. Bureau of Labor Statistics, "Employer Costs for Employee Compensation—March 2017," news release, March 17, 2017, http:// www.bls.gov.

83. Bureau of Labor Statistics, "Employer Costs for Employee Compensation—December 2018," news release, March 19 2019, http://www.bls.gov.

84. Company website, "What Are Salary Estimates in Job Listings?" Glassdoor, January 16, 2019, www.glassdoor.com; Company website, "About Us," www.salary.com, accessed March 20, 2019.

85. A. Nyberg, J. Pieper, and C. Trevor, "Pay-for-Performance's Effect on Future Employee Performance: Integrating Psychological and Economic Principles toward a Contingency Perspective," *Journal of Management* 42 (2016), pp. 1753-83; S. Gross and J. Bacher, "The New Variable Pay Programs: How Some Succeed, Why Some Don't," *Compensation and Benefits Review* 25, no. 1 (January-February 1993), p. 51; G. Milkovich, J. Newman, and B. Gerhart, *Compensation,* 11th ed. (New York: McGraw-Hill/Irwin, 2013); B. Gerhart and M. Fang, "Pay for (Individual) Performance: Issues, Claims, and the Role of Sorting Effects," *Human Resource Management Review* 24 (2014), pp. 41-52; L. Bareket-Bojmel, G. Hochman, and D. Ariely,

"It's (Not) All about the Jacksons: Testing Different Types of Short-Term Bonuses in the Field," *Journal of Management* 43 (2017), pp. 534–54.

86. H. Peterson, "Walmart Touts $1,000 Cash Bonus for Employees—but There's a Catch," *Business Insider,* March 9, 2018, https://www.businessinsider.com.

87. Company website, "Benefits," New Belgium Brewing Company, https://www.newbelgium.com.

88. Organization website, "Executive Paywatch," AFL-CIO, accessed March 20, 2019, www.aflcio.org; D. Hembree, "CEO PaySkyrockets to 361 Times That of the Average Worker," *Forbes,* May 22, 2018, www.forbes.com.

89. B.Connelly, K.T. Haynes, L. Tihanyi, D. Gamache, and C. Devers, "Minding the Gap: Antecedents and Consequences of Top Management-to-Worker Pay Dispersion," *Journal of Management* 42 (2016), pp. 862–85.

90. M. J. Conyon, "Executive Compensation and Incentives," *Academy of Management Perspectives* 20,no. 1 (February 2006), pp. 25–44.

91. J. D. Glater, "Stock Options Are Adjusted after Many Share Prices Fall," *The New York Times,* March 27, 2009, http://www.nytimes.com; Carol Bowie, "Post-Crisis Trends in U.S. Executive Pay," Harvard Law School Forum on Corporate Governance and Financial Regulation, February 27, 2012, https://blogs.law.harvard.edu; Scott Thurm, "'Pay for Performance' No Longer a Punchline," *The Wall Street Journal,* March 20, 2013, http://online.wsj.com.

92. U.S. Congress, "H.R. 1628—American Health Care Act of 2017," www.congress.gov, accessed March 3, 2019.

93. J. Marte, "Nearly a Quarter of Fortune 500 Companies Still Offer Pensions to New Hires," *The Washington Post,* September 5, 2014, http://www.washingtonpost.com.

94. E. C. Kearns and M. Gallagher, eds., *The Fair Labor Standards Act* (Washington, DC: BNA, 1999).

95. C. Fay and H. W. Risher, "Contractors, Comparable Worth and the New OFCCP: Deja Vu and More," *Compensation and Benefits Review* 32, no. 5 (September–October 2000), pp. 23–33; G. Flynn, "Protect Yourself from an Equal-Pay Audit," *Workforce* 78, no. 6 (June 1999), pp. 144–46.

96. G. W. Bohlander, S. A. Snell, and A. W. Sherman Jr., *Managing Human Resources,* 12th ed. (Mason, OH: South-Western Publishing, 2001).

97. Organization website, "State Equal Pay Laws," National Conference of State Legislatures, August 23, 2016, www.ncsl.org.

98. "US Mine Disasters Fast Facts," CNN Library, February 27, 2019, www.cnn.com.

99. Mine Safety and Health Administration, "Mine Safety and Health at a Glance: 1978–2017," news release, http://www.msha.gov.

100. "Death on the Job: The Toll of Neglect," AFL-CIO, April 2018, https://aflcio.org.

101. L. Kahn, *Primer of Labor Relations,* 25th ed. (Washington, DC: Bureau of National Affairs Books, 1994); A. Sloane and F. Witney, *Labor Relations* (Englewood Cliffs, NJ: Prentice-Hall, 1985).

102. S. Premack and J. E. Hunter; "Individual Unionization Decisions," *Psychological Bulletin* 103 (1988), pp. 223–34; L. Troy, *Beyond Unions and Collective Bargaining* (Armonk, NY: M. E. Sharpe, 1999); J. A. McClendon, "Members and Nonmembers: Determinants of Dues-Paying Membership in a Bargaining Unit," *Relations Industrielles* 55, no. 2 (Spring 2000), pp. 332–47.

103. M. Cardador, B. Grant, J. Lamare, and G. Northcraft, "To Be or Not to Be Unionized? A Social Dilemma Perspective on Worker Decisions to Support Union Organizing," *Human Resource Management Review* 27 (2017), pp. 554–68.

104. R. Sinclair and L. Tetrick, "Social Exchange and Union Commitment: A Comparison of Union Instrumentality and Union Support Perceptions," *Journal of Organizational Behavior* 16, no. 6 (November 1995), pp. 669–79. See also S. Premack and J. E. Hunter; "Individual Unionization Decisions," *Psychological Bulletin* 103 (1988), pp. 223–34.

105. D. Lewin and Richard B. Peterson, *The Modern Grievance Procedure in the United States* (Westport, CT: Quorum Books, 1998).

106. G. Bohlander and D. Blancero, "A Study of Reversal Determinants in Discipline and Discharge Arbitration Awards: The Impact of Just Cause Standards," *Labor Studies Journal* 21, no. 3 (Fall 1996), pp. 3–18.

107. Betsy Mikel, "Google Used a Curious Strategy to Recruit Employees with a Hard-to-Find Personality Trait," *Inc.,* https://www.inc.com/betsy-mikel/google-looked-for-1-personality-trait-when-hiring-its-early-employees.html accessed March 25, 2019.

108. Ruth Umoh, "The No. 1 Trait Google Looks for in 'Ideal' Job Candidates," *CNBC,* May 10, 2018, https://www.cnbc.com/2018/05/10/googles-ideal-job-candidate-has-this-trait.html.

109. Ruth Umoh, "Top Google Recruiter: Google Uses This 'Shocking' Strategy to Hire the Best Employees," *CNBC,* January 10, 2018, https://www.cnbc.com/2018/01/10/google-uses-this-shocking-strategy-to-hire-the-best-employees.html.

CHAPTER 11
Managing Diversity and Inclusiveness

E pluribus unum (Out of many, one)

Sollina Images LLC/Blend Images

learning objectives

After studying Chapter 11, you will be able to:

LO 11-1 Describe how changes in the U.S. workforce make diversity a critical organizational and managerial issue.

LO 11-2 Distinguish between affirmative action and managing diversity.

LO 11-3 Explain how diversity, if well managed, can give organizations a competitive edge.

LO 11-4 Identify challenges associated with managing a diverse workforce.

LO 11-5 Define monolithic, pluralistic, and multicultural organizations.

LO 11-6 List actions managers and their organizations can take to cultivate diversity.

chapter outline

Diversity: A Brief History

Diversity Today
The Changing Workforce

Understanding Diversity and Inclusion
Advantage through Diversity and Inclusion
Managing Diversity and Inclusion

Multicultural Organizations

Cultivating Inclusiveness
Top Management's Leadership and Commitment
Organizational Assessment
Attracting Employees
Training Employees
Retaining Employees

Management in Action

JULIE SWEET: INNOVATING BY INCLUSION AT ACCENTURE

In 2010, as a partner at one of the most prestigious law firms in the United States, Julie Sweet was by any measure very successful. Then one day she simply decided to start over. She accepted a position as general counsel at Accenture, a global management consulting firm that partners with more than three-quarters of *Fortune* 500 companies to drive innovative and creative solutions to the world's most pressing challenges. Five years later Sweet became the CEO of Accenture North America[1] and recently she became CEO of Accenture.

Accenture has seen strong growth on all fronts. Since 2015, its annual revenue has increased to $40 billion in 2018, an increase of nearly 25 percent, and its stock has nearly doubled. It has offices in 52 countries and offers strategic advice and solutions to businesses in over 40 industries, holding more than 6,800 patents or pending patents.[2] So what's been the secret to Accenture's success? According to Sweet, the answer is simple: Accenture's diverse workforce. The company known for its innovative consulting solutions is also innovating in the areas of diversity and inclusion.

Sweet has made diversity and inclusion a priority at Accenture North America. She believes that these pillars aren't simply a matter of sound ethics; it's sound business. The innovative solutions that Accenture delivers to its clients worldwide are enabled by the diversity of perspectives that comprise the firm's workforce. In

D Dipasupil/Getty Images for Fortune

addition to generating a better product for its clients, Sweet believes fully that a diverse workforce helps Accenture attract and retain the very best talent.[3]

Accenture's record in this area is, indeed, impressive. It's been ranked in Thomson Reuters Diversity and Inclusion Index for three years in a row, claiming first in 2018.[4] And Sweet has no plans to ease up on her emphasis on inclusion. Of the 469,000 employees working for Accenture worldwide, 42 percent are currently women. Sweet has set an ambitious goal of complete gender parity by 2025. She believes they are right on track.[5]

As you read this chapter, think about how bringing together a diverse group and leading it toward a common purpose can be challenging but also a source of opportunity. Consider how diversity and inclusion works as not just a human resources strategy but, as Sweet says, a business strategy.

diverse workforce

One in which there are both similarities and differences among employees in terms of age, cultural background, physical abilities and disabilities, race, religion, sex, and sexual orientation.

Historically, white, American-born males dominated the U.S. workforce, and businesses catered to their needs. Chapter 10 discussed equal opportunity and fair treatment in the workplace. Here, we discuss why and how a proactive approach to developing and managing a **diverse workforce** is not just a legal obligation but also an arena for taking ethical actions and creating real advantage for your organization.

Few societies have access to the range of talents available in the United States, with its immigrant tradition and diverse population. Yet getting people from widely divergent backgrounds to work together effectively is not easy. For these reasons, managing diversity is both a big challenge and big opportunity.

Managing diversity requires attending carefully to basic HRM activities such as recruiting, training, and promoting people with different backgrounds and perspectives. It also requires more than just hiring women and minorities and making sure they are treated fairly and encouraged to succeed. It means understanding and deeply valuing employee differences—managing *inclusively*[6]—in ways that build a more effective and profitable organization. A recent McKinsey study found that companies that were more inclusive achieved better than 20 percent higher financial performance than their less diverse counterparts.[7]

Diversity: A Brief History

managing diversity

Managing a culturally diverse workforce by recognizing the characteristics common to specific groups of employees while dealing with employees as individuals and supporting, nurturing, and utilizing their differences to the organization's advantage; see also *diversity*.

Many legal rights—equal opportunity, fair treatment in housing, the illegality of religious, racial, and sex discrimination—received their initial impetus from the civil rights movement.

American Photo Archive/Alamy Stock Photo

Managing diversity is not a new management issue. From the late 1800s to the early 1900s, most of the groups immigrating to the United States were from Italy, Poland, Ireland, and Russia. Many considered them outsiders because most did not speak English and had different customs and work styles. They struggled to gain acceptance in industries such as steel, coal, automobile manufacturing, insurance, and finance.

In the 1800s, it was considered poor business practice for white Protestant-dominated insurance companies to hire Irish, Italians, Catholics, or Jews. As late as the 1940s, and in some cases later yet, colleges routinely discriminated against immigrants, Catholics, black people, and Jews, and established strict quotas if admitting any at all. Discrimination severely diminished the employment prospects of many groups, and it wasn't until the 1960s that the struggle for acceptance by successful white ethnic and religious groups made notable progress.

Women's struggle for acceptance in the workplace was in some ways even more difficult. When the women's rights movement was launched in 1948 in Seneca Falls, New York, most occupations were off-limits to women, and colleges and professional schools were totally closed to them. Women could not vote and lost all property rights once they were married.

In the first part of the 20th century, a widespread, persistent assumption held that certain jobs were done only by men, and other jobs only by women. When women began entering professional schools, they were subject to severe quotas. As recently as the 1970s, classified ad sections in newspapers listed different jobs by sex, with sections headed "Help Wanted—Males" and "Help Wanted—Females." Women who wanted a bank loan needed a male cosigner, and married women could not get credit cards in their own name.[8]

Only when the Civil Rights Act of 1964 and other legislation arrived was this kind of sex discrimination gradually eliminated. Women still are underrepresented at the most senior levels of corporate life, and major disparities still exist in other areas such as pay. But now increasing numbers of women occupy most jobs once considered the exclusive province of men, including frontline military units as well as the executive suite.

The most difficult and wrenching struggle for equality involved America's nonwhite minorities. Rigid racial segregation remained a fact of American life for 100 years after the end of the Civil War. Black voting rights, particularly in the South, often were viciously suppressed, and racial discrimination in education, and employment persisted.

Years of difficult, courageous protest and struggle gradually began to eat away at both legal and social barriers to equality. Organizations such as the National Association for the Advancement of Colored People (NAACP), formed by a group of blacks and whites, began to use America's court system and the Constitution to bring equality to African Americans and other people of color. The unanimous *Brown v. Board of Education* Supreme Court decision in 1954 declared segregation unconstitutional, setting the stage for other legislation including the Civil Rights Act of 1964.

Consequences of America's bitter racial legacy are still with us; the struggle for equality is far from complete. But many of the rights most of us take for granted today—equal opportunity, fair treatment in housing, the illegality of religious, racial, and sex discrimination—received their greatest impetus from the civil rights movement.

Today nearly half of the U.S. workforce consists of women, 17 percent of U.S. workers identify themselves as Hispanic or Latino, and 12 percent African American. Women own nearly 40 percent of small businesses in the United States, employing about 9 million people.[9]

> The traditional American image of diversity has been one of assimilation.

The traditional American image of diversity has been one of **assimilation**. The United States has long been praised as the world's melting pot, a country in which ethnic and racial differences blended ideally into an American purée. In real life, many see not a melting pot but a mixing bowl. Progress, setbacks, and periods of strain appear, fade, and reappear; progress comes not naturally but only with concerted and sustained effort.

assimilation

The absorption into the cultural tradition of a population or group.

Diversity Today

Diversity refers to far more than skin color and gender. It is a broad term used to refer to all kinds of differences, as summarized in Exhibit 11.1. These differences include education, political belief, religion, and income in addition to gender, race, ethnicity, and nationality.[10]

Members of a demographic group or people who have been through similar important experiences share some common values, attitudes, and perspectives. At the same time, much diversity exists within each category. Every group is made up of individuals, each unique in personality, education, and opinions. There may be more differences among, say, three Asian American people from Thailand, Hong Kong, and Korea than among a white person, an African American person, and an Asian American person all born in Chicago. And not all white males behave alike, nor do people from the same hometown share the same personal or professional goals and values.

Therefore managing diversity requires awareness of aspects common to a group of employees while also working with each employee as an individual. Managing diversity means not just tolerating or accommodating all sorts of differences, but supporting, nurturing, integrating, and using these differences to the organization's advantage. Knowing that U.S. companies must learn to manage a diverse workforce better than their competitors, JCPenney has a professional development program called "Emerging Leaders" that pairs racially diverse managers with an outside career coach and an internal sponsor to maximize career success.[11]

Although many companies initially instituted diversity programs to prevent discrimination, more now see these programs as a crucial way to expand their pool of talent and customer bases worldwide. These potential benefits are making diversity initiatives standard practice among industry-leading companies. Exhibit 11.2 lists some of initiatives that leading diversity-embracing companies are doing.

LO 11-1 Describe how changes in the U.S. workforce make diversity a critical organizational and managerial issue.

diversity

A broad term used to refer to all kinds of differences. These differences include education, political belief, religion, and income in addition to gender, race, ethnicity, and nationality

The Changing Workforce

Although white, American-born males still constitute the largest percentage of workers—about 80 percent of U.S. workers are white, and more than half of them are male—their share of the labor force is declining. The number of white male workers will continue growing, but the numbers of Asian American, African American, and Hispanic American workers will grow faster.[12] This parallels trends in the overall U.S. population.

EXHIBIT 11.1
Components of a
Diversified Workforce

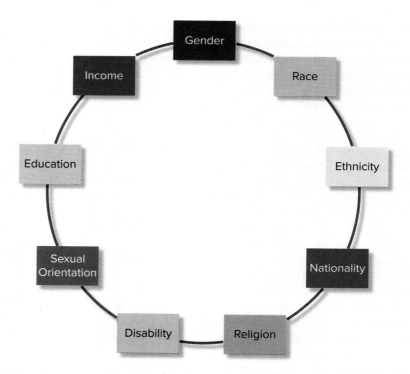

About one in three U.S. residents is a racial or ethnic minority. The largest and fastest-growing minority group is Hispanics, closely followed by Asian Americans. In several states—California, Hawaii, New Mexico, and Texas—and the District of Columbia, these minority groups plus Native Americans and Pacific Islanders combine to make a population that is "majority minority."[13]

The U.S. Census Bureau projects that by 2045, these one-time minority groups will collectively represent a majority of the U.S. population.[14]

Gender Issues   Social changes during the 1960s and 1970s, coupled with financial necessity, greatly increased the number of women entering the workforce. Consider:

- Women make up about 47 percent of the workforce.
- Approximately 54 percent of marriages are dual-earner marriages.
- Nearly one of every four married women in two-income households earns more than her husband does.
- The percentage of women in the labor force earning college degrees has nearly quadrupled over the past 45 years.[15]

EXHIBIT 11.2
Examples of Diversity
Initiatives in Companies

Company Name	Diversity Initiatives
Kaiser Permanente	Placing women in executive positions
EY	Offering mentoring programs
Comcast NBCUniversal	Using diverse suppliers
Northrup Grumman	Employing veterans
Abbvie	Including LGBT employees
Johnson & Johnson	Sponsoring diversity councils
AT&T	Organizing employee resource groups
Accenture	Including people with disabilities

SOURCE: Adapted from "The 2018 DiversityInc Top 50 Companies for Diversity," DiversityInc, https://www.diversityinc.com/di_top_50/, accessed March 21, 2019.

For anyone holding dual responsibilities, balancing work and family presents an enormous challenge. Although men's roles in our society have been changing, women still adopt the bulk of family responsibilities, including household responsibilities, child care, and care of elderly parents. Yet some companies still expect their employees, particularly at the managerial level or in certain professions, to put in long hours and sacrifice their personal lives for the sake of their work. Not only can these expectations put many women at a career disadvantage, but they also cause companies to lose valuable talent.

Companies that offer their employees the opportunity to balance work and family are better able to recruit and retain women and sometimes men. These companies offer family-friendly benefits such as onsite child care, in-home care for elderly family members, increased maternity leave, job sharing, and flexible work schedules, and they permit more work from home.

The average full-time working woman earns about 83 percent as much as men in the same job. A long-standing, persistent gap exists between male and female workers' earnings, even after adjusting for age, marital status, geographic region, college major and GPA, type and selectivity of undergraduate school, type of occupation, economic sector, number of hours worked, and months between graduation and starting work. Importantly, differences in performance evaluations do not explain the pay differences.[16]

While career interruptions to care for family reduce women's long-term earnings,[17] another possible explanation for the wage gap is that women may not be negotiating pay as effectively as men. This hurdle is complicated by evidence that some negotiation tactics that work for men can backfire when women use them, but women tend to benefit by doing more research into pay scales and expressing their pay requirements in a pleasant tone, backed up with evidence of their worth.[18]

Another concern is the low representation of women in top jobs. As women and minorities move up the corporate ladder, they encounter a **glass ceiling**: an invisible barrier that makes it difficult for women and minorities to move beyond a certain hierarchical level. At this writing, just 24 women are chief executives of S&P 500 companies—that's 24 out of 500. Among all board members of those companies, about 21 percent are women.[19] Still, one positive trend is that women's leadership is beginning to be seen at companies in a broader range of industries. Exhibit 11.3 lists top women executives and their companies.

To help break through the glass ceiling, Accenture sponsors monthly networking events and offers flexible schedules and part-time arrangements. Employers sometimes match employees with mentors to help them navigate the corporate environment. Whatever the source of career

> Full-time working women on average earn about 83 percent as much as men in the same job.

Irene Rosenfeld has broken through the glass ceiling as chair and CEO of Mondelez International, overseeing the company with revenues of over $30 billion.

Chris Ratcliffe/Bloomberg/ Getty Images

glass ceiling

An invisible barrier that makes it difficult for women and minorities to move beyond a certain hierarchical level.

EXHIBIT 11.3
Top Women Executives and Their Companies

Rank	Name	Company	Title
1	Marillyn Hewson	Lockheed Martin	Chair, president, and CEO
2	Mary Barra	General Motors	Chair and CEO
3	Abigail Johnson	Fidelity Investments	Chair and CEO
4	Ginny Rometty	IBM	Chair, president, and CEO
5	Gail Boudreaux	Anthem	President and CEO
6	Sheryl Sandberg	Facebook	COO
7	Safra Catz	Oracle	Co-CEO
8	Phebe Novakovic	General Dynamics	Chair and CEO
9	Ruth Porat	Google, Alphabet	SVP and CFO
10	Susan Wojcicki	Google, Alphabet	CEO, YouTube

SOURCE: Adapted from "The Most Powerful Women in Business," *Fortune*, 2018, http://www.fortune.com.

EXHIBIT 11.4
Top Companies for Women

Accenture	Intel
Bank of America	Marriott International
General Mills	Procter & Gamble
Hewlett-Packard	Sony Electronics

SOURCE: Adapted from "2018 Working Mother 100 Best Companies," *Working Mother*, www.workingmother.com.

sexual harassment

Unwelcome sexual conduct that is a term or condition of employment.

obstacles, empowerment programs can help. Exhibit 11.4 lists eight companies where women are thriving as a result of proactive leadership, mentoring programs, and hiring initiatives.

In recent years more people are drawing attention publicly to the serious problem of **sexual harassment**: unwelcome sexual conduct falling into two categories. The first, *quid pro quo harassment,* occurs when submission to or rejection of sexual conduct is used as a basis for employment decisions.

The second type, *hostile environment,* occurs when unwelcome sexual conduct "has the purpose or effect of unreasonably interfering with job performance or creating an intimidating, hostile, or offensive working environment." Behaviors that can cause a hostile work environment include persistent or pervasive displays of pornography, lewd or suggestive remarks, or demeaning taunts or jokes. Both categories of harassment violate Title VII of the Civil Rights Act of 1964.

Regardless of the sex of the harasser and the victim—in a recent year, more than 15 percent of complaints filed with the federal government came from males—if an employee files a complaint of sexual harassment with the Equal Employment Opportunity Commission (EEOC), the commission may investigate. If it finds evidence for the complaint, it may request mediation, seek a settlement, or file a lawsuit. Companies fear these lawsuits, with stiff potential fines and negative publicity that can damage the company's reputation and ability to recruit the best employees.

Harassment via a hostile work environment is now more common than quid pro quo harassment. The former may involve more subjective standards, but managers must maintain an appropriate work environment by ensuring everyone knows what conduct is and is not appropriate and that misconduct has serious consequences. Even when managers do not themselves engage in harassment, they and their employers can be held liable if a lawsuit is filed and they have failed to prevent harassment or to take appropriate action after receiving legitimate complaints. Also important to know is that the "hostile work environment" standard applies to same-sex harassment as well as to non-gender-related cases, such as a pattern of racial or ethnic slurs.

Teenage employees are particularly vulnerable because they are inexperienced, hold lower-status jobs, and often feel hesitant or embarrassed to speak up. The federal EEOC has made this concern a priority and launched a teen-focused page called "Youth at Work" on its website (http://www.youth.eeoc.gov). The National Restaurant Association and National Retail Federation also have stepped up efforts to protect teens from harassment.[20]

> A strong commitment to valuing diversity can reduce sexual harassment.

One way managers can help their companies prevent harassment, or avoid punitive damages if an unfounded lawsuit is filed, is to make sure their organizations have an effective and comprehensive policy on harassment. Companies such as Kaiser Permanente, AT&T, New York Life, and Hilton know that a strong commitment to valuing diversity leads to fewer problems with sexual harassment.[21]

Gender issues do not apply only to women. In some ways, the changing status of women has given men the opportunity to redefine their roles, expectations, and lifestyles. Some men are deciding that there is more to life than corporate success and choosing to scale back work hours to spend more time with their families. Men as well as women want to achieve a balance between career and family.

Employees who are lesbian, gay, bisexual, or transgender (LGBT) are affected by the same issues. They want to avoid discrimination and harassment too, of course, to obtain benefits for a same-sex spouse or domestic partner, or to feel free not to be secretive about this aspect of who they are. Treatment of LGBT employees is an area of ongoing change, both in societal attitudes and in the law. For example, a few years ago, couples in a same-sex relationship would be categorized legally as single, but now some states have laws allowing them to marry or register as domestic partners and to adopt children together.

More than 90 percent of *Fortune* 500 companies have policies protecting employees on the basis of sexual orientation.[22] In situations where laws, policies, and social norms are in a state of flux, employers must be especially attentive to what is required and how employees, customers, and other stakeholders are affected by company policies and practices.

Minorities and Immigrants   Organizations that do not take full advantage of the skills and capabilities of minorities and immigrants are severely limiting their potential talent pools and their ability to understand and capture diverse markets. As minority shares of the population grow, so do these groups' purchasing power. And if you sell to businesses, you probably deal with minority-owned companies because the number of businesses started by Asian American, African American, and Hispanic entrepreneurs is growing much faster than the overall growth in new companies. Immigrants founded more than half of the companies that started in California's high-tech Silicon Valley; in a recent year, half of patent applications in the United States identified an immigrant as the inventor or a co-inventor.[23]

In many urban areas with large Asian, Hispanic, or African American populations, banks have deliberately increased the diversity of their managers and tellers to reflect the population mix in the community and attract additional business. Such diversity—and effective collaboration among diverse employees—creates better customer service that helps banks compete successfully. For example, tellers approached by new immigrants who do not yet speak English immediately call on their bilingual colleagues for help. The bilingual colleagues also are better able to assist bank customers with special problems such as income transfers from abroad.

Exhibit 11.5 gives signs of progress in the top ranks. Even so, evidence shows troubling racial disparities in employment and earnings. Unemployment rates are higher for black and Hispanic workers than for whites—twice as high in the case of black men. Earnings of black

EXHIBIT 11.5   Some Top Executives of Color

Name(s)	Company Name	Title
Ajay Banga	Mastercard	President and CEO
Jin Sook and Do Won Chang	Forever 21	Co-founders and owners
Gisel Ruiz	Sam's Club	Executive vice president and COO
John Thompson	Microsoft	Chair
Marvin Ellison	Lowe's	President and CEO
Kenneth Frazier	Merck	CEO and chair
Ann-Marie Campbell	The Home Depot	Executive vice president
David Huntley	AT&T	Senior executive vice president and chief compliance officer
Orlando Ashford	Holland America Line	President
Arnold Donald	Carnival Corporation	CEO

SOURCES: Company website, "Our People," https://newsroom.mastercard.com; "Billionaires 2019," *Forbes,* www.forbes.com; Company website, "Gisel Ruiz: Executive Vice President and Chief Operating Officer, Sam's Club," www.walmart.com; Company website, "Leadership," www.microsoft.com; Shoulberg, W., "How Did Marvin Ellison Do on His First Quarterly Report Card at Lowe's?" *Forbes,* August 29, 2018, www.forbes.com; Company website, "Leadership," www.merck.com; Company website, "The Home Depot Leadership," www.homedepot.com; Company website, "Corporate Governance," www.att.com; Company website, "Meet Holland America Line President Orlando Ashford," July 15, 2015, www.hollandamerica.com; Company website, "Governance," www.carnivalcorp.com.

EY has been named as one of the best companies for valuing diversity, based on how it ranked in four key areas: CEO commitment, human capital, corporate and organizational communications, and supplier diversity.

Lars Niki

and Hispanic workers consistently trail those of white and Asian workers, and African Americans and Hispanic Americans are underrepresented in management and professional occupations.[24] This underrepresentation perpetuates the problem because it leaves aspiring young minorities with fewer role models or mentors that are so important to people's careers.

Discrimination accounts for at least some of the disparities in employment and earnings. In one recent study—and there are other such findings—fictitious résumés were used to respond to help-wanted ads in Boston and Chicago newspapers. Résumés with "white-sounding names" were 50 percent more likely to get a callback for an interview than the same résumés with African American names. Despite equivalence in credentials, the often unconscious assumptions about different racial groups are very difficult to overcome.[25]

Virtually every large organization has policies and programs dedicated to increasing minority representation, including compensation systems that reward managers for increasing diversity. Major companies such as FedEx, Xerox, Royal Dutch Shell, PNC Financial, and Sun Microsystems have corporate diversity officers who help managers to attract, retain, and promote minority and women executives. Many organizations support minority internships and MBA programs. Microsoft sponsors summer internship programs for minority undergraduate students pursuing computer science or software engineering degrees. Lockheed Martin partners with the American Management Association's Operation Enterprise on two-week paid summer internship programs for high school and college students. Ideally these internships turn into full-time employment.

Mental and Physical Disabilities   The largest unemployed minority population in the United States is people with disabilities. It includes people of all ethnic backgrounds, cultures, and ages. The share of the population with a disability is growing as the average worker gets older and heavier.[26] According to U.S. government statistics, about 19 percent of people with disabilities are employed compared to 66 percent of people without.[27] One-third are employed on a part-time basis.[28] People with a disability are more likely to have jobs if they have higher education levels, and more likely than workers without disabilities to have a part-time job because they can't find full-time work.[29]

The Americans with Disabilities Act Amendments Act (ADAAA) defines a disability as a physical or mental impairment that substantially limits one or more major life activities. Examples of such physical or mental impairments include those resulting from orthopedic, visual, speech, and hearing impairments; cerebral palsy; epilepsy; multiple sclerosis; HIV infections; cancer; heart disease; diabetes; mental retardation; psychological illness; particular learning disabilities; drug addiction; and alcoholism.[30]

New assistive technologies are making it easier for companies to comply with the ADAAA and for those with disabilities to be productive on the job. In many cases, state governments pay for special equipment or other accommodations.

Accommodations can result in unanticipated fringe benefits, too. The National Industries for the Blind (NIB), a Virginia company that markets products under the Skilcraft brand name, is a case in point. It employees 6,000 people who are visually impaired. Because the company's warehouse pickers have trouble reading instructions on paper, NIB installed a voice technology system that conveys instructions to workers through headsets. An added benefit is that the technology has raised the productivity of the entire operation. Accuracy has improved, and workers—both blind and sighted—are able to pick and ship orders faster using the headsets.

For most businesses, people with disabilities represent an unexplored but productive labor market. Employers frequently find that employees with disabilities are more dependable than other employees, miss fewer days of work, and exhibit lower turnover. Companies receive tax credits for hiring workers with disabilities. And such practices send important signals to other employees and outside stakeholders of a strong desire for an inclusive organization.

Education Levels   When the United States was an industrial economy, many jobs required physical strength, stamina, and skill in a trade, rather than college degrees. In today's service and technology economy, more positions require a college education and even a graduate or professional degree, and prospective employees have responded by applying to college in record numbers. One result is rising shares of African American, Hispanic, and female graduates.

People with degrees in science and technology are in especially high demand. Employers often expand their search for scientists and computer professionals overseas, but visa requirements limit that supply. On the other side of the spectrum, in the current labor pool almost 22 percent of foreign-born workers have not completed high school, compared with just 4 percent of native-born workers.[31]

> The share of workers with a bachelor's degree has more than doubled since 1970.

Age   Approximately 10,000 Boomers (those born between 1946 and 1964) are retiring each day in the United States.[32] Industries most at risk of losing this talent include health care (hospitals and nursing facilities), transportation, social assistance, and mining and construction.[33] At the same time, the Bureau of Labor Statistics projects that entry-level workers will be in short supply.

On the plus side, almost 70 percent of workers between the ages of 45 and 74 say that they intend to work in retirement. Retirees often return to the workforce at the behest of their employers, who don't want to lose the knowledge accumulated by longtime employees, their willingness to work nontraditional shifts, and their reliable work habits, which have a positive effect on the entire work group.

To prevent an exodus of talent, employers need strategies to help retain, attract, and motivate skilled and knowledgeable older workers.[34] Phased retirement plans allow older employees to work fewer hours per week. Other strategies include workplace adaptations to help older workers cope with physical problems such as poor vision, hearing, and mobility. This is quite different from previous practice when companies gave older workers incentives to leave in order to reduce overhead and perhaps hire less expensive replacements. Now, a strong majority of employers view their older workers as valuable resources for training, mentoring, and sharing knowledge.[35]

At the same time, companies need to compete hard for the smaller pool of young talent, who know the job market and expect the working conditions they value. Bruce Tulgan, founder of Rainmaker Thinking, which specializes in researching generational differences, says that today's young workers tend to be "high-maintenance" but also "high-performing," having learned information technologies so thoroughly.[36]

Therefore top employers scramble to design work arrangements that are stimulating, involve teamwork, keep work hours reasonable, and provide plenty of positive feedback. Employers also are updating their recruiting tactics to reach young workers where they are—through social media. Most recruiters post job opportunities on Facebook, Instagram, LinkedIn, and Twitter.[37]

affirmative action

Special efforts to recruit and hire qualified members of groups that have been discriminated against in the past.

Understanding Diversity and Inclusion

A few decades ago, companies in the United States introduced **affirmative action**: legally mandated efforts to recruit and hire qualified members of groups that were discriminated against in the past. The intent was not to prefer these group members to the exclusion of others, but to correct for the long history of discriminatory practices and exclusion. Viewed from this perspective, amending these wrongs is moral and ethical as well as a legal necessity.

LO 11-2   Distinguish between affirmative action and managing diversity.

Inclusiveness Works

Avoiding Age Discrimination

Many companies are trying to adjust to the life experience and work expectations of younger employees. To do so, firms are reassessing management practices, work hours, and benefits programs. All of these measures to be more inclusive of younger people are valuable, yet managers must also be careful to not exclude older employees in the process.

Age discrimination is a problem in many organizations today. An AARP report found that nearly two out of three workers over the age of 45 has encountered age discrimination. Among those who reported bias, more than 90 percent believed that such discrimination is common.[38]

Moreover, the number of age discrimination claims is actually increasing. With a graying workforce, this is a problem unlikely to go away anytime soon. In fact, by 2022, more than a third of the workforce is expected to be age 50 or over, when age discrimination becomes most prevalent.[39]

So what can managers do to avoid age discrimination? The most basic step is to avoid asking questions related to age, such as when someone plans to marry, retire, or have children. It's also critical to have a balanced workforce in relation to age, so there is no particular age that feels like a disempowered minority in relation to the broader workforce.

Plus, education and communication are critical. Smart managers create opportunities for employees of different ages to get to know one another in meaningful ways.[40] Acknowledging each individual employee's value and contributions is, after all, what a truly inclusive workplace is all about.

1. What are some advantages and disadvantages of pursuing a workforce that is balanced among all age groups?
2. If you were a manager of a workforce diverse in age, what kind of activities do you think would be helpful to get older and younger workers to interact meaningfully?

Managing diversity involves making changes to remove obstacles that keep people from reaching their full potential.

Mark Bowden/Getty Images

Nevertheless, the legislated approach created fragmented efforts that have not fully achieved the integrative goals of diversity. Employment discrimination persists; even after decades of government legislation, equal employment opportunity (EEO) and affirmative action laws have not adequately improved the upward mobility of women and minorities. To move beyond correcting past wrongs and create truly inclusive organizations requires a change in organization culture to one in which diversity contributes directly to stronger team and organizational performance.

Diversity and inclusiveness are not the same things. Diversity implies bringing in multiple distinctive categories of people sharing human commonalities (not a diversity of job titles or ranks). **Inclusion** is much more; it offers people a fair opportunity to participate and contribute fully and the support to be authentically themselves. Inclusion in practice means providing reasonable access to decision-making processes, organizational resources, and upward mobility opportunities.[41] The bottom line is this: People in inclusive workplaces (1) feel safe (not just physically, but also psychologically) when sharing different opinions and views with others; (2) feel as though they belong, via their genuine involvement in work groups; and (3) feel respected and valued by colleagues.[42]

As you can imagine, diversity creates opportunity to innovate and strengthen the organization, but inclusion is what really brings its potential advantages to fruition for both people and organization. Employers are legally mandated to pursue and demonstrate diversity, while inclusion develops over time from voluntary action and continuous effort.[43]

Diversity is important, but inclusiveness is critical.

Advantage through Diversity and Inclusion

Diversity in an organization's upper ranks relates to superior financial performance, as shown by a number of studies. Investors' preferences for organizations play a role along with superior diversity management. Whether and how women on boards of directors relate to firm financial performance is complex and difficult to discern, but the findings seem mostly positive.[44] One recent study shows that female board members can help to deter securities fraud.[45] Diversity can provide an organizational strength, especially if managers know how to leverage it.[46]

Attracting, Motivating, and Retaining Employees   Companies with a reputation for providing opportunities for diverse employees will have an advantage in the labor market, and will be sought out by the most qualified employees. Firms that earn a spot on popular rankings like *Fortune*'s Best Companies for Diversity or *Working Mother's* 100 Best Companies stand out to potential applicants. When employees believe their differences are not merely tolerated but valued, they may become more loyal, productive, and committed.

Understanding Differentiated Markets   Companies such as Humana, Abbott Laboratories, Kellogg Company, Toyota Motor, and CVS Health are committed to diversity because as the workforce changes, so does their customer base. Just as diverse groups prefer to work for employers that value diversity, they may prefer to patronize such organizations.

A diverse workforce can provide a company with greater knowledge of the preferences and consuming habits of a diversified marketplace. This knowledge helps in designing products and developing marketing campaigns to meet consumers' needs. In addition, for at least some goods and services, a multicultural sales force can help sell to diverse groups. A diverse workforce also can give a company an edge in a global economy by helping to understand other customs, cultures, and market needs.

Creative Problem Solving   Work team diversity promotes creativity and innovation because people from different backgrounds bring different perspectives. Diverse groups have a broader base of experience from which to approach a problem; when effectively managed, they invent more options and create more solutions than homogeneous groups do. In addition, diverse groups are freer to deviate from traditional approaches and practices. Diversity also can help minimize groupthink (recall Chapter 3).[47]

Many law firms routinely have diverse legal teams working together on cases. Complex cases often require fresh "out-of-the-box" ideas, and a group of lawyers from the same background who all think alike may not be as innovative as a more diverse team. In jury trials, the impression that a legal team makes on a jury can help or badly hurt the client, and a visibly diverse legal team is likely to impress a diverse jury.

Organizational Flexibility   Managing diversity requires a corporate culture that tolerates many styles and approaches. Less restrictive policies and less standardized operating methods enable greater flexibility and thus quicker response to environmental changes. Procter & Gamble values diversity as key to fulfilling its strategy: "Everyone valued, everyone included, everyone performing at their peak."[48]

Managing Diversity and Inclusion

Every year, thousands of lawsuits are filed over issues of discrimination and unfair treatment, some involving the largest and most respected firms.[49] Recently settled governmental EEOC lawsuits include Albertsons' for subjecting Hispanic employees to harassment and a

LO 11-3 Explain how diversity, if well managed, can give organizations a competitive edge.

inclusion

Offering to a diverse workforce a fair opportunity to participate and contribute fully, support to be authentically themselves, and reasonable access to decision-making processes.

Bottom Line

A diverse workforce can lead to greater responsiveness. *Why might a customer who wants something new get a faster response from a company that tolerates different styles?*

LO 11-4 Identify challenges associated with managing a diverse workforce.

Social Entrepreneurship

A Popular Business Model

Social entrepreneurship has grown in popularity in recent years. It's become especially relevant with younger entrepreneurs who are looking for more than just profit; they're looking to make a difference. In a recent survey, 94 percent of early career employees said they want to use their skills to benefit good causes.[50]

Forty-two percent of existing social enterprises were created in the past 10 years.[51] And the young innovators who are launching them are doing so for a host of reasons. Many are happy to be part of an endeavor that has meaningful and lasting social impact. It also helps keep them motivated.[52] In short, it's more than just business to them, it's a way of life.

Take, for example, Angela Damiani. She's the co-founder and CEO of NEWaukee, a Milwaukee-based firm that specializes in creating meaningful, authentic social engagements around the city. The events NEWaukee sponsors help connect local businesses to the communities they serve. Damiani is fueled by what she describes as a "connection crisis" in the digital age, whereby people are becoming more isolated and, as result, less happy. She explains her thoughts on the NEWaukee website:

> Through thousands of events and programs, NEWaukee has connected people to place. Why? Because through meaningful invitation and thoughtful execution of unique experiences, people find things: a career, an opportunity, a relationship, a friend, a cause, a purpose, or a passion. Now more than ever, people need a thoughtful invitation to get offline and meet one another in person.[53]

Angela Damiani

What does such an event look like? For the past six years, NEWaukee has hosted the summer "Night Market" in the downtown area that brings city residents together to interact with each other and with local businesses, who also get a chance to promote and sell their products and services.[54]

Such inclusive environments are meant to add enrichment and opportunity to people's lives, and NEWaukee has created a business of it using a social enterprise model.

1. Do you think social entrepreneurship will become a mainstream business model? Why or why not?
2. Do you think that young people today are in fact more civic minded? Do you yourself want to make a difference in people's lives?

4 PM production/Shutterstock

hostile work environment, American Airlines and Envoy Air paying $9.8 million for denying reasonable accommodations, and Llanerch Country Club for laying off a 59-year-old employee and "looking to staff in a younger direction."[55]

Even when there is no overt discrimination in hiring, pay, and firing, managing diversity can be challenging. Minorities and women often find themselves in an environment that does not give them the opportunity to do their best work. And managers with all the goodwill in the world find it harder than they expected to get people from different backgrounds to work together for a common goal.[56]

Managing diversity requires identifying and overcoming difficulties, including unexamined assumptions, lower cohesiveness, miscommunications, mistrust and tension, and stereotyping. As you read the following, practice putting yourself in other people's shoes to better understand their thoughts, feelings, and actions. You can view these topics through two lenses that are important to everyone at work and in life: fairness and stress. Poor diversity management practices often cause people to be treated unfairly or unjustly experience higher job stress (which can spill over into life more broadly).[57]

Unexamined Assumptions   For most of us, seeing the world from someone else's perspective is difficult because our own assumptions and viewpoints seem so normal and familiar. For example, heterosexual employees may not even think about whether to put a photo of their loved ones on their desks; it is a routine, even automatic decision, repeated in a million workplaces across the country. But for many LGBT employees in some environments, displaying (or even considering) such photos can cause considerable anxiety.

Other unexamined assumptions involve the roles of women and men. For example, many people assume that women will shoulder the burden of caring for children, even if it conflicts with the demands of work. In an experiment, employers were less likely to invite the fictional candidate for an interview when the résumé implied the candidate was a parent—but only if the name was female.[58] Because the résumés were otherwise identical, the results suggest that people make assumptions about mothers that do not apply to fathers or to childless women.

In organizations that are oblivious to such assumptions and do not actively help people feel welcome and valued, managers will find it more difficult to develop an enthusiastically shared sense of purpose.

Lower Cohesiveness   Diversity can create a lack of cohesiveness. *Cohesiveness* refers to how tightly knit the group is and the degree to which group members perceive things and behave in similar or mutually agreed-upon ways. Because of differences, diverse groups typically are less cohesive than homogeneous groups. Mistrust, miscommunication, stress, and attitudinal differences reduce cohesiveness, which in turn can diminish productivity.

This may be one explanation for the results of a study that showed greater turnover among store employees who feel they are greatly outnumbered by co-workers from other racial or ethnic groups.[59] In a diverse group, managers should take the lead in building cohesiveness by establishing common goals and values. Group cohesiveness will be discussed in greater detail in Chapter 14.

Communication Problems   Communication difficulties include misunderstandings, inaccuracies, inefficiencies, and slowness. Speed is lost when not all group members are fluent in the same language or when additional time is required to explain things. Sometimes diversity decreases communication, as when white male managers feel less comfortable giving feedback to women or minorities for fear of how criticism may be received. If managers don't deliver helpful feedback, employees will not know how to improve their performance.

Diversity also can lead to errors and misunderstandings. Group members may assume they interpret things similarly when in fact they do not, or they may disagree because of their different frames of reference.[60] For example, if managers do not actively encourage and accept the expression of different points of view, some employees may be afraid to speak up at meetings, leaving the manager with a false impression that consensus has been reached. We discuss communication in depth in Chapter 15.

Mistrust and Tension   People prefer to associate with others who are like themselves. This is a normal, understandable tendency. Feeling excluded from joining colleagues at business lunches or after-hour gatherings is isolating and frustrating and can lead to misunderstandings, mistrust, and ineffective work relationships. Tensions may develop between people of different ages; what one generation might see as a tasteless tattoo is for others a creative example of body art. Such disagreements can cause stress, tension, and resentment, making it more difficult to agree on work issues.

Stereotyping   We learn to see the world in a certain way based on our backgrounds and experiences. Our interests, values, and cultures act as filters and distort, block, and select what we see and hear. We see and hear what we expect to see and hear. Group members often inappropriately stereotype colleagues rather than accurately perceiving their contributions, capabilities, aspirations, and motivations.

Such stereotypes usually are negative or condescending. Women may be stereotyped as not dedicated to their careers, and older workers[61] as incapable and unwilling to learn new skills. But even so-called positive stereotypes can be burdensome. The common stereotype that Asian Americans are good at math may leave unrecognized other positive attributes. Many people dislike being stereotyped at all, even positively, preferring to be understood and treated as individuals.

Stereotypes may lead organizations to miss the opportunity to hire qualified candidates[62] and can cost the organization dearly by stifling employees' motivation so that they don't contribute fully. Managers want their employees to perform to their full ability, but stereotypes that dampen individual employees' ambition and performance detract from the organization's success.

Managers unaware of stereotyping—by themselves or others—may not recognize its effects on how people are treated. Employees stereotyped negatively will be given work assignments that are less important than those given to co-workers. Those assignments will underuse people's skills, frustrate them, perhaps reduce their commitment, and cause higher turnover.[63]

Leveraging Differences   For all these reasons, and more, managing diversity is not easy. Managers are not immune to the biases, stereotypes, inexperience, and tensions that make communication, teamwork, and leadership in a diverse workforce challenging. But they do need to confront these issues and develop the necessary strategies and skills if they and their organizations are to succeed in our multicultural environment.

One constructive way to begin is with what Professor Martin Davidson calls "leveraging difference." This approach sees diversity not as a problem to be tolerated or solved but as a resource the organization can capitalize on, even though doing so can be difficult. Leveraging difference starts with recognizing that we all bring something different, contributing a wide variety of strengths, values, and ways of thinking and problem solving. To capitalize on these differences, Exhibit 11.6 offers suggestions applicable to the whole spectrum of organizational activities such as innovating, learning, working as a team, and interacting with customers.[64]

EXHIBIT 11.6   Leveraging Employee Differences

	Key Individual Practices	Key Organizational Practices
Seeing	• Adopt a stance that relevant differences are ubiquitous. • Attend to points of conflict. • Observe silence.	• Attend to intergroup tension. • Reduce the climate of secrecy.

Understanding	• Build skill in acquiring data.
	  – Listen.
	  – Ask questions.
	  – Learn and share your own story.
	• Include people who are different in your inner circle or network.
		• Acquire information via survey and other data gathering.
		• Create and institutionalize inclusive structures.

Valuing	• Lower the levels of unnecessary carefulness when dealing with differences. • Be willing to persist in the midst of conflict and its accompanying discomfort. • Incorporate data into your worldview.	• Reward and hold employees accountable for engaging in difference-related activities. • Recruit and develop people who add diversity to the organization.

SOURCE: Davidson, M. N., *The End of Diversity as We Know It: Why Diversity Efforts Fail and How Leveraging Difference Can Succeed.* San Francisco: Berrett-Kohler Press, 2011.

Management in Action

AT ACCENTURE, BEING INCLUSIVE IS A TOP PRIORITY

Accenture emphasizes its core values as a driver of its culture and success, and those values need to be exhibited in the individual behaviors of its workforce. On the Inclusion and Diversity page of its corporate website, Accenture's values state:

> We have an unwavering commitment to diversity with the aim that every one of our people has a full sense of belonging within our organization. As a business imperative, every person at Accenture has the responsibility to create and sustain an inclusive environment.[65]

Julie Sweet, CEO of Accenture, has tried to embody these values since taking over in 2015. One of her first initiatives was to create an inclusive work environment by eliminating obstacles that hindered openness and more personal communication. She did away with one of the staple communication conventions of American business: the corporate memo. She now does live-streaming conversations or, when time simply doesn't allow, pre-taped video messages.

To her, either are better ways to communicate with her team comprised of over 50,000 employees. "It is very hard to transform your culture and your workforce to be a relevant company in the digital world if all of your processes are stuck in the traditional world," she says.[66] Sweet wants to foster an environment of honesty and trust, where everyone feels they have a voice. Being authentic and more present are two important components to building that kind of environment, and Sweet feels that the live-streaming conversations are a way to achieve that goal. There's often time at the end of the live stream for employees to ask questions.

Not only was Accenture ranked first in 2018 for diversity and inclusion, it once again made *Fortune*'s list of the World's Most Admired Companies in 2019.[67] Clearly, such recognition can't be explained by one small management initiative. But when you live by the credo that every individual counts, such seemingly minor initiatives will, eventually, help Accenture be world class.

- Do you agree that every individual in an organization counts? Explain your thinking.
- To what degree do you think more open, personalized communication fosters an inclusive workplace environment?

Multicultural Organizations

To capitalize on the benefits and minimize the costs of a diverse workforce, one of the first things managers need to do is examine prevailing assumptions about people and cultures. Exhibit 11.7 shows some assumptions that might exist. Based on these assumptions, we can classify organizations as one of three types and describe their implications for managers.

Some organizations are **monolithic**, having very little diversity or inclusiveness. For example, a firm might favor hiring alumni of the same school. In monolithic organizations, groups other than the norm (if represented) work primarily in low-status jobs. Minority group members must adopt the norms of the majority to survive. This fact, coupled with small numbers, keeps conflicts among groups low. Discrimination and prejudice can prevail, integration between groups is almost nonexistent, and minority group members do not identify strongly with the company.

Most large U.S. companies made the transition from monolithic to pluralistic organizations in the 1960s and 1970s because of changing demographics and societal forces such as the civil rights and women's movements. **Pluralistic organizations** have a more diverse employee population and use an affirmative action approach to managing diversity: They actively try to hire and train a diverse workforce and to avoid discrimination. They integrate groups more fully than do monolithic organizations, but like monolithic organizations they often have minority group members clustered at certain levels or in particular functions within the organization.

LO 11-5 Define monolithic, pluralistic, and multicultural organizations.

monolithic organization

An organization that has a low degree of structural integration—employing few women, minorities, or other groups that differ from the majority—and thus has a highly homogeneous employee population.

pluralistic organization

An organization that has a relatively diverse employee population and makes an effort to involve employees from different gender, racial, or cultural backgrounds.

EXHIBIT 11.7   Diversity Assumptions and Implications

Common and Misleading Assumptions		More Appropriate Assumptions	
Homogeneity	*Melting pot myth:* We are all the same.	Heterogeneity	*Image of cultural pluralism:* We are not all the same; groups within society differ across cultures.
Similarity	*Similarity myth:* "They" are all just like me.	Similarity and difference	*They are not just like me:* Many people differ from me culturally. Most people exhibit both cultural similarities and differences when compared with me.
Parochialism	*Only-one-way myth:* Our way is the only way. We do not recognize any other way of living or working.	Equifinality	*Our way is not the only way:* There are many culturally distinct ways of reaching the same goal, of working, and of living one's life.
Ethnocentrism	*One-best-way myth:* Our way is the best way. All other approaches are inferior versions of our way.	Culture contingency	*Our way is one possible way:* There are many and equally good ways to reach the same goal. The best way depends on the culture of the people involved.

SOURCE: Adler, Nancy J., "Diversity Assumptions and Their Implications for Management," *Handbook of Organization*, 1996.

Because of training programs and greater cultural integration, the pluralistic organization shows less prejudice and some acceptance of minority group members into the informal network. Improved employment opportunities help group members identify more strongly with the organization. Sometimes some majority group members' resentments toward women and minorities create more conflict than exists in the monolithic organization.

The pluralistic organization does not adequately address the cultural aspects of integration. In contrast, **multicultural organizations** both are diverse and value differences. These organizations fully integrate gender, racial, and minority group members, both formally and informally. Rather, managers value and leverage the varieties of experiences and knowledge employees bring to help the company achieve agreed-upon strategies and goals.[68]

The truly multicultural organization is marked by an absence of prejudice and discrimination and by low levels of intergroup conflict. It forges a synergistic environment in which all members contribute to their maximum potential, and fully realizes diversity advantages.[69]

multicultural organization

An organization that values cultural diversity and seeks to utilize and encourage it.

Cultivating Inclusiveness

LO 11-6 List actions managers and their organizations can take to cultivate diversity.

Plans for becoming multicultural and making the most of a diverse workforce should include (1) securing top management's leadership and commitment, (2) assessing the organization's progress toward goals, (3) attracting employees, (4) training employees in diversity, and (5) retaining employees.

Top Management's Leadership and Commitment

If top management is not visibly committed to diversity programs, others in the organization will not take the effort seriously. One way to communicate this commitment to all employees—as well as to the external environment—is to incorporate diversity values into the corporate mission statement and into strategic plans and objectives. Managerial compensation can be linked directly to accomplishing diversity goals. Adequate funding must be allocated to the diversity effort to ensure its success. Also, top management can set an example by confronting discriminatory actions and microaggressions, participating personally in diversity programs, and making participation mandatory for all managers.

As mentioned earlier, some organizations have corporate offices or committees to coordinate the companywide diversity effort. Among many examples, the City of Boston has a chief diversity officer, and Avon has a director of multicultural planning and design.

The work of managing diversity cannot be done by top management or diversity directors alone. Many rely on minority advisory groups or task forces to monitor organizational policies, practices, and attitudes; assess their impact on the diverse groups within the organization; and provide feedback and suggestions.

General Electric provides mentorship through employee resource groups like the African American Forum, Hispanic Forum, and Women's Network. Caterpillar also has numerous employee resource groups that offers mentoring and education about cultural differences to celebrate workplace diversity.

As you can see, progressive companies are moving from asking managers what they think minority employees need and toward asking the employees themselves what they need.

Michael Jordan, Basketball Hall of Fame inductee, is one of the high-profile minority team owners in the NBA.

Streeter Lecka/Getty Images

Organizational Assessment

The next step in managing diversity is to establish an ongoing assessment of the organization's workforce, culture, policies, and practices in areas such as recruitment, promotions, benefits, and compensation. Managers evaluate whether they are attracting their share of diverse candidates from the labor pool and whether the current workforce composition is meeting customer needs. The objective is to identify areas with problems or opportunities and to make recommendations. Etsy, the social commerce website for handcrafted and vintage items, determined that 80 percent of its customers were women but only about 3 percent of its engineers were women. Marc Hedlund, former senior vice president of engineering, determined—easily, with the data—that Etsy needed to bring in more female engineers and develop their customer skills.[70]

Women and Asian Americans can be at a disadvantage when an organization values aggressiveness. Such a culture might exclude—from hiring, or full inclusion—those who do not exhibit high levels of aggressiveness. Managers could then decide that the organization's "values" need to change so that other personal styles are equally acceptable.

Managers can change their own behaviors to reflect such a change—for example, by asking everyone in meetings for their thoughts instead of letting more assertive participants dominate. Corporate norms should be identified and evaluated regarding their real value and their impact on people.

Attracting Employees

Companies can attract a diverse, qualified workforce by using effective recruiting practices, accommodating employees' work and family needs, and offering alternative work arrangements.

Recruiting   Developing a reputation for hiring and promoting all types of people can be a strong recruiting tool. Xerox gives prospective employees an article that rates the company as one of the best places for African Americans to work. Hewlett-Packard ensures that its female candidates are familiar with its high rating by *Working Woman* magazine.

Some employers work hard to attract female applicants, ensure that their talents are used to full advantage, and to keep (avoid losing) their best people. With more than 80 percent of its customers female, Etsy's solution was to position itself as a company that values women. It offers female engineers $5,000 grants to attend a programming retreat in New York, bringing a flood of Etsy-appreciating women to learn the skills Etsy needs. The company also shifted its focus from hiring senior engineers to hiring junior engineers and training them to lead. The focus on diversity not only increased the share of female engineers, but

Karl DeBlaker/AP Images

also has attracted male engineers who value the company's culture and work well in teams. Within six years, the number of women in engineering positions grew from 4 to 29 percent.[71]

Many minority group members, people with disabilities, and those who are economically disadvantaged are physically isolated from job opportunities. Companies can bring information about job opportunities to the source of labor, or they can transport the labor to the jobs. Melwood is a nonprofit that provides job opportunities for people with disabilities, and it will transport people to and from their jobs. Shelters to Shutters helps people transition out of homelessness and into economic independence by engaging the real estate industry to provide employment and housing opportunities. The Federal Interagency Reentry Council helps people released from prison by helping them find employment opportunities.

Accommodating Work and Family Needs   Many job seekers put family needs first. Corporate work and family policies have a big impact on recruiting success and failure. SAS, the business analytics software company in North Carolina, helps employees manage the stresses of everyday life and offers deeply discounted child care.[72]

Employers offering onsite child care report lower turnover and absenteeism and higher morale. Many companies assist with care for elderly dependents, care for sick family members, parental leaves of absence, and benefits tailored to individual family needs. Some companies accommodate dual-career couples by limiting relocation requirements or providing job search assistance to relocated spouses.

Alternative Work Arrangements   Many employers offer flexible work schedules and arrangements. General Electric Aviation invites its engineers to develop and submit a plan to reduce onsite work hours and work offsite. Approval of the flexible work plan depends on each engineer's job duties and the company's ability to accommodate the request.[73] Other creative work arrangements include compressed workweeks (e.g., four 10-hour days) and job sharing, in which two part-time workers share one full-time job.

Training Employees

Traditionally, most management training was based on the unstated assumption of a homogeneous, often white-male, full-time workforce. But diversity creates an additional layer of complexity.[74] Diversity training programs attempt to identify and reduce hidden biases and develop the skills needed to manage effectively in a diversified workforce.

Most U.S. organizations sponsor some sort of diversity training, typically of two types: awareness building and skill building.

Awareness Building   Diversity training must increase awareness of the meaning and importance of valuing diversity.[75] The aim is to sensitize employees to the assumptions they make about others and the way those assumptions affect their behaviors, decisions, and judgments. For example, a male employee who has never reported to a female manager may feel awkward the first time he is required to do so. Awareness building can reveal this concern in advance and help people address it.

To build awareness, trainers teach people about myths, stereotypes, and cultural differences as well as the organizational barriers that inhibit the full contributions of all employees. They offer a better understanding of corporate culture, requirements for success, and important behaviors that affect opportunities for advancement.

In most companies, the rules for success are ambiguous, unwritten, and perhaps inconsistent with written policy. A common problem for women, minorities, immigrants, and young employees is that they are unaware of unofficial rules that are obvious to people in the mainstream. For example, organizations often have informal networks and power

The Digital World

Using AI to Hire a More Diverse Workforce

Can artificial intelligence (AI) help companies hire a more diverse workforce? Chatbots have been used by HR for years to help potential employees walk through the application process and initial interviewing.[76] Today, some companies go a step further by using AI-enabled HR technology to help remove bias from the process. The technology provides hiring managers with data to make more objective decisions based less on feelings or impressions, which are often biased.[77]

For example, AI-enabled HR technology like Harver uses data and predictive analytics to evaluate which candidates will be most likely to succeed in different positions.[78] The technology also helps remove bias in job postings, create more inclusive interview panels, and recommend appropriate salaries regardless of ethnicity or gender.[79]

Although the technology shows promise, experts warn that the recommendations it makes are only as sound as the data provided. Still, AI algorithms tend to do a better job than humans at picking out candidates who are the right fit for the job.[80]

1. Do you think AI would be more helpful in the hiring process for some industries than others? Where do you see AI being a good fit?

2. What do you make of the research claiming that AI tends to do a better job than humans at candidate selection? Do you see any potential drawbacks, or do you think it should be implemented on a wider scale?

---

structures that may not be apparent or readily available to all. As a result, some are less likely than others to know where to go when they need approvals, support, and allies.

Skill Building   Diversity training that merely identifies problems without giving participants the tools they need to act is not good enough. Skill building helps people deal more effectively with one another and with diverse customers. Most of the skills taught are interpersonal, such as active listening, coaching, and giving feedback.

Ideally, organizational assessment determines the skills taught; the training is tailored to needs. Tying the training to business goals increases its usefulness and allows managers to assess whether it is working.

The best training relates to the actual challenges employees encounter in the workplace. For example, employees in a hospital diversity training program might practice how to handle a white patient who asks to be treated only by a white doctor and a male patient who wants to be treated only by a male doctor. Training ABC and American Training Resources are among the companies that offer such products.

Retaining Employees

Replacing qualified and experienced workers is difficult and costly, so retaining good people is vitally important. Most executives know that failing to attend to diversity and inclusion contributes to employee turnover.[81] Strategies such as the following can help.[82]

Support Groups   Support groups, sometimes called affinity groups, provide emotional and career support for members who traditionally have not been included in the majority's informal groups. They also can help diverse employees understand work norms and the corporate culture.

At Apple headquarters in Cupertino, California, support groups include a Jewish cultural group, a gay/lesbian group, an African American group, and a technical women's group. Avon encourages employees to organize into African American, Hispanic American, and Asian American networks by granting them official recognition and assigning a senior manager to provide advice. These groups help new employees adjust and provide direct feedback to management about particular concerns.

> **Bottom Line**
> Managers should assume that everyone likes to feel valued. *What makes you feel that your employer values who you are and what you contribute?*

Mentoring   Many people are puzzled by the apparent inability of women to move up beyond a certain point on the corporate ladder (the glass ceiling).[83] Sexism is an obvious explanation in some, but not all, cases. A recent study found that men did *not* rate women lower than other men on job performance or promotability but *did* consider women's careers more likely than men's to "derail"—go off track or plateau or end prematurely. Men felt women's futures were less promising than other men's because of "ineffective interpersonal behaviors" like ordering people around rather than trying to get them on board. But ironically, men in the study observed such behaviors slightly less often in women than in other men.[84] Such actions are not automatic, of course; individuals differ, as do the nature of relationships over time. But overall, men who anticipated less rosy futures for women were more likely to withdraw as their mentors or sponsors.[85]

Having good mentors is perhaps more important for women and minorities than for men. To help these groups enter the informal network that provides exposure to top management and access to information, many companies use formal mentoring programs. **Mentors** are higher-level managers who coach, advise, and help people meet top managers and learn the norms and values of the organization. If your employer doesn't make sure you have formal mentoring, you should take it upon yourself to ask others' advice and find your own mentors.

In Canada, EY established several mentoring programs for women, minorities, and immigrants. Mentors work with employees to help them gain relevant experience, new skills, and connections with senior leaders. EY sees these mentorships as ways not only to strengthen employees' contributions, but also to fill its talent pipeline with future leaders. In an unusual twist on mentorship, EY also has a reverse mentoring program in which women and minority employees discuss with leaders issues related to diversity at the company.[86]

---

mentors

Higher-level managers who help ensure that high-potential people are introduced to top management and socialized into the norms and values of the organization.

Career Development and Promotions   Because they hit a glass ceiling, many talented people leave their employers for better opportunities elsewhere. Firms such as Deloitte and Honeywell use teams to evaluate the career progress of women, minorities, and employees with disabilities and to find promotion opportunities. One important step is to make sure deserving employees can work in line positions. Women in particular often work in staff positions, such as human resources, with less bottom-line opportunity to show they can earn money for their employers. Career development programs that give exposure and experience in line jobs can make senior management positions more attainable.

Systems Accommodation   Managers can support diversity by recognizing cultural and religious holidays, accepting different modes of dress, and accommodating dietary restrictions. Accommodations for disability likely will become increasingly important as the median age of the workforce continues to rise. In addition, the average weight of U.S. workers is increasing; this relates to health consequences such as heart disease, joint problems, and diabetes and to workplace injury claims and absences due to injuries.[87] Managers can work to maintain safe workplaces and offer benefits that encourage healthy lifestyles.

Accountability   Performance appraisal and reward systems should reinforce effective diversity management. At PepsiCo, each executive reporting to the CEO is responsible for employee development of a particular group. The executive must identify leadership talent, learn group members' concerns, identify areas where support is needed, and create plans for addressing these issues.[88] PepsiCo has earned several recent awards for its diversity management efforts.[89]

For decades, U.S. corporations strove to integrate their workforces because of regulatory and social responsibility pressures. Today globalization, changing demographics, and the expansion of ethnic markets at home have made managing a diverse workforce a bottom-line issue. The best managers and organizations know that to be competitive, they should make genuine inclusion a strategic priority so as to attract, develop, keep, and apply the knowledge of the very best talent.

Management in Action

SWEET: HOW TO BUILD AN INCLUSIVE ENVIRONMENT

Creating diverse and inclusive workforces has proven challenging to many organizations across a wide array of industries. Accenture, being ranked first among all companies for diversity and inclusion, clearly has found a way to overcome many of these obstacles. In fact, to Julie Sweet, CEO of Accenture, it's fairly straightforward.

"I don't think it's rocket science," she said in a recent interview with *The New York Times.* "You first have to decide if diversity is a business priority. If it is, then you need to treat it like a business priority. You set goals, have accountable leaders, you measure progress, and you have an action plan. If you do those four things, you will make progress."[90]

And Accenture has indeed set goals and made progress on a range of fronts. Accenture is on its way to reaching its goal of gender parity by 2025. In recent years, the organization has added thousands of employees from diverse backgrounds to its workforce. It has set a goal of hiring 5,000 veterans or military spouses by 2020, and close to 5 percent of its workforce has self-identified as a person with a disability.[91]

- Suppose you were charged with increasing the diversity at Accenture. What specific recommendations would you make as part of its action plan?
- Many firms struggle with achieving a more diverse and inclusive workplace. What do you see as the primary obstacles to progress on this front?

KEY TERMS

affirmative action, p. 341

assimilation, p. 335

diverse workforce, p. 334

diversity, p. 335

glass ceiling, p. 337

inclusion, p. 342

managing diversity, p. 334

mentors, p. 352

monolithic organization, p. 347

multicultural organization, p. 348

pluralistic organization, p. 347

sexual harassment, p. 338

RETAINING WHAT YOU LEARNED

In Chapter 11, you learned that the U.S. workforce is becoming more diverse. A skills gap exists because typical workers often lack the skills to fill jobs that are being created. To fill this gap and achieve competitive advantage, managers need to recruit, develop, motivate, and retain a diverse workforce. Affirmative action is used to correct past exclusion of women and minorities from organizations. Managing diversity takes a broader approach aimed at supporting, nurturing, and using employee differences to the organization's advantage. Managing diversity can result in enhanced talent management practices, marketing strategies to reach diverse consumers, innovation and problem solving, and organizational flexibility. Challenges associated with managing a diverse workforce include decreased group cohesiveness, communication problems, mistrust and tension, and stereotyping. Based on prevailing assumptions about people and cultures, organizations take one of the following forms: (1) monolithic, (2) pluralistic, or (3) multicultural. In order to cultivate diversity, managers and organizations need to support and commit to it. A thorough assessment needs to be completed before programs can be designed to attract, develop, motivate, and retain diverse talent.

LO 11-1   Describe how changes in the U.S. workforce make diversity a critical organizational and managerial issue.

- The labor force is getting older and more racially and ethnically diverse, with a higher proportion of women. Exhibit 11.1 (reproduced below) illustrates the components of a diversified workforce.
- The jobs that are being created frequently require higher skills than the typical worker can provide; thus we are seeing a growing skills gap.
- To be competitive, organizations can no longer take the traditional approach of depending on white males to form the core of the workforce.
- Today managers must search widely to make use of talent wherever it can be found. As the labor market changes, organizations that recruit, develop, motivate, and retain a diverse workforce will have a competitive advantage.

LO 11-2   Distinguish between affirmative action and managing diversity.

- Affirmative action is designed to correct past exclusion of women and minorities from U.S. organizations.
- Despite the accomplishments of affirmative action, it has not eliminated barriers that prevent people from reaching their full potential.
- Managing diversity goes beyond hiring people who are different from the norm and seeks to support, nurture, and capitalize on employee differences to the organization's advantage.

LO 11-3   Explain how diversity, if well managed, can give organizations a competitive edge.

- Managing diversity is a bottom-line issue. If managers are effective at managing diversity, they will have an easier time attracting, retaining, and motivating the best employees.
- Diverse workforces will more effectively market to and serve diverse consumer groups in the United States and globally; they will be more creative, more innovative, and better able to solve problems.
- In addition, they potentially increase their employers' flexibility and responsiveness to environmental change.

LO 11-4   Identify challenges associated with managing a diverse workforce.

- Diversity challenges for managers include decreased group cohesiveness, communication and teamwork problems, mistrust and tension, and stereotyping.
- These challenges can be turned into advantages by means of training and many other management strategies and tactics.

LO 11-5   Define monolithic, pluralistic, and multicultural organizations.

- These categories are based on the organization's prevailing assumptions about people and cultures.
- Monolithic organizations have a low intergroup integration and relatively homogeneous workforces.
- Pluralistic organizations have a more diverse employee population and try to more fully involve different employee groups (e.g., engaging in affirmative action and avoiding discrimination).

EXHIBIT 11.1 (revisited)   Components of a Diversified Workforce

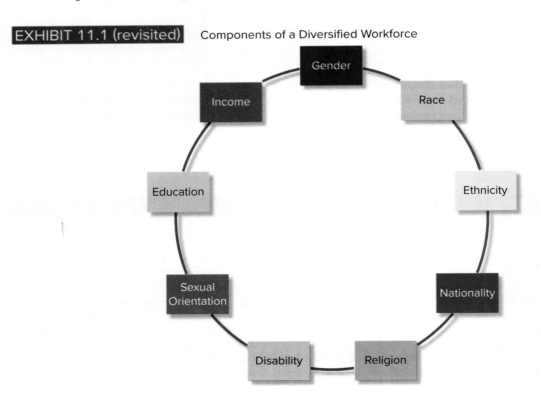

- Multicultural organizations not only have diversity but value it. They fully integrate men and women of various racial and ethnic groups as well as people with different types of experience and expertise.
- Conflict is greatest (all else equal) in pluralistic organizations.

LO 11-6 List actions managers and their organizations can take to cultivate diversity.

- To be successful, efforts to manage diversity must have top management support and commitment.

- Organizations should first undertake a thorough assessment of their cultures, policies, and practices, as well as the demographics of their labor pools and customer bases.
- Only after this diagnosis has been completed is a company in position to initiate programs designed to attract, develop, motivate, and retain the most talented and diverse workforce possible.

DISCUSSION QUESTIONS

1. What are some differences among affirmative action, diversity, and inclusiveness?
2. What opportunities do you see as a result of changes in our nation's workforce?
3. Is prejudice declining in our society? In our organizations? Why or why not?
4. What distinctions can you make between affirmative action and managing diversity?
5. How can managers overcome obstacles to diversity such as mistrust and tension, stereotyping, and communication problems?
6. How can organizations meet the special needs of different groups (e.g., work and family issues) without appearing to show favoritism?
7. How can diversity and inclusiveness give a company a competitive edge? Can they really make a difference in the bottom line? How?
8. Why are these issues sometimes difficult to talk about? What could make conversations both more comfortable and productive?

EXPERIENTIAL EXERCISES

11.1   Being Different

OBJECTIVES

1. To increase your awareness of the feeling of being different.
2. To understand better the context of being different.

INSTRUCTIONS

1. Working alone, complete the Being Different Worksheet.
2. In small groups, compare worksheets and prepare answers to the discussion questions.

3. When the class reconvenes, group spokespersons present group findings.

DISCUSSION QUESTIONS

1. Were there students who experienced being different in situations that surprised you?
2. How would you define "being different"?
3. How can this exercise be used to good advantage?

Being Different Worksheet

Think back to a recent situation in which you experienced "being different" and answer the following questions:

1. Describe the situation in which you experienced being different.

_____

_____

2. Explain how you felt.

_____

_____

3. What did you do as a result of being different? (That is, in what way was your behavior changed by the feeling of being different?)

_____

_____

4. What did others in the situation do? How do you think they felt about the situation?

_____

_____

5. How did the situation turn out in the end?

_____

_____

6. As a result of that event, how will you probably behave differently in the future? In what way has the situation changed you?

_____

_____

11.2   Gender Stereotypes

PART I

Your instructor will divide the group into smaller groups based on gender, resulting in male-only and female-only groups. Groups are to brainstorm a list in response to the following statements. It is not necessary for all members to agree with everything the group generates. Add all inputs to the list.

Female groups complete the following:
- All men are _____
- Men think all women are _____

Male groups complete the following:
- All women are _____
- Women think all men are _____

PART II

After generating your lists, your groups will present a role-play to the class based on the following scenarios by switching gender roles (females portray males, and males portray females):

Two friends (of the same gender) meeting each other back at school for the first time this year.

A person flirting with a member of the opposite sex at a party. (Females play a male flirting with a female; males play a female flirting with a male.)

QUESTIONS

1. What aspects of the role-plays were accurate, distorted, or inaccurate?
2. How did you feel portraying the opposite gender, and how did it feel to see your gender portrayed?
3. On what stereotypes or experiences were these role-plays based?

PART III

Your group will now write its brainstorm lists on the board for discussion. Remember that these lists are a product of a group effort and are generally based on stereotypes and not necessarily the view of any one individual.

Analyze the lists for positive and negative results in both personal and professional settings. Generate a list of ways to dispel, reduce, or counter negative stereotypes.

QUESTIONS

1. What similarities, patterns, or trends developed from the groups?
2. How do you feel about the thoughts presented about your gender?
3. What implications do these thoughts have on actions and situations in the work environment?
4. What can you do to reduce the negative effects of these stereotypes? What can you do to help dispel these stereotypes? (Brainstorm with your group or class.)

SOURCES: Portions of this exercise were adapted from concepts in Fritz, S. F. et al., *Interpersonal Skills for Leadership*. Englewood Cliffs, NJ: Prentice Hall, 1999; Shani, A. B. and Lau, J. B., *Behavior in Organizations: An Experiential Approach,* 6th ed. New York: Irwin, 1996.

11.3   He Works, She Works

INSTRUCTIONS

1. Complete the He Works, She Works Worksheet. In the appropriate spaces, write what you think the stereotyped responses would be. Do not spend too much time considering any one item. Rather, respond quickly and let your first impression or thought guide your answer.

2. Compare your individual responses with those of other class members or participants. It is interesting to identify and discuss the most frequently used stereotypes.

He Works, She Works Worksheet

The family picture is on *his* desk: *He's a solid, responsible family man.*

His desk is cluttered: _____

He's talking with co-workers: _____

He's not at his desk: _____

He's not in the office: _____

The family picture is on *her* desk: *Her family will come before her career.*

Her desk is cluttered: _____

She's talking with co-workers: _____

She's not at her desk: _____

She's not in the office: _____

The family picture is on *his* desk: *He's a solid, responsible family man.*

He's having lunch with the boss: _____

The boss criticized *him:* _____

He got an unfair deal: _____

He's getting married: _____

He's going on a business trip: _____

He's leaving for a better job: _____

The family picture is on *her* desk: *Her family will come before her career.*

She's having lunch with the boss: _____

The boss criticized *her:* _____

She got an unfair deal: _____

She's getting married: _____

She's going on a business trip: _____

She's leaving for a better job: _____

SOURCE: Luthans, F., *Organizational Behavior.* New York: McGraw-Hill, 1989.

Concluding Case

NICHE HOTEL GROUP

Monique Johnson was thrilled about her new position as vice president of human resources for Niche Hotel Group (NHG). The hotel chain has distinctive properties in cities throughout the United States, attracting a young, international clientele with casual but elegant surroundings and popular sushi bars. Besides the chance to stay at these establishments as she toured the country, Monique would have opportunities to meet the members of NHG's talented and diverse workforce. In addition, she was proud to advance NHG's practice of valuing diversity, including respect for all people regardless of age, sex, race, ethnicity, nationality, disability status, sexual orientation, and gender identity. She felt sure those values would be upheld because the commitment came from the top. In fact, NHG's chief executive, Mike Jepsen, had asked Monique to meet with him every month to review the company's performance in attracting and developing talent.

For several months, Monique's work progressed as she had expected. Then she heard some disturbing news. One of the hotel's managers, April Lee, called her to say she had received complaints that an assistant manager in the hotel's sushi bar had been embarrassing some of the male servers. When April met with the servers to investigate, they described being teased because they were gay but said they had not bothered to complain. Two of the servers admitted that they believed complaining would be futile. As white, male employees, they said, they doubted they would be taken seriously, because NHG's management tended to favor its female and minority employees. April worried that the servers might quit, take legal action, or both before the situation could be sorted out. Monique reviewed with April the basic legal requirements and company policy for handling this type of problem, and she offered to fly out to April's hotel after her monthly meeting with the CEO.

That Thursday, Monique briefed Mike about the situation at April's hotel. Mike sighed, "Here we go again." In response to Monique's puzzled look, he explained, "We've had mandatory diversity training three times for every NHG

employee. But it's never enough. Sooner or later, someone hurts someone else's feelings, and we have to bring back the trainers. I guess we just have to keep doing it until everyone respects everyone else's differences."

"You've done diversity training three times without creating a positive climate for diversity?" replied Monique. Mike nodded his head ruefully and then asked if she had a better idea. "Maybe it's time to stop focusing on categorizing people and to start thinking about how each of us is working as part of a team, how each of us is contributing to our mission. Maybe we need to train in something else—say, communication—how we talk and how well we listen."

DISCUSSION QUESTIONS

1. Do you think communication training would be an effective way to create a more inclusive and tolerant workplace? Why or why not?

2. Why do you think diversity training has not always prevented problems at NHG?

3. NHG is in the hospitality industry, which spans many types of skills and workers, in addition to a diverse array of geographic and cultural regions. Do you think achieving inclusiveness on such a vast scale is possible? Why or why not?

ENDNOTES

1. Mark Abadi, "The CEO of a Consulting Firm Says If 'You Can See Your Future' at Work, You May Not Be in the Right Career," *Business Insider,* January 4, 2019, https://www.businessinsider.com/accenture-julie-sweet-switch-careers-2019-1.

2. Accenture website, "Accenture—About," https://www.accenture.com/us-en/about/company-index accessed March 31, 2019.

3. Damanick Dantes, "Accenture CEO: Diversity and Inclusion Start from Within," *Fortune,* January 8, 2019, http://fortune.com/2019/01/08/accenture-ceo-julie-sweet-ceo-initiative/.

4. Janice Gassam, "The 10 Most Diverse Companies of 2018," *Forbes,* October 11, 2018, https://www.forbes.com/sites/janicegassam/2018/10/11/the-10-most-diverse-companies-of-2018/#55a381911404.

5. Damanick Dantes, "Accenture CEO: Diversity and Inclusion Start from Within," *Fortune,* January 8, 2019, http://fortune.com/2019/01/08/accenture-ceo-julie-sweet-ceo-initiative/.

6. M. E. Mor Barak, *Managing Diversity: Toward a Globally Inclusive Workplace,* 3rd ed. (Thousand Oaks, CA: Sage, 2014).

7. "Delivering through Diversity," *McKinsey Report,* January 2018, www.mckinsey.com.

8. B. Eisenberg and M. Ruthsdotter, "Living the Legacy: The Women's Rights Movement 1848–1998," National Women's History Project, http://www.legacy98.org/move-hist.html.

9. Bureau of Labor Statistics, "2018 Labor Force Statistics from the Current Population Survey," http://www.bls.gov/cps; "The Megaphone of Main Street: *Women's Entrepreneurship,* Spring 2018," SCORE Association, August 23, 2018, www.score.org.

10. Shung J. Shin, Tae-Yeol Kim, Jeong-Yeon Lee, and Lin Bian, "Cognitive Team Diversity and Individual Team Member Creativity: A Cross-Level Interaction," *Academy of Management Journal* 55 (February 2012), pp. 197–212; David A. Harrison and Katherine J. Klein, "What's the Difference? Diversity Constructs as Separation, Variety, or Disparity in Organizations," *Academy of Management Review* 32 (October 2007), pp. 1199–1228; Scott E. Page, "Making

the Difference: Applying a Logic of Diversity," *Academy of Management Perspectives* 21 (November 2007), pp. 6–20.

11. "The 2018 DiversityInc. Top 50 Companies for Diversity," *DiversityInc,* www.diversityinc.com, accessed March 9, 2019.

12. Bureau of Labor Statistics, "Table 3.4: Civilian Labor Force by Age, Sex, Race, and Ethnicity, 1996, 2006, 2016, and Projected 2026," news release, October 24, 2017, http://www.bls.gov.

13. "Quick Facts," U.S. Census Bureau, https://census.gov, accessed March 10, 2019; "Older People Projected to Outnumber Children for First Time in U.S. History," U.S. Census Bureau (press release), March 13, 2018, https://census.gov.

14. J. Vespa et al., "Demographic Turning Points for the United States: Population Projections for 2020 to 2060," U.S. Census Bureau, March 2018, https://www.census.gov.

15. Bureau of Labor Statistics, "2018 Labor Force Statistics from the Current Population Survey," http://www.bls.gov/cps; Bureau of Labor Statistics, "Women in the Labor Force: A Databook," December 2018, http://www.bls.gov; M. Heggeness, "Spouses Report Earnings Differently When Wives Earn More," U.S. Census Bureau, July 16, 2018, https://www.census.gov.

16. A. Joshi, J. Son, and H. Roh, "When Can Women Close the Gap? A Meta-analytic Test of Sex Differences in Performance and Rewards," *Academy of Management Journal* 58 (2015), pp. 1516–45.

17. A. Brown and E. Patten, "The Narrowing, but Persistent, Gender Gap in Pay," Pew Research, April 3, 2017, http://www.pewresearch.org.

18. B. Cronin, "Negotiating Tactics Play Role in Gender Pay Gap," *The Wall Street Journal,* April 1, 2013, http://www.wsj.com; Bureau of Labor Statistics, "Labor Force Characteristics by Race and Ethnicity, 2011," Report 1036, August 2012, http://www.bls.gov; AAUW, "The Simple Truth about the Gender Pay Gap," 2013, http://www.aauw.org; Jessica Bennett, "How to Attack the Gender Wage Gap? Speak Up," *The New York Times,* December 15, 2012, http://www.nytimes.com.

19. Catalyst, "Women CEOs of the S&P 500," http://www.catalyst.org, accessed March 20, 2017.

20. "National Restaurant Association Offers Training DVDs on Harassment Prevention, Social Media Use, and Customer Service," National Restaurant Association, press release, April 22, 2014, http://www.restaurant.org.

21. "The 2018 DiversityInc. Top 50 Companies forDiversity," *DiversityInc*, www.diversityinc.com, accessed March 9, 2019.

22. "Discrimination in Employment Issues for LGBT Individuals," American Bar Association, March 29, 2018, https://www.americanbar.org; D. Wilkie, "More Than Half of LGBT Workers Closeted," Society for Human Resource Management, May 15, 2014, http://www.shrm.org.

23. J. Quittner, "Not Made in America: Where U.S. Innovation Really Comes From," *Inc.,* April 10, 2014, www.inc.com; "The United States of Entrepreneurs," *The Economist,* March 14, 2009, http://www.economist.com.

24. Bureau of Labor Statistics, "Labor Force Characteristics by Race and Ethnicity, 2015," September 2016, www.bls.gov.

25. M. Bertrand and S. Mullainathan, "Are Emily and Greg More Employable Than Lakisha and Jamal?" NBER Working Paper No. 9873, July 2003, http://www.nber.org.

26. "Persons with a Disability: Labor Force Characteristics Summary," Bureau of Labor Statistics, June 21, 2016, www.bls.gov; D. Pattison and H. Waldron, "Growth in New Disabled-Worker Entitlements, 1970–2008," *Social Security Administration Bulletin* 73, no. 4 (2013), http://www.ssa.gov.

27. Bureau of Labor Statistics, "Persons with a Disability: Labor Force Characteristics Summary," news release, February 26, 2019, https://www.bls.gov.

28. Bureau of Labor Statistics, "Persons with a Disability: Labor Force Characteristics Summary," news release, February 26, 2019, https://www.bls.gov.

29. U.S. Bureau of the Census, "Anniversary of Americans with Disabilities Act: July 26," Facts for Features CB11-FF.14, May 31, 2011, http://www.census.gov; Bureau of Labor Statistics, "Persons with a Disability: Labor Force Characteristics—2009," news release, August 25, 2010, http://www.bls.gov/cps.

30. Equal Employment Opportunity Commission, "Disability Discrimination," http://www.eeoc.gov; EEOC, "Notice Concerning the Americans with Disabilities Act (ADA) Amendments Act of 2008," http://www.eeoc.gov; EEOC, "ADA Charge Data by Impairments/Bases: Resolutions, FY1997–FY2008," http://www.eeoc.gov.

31. Bureau of Labor Statistics, "Labor Force Characteristics of Foreign-Born Workers Summary," news release, May 17, 2018, https://www.bls.gov.

32. P. Taylor and the Pew Research Center, *The Next America* (New York: Public Affairs, 2014).

33. The Conference Board, "Growing Labor Shortages on the Horizon in Mature Economies," press release, September 2, 2014, http://www.conference-board.org.

34. C. Kulik, S. Perera, and C. Cregan, "Engage Me: The Mature-Age Worker and Stereotype Threat," *Academy of Management Journal* 59 (2016), pp. 2132–56.

35. S. Vernon, "Will Boomers Really Be Able to Work Past 65?" *CBS News,* January 6, 2015, http://www.cbsnews.com.

36. P. Shergill, "Managing High-Performing but Demanding Gen Y," *HR Magazine,* August 22, 2014, http://www.hrmagazine.co.uk; N. A. Hira, "Attracting the Twenty-Something Worker," *Fortune,* May 15, 2007, http://money.cnn.com.

37. A. Doyle, "Best Social Media Sites for Job Searching," *The Balance Careers,* February 2, 2019, www.thebalancecareers.com.

38. Kenneth Terrell, "Age Discrimination Common in Workplace, Survey Says," AARP, August 2, 2018, https://www.aarp.org/work/working-at-50-plus/info-2018/age-discrimination-common-at-work.html.

39. Bonnie Marcus, "What Should You Do When Faced with Age Discrimination at Work?" *Forbes,* February 22, 2019, https://www.forbes.com/sites/bonniemarcus/2019/02/22/what-should-you-do-when-faced-with-age-discrimination-at-work/#6e94122573d4.

40. Katharine Paljug, "How Employers Can Avoid Age Discrimination," *Business News Daily,* May 2, 2018, https://www.businessnewsdaily.com/10726-how-businesses-can-avoid-age-discrimination.html.

41. M. Mor Barak and M. Cherin, "A Tool to Expand Organizational Understanding of Workforce Diversity," *Administration in Social Work* 22 (1998), pp. 47–64.

42. L. Shore, J. Cleveland, and D. Sanchez, "Inclusive Workplaces: A Review and Model," *Human Resource Management Review* 28 (2018), pp. 176–89.

43. M. F. Winters, "From Diversity to Inclusion: An Inclusion Equation," in B. M. Ferdman and B. R. Deane, eds., *Diversity at Work: The Practice of Inclusion* (San Francisco, CA: Jossey-Bass, 2014), pp. 205–28.

44. C. Post and K. Byron, "Women on Boards and Firm Financial Performance: A Meta-Analysis," *Academy of Management Journal* 58 (2015), pp. 1546–71.

45. D. Cumming, T. Y. Leung, and O. Rui, "Gender Diversity and Securities Fraud," *Academy of Management Journal* 58 (2015), pp. 1572–93.

46. See, for example, R. Riccò and M. Guerci, "Diversity Challenge: An Integrated Process to Bridge the 'Implementation Gap,'" *Business Horizons* 57 (2014), pp. 235–45; C. Francoeur, R. Labelle, and B. Sinclair-Desgagné, "Gender Diversity in Corporate Governance and Top Management," *Journal of Business Ethics* 81, no. 1 (2008), pp. 83–95; A. McMillan-Capehart, J. R. Aaron, and B. N. Cline, "Investor Reactions to Diversity Reputation Signals," *Corporate Reputation Review* 13 (2010), pp. 184–97; P. Wang and J. L. Schwarz, "Stock Price Reactions to GLBT Nondiscrimination Policies," *Human Resource Management* 49, no. 2 (2010), pp. 195–216; R. C. Anderson, D. M. Reeb, A. Upadhyay, and W. Zhao, "The Economics of Director Heterogeneity," *Financial Management* 40, no. 1 (2011), pp. 5–38; M. Davidson, "Leveraging Difference for Organizational Excellence: Managing Diversity Differently," technical note UVA-OB-0767 (Charlottesville, VA: Darden Business Publishing, 2002); Eric Kearney, Diether Gebert, and Sven C. Voelpel, "When and How Diversity Benefits Teams: The Importance of Team Members' Need for Cognition," *Academy of Management Journal* 52 (June 2009), pp. 581–98.

47. A. Diaz-Uda, C. Medina, and B. Schill, "Diversity's New Frontier: Diversity of Thought and the Future of the Workforce," Deloitte University Press, July 23, 2013, http://www.dupress.com; N. Adler, *International Dimensions of Organizational Behavior,* 3rd ed. (Boston: PWS-Kent, 1997); T. Cox and S. Blake, "Managing Cultural Diversity: Implications for Organizational Competitiveness," *Academy of Management Executives* 5 (August 1991), pp. 45–56.

48. Procter & Gamble, "Fulfilling Our Potential," corporate Purpose & People website, http://www.pg.com/en_US/company/purpose_people/diversity_inclusion.

49. See www.eeco.gov.

50. Sara Horowitz, "94 Percent of Millennials Want to Use Their Skills for Good," *Huffington Post,* December 6, 2017, https://www.huffpost.com/entry/94-of-millennials-want-to_b_5618309.

51. Robin Meyerhoff, "Why Social Entrepreneurs and Big Business Need Each Other More Than Ever," *Forbes,* November 1, 2018, https://www.forbes.com/sites/sap/2018/11/01/why-social-entrepreneurs-and-big-business-need-each-other-more-than-ever/#7bd0367245b4.

52. Mei Mei Fox, "5 Reasons Why Social Entrepreneurship Is the New Business Model," *Forbes,* August 8, 2016, https://www.forbes.com/sites/meimeifox/2016/08/08/5-reasons-why-social-entrepreneurship-is-the-new-business-model/#4e001e7c44ca.

53. Angela Damiani, "A Reflection on Ten Years and Where We Go Next," NEWaukee, https://www.newaukee.com/news/10-year-reflection/ accessed March 31, 2019.

54. Stephanie Staudinger, "NEWaukee Night Market to Return for Sixth Year," CBS 58, March 4, 2019, https://www.cbs58.com/news/newaukee-night-market-to-return-for-sixth-year.

55. U.S. Equal Employment Opportunity Commission, www.eeoc.gov., accessed March 11, 2019.

56. B. Kreissl, "Managing a Multigenerational Workforce," *Canadian HR Reporter* 28 (2015), pp. 19–20; R. R. Thomas Jr., "From Affirmative Action to Affirming Diversity," *Harvard Business Review,* March–April 1990.

57. L. Dhanani, J. Beus, and D. Joseph, "Workplace Discrimination: A Meta-Analytic Extension, Critique, and Future Research Agenda," *Personnel Psychology* 71 (2018), pp. 147–79.

58. S. Correll, S. Bendard, and I. Paik, "Getting a Job: Is There a Motherhood Penalty?" *American Journal of Sociology* 112, no. 5 (2007), pp. 1297–1338; K. Jesella, "Mom's Mad, and She's Organized," *The New York Times,* February 22, 2007, http://www.nytimes.com.

59. G. Avalos, "Study Looks at Diversity, Turnover," *Contra Costa Times* (Walnut Creek, CA), October 13, 2006, Business & Company Resource Center, http://galenet.galegroup.com; Aparna Joshi and Hyuntak Roh, "The Role of Context in Work Team Diversity Research: A Meta-Analytic Review," *Academy of Management Journal* 52 (June 2009), pp. 559–627.

60. N. Adler, *International Dimensions of Organizational Behavior,* 3rd ed. (Boston: PWS-Kent, 1997); T. Cox and S. Blake, "Managing Cultural Diversity: Implications for Organizational Competitiveness," *Academy of Management Executives* 5 (August 1991), pp. 45–56; Brian Blume, Timothy Baldwin, and Katherine Ryan, "Communication Apprehension: A Barrier to Students' Leadership, Adaptability, and Multicultural Appreciation," *Academy of Management Learning and Education* 12 (September 12, 2012), pp. 158–72.

61. C. Kulik, S. Perera, and C. Cregan, "Engage Me: The Mature-Age Worker and Stereotype Threat," *Academy of Management Journal* 59 (2016), pp. 2132–56.

62. J. Nanley, A. Pugh, N. Romero, and A. Seals, "An Examination of Racial Discrimination in the Labor Market for Recent College Graduates: Estimates from the Field," Auburn University Department of Economics Working Paper Series no. 2014–06, http://www.http:// cla.auburn.edu/econwp/.

63. N. Adler, *International Dimensions of Organizational Behavior,* 3rd ed. (Boston: PWS-Kent, 1997).

64. M. Davidson, "Leveraging Difference for Organizational Excellence: Managing Diversity Differently," technical note UVA-OB-0767 (Charlottesville, VA: Darden Business Publishing, 2002).

65. Accenture Website "Inclusion and Diversity," https://www.accenture.com/us-en/about/inclusion-diversity-index accessed March 31, 2019.

66. Marguerite Ward, "The CEO of a $16 Billion Business Explains Why She Banned Corporate Memos," *CNBC,* November 28, 2016, https://www.cnbc.com/2016/11/28/ceo-of-a-14-billion-business-banned-corporate-memos.html.

67. "The World's Most Admired Companies," *Fortune,* http://fortune.com/worlds-most-admired-companies/list accessed March 31, 2019.

68. K. A. Jehn, "Workplace Diversity, Conflict, and Productivity: Managing in the 21st Century," SEI Center for Advanced Studies in Management, Wharton School, University of Pennsylvania, Diversity, http://mktg-sun.wharton.upenn.edu/SEI/diversity.html; Anne Nederveen Pieterse, Daan van Knippenberg, and Dirk van Dierendonck, "Cultural Diversity and Team Performance: The Role of Team Member Goal Orientation," *Academy of Management Journal* 56 (July 20, 2012), pp. 782–804.

69. A. J. Murrell, F. J. Crosby, and R. J. Ely, *Mentoring Dilemmas: Developmental Relationships within Multicultural Organizations* (Mahwah, NJ: Erlbaum, 1999). See a review of this book by M. L. Lengnick-Hall, "Mentoring Dilemmas: Developmental Relationships within Multicultural Organizations," *Personnel Psychology* 53, no. 1 (Spring 2000), pp. 224–27.

70. Brett Berson, Jack Zenger, Kellan Elliott-McCrea, and Joseph Folkman, "Why Recruiting Women Requires Creativity," *Build,* February 25, 2013, http://thebuildnetwork.com.

71. J. Silverman, "Doing Well While Doing Good, an Update on Our Progress," Etsy (news release), August 7, 2018, www.etsy.com; Company website, "Etsy Hacker Grants," www.etsy.com, accessed March 11, 2019; R. Rosen, "Etsy CTO: Prioritizing Diversity in Our Hiring Fielded Better Women and Men," *The Atlantic,* February 7, 2013, http://www.theatlantic.com.

72. K. Jones, "The Most Desirable Employee Benefits," *Harvard Business Review,* February 15, 2017, www.hbr.org.

73. Society of Women Engineers, "Establishing a Flexible Career Arrangement Porgram," February 13, 2014, http://www.societyofwomenengineers.com; M. D. Lee, S. M. MacDermid, and M. L. Buck, "Organizational Paradigms of Reduced-Load Work: Accommodation, Elaboration, and Transformation," *Academy of Management Journal* 43, no. 6 (December 2000), pp. 1211–34.

74. L. E. Overmyer Day, "The Pitfalls of Diversity Training," *Training and Development* 49, no. 12 (December 1995), pp. 24–29; S. Rynes and B. Rosen, "A Field Survey of Factors Affecting the Adoption and Perceived Success of Diversity Training," *Personnel Psychology* 48, no. 2 (Summer 1995), pp. 247–70; L. Ford, "Diversity: From Cartoons to Confrontations," *Training & Development* 54, no. 8 (August 2000), pp. 70–71; J. M. Ivancevich and J. A. Gilbert, "Diversity Management: Time for a New Approach," *Public Personnel Management* 29, no. 1 (Spring 2000), pp. 75–92; Katerina Bezrukova, Karen A. Jehn, and Chester S. Spell, "Reviewing Diversity Training: Where We Have Been and Where We Should Go," *Academy of Management Learning and Education* 11 (June 2012), pp. 207–27.

75. "How to Increase Workplace Diversity," *The Wall Street Journal,* April 7, 2009, http://www.wsj.com; M. Burkart, "The Role of Training in Advancing a Diversity Initiative," *Diversity Factor* 8, no. 1 (Fall 1999), pp. 2–5.

76. Harver.com, "5 Fascinating Uses of AI in Recruitment," https://harver.com/blog/uses-ai-in-recruitment/., accessed April 1, 2019.

77. Rogerio Rizzi, "AI Helping Organizations Overcome Bias and Embrace an Inclusive Culture," November 20, 2018, https://www.digitalistmag.com/future-of-work/2018/11/20/ai-helping-organizations-overcome-bias-embrace-inclusive-culture-06194307.

78. "5 Fascinating Uses of AI in Recruitment," Harver, https://harver.com/blog/uses-ai-in-recruitment/, accessed April 1, 2019.

79. Rogerio Rizzi, "AI Helping Organizations Overcome Bias and Embrace an Inclusive Culture," November 20, 2018, https://www.digitalistmag.com/future-of-work/2018/11/20/ai-helping-organizations-overcome-bias-embrace-inclusive-culture-06194307.

80. Rudina Seseri, "How AI Is Changing the Game for Recruiting," *Forbes,* January 29, 2018, https://www.forbes.com/sites/valleyvoices/2018/01/29/how-ai-is-changing-the-game-for-recruiting/#6d2773f11aa2.

81. Korn Ferry, "Executive Survey Finds a Lack of Focus on Diversity and Inclusion Key Factors in Employee Turnover," press release, March 2, 2015, http://www.kornferry.com.

82. D. M. Robinson and T. Reio Jr., "Benefits of Mentoring African-American Men," *Journal of Managerial Psychology* 27 (2012), pp. 406–21; "How Bad Is the Turnover Problem?" *HR Focus,* March 2007, Business & Company Resource Center, http://galenet.galegroup.com; B. Thomas, "Black Entrepreneurs Win, Corporations Lose," *BusinessWeek,* September 20, 2006, General Reference Center Gold, http://find.galegroup.com; P. Shurn-Hannah, "Solving the Minority Retention Mystery," *The Human Resource Professional* 13, no. 3 (May–June 2000), pp. 22–27.

83. S. H. Jeong and D. A. Harrison, "Glass Breaking, Strategy Making, and Value Creating: Meta-Analytic Outcomes of Women as CEOs and TMT Members," *Academy of Management Journal* 60 (2017), pp. 1219–62.

84. J. Bono, P. Braddy, Y. Liu, et al., "Dropped on the Way to the Top: Gender and Managerial Derailment," *Personnel Psychology* 70 (2017), pp. 729–68.

85. J. Bono, P. Braddy, Y. Liu, et al., "Dropped on the Way to the Top: Gender and Managerial Derailment," *Personnel Psychology* 70 (2017), pp. 729–68.

86. "6 Tips on Working with Much Younger Colleagues," *Forbes,* March 27, 2017, www.forbes.com.

87. K. Van Nuys, D. Globe, D. Ng-Mak, H. Cheung, J. Sullivan, and D. Goldman, "The Association between Employee Obesity and Employer Costs: Evidence from a Panel of U.S. Employers," *American Journal of Health Promotion* 28 (May–June 2014), pp. 277–85.

88. R. Rodriguez, "Diversity Finds Its Place," *HR Magazine,* August 2006, Business & Company Resource Center, http://galenet.galegroup.com; C. Clifford, "PepsiCo CEO: Hiring More Women and People of Color Is a 'Business Imperative,'" *CNBC,* October 17, 2016, www.cnbc.com.

89. PepsiCo, "Diversity & Engagement," http://www.pepsic.com, accessed April 11, 2017.

90. David Gelles, "Julie Sweet of Accenture Could See Her Future," *The New York Times,* January 2, 2019, https://www.nytimes.com/2019/01/02/business/julie-sweet-accenture-corner-office.html.

91. Accenture website, "Inclusion and Diversity—Workforce Demographic in the United States," https://www.accenture.com/us-en/company-us-diversity#block-our-workforce-demographics-united-states.

PART THREE   SUPPORTING CASE

Zappos

At the turn of the millennium, Zappos, a Las Vegas–based Internet retailer, was a start-up struggling to survive. The company wanted to be *the* online destination for buying shoes, but customers hesitated to pick out shoes online. The company hired a 27-year-old business consultant named Tony Hsieh to figure out what would save Zappos.

Hsieh, a first-generation Taiwanese American with a degree in computer science, already had a couple of successful business start-ups under his belt. Undeterred by Zappos's weak performance, he set an ambitious goal: Zappos would become the largest shoe retailer on the Internet. How? Not by focusing on mainly price or even selection, but by enhancing a company culture designed to make employees happy. Happy employees, Hsieh believed, would deliver superior service. And when customers take a chance on picking out shoes from a website, they want to trust that the seller will ensure they are satisfied with everything about the purchase, from shoe style and fit to fast delivery and an easy returns policy.

The approach quickly began to stimulate sales, and just a year after he started advising Zappos, Hsieh was named chief executive. He worked for the startlingly small salary of $36,000. That arrangement didn't bother Hsieh because he is more motivated by creating a great organization than by earning money. After all, his previous business, LinkExchange, brought him $265 million when he sold it to Microsoft.

The Zappos culture is built on 10 core values:

1. Deliver WOW (an emotional impact and powerful story to tell) through service.
2. Embrace and drive change.
3. Create fun and a little weirdness.
4. Be adventurous, creative, and open-minded.
5. Pursue growth and learning.
6. Build open and honest relationships with communication.
7. Build a positive team and family spirit. ("Family" refers to Zappos co-workers.)
8. Do more with less.
9. Be passionate and determined.
10. Be humble.

These somewhat unconventional values are essential hiring criteria, and the company's career website directs potential applicants to read the values—which are described in whimsical terms—and apply for a job only if they want to be part of this "best thing about the Zappos family." In fact, at the end of the orientation process, employees are offered $3,000 to quit if they feel they aren't a good fit with the company values, and displaying a lack of the values is grounds for being discharged. According to Hsieh, hiring people who share the core values makes it easy to form real friendships, and those relationships, in turn, create an environment in which people think creatively.

The Zappos human resources department, under the leadership of Hollie Delaney, a Salt Lake City native, ensures that job candidates start to experience and participate in this unconventional, fun culture during the application and selection process. An online application invites them to submit video cover letters with their applications, and interviews are conducted in a room that looks like the set of a TV talk show, where candidates might answer a question such as "What's your theme song?" Employees evaluating candidates consider not only work history, but also the way candidates interact during lunch. They even take into account the observations of the shuttle drivers who take visiting job candidates back to their hotel. Once on board, employees might discover that fun and a little weirdness at the company includes an opportunity to dye Hsieh's or another manager's hair blue or shave his or her head at the annual Bald & Blue Day. And the commitment to wowing customers spills over into work relationships: Given a chance to reward colleagues' good behavior with a $50 monthly bonus, many employees held off, waiting to see exceptional behavior.

Recently performance appraisals also were brought into line with the focus on values. Employees are rated not just on task accomplishment, but also on how well they represent the core values. Managers are expected to describe specific instances of employees demonstrating the values at work, and employees who score low on a measure have the chance to receive training in that value. Outside the formal appraisal process, employees also continue to receive regular feedback on task-related measures such as percentage of hours spent talking to customers.

Delaney acknowledges that the company's values result in a work environment that is loud, hardworking, and full of change—conditions that aren't for everyone. Pay also isn't necessarily high, especially for call center workers. But for those who share the values, this kind of workplace is exhilarating. There also are plenty of rewards and perks, including profit sharing, a nap room, and access to a life coach who counsels employees as they sit on a velvet throne.

With this approach to human resources management, Hsieh helped Zappos grow into a billion-dollar company, which was eventually acquired by Amazon for $1.2 billion. Hsieh negotiated a deal in which Amazon promised to let Zappos continue operating independently, in accordance with its distinctive culture.

Unfortunately, although the 2008 financial crisis didn't keep sales at Zappos from rising, the ongoing economic slowdown eventually hurt, and Zappos laid off some of its workers, letting them down as gently as it could with generous severance packages. Even so, Zappos, unlike many businesses, hasn't outsourced its call center, located in Kentucky, because those employees need to be a part of the company culture. After all, they are the ones who talk directly with customers, and they're trained to wow customers—for example, encouraging them to try multiple sizes because shipping is free in both directions. What's next for this innovative e-retailer? Several reports are emerging that Zappos is moving away from using a hierarchical, traditional management approach with titles and detailed employee job descriptions. Zappos hopes that empowering its diverse employees will keep it at the forefront of employees' minds as a great place to work.

QUESTIONS

1. Evaluate whether you think Zappos is a responsive organization. How do you expect its recent downsizing to affect its responsiveness?

2. How does human resources management reinforce Zappos's core values?

3. How well do you think Zappos's human resources strategy supports the valuing of employee diversity? What diversity issues does Zappos need to address?

SOURCES: Greenfield, R., "Zappos CEO Tony Hsieh: Adopt Holacracy or Leave," *Fast Company,* March 30, 2015, http://www.fastcompany.com; Rodriguez, G., "The Great Zappos 'Circles' Experiment and Why It Really Matters," *Forbes,* January 15, 2014, http://www.forbes.com; Blodget, H., "Zappos CEO Tony Hsieh Making $36,000 a Year Working for Amazon," *Yahoo Finance,* September 10, 2010, http://finance.yahoo.com; Zappos, Jobs web page, http://about.zappos.com/jobs/; Gurchiek, K., "Delivering HR at Zappos," *HR Magazine,* June 2011, http://www.shrm.org; O'Brien, J. M., "Zappos Knows How to Kick It," *Fortune,* January 22, 2009, http://money.cnn.com; Pyrillis, R., "The Reviews Are In," *Workforce Management,* May 1, 2011, Business & Company Resource Center, http://galenet.galegroup.com.

CHAPTER 12
Leadership

> Every soldier has a right to competent command.
>
> —Julius Caesar

Matej Kastelic/Alamy Stock Photo

learning objectives

After studying Chapter 12, you will be able to:

LO 12-1 Discuss what it means to be a leader.

LO 12-2 Summarize what people want and organizations need from their leaders.

LO 12-3 Explain how a good vision helps you be a better leader.

LO 12-4 Identify sources of power in organizations.

LO 12-5 List personal characteristics that contribute to leader effectiveness.

LO 12-6 Describe behaviors that will make you a better leader and know when situations call for them.

LO 12-7 Distinguish between charismatic and transformational leadership.

LO 12-8 Describe types of opportunities to lead.

LO 12-9 Discover how to further your own leadership development.

chapter outline

Management in Action

KENNETH FRAZIER: A LEADER FOCUSING ON THE LONG TERM

Kenneth Frazier belongs to a very small and select group. As chairman and CEO of Merck & Co., a multinational pharmaceutical company, he is one of only three African American CEOs of a *Fortune* 500 company. Born in Philadelphia and having earned his law degree from Harvard Law School, he joined Merck in 1992 as vice president and general counsel of the Astra Merck Group. In 2007, he was chosen to lead Merck's Global Human Health division; in 2010, he was named president of Merck, and in 2011, he was named CEO, where he's been ever since.

Frazier took over as CEO during a challenging time in Merck's long history. A spate of events caused the company's stock to slide. In 2008, it paid out nearly $5 billion to settle thousands of lawsuits.[1] The U.S. economy was still in the early stages of recovering from the Great Recession, and there was industrywide uncertainty about the impact the newly passed Affordable Care Act would have. Meanwhile, Merck's reputation was still tarnished from the Vioxx scandal in which Merck was accused of marketing and promoting a drug that was known to increase the risk of heart attacks.

Contrary to the volatility of the 2000s, Frazier's leadership over the past decade has been a steadying force. Since taking over as CEO, Merck's stock has nearly tripled; in 2018, its revenue was over $42 billion, the fourth consecutive year of growth.[2] Not that these short-term results matter much to Frazier. The guiding philosophy of his leadership has been to focus on long-term sustainability and health, both for shareholders and society.

Bennett Raglin/NAACP LDF/Getty Images

Frazier's decisions surrounding the development of one of its cornerstone cancer drugs, Keytruda, exemplifies his approach. In the early trial phases in 2013, Frazier was very cautious, calling for an extension of clinical studies. The market reacted negatively and Merck's stock took a hit. In fact, Merck has conducted over 700 clinical trials for Keytruda, far more than other drug in its class.[3]

The long-term result? Doctors and medical professionals view Keytruda as a major advance in immunotherapy drugs, effective in patients with a variety of cancers and helping them live longer lives. The drug is also generating billions of dollars in global sales and is a prime reason Merck's stock is soaring again. As Frazier puts it: "Keep your eyes on the prize. Manage to the long term, not to what Wall Street says it wants in the short term."[4]

Kenneth Frazier is having a profound effect on Merck's management strategy and objectives, as well as its performance. In fact, the company even raised the mandatory retirement age of 65 for CEOs so Frazier could continue in his role.[5] As you read this chapter, compare Frazier's long-term approach with the kinds of practices recommended for successful leadership.

People get excited about the topic of leadership. They want to know what makes a great leader. Managers in all industries are interested in this question. They believe the answer will bring improved organizational performance and personal career success. They hope to acquire the skills that will transform an average manager into a true leader.

Based on the idea that leadership can be learned, many large organizations such as First Data Corp., BAE Systems, Comcast-NBCUniversal, and PwC actively recruit retired military personnel in the belief that military training and experience prepare people to lead.[6] Of course you don't have to join the armed services to acquire leadership skills. According to one source, "Leadership seems to be the marshaling of skills possessed by a majority but used by a minority. But it's something that can be learned by anyone, taught to everyone, denied to no one."[7]

LO 12-1 Discuss what it means to be a leader.

What is leadership? To start, a leader is one who influences others to attain goals. The greater the number of followers, the greater the influence. And the more successful the attainment of worthy goals, the more evident the leadership. But we must explore beyond this bare definition to capture the excitement and intrigue that devoted followers and students of leadership feel when they see a great leader in action, to understand what organizational leaders really do, and to learn what it takes to become a truly outstanding leader.

Outstanding leaders combine good strategic substance and effective interpersonal processes to formulate and implement strategies that produce results and sustainable competitive advantage.[8] They may launch enterprises, build organization cultures, win wars, or otherwise change the course of events.[9] They are strategists who seize opportunities others overlook, but "they are also passionately concerned with detail—all the small, fundamental realities that can make or mar the grandest of plans."[10]

What Do We Want from Our Leaders?

LO 12-2 Summarize what people want and organizations need from their leaders.

What do people want from their leaders? Broadly speaking, people want their leaders to help them (and not hinder them) as they pursue their goals.[11] These goals include not just more pay and promotions but support for their personal development; clearing of obstacles so they can perform at high levels; and treatment that is respectful, fair, and ethical. Leaders serve people best when they help them develop their own initiative and good judgment, enable them to grow, and help them become better contributors. People want competence and proper management—the kinds of things found in this chapter and others throughout this book.

Meanwhile, and into the future, organizations need people at all levels to lead. They need leaders throughout the organization to do the things that their people want, but also to help create and implement strategic direction. Thus organizations place people in formal leadership positions to achieve both personal and organizational goals.

> Organizations need people at all levels to be leaders.

Shireen Yates, co-founder and CEO of Nima, learned that her company accomplished more when she delegated more control to her team. According to Yates: "I grew by being able to set a direction but really empower the team to feel like they have full ownership in achieving the objectives and moving things forward."[12]

Nima, which makes portable sensors that detect allergens like gluten and peanuts in food, has experienced an increase is sales among allergy sufferers.[13] Users can rate restaurants and upload the allergen data to Nima's database for other users to see.[14]

These two perspectives—what people want and what organizations need—are neatly combined in a set of five key behaviors identified by James Kouzes and Barry Posner, two well-known authors and consultants (see Exhibit 12.1).

You will read about these and other aspects of leadership in this and the following chapters. The topics we discuss will help you become a better leader, and give you benchmarks you can use to assess the competence and fairness with which your boss manages you.

Inclusiveness Works

Including the LGBTQ Community

Approximately 4.5 percent of the U.S. population identifies as lesbian, gay, bisexual, transgender, and queer.[15] As acceptance and tolerance for all individuals in society continues to grow, this percentage is likely to increase. And though progress has been made, there is still a long road to equality and many challenges facing the LGBTQ community.

Although LGBTQ individuals have faced violence and discrimination throughout U.S. history, they are still not a protected class under federal law, and only about half of the states provide nondiscrimination laws in the workplace.[16] It should come as little surprise, then, that a recent study reported that upward of 25 percent of individuals identifying as LGBTQ were discriminated against in the workplace.[17]

It's important to remember that discrimination can occur in explicit ways, such as being fired, demoted, or harassed. But it can also occur in subtle ways, such as being excluded by co-workers or feeling unaccepted due to formal organizational policies and culture.

There are steps leaders can take to create a workplace environment that can address these challenges. Having a written policy that prohibits harassment and promotes tolerance is a good first step, but employees should also be trained on company policies and values, including unconscious biases that they may harbor.[18] In addition, the organization can proactively account for the health and well-being of LGBTQ employees by providing health care plans that include specialized services that address their needs.[19]

Considering employees' wants and needs both inside and outside the workplace is more likely to lead to feelings of inclusion and a more cohesive and productive organization.

1. How does promoting inclusion for the LGBTQ community illustrate the leadership behaviors listed in Exhibit 12.1?
2. If you were the leader of an organization, how would you create an environment that promotes acceptance and inclusion for all individuals?

---

1. **Challenge the process.** They challenge conventional beliefs and practices, and they create constructive change.

2. **Inspire a shared vision.** They appeal to people's values and motivate them to care about an important mission.

3. **Enable others to act.** They give people access to information and give them the power to perform to their full potential.

4. **Model the way.** They don't just tell people what to do—they are living examples of the ideals they believe in.

5. **Encourage the heart.** They show appreciation, provide rewards, and use various approaches to motivate people in positive ways.

EXHIBIT 12.1
What Do the Best Leaders Do?

SOURCE: Adapted from Kouzes, J. and Posner, B., *The Leadership Challenge,* 2nd ed. San Francisco: Jossey-Bass, 1995.

Vision

A vision is not just a picture of what could be; it is an appeal to our better selves, a call to become something more," stated Rosabeth Moss Kanter of the Harvard Business School.[20] Having a vision for the future and communicating that vision to others are known to be essential components of great leadership. "We want to open up space for humanity, and in order to do that, space must be affordable," said Elon Musk, CEO of SpaceX (and Tesla)."[21] Sir Richard Branson, CEO of the Virgin Group, envisions that by 2050 the entire world will be powered by renewable energy.[22] Practicing business people are not alone in understanding the importance of vision; academic research shows that communicating a clear vision leads to higher organizational performance.[23]

LO 12-3 Explain how a good vision helps you be a better leader.

Imagine trying to complete a challenging jigsaw puzzle without the vision of what you're working toward.

Tetra Images/Getty Images

vision

A mental image of a possible and desirable future state of the organization.

Bottom Line

You can't perform in the long run if you don't have a vision of what you want to accomplish. *Do you have to be a top-level executive to have a vision?*

Not just any vision will do.

Bottom Line

Imagine a world with clean air, clean water, and enough food for all. In many businesses around the world, managers with vision are working toward making parts of that fantasy a reality. *What is your vision for a better future?*

A **vision** is a mental image of a possible and desirable future state of the organization. It expresses the leader's ambitions for the organization.[24] A leader can create a vision that describes high performance aspirations, the nature of corporate or business strategy, or even the kind of workplace worth building. The best visions are both ideal and unique.[25]

If a vision conveys an *ideal,* it communicates a standard of excellence and a clear choice of positive values. If the vision is also *unique,* it communicates and inspires pride in being different from other organizations. The choice of language is important; the words should imply a combination of realism and optimism, an action orientation, and resolution and confidence that the vision will be attained.[26]

Visions can be small or large and can exist at any organizational level as well as at the very top. The important points are that (1) a vision is necessary for effective leadership; (2) a manager or team can develop a vision for any job, work unit, or organization; and (3) many people, including managers who do not develop into effective leaders, do not develop a clear vision—instead they focus on performing or surviving on a day-by-day basis.

Put another way, leaders must know what they want.[27] And other people must understand what that is. The leader must be able to articulate the vision, clearly and often. Other people throughout the organization should understand the vision and be able to state it clearly themselves. That's a start. But the vision means nothing until the leader and followers take action to turn the vision into reality.[28]

One leader who articulated and modeled a clear vision was George Buckley, former chief executive of 3M Company, the innovative manufacturer best known for its Scotch tape, Post-it Notes and sandpaper. When the economy turned sour, other manufacturers slashed spending on research and development (R&D), but Buckley wanted to retain 3M's commitment to innovation. So even as he tied R&D spending to revenues (R&D spending fell, but not faster than revenues), he challenged his R&D staff to make products cheaper to produce.

Buckley even convinced them that the effort could be satisfying. He accomplished this by recognizing that what drives researchers is a belief that what they do is intellectually stimulating and significant. For example, when Buckley asked the leader of 3M's abrasives business what innovations were in the pipeline, the unit's head commented that abrasives were "not considered sexy." Buckley replied, "Why not? I think abrasives are sexy. Why can't abrasives be sexy?" Eventually, as researchers saw how their innovations were helping the company serve its markets, they grew enthusiastic about Buckley's vision.[29]

A metaphor reinforces the important concept of vision.[30] Putting a jigsaw puzzle together is much easier if you have the picture on the box cover in front of you. Without the picture, or vision, the lack of direction is likely to result in frustration and failure. That is what communicating a vision is all about: making clear where you are heading.

Not just any vision will do. Visions can be inappropriate, or fail, for a variety of reasons (see Exhibit 12.2).[31] First, an inappropriate vision may reflect merely the leader's personal needs. Such a vision can be unethical, or it may fail because of lack of acceptance by the market or by those who must implement it. Second (and related to the first), an inappropriate vision may ignore stakeholder needs. Third, the leader must stay abreast of environmental changes. Although effective leaders maintain confidence and persevere despite obstacles, the time may come when the facts dictate that the vision must change. You will learn more about change and how to manage it later in the book.

Where do visions come from?[32] Leaders should be sensitive to emerging opportunities, develop the right capabilities or worldviews, and not be overly invested in the status quo. You can capitalize on networks of insightful people who have ideas about the future. Some visions are accidental; a company may stumble into an opportunity, and the leader may get credit for foresight. Some leaders and companies launch many new initiatives and, through trial and error, occasionally hit home runs. If people talk about and learn from these successes, a good vision can emerge.

Management in Action

FRAZIER'S VISION FOR MERCK

MANAGER'S BRIEF

PROGRESS REPORT

ONWARD

Great leaders have vision, and great visions transcend the bottom line of a single organization. Kenneth Frazier has demonstrated this core principal in his time as the CEO of Merck & Co., one of the top five pharmaceutical companies in the world.

Many executives feel pressured into making decisions that will promote short-term and solid returns for shareholders. Frazier has eschewed that pressure and instead focused on long-term progress and sustainability. "The revenue and shareholder value we create are an imperfect proxy for the value we create for patients and society," he says. "While a fundamental responsibility of business leaders is to create value for shareholders, I think businesses also exist to deliver value to society. . . . Our salient purpose in the world is to deliver medically important vaccines and medicines that make a huge difference for humanity."[33]

To measure this value beyond the latest earnings report, Frazier says he relies on two key metrics: "How many people do we help? How much help do we give them?"[34] These are the two questions that guide his decision making, and the impact has been substantial.

Despite immense pressures to bring the drug to market faster, Frazier extended early-phase clinical trials for the immunotherapy cancer drug Keytruda, which is now helping thousands of individuals suffering from a variety of cancers around the world.

Keytruda has been profitable for Merck, but not all drugs that it develops will be. Merck has also developed a drug to possibly eradicate the spread of Ebola, a lethal fast-spreading virus that has terrorized people in various parts of Africa for decades. Between 2014 and 2016, Ebola took the lives of more than 11,000 people. Since then, Merck has invested tens of millions of dollars developing v920, a vaccine to fight Ebola. In May 2018, the virus emerged once again. But this time, only 33 people died, and the outbreak ended almost as quickly as it appeared. Medical professionals are primarily crediting Merck's vaccine with this remarkable progress, and perhaps it will even be a tipping point in fighting not only Ebola, but also other viral epidemics.[35]

Because v920 is deployed to primarily impoverished people in underdeveloped parts of the world, Merck stands to earn little if anything from the vaccine. But by Frazier's two metrics, the company has achieved immeasurable success—so much so that *Fortune* magazine ranked Merck second in its annual Change the World list, which recognizes companies that are trying to help the planet and tackle social problems.[36] That's a vision worth following.

- What do you think of the two metrics that guide Kenneth Frazier's vision? Where do you see the CEO's primary responsibility being? To shareholders or society?
- "Responsible leadership" is a label sometimes used to describe leaders who care about and act on behalf of social issues. You learned in Chapter 5 about ethics, CSR, and sustainability; how does Kenneth Frazier exhibit responsible leadership?

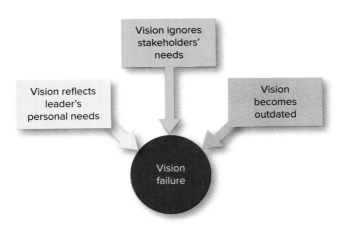

EXHIBIT 12.2
Reasons Why
Visions Fail

SOURCE: Adapted from Conger, J. A., "The Dark Side of Leadership," *Organizational Dynamics* 19 (Autumn 1990), 44–55.

Leading and Managing

Rawpixel.com/Shutterstock

Effective managers are not necessarily true leaders. Many administrators, supervisors, and even top executives perform their responsibilities successfully without being great leaders. But these positions afford an opportunity for leadership and greater positive impact. The ability to lead effectively, then, will set the excellent managers apart from the rest.

Whereas management must deal with the ongoing, day-to-day complexities of organizations, true leadership includes effectively orchestrating important change.[37] Managing requires planning and budgeting routines; leading includes setting the direction (creating a vision) for the firm. Management requires structuring the organization, staffing it with capable people, and monitoring results; leadership goes beyond these functions by inspiring people to accomplish a great vision. Great leaders keep people focused on moving the organization toward its ideal future, motivating them to overcome whatever obstacles lie in the way.

> Good leadership is all too rare.

Good leadership, unfortunately, is all too rare. Managers may focus on the activities that earn them praise and rewards, such as actions that increase the company's stock price, rather than making tough ethical choices or investing in long-term projects and sustainable advantage. Some new managers, learning that quick wins will help them establish their credibility as leaders, push a pet project while neglecting the negative impact on the people they were assigned to lead. This approach tends to backfire because employees distrust this type of manager and lose any commitment they might have had to the team's long-term success. Successful leaders, in contrast, enlist the team in scoring collective wins that result from working together toward a shared vision.[38]

It is important to be clear here about several things. First, management and leadership are both vitally important. To highlight the need for more leadership is not to minimize the importance of management or managers. But leadership involves unique processes that are distinguishable from basic management processes.[39] Moreover, just because they involve different processes does not mean that they require different, separate people. The same individual can exemplify effective managerial processes, leadership processes, both, or neither.

Some people dislike the idea of distinguishing between management and leadership, maintaining that it is artificial or derogatory toward the managers and the management processes that make organizations run. An alternative distinction is between supervisory and strategic leadership.[40] **Supervisory leadership** is behavior that provides guidance, support, and corrective feedback for day-to-day activities. **Strategic leadership** gives purpose and meaning to organizations.

Strategic leadership involves anticipating and envisioning a viable future for the organization and working with others to initiate changes that create that future.[41]

supervisory leadership

Behavior that provides guidance, support, and corrective feedback for day-to-day activities.

strategic leadership

Behavior that gives purpose and meaning to organizations, envisioning and creating a positive future.

Leading and Following

Organizations succeed or fail not only because of how well they are led, but because of how well followers follow. Just as managers are not necessarily good leaders, people are not always good followers. One leadership scholar stated, "Executives are given subordinates; they have to earn followers."[42] But it's also true that good followers help produce good leadership.

As a manager, you will be asked to perform the roles of both leader and follower. As you lead the people who report to you, you will report to your boss. You will be a member of some teams and task forces, and you may head others. Although the official leadership roles get the glamour and therefore are the positions that many people covet, followers must perform their responsibilities conscientiously and well.

1. **Volunteering** to handle tasks or help accomplish goals.
2. **Accepting** assignments in a willing manner.
3. **Exhibiting** loyalty to the group.
4. **Voicing** differences of opinion, but supporting the group's decisions.
5. **Offering** suggestions.
6. **Maintaining** a positive attitude, even in confusing or trying times.
7. **Working** effectively as a team member.

EXHIBIT 12.3
Behaviors of Effective
Followers

SOURCE: Adapted from Holden Leadership Center, University of Oregon, http://leadership.uoregon.edu/resources/exercises_tips/skills/followership.

Good followership doesn't mean merely obeying orders, although some bosses may view it that way. Simply obeying can hurt your employer and people when the boss is wrong. It also neglects the important point, elaborated later, that leadership is valuable at all organizational levels. Think, for instance, of teammates who inspire one another; not all leadership comes from just the coaches.

Leadership can even flow from direct report to boss, as when an employee or player influences a boss or coach to change a decision or practice activity. People throughout organizations have options that they can take or leave,[43] for instance to passively accept decisions and orders, express opinions, take initiative, resist or undermine the leader, or even overthrow a leader altogether (by ethical means or otherwise).

Exhibit 12.3 lists additional behaviors of effective followers. The most effective followers are capable of independent thinking and at the same time are actively committed to organizational goals.[44] These ideas are not just academic exercises; they are useful things for you to consider and apply as appropriate.

The best followers master skills that are useful to their organizations, and they hold performance standards that are higher than required. Effective followers may not get the glory, but they know their contributions to the organization are valuable. And as they make those contributions, they study leaders in preparation for their own leadership roles.[45]

Effective followers also distinguish themselves from ineffective ones by their enthusiasm and commitment to the organization and to a person or purpose—an idea, a product—other than themselves or their own interests.

Power and Leadership

Central to effective leadership is **power**—the ability to influence other people.[46] In organizations, this influence often means the ability to get things done or accomplish one's goals despite resistance from others.

LO 12-4 Identify sources of power in organizations.

power

The ability to influence others.

Sources of Power

One of the earliest and still most useful approaches to understanding power identifies five important potential sources of power.[47] Exhibit 12.4 shows those power sources.

Legitimate Power   The leader with *legitimate power* has the right, or the authority, to tell others what to do; employees are obligated to comply with legitimate orders. For example, a supervisor tells an employee to remove a safety hazard, and the employee removes the hazard because he has to obey the authority of his boss. In contrast, when a staff person (e.g., social media manager) lacks the authority to give an order to a line manager (e.g., sales director), the staff person has no legitimate power over the manager. As you might guess, managers have more legitimate power over their direct reports than they do over their peers, bosses, and others inside or outside their organizations.[48]

EXHIBIT 12.4
Sources of Leader Power

SOURCE: Adapted from French, J. R. P. and Raven, B., "The Bases of Social Power," *Studies in Social Power,* ed. D. Cartwright. Ann Arbor, MI: Institute for Social Research, 1959.

Reward Power   The leader who has *reward power* influences others because she controls valued rewards; people comply with the leader's wishes in order to receive those rewards. For example, a manager works hard to achieve her performance goals to get a positive performance review and a big pay raise from her boss. On the other hand, if company policy dictates that everyone receive the same salary increase, a leader's reward power decreases because he or she is unable to give higher raises.

Coercive Power   The leader with *coercive power* has control over punishments; people comply to avoid those punishments. For instance, a manager implements an absenteeism policy that administers disciplinary actions to offending employees. A manager has less coercive power if, say, a union contract limits her ability to punish. In general, lower-level managers have less legitimate, coercive, and reward power than do middle and higher-level managers.[49]

Referent Power   The leader with *referent power* has personal characteristics that appeal to others; people comply because of admiration, personal liking, a desire for approval, or a desire to be liked by the leader. For example, young, ambitious managers emulate the work habits and personal style of a successful, charismatic executive. An executive who is incompetent, disliked, and less respected has little referent power.

Expert Power   The leader who has *expert power* has certain expertise or knowledge; people comply because they believe in, can learn from, or can otherwise gain from that expertise. For example, a seasoned sales manager gives her salespeople some tips on how to close a deal. The salespeople then alter their sales techniques because they respect the manager's expertise. However, this manager may lack expert power in other areas, such as finance; thus her salespeople may ignore her advice concerning financial matters.

Monkey Business Images/
Shutterstock

People who are in a position that gives them the right to tell others what to do, who can reward and punish, who are well liked and admired, and who have expertise on which other people can draw will be powerful members of the organization.

What does having authority and power over others "do" to people?[50] A fascinating stream of research by Northwestern University's Adam Galinsky and colleagues provides evidence-based answers. Formal power holders tend to pay more attention to the big picture than details, less likely to take others' perspectives into account, judge other people's ethics more strongly than their own, have more confidence in their own knowledge than in others', be more optimistic than others, be more action oriented, express themselves more freely, and more often violate social norms while feeling less guilty about doing so.

Tendencies, of course, don't describe every official power holder. It's worth reading them again and thinking about them from a personal perspective: which ones might describe you, and which ones do you want to embrace or avoid?

All of the power sources discussed above are important. Although it is easy to assume that the most powerful bosses are those who have high legitimate power and control major rewards and punishments, it is important not to underestimate the more personal sources such as expert and referent powers. Additional personal sources of power that do not necessarily stem from one's position or level within an organization include access to information, holding a position located close to powerful others, and having a strong informal network.[51]

Traditional Approaches to Understanding Leadership

Three traditional approaches to studying leadership are the trait approach, the behavioral approach, and the situational approach.

Leader Traits

The **trait approach** is the oldest leadership perspective; it focuses on individual leaders and attempts to determine the personal characteristics (traits) that great leaders share. What set Margaret Thatcher, Nelson Mandela, Julius Caesar, and George Washington apart from the crowd? The trait approach assumes the existence of a leadership personality and assumes that leaders are born, not made.

From 1904 to 1948, researchers conducted more than 100 leadership trait studies.[52] At the end of that period, management scholars concluded that no particular set of traits is necessary for a person to become a successful leader. Enthusiasm for the trait approach diminished, but some research on traits continued. By the mid-1970s, a more balanced view emerged: Although no traits ensure leadership success, certain characteristics are potentially useful. The current perspective is that some some personal characteristics—many of which a person need not be born with but can strive to acquire—contribute to leader effectiveness (see Exhibit 12.5).[53]

LO 12-5 List personal characteristics that contribute to leader effectiveness.

trait approach

A leadership perspective that attempts to determine the personal characteristics that great leaders share.

EXHIBIT 12.5
Personal Attributes That Aid Leader Effectiveness

1. *Drive.* Drive refers to a set of characteristics that reflect a high level of effort. Drive includes high need for achievement, constant striving for improvement, ambition, energy, tenacity (persistence in the face of obstacles), and initiative. In several countries, the achievement needs of top executives were shown to relate to the growth rates of their organizations.[54] But the need to achieve can be a drawback if leaders focus on personal achievement and get so personally involved with the work that they do not delegate enough work to others.

2. *Leadership motivation.* Great leaders have more than drive; they *want to lead.* In this regard, it helps to be extroverted—extroversion is related to both leader emergence and leader effectiveness.[55] However—and this is a huge point—introverts have great strengths that can contribute to effective leadership, and extroversion can backfire. For example, the assertiveness of extroverted leaders can quash the contributions of group members. Extroverts sometimes should adopt a more reserved, quiet style.[56]

    If you consider yourself to be introverted, as so many of us do, you might want to heed the words of Mahatma Gandhi: "In a gentle way, you can shake the world." And listen to author Susan Cain, who writes that introverts are underrated as leaders and are the people who can help us "think deeply, strategize, solve complex problems, and spot canaries in your coal mine."[57]

    Also important is a high need for power, a preference to be in leadership rather than follower positions.[58] A high power need induces people to want to influence others, and sustains interest and satisfaction in the leadership process. When the power need is exercised in moral and socially constructive ways, rather than to the detriment of others, leaders inspire more trust, respect, and commitment to their vision.

3. *Integrity.* Integrity is the correspondence between actions and words. Honesty and credibility, in addition to being desirable characteristics in their own right, are especially important for leaders because these traits inspire trust in others.

4. *Self-confidence.* Self-confidence is important for a number of reasons. The leadership role is challenging, and setbacks are inevitable. Self-confidence allows a leader to overcome obstacles, make decisions despite uncertainty, and instill confidence in others. Of course you don't want to overdo this; arrogance and cockiness have triggered more than one leader's downfall.

5. *Knowledge of the business.* Effective leaders have a high level of knowledge about their industries, companies, and technical matters. Leaders must be able to interpret vast quantities of information. Advanced degrees are useful in a career, but ultimately less important than acquired expertise in matters relevant to the organization.[59]

6. *Dark traits.* Recent years have generated a great deal of interest in the dark side of leadership. The "Dark Triad" traits[60] are Machiavellianism (manipulative belief in expediency over principle), narcissism (inflated view of self, self-love, and fantasies of control, admiration, and successes), and psychopathy (the most serious; lack of empathy, lack of remorse, and guilt when harming others). Consider also three less-studied but severely labeled "Nightmare Traits": dishonesty, disagreeableness, and carelessness.[61]

behavioral approach

A leadership perspective that attempts to identify what good leaders do—that is, what behaviors they exhibit.

Finally, one personal quality may be the most important: the ability to perceive the needs and goals of others and to adjust one's personal leadership approach accordingly.[62] Effective leaders do not rely on one leadership style; rather, they are capable of using different styles as the situation warrants.[63] This quality—flexibility—is the cornerstone of the situational approaches to leadership, which you will read about shortly.

> Arrogance and hubris have triggered more than one leader's downfall.

LO 12-6 Describe behaviors that will make you a better leader and know when situations call for them.

Leader Behaviors

The **behavioral approach** to leadership attempts to identify what good leaders do. Should leaders focus on getting the job done, or on keeping their followers happy? Should they make decisions autocratically or democratically? In the behavioral approach, personal characteristics are considered less important than the actual behaviors that leaders exhibit.

Three general categories of leadership behavior have received particular attention: behaviors related to task performance, group maintenance, and employee participation in decision making.

Task Performance   Leadership requires getting the job done. **Task performance behaviors** are the leader's efforts to ensure that teams, organizations, or individuals achieve their work goals. This dimension is variously referred to as *concern for production, directive leadership, initiating structure,* or *closeness of supervision.* It includes a focus on work speed, quality and accuracy, quantity of output, and rule following.[64] For example, an IT manager may spend extra one-on-one time with newly hired team members to help them understand their roles and objectives. This type of leader behavior improves individual and group performance and therefore the leader's own performance.[65]

Group Maintenance   Leadership is inherently an interpersonal, group activity.[66] In exhibiting **group maintenance behaviors**, leaders take action to ensure the satisfaction of group members, develop and maintain harmonious work relationships, and preserve the social stability of the group. This dimension is sometimes referred to as *concern for people, supportive leadership,* or *consideration.* It includes a focus on people's feelings and comfort, appreciation of them, and stress reduction.[67] The same IT manager may check in with the new team members and ask how they're doing or see if they need anything. Such leader behavior improves follower satisfaction, motivation, and leader effectiveness.[68]

What specific behaviors do performance- and maintenance-oriented leadership imply? To help answer this question, assume you are asked to rate your boss on these two dimensions. If a leadership study were conducted in your organization, you would be asked to fill out a questionnaire similar to the one in Exhibit 12.6. The behaviors indicated in the first

Task Performance Leadership

1. Is your superior strict about observing regulations?
2. To what extent does your superior give you instructions and orders?
3. Is your superior strict about the amount of work you do?
4. Does your superior urge you to complete your work by a specified time?
5. Does your superior try to make you work to your maximum capacity?
6. When you do an inadequate job, does your superior focus on the inadequate way the job is done?
7. Does your superior ask you for reports about the progress of your work?
8. How precisely does your superior work out plans for goal achievement each month?

Group Maintenance Leadership

1. Can you talk freely with your superior about your work?
2. Does your superior generally support you?
3. Is your superior concerned about your personal problems?
4. Do you think your superior trusts you?
5. Does your superior give you recognition when you do your job well?
6. When a problem arises in your workplace, does your superior ask your opinion about how to solve it?
7. Is your superior concerned about your future benefits, such as promotions and pay raises?
8. Does your superior treat you fairly?

SOURCE: Misumi, J. and Peterson, M., "The Performance-Maintenance (PM) Theory of Leadership: Review of a Japanese Research Program," *Administrative Science Quarterly* 30, no. 2 (June 1985).

Bottom Line

Task performance behaviors focus on achieving work goals. *What shows you that a manager cares about task performance?*

task performance behaviors

Actions taken to ensure that teams, organizations, or individuals achieve their work goals.

group maintenance behaviors

Actions taken to ensure the satisfaction of group members, develop and maintain harmonious work relationships, and preserve the social stability of the group.

EXHIBIT 12.6

Questions Assessing Task Performance and Group Maintenance Leadership

set of questions represent performance-oriented leadership; those indicated in the second set represent maintenance-oriented leadership.

Leader–member exchange (LMX) theory highlights the importance of leader behaviors not just toward the group as a whole but toward individuals on a personal basis.[69] The focus in the original formulation, which has since been expanded, is primarily on the leader behaviors historically considered group maintenance.[70] According to LMX theory, and as supported by research evidence, maintenance behaviors such as trust, open communication, mutual respect, mutual obligation, and mutual loyalty form the cornerstone of relationships that are satisfying and perhaps more productive.[71]

Remember, though, the potential for cross-cultural differences. Maintenance behaviors are important everywhere, but the specific behaviors can differ from one culture to another.[72] For example, in the United States, maintenance behaviors include dealing with people face-to-face; in Japan, written memos are preferred over giving directions face-to-face, thus avoiding confrontation and permitting face-saving in the event of disagreement.[73]

Participation in Decision Making   How should a leader make decisions? More specifically, to what extent should leaders involve their people in making decisions?[74] As a dimension of leadership behavior, **participation in decision making** can range from autocratic to democratic. **Autocratic leadership** makes decisions and then announces them to the group. **Democratic leadership** solicits input from others. Democratic leadership seeks information, opinions, and preferences, sometimes to the point of meeting with the group, leading discussions, and using consensus or majority vote to make the final choice.

The Effects of Leader Behavior

How the leader behaves influences people's attitudes and performance. Studies of these effects focus on autocratic-versus-democratic decision styles or on performance-versus-maintenance-oriented behaviors.

Decision Styles   The classic study comparing autocratic and democratic styles found that a democratic approach resulted in the most positive attitudes, whereas an autocratic approach resulted in somewhat higher performance.[75] A **laissez-faire** style, in which the leader essentially made no decisions, led to more negative attitudes and lower performance. These results seem logical, and probably represent the prevalent beliefs among managers about the general effects of these approaches.

Democratic styles, appealing though they may seem to some, are not always the most appropriate. When speed is of the essence, democratic decision making may be too slow, or people may want decisiveness from their leader.[76] Whether a decision should be made autocratically or democratically depends on the characteristics of the leader, the followers, and the situation.[77] Thus a situational approach to leader decision styles, discussed later in the chapter, is appropriate.

Performance and Maintenance Behaviors   The performance and maintenance dimensions of leadership are independent of each other. In other words, a leader can behave in ways that emphasize one, both, or neither of these dimensions.

> A leader can behave in ways that emphasize one, both, or neither of these behaviors.

A team of Ohio State University researchers investigated the effects of leader behaviors in a truck manufacturing plant of International Harvester.[78] Generally, supervisors who were high on maintenance behaviors (which the researchers termed *consideration*) had fewer grievances and less turnover in their work units than supervisors who were low on this dimension. The opposite held for task performance behaviors (which the research team called *initiating structure*). Supervisors high on this dimension had more grievances and higher turnover rates.

When maintenance and performance leadership behaviors were considered together, the results were more complex. But one conclusion was clear: When a leader is high on

---

leader–member exchange (LMX) theory

Highlights the importance of leader behaviors not just toward the group as a whole but toward individuals on a personal basis.

participation in decision making

Leader behaviors that managers perform in involving their employees in making decisions.

autocratic leadership

A form of leadership in which the leader makes decisions on his or her own and then announces those decisions to the group.

democratic leadership

A form of leadership in which the leader solicits input from subordinates.

laissez-faire

A leadership philosophy characterized by an absence of managerial decision making.

performance-oriented behaviors, he or she should also be maintenance oriented. Otherwise, the leader will face high rates of employee turnover and grievances.

At about the same time the Ohio State studies were conducted, a research program at the University of Michigan was studying the impact of the same leader behaviors on groups' job performance.[79] Among other things, the researchers concluded that the most effective managers engaged in what they called task-oriented behavior: planning, scheduling, coordinating, providing resources, and setting performance goals. Effective managers also exhibited more relationship-oriented behavior: demonstrating trust and confidence, being friendly and considerate, showing appreciation, keeping people informed, and so on. As you can see, these dimensions of leader behavior are essentially the task performance and group maintenance dimensions.

After publication of the Ohio State and Michigan findings, it became popular to talk about the ideal leader as one who is always both performance and maintenance oriented. The best-known leadership training model to follow this style is Blake and Mouton's Leadership Grid.[80] In grid training, managers are rated on their performance-oriented behavior (called *concern for production*) and maintenance-oriented behavior (*concern for people*). Then their scores are plotted on the grid shown in Exhibit 12.7. The highest score is a 9 on both dimensions.

As the figure shows, joint scores can fall at any point on the grid. Managers who did not score a 9,9—for example, those who were high on concern for people but low on concern for production—would then receive training on how to become a 9,9 leader.

For a long time, grid training was warmly received by U.S. business and industry. Later, however, it was criticized for embracing a simplistic, one-best-way style of leadership and ignoring the possibility that 9,9 is not best under all circumstances. However, recent research continues to make clear the importance of both of these leader behaviors.[81] So if the manager is uncertain how to lead individuals or teams, it probably is best to exhibit behaviors that help both task performance and group maintenance.[82]

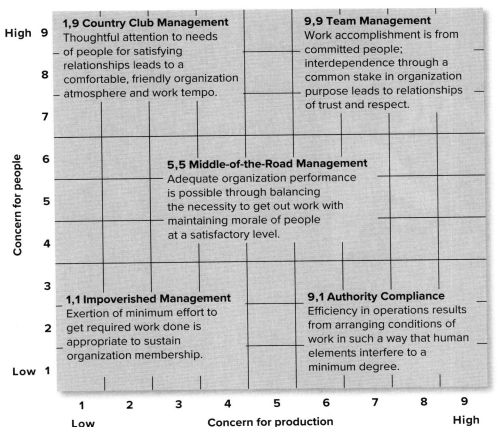

EXHIBIT 12.7
The Leadership Grid

1,9 Country Club Management
Thoughtful attention to needs of people for satisfying relationships leads to a comfortable, friendly organization atmosphere and work tempo.

9,9 Team Management
Work accomplishment is from committed people; interdependence through a common stake in organization purpose leads to relationships of trust and respect.

5,5 Middle-of-the-Road Management
Adequate organization performance is possible through balancing the necessity to get out work with maintaining morale of people at a satisfactory level.

1,1 Impoverished Management
Exertion of minimum effort to get required work done is appropriate to sustain organization membership.

9,1 Authority Compliance
Efficiency in operations results from arranging conditions of work in such a way that human elements interfere to a minimum degree.

Concern for people — High 9, 8, 7, 6, 5, 4, 3, 2, Low 1

Concern for production — Low 1 2 3 4 5 6 7 8 9 High

SOURCE: Blake, Robert Rogers and McCanse, Anne Adams, *The Leadership Grid Figure from Leadership Dilemmas— Grid Solutions*. Houston, TX: Gulf Publishing Company, 1991, p. 29.

In fact, a wide range of effective leadership styles exists. Organizations that understand the need for diverse leadership styles will have a competitive advantage in the modern business environment over those that believe there is only one best way.

Situational Approaches to Leadership

situational approach

Leadership perspective proposing that universally important traits and behaviors do not exist and that effective leadership behavior varies from situation to situation.

According to proponents of the **situational approach** to leadership, universally important traits and behaviors don't exist. They believe effective leader behaviors vary from situation to situation. The leader should first analyze the situation and then decide what to do. In other words, look before you lead.

A head nurse in a hospital described her situational approach to leadership:

> My leadership style is a mix of all styles. In this environment I normally let people participate. But in a code blue situation where a patient is dying I automatically become very autocratic: "You do this; you do that; you, out of the room; you all better be quiet; you, get Dr. Mansfield." The staff tell me that's the only time they see me like that. In an emergency like that, you don't have time to vote, talk a lot, or yell at each other. It's time for someone to set up the order.
>
> I remember one time, one person saying, "Wait a minute, I want to do this." He wanted to do the mouth-to-mouth resuscitation. I knew the person behind him did it better, so I said, "No, he does it." This fellow told me later that I hurt him so badly to yell that in front of all the staff and doctors. It was like he wasn't good enough. So I explained it to him: "That's the way it is. A life was on the line. I couldn't give you warm fuzzies. I couldn't make you look good because you didn't have the skills to give the very best to that patient who wasn't breathing anymore."[83]

Look (and think) before you lead.

This nurse has her own intuitive situational approach to leadership. She knows the potential advantages of the participatory approach to decision making, but she also knows that in some circumstances she must make decisions herself.

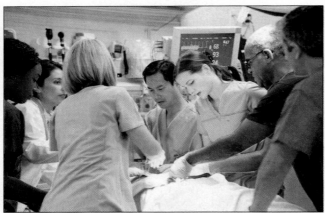

Nurses experience situational leadership on a daily basis. How would you handle a leadership role under pressure?

monkeybusinessimages/Getty Images

The first situational model of leadership—still highly useful—was proposed in 1958 by Tannenbaum and Schmidt. In their classic *Harvard Business Review* article, these authors described how managers should consider three factors before deciding how to lead: forces in the manager, forces in the subordinate, and forces in the situation.[84]

Forces in the manager include the manager's personal values, inclinations, feelings of security, and confidence in subordinates. Forces in the subordinate include his or her knowledge and experience, readiness to assume responsibility for decision making, interest in the task or problem, and understanding and acceptance of the organization's goals. Forces in the situation include the type of leadership style the organization values, the degree to which the group works effectively as a unit, the problem itself and the type of information needed to solve it, and the amount of time the leader has to make the decision.

Consider which of these forces makes an autocratic style most appropriate and which dictates a democratic, participative style. By engaging in this exercise, you are constructing a situational theory of leadership.

Although the Tannenbaum and Schmidt article was published more than a half century ago, most of its arguments remain valid. Since that time, other situational models have emerged. We will focus here on four: the Vroom model for decision making, Fiedler's contingency model, Hersey and Blanchard's situational theory, and path–goal theory.

Vroom model

A situational model that focuses on the participative dimension of leadership.

The Vroom Model of Leadership   This situational model follows in the tradition of Tannenbaum and Schmidt. The **Vroom model** emphasizes the participative dimension of leadership: how leaders go about making decisions. The model uses the basic situational approach of assessing the situation before determining the best leadership style.[85]

The Vroom model operates as a decision tree in which you answer a series of questions one at a time, choosing high or low for each; the specifics are not important here. Eventually you reach 1 of 14 possible endpoints. For each endpoint, the model states which of five decision styles is most appropriate. Several decision styles may work, but the style recommended is the one that takes the least amount of time.

The five leader decision styles—decide alone, consult individuals, consult multiple group members, facilitate a whole-group decision, and delegate to others—indicate that there are several shades of participation, not just autocratic or democratic.

Of course not every managerial decision warrants this complicated analysis. But the model becomes less complex after you work through it a couple of times. Also, using the model for major decisions ensures that you consider the important situational factors and alerts you to the most appropriate style to use.

Fiedler's Contingency Model   According to **Fiedler's contingency model of leadership effectiveness**, effectiveness depends on two factors: the personal style of the leader and the degree to which the situation gives the leader power, control, and influence over the situation.[86] Exhibit 12.8 illustrates the contingency model. The upper half of the figure shows the situational analysis, and the lower half indicates the appropriate style. In the upper portion, three questions are used to analyze the situation:

1. Are leader–member relations good or poor? (To what extent is the leader accepted and supported by group members?)
2. Is the task structured or unstructured? (To what extent do group members know what their goals are and how to accomplish them?)
3. Is the leader's position power strong or weak (high or low)? (To what extent does the leader have the authority to reward and punish?)

Fiedler's contingency model of leadership effectiveness

A situational approach to leadership postulating that effectiveness depends on the personal style of the leader and the degree to which the situation gives the leader power, control, and influence over the situation.

EXHIBIT 12.8   Fiedler's Analysis of Situations in Which the Task- or Relationship-Motivated Leader Is More Effective

Leader–member relations	Good				Poor			
Task structure	Structured		Unstructured		Structured		Unstructured	
Leader position power	High	Low	High	Low	High	Low	High	Low
Favorable for leader → Unfavorable for leader								
Type of leader most effective in the situation	1 Task-motivated	2 Task-motivated	3 Task-motivated	4 Relation-ship-motivated	5 Relation-ship-motivated	6 Relation-ship-motivated	7 Relation-ship-motivated	8 Task-motivated

SOURCE: Organ, Dennis and Bateman, Thomas, *Organizational Behavior,* 4th ed. New York: McGraw-Hill, 1990.

These three sequential questions create a decision tree (from top to bottom in the figure) in which a situation is classified into one of eight categories. The lower the category number, the more favorable the situation is for the leader; the higher the number, the less favorable the situation. Fiedler originally called this variable "situational favorableness," and later "situational control." Situation 1 is the best: relations are good, task structure is high, and power is high. In the least favorable situation (8), in which the leader has very little situational control, relations are poor, tasks lack structure, and the leader's power is weak.

Different situations dictate different leadership styles. Fiedler measured leadership styles with an instrument assessing the leader's least preferred co-worker (LPC); that is, the attitude toward the follower the leader liked the least. This was considered an indication more generally of leaders' attitudes toward people. If a leader can single out the person she likes the least, but her attitude is not all that negative, she would receive a high score on the LPC scale. Leaders with more negative attitudes toward others would receive low LPC scores.

Based on the LPC score, Fiedler considered two leadership styles. **Task-motivated leadership** places primary emphasis on completing the task and is more likely exhibited by leaders with low LPC scores. **Relationship-motivated leadership** emphasizes maintaining good interpersonal relationships and is more likely from high-LPC leaders. These leadership styles correspond to task performance and group maintenance leader behaviors, respectively.

The lower part of Exhibit 12.8 indicates which style is situationally appropriate. For situations 1, 2, 3, and 8, a task-motivated leadership style is more effective. For situations 4 through 7, relationship-motivated leadership is more appropriate.

Fiedler's theory was not always supported by research. It is better supported if three broad rather than eight specific levels of situational control are assumed: low, medium, and high. The theory was quite controversial in academic circles; among other arguable things, it assumed that leaders cannot change their styles but must be assigned to situations that suit their styles. Most important, it initiated and continues to emphasize the importance of finding a fit between the situation and the leader's style.

Hersey and Blanchard's Situational Theory   Hersey and Blanchard developed a situational model that added another factor the leader should take into account before deciding whether task performance or maintenance behaviors are more important. Originally called the *life-cycle theory of leadership,* **Hersey and Blanchard's situational theory** highlights the maturity of the followers as the key situational factor.[87] **Job maturity** is the level of the follower's skills and technical knowledge relative to the task being performed; **psychological maturity** is the follower's self-confidence and self-respect. High-maturity followers have both the ability and the confidence to do a good job.

The theory proposes that the more mature the followers, the less the leader needs to engage in task performance behaviors. The required amount of maintenance behavior is a bit more complex; maintenance behaviors are not important with followers of low or high levels of maturity but are important for followers of moderate maturity. For low-maturity followers, the emphasis should be on performance-related leadership; for moderate-maturity followers, performance leadership is somewhat less important and maintenance behaviors become more important; and for high-maturity followers, neither dimension of leadership behavior is important.

Little academic research has been done on this situational theory, but the model is well known and popular in management training seminars. Regardless of its scientific validity, Hersey and Blanchard's model provides a reminder that it is important to treat different people differently. Moreover, it suggests the importance of treating the same individual differently from time to time as he or she changes jobs or acquires more maturity in his or her particular job.[88]

Path–Goal Theory   Perhaps the most comprehensive and generally useful situational model of leadership effectiveness is path–goal theory. Developed by Robert House, **path–goal theory** gets its name from its concern with how leaders influence followers' perceptions of their work goals and the paths they follow toward goal attainment.[89]

---

task-motivated leadership

Leadership that places primary emphasis on completing a task.

---

relationship-motivated leadership

Style in which leader focuses on interpersonal relationships for measuring performance.

Hersey and Blanchard's situational theory

A life-cycle theory of leadership postulating that a manager should consider an employee's psychological and job maturity before deciding whether task performance or maintenance behaviors are more important.

---

job maturity

The level of the employee's skills and technical knowledge relative to the task being performed.

---

psychological maturity

An employee's self-confidence and self-respect.

---

path–goal theory

A theory that concerns how leaders influence subordinates' perceptions of their work goals and the paths they follow toward attainment of those goals.

EXHIBIT 12.9
The Path–Goal Framework

The key situational factors in path–goal theory are (1) personal characteristics of followers and (2) environmental pressures and demands with which followers must cope to attain their work goals. These factors determine which leadership behaviors are most appropriate.

The four pertinent leadership behaviors are as follows:

1. *Directive leadership,* a form of task performance-oriented behavior.
2. *Supportive leadership,* a form of group maintenance-oriented behavior.
3. *Participative leadership,* or decision style.
4. *Achievement-oriented leadership,* or behaviors geared toward motivating people, such as setting challenging goals and rewarding good performance.

These situational factors and leader behaviors are merged in Exhibit 12.9. As you can see, appropriate leader behaviors—as determined by characteristics of followers and the work environment—lead to effective performance.

The theory also specifies which follower and environmental characteristics are important. There are three key follower characteristics. *Authoritarianism* is the degree to which individuals respect, admire, and defer to authority. *Locus of control* is the extent to which individuals see the environment as responsive to their own behavior. People with an *internal* locus of control believe that what happens to them is their own doing; people with an *external* locus of control believe that it is just luck or fate. Finally, *ability* is people's beliefs about their own abilities to do their assigned jobs.

Path–goal theory states that these personal characteristics determine the appropriateness of various leadership styles. For example, the theory makes the following propositions:

- A directive leadership style is more appropriate for highly authoritarian people because such people respect authority.
- A participative leadership style is more appropriate for people who have an internal locus of control because these individuals prefer to have more influence over their own work (and lives).
- A directive style is more appropriate when subordinates' ability is low. The directive style helps people understand what has to be done.

Appropriate leadership style is also determined by three important environmental factors: people's tasks, the formal authority system of the organization, and the primary work group:

- Directive leadership is inappropriate if tasks already are well structured.
- If the task and the authority or rule system are dissatisfying, directive leadership will create greater dissatisfaction.
- If the task or authority system is dissatisfying, supportive leadership is especially appropriate because it offers one positive source of gratification in an otherwise negative situation.
- If the primary work group provides social support to its members, supportive leadership is less important.

Path–goal theory offers many more propositions. In general, the theory suggests that the functions of the leader are to (1) make the path to work goals easier to travel by providing coaching and direction, (2) reduce frustrating barriers to goal attainment, and (3) increase opportunities for personal satisfaction by increasing payoffs to people for achieving performance goals. The best way to do these things depends on your people and on the work situation. Again, analyze and then adapt your style accordingly.

Substitutes for Leadership   Sometimes leaders don't have to lead, or situations constrain their ability to lead effectively. The situation may be one in which leadership is unnecessary or has little impact. **Substitutes for leadership** can provide the same influence on people that leaders otherwise would have.

Certain follower, task, and organizational factors are substitutes for task performance and group maintenance leader behaviors.[90] For example, group maintenance behaviors are less important and have less impact if people already have a closely knit group, they have a professional orientation, the job is inherently satisfying, or there is great physical distance between leader and followers. Thus, physicians who are strongly concerned with professional conduct, enjoy their work, and work independently do not need social support from hospital administrators.

Task performance leadership is less important and will have less of a positive effect if people have a lot of experience and ability, feedback is supplied to them directly from the task or customer or co-worker, or the rules and procedures are rigid. If these factors are operating, the leader does not have to tell people what to do or how well they are performing.

The concept of substitutes for leadership does more than indicate when a leader's attempts at influence will and will not work. It provides useful and practical prescriptions for how to manage more efficiently.[91] If the manager can develop the work situation and employees to the point that a number of these substitutes for leadership are operating, she does not need to spend as much time in direct attempts to influence people. The leader will be free to spend more time on other important activities.

A study in China found substitutes for leadership to improve both job satisfaction and performance among knowledge workers.[92] Overall, though, substitutes for leadership may be better predictors of commitment and satisfaction than of performance.[93] These substitutes are helpful, but you can't put substitutes in place and think you've completed your job as leader.

These leadership substitutes can fill in for certain leader behaviors, but they do not completely replace the leaders themselves. Some maintain another potential leadership substitute is artificial intelligence. Automated decision making is not new, but as AI decision making advances, it will become a game changer for the management profession.[94] What do you think, can technology ever substitute completely for human leadership?

And as a follower, consider this: If you're not "getting" good leadership from above, and if good substitutes are not in place, create your own substitute for others' leadership: self-leadership. As but one example, proactive employees can inject ethical behavior into a work environment where the boss is not creating a culture of ethics.[95] Whatever you care about most, you have the options—and can take the initiative—to motivate yourself, lead yourself, and create positive change.

substitutes for leadership

Factors in the workplace that can exert the same influence on employees as leaders would provide.

Contemporary Perspectives on Leadership

LO 12-7 Distinguish between charismatic and transformational leadership.

So far you have learned the major classic approaches to understanding leadership, all of which remain useful today. Now we will discuss some newer developments that are revolutionizing our understanding of this vital aspect of management.

Charismatic Leadership

Like many great leaders, Ronald Reagan had charisma. So did John F. Kennedy. Thomas Watson, Richard Branson, Oprah Winfrey, Steve Jobs, and Mark Cuban are good examples of charismatic leaders in business.

Charisma is an elusive concept; it is easy to spot but hard to define, and scholars continue to debate it.[96] What *is* charisma, and how does one acquire it? According to one definition, "Charisma packs an emotional wallop for followers above and beyond ordinary esteem, affection, admiration, and trust. . . . The charismatic is an idolized hero, a messiah, and a savior."[97]

As you can see from this quotation, many people, particularly North Americans, value charisma in their leaders. But some people don't like the term *charisma;* it can be associated with the negative charisma of evil leaders whom people follow blindly.[98] Nevertheless, charismatic leaders who display appropriate values and use their charisma for appropriate purposes serve as ethical role models for others.[99]

Charismatic leaders are dominant and exceptionally self-confident, and have a strong conviction in the moral righteousness of their beliefs.[100] They strive to create an aura of competence and success and communicate high expectations for and confidence in followers. Ultimately, charismatic leaders somehow satisfy other peoples' needs and help reduce their stress.[101] Even people who have no direct contact with a leader can perceive him or her as charismatic, because other followers spread the word.[102]

And guess what: People can learn to be more charismatic.[103]

The charismatic leader articulates ideological goals and makes sacrifices in pursuit of those goals.[104] Martin Luther King Jr. had a dream for a better world, and John F. Kennedy spoke of landing a human on the moon. In other words, such leaders have a compelling vision. The charismatic leader also arouses a sense of excitement and adventure. He or she is an eloquent speaker who exhibits superior verbal skills, which help communicate the vision and motivate followers. Spotify CEO Daniel Ek has said he was not naturally charismatic, but he took steps to improve his communication style by explaining things more clearly and concisely and by being transparent about his shortcomings with his employees.[105]

Leaders who do these things inspire in their followers trust, confidence, acceptance, obedience, emotional involvement, affection, admiration, and higher performance.[106] A study of firefighters found them to be happier when working for charismatic officers who expressed positive attitudes.[107] Having charisma not only helps CEOs inspire employees, but also may inspire them to influence external stakeholders, including customers and investors.[108] Evidence for the positive effects of charismatic leadership has been found in a wide variety of groups, organizations, and management levels, and in countries including India, Singapore, the Netherlands, China, Japan, and Canada.[109]

In small firms, CEO charisma combined with strong HRM practices generates high organizational performance. Leader charisma also improves corporate financial performance, particularly under conditions of uncertainty—that is, in risky circumstances or when environments are changing and people have difficulty understanding what to do.[110] Uncertainty is stressful, and it makes people more receptive to the ideas and actions of charismatic leaders. By the way, as an organization's performance improves under a person's leadership, that person becomes seen as more charismatic as a result of the higher performance.[111]

Transformational Leadership

Charisma contributes to transformational leadership. **Transformational leaders** motivate people to transcend their personal interests for the sake of the larger community.[112] They generate excitement and revitalize organizations. At Amazon, chief executive Jeff Bezos generates excitement with his zeal to create a great customer experience coupled with determination to focus on the long term, no matter how hard investors press for quick profits. His vision keeps employees innovating and gives them a sense of purpose greater than quarterly financial performance.[113]

The transformational process moves beyond the more traditional *transactional* approach to leadership. **Transactional leaders** view management as a series of transactions in which they use their legitimate, reward, and coercive powers to give commands and exchange rewards for services rendered. Unlike transformational leadership, transactional leadership is dispassionate; it does not excite, transform, empower, or inspire people to focus on the interests of the group or organization. Transactional approaches may be more effective for individualists than for collectivists (recall Chapter 6).[114]

Martin Luther King Jr. was a brilliant, charismatic leader who had a compelling vision, a dream for a better world.

Trinity Mirror/Mirrorpix/Alamy Stock Photo

charismatic leader

A person who is dominant, self-confident, convinced of the moral righteousness of his or her beliefs, and able to arouse a sense of excitement and adventure in followers.

transformational leader

A leader who motivates people to transcend their personal interests for the good of the group.

transactional leaders

Leaders who manage through transactions, using their legitimate, reward, and coercive powers to give commands and exchange rewards for services rendered.

Generating Excitement   Transformational leaders generate excitement in several ways.[115] First, they are charismatic, as described earlier. Second, they give their followers individualized attention. Transformational leaders delegate challenging work to deserving people, keep lines of communication open, and provide one-on-one mentoring to develop their people. They do not treat everyone alike because not everyone *is* alike.

Third, transformational leaders are intellectually stimulating. They arouse in their followers an awareness of problems and potential solutions. They articulate the organization's opportunities, threats, strengths, and weaknesses. They stir the imagination and generate insights. Therefore, problems are recognized, and high-quality solutions are identified and implemented with the full commitment of followers.

Level 5 leadership

A combination of strong professional will (determination) and humility that builds enduring greatness.

Additional Strategies   Many additional strategies contribute to transformational leadership.[116] First, transformational leaders have a vision—a goal, an agenda, or a results orientation that grabs people's attention. Second, they communicate their vision; through words, manner, or symbolism, they convey a compelling image of the ultimate goal. Transformational leadership is most effective in motivating followers when they can see directly the meaningful consequences of the leader's vision, such as by interacting with those who benefit from their work.[117]

> Transformational leaders strive for success rather than merely try to avoid failure.

Cindy Ord/Getty Images

Bottom Line

Transformational leadership is good for people and good for the bottom line. *Why might improving employees' personal development be good for a company?*

authentic leadership

A style in which the leader is true to himself or herself while leading.

Third, transformational leaders build trust by being consistent, dependable, and persistent. They position themselves clearly by choosing a direction and staying with it, thus projecting integrity. Finally, they have positive self-regard. They do not feel self-important or complacent; rather, they recognize their personal strengths, compensate for their weaknesses, nurture and continually develop their talents, and know how to learn from failure. They strive for success rather than merely try to avoid failure.

Transformational leadership has been identified in industry, the military, and politics.[118] Besides Amazon's Jeff Bezos, transformational leaders in business include Mary Barra (CEO of General Motors), Reed Hastings (CEO of Netflix), Mark Bertolini (CEO of Aetna), Shantanu Narayen (CEO of Adobe), and Indra Nooyi (former CEO of PepsiCo).[119]

Transformational leadership exhibited by CEOs predicts firm performance, at least for small and midsized firms.[120] In public schools, transformational leadership improved student test scores, in part through stimulating engagement from multiple stakeholders.[121]

A concept well known among executives, **Level 5 leadership**, is considered by some to be the ultimate leadership style. Level 5 leadership is a combination of strong professional will (determination) and personal humility that builds enduring greatness.[122] A Level 5 leader is relentlessly focused on the organization's long-term success while also behaving modestly, directing attention toward the organization rather than himself or herself.

Humble CEOs are more likely[123] to have management teams that collaborate, share information, make decisions together, and share a vision—plus, higher-performing firms. Examples include IBM's former chief executive Louis Gerstner and former talk show host and founder of OWN cable network, Oprah Winfrey. Gerstner is widely credited for turning around a stodgy IBM by shifting its focus from computer hardware to business solutions. Following his retirement, Gerstner wrote a memoir that details what happened at the company but says little about himself. Level 5 leadership is seen as a way to transform organizations to make them great.[124]

Finally, consider the potential power of **authentic leadership**, rooted in the ancient Greek philosophy: "To thine own self be true."[125] Specifically, authentic leaders exhibit[126] (1) self-awareness, understanding their strengths and weaknesses and impact on other people; (2) transparency, openly and sharing information including being honest about themselves; (3) belief in evidence, processing data as objectively as possible; and (4) morality, aligning their behavior with their internal values. These characteristics operate together to have a wide variety of positive effects on followers.[127]

Authentic leaders are ethically mature; people view leaders who exhibit moral reasoning as more transformational than leaders who do not.[128] Importantly, these leader behaviors flow down from one organizational level to the next[129]—leaders' actions have an impact beyond their immediate, direct reports.

Pseudotransformational leaders are the opposite: They talk a good game, but they ignore followers' real needs as their own self-interests (power, prestige, control, wealth, fame) take precedence.[130]

Many Opportunities to Lead

A common view of leaders is that they are superheroes acting alone, swooping in to save the day. But especially in these complex times, leaders cannot and need not act alone. Effective leadership must permeate the organization, not reside in one or two superstars at the top. The top leader's job becomes one of spreading leadership abilities throughout the firm.[131]

Make people responsible for their own performance. Create an environment in which each person can figure out what needs to be done and then do it well. Point the way and clear the path so that people can succeed. Give them the credit they deserve. Make heroes out of *them*.

Thus, what is required of leaders is not just to manage resources efficiently, but to effectively unleash people's full potential.

This perspective uncovers a variety of nontraditional leadership roles that are emerging as vitally important.[132] For example, the term **servant-leader** was coined by Robert Greenleaf, a retired AT&T executive. Servant-leadership is concerned primarily with the people in the organization and other stakeholders in the broader community. Servant-leaders care about people's needs as ends in themselves rather than a means to meeting organizational goals. Servant-leaders strive for personal authenticity as a means to serve a higher calling and make a positive difference for others.[133]

The servant-leader's relationship with employees is akin to serving customers. Leaders at Southwest Airlines, UPS, and Ritz-Carlton adhere to this philosophy.[134] Servant-leaders strive to be self-aware, genuine, open with others, and ethical, and care about their followers' personal well-being and their local communities. For those who want to both lead and serve others, servant-leadership is a way to relate to others and serve their needs, while motivating performance and strengthening the organization.[135]

Cheryl Bachelder provides a good example. When she became CEO of Popeyes Louisiana Kitchen, she knew things had to change in order to reverse the company's sliding stock price. Through active listening, Bachelder learned how best to serve the needs of franchise owners. The turnaround was dramatic as average store sales increased by 25 percent, and the company's stock price rose from $13 per share when she took over in 2007 to around $80 per share 10 years later.[136]

A concept related to servant-leadership is **responsible leadership**, focusing on decision-making processes and choices that support corporate social responsibility (Chapter 5).[137] The nearby "Social Entrepreneurship" box describes how Elizabeth Hausler serves others by harnessing the energies of multiple organizations and individuals to build affordable, disaster-proof homes.

Additional opportunities abound for leadership that is not classically top-down. **Lateral leadership** does not involve a hierarchical, superior–subordinate relationship but, instead, invites colleagues at the same level to solve problems together.[138] You alone can't provide a solution to every problem, but you can create processes through which people work collaboratively. It's not about you as a leader solving problems; it's about creating better interpersonal processes for finding solutions. Similarly, **intergroup leaders** lead collaborative performance between different groups or organizations.[139] Examples are interdepartmental cooperation, joint ventures, public–private partnerships, and collaborations that cross national, cultural, and religious boundaries.

pseudotransformational leaders
Leaders who talk about positive change but allow their self-interests to take precedence over followers' needs.

LO 12-8 Describe types of opportunities to lead.

servant–leader
A leader who serves others' needs while strengthening the organization.

responsible leadership
Style in which leader focuses on decision-making processes and choices that support corporate social responsibility.

lateral leadership
Style in which colleagues at the same hierarchical level are invited to collaborate and facilitate joint problem solving.

intergroup leader
A leader who leads collaborative performance between groups or organizations.

Social Entrepreneurship

Engineering Disaster-Resilient Homes

Elizabeth Hausler grew up in Plano, Illinois, where she spent formative summers working as a bricklayer in her father's business. Inspired by the experience, she became an engineer. In 2001, she was moved by news of a severe earthquake in Gujarat, India, that killed thousands and injured many more. In that moment, Hausler came to a realization about natural disasters: What made the difference between homes that could withstand a disaster and those that could not was architectural engineering.

On a trip to Gujarat a few years later, Hausler learned that "if we want people to engage with us about how to build a safe house that will withstand the next earthquake or typhoon, we have to get the architecture right. We have to work with homeowners."[140] Energized to put her engineering skills to use to reduce the scale of loss from unsafe buildings, Hausler founded a nonprofit called Build Change. Its mission is to greatly reduce deaths, injuries, and economic losses caused by housing and school collapses due to earthquakes and typhoons in emerging nations.[141]

Since 2004, the organization has built over 57,000 disaster-resilient buildings for over 300,000 people in China, Haiti, Nepal, and the Philippines—and created nearly 20,000 new jobs in the process.[142]

"Elizabeth Hausler's expertise in and passion for prevention of disaster-related deaths runs throughout the Build Change organization," says Shivani Garg Patel of the Skoll Foundation, which recently gave Hausler its Award for Social Entrepreneurship. "The team aims to change the status quo at all levels of the local system—from the homeowner, to builder, to aid agency and government leader—and they dig in to ensure safe houses and schools for the most vulnerable."[143]

Hausler's use of her engineering talent and her unique vision for Build Change exemplify transformational leadership. Her organization is succeeding in many ways, not only saving lives and homes but also nurturing new talent. And, local communities benefit financially. "For every dollar invested in prevention," says Hausler, "we can save $7 in rebuilding and reconstruction costs."[144] In effect, Hausler is transforming the lives of those in her organization as well as those in the communities they serve.

- What makes Elizabeth Hausler such an effective leader?
- To what degree is Hausler a servant–leader? A Level 5 leader?

---

shared leadership

Rotating leadership, in which people rotate through the leadership role based on which person has the most relevant skills at a particular time.

With work often being team-based (see Chapter 14), **shared leadership** occurs when leadership rotates to the person with the key knowledge, skills, and abilities for the issue facing the team at a particular time.[145] Shared leadership is most important when tasks are interdependent, are complex, and require creativity. High-performing teams engaged in such work exhibit more shared leadership than poorly performing teams.[146] In consulting teams, the higher the shared leadership, the higher their clients rated the teams' performance.[147]

The role of hierarchical leader remains important—the formal leader still designs the team, manages its external boundaries, provides task direction, emphasizes the importance of the shared leadership approach, and engages in the transactional and transformational activities described in this chapter. But at the same time, the metaphor of geese in V-formation adds strength to the group; the lead goose periodically drops to the back, and another goose steps up and takes its place at the forefront.

You don't need to always be lead goose. But you can and should be when appropriate opportunities appear.

A Note on Courage

To be a good leader, you need the courage[148] to create a vision of greatness for your unit; identify and manage allies, adversaries, and fence sitters; and execute your vision, often against opposition. This does not mean you should commit career suicide by alienating too many powerful people; it does mean taking reasonable risks, with the good of the firm at heart, to produce constructive change.

Alan Mulally needed courage when he left Boeing to take charge of Ford Motor Company when a series of poor decisions had made Ford a money-losing company. Many of Ford's managers were skeptical of Mulally as their new CEO because he came from outside the automobile industry. Nevertheless, Mulally plunged ahead with decisions that were controversial at the time. He borrowed heavily and determined that the company would go forward with greater focus by offering fewer brands and models, with each being the best in its class. A few years later, Mulally's courageous efforts looked brilliant; Ford's borrowing gave the company resources to draw on when other automakers were accepting government loans to survive a financial crisis, and within a few years, Ford was recording record profits.[149]

Fulfilling your vision will require some of the following acts of courage:[150] (1) seeing things as they are and facing them head-on, making no excuses and harboring no wishful illusions; (2) saying what needs to be said to those who need to hear it; and (3) persisting despite resistance, criticism, abuse, and setbacks. Courage includes stating the realities, even when they are harsh, and publicly stating what you will do to help and what you want from others. This means laying the cards on the table honestly: Here is what I want from you . . . what do you want from me?[151]

Developing Your Leadership Skills

You may or may not yet have experiences that have taught you about leadership. Leadership develops throughout one's career and in every life domain.[152] But more important than having worked in leadership roles is to work with purpose to learn and develop. Great musicians and great athletes don't become great on natural gifts alone. They pay their dues by practicing, learning, sacrificing, and being coachable. Leaders in a variety of fields, when asked how they became the best leader possible, offered the following comments:[153]

LO 12-9 Discover how to further your own leadership development.

- "I've observed methods and skills of my bosses that I respected."
- "By taking risks, trying, and learning from my mistakes."
- "Reading autobiographies of leaders I admire to try to understand how they think."
- "Lots of practice."
- "By making mistakes myself and trying a different approach."
- "By being put in positions of responsibility that other people counted on."

How Do I Start?

How do you go about developing your leadership abilities? You don't have to wait until you land a management job or even finish your education. You can begin establishing credibility by behaving with integrity, learning from your mistakes, and becoming competent in your chosen field. You should look for— and then seize—opportunities to take actions that will help the groups you already belong to. Even before you are a supervisor, you can practice listening carefully when you are in a group and by sharing what you know so that the whole group will be better informed. Begin building a network of personal contacts by reaching out to others to offer help, not just to request it.[154]

When you are searching for your next job, look for a position with an employer that is committed to developing leadership talent. Ideally, leadership development is connected to opportunities to practice the skills you are learning about here, so ask about chances to lead a project or a team, even for short periods of time.[155] Companies that excel at leadership development include SAS, Bonobos, Randstad US, Paychex, Schneider Electric, and Marriott International.[156]

More specifically, here are some developmental experiences you should seek:[157]

Challenges expand knowledge and experiences. Being open to new ideas allows managers to learn, grow, and succeed even though the challenge may be out of their comfort zone.

Karl Weatherly/Getty Images

- *Assignments:* Building something from nothing; fixing or turning around a failing operation; taking on project or task force responsibilities; accepting international assignments.

The Digital World

How AI Is Affecting Leadership

Leaders today know the business world is constantly changing, increasingly global, and extremely fast paced. New forms of technology are also revolutionizing the ways leaders behave. Artificial intelligence, for example, is changing the leadership landscape in a number of ways:

1. AI is changing the focus of business. Leaders now need to consider how AI can transform the nature of the work their organizations do, not just now but in the future. In fact, research suggests that AI will have a $15.7 billion impact on the economy as early as 2030.[158]
2. AI is greatly reducing the need for humans to process facts and data. These "hard" elements of leadership that rely on cognitive processing of information are becoming less important. Meanwhile, the "soft" skills that only humans can bring to the table, such as personality and the ability to

form and communicate a vision for the future, are taking precedence.[159]
3. AI is allowing for better decision making. By using AI-enabled predictive analytics, leaders can help their organizations make better, more agile decisions that are grounded in data rather than gut feelings, which can often be wrong.[160]

What skills do leaders need to succeed in the AI landscape? One expert says the three skills that are most important for leaders are adaptability, vision, and engagement.[161] Leaders who want to succeed understand at least one thing: The future of AI is now.

1. What other ways do you see AI affecting leadership roles now and in the future?
2. What other skills do you think leaders will need in the future, and why?

- *Other people:* Having exposure to positive role models; increasing visibility to others; working with people of diverse backgrounds.
- *Hardships:* Overcoming ideas that fail and deals that collapse; confronting others' performance problems; breaking out of a career rut.
- *Other events:* Formal courses; challenging job experiences; supervision of others; experiences outside work.

What Are the Keys?

The most effective developmental experiences have three components: assessment, challenge, and support.[162] *Assessment* includes information that gives you an understanding of where you are now, what your strengths are, your current levels of performance and leadership effectiveness, and your primary development needs. You can think about what your past feedback has been, what previous successes and failures you have had, how people have reacted to your ideas and actions, what your personal goals are, and what strategies you should implement to make progress. You can seek answers from your peers at work, bosses, family, friends, customers, and anyone else who knows you and how you work. The information you collect will help clarify what you need to learn, improve, or change.[163]

The most potent developmental experiences provide *challenge*—they stretch you. We all think and behave in habitual, comfortable ways. This is natural and perhaps sufficient to survive. But you've probably heard people say how important it can be to get out of your comfort zone—to tackle situations that require new skills and abilities, that are confusing or ambiguous, or that you simply would rather not deal with. Sometimes the challenge comes from lack of experience; other times, it requires changing old habits.

It may be uncomfortable, but this is how great managers learn. Remember, some people don't bother to learn, or outright refuse to learn. Make sure you think about your experiences along the way and reflect on them afterward, introspectively and in discussion with others.

You receive *support* when others send the message that your efforts to learn and grow are valued. Without support, challenging developmental experiences can be overwhelming. With support, it is easier to handle the struggle, stay on course, open up to learning, and actually learn from experiences. Support can come informally from other people; more

Management in Action

KENNETH FRAZIER: LEADERSHIP THROUGH EXPERIENCE

Kenneth Frazier grew up in humble and sometimes difficult conditions in the inner city of Philadelphia. His mother died when he was 12, and he was then raised by his father, a stern man who made ends meet working as a janitor. "If you grew up in a neighborhood like mine," Frazier says, "you were forced to decide early on what you stood for in life, because there were a lot of peer pressures that could take you the wrong way."[164]

Frazier's father set high standards in their home and stressed education above all else, and Frazier was one of few African American children from his neighborhood who was bused to a predominantly white school during a time when racial segregation was prevalent. He credits the high standards he was forced to meet both at school and at home with serving as the foundation of his leadership skills.

Within a few years of joining Merck, Frazier worked for the legal department in public affairs, which entailed gaining knowledge about many aspects of the firm's operations. "I realized . . . what's most important is to be a learner. Many people know a lot about a little, but there are only a few people who know a little about a lot and

can see the company more broadly. This was critical to the idea of why I eventually became CEO."[165]

For Frazier, the ability to effectively communicate strategy and vision to those who need to execute it is an invaluable tool for a leader. He credits his experiences growing up, including those that were more challenging, as well as his experience working as a prosecutor before his time at Merck. "I think it helped me a lot as a jury trial lawyer to have been raised where I was raised," he says, "because for me, talking to the normal, average person wasn't a hard thing. I didn't feel like I had to talk down to them. I understood them."[166]

That kind of communication skill set has served him well in a position that requires him to deliver for an eclectic group of stakeholders—while also trying to heal the world.

- Frazier has clearly used his experiences in life to develop his leadership skills. In what way have you capitalized on your life experiences to develop such skills?
- What evidence, if any, do you see that Frazier is a charismatic leader? A transformational leader? An authentic leader? A servant–leader?

formally through the procedures of the organization; and through learning resources in the forms of training, constructive feedback, talking with others, and so on.

What develops in leadership development? Through such experiences, you can acquire more self-awareness and self-confidence, a broader perspective on the organizational system, creative thinking, the ability to work more effectively in complex social systems, and the ability to learn, grow, and make an impact.

KEY TERMS

authentic leadership, p. 384

autocratic leadership, p. 376

behavioral approach, p. 374

charismatic leader, p. 383

democratic leadership, p. 376

Fiedler's contingency model of leadership effectiveness, p. 379

group maintenance behaviors, p. 375

Hersey and Blanchard's situational theory, p. 380

intergroup leader, p. 385

job maturity, p. 380

laissez-faire, p. 376

lateral leadership, p. 385

leader–member exchange (LMX) theory, p. 376

Level 5 leadership, p. 384

participation in decision making, p. 376

path–goal theory, p. 380

power, p. 371

pseudotransformational leaders, p. 385

psychological maturity, p. 380

relationship-motivated leadership, p. 380

responsible leadership, p. 385

servant–leader, p. 385

shared leadership, p. 386

situational approach, p. 378

strategic leadership, p. 370

substitutes for leadership, p. 382

supervisory leadership, p. 370

task-motivated leadership, p. 380

task performance behaviors, p. 375

trait approach, p. 373

transactional leaders, p. 383

transformational leader, p. 383

vision, p. 368

Vroom model, p. 378

RETAINING WHAT YOU LEARNED

In Chapter 12, you learned what it means to be a leader. You also learned that leaders are needed at all levels of organizations and that people want leaders to help them achieve their goals. The best leaders have and share effectively a compelling vision that motivates others to achieve more than they thought was possible. Having and using power are important tools for any leader. Leaders can draw on five types of power—legitimate, reward, coercive, referent, and expert—to influence others. While there are several personal characteristics associated with leaders, the most important skill is the ability to perceive the situation accurately and then change behavior accordingly. Several leadership theories describe the interaction of leaders and the situation at hand, including Vroom's model, Fiedler's contingency model, Hersey and Blanchard's situation theory, and House's path–goal theory. Charismatic leaders are dominant and self-confident, and communicate high expectations for and confidence in their followers. Transformational leaders translate vision into reality by inspiring followers to transcend their individual interests for the good of the larger community. Many nontraditional opportunities to lead include servant, intergroup, shared, or lateral leadership. Furthermore, you can ask for developmental assignments or activities that include assessment, challenge, and support.

LO 12-1   Discuss what it means to be a leader.

- A leader is one who influences others to attain goals.
- Leaders orchestrate change, set direction, and motivate people to overcome obstacles and move the organization toward its ideal future.

LO 12-2   Summarize what people want and organizations need from their leaders.

- People want help in achieving their goals, and organizations need leaders at all levels.
- Exemplary leaders challenge the process, inspire a shared vision, enable others to act, model the way, and encourage the heart.

LO 12-3   Explain how a good vision helps you be a better leader.

- Outstanding leaders have vision. A vision is a mental image of an appealing, attainable future that goes beyond the ordinary and perhaps beyond what others thought possible.
- The vision provides the direction in which the leader wants the organization to move and inspiration for people to pursue it.

LO 12-4   Identify sources of power in organizations.

- Having power and using it appropriately are essential to effective leadership. Managers at all levels of the organization have five potential sources of power.
- Legitimate power is the company-granted authority to direct others.
- Reward power is control over rewards valued by others in the organization.

- Coercive power is control over punishments that others want to avoid.
- Referent power consists of personal characteristics that appeal to others, who model their behavior on the leader's and seek the leader's approval.
- Expert power is expertise or knowledge that can benefit others.

LO 12-5   List personal characteristics that contribute to leader effectiveness.

- Useful leader characteristics include drive, leadership, motivation, integrity, self-confidence, and knowledge of the business.
- Perhaps the most important skill is flexibility: the ability to perceive the situation accurately and then change behavior accordingly.

LO 12-6   Describe behaviors that will make you a better leader and know when situations call for them.

- Important leader behaviors include task performance behaviors, group maintenance behaviors, and decision making.
- According to the Vroom model, decision making options include deciding alone, consulting individuals, consulting multiple group members, facilitating a whole-group process, or delegating to others, depending on factors such as the significance of the decision and the importance of followers' commitment.
- Fiedler's contingency model says that a task-motivated leader is more successful when leader–member relations are good and the task is highly structured, or with an unstructured task but low position power for the leader, or with poor leader–member relations when the task structure and leader's position power are both low. In other situations, a relationship-oriented leader will perform better.
- Hersey and Blanchard's situational theory says that task performance behaviors become less important as the follower's job maturity and psychological maturity increase.
- Path–goal theory assesses characteristics of the followers, the leader, and the situation; it then indicates the appropriateness of directive, supportive, participative, or achievement-oriented leadership behaviors.

LO 12-7   Distinguish between charismatic and transformational leadership.

- To have charisma is to be dominant and self-confident, to have a strong conviction of the righteousness of your beliefs, to create an aura of competence and success, and to communicate high expectations for and confidence in your followers. Charisma is one component of transformational leadership.

- Transformational leaders translate a vision into reality by inspiring people to transcend their individual interests for the good of the larger community.
- They do this through charisma, individualized attention to followers, intellectual stimulation, formation and communication of their vision, building of trust, and positive self-regard.

LO 12-8   Describe types of opportunities to lead.

- There's plenty of opportunity to be a leader; being a manager of others who report to you is just the traditional one.
- You also can find or create opportunities to be a servant–leader or intergroup leader, and engage in shared leadership and lateral leadership. A servant–leader serves others' needs while strengthening the organization.
- Intergroup leaders facilitate collaborative performance between different groups or organizations.

- Shared leadership involves taking on a leadership role when your skills are most relevant to a particular situation.
- Lateral leadership is inspiring people to work collaboratively and solve problems together.

LO 12-9   Discover how to further your own leadership development.

- You can develop your own leadership skills not only by understanding what effective leadership is all about, but also by seeking challenging developmental experiences.
- Such important life experiences come from taking challenging assignments, through exposure to working with other people, by overcoming hardships and failures, by taking formal courses, and via many other actions.
- The most important elements of a good developmental experience are assessment, challenge, and support.

DISCUSSION QUESTIONS

1. What behaviors do you expect from a good leader?
2. Is there a difference between effective management and effective leadership? Explain.
3. Identify someone you think is an effective leader. What makes him or her effective?
4. Do you think most managers can be transformational leaders? Why or why not?
5. In your own words, define courage. What is the role of courage in leadership? Give examples of acts of leadership you consider courageous.
6. Do you think men and women differ in their leadership styles? If so, how?
7. Who are your heroes? What makes them heroes, and what can you learn from them?
8. Assess yourself as a leader based on what you have read in this chapter. What are your strengths and weaknesses?

9. Identify some developmental experiences you have had that may have strengthened your ability to lead. What did those experiences teach you? Be specific.
10. Consider a job you hold or held in the past. Consider how your boss managed you. How would you describe him or her as a leader? What substitutes for leadership would you have enjoyed seeing put into place?
11. Consider a group or an organization in which you are a leader or a member. What could great transformational leadership accomplish?
12. Name some prominent leaders whom you would describe as authentic and inauthentic and discuss.
13. Name some leaders you consider servant–leaders and discuss.
14. Identify some opportunities for you to exhibit shared, lateral, and other forms of leadership that are not "top-down."

EXPERIENTIAL EXERCISES

12.1   Using the Five Sources of Power at Work

OBJECTIVE

To explore how power can be applied to organizational challenges to create positive outcomes.

INSTRUCTIONS

Read each of the scenarios (below) and choose one of the five sources of power to resolve the challenge in each scenario.

Five Sources of Power Worksheet

Five Sources of power:

1. *Legitimate—Leader draws authority from a position/ title.*
2. *Reward—Leader controls valued outcomes like pay raises.*
3. *Coercive—Leader can doll out punishments.*

4. *Referent—Leader influences through appealing personal characteristics.*

5. *Expert—Leader possesses experience and knowledge that is valued.*

Scenario 1:

Assume you're a supervisor of a technical support department at a website hosting company. You want your staff to complete a large project within the next two months. Usually, such a project would take about three months to accomplish. To persuade your staff to rise to this challenge, you offer each of them three additional paid vacation days. Your staff enjoys taking three-day weekends, so the incentive should motivate them to finish the project within the shorter time frame.

As the supervisor, you are using _____ power to motivate your staff.

Scenario 2:

Assume you work at a local restaurant. As a part-time employee working your way through college, you are not interested in becoming a manager. Even so, sometimes you wish you were in charge. Just yesterday, your manager asked if you would be willing to work two extra days per week for the next month. After you explained that you could work only your usual three days per week due to college and other commitments, your boss threatened to cut your hours indefinitely. Given how much you need the money, you grudgingly agreed to work the two extra days per week.

Your manager is using _____ power to persuade you to work the two extra days per week.

Scenario 3:

Assume you were recently promoted to assistant manager of the bank in your hometown. You are friends with the employees who now report to you. You notice that they still treat you like a buddy and do not seem to respect you in your new role. You decide that it will be in everyone's best interest if you assert yourself by reminding them that you are now their manager (and not their buddy). This is a challenging task, but you feel the need to have their respect now that you are the manager.

You are using _____ power to encourage employees to respect you in your new role as assistant manager.

Scenario 4:

Assume you are an experienced marketer of outdoor adventure trips. You recently changed jobs. While working for your previous employer, Good Time Adventures, you created several successful marketing programs that resulted in a 30 percent increase in sales over a three-year period. Now that you recently joined Eco Tours & Adventures, none of your co-workers knows the extent of your marketing knowledge. Your goal is to increase your power within the company. You decide to develop a really impactful and creative marketing campaign unlike any used by Eco Tours & Adventures in the past.

You are using _____ power to increase your influence at Eco Tours & Adventures.

Scenario 5:

Assume you are a salesperson and just found out that your organization's largest client is thinking about moving its business to one of your competitors. If this happens, you will lose about 25 percent of your commission this year, not to mention the loss of revenue to your company. You decide to rush over to see your contact at the client company. You spend two hours listening to why the client might leave and ask repeatedly what your company can do to make things right. You are nervous, but still use your charm and sense of humor to convince your contact that you and your company deserve one more chance. Your contact agrees to get you a meeting with the CEO and to put in a good word for your company. She says she is doing this because she likes you (professionally) and doesn't want to see you lose the business.

You are using _____ power to convince your contact that you and your company deserve another chance.

Concluding Case

LEADERSHIP CHANGE HURTS BREITT, STARR & DIAMOND LLC

Josh Breitt, Rachel Starr, and Justin Diamond started an advertising agency to serve the needs of small businesses selling in and around their metropolitan area. Breitt contributed a talent for writing scripts and wooing clients. Starr brought a wealth of media contacts, and Diamond handled art and graphic design. Their quirky ad campaigns soon attracted a stream of projects from car dealers, community banks, and small retailers. Since the agency's first year, these clients keep the doors open while the firm wins contracts from other companies. Breitt, Starr & Diamond (BS&D) prospered by helping clients stay current, and the agency grew to meet demand, adding two administrative assistants, three salespeople, a social media expert, and a retired human resource manager, who works 10 hours per week.

As the firm grew, the partners were being pulled away from their areas of expertise to answer questions from the staff and solve problems about how to coordinate work, define jobs, and set priorities. They realized that none of them had any management training—and had no desire to be a manager. They decided to hire a manager of operations to be responsible for supervising employees, making sure expenses didn't go over budget, and planning the resources needed for further growth.

The partners interviewed several candidates and hired Brad Howser, a longtime manager for a four-physician medical office. He quickly began to make changes. Howser required all employees to start by 9:00 each morning. Some of the staff complained that flexible hours were necessary for their child care arrangements, but Howser was unyielding. He also believed the firm was spending too much on office supplies, so all purchases would be made by him and any requests needed to be submitted in writing on a form he supplied to the staff. Finally, to promote what he called "team spirit," Howser began scheduling weekly Monday morning staff meetings. He would offer motivational thoughts based on his experience and invite employees to share any work-related concerns or ideas they might have. Generally, the employees chose not to share.

Initially, the partners were impressed with Howser's vigorous approach to his job. They felt more productive than they had been in years because Howser was handling employee concerns. Then the top salesperson quit, followed by the social media expert. Then another salesperson asked if she might meet with the partners. "Is it something you should be discussing with Brad?" Rachel asked her. The bookkeeper replied that, no, it was *about* Brad. All the employees were unhappy with him, and more were likely to leave.

DISCUSSION QUESTIONS

1. What leader behaviors did Brad Howser exhibit? How well did they fit the needs of the ad agency and the expectations of the staff?

2. Assume that hiring a manager of operations was a good idea. What leadership style would have been more effective in this position? Why?

3. Consider your own leadership style. What are some of your behavioral tendencies, and how might you change your approach to situations like the one at BSD?

ENDNOTES

1. "Merck Agrees to Pay $830 Million to Settle Vioxx Securities Lawsuit," Reuters, January 15, 2016, https://www.reuters.com/article/us-merck-vioxx-settlement-idUSKCN0UT1PX.

2. "Total Revenue of Merck & Co. from 2006 to 2018 (in Million U.S. Dollars)," *Statista,* https://www.statista.com/statistics/272350/revenue-of-merck-and-co/, accessed April 2, 2019.

3. Peter Loftus, "Why Merck Is Betting Big on One Cancer Drug," *The Wall Street Journal,* April 15, 2018, https://www.wsj.com/articles/why-merck-is-betting-big-on-one-cancer-drug-1523790000.

4. Adi Ignatius, "'Businesses Exist to Deliver Value to Society,'" *Harvard Business Review,* March–April 2018, https://hbr.org/2018/03/businesses-exist-to-deliver-value-to-society.

5. "Merck's Frazier to Remain CEO beyond 2019," Reuters, September 26, 2018, https://www.cnbc.com/2018/09/26/mercks-frazier-to-remain-ceo-beyond-2019.html.

6. "Best for Vets Employers 2018," *Military Times,* https://rebootcamp.militarytimes.com, accessed March 13, 2019.

7. W. Bennis and B. Nanus, *Leaders* (New York: Harper & Row, 1985), p. 27.

8. J. Petrick, R. Schere, J. Brodzinski, J. Quinn, and M. Fall Ainina, "Global Leadership Skills and Reputational Capital: Intangible Resources for Sustainable Competitive Advantage," *Academy of Management Executive,* February 1999, pp. 58–69.

9. W. Bennis and B. Nanus, *Leaders* (New York: Harper & Row, 1985).

10. W. Bennis and B. Nanus, *Leaders* (New York: Harper & Row, 1985), p. 144.

11. E. E. Lawler III, *Treat People Right! How Organizations and Individuals Can Propel Each Other into a Virtual Spiral of Success* (San Francisco: Jossey-Bass, 2003); G. Llopis, "The 6 Most Important Things Employees Need from Their Leaders to Realize High Potential," *Forbes,* September 30, 2013, http://www.forbes.com.

12. Alejandra Cancino, "Deliberate Change of Pace Works for ITW Attorney," *Chicago Tribune,* May 6, 2013, sec. 2, pp. 1, 4.

13. N. Zipkin, "Why Entrepreneurs Should Question Everything and Everyone, Even the Experts," *Entrepreneur,* September 1, 2017, www.entrepreneur.com.

14. "Coffee's Cultural Appeal and the Peanut Sensor," *Modern Restaurant Management,* September 10, 2018, www.moderrestaurantmanagement.com.

15. Frank Newport, "In U.S., Estimate of LGBT Population Rises to 4.5%," *Gallup,* May 22, 2018, https://news.gallup.com/poll/234863/estimate-lgbt-population-rises.aspx.

16. MAP, "Non-discrimination Laws," http://www.lgbtmap.org/equality-maps/non_discrimination_laws, accessed April 3, 2019.

17. Sejal Singh and Laura E. Durso, "Widespread Discrimination Continues to Shape LGBT People's Lives in Both Subtle and Significant Ways," Center for American Progress, May 2, 2017, https://www.americanprogress.org/issues/lgbt/news/2017/05/02/429529/widespread-discrimination-continues-shape-lgbt-peoples-lives-subtle-significant-ways/.

18. Michaela Krejcova, "The Value of LGBT Equality in the Workplace," GLAAD, February 26, 2015, https://www.glaad.org/blog/value-lgbt-equality-workplace.

19. Stephanie Dwilson, "LGBTQ Health and the Benefits of Diversity in the Workplace," *The Benefits Guide,* June 1, 2018, https://thebenefitsguide.com/lgbtq-health-and-the-benefits-of-diversity-in-the-workplace/.

20. P. Fitch, "The Value of Vision," *Canadian Journal of Hospital Pharmacy* 70, no. 6 (November–December 2017), pp. 472–73.

21. J. Cheng and R. Harrington, "12 of the Smartest Things Elon Musk Has Said about the Future of Our Planet," *Business Insider,* March 5, 2018, www.buisnessinsider.com.

22. "Branson Outlines World Powered by Wind, Solar Power," *Phys.org,* September 25, 2015, www.phys.org.

23. A. M. Carton, C. Murphy, and J. R. Clark, "A (Blurry) Vision of the Future: How Leader Rhetoric about Ultimate Goals Influences Performance," *Academy of Management Journal* 57 (2014), pp. 1544–70; A. Ruvio, Z. Rosenblatt, and R. Hertz-Lazarowitz, "Entrepreneurial Leadership Vision in Nonprofit vs. For-Profit Organizations," *Leadership Quarterly* 21 (2010), pp. 144–58; J. Baum, E. A. Locke, and S. Kirkpatrick, "A Longitudinal Study of the Relation of Vision and Vision Communication to Venture Growth in Entrepreneurial Firms," *Journal of Applied Psychology* 83 (1998), pp. 43–54.

24. E. C. Shapiro, *Fad Surfing in the Boardroom* (Reading, MA: Addison-Wesley, 1995).

25. J. Kouzes and B. Posner, *The Leadership Challenge,* 2nd ed. (San Francisco: Jossey-Bass, 1995).

26. J. Kouzes and B. Posner, *The Leadership Challenge,* 2nd ed. (San Francisco: Jossey-Bass, 1995).

27. W. Bennis and R. Townsend, *Reinventing Leadership* (New York: William Morrow, 1995).

28. W. Bennis and R. Townsend, *Reinventing Leadership* (New York: William Morrow, 1995).

29. D. Mattioli and K. Maher, "At 3M, Innovation Comes in Tweaks and Snips," *The Wall Street Journal,* March 1, 2010, http://online.wsj.com.

30. J. Kouzes and B. Posner, *The Leadership Challenge,* 2nd ed. (San Francisco: Jossey-Bass, 1995).

31. J. A. Conger, "The Dark Side of Leadership," *Organizational Dynamics* 19 (Autumn 1990), pp. 44–55.

32. J. Conger, "The Vision Thing: Explorations into Visionary Leadership," in *Cutting Edge Leadership 2000,* ed. B. Kellerman and L. Matusak (College Park, MD: James MacGregor Burns Academy of Leadership, 2000).

33. Adi Ignatius, "'Businesses Exist to Deliver Value to Society,'" *Harvard Business Review,* March–April 2018, https://hbr.org/2018/03/businesses-exist-to-deliver-value-to-society.

34. Adi Ignatius, "'Businesses Exist to Deliver Value to Society,'" *Harvard Business Review,* March–April 2018, https://hbr.org/2018/03/businesses-exist-to-deliver-value-to-society.

35. Clifton Leaf, "Deploying the Profit Motive to Beat Ebola," *Fortune,* August 20, 2018, http://fortune.com/2018/08/20/merck-ebola-outbreak-vaccine/.

36. "Change the World," *Fortune,* http://fortune.com/change-the-world/, accessed April 2, 2019.

37. J. P. Kotter, "What Leaders Really Do," *Harvard Business Review* 68 (May–June 1990), pp. 103–11.

38. J. Jensen, "From Me to We," *Leadership Excellence* 3, no. 1 (2014), pp. 65–66; M. E. Van Buren and T. Safferstone, "Collective Quick Wins," *Computerworld,* January 26, 2009, pp. 24–25.

39. G. Yukl, *Leadership in Organizations,* 3rd ed. (Englewood Cliffs, NJ: Prentice Hall, 1994).

40. R. House and R. Aditya, "The Social Scientific Study of Leadership: Quo Vadis?" *Journal of Management* 23 (1997), pp. 409–73.

41. K. Boal and P. Schultz, "Storytelling, Time, and Evolution: The Role of Strategic Leadership in Complex Adaptive Systems," *Leadership Quarterly* 18 (2007), pp. 411–28; R. D. Ireland and M. A. Hitt, "Achieving and Maintaining Strategic Competitiveness in the 21st Century: The Role of Strategic Leadership," *Academy of Management Executive,* February 1999, pp. 43–57.

42. J. Gardner, "The Heart of the Matter: Leader–Constituent Interaction," in *Leading & Leadership,* ed. T. Fuller (Notre Dame, IN: University of Notre Dame Press, 2000), pp. 239–44, quote at p. 240.

43. M. Uhl-Bien, M., R. Riggio, K. Lowe, and M. Carsten, "Followership Theory: A Review and Research Agenda," *The Leadership Quarterly* 25 (2014), pp. 83–104.

44. R. E. Kelly, "In Praise of Followers," *Harvard Business Review* 66 (November–December 1988), pp. 142–48.

45. R. E. Kelly, "In Praise of Followers," *Harvard Business Review* 66 (November–December 1988).

46. C. Manz and D. Gioia, "The Interrelationship of Power and Control," *Human Relations* 36, no. 5 (1983), pp. 459–76.

47. J. R. P. French and B. Raven, "The Bases of Social Power," in *Studies in Social Power,* ed. D. Cartwright (Ann Arbor, MI: Institute for Social Research, 1959).

48. G. Yukl and C. Falbe, "Importance of Different Power Sources in Downward and Lateral Relations," *Journal of Applied Psychology* 76 (1991), pp. 416–23.

49. G. Yukl and C. Falbe, "Importance of Different Power Sources in Downward and Lateral Relations," *Journal of Applied Psychology* 76 (1991), pp. 416–23.

50. R. E. Sturm and J. Antonakis, "Interpersonal Power: A Review, Critique, and Research Agenda," *Journal of Management,* 41, (2015), pp. 136–63.

51. S. Badal, "For Great Business Builders, Knowledge Is Power," *Gallup Business Journal,* September 30, 2014, http://www.gallup.com; L. Bryan, E. Matson, and L. Weiss, "Harnessing the Power of Informal Employee Networks," *McKinsey Report* 4 (2007), pp. 44–55.

52. R. M. Stogdill, "Personal Factors Associated with Leadership: A Survey of the Literature," *Journal of Psychology* 25 (1948), pp. 35–71.

53. G. Moran, "Leadership: Nature or Nurture?" *Entrepreneur,* October 14, 2013, http://www.entrepreneur.com; S. Kirkpatrick and E. Locke, "Leadership: Do Traits Matter?" *The Executive* 5 (May 1991), pp. 48–60.

54. G. A. Yukl, *Leadership in Organizations,* 2nd ed. (Englewood Cliffs, NJ: Prentice-Hall, 1989).

55. T. Judge, J. Bono, R. Ilies, and M. Gerhardt, "Personality and Leadership: A Qualitative and Quantitative Review," *Journal of Applied Psychology* 87 (2002), pp. 765–80.

56. A. Grant, F. Gino, and D. Hofmann, "Reversing the Extroverted Leadership Advantage: The Role of Employee Proactivity," *Academy of Management Journal* 54 (2011), pp. 528–50.

57. S. Cain, *Quiet: The Power of Introverts in a World That Can't Stop Talking* (New York: Broadway Books, 2013); L. A. Clack, "Book Review: Quiet: The Power of Introverts in a World That Can't Stop Talking," *Frontiers in Psychology* 8 (2017), p. 185.

58. R. Foti and N. M. A. Hauenstein, "Pattern and Variable Approaches in Leadership Emergence and Effectiveness," *Journal of Applied Psychology* 92 (2007), pp. 347–55.

59. J. P. Kotter, *The General Managers* (New York: Free Press, 1982).

60. J. LeBreton, L. Shiverdecker, and E. Grimaldi, "The Dark Triad and Workplace Behavior," *Annual Review of Organizational Psychology and Organizational Behavior* 5 (2018), pp. 387–414.

61. R. de Vries, "Three Nightmare Traits in Leaders," *Frontiers in Psychology,* June 4, 2018, www.frontiersinpsychology.com.

62. T. Manning, "The Art of Successful Influence: Matching Influence Strategies and Styles to the Context," *Industrial and Commercial Training* 44 (2012), pp. 26–34; S. Zaccaro, R. Foti, and D. Kenny, "Self-Monitoring and Trait-Based Variance in Leadership: An Investigation of Leader Flexibility across Multiple Group Situations," *Journal of Applied Psychology* 76 (1991), pp. 308–15.

63. D. Goleman, "Leadership That Gets Results," *Harvard Business Review,* March–April 2000, pp. 78–90.

64. J. Misumi and M. Peterson, "The Performance-Maintenance (PM) Theory of Leadership: Review of a Japanese Research Program," *Administrative Science Quarterly* 30 (June 1985), pp. 198–223.

65. T. Judge, R. Piccolo, and R. Ilies, "The Forgotten Ones? The Validity of Consideration and Initiating Structure in Leadership Research," *Journal of Applied Psychology* 89 (2004), pp. 36–51.

66. G. Thomas, R. Martin, and R. Riggio, "Leading Groups: Leadership as a Group Process," *Group Processes & Intergroup Relations* 16 (2013), pp. 3–16.

67. J. Misumi and M. Peterson, "The Performance-Maintenance (PM) Theory of Leadership: Review of a Japanese Research Program," *Administrative Science Quarterly* 30 (June 1985), pp. 198–223.

68. T. Judge, R. Piccolo, and R. Ilies, "The Forgotten Ones? The Validity of Consideration and Initiating Structure in Leadership Research," *Journal of Applied Psychology* 89 (2004), pp. 36–51.

69. G. Graen and M. Uhl-Bien, "Relationship-Based Approach to Leadership: Development of Leader-Member Exchange (LMX) Theory of Leadership over 25 Years: Applying a Multi-Level Multi-Domain Perspective," *Leadership Quarterly* 6, no. 2 (1995), pp. 219–47.

70. R. House and R. Aditya, "The Social Scientific Study of Leadership: Quo Vadis?" *Journal of Management* 23 (1997), pp. 409–73.

71. C. R. Gerstner and D. V. Day, "Meta-Analytic Review of Leader-Member Exchange Theory: Correlates and Construct Issues," *Journal of Applied Psychology* 82 (1997), pp. 827–44.

72. T. Rockstuhl, J. Dulebohn, S. Ang, and L. Shore, "Leader-Member Exchange (LMX) and Culture: A Meta-analysis of Correlates of LMX Across 23 Countries," *Journal of Applied Psychology* 97 (2012), pp. 1097–1130.

73. J. Misumi and M. Peterson, "The Performance-Maintenance (PM) Theory of Leadership: Review of a Japanese Research Program," *Administrative Science Quarterly* 30 (June 1985), pp. 198–223.

74. M. Mills and S. Culberston, "High-Involvement Work Practices: Are They Really Worth It?" *Academy of Management Perspectives* 23 (2009), pp. 93–95; J. Wagner III, "Participation's Effect on Performance and Satisfaction: A Reconsideration of Research," *Academy of Management Review,* April 1994, pp. 312–30.

75. R. White and R. Lippitt, *Autocracy and Democracy: An Experimental Inquiry* (New York: Harper & Brothers, 1960).

76. R. Charan, "Conquering a Culture of Indecision," *Harvard Business Review* 84 (2006), pp. 108–17; J. Muczyk and R. Steel, "Leadership Style and the Turnaround Executive," *Business Horizons,* March–April 1999, pp. 39–46.

77. A. Tannenbaum and W. Schmidt, "How to Choose a Leadership Pattern," *Harvard Business Review* 36 (March–April 1958), pp. 95–101.

78. E. Fleishman and E. Harris, "Patterns of Leadership Behavior Related to Employee Grievances and Turnover," *Personnel Psychology* 15 (1962), pp. 43–56.

79. R. Likert, *The Human Organization: Its Management and Value* (New York: McGraw-Hill, 1967).

80. R. Blake and J. Mouton, *The Managerial Grid* (Houston: Gulf, 1964).

81. M. Ceri-Booms, P. Curseu, and L. Oerlemans, "Task and Person-Focused Leadership Behaviors and Team Performance: A Meta-Analysis," *Human Resource Management Review* 27 (2017), pp. 178–92.

82. J. Misumi and M. Peterson, "The Performance-Maintenance (PM) Theory of Leadership: Review of a Japanese Research Program," *Administrative Science Quarterly* 30 (June 1985), pp. 198–223.

83. J. Wall, *Bosses* (Lexington, MA: Lexington Books, 1986), p. 103.

84. A. Tannenbaum and W. Schmidt, "How to Choose a Leadership Pattern," *Harvard Business Review* 36 (March–April 1958), pp. 95–101.

85. To practice using the decision tree, please see V. H. Vroom, "Leadership and the Decision-Making Process," *Organizational Dynamics,* Spring 2000, pp. 82–93.

86. F. E. Fiedler, *A Theory of Leadership Effectiveness* (New York: McGraw-Hill, 1967).

87. P. Hersey and K. Blanchard, *The Management of Organizational Behavior* (Englewood Cliffs, NJ: Prentice Hall, 1984).

88. G. Yukl, *Leadership in Organizations,* 3rd ed. (Englewood Cliffs, NJ: Prentice Hall, 1994).

89. R. J. House, "Path–Goal Theory of Leadership: Lessons, Legacy, and a Reformulated Theory," *Leadership Quarterly* 7 (1996), pp. 323–52; R. J. House, "A Path–Goal Theory of Leader Effectiveness," *Administrative Science Quarterly* 16 (1971), pp. 321–39.

90. J. Howell, D. Bowen, P. Dorfman, S. Kerr, and P. Podsakoff, "Substitutes for Leadership: Effective Alternatives to Ineffective Leadership," *Organizational Dynamics* 19 (Summer 1990), pp. 21–38.

91. R. G. Lord and W. Gradwohl Smith, "Leadership and the Changing Nature of Performance," in *The Changing Nature of Performance,* ed. D. R. Ilgen and E. D. Pulakos (San Francisco: Jossey-Bass, 1999).

92. X.-D. Xu, J. A. Zhong, and X.-Y. Wang, "The Impact of Substitutes for Leadership on Job Satisfaction and Performance," *Social Behavior and Personality* 41 (2013), pp. 675–85.

93. S. Dionne, F. Yammarino, L. Atwater, and L. James, "Neutralizing Substitutes for Leadership Theory: Leadership Effects and Common-Source Bias," *Journal of Applied Psychology* 87 (2002), pp. 454–64.

94. S. Purohit, "What If Project Managers Get Replaced by Bots and AI?" eLearning Industry, November 10, 2018, www.elearningindustry.com; J. Moulds, "Robot Managers: The Future of Work or a Step Too Far?" *The Guardian,* April 6, 2018, www.theguardian.com.

95. M. Velez and P. Neves, "Shaping Emotional Reactions to Ethical Behaviors: Proactive Personality as a Substitute for Ethical Leadership," *Leadership Quarterly* 29 (2018), pp. 663–73.

96. D. Van Knippenberg and S. Sitkin, "A Critical Assessment of Charismatic Transformational Leadership Research: Back to the Drawing Board?" *Academy of Management Annals* 7 (2013), pp. 1–60.

97. B. M. Bass, *Leadership and Performance beyond Expectations* (New York: Free Press, 1985).

98. T. Chamorro-Premuzic, "The Dark Side of Charisma," *Harvard Business Review,* November 16, 2012, http://www.hbr.org; Y. A. Nur, "Charisma and Managerial Leadership: The Gift That Never Was," *Business Horizons,* July–August 1998, pp. 19–26; R. J. House, "A 1976 Theory of Charismatic Leadership," in *Leadership: The Cutting Edge,* ed. J. G. Hunt and L. L. Larson (Carbondale: Southern Illinois University Press, 1977).

99. M. Brown and L. Trevino, "Socialized Charismatic Leadership, Values Congruence, and Deviance in Work Groups," *Journal of Applied Psychology* 91 (2006), pp. 954–62.

100. M. Potts and P. Behr, *The Leading Edge* (New York: McGraw-Hill, 1987).

101. M. A. LePine, Y. Zhang, E. R. Crawford, and B. L. Rich, "Turning Their Pain to Gain: Charismatic Leader Influence on Follower Stress Appraisal and Job Performance," *Academy of Management Journal* 59 (2016) pp. 1036–59; J. Howell and B. Shamir, "The Role of Followers in the Charismatic Leadership Process: Relationships and Their Consequences," *Academy of Management Review* 30 (2005), pp. 96–112.

102. B. Galvin, P. Balkundi, and D. Waldman, "Spreading the Word: The Role of Surrogates in Charismatic Leadership Processes," *Academy of Management Review* 35 (2010), pp. 477–94; B. Galvin, P. Balkundi, and D. Waldman, "Can Charisma Be Taught? Tests of Two Interventions," *Academy of Management Review* 35 (2010), pp. 477–94.

103. B. Galvin, P. Balkundi, and D. Waldman, "Can Charisma Be Taught? Tests of Two Interventions," *Academy of Management Review* 35 (2010), pp. 477–94; M. Fenley and S. Liechti, *Academy of Management Learning & Education* 10 (2011), pp. 374–96.

104. S. Yorges, H. Weiss, and O. Strickland, "The Effect of Leader Outcomes on Influence, Attributions, and Perceptions of Charisma," *Journal of Applied Psychology* 84 (1999), pp. 428–36.

105. J. Stillman, "Spotify CEO: How I Learned to Lead with Zero Natural Charisma," *Inc.,* August 23, 2018, https://www.inc.com.

106. D. A. Waldman and F. J. Yammarino, "CEO Charismatic Leadership: Levels-of-Management and Levels-of-Analysis Effects," *Academy of Management Review* 24 (1999), pp. 266–85.

107. A. Erez, V. F. Misangyi, D. E. Johnson, M. A. LePine, and K. C. Halverson, "Stirring the Hearts of Followers: Charismatic Leadership as the Transferral of Affect," *Journal of Applied Psychology* 93 (2008), pp. 602–16.

108. D. Cossin and J. Caballero, "Transformational Leadership Background Literature Review," IMD Global Board Center, June 2013, www.imd.org; A. Fanelli and V. Misangyi, "Bringing Out Charisma: CEO Charisma and External Stakeholders," *Academy of Management Review* 31 (2006), pp. 1049–61.

109. R. House and R. Aditya, The Social Psychological Study of Leadership: Quo Vadis? *Journal of Management* 23, (1997), pp. 409–73.

110. D. A. Waldman, G. G. Ramirez, R. J. House, and P. Puranam, "Does Leadership Matter? CEO Leadership Attributes and Profitability under Conditions of Perceived Environmental Uncertainty," *Academy of Management Journal* 44 (2001), pp. 134–43.

111. S. Boehm, D. Dwertmann, H. Bruch, and B. Shamir, "The Missing Link? Investigating Organizational Identity Strength and Transformational Leadership Climate as Mechanisms That Connect CEO Charisma with Firm Performance," *Leadership Quarterly* 26 (2015), pp. 156–71; B. Agle, N. Nagarajan, J. Sonnenfeld, and D. Srinivasan, "Does CEO Charisma Matter? An Empirical Analysis of the Relationships among Organizational Performance, Environmental Uncertainty, and Top Management Team Perceptions of CEO Charisma," *Academy of Management Journal* 49 (2006), pp. 161–74.

112. J. M. Howell and K. E. Hall-Merenda, "The Ties That Bind: The Impact of Leader-Member Exchange, Transformational and Transactional Leadership, and Distance on Predicting Follower Performance," *Journal of Applied Psychology* 84 (1999), pp. 680–94; B. M. Bass, "Leadership: Good, Better, Best," *Organizational Dynamics,* Winter 1985, pp. 26–40.

113. B. Thompson, "Take a Tip from Bezos: Customers Always Need a Seat at the Table," *Entrepreneur,* May 28, 2014, http://www.entrepreneur.com; Adam Lashinsky, "Amazon's Jeff Bezos: The Ultimate Disrupter," *Fortune,* November 16, 2012, http://management.fortune.cnn.com.

114. D. I. Jung and B. J. Avolio, "Effects of Leadership Style and Followers' Cultural Orientation on Performance in Group and Individual Task Conditions," *Academy of Management Journal* 42 (1999), pp. 208–18.

115. B. M. Bass, *Leadership and Performance beyond Expectations* (New York: Free Press, 1985).

116. W. Bennis and B. Nanus, *Leaders: Strategies for Taking Charge.* (New York: HarperBusiness, 2012).

117. A. M. Grant, "Leading with Meaning: Beneficiary Contact, Prosocial Impact, and the Performance Effects of Transformational Leadership," *Academy of Management Journal* 55 (2012), pp. 458–76.

118. B. Bass, B. Avolio, and L. Goodheim, "Biography and the Assessment of Transformational Leadership at the World-Class Level," *Journal of Management* 13 (1987), pp. 7–20.

119. D. Novak, "Follow Indra Nooyi's Example: Become a Leader People Are Excited to Follow," *CNBC,* September 12, 2018, www.cnbc.com; M. Matousek, "Mary Barra Was Called a 'Lightweight' When She Became CEO of GM—Here's How She Transformed the Company and Silenced Her Doubters," *Business Insider,* January 11, 2018, www.businessinsider.com; S. Anthony and E. Schwartz, "What the Best Transformational Leaders Do," *Harvard Business Review,* May 8, 2017, https://hbr.org.

120. Y. Ling, Z. Simisek, M. Lubatkin, and J. F. Veiga, "The Impact of Transformational CEOs on the Performance of Small to

Medium-Sized Firms: Does Organizational Context Matter?"
Journal of Applied Psychology 93 (2008), pp. 923-34.

121. R. Sun and A. Henderson, "Transformational Leadership and Organizational Processes: Influencing Public Performance," *Public Administration Review* 77 (2017), pp. 554-65.

122. J. Collins, "Level 5 Leadership," *Harvard Business Review* 1 (2001), pp. 66-76; J. Kline Harrison and M. William Clough, "Characteristics of 'State of the Art' Leaders: Productive Narcissism versus Emotional Intelligence and Level 5 Capabilities," *Social Science Journal* 43 (2006), pp. 287-92.

123. A. Ou, D. Waldman, and S. Peterson, "Do Humble CEOs Matter? An Examination of CEO Humility and Firm Outcomes," *Journal of Management* 44 (2018), pp. 1147-73.

124. G. Satell, "Why Tim Cook's 'Level 5 Leadership' Might Not Be Enough to Secure Apple's Future," *Forbes*, June 4, 2013, http://www.forbes.com; D. Vera and M. Crossan, "Strategic Leadership and Organizational Learning," *Academy of Management Review* 29 (2004), pp. 222-40.

125. F. Luthans, *Organizational Behavior*, 10th ed. (New York: McGraw-Hill/Irwin, 2005); F. Luthans and B. Avolio, "Authentic Leadership Development," in *Positive Organizational Scholarship*, ed. K. Cameron, J. Dutton, and R. Quinn (San Francisco: Berrett-Koehler, 2003), pp. 241-58.

126. B. Avolio, T. Wernsing, and W. Gardner, "Revisiting the Development and Validation of the Authentic Leadership," *Journal of Management* 44 (2018), pp. 399-411.

127. B. Avolio, T. Wernsing, and W. Gardner, "Revisiting the Development and Validation of the Authentic Leadership," *Journal of Management* 44 (2018), pp. 399-411.

128. N. Turner, J. Barling, O. Epitropaki, V. Butcher, and C. Milner, "Transformational Leadership and Moral Reasoning," *Journal of Applied Psychology* 87 (2002), pp. 304-11.

129. D. M. Mayer, M. Kuenzi, R. Greenbaum, M. Bardes, and R. Salvador, "How Low Does Ethical Leadership Flow? Test of a Trickle-Down Model," *Organizational Behavior and Human Decision Processes* 108 (2009), pp. 1-13.

130. B. M. Bass, "Thoughts and Plans," in *Cutting Edge Leadership 2000*, ed. B. Kellerman and L. R. Matusak (College Park, MD: James MacGregor Burns Academy of Leadership, 2000), pp. 5-9; J. Spangenburg, "The Effect of a Pseudo-transformational Leader: Whitewater Rafting in a Hurricane," *International Journal of Management & Information Systems* 16 (2012), https://clutejournals.com/index.php/IJMIS/article/view/7309, p. 325.

131. W. Bennis, "The End of Leadership: Exemplary Leadership Is Impossible without Full Inclusion, Initiatives, and Cooperation of Followers," *Organizational Dynamics*, Summer 1999, pp. 71-79.

132. J. Hoch, W. Bommer, J. Dulebohn, and D. Wu, "Do Ethical, Authentic, and Servant Leadership Explain Variance above and beyond Transformational Leadership? A Meta-analysis," *Journal of Management* 44 (2018), pp. 501-29; "What Is Servant Leadership?" Robert K. Greenleaf Center for Servant Leadership, https://www.greenleaf.org; Larry W. Boone and Sanya Makhani, "Five Necessary Attitudes of a Servant Leader," *Review of Business* 83, no. 1 (Winter 2012), pp. 83-96.

133. N. Eva, M. Robin, S. Sendjaya, D. van Dierendonck, and R. Liden, "Servant Leadership: A Systematic Review and Call for Future Research," *Leadership Quarterly* 30 (2019), pp. 111-32.

134. F. Hanson, "Why Every Entrepreneur Should Be a Servant Leader," *Entrepreneur*, May 10, 2018, https://www.entrepreneur.com.

135. M. Chiniara and K. Bentein, "Linking Servant Leadership to Individual Performance: Differentiating the Mediating Role of Autonomy, Competence and Relatedness Need Satisfaction," *Leadership Quarterly* 27 (2016), pp. 124-41; R. Liden, S. Wayne, C. Liao, and J. Meuser, "Servant Leadership and Serving Culture: Influence on Individual and Unit Performance," *Academy of Management Journal* 57 (2014), pp. 1434-52; D. Parris and J. Peachey, "A Systematic Literature Review of Servant Leadership Theory in Organizational Contexts," *Journal of Business Ethics* 113 (2013), pp. 377-93; D. Van Dierendonck, "Servant Leadership: A Review and Synthesis," *Journal of Management* 37 (2011), pp. 1228-61.

136. "Popeyes Louisiana Kitchen Inc.," *Google Finance*, March 27, 2017, www.google.com; J. Goudreau, "The CEO of Popeyes

137. D. Waldman and R. Balven, "Responsible Leadership: Theoretical Issues and Research Directions," *Academy of Management Perspectives* 28 (2014), pp. 224-34; L. J. Christensen, L. Jones. A. Mackey, and D. Whetten, "Taking Responsibility for Corporate Social Responsibility: The Role of Leaders Leaders in Creating, Implementing, Sustaining, or Avoiding Socially Responsible Firm Behaviors," *Academy of Management Perspectives* 28 (2014), pp. 164-78.

138. C. L. Pearce, "The Future of Leadership: Combining Vertical and Shared Leadership to Transform Knowledge Work," *Academy of Management Executive*, February 2004, pp. 47-57.

139. M. Hogg, D. van Knippenberg, and D. E. Rasst III, "Intergroup Leadership in Organizations: Leading across Group and Organizational Boundaries," *Academy of Management Review* 37 (2012), pp. 232-55; T. Pittinsky (ed.), *Crossing the Divide: Intergroup Leadership in a World of Difference* (Cambridge, MA: Harvard Business Publishing, 2009); T. Pittinsky and S. Simon, "Intergroup Leadership," *Leadership Quarterly* 18 (2007), pp. 586-605.

140. C. L. Pearce, "The Future of Leadership: Combining Vertical and Shared Leadership to Transform Knowledge Work," *Academy of Management Executive*, February 2004, pp. 47-57.

141. "Build Change, Home," https://www.buildchange.org/, accessed April 3, 2019.

142. "Build Change, Home," https://www.buildchange.org/, accessed April 3, 2019.

143. "Meet the 2017 Skoll Awardees for Social Entrepreneurship," Skoll, March 27, 2017, http://skoll.org/2017/03/27/meet-2017-skoll-awardees-social-entrepreneurship/.

144. "Meet the 2017 Skoll Awardees for Social Entrepreneurship," Skoll, March 27, 2017, http://skoll.org/2017/03/27/meet-2017-skoll-awardees-social-entrepreneurship/.

145. D. Wang, D. Waldman, and Z. Zhang, "A Meta-analysis of Shared Leadership and Team Effectiveness," *Journal of Applied Psychology* 99 (2014), pp. 181-98; C. L. Pearce, "The Future of Leadership: Combining Vertical and Shared Leadership to Transform Knowledge Work," *Academy of Management Executive*, February 2004, pp. 47-57.

146. L. D'Innocenzo, J. Mathieu, and M. Kukenberger, "Meta-analysis of Different Forms of Shared Leadership-Team Performance Relations," *Journal of Management* 42 (2016), pp. 1964-91; V. Nicolaides, K. LaPort, T. Chen, A. Tomassetti, E. Weis, S. Zaccaro, and J. Cortina, "The Shared Leadership of Teams: A Meta-analyses of Proximal, Distal, and Moderating Relationships," *Leadership Quarterly* 25 (2014), pp. 923-42.

147. J. Carson, P. Tesluk, and J. Marrone, "Shared Leadership in Teams: An Investigation of Antecedent Conditions and Performance," *Academy of Management Journal* 50 (2007), pp. 1217-34.

148. M. M. Koerner, "Courage as Identity Work: Accounts of Workplace Courage," *Academy of Management Journal* 57 (2014), pp. 63-93.

149. S. Caldicott, "Why Ford's Alan Mulally Is an Innovation CEO for the Record Books," *Forbes*, June 25, 2014, http://www.forbes.com; J. Reed and B. Simon, "Adroit in Detroit," *Financial Times*, January 25, 2011, Business & Company Resource Center, http://galenet.galegroup.com; "Epiphany in Dearborn: Ford," *The Economist*, December 11, 2010, Business & Company Resource Center, http://galenet.galegroup.com; J. LaReau, "Ford Slashes Debt, Spends on Operations," *Automotive News*, January 31, 2011, Business & Company Resource Center, http://galenet.galegroup.com.

150. P. Block, *The Empowered Manager* (San Francisco: Jossey-Bass, 1991).

151. P. Block, *The Empowered Manager* (San Francisco: Jossey-Bass, 1991).

152. M. Hammond, R. Clapp-Smith, and M. Palansky, "Beyond (Just) the Workplace: A Theory of Leader Development across Multiple Domains," *Academy of Management Review* 42 (2017), pp. 481-98.

153. J. Kouzes and B. Posner, *The Leadership Challenge*, 2nd ed. (San Francisco: Jossey-Bass, 1995).

154. L. W. Boone and M. S. Peborde, "Developing Leadership Skills in College and Early Career Positions," *Review of Business*, Spring 2008, Business & Company Resource Center, http://galenet.galegroup.com.

155. A. Gaines, "Straight to the Top," *American Executive,* August 2008, Business & Company Resource Center, http://galenet.galegroup.com; S. J. Allen and N. S. Hartman, "Leadership Development: An Exploration of Sources of Learning," *SAM Advanced Management Journal,* Winter 2008, pp. 10–19, 62–63.

156. Thottam, "10 Companies with Awesome Training and Development Programs," *Monster,* www.monster.com, accessed March 23, 2019.

157. M. McCall, *High Flyers* (Boston: Harvard Business School Press, 1998).

158. Daniel Araya, "Who Will Lead in the Age of Artificial Intelligence?" *Forbes,* January 1, 2019, https://www.forbes.com/sites/danielaraya/2019/01/01/who-will-lead-in-the-age-of-artificial-intelligence/#53d7fd706f95.

159. Tomas Chamorro-Premuzic, Michael Wade, and Jennifer Jordan, "As AI Makes More Decisions, the Nature of Leadership Will Change," January 22, 2018, https://hbr.org/2018/01/as-ai-makes-more-decisions-the-nature-of-leadership-will-change%20and%20https://emerj.com/partner-content/the-impact-of-ai-on-business-leadership-and-the-modern-workforce/.

160. Sam Bourton, Johanne Lavoie, and Tiffany Vogel, "Will Artificial Intelligence Make You a Better Leader?" April 2018, https://www.mckinsey.com/business-functions/organization/our-insights/will-artificial-intelligence-make-you-a-better-leader; "5 Ways AI Can Transform Leadership," *HR Technologist,* November 16, 2018, https://www.hrtechnologist.com/articles/leadership-succession/5-ways-ai-can-transform-leadership/.

161. Jason Albanese, "The 3 Skills Leaders Need to Succeed in the Age of Artificial Intelligence," *Inc.,* https://www.inc.com/jason-albanese/the-3-skills-leaders-need-to-succeed-in-age-of-artificial-intelligence.html, accessed April 1, 2019.

162. E. Van Velsor, C. D. McCauley, and R. Moxley, "Our View of Leadership Development," in *Center for Creative Leadership Handbook of Leadership Development,* ed. C. D. McCauley, R. Moxley, and E. Van Velsor (San Francisco: Jossey-Bass, 1998), pp. 1–25.

163. D. S. DeRue and N. Wellman, "Developing Leaders via Experience: The Role of Developmental Challenge, Learning Orientation, and Feedback Availability," *Journal of Applied Psychology* 94 (2009), pp. 859–75.

164. Adi Ignatius, "'Businesses Exist to Deliver Value to Society,'" *Harvard Business Review,* March–April 2018, https://hbr.org/2018/03/businesses-exist-to-deliver-value-to-society.

165. Ann C. Mule, Veta T. Richardson, and Brent Thomas, "On Leadership: An Interview with Kenneth Frazier," Association of Corporate Counsel, November 16, 2017, https://www.weinberg.udel.edu/content-sub-site/Documents/For-Events/ACC-Ken_Frazier-QA-Article-MGP-11.16.17-sm1.pdf.

166. Catherine Dunn, "Merck CEO Ken Frazier Rose from Humble Beginnings in North Philly to Run a Big Pharma Company," *Philadelphia Inquirer,* November 21, 2018, https://www.philly.com/philly/business/merck-ceo-ken-frazier-trump-drug-prices-20181121.html.

CHAPTER 13
Motivating for Performance

> The worst mistake a boss can make is not to say well done.
>
> —John Ashcroft, Business Executive
>
> The reward of a thing well done is to have done it.
>
> —Ralph Waldo Emerson

Rawpixel.com/Shutterstock

learning objectives

After studying Chapter 13, you will be able to:

LO 13-1   Identify the kinds of behaviors managers need to motivate in people.

LO 13-2   List principles for setting goals that motivate employees.

LO 13-3   Summarize how to reward good performance effectively.

LO 13-4   Describe the key beliefs that affect people's motivation.

LO 13-5   Discuss ways in which people's individual needs affect their behavior.

LO 13-6   Define ways to create jobs that motivate.

LO 13-7   Summarize how people assess fairness and how to achieve fairness.

LO 13-8   Identify causes and consequences of a (dis)satisfied workforce.

chapter outline

Motivating for Performance

Setting Goals
Goals That Motivate
Stretch Goals

Limitations of Goal Setting
Set Your Own Goals

Reinforcing Performance
(Mis)Managing Rewards and
Punishments

Managing Mistakes
Providing Feedback

Performance-Related Beliefs
The Effort-to-Performance
Link
The Performance-to-
Outcome Link

Impact on Motivation
Managerial Implications of
Expectancy Theory

Understanding People's Needs
Maslow's Needs
Alderfer's ERG Theory
McClelland's Needs

Don't Forget: People Can
Differ

Designing Motivating Jobs
Job Rotation, Enlargement,
and Enrichment
Herzberg's Two-Factor
Theory

The Hackman and Oldham
Model of Job Design
Empowerment and
Engagement

Achieving Fairness
Assessing Equity
Restoring Equity

Procedural Justice

Employee Satisfaction and Well-being
Quality of Work Life

Psychological Contracts

Management in Action

WHAT MAKES SAS A FAMOUSLY GREAT PLACE TO WORK?

SAS (named after its first product, Statistical Analysis Software) has grown since its 1976 founding into the world's leader in data analytics software. The company consistently reports over $3 billion in annual revenue and has approximately 14,000 employees worldwide. For decades, SAS has been known as one of the best places to work, listed once again in *Fortune*'s World's Best Workplaces for 2018.[1]

An employee summed up his appreciation of the company this way: "SAS does so much for the employees. I always feel this is my second home. I want to give my best to this company and would like to help in any way possible to make this company more successful."[2]

However, if you talk to SAS's leaders, you hear less about benefits and more about the company's values, which shape its work environment. As the director of recreation and employee services said, "When people are treated as if they're important and truly make a difference, their loyalty and engagement soar."[3] SAS emphasizes appreciating what workers contribute, building their trust, and empowering them to make decisions in their area of responsibility.

SAS Software Co.

SAS's co-founder and chief executive, James Goodnight, believes this treatment is the primary way SAS unleashes creativity. "Ninety-five percent of my assets drive out of the gate every evening," says Goodnight. "It's my job to maintain a work environment that keeps those people coming back every morning."[4] That SAS gets it right is evident in the company's success.

SAS stands out as a company that offers generous benefits to its workers. As you read this chapter, consider whether generosity is enough to bring out employees' best work, aimed at the company's goals and priorities. If not, what other efforts should managers make?

This chapter tackles an age-old question: How can a manager motivate people to work hard and perform at their best levels? SAS demonstrates that treating employees as valued contributors to the organization can be a key part of motivating them.

A sales manager in one company had a different approach to this question. Each month, the person with the worst sales performance took home a live goat for the weekend. The manager hoped the goat-of-the-month employee would be so embarrassed that he or she would work harder the next month to increase sales.[5]

This sales manager may get high marks for creativity. But if he is graded by results, as he grades his salespeople, he will fail. He may succeed in motivating a few of his people to increase sales, but some good people will be motivated to quit the company.

Motivating for Performance

LO 13-1 Identify the kinds of behaviors managers need to motivate in people.

Understanding why people do the things they do on the job can be a difficult task. Predicting their response to management's latest productivity program is harder yet. Fortunately, enough is known about motivation to give the thoughtful manager practical, effective techniques for increasing people's effort and performance.

Motivation refers to forces that energize, direct, and sustain a person's efforts. All behavior, except involuntary reflexes such as eye blinks (which have little to do with management), is motivated. A highly motivated person will work hard toward achieving performance goals. With adequate ability, understanding of the job, and access to necessary resources, someone who is motivated will be a strong performer.

motivation

Forces that energize, direct, and sustain a person's efforts.

Managers must know what behaviors they want people to exhibit. Although productive people appear to do a seemingly limitless number of things, most of the important activities can be grouped into five general categories.[6] As shown in Exhibit 13.1, managers must motivate people to (1) join the organization, (2) remain in the organization, and (3) come to work regularly. On these points, you should reject the common notion that loyalty is dead and accept the challenge of creating an environment that will attract and energize people so that they commit to the organization.[7]

Of course, companies also want people to (4) perform—that is, once employees are at work, they should work hard to contribute high output and high quality. Finally,

EXHIBIT 13.1

Managers Must Motivate People to Engage in Key Behaviors

managers want employees to (5) exhibit good citizenship. Good citizens contribute above and beyond the call of duty by doing extra things that help the company. The importance of citizenship behaviors may be less obvious than sheer productive output, but these behaviors help the organization function smoothly. They also make managers' lives easier.

Setting Goals

Setting work-related goals is an extremely common approach to motivating employees. In fact, it is perhaps the most important, valid, and useful single approach to motivating performance. However, goal setting needs to be done properly, or it will backfire.

Goal-setting theory states that people have conscious goals that energize them and direct their thoughts and behaviors toward a particular end.[8] Keeping in mind the principle that goals motivate, managers set goals for employees or collaborate with employees to set goals together. For example, in order to keep the United States safe, the Department of Homeland Security (DHS) sets goals to prevent cyber and all other types of terrorist attacks.[9]

Goal setting works for any job in which people have control over their performance.[10] You can set goals for performance quality and quantity, and behavioral goals such as cooperation or teamwork.[11] In fact, you can set goals for whatever is important.[12]

Goals That Motivate

The most powerful goals are meaningful; important purposes that appeal to people's higher values add extra motivating power.[13] Starbucks cares deeply about the environment. New Belgium Brewery is dedicated to continuously improving its sustainability initiatives. Honest Tea sells organic and natural beverages but also wants to improve people's health and well-being. Hobby Lobby and Chick-fil-A have religious commitments that appeal to their employees, and Huntsman Corporation has goals of paying off corporate debt but also relieving human suffering—it sponsors cancer research and a number of charities.

Meaningful goals also can be based on data about competitors; exceeding competitors' performance can stoke people's competitive spirit and desire to win in the marketplace.[14] This point is not just about the values companies espouse and the lofty goals they pursue; it's also about leadership at a more personal level. Followers of transformational leaders view their work as more important and as highly congruent with their personal goals compared with followers of transactional leaders[15] (recall Chapter 12).

The most motivating performance goals are acceptable to employees. This means, among other things, that they should not conflict with people's personal values and that people have reasons to pursue them. Allowing people to participate in setting their work goals—as opposed to the boss setting their goals for them—is often a great way to generate goals that people accept and pursue willingly.

Acceptable, maximally motivating goals are challenging but attainable. They should be high enough to inspire better performance but not so high that people can never reach them. Ideal goals are not merely general prompts to improve performance, do one's best, increase productivity, or reduce the time customers must wait to receive service. Rather, the goals should be specific regarding target and time frame. Notejoy, an organizational collaboration platform, has its employees develop and host five webinars in a given quarter with at least fifteen attendees per webinar and an 80 percent or higher satisfaction rating on its content.[16]

Deadlines and measurable performance goals are specific, quantifiable goals that employees are motivated to achieve. Walmart, HP, and others use the acronym SMART (see Exhibit 13.2) to create motivating goals: specific, measurable, achievable, results-based, and time-specific.[17]

LO 13-2 List principles for setting goals that motivate employees.

Bottom Line
You can set goals related to cost, quality, speed, service, innovation, sustainability—anything that's important. *What is one goal you have set for yourself as a student? If you haven't set any goals, you could start by setting one now for this course.*

goal-setting theory

A motivation theory stating that people have conscious goals that energize them and direct their thoughts and behaviors toward a particular end.

EXHIBIT 13.2
SMART Goals Motivate

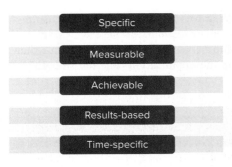

- Specific
- Measurable
- Achievable
- Results-based
- Time-specific

SOURCE: Adapted from Shaw, K. N., "Changing the Goal-Setting Process at Microsoft," *Academy of Management Executive* 4 (November 2004), pp. 139–43.

Stretch Goals

stretch goals

Targets that are particularly demanding, sometimes even thought to be impossible.

Some firms and bosses set **stretch goals**—targets that are exceptionally demanding and that some people would never even think of. Two important types of stretch goals are *vertical* stretch goals, aligned with current activities including productivity and financial results, and *horizontal* stretch goals, which involve people's professional development such as attempting and learning new, difficult things.[18] Impossible though stretch goals may seem to some, they sometimes are in fact attainable.

Stretch goals can generate a major shift away from mediocrity and toward tremendous achievement. But if people try in good faith but don't meet their stretch goals, don't punish them—remember how difficult their goals are! Base your assessment on how much performance has improved, how the performance compares with others, and how much progress has been made.[19]

> Goals can generate manipulative game-playing and unethical behavior.

Limitations of Goal Setting

Goal setting is an extraordinarily powerful management technique. But even specific, challenging, attainable goals work better under some conditions than others. If people lack relevant ability and knowledge, a better course might be simply to urge them to do their best or to set a goal to learn rather than a goal to achieve a specific performance level.[20]

Individual performance goals can be dysfunctional if people work in a group and cooperation among team members is essential to group performance.[21] Goals aimed at maximizing individual performance can create competition and reduce cooperation, thereby hurting group performance. On the other hand, group-centric goals aimed at maximizing the individual's contributions to the group's performance have a positive effect.[22] If cooperation is important, performance goals should be established for the team.

Goals can generate manipulative game-playing and unethical behavior. For example, people can sometimes find ingenious ways to set easy goals and convince their bosses that they are difficult.[23] Or they may find ways to meet goals simply to receive a reward, without necessarily performing in other desirable ways. In big law firms, it's common for lawyers to keep detailed records of their time and to be rewarded for billing, say, 1,800 hours per year. This system invites inefficient work and creates a dismal, demotivating environment for any lawyer who chose the profession out of concern for clients or love of the law.[24]

People who aren't on track to meet their goals are more likely to act unethically than are people who are trying to do their best but have no specific performance goals.[25] This is particularly true when people fall just short of reaching their goals.[26]

Financial reports provide an example familiar to business executives. Some executives have mastered the art of earnings management—precisely meeting Wall Street analysts' earnings estimates or beating them by a single penny.[27] The media trumpet, and investors reward, companies that meet or beat the estimates. Managers sometimes meet this goal by either manipulating the numbers or initiating whispering campaigns to persuade analysts to lower their estimates, making them more attainable. The marketplace wants short-term, quarterly performance, but long-term viability is more important to a company's ultimate success.

It is important *not* to establish a single productivity goal if there are other important dimensions of performance.[28] Productivity goals will likely enhance productivity, but they may also cause employees to neglect other areas, such as learning, tackling new projects, or developing creative solutions to job-related problems. If acquiring knowledge and skills is important, you can add a specific and challenging learning goal such as "identify 10 ways to develop relationships with end users of our products." A manager who wants to motivate creativity can establish creativity goals along with productivity goals for individuals or for brainstorming teams.[29]

Set Your Own Goals

Goal setting works for yourself as well—it's a powerful tool for self-management. Set goals for yourself; don't just try hard or hope for the best. Create a statement of purpose for yourself comprising three elements: an inspiring distant vision, a mid-distant goal along the way (worthy in its own right), and near-term objectives to start working on immediately.[30] So if you are going into business, you might articulate your goal for the type of businessperson you want to be in five years, the types of jobs that could create the opportunities and teach you what you need to know to become that businessperson, and the specific schoolwork and job search activities that can get you moving in those directions. On the job, apply SMART and other goal-setting advice for yourself.

Setting unprecedented goals can push a person to reach a higher level of achievement.

photobac/123RF

Reinforcing Performance

Goals are universal motivators. So are the processes of reinforcement described in this section. In 1911, psychologist Edward Thorndike formulated the **law of effect**: behavior that is followed by positive consequences probably will be repeated.[31] This powerful law of behavior laid the foundation for countless investigations into the effects of the positive consequences, called **reinforcers**, that motivate behavior. **Organizational behavior modification** (or **OB mod**) attempts to influence people's behavior, and improve performance,[32] by systematically managing work conditions and the consequences of people's actions.

Four key consequences of behavior either encourage or discourage people's behavior (see Exhibit 13.3):

1. **Positive reinforcement**—applying a positive consequence that increases the likelihood that the person will repeat the behavior that led to it. Examples of positive reinforcers include a boss thanking an employee, letters of commendation, favorable performance evaluations, and pay raises.[33]
2. **Negative reinforcement**—removing or withholding an undesirable consequence. For example, a manager takes an employee (or a school takes a student) off probation because of improved performance.
3. **Punishment**—administering an aversive consequence. Examples include criticizing or shouting at an employee, assigning an unappealing task, and sending a worker home without pay.

LO 13-3 Summarize how to reward good performance effectively.

law of effect

A law formulated by Edward Thorndike in 1911 stating that behavior that is followed by positive consequences will likely be repeated.

reinforcers

Positive consequences that motivate behavior.

organizational behavior modification (OB mod)

The application of reinforcement theory in organizational settings.

---

positive reinforcement

Applying consequences that increase the likelihood that a person will repeat the behavior that led to it.

negative reinforcement

Removing or withholding an undesirable consequence.

punishment

Administering an aversive consequence.

EXHIBIT 13.3
Behavior, Consequences, and Effects

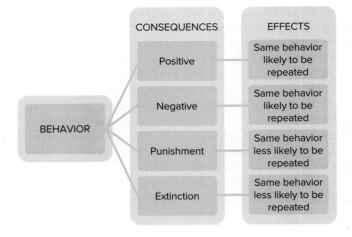

extinction

Withdrawing or failing to provide a reinforcing consequence.

Whereas negative reinforcement can involve the *threat* of punishment and then not delivering the punishment when employees perform satisfactorily, punishment is the actual delivery of the aversive consequence.

4. **Extinction**—withdrawing or failing to provide a reinforcing consequence. When this occurs, motivation is reduced and the behavior is *extinguished,* or eliminated. Ways that managers may unintentionally extinguish desired behaviors include not giving a compliment for a job well done, forgetting to say thanks for a favor, and setting impossible performance goals so a person never experiences success.

Extinction can be used intentionally on undesirable behaviors, too. The manager might ignore long-winded opining during a meeting or fail to acknowledge unimportant emails in the hope that they will discourage the employees from continuing.

The first two consequences, positive and negative reinforcement, are positive for the person receiving them—the person either gains something or avoids something negative. Therefore, the person who experiences them will be motivated to behave in the ways that led to the reinforcement. The last two consequences, punishment and extinction, are negative for the person receiving them: motivation to repeat the behavior that led to the undesirable results will drop.

Managers should be careful to match consequences to what employees will actually find desirable or undesirable. When a supervisor punished an employee for tardiness by suspending him for three days, the employee was delighted. It was fishing season.[34]

(Mis)Managing Rewards and Punishments

You've learned about the positive effects of a transformational leadership style, but giving rewards (a transaction) to high-performing people also is essential.[35] Unfortunately, sometimes organizations and managers reinforce the wrong behaviors.[36] As discussed in Chapter 10, stock options are intended to reinforce behaviors that add to the company's value, but stock options also can motivate decisions that artificially deliver short-term gains in stock prices but hurt the company in the long run. Likewise, programs that punish employees for absenteeism beyond a certain limit may actually encourage them to be absent. People may use up all their allowable absences and fail to come to work regularly until they reach the point at which their next absence will result in punishment.

Sometimes employees are reinforced with admiration for multitasking. This behavior may look efficient and send a signal that the employee is busy and valuable, but multitasking slows down the brain's efficiency and causes mistakes.[37] Scans of brain activity show that the brain is not able to concentrate on two tasks at once; it needs time to switch among the multitasker's activities. As a

Sometimes organizations and managers reinforce the wrong behaviors.

result, managers who praise the hard work of multitaskers may be unintentionally reinforcing inefficiency and failure to think deeply about problems.

The reward system should support the firm's strategy, defining people's performance in ways that pursue strategic objectives.[38] Reward employees for developing themselves in strategically important ways—for building new skills that are critical to strengthening core competencies and creating value.

Managers can be creative in their use of reinforcers. Ryan LLC, an international tax services company, took several steps to reward its employees. The firm is flexible about when and where employees do their work. Ryan also offers 12 weeks of paid pregnancy leave, paid 4-week sabbaticals every five years, and subsidies for employee health club memberships.[39]

At 10:30 every morning, when Richard Sheridan, CEO, passes the Viking helmet, Menlo Innovations employees must talk about their day.

Andre J. Jackson/MCT/Newscom

Innovative managers use nonmonetary rewards, including intellectual challenge, meaningful responsibilities, autonomy, recognition, and greater influence over decisions. These and other rewards for high-performing employees, when creatively devised and applied, can continue to motivate when pay and promotions are scarce. Employees at Menlo Innovations, a custom software design firm, are empowered to call for companywide meetings by shouting, "Hey, Menlo!" All employees (who work in the same large room) stop what they're doing, listen to their colleague, respond (if needed), and then get back to work. These impromptu meetings are effective and may last only about one or two minutes.

Another reward of working at Menlo is the ability to work in pairs. CEO Richard Sheridan believes strongly that paired employees who can ask one another "Hey, what about this?" while writing software can increase quality and creativity. By creating such a rewarding organization culture, Sheridan hopes that all of Menlo's employees will experience joy.[40]

Managing Mistakes

How managers react to people's mistakes has a big impact on motivation. Punishment is appropriate sometimes, as when people violate the law, ethical standards, safety rules, or standards of interpersonal treatment, or when they perform like a slacker. But sometimes managers punish people when they shouldn't—when poor performance isn't the person's fault or when managers take out their frustrations on the wrong people.

Managers who overuse punishment or use it inappropriately create a climate of fear in the workplace.[41] Fear causes people to focus on the short term, sometimes creating problems in the longer run. Fear also creates a focus on oneself rather than on the group and the organization.

Recognize that everyone makes mistakes and that failures can be beneficial when people discuss and learn from them.[42] Don't punish, but appreciate, people for honestly delivering bad news to their bosses. Treat failure to act responsibly as a failure but don't punish unsuccessful, good-faith efforts. If you're a leader, talk about your mistakes with your people and show how you learned from them. Give people second chances and maybe third chances. Encourage people to try new things and don't punish them if what they try in good faith just doesn't work out.

Managers who inappropriately yell at their staff or overuse punishment often create a climate of fear and anxiety in the workplace. How would you deal with a situation like this?

Shannon Fagan/Image Source

Providing Feedback

Most managers don't provide enough useful feedback, and most people don't ask for feedback enough.[43] As a manager, you should consider all potential causes of poor performance, pay full attention when employees ask for feedback or want to discuss performance issues, and provide constructive feedback.

> *Try not to be afraid of receiving feedback; in fact, you should actively seek it.*

Feedback can be offered in many ways.[44] You can provide statistics on work that the person has directly influenced. Customers sometimes give feedback directly; you also can request customer feedback and give it to the employee. A manufacturing firm—high tech or otherwise—can put the phone number or website of the production team on the product so customers can contact the team directly. And recalling Chapter 10, bosses can give regular, ongoing feedback—it helps correct problems immediately, provides immediate reinforcement for good work, and prevents surprises when the formal review comes.

For yourself, try not to be afraid of receiving feedback; in fact, you should actively seek it. But whether or not you seek the feedback, when you get it, don't ignore it. Try to avoid negative emotions such as anger, hurt, defensiveness, or resignation. Think, It's up to me to get the feedback I need; I need to know these things about my performance and my behavior; learning what I need to know about myself will help me identify needs and create new opportunities; it serves my interest best to know rather than not know; taking initiative on this gives me more power and influence over my career.[45]

Bottom Line

Make sure that you reward the right things, not the wrong things. Sound obvious? You'd be surprised how often this principle is violated! *What is rewarding, and not rewarding, about feedback from your manager?*

Performance-Related Beliefs

LO 13-4 Describe the key beliefs that affect people's motivation.

expectancy theory

A theory proposing that people will behave based on their perceived likelihood that their effort will lead to a certain outcome and on how highly they value that outcome.

expectancy

Employees' perception of the likelihood that their efforts will enable them to attain their performance goals.

In contrast to reinforcement theories, which describe the processes by which factors in the work environment affect people's behavior, expectancy theory considers some of the performance-related thoughts in people's heads. According to **expectancy theory**, the person's work efforts lead to some level of performance.[46] Then, performance leads to one or more outcomes for the person. This process is shown in Exhibit 13.4. People develop two important beliefs linking these events: expectancy, which links effort to performance, and instrumentality, which links performance to outcomes.

The Effort-to-Performance Link

The first belief, **expectancy**, is people's perceived likelihood that their efforts will enable them to attain their performance goals. An expectancy can be high (up to 100 percent), such as when a student is confident that if she studies hard, she will get a good grade on the final. An expectancy can also be low (down to a 0 percent likelihood), such as when a suitor is convinced that his dream date will never go out with him.

All else equal, high expectancies create higher motivation than do low expectancies. In the preceding examples, the student is more likely to study hard for the exam than the suitor is to pursue the dream date, even though both want their respective outcomes.

Expectancies can vary among individuals, even in the same situation. For example, a sales manager might initiate a competition in which the top salesperson wins a free trip to Hawaii. In such cases, the few top people, who have performed well in the past, will be

EXHIBIT 13.4
Basic Concepts of Expectancy Theory

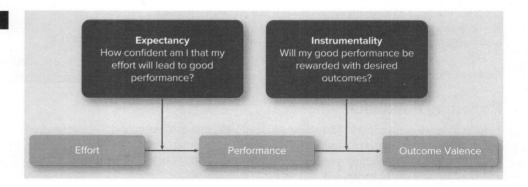

more motivated by the contest than will the historically average and below-average performers. The top people will have higher expectancies—stronger beliefs that their efforts can help them win the competition.

The Performance-to-Outcome Link

The example of the sales contest illustrates how performance results in some kind of **outcome**, or consequence, for the person. Actually, it often results in several outcomes. For example, turning in the best sales performance could lead to (1) a competitive victory, (2) the free trip to Hawaii, (3) feelings of achievement, (4) recognition from the boss, (5) status throughout the company, and (6) resentment from other salespeople.

Winning a competition for a free trip to Hawaii would be great, but what about all the losers?

Inti St. Clair/Spaces Images/Blend Images LLC

But how certain is it that performance will result in all of those outcomes? Will winning the contest really lead to resentment? Will it really lead to increased status?

These questions address the second key belief described by expectancy theory: instrumentality.[47] **Instrumentality** is the perceived likelihood that performance will be followed by a particular outcome. Like expectancies, instrumentalities can be high (up to 100 percent) or low (approaching 0 percent). For example, you can be fully confident that if you do a good job, you'll get a promotion; or you can feel that no matter how well you do, the promotion will go to someone else.

Each outcome has an associated valence. **Valence** is the value the person places on the outcome. Valences can be positive, as a Hawaiian vacation would be for most people, or negative, as in the case of the other salespeople's resentment.

Impact on Motivation

For motivation to be high, expectancy, instrumentalities, and total valence of all outcomes must all be high. People will not be highly motivated if any of the following conditions exist:

1. They believe they can't perform well enough to achieve the positive outcomes that they knows the company provides to good performers (high valence and high instrumentality but low expectancy).
2. They know they can do the job and are fairly certain what the ultimate outcomes will be (say, a promotion and a transfer). However, they don't want those outcomes or believe other, negative outcomes outweigh the positive (high expectancy and high instrumentality but low valence).
3. They know they can do the job and want several important outcomes (a favorable performance review, a raise, and a promotion). But they believe that no matter how well they perform, the outcomes will not be forthcoming (high expectancy and positive valences but low instrumentality).

Managerial Implications of Expectancy Theory

Expectancy theory helps the manager zero in on key leverage points for influencing motivation. Three implications are crucial:

1. *Increase expectancies.* Provide a work environment that facilitates good performance and set realistically attainable performance goals. Provide training, support, required resources, and encouragement so that people are confident they can perform at the levels expected of them. Recall from Chapter 12 that some leaders excel at boosting their followers' confidence.
2. *Identify positively valence outcomes.* Understand what people want to get out of work. Think about what their jobs provide them and what is not provided, but could be.

outcome

A consequence a person receives for his or her performance.

instrumentality

The perceived likelihood that performance will be followed by a particular outcome.

valence

The value an outcome holds for the person contemplating it.

Consider how people may differ in the valences they assign to outcomes. Know the need theories of motivation, described in the next section, and their implications for identifying important outcomes.

3. *Make performance instrumental toward positive outcomes.* Make sure that good performance is followed by personal recognition and praise, favorable performance reviews, pay increases, and other positive results. Also, make sure that working hard and doing things well will have as few negative results as possible. It is useful to realize, too, that bosses usually control rewards and punishments, but others do so as well. Peers, direct reports, customers, and others tend to provide outcomes in the form of compliments, help, criticism, and other social punishments.

Organizations set up formal reward systems as well. Austin-based YouEarnedIt created an app designed to increase employee happiness and engagement at work. The app empowers employees to recognize one another's contributions and hard work. The idea of having employees provide one another with real-time, meaningful recognition on a daily basis is catching on. YouEarnedIt's clients include Anheuser-Busch, Goodwill, and J. Walter Thompson.[48] As you read "Management in Action: Progress Report," consider whether similar ideas would motivate employees at SAS.

Management in Action

GETTING EMPLOYEES TO BACK THE SAS MISSION

James Goodnight, a statistician, co-founded SAS with colleagues from North Carolina State University. Since his first experiences of programming a computer while in college, he had recognized the joy of creating something that would benefit others. Goodnight wants his employees to feel the same sense of accomplishment. He starts with treating every employee with respect.

To see how this works, consider how SAS has recently innovated in a couple of important areas of computing. One is the rapid switch of the computer industry to cloud computing. SAS grew up when big organizations invested in large, powerful computers, and its software was written for those systems. With the rise of the Internet, data have streamed in from many sources in real time, and computing systems are being reworked to process the data in parallel on multiple computers that do not necessarily reside at the organization using the data. A few years ago, SAS introduced Viya, its next-generation, open-architecture data platform that is built for the cloud and real-time parallel processing, prompting Goodnight to declare, "We're ready for big data."[49]

SAS has also expanded its cloud services by investing and innovating in the AI space. The company just announced a $1 billion investment in artificial intelligence

and technologies that will further strengthen its position in such fields as advanced analytics and machine learning.[50] In fact, SAS recently partnered with Siemens Healthineers to explore how artificial intelligence can improve cardiac MRI diagnostics.[51] The goal is to allow medical professionals to make real-time cardiovascular diagnoses that can save time, resources, and ultimately lead to better patient outcomes.

Some observers wondered whether SAS could make the transition from hardware to software systems and services. But because SAS attracts the best people (thanks to its reputation for treating employees well), hires for creativity, and makes it easy to stay on the job (thanks to corporate perks such as subsidized cafeterias and onsite haircuts), SAS has no trouble convincing employees to push hard toward reaching ambitious goals. On SAS's website, Goodnight describes his philosophy quite plainly: "Treat employees like they make a difference and they will."[52]

- What kinds of reinforcement and feedback do you think would be most useful and productive with SAS employees?
- How should SAS's managers apply the implications of expectancy theory to keep the company innovative?

Understanding People's Needs

The manager who appropriately applies goal-setting, reinforcement, and expectancy theories is creating essential motivating elements in the *work environment*. But motivation also is affected by characteristics of the *person*. Several important theories describe the kinds of needs that people want to satisfy. The extent to which and the ways in which a person's needs are met or not met at work affect his or her behavior on the job.

The best-known approaches to understanding people's needs are Maslow's hierarchy, Alderfer's ERG theory, and McClelland's needs.

LO 13-5 Discuss ways in which people's individual needs affect their behavior.

Maslow's Needs

Exhibit 13.5 shows a set of human needs famously described by psychologist Abraham Maslow.[53] The needs are

1. *Physiological* (food, water, sex, and shelter).
2. *Safety or security* (protection against threat and deprivation).
3. *Social or belongingness* (friendship, affection, and love).
4. *Esteem or ego* (independence, achievement, freedom, status, and recognition).
5. *Self-actualization* (realizing one's full potential, becoming everything one is capable of being).

Maslow's need hierarchy is commonly understood as operating from the bottom to the top of a pyramid, because people need to satisfy the lower needs before they try to satisfy the higher needs. When people have nothing and struggle to survive, they concern themselves with their physical and safety needs.

You might recognize this famous pyramid from elsewhere, although Maslow himself did not present his theory in this fashion.[54] Maslow understood that for people not dealing with day-to-day survival, all needs can motivate, sometimes separately and other times simultaneously. In the modern workplace, physiological and safety needs generally are well satisfied, making social, ego, and self-actualization needs important. But safety issues are still very important in manufacturing, mining, health care, and other work environments.

Maslow's need hierarchy

A conception of human needs organizing needs into a hierarchy of five major types.

EXHIBIT 13.5
Maslow's Need Hierarchy

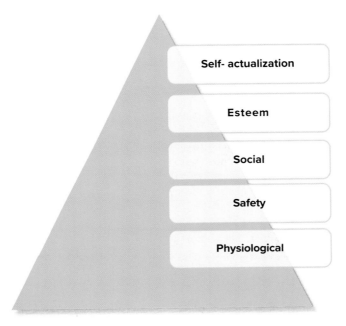

SOURCE: Organ, D. and Bateman, T., *Organizational Behavior,* 4th ed. New York: McGraw-Hill, 1991.

> Safety issues are still very important in manufacturing, mining, health care, and other work environments.

Maslow maintained that once a need is satisfied, it is no longer a powerful motivator. For example, labor unions negotiate for higher wages, benefits, safety standards, and job security. These bargaining issues relate directly to the satisfaction of Maslow's lower-level needs. After these needs are reasonably satisfied, the higher-level needs—social, ego, and self-actualization—become dominant concerns.

Maslow's hierarchy is important and useful, even if not complex enough to be a complete theory of human motivation.[55] Maslow made at least three major and practical contributions. First, he identified important need categories, which can help managers create effective positive outcomes. Second, it is helpful to think of two general levels of needs, in which lower-level needs must be satisfied before higher-level needs become important. Third, Maslow alerted managers to the importance of personal growth and self-actualization.

Self-actualization is the best-known concept from this theory. According to Maslow, the average person is only 10 percent self-actualized. In other words, most of us are living our lives and working at our jobs with a large untapped reservoir of potential. The implication is clear: Managers should create work environments that provide training, resources, autonomy, responsibilities, and challenging assignments. This type of environment gives people a chance to use their skills and abilities in creative ways and allows them to achieve more of their full potential.

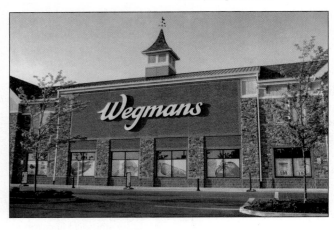

So, treat people not merely as a cost to be controlled but an asset to be developed.[56] Many companies have programs that provide personal growth experiences for their people. For example, associates at W. L. Gore are encouraged to reach their full potential by developing their talents, enjoying their work, and directing their own work activities.[57]

Organizations gain by making full use of their human resources, and employees gain by capitalizing on opportunities to meet their higher-order needs on the job. Wegmans Food Markets, known for its high-quality workforce, invests heavily in training and developing its people. It spends $50 million each year to allow employees to travel to supplier partners and to participate in programs such as department universities, workshops, Dale Carnegie training, cooking technique certifications, and more.[58] Employees feel secure in their jobs, enjoy friendships with co-workers and customers, and experience a sense of achievement.

Alderfer's ERG Theory

Maslow's theory has general applicability, but Alderfer aimed his ERG theory expressly at understanding people's needs at work.[59]

Alderfer's ERG theory

A human needs theory postulating that people have three basic sets of needs that can operate simultaneously.

Alderfer's ERG theory postulates three sets of needs: existence, relatedness, and growth. Existence needs are all material and physiological desires. Relatedness needs involve relationships with other people and are satisfied through the process of mutually sharing thoughts and feelings. Growth needs motivate people to change themselves or their environment productively or creatively. Satisfaction of the growth needs comes from fully using personal capacities and developing new capacities.

What similarities do you see between Alderfer's and Maslow's needs? Roughly speaking, existence needs subsume physiological and security needs, relatedness needs are similar to social and esteem needs, and growth needs correspond to self-actualization.

ERG theory proposes that several needs can operate at once. Whereas Maslow said that self-actualization is important to people only after other sets of needs are satisfied, Alderfer suggests that employees can be motivated on the job to satisfy existence, relatedness, and growth needs at the same time.

Maslow's theory is better known to American managers than Alderfer's, but ERG theory has more research support.[60] Both have practical value in that they remind managers of the types of reinforcers or outcomes that can be used to motivate people. Regardless of whether a manager prefers the Maslow or the Alderfer theory, she can motivate people by helping them satisfy their needs, particularly by offering opportunities for self-actualization and growth.

McClelland's Needs

David McClelland also identified a number of basic needs that motivate people. The most important needs for managers, according to McClelland, are the needs for achievement, affiliation, and power.[61] Different needs predominate for different people. As you read about these needs, think about yourself—which ones are most and least important to you?

The *need for achievement* is characterized by a strong orientation toward accomplishment and an obsession with success and goal attainment. Most managers and entrepreneurs in the United States have high levels of this need and like to see it in their employees.

The *need for affiliation* reflects a strong desire to interact with and be liked by other people. Individuals who have high levels of this need are oriented toward getting along with others and may be less concerned with achieving at high levels.

The *need for power* is a desire to influence or control other people. This need can be a negative force—termed *personalized power*—if it is expressed by aggressively manipulating and exploiting others. People high on the personalized power need want power purely for the pursuit of their own goals. But the need for power also can be a positive motive—called *socialized power*—because it can be channeled toward constructively helping people, organizations, and societies.

Low need for affiliation and moderate to high need for power are associated with managerial success for both higher- and lower-level managers.[62] One reason the need for affiliation is not necessary for leadership success is that people high on this need have difficulty making tough but necessary decisions that will make some people unhappy.

Don't Forget: People Can Differ

A 2014 survey found that employees in Canada were most attracted by competitive pay, work–life balance, and opportunities for advancement; in Germany by autonomy, in Japan by high-quality co-workers; in the Netherlands by a collaborative work environment; and in the United States by competitive health benefits. No single human need or work environment is always the most motivating; managers can customize their approaches by considering how individuals differ both within and between cultures, and over time.

Designing Motivating Jobs

Here's an example of a reward that didn't motivate. One of Mary Kay Ash's former employers gave her a sales award: a flounder-fishing light. Unfortunately, she didn't fish. Fortunately, she later was able to design her own organization, Mary Kay Cosmetics, around intrinsic as well as extrinsic motivators that mattered to her people.[63]

Jobs can be rewarding both extrinsically and intrinsically.[64] **Extrinsic rewards** are given to people by the boss, the company, or some other person. In contrast, a person derives an **intrinsic reward** directly from performing the job itself. An interesting project, an intriguing subject that is fun to study, a completed sale, helping a co-worker achieve a difficult task, and the discovery of the perfect solution to a difficult problem all can give people the feeling that they have done something meaningful and well. As an example, the nearby "Social Entrepreneurship" box discusses how one organization is providing intrinsic rewards to veterans in the form of a renewed sense of purpose.

If you have learned elsewhere that extrinsic rewards are bad things because they decrease intrinsic motivation, be aware that those findings come primarily from laboratory research using students. In the world of working adults, the two types of rewards together[65] can

LO 13-6 Define ways to create jobs that motivate.

extrinsic reward

Reward given to a person by the boss, the company, or some other person.

intrinsic reward

Reward a worker derives directly from performing the job itself.

Social Entrepreneurship

Veterans on a Mission

Shortly after returning from his deployments in Iraq and Afghanistan, Marine veteran Jake Wood co-founded Team Rubicon. Staffed by veterans, his organization bridges the gap between the moment a natural disaster happens and the time at which conventional aid organizations respond. Wood seeks to solve two problems. The first is that many aid organizations are not equipped or trained to respond rapidly during the crucial window of time immediately following a disaster. The second is the suboptimal way that many veterans are reintegrated into society after serving in the military. Veterans have a unique set of skills and experiences that are ideal for disaster relief situations. Many veterans also say they miss the intense sense of teamwork they felt while they were serving.

Team Rubicon provides veterans with three things they lose after leaving the military:

1. *Purpose:* Doing important, meaningful work, in this case helping survivors of natural disasters.
2. *Community:* Continuing to protect and serve others through cohesive team efforts.
3. *Identity:* Providing a sense of accomplishment and self-worth gained from understanding the difference one person can make.

Since its founding in 2010 when it formed to provide relief in the initial days following the earthquake in Haiti, Team Rubicon has made a positive impact on survivors of many disasters around the world, including the contaminated water emergency in Flint, Michigan; the surge of refugees in Greece; an outbreak of Ebola in Sierra Leone; a dam failure in Nevada; the devastating wildfire in Gatlinburg, Tennessee; and Hurricane Harvey, which devastated southeastern Texas. Team Rubicon has responded to more than

Justin Sullivan/Getty Images

250 disasters with the help of over 80,000 volunteers, nearly 80 percent of them veterans.[66]

Disaster relief missions are highly motivating for veterans, and their skills bring victims badly needed assistance, medical supplies, and other forms of relief until organizations like the Red Cross arrive. Not only do Team Rubicon staff and volunteers bring assistance, they end up saving lives. The critical aid Team Rubicon provides to those in crisis around the world was recognized in 2018 when co-founder Jake Wood was presented with ESPY's Pat Tillman Award for Service.[67]

- What types of rewards are likely to keep veterans who work for Team Rubicon motivated: extrinsic, intrinsic, or both? Why?

- How and to what degree do you think Team Rubicon will make a positive impact on natural disaster victims?

motivate powerfully. People expect extrinsic rewards for their work; they will be all the more motivated if their jobs are intrinsically rewarding as well.

Intrinsic rewards are essential to the motivation that drives creativity.[68] A challenging problem, a chance to create something new, and work that is exciting in and of itself can provide intrinsic motivation that inspires people to devote time and energy to the task. So do managers who allow people some freedom to pursue the tasks that interest them most. The opposite situations result in routine, habitual behaviors that interfere with creativity.[69] In manufacturing facilities, researchers found that employees initiated more applications for patents, made more novel and useful suggestions, and were rated by their managers as more creative when their jobs were challenging and their managers did not control their activities closely.[70]

Some managers and organizations create environments that quash creativity and motivation.[71] The classic example of a demotivating job is the highly specialized assembly line job; each worker performs one boring operation before passing the work along to the next worker. Such specialization, the mechanistic approach to job design, was the prevailing practice in the United States through most of the 20th century.[72] But jobs that are too simple and routine result in employee dissatisfaction, absenteeism, and turnover.

Especially in industries that depend on highly motivated knowledge workers, keeping talented employees may require letting them design their own jobs so their work is more interesting than it would be elsewhere. [73] Designing jobs in the following ways can make them more intrinsically motivating.

Job Rotation, Enlargement, and Enrichment

With **job rotation**, workers who otherwise would spend all their time in one routine task can instead move from one task to another. Rather than working in a single section of a department store, an employee might rotate (with training) through housewares, shoes, and toys. Job rotation is intended to alleviate boredom by giving people different things to do at different times.

As you may guess, however, the person may just be changing from one boring job to another. But job rotation can benefit everyone when done properly, with people's input and career interests in mind. Blue Cross and Blue Shield of North Carolina hires college graduates straight out of school to join its Rotational Development Program, a full-time, two-year program that focuses on developing future leaders.[74]

Job enlargement is similar to job rotation in that people are given different tasks to do. But whereas job rotation involves doing one task at one time and changing to a different task at a different time, job enlargement means that the worker has multiple tasks at the same time. Thus an assembly worker's job is enlarged if he or she is given two tasks rather than one to perform. At a financial services firm, enlarged jobs led to higher job satisfaction, better error detection by clerks, and improved customer service.[75]

With job enlargement, the person's additional tasks are at the same level of responsibility. **Job enrichment**, however, creates more profound changes by adding higher levels of responsibility. This practice includes giving people not only more tasks but higher-level ones, such as making more important decisions. The first approach to job enrichment was Herzberg's two-factor theory, followed by the Hackman and Oldham model.

Herzberg's Two-Factor Theory

Frederick Herzberg's **two-factor theory** distinguished between two broad categories of factors that affect people in their jobs.[76] The first category, **hygiene factors**, are characteristics of the workplace: company policies, working conditions, pay, co-workers, supervision, and so forth. These factors can make people unhappy if they are poorly managed. If they are well managed and viewed as positive by employees, the employees will no longer be dissatisfied. However, no matter how good these factors are, they will not make people truly satisfied or motivated to do a good job.

According to Herzberg, the key to true job satisfaction and motivation to perform lies in the second category: the motivators. The **motivators** describe the job itself—that is, what people *do* at work. Motivators are the nature of the work itself, the actual job responsibilities, opportunity for personal growth and recognition, and the feelings of achievement the job provides when people perform well. When these factors are present, jobs are both satisfying and motivating for most people.

Herzberg's theory has been criticized by many scholars, and for that reason we will not go into more detail about the theory. But Herzberg was a pioneer in the area of job design and still is a respected name. Furthermore, even if the specifics of his theory do not hold up to scientific scrutiny, he made several important contributions. First, Herzberg's theory highlights the important distinction between extrinsic rewards (hygiene factors) and intrinsic rewards (motivators). Second, it reminds managers not to count solely on extrinsic factors to motivate workers, but to focus on intrinsic rewards as well. Third, it set the stage for later theories, such as the Hackman and Oldham model, that explain more precisely how managers can enrich people's jobs.

Intrinsic rewards are essential to the motivation underlying creativity.

Bottom Line

Intrinsic rewards and the freedom to be creative are keys to creativity. *Why might an employee be more creative when a job is intrinsically rewarding?*

job rotation

Changing from one task to another to alleviate boredom.

job enlargement

Giving people additional tasks at the same time to alleviate boredom.

job enrichment

Changing a task to make it inherently more rewarding, motivating, and satisfying.

two-factor theory

Herzberg's theory describing two factors affecting people's work motivation and satisfaction.

hygiene factors

Characteristics of the workplace, such as company policies, working conditions, pay, and supervision, that can make people dissatisfied.

motivators

Factors that make a job more motivating, such as additional job responsibilities, opportunities for personal growth and recognition, and feelings of achievement.

The Hackman and Oldham Model of Job Design

Following Herzberg's work, Hackman and Oldham proposed a more complete model of job design.[77] Exhibit 13.6 illustrates their model. As you can see, well-designed jobs lead to high motivation, high-quality performance, high satisfaction, and low absenteeism and turnover. These outcomes occur when people experience three critical psychological states shown in the middle column of the figure:

1. They believe they are doing something meaningful because their work is important to other people.
2. They feel personally responsible for how the work turns out.
3. They learn how well they perform their jobs.

These psychological states occur when people are working on enriched jobs—that is, jobs that offer the following five core dimensions:

1. *Skill variety*—different job activities involving several skills and talents. SAS, a business analytics software company, wants its knowledge workers to continually grow by adding new skills. The goal is to keep employees "challenged, motivated, and engaged."[78]
2. *Task identity*—the completion of a whole, identifiable piece of work. At State Farm Insurance, agents are independent contractors who sell and provide service for State Farm products exclusively. They have built and invested in their own businesses. As a result, agent retention and productivity are far better than industry norms.[79]
3. *Task significance*—an important, positive impact on the lives of others. A study of lifeguards found dramatic improvements in their performance if they were taught about how lifeguards make a difference by preventing deaths. Lifeguards who were told simply that the job can be personally enriching showed no such improvements.[80]
4. *Autonomy*—independence and discretion in making decisions. 3M encourages employees to spend up to 15 percent of their time pursuing exciting, innovative ideas. The company's strategy has resulted in several innovations, including Post-it

EXHIBIT 13.6

The Hackman and Oldham Model of Job Enrichment

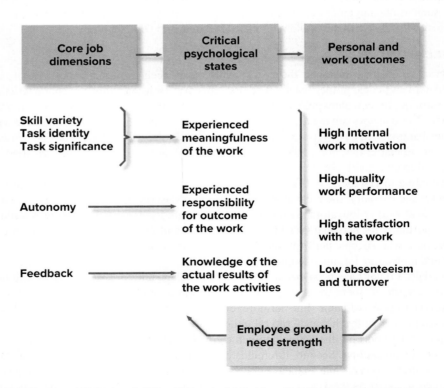

SOURCE: Hackman, J. Richard, et al., "A New Strategy for Job Enrichment," *California Management Review* 17, no. 4 (Summer 1975), pp. 57–71.

Notes. Former president and chairman, William McKnight put it succinctly: "Hire good people and leave them alone."[81]

5. *Feedback*—information about job performance. Many companies provide information on productivity, quality, and other performance indicators. Ride-sharing firms like Uber and Lyft encourage customers to submit online reviews of their trip experience—thousands of reviews every day—which is a powerful source of motivation for drivers.

The most effective job enrichment increases all five core dimensions.

A person's growth need strength will help determine how effective a job enrichment program might be. **Growth need strength** is the degree to which an individual wants personal and psychological development. Job enrichment would be more successful for people with high growth need strength. But very few people respond negatively to job enrichment.[82]

Empowerment and Engagement

We frequently hear managers talk about empowering their people.[83] Individuals may—or may not—feel empowered, and groups can have a culture of empowerment that predicts work unit performance.[84] **Empowerment** is the process of sharing power with employees, thereby enhancing their confidence in their ability to perform their jobs and their belief that they are influential contributors to the organization.

Unfortunately, empowerment doesn't always live up to its hype. One problem is that managers undermine it by sending mixed messages such as "Do your own thing—the way we tell you."[85] But empowerment can be profoundly motivating when done properly.[86]

To empower people,[87] management must create an environment in which all the employees feel they have real influence over performance standards and business effectiveness within their areas of responsibility. An empowering work environment provides people with information necessary for them to perform at their best, knowledge about how to use the information and how to do their work, power to make decisions that give them control over their work, and the rewards they deserve for the contributions they make.[88]

Empowerment done well leads to higher levels of **employee engagement** and overall performance.[89] Engaged employees invest their physical, mental, and emotional energy into performing their jobs, including working hard and producing, taking initiative, and contributing additional citizenship behaviors. They persevere in achieving their goals and their leader's vision even in the face of obstacles. Ultimately, managed well, they and their units perform at higher levels.[90]

Genuine empowerment—as opposed to its common use as an empty buzzword—engages employees by changing their beliefs from feeling powerless to believing strongly in their own personal effectiveness.[91] People engage because empowering circumstances allow them to feel self-determined: fulfilling their desires for autonomy, relatedness, and competence.[92] When the job fits their values, empowered employees perceive meaning in their work. And they know they have an impact because they have some influence over important strategic, administrative, or operating decisions or outcomes on the job.

When speaking of times when they felt disempowered, people mentioned the following:[93]

- Her reaction to my mistakes made me doubt my abilities. The more upset she got with me, the more responsibilities she took away from me. My confidence was shot.
- Orientation really sounded like "A Hundred Ways You Can Get Fired."
- One HR manager added ten days to the hiring process because he required that his HR staff obtain his signature at certain milestones during the hiring process. His lack of trust made employee empowerment a joke.

In contrast, people felt empowered in the following examples:

- In my current role I have a lot of autonomy, and for me, it is very motivating.
- Once my boss saw that I had a very strong grasp of my role, she welcomed my ideas to expand it. I was encouraged to experiment and find ways to make my role more valuable to the company.
- The initiative wasn't a "company project." It was "my project."

---

growth need strength

The degree to which individuals want personal and psychological development.

---

empowerment

The process of sharing power with employees, thereby enhancing their confidence in their ability to perform their jobs and their belief that they are influential contributors to the organization.

---

employee engagement

When employees invest their physical, mental, and emotional energy into performing their jobs, including working hard and producing, taking initiative, and contributing additional citizenship behaviors.

Bottom Line

Job enrichment and empowerment don't work magic overnight; people may resist the new approaches and make mistakes along the way. But done right, their potential to achieve real results is undeniable. *What might be some differences between empowerment "done right" and "done wrong"?*

Inclusiveness Works

Improving D&I Initiatives with Intrinsic Motivation

Diversity and inclusion (D&I) initiatives are becoming commonplace, which is good news. The bad news, however, is that many of these initiatives aren't doing much to increase diversity or inclusion. In fact, a *Harvard Business Review* article states that in some instances, programs designed to increase diversity are instead resulting in less diversity and reinforcing cultural stereotypes. And when positive results do show up, the benefits seem to be fleeting, disappearing shortly after a D&I training program concludes.[94] How can this be?

The answer, it seems, might reside in how management motivates (or demotivates) its employees to engage with D&I initiatives. It shouldn't come as too much of a surprise that what makes for more rewarding and empowering jobs includes more rewarding and empowering D&I initiatives—intrinsic rewards.

Too often D&I programs are mandated by top management. Employees take a training course or comply with some legal requirement stating they have done what they were told to do. In effect, employees are disempowered; they have no agency in the matter.[95] Not only that, but most D&I programs are framed as something that's done for the good of the organization, not the employees themselves. In either case, there's little or no intrinsic reward to embracing the programs.

The irony is that our beliefs about diversity and inclusion are deeply personal, rooted in us since we were children. So D&I programs should be about reaching one's greatest potential. When we're the master of our own beliefs and behaviors we engage on an intrinsic level, whereby lessons are internalized and adopted for the long term.[96] Research finds that giving employees more choice in when and how to engage in D&I initiatives adds to this sense of agency and intrinsic purpose, ultimately leading to better results.[97]

- How do you think encouraging more intrinsic motivation in employees will lead to greater engagement in D&I programs?
- Why do you think so many D&I initiatives are unsuccessful? What factors drive the success and failure of such programs?

You should not be surprised when a new empowerment program causes some problems, at least in the short term. This occurs with virtually any change, including changes for the better. It's important to remember that with empowerment comes responsibility, and employees don't necessarily like the extra accountability at first.[98] People may make mistakes at first, especially until they receive training. And because more training is needed, costs are higher.

Furthermore, because people acquire new skills, engage more fully, and make greater contributions, they may expect or demand higher wages. But if they are well trained and truly empowered, they will deserve them—and both they and the company will benefit.

Achieving Fairness

LO 13-7 Summarize how people assess fairness and how to achieve fairness.

---

equity theory

A theory stating that people assess how fairly they have been treated according to two key factors: outcomes and inputs.

Ultimately, one of the most important issues in motivation is how people view their contributions to the organization and what they receive from the organization. Ideally, they will view their relationship with their employer as a well-balanced, mutually beneficial exchange. People assess (1) the contributions they make in their work, and (2) the positive and negative outcomes they receive—overall, how fairly the organization treats them.[99]

The starting point for understanding how people interpret their contributions and outcomes is equity theory.[100] **Equity theory** proposes that when people assess how fairly they are treated, they consider two key factors: outcomes and inputs. Outcomes, as in expectancy theory, refer to the various things the person receives on the job: recognition, pay, benefits, satisfaction, security, job assignments, punishments, and so forth. Inputs refer to the contributions the person makes to their employer: effort, time, talent, performance, extra commitment, good citizenship, and so forth. People have a general expectation that the outcomes they receive will reflect, or be proportionate to, the inputs they provide—a fair day's pay (and other outcomes) for a fair day's work (broadly defined by how people view all their contributions).

But this comparison of outcomes to inputs is not the whole story. People also pay attention to the outcomes and inputs others receive. At salary review time, for example, most people—from executives on down—try to pick up clues that will tell them who got the highest raises. As described in the following section, they compare ratios, try to restore equity if necessary, and derive more or less satisfaction based on how fairly they believe they have been treated.

Equity theory suggests that people compare the ratio of their outcomes to inputs against the outcome-to-input ratio of some comparison person. How would you deal with someone you perceive to be a slacker who gets promoted over you?

imtmphoto/Shutterstock

Assessing Equity

Equity theory states that people compare the ratio of their own outcomes to inputs against the outcome-to-input ratio of some comparison person. The comparison person can be a fellow student, a co-worker, a boss, or an average industry pay scale. Stated more succinctly, people compare their own outcomes and inputs to those of a comparison person (see Exhibit 13.7). If the ratios are equivalent, people believe the relationship is equitable, or fair. Equity causes people to be satisfied with their treatment. But the person who believes his or her ratio is lower than another's will feel inequitably treated. Inequity causes dissatisfaction and leads to an attempt to restore balance to the relationship.

Inequity and the negative feelings it creates can appear anywhere. As a student, perhaps you have been in the following situation. You stay up all night and get a C on the exam. Meanwhile another student studies a couple of hours, goes out for the rest of the evening, gets a good night's sleep, and gets a higher grade. You perceive your inputs (time spent studying) as much greater than the other student's, but your outcomes (exam grade) are lower. It doesn't feel fair, and you are not happy.

In business, the same thing can happen with pay raises. One manager puts in long weeks, has a degree from a prestigious university, and believes she is destined for the top. When her archrival—whom she perceives as less deserving ("she never comes into the office on weekends, and all she does when she is here is butter up the boss")—gets the higher raise or the promotion, she feels serious inequity.

Assessments of equity are not made objectively. They are subjective perceptions or beliefs. In the preceding examples, the person who got the higher raise probably felt she deserved it. Even if she admits she doesn't put in long workweeks, she may convince herself she doesn't need to

EXHIBIT 13.7   Equity Theory

Comparing Your Ratio to Other's Ratio			Your Likely Perception	Actions You May Take to Restore Equity
$\frac{\text{Your Outcomes}}{\text{Your Inputs}}$	=	$\frac{\text{Other's Outcomes}}{\text{Other's Inputs}}$	Equitably treated.	No action necessary.
$\frac{\text{Your Outcomes}}{\text{Your Inputs}}$	<	$\frac{\text{Other's Outcomes}}{\text{Other's Inputs}}$	Inequitably treated. Feel underrewarded.	Reduce your inputs (e.g., exert less effort). Try to increase your outcomes (e.g., ask for a raise). Change your perception of inputs or outcomes (e.g., maybe so-and-so really did deserve the bonus).
$\frac{\text{Your Outcomes}}{\text{Your Inputs}}$	>	$\frac{\text{Other's Outcomes}}{\text{Other's Inputs}}$	Inequitably treated. Feel overrewarded.	Increase your inputs by putting in extra effort. Help other person increase her outcomes (e.g., urge her to ask for a larger bonus).

because she's so talented. The student who got the higher grade may believe it was a fair, equitable result because (1) she kept up all semester, while the other student did not, and (2) she's extra-smart. (Ability and experience, not just time and effort, can be seen as inputs.)

Restoring Equity

People who feel inequitably treated and dissatisfied are motivated to do something to restore equity. They have a number of options to change the ratios, or reevaluate the situation and decide it is equitable after all.

The equity equation shown earlier indicates a person's options for restoring equity. People who feel inequitably treated can reduce their inputs by giving less effort, performing at lower levels, or quitting. ("Well, if that's the way things work around here, there's no way I'm going to work that hard [or stick around].") Or they can attempt to increase their outcomes. ("My boss [or teacher] is going to hear about this. I deserve more; there must be some way I can get more.")

On the positive side, employees can also put forth extra effort to keep a situation equitable for the group. When people see their colleagues working hard to meet an important deadline, they may be inclined to work harder themselves.

Other ways of restoring equity focus on changing the other person's ratio. A person can decrease others' outcomes. An employee may sabotage work to create problems for his company or his boss.[101] A person can change her perceptions of inputs or outcomes. ("That promotion isn't as great a deal as he thinks. The pay is not that much better, and the headaches will be unbelievable.") It is also possible to increase others' inputs, particularly by changing perceptions. ("The more I think about it, the more I see he deserved it. He's worked hard all year, he's competent, and it's about time he got a break.")

Thus a person can restore equity in a number of ways by behaviorally or perceptually changing inputs and outcomes.

Procedural Justice

procedural justice

Using fair processes in decision making and making sure others know that the process was as fair as possible.

Inevitably, managers make decisions that have outcomes more favorable for some than for others. Those with favorable outcomes will be pleased; those with worse outcomes, all else equal, will be displeased. But managers desiring to put salve on the wounds—say, of people they like or respect or want to keep and motivate—still can take actions to reduce the dissatisfaction. The key is for people to believe that managers provide **procedural justice**—using fair process in decision making.[102] When people perceive procedural fairness, they are more likely to support decisions and decision makers.[103] For example, nurses who perceived their performance evaluations as fair were more likely to remain in their jobs.[104]

You can increase people's beliefs that the process was fair by making the process open and visible; stating decision criteria in advance rather than after the fact; making sure that the most appropriate people—those who have valid information and are viewed as trustworthy—make the decisions; giving people a chance to participate in the process; and providing an appeal process that allows people to question decisions safely and receive complete answers.[105] However, the impact of procedural justice can differ by country and culture[106]—for instance, the impact is strongest among nations characterized by individualism, uncertainty avoidance, and low power distance (recall Chapter 6).[107]

At an elevator plant in the United States, an army of consultants arrived one day, unexplained and annoying.[108] The rumor mill kicked in; employees thought the plant was to be shut down or that some of them would be laid off. Three months later, management unveiled its new plan, involving a new method of manufacturing based on teams. As the changes were implemented, management did not adequately answer questions about the purpose of the changes, employees resisted, conflicts arose, and the formerly popular plant manager lost the trust of his people. Costs skyrocketed, and quality plummeted.

Concerned, management conducted a survey. Employees were skeptical that the results would lead to any positive changes and were worried that management would be angry that people had voiced their honest opinions. But management reacted by saying, "We were wrong, we screwed up, we didn't use the right process." They went on to share with employees critical business information, the limited options available, and the dire consequences if the company didn't change.

Employees saw the dilemma and came to view the business problem as theirs as well as management's, but they were scared that some of them would lose their jobs. Management retained the right to lay people off if business conditions grew worse but also made several promises: no layoffs as a result of changes made, cross-training programs for employees, no replacements of departing people until conditions improved, a chance for employees to serve in new roles as consultants on quality issues, and sharing of sales and cost data on a regular basis.

The news was bad, but people understood it and began to accept a greater share of responsibility along with management. Trust and commitment began to return, as did stronger performance.

Employee Satisfaction and Well-Being

If people feel fairly treated from the outcomes they receive and the processes used, they will be satisfied. A satisfied worker is not necessarily more productive than a dissatisfied one; sometimes people are happy with their jobs because they don't have to work hard! But job dissatisfaction, aggregated across many individuals, creates a workforce that is more likely to exhibit (1) higher turnover; (2) higher absenteeism; (3) less good citizenship;[109] (4) more grievances and lawsuits; (5) strikes; (6) stealing, sabotage, and vandalism; (7) poorer mental and physical health (which can mean higher job stress, higher insurance costs, and more lawsuits);[110] (8) more injuries;[111] (9) poor customer service;[112] and (10) lower productivity and profits.[113] All of these consequences of dissatisfaction, either directly or indirectly, are costly to organizations.

Sadly, most people are dissatisfied with their jobs, with the greatest dissatisfaction among lower wage earners and workers aged 25 and younger.[114]

Regarding how it affects job performance, job satisfaction is especially important for relationship-oriented service employees such as realtors, hair stylists, and stockbrokers. Customers develop (or don't develop) a commitment to a specific service provider. Satisfied service providers are less likely to quit the company and more likely to provide an enjoyable customer experience.[115]

Quality of Work Life

Quality of work life is a decades-old but still highly useful concept. **Quality of work life (QWL) programs** create a workplace that enhances employee job satisfaction and overall physical and mental well-being.[116] The general goal of QWL programs is to satisfy the full range of employee needs. Promoting QWL is a social and political cause that sprang originally from the establishment of democratic societies and basic human rights.[117]

Traditionally, QWL has at least eight categories:[118]

1. Adequate and fair compensation.
2. A safe and healthy environment.
3. Jobs that develop human capacities.
4. A chance for personal growth and security.
5. A social environment that fosters personal identity, freedom from prejudice, a sense of community, and upward mobility.
6. Constitutionalism, or the rights of personal privacy, dissent, and due process.
7. A work role that minimizes infringement on personal leisure and family needs.
8. Socially responsible organizational actions.

Organizations differ drastically in their attention to QWL. Critics claim that QWL programs don't necessarily inspire employees to work harder if the company does not tie rewards directly to their job performance. Advocates of QWL claim that it improves

LO 13-8 Identify causes and consequences of a (dis)satisfied workforce.

Bottom Line

One satisfied employee doesn't necessarily produce well on every performance dimension. But an organization full of people with high job satisfaction will likely perform well in many ways. *In a company with a strategy focused on low cost, how is employee satisfaction important?*

quality of work life (QWL) programs

Programs designed to create a workplace that enhances employee well-being.

The Digital World

Using Technology to Motivate

In today's competitive business landscape, companies try to find creative new ways to engage, motivate, and retain their employees that go beyond bonuses, free lunches, and workplace gyms. Companies are finding that one powerful way to motivate employees involves technology. Here are just a few ways companies are using technology to motivate their employees:

- Some companies are using apps like Google Drive, Slack, and Dropbox to enable employees to connect, collaborate, and communicate with each other in simple ways that were not possible before.[119] By making collaboration easier, companies motivate their employees to stay connected and committed to a team.
- Today, almost all employees use mobile devices to connect with their workplaces no matter where they are. Such mobility enables—and motivates—employees to work from offsite locations when and where they want, providing the flexibility that many workers seek from their jobs.[120]
- Augmented and virtual reality training are also engaging workers in fun and new ways, helping them to acquire needed on-the-job skills in a way that motivates them to continue learning.[121]
- Companies are also turning to HR software to provide employees with better real-time performance feedback, helping to promote desired behaviors and a sense of engagement.[122]

Using technology to motivate employees works best in a culture that truly values its people, not just through its perks but in the way company leaders view and treat their employees.[123]

1. Of the four ways of employing technology to enhance motivation discussed here, which do you think would be the most effective? Why?
2. In what ways does technology motivate you? At school? At work?

organizational effectiveness and productivity overall. The term *productivity,* as applied by QWL programs, means much more than each person's quantity of work output.[124] It also includes attendance, work quality, innovation, citizenship behaviors, and countless other contributions that committed people make.

All in all, people's satisfaction and well-being have many important consequences, beneficial to both employees and employers.[125] These range from better attitudes and health to work behaviors and performance, and ultimately include firm value[126] and other business outcomes.[127] Win–win solutions are indeed possible in a well-managed workplace.

Psychological Contracts

psychological contract

A set of perceptions of what employees owe their employers, and what their employers owe them.

The relationship between individuals and employing organizations typically is formalized by a written contract. But in employees' minds, there also exists a **psychological contract**—a set of perceptions of what they owe their employers and what their employers owe them.[128] This contract, whether it is seen as being upheld or violated—and whether the parties trust one another or not—has important implications for how people judge equity, fairness, and justice, how satisfied and motivated they are, and organizational effectiveness. Experiencing significant breach of psychological contract will harm those things and people's physical and mental health.[129]

The nature of the employer–employee relationship, and what each expects from the other, changes as the times change.[130] Historically, in big companies, the employment relationship was stable and predictable. But mergers, layoffs, and other disruptions tore apart the old deal.[131] As one executive put it, "The 'used-to-be's' must give way to the realities of 'What is and what will be.'"[132]

The fundamental used-to-be of traditionally managed organizations was that employees were expected to be loyal, and employers would provide secure employment. But now the implicit contract goes something like this:[133] If people stay, do their own jobs plus someone else's (who has been downsized), and do additional things such as participating in task forces, the company will try to provide a job (if it can), provide gestures that it cares, and keep providing more or less the same pay (with periodic small increases).

The likely result of this not-very-satisfying arrangement: uninspired people and a business trying to survive. Career advisers tell disillusioned employees to think of themselves as free agents and to change jobs when a new option beckons.

But a better deal is possible, for both employers and employees.[134] Ideally, your employer will provide continuous skill updating and an invigorating work environment in which you can use your skills and are motivated to stay even if you have other job options.[135] The employer says, in essence, "If you make us more valuable, we'll make you more valuable," and the employee says, "If you help me grow, I'll help the company grow." The company benefits from your contributions, and you thrive in your work while you also become more marketable if and when you decide to look elsewhere. Employment is an alliance—perhaps temporary, perhaps long term—aimed at helping both employer and employee succeed.[136] The results of such a contract are much more likely to be a mutually beneficial and satisfying relationship and a high-performing, successful organization.

Finally, consider how these ideas for motivation apply at SAS. Read the "Management in Action: Onward" feature, and ask yourself whether old-fashioned stable employment relationships can—or should—be the norm.

Management in Action

HOW THE SAS CULTURE LEADS TO EMPLOYEE SATISFACTION

MANAGER'S BRIEF

PROGRESS REPORT

ONWARD

Jennifer Mann, SAS's executive vice president of human resources, says, "At SAS, our goal is to offer meaningful work for our employees, an empowering management philosophy, and a world-class work environment."[137] Mann sees a welcoming and respectful workplace as foundational to the company's success.

What convinces employees that SAS values their contributions? We have already talked about employee benefits, but it's the culture of SAS that seems to be the biggest difference. And that culture starts at the top. CEO James Goodnight puts his time and money on the line for his people.

In 2008, for example, as a financial crisis gave way to the Great Recession, other software companies announced major layoffs, and SAS employees became nervous. Goodnight spoke to all of them via webcast, saying there would be no layoffs; they just all needed to be more frugal. Not only did the company weather that economic downturn, it continued growing and developed new products to launch as the economy recovered. Loyalty is a two-way street. Goodnight shows his loyalty to his employees, and in return, they demonstrate their loyalty to him and SAS's vision as a whole. It's not a coincidence that SAS has a very low turnover rate of approximately 5 percent compared to an industry average that is typically more than 20 percent.

The culture of SAS also respects employees' time. The company's standard workweek is just 35 hours. "I don't expect people to work 60 to 70 hours a week. It's been my experience, much past 40 hours a week and you're writing pretty worthless code, which you spend the next day unraveling," says Goodnight.[138] The company's onsite facilities and beautiful grounds make it easy for employees to take a break to work out, get a haircut or massage, or go for a hike. Managers don't worry that employees will goof off; they find that trust motivates employees to work hard to please customers and help the company succeed. A similar attitude of trust applies to sick days at SAS, which are unlimited.

SAS also ensures that work is meaningful. Goodnight reminds employees that SAS software is useful to people all over the world. Programmers' work is designed so they feel ownership of their creations. Even the landscapers at headquarters are assigned to particular plots, so these employees enjoy imparting beauty to that parcel and feel the same identification with the company as any programmer does.[139] As Keisha Simpson, an SAS IT manager, states on the company website, "'SAS' culture allows its employees to set and achieve limitless goals."[140]

- How closely aligned do you feel employee satisfaction is to productivity? To what degree does a firm's culture contribute to employee satisfaction?
- If you were trying to motivate a workforce, what strategies would you use?

KEY TERMS

Alderfer's ERG theory, p. 410

employee engagement, p. 415

empowerment, p. 415

equity theory, p. 416

expectancy, p. 406

expectancy theory, p. 406

extinction, p. 404

extrinsic reward, p. 411

goal-setting theory, p. 401

growth need strength, p. 415

hygiene factors, p. 413

instrumentality, p. 407

intrinsic reward, p. 411

job enlargement, p. 413

job enrichment, p. 413

job rotation, p. 413

law of effect, p. 403

Maslow's need hierarchy, p. 409

motivation, p. 400

motivators, p. 413

negative reinforcement, p. 403

organizational behavior modification (OB mod), p. 403

outcome, p. 407

positive reinforcement, p. 403

procedural justice, p. 418

psychological contract, p. 420

punishment, p. 403

quality of work life (QWL) programs, p. 419

reinforcers, p. 403

stretch goals, p. 402

two-factor theory, p. 413

valence, p. 407

RETAINING WHAT YOU LEARNED

In Chapter 13, you learned that managers can motivate employees in a variety of ways. Goals that are specific, quantifiable, and challenging are powerful tools for motivating individuals and teams. Organizations develop programs that use different types of reinforcement to influence employees' behaviors. Managers should reinforce appropriate behaviors, manage mistakes properly, and provide useful feedback. Expectancy theory states that employees are motivated when they believe they can perform a job well and their performance will be rewarded with a valued outcome. People's needs affect their behaviors at work. Maslow and Alderfer offered similar need theories of motivation. McClelland said people vary in the extent to which they need achievement, affiliation, and power. Managers can create motivating jobs by making them intrinsically rewarding. Jobs can be enriched by building in skill variety, task identity, task significance, autonomy, and feedback. Employees with jobs that have the necessary information, knowledge, power, and rewards feel empowered. Equity theory explores how an individual's perceptions of fairness can lead to either feeling satisfied or dissatisfied at work. A satisfied workforce has many advantages for the firm, including lower absenteeism and turnover; fewer grievances, lawsuits, and strikes; lower health costs; and higher-quality work. A psychological contract is a set of perceptions of what employees think they owe their employer and what they think their employer owes them.

LO 13-1   Identify the kinds of behaviors managers need to motivate in people.

- All important work behaviors are motivated.
- Managers need to motivate employees to join and remain in the organization and to exhibit high attendance, job performance, and citizenship.

LO 13-2   List principles for setting goals that motivate employees.

- Goal setting is a powerful motivator. Specific, quantifiable, and challenging but attainable goals motivate high effort and performance.

- Goal setting can be used for teams as well as for individuals.
- Care should be taken to avoid setting single goals to the exclusion of other important dimensions of performance.
- Managers also should keep sight of the other potential downsides of goals.

LO 13-3   Summarize how to reward good performance effectively.

- Organizational behavior modification programs influence work behavior by arranging consequences for people's actions.
- Most programs use positive reinforcement as a consequence, but other important consequences are negative reinforcement, punishment, and extinction.
- Care must be taken to reinforce appropriate, not inappropriate, behavior.
- Innovative managers use a wide variety of rewards for good performance.
- They also understand how to manage mistakes and provide useful feedback.

LO 13-4   Describe the key beliefs that affect people's motivation.

- Expectancy theory describes three important work-related beliefs.
- Motivation is a function of people's (1) expectancies, or effort-to-performance links; (2) instrumentalities, or performance-to-outcome links; and (3) valences that they attach to the outcomes of performance.

LO 13-5   Discuss ways in which people's individual needs affect their behavior.

- According to Maslow, important needs arise at five levels of a hierarchy: physiological, safety, social, ego, and self-actualization needs.

- Focusing more on the context of work, Alderfer's ERG theory described three sets of needs: existence, relatedness, and growth.
- McClelland stated that people vary in their needs for achievement, affiliation, and power.
- Because people are inclined to satisfy their own needs, these theories tell managers the kinds of rewards that motivate people.

LO 13-6 Define ways to create jobs that motivate.

- One approach to motivating people is to create intrinsic motivation through redesigning jobs.
- Jobs can be enriched by building in more skill variety, task identity, task significance, autonomy, and feedback.
- Empowerment includes perceived meaning, competence, self-determination, and impact. These qualities come from an environment in which people have necessary information, knowledge, power, and rewards.

LO 13-7 Summarize how people assess fairness and how to achieve fairness.

- Equity theory states that people compare their inputs and outcomes to the inputs and outcomes of others.

- Perceptions of equity (fairness) are satisfying; feelings of inequity (unfairness) are dissatisfying and motivate people to change their behavior or their perceptions to restore equity.
- In addition to fairness of outcomes, as described in equity theory, fairness is also appraised and managed through procedural justice.

LO 13-8 Identify causes and consequences of a (dis)satisfied workforce.

- A satisfied workforce has many advantages for the firm, including: lower absenteeism and turnover; fewer grievances, lawsuits, and strikes; lower health costs; and higher-quality work.
- One general approach to generating higher satisfaction for people is to implement a quality of work life program. QWL seeks to provide a safe and healthy environment, opportunity for personal growth, a positive social environment, fair treatment, and other improvements in people's work lives.
- These and other benefits from the organization, exchanged for contributions from employees, create a psychological contract.
- Over time, how the psychological contract is upheld or violated will influence people's satisfaction and motivation.

DISCUSSION QUESTIONS

1. Think of a significant mistake you've seen someone make on a job. How did the boss handle it, and what was the effect?

2. It is difficult for managers to empower their people successfully, in part because the process is not simple but complex. Discuss in depth.

3. Think of a job you hold or held in the past. How would you describe the psychological contract? How does (did) this affect your attitudes and behaviors on the job?

4. If a famous executive or sports figure were to give a passionate motivational speech, trying to persuade people to work harder, what do you think the impact would be? Why?

5. Give some examples of situations in which you wanted to do a great job but were prevented from doing so. What was the impact on you, and what would this teach you as you try to motivate other people to perform?

6. Discuss the similarities and differences between setting goals for other people and setting goals for yourself. When does goal setting fail, and when does it succeed?

7. Identify four examples of people inadvertently reinforcing the wrong behaviors or punishing or extinguishing good behaviors.

8. Assess yourself on McClelland's three needs. On which need are you highest, and on which are you lowest? What are the implications for you as a manager?

9. Identify a job you have held and appraise it on Hackman and Oldham's five core job dimensions. Also describe the degree to which it made you feel empowered. As a class, choose one job and discuss together how it could be changed to be more motivating and empowering.

10. Using expectancy theory, analyze how you have made and will make personal choices, such as a major area of study, a career to pursue, or job interviews to seek.

11. Describe a time when you felt unfairly treated and explain why. How did you respond to the inequity? What other options might you have had?

12. Provide examples of how outcomes perceived as unfair can decrease motivation. Then discuss how procedural justice, or fair process, can help overcome the negative effects.

13. Describe what you expect of your psychological contract with your employer after your graduation. How will you deal if it doesn't meet your expectations?

14. Set some goals for yourself, considering the relevant discussion in the chapter.

EXPERIENTIAL EXERCISES

13.1   Assessing Yourself

Circle the response that most closely correlates with each of the following items:

	Agree	Neither	Agree nor	Disagree	Disagree
1. I have developed a written list of short- and long-term goals I would like to accomplish.	1	2	3	4	5
2. When setting goals for myself, I give consideration to what my capabilities and limits are.	1	2	3	4	5
3. I set goals that are realistic and attainable.	1	2	3	4	5
4. My goals are based on my hopes and beliefs, not on those of my parents, friends, or significant other.	1	2	3	4	5
5. When I fail to achieve a goal, I get back on track.	1	2	3	4	5
6. My goals are based on my personal values.	1	2	3	4	5
7. I have a current mission statement and have involved those closest to me in formulating it.	1	2	3	4	5
8. I regularly check my progress toward achieving the goals I have set.	1	2	3	4	5
9. When setting goals, I strive for performance, not outcomes.	1	2	3	4	5
10. I have a support system in place—friends, family members, and/or colleagues who believe in me and support my goals.	1	2	3	4	5
11. I apply SMART characteristics to my goals.	1	2	3	4	5
12. I prioritize my goals, focusing only on the most important or valuable ones at a particular point in time.	1	2	3	4	5
13. I reward myself when I achieve a goal or even when I reach a particular milestone.	1	2	3	4	5
14. I revisit my goals periodically and add and modify goals as appropriate.	1	2	3	4	5

Sum your circled responses. If your total is 42 or higher, you might want to explore ways to improve your skill in the area of goal setting.
SOURCE: de Janasz, Suzanne C., Dowd, Karen O. and Schneider, Beth Z., *Interpersonal Skills in Organizations.* New York: McGraw-Hill, 2012, p. 56.

13.2   Personal Goal Setting

1. In the spaces provided, brainstorm your goals in the following categories. Write down as many as you wish including short-, mid-, and long-term goals.

   Academic, intellectual

   Health, fitness

   Social: family, friends, significant other, community

   Career, job

   Financial

   Other

2. Of the goals you have listed, select from each of the six categories the two most important goals that you would like to pursue in the short term (next 6–12 months). Write these here.

   a. _____

   b. _____

   c. _____

d. _____

e. _____

f. _____

g. _____

h. _____

i. _____

j. _____

k. _____

l. _____

3. From the 12 goals listed, choose the 3 that are the most important to you at this time: the 3 you commit to work on in the next few months. Write a goal statement for each one, using the following guidelines:

   Begin each with the word "To . . ."

   Be specific.

Quantify the goal if possible.

Each goal statement should be realistic, attainable, and within your control.

Each goal statement should reflect your aspirations—not those of others such as parents, roommates, significant others, and the like.

a. _____
   _____

b. _____
   _____

c. _____
   _____

4. On a separate sheet of paper, develop an action plan for each goal statement. For each action plan, list the steps you will take to accomplish the goal.

   Include dates (by when) and initials (who's responsible) for each step.

Visualize completing the goal and, working backward, specify each step necessary between now and then to reach the goal.

Identify any potential barriers you might experience in attaining the goal. Problem solve around these obstacles and convert them into steps in your action plan.

Identify the resources you will need to accomplish these goals and build steps to acquire the necessary information into your action plan.

5. Transfer the dates of each step for each goal in your action plan to a daily calendar.

6. Keep an ongoing daily or weekly record of the positive steps you take toward meeting each goal.

SOURCE: de Janasz, Suzanne C., Dowd, Karen O. and Schneider, Beth Z., *Interpersonal Skills in Organizations.* New York: McGraw-Hill, 2012, pp. 75-76. Copyright ©2012 McGraw-Hill Global Education Holdings LLC. All rights reserved. Used with permission.

13.3   What Do Students Want from Their Jobs?

OBJECTIVES

1. To demonstrate individual differences in job expectations.
2. To illustrate individual differences in need and motivational structures.
3. To examine and compare extrinsic and intrinsic rewards.

INSTRUCTIONS

1. Working alone, complete the "What I Want from My Job" survey.
2. In small groups, compare and analyze differences in the survey results and prepare group responses to the discussion questions.

3. After the class reconvenes, group spokespersons present group findings.

DISCUSSION QUESTIONS

1. Which items received the highest and lowest scores from you? Why?
2. On which items was there most and least agreement among students? What are the implications?
3. Which job rewards are extrinsic, and which are intrinsic?
4. Were more response differences found in intrinsic or in extrinsic rewards?
5. In what ways do you think blue-collar workers' responses would differ from those of college students?

What I Want from My Job

Determine what you want from a job by circling the level of importance of each of the following job rewards:

	Very Important	Important	Indifferent	Unimportant	Very Unimportant
1. Advancement opportunities	5	4	3	2	1
2. Appropriate company policies	5	4	3	2	1
3. Authority	5	4	3	2	1
4. Autonomy and freedom on the job	5	4	3	2	1
5. Challenging work	5	4	3	2	1
6. Company reputation	5	4	3	2	1
7. Fringe benefits	5	4	3	2	1
8. Geographic location	5	4	3	2	1
9. Good co-workers	5	4	3	2	1

(Continued)

	Very Important	Important	Indifferent	Unimportant	Very Unimportant
10. Good supervision	5	4	3	2	1
11. Job security	5	4	3	2	1
12. Money	5	4	3	2	1
13. Opportunity for self-development	5	4	3	2	1
14. Pleasant office and working conditions	5	4	3	2	1
15. Performance feedback	5	4	3	2	1
16. Prestigious job title	5	4	3	2	1
17. Recognition for doing a good job	5	4	3	2	1
18. Responsibility	5	4	3	2	1
19. Sense of achievement	5	4	3	2	1
20. Training programs	5	4	3	2	1
21. Type of work	5	4	3	2	1
22. Working with people	5	4	3	2	1

Concluding Case

BIG BISON RESORTS: FINDING THE RIGHT MOTIVATORS

Frank Schuman, vice president of human resources for Big Bison Resorts, heard laughter as he approached the chief executive's office door. As he stepped into the room, he saw CEO Janette Briggs seated behind her desk, telling two other executives a story that they were obviously enjoying.

"Oh, Frank! Good!" exclaimed Janette when she saw him enter. "I was just telling Pedro and Marlys about my great adventure in TV land." Janette had been away for the past two weeks, taping *Executive in Disguise,* a popular reality TV show in which top managers don disguises and act as lower-tier service employees and perform their everyday tasks and duties.

"How did it go?" asked Frank.

"It was eye-opening," Janette replied. "After spending all that time in our kitchens and cleaning the guest rooms and pools, I see our people and their jobs in a totally new way."

"Is that why you called me here?" Frank asked. "I thought you wanted to review our plans for the new Employee of the Month program we're starting."

"See, that's the issue. After working directly with our frontline staff, I'm having doubts about putting resources into Employee of the Month," replied Janette. "Have a seat, Frank, and let me share what I saw over the past two weeks."

"I've been telling Marlys and Pedro what it's like to work in one of our kitchens. The pace is unbelievable. The workload is incredible. And the teamwork is out of this world. Frank, I was amazed, and you would be, too. I know how to make a grilled cheese sandwich, but these folks do a lot more than cook. They're planning and controlling on the fly: How many salads? How many pancakes? How can we make all that without any waste? There's no supervisor on the line; they're *all* thinking like managers—how to please customers, control costs.

Honestly, our managers could take lessons from them on teamwork and quality control."

"It sounds like we have a lot of Employees of the Month," Frank said hopefully. Maybe the program wouldn't be canceled after all, and his group's efforts wouldn't have been wasted.

"No," said Janette. "The point is, we've tried so many programs to boost productivity. As you know, we were looking at bonuses last year, but then the economy slumped and business dropped off. But we have to do something. That's why I called you in. We need your HR expertise. What do people want? I thought it would be pay, prizes, that sort of thing. And you agreed with me. But really, Frank, are those the right motivators? The people I worked with the past two weeks—they're so good at what they do, and they're constantly thinking up ways to make our guests happy. They already take pride in what they accomplish. We need to decide how to design their jobs better so they can accomplish more without us getting in their way with, well, Employee of the Month ceremonies."

"OK," replied Frank, "now that you've put it that way, I have to ask if maybe what we *don't* want to do is decide what will make their jobs better."

Janette looked puzzled. "So you're saying we *shouldn't* make their jobs better?"

"What I mean," replied Frank, "is that we need to *listen* before we *decide.*"

DISCUSSION QUESTIONS

1. What kinds of behavior would an Employee of the Month program, as described here, reinforce at Big Bison Resorts? How might the company apply the principles of goal setting, reinforcement, and expectancy theories more effectively?

2. How might the company get input from employees to make people's jobs more motivating? What impact would this effort have on the company's performance?

3. How would Big Bison's employees perceive the equity of the Employee of the Month program? Compare their potential reactions with the response you would expect from involving employees in improving their jobs.

4. Think about a previous job you have held or hold currently. If you had the power to make such decisions, what would you do to make the job more motivating for employees?

ENDNOTES

1. "2018 World's Best Workplaces," *Fortune,* http://fortune.com/2018/10/15/worlds-best-workplaces-2018/, accessed April 10, 2019.

2. Mark C. Crowley, "How SAS Became the World's Best Place to Work," *Fast Company,* January 22, 2013, https://www.fastcompany.com/3004953/how-sas-became-worlds-best-place-work.

3. Mark C. Crowley, "How SAS Became the World's Best Place to Work," *Fast Company,* January 22, 2013, https://www.fastcompany.com/3004953/how-sas-became-worlds-best-place-work.

4. Mark C. Crowley, "How SAS Became the World's Best Place to Work," *Fast Company,* January 22, 2013, https://www.fastcompany.com/3004953/how-sas-became-worlds-best-place-work.

5. R. Kreitner and F. Luthans, "A Social Learning Approach to Behavioral Management: Radical Behaviorists 'Mellowing Out,'" *Organizational Dynamics,* Autumn 1984, pp. 47–65.

6. D. Katz and R. L. Kahn, *The Social Psychology of Organizations* (New York: Wiley, 1966).

7. C. A. Bartlett and S. Ghoshal, "Building Competitive Advantage through People," *Sloan Management Review,* Winter 2002, pp. 34–41.

8. E. Locke, "Toward a Theory of Task Motivation and Incentives," *Organizational Behavior and Human Performance* 3 (1968), pp. 157–89.

9. Department of Homeland Security, "Fiscal Years 2019–2022 Strategic Plan," http://www.dhs.gov, accessed March 16, 2019.

10. E. A. Locke, "Guest Editor's Introduction: Goal-Setting Theory and Its Applications to the World of Business," *Academy of Management Executive* 4 (November 2004), pp. 124–25.

11. G. P. Latham, "The Motivational Benefits of Goal-Setting," *Academy of Management Executive* 4 (November 2004), pp. 126–29.

12. E. A. Locke, "Linking Goals to Monetary Incentives," *Academy of Management Executive* 4 (November 2004), pp. 130–33.

13. E. E. Lawler III, *Treat People Right!* (San Francisco: Jossey-Bass, 2003).

14. E. E. Lawler III, *Treat People Right!* (San Francisco: Jossey-Bass, 2003).

15. J. Bono and T. Judge, "Self-Concordance at Work: Toward Understanding the Motivational Effects of Transformational Leaders," *Academy of Management Journal* 46 (2003), pp. 554–71.

16. Ada Chen Rekhi, Notejoy, https://fitsmallbusiness.com/smart-goals-examples/, accessed March 31, 2019.

17. "Setting an Emissions Target," Walmart, March 18, 2018, https://www.walmartsustainabilityhub.com; "HP Announces Supply Chain Goals to Enhance Environmental and Social Impact," Hewlett-Packard (press), June 14, 2017, https://press.ext.hp.com.

18. S. Kerr and S. Laundauer, "Using Stretch Goals to Promote Organizational Effectiveness and Personal Growth: General Electric and Goldman Sachs," *Academy of Management Executive* 4 (November 2004), pp. 134–38.

19. S. Kerr and S. Laundauer, "Using Stretch Goals to Promote Organizational Effectiveness and Personal Growth: General Electric and Goldman Sachs," *Academy of Management Executive* 4 (November 2004), pp. 134–38.

20. G. P. Latham, "The Motivational Benefits of Goal-Setting," *Academy of Management Executive* 4 (November 2004), pp. 126–29.

21. T. Mitchell and W. Silver, "Individual and Group Goals When Workers Are Interdependent: Effects on Task Strategies and Performance," *Journal of Applied Psychology* 75 (1990), pp. 185–93.

22. A. Kleingeld, H. van Mierlo, and L. Arends, "The Effect of Goal Setting on Group Performance: A Meta-Analysis," *Journal of Applied Psychology* 96 (2011), pp. 1289–1304.

23. G. P. Latham, "The Motivational Benefits of Goal-Setting," *Academy of Management Executive* 4 (November 2004), pp. 126–29.

24. "2018 Report on the State of the Legal Market," Legal Executive Institute, http://www.legalexecutiveinstitute.com, accessed March 17, 2019; "A Millennial Explains How Law Firms Can Attract and Keep His Generation of Lawyers," American Bar Association, May 23, 2018, https://www.americanbar.org.

25. D. Welsh and L. Ordóñez, "The Dark Side of Consecutive High Performance Goals: Linking Goal Setting, Depletion, and Unethical Behavior," *Organizational Behavior and Human Decision Processes* 123 (2014), pp. 79–89.

26. M. Schweitzer, L. Ordonez, and B. Douma, "Goal Setting as a Motivator of Unethical Behavior," *Academy of Management Journal* 47 (2004), pp. 422–32.

27. T. Gryta, S. Ng, and T. Francis, "Companies Routinely Steer Analysts to Deliver Earnings Surprises," *The Wall Street Journal,* August 4, 2016, www.wsj.com; C. Beaudoin, A. Cianci, and G. Tsakumis, "The Impact of CFOs' Incentives and Earnings Management Ethics on Their Financial Reporting Decisions: The Mediating Role of Moral Disengagement," *Journal of Business Ethics* 128 (2015), pp. 505–18.

28. G. Seijts and G. Latham, "Learning versus Performance Goals: When Should Each Be Used?" *Academy of Management Executive* 19 (February 2005), pp. 124–31; P. C. Early, T. Connolly, and G. Ekegren, "Goals, Strategy Development, and Task Performance: Some Limits on the Efficacy of Goal Setting," *Journal of Applied Psychology* 74 (1989), pp. 24–33; C. E. Shalley, "Effects of Productivity Goals, Creativity Goals, and Personal Discretion on Individual Creativity," *Journal of Applied Psychology* 76 (1991), pp. 179–85.

29. R. C. Litchfield, "Brainstorming Reconsidered: A Goal-Based View," *Academy of Management Review* 33 (2008), pp. 649–68.

30. R. Fisher and A. Sharp, *Getting It Done* (New York: HarperCollins, 1998).

31. E. Thorndike, *Animal Intelligence* (New York: Macmillan, 1911).

32. A. D. Stajkovic and F. Luthans, "Differential Effects of Incentive Motivators on Work Performance," *Academy of Management Journal* 44 (2001), pp. 580–90.

33. B. Sims Jr., "Want Your Team to Perform Better? Try Positive Reinforcement," *Entrepreneur,* February 6, 2014, http://www.entrepreneur.com; J. Zaslow, "The Most-Praised Generation Goes to Work," *The Wall Street Journal,* April 20, 2007, http://online.wsj.com.

34. Adam Madison, "Positive Results," *Rock Products,* September 1, 2008, Business & Company Resource Center, http://galenet.galegroup.com.

35. T. Judge and R. Piccolo, "Transformational and Transactional Leadership: A Meta-Analytic Test of Their Relative Ability," *Journal of Applied Psychology* 89 (2004), pp. 755–68.

36. S. Kerr, "On the Folly of Rewarding a While Hoping for B," *Academy of Management Journal* 18 (1975), pp. 769–83.

37. D. Levitin, "Why the Modern World Is Bad for Your Brain," *The Guardian,* January 18, 2015, http://www.theguardian.com; T. Bradberry, "Multitasking Damages Your Brain and Career, New Studies Suggest," *Forbes,* October 8, 2014, http://www.forbes.com; S. Lohr, "Science Finds Advantage in Focusing, Not Multitasking," *Chicago Tribune,* March 25, 2007, sec. 1, p. 10.

38. E. E. Lawler III, *Rewarding Excellence* (San Francisco: Jossey-Bass, 2000).

39. C. Meyer, "Money Isn't Everything: Nonfinancial Rewards That Retain the Best Workers," *Journal of Accountancy,* June 20, 2016, www.journalofaccountancy.com.

40. R. Sheridan, *Joy, Inc.: How We Build a Workplace People Love* (New York: Portfolio/Penguin, 2015); M. May, "Creating a Company Culture of Joy," American Express Open Forum, January 15, 2014, www.americanexpress.com.

41. J. Pfeffer and R. Sutton, *The Knowing–Doing Gap* (Boston: Harvard Business School Press, 2000).

42. R. Khanna, I. Guler, and A. Nerkar, "Fail Often, Fail Big, and Fail Fast? Learning from Small Failures and R&D Performance in the Pharmaceutical Industry," *Academy of Management Journal* 59 (2016), pp. 436–59.

43. A. Vaccaro, "The Best Leaders Ask for More Feedback," *Inc.,* December 24, 2013, http://www.inc.com; S. Moss and J. Sanchez, "Are Your Employees Avoiding You? Managerial Strategies for Closing the Feedback Gap," *Academy of Management Executive* 18, no. 1 (February 2004), pp. 32–44.

44. E.E. Lawler III (2003). *Treat people right.* San Francisco: Jossey-Bass.

45. R. Cheramie, "An Examination of Feedback-Seeking Behaviors: The Feedback Source and Career Success," *Career Development International* 18 (2013), pp. 712–31; S. B. Silverman, C. E. Pogson, and A. B. Cober, "When Employees at Work Don't Get It: A Model for Enhancing Individual Employee Change in Response to Performance Feedback," *Academy of Management Executive* 19, no. 2 (May 2005), pp. 135–47; J. Jackman and M. Strober, "Fear of Feedback," *Harvard Business Review,* April 2003, pp. 101–7.

46. V. H. Vroom, *Work and Motivation* (New York: Wiley, 1964).

47. R. E. Wood, P. W. B. Atkins, and J. E. H. Bright, "Bonuses, Goals, and Instrumentality Effects," *Journal of Applied Psychology* 84 (1999), pp. 703–20.

48. "Our Story," YouEarnedIt, https://youearnedit.com, accessed March 13, 2019.

49. Bruce Rogers, "Tech Titan Jim Goodnight Positions SAS for the Future," *Forbes,* October 31, 2016, https://www.forbes.com/sites/brucerogers/2016/10/31/tech-titan-jim-goodnight-positions-sas-for-the-future/#4c375f514e55.

50. "SAS Announces $1 Billion Investment in Artificial Intelligence (AI)," *PR Newswire,* March 17, 2019, https://www.prnewswire.com/news-releases/sas-announces-1-billion-investment-in-artificial-intelligence-ai-300813597.html.

51. Mike Miliard, "Siemens, SAS Join Forces for AI-Enabled IoT Analytics," *Healthcare IT News,* April 3, 2019, https://www.healthcareitnews.com/news/siemens-sas-join-forces-ai-enabled-iot-analytics.

52. SAS, "About SAS," https://www.sas.com/en_us/company-information/leadership.html accessed April 10, 2019.

53. A. H. Maslow, "A Theory of Human Motivation," *Psychological Review,* July 1943, pp. 370–96.

54. T. Bridgman, S. Cummings, and J. Ballard, "Who Built Maslow's Pyramid? A History of the Creation of Management Studies' Most Famous Symbol and Its Implications for Management Education," *Academy of Management Learning & Education,* 18 (2019), https://doi.org/10.5465/amle.2017.0351.

55. M. Wahba and L. Birdwell, "Maslow Reconsidered: A Review of Research on the Need Hierarchy Theory," *Organizational Behavior and Human Performance* 15 (1976), pp. 212–40.

56. M. Marchington and M. Marchington, "Human Resource Management (HRM): Too Busy Looking Up to See Where It Is Going Longer Term?" *Human Resource Management Review* 25 (2015), pp. 176–87.

57. "Our Beliefs & Principles," W. L. Gore, https://www.gore.com, accessed March 13, 2019.

58. "It's the Actions That Count: Find Out Why Our Employees Enjoy Coming into Work Every Day," Wegmans Food Markets, https://jobs.wegmans.com, accessed March 17, 2019.

59. C. Alderfer, *Existence, Relatedness, and Growth: Human Needs in Organizational Settings* (Glencoe: IL: Free Press, 1972).

60. C. Pinder, *Work Motivation* (Glenview, IL: Scott, Foresman, 1984).

61. D. McClelland, *The Achieving Society* (New York: Van Nostrand Reinhold, 1961).

62. D. McClelland and R. Boyatzis, "Leadership Motive Pattern and Long-Term Success in Management," *Journal of Applied Psychology* 67 (1982), pp. 737–43.

63. E. E. Lawler III and D. Finegold, "Individualizing the Organization: Past, Present, and Future," *Organizational Dynamics,* Summer 2000, pp. 1–15.

64. B. Gerhart and M. Fang, "Pay, Intrinsic Motivation, Extrinsic Motivation, Performance, and Creativity in the Workplace: Revisiting Long-Held Beliefs," *Annual Review of Organizational Psychology and Organizational Behavior* 2 (2015), pp. 489–521.

65. B. Gerhart and M. Fang, "Pay, Intrinsic Motivation, Extrinsic Motivation, Performance, and Creativity in the Workplace: Revisiting Long-Held Beliefs," *Annual Review of Organizational Psychology and Organizational Behavior* 2 (2015), pp. 489–521; C. Cerasoli, J. Nicklin, and M. Ford, "Intrinsic Motivation and Extrinsic Incentives Jointly Predict Performance: A 40-Year Meta-Analysis," *Psychological Bulletin* 140 (2014), pp. 980–1008.

66. Team Rubicon, "Stories and Impact," https://teamrubiconusa.org/stories-impact/ accessed April 11, 2019.

67. Enjoli Francis and Eric Noll, "Co-founder and CEO of Team Rubicon to Be Presented with ESPY's Pat Tillman Award for Service," *ABC News,* July 18, 2018, https://abcnews.go.com/US/cofounder-ceo-team-rubicon-presented-espys-pat-tillman/story?id=56668477.

68. T. M. Amabile, "A Model of Creativity and Innovation in Organizations," in *Research in Organizational Behavior,* ed. B. M. Staw and L. L. Cummings (Greenwich, CT: JAI Press, 1988), pp. 10, 123–67.

69. N. Madjar, E. Greenberg, and Z. Chen, "Factors for Radical Creativity, Incremental Creativity, and Routine, Noncreative Performance," *Journal of Applied Psychology* 96 (2011), pp. 730–43; C. M. Ford, "A Theory of Individual Creative Action in Multiple Social Domains," *Academy of Management Review* 21 (1996), pp. 1112–42.

70. G. Oldham and A. Cummings, "Employee Creativity: Personal and Contextual Factors at Work," *Academy of Management Journal* 39 (1996), pp. 607–34.

71. A. Fisher, "How Companies Kill Creativity," *Fortune,* October 17, 2013, http://www.fortune.com; T. Amabile, R. Conti, H. Coon, J. Lazenby, and M. Herron, "Assessing the Work Environment for Creativity," *Academy of Management Journal* 39 (1996), pp. 1154–84.

72. M. Campion and G. Sanborn, "Job Design," in *Handbook of Industrial Engineering,* ed. G. Salvendy (New York: Wiley, 1991).

73. E. E. Lawler III and D. Finegold, "Individualizing the Organization: Past, Present, and Future," *Organizational Dynamics* 29, no. 1 (2000), pp. 1–15.

74. "Students & Recent Grads," Blue Cross and Blue Shield of North Carolina, https://www.bluecrossnc.com, accessed March 13, 2019.

75. M. Campion and D. McClelland, "Interdisciplinary Examination of the Costs and Benefits of Enlarged Jobs: A Job Design Quasi-Experiment," *Journal of Applied Psychology* 76 (1991), pp. 186–98.

76. F. Herzberg, *Work and the Nature of Men* (Cleveland: World, 1966).

77. J. R. Hackman, G. Oldham, R. Janson, and K. Purdy, "A New Strategy for Job Enrichment," *California Management Review* 16 (Fall 1975), pp. 57–71.

78. I. Thottam, "10 Companies with Awesome Training and Development Programs," *Monster,* www.monster.com, accessed April 2, 2019.

79. R. Rechheld, "Loyalty-Based Management" *Harvard Business Review,* March–April 1993, pp. 64–73.

80. "Motivation in Today's Workplace: The Link to Performance," *HR Magazine,* July 2010, pp. 1–9.

81. "3M Careers," https://www.3m.com/3M/en_US/careers-us/culture/15-percent-culture/, accessed April 1, 2019.

82. M. Campion and G. Sanborn, "Job Design," in *Handbook of Industrial Engineering,* ed. G. Salvendy (New York: Wiley, 1991).

83. Y. Yin, Y. Wang, and Y. Lu, "Why Firms Adopt Empowerment Practices and How Such Practices Affect Firm Performance," *Human Resource Management Review* 29 (2019), pp. 111–24.

84. S. Seibert, S. Silver, and W. A. Randolph, "Taking Empowerment to the Next Level: A Multiple-Level Model of Empowerment, Performance, and Satisfaction," *Academy of Management Journal* 47 (2004), pp. 332–49.

85. C. Argyris, "Empowerment: The Emperor's New Clothes," *Harvard Business Review,* May–June 1998, pp. 98–105.

86. R. Forrester, "Empowerment: Rejuvenating a Potent Idea," *Academy of Management Executive,* August 2000, pp. 67–80; N. Lorinkova, M. Pearsall, and H. P. Sims Jr., "Examining the Differential Longitudinal Performance of Directive versus Empowering Leadership in Teams," *Academy of Management Journal* 56 (2012), pp. 573–96; D. Liu, S. Zhang, L. Wang, and T. Lee, "The Effects of Autonomy and Empowerment on Employee Turnover: Test of a Multilevel Model in Teams," *Journal of Applied Psychology* 96 (2011), pp. 1305–16; M. T. Maynard, L. Gilson, and J. Mathieu, "Empowerment–Fad or Fab? A Multilevel Review of the Past Two Decades of Research," *Journal of Management* 38 (2012), pp. 1231–81; X. Zhang and K. Bartol, "Linking Empowering Leadership and Employee Creativity: The Influence of Psychological Empowerment, Intrinsic Motivation, and Creative Process Engagement," *Academy of Management Journal* 53 (2010), pp. 107–28.

87. M. M. Butts, R. J. Vandenberg, D. M. DeJoy, B. S. Schaffer, and M. G. Wilson, "Individual Reactions to High Involvement Work Processes: Investigating the Role of Empowerment and Perceived Organizational Support," *Journal of Occupational Health Psychology* 14 (2009), pp. 122–36; Price Waterhouse Change Integration Team, *Better Change* (Burr Ridge, IL: Richard D. Irwin, 1995).

88. E. E. Lawler III, *The Ultimate Advantage: Creating the High Involvement Organization* (San Francisco: Jossey-Bass, 1992).

89. W. A. Kahn, "Psychological Conditions of Personal Engagement and Disengagement at Work," *Academy of Management Journal* 33 (1990), pp. 692–724; W. Macey and B. Schneider, "The Meaning of Employee Engagement," *Industrial and Organizational Psychology: Perspectives on Science and Practice* 1 (2008), pp. 3–30; D. Cossin and J. Caballero, "Transformational Leadership Background Literature Review," IMD Global Board Center, June 2013, www.imd.org; A. Fanelli and V. Misangyi, "Bringing Out Charisma: CEO Charisma and External Stakeholders," *Academy of Management Review* 31 (2006), pp. 1049–61.

90. D'Innocenzo, M. Lucian, J. Mathieu, et al., "Empowered to Perform: A Multilevel Investigation of the Influence of Empowerment on Performance in Hospital Units," *Academy of Management Journal* 58 (2016), pp. 1290–1307.

91. R. C. Liden, S. J. Wayne, and R. T. Sparrowe, "An Examination of the Mediating Role of Psychological Empowerment on the Relations between the Job, Interpersonal Relationships, and Work Outcomes," *Journal of Applied Psychology* 85 (2000), pp. 407–16.

92. M. Gagne and E. Deci, "Self-Determination Theory and Work Motivation," *Journal of Organizational Behavior* 26 (2005), pp. 331–62; A.A. Van den Broeck, C.-H. Chang, and C. Rosen, "A Review of Self-Determination Theory's Basic Psychological Needs at Work," *Journal of Management* 42 (2016), pp. 1195–1229.

93. T. Koren, "What Happened When I Finally Had a Manager Who Trusted Me," *LeadWise,* May 1, 2017, https://journal.leadwise.co/; M. Solomon, "To Transform Your Company Culture, Change Your POV: Hyatt CEO's Perspective," *Forbes,* May 11, 2015, https://www.forbes.com; S. Heathfield, "Empowering Employees to Make Decisions," *The Balance Careers,* January 28, 2019, https://www.thebalancecareers.com; C. Nielson, "Autonomy: Empowering the Individual to Do Their Best Work," *DecisionWise,* April 9, 2018, https://www.decision-wise.com; T. Matlett, "6 Ways to Encourage Autonomy with Your Employees," *Entrepreneur,* March 4, 2016, https://www.entrepreneur.com.

94. Frank Dobbin and Alexandra Kalev, "Why Diversity Programs Fail," *Harvard Business Review,* July–August 2016, https://hbr.org/2016/07/why-diversity-programs-fail.

95. Santiago Jaramillo, "Four Steps to Motivating a Multigenerational Workforce," *Forbes,* December 18, 2017, https://www.forbes.com/sites/forbeshumanresourcescouncil/2017/12/18/four-steps-to-motivating-a-multigenerational-workforce/#41a50a706022.

96. Kim Elsesser, "Is This the Answer to Diversity and Inclusion?" *Forbes,* January 28, 2019, https://www.forbes.com/sites/kimelsesser/2019/01/28/is-this-the-answer-to-diversity-and-inclusion/#1353cd17523f.

97. Frank Dobbin and Alexandra Kalev, "Why Diversity Programs Fail," *Harvard Business Review,* July–August 2016, https://hbr.org/2016/07/why-diversity-programs-fail.

98. W. A. Randolph and M. Sashkin, "Can Organizational Empowerment Work in Multinational Settings?" *Academy of Management Executive* 16 (2002), pp. 102–15.

99. J. Colquitt and K. Zipay, "Justice, Fairness, and Employee Reactions," *Annual Review of Organizational Psychology and Organizational Behavior* 2 (2015), pp. 75–99.

100. J. Adams, "Inequality in Social Exchange," in. *Advances in Experimental Social Psychology,.* ed. L. Berkowitz (New York: Academic Press, 1965).

101. T. Weiss, "How to Prevent IT Sabotage Inside Your Company," *CIO,* August 19, 2011, http://www.cio.com; D. Skarlicki, R. Folger, and P. Tesluk, "Personality as a Moderator in the Relationships between Fairness and Retaliation," *Academy of Management Journal* 42 (1999), pp. 100–08.

102. A. M. Ryan and J. Wessel, "Implications of a Changing Workforce and Workplace for Justice Perceptions and Expectations," *Human Resource Management Review* 25 (2015), pp. 162–75.

103. J. Brockner, "Making Sense of Procedural Fairness: How High Procedural Fairness Can Reduce or Heighten the Influence of Outcome Favorability," *Academy of Management Review* 27 (2002), pp. 58–76; D. De Cremer and D. van Knippenberg, "How Do Leaders Promote Cooperation? The Effects of Charisma and Procedural Fairness," *Journal of Applied Psychology* 87 (2002), pp. 858–66.

104. M. Armstrong-Stassen, M. Freeman, S. Cameron, and D. Rajacic, "Nurse Managers' Role in Older Nurses' Intention to Stay," *Journal of Health Organization and Management* 29 (2015), pp. 55–74.

105. E. E. Lawler III, *Treat People Right!* (San Francisco: Jossey-Bass, 2003).

106. S. Persson and D. Wasieleski, "The Seasons of the Psychological Contract: Overcoming the Silent Transformations of the Employer-Employee Relationship," *Human Resource Management Review* 25 (2015), pp. 368–83.

107. R. Shao, D. Rupp, D. Skarlicki, and K. Jones, "Employee Justice across Cultures: A Meta-Analytic Review," *Journal of Management* 39 (2013), pp. 263–301.

108. W. C. Kim and R. Mauborgne, "Fair Process: Managing in the Knowledge Economy," *Harvard Business Review,* July–August 1997, pp. 65–75.

109. T. Bateman and D. Organ, "Job Satisfaction and the Good Sold: The Relationship between Affect and Employee 'Citizenship,'" *Academy of Management Journal,* 1983, pp. 587–95.

110. A. de Castro, G. Gee, and D. Takeuchi, "Relationship between Job Dissatisfaction and Physical and Psychological Health among Filipino Immigrants," *American Association of Occupational Health Nurses Journal* 56 (2008), pp. 33–40; D. Henne and E. Locke, "Job Dissatisfaction: What Are the Consequences?" *International Journal of Psychology* 20 (1985), pp. 221–40.

111. J. Barling, E. K. Kelloway, and R. Iverson, "High-Quality Work, Job Satisfaction, and Occupational Injuries," *Journal of Applied Psychology* 88 (2003), pp. 276–83.

112. D. Bowen, S. Gilliland, and R. Folger, "HRM and Service Fairness: How Being Fair with Employees Spills Over to Customers," *Organizational Dynamics,* Winter 1999, pp. 7–23.

113. J. Harter, F. Schmidt, and T. Hayes, "Business-Unit-Level Relationship between Employee Satisfaction, Employee Engagement, and Business Outcomes: A Meta-Analysis," *Journal of Applied Psychology* 87 (2002), pp. 268–79.

114. S. Adams, "Most Americans Are Unhappy at Work," *Forbes,* June 20, 2014, http://www.forbes.com; The Conference Board, "U.S. Workers More Satisfied? Just Barely," press release, June 18, 2014, http://www.conference-board.org.

115. Heiner Evanschitzky, Christopher Groening, Vikas Mittal, and Maren Wunderlich, "How Employer and Employee Satisfaction Affect Customer Satisfaction: An Application to Franchise Services," *Journal of Service Research* 14, no. 2 (May 2011), pp. 136–48; "Motivation in Today's Workplace: The Link to Performance," *HR Magazine,* July 2010, pp. 1–2, 4.

116. G. Grote and D. Guest, "The Case for Reinvigorating Quality of Working Life Research," *Human Relations* 70 (2017), pp. 149–67; S. Sonnentag, "Dynamics of Well-Being," *Annual Review of Organizational Psychology and Organizational Behavior* 2 (2015), pp. 261–93.

117. G. Grote and D. Guest, "The Case for Reinvigorating Quality of Working Life Research," *Human Relations* 70 (2017), pp. 149–67.

118. R. E. Walton, "Improving the Quality of Work Life," *Harvard Business Review,* May–June 1974, pp. 12, 16, 155; G. Grote and D. Guest, "The Case for Reinvigorating Quality of Working Life Research," *Human Relations* 70 (2017), pp. 149–67.

119. Matt Straz, "4 Ways to Use Technology In the Workplace to Motivate Employees," *Entrepreneur,* February 23, 2015, https://www.entrepreneur.com/article/242961.

120. "How Great Leaders Use Technology to Motivate Employees," June 23, 2016, https://mytechdecisions.com/compliance/how-great-leaders-use-technology-to-motivate-employees/.

121. "How Great Leaders Use Technology to Motivate Employees," June 23, 2016, https://mytechdecisions.com/compliance/how-great-leaders-use-technology-to-motivate-employees/.

122. Matt Straz, "4 Ways to Use Technology In the Workplace to Motivate Employees," *Entrepreneur,* February 23, 2015, https://www.entrepreneur.com/article/242961.

123. Mark Donahue, "Retain Your Employees and Make Them More Productive by Adopting a Village Worldview," *Forbes,* April 11, 2019, https://www.forbes.com/sites/forbesleadershipcollective/2019/04/11/retain-your-employees-and-make-them-more-productive-by-adopting-a-village-worldview/#76e595093ad0.

124. E. E. Lawler III, "Strategies for Improving the Quality of Work Life," *American Psychologist* 37 (1982), pp. 486–93; J. L. Suttle, "Improving Life at Work: Problems and Prospects," in *Improving Life at Work,* ed. J. R. Hackman and J. L. Suttle (Santa Monica, CA: Goodyear, 1977); B. Erdogan, T. Bauer, D. Truxillo, et al., "Whistle While You Work: A Review of the Life Satisfaction Literature," *Journal of Management* 38 (2012), pp. 1038–83.

125. P. B. Warr, "Well-Being and the Workplace," in D. Kahneman, E. Diener, and N. Schwarz, eds., *Well-Being: The Foundations of Hedonic Psychology* (New York: Russell Sage Foundation, 1999); T. A. Wright and R. Cropanzano, "The Role of Psychological Well-Being in Job Performance: A Fresh Look at an Age-Old Quest," *Organizational Dynamics* 33 (2004), pp. 338–51; G. Grote and D. Guest, "The Case for Reinvigorating Quality of Working Life Research," *Human Relations* 70 (2017), pp. 149–67.

126. A. Edmans, "The Link between Job Satisfaction and Firm Value, with Implications for Corporate Social Responsibility," *Academy of Management Perspectives* 26 (2012), pp. 1–19.

127. T. Wright and D. Bonett, "Job Satisfaction and Psychological Well-Being as Nonadditive Predictors of Workplace Turnover," *Journal of Management* 33 (2007), 141–60; J. K. Harter, F. L. Schmidt, and C. L. M. Keyes, "Well-Being in the Workplace and Its Relationship to Business Outcomes: A Review of the Gallup Studies," in *Flourishing: The Positive Person and the Good Life,* ed. C. L. M. Keyes and J. Haidt (Washington DC: American Psychological Association, 2003), pp. 205–24.

128. S. L. Robinson, "Trust and Breach of the Psychological Contract," *Administrative Science Quarterly* 41 (1996), pp. 574–99.

129. J. Robbins, M. Ford, and L. Tetrick, "Perceived Unfairness and Employee Health: A Meta-Analytic Integration," *Journal of Applied Psychology* 97 (2012), pp. 235–72; M. Dahl, "Organizational Change and Employee Stress," *Management Science* 57 (2011), pp. 240–56.

130. A. M. Ryan and J. Wessel, "Implications of a Changing Workforce and Workplace for Justice Perceptions and Expectations," *Human Resource Management Review* 25 (2015), pp. 162–75.

131. L. Grunberg, S. Moore, E. Greenberg, and P. Sikora, "The Changing Workplace and Its Effects A Longitudinal Examination of Employee Responses at a Large Company," *Journal of Applied Behavioral Science* 44 (2008), pp. 215–36; D. Rousseau, "Changing the Deal While Keeping the People," *Academy of Management Executive* 10 (1996), pp. 50–58.

132. E. Ridolfi, "Executive Commentary," *Academy of Management Executive* 10 (1996), pp. 59–60.

133. E. E. Lawler III, *From the Ground Up* (San Francisco: Jossey-Bass, 1996).

134. E. E. Lawler III, *From the Ground Up* (San Francisco: Jossey-Bass, 1996).

135. S. Ghoshal, C. Bartlett, and P. Moran, "Value Creation: The New Management Manifesto," *Financial Times Mastering Management Review,* November 1999, pp. 34–37.

136. R. Hoffman, B. Casnocha, and C. Yen, "Tours of Duty: The New Employer–Employee Contract," *Harvard Business Review,* June 2013, pp. 48–58.

137. SAS, "About SAS," https://www.sas.com/en_us/company-information/leadership/jenn-mann.html accessed April 10, 2019.

138. Mark C. Crowley, "How SAS Became the World's Best Place to Work," *Fast Company,* January 22, 2013, https://www.fastcompany.com/3004953/how-sas-became-worlds-best-place-work.

139. Bruce Rogers, "Tech Titan Jim Goodnight Positions SAS for the Future," *Forbes,* October 31, 2016, https://www.forbes.com/sites/brucerogers/2016/10/31/tech-titan-jim-goodnight-positions-sas-for-the-future/#1591edce4e55.

140. SAS, "About SAS," https://www.sas.com/en_us/careers/culture.html accessed April 10, 2019.

CHAPTER 14
Teamwork

No one can whistle a symphony. It takes an orchestra to play it.

—Halford E. Luccock

Adam Hester/Blend Images

learning objectives

After studying Chapter 14, you will be able to:

LO 14-1   Discuss how teams can contribute to an organization's effectiveness.

LO 14-2   Describe different types of teams.

LO 14-3   Summarize how groups become teams.

LO 14-4   Explain why groups sometimes fail.

LO 14-5   Describe how to build an effective team.

LO 14-6   List methods for managing a team's relationships with other teams.

LO 14-7   Identify ways to manage conflict.

chapter outline

The Contributions of Teams

Types of Teams
Self-Managed Teams

How Groups Become Real Teams
Group Processes
Critical Periods
Teaming Challenges
Why Groups Sometimes Fail

Building Effective Teams
Performance Focus
Motivating Teamwork
Member Contributions
Norms
Roles
Cohesiveness
Building Cohesiveness and High-Performance Norms

Managing Lateral Relationships
Managing Outward
Lateral Role Relationships
Managing Conflict
Conflict Styles
Being a Mediator
Virtual and E-conflict

Management in Action

TEAMWORK AT WHOLE FOODS MARKET

Whole Foods Market has a purpose beyond profits, and even a purpose beyond selling organic vegetables and cheeses. The chain of 500 health-food stores in North America and the United Kingdom seeks to "nourish people and the planet."[1] This mission shapes the selection of merchandise grown organically and sustainably, including fresh produce, meats and fish, and whole grains, all attractively displayed. It also shapes the way the company treats its 90,000-plus employees.

Managing employees is based on key values: personal responsibility, diversity, and commitment to the organization's purpose. To sustain this combination of values, the company operates as a set of teams, with every employee being a team member. A team may have between 6 and 100 members, with the large teams divided into subteams. The leader of each team in a store is a member of the store's leadership team, and the head of each store leadership team is a member of a regional team. At the top of the Whole Foods hierarchy is an executive team.

Each employee is responsible for participating in decisions related to his or her team's work. Team members have a vote in which employees are part of the team and what benefits will be included in their compensation packages.

Team spirit and empowerment at Whole Foods have laid a strong foundation for business success. CEO John Mackey says living out the store's values creates a climate that frees employees to innovate and be creative without fear. One of Whole Foods's core values is premised on teamwork. As stated on the company website: "Our success is dependent upon the collective

David Paul Morris/Getty Images

energy, intelligence, and contributions of all of our Team Members. We design and provide safe and empowering environments where highly motivated people can flourish and reach their highest potential."[2]

Whole Foods is regularly listed as one of the best companies to work for. In 2018, it was ranked by *Forbes* as one of America's best employers.[3] There's little surprise, then, that Whole Foods reports employee turnover of just 15 percent per year, whereas the industry standard is almost 40 percent.[4] Many attribute this to the company's ability to foster a strong, team-oriented culture. And after year upon year of strong growth, Whole Foods became the world's largest supermarket chain specializing in natural and organic foods, with far more room to grow now that it is a part of the Amazon empire.

Whole Foods Market expresses a strong commitment to its employees, empowers them to make decisions, and expects a high level of commitment to serving customers. As you read this chapter, consider additional ingredients that can help ensure truly effective teamwork.

Sometimes teams work, and sometimes they don't. The goal of this chapter is to help make sure that your teams (and you) succeed. Empowerment at Whole Foods Market illustrates one way a company can apply teamwork with extraordinary results.

Teams transform the ways organizations do business.[5] Almost all companies now use teams to produce goods and services, to manage projects, and to make decisions and run the company.[6] For you, this has two vital implications. First, you *will* be working in and sometimes managing teams. Second, the ability to work in and lead teams is valuable to your employer and important to your career. Fortunately, coursework focusing on team training really can enhance students' teamwork knowledge and skills.[7]

The Contributions of Teams

LO 14-1 Discuss how teams can contribute to an organization's effectiveness.

Bottom Line

Well-managed teams are powerful forces that can deliver all desired results. *What do you think makes a team more powerful than a set of individuals?*

work teams

Teams that make or do things like manufacture, assemble, sell, or provide service.

Companies are increasingly using teams to achieve competitive advantage.[8] Used properly, teams can be powerfully effective as a building block for organization structure. Organizations such as Semco, W. L. Gore, and Kollmorgen are structured entirely around teams. 3M's breakthrough products emerge through the use of teams that are small entrepreneurial businesses within the larger corporation.

Teams can increase productivity, improve quality, and reduce costs. At California's Papa & Barkley company, teams increase productivity to manage a 15 percent growth in business every month.[9] Tarang Amin credits teamwork for increasing quality and helping him build successful brands such as Bounty, Pantene, and e.l.f. Cosmetics.[10]

Teams also can enhance speed and be powerful forces for innovation, change, and creativity.[11] Amazon, 3M, Boeing, and many other companies use teams to create new products faster. Cisco relies on teams to keep the firm competitive in the ever-changing field of technology. Nestlé's InGenius program allows employees to collaborate with other employees and external partners to pitch new innovative ideas for business opportunities. It has implemented 48 business ideas in 5 years.[12]

Teams also provide many benefits for their members.[13] You will learn a lot from your teammates, and they from you. Members learn about the company and themselves and acquire new skills and performance strategies. The team can satisfy important personal needs, such as affiliation and esteem. Other needs are met as team members receive tangible organizational rewards that they could not have achieved working alone. Moreover, teams help individuals develop their networks.[14]

Teams improve the quality of decision making and are powerful forces for innovation, change, and creativity.

Team members can provide one another with feedback; identify opportunities for growth and development; and train, coach, and mentor.[15] A marketing representative can learn about financial modeling from a colleague on a new-product development team, and the financial expert can learn about consumer marketing. Experience working together in a team, and developing strong problem-solving capabilities, is a vital supplement to specific job skills or functional expertise. And—a big advantage—you can transfer your teamwork skills to new positions.

Types of Teams

LO 14-2 Describe different types of teams.

Your employer might have hundreds of groups and teams, and the variety of different types is vast.[16] Following are a few of the most common.[17] **Work teams** make or do things such as manufacture, assemble, sell, or provide service. Each is a clearly defined part of the formal organization structure, and composed of a full-time, stable membership. Work teams are what most people think of when they think of teams in organizations.[18]

Project and development teams work on long-term projects, sometimes over a period of years. They have specific assignments, such as research or new-product development, and members usually must contribute expert knowledge and judgment. These teams work toward a one-time product, disbanding once their work is completed. Then new teams are formed for new projects.

Parallel teams operate separately from the regular work structure of the firm on a temporary basis. Members often come from different units or jobs and are asked to do work that is not being done by the standard structure. Their charge is to recommend solutions to specific problems. They usually do not have authority to act, however. Examples include task forces and quality or safety teams formed to study a particular problem.

For example, in response to the U.S. Department of Education and Justice's recent decision to "rescind guidance regarding transgender students," members of Congress relaunched a bipartisan task force to help preserve the rights of transgender students. Today, the task force seeks to protect the rights of the transgender community as a whole.[19]

Management teams coordinate and provide direction to the subunits under their jurisdiction and integrate work among subunits.[20] Management teams are based on authority stemming from hierarchical rank and are responsible for the overall performance of business units. At the top of the organization resides the top management team (TMT) that establishes strategic direction and manages the firm's overall performance.

Transnational teams are composed of multinational members whose activities span multiple countries.[21] Such teams differ from other work teams by being multicultural and by often being geographically dispersed while working on highly complex projects having considerable impact on company objectives.

Transnational teams tend to be **virtual teams**,[22] communicating electronically more than face-to-face, although other types of teams may operate virtually as well. As you can imagine, virtuality can help or hinder a group's performance.[23] Virtual teams face difficult challenges: building trust, cohesion, and team identity and overcoming the isolation of virtual team members.[24] It won't surprise you that, recalling the leadership chapter, virtual team leaders must to tend to the people as well as the task.[25] Further, team members can share the leadership in empowered teams.[26] Exhibit 14.1 shows a few other tactics that managers can use to strengthen virtual teams. As discussed in "Inclusiveness Works," universities are experimenting with ways to train students to work effectively in global virtual teams.

In today's fast-changing, unpredictable environment, **teaming** is a strategy of teamwork on the fly.[27] In teaming, organizations create many temporary, changing teams, and you might feel like you are in a shifting series of temporary pick-up basketball games, working with different teammates and facing different challenges. You will leave one team when it has achieved (or failed at), its goal and join new teams when new opportunities arise. Because no two projects are alike, people need to get up to speed quickly on brand-new topics again and again. Because solutions can come from anywhere, team members can, too.

project and development teams

Teams that work on long-term projects but disband once the work is completed.

parallel teams

Teams that operate separately from the regular work structure and are temporary.

management teams

Teams that coordinate and provide direction to the subunits under their jurisdiction and integrate work among subunits.

transnational teams

Teams composed of multinational members whose activities span multiple countries. Such teams differ from other work teams by being multicultural and by often being geographically dispersed, being psychologically distant, and working on highly complex projects having considerable impact on company objectives.

virtual teams

Teams that are physically dispersed and communicate electronically more than face-to-face.

teaming

A strategy of teamwork on the fly, creating many temporary, changing teams.

The 29-person product development team at Omnica is responsible for rapidly and efficiently producing medical and high-tech products for their clients.

Omnica

Inclusiveness Works

Empathy in Teams Helps Cohesion and Inclusiveness

Organizations around the United States spend about $8 billion a year on D&I initiatives.[28] Unfortunately, the return on these investments isn't what many managers would like. One strategy that is often overlooked in creating inclusive workplace teams is fostering and practicing empathy.

Empathy is recognizing and trying to understand the emotions, perspectives, and life experiences of others.[29] Often we make sense of the complex environments we inhabit by organizing the world into categories. Organizing people into categories, or groups, however, leads to stereotyping, and so long as we think of another as a "type" we will struggle to see him or her as a person. Striving for empathy can help break through the cognitive walls that often divide us.

So how can we learn to empathize? One way is to create opportunities for sharing among team members. Managers can plan structured team-building exercises that require sharing personal values and experiences.[30] It helps if the exercises focus on real team goals, not solely the purpose of "getting to know each other." The more team members understand one another's perspectives, the more they begin to see beyond "types" and develop better relationships and stronger team cohesion.

It's important to encourage open and honest communication among members. The team can discuss and establish norms for how the team will conduct itself such as preferred ways of giving and receiving feedback.[31] Sharing thoughts in a systematic way engenders trust and respect for other viewpoints— hallmarks of cohesive teams.

- Provide an example of a time when you productively empathized with someone. Do you think the same process can translate to the workplace? Explain.

- Imagine you're the leader of a new team tasked with creating a promotion for a smartphone. The team includes members from diverse functions, genders, socioeconomic statuses, and ethnic backgrounds. How would you generate a discussion that relates to the team's task but also helps develop empathy among members?

Self-Managed Teams

self-managed teams

Autonomous work groups in which workers are trained to do all or most of the jobs in a unit, have no immediate supervisor, and make decisions previously made by frontline supervisors.

Traditional work groups have no managerial responsibilities;[32] the frontline manager plans, organizes, staffs, directs, and controls them, and other groups provide support activities, including quality control and maintenance. But one important trend has been to give teams more autonomy so that workers are trained to do all or most of the jobs in the unit, and they make decisions previously made by their bosses.[33] People sometimes resist these **self-managed teams**, in part because they don't want so much responsibility and the change is difficult.[34] Moreover, poorly managed conflict is a particular problem in self-managed teams.[35] But compared with traditionally managed teams, self-managed teams tend to be more productive, have lower costs, provide better customer service, provide higher quality, have better safety records, and are more satisfying for members.

EXHIBIT 14.1

Best Practices of Virtual Team Leaders

1. Establish and maintain trust through the use of communication technology.
2. Ensure diversity in the team is understood, appreciated, and leveraged.
3. Manage virtual work cycles and meetings.
4. Monitor team progress through the use of technology.
5. Enhance external visibility of the team and its members.
6. Ensure individuals benefit from participating in virtual teams.

Source: Adapted from Malhotra, A., Majchrzak, A. and Rosen, B., "Leading Virtual Teams," *Academy of Management Perspectives,* February 2007, pp. 60–70.

Autonomous work groups control decisions about and execution of a complete range of tasks—acquiring raw materials and performing operations, quality control, maintenance, and shipping. They are fully responsible for an entire product or an entire part of a production process. **Self-designing teams** do all of that and go one step further—they also have control over the design of the team. They decide themselves whom to hire, whom to fire, and what tasks the team will perform.

Autonomous teams are known to improve the organization's financial and overall performance.[36] For example, Spotify develops new products through the use of "squads," which are cross-functional, self-organized teams of no more than eight people. This framework promotes flexibility and allows the company to be 100 percent agile.[37]

In trying to take such practices to operations outside the United States, managers need to recognize that cultural differences may affect how employees react to being given decision-making authority. As you learn more about the self-managed teams at Whole Foods Market, described in "Management in Action: Progress Report," consider whether they would continue to be equally effective if the company expanded into other countries with different cultures, and what you might do to help make sure they work well.

autonomous work groups

Groups that control decisions about and execution of a complete range of tasks.

self-designing teams

Teams with the responsibilities of autonomous work groups, plus control over hiring, firing, and deciding what tasks members perform.

Management in Action

SELF-MANAGED TEAMS AT WHOLE FOODS MARKET

To spur innovation and strengthen commitment, Whole Foods Market empowers its 90,000 employees to participate in planning and decision making with their teams. Within a store, teams are organized by department such as meat, produce, and dairy. They make decisions about product selection, pricing, promotion, and merchandising (the way products are displayed to entice buyers), as well as efforts to improve efficiency. They also contribute to decisions about hiring and compensation.[38]

The company is widely known for team member involvement in hiring decisions, but employees support rather than control the entire hiring process. A human resource employee at each store or other facility screens job applications and selects candidates with the necessary skills and concern for customer service. Candidates who pass the initial screening may be interviewed by one or more store leaders. (Applicants to lead teams generally interview with a group.)

Each employee hired begins an orientation period, during which he or she has probationary status. After the new employee has worked for 1 to 3 months, the team meets to decide whether to keep the person on the team, based on whether he or she meets the job requirements, follows company policies and procedures, provides excellent customer service, and works well with the team. Two-thirds must vote in favor of keeping the employee; otherwise, the person can try to join another team or will have to leave the company.[39]

Rewards, too, are linked to teamwork. Most incentive pay, such as bonuses, is tied to team performance, and teams exist throughout the hierarchy. But Whole Foods offers its team members more than just strong benefits packages and incentives. It offers them a shared vision. As Andres Traslavina, director of global executive recruiting at Whole Foods Market, puts it, "People choose to work here because they believe in our mission, values, and purpose. They also make this choice because these ideals align with their own. . . . Once they become part of our community, they build meaningful relationships with Team Members that feel like family."[40]

- What advantages does teamwork offer to Whole Foods Market?
- Why do you think human resource professionals conduct the initial screening process for new hires? What might be the consequences of having the store teams carry out the entire process of hiring and rewarding team members?

MANAGER'S BRIEF

PROGRESS REPORT

ONWARD

Teams at Lockheed Martin have achieved success in terms of on-time delivery and high production standards, allowing the company to meet customer demand.

508 collection/Alamy Stock Photo

How Groups Become Real Teams

LO 14-3 Summarize how groups become teams.

team

A small number of people with complementary skills who are committed to a common purpose, set of performance goals, and approach for which they hold themselves mutually accountable; see also *groups.*

The words *group* and *team* often are used interchangeably.[41] Modern managers sometimes use the word *teams* to the point that it has become a cliché; often they talk about teams even when there is no real teamwork.

It's useful to make a distinction between groups and teams. A *working group* is a collection of people who work in the same area or have been drawn together to undertake a task, but do not necessarily come together as a unit and achieve significant performance improvements. A real **team** is formed of people (usually a small number) with complementary skills who trust one another and are committed to a common purpose, common performance goals, and a common approach for which they hold themselves mutually accountable.[42]

Groups become true teams via basic group processes, critical time periods, and the management practices described throughout this chapter.

Group Processes

Assume you are the leader of a newly formed group—actually just a bunch of people. What will you face as you attempt to develop your group into a high-performing team? If groups are to develop successfully, they will engage in various processes, including the stages detailed in Exhibit 14.2

To be clear: This is an idealized version, describing genuine teamwork and performance. But many teams don't make it that far, or do so but only at mediocre levels, or don't do much during forming and disintegrate quickly. Moving from group of co-workers to

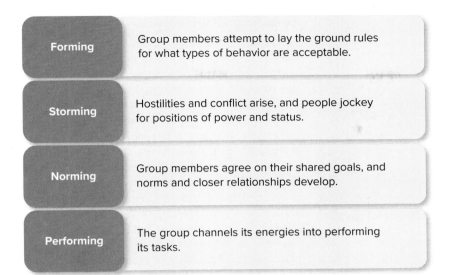

SOURCE: Adapted from Tuckman, B. W., "Developmental Sequence in Small Groups," *Psychological Bulletin* 63 (1965), pp. 384–99.

high-performing team requires certain strategies and tactics; the process must be managed strategically and well.

Virtual groups, too, can go through these stages of group development.[43] The forming stage is characterized by unbridled optimism: "I believe we have a great team and will work well together. We all understand the importance of the project and intend to take it seriously." Optimism turns into reality shock in the storming stage: "No one has taken a leadership role. We have not made the project the priority that it deserves." The norming stage comes at about the halfway point in the project life cycle, in which people refocus and recommit: "You must make firm commitments to a specific time schedule." The performing stage is the dash to the finish as teammates show the discipline needed to meet the deadline.

This is the most famous of several life-cycle models of team development.[44] Groups don't necessarily go through those processes in that particular sequence, but all the processes are important. From a leadership perspective, it helps to know the two most dynamic periods of development: (1) a *transition phase* of planning and establishing the group's mission, goals, and processes and (2) an *action phase* in which the team executes the work activities that contribute directly to it performance goals.[45] Think about how often your study or project groups dive into their work without adequately tackling the transition phase and the problems that arise because they skipped it.

Critical Periods

Groups pass through critical periods, or times when they are particularly open to formative experiences.[46] The first such critical period is in the forming stage, at the first meeting, when the group establishes rules and roles that set longer-lasting precedents. A second critical period is the midway point between the initial meeting and a deadline (such as completing a project or making a presentation). At this point, the group has enough experience to understand its work; it comes to realize that time is becoming a scarce resource and it must get on with it; and there is enough time left to change its approach if necessary.

In the initial meeting, the group should establish desired norms, roles, and other determinants of effectiveness that are discussed throughout this chapter. At the second critical period (the midpoint), groups should renew or open lines of communication with outside constituencies. The group can use fresh information from its external environment to revise its approach to performing its task and ensure that it meets customer needs. Without these activities, groups may get off on the wrong foot from the beginning, and members may never revise their behavior in a needed direction.[47]

g-stockstudio/Shutterstock

Teaming Challenges

Fast-forming, fast-acting, temporary groups do not have the luxury of time to allow all necessary team processes to develop naturally. Practices that are particularly helpful in this context[48] include (1) emphasizing the team's purpose, including why it exists, what's at stake, and what its shared values are; (2) building **psychological safety**,[49] making clear that people need to and can speak up freely, be honest, disagree, offer ideas, raise issues, share their knowledge, ask questions, or show fallibility without fear that others will think less of them or criticize them; (3) embracing failure, understanding that mistakes are inevitable, errors should be acknowledged, and learning as we go is a way to create new knowledge while we execute; and (4) putting conflict to work by explaining how we arrive at our views, expressing interest in one another's thinking and analyses, and attempting fully to understand and capitalize on others' diverse perspectives.[50]

The leader—and team members who want to help the team perform well—should ask for, expect, and model these behaviors.

LO 14-4 Explain why groups sometimes fail.

Why Groups Sometimes Fail

Groups do not always develop smoothly, become a well-oiled team, and deliver superb performance.[51] Some groups never do work out. Such groups can be frustrating for managers and members, who conclude that teams are a waste of time and that the difficulties are not worth the trouble.

It is not easy to build high-performance teams. *Teams* is often just a word management uses to describe merely putting people into groups. "Teams" sometimes are launched with little or no training or support systems. Both managers and group members need new skills to make a group work, including negotiating goals that everyone can get behind, delivering

psychological safety

When employees feel they can speak up honestly and freely without fear.

The Digital World

Are You Ready for Global Virtual Teamwork?

Approximately 1.3 billion people worldwide are engaged in virtual work.[52] Companies equip their employees for virtual teamwork with advanced videoconferencing software and instant messaging, as well as mobile devices like smartphones and tablets. In fact, according to a recent survey, more than half (51 percent) of early career employees believe that virtual teams and enhanced communications technology will make meeting face-to-face obsolete in the future.[53]

Virtual teamwork skills fall into two broad areas: (1) using online sharing tools like Google Docs, Slack, Yammer, and Dropbox and communication technology like online chat; and (2) cross-cultural skills such as adapting to different language and values, overcoming stereotypes, and coordinating across different time zones.[54]

To prepare students to work effectively in global virtual teams upon entering the workforce,

instructors from several universities in multiple countries engaged in a large-scale collaboration project. More than 6,000 business students were assigned to mostly seven-member, multinational teams. Working together virtually, the teams were tasked with developing a proposal for creating a new product for a client company and analyzing how the product would be brought to market. Instructors graded the projects, and feedback was collected from the students regarding how much they learned. Research found that the global virtual team assignments helped students:[55]

- Improve their understanding of the challenges associated with global virtual teamwork;
- Change their attitudes toward different cultures (reduction in perceived differences); and
- Use more effective behaviors with regard to team leadership, coordination, and communication.

on promises made, speaking up in groups to share ideas and build cooperation, recognizing and getting along with people's different work styles, and finding constructive ways to deal with conflict.[56] Giving up some authority and control is very difficult for managers from traditional systems, but they have to realize they will gain control in the long run by creating stronger, better-performing units.

Teams should be properly empowered,[57] as discussed in Chapter 13. The benefits of teams are reduced when they are not allowed to make important decisions—in other words, when management doesn't trust them with important responsibilities. If teams must acquire permission for every innovative idea, they will revert to making safe, traditional decisions.[58]

Empowerment enhances team performance even among virtual teams. Empowerment for virtual teams includes thorough training in using the technologies and strong technical support from management. Some virtual teams have periodic face-to-face interactions, which help performance; empowerment is particularly helpful for virtual teams that don't often meet face-to-face.[59]

> Empowerment enhances team performance even among virtual teams.

To be successful, team members must apply clear thinking and appropriate practices. The difference between success and failure often lies with whether people can join new groups and contribute quickly in ways that develop a high-performing team. Moreover, in fast-moving environments, people must do the same *repeatedly* as team assignments come, go, and come again as new challenges arise. Teamwork fails when individuals have not considered what they must contribute to their teams and how to bring out the best in one another.

Building Effective Teams

All the processes just described form the building blocks of an effective work team. But what does it really mean for a team to be effective? Team effectiveness is defined by three criteria:[60]

LO 14-5 Describe how to build an effective team.

1. *Team productivity.* The output of the team meets or exceeds the standards of quantity and quality expected by the customers, inside and outside the organization, who receive the team's goods or services.
2. *Member satisfaction.* Team members realize satisfaction of their personal needs.
3. *Member commitment.* Team members remain committed to working together again; that is, the group doesn't burn out and disintegrate after a grueling project. Looking back, the members are glad they were involved. In other words, effective teams remain viable and have good prospects for repeated success in the future.[61]

Performance Focus

The core of effective teamwork is commitment to a common purpose.[62] The best teams are those that face an important performance challenge share a common understanding and appreciation of their collective purpose. Without this, a group will be just a bunch of individuals.

The best teams also work hard at developing a common understanding of how they will work together to achieve their purpose.[63] They discuss and agree on details such as how they will allocate tasks and how they will make decisions. The team should examine its performance strategies and be open to changing them when appropriate.

Teams usually standardize at least some processes, but they should be willing to try creative new ideas if the situation calls for them.[64] With a clear, strong, motivating purpose and effective performance strategies, people pull together into a powerful force that has a chance to achieve extraordinary things.

The team's general purpose should be translated into specific, measurable performance goals.[65] You learned in Chapter 13 about how goals motivate individual performance. Performance can be defined by collective end products instead of an accumulation of individual products.[66] Team-based performance goals help define and distinguish the team's product, encourage communication within the team, energize and motivate team members, provide feedback on progress, signal team victories (and defeats), and ensure that people

focus clearly on team results. It is not simple in practice, but teams with both difficult goals and incentives to attain them tend to achieve the highest performance levels.[67]

The best team-based measurement systems inform top management of the team's level of performance, and help the team understand its own processes and gauge its own progress. Ideally, the team plays the lead role in designing its own measurement system. This responsibility is a great indicator of whether the team is truly empowered.[68]

Teams, like individuals, need feedback on their performance. Feedback from customers is especially crucial. Some customers for the team's products are inside the organization. Teams should be responsible for satisfying customers and should be given or should seek performance feedback.

Better yet, when possible, teams should interact directly with external customers who make the ultimate buying decisions about their goods and services. External customers typically provide the most honest, crucial, and useful performance feedback.[69]

Motivating Teamwork

Sometimes people work less hard and are less productive when they are members of a group. Such **social loafing** occurs when individuals believe that their contributions are not important, others will do the work for them, their lack of effort will go undetected, or they will be the lone sucker if they work hard but others don't. Perhaps you have seen social loafing in some of your student teams.[70]

Conversely, sometimes individuals work harder when they are members of a group than when they are working alone. This **social facilitation effect** occurs because individuals usually are more motivated when others are present, they are concerned with what others think of them, and they want to maintain a positive self-image.

A social facilitation effect is maintained—and a social loafing effect can be avoided—when group members know each other, they can observe and communicate with one another, clear performance goals exist, the task is meaningful to the people working on it, they believe that their efforts matter and others will not take advantage of them, and the culture supports teamwork.[71] Thus, under ideal circumstances, everyone works hard, contributes in concrete ways to the team's work, and is accountable to teammates.

> Accountability to one another, rather than just to the leader, is an essential aspect of good teamwork.

Accountability to one another, rather than just to the boss, is an essential aspect of good teamwork. Accountability inspires mutual commitment and trust.[72] Trust in your teammates—and their trust in you—may be the ultimate key to effectiveness.

Team effort also comes from designing the team's task to be motivating. You learned techniques for creating motivating tasks in Chapter 13. Tasks are motivating when they use a variety of member skills and provide high task variety, identity, significance, autonomy, and performance feedback.

Ultimately, teamwork is motivated by tying rewards to team performance.[73] Further, combining individual and shared rewards can reduce social loafing and increase team performance.[74]

It is not easy to move from a system of rewards based on individual performance to one based on team performance and cooperation. It also may not be appropriate unless people are truly interdependent and must collaborate to attain true team goals.[75] Team-based rewards, provided by about 30 percent of companies, often are combined with regular salaries and rewards based on individual performance.[76] At FIFTEEN, a marketing and advertising agency based in New York, employees work as a team, and when someone brings in a new client, the entire team shares up to 5 percent of net billings for the first three years.[77]

If team performance is difficult to measure validly, then desired behaviors, activities, and processes that indicate good teamwork can be rewarded. Individuals in teams can be given differential rewards based on teamwork indicated by each person's active participation, cooperation, leadership, and other contributions to the team.

If team members are to be rewarded differentially, such decisions are better *not* left only to the boss.[78] They should be made by the team itself, through peer ratings or multirater evaluation systems. Why? Team members are in a better position to know how teams really operate, and make more valid reward allocations.

Social Entrepreneurship

Is Co-working Here to Stay?

Social entrepreneurs are often freelancers and remote workers who prefer not to work at home. As such, they often turn to nontraditional work locations to get their work done. Growing in popularity since the mid-2000s, co-working offers space in which to work and connect with other people on a temporary basis (daily, weekly, monthly). Such interactions facilitate the exchange of business ideas, advice, and new project opportunities. "Having a place that's relaxed and comfortable is very good for creative type work," says David James, co-founder of Cowork Café. "There's a certain feeling that you get in a place like this you can't get in an office-type building."[79]

One new co-working trend is to use space that is typically empty during the workday, such as high-end restaurants that are open to the public only at dinnertime. A start-up called Spacious offers such space in several New York City restaurants. Another option is to use surplus retail space; a handful of Staples stores in the Boston area offer workspaces for rent in a partnership with a co-working company called Workbar.[80]

Co-working providers that share restaurant or retail space must limit user benefits to avoid disrupting the intended use of the location. Others that offer their own space now offer lockers and storage space, dedicated workspaces (usually for a premium), and a growing list of amenities such as gyms, cafés and bars, and classes and workshops.

As our work becomes more digital and portable, the market for co-working space continues to grow at faster rates. Currently, the gig economy—comprised of freelancers, entrepreneurs, and contract workers—makes up about a third of the overall economy.[81]

MANDEL NGAN/Getty Images

Clearly, co-working accommodates such lifestyles. But even some larger companies like Cisco and KPMG are housing their employee teams in co-working spaces.[82]

Co-working also embodies the values of community, sustainability, collaboration, and diversity—many of the same values that infuse the social entrepreneurial spirit. It's little wonder that co-working is becoming an increasingly attractive option for entrepreneurs from all walks of life.[83]

- Do you think co-working can help entrepreneurs or remote workers feel like part of a team? Could this be important? Why or why not?

- What do you think the owners of co-working spaces can do to promote collaboration and information sharing among their clients?

Member Contributions

Team members should be selected and trained so that they become effective contributors. Unilever and Procter & Gamble select team members based on the results of tests designed to predict how well they will contribute to team success in an empowered environment. The skills teams need teams include (1) technical or functional expertise, (2) problem-solving and decision-making skills, and (3) interpersonal skills. Some managers and teams mistakenly overemphasize some skills, particularly technical or functional ones, and underemphasize the others. For the best team performance, all three types of skills should be represented, and developed, among team members.

The "Social Entrepreneurship" box discusses an innovative way in which individuals contribute to one another's success.

Norms

norms

Shared beliefs about how people should think and behave.

Norms are shared beliefs about how people should think and behave. For example, some people like to keep information and knowledge to themselves, but teams should try to establish a norm of knowledge sharing because it can improve performance.[84] Teams perform

The mission of Cassini Imaging Science Team is to guide the cameras that take photos of the outer reaches of space. Though the team is widely dispersed (members' locations include New York, California, and Belgium), they are united by a shared sense of purpose and a high value placed on scientific knowledge and technical excellence.

Sources: NASA, ESA and A. Nota

roles

Different sets of expectations for how different individuals should behave.

task specialist role

An individual who has more advanced job-related skills and abilities than other group members possess.

team maintenance role

Individual who develops and maintains team harmony.

better when they think and talk about their tasks and about how they interact with and depend on one another.[85]

From the organization's standpoint, norms can be positive or negative. In some teams, everyone works hard; in other groups, employees are anti-management and do as little work as possible. Some groups develop norms of taking risks, others of being conservative.[86] A norm could dictate that employees speak either favorably or critically of the company. Team members may show concern about poor safety practices, drug and alcohol abuse, and employee theft, or they may not care about these issues (or may even condone such practices). Health consciousness is the norm among executives at some companies, but smoking is a norm at tobacco companies. Some groups have norms of distrust and of being closed toward one another; but as you might guess, norms of trust and open discussion about conflict are better for group performance.[87]

A professor described his consulting experiences at two companies that exhibited different norms in their management teams.[88] Years ago at Federal Express Corporation, a young manager interrupted the professor's talk by proclaiming that a recent decision by top management ran counter to the professor's point about corporate planning. He was challenging top management to defend its decision. A hot debate ensued, and after an hour everyone went to lunch without a trace of hard feelings. But at another corporation, the professor opened a meeting by asking a group of top managers to describe the company's culture. There was silence. He asked again. More silence. Then someone passed him an unsigned note that read, "Dummy, can't you see that we can't speak our minds? Ask for the input anonymously, in writing." As you can see, norms are important and can vary greatly from one group to another.

Roles

Roles are different sets of expectations for how different individuals should behave. Whereas norms apply generally to all team members, different roles exist for different members within the norm structure.

Two important sets of roles must be performed.[89] **Task specialist roles** are filled by individuals who have particular job-related skills and abilities. These employees keep the team moving toward accomplishment of the objectives. **Team maintenance roles** develop and maintain harmony within the team. They boost morale, give support, provide humor, soothe hurt feelings, and generally exhibit a concern with members' well-being.

Note the similarity between these roles and the important task performance and group maintenance leadership behaviors you learned about in Chapter 12. Some of these roles will be more important than others at different times and under different circumstances. But these behaviors need not be carried out only by one or two leaders; any member of the team can assume them at any time. Both types of roles can be performed by different people at different times to create and maintain an effectively functioning team.

Beyond what you read about in Chapter 12, what roles should team leaders perform? Superior leaders are better at relating, scouting, persuading, and empowering than are average team leaders.[90] *Relating* includes exhibiting more social and political awareness, caring for team members, and building trust. *Scouting* means seeking information from managers, peers, and specialists, and investigating problems systematically. *Persuading* means not only influencing the team members but also obtaining external support for teams. *Empowering* includes delegating authority, being flexible regarding team decisions, and coaching. Leaders also should roll up their sleeves and do real work to accomplish team goals, not just supervise.[91]

Finally, recall from Chapter 12 the importance of shared leadership, in which group members rotate or share leadership roles.[92]

Cohesiveness

One of the most important properties of a team is **cohesiveness**:[93] how attractive the team is to its members, how motivated members are to remain in the team, and how much team members influence one another. In general, it refers to how tightly knit the team is.

The Importance of Cohesiveness   Cohesiveness is important for two primary reasons. First, it contributes to member satisfaction. In a cohesive team, members communicate and get along well with one another. They feel good about being a part of the team. Even if their jobs are unfulfilling or the organization is oppressive, people gain some satisfaction from enjoying their co-workers.

Second, cohesiveness has a major impact on performance. Sports fans read about this all the time. When teams are winning, players talk about the team being close, getting along well, and knowing one another's games. In contrast, players attribute losing to problems within the team.

Cohesiveness clearly can have a positive effect on performance.[94] But this interpretation is simplistic; exceptions to this intuitive relationship do occur. Tightly knit work groups also can be disruptive to the organization, such as when they sabotage the assembly line, get their boss fired, or enforce low performance norms.

When does high cohesiveness lead to good performance, and when does it result in poor performance? The ultimate outcome depends on the task and on whether the group has high or low performance norms.

The Task   If the task is to make a decision or solve a problem, cohesiveness can lead to poor performance. Groupthink (Chapter 3) occurs when a tightly knit group is so cooperative that agreeing with one another's opinions and refraining from criticizing others' ideas become norms. For a cohesive group to make good decisions, it should establish a norm of constructive disagreement. This type of debating is important for groups up to the level of boards of directors.[95] In top management teams it improves the companies' financial performance.[96]

But the effect of cohesiveness on performance can be positive, particularly if the task is to produce some tangible production output. In day-to-day work groups for which decision making is not the primary task, cohesiveness can enhance performance. However, that depends on the group's performance norms.[97]

Performance Norms   Some groups are better than others at ensuring that their members behave the way the group prefers. Cohesive groups are more effective than non-cohesive groups at norm enforcement. But the next question is, Do they have norms of high or low performance?

As Exhibit 14.3 shows, the highest performance occurs when a cohesive team has high-performance norms. But if a highly cohesive group has low-performance norms, that group will have the worst performance. But in the group's eyes, it will have succeeded in achieving its goal of poor performance.

cohesiveness

The degree to which a group is attractive to its members, members are motivated to remain in the group, and members influence one another.

Bottom Line

Cohesive groups are better than non-cohesive groups at attaining the goals they want to attain; as a manager, you need to ensure that your team's goals represent good business results. *What happens if a team leader builds a cohesive team but fails to set the right goals?*

EXHIBIT 14.3

Cohesiveness, Performance Norms, and Group Performance

Performance norms

	Low	**High**
High (Cohesiveness)	High goal attainment (group's perspective) and lowest task performance (management's perspective)	High goal attainment and task performance
Low (Cohesiveness)	Poor goal attainment and task performance	Moderate goal attainment and task performance

Non-cohesive groups with high-performance norms can be effective from the company's standpoint. However, they won't be as productive as they would be if they were more cohesive. Non-cohesive groups with low-performance norms perform poorly, but they will not ruin things for management as effectively as can cohesive groups with low-performance norms.

Building Cohesiveness and High-Performance Norms

So, managers should build teams that are cohesive and have high-performance norms. The following actions can help create such teams:[98]

1. *Recruit members with similar attitudes, values, and backgrounds.* Similar individuals are more likely to get along with one another. Don't do this, though, if the team's task requires diverse skills and inputs. For example, a homogeneous committee or board might make poor decisions because it will lack different information and viewpoints and may succumb to groupthink. Educational diversity and national diversity provide more benefits than limitations to groups' information use and application.[99]

2. *Maintain high entrance and socialization standards.* Teams and organizations that are difficult to get into have more prestige. Individuals who survive a difficult interview, selection, or training process will be proud of their accomplishment and feel more attachment to the team.

3. *Keep the team small* (but large enough to get the job done). The larger the group, the less important members may feel. Small teams make individuals feel like large contributors. Amazon uses a two-pizza rule when deciding how many people should be on a team. If two pizzas can feed the team (usually between 5 and 8 members), then the team is not too big.[100]

4. *Help the team succeed, and publicize its successes.* You can empower teams as well as individuals.[101] Be a path–goal leader who facilitates success; the experience of winning brings teams closer together. Then, if you inform superiors of your team's successes, members will believe they are part of an important, prestigious unit. Teams that get into a good performance track continue to perform well as time goes on; groups that don't often enter a downward spiral in which problems compound over time.[102]

5. *Be a participative leader.* Participation in decisions gets team members more involved with one another and striving toward goal accomplishment. Too much autocratic decision making from above can alienate the group from management.

6. *Present a challenge from outside the team.* Competition with other groups makes team members band together to defeat the enemy (witness what happens to school spirit before a big game against an arch-rival). Some of the greatest teams in business and in science have been focused on winning a competition.[103]

   But don't *you* become the outside threat. If team members dislike you as a boss, they will become more cohesive—but their performance norms will be against you, not with you.

7. *Tie rewards to team performance.* To a large degree, teams are motivated just as individuals are—they do the activities that are rewarded. Make sure that high-performing teams get the rewards they deserve and that poorly performing groups get fewer rewards. Bear in mind that not just monetary rewards but also recognition for good work are powerful motivators. If you recognize and celebrate team accomplishments, cohesiveness is likely to increase. Ideally, being a member of a high-performing team, recognized as such throughout the organization, becomes a badge of honor.[104]

But don't forget: Strong cohesiveness encouraging too much agreeableness can be dysfunctional. For problem solving and decision making, the team should establish norms promoting an open, constructive atmosphere including honest disagreement over issues without personal conflict and animosity.[105]

Managing Lateral Relationships

Teams do not function in a vacuum; they are interdependent with other teams. For example, **boundary-spanning** teams are responsible for interfacing with other teams to eliminate production bottlenecks, implement new processes, and work with suppliers on quality issues.[106] Boundary-spanning activities[107] are those that entail dealing with people outside the group.

Managing Outward

Several vital roles (see Exhibit 14.4) link teams to their external environments—that is, to other individuals and groups both inside and outside the organization. One type of role that spans team boundaries is the **gatekeeper**, a team member who stays abreast of current information in scientific and other fields and informs the group of important developments. Information useful to the group also includes information about resources, trends, and political support throughout the corporation or the industry.[108]

General team strategies for managing outward include informing, parading, and probing.[109] The **informing** strategy entails making decisions with the team and then telling outsiders of the team's intentions. **Parading** is to emphasize internal team building and achieve external visibility simultaneously. **Probing** focuses most on external relations. This strategy requires team members to interact frequently with outsiders; diagnose the needs of customers, clients, and higher-ups; and experiment with solutions before taking action.

The appropriate balance between an internal and external strategic focus and between internal and external roles depends on the team's strategy and how much members need information, support, and resources from outside. When teams depend highly on outsiders, probing is the best strategy. Parading teams perform at an intermediate level, and informing teams are likely to fail. They are too isolated from the outside groups on which they depend.

Informing or parading strategies are more effective for teams that are less dependent on outside groups—for example, established teams working on routine tasks in stable environments. But for most important work teams—task forces, new-product teams, and strategic decision-making teams tackling unstructured problems in rapidly changing external environments— interfacing effectively with the outside is vital.

Lateral Role Relationships

To repeat—teams do not function in a vacuum; they are interdependent with other teams. These interdependencies create conflicts both between and within teams,[110] and therefore

LO 14-6 List methods for managing a team's relationships with other teams.

boundary-spanning

Interacting with people in other groups, thus creating linkages between groups.

gatekeeper

A team member who keeps abreast of current developments and provides the team with relevant information.

informing

A team strategy that entails making decisions with the team and then informing outsiders of its intentions.

parading

A team strategy that entails simultaneously emphasizing internal team building and achieving external visibility.

probing

A team strategy that requires team members to interact frequently with outsiders, diagnose their needs, and experiment with solutions.

EXHIBIT 14.4

Teams Link to the External Environment in Different Ways

SOURCE: Adapted from D. G. Ancona, "Outward Bound: Strategies for Team Survival in an Organization," *Academy of Management Journal* 33 (1990), pp. 334–65.

Different teams, like different individuals, have roles to perform.

require coordination and leadership.[111] To understand the process and make it more productive, it helps to know the different types of lateral role relationships.

Different teams, like different individuals, have roles to perform. As teams carry out their roles, several distinct patterns of working relationships develop:[112]

1. *Workflow relationships* emerge as materials are passed from one group to another. A group commonly receives work from one unit, processes it, and sends it to the next unit in the sequence. Your group, then, will come before some groups and after others in the process.

2. *Service relationships* exist when top management centralizes an activity to which a large number of other units must gain access. Common examples include technology services and administrative staff. Such units assist others to help them accomplish their goals.

3. *Advisory relationships* exist when teams with problems call on centralized sources of expert knowledge. For example, staff members in the human resources or legal department advise work teams when needed.

4. *Audit relationships* develop when people not directly in the chain of command evaluate the methods and performances of other teams. Financial auditors check the books, and technical auditors assess the methods and quality of the work.

5. *Stabilization relationships* involve auditing before the fact. In other words, teams sometimes must obtain clearance from others—for example, for large purchases—before they take action.

6. *Liaison relationships* involve intermediaries between teams. Managers often are called on to mediate conflict between two organizational units. Public relations people, sales managers, purchasing agents, and others who work across organizational boundaries serve in liaison roles as they maintain communications between the organization and the outside world.

By assessing each working relationship with another unit (from whom do we receive work, and to whom do we send work? what permissions do we control, and to whom must we go for authorizations?), teams can better understand whom to contact and when, where, why, and how to do so. Coordination throughout the working system improves, problems are avoided or short-circuited before they get too serious, and performance improves.[113]

LO 14-7 Identify ways to manage conflict.

Managing Conflict

The complex maze of interdependencies provides many opportunities for conflict to arise. Some conflict is constructive for the organization. Typically, conflict can foster creativity when it is about ideas rather than personalities. On the other hand, team members can work to maintain harmony during meetings, but unresolved differences can spill over into nasty conflicts outside the office.[114]

Many factors cause great potential for destructive conflict: the sheer number and variety of interpersonal contacts, ambiguities in jurisdiction and responsibility, differences in goals, competition for scarce resources, different perspectives held by members of different units, and varying time horizons in which some units attend to long-term considerations and others focus on short-term need. For many reasons, and very commonly, subgroups form along conflict fault lines.[115]

Both demographic and cross-functional diversity lead initially to problems such as stress, lower cooperation, and lower cohesiveness.[116] Transformational leadership (Chapter 13), effective diversity management (Chapter 11), and constructive conflict management (discussed next) can reduce the problems and help realize the often-untapped potential benefits of groups.[117]

Conflict Styles

People inevitably disagree and have deeper conflicts, and must decide how to manage them. The aim should be to make the conflict productive—that is, to make those involved believe they have benefited rather than lost from the conflict.[118] People believe they have benefited from a conflict when (1) a new solution is implemented, the problem is solved, and it is unlikely to emerge again; and (2) work relationships have been strengthened and people believe they can work together productively in the future.

People handle conflict in different ways. You have your own style; others' styles may be similar or may differ. Styles depend in part on the home country's cultural norms. For example, as you learned in Chapter 6, people from some cultures are more concerned with collective than with individual interests, and they are more likely than managers in the United States to turn to higher authorities to make decisions rather than resolve conflicts themselves.[119]

Teams inevitably face conflicts and must decide how to manage them.
Juice Images/Glow Images

Culture aside, any team or individual has several options regarding how to deal with conflicts.[120] These personal styles of dealing with conflict, shown in Exhibit 14.5, differ based on how much people strive to satisfy their own concerns (the assertiveness dimension) and how much they focus on satisfying the other party's concerns (the cooperation dimension).

For example, a common approach to conflict is **avoidance**. Here, people do nothing to satisfy themselves or others. They ignore the problem by doing nothing at all or address it by merely smoothing over or deemphasizing the disagreement. This, of course, fails to solve the problem or clear the air. In a large retail company, employees in the marketing department were tired of dealing with the limits placed on them by the security team of the company's information technology (IT) department. Marketing wanted more communication with consumers, while IT security was obsessed with protecting the company's data from unauthorized access. Avoiding direct conflict, but feeling good about taking action, the marketing group set up a website without telling anyone in IT security.[121]

Accommodation means cooperating on behalf of the other party but not being assertive about one's own interests. **Compromise** involves moderate attention to both parties' concerns, being neither highly cooperative nor highly assertive. This style results in satisficing

avoidance

A reaction to conflict that involves ignoring the problem by doing nothing at all or deemphasizing the disagreement.

accommodation

A style of dealing with conflict involving cooperation on behalf of the other party but not being assertive about one's own interests.

compromise

A style of dealing with conflict involving moderate attention to both parties' concerns.

EXHIBIT 14.5

Conflict Management Strategies

Cooperation

	Uncooperative	Cooperative
Assertive	Competing	Collaborating
		Compromising
Unassertive	Avoiding	Accommodating

Assertiveness

SOURCE: Thomas, K., "Conflict and Conflict Management," *Handbook of Industrial and Organizational Psychology*, ed. M. D. Dunnette. Skokie, IL: Rand McNally, 1976.

competing

A style of dealing with conflict involving strong focus on one's own goals and little or no concern for the other person's goals.

collaboration

A style of dealing with conflict emphasizing both cooperation and assertiveness to maximize both parties' satisfaction.

superordinate goals

Higher-level goals taking priority over specific individual or group goals.

mediator

A third party who intervenes to help others manage their conflict.

but not optimizing solutions. **Competing** is when people focus strictly on their own wishes and are unwilling to recognize the other person's concerns. Finally, **collaboration** emphasizes both cooperation and assertiveness. The goal is to maximize satisfaction for both parties.

At the retail company in the previous example, a consulting firm called Solutionary "forced" the marketing and IT groups to collaborate. The consultants discovered the marketing group's secret website during a routine test. Then they hacked into the company's network and altered some information including some store prices. The hacking incident brought together the IT security people and the marketing people to find a solution that would meet marketing goals without compromising the company's data.[122]

Different approaches are necessary at different times.[123] For example, *competing* can be necessary for cutting costs or dealing with other scarce resources. *Compromise* may be useful when people are under time pressure, when they need to achieve a temporary solution, or when collaboration fails. People should *accommodate* when they learn they are wrong or to minimize loss when they are outmatched. Even *avoiding* may be appropriate if the issue is trivial or resolving the conflict should be someone else's responsibility.

But when the conflict concerns important issues, when both sets of concerns are valid and important, when a creative solution is needed, and when commitment to the solution is vital to implementation, *collaboration* is the ideal approach. Collaboration is an open-minded discussion aimed at making the conflict constructive rather than destructive.[124]

An important technique is to invoke **superordinate goals**—higher-level organizational goals toward which everyone should be striving and that ultimately need to take precedence over personal or unit preferences.[125] Collaboration offers the best chance of reaching mutually satisfactory solutions based on the ideas and interests of all parties and of maintaining and strengthening work relationships.

Being a Mediator

Managers spend a lot of time trying to resolve conflict between other people. You already may have served as a **mediator**, a third party intervening to help settle a conflict between other people. Third-party intervention, done well, can improve working relationships and help the parties improve their own conflict management, communication, and problem-solving skills.[126]

Some insights into how to be effective as a mediator came from a study of human resource (HR) managers and the conflicts with which they deal.[127] HR managers encounter every type of conflict imaginable: interpersonal difficulties from minor irritations to jealousy to fights; operations issues, including union issues, work assignments, overtime, and sick leave; discipline over infractions ranging from drug use and theft to sleeping on the job; sexual harassment and racial bias; pay and promotion issues; and feuds or strategic conflicts among divisions or individuals at the highest organizational levels.

In the study, the HR managers successfully settled most of the disputes. These managers typically follow a four-stage strategy, summarized in Exhibit 14.6. They *investigate* by interviewing the disputants and others and gathering more information. While talking with the disputants, they seek both parties' perspectives, remaining as neutral as possible. The discussion should stay issue oriented, not personal. They *review the findings* to determine how best to resolve the dispute, often in conjunction with the disputants' bosses. They do not assign blame prematurely; at this point they explore solutions.

> HR managers encounter every type of conflict imaginable.

They take action by *applying solutions* and explaining their decisions and the reasoning, and advise or train the disputants to avoid future incidents. And they *follow up* by making sure everyone understands the solution, documenting the conflict and the resolution, and monitoring the results by checking back with the disputants and their bosses. Throughout, the objectives of the HR people are to be fully informed so that they understand the

EXHIBIT 14.6

A Four-Stage Model of
Dispute Resolution

SOURCE: Adapted from Blum, M. and Wall, J. A. Jr., "HRM: Managing Conflicts in the Firm," *Business Horizons*, May–June 1997, pp. 84–87.

conflict; to be active and assertive in trying to resolve it; to be as objective, neutral, and impartial as humanly possible; and to be flexible by modifying their approaches according to the situation.

Here are some other recommendations for managing conflict well.[128] Don't allow dysfunctional conflict to build, or hope or assume that it will go away. Address it before it escalates. Try to resolve it, and if the first efforts don't work, try others. And remember our discussion of procedural justice (Chapter 13). Even if disputants are not happy with your decisions, it helps to strive for fairness, making a good-faith effort, and giving them a voice in the proceedings. Caring about others' goals as well as your own will help ensure a collaborative process. Remember, too, that you may be able to ask HR specialists to help with difficult conflicts.

Virtual and E-conflict

When teams are geographically dispersed, as with virtual teams, team members tend to experience more conflict and less trust.[129] One study showed how different conflict styles affect the success of virtual teams.[130] Avoidance hurt performance. Accommodation—conceding to others to maintain harmony rather than assertively attempting to negotiate integrative solutions—had no effect on performance. Collaboration had a positive effect on performance.

The researchers also uncovered two surprises: compromise hurt performance, and competition helped performance. Compromises hurt because they often are watered-down, middle-of-the-road, suboptimal solutions. Competitive behavior was useful because the virtual teams were temporary and under time pressure, so having some individuals behave dominantly and impose decisions to achieve efficiency helped more than it hurt.

When people have problems in business-to-business (B2B) e-commerce—for example, costly delays—they tend to behave competitively and defensively rather than collaboratively.[131] Technical problems and recurring problems test people's patience. Conflict will escalate unless people use more cooperative, collaborative styles. There's a lot at stake considering the B2B market is expected to reach $1.82 trillion worldwide by 2023.[132]

Try to prevent conflicts before they arise; for example, make sure your information system is running smoothly before linking with others. Monitor and reduce or eliminate problems as soon as possible. When problems do appear, express your willingness to cooperate, and then actually be cooperative. Even technical problems require the social skills of good management.

In the end, of course, conflicts in the complex web of human relationships are unavoidable, whether virtually or face-to-face. As you read "Management in Action: Onward," think about what Whole Foods needs to keep diverse employees working together constructively.

Management in Action

BALANCING TEAMWORK AND DIVERSITY AT WHOLE FOODS MARKET

What unifies employees at Whole Foods Market is the sense of mission and shared values. Team members develop a sense of purpose, and the team monitors performance, making sure everyone contributes. In addition, unlike many retailers, Whole Foods schedules most of its employees for full-time work; this helps them learn about their jobs, build stronger relationships, and develop a greater commitment to the organization.

In addition to teamwork, Whole Foods stresses its commitment to hiring employees from many different backgrounds. In 2019, Whole Foods was once again ranked in *Forbes's* "Best Employers for Diversity."[133] Compared with other supermarkets, its dress code offers wide latitude for personal style. To counteract misunderstandings that can occur when people come from different backgrounds and express themselves differently, the company expects team members to communicate frequently and respectfully and to show appreciation for what others contribute.

But bringing together a diverse group of people with a wide range of experiences and perspectives actually poses a challenge to team cohesiveness. Management needs to be mindful of balancing the two. CEO John Mackey sees a role for competition in fostering cohesion and collaboration. The company encourages teams to compete with one another to be best at what they do.

For example, the produce teams might strive to have the biggest sales increase in their region or among all the company's stores. Shared team goals bridge individual differences and generate team cohesion.

Whole Foods strikes this balance in another way as well. For as much of an emphasis as Whole Foods puts on teamwork, it also promotes and empowers the value of the individual. By doing away with rigid codes for storewide uniforms, Whole Foods allows its employees to express their true selves in the workplace that may embody different cultural backgrounds and upbringings. It also empowers each employee to make decisions.[134] Shared responsibility is a core leadership principle, as stated on its website: "Team Members have the responsibility for their own successes and failures. Individual creativity and experimentation are essential and mistakes are opportunities to learn and grow."[135]

By empowering and valuing the individual, Whole Foods is able to uphold two key principles: teamwork and diversity.

- Whole Foods empowers the individual to help bring a diverse workforce together. What other strategies can be employed to reach this same end?
- In 2017, Amazon bought Whole Foods. How is it doing? Has the culture changed or remained the same?

KEY TERMS

accommodation, p. 449

autonomous work groups, p. 437

avoidance, p. 449

boundary-spanning, p. 447

cohesiveness, p. 445

collaboration, p. 450

competing, p. 450

compromise, p. 449

gatekeeper, p. 447

informing, p. 447

management teams, p. 435

mediator, p. 450

norms, p. 443

parading, p. 447

parallel teams, p. 435

probing, p. 447

project and development teams, p. 435

psychological safety, p. 440

roles, p. 444

self-designing teams, p. 437

self-managed teams, p. 436

social facilitation effect, p. 442

social loafing, p. 442

superordinate goals, p. 450

task specialist role, p. 444

team, p. 438

teaming, p. 435

team maintenance role, p. 444

transnational teams, p. 435

virtual teams, p. 435

work teams, p. 434

RETAINING WHAT YOU LEARNED

In Chapter 14, you learned that teams can help organizations be more effective, productive, and innovative. Compared to the past, teams now have more authority and may be self-managed. Teams come in several shapes and sizes, including work teams, project and development teams, parallel teams, management teams, transnational teams, and virtual teams. Groups that keep developing may go through stages: forming, storming, norming, and performing. A group generally becomes a team when team members commit to a purpose, pursue goals, and hold themselves accountable to one another. Moving from a traditional structure to a team-based approach tends to be challenging for many companies. Ways to build high-performance teams include establishing a common purpose, setting measurable goals, and making sure everyone works hard and contributes in meaningful ways. Team members perform important roles such as gatekeeping, informing, parading, and probing. Inevitably, conflict arises on teams. Five basic interpersonal approaches to managing conflict are avoidance, accommodation, compromise, competition, and collaboration. Techniques for managing conflict between other parties include acting as a mediator.

LO 14-1   Discuss how teams can contribute to an organization's effectiveness.

- Teams are building blocks for organization structure and forces for productivity, quality, cost savings, speed, change, and innovation.
- They potentially provide many benefits for both the organization and individual members.

LO 14-2   Describe different types of teams.

- Compared with traditional work groups that were closely supervised, today's teams have more authority and often are self-managed.
- Teams now are used in many more ways, for many more purposes, than in the past. Types of teams include work teams, project and development teams, parallel teams, management teams, transnational teams, and virtual teams.
- Work teams range from traditional groups with low autonomy to self-designing teams with high autonomy.

LO 14-3   Summarize how groups become teams.

- Groups carry on a variety of important developmental processes, including forming, storming, norming, and performing (see Exhibit 14.2).
- A true team has members who complement one another; who are committed to a common purpose, performance goals, and approach; and who hold themselves accountable to one another.

LO 14-4   Explain why groups sometimes fail.

- Teams do not always work well. Some companies underestimate the difficulties of moving to a team-based approach.

- Teams require training, empowerment, and a well-managed transition to make them work.
- Groups often fail to become effective teams unless managers and team members commit to the idea, understand what makes teams work, and implement appropriate practices.

LO 14-5   Describe how to build an effective team.

- Create a team with a high-performance focus by establishing a common purpose, translating the purpose into measurable team goals, designing the team's task so it is intrinsically motivating, designing a team-based performance measurement system, and providing team rewards.
- Work to develop a common understanding of how the team will perform its task. Make it clear that everyone has to work hard and contribute in concrete ways.
- Establish mutual accountability and build trust among members.
- Examine the team's strategies periodically and be willing to adapt.
- Make sure members contribute fully by selecting them appropriately, training them, and ensuring that all important roles are carried out.
- Take steps to establish team cohesiveness and high-performance norms.

LO 14-6   List methods for managing a team's relationships with other teams.

- Don't manage inside the team only. Manage the team's relations with outsiders, too.
- Perform important roles such as gatekeeping, informing, parading, and probing.
- Identify the types of lateral role relationships you have with outsiders. This can help coordinate efforts throughout the work system.

LO 14-7   Identify ways to manage conflict.

- Managing lateral relationships well can prevent some conflict. But conflict arises because of the sheer number of contacts, ambiguities, goal differences, competition for scarce resources, and different perspectives and time horizons.
- Five basic interpersonal approaches to managing conflict can be used: avoidance, accommodation, compromise, competition, and collaboration. You should be willing and able to use them all, depending on the situation.
- Superordinate goals are higher-level organizational goals that can help generate a collaborative relationship if conflicting parties commit to them.
- As a manager, you undoubtedly will need to act as a mediator between conflicting parties; the chapter offers a number of useful strategies and tactics.

DISCUSSION QUESTIONS

1. Why do you think some people resist the idea of working in teams? How would you help them to be more engaged?

2. Consider a team project at school in which you participated. How effective was the teamwork? How could it have been improved?

3. Experts say that teams are a means, not an end. What do you think they mean? Why do some companies create teams to accomplish work that could easily be done by individuals? How can this pitfall be avoided?

4. Choose a sports team with which you are familiar. Assess its effectiveness and discuss the factors that contribute to its successes and failures.

5. Assess the effectiveness, as in Question 4, of a student group with which you have been affiliated. Could anything have been done to make it more effective?

6. Consider the various roles members have to perform for a team to be effective. Which roles would play to your strengths, and which to your weaknesses? How can you become a better team member?

7. Discuss personal examples of virtual conflict and how they were managed, well or poorly.

8. What do you think is your most commonly used style in handling conflict? Least common? What can you do to expand your repertoire and become better at conflict management?

9. Generate real examples of how superordinate goals have helped resolve a conflict. Identify some current conflicts and provide some specific ideas for how superordinate goals could help.

10. How might self-managed teams operate differently in different cultures? What are the advantages, disadvantages, and implications of homogeneous versus highly diverse self-managed teams?

EXPERIENTIAL EXERCISES

14.1   Student Project Group Development

OBJECTIVE
To explore how student project groups develop through various stages.

INSTRUCTIONS
1. Think about the last time you were assigned to a student group to complete a course-related project.

2. Next, write down how your group experienced (if at all) each of the four stages of group development: forming, storming, norming, and performing.

3. The instructor assigns students into groups of three and asks team members to share their answers with one another.

Student Project Group Processes Worksheet

Process	To what degree did your student project group experience this stage? Explain.
Forming	
Storming	
Norming	
Performing	

14.2 Which Style of Conflict Resolution Would You Use?

OBJECTIVE

To explore which conflict styles students would use in a variety of workplace scenarios.

INSTRUCTIONS

1. Read each of the following workplace scenarios.

2. Next, choose the conflict style being used by the individual in the scenario.

3. Describe why you think the conflict style will (or will not) help resolve the situation.

Conflict Styles

—*Avoidance*
—*Accommodation*
—*Compromise*
—*Competing*
—*Collaboration*

CONFLICT STYLE WORKSHEET

Scenario 1: While at work, Maria and her co-worker notice that a laptop is missing from an employee's cubicle (note that the employee is on vacation). Maria's first impulse is to report the missing laptop to the manager. However, her co-worker thinks there may be an innocent reason for the missing laptop. He wants Maria to join him in speaking with employees who are in the office. Maria agrees to team up with her co-worker but insists that if after 1 hour they haven't found the missing laptop, they would inform the manager.

Maria is using the _____ conflict style.

To what degree will this style help (or not help) resolve the situation?

_____

_____

_____

Scenario 2: Assume Paul is waiting to hear from his boss whether he is finally going to receive the promotion that he has been promised. Paul's boss just found out that the budget for the new position for which Paul was slotted has been cut. Consequently, he will not receive the promotion. His boss thinks she can get Paul a job transfer and promotion in another division in the company. She needs a few days to make it happen and doesn't want to discuss the situation with Paul until it is a done deal. Paul's boss intends to keep him busy with projects over the next few days until she finds out whether Paul receives the alternate promotion.

Paul's boss is using the _____ conflict style until she hears back from her contact in the other division.

To what degree will this style help (or not help) resolve the situation?

_____

_____

_____

Concluding Case

UN-TEAMWORK AT QUADRA

Based in Alabama, Quadra Drilling Systems sells drilling equipment around the world. Its factories in Brazil, China, the Czech Republic, India, and South Africa run multiple shifts to keep up with strong demand in developing nations. Quadra is very profitable, but environmental groups have expressed concern about its negative impact on climate change. As executives developed a response, they realized that achieving more sustainable resource use could make the company more efficient and create a more favorable business environment for the long term.

The executives decided to form a group called the Quadra Green Team, made up of representatives in each of its locations. Each facility's managers chose three employees—one each from engineering, production, and finance—with leadership skills, English-language ability, and knowledge about environmental sustainability.

To save money as well as fuel, the Green Team operates as a virtual team. Its members connect by videoconferencing once a month. Between meetings, they share thoughts via email and Google Docs.

In the initial phases, all the Green Team members were enthusiastic. But over time, several members became concerned that the team didn't have a firm plan to establish measurable goals within a specific timeline. One meeting ended up being devoted to the team debating whether to establish an action plan or refine the ideas already submitted. Frustrated, the South African representatives took one idea to their facility's management for approval and began to implement it without telling the rest of the team.

Shortly thereafter, the representatives in India and the Czech Republic were openly complaining that meetings were always scheduled at times convenient for the employees in the U.S. headquarters. The Chinese team members agreed. The debate about whether headquarters should always schedule meetings lasted for 45 minutes, after which no one was in any mood to discuss sustainability.

Two of the Alabama team representatives took their frustration to their managers. The executive team investigated and decided the team needed to be unified behind a common goal. They directed the team to present three resource-saving ideas by the end of the year, and they offered incentives to promote teamwork. The team members are each allocated 100 points a month. Whenever one team member appreciates another's actions, he or she gives that person points. All team members' point scores are viewable by the whole team. At the end of the year, the points earned by each employee will be exchanged for cash rewards in the local currency. The executives hope the program will motivate greater cooperation.

DISCUSSION QUESTIONS

1. What went wrong in the formation of the Green Team? What should Quadra have done differently?

2. What conditions contribute to this team's cohesiveness? What reduces cohesiveness?

3. What do you think of the points plan? How should Quadra's executives help the Green Team manage its conflict?

ENDNOTES

1. Whole Foods website, "Our Core Values," https://www.wholefoodsmarket.com/mission-values/core-values, accessed April 11, 2019.

2. Whole Foods website, "Our Core Values," https://www.wholefoodsmarket.com/mission-values/core-values, accessed April 11, 2019.

3. Forbes, "America's Best Employers," https://www.forbes.com/companies/whole-foods-market/#3cb32b4e34df, accessed April 11, 2019.

4. Russ Buchanan, "Employee Turnover in a Grocery," Small Business Chronicle, http://smallbusiness.chron.com/employee-turnover-grocery-15810.html, accessed April 11, 2019.

5. J. Martin and K. Eisenhardt, "Rewiring: Cross-Business-Unit Collaborations in Multibusiness Organizations," Academy of Management Journal 53 (2010), pp. 265–301; E. C. Wenger and W. M. Snyder, "Communities of Practice: The Organizational Frontier," Harvard Business Review, January–February 2000, pp. 139–45.

6. "How Companies Use Teams to Drive Performance," Ernst & Young Insights, http://www.ey.com, accessed May 23, 2015; S. Cohen and D. Bailey, "What Makes Teams Work: Group Effectiveness Research from the Shop Floor to the Executive Suite," Journal of Management 23 (1997), pp. 239–90.

7. G. Chen, L. Donahue, and R. Klimoski, "Training Undergraduates to Work in Organizational Teams," Academy of Management Learning and Education 3 (2004), pp. 27–40.

8. T. McDowell, D. Agarwal, D. Mille, T. Okamoto, and T. Page, "Organization Design: The Rise of Teams," Deloitte, February 29, 2016, www.dupress.deloitte.com;T. O'Neill and E. Salas, "Creating High Performance Teamwork in Organizations," Human Resource Management Review 28 (2018), pp. 325–31.

9. J. Weed, "California's Papa & Barkley Cannabis Company Grows with Teamwork," Forbes, June 22, 2018, https://www.forbes.com.

10. S. Siang, "How Mentors, Teamwork and Lessons from Failure Led to Success for CEO of e.l.f. Cosmetics," Forbes, March 11, 2019, https://www.forbes.com.

11. M. Mace, "Google Logic: Why Google Does the Things It Does the Way It Does," The Guardian, July 9, 2013, http://www.theguardian.com; A. Somech and A. Drach-Zahavy, "Translating Team Creativity to Innovation Implementation: The Role of Team Composition and Climate for Innovation," Journal of Management 39 (2013).

12. Company website, "InGenius: Accelerator Program within Nestlé, Focusing on Employee-Driven Innovation," Nestlé, http://ingenius-accelerator.nestle.com, accessed March 21, 2019.

13. D. Nadler, J. R. Hackman, and E. E. Lawler III, Managing Organizational Behavior (Boston: Little, Brown, 1979).

14. A. C. Edmondson, "Teamwork on the Fly," Harvard Business Review, April 2012, pp. 72–80.

15. L. Gratton and T. Erickson, "Eight Ways to Build Collaborative Teams," Harvard Business Review, November 2007, http://www.hbr.com; M. Cianni and D. Wnuck, "Individual Growth and Team Enhancement: Moving toward a New Model of Career Development,"

Academy of Management Executive 11 (1997), pp. 105–15.

16. J. Hollenbeck, B. Beersma, and M. Schouten, "Beyond Team Types and Taxonomies: A Dimensional Scaling Conceptualization for Team Description," Academy of Management Review 37 (2012), pp. 82–106.

17. S. Cohen, "New Approaches to Teams and Teamwork," in J. Galbraith, E. E. Lawler III, and Associates, Organizing for the Future (San Francisco: Jossey-Bass, 1993).

18. S. Cohen and D. Bailey, "What Makes Teams Work: Group Effectiveness Research from the Shop Floor to the Executive Suite," Journal of Management 23 (1997), pp. 239–90.

19. M. O'Hara, "Congress Relaunches Transgender Equality Task Force," NBC News, March 2, 2017, www.nbc.com; S. McBride, "Parents of Transgender Children Call on Congress to Pass the Equality Act," The Human Rights Campaign, January 30, 2019, www.hrc.org.

20. L. Mullins, "Integration Crew for Maryland Bank," American Banker, February 13, 2007, General Reference Center Gold, http://find.galegroup.com; P. C. Earley and C. B. Gibson, MultinationalWork Teams (Mahwah, NJ: Erlbaum, 2002), p. 214.

21. K. Lagerstrom and M. Andersson, "Creating and Sharing Knowledge within a Transnational Team—The Development of a Global Business System," Journal of World Business 38 (2003), pp. 84–95; C. Snow, S. Snell, S. Davison, and D. Hambrick, "Use Transnational Teams to Globalize Your Company," Organizational Dynamics, Spring 1996, pp. 50–67.

22. L. Gilson, M. Travis, N. C. J. Young, M. Vartiainen, and M. Hakonen, "Virtual Teams Research: 10 Years, 10 Themes, and 10 Opportunities," Journal of Management 41 (2015), pp. 1313–37; J. Dulebohn and J. Hoch, "Virtual Teams in Organizations," Human Resource Management Review 27 (2017), pp. 569–74.

23. J. Schaubroeck and A. Yu, "When Does Virtuality Help or Hinder Teams? Core Team Characteristics as Contingency Factors," Human Resource Management Review 27 (2017), pp. 635–47.

24. B. Kirkman, B. Rosen, C. Gibson, P. Tesluk, and S. McPherson, "Five Challenges to Virtual Team Success: Lessons from Sabre, Inc.," Academy of Management Executive 16 (2002), pp. 67–80.

25. B. Liao, "Leadership in Virtual Teams: A Multilevel Perspective," Human Resource Management Review 27 (2017), pp. 648–59.

26. N. Hill and K. Bartol, "Empowering Leadership and Effective Collaboration in Geographically Dispersed Teams," Personnel Psychology 69 (2016), pp. 159–98.

27. A. C. Edmondson, "Teamwork on the Fly," Harvard Business Review, April 2012, pp. 72–80.

28. Kim Elsesser, "Is This the Answer to Diversity and Inclusion?" Forbes, January 28, 2019, https://www.forbes.com/sites/kimelsesser/2019/01/28/is-this-the-answer-to-diversity-and-inclusion/#1353cd17523f.

29. Mindtools, "Empathy at Work: Developing Skills to Understand Other People," https://www.mindtools.com/pages/article/EmpathyatWork.htm, accessed April 11, 2019.

30. Peter Lee, "3 Simple Ways to Build an Inclusive Team," *Medium,* May 18, 2018, https://medium.com/@innovativepete/3-simple-ways-to-build-an-inclusive-team-1e1a2a4b6aa4.

31. Sonia Thompson, "Follow These 5 Steps to Build a High-Performing Inclusive Team—Even If You've Struggled in the Past," *Inc.,* https://www.inc.com/sonia-thompson/follow-these-5-steps-to-build-a-high-performing-inclusive-team-even-if-youve-struggled-in-past.html, accessed April 11, 2019.

32. R. Banker, J. Field, R. Schroeder, and K. Sinha, "Impact of Work Teams on Manufacturing Performance: A Longitudinal Field Study," *Academy of Management Journal* 39 (1996), pp. 867–90.

33. M. Muethel and M. Hoegl, "Shared Leadership Effectiveness in Independent Professional Teams," *European Management Journal* 31 (2013), pp. 423–32; D. Yeatts, M. Hipskind, and D. Barnes, "Lessons Learned from Self-Managed Work Teams," *Business Horizons,* July–August 1994, pp. 11–18.

34. B. Kirkman and D. Shapiro, "The Impact of Cultural Values on Job Satisfaction and Organizational Commitment in Self-Managing Work Teams: The Mediating Role of Employee Resistance," *Academy of Management Journal* 44 (2001), pp. 557–69.

35. C. Langfred, "The Downside of Self-Management: A Longitudinal Study of the Effects of Conflict on Trust, Autonomy, and Task Interdependence in Self-Managing Teams," *Academy of Management Journal,* 2007, pp. 885–900.

36. M. Johnson, J. Hollenbeck, D. DeRue, C. Barnes, and D. Jundt, "Functional versus Dysfunctional Team Change: Problem Diagnosis and Structural Feedback for Self-Managed Teams," *Organizational Behavior and Human Decision Processes* 122 (2013), pp. 1–11; S. Sarker, S. Sarker, S. Kirkeby, and S. Chakraborty, "Path to 'Stardom' in Globally Distributed Hybrid Teams: An Examination of a Knowledge-Centered Perspective Using Social Network Analysis," *Decision Sciences* 42 (2011), 339–70; B. Macy and H. Isumi, "Organizational Change, Design, and Work Innovation: A Meta-Analysis of 131 North American Field Studies—1961–1991," *Research in Organizational Change and Development* 7 (1993), pp. 235–313.

37. T. Fernandes, "Spotify Squad Framework—Part 1," *Medium,* March 6, 2017, https://medium.com.

38. Whole Foods website, "Our Core Values," https://www.wholefoodsmarket.com/mission-values/core-values, accessed April 11, 2019.

39. David Burkus, "Why Whole Foods Builds Its Entire Business on Teams," *Forbes,* June 8, 2016, https://www.forbes.com/sites/davidburkus/2016/06/08/why-whole-foods-build-their-entire-business-on-teams/#386ddaa03fa1.

40. Greenhouse, "Greenhouse OPEN Speaker Series: How Whole Foods Market Approaches Hiring, with Director of Global Executive Recruiting, Andres Traslavina," February 8, 2018, http://www.greenhouse.io/blog/greenhouse-open-speaker-series-learn-why-diversity-inclusion-is-top-of-mind-for-whole-foods-market-director-of-global-executive-recruiting-andres-traslavina.

41. S. Cohen and D. Bailey, "What Makes Teams Work: Group Effectiveness Research from the Shop Floor to the Executive Suite," *Journal of Management* 23 (1997), pp. 239–90.

42. J. Katzenbach and D. Smith, "The Discipline of Teams," *Harvard Business Review,* March–April 1993, pp. 111–20.

43. D. Mukherjee, S. Lahiri, D. Mukherjee, and T. Billing, "Leading Virtual Teams: How Do Social, Cognitive, and Behavioral Capabilities Matter?" *Management Decision* 50 (2012), pp. 273–90; S. Furst, M. Reeves, B. Rosen, and R. Blackburn, "Managing the Life Cycle of Virtual Teams," *Academy of Management Executive,* May 2004, pp. 6–20. Quotes in this paragraph are from pp. 11 and 12.

44. S. Humphrey and F. Aime, "Team Microdynamics: Toward an Organizing Approach to Teamwork" *Academy of Management Annals* 8 (2014), pp. 443–503.

45. M. Marks, J. Mathieu, and S. Zaccaro, "A Temporally Based Framework and Taxonomy of Team Processes," *Academy of Management Review* 26 (2011), pp. 356–76; F. Morgeson, D. S. DeRue, and E. Karam, "Leadership in Teams: A Functional Approach to Understanding Leadership Structures and Processes," *Journal of Management* 36 (2010), pp. 5–39.

46. C. J. G. Gersick, "Time and Transition in Work Teams: Toward a New Model of Group Development," *Academy of Management Journal* 31 (1988), pp. 9–41.

47. J. R. Hackman, *Groups That Work (and Those That Don't)* (San Francisco: Jossey-Bass, 1990).

48. J. R. Hackman, *Groups That Work (and Those That Don't)* (San Francisco: Jossey-Bass, 1990); A. C. Edmondson, "Teamwork on the Fly," *Harvard Business Review,* April 2012, pp. 72–80.

49. A. Newman, R. Donahue, and N. Eva, "Psychological Safety: A Systematic Review of the Literature," *Human Resource Management Review* 27 (2017), pp. 521–35; M. Frazier, S. Fainshmidt, R. Klinger, A. Pezeshkan, and V. Vracheva, "Psychological Safety: A Meta-Analytic Review and Extension," *Personnel Psychology* 70 (2017), pp. 113–65; C. Roussin, T. MacLean, and J. Rudolph, "The Safety in Unsafe Teams: A Multilevel Approach to Team Psychological Safety," *Journal of Management* 42 (2016), pp. 1409–33.

50. I. Hoever, D. van Knippenberg, W. van Ginkel, and H. Barkema, "Fostering Team Creativity: Perspective Taking as Key to Unlocking Diversity's Potential," *Journal of Applied Psychology* 97 (2012), pp. 982–96.

51. R. Cross, "Looking before You Leap: Assessing the Jump to Teams in Knowledge-Based Work," *Business Horizons,* September–October 2000, pp. 29–36.

52. Tammy Johns and Lynda Gratton, "The Third Wave of Virtual Work," https://hbr.org/2013/01/the-third-wave-of-virtual-work, accessed April 11, 2019.

53. "Dell and Intel Future Workforce Study Provides Key Insights into Technology Trends Shaping the Modern Global Workplace," Dell, July 18, 2016, www.dell.com.

54. J. Ferri-Reed, "Building Innovative Multi-Generation Teams," *Journal of Quality and Participation* 37 (October 2014), pp. 20–22; R. Shehadi and D. Karam, "Five Essential Elements of the Digital Workplace," *Forbes,* March 31, 2014, http://www.forbes.com; T. Johns and L. Grafton, "The Third Wave of Virtual Work," *Harvard Business Review,* January 1, 2013, http://www.hbr.org.

55. V. Taras, D. Caprar, D. Rottig, R. Sarala, N. Zakaria, F. Zhao, et al., "A Global Classroom? Evaluating the Effectiveness of Global Virtual Collaboration as Teaching Tool in Management Education," *Academy of Management Learning & Education* 12 (2013), pp. 414–35.

56. Geoff Colvin, "The Art of the Self-Managing Team," *Fortune,* December 5, 2012, http://management.fortune.cnn.com; Chana R. Schoenberger, "How to Get People to Work Together," *The Wall Street Journal,* September 7, 2012, http://blogs.wsj.com; John Baldoni, "The Secret to Team Collaboration: Individuality," *Inc.,* January 18, 2012, http://www.inc.com.

57. N. Lorinkova, M. Pearsall, and H. P. Sims Jr., "Examining the Differential Longitudinal Performance of Directive versus Empowering Leadership in Teams," *Academy of Management Journal* 56 (2013), pp. 573–96; M. T. Maynard, L. Gilson, and J. Mathieu, "Empowerment—Fad or Fab? A Multilevel Review of the Past Two Decades of Research," *Journal of Management* 38 (2012), pp. 1231–81; S. Seibert, G. Wang, and S. Courtright, "Antecedents and Consequences of Psychological and Team Empowerment in Organizations: A Meta-Analytic Review," *Journal of Applied Psychology* 96 (2011), pp. 981–1003; G. Chen, P. N. Sharma, S. Edinger, D. Shapiro, and J.-L. Farh, "Motivating and Demotivating Forces in Teams: Cross-Level Influences of Empowering Leadership and Relationship Conflict," *Journal of Applied Psychology* 96 (2011), pp. 541–57.

58. A. Nahavandi and E. Aranda, "Restructuring Teams for the Reengineered Organization," *Academy of Management Executive,* November 1994, pp. 58–68.

59. B. Kirkman, B. Rosen, P. Tesluk, and C. Gibson, "The Impact of Team Empowerment on Virtual Team Performance: The Moderating Role of Face-to-Face Interaction," *Academy of Management Journal* 47 (2004), pp. 175–92.

60. D. Nadler, J. R. Hackman, and E. E. Lawler III, *Managing Organizational Behavior* (Boston: Little, Brown, 1979).

61. D. Nadler, J. R. Hackman, and E. E. Lawler III, *Managing Organizational Behavior* (Boston: Little, Brown, 1979).

62. J. Katzenbach and D. Smith, "The Discipline of Teams," *Harvard Business Review,* March–April 1993, pp. 111–20.

63. J. Katzenbach and D. Smith, "The Discipline of Teams," *Harvard Business Review,* March–April 1993, pp. 111–20.

64. L. Gibson, J. Mathieu, C. Shalley, and T. Ruddy, "Creativity and Standardization: Complementary or Conflicting Drivers of Team

Effectiveness?" *Academy of Management Journal* 48 (2005), pp. 521–31.

65. C. Meyer, "How the Right Measures Help Teams Excel," *Harvard Business Review,* May–June 1994, pp. 95–103.

66. J. R. Katzenbach and J. A. Santamaria, "Firing Up the Front Line," *Harvard Business Review,* May–June 1999, pp. 107–17.

67. D. Blumenthal, Z. Song, A. Jena, and T. Ferris, "Guidance for Structuring Team-Based Incentives in Health Care," *American Journal of Managed Care* 19 (2013), pp. 64–70; D. Knight, C. Durham, and E. Locke, "The Relationship of Team Goals, Incentives, and Efficacy to Strategic Risk, Tactical Implementation, and Performance," *Academy of Management Journal* 44 (2001), pp. 326–38; A. Kleingeld, H. van Mierlo, and L. Arends, "The Effect of Goal Setting on Group Performance: A Meta-Analysis," *Journal of Applied Psychology* 96 (2011), pp. 1289–1304; C. Barnes, J. Hollenbeck, D. Jundt, D. S. De Rue, and S. Harmon, "Mixing Individual Incentives and Group Incentives: Best of Both Worlds or Social Dilemma?" *Journal of Management* 37 (2011), pp. 1611–35.

68. B. L. Kirkman and B. Rosen, "Powering Up Teams," *Organizational Dynamics* (Winter 2000), pp. 48–66.

69. E. E. Lawler III, *From the Ground Up* (San Francisco: Jossey-Bass, 1996).

70. M. Schippers, "Social Loafing Tendencies and Team Performance: The Compensating Effect of Agreeableness and Conscientiousness," *Academy of Management Learning & Education* 13 (2014), pp. 62–81; A. Jassawalla, H. Sashittal, and A. Maishe, "Students' Perceptions of Social Loafing: Its Antecedents and Consequences in Undergraduate Business Classroom Teams," *Academy of Management Learning and Education,* 2009, pp. 42–54.

71. M. Erez, "Is Group Productivity Loss the Rule or the Exception? Effects of Culture and Group-Based Motivation," *Academy of Management Journal* 39 (1996), pp. 1513–37; A. Mas and E. Moretti, "Peers at Work," *The American Economic Review* 99 (2009), pp. 112–45.

72. J. Katzenbach and D. Smith, "The Discipline of Teams," *Harvard Business Review,* March–April 1993, pp. 111–20.

73. Y. Garbers and U. Konradt, "The Effect of Financial Incentives on Performance: A Quantitative Review of Individual and Team-Based Financial Incentives," *Journal of Occupational and Organizational Psychology* 87 (2014), pp. 102–37; M. Johnson, J. Hollenbeck, S. Humphrey, D. Ilgen, D. Jundt, and C. Meyer, "Cutthroat Cooperation: Asymmetrical Adaptation to Changes in Team Reward Structures," *Academy of Management Journal,* 2006, pp. 103–19.

74. M. J. Pearsall, M. S. Christian, and A. P. J. Ellis, "Motivating Interdependent Teams: Individual Rewards, Shared Rewards, or Something Between?" *Journal of Applied Psychology* 95 (2010), pp. 183–91.

75. R. Wageman, "Interdependence and Group Effectiveness," *Administrative Science Quarterly* 40 (1995), pp. 145–80.

76. S. Grant, "What the Best Companies Get Right about Salaries," *Bloomberg,* March 1, 2016, www.bloomberg.com.

77. L. Handrick, "Top 25 Employee Incentive Programs from the Pros," FitSmallBusiness, July 18, 2018, https://fitsmallbusiness.com.

78. E. E. Lawler III, *From the Ground Up* (San Francisco: Jossey-Bass, 1996).

79. Susan Johnston Taylor, "Are Empty High-End Restaurants the Next Coworking Trend?" *Fast Company,* July 8, 2016, https://www.fastcompany.com/3061602/why-freelancers-are-paying-to-work-in-high-end-restaurants-before-they-op.

80. Susan Johnston Taylor, "Are Empty High-End Restaurants the Next Coworking Trend?" *Fast Company,* July 8, 2016, https://www.fastcompany.com/3061602/why-freelancers-are-paying-to-work-in-high-end-restaurants-before-they-op.

81. "Coworking, Social Entrepreneurship & Trends to Look for in 2018," CO Hatch, May 29, 2018, https://www.cohatch.com/blog/2017-year-in-review-coworking-social-entrepreneurship-trends-to-look-for-in-2018.

82. Don Ball, "The Stats on Co-working Spaces Are Even Better Than What They Seem," *Entrepreneur,* June 12, 2018, https://www.entrepreneur.com/article/314191.

83. Kjersti Sjaatil, "Are Coworking Spaces Shaping Entrepreneurship Cultures? A Case Study of Tøyen Startup Village," *Medium,* September 2, 2018, https://medium.com/datadriveninvestor/

are-coworking-spaces-shaping-entrepreneurship-cultures-a-case-study-of-t%C3%B8yen-startup-village-4f822163f386.

84. A. Grant, "Givers Take All: The Hidden Dimension of Corporate Culture," *McKinsey Quarterly* (2013), pp. 52–65; A. Srivastava, K. Bartol, and E. Locke, "Empowering Leadership in Management Teams: Effects on Knowledge Sharing, Efficacy, and Performance," *Academy of Management Journal,* 2006, pp. 1239–51.

85. L. A. DeChurch and J. R. Mesmer-Magnus, "The Cognitive Underpinnings of Effective Teamwork: A Meta-Analysis," *Journal of Applied Psychology* 95 (2010), pp. 32–53.

86. J. M. Levine, E. T. Higgins, and H. Choi, "Development of Strategic Norms in Groups," *Organizational Behavior and Human Decision Processes* 82 (2000), pp. 88–101.

87. M. Duffy, K. Scott, J. Shaw, B. Tepper, and K. Aquino, "A Social Context Model of Envy and Social Undermining," *Academy of Management Journal* 55 (2012), pp. 643–66; K. Jehn and E. Mannix, "The Dynamic Nature of Conflict: A Longitudinal Study of Intragroup Conflict and Group Performance," *Academy of Management Journal* 44 (2001), pp. 238–51.

88. J. O'Toole, *Vanguard Management: Redesigning the Corporate Future* (New York: Doubleday, 1985).

89. R. F. Bales, *Interaction Process Analysis: A Method for the Study of Small Groups* (Reading, MA: Addison-Wesley, 1950).

90. V. U. Druskat and J. Wheeler, "Managing from the Boundary: The Effective Leadership of Self-Managing Work Teams," *Academy of Management Journal* 46 (2003), pp. 435–57.

91. J. R. Katzenbach and D. K. Smith, *The Wisdom of Teams* (Boston: Harvard Business School Press, 1993).

92. V. Nicolaides, K. LaPort, T. Chen, A. Tomassetti, E. Weis, S. Zaccaro, and J. Cortina, "The Shared Leadership of Teams: A Meta-analysis of Proximal, Distal, and Moderating Relationships," *Leadership Quarterly* 25 (2014), 923–42; J. Carson, P. Tesluk, and J. Marrone, "Shared Leadership in Teams: An Investigation of Antecedent Conditions and Performance," *Academy of Management Journal,* 2007, pp. 1217–34.

93. S. E. Seashore, *Group Cohesiveness in the Industrial Work Group* (Ann Arbor: University of Michigan Press, 1954).

94. S. Wise, "Can a Team Have Too Much Cohesion? The Dark Side to Network Density," *European Management Journal* 32 (2014), pp. 703–11; B. Mullen and C. Cooper, "The Relation between Group Cohesiveness and Performance: An Integration," *Psychological Bulletin* 115 (1994), pp. 210–27.

95. R. Hasson, "How to Resolve Board Disputes More Effectively," *MIT Sloan Management Review* 48 (2006), pp. 77–80; D. P. Forbes and F. J. Milliken, "Cognition and Corporate Governance: Understanding Boards of Directors as Strategic Decision-Making Groups," *Academy of Management Review* 24 (1999), pp. 489–505.

96. T. Simons, L. H. Pelled, and K. A. Smith, "Making Use of Difference: Diversity, Debate, and Decision Comprehensiveness in Top Management Teams," *Academy of Management Journal* 42 (1999), pp. 662–73.

97. S. E. Seashore, *Group Cohesiveness in the Industrial Work Group* (Ann Arbor: University of Michigan Press, 1954).

98. B. Lott and A. Lott, "Group Cohesiveness as Interpersonal Attraction: A Review of Relationships with Antecedent and Consequent Variables," *Psychological Bulletin,* October 1965, pp. 259–309.

99. K. Dahlin, L. Weingart, and P. Hinds, "Team Diversity and Information Use," *Academy of Management Journal* 48 (2005), pp. 1107–23.

100. R. Gillett, "Productivity Hack of the Week: The Two Pizza Approach to Productive Teamwork," *Fast Company,* October 24, 2014, http://www.fastcompany.com.

101. B. L. Kirkman and B. Rosen, "Beyond Self-Management: Antecedents and Consequences of Team Empowerment," *Academy of Management Journal* 42 (1999), pp. 58–74.

102. J. R. Hackman, *Groups That Work (and Those That Don't)* (San Francisco: Jossey-Bass, 1990).

103. W. Bennis, *Organizing Genius* (Reading, MA: Addison-Wesley, 1997).

104. M. Cianni and D. Wnuck, "Individual Growth and Team Enhancement: Moving toward a New Model of Career

Development," *Academy of Management Executive* 11 (1997), pp. 105–15.

105. T. O'Neill and M. McLarnon, "Optimizing Team Conflict Dynamics for High Performance Teamwork," *Human Resources Management Review* 28 (2018), pp. 378–94.

106. R. S. Wellins and W. C Byham, *Inside Teams: How 20 World-Class Organizations Are Winning through Teams* (San Francisco: Jossey-Bass, 1996).

107. J. A. Marrone, "Team Boundary Spanning: A Multilevel Review of Past Research and Proposals for the Future," *Journal of Management* 36 (2010), pp. 911–40.

108. D. G. Ancona, "Outward Bound: Strategies for Team Survival in an Organization," *Academy of Management Journal* 33 (1990), pp. 334–65.

109. D. G. Ancona, "Outward Bound: Strategies for Team Survival in an Organization," *Academy of Management Journal* 33 (1990), pp. 334–65.

110. L. Van Bunderen, L. Greer, and D. Van Knippenberg, "When Interteam Conflict Spirals into Intrateam Power Struggles: The Pivotal Role of Team Power Structures," *Academy of Management Journal* 61 (2018), pp. 1100–30.

111. T. De Vries, J. Hollenbeck, R. Davison, F. Walter, and G. Van der Vegt, "Managing Coordination in Multiteam Systems: Integrating Micro and Macro Perspectives," *Academy of Management Journal* 59 (2016), pp. 1823–44; W. De Vries, F. Walter, G. Van der Vegt, and P. Essens, "Antecedents of Individuals' Interteam Coordination: Broad Functional Experiences as a Mixed Blessing," *Academy of Management Journal* 57 (2014), pp. 1334–59; H. Bruns, "Working Alone Together: Coordination in Collaboration Across Domains of Expertise," *Academy of Management Journal* 56 (2013), pp. 62–83; M. Hogg, D. van Knippenberg, and D. Rast III, "Intergroup Leadership in Organizations: Leading across Group and Organizational Boundaries," *Academy of Management Review* 37 (2012), pp. 232–55.

112. L. Sayles, *Leadership: What Effective Managers Really Do, and How They Do It* (New York: McGraw-Hill, 1979).

113. L. Sayles, *Leadership: What Effective Managers Really Do, and How They Do It* (New York: McGraw-Hill, 1979).

114. M. Holt, "Risks of Not Confronting Conflict in the Workplace," *Chron (Houston Chronicle),* http://www.smallbusiness.chron.com, accessed May 25, 2015; M. Myatt, "5 Keys of Dealing with Workplace Conflict," *Forbes,* February 22, 2012, http://www.forbes.com; P. Lencioni, "How to Foster Good Conflict," *The Wall Street Journal,* November 13, 2008, http://online.wsj.com.

115. A. Caron and T. Cummings, "A Theory of Subgroups in Work Teams," *Academy of Management Review* 37 (2012), pp. 441–70.

116. D. Staples and L. Zhao, "The Effects of Cultural Diversity in Virtual Teams versus Face-to-Face Teams," *Group Decision and Negotiation* 15 (2006), pp. 389–406; J. Chatman and F. Flynn, "The Influence of Demographic Heterogeneity on the Emergence and Consequences of Cooperative Norms in Work Teams," *Academy of Management Journal* 44 (2001), pp. 956–74; R. T. Keller, "Cross-Functional Project Groups in Research and New Product Development: Diversity, Communications, Job Stress, and Outcomes," *Academy of Management Journal* 44 (2001), pp. 547–55.

117. J.-L. Farh, C. Lee, and C. Farh, "Task Conflict and Team Creativity: A Question of How Much and When," *Journal of Applied Psychology,* 2010, pp. 1173–80; J. Shaw, J. Zhu, M. Duffy, K. Scott, H. A. Shih, and E. Susanto, "A Contingency Model of Conflict and Team Effectiveness," *Journal of Applied Psychology* 96 (2011), pp. 391–400; F. R. C. de Wit, L. Greer, and K. Jehn, "The Paradox of Intergroup Conflict: A Meta-Analysis," *Journal of Applied Psychology* 97 (2012), pp. 360–90; S. Thatcher and P. Patel, "Group Faultlines: A Review, Integration, and Guide for Research," *Journal of Management* 38 (2012), pp. 969–1009; I. Hoever, D. van Knippenberg, W. van Ginkel, and H. Barkema, "Fostering Team

Creativity: Perspective Taking as Key to Unlocking Diversity's Potential," *Journal of Applied Psychology* 97 (2012), pp. 982–96.

118. D. Tjosvold, *Working Together to Get Things Done* (Lexington, MA: Lexington Books, 1986).

119. T. Kim, C. Wang, M. Kondo, and T. Kim, "Conflict Management Styles: The Differences among the Chinese, Japanese and Koreans," *International Journal of Conflict Management* 18 (2007), pp. 23–41; C. Tinsley and J. Brett, "Managing Workplace Conflict in the United States and Hong Kong," *Organizational Behavior and Human Decision Processes* 85 (2001), pp. 360–81.

120. K. W. Thomas, "Conflict and Conflict Management," in *Handbook of Industrial and Organizational Psychology,* ed. M. D. Dunnette (Chicago: Rand McNally, 1976).

121. D. Tynan, "IT Turf Wars," *InfoWorld.com,* February 14, 2011, Business & Company Resource Center, http://galenet.galegroup.com.

122. D. Tynan, "IT Turf Wars," *InfoWorld.com,* February 14, 2011, Business & Company Resource Center, http://galenet.galegroup.com.

123. K. Conerly and A. Tripathi, "What Is Your Conflict Style? Understanding and Dealing with Your Conflict Style," *Journal for Quality and Participation* 27 (2004), pp. 16–20; K. W. Thomas, "Toward Multidimensional Values in Teaching: The Example of Conflict Behaviors," *Academy of Management Review,* 1977, pp. 484–89.

124. D. Tjosvold, A. Wong, and N. Chen, "Constructively Managing Conflicts in Organizations," *Annual Review of Organizational Psychology and Organizational Behavior* 1 (2014), pp. 545–68.

125. R. Lau and A. Cobb, "Understanding the Connections between Relationship Conflict and Performance: The Intervening Roles of Trust and Exchange," *Journal of Organizational Behavior* 31 (2010), pp. 898–917; C. O. Longenecker and M. Neubert, "Barriers and Gateways to Management Cooperation and Teamwork," *Business Horizons,* September–October 2000, pp. 37–44.

126. P. S. Nugent, "Managing Conflict: Third-Party Interventions for Managers," *Academy of Management Executive* 16 (2002), pp. 139–54.

127. M. Blum and J. A. Wall Jr., "HRM: Managing Conflicts in the Firm," *Business Horizons,* May–June 1997, pp. 84–87.

128. J. Leon-Perez, F. Medina, A. Arenas, and L. Munduate, "The Relationship between Interpersonal Conflict and Workplace Bullying," *Journal of Managerial Psychology* 30 (2015), pp. 250–63; J. A. Wall Jr. and R. R. Callister, "Conflict and Its Management," *Journal of Management* 21 (1995), pp. 515–58.

129. J. Polzer, C. B. Crisp, S. Jarvenpaa, and J. Kim, "Extending the Faultline Model to Geographically Dispersed Teams: How Collocated Subgroups Can Impair Group Functioning," *Academy of Management Journal* 49 (2006), pp. 679–92; T. Brake, "Tips for Managing Conflict on Virtual Teams," *Training Magazine,* March 22, 2016, www.trainingmag.com.

130. F. Siebdrat, M. Hoegl, and H. Ernst, "How to Manage Virtual Teams," *MIT Sloan Management Review* 50 (2009), pp. 63–68; M. Montoya-Weiss, A. Massey, and M. Song, "Getting It Together: Temporal Coordination and Conflict Management in Global Virtual Teams," *Academy of Management Journal* 44 (2001), pp. 1251–62.

131. R. Standifer and J. A. Wall Jr., "Managing Conflict in B2B Commerce," *Business Horizons,* March–April 2003, pp. 65–70.

132. "US B2B eCommerce Will Hit $1.8 Trillion by 2023," Forrester, January 28, 2019, www.forrester.com.

133. "Best Employers for Diversity 2019," *Forbes,* https://www.forbes.com/companies/whole-foods-market/#275822af34df, accessed April 11, 2019.

134. Greenhouse, "Greenhouse OPEN Speaker Series: How Whole Foods Market Approaches Hiring, with Director of Global Executive Recruiting, Andres Traslavina," February 8, 2018, http://www.greenhouse.io/blog/greenhouse-open-speaker-series-learn-why-diversity-inclusion-is-top-of-mind-for-whole-foods-market-director-of-global-executive-recruiting-andres-traslavina.

135. Whole Foods website, "Our Leadership Principles," https://www.wholefoodsmarket.com/our-leadership-principles, accessed April 11, 2019.

CHAPTER 15
Communicating

The single biggest problem with communication is the illusion that it has taken place.

—G. B. Shaw

Monkey Business Images/Shutterstock

learning objectives

After studying Chapter 15, you will be able to:

LO 15-1 Discuss important advantages of two-way communication.

LO 15-2 Identify communication problems to avoid.

LO 15-3 Describe when and how to use the various communication channels.

LO 15-4 Summarize ways to become a better sender and receiver of information.

LO 15-5 Explain how to improve downward, upward, and horizontal communication.

LO 15-6 Summarize how to work with the company grapevine.

LO 15-7 Describe the boundaryless organization and its advantages.

chapter outline

Interpersonal Communication
 One-Way versus Two-Way Communication
 Communication Pitfalls
 Oral and Written Channels
 Digital Communication and Social Media
 Media Richness

Improving Communication Skills
 Improving Sender Skills
 Improving Receiver Skills

Organizational Communication
 Downward Communication
 Upward Communication
 Horizontal Communication
 Informal Communication
 Transparency

Management in Action

COMMUNICATING, SOUNDCLOUD STYLE

What's the largest music and audio platform on the Internet? It's not Spotify. It's not Pandora. It's not Amazon. The answer is SoundCloud, the music- and audio-sharing platform that Alexander Ljung and Eric Wahlforss founded in a Berlin nightclub in 2008.

The company has grown into a highly valued resource not only for established and aspiring musicians, but also for their fans, who can connect with them on the site. SoundCloud also goes beyond music, providing content for those who enjoy listening to university lectures, comedy acts, radio shows, and arts reviews. SoundCloud currently hosts more than 135 million high-quality tracks accessed by more than 175 million users, and it employs 300 people in two countries: Germany, where it's headquartered, and the United Kingdom.[1]

Ljung and Wahlforss built the company culture as a collaborative and entrepreneurial environment that minimizes hierarchy and top-down management. "The aim of the organization/process is getting out of the way as much as possible for people to actually get the job done," says Wahlforss. Thus, product teams are responsible for creating their own workflows and communication flows, and product managers are charged with communicating their vision of the product to team members and ensuring that everyone takes ownership of it. "We aim to empower our employees rather than to control them," Wahlforss explains.[2]

SoundCloud's flat organization and hands-off management style depend on a healthy flow of

Simon Dawson/Getty Images

communication within and between the company's functional groups, as well as across four different time zones. That flow is supported by a company intranet and chat platform, and by regular "All Hands" meetings that everyone is expected to attend (remotely or in person in Berlin).[3]

The communications manager chooses a theme for each meeting, and he or she or one of his or her team prepares an agenda, selects the speakers, and serves as host. Planning begins a few weeks in advance, and a run-through ensures that speakers are prepared and polished. The manager surveys all employees after every meeting, asking three brief questions: Was the meeting valuable? What did you like best? How can we improve the meeting?[4]

SoundCloud's All Hands meetings are so popular that some remote employees now meet for breakfast so they can participate in the Berlin event in real time rather than watch taped footage later. As you read this chapter, consider how free-flowing communication among employees can build commitment and empowerment.

Communicating effectively contributes mightily to people's job performance and organizational effectiveness.[5] It is a primary means by which managers carry out the responsibilities described throughout this book, such as making group decisions, sharing a vision, interacting with external stakeholders, motivating employees, and leading teams. In this chapter, we present important communication concepts and practical guidelines for improving your own effectiveness. We also discuss communication throughout the organization.

Interpersonal Communication

communication

The transmission of information and meaning from one party to another through the use of shared symbols.

Communication is the transmission of information and meaning from one party to another through the use of shared symbols. Exhibit 15.1 shows a general model of how one person communicates with another.

The sender initiates the process by conveying information to the receiver—the person for whom the message is intended. The sender has a meaning she wishes to convey and encodes the meaning into symbols (chosen words). Then the sender transmits, or sends, the message through some channel, such as a verbal or written medium.

The receiver decodes the message (reads it) and attempts to interpret the sender's meaning. The receiver may provide feedback to the sender by encoding a message in response to the sender's message.

This sounds simple, but noise, or interference in the process, often blocks understanding. Noise could be anything that interferes with accurate communication: poor phone reception, poor listening while distracted by other things, or simple fatigue or stress.

The model in Exhibit 15.1 is more than a theoretical treatment of the process: it points out the key ways in which communications can break down. Mistakes can occur at each stage of the model. A manager who is alert to potential problems can perform each step carefully to ensure more effective communication. The model also helps explain the topics discussed next: the differences between one-way and two-way communication, communication pitfalls, mixed signals and misperception, and types of communication channels.

LO 15-1 Discuss important advantages of two-way communication.

One-Way versus Two-Way Communication

one-way communication

A process in which information flows in only one direction—from the sender to the receiver, with no feedback loop.

In **one-way communication**, information flows in only one direction—from the sender to the receiver, without the feedback loop. A manager sends an e-mail and sees no replies. An employee phones the information technology (IT) department and leaves a message requesting repairs for her computer. A supervisor yells about an employee's mistake and then storms away.

When receivers do respond to senders—Person B becomes the sender and Person A the receiver—it's now **two-way communication**. The manager's e-mail invites the receiver to reply with any questions, the IT department returns the employee's call and asks for details about the computer problem, and the supervisor calms down and listens to the employee's explanation.

two-way communication

A process in which information flows in two directions—the receiver provides feedback, and the sender is receptive to the feedback.

True two-way communication means not only that the receiver provides feedback but also that the sender is receptive to the feedback. In these constructive exchanges, information is shared between both parties, rather than merely delivered from one person to the other.

EXHIBIT 15.1

A General Model of Communication

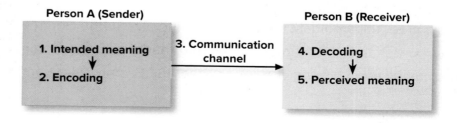

Because it is faster and easier for the sender, one-way communication is very common. A busy executive finds it easier to dash off an e-mail message than to discuss a problem in person with a subordinate. Also, he doesn't have to deal with questions or challenges from someone who disagrees.

Two-way communication is more difficult and time-consuming than one-way communication. However, it is more accurate: fewer mistakes occur, and fewer problems arise later. When receivers have a chance to ask questions, share concerns, and make suggestions or modifications, they understand more precisely what the sender is communicating and what they should do with the information.[6] Effectively sharing information among teammates is a prime contributor to performance.[7]

As discussed in Chapter 10, performance appraisals typically consist of two-way communication between employees and their managers, usually once per year. About one-third of companies—for example, Adobe, Gap, IBM, and OppenheimerFunds—are breaking with tradition by providing employees with more "frequent, informal check-ins."[8] It's a good example of two-way communication at its best. Managers can provide constructive suggestions to improve job performance, and employees can ask questions that relate to their current projects, maximizing on-the-job training.[9]

Communication Pitfalls

LO 15-2 Identify communication problems to avoid.

As we know from personal experience, the sender's intended message does not always get across to the receiver. You are operating under an illusion if you think there is a perfect correlation between what you say and what people hear.[14] Errors can occur in every stage of the communication process. In the encoding stage, people leave out facts or write

Inclusiveness Works

Becoming More Inclusive through Storytelling

Accumulating evidence indicates that organizations with diverse and inclusive workplaces are more profitable.[10] The reason for this is simple. As Miguel Castro, senior director and lead for the Culture & Identity, Global Diversity & Inclusion Office at SAP, says, "When people are comfortable and can express themselves in an authentic way, they are more likely to perform better, which increases engagement and contributes to the organization as a whole."[11]

To encourage employees from all backgrounds to feel comfortable in the workplace, some organizations are turning to one of the most fundamental means of human communication: storytelling. Sharing stories is an intimate activity that requires trust and respect, but it also fosters understanding and empathy, a key component of an inclusive workplace. Firms are beginning to focus their efforts on finding ways for employees to share true stories that can help deliver on the challenging goals of D&I initiatives.

Elena Valentine is a filmmaker, design researcher, and CEO of Skill Scout, and she's turning her attention to filming employee stories as a way to create more inclusive environments. She recently conducted a workshop on the strategy, stating, "At the heart of inclusion is the feeling of connection and belongingness. . . . I've seen the power storytelling has to make meaningful connections in the workplace."[12]

Many organizations are starting to feel the same way. For example, SAP, a market leader in enterprise application software, recently launched "We Are One," which is an employee-driven event that focuses on sharing diverse life experiences. And the business-networking firm LinkedIn has launched #ProudAtWork, a campaign that encourages employees from all company levels and units to share stories about their feelings of belonging in the workplace.[13]

- Do you believe storytelling really will help promote inclusiveness in the workplace? What are the benefits? What are the risks?

- Have you noticed that storytelling brings people closer together or further apart? Explain your answer.

Bottom Line

Don't expect to deliver results without communicating effectively with all relevant stakeholders. *How can two-way communication with your supervisor help you deliver your best work as an employee?*

perception

The process of receiving and interpreting information.

filtering

The process of withholding, ignoring, or distorting information.

LO 15-3 Describe when and how to use the various communication channels.

confusing phrases. In the transmission stage, a message may get lost in a cluttered inbox or bullet points on PPT slides could be too small to read from the back of the room.

Decoding problems arise when the receiver doesn't pay attention or reads too quickly and overlooks a key point. And of course receivers can misinterpret the message: A listener takes a general statement by the boss too personally, or a sideways glance is taken the wrong way.

More generally, people's perceptual and filtering processes create misinterpretations. **Perception** is the process of receiving and interpreting information. As you know, such processes are not perfectly objective. They are subjective because people's self-interested motives and attitudes create biased interpretations. People often assume that others share their views and care more about their own views than those of others.[15] But perceptual differences get in the way of shared consensus.

To remedy this, it helps to remember that others' viewpoints are legitimate and to incorporate others' perspectives into your interpretation of issues.[16] Understanding others' viewpoints is fundamental to working collaboratively. And your ability to take others' perspectives—to really to understand the viewpoints of customers or your boss and colleagues—can strengthen your job performance.[17]

Filtering is the process of withholding, ignoring, or distorting information. Senders do this when they tell the boss what they think the boss wants to hear or give unwarranted compliments rather than honest criticism. Receivers also filter information; they may fail to recognize a message's importance or attend to some aspects of it but not others. Probably you have heard the saying: "So-and-so hears only what he wants to hear (or sees only what he wants to see)."

Sometimes managers, so as not to demotivate or start an argument, soften or distort the fact that an employee needs to correct a problem behavior. A manager may sugarcoat the feedback by saying, "That wasn't bad" or "You'll get the hang of it after a while." Honesty, including better ideas or suggestions, works better.[18]

Due to filtering and perceptual differences, you cannot assume the other person means what you think he means or understands the meanings you intend. Managers need to interpret signals and adjust their own communication styles and perceptions to the people with whom they interact.[19]

Oral and Written Channels

Communication move through a variety of channels including oral, written, and digital. Each has advantages and disadvantages.

Oral communication includes face-to-face discussions, phone conversations, meetings, and formal presentations and speeches. Its advantages are that questions can be asked and answered, feedback can be immediate and direct, receivers can sense the sender's sincerity (or lack thereof), and oral communication often is more persuasive than written. However, oral communication has disadvantages too: It can lead to spontaneous, ill-considered statements (and regret), and there is no permanent record of it unless you make an effort to record it.

Written communication includes e-mails, memos, reports, spreadsheets, product brochures, and other documents. Advantages to using written messages are that you can revise and perfect them and save them in a permanent record. Your message stays the same even if relayed through many people, and receivers have more time to analyze the message. Disadvantages are that the sender has no control over where, when, or if the message is read; the sender does not receive immediate feedback; the receiver may not understand parts of the message; and the message might not contain all the information others need.[20]

You should weigh these considerations when deciding whether to communicate orally or in writing. Also, sometimes use both channels, such as following up a meeting with confirming notes, or writing an e-mail to prepare someone for your phone call.

Digital Communication and Social Media

Employers are catching up with consumers in their use of social media. For example, a recent survey of the *Fortune* 500 companies found that about 60 percent of CEOs are not active on any social media channel like LinkedIn, Twitter, or YouTube.[21]

Other CEOs are using social media to become industry thought leaders and generate lots of free advertising for their brands.[22] Take John Legere, CEO of T-Mobile, who has garnered over 5 million followers on his Twitter account where he displays his outsized personality and posts about company products.[23]

Advantages The obvious advantages of digital communications are sharing more information and quickly delivering it to large numbers of people. In virtual teams, maximum effectiveness comes from knowing and using the most appropriate technologies, including videoconferencing and other face-to-face methods.[24]

For example, Microsoft's SharePoint allows companies to create websites that enable employees to collaborate on web pages, documents, lists, calendars, and data. Hitachi Solutions Europe helps client companies create SharePoint platforms to quickly respond to changing business needs and reduce their training costs.[25] Amazon, Tesla, and Airbnb use the online platform Incogneato to gather ideas anonymously before participants meet in person to discuss.[26] This approach tends to yield a wider range of potential solutions.

Some research indicates that more data sharing and critical argumentation occur with a group decision support system than is found in face-to-face meetings, resulting in higher-quality decisions.[27] But anonymity tempts participants to make careless, rude, or ill-advised statements, so employers may require identities to be revealed or limit access to social networking technologies. However, companies see services such as LinkedIn, Twitter, and Facebook as necessary for staying in touch with the hundreds of millions of people who use these services—especially younger generations of co-workers and customers who are likelier to check tweets and texts than voice mail and email.[28] Complicating this trend is how employees use their own mobile devices and applications in the workplace.

Disadvantages Disadvantages of digital communication include the inability to pick up subtle, nonverbal, or inflectional cues about what the communicator is thinking or conveying, and difficulties in solving complex problems that require extended, face-to-face interactions. Plus, people are more willing to lie online.[29] In online bargaining—even before it begins—negotiators distrust one another more than in face-to-face negotiations. After the negotiation (compared with face-to-face negotiators), people usually are dissatisfied with economically equivalent outcomes.[30]

Although organizations rely heavily on digital communications for group decision making, face-to-face groups generally develop more trust among members, take less time, make higher-quality decisions, and are more satisfying for members.[31] Email is most appropriate for routine messages that do not require the exchange of large quantities of complex information. It is less suitable for communicating confidential information, resolving conflicts, or negotiating.[32]

Employees sometimes are laid off via email and even text messages.[33] Not only do these impersonal channels cause hurt feelings, but an upset employee can easily forward messages, creating a snowball effect that can embarrass everyone involved.

Email is one of the most convenient forms of communication, but what are some of the pitfalls? How often have you sent an email, whether personal or professional, and found that someone misinterpreted the message?

GaudiLab/Shutterstock

Bottom Line
Imagine the savings of money and natural resources you could create if your company sought and used the most cost-effective ways to communicate. *What forms of digital communication do you use (on the job or for personal use)?*

Cisco employees in New York (left) and San Jose, California (on-screen), meeting via monitor. What are the advantages and disadvantages to using this type of technology to communicate?

Ariel Skelley/Blend Images LLC

Companies worry about leaks and negative portrayals, and may require employees to agree to specific guidelines before they post information on company review sites like Glassdoor.com or Salary.com.

Unisys, Sprint, and Hewlett-Packard train employees use social media in a productive manner. Guidelines for social media use include the following: (1) Use reasonable etiquette and treat people respectfully, (2) identify and represent yourself (usually you are not representing your employer), (3) be factual and don't violate company disclosure policies, and (4) review the message before posting it (remember, it will become a permanent record).[34]

Digital channels invite misinterpretations and nasty messages. People hurl insults, vent frustration, snitch on co-workers to the boss, and otherwise breach protocol. The lack of nonverbal cues can result in kidding remarks being taken seriously, causing resentment and regret.[35] People see negative meanings in neutral messages[36] and are more likely to feel justified in lying.[37] Confidential messages—including details about people's personal lives and insulting, embarrassing remarks—can become public knowledge through digital leaks.

Different people and sometimes different business units latch onto different channels as their medium of choice. And emails and other forms of digital communication sometimes are seen by people they weren't intended for. Be careful with whether you click Reply or Reply to All. Most companies save all digital messages and can use them in court cases to indict individuals or companies.

Digital messages sent from work and on company-provided devices are private property—but they are private property of the system's owner, not of the sender. Here's a golden rule (like the sunshine rule in the ethics chapter): Don't hit Send or post a comment unless you'd be comfortable having the contents become public and read by your mother or a competitor.

> Digital communication like texts and emails are the property of the system's owner, not of the sender.

Managing the Digital Load   Digital communication media are essential, but the sheer volume and variety of sources can be overwhelming.[38] For example, a recent study found that business people send and receive about 125 emails per day.[39] Fortunately, a few rules of thumb can help.

With information overload, the challenge is to separate the truly important from the unimportant. Take control over your time by deciding how often you need to check email, texts, and social media updates, and turn off the notifications and badges when you are doing other things.[40] When you check messages, reply immediately if you can, so you handle each message only once, and use organizational tools such as file folders. Avoid burdening others by copying them on messages they do not need to see.

Social media offer more efficient communication tools than email. You can post answers to business questions on social media sites where it is far simpler to address the usual follow-up questions and forwards that accompany email discussions.[41]

Management also has a role to play. Employees check messages and emails constantly if they believe (perhaps correctly) that this is what their bosses or customers expect of them. Managers can help employees by establishing a "standard response time" policy that sets acceptable guidelines.[42]

Some organizations recognize the downsides of digital media overuse. To help employees stop feeling connected to work 24/7, health care consulting firm Vynamic implemented a policy prohibiting work-related communication from 10 p.m. to 6 a.m. during the week and all weekend. It's called "ZZZ-mail, as in catching some zzz's."[43] In New York City, legislatures are considering passing a bill that would ban employers from sending after-hours work emails to employees.[44]

The Virtual Office   Based on the philosophy that management's focus should be on what people do, not on where they are, the **virtual office** is a mobile office in which people can work anywhere—their home, car, airport, coffee houses, customers' offices—as long as they have the tools to communicate with customers and colleagues. Consulting firm Deloitte gives many of its employees the choice to work up to five days a week outside the office. When desired, employees can reserve a workspace at the company for the day, a concept known as "hotdesking."[45]

In the short run, at least, the benefits of virtual offices appear substantial. Saving money on rent and utilities is an obvious advantage. Deloitte saved 30 percent in office rental and energy costs.[46] A virtual office gives employees access to whatever information they need from the company, whether they are in a meeting, visiting a client, or working from home.[47] Hiring and retaining talented people is easier because virtual offices support scheduling flexibility and may make it possible to keep an employee who wants to relocate—for example, with a spouse taking a new job in another city.

Web-hosting company Automattic, based in San Francisco, takes the virtual office to an extreme, and its people love it. Employees work at their homes in 28 states and 53 countries. For meetings, participants sign in to the Skype or Google+ Hangouts video chat service. If a topic is sensitive or a misunderstanding occurs, employees place a phone call (the traditional way or using Skype). For an informal chat, they often use the ICQ instant-messaging system.

Automattic has not abandoned face-to-face communication. Teams are encouraged to meet at least once a year in mutually agreed-on locations. And at a different location each year, the company hosts a weeklong grand meetup for everyone to gather, get (re) acquainted, and talk strategy.[48]

What will be the longer-term impact on productivity and morale? We may be in danger of losing too many human moments, those authentic encounters that happen only when people are physically together.[49] Some people hate working at home. Some send texts or emails in the middle of the night—and others receive and reply to them. Some work around the clock and still feel they are not doing enough. The long hours of being constantly close to the technical tools of work can cause burnout.

And some companies are learning that direct supervision at the office is necessary to maintain the quality of work, especially when employees are inexperienced and need guidance. The virtual office requires changes in how human beings work and interact, and presents technical challenges. So, although it is much hyped and useful, it will not completely replace real offices and face-to-face work.

virtual office

A mobile office in which people can work anywhere, as long as they have the tools to communicate with customers and colleagues.

The Digital World

Gmail Predicts What You Want to Say

Business is often conducted via email. Research shows that 86 percent of business professionals list email as their preferred communication medium. Meanwhile, business users send an average of over 120 emails per day, contributing to a worldwide total of over 269 billion emails sent every 24 hours.[50]

Google is taking the efficiency of email a step further by incorporating artificial intelligence (AI) into its popular email service Gmail. With an AI-enabled feature called Smart Compose, as sentences are written, Gmail suggests forthcoming words and phrases. If users want to accept Gmail's suggestions, they click the Tab key; to ignore them, they continue typing.[51]

The AI feature is still learning, as evidenced by some initial challenges. After the feature revealed a gender bias, Google programmers blocked Smart Compose from using gender-based pronouns in its suggestions.[52] Despite such growing pains, Google plans to invest in more AI features in its future products.

1. Have you used Google's Smart Compose feature? If so, what did you think of it?
2. In what other ways can you imagine AI helping to improve business communication?

Media Richness

media richness

The degree to which a communication channel conveys information.

Some communication channels convey more information than others. The amount of information a medium conveys is called **media richness**.[53] (See Exhibit 15.2 for a comparison.) The more information or cues a medium sends to the receiver, the richer the medium is.[54]

The richest media are more personal than technological, provide quick feedback, allow lots of descriptive language, and send different types of cues. Face-to-face communication is the richest medium because it offers a variety of cues in addition to words: tone of voice, facial expression, body language, and other nonverbal signals. It also allows more descriptive language than, say, an email does. In addition, it affords more opportunity for the receiver to give feedback to and ask questions of the sender, turning one-way into two-way communication.

A phone conversation is less rich than face-to-face communication, and email and texts are less rich yet. In general, you should send difficult and unusual messages through richer media, transmit simple and routine messages through less rich media, and use multiple media for important messages that you want to ensure people attend to, understand, and remember.[55] You should also consider factors such as which medium your receiver prefers, the preferred communication style in your organization, and cost.[56]

EXHIBIT 15.2
Differences in Media Richness

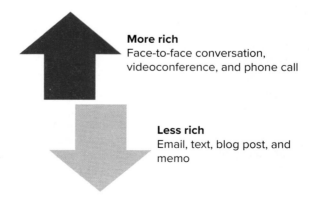

More rich
Face-to-face conversation, videoconference, and phone call

Less rich
Email, text, blog post, and memo

Management in Action

SOUNDCLOUD USES MULTIPLE CHANNELS

SoundCloud, the largest music and audio platform on the Internet, takes the quality of its internal communications so seriously that it has put a top manager directly in charge of them. It's the communications manager's job to help the company's 300 employees keep effortlessly in touch even though they work in two countries: Germany and the UK.

SoundCloud's flat structure and minimal organizational hierarchy mean employees carry a great deal of responsibility for communicating with each other, and the company's growth and location in four time zones have raised challenges that called for creative solutions. Fortunately, the company has many communication channels to rely on.

SoundCloud's regular All Hands meeting takes place a few times each quarter and focuses on a theme, such as new products, quarterly objectives, or strategy. All employees are expected to attend, whether remotely in real time or via recorded video or, in Berlin, in person. The IT team helps maintain high production values, checking sound quality and camera angles, to make viewing the meetings as engaging as possible for SoundCloud's remote employees. Employees can participate in the All Hands Q&A sessions directly or by submitting questions through the company's

intranet or chat platform, however they feel comfortable, so the boldest and the shyest can all be heard from.[57]

Other kinds of meetings that occur throughout the company are Town Halls and Open Houses. In Town Halls, team members gather to discuss goals and performance and to kick off new projects or celebrate completed ones. Open Houses are small and informal; they can center on new or surprising user research findings, product prototypes, or progress reports on new-product launches.[58]

For real-time communications, SoundCloud relies on Slack, the collaborative messaging platform, as well as Skype to connect the company's four far-flung offices. Slack also serves a social function, hosting separate discussion groups and channels for special interests and hobbies that bring together people from all over the company.

- What benefits does SoundCloud enjoy from implementing so many different communication channels?
- How well do you think the company is supporting its employees' need to communicate across four different locations? What additional communication channels or tools could it add?

Improving Communication Skills

Employers are dismayed by college graduates' poor communication skills. A demonstrated ability to communicate effectively will make you a more attractive job candidate. You can do many things to improve your communication skills, both as a sender and as a receiver.

LO 15-4 Summarize ways to become a better sender and receiver of information.

Improving Sender Skills

To start, be aware that honest, direct, straight talk is important but all too rare. CEOs sometimes spin their messages for different audiences—the investment community, employees, government, or the board. This may or may not be straight talk: the focus of the messages can differ, but inconsistencies cause difficulties. People want to be able to identify a leader's perspective, reasoning, and intentions.[59]

Beyond this basic point, senders can improve their skills in persuasion, writing, language, and nonverbal signaling

Presentation and Persuasion Skills   Throughout your career, you will be called upon to state your case on a variety of issues. You will have information and perhaps an opinion or proposal to present to others. Exhibit 15.3 offers some useful tips on formal presentations; the following discussion focuses on other keys to persuasion.

EXHIBIT 15.3
Ten Ways to Add Power to Your Presentations

"All the great speakers were bad speakers at first." Ralph Waldo Emerson

1. *Spend adequate time on the **content** of your presentation.* Know your content inside and out; you'll be able to discuss it conversationally and won't be tempted to memorize. If you believe in what you're saying and *own* the material, you will convey enthusiasm and will be more relaxed.

2. *Clearly understand the **objective** of your presentation.* Answer this question with one sentence: "What do I want the audience to believe following this presentation?" Everything else in a presentation—the structure, the words, the visuals—should support your objective.

3. ***Tell** the audience the **purpose** of the presentation.* As the saying goes, "Tell them what you're going to tell them, then tell them, then tell them what you've told them." Use a clear preview statement early on to help the audience know where you're taking them.

4. *Provide **meaning**, not just data.* Today information is widely available; you won't impress people by overloading them with data. People have limited attention spans and want presenters to help clarify the meaning of data.

5. ***Practice, practice, practice.*** Appearing polished and relaxed during a presentation requires rehearsal time. Practice making your points in a variety of ways. Above all, don't memorize a presentation's content.

6. *Remember that a presentation is more like a **conversation** than a speech.* Keep your tone conversational, yet professional. Audience members will be much more engaged if they feel you are talking with them rather than at them. Rely on PowerPoint slides to jog your memory.

7. *Remember the incredible power of **eye contact**.* Look at individual people in the audience. Try to have a series of one-on-one conversations with people in the room. This will calm you and help you connect with your audience.

8. ***Allow imperfection.*** If you forget what you were going to say, simply pause, look at your notes or slides, and go on. Don't effusively apologize or giggle or look mortified. An audience doesn't know your material nearly as well as you do and won't notice many mistakes.

9. *Be prepared to **answer tough questions**.* Try to anticipate the toughest questions you might receive. Plan your answers in advance. If you don't have an answer, acknowledge the fact and offer to get the information later.

10. *Provide a crisp **wrap-up, question-and-answer session, and summary**.* Set up the Q&A session by saying, "We'll take questions for 10 minutes and then have a few closing remarks." This prevents your presentation from just winding down to a weak ending. Also, if you receive hostile or hard-to-answer questions, you'll have a chance to have the final word. Follow the Q&A with a brief summary statement.

SOURCE: Hamilton, Lynn, University of Virginia, class handout. Used with permission.

Typically, your goal will be to sell your idea. In other words, your challenge will be to persuade others to go along with your personal recommendation. As a leader, you will find that some of your toughest challenges arise when people do not want to do what has to be done. Leaders have to be persuasive to get people on board.[60]

Persuasion is not what many people think: merely selling an idea or convincing others to see things your way. Don't assume that it takes a "my way or the highway" approach, with a one-shot effort to make a hard sell without compromise.[61] Usually it is more constructive to consider persuasion a process of learning from each other and negotiating a shared solution.

> Persuasion is not what many people think it is.

Persuasive speakers are seen as authentic, which happens when speakers are open with the audience, make a connection, demonstrate passion, and show they are listening as well as speaking. As a speaker, you can practice this kind of authenticity by adopting the body language you use when you're around people you're comfortable with, planning how to engage directly with your listeners, identifying the reasons you care about your topic, and watching for nonverbal cues plus fully engaging when you listen to audience comments and questions.[62]

The most powerful and persuasive messages are simple and informative, are told with stories and anecdotes, and convey excitement.[63] People are more likely to remember and buy into your message if you express it as a story that is simple, surprising, concrete, and credible and that includes emotional content.

Brad Heidrich, a senior research scientist for Janssen Pharmaceutical (a Johnson & Johnson company), communicates his life's passion in a compelling manner. He summarized his goal to discover and develop treatments for blood cancers: "The patients really drive me. . . . When we sit in meetings with senior leadership, the one thing we always talk about is what we can do for patients and how quickly."[64] As a survivor of childhood cancer, Heidrich communicates from his heart with urgency.

Writing Skills   Effective writing is more than correct spelling, punctuation, and grammar (although these help). Good writing above all requires clear, logical thinking.[65] The act of writing can be a powerful thinking aid because you have to think about what you really want to say and what the logic is behind your message.[66]

You want people to find your writing readable and interesting. Strive for clarity, organization, readability, and brevity.[67] Brevity is much appreciated by readers who are overloaded with things to read. Help email recipients manage the flood of information by providing specific subject lines, putting your main point at the beginning of the message, limiting paragraphs to five lines or less, and avoiding sarcasm or caustic humor (which can be misinterpreted, especially when readers are scanning messages in a hurry).[68]

Your first draft rarely is as good as it could be. If you have time, revise it. Go through your entire message and delete all unnecessary words, sentences, and paragraphs. Use specific, concrete words rather than abstract phrases. Instead of saying, "A period of unfavorable weather set in," say, "It rained every day for a week."

Language   Word choice can enhance or interfere with communication effectiveness. For example, jargon is a form of shorthand and can make communication more effective when both the sender and the receiver know the buzzwords. But when the receiver is unfamiliar with the jargon, misunderstandings result. This occurs often when people from different functional areas or disciplines communicate with one another. As in writing, simplicity usually helps.

Whether speaking or writing, you should consider the receiver's background—cultural as well as technical—and adjust your language accordingly. When you are receiving, don't assume that your understanding is the same as the speaker's intentions.

The meaning of words also can vary by culture. Japanese people use the simple word *hai* (yes) to convey that they understand what is being said; it does not necessarily mean that they agree. Asian business people rarely use the direct "no," using more subtle or tangential ways of disagreeing.[69] Similarly, Japanese speakers apologize more often than Americans; the Japanese know an apology's potential to repair damaged relationships. In the United States, many view apologies as weak or admissions of guilt and, therefore, avoid them.

Not just individuals, but organizations as a whole can benefit from multilingual capabilities.[70] Global teams fail when members have difficulties communicating because of language, cultural, and geographic barriers. Diversity harms team functioning at first. But when they develop ways to interact and communicate, teams develop a common identity and perform well.[71]

When conducting business overseas, try to learn as much as possible about the other country's language

Global teams fail when members have difficulty communicating because of language, cultural, and geographic barriers. What could you do to overcome these barriers?

Andrey_Popov/Shutterstock

> Learning host country languages and customs will give you an edge over competitors who do not.

and customs. Americans are less likely to do this than people from some other cultures, but a language strategy is becoming a key component of managing talent globally.[72] Those who do learn one or more foreign languages will have an edge over their competitors who do not.[73] Making the effort to learn the local language builds rapport, sets a proper tone for doing business, aids in adjustment to culture shock, and can help you "get inside" the other culture.[74] You will learn more about how people think, feel, and behave, both in their lives and in their business dealings.

Isadora Getty Buyou/Image Source

Nonverbal Skills   People send and interpret signals other than those that are spoken or written. Nonverbal messages can support or undermine the stated message, and convey information about emotions, power, relationships, and more.[75] In employees' eyes, managers' actions can speak louder than the words they choose.

In conversation, except when you intend to convey a negative message, you should give nonverbal signals that express warmth, respect, concern, a feeling of equality, and a willingness to listen. Negative nonverbal signals show coolness, disrespect, lack of interest, and a feeling of superiority.[76] The following suggestions can help you send positive nonverbal signals.

First, use time properly. Don't keep your employees (or teammates, or bosses!) waiting to see you. Devote sufficient time to your meetings with them and communicate frequently to show your interest. Second, make your office arrangement conducive to open communication. A seating arrangement that avoids separation of people helps establish a warm, cooperative atmosphere (in contrast, an arrangement in which you sit behind your desk and your subordinate sits before you creates a more intimidating, authoritative environment).[77] Third, remember your nonverbals; body language, facial expressions and tone of voice convey a lot.[78]

Several nonverbal signals convey a positive attitude toward the other person: assuming a position close to the person; maintaining eye contact; smiling; having an open body orientation, such as facing the other person directly; uncrossing the arms; and leaning forward to convey interest in what the other person is saying. To show confidence, managers (and employees, too) should make eye contact, use a firm handshake, dress professionally, and speak in an appropriate tone of voice.[79]

Silence is an interesting nonverbal signal. The average American is said to spend about twice as many hours per day in conversation as the average Japanese.[80] North Americans tend to talk to fill silences; Japanese allow long silences to develop, believing they can get to know people better. Japanese believe that two people with good rapport will know each other's thoughts. The need to use words implies a lack of understanding.

Improving Receiver Skills

Once you become effective at sending oral, written, and nonverbal messages, you are halfway toward becoming a complete communicator. However, you must also develop adequate receiving capabilities. Receivers need good listening, reading, and observational skills.

Listening   Although people often assume that good listening is easy and natural, in fact it is difficult and not nearly as common as needed. Consultant Bernard Ferrari saw this challenge in a meeting of an company's chief marketing officer (CMO) and the team that had introduced a new product that was not selling. The CMO listened carefully as the engineers exclaimed how great the product was. She then asked what customers were saying that might explain the lack of orders. The engineers admitted they had not spoken with any customers; rather, they had been careful not to leak any information while the product was under development and assumed that customers would immediately see its value after being

Social Entrepreneurship

Communicating Success to Create Change

Everyone loves success stories, but for social enterprises, communicating such success serves a critical function. More than mere facts, analysis, or numerical data, a success story informs stakeholders about the work of the organization, builds its commitment and advocacy, spreads the word about the organization's impact, and can even help secure the funding needed to survive. Success stories can establish a shared vision with readers or listeners, and motivate them to join the social enterprise's campaign or become part of its community.

As Barbara Safani of Career Solvers says, "Impactful communication facilitates change. . . . It creates a common language that everyone can relate to and want to be a part of."[81] Success stories about people whose lives have been changed by a social enterprise are especially powerful, and some firms specialize in helping social enterprises uncover and communicate these victories. The Sundance Institute's Stories of Change program brings independent filmmakers and social entrepreneurs together "to support the creation of compelling films about solutions to urgent social issues that enlighten and inspire audiences."[82]

Another resource is the Social Enterprise Alliance, a membership organization for social enterprises that helps them spread success stories like that of Tevin, a young New Orleans man. Tevin received training and job placement as a chef from a social enterprise called Liberty's Kitchen, but he still cherished the dream of becoming an artist. With the help of a mentor that Liberty's Kitchen found for him, Tevin enrolled in a community college design program. He is working toward a degree while serving as a youth mentor himself. Liberty's Kitchen's blog tells his story and those of many others.[83]

1. How can success stories offer a more powerful communication tool than a straightforward presentation of data, analyses, and facts?
2. What do social enterprises need to know about their audiences in order to successfully communicate stories of their success?

introduced to the market. Because the CMO took time to listen to the engineers, instead of jumping to conclusions about their product, she and the engineers were able to devise a product communication and rollout plan, and orders soon began flowing in.[84]

A basic technique called reflection helps people listen well.[85] **Reflection** is a process by which a person states what he or she believes the other person says or means. This technique places a greater emphasis on listening than on talking. When the listener reflects to the speaker, who then signals accuracy or corrects misunderstandings, the result is more effective two-way communication.

Besides using reflection, you can improve your listening by practicing the techniques described in Exhibit 15.4. (Note the date of the original source; some things don't change!) For managers, the stakes are high; failure to listen not only causes managers to miss good ideas but even drives employees to quit.[86]

Listening begins with personal contact. Staying in the office, keeping the door closed, and eating lunch at your desk are sometimes necessary to get pressing work done, but that is no way to stay on top of what's going on. Better to walk the halls, initiate conversations, and go to lunch even with people outside your area.[87] Barbara Corcoran, founder of her namesake company and "shark" on ABC's TV show *Shark Tank,* regularly asks her employees "How's it going?" She appreciates when employees provide constructive criticism. Corcoran advises you can only get this feedback through active listening.[88]

When a manager takes time to really listen to and get to know people, those same people think, "She's showing an interest in me" or "He's letting me know that I matter" or "She values my ideas and contributions." Trust develops.

Listening and learning from others are even more important for innovation than for routine work. Successful change and innovation come through lots of human contact and conversation.

reflection

Process by which a person states what he or she believes the other person says or means.

EXHIBIT 15.4
Ten Keys to Effective Listening

1. *Find an area of interest.* Even if you decide the topic is dull, ask yourself, "What is the speaker saying that I can use?"

2. *Judge content, not delivery.* Don't get caught up in the speaker's personality, mannerisms, speaking voice, or clothing. Instead, try to learn what the speaker knows.

3. *Hold your fire.* Rather than getting immediately excited by what the speaker seems to be saying, withhold evaluation until you understand the speaker's message.

4. *Listen for ideas.* Don't get bogged down in all the facts and details; focus on central ideas.

5. *Be flexible.* Have several systems for note taking and use the system best suited to the speaker's style. Don't take too many notes or try to force everything said by a disorganized speaker into a formal outline.

6. *Resist distraction.* Close the door, shut off the radio, move closer to the person talking, or ask him or her to speak louder. Don't look out the window or at papers on your desk.

7. *Exercise your mind.* Some people tune out when the material gets difficult. Develop an appetite for a good mental challenge.

8. *Keep your mind open.* Many people get overly emotional when they hear words referring to their most deeply held convictions—for example, *union, subsidy, import, Republican* or *Democrat,* and *big business.* Try not to let your emotions interfere with comprehension.

9. *Capitalize on thought speed.* Take advantage of the fact that most people talk at a rate of about 125 words per minute, but most of us think at about four times that rate. Use those extra 400 words per minute to think about what the speaker is saying rather than turning your thoughts to something else.

10. *Work at listening.* Spend some energy. Don't just pretend you're paying attention. Show interest. Good listening is hard work, but the benefits outweigh the costs.

SOURCE: Nichols, Ralph G., "Listening Is a 10-Part Skill," in *Readings in Interpersonal and Organizational Communication* ed. R. C. Huseman, C. M. Logue, and D. L. Freshley (Boston: Allyn & Bacon, 1977).

Reading Illiteracy is a significant problem in the United States as well as in other countries. Even if illiteracy is not a problem in your organization, reading mistakes are common and costly. As a receiver, for your own benefit, read messages as soon as possible, before it's too late to respond. You may skim most of your reading materials, but read important messages, documents, and passages slowly and carefully. Note important points for later referral.

Consider taking courses to increase your reading speed and comprehension skills. And don't limit your reading to items about your particular job skills or technical expertise; read materials that fall outside your immediate concerns. You never know when a creative idea that will help you in your work will be inspired by a novel, a biography, a sports story, or an article about a problem in another business or industry.

Observing The best communicators are also good at observing and interpreting nonverbal communications. (As Yogi Berra said, "You can observe a lot by watching.") For example, by reading nonverbal cues, a presenter can determine how her talk is going and adjust her approach if necessary. Some companies train their sales forces to interpret the nonverbal signals of potential customers. People can decode nonverbal signals to determine whether a sender is being truthful or deceitful. Deceitful communicators tend to maintain less eye contact, make either more or fewer body movements than usual, and smile either too much or too little. Verbally, they offer fewer specifics than do truthful senders.[89]

A vital source of useful observations comes from personally visiting people, plants, and other sites to get a firsthand view.[90] Many corporate executives rely heavily on reports from the field and don't travel to remote locations to observe firsthand what is going on. But reports are no substitute for actually seeing things happen in practice. Frequent visits to the field and careful observation offer deeper understanding of current operations, future prospects, and ideas for how to exploit capabilities fully.[91]

Of course, you must accurately interpret what you observe. An American employee working at Razorfish in Shanghai was surprised to discover how much he was expected to socialize with his Chinese boss. Beyond attending occasional happy hours and lunches, the employee observed: "In China, it's really expected that you become friends with your boss and you go out and socialize in a way that doesn't happen in the U.S."[92]

Japanese are skilled at interpreting every nuance of voice and gesture, putting most Westerners at a disadvantage.[93] When one is conducting business in other countries, local guides can be invaluable not only to interpret language, but to decode behavior at meetings, spot subtle hints and nonverbal cues, identify who the key people are, and tell you how the decision-making process operates.

Organizational Communication

Communicating poorly or well affects individuals, relationships, groups and teams, and entire organizations.[94] Every minute of every day, countless bits of information are transmitted in small interactions and through every corner of every organization. The flow of information affects performance at every level. Communications travel downward, upward, horizontally, and informally.

LO 15-5 Explain how to improve downward, upward, and horizontal communication.

Downward Communication

Downward communication refers to the flow of information from higher to lower levels in the organization's hierarchy. Examples include a manager giving an assignment to an assistant, a supervisor making an announcement to his subordinates, and a company president delivering a talk to her management team. Downward communication that provides relevant information can strengthen employee identification with the company, stimulate supportive attitudes, and help motivate decisions consistent with the organization's objectives.[95]

People must receive useful information to perform their jobs and become—and remain—loyal members of the organization. But they often lack adequate information.[96] One reason is a lack of openness between managers and employees. Managers may believe "No news is good news," "I don't have time to keep them informed of everything they want to know," or "It's none of their business, anyway." Some managers withhold information even if sharing it would be useful.

A second reason is filtering, introduced earlier. When messages are passed from one person to another, some information is left out. When a message passes through many people, each transmission may cause further information loss. The message also gets distorted as people add their own words or interpretations.

As communications cascade downward from one person to another through successive organizational levels, much information is lost. The hypothetical data in Exhibit 15.5 suggest that by the time messages reach lower levels, receivers may get very little useful information. The more authority levels through which communication pass, the more information will be lost or distorted. Flatter organizations with fewer hierarchical levels benefit from less filtering.

Fuse/Getty Images

downward communication

Information that flows from higher to lower levels in the organization's hierarchy.

As messages are communicated downward through successive organizational levels, much information is lost.

EXHIBIT 15.5
Information Loss in
Downward Communication

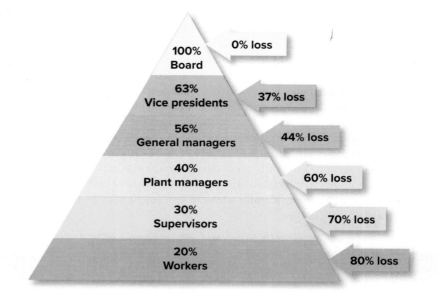

Coaching

Coaching   Some of the most important downward communications occur when managers give performance feedback to their direct reports. We discussed earlier the importance of giving feedback and positive reinforcement when it is deserved. It is also important to explicitly discuss poor performance and how to improve. Coaching is often the best way to help them change and succeed.

    Coaching is dialogue with a goal of helping someone become more effective and achieve their full potential on the job.[97] Coaching is not just for poor performers; as even the greatest athletes know, it suits anyone who is already good and aspires to excellence. Even CEOs desire coaching, typically from outside consultants, especially in the areas of managing conflict, delegating, building teams, and mentoring.[98]

    Good coaching helps you think through problems and opportunities, identify options, and learn from experience. Good coaches ask good questions, listen well, provide input, and encourage people to also think for themselves. Effective coaching requires honesty, calmness, and support—all aided by a sincere desire to help. The ultimate and longest-lasting help may be to show people how to keep learning as they coach themselves through their future challenges.

Downward Communication in Difficult Times

Downward Communication in Difficult Times   Managers frequently need to deliver bad news,[99] and proper downward communication can be particularly valuable during difficult times. During corporate mergers and acquisitions, people are anxious as they wonder how the changes will affect them. Ideally and ethically, top management communicates with employees about the change as early as possible.

    But some argue against that approach, maintaining that telling employees about a coming reorganization might cause too many to quit. Then too, top management often isolates itself, prompting rumors and anxiety. CEOs and other senior execs are surrounded by lawyers, investment bankers, and so on—people who are paid to make the deal happen, not to make it work.

    Yet with the people who are affected by the deal, it's important to increase, not decrease, communication.[100]

    In a merger of two *Fortune* 500 companies, two plants received very different information.[101] All employees at both plants received the initial letter from the CEO announcing the merger. But after that, one plant was kept in the dark while the other received continual information about what was happening. Top management told employees about the layoffs; transfers; promotions and demotions; and changes in pay, jobs, and benefits.

---

coaching

Dialogue with a goal of helping another be more effective and achieve his or her full potential on the job.

Which plant do you think fared better as the difficult transitional months unfolded? In both plants, the merger hurt employees' job satisfaction and commitment to the organization and increased their belief that the company was untrustworthy, dishonest, and uncaring. In the plant where employees got little information, these problems persisted for a long time. But in the plant where employees received complete information, the situation stabilized and attitudes improved toward their former levels. Full communication helped employees survive an anxious period and offered symbolic value by signaling management's care and concern for employees. Without such communications, employee reactions to a merger or acquisition may be so negative that they undermine the corporate strategy and future performance.

Open-Book Management   Executives often are proud of their newsletters, staff meetings, videos, and other vehicles of downward communication. Commonly, the information provided concerns company sports teams, birthdays, and new copy machines. But a more unconventional philosophy is **open-book management**: the practice of sharing with employees at all organizational levels vital information traditionally meant for management's eyes only. This information includes financial goals, income statements, budgets, sales, forecasts, and other relevant data about company performance and prospects. This practice is dramatically different from the usual closed-book approach in which people may or may not have a clue about how the company is doing, may or may not believe the things that management tells them, and may or may not believe that their personal performance makes a difference.

Open-book management is controversial because many managers prefer to keep such information to themselves. Sharing strategic plans and financial information with employees could lead to leaks to competitors or to employee dissatisfaction with their pay. Father of scientific management Frederick Taylor, early in the 20th century, would have considered it idiotic to open the books to all employees.[102]

Rob Tolleson at CPO Commerce credits open-book management with saving his company from collapse. Due to a major IT malfunction, the online vendor of power tools struggled to figure out how to fulfill customers' orders. Employees, who had full access to company information, were able to work together for weeks to develop creative solutions until the company could stabilize itself.[103] And Integrated Project Management Company, a professional services company that practices open-book management, ranked 8th in *Fortune*'s 2018 "Best Companies to Work For in Chicago."[104]

However, the practice remains uncommon; only an estimated 4,000 U.S. firms are true believers.[105] Most firms apparently consider it too risky and/or too difficult. But managers in every company should consider carefully whether they provide their people with too much information, or too little.

Upward Communication

Upward communication travels from lower to higher ranks in the hierarchy. Good upward communication is important for several reasons.[106] First, managers learn what's going on. Management gains a more accurate picture of subordinates' work, accomplishments, problems, plans, attitudes, and ideas. Second, employees gain from the opportunity to communicate upward. People can relieve some of their frustrations and gain a stronger sense of participation in the enterprise. Third, effective upward communication facilitates downward communication as good listening becomes a two-way street.

The problems common in upward communication are similar to those for downward communication. Managers are bombarded with information and may neglect or miss information from below. Furthermore, some employees are not always open with their bosses; in other words, filtering occurs upward as well as downward. People tend to share only good news with their bosses and suppress bad news because they (1) want to appear competent; (2) mistrust their boss and fear being punished, even if the reported problem is not their fault; or (3) believe they are helping their boss if they shield him or her from problems.

open-book management

Practice of sharing with employees at all levels of the organization vital information previously meant for management's eyes only.

Bottom Line

The more management communicates revenue, cost, quality, sustainability, and other data, the more people will pay attention to those aspects of performance and find new ways to improve. *For employees to be motivated by open-book management, what kinds of information would they need besides sales and profit numbers?*

upward communication

Information that flows from lower to higher levels in the organization's hierarchy.

For these and other reasons,[107] managers may not learn about important problems. As one leadership expert put it, "If the messages from below say you are doing a flawless job, send back for a more candid assessment."[108]

Managing Upward Communication   Generating useful information from below requires managers to both facilitate and motivate upward communication. They could have an open-door policy and encourage people to use it, have lunch or coffee with employees, use surveys, institute a suggestion program, or hold town hall meetings. They can ask for advice, make informal plant visits, really think about and respond to employee suggestions, and distribute summaries of new ideas and practices inspired by employee ideas and actions.[109]

Some executives practice MBWA (management by wandering around). That term refers simply to getting out of the office, walking around, and talking frequently and informally with employees.[110] Over his 40-year career with Marriott Corporation, Bill Marriott would walk through many of the firm's hotels to speak with employees and to ensure they were delivering consistent, high-quality customer service.[111]

Useful upward communication must be reinforced and not punished. The person who tries to talk to the manager about an important issue must not be brushed off repeatedly. An announced open-door policy must truly be open door. Ideally, people trust their bosses and know that they will not hold a grudge against whoever delivers negative information. Managers should truly listen and learn, not punish the messenger for being honest, and take action on valid ideas.

What will be your own tendencies regarding what you do and don't convey to your boss? A useful consideration is that exercising **voice**—speaking up with good intentions about work-related issues, rather than remaining silent—is that others will perceive your comments as either positive (good ideas and opportunities, usually presented in positive tone) or negative (problems, sometimes presented in negative tone and prompting defensiveness).[112] Both types are potentially useful, but bear in mind the importance of presenting them appropriately and offering positive ideas, not just criticism.

voice

When people speak up with good intentions about work-related issues, rather than remaining silent.

Horizontal Communication

Much information needs to be shared among people on the same hierarchical level. Such **horizontal communication** can take place among people in the same work team or in different departments. For example, a purchasing agent discusses a problem with a production engineer, and a task force of department heads meets to discuss a widespread concern. Communicating with others outside the firm, including potential investors, is another vital type of horizontal communication.[113]

horizontal communication

Information shared among people on the same hierarchical level.

Horizontal communication serves several important functions.[114] It shares information, coordinates activities, and allows problem solving among units. Effective dialogue between disagreeing individuals and units helps resolve conflict constructively.[115] Facilitating interactions provides social and emotional support to people and improves morale and effectiveness.

Managing Horizontal Communication   The need for horizontal communication is similar to the need for integration, discussed in Chapter 8. Particularly in complex environments, in which decisions in one unit affect another, information must be shared horizontally. Google provides space for ongoing horizontal communication in Google Cafés, which are designed to encourage more interaction among employees within and between teams.[116]

Applied Materials, a semiconductor equipment manufacturer in Santa Clara, California, took a sophisticated approach to managing horizontal communication. To improve the caliber and efficiency of its information technology (IT) group, the company outsourced routine tasks, cut the in-house IT workforce, and focused the remaining IT employees on supporting strategy. The IT workers were expected to collaborate with each other (and with customers) to develop and implement creative projects.

Applied Materials surveyed its IT staff to determine their communication patterns. About half of the IT people were communication hubs—that is, many colleagues consulted with them for ideas and questions. Those highly networked employees weren't necessarily managers; they were people at all levels whom others trusted and respected. The company assembled a team of 12 highly networked IT employees to share insights about what affected collaboration in the company. This team identified barriers, and Applied Materials used that information to provide coaching in better communication. A follow-up survey showed that more employees had become highly networked.[117]

Informal Communication

Communications differ in their levels of formality. Formal communications are official, management-sanctioned episodes of information transmission. They often are preplanned and necessary for performing some task.

Informal communication is more unofficial. People gossip[118]; employees complain about their bosses; friends talk about their favorite sports teams; work teams tell newcomers how to get by.[119]

The **grapevine** is the social network of informal communications. Informal networks provide people with information, help them solve problems, and teach them how to do their work. You should develop a good network of people willing and able to help.[120] However, the grapevine can be destructive when misinformation proliferates and harms people and operations.[121]

What does this mean for you personally? Don't overindulge in gossip, digital or otherwise. But don't avoid the grapevine, either.[122] Listen, but evaluate before believing what you hear. Who is the source, and how credible? Does the rumor make sense? Is it consistent or inconsistent with other things you know or have heard? Seek more information, but don't stir the pot.

Managing Informal Communication   Rumors start over any number of topics, including who's leaving, who's getting a promotion, salaries, job security, and costly mistakes. Rumors can destroy people's faith and trust in the company—and in each other. But the grapevine cannot be eliminated, so managers need to work with it.

The grapevine can be managed in several ways.[123] First, the manager who hears a story that could get out of hand should talk to the key people involved to get the facts and their perspectives. Don't allow malicious gossip.

Second, managers can prevent rumors from starting by explaining important events, providing facts, and working to establish open communications and trust over time. These efforts are especially important during times of uncertainty, such as after a merger or layoff or when sales slow down, because anxiety gives birth to rumors.

Third, neutralize rumors once they have started. Disregard a rumor if it is ridiculous, confirm parts that are true, make public comments ("no comment" is seen as a confirmation of the rumor), deny the rumor if the denial is based in truth (don't make false denials), make sure communications about the issue are consistent, select a spokesperson of appropriate rank and knowledge, and hold town meetings if necessary.[124]

Transparency

Many executives and management scholars today consider open access to information in all directions to be an organizational imperative. You will often hear the relevant term **transparency**: people's beliefs that the information their employer and others send them is of high quality, as defined by *accuracy, timeliness,* and full *disclosure* of relevant information.[125] "Relevant" indicates that not all information—for instance, company secrets or confidential conversations—should be or needs to be shared. Ideally, all relevant stakeholders, internal and external, use those three quality criteria to achieve transparency with one another.

LO 15-6 Summarize how to work with the company grapevine.

grapevine

Informal communication network.

transparency

People's beliefs that the information their employer and others send them is of high quality, as defined by accuracy, timeliness, and full disclosure of relevant information.

It's hard to know how rumors get started, but we do know they happen.

Bill Varie/Getty Images

LO 15-7 Describe the boundaryless organization and its advantages.

Jack Welch, when he was CEO of General Electric, coined the now-famous word *boundarylessness*. A **boundaryless organization** is one that has few major obstacles to information flow. Instead of metaphorical barriers separating people and places, in "boundarylessness" organizations, ideas, information, and decisions move quickly to wherever they are needed.[126]

This free flow does not imply a random free-for-all of unlimited communication and information overload. It implies information available *as needed* moving *fast and easily* enough that the organization functions far better as a whole than as separate parts.

GE's chief learning officer used the metaphor of the organization as a house having three kinds of boundaries: the floors and ceilings, the walls that separate the rooms, and the outside walls. These barriers correspond to the boundaries between different organizational levels, different units, and the organization and its external stakeholders—for example, suppliers and customers.[127]

GE's famous Workout program is a series of meetings for people across multiple hierarchical levels, characterized by extremely frank, tough discussions that break down even vertical boundaries. From 2007 to 2018, nearly 1.5 million GE people have been through a Workout program.[128] Customers and suppliers participate in Workout programs as well, breaking down external boundaries.

Boundarylessness facilitates dialogue by turning barriers—physical and psychological—into permeable membranes. As the GE people put it, people from different parts of the organization need to learn both "how to talk" and "how to walk."[129] That is, dialogue is essential, but it must be followed by commensurate action.

Consistency between words and action is one type of integrity, which creates trust. Transparency, too, strengthens people's trust in an organization and in one another. Taken together, these are vital contributors to personal, team, and organizational effectiveness.[130]

boundaryless organization

Organization in which there are few major obstacles to information flow.

Management in Action

SOUNDCLOUD: REINVENTING COMMUNICATION BETWEEN ARTISTS AND LISTENERS

SoundCloud is the largest music and audio platform on the Internet, but like other companies it experienced growing pains. Part of SoundCloud's challenge was identifying its core strength. Many other and often better-known platforms, such as Amazon, Apple, and Spotify, offer streaming services of mainstream artists. SoundCloud's niche strength has always been in its ability to enable music artists to create and connect with listeners. It wasn't until recently, however, that the firm made this its primary focus.

As CEO Kerry Trainor puts it, "We want to be the first place that creators come to share their work with the world, and build and grow their careers. . . . We also are where passionate music listeners who want to discover something truly new come to connect with creators."[131]

Over the years, SoundCloud has helped launch some of music's biggest artists, like Kehlani, Lil Uzi Vert, and, perhaps most notably, Post Malone, who originally launched his Billboard top 100 hit "White Iverson" from his SoundCloud account.[132] SoundCloud is now investing heavily in developing tools that will further enable artists to create and connect with listeners. It recently announced a new software integration that will allow DJs to stream and mix any of SoundCloud's 200 million tracks instantly. The goal, according to CEO Trainer, is to create new music in real-time, what he calls "streaming workflows": "Until recently, digital workflows for DJs were limited to downloads and physical media, but streaming workflows are the future."[133] If it works, SoundCloud will revolutionize the way music artists communicate with their audiences.

- What similarities and differences do you see between the way an organization communicates internally and how it communicates with its market? How might an organization be poor in one but strong in another? Explain.
- Check in on SoundCloud's progress as it creates new ways for artists to communicate and connect with listeners. To what degree is it succeeding or failing in its strategy?

KEY TERMS

RETAINING WHAT YOU LEARNED

In Chapter 15, you learned that there are key differences between one-way and two-way communication flows. One-way communication is faster and easier than two-way communication, but two-way communication is more accurate and results in better performance. Problems in communication can occur in all stages: encoding, transmission, decoding, and interpreting. Noise can complicate communication. Subjective perceptions and filtering are potential sources of error. Communications are sent through oral, written, and digital channels. People should weigh the advantages and disadvantages of each channel before sending a message. Digital media have a major impact on interpersonal and organizational communications. Media richness is one factor to consider as you decide which channels to use and how to use them. You can improve your writing and speaking skills in many ways. You also can actively manage downward, upward, and horizontal communications. The informal flow of communication (the grapevine) is important as well, and it too needs to be managed actively. Boundaries exist between different organizational levels, units, and organizations and external stakeholders. The boundaryless organization is one without major barriers to the flow of important communications.

LO 15-1 Discuss important advantages of two-way communication.

- One-way communication flows from the sender to the receiver with no feedback loop.
- In two-way communication, each person is both a sender and a receiver as both parties provide and react to information.
- One-way communication is faster and easier but less accurate than two-way; two-way communication is slower and more difficult but is more accurate and results in better performance.

LO 15-2 Identify communication problems to avoid.

- The communication process involves a sender who conveys information to a receiver.
- Problems in communication can occur in all stages: encoding, transmission, decoding, and interpreting.
- Noise in the system further complicates communication, creating more distortion. Moreover, feedback may be unavailable or misleading.

- Subjective perceptions and filtering add to the possibility of error.

LO 15-3 Describe when and how to use the various communication channels.

- Communications are sent through oral, written, and digital channels. All have important advantages and disadvantages that you should consider before choosing a channel.
- Digital media have a huge impact on interpersonal and organizational communications and make possible the virtual office.
- Key advantages of digital media are speed, cost, and efficiency, but the downsides are also significant, including information overload.
- Media richness, or how much and what sort of information a channel conveys, is one factor to consider as you decide which channels to use and how to use them both efficiently and effectively.

LO 15-4 Summarize ways to become a better sender and receiver of information.

- Practice writing, be critical of your work, and revise.
- Train yourself as a speaker. Use language carefully and well and work to overcome cross-cultural language differences. Be alert to the nonverbal signals that you send, including your use of time as perceived by other people.
- Know the common bad listening habits and work to overcome them. Read widely and engage in careful, firsthand observation and interpretation.

LO 15-5 Explain how to improve downward, upward, and horizontal communication.

- Actively manage communications in all directions. Engage in two-way communication more than one-way. Make information available to others.
- Useful approaches to downward communication include coaching, special communications during difficult periods, and open-book management.
- You should also both help and motivate people to communicate upward.
- Many mechanisms exist for enhancing horizontal communications.

LO 15-6   Summarize how to work with the company grapevine.

- The informal flow of information is important, just as formal communication is, to organizational effectiveness and employee morale.
- Managers must understand that the grapevine cannot be eliminated and should be managed actively.
- Many of the suggestions for managing formal communications apply also to managing the grapevine. Moreover, managers can take steps to prevent rumors or neutralize the ones that arise.

LO 15-7   Describe the boundaryless organization and its advantages.

- Boundaries—psychological if not physical—exist between different organizational levels, units, and organizations and external stakeholders.
- The boundaryless organization has no major barriers to the flow of important communications. Ideas, information, decisions, and actions move to where they are most needed.
- Relevant information should be available as needed so that the organization as a whole functions far better than as separate parts.

DISCUSSION QUESTIONS

1. Think of an occasion when you faced a miscommunication problem. What do you think caused the problem? How do you think it should have been handled better?

2. Have you ever *not* given someone information or opinions that perhaps you should have? Why? Was it the right thing to do? Why or why not? What would cause you to be glad that you provided (or withheld) negative or difficult information? What would cause you to regret providing/withholding it?

3. Think back to discussions you have heard or participated in. Consider the differences between one-way and two-way communication. How can two one-ways be turned into a true two-way?

4. Share with the class some of your experiences—both good and bad—with digital media.

5. Report examples of mixed signals you have received (or sent). How can you reduce the potential for misunderstanding and misperception as you communicate with others?

6. What makes you want to say to someone, "You're not listening"?

7. What do you think about the practice of open-book management? What would you think about it if you were running your own company?

8. Discuss organizational rumors you have heard: what they were about, how they got started, how accurate they were, and how people reacted to them. What lessons can you learn from these episodes?

9. Refer to the section "The Virtual Office." What do you think will be the long-term impact of the mobile office on job satisfaction and performance? If you were a manager, how would you maximize the benefits and minimize the drawbacks? If you worked in this environment, how would you manage yourself to maximize your performance and avoid burnout?

10. Have you ever made or seen mistakes due to people not speaking a common language well? How do you or will you deal with others who do not speak the same language as you?

11. Have you ever tried to coach someone? What did you do well, and what mistakes did you make? How can you become a better coach?

12. Have you ever been coached by someone? What did he or she do well, and what mistakes were made? How was it for you to be on the receiving end of the coaching, and how did you respond? What is required to be successful as the receiver of someone else's coaching attempts?

13. Think about how companies communicate with Wall Street and the media and how analysts on TV communicate with viewers. What concepts from the chapter apply, and how can you become a more astute consumer of such information?

EXPERIENTIAL EXERCISES

15.1   Interpreting Nonverbal Communication

OBJECTIVE

To become more skilled at interpreting meanings associated with nonverbal communication.

INSTRUCTIONS

Assume your boss exhibits each of the four behaviors listed below over the course of a month. Read each behavior and then record your interpretation of what it most likely means.

Nonverbal Communication Interpretation Worksheet

Your manager . . .	You interpret this behavior to mean . . .
Arrives at the office earlier than usual and has a worried look on her face.	
Spends more time than any other manager when training new employees.	
Wears freshly pressed suits to work each day.	
Looks at her phone to read texts and emails several times per hour, even during meetings and one-on-one conversations.	

SOURCE: Adapted from Jauch, Laurence R., et al., *The Managerial Experience: Cases, Exercises, and Readings,* 5th ed. Boston: South-Western, 1989.

15.2   Listening Skills Survey

OBJECTIVES

1. To measure your skills as a listener.
2. To gain insight into the factors that determine good listening habits.
3. To demonstrate how you can become a better listener.

INSTRUCTIONS

1. Working alone, complete the Listening Skills Survey.
2. In small groups, compare scores, discuss survey test items, and prepare responses to the discussion questions.

3. After the class reconvenes, group spokespersons present group findings.

DISCUSSION QUESTIONS

1. In what ways did students' responses on the survey agree or disagree?
2. What do you think accounts for the differences?
3. How can the results of this survey be put to practical use?

Listening Skills Survey

To measure your listening skills, complete the following survey by circling the degree to which you agree with each statement.

	Strongly Agree	Agree	Neither Agree nor Disagree	Disagree	Strongly Disagree
1. I tend to be patient with the speaker, making sure she or he is finished speaking before I respond in any fashion.	5	4	3	2	1
2. When listening, I don't doodle or fiddle with papers and things that might distract me from the speaker.	5	4	3	2	1
3. I attempt to understand the speaker's point of view.	5	4	3	2	1
4. I try not to put the speaker on the defensive by arguing or criticizing.	5	4	3	2	1
5. When I listen, I focus on the speaker's feelings.	5	4	3	2	1

(Continued)

	Strongly Agree	Agree	Neither Agree nor Disagree	Disagree	Strongly Disagree
6. I do not let a speaker's annoying mannerisms distract me.	5	4	3	2	1
7. While the speaker is talking, I watch carefully for facial expressions and other types of body language.	5	4	3	2	1
8. I never talk when the other person is trying to say something.	5	4	3	2	1
9. During a conversation, a period of silence doesn't seem awkward to me.	5	4	3	2	1
10. I want people to give me the facts and reasoning behind the idea so that I can make up my own mind.	5	4	3	2	1
11. When the speaker is finished, I respond to his or her feelings.	5	4	3	2	1
12. I don't evaluate the speaker's words until she or he is finished talking.	5	4	3	2	1

15.3   Active Listening

This exercise involves triads. Each triad counts off into threes: 1, 2, 3, 1, 2, 3, and so on. In the first round, all the 1s in their respective triads take the pro position (see the topics given later in the exercise), all the 2s take the con position, and all the 3s act as observers. After a topic is given, two individuals representing opposing viewpoints have one minute to collect their thoughts and then five to seven minutes to arrive at a mutually agreeable position on that topic.

The observer should use the Listening Feedback Form to capture actual examples of what the individuals said or did that indicated active and less-than-active listening. When time is called, the pro individuals share their opinion of which listening behaviors they performed well and which

ones they'd like to improve. Then the con individuals do the same. Finally, the observers share their observations and insights, using examples to reinforce their feedback.

If additional rounds are used, rotate the roles so that each person plays a speaking role and, if possible, an observing role.

Round 1:
Topic selected: _____
Notes:

Round 2:
Topic selected: _____
Notes:

Listening Feedback Form

Indicators of Active Listening	Pro	Con
1. Asked questions for clarification		
2. Paraphrased the opposing view		
3. Responded to nonverbal cues (e.g., body posture, tone of voice)		
4. Appeared to move toward a mutually satisfying solution		
Indicators of Less-Than-Active Listening		
5. Interrupted before allowing the other person to finish		
6. Was defensive about her or his position		
7. Appeared to dominate the conversation		
8. Ignored nonverbal cue		

Potential topics to be used:

1. Gun control
2. Capital punishment
3. Race as a criterion for college admission
4. Prison reform
5. U.S. intervention in wars outside the United States
6. Legalization of marijuana
7. Mandatory armed forces draft
8. Interracial adoption
9. Premarital and extramarital sex

10. Prayer in schools

11. Diversity in the workplace

12. Pornography on the Internet

QUESTIONS

1. Did you arrive at a mutually agreeable solution? What helped you get there?

2. What were some factors that hindered this process?

3. How comfortable did you feel arguing the position you were given? How did this influence your ability to listen actively?

4. If the position you were given was exactly opposite your values or beliefs, do you see this topic differently now than before the exercise?

5. What steps can you take to improve your ability to listen actively to friends or associates, especially when you don't agree with their viewpoint?

Concluding Case

COMMUNICATING AT BEST TRUST BANK

Best Trust has grown to one of the world's top 25 banks by building on its broad name recognition and reputation for integrity. Its 73,000-employee workforce spans 47 countries.

One of those employees is Paul Wysinsky, who in the 1980s took an entry-level job as a bank teller. Paul developed a track record of satisfying customers, working efficiently, and cooperating well with others on his team. He took business courses during the evening, earned a master's degree, and worked his way up through middle management positions. Twenty years later, he was offered a vice president's job in the human resources division, responsible for recruiting and retaining Best Trust's employees in Houston, Texas. Paul tackled the new responsibilities so well that he was soon promoted to run all of HR.

The nature of Paul's work communications changed considerably as he rose through the ranks. When Paul was a teller, his favorite responsibility was greeting customers and listening to their needs and concerns. When customers were upset about a problem, he would initially get nervous, but with experience, he became an expert at listening attentively, helping the customer find the best possible solution and speaking in a respectful tone that almost always soothed any frayed nerves.

Now that Paul is an executive vice president, he rarely talks with Best Trust's customers, and more of his communications are structured and formal. Although he cares about attracting, motivating, and retaining employees in all positions, he knows he cannot possibly have a dialogue with 73,000 people in dozens of countries. In fact, he can't even have personal conversations with all of the HR employees—Best Trust has more than 800 of them, including several at each facility.

Consequently, Paul looks for a variety of ways to communicate. He meets weekly with all the department and functional heads involved in formulating strategy. The meeting's agenda includes reviewing HR issues such as leadership development, succession planning, diversity management, and employee satisfaction. Paul is well prepared because he meets at least weekly with each of the managers who report directly to him. In these one-on-one meetings, Paul and the manager review progress on the issues handled by that manager. Paul also uses these meetings to learn what challenges the manager is facing so he can offer coaching and encouragement.

Talking one on one to employees can feel like an escape from one of the chief annoyances of his job: poorly written messages from many of the bank's middle managers. It seems that Best Trust has excelled at finding people with strong analytic and customer service skills, but many of these people stumble at presenting an idea or summarizing their progress in emails and reports. Paul feels intense time pressure, and if he gets a suggestion but can't figure out the main idea in the first couple of sentences, he simply passes it to one of his managers for a possible follow-up. Paul suspects that good ideas and real problems are being missed. Rambling reports and long-winded presentations loaded with jargon seem to have become a norm at Best Trust, and Paul is thinking about adding a new training program to improve writing and communication skills.

To report news about the bank's policies, benefits, and other initiatives, Paul uses a variety of media. He gives presentations at events such as the employee recognition gathering and at branches around the world. Four times a year, he records a video that is posted on the bank's intranet. Also on the intranet, Paul leads regular town hall meetings, a live video feed that allows employees to post questions and ideas, which Paul and other executives answer in real time.

Paul also has a whole set of policy concerns related to employee Internet use, such as whether to allow employees to access social media and how closely to monitor blogs and other public information for company-related posts. When Paul thinks about it, he realizes that his communication skills have barely grown as fast as the communication demands of his work.

QUESTIONS

1. How has the media richness of Paul's communications changed since the days when he was a teller? Why do you think he misses communicating one on one with customers?

2. What sender and receiver skills are described in this case? Which ones need improvement? Offer suggestions for improving the weak skills.

3. How might Paul improve upward communication and the communication culture more generally at Best Trust?

ENDNOTES

1. Hugh McIntyre, "The Top 10 Streaming Music Services by Number of Users," *Forbes,* May 25, 2018, https://www.forbes.com/sites/hughmcintyre/2018/05/25/the-top-10-streaming-music-services-by-number-of-users/#75e7028a5178.

2. Ariston Anderson, "SoundCloud: On Startup Culture, Entrepreneurial Employees & Hackdays," 99u.com, n.d., http://99u.com/articles/7191/soundcloud-on-startup-culture-entrepreneurial-employees-hackdays, accessed April 19, 2017.

3. "How SoundCloud Keeps Communication Flowing across Four Offices in 4 Time Zones," FirstRound.com, http://firstround.com/review/how-soundcloud-keeps-communication-flowing-across-4-offices-in-4-time-zones/, accessed April 12, 2019.

4. "How SoundCloud Keeps Communication Flowing across Four Offices in 4 Time Zones," FirstRound.com, http://firstround.com/review/how-soundcloud-keeps-communication-flowing-across-4-offices-in-4-time-zones/, accessed April 12, 2019.

5. M. Venus, D. Stam, and D. van Knippenberg, "Leader Emotion as a Catalyst of Effective Leader Communication of Visions, Value-Laden Messages, and Goals," *Organizational Behavior and Human Decision Processes* 122 (2013), pp. 53–68; L. Penley, E. Alexander, I. E. Jernigan, and C. Henwood, "Communication Abilities of Managers: The Relationship to Performance," *Journal of Management* 17 (1991), pp. 57–76.

6. W. V. Haney, "A Comparative Study of Unilateral and Bilateral Communication," *Academy of Management Journal* 7 (1964), pp. 128–36.

7. J. R. Mesmer-Magnus and L. A. DeChurch, "Information Sharing and Team Performance: A Meta-Analysis," *Journal of Applied Psychology* 94 (2009), pp. 535–46.

8. P. Cappelli and A. Tavis, "The Performance Management Revolution," *Harvard Business Review,* October 2016, www.hbr.org.

9. P. Cappelli and A. Tavis, "The Performance Management Revolution," *Harvard Business Review,* October 2016, www.hbr.org.

10. Karsten Strauss, "More Evidence That Company Diversity Leads to Better Profits," *Forbes,* January 25, 2018, https://www.forbes.com/sites/karstenstrauss/2018/01/25/more-evidence-that-company-diversity-leads-to-better-profits/#2d95728a1bc7; Anna Powers, "A Study Finds That Diverse Companies Produce 19% More Revenue," *Forbes,* June 27, 2018, https://www.forbes.com/sites/annapowers/2018/06/27/a-study-finds-that-diverse-companies-produce-19-more-revenue/#1506933d506f.

11. Nicole Fallon, "A Culture of Inclusion: Promoting Workplace Diversity and Belonging," *Business News Daily,* June 30, 2017, https://www.businessnewsdaily.com/10055-create-inclusive-workplace-culture.html.

12. Anthony Paradiso, "Inclusive Storytelling with Transparency and Authenticity with #SHRMDIV Presenter, Elena Valentine," SHRM, October 11, 2018, https://blog.shrm.org/blog/inclusive-storytelling-with-transparency-and-authenticity-with-shrmdiv-pres-0.

13. Nicole Fallon, "A Culture of Inclusion: Promoting Workplace Diversity and Belonging," *Business News Daily,* June 30, 2017, https://www.businessnewsdaily.com/10055-create-inclusive-workplace-culture.html.

14. I. Wickelgren, "Speaking Science: Why People Don't Hear What You Say," *Scientific American,* November 8, 2012, http://www.scientificamerican.com; M. McCormack, "The Illusion of Communication," *Financial Times Mastering Management Review,* July 1999, pp. 8–9.

15. F. Flynn and S. Wiltermuth, "Who's with Me? False Consensus, Brokerage, and Ethical Decision Making in Organizations," *Academy of Management Journal* 53 (2010), pp. 1074–89; R. Cross and S. Brodt, "How Assumptions of Consensus Undermine Decision Making," *Sloan Management Review* 42 (2001), pp. 86–94.

16. S. Mohammed and E. Ringseis, "Cognitive Diversity and Consensus in Group Decision Making: The Role of Inputs, Processes, and Outcomes," *Organizational Behavior and Human Decision Processes* 85 (2001), pp. 310–35.

17. S. Parker and C. Axtell, "Seeing Another Viewpoint: Antecedents and Outcomes of Employee Perspective Taking," *Academy of Management Journal* 44 (2001), pp. 1085–1100.

18. C. Folz, "How to Deliver Bad News," Society for Human Resource Management, August 25, 2016, www.shrm.org.

19. Novo Nordisk website, "Our Triple Bottom Line," http://www.novonordisk.com, accessed June 8, 2015; J. Ochs, "Defining 'Social Enterprise,'" *Minnesota Business Magazine,* December 17, 2014, http://www.minnesotabusiness.com; J. Jervis, "Social Enterprises: Popular but Confusing, Says Study," *The Guardian,* January 8, 2013, http://www.theguardian.com; A. Field, "Salesforce.com's Thwarted Efforts to Trademark Social Enterprise Should Be a Wake Up Call," *Forbes,* September 11, 2012, http://www.forbes.com.

20. T. W. Comstock, *Communicating in Business and Industry* (Albany, NY: Delmar, 1985).

21. R. Erskine, "Is Your CEO on Social Media? If Not, Your Business May Be at Risk," *Forbes,* September 17, 2018, www.forbes.com.

22. C. Conner, "How Top CEOs Leverage Social Media to Build a Following and Brand Loyalty," *Forbes,* March 11, 2018, www.forbes.com.

23. C. Conner, "How Top CEOs Leverage Social Media to Build a Following and Brand Loyalty," *Forbes,* March 11, 2018, www.forbes.com.

24. S. Marlow, C. Lacerenza, and E. Salas, "Communication in Virtual Teams: A Conceptual Framework and Research Agenda," *Human Resource Management Review* 27 (2017), pp. 575–89.

25. Microsoft Support, https://support.office.com, accessed June 2, 2015; Hitachi Solutions Europe, Ltd., http://uk.hitachi-solutions.com, accessed June 2, 2015.

26. Company website, Incogneato, https://www.incognea.to, accessed April 4, 2019.

27. S. S. K. Lam and J. Schaubroeck, "Improving Group Decisions by Better Pooling Information: A Comparative Advantage of Group Decision Support Systems," *Journal of Applied Psychology* 85 (2000), pp. 565–73.

28. J. Goudreau, "How to Communicate in the New Multigenerational Office," *Forbes,* February 14, 2013, http://www.forbes.com; M. Schmulen, "Memo to the Boss: Twitter's Not a Time Suck," *Fortune,* January 19, 2010, http://tech.fortune.cnn.com; D. Lindorff, "Facing Up to Facebook," *Treasury & Risk,* April 2011, Business & Company; J. Goudreau, "How to Communicate in the New Multigenerational Office," *Forbes,* February 14, 2013, http://www.forbes.com; M. Schmulen, "Memo to the Boss," Resource Center, http://galenet.galegroup.com; S. Ali, "Why No One under 30 Answers Your Voicemail," *DiversityInc,* August 27, 2010, http://www.diversityinc.com.

29. M. Drouin, D. Miller, S. Wehle, and E. Hernandez, "Why Do People Lie Online? 'Because Everyone Lies on the Internet,'" *Computers in Human Behavior* 64 (2016), pp. 134–42; S. Aral, "The Problem with Online Ratings," *MIT Sloan Management Review* 55 (2014), pp. 47–52; C. Naquin, T. Kurtzberg, and L. Belkin, "The Finer Points of Lying Online: E-Mail versus Pen and Paper," *Journal of Applied Psychology* 95 (2010), pp. 387–94.

30. C. Naquin and G. Paulson, "Online Bargaining and Interpersonal Trust," *Journal of Applied Psychology* 88 (2003), pp. 113–20.

31. N. Hill, K. Bartol, P. Tesluk, and G. Langa, "Organizational Context and Face-to-Face Interaction: Influences on the Development of Trust and Collaborative Behaviors in Computer-Mediated Groups," *Organizational Behavior and Human Decision Processes* 108 (2009), pp. 187–201; B. Baltes, M. Dickson, M. Sherman, C. Bauer, and J. LaGanke, "Computer-Mediated Communication and Group Decision Making: A Meta-Analysis," *Organizational Behavior and Human Decision Processes* 87 (2002), pp. 156–79.

32. E. Martinez-Moreno, P. González-Navarro, A. Zornoza, and P. Ripoll, "Relationship, Task and Process Conflicts and Team Performance: The Moderating Role of Communication Media," *International Journal of Conflict Management* 20 (2009), pp. 251–68; R. Rice and D. Case, "Electronic Message Systems in the University: A Description of Use and Utility," *Journal of Communication* 33 (1983), pp. 131–52; C. Steinfield, "Dimensions of Electronic Mail Use in an Organizational Setting," *Proceedings of the Academy of Management,* San Diego, 1985.

33. A. Farnham, "Kicked to Curb by Text: New, Awful Way to Be Fired," *ABC News,* July 16, 2013, http://www.abcnews.com; M. Gardner, "You've Got Mail: 'We're Letting You Go,'" *Christian Science Monitor,* September 18, 2006, http://www.csmonitor.com; Linton Weeks,

"Read the Blog: You're Fired," *National Public Radio,* December 8, 2008, http://www.npr.org.

34. J. Meister, "To Do: Update Company's Social Media Policy ASAP," *Forbes,* February 7, 2013, http://www.forbes.com.

35. J. DeMers, "Communication in 2015: Text, Voice, Video or In-Person?" *Inc.* January 29, 2015, www.inc.com; K. Ferrazzi, "How to Avoid Virtual Communication," *Harvard Business Review,* April 12, 2013, http://www.hbr.org.

36. K. Byron, "Carrying Too Heavy a Load? The Communication and Miscommunication of Emotion by Email," *Academy of Management Review* 33 (2008), pp. 309–27.

37. C. Naquin, T. Kurtzberg, and L. Belkin, "The Finer Points of Lying Online: E-mail versus Pen and Paper," *Journal of Applied Psychology* 95, no. 2 (2010), pp. 387–94.

38. G. Moran, "6 Ways to Tame Your Email Overload," *Fast Company,* March 2, 2016, www.fastcompany.com; A. Hopp, "Overwhelming Communication," *Training Journal,* April 23, 2014, http://www.trainingjournal.com.

39. Company website, "Email Statistics Report," The Radicati Group, www.radicati.com, accessed April 5, 2019.

40. N. Fallon, "12 Easy Ways to Be More Productive at Work," *Business News Daily,* April 20, 2017, www.businessnewsdaily.com; Robby Macdonell, "Can We Talk for a Minute about Why Email Sucks So Much?" *RescueTime Blog,* February 16, 2013, http://blog.rescuetime.com.

41. M. Chui, J. Manyika, J. Bughin, et al., "The Social Economy: Unlocking Value and Productivity through Social Technologies" McKinsey Global Institute, July 2012, http://www.mckinsey.com.

42. L. Vanderkam, "What Is an Appropriate Response Time to Email?" *Fast Company,* March 29, 2016, www.fastcompany.com; C. Conner, "Why Every Organization Needs a Standard Response Time Policy," *Forbes,* August 16, 2013, http://www.forbes.com.

43. P. Ebben, "Company Bans After-Work Emails to Improve Employee Work–Life Balance," 4 WBZ Boston CBS Local News, April 24, 2018, www.bostoncbslocal.com.

44. H. Fernandez, "Work Email Ban after Hours in New York City May Become Law," *Fox Business,* March 26, 2018, www.foxbusiness.com.

45. Company website, "Workplace Flexibility Takes Control of Letting," Deloitte, gohttps://www2.deloitte.com/us/en/pages/human-capital/solutions /workplace-flexibility-services.html, accessed April 5, 2019; J. Pochepan, "Here's What Happens When You Take Away Dedicated Desks for Employees," *Inc.,* May 10, 2018, www.inc.com.

46. S. Kejriwal and S. Mahajan, "Smartbuildings: How IoT Technology Aims to Add Value for Real Estate Companies," Deloitte, www2.deloitte.com, accessed April 5, 2019.

47. P. Economy, "5 Ways to Get the Most from Virtual Employees," *Inc.,* June 13, 2014, http://www.inc.com; T. Mackintosh, "Is This the Year You Move to a Virtual Office?" *Accounting Technology,* May 2007, General Reference Center Gold, http://find.galegroup.com.

48. Company website, "Work with Us," http://automattic.com/work-with-us/, accessed May 3, 2015; Rachel Emma Silverman, "Step into the Office-less Company," *The Wall Street Journal,* September 4, 2012, http://online.wsj.com; Verne Kopytoff, "Why Some Company Offices Are Virtual," *Bloomberg Businessweek,* September 10, 2012, EBSCOhost, http://web.ebscohost.com; Automattic, "Work with Us," http://automattic.com.

49. E. Hallowel, "The Human Moment at Work," *Harvard Business Review,* January–February 1999, http://www.hbr.org.

50. The Radicati Group, "Email Statistics Report 2017–2021," http://www.radicati.com/wp/wp-content/uploads/2017/01/Email-Statistics-Report-2017-2021-Executive-Summary.pdf; Hubspot, "The Ultimate List of Marketing Statistics for 2018," https://www.hubspot.com/marketing-statistics.

51. James Vincent, "Google Removed Gendered Pronouns from Gmail's Smart Compose to Avoid AI Bias," *The Verge,* November 27, 2018, https://www.theverge.com/2018/11/27/18114127/google-gmail-smart-compose-ai-gender-bias-prounouns-removed.

52. Rob Thuron, "New AI-Powered Gmail Feature Can Write Emails for You," *TechSpot,* May 9, 2018, https://www.techspot.com/news/74533-new-ai-powered-gmail-feature-can-write-emails.html.

53. R. Lengel and R. Daft, "The Selection of Communication Media as an Executive Skill," *Academy of Management Executive* 2 (1988), pp. 225–32.

54. J. R. Carlson and R. W. Zmud, "Channel Expansion Theory and the Experiential Nature of Media Richness Perceptions," *Academy of Management Journal* 42 (1999), pp. 153–70.

55. J. Fulk and B. Boyd, "Emerging Theories of Communication in Organizations," *Journal of Management* 17 (1991), pp. 407–46.

56. J. Fulk and B. Boyd, "Emerging Theories of Communication in Organizations," *Journal of Management* 17 (1991), pp. 407–46.

57. "How SoundCloud Keeps Communication Flowing across Four Offices in 4 Time Zones," *FirstRound.com,* http://firstround.com/review/how-soundcloud-keeps-communication-flowing-across-4-offices-in-4-time-zones/, accessed April 12, 2019.

58. "How SoundCloud's All Hands Meetings Keep Its Four Offices Aligned," *Future of Work,* https://academy.nobl.io/how-soundclouds-all-hands-meetings-keep-its-four-offices-aligned, accessed April 12, 2019.

59. L. Bossidy and R. Charan, *Confronting Reality: Doing What Matters to Get Things Right* (New York: Crown Business, 2004).

60. C. Beers, "Leading through the Power of Persuasion," *Fast Company,* November 8, 2012, http://www.fastcompany.com; M. McCall, M. Lombardo, and A. Morrison, *The Lessons of Experience: How Successful Executives Develop on the Job* (Lexington, MA: Lexington, 1988).

61. J. A. Conger, "The Necessary Art of Persuasion," *Harvard Business Review,* May–June 1998, pp. 84–95.

62. N. Morgan, "How to Become an Authentic Speaker," *Harvard Business Review,* November 2008, pp. 115–19.

63. N. Nohria and B. Harrington, *Six Principles of Successful Persuasion* (Boston: Harvard Business School Publishing Division, 1993).

64. K. Mascia, "He Beat Childhood Cancer. Now He's Trying to Save Lives as a Cancer Researcher," March 12, 2019, Johnson & Johnson Personal Stories, www.jnj.com.

65. H. K. Mintz, "Business Writing Styles for the 70's," *Business Horizons,* August 1972, in *Readings in Interpersonal and Organizational Communication,* ed. R. C. Huseman, C. M. Logue, and D. L. Freshley (Boston: Allyn & Bacon, 1977).

66. C. D. Decker, "Writing to Teach Thinking," *Across the Board,* March 1996, pp. 19–20.

67. M. Forbes, "Exorcising Demons from Important Business Letters," *Marketing Times,* March–April 1981, pp. 36–38.

68. R. Gillett, "Here's Why No One Gets Your Sarcastic Emails," *Fast Company,* May 30, 2014, http://www.fastcompany.com; T. Flood, "Top Ten Mistakes Managers Make with Email," *The Wall Street Journal,* February 3, 2010, http://online.wsj.com.

69. G. Ferraro, "The Need for Linguistic Proficiency in Global Business," *Business Horizons,* May–June 1996, pp. 39–46; William W. Maddux, Peter H. Kim, Tetsushi Okumura, and Jeanne M. Brett, "Why 'I'm Sorry' Doesn't Always Translate," *Harvard Business Review,* June 2012, p. 26.

70. D. Welch and L. Welch, "Developing Multilingual Capacity: A Challenge for the Multinational Enterprise," *Journal of Management* 44 (2018), pp. 854–59.

71. P. C. Early and E. Mosakowski, "Creating Hybrid Team Cultures: An Empirical Test of Transnational Team Functioning," *Academy of Management Journal* 43 (2000), pp. 26–49.

72. T. Neeley and R. Kaplan, "What's Your Language Strategy?" *Harvard Business Review,* September 2014, www.hbr.org.

73. B. Rashid, "3 Corporate Benefits of Learning a Foreign Language and Why You Should Care," *Forbes,* June 12, 2017, www.forbes.com; C. Chu, *The Asian Mind Game* (New York: Rawson Associates, 1991).

74. G. Ferraro, "The Need for Linguistic Proficiency in Global Business," *Business Horizons,* May–June 1996, pp. 39–46.

75. S. Bonaccio, J. O'Reilly, S. O'Sullivan, and F. Chiocchio, "Nonverbal Behavior and Communication in the Workplace: A Review and an Agenda for Research," *Journal of Management* 42 (2016), pp. 1044–74.

76. T. W. Comstock, *Communicating in Business and Industry* (Albany, NY: Delmar, 1985).

77. M. Korda, *Power: How to Get It, How to Use It* (New York: Random House, 1975).

78. A. Mehrabian, "Communication without Words," "The Hidden Message Managers Send," *Harvard Business Review,* November–December 1979, pp. 135–48.

79. G. Ferraro, "The Need for Linguistic Proficiency in Global Business," *Business Horizons,* May–June 1996, pp. 39–46.

80. Social Impact Stories, http://www.social-impact-stories.com/about, accessed April 21, 2017; Renyung Ho, "The Power of Storytelling for Social Business," *Conscious* magazine, n.d., http://consciousmagazine.co/the-power-of-storytelling-for-social-businesses/, accessed April 21, 2017; "Stories of Change," http://www.sundance.org/support/storiesofchange, accessed April 21, 2017; Jeff Bladt and Bob Filbin, "A Data Scientist's Real Job: Storytelling," March 27, 2013, https://hbr.org/2013/03/a-data-scientists-real-job-sto; "Social Enterprise Stories," https://socialenterprise.us/story-telling/, accessed April 21, 2017; organization website, Liberty's Kitchen, http://www.libertyskitchen.org/blog/, accessed April 21, 2017.

81. Forbes Coaches Council, "What Is Impactful Communication and Why Is It Important for Your Company?" *Forbes,* May 13, 2016, https://www.forbes.com/sites/forbescoachescouncil/2016/05/13/what-is-impactful-communication-and-why-is-it-important-for-your-company/#1b7b61024cdf.

82. Sundance Institute, "Sundance Stories of Change," https://www.sundance.org/support/storiesofchange/dashboard, accessed April 12, 2019.

83. Liberty's Kitchen, "Liberty's Kitchen Archive," http://www.libertyskitchen.org/blog/, accessed April 12, 2019.

84. Bernard T. Ferrari, "The Executive's Guide to Better Listening," *McKinsey Quarterly,* February 2012, https://www.mckinseyquarterly.com.

85. A. Athos and J. Gabarro, *Interpersonal Behavior* (Englewood Cliffs, NJ: Prentice-Hall, 1978).

86. M. K. Pratt, "Five Ways to Drive Your Best Workers Out the Door," *Computerworld,* August 25, 2008, pp. 26–27, 30.

87. J. Kouzes and B. Posner, *The Leadership Challenge* (San Francisco: Jossey-Bass, 1995).

88. "11 highly effective ways to connect with employees," *CNBC,* January 4, 2018, www.cnbc.com.

89. G. Graham, J. Unruh, and P. Jennings, "The Impact of Nonverbal Communication in Organizations: A Survey of Perceptions," *Journal of Business Communications* 28 (1991), pp. 45–62.

90. G. Graham, J. Unruh, and P. Jennings, "The Impact of Nonverbal Communication in Organizations: A Survey of Perceptions," *Journal of Business Communications* 28 (1991), pp. 45–62.

91. E. Goodson, "Read a Plant—Fast," *Harvard Business Review,* May 2002, pp. 105–13; D. Upton and S. Macadam, "Why (and How) to Take a Plant Tour," *Harvard Business Review,* May–June 1997, pp. 97–106.

92. H. Seligson, "For American Workers in China, a Culture Clash," *The New York Times,* December 23, 2009, http://www.nytimes.com.

93. C. Chu, *The Asian Mind Game* (New York: Rawson Associates, 1991).

94. J. Keyton, "Communication in Organizations," *Annual Review of Organizational Psychology and Organizational Behavior* 4 (2017), pp. 501–26.

95. A. Smidts, A. T. H. Pruyn, and C. B. M. van Riel, "The Impact of Employee Communication and Perceived External Prestige on Organizational Identification," *Academy of Management Journal* 49 (2001), pp. 1051–62.

96. X. Qin, R. Ren, Z. Zhang, and R. Johnson, "Fairness Heuristics and Substitutability Effects: Inferring the Fairness of Outcomes, Procedures, and Interpersonal Treatment When Employees Lack Clear Information," *Journal of Applied Psychology* 100 (2015), pp. 749–66; J. Koehler, K. Anatol, and R. Applebaum, *Organizational Communication: Behavioral Perspectives* (Orlando, FL: Holt, Rinehart & Winston, 1981).

97. J. Waldroop and T. Butler, "The Executive as Coach," *Harvard Business Review,* November–December 1996, pp. 111–17; S. Toye, "Coaching Comes of Age," *Training Journal,* 2015, pp. 21–24; D. T. Hall, K. L. Otazo, and G. P. Hollenbeck, "Behind Closed Doors: What Really Happens in Executive Coaching," *Organizational Dynamics,* Winter 1999, pp. 39–53; D. O'Neil, M. Hopkins, and D. Bilimoria, "A Framework for Developing Women Leaders: Applications to Executive Coaching," *Journal of Applied Behavioral Science* 51 (2015), pp. 253–76.

98. D. Larcker, S. Miles, B. Tayan, and M. Gutman, "2013 Executive Coaching Survey," The Miles Group and Stanford University,

August 2013, http://www.gsb.stanford.edu/faculty-research/publications/2013-executive-coachingsurvey.

99. R. J. Bies, "The Delivery of Bad News in Organizations: A Framework for Analysis," *Journal of Management* 39 (2013), pp. 136–62.

100. J. Gutknecht and J. B. Keys, "Mergers, Acquisitions, and Takeovers: Maintaining Morale of Survivors and Protecting Employees," *Academy of Management Executive,* August 1993, pp. 26–36.

101. D. Schweiger and A. DeNisi, "Communication with Employees Following a Merger: A Longitudinal Field Experiment," *Academy of Management Journal* 34 (1991), pp. 110–35.

102. J. Case, "Opening the Books," *Harvard Business Review,* March–April 1997, pp. 118–27.

103. "How Total Transparency Saved My Company," *Inc.,* March 2014, http://www.inc.com.

104. "The Best Companies to Work for in Chicago," *Fortune,* May 22, 2018, www.fortune.com.

105. S. Stevenson, "We Spent *What* on Paper Clips?" *Slate,* May 19, 2014, http://www.slate.com; "Hilcorp Hits #15 on Fortune's 100 Best Companies to Work For List," press release on, January 23, 2014, http://www.hilcorp.com; P. Patel, "Houston's Top Workplaces 2010: No. 1 Midsize Company, Hilcorp Energy Company," *Houston Chronicle,* November 7, 2010, www.houstonchronicle.com.

106. W. V. Ruch, *Corporate Communications* (Westport, CT: Quorum, 1984).

107. L. Tost, F. Gino, and R. Larrick, "When Power Makes Others Speechless: The Negative Impact of Leader Power on Team Performance," *Academy of Management Journal* 56 (2013), pp. 1465–86.

108. J. Gardner, "The Heart of the Matter: Leader-Constituent Interaction," in *Leading & Leadership,* ed. T. Fuller (Notre Dame, IN: Notre Dame University Press, 2000), pp. 239–44.

109. R. Ashkenas, D. Ulrich, T. Jick, and S. Kerr, *The Boundaryless Organization* (San Francisco: Jossey-Bass, 1995).

110. W. V. Ruch, *Corporate Communications* (Westport, CT: Quorum, 1984).

111. H. Touryalai, "Marriott's Upgrade: New CEO Arne Sorenson Freshens Up the Brand for Millennials," *Forbes,* June 26, 2013, http://www.forbes.com.

112. M. Chamberlin, D. Newton, and J Lepine, "A Meta-Analysis of Voice and Its Promotive and Prohibitive Forms: Identification of Key Associations, Distinctions, and Future Research Directions," *Personnel Psychology* 70 (2017), pp. 11–71.

113. A. Hutton, "Four Rules for Taking Your Message to Wall Street," *Harvard Business Review,* May 2001, pp. 125–32.

114. R. Applebaum, J. Koehler, and K. Anatol. *Organizational Communication: Behavioral Perspectives,* Boston: Houghton Mifflin Harcourt, 1981).

115. D. Tjosvold, A. S. H. Wong, and N. Y. F. Chen, "Constructively Managing Conflicts in Organizations," *Annual Review of Organizational Psychology and Organizational Behavior* 1 (2014), pp. 545–68.

116. E. Huynh, "Google's Innovative Workplace," *Medium,* March 6, 2018, https://medium.com.

117. T. Harbert, "Teamwork for Techies," *Computerworld,* December 20, 2010, pp. 24–27.

118. L.-Z. Wu, T. Birtch, F. F. T. Chiang, and H. Zhang, "Perceptions of Negative Workplace Gossip: A Self-Consistency Theory Framework," *Journal of Management* 44 (2018), pp. 1873–98.

119. N. B. Kurland and L. H. Pelled, "Passing the Word: Toward a Model of Gossip and Power in the Workplace," *Academy of Management Review* 25 (2000), pp. 428–38.

120. T. Grosser, V. Lopez-Kidwell, G. Labianca, and L. Ellwardt, "Hearing It through the Grapevine: Positive and Negative Workplace Gossip," *Organizational Dynamics* 41 (2012), 52–61; L. Abrams, R. Cross, E. Lesser, and D. Levin, "Nurturing Interpersonal Trust in Knowledge-Sharing Networks," *Academy of Management Executive* 17 (November 2003), pp. 64–77.

121. R. L. Rosnow, "Rumor as Communication: A Contextual Approach," *Journal of Communication* 38 (1988), pp. 12–28.

122. L. Burke and J. M. Wise, "The Effective Care, Handling, and Pruning of the Office Grapevine," *Business Horizons,* May–June 2003, pp. 71–76.

123. K. Davis, "The Care and Cultivation of the Corporate Grapevine," *Dun's Review,* July 1973, pp. 44–47.

124. N. Difonzo, P. Bordia, and R. Rosnow, "Reining in Rumors," *Organizational Dynamics,* Summer 1994, pp. 47–62.

125. A. Schnackenberg and E. Tomlinson, "Organizational Transparency: A New Perspective on Managing Trust in Organization-Stakeholder Relationships," *Journal of Management* 42 (2016), pp. 1784–1810.

126. R. Ashkenas, D. Ulrich, T. Jick, and S. Kerr, *The Boundaryless Organization, Breaking the Chains of Organizational Structure* (San Francisco: Jossey-Bass, 1995).

127. R. M. Hodgetts, "A Conversation with Steve Kerr," *Organizational Dynamics,* Spring 1996, pp. 68–79.

128. "Number of Employees at General Electric in the U.S. from 2007 to 2018 (in 1,000s)," *Statistica,* www.statistica.com, accessed April 5, 2019.

129. R. Ashkenas, D. Ulrich, T. Jick, and S. Kerr, *The Boundaryless Organization, Breaking the Chains of Organizational Structure* (San Francisco: Jossey-Bass, 1995).

130. A. Schnackenberg and E. Tomlinson, "Organizational Transparency: A New Perspective on Managing Trust in Organization-Stakeholder Relationships," *Journal of Management* 42 (2016), pp. 1784–1810.

131. KC Ifeanyi, "After a Terrible, Horrible, No Good, Very Bad 2017, SoundCloud Is on the Mend with More Features," *Fast Company,* February 19, 2019, https://www.fastcompany.com/90309061/after-a-terrible-horrible-no-good-very-bad-2017-soundcloud-is-on-the-mend-with-more-features.

132. Carley Marie, "How Post Malone Went from SoundCloud Star to Rockstar," The Versed, September 16, 2018, https://www.theversed.com/91853/post-malone-went-soundcloud-star-rockstar/#.LkMtUEXY8P.

133. Daniel Sanchez, "SoundCloud Unveils a Slew of DJ Software Partnerships: 'Streaming Workflows Are the Future,'" *Digital Music News,* October 18, 2018, https://www.digitalmusicnews.com/2018/10/18/latest-soundcloud-real-time-dj-mixing-streaming/.

PART FOUR SUPPORTING CASE

Leading and Motivating When Disaster Strikes: Magna Exteriors and Interiors

Magna Exteriors and Interiors Corporation manufactures vehicle components that give car or truck models their distinctive looks. Some of Magna's exterior products are trim, roof systems, body panels, and front and rear end fascia; interior products include trim, cockpit systems, and cargo management systems. Nowadays auto companies don't make all these components but, instead, create the designs and handle the final assembly of components from suppliers such as Magna, delivered to the auto company as needed to meet production plans.

Magna Exteriors and Interiors is a unit of Magna International, which describes itself as "the most diversified automotive supplier in the world." Magna has 263 manufacturing operations plus sales and engineering centers in 26 countries of North America, South America, Africa, Europe, and Asia. These meet the needs of more than two dozen customers, including General Motors, Ford, Chrysler, Toyota, Mack, Harley-Davidson, and Volkswagen. The customers sell different kinds of vehicles, and it is expensive to build and transport large components, so Magna's factories need to be close to customers both geographically and in their working relationships.

Meeting these requirements suddenly became a problem for Magna's factory in Howell, Michigan, on a recent Wednesday evening in March. A fire started on an assembly line at the facility, which makes interior trim such as rear window trays, door panels, and skins for instrument panels. Fortunately, the hundred workers who were finishing up the afternoon shift all escaped safely.

The Howell facility employs about 450 workers. Its customers include 16 GM, Ford, Chrysler, Nissan, and Mazda assembly plants. Forecasting a shortage of parts, some of its customers slowed production and canceled shifts in the days immediately after the fire. Magna's managers knew they needed to scramble, or employees would be out of work and important customers would be lost. Robert Brownlee, president of Magna Exteriors and Interiors North America, decided the Howell facility should be running again within just two days. Meeting that goal would require an all-out effort.

While the firefighters were still battling the blaze, Brownlee conferred by phone with his top managers, figuring out what they should do first. Because they couldn't yet assess the extent of the damages, they had to work with a worst-case scenario: destruction of the entire building. They identified four Magna facilities making similar products, where they could ship the Howell plant's tooling on flatbed trucks if need be. That night, Brownlee directed all four of the plants to increase production and build up their inventories in case they would be needed for the Howell plant's customers.

Next the managers set up a reconstruction team, including electricians, pipe fitters, millwrights, mechanics, tool-makers, and information technology specialists. The team assembled in Howell with a structural engineer, awaiting permission to enter the damaged building. On Thursday night, about 24 hours after the fire, the fire department let the team enter the plant. The structural engineer determined that the fire had been contained in one part of the plant. About 30 percent of the plant, representing one out of four production sectors, was destroyed beyond repair. One of the four remaining production sectors had largely escaped damage.

Now the clock was ticking on Brownlee's two-day recovery goal. On Friday morning, workers pulled damaged tooling out of the rubble and had it moved to Brighton, a city 12 miles away, where they cleaned it and set up a temporary assembly line in a Magna warehouse. Back in Howell, the reconstruction team was building a temporary wall to seal off the undamaged part of the facility and repairing the roof. The heating and electrical systems were destroyed, so they brought in a dozen diesel generators to power heaters and lighting. Until the roof was repaired, they coped with Michigan's wintry March weather by wearing snowmobile suits while clearing out debris and damaged products, working around the clock.

The next morning, spirits rose when power was restored to the least-damaged sector, and the lights came back on. Workers continued to repair, clean, and rewire the tooling. By Saturday night, workers were able to restart some of the machinery and do test runs. Unfortunately, they ran into problems with each attempt. Managers were scrambling to keep on top of the plant reconstruction and the attempts to restart machinery. Brownlee saw that this was too much responsibility. He called together the managers, put each one in charge of relaunching one product line, and directed them to put a subordinate in charge of every other duty, including reconstruction.

The efforts to restart continued as representatives from every customer monitored the progress. Magna gave customers daily updates, and as each assembly line resumed, the relevant customer's representative signed off as part of the quality-control practices. By Sunday, limited production had begun at the Howell plant. Six days after the fire department determined that the fire was extinguished, the Howell plant was running at 80 percent of capacity, and its temporary line in Brighton handled the remaining production.

In a statement to the media, the company publicly thanked "the Magna Howell employees who continue to do whatever it takes to meet customer requirements; the Magna group office employees and Magna employees from numerous other divisions who have come to support the effort," the company's contractors and customers, the community's firefighters, and others who helped after the fire.

QUESTIONS

1. As a leader, what vision did Robert Brownlee offer? What combination of task performance and group maintenance behaviors did he use? Was this the appropriate combination after the fire? Why or why not?

2. What do you think the Magna managers and employees were motivated by most after the fire? Why?

3. Management set up a cross-functional reconstruction team, but there is no evidence that this was a self-managed team. Would a self-managed team have been more effective? Why or why not?

SOURCES: Sedgwick, D., "Five-Alarm Planning," *Crain's Detroit Business*, April 18, 2011, Business & Company Resource Center, http://galenet. galegroup.com; Magna International, "About Magna Exteriors and Interiors," http://www.magna.com; Van Alphen, T., "Magna Plant Resumes Full Deliveries after Fire," *Toronto Star*, March 10, 2011, http://www.thestar.com; Magna International, "Magna Atreum Howell Plant Back in Business Six Days after Fire," news release, March 9, 2011, http://www.magna.com.

CHAPTER 16
Managerial Control

A budget is telling your
money where to go instead of
wondering where it went.
—Dave Ramsey

Corbis/age fotostock

learning objectives

After studying Chapter 16, you will be able to:

LO 16-1   Explain why companies develop control systems.

LO 16-2   Summarize how to design a basic bureaucratic
control system.

LO 16-3   Describe the purposes for using budgets as a
control device.

LO 16-4   Define basic types of financial statements and
financial ratios used as controls.

LO 16-5   List procedures for implementing effective control
systems.

LO 16-6   Identify ways in which organizations use market
control mechanisms.

LO 16-7   Discuss the use of clan control in an empowered
organization.

chapter outline

Bureaucratic Control Systems
The Control Cycle
Approaches to Bureaucratic Control
Management Audits
Budgetary Controls
Financial Controls
Problems with Bureaucratic Control
Designing Effective Control Systems

The Other Controls: Markets and Clans
Market Control
Clan Control: The Role of Empowerment
and Culture

Management in Action

TRACKING EMPLOYEES TO CONTROL HEALTH CARE COSTS

Providing employee health insurance is a major expense for most companies. In addition, health problems caused by employee obesity cost U.S. companies about $73 billion (including the cost of lost productivity) every year.[1] Companies are eager to find ways to reduce these expenses.

One solution is to try to prevent employees from becoming unhealthy in the first place; health insurance costs would drop, and workers would file fewer claims to treat preventable conditions. More than 80 percent of large U.S. companies now have wellness programs to help employees lose weight, stop smoking, eat healthier, manage stress, or work more safely. Some run fitness contests or offer financial rewards, and others offer onsite gyms and healthy cafeteria offerings to encourage employee health.[2]

How are employers measuring the results of these efforts? One way is to use fitness trackers. Among the corporate giants that have given Fitbit devices to their employees are Bank of America, IBM, Target, Time Warner, and Barclays. Fitbit has even created a wellness division to train corporate clients to monitor and improve their employees' overall health.

At IBM, 96 percent of the 40,000 employees who were given Fitbits used them throughout the company's fitness challenge, and 63 percent continued using them after. For some companies, like the cloud-services start-up Appirio in San Francisco, tracking devices led to cost savings. After outfitting about 400 workers with Fitbits, the company shaved more than $250,000 from its annual employee health insurance bill.[3]

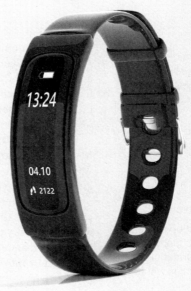

rawf8/Shutterstock

Employees generally like wellness programs, as long as the programs are flexible and can be customized to their personal wants and needs. Indiana University Health Center ran a weight loss challenge that included discounted Fitbits. Said one employee who lost 30 pounds and lowered his cholesterol during the program, "I racked up enough points for a free exercise ball and a slight discount on my insurance. But by far the biggest reward was my health."[4]

Some companies also monitor employees' use of email, social media, and the Internet, and even their weight loss progress and physical location. As you read this chapter, think about the kinds of control measures and processes that can help a company manage all its costs, including the cost of maintaining a healthy and productive workforce.

LO 16-1 Explain why companies develop control systems.

At Teco Energy, 170 team members alertly find ways to reduce waste and improve customer services. Teco also assigns improvement projects to teams to *prevent* problems.[5] It assigns a production engineer to design teams to ensure production efficiencies, reducing defects as well as costs.[6]

Spotting and preventing problems are two sides of the same coin: controlling employee behavior and performance. Left on their own, people may work in ways that they believe to be beneficial in some way, but hurt overall organizational performance. Employees simply wasting time online (shopping, checking scores, watching funny cat videos . . .) cost U.S. employers about $85 *billion* each year![7]

Bottom Line
Control helps to attain any management objective.

Even well-intentioned people may not know whether they are directing their efforts toward the activities that are most important. Thus control done well is a strong force that keeps the organization together and heading in the right direction.

The best managers exert control without micromanaging.

Once managers form plans and strategies, they must ensure that the plans are carried out. They must make sure that people are doing what needs to be done, and are not doing inappropriate things. As problems arise, management must take corrective action. This process is the control function of management.

control

Any process that directs the activities of individuals toward the achievement of organizational goals.

Effective planning facilitates control, and control facilitates planning. Planning lays out a framework for the future and provides a blueprint for control. Control systems then regulate resource allocation and use and facilitate the next planning cycle. Managers today must control their people, inventories, quality, and costs, to mention just a few of their responsibilities.

Control is defined as any process that directs activities toward organizational goals. It is how effective managers make sure that activities are going as planned. Some managers don't want to admit it (see Exhibit 16.1), but control problems—the lack thereof, or the wrong kinds—can cause irreparable damage.

bureaucratic control

The use of rules, regulations, and authority to guide performance.

Managers can use three broad strategies for achieving organizational control: bureaucratic, market, and clan controls.[8] **Bureaucratic control** is the use of rules, regulations, and formal authority to guide performance. It includes such items as budgets, statistical reports, and performance appraisals to regulate behavior and results.

market control

Control based on the use of pricing mechanisms and economic information to regulate activities within organizations.

Market control uses pricing mechanisms to regulate activities as though they were economic transactions. Business units are profit centers that trade resources (services or goods) with one another via such mechanisms. Managers who run these units are responsible for and evaluated by profit and loss.

clan control

Control based on the norms, values, shared goals, and trust among group members.

Those first two control types share an assumption that the interests of organizations and employees diverge. **Clan control** (or *cultural control*), is based on a belief that employees share the values, expectations, and goals of the organization and behave and perform accordingly. Formal controls are less necessary when organizational members have common values and

---

EXHIBIT 16.1

Symptoms of an Out-of-Control Company

- **Lax top management**—senior managers do not emphasize or value the need for controls, or they set a bad example.
- **Absence of policies**—the firm's expectations are not established in writing.
- **Lack of agreed-upon standards**—organization members are uncertain about what needs to be achieved.
- **"Shoot the messenger" management**—employees feel their careers would be at risk if they reported bad news.
- **Lack of periodic reviews**—managers do not assess performance on a regular, timely basis.
- **Bad information systems**—key data are not measured and reported in a timely and easily accessible way.
- **Lack of ethics in the culture**—organization members have not internalized a commitment to integrity.

Control System	Features and Requirements
Bureaucratic control	Uses formal rules, standards, hierarchy, and legitimate authority. Works best where tasks are clear and workers are independent.
Market control	Uses prices, competition, profit centers, and exchange relationships. Works best where tangible outputs are specified and markets can be established between parties.
Clan control	Uses culture, shared values, beliefs, expectations, and trust. Works best where there is no one best way to do a job, and employees are empowered to make decisions.

EXHIBIT 16.2
Control Systems and Characteristics

SOURCES: Ouchi, W. G., "A Conceptual Framework for the Design of Organizational Control Mechanisms," *Management Science* 25 (1979), pp. 833–48; Ouchi, W. G., "Markets, Bureaucracies, and Clans," *Administrative Science Quarterly* 25 (1980), pp. 129–41; Robey, R. D. and Sales, C. A., *Designing Organizations* (Burr Ridge, IL: Richard D. Irwin, 1994).

goals, and trust one another. Clan control stems from informal interpersonal processes influenced by culture, leaders, and teams (e.g., group norms and cohesiveness).

Exhibit 16.2 summarizes the main features of bureaucratic, market, and clan controls. Bureaucratic controls are ubiquitous, and therefore we give them the most attention; we discuss market and clan controls toward the end of the chapter.

Bureaucratic Control Systems

Bureaucratic (or formal) control systems measure progress toward performance goals and apply corrective measures as needed to ensure that performance achieves managers' objectives. Control systems detect and correct significant variations, or discrepancies, in the results of planned activities.

LO 16-2 Summarize how to design a basic bureaucratic control system.

The Control Cycle

As Exhibit 16.3 shows, a typical control system has four major steps:

1. Setting performance standards.
2. Measuring performance.
3. Comparing performance against the standards and determining deviations.
4. Taking action to correct problems and reinforce successes.

EXHIBIT 16.3
The Control Cycle

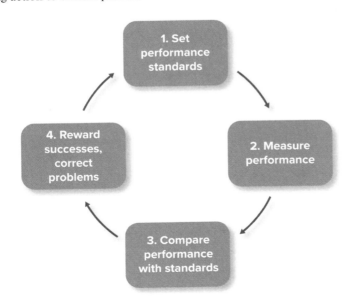

standard

Expected performance for a given goal: a target that establishes a desired performance level, motivates performance, and serves as a benchmark against which actual performance is assessed.

Bottom Line

Standards should be set for all bottom-line goals. *Give an example of a standard for sustainability.*

Step 1: Setting Performance Standards   Every organization has goals for profitability, customer satisfaction, costs, and so on. A **standard** is the targeted level of performance for a particular goal. Standards establish desired performance levels, motivate performance, and serve as benchmarks against which to assess actual performance. Standards can be set for any activity—financial activities, operating activities, legal compliance, charitable contributions,[9] and social impact (see the nearby "Social Entrepreneurship" box).

Performance standards can be set with respect to (1) quantity, (2) quality, (3) time used, and (4) cost. Production activities include volume of output (quantity), defects (quality), on-time availability of finished goods (time use), and dollar expenditures for raw materials and direct labor (cost). Customer service can be measured by the same standards—adequate supply and availability of products, quality of service, speed of delivery, and cost.

Step 2: Measuring Performance   The second step in the control process is to measure performance levels. Managers can count units produced, websites viewed, days absent,

Social Entrepreneurship

Beyond Counting: Measuring Social Impact

Nobel laureate Mohammed Yunus, founder of Grameen Bank, set a high standard when he declared that "social business" could lead to a "world without poverty."[10] But social enterprises can't assess their impact unless they know how to measure it.

Many social enterprises measure their impact by counting the number of people who receive the enterprise's product or service. For example, TOMS counts the shoes it donates annually to impoverished children (currently more than 86 million pairs throughout the world).[11] Root Capital measures the amount of money it lends (currently $1.3 billion to help improve the lives of more than 1.3 million small-scale farmers and 5.9 million family members).[12]

Both organizations are making a social impact, but the questions remain: What *exactly* is the impact they are having on their recipients? How many recipients wear the shoes or use the loan money as intended? To what degree did the recipients fare better than comparable individuals who didn't receive free shoes or a loan?

Despite its popularity, counting outcomes is an incomplete measure. More comprehensive assessments of social impact include:

1. *Impact Value Chain (IVC).* Developed by Professor Catherine Clark, the IVC takes a holistic approach to measuring social impact. Social enterprises can measure their impact by evaluating the entire process or value chain, including inputs, outputs, and outcomes.
2. *Progress Out of Poverty Index (PPI).* Created by the Grameen Foundation, the PPI "provides a

Casimiro/Alamy Stock Photo

relatively low-cost and efficient way to evaluate the poverty level of a given community."
3. *B Impact Assessment (BIA).* Developed by B-Lab, a nonprofit that certifies benefit corporations, the BIA evaluates an organization's "impact on its workers, community, environment, and customers."[13]

Some argue that we need specific measures customized to each social enterprise's goals. With better measures, we can more truly know when and how a social enterprise changes the world.

- Can you think of other ways TOMS or Root Capital could assess their social impact?

- Dive a little deeper by doing a bit of research. Which of the three measures (IVC, PPI, or BIA) do you think is the most accurate way to measure social impact? Why?

samples distributed, and dollars earned. Performance data commonly are obtained from three sources: written reports, oral reports, and personal observations.

Written reports are not only developed by people, but are often computer- and AI-generated. Thanks to computers' data-gathering and analysis capabilities and decreasing costs of cloud storage, both large and small companies can gather and retain huge amounts of performance data. One particularly efficient application, dashboards, help managers monitor several organizational performance indicators in realtime. Dashboards typically illustrate the data in easy to analyze charts and other visual graphics.[14]

One common example of oral reports occurs when a salesperson contacts his or her immediate manager at the close of each business day to report the accomplishments, problems, or customers' reactions during the day. The manager can ask questions to gain additional information or clear up any misunderstandings. When necessary, the discussion can identify possible corrective actions.

Personal observation involves going to the area where activities take place and watching what is occurring. Managers can directly observe work methods, employees' nonverbal signals, and the general operation. Personal observation gives a detailed picture of what is going on, but it has some disadvantages. It does not provide accurate quantitative data; the limited information usually is general and subjective. Plus, employees can misunderstand the purpose of personal observation as mistrust.

At the Baccarat factory in France, the workers in the quality control area are responsible for the quality and selection of these fine-cut crystal glasses.

asiseeit/Getty Images

Still, many managers believe in the value of firsthand observation. Personal contact can increase leadership visibility and upward communication. It also can provide valuable information to supplement written and oral reports.

The Digital World

Technology Provides More Thorough and Timely Performance Reviews

Timing matters in feedback control. The shorter the time lag between performance and feedback, the quicker problems are corrected. To that end, companies like the Gap, Deloitte, and GE are doing away with annual performance evaluations in favor of more frequent coaching and app-based feedback systems.[15] Some attribute this change in part to younger employees' desire for greater responsibility and a "feedback-rich" culture in which learning is continuous. Others suggest that fast-changing business environments require more frequent dialogue between managers and employees to ensure alignment between employees' actions and the firm's business strategy.[16]

Software maker Adobe used to spend more than 80,000 hours per year administering traditional performance evaluations. Now, every three months, a manager or employee requests a "check-in" to discuss performance.[17] Prior to the meeting, fellow employees provide performance feedback. Adobe's goal is to "make coaching and developing a continuous, collaborative process between managers and employees."[18] Since launching the new performance feedback system, Adobe reported a 30 percent reduction in its voluntary employee turnover.

1. Organizations that want to align talent with evolving business strategies must provide frequent coaching and developmental feedback. How often do you think organizations should provide feedback to their employees? Why?
2. Do you think the costs of technology plus frequent personal feedback from multiple sources can become too expensive to be worth it for companies? Why or why not?

It is important to acquire performance data on a timely basis. For example, consumer goods companies such as Procter & Gamble, Colgate Palmolive, and Campbell Soup carefully track new-product sales in selected local markets first so they can make adjustments before a national rollout. Unavailable information is useless information.

Step 3: Comparing Performance with the Standard

Now, armed with relevant data, the manager can evaluate the performance. For some activities, small deviations from standard are acceptable, whereas in others a slight deviation may be serious. In many manufacturing processes, a significant deviation in either direction (e.g., drilling a hole that is too small or too large) is unacceptable. In other cases, a deviation in one direction, such as sales or customer satisfaction that fall below the target level, is a problem, but a deviation in the other, exceeding the sales target or customer expectations, means employees are delivering better-than-expected results.

> Managers save time and effort by applying the principle of exception.

The managerial **principle of exception** states that control is enhanced by concentrating on the exceptions to—that is, significant deviations from—the expected result or standard. In comparing performance with the standard, managers need to attend to the exception—for example, a few defective components produced on an assembly line, or the feedback from customers who are upset (or delighted) with a service.

Identifying and correcting exceptions or product defects can sometimes mean the different between life and death. Many severe allergy sufferers carry EpiPens in case they need to self-administer an emergency treatment. In 2018, the product was in short supply in the United States due to manufacturing delays at Pfizer's Brentwood, Missouri, plant. The manufacturer has been addressing complaints from the Food and Drug Administration that the EpiPen failed to function during emergencies, resulting in patient deaths.[19]

Applying this principle, only exceptional cases require attention and action. This principle is important in controlling. The manager is not concerned with performance that equals or closely (adequately) approximates the expected results. Managers can save much time and effort by using the principle of exception.

Step 4: Taking Action to Correct Problems and Reinforce Successes

The last step in the control process is to take appropriate action on significant deviations. This step ensures that operations are adjusted to better achieve the planned results or, if the performance news is good, to keep achieving and perhaps learning from those exceptional results. When discovering significant variances, managers should take immediate and vigorous action.

Chipotle is taking food safety control to the next level. The fast casual chain recently announced the rollout of Zenput, a mobile food-safety protocol platform used by KFC, Domino's, and others to ensure that all employees at Chipotle's nearly 2,500 stores adhere to food management standards and procedures. This rollout comes in the wake of another food-safety event at a Powell, Ohio, restaurant where 600 people reported illnesses after eating there.[20] Since the end of 2015, Chipotle has experienced other food-safety events.[21]

The best corrective action depends on the nature of the problem. To solve a systemic problem, such as major delays in work flow, often a functionally diverse team approach is most effective. As you know, teams can bring greater resources, creative ideas, and grounded perspectives to problem solving. Knowledgeable team members can prevent managers from implementing simplistic solutions that don't address a problem's underlying causes. A diverse, informed team is more likely to take into account the effects of a proposed solution throughout the organization, preventing new problems from arising. As a result, the corrective action will probably be more effective.

Sometimes managers can play a direct role in problem solving by being plugged into the current work environment. Amanda Andrade, chief people officer at Veterans United Home Loans in Columbia, Missouri, takes this to heart. Andrade consistently assesses employee and company strengths and disconnects. She and her team are quick to take action. According to Andrade: "Then we make a plan to capitalize on the strengths and fix the disconnects."[22]

principle of exception

A managerial principle stating that control is enhanced by concentrating on the exceptions to or significant deviations from the expected result or standard.

1. What were our intended results?	2. What were our actual results?	3. What caused our results?	4. What will we sustain? Improve?
(What was planned?)	(What really happened?)	(Why did it happen?)	(What can we do better next time?)

EXHIBIT 16.4
Questions for an After-Action Review

After taking corrective action, some managers conduct an **after-action review**, using the four questions shown in Exhibit 16.4 to guide a frank and open-minded discussion aimed at continuous improvement.[23] The U.S. Army developed this process to help soldiers learn from their experiences, and the method applies equally well in business.

Employees at the J. M. Huber Corporation conduct a review after every planned project and major unplanned event and post lessons learned in an online database. In the public sector as well, emergency response teams improve their performance via after-action reviews. These reviews are most effective when scheduled regularly and when participation is mandatory for everyone involved. A post-action review can lead to better decision making, higher situational awareness, and enhanced organizational learning.[24]

after-action review

A frank and open-minded discussion of four basic questions aimed at continuous improvement.

Approaches to Bureaucratic Control

Three approaches to bureaucratic control are feedforward, concurrent, and feedback. **Feedforward control** takes place before operations begin and includes policies, procedures, and rules designed to ensure that planned activities are carried out properly. Examples include inspection of raw materials and proper selection and training of employees. **Concurrent control** takes place while plans are being carried out; it includes directing, monitoring, and fine-tuning activities as they occur. **Feedback control** uses information about results to correct deviations after they arise.

feedforward control

The control process used before operations begin, including policies, procedures, and rules designed to ensure that planned activities are carried out properly.

Feedforward Control Feedforward control (sometimes called *preliminary control*) is future oriented; its aim is to *prevent* problems before they arise. Instead of waiting for results and comparing them with goals, a manager can exert control by limiting activities in advance. Formal rules and procedures prescribe people's actions before they occur.

For example, human resource policies defining what forms of body art are acceptable to display at work can avoid awkward case-by-case conversations about particular people.[25] Or a company might dictate that managers adhere to clear ethical and legal guidelines when making decisions. Legal experts advise companies to establish policies forbidding disclosure of proprietary information or making clear that employees are not speaking for the company when they post messages on blogs, microblogging sites, and social networking sites.

Some firms, concerned about the pitfalls of workplace romance, have sought a solution in feedforward control. Romantic activities between a supervisor and subordinate create a conflict of interest or lead to sexual harassment. Other employees might infer from lack of action that the company allows a culture of harassment or sanctions personal relationships as a path to advancement. And relationship ups and downs can affect everyone's mood and motivation.

Controls aimed at preventing such problems include training in appropriate behavior (including how to avoid sexual harassment) and even requiring executives and their romantic interests to sign "love contracts" stating that the relationship is voluntary and welcome. The company keeps a copy of the contract in case the relationship dissolves and an unhappy employee blames the company for allowing it in the first place.[26]

concurrent control

The control process used while plans are being carried out, including directing, monitoring, and fine-tuning activities as they are performed.

feedback control

Control that focuses on the use of information about previous results to correct deviations from the acceptable standard.

Concurrent Control   Concurrent control takes place while plans are carried out and is the heart of any control system. On a manufacturing floor, materials must be available when and where needed, and breakdowns in the production process must be repaired immediately. In an airline terminal, the baggage must get to the right airplanes before flights depart. An online financial institution has to ensure that customers can access their checking, savings, and other bank accounts 24/7. Concurrent control also is in effect when supervisors monitor employees to ensure they work efficiently and carefully.

Information technology provides powerful concurrent controls, giving managers immediate access to data from the most remote corners of their companies. For example, managers update budgets instantly based on a continuous flow of performance data. In production facilities, monitoring systems that track errors per hour, machine speeds, and other measures allow managers to correct small production problems before they become disasters. Point-of-sale terminals in store checkout lines send sales data to a retailer's headquarters to show which products are selling in which locations.

Concurrent control also applies in service settings. As part of its efforts to transform safety, quality, and efficiency, Virginia Mason Medical Center authorized employees to issue personal safety alerts (PSAs). If any employee has a concern or question about a patient's safety, that employee calls an alert. The PSA system has both improved the hospital's safety performance and lowered its costs for professional liability insurance.[27]

> Timing is an important aspect of feedback control.

Feedback Control   Feedback control involves gathering performance data, using it to identify performance below standard, and then taking corrective action as needed. When supervisors monitor ongoing behavior, they are exercising concurrent control. When they check results to discover and then correct improper performance, they are using feedback as a means of control. An example would be how supervisors frequently check for customer service errors in recorded conversations between customers and representatives of call centers. That is why when you call an insurance or credit card company for assistance, you probably hear a recording indicating the call will be recorded for quality control or security purposes.

Timing matters greatly in feedback control. Long time lags often occur between performance and feedback, such as when actual spending is compared with the quarterly budget or when an employee's annual performance is compared to goals set a year earlier. Performance feedback after shorter time lags allows faster problem identification and corrections, preventing more serious harm.[28]

Some feedback processes are under real-time (concurrent) control, as with computer-controlled robots on assembly lines. Such units have sensors that continually determine whether they are in the correct positions to perform their functions. If they are not, a built-in control device makes immediate corrections.

In other situations, feedback processes take more time. Hertz uses feedback including customer ratings of service and car quality. Compliments and complaints help the company reinforce or correct practices at particular facilities. If a customer is upset about something, Hertz wants to know as soon as possible so it can correct the problem.

Six Sigma   A particularly robust and powerful application of feedback control is six sigma, introduced in Chapter 9. Six sigma is designed to reduce defects in all organization processes—not just product defects but anything that might make customers unhappy. Sigma is the Greek letter used in statistics to designate the estimated standard deviation, or variation, in a process. It indicates how often defects in a process are likely to occur. The higher the sigma number, the lower the level of variation or defects. Exhibit 16.5 shows that a two-sigma-level process has more than 300,000 defects per million opportunities (DPMO)—not a well-controlled process. A three-sigma-level process has 66,807 DPMO, which is roughly a 93 percent level of accuracy. Many organizations operate at this level, which on its face does not sound too bad until we consider its implications—for example, 7 pieces of airline

Inclusiveness Works

Making a Measurable Impact with D&I Initiatives

Julie Sweet is the CEO of Accenture, an organization that is consistently one of the top rated in the world for its diverse and inclusive workplace.[29] In a recent interview with *The New York Times,* Sweet shared her thoughts: "You first have to decide if diversity is a business priority. If it is, then you need to treat it like a business priority. You set goals, have accountable leaders, you measure progress, and you have an action plan."[30]

Although Sweet's approach sounds simple enough to implement, different groups define "diversity" and "inclusion" differently. For example, some workers think of workplace diversity as equal and fair representation based on conventional demographics, such as gender, race, and age, apart from business outcomes. Other workers view diversity as an integration of various backgrounds and perspectives that is integral to business outcomes.[31]

As markets and workplaces become increasingly globalized, D&I initiatives are shifting from a corporate "reporting goal" to a CEO-level business priority. As such, organizations are shifting away from measuring D&I based merely on a demographic profile to measuring D&I in all facets of operations, from recruitment to promotion and pay. And as firms invest more in proactive D&I initiatives, managers are being held accountable with metrics that measure how their results compare with other departments.[32]

As one HR professional says, "Diversity isn't scary and it's not about being PC. It's a real business opportunity to understand different business groups and make sure you support them."[33] Effective measurement practices are critical to progress.

- Every chapter in this book has a feature about diversity and inclusion. By now, how do you define them? How would your definition influence the way you implemented and measured D&I initiatives?
- What measures can you think of that might effectively capture D&I progress?

baggage lost for every 100 processed. The additional costs to organizations of such inaccuracy are enormous. As you can see in the exhibit, even at just above a 99 percent defect-free rate, or 6,210 DPMO, the accuracy level can be unacceptable.[34]

Recalling Chapter 9, at a six-sigma level a process produces fewer than 3.4 defects per million, or a 99.99966 percent level of accuracy. Six-sigma companies have close to zero defects plus substantially lower production costs and cycle times, leading to much higher customer satisfaction.

This methodology isn't just for the factory floor. For instance, accountants have used six sigma to improve the quality of their audits investigating risks faced by their clients.[35]

The six-sigma approach begins by defining the outputs and information that flow through each stage of the process and then measuring performance at each stage. Tools for analyzing results include looking for the root causes of problems. Suppose some customers are

Bottom Line

Six sigma aims for defect-free performance. *How would attempting and achieving six-sigma quality influence costs?*

Sigma Level	DPMO	Is Four Sigma Good Enough?
2σ	308,537	Consider these everyday examples of four-sigma quality . . .
3σ	66,807	• 20,000 lost articles of mail per hour.
4σ	**6,210**	• Unsafe drinking water 15 minutes per day.
5σ	233	• 5,000 incorrect surgical operations per week.
6σ	3.4	• 200,000 wrong prescriptions each year.
		• No electricity for 7 hours each month.

EXHIBIT 16.5

Relationship between Sigma Level and Defects per Million Opportunities

SOURCE: Rancour, Tom and McCracken, Mike, "Applying 6 Sigma Methods for Breakthrough Safety Performance," *Professional Safety* 45, no. 10 (October 2000), pp. 29–32.

dissatisfied with a company's customer service. Asking "why?" over and over (famously, thanks to Toyota, asking "why?" five times) could reveal that customers are dissatisfied because phone calls go unanswered, which happens because support staff can't keep up with the call volume because the department is understaffed, which is the result of a hiring freeze, which is the result of budget cuts, which were implemented after sales revenue dropped.

A good solution should somehow address the budget restrictions, either by increasing the budget or by learning how a small department can better satisfy customers. After changing and evaluation the new processes, this cycle continues until the desired quality level is achieved. This is how the six-sigma process creates continuous improvement.

Six sigma doesn't automatically and always deliver better business results.[36] It focuses only on how to eliminate defects in a process, not whether the process is the best one for the bottom line. At Home Depot, six sigma improved customer checkout processes and decisions about where to place products in stores, but the effort took store workers away from customers. At 3M, driving efficiency through six sigma slowed down the flow of innovative ideas. One way to apply the strengths of six sigma and minimize its drawbacks is to create goals and control processes for new products that are different from those for mature products.

Management Audits

Management audits evaluate the effectiveness and efficiency of the organization's various systems, from social responsibility programs to accounting systems. Managers conduct external and internal audits: external audits of other companies and internal audits of their own companies. Some of the same tools and approaches are used for both types.[37]

External Audits   An **external audit** occurs when one organization evaluates another organization. Commonly an external body such as a CPA firm conducts financial and accounting audits. But any company can conduct external audits of competitors or other companies for its own strategic purposes. This type of analysis (1) investigates other organizations for possible merger or acquisition, (2) determines the soundness of a company being considered as a supplier, or (3) discovers the strengths and weaknesses of a competitor to maintain or better exploit the competitive advantages of the investigating organization.

External audits provide essential feedback control when they identify evidence of legal and ethical lapses that could harm the organization and its reputation. They also provide feedforward control because they can prevent problems from occurring in the future. When a company seeking to buy other businesses gathers accurate information about candidates, it is more likely to acquire the best companies and avoid unsound acquisitions.

Internal Audits   Your employer might assign a group to conduct an **internal audit** to assess (1) what the company has done for itself, and (2) what it has done for its customers or other recipients of its goods or services. The audit can assess financial stability, production efficiency, sales effectiveness, human resources development, earnings growth, energy use, public relations, civic responsibility, and other effectiveness criteria. An audit is intended to improve a company's risk management, control, and governance processes.[38]

Management audits uncover common undesirable practices such as unnecessary work, work duplication, poor inventory control, uneconomical use of equipment and machines, procedures that are costlier than necessary, and wasted resources. Strong audit committees do a better job of finding and eliminating undesirable practices.[39] Stock prices of companies with highly rated audit committees tend to rise faster than shares of companies with lower-rated internal auditors.

Sustainability Audits and the Triple Bottom Line   Companies that are serious about sustainability conduct audits to evaluate how effectively they are serving all stakeholders and protecting the environment. Sustainability audits typically evaluate performance in terms of a **triple bottom line**—that is, the company's financial performance, environmental impact, and impact on people in the company and the communities where it operates. Adapting a slogan coined by Shell in the 1990s, an easy way to remember the three bottom lines is *profit, planet,* and *people.*[40]

Novo Nordisk, a health care company, has incorporated a triple bottom line approach into its bylaws, mandating that all three goals remain front and center. The firm is dedicated to making innovative insulin products available and affordable, while moving to from a "take-make-dispose" business model to a one that has zero environmental impact.[41]

In practice, reporting a triple bottom line is not standardized and regulated the way financial reporting is. A company might report its profitability in the traditional way, its environmental impact in terms of efficiency of resource use, and its human impact in terms of general policies. Specific practices vary, but a sustainability audit can be a first step toward measuring and reinforcing sustainable business practices.

Budgetary Controls

Budgetary controls tie together feedforward control, concurrent control, and feedback control, depending on the point at which they are applied. Budgetary control is the process of finding out what's being done and comparing the results with the corresponding budget data to verify accomplishments or remedy differences. Budgetary control is commonly called **budgeting**.

Fundamental Budgetary Considerations   In business, budgetary control begins with an estimate of sales and expected income. Exhibit 16.6 shows a budget with a forecast of expected sales (the sales budget) on the top row, followed by several categories of estimated expenses for the first three months of the year. In the bottom row, the profit estimate is determined by subtracting each month's budgeted expenses from the sales in that month's sales budget. Columns next to each month's budget provide space to enter the actual accomplishments so that managers can readily compare expected amounts and actual results.

Although we focus here on the flow of money into and out of the company, budgeting information is not confined to to dollars. The entire enterprise and any of its units can create budgets for their activities, using units other than money as appropriate. For example, many organizations use production budgets forecasting physical units produced and shipped, and labor can be budgeted in skill levels or required work hours.

A primary consideration is the length of the budget period. All budgets are prepared for a specific time period. Many budgets cover one, three, or six months or one year.

The length of time chosen depends on the primary purpose and the normal cycle of activity. For example, seasonal variations should be included for production and for sales. The budget period commonly coincides with other control tools such as managerial reports, balance sheets, and statements of profit and loss. The choice of budget period also should consider how accurately reasonable forecasts can be made.

LO 16-3   Describe the purposes for using budgets as a control device.

budgeting

The process of investigating what is being done and comparing the results with the corresponding budget data to verify accomplishments or remedy differences; also called *budgetary controlling.*

EXHIBIT 16.6   A Sales Expense Budget

	January		February		March	
	Expectancy	Actual	Expectancy	Actual	Expectancy	Actual
Sales	$1,200,000		$1,350,000		$1,400,000	
Expenses						
General overhead	310,000		310,000		310,000	
Selling	242,000		275,000		288,000	
Producing	327,000		430,500		456,800	
Research	118,400		118,400		115,000	
Office	90,000		91,200		91,500	
Advertising	32,500		27,000		25,800	
Estimated gross profit	80,100		97,900		112,900	

Budgetary control proceeds through several stages. Establishing expectancies starts with the broad plan for the company and the estimate of sales, and it ends with budget approval and publication. Next, the budgetary operations stage deals with comparing results with expectancies. The last stage, as in any control process, involves responding appropriately by reinforcing successes and correcting problems.

In a small company, budgeting responsibility generally rests with the owner. In bigger companies, practices vary, with a member of top management often serving as the chief budget coordinator. Usually the chief financial officer (CFO) has these duties. This executive resolves conflicting interests, recommends adjustments when needed, and gives official sanction to the budgetary procedures.

Types of Budgets   Common types of budgets are:

- *Sales budget.* Usually data for the sales budget include forecasts of sales by month, sales area, and product.
- *Production budget.* The production budget commonly is expressed in physical units. Required information for preparing this budget includes types and capacities of machines, quantities to produce, and availability of materials.
- *Cost budget.* The cost budget is used for areas of the organization that incur expenses but no revenue, such as human resources and other support departments. Costs may be fixed, or independent of the immediate level of activity (such as rent), or variable, rising or falling with the level of activity (such as raw materials).
- *Cash budget.* The cash budget is essential to every business. It should be prepared after all other budget estimates are completed. The cash budget shows the anticipated receipts and expenditures, the amount of working capital available, the extent to which outside financing may be required, and time periods and amounts of cash available.
- *Capital budget.* The capital budget is used for the cost of fixed assets such as plants and equipment. Such costs are usually treated not as regular expenses but as investments because of their long-term nature and importance to productivity.
- *Master budget.* The master budget includes all the major activities of the business. It brings together and coordinates all the activities of the other budgets. Think of it as a budget of budgets.

Traditionally, senior management imposed budgets top-down, by setting specific targets for the entire organization at the beginning of the budget process. Now the budget process is likely also to be bottom-up, with top management setting the general direction but with lower-level and middle-level managers developing budget specifics and submitting them for approval. When the budgets are consolidated, senior managers determine whether overall budget objectives are being met. Then they either approve the budget or send it back down the organization for refinements.

accounting audits

Procedures used to verify accounting reports and statements.

Accounting records must be inspected periodically to ensure that they were prepared properly. **Accounting audits**, designed to verify accounting reports and statements, are essential to the control process. This audit is performed by public accounting firms. Knowing that accounting records are accurate, true, and in keeping with generally accepted accounting principles (GAAP) creates confidence that a reliable base exists for sound overall controlling purposes.

activity-based costing (ABC)

A method of cost accounting designed to identify streams of activity and then to allocate costs across particular business processes according to the amount of time employees devote to particular activities.

Activity-Based Costing   Traditional cost accounting methods may be inappropriate today because they are based on outdated methods of rigid hierarchical organizations. Instead of assuming that organizations are bureaucratic machines with separate component functions such as human resources,[42] purchasing, and marketing, companies such as UPS and General Motors use **activity-based costing (ABC)** to allocate costs across business *processes* rather than functions.

ABC starts with the assumption that organizations are collections of people performing many different but related activities to satisfy customer needs. The ABC system identifies those activity streams and then assigns expenses to those areas of activity. In a

Administrative expenses			Laboratory	Radiology	Dr. Kent (240 visits)	Dr. Olson (200 visits)	Dr. Lane (160 visits)
Office salaries							
Direct	1,500				600	500	400
Payroll and personnel	1,000		119	39	337	254	251
Supervision	2,000		238	79	673	508	502
Unutilized*	500	Expenses allocated to services provided					
Advertising	600				200	200	200
Rent	1,000		125	125	250	250	250
Utilities	200		25	25	50	50	50
Office supplies	300				100	100	100
Building insurance	100		12	13	25	25	25
Telephone	600				200	200	200
Depreciation	300				100	100	100
Total	**8,100**		**519**	**281**	**2,535**	**2,187**	**2,078**

*Not allocated.

SOURCE: Based on Schuneman, Pam, "Master the 'ABCs' of Activity-Based Costing," *Managed Care,* May 1997, http://www.managedcaremag.com.

EXHIBIT 16.7
Activity-Based Costing Example: ABC Medical Clinic

manufacturing company, a group of employees might process sales orders, buy parts, and request engineering changes. The expenses for their salaries and fringe benefits are divided among these activities according to the amount of time spent on each.

A similar approach, illustrated in Exhibit 16.7, is to allocate costs of providing support services to the business functions served. In this example, a medical clinic, administrative expenses such as office workers' salaries, rent, and utilities are divided among the doctors' practices and the clinic's laboratory and radiology services. Options for allocating these expenses include the number of employees in each group, the number of patients seen, and the square footage each group occupied.

Traditional and ABC systems reach the same bottom line. However, because the ABC method allocates costs across business processes, it provides a more accurate picture of how costs should be charged to products (goods and services).[43]

This greater accuracy can give managers a more realistic picture of how the organization actually is allocating its resources. It can highlight where wasted activities are occurring or whether activities cost too much relative to the benefits provided. Managers can then take corrective action.

Financial Controls

In addition to budgets, businesses commonly use other statements for financial control. Two financial statements that help control overall organizational performance are the balance sheet and the profit and loss statement.

The Balance Sheet   The **balance sheet** shows the financial picture of a company at a given time. This statement itemizes three elements: (1) assets, (2) liabilities, and (3) stockholders' equity. **Assets** are the values of the various items the corporation owns. **Liabilities** are the amounts the corporation owes to various creditors. **Stockholders' equity** is the amount accruing to the corporation's owners. The relationship among these three elements is as follows:

$$\text{Assets} = \text{Liabilities} + \text{Stockholders' equity}$$

Exhibit 16.8 shows an example of a balance sheet. During the year, the company grew because it enlarged its building and acquired more machinery and equipment by means of long-term debt in the form of a first mortgage. Additional stock was sold to help finance the expansion. At the same time, accounts receivable were increased, and work in process was reduced.

balance sheet

A report that shows the financial picture of a company at a given time and itemizes assets, liabilities, and stockholders' equity.

assets

The values of the various items the corporation owns.

Bottom Line
Activity-based costing can highlight overspending. *When a certain activity is the most costly, how would you decide whether it's a case of overspending?*

LO 16-4   Define basic types of financial statements and financial ratios used as controls.

liabilities

The amounts a corporation owes to various creditors.

stockholders' equity

The amount accruing to the corporation's owners.

EXHIBIT 16.8

A Comparative Balance
Sheet

Comparative Balance Sheet for the Years Ending December 31		
	This Year	Last Year
Assets		
Current assets:		
Cash	$ 161,870	$ 119,200
U.S. Treasury bills	250,400	30,760
Accounts receivable	825,595	458,762
Inventories:		
Work in process and finished products	429,250	770,800
Raw materials and supplies	251,340	231,010
Total current assets	1,918,455	1,610,532
Other assets:		
Land	157,570	155,250
Building	740,135	91,784
Machinery and equipment	172,688	63,673
Furniture and fixtures	132,494	57,110
Total other assets before depreciation	1,202,887	367,817
Less: Accumulated depreciation and amortization	67,975	63,786
Total other assets	1,134,912	304,031
Total assets	$3,053,367	$1,914,563
Liabilities and stockholders' equity		
Current liabilities:		
Accounts payable	$ 287,564	$ 441,685
Payrolls and withholdings from employees	44,055	49,580
Commissions and sundry accruals	83,260	41,362
Federal taxes on income	176,340	50,770
Current installment on long-term debt	85,985	38,624
Total current liabilities	667,204	622,021
Long-term liabilities:		
15-year, 9 percent loan, payable in each of the years 2021–2036	210,000	225,000
5 percent first mortgage	408,600	
Registered 9 percent notes payable		275,000
Total long-term liabilities	618,600	500,000
Stockholders' equity:		
Common stock: authorized 1,000,000 shares, outstanding last year 492,000 shares, outstanding this year 700,000 shares at $1 par value	700,000	492,000
Capital surplus	981,943	248,836
Earned surplus	75,620	51,706
Total stockholders' equity	1,757,563	792,542
Total liabilities and stockholders' equity	$3,053,367	$1,914,563

Observe that Total assets ($3,053,367) = Total liabilities ($677,204 + $618,600) + Stock-holders' equity ($700,000 + $981,943 + $75,620).

Summarizing balance sheet items over time uncovers important trends and gives managers further insight into overall performance and areas in need of adjustments. For example, this company might find it prudent to slow down its expansion plans.

The Profit and Loss Statement   The **profit and loss statement** is an itemized financial statement of the income and expenses of a company's operations. Exhibit 16.9 shows a comparative statement of profit and loss for two consecutive years. In this illustration, the company's operating revenue increased. Expenses also went up but at a lower rate, resulting in a higher net income.

Some managers draw up tentative profit and loss statements and use them as goals. Then performance is measured against these goals or standards. From comparative statements of this type, a manager can identify trouble areas and correct them.

Controlling by profit and loss is commonly used for the entire enterprise and, in the case of a diversified corporation, its divisions. However, if controlling is by departments, as in a decentralized organization in which managers have control over both revenue and expense, each department has a profit and loss statement. Each department's output is measured, and each is charged a cost, including overhead. Expected net income is the standard for assessing departmental performance.

Financial Ratios   An essential approach to monitoring an enterprise's overall performance is to use key financial ratios. Ratios help indicate strengths and weaknesses in a company's operations. Key ratios are calculated from selected items on the profit and loss statement and the balance sheet. We describe three categories of financial ratios: liquidity, leverage, and profitability:

- *Liquidity ratios.* Liquidity ratios indicate a company's ability to pay short-term debts. The most common liquidity ratio is *current assets to current liabilities,* called the **current ratio** or *net working capital ratio.* This ratio indicates the extent to which current assets can decline and still be adequate to pay current liabilities. Referring back to Exhibit 16.8, the liquidity ratio there is about 2.86 ($1,918,455/$667,204). The company's current assets are more than capable of supporting its current liabilities.

profit and loss statement
An itemized financial statement of the income and expenses of a company's operations.

current ratio
A liquidity ratio that indicates the extent to which short-term assets can decline and still be adequate to pay short-term liabilities.

EXHIBIT 16.9
Comparative Statement of Profit and Loss for the Years Ending June 30

	This Year	Last Year	Increase or Decrease
Income:			
Net sales	$253,218	$257,636	$4,418*
Dividends from investments	480	430	50
Other	1,741	1,773	32*
Total	255,439	259,839	4,400*
Deductions:			
Cost of goods sold	180,481	178,866	1,615
Selling and administrative expenses	39,218	34,019	5,199
Interest expense	2,483	2,604	121*
Other	1,941	1,139	802
Total	224,123	216,628	7,495
Income before taxes	31,316	43,211	11,895*
Provision for taxes	3,300	9,500	6,200*
Net income	$ 28,016	$ 33,711	$5,695*

*Decrease

debt–equity ratio

A leverage ratio that indicates the company's ability to meet its long-term financial obligations.

return on investment (ROI)

A ratio of profit to capital used, or a rate of return from capital.

management myopia

Focusing on short-term earnings and profits at the expense of longer-term strategic requirements.

- *Leverage ratios.* Leverage ratios show the funds in the business supplied by creditors and shareholders. An important example is the **debt–equity ratio**, which indicates the company's ability to meet its long-term financial obligations. In Exhibit 16.8, the debt–equity ratio is only 0.35 ($618,600/$1,757,563). The company has financed its expansion almost entirely by issuing stock rather than by incurring long-term debt.
- *Profitability ratios.* Profitability ratios indicate management's ability to generate a financial return on sales or investment. For example, **return on investment (ROI)** is a ratio of profit to capital used, or a rate of return from capital (equity plus long-term debt). This ratio allows managers and shareholders to assess how well the firm is doing compared with other investments. If the net income of the company in Exhibit 16.8 were $300,000 this year, its return on capital would be 12.6 percent [$300,000/ ($1,757,563/$618,600)]—normally a very reasonable rate of return.

Using Financial Ratios   Although financial ratios provide useful performance standards and indicators, relying on them exclusively is unwise. Because ratios usually are based on short time horizons (monthly, quarterly, or yearly), they often cause **management myopia**—focusing on short-term earnings and profits at the expense of longer-term strategic requirements.[44] Control systems using longer-term performance targets (e.g., 3 to 6 years) can reduce management myopia and focus attention farther into the future.

A second negative impact of ratios is that they relegate other important considerations to secondary positions. Research and development, management development, progressive human resource practices, and other activities may receive insufficient attention.

Therefore managers should supplement financial ratios with additional control measures. Controls can hold managers accountable for market share, number of patents granted, sales of new products, human resource development, and other performance indicators.

Problems with Bureaucratic Control

People are not machines that automatically fall into line as the designers of control systems intend. In fact, control systems easily can lead to dysfunctional behavior. A control system

> A new control system won't work well without considering how people will react to it.

cannot be effective without considering how people react to it. Managers should know at least three potential behavioral problems: rigid bureaucratic behavior, tactical behavior, and resistance.[45]

Rigid Bureaucratic Behavior   People want to look good on what the control system measures. This focuses them on what management requires, but can result in rigid, inflexible behavior geared toward doing *only* what the system demands. For example, we noted earlier that six sigma emphasizes efficiency over innovation. After 3M began using six sigma extensively, it fell below its goal of having at least one-third of sales come from new products.

So when George Buckley took the CEO post, he relied less on efficiency controls. Buckley explained, "Invention is by its very nature a disorderly process."[46] The control challenge, of course, is for 3M to be both efficient and creative.

Rigid bureaucratic behavior can help employees stay out of trouble by sticking strictly to the rules. Unfortunately, this can make the entire organization slow to act, leading to poor customer service.

Probably you have been victimized by rigid bureaucratic behavior. Reflect for a moment on this classic story of a nightmare at a hospital:

> At midnight, a patient with eye pains enters an emergency room at a hospital. At the reception area, he is classified as a non-emergency case and referred to the hospital's eye clinic. Trouble is, the eye clinic doesn't open until the next morning. When he arrives at the clinic, the nurse asks for his referral slip, but the emergency room doctor had forgotten to give it to him. The patient has to return to the emergency room and wait for another physician to screen him. The physician refers him back to the eye clinic and to a social worker to arrange payment. Finally, a third doctor looks into his eye, sees a small piece of metal, and removes it—a 30-second procedure.[47]

Management in Action

BALANCING THE PROS AND CONS OF EMPLOYEE TRACKING

As more companies are beginning to track and monitor their employees, employers are beginning to weigh the pros and cons of such monitoring.

Some monitoring of employees offers clear net benefits. For example, biometric data can prevent sleep-deprived workers from undertaking dangerous tasks. Tracking can also confirm or refute long-standing assumptions in a whole host of critical areas. For example, the company Humanyze developed a system that uses sensors to record employees' communications, behavior, and body language. It's part of a fast-growing industry called "people analytics."[48] One study using Humanyze's platform showed that men and women acted almost exactly the same in the workplace, yet women were ultimately not advanced as often to senior positions as men were. The study found that bias, not behavior, accounted for the different outcomes.[49]

Potentially offsetting the knowledge gained by tracking, the practice can also have intended consequences. While fitness tracking devices and other employee monitoring methods can improve health or productivity, they also can raise privacy concerns and make employees feel pressured to participate. Employees may want to opt out of contests or challenges, for instance, to avoid public shaming when struggling to lose weight or quit smoking. People might also feel pressured and experience undue stress by negative reinforcement tools, like higher insurance premiums for those who fall short of health goals. Even intended positive reinforcement, such as financial rewards for meeting challenges, can cause stress.

Ideally, companies inform employees about what they monitor and obtain their individual consent. Companies can monitor social media but cannot force current or former employees to disclose their social media passwords. But monitoring practices face few other constraints. Many worry that tracking and recording devices can be misused and lead to discriminatory practices that exceed normal management controls.[50]

- What other downsides to employee tracking exist? What would you suggest companies do to avoid these issues?
- Do the potential benefits of employee monitoring outweigh the potential negative aspects? Why or why not?

Stories like these have given bureaucracy a bad name. Some managers will not even use the term *bureaucratic control* because of its negative connotations. Problems occur when a system is viewed not as a tool that helps run the business, but one that dictates rigid, inflexible behavior.

Tactical Behavior   People sometimes engage in tactics aimed at beating the system. A common type of tactical behavior is to manipulate information or report false performance data. People can provide two kinds of invalid data: about what *has* been done and about what *can* be done.

False reporting about the past is less common because it is easier to spot the discrepancy and identify the culprit, in contrast to someone giving an erroneous prediction or estimate of what might happen in the future. But people do sometimes intentionally feed false information into management information systems to cover up errors or poor performance or to manipulate the system to get their way.

An employee at a large financial services firm was told by her new manager that as long as he continued to do a great job, he would have nothing to worry about regarding his job security. Nearly a year passed with minimal contact with the manager, so the employee took this as a good sign. About 10 months after the initial meeting, the manager surprised the employee by giving him a very negative performance review, even though the manager never previously complained about the employee's work. The employee transferred out of the department to work for a different manager. Later, the employee learned that the manager lied about his performance so the position could be given to someone else.[51]

More commonly, people falsify their predictions or requests for the future. When asked to give budgetary estimates, they often ask for larger amounts than they need. On the other hand, people sometimes submit unrealistically *low* estimates when they believe that will help them get a budget or a project approved. Budget-setting sessions can become tugs of war between subordinates trying to get slack in the budget and superiors attempting to minimize slack.

Managers use similar tactics when they negotiate low performance goals for themselves so they will have little trouble meeting them; salespeople when they make low sales forecasts so they will look good by exceeding them; and workers when they slow down the work pace while analysts are setting work pace standards. In these sorts of cases, people care about their own performance numbers more than the overall performance of their departments or companies.

Resistance to Control   People often resist control systems, for several reasons. First, control systems make employees more accountable for their actions and performance. Control systems decrease people's autonomy, uncover mistakes, and can feel like threats to job security and status.

Second, control systems can change expertise and power structures. Management information systems can more quickly make the costing, purchasing, and production decisions that managers made previously. As a result, people can lose decision-making authority, power, and expertise.

Third, control systems can change the organization's social structure. They can create competition and disrupt social groups and friendships. People may end up competing against those with whom they formerly had comfortable, cooperative relationships. People often resist control systems that reduce their social need satisfaction.

Additionally, control systems can invade privacy, lead to lawsuits, and cause low morale.

LO 16-5 List procedures for implementing effective control systems.

Designing Effective Control Systems

Effective control systems maximize potential benefits and minimize dysfunctional behaviors. To achieve this, management needs to design control systems that

1. Establish valid performance standards.
2. Provide adequate information to employees.
3. Ensure acceptability to employees.
4. Encourage open communication.
5. Use multiple approaches.

Establish Valid Performance Standards   The most effective standards, as you know, are expressed in quantitative terms; they are objective rather than subjective. Furthermore, the system should incorporate all important aspects of performance because people often neglect unmeasured behaviors. In addition, the best standards are not readily susceptible to sabotage or cheating.

Management also must defend against another problem: too many measures that create overcontrol and employee resistance. To make multiple controls tolerable, managers can emphasize the most important areas. They can prioritize; for example, purchasing agents might rank performance targets this way: quality, availability, cost, and inventory level. Managers also can set tolerance ranges, for example, by specifying optimistic, expected, and minimum levels.

Some companies' budgets set cost targets only. This causes managers to control spending, but to neglect earnings. At Emerson Electric, profit and growth are key measures. If an unanticipated opportunity to increase market share arises, managers can spend what they need to go after it. The phrase "it's not in the budget" is less likely to stifle people at Emerson than it is at most other companies. A company that focused only on sales volume without also looking at profitability might soon go out of business.

This point applies as well to nonfinancial performance dimensions. At many customer service call centers, control aims to maximize efficiency by focusing on the average time each agent spends handling phone calls. But the business objectives of call centers should also include other measures such as cross-selling products, improving customer satisfaction, and encouraging repeat business. Customer service agents at TD Bank are evaluated by their ability to "achieve first-call issue resolution and receive favorable customer feedback—not by how quickly they can get the customer off the phone."[52]

Provide Adequate Information   Management must communicate to employees the importance and nature of the control system. Then people must receive performance feedback. Feedback enables them to correct their own deviations from performance standards.

In general, a manager designing a control system should evaluate the information system with the following questions:

1. Does it provide people with data relevant to the decisions they need to make?
2. Does it provide the right amount of information to decision makers throughout the organization?
3. Does it provide enough information to each part of the organization about how other, related parts of the organization are functioning?[53]

Ensure Acceptability to Employees   People will work well within the system if they accept it. They are more likely to accept systems that have reasonable, achievable performance standards but are not overly controlling. Ideally, the control system will emphasize positive behavior rather than focus solely on controlling negative behavior.

In more than two decades, Johnson & Johnson's Ethicon San Lorenzo facility has never had to recall a product. The company makes sutures, meshes, and other supplies for surgery—an industry in which quality must be perfect and recalls are all too common. To achieve these outstanding results, the company created the Do It Right Framework, which includes training, employee involvement in process improvements, and open communication about company objectives.

Importantly, employees should understand how their work matters. Every employee sees a video about Ethicon's work, highlighted by a cardiovascular surgeon describing how he uses the products and why their quality affects patients' recovery. Doing the job right is something employees genuinely care about.[54]

One of the best ways to establish reasonable standards and gain employee acceptance is to set standards participatively. As you learned in Chapter 4, participation in decision making secures people's understanding and cooperation and results in better decisions. Allowing employees to collaborate in decisions that affect their jobs will help overcome resistance to the system. In addition, employees on the front line are more likely to know which standards are most important and practical, and they can inform their bosses about issues. Moreover, when deviations from standards occur, it's easier to obtain cooperation in problem solving if standards were established collaboratively.

Encourage Open Communication   Employees should feel willing and able to report deviations so that problems can be addressed. You read about upward communication in the previous chapter. If people feel that their bosses want to hear only good news, or fear reprisal for reporting bad news (even if it is not their fault), then controls become less effective. Problems go unreported and over time become more expensive or difficult to solve. But if managers create an environment of openness and honesty, and appreciate it when employees convey problems in a timely fashion, then the control system is far more likely to work to its potential.

Use Multiple Approaches   No single control system will suffice. Multiple controls are necessary. For example, banks need controls on risk so that they don't lose too much money from defaulting borrowers, plus profit controls including sales budgets that aim for growth in accounts and customers.

As you now know, control systems should include both financial and nonfinancial performance targets and incorporate aspects of feedforward, concurrent, and feedback control. Many companies use **strategy maps** to show how they plan to convert their various assets into

strategy map

A depiction of how how an organization plans to convert its various assets into desired outcomes.

EXHIBIT 16.10   A Strategy Map and Balanced Scorecard for Performance Improvement at a Hospital

Strategy Map

Financial	Steady growth	Return on investor capital	Productivity
Customer Satisfaction	Service leadership	Patient satisfaction	Operational excellence
Business Processes	Improve quality and timeliness of services	Continuously improve staff's skills	Improve patient value
Learning & Growth	Promote culture of quality service	Align employee competencies with strategy	Implement technology to support innovation

Balanced Scorecard

Objectives	Measurement	Target
Grow sales revenue Increase profit	Balance sheet Profit and loss statement	10% annually 5% annually
Increase satisfaction Attract repeat patients	Satisfaction surveys Track in database	90% highly satisfied 80% return rate
Increase expertise of staff Reduce error rates	Completion rate of online training modules Number of incorrect dosages	90% passed with score of 85% or higher 2% or lower
Communicate importance of high quality Develop succession plan	Number of emails and mentions during meetings Percentage completed and times updated	One email and mention per week 90% by year-end and one time per month

SOURCES: Adapted from Kaplan, R. S. and Norton, D. P., "Having Trouble with Your Strategy? Then Map It," *Harvard Business Review,* September–October 2000, pp. 167–72; Kaplan, R. S. and Norton, D. P., *The Balanced Scorecard: Translating Strategy into Action.* Boston: Harvard Business School Press, 1996, p. 76.

balanced scorecard

Control system combining four sets of performance measures: financial, customer satisfaction, business processes, and learning and growth.

desired outcomes.[55] Related to these maps is the **balanced scorecard**, which holds managers responsible for a combination of four sets of performance measures (see Exhibit 16.10): (1) financial, (2) customer satisfaction, (3) business processes, and (4) learning and growth.[56] The general goal is to broaden management's horizon beyond short-term financial results in order to sustain long-term success.

Michael Boo, chief strategy officer of the National Marrow Donor Program (NMDP), wanted to develop new ways of reaching the nonprofit's vision of 10,000 bone marrow transplants per year. Such transplants can prolong the lives of individuals with leukemia and other life-threatening diseases. He and colleagues developed a balanced scorecard with four perspectives: stakeholder, financial performance, processes, and people/knowledge/technology. In the first year, the NMDP made headway against its ambitious goal, averaging nearly 500 transplants each month.[57]

Effective control requires using many of the other techniques and practices of good management. To gain employee acceptance, managers also rely on other communication and motivational tools that we discussed in earlier chapters, such as group decision making and positive reinforcement.

The Other Controls: Markets and Clans

Formal bureaucratic control systems are pervasive (and the most talked about in management textbooks), but they alone don't ensure optimal control. Market controls and clan controls offer more flexible, and potent, approaches to regulating performance.

Market Control

Unlike bureaucratic controls, market controls use economic forces—and the pricing mechanisms that accompany them—to regulate performance. The system works like this: When a person or unit produces a good or service that others value, a price for it can be negotiated. As a market for these transactions becomes established, two things happen:

- The price indicates the value of the good or service.
- Price competition controls productivity and performance.

The basic principles underlying market controls operate at the corporate level, the business unit (or department) level, and the individual level. Exhibit 16.11 shows a few ways in which organizations use market controls.

LO 16-6 Identify ways in which organizations use market control mechanisms.

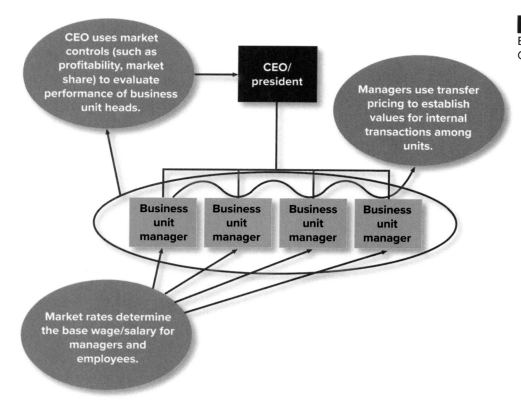

EXHIBIT 16.11
Examples of Market Control

CEO uses market controls (such as profitability, market share) to evaluate performance of business unit heads.

CEO/president

Managers use transfer pricing to establish values for internal transactions among units.

Business unit manager

Business unit manager

Business unit manager

Business unit manager

Market rates determine the base wage/salary for managers and employees.

Bottom Line

Market controls help maintain low prices. *You manage the tech support unit for your company. How might market controls affect your costs?*

transfer price

Price charged by one unit for a good or service provided to another unit within the organization.

Market Controls at the Corporate Level   Large, diversified companies use market controls to regulate independent business units. Conglomerates that act as holding companies treat business units as profit centers that compete with one another. Top executives use profit and loss data to evaluate unit performance. They delegate (decentralize) power and decision making to the business units, and market controls help ensure that unit managers' performance is in line with corporate objectives.

Market Controls at the Business Unit Level   Market control is used within business units to regulate exchanges among departments and functions. Transfer pricing is a method that organizations use to try to create market forces for internal transactions. A **transfer price** is the charge by one unit for a good or service that it supplies to another unit of the same organization. For example, in automobile manufacturing, a transfer price is affixed to components and subassemblies before they are shipped to subsequent business units for final assembly. Ideally, the transfer price reflects the price that the receiving business unit would have to pay for that product or service in the external marketplace.

As organizations have options to outsource and get goods and services from external partners, market controls such as transfer prices provide incentives to keep costs down and quality up. Managers stay in close touch with prices in the marketplace to make sure their own costs are in line, and they try to improve the service they provide to increase their department's value to the organization.

Consider a common example in which training and development can be done internally by the human resources department or outsourced to a consulting firm. If the human resources department cannot supply quality training at a reasonable price, the department's internal value drops—and managers generally don't want that to happen. To state this more positively: A manager or unit can add value—and benefit accordingly—by competing with outside suppliers and delivering a better product internally at lower cost.

Market Controls at the Individual Level   Market controls are used also at the individual level. For example, when organizations hire employees, the supply and demand for particular skills influence the wages employees can expect to receive. Employers pay higher wages to people with skills most valued by labor markets. Wages don't perfectly reflect external market rates—internal considerations pertain as well—but the market rate is often the best indicator of an employee's potential worth to a firm.

It would seem that market controls play an important role in professional athletes' salaries. But do the absurdly high salaries that some players make truly indicate a player's skill—or something else? If the player doesn't live up to expectations, or has a bad year, should the team cut his pay?

Alexey Stiop/Shutterstock

External market forces apply at executive levels as well. Board members use market controls to manage CEOs. Ironically, CEOs usually are seen as the ones controlling everyone else in the company; but the CEO is accountable to the board of directors, and the board must devise ways to ensure that the CEO acts in its interest.

You read about CEO compensation in Chapter 10. While compensation committees and boards decide the details, what other companies are doing for their CEOs is a major determinant. Compensation fads come and go, trends rise and fall, and top executive behaviors change in accord with these control systems. Examples include stock-based features that motivate longer or shorter time horizons and decisions and the use (or not) of the balanced scorecard.

Clan Control: Roles for Empowerment and Culture

Managers are discovering that control systems based solely on bureaucratic and market mechanisms are insufficient for directing and fully engaging today's workforce. There are several reasons for this:

LO 16-7 Discuss the use of clan control in an empowered organization.

- *Employees' jobs have changed.* The nature of work is changing. More work is knowledge-based and difficult to monitor. There is no one best way to work, and standardizing jobs is difficult. Close supervision is unrealistic in part because it is nearly impossible to supervise activities such as thinking and creative problem solving.
- *Management has changed.* Supervisors used to know more about jobs than employees did. Today many employees know more about their jobs than anyone else does. This is the shift from touch labor to knowledge work. When real expertise in organizations exists at the very lowest levels, hierarchical control is less practical.[58]
- *The employment relationship has changed.* The social contract at work is being renegotiated. It used to be that employees were most concerned about pay, job security, and work hours. Now more employees want to be more fully engaged in their work, taking part in decision making, devising solutions to unique problems, and doing challenging assignments. They want to use their brains.

For these reasons, empowerment (Chapter 13) and appropriate democratic approaches[59] can be vital elements of a manager's control repertoire. With no one best way to approach a job and no way to scrutinize knowledge activities all day, managers empower employees to make decisions and trust that they will act in the best interests of the firm. But this does not mean giving up control. It means creating a strong culture of high standards and integrity so that employees will exercise effective control on their own.

Recall our discussion of organization culture in Chapter 2. A culture that encourages the wrong behaviors will severely hinder efforts to impose controls. But if managers create a strong culture that encourages constructive behaviors, one in which everyone understands and accepts management's values and expectations, then clan control can be highly effective.[60] Employees then are working within a guiding framework of values and use their best judgment.

As an example, Starbucks relies partly on clan control to shape and guide employee behavior.[61] It emphasizes satisfying customers more than pleasing the bosses. Good-faith work that results in a mistake is tolerated as the unavoidable by-product of dealing with uncertainty and is viewed as an opportunity to learn. And team members learn together.

Clan control can be a double-edged sword. It takes a long time to develop and even longer to change. This provides stability and direction during periods of upheaval. Yet if managers want to establish a new culture—a better version of clan control—they must help employees unlearn the old values and behaviors and embrace the new. We will talk more about this change process in the final chapter of this book.

Bottom Line

Clan control can ensure that employees meet performance standards. *What examples have you seen?*

Management in Action

FUTURE TRENDS IN EMPLOYEE MONITORING

Employers have a growing range of options for tracking, recording, and crunching employee data. For instance, office spaces are now equipped with networks of sensors, installed in computers or lighting or heating fixtures, that can detect people's motions and energy use in real time. Other systems can tell when a keyboard has been inactive for 15 minutes or when an employee visits a non-work-related website. The restaurant industry mines vast quantities of data about average serving time and tables turned per hour, among other things. Managers can counsel and train participating wait staff, increasing both tips and profits.[62]

Some companies collect health or productivity statistics and identify, for instance, who should be advised about the risk of diabetes or who might value a recommendation for an obstetrician. Credit scores, Internet search data, and even the stores where employees shop can identify healthy employees who keep doctors' appointments and ride bikes to work, as well as those who buy video games

and could use counseling about weight loss. "All sorts of monitoring takes place for all sorts of reasons," says Lewis Maltby, president of the National Workrights Institute. "Virtually every company conducts electronic monitoring."[63]

A recent survey of 1,000 workers found 54 percent of workers who were tracked felt positively about the experience.[64] Perhaps they valued their employers' ability to locate them in an emergency and were less concerned that their privacy could be invaded or the monitoring system hacked. As one younger worker said regarding the monitoring of his personal data, "It's part of the generation. We're used to it."[65]

- How do you feel about the prospect of employees being able to monitor some of your activities outside of the workplace? What are some risks and rewards?
- Are young people so accustomed to having their personal data used in various ways that extensive workplace tracking is likely not to be an issue in the future? Explain your answer.

KEY TERMS

accounting audits, p. 504

activity-based costing (ABC), p. 504

after-action review, p. 499

assets, p. 505

balance sheet, p. 505

balanced scorecard, p. 512

budgeting, p. 503

bureaucratic control, p. 494

clan control, p. 494

concurrent control, p. 499

control, p. 494

current ratio, p. 507

debt–equity ratio, p. 508

external audit, p. 502

feedback control, p. 499

feedforward control, p. 499

internal audit, p. 502

liabilities, p. 505

management audit, p. 502

management myopia, p. 508

market control, p. 494

principle of exception, p. 498

profit and loss statement, p. 507

return on investment (ROI), p. 508

standard, p. 496

stockholders' equity, p. 505

strategy map, p. 511

transfer price, p. 514

triple bottom line, p. 502

RETAINING WHAT YOU LEARNED

In Chapter 16, you learned that companies develop control systems in order to keep employees focused on achieving organizational goals. The basic bureaucratic control system includes setting performance standards, measuring performance, comparing performance to standards, and eliminating unfavorable deviations. Performance standards should cover issues such as quantity, quality, time, and cost. Budgets are a control mechanism that act as an initial guide for allocating resources and using funds. Many companies are changing how they prepare budgets, with activity-based costing, to eliminate waste and improve business processes. Balance sheets compare the value of company assets to the obligations the company owes to owners and creditors. Profit and loss statements show company income relative to costs incurred. Financial ratios provide goals for managers as well as standards against which to evaluate performance. Managers use a variety of procedures to maximize the effectiveness of control systems. Market controls can be used at the level of the corporation, the business unit or department, and the individual. To be responsive to customers, companies are increasingly using clan control to harness the expertise of employees and give them the freedom to act on their own initiative.

LO 16-1   Explain why companies develop control systems.

- Left to their own devices, employees may act in ways that do not benefit the organization.
- Control systems are designed to eliminate idiosyncratic behavior and keep employees directed toward achieving the goals of the firm.
- Control systems are a steering mechanism for guiding resources and for guiding each individual to act on behalf of the organization.

LO 16-2   Summarize how to design a basic bureaucratic control system.

- The design of a basic control system involves four steps: (1) setting performance standards, (2) measuring performance, (3) comparing performance with the standards, and (4) eliminating unfavorable deviations by taking corrective action.
- Performance standards should be valid and should cover issues such as quantity, quality, time, and cost.
- Once performance is compared with standards, the principle of exception suggests that the manager needs to attend to and take action on the exceptional cases of significant deviations. Then the manager should take the action most likely to solve the problem.

LO 16-3   Describe the purposes for using budgets as a control device.

- Budgets combine the benefits of feedforward, concurrent, and feedback controls. They serve as an initial guide for allocating resources, a reference point for using funds, and a feedback mechanism for comparing actual levels of sales and expenses with their expected levels.
- Recently companies have modified their budgeting processes to allocate costs over basic processes (such as customer service) rather than to functions or departments.
- By changing the way they prepare budgets, many companies have discovered ways to eliminate waste and improve business processes.

LO 16-4   Define basic types of financial statements and financial ratios used as controls.

- The basic financial statements are the balance sheet and the profit and loss statement.
- The balance sheet compares the value of company assets to the obligations the company owes to owners and creditors.
- The profit and loss statement shows company income relative to costs incurred. In addition to these statements, companies look at liquidity ratios (whether the company can pay its short-term debts), leverage ratios (the extent to which the company is funding operations by going into debt), and profitability ratios (profit relative to investment). These ratios provide goals for managers as well as standards against which to evaluate performance.

LO 16-5   List procedures for implementing effective control systems.

- To maximize the effectiveness of controls, managers should (1) establish valid performance standards, (2) provide adequate information to employees, (3) ensure acceptability, (4) maintain open communication, and (5) use multiple approaches (such as bureaucratic, market, and clan control).

LO 16-6   Identify ways in which organizations use market control mechanisms.

- Market controls are useful at the level of the corporation, the business unit or department, or the individual.
- At the corporate level, business units are evaluated against one another based on profitability. At times, less profitable businesses are sold while more profitable businesses receive more resources.
- Within business units, transfer pricing can be used to approximate market mechanisms to control transactions among departments.
- At the individual level, market mechanisms control the wage rate of employees, including top executives.

LO 16-7   Discuss the use of clan control in an empowered organization.

- Approaching control from a centralized, mechanistic viewpoint is increasingly impractical. In today's organizations, it is difficult to program one best way to approach work, and it is often difficult to monitor performance.
- To be responsive to customers, companies can use clan control to harness the expertise of employees and give them the freedom to act on their own initiative.

DISCUSSION QUESTIONS

1. What controls can you identify in the management of your school or at a company where you have worked? How might the organization's performance change if those controls were not in place?

2. How are leadership and control different? How are planning and control different?

3. Imagine you are the sales manager of a company that sells medical supplies to hospitals nationwide.

You have 10 salespeople reporting to you and you're responsible for achieving a certain level of sales each year. How might you go about taking each step in the control cycle?

4. In the situation described in Question 3, what actions would you need to take if sales fell far below the budgeted level? What, if any, actions would you need to take if sales far exceeded the sales budget? If sales are right on target, does effective controlling require any response from you?

5. Besides sales and expenses, identify five other important control measures for a business. Include at least one nonfinancial measure.

6. What are the pros and cons of bureaucratic controls such as rules, procedures, and close supervision?

7. Suppose a company at which executives were rewarded for meeting targets based only on profits and stock price switches to a balanced scorecard that adds measures for customer satisfaction, employee engagement, employee diversity, and ethical conduct. How would you expect executives' behaviors to change in response to the new control system?

How would you expect the company's performance to change?

8. Google uses Google Apps, such as Gmail, Google Calendar, and Docs & Spreadsheets, as collaboration tools for employees. Describe how the company could use controls to determine whether Google employees will use these software programs or competing software (e.g., Word and Excel).

9. How effective is clan control as a control mechanism? What are its strengths and limitations? When should a manager rely primarily on clan control?

10. Does empowerment imply that management loses control? Why or why not?

11. Some people use the concept of personal control to describe the application of business control principles to individual careers. Thinking about your school performance and career plans, which steps of the control process (Exhibit 16.3) have you been applying effectively? How do you keep track of your performance in meeting your career and life goals? How do you measure your success? Does clan control help you meet your personal and professional goals?

EXPERIENTIAL EXERCISES

16.1   SAFETY PROGRAM

OBJECTIVE

To understand some of the specific activities that fall under the management functions of planning, organizing, controlling and staffing, and directing.

INSTRUCTIONS

Read the following case and then evaluate the likely success of this managerial control effort. Specifically, how well did the manager review the source of the problems? How well designed is the new control system? How effectively is the manager building employee commitment to using the control mechanisms? How could this manager improve the control process? Summarize your findings and recommendations in a paragraph or two.

MANAGING THE VAMP CO. SAFETY PROGRAM

If there are specific things that a manager does, how are they done? What does it look like when one manages? The following describes a typical situation in which a manager performs managerial functions:

As production manager of the Vamp Stamping Company, you've become quite concerned over the metal stamping shop's safety record. Accidents that resulted in operators' missing time on the job have increased quite rapidly in the past year. These more serious accidents have jumped from 3 percent of all accidents reported to a current level of 10 percent.

Because you're concerned about your workers' safety as well as the company's ability to meet its customers'

orders, you want to reduce this downtime accident rate to its previous level or lower within the next 6 months.

You call the accident trend to the attention of your production supervisors, pointing out the seriousness of the situation and their continuing responsibility to enforce the gloves and safety goggles rules. Effective immediately, every supervisor will review his or her accident reports for the past year, file a report summarizing these accidents with you, and state their intended actions to correct recurring causes of the accidents. They will make out weekly safety reports as well as meet with you every Friday to discuss what is being done and any problems they are running into.

You request the union steward's cooperation in helping the safety supervisor set up a short program on shop safety practices.

Because the machine operators are having the accidents, you encourage your supervisors to talk to their workers and find out what they think can be done to reduce the downtime accident rate to its previous level.

While the program is going on, you review the weekly reports, looking for patterns that will tell you how effective the program is and where the trouble spots are. If a supervisor's operators are not decreasing their accident rate, you discuss the matter in considerable detail with the supervisor and his or her key workers.

SOURCE: Herbert, Theodore T., *The New Management: Study Guide,* 4th ed. Upper Saddle River, NJ: Prentice Hall, 1987, p. 41.

16.2   Feedforward, Concurrent, and Feedback Control

OBJECTIVES

1. To demonstrate the need for control procedures.
2. To gain experience in determining when to use feedforward, concurrent, and feedback controls.

INSTRUCTIONS

1. Read the text materials on feedforward, concurrent, and feedback control.
2. Read the Control Problem Situation and be prepared to resolve those control problems in a group setting.
3. Your instructor will divide the class into small groups. Each group completes the Feedforward, Concurrent, and Feedback Control Worksheet by achieving consensus on the types of control that should be applied in each situation. The group also develops responses to the discussion questions.
4. After the class reconvenes, group spokespersons present group findings.

DISCUSSION QUESTIONS

1. For which control(s) was it easier to determine application? For which was it harder?
2. Would this exercise be better assigned to groups or to individuals?

CONTROL PROBLEM SITUATION

Your management consulting team has just been hired by Technocron International, a rapidly growing producer of electronic surveillance devices that are sold to commercial and government end users. Some sales are made through direct selling, and some through industrial resellers. Direct-sale profits are being hurt by what seem to be exorbitant expenses paid to a few of the salespeople, especially those who fly all over the world in patterns that suggest little planning and control.

There is trouble among the resellers because standard contracts have not been established, and each reseller has an entirely different contractual relationship. Repayment schedules vary widely from customer to customer. Also, profits are reduced by the need to customize most orders, making mass production almost impossible. However, no effort has been made to create interchangeable components. There are also tremendous inventory problems. Some raw materials and parts are bought in such small quantities that new orders are being placed almost daily. Other orders are so large that there is hardly room to store everything. Many of these purchased components are later found to be defective and unusable, causing production delays. Engineering changes are made that make large numbers of old components still in storage obsolete. Some delays result from designs that are very difficult to assemble, and assemblers complain that their corrective suggestions are ignored by engineering.

To save money, untrained workers are hired and assigned to experienced worker-buddies who are expected to train them on the job. However, many of the new people are too poorly educated to understand their assignments, and their worker-buddies wind up doing a great deal of their work. This, along with the low pay and lack of consideration from engineering, is causing a great deal of worker unrest and talk of forming a union. Last week alone nine new worker grievances were filed, and the U.S. Equal Employment Opportunity Commission has just announced intentions to investigate two charges of discrimination on the part of the company. There is also a serious cash flow problem because a number of long-term debts are coming due at the same time. The cash flow problem could be relieved somewhat if some of the accounts payable could be collected.

The CEO manages corporate matters through five functional divisions: operations, engineering, marketing, finance, and human resources management and general administration.

Feedforward, Concurrent, and Feedback Control Worksheet

Technocron International is in need of a variety of controls. Complete the following matrix by noting the feedforward, concurrent, and feedback controls that are needed in each of the five functional divisions.

Divisions	Feedforward Controls	Concurrent Controls	Feedback Controls
HRM and general administration	_____	_____	_____
Operations	_____	_____	_____
Engineering	_____	_____	_____
Marketing	_____	_____	_____
Finance	_____	_____	_____

Concluding Case

GROWING GRIZZLY BEAR LODGE

Diane and Rudy Conrad own a small lodge outside Yellowstone National Park. Their lodge has 15 rooms and can accommodate up to 50 guests. Their busy season runs from May through September, but they remain open until Thanksgiving and reopen in April. Currently their annual revenue is $320,000. With expenses running at $230,000—including mortgage, payroll, utilities, maintenance, and so forth—the Conrads' annual income is $90,000.

Diane and Rudy include in the room rate a continental breakfast on weekdays and a full breakfast on weekends. They currently employ one cook and two wait staff for the breakfasts on weekends, handling the other breakfasts themselves. They also have several housekeeping staff members, a groundskeeper, and a front-desk employee. The Conrads take pride in the efficiency of their operation, including the loyalty of their employees, which they attribute to their own form of clan control. If a guest needs something—whether it's a breakfast catered to a special diet or an extra set of towels—Grizzly Bear workers are empowered to provide it. This proactive approach is especially helpful given that many of their guests are families with children.

The Conrads recently decided to expand their business. They bought the property next door, giving them space to build an additional 20 rooms. They want to expand without cutting back on their signature personalized service. In addition to hiring more staff to handle the larger facility, they are collaborating with local businesses to offer guided rafting, fishing, hiking, and horseback riding trips. They are also expanding their food service to include dinner during the busy season, which means renovating the restaurant area of the lodge and hiring more staff.

Ultimately, the Conrads would like the lodge to be open year-round, offering guests opportunities to cross-country ski, snowmobile, and hike. They also plan to offer holiday packages. The Conrads report that staff members are enthusiastic about their plans and want to stay with them through the expansion. "This is our dream business," says Diane. "We're only at the beginning."

QUESTIONS

1. How can the Conrads use feedforward, concurrent, and feedback controls now and in the future to ensure their guests' satisfaction?
2. What budgetary considerations would the Conrads have as they plan their expansion?
3. How could the Conrads use market controls to plan and implement their expansion?

ENDNOTES

1. Ian Kudel, Joanna C. Huang, and Rahul Ganguly, "Impact of Obesity on Work Productivity in Different US Occupations," *Journal of Occupational and Environmental Medicine,* January 2018, https://www.ncbi.nlm.nih.gov/pmc/articles/PMC5770108/.
2. Stefanie Valentic, "More Employers Offer Health and Wellness Programs," *EHS Today,* January 12, 2018, https://www.ehstoday.com/health/more-employers-offer-health-and-wellness-programs-infographic.
3. Christina Farr, "How Fitbit Became the Next Big Thing in Corporate Wellness," *Fast Company,* April 18, 2016, https://www.fastcompany.com/3058462/how-fitbit-became-the-next-big-thing-in-corporate-wellness.
4. "What Matters to Employees in Wellness Programs?" *Wellsource,* July 23, 2018.
5. Company website, "Continuous Improvement," Teco Energy, tecoenergy.com, accessed April 30, 2017.
6. Company website, "Continuous Improvement," Teco Energy, www.tacoenergy.com, accessed April 30, 2017.
7. C. Zakrzewski, "The Key to Getting Workers to Stop Wasting Time Online," *The Wall Street Journal,* March 13, 2016, www.wsj.com.
8. W. G. Ouchi, "Markets, Bureaucracies, and Clans," *Administrative Science Quarterly* 25 (1980), pp. 129–41; R. Simons, A. Davila, and R. S. Kaplan, *Performance Measurement & Control Systems for Implementing Strategy* (Englewood Cliffs, NJ: Prentice Hall, 2000).
9. E. D. Pulakos, S. Arad, M. A. Donovan, and K. E. Plamondon, "Adaptability in the Workplace: Development of a Taxonomy of Adaptive Performance," *Journal of Applied Psychology* 85, no. 4 (August 2000), pp. 12–24; K. A. Merchant and T. Sandino, "Four Options for Measuring Value Creation: Strategies for Managers to Avoid Potential Flaws in Accounting Measures of Performance," *Journal of Accountancy* 208, no. 2 (2009), pp. 34–38.
10. Grameen Bank, "Magazine Archives," http://www.grameen.com/magazine-archives/, accessed April 16, 2019.
11. TOMS, "Giving Shoes," http://www.toms.com/what-we-give-shoes, accessed April 16, 2019.
12. Root Capital, "Our Impact," https://rootcapital.org/our-impact/, accessed April 16, 2019.
13. Kate Ruff and Sara Olsen, "The Next Frontier in Social Impact Measurement Isn't Measurement At All," *Stanford Social Innovation Review,* May 10, 2016, https://ssir.org/articles/entry/the_next_frontier_in_social_impact_measurement_isnt_measurement_at_all.
14. G. Anadiotis, "Business Analytics: The Essentials of Data-Driven Decision-Making," *ZDNet,* June 11, 2018, www.zdnet.com.
15. Lisa Bodell, "It's Time to Put Performance Reviews on Notice," *Forbes,* April 27, 2018, https://www.forbes.com/sites/lisabodell/2018/04/27/why-performance-reviews-are-irrelevant-today/#2dfffbc84b63; *Impraise Blog,* "How GE Renews Performance Management: From Stack Ranking to Continuous Feedback," https://blog.impraise.com/360-feedback/how-ge-renews-performance-management-from-stack-ranking-to-continuous-feedback-360-feedback, accessed April 11, 2019.
16. B. Miller, "Banish 'Annual' from Your Performance Review Vocabulary," *Entrepreneur*, October 10, 2014, http://www.entrepreneur.com; Deloitte, "Performance Management Is Broken," *Global Human Capital Trends 2014: Engaging the 21st Century Workforce,* http://www2.deloitte.com.

17. Adobe, "How Abode Retired Performance Reviews and Inspired Great Performance," https://www.adobe.com/check-in.html#m36c0cc 8c2935ed72c577471a2ab09fcc, accessed April 11, 2019.

18. Lisa Barry, Stacia Garr, and Andrew Liakopoulos, "Performance Management Is Broken: Replace 'Rank and Yank' with Coaching and Development," March 4, 2014, http://dupress.com/articles/ hc-trends-2014-performance-management/.

19. J. Rockoff and P. Loftus, "Pfizer Plant's Troubles Curb EpiPen Supply," *The Wall Street Journal,* May 10, 2018, www.wsj.com.

20. D. Klein, "Chipotle Goes Mobile with New Food-Safety Platform," *QSR,* September 2018, www.qsrmagazing.com.

21. S. Czarnecki, "Timeline of a Crisis: When Chipotle's New Crisis Met Its Old One," *PRWeek,* January 17, 2017, www.prweek.com.

22. J. Arnold, "Creating an Optimal Employee Experience," Society for Human Resource Management, May 21, 2018, www.shrm.org.

23. Todd Henshaw, "Nano Tools for Leaders: After Action Reviews," *Wharton@Work,* April 2012, http://executiveeducation.wharton. upenn.edu; John Kello, "Upon Further Review: Benefits of Brief Post-Shift Huddles," *Industrial Safety & Hygiene News,* August 2012, p. 30; Stephen C. Harper, "Survival of the Swiftest," *Industrial Management,* January 2012, pp. 16–20.

24. J. Boss, "Don't Skimp on the After Action Review: 6 Ways an AAR Will Catapult Your Situational Awareness," *Forbes,* December 1, 2016, www.forbes.com.

25. "Dress & Appearance: Tattoos/Piercings: May Employers Have Dress Code Requirements That Prohibit All Visible Tattoos and Piercings?" Society for Human Resource Management, May 25, 2015, www.shrm.org; B. Miller, K. Nicols, and J. Eure, "Body Art in the Workplace: Piercing the Prejudice?" *Personnel Review* 38, no. 6 (2009), pp. 621–40.

26. M. Gwin, "Love Contracts: What Restaurant Owners Should Know about Consensual Relationships between Employees," *Modern Restaurant Management,* August 2, 2018, www.modern restaurantmanagement.com; M. Berman-Gorvine, "Let Love Bloom at Work, but Very Carefully," *Bloomberg BNA,* January 30, 2017, www.bna.com; "Office Romances and 'Love Contract?'" *National Law Review,* February 2, 2016, www.natlawreview.com.

27. Gary S. Kaplan, "Pursuing the Perfect Patient Experience," *Frontiers of Health Services Management,* Spring 2013, pp. 16–27. For an additional example in another type of organization, see David T. Goomas, Stuart M. Smith, and Timothy D. Ludwig, "Business Activity Monitoring: Real-Time Group Goals and Feedback Using an Overhead Scoreboard in a Distribution Center," *Journal of Organizational Behavior Management* 31 no. 3 (2011), pp. 196–209.

28. M. Kownatzki, J. Walter, S. Floyd, and C. Lechner, "Corporate Control and the Speed of Strategic Business Unit Decision Making," *Academy of Management Journal* 56 (2013), pp. 1295–1324; V. U. Druskat, "Effects and Timing of Developmental Peer Appraisals in Self-Managing Work Groups," *Journal of Applied Psychology* 84, no. 1 (February 1999), p. 58; Baard Kuvaas, "The Interactive Role of Performance Appraisal Reactions and Regular Feedback," *Journal of Managerial Psychology* 26 no. 2 (2011), pp. 123–37.

29. Janice Gassam, "The 10 Most Diverse Companies of 2018," *Forbes,* October 11, 2018, https://www.forbes.com/sites/janicegassam/ 2018/10/11/the-10-most-diverse-companies-of-2018/#55a381911404.

30. David Gelles, "Julie Sweet of Accenture Could See Her Future," *The New York Times,* January 2, 2019, https://www.nytimes.com/ 2019/01/02/business/julie-sweet-accenture-corner-office.html.

31. Kayla Kozan, "Diversity and Inclusion: A Beginner's Guide for HR Professionals," *Ideal,* February 24, 2019, https://ideal.com/ diversity-and-inclusion/.

32. Juliet Bourke, Stacia Garr, Ardie van Berkel, and Jungle Wong, "Diversity and Inclusion: The Reality Gap," *Deloitte Insights,* February 28, 2017, https://www2.deloitte.com/insights/us/en/focus/human-capital-trends/2017/diversity-and-inclusion-at-the-workplace.html.

33. Rachel Willcox, "The Benefits of Monitoring Diversity," *Economia,* February 8, 2017, https://economia.icaew.com/features/february-2017/ the-benefits-of-monitoring-diversity.

34. S. Waddock and N. Smith, "Corporate Responsibility Audits: Doing Well by Doing Good," *Sloan Management Review* 41, no. 2 (Winter 2000), pp. 75–83; L. L. Bergeson, "OSHA Gives Incentives for Voluntary Self-Audits," *Pollution Engineering* 32, no. 10 (October 2000), pp. 33–34; Scott M. Shafer and Sara B. Moeller, "The Effects of Six

Sigma on Corporate Performance: An Empirical Investigation," *Journal of Operations Management* 30, no. 7–8 (November 1, 2012), pp. 521–32.

35. S. Aghili, "A Six Sigma Approach to Internal Audits," *Strategic Finance,* February 2009, Business & Company Resource Center, http://galenet.galegroup.com.

36. See, for example, "Ways to Avoid a Six Sigma Project Failure," Villanova University, January 19, 2016, www.villanovau.com;Ryan Huang, "Six Sigma 'Killed' Innovation in 3M," *ZDNet,* March 14, 2013, http://www.zdnet.com.

37. "Unlocking the Strategic Value of Internal Audit," Ernst & Young/*Forbes Insight,* 2010, http://www.forbes.com; T. Rancour and M. McCracken, "Applying 6 Sigma Methods for Breakthrough Safety Performance," *Professional Safety* 45, no. 10 (October 2000), pp. 29–32; G. Eckes, "Making Six Sigma Last," *Ivey Business Journal,* January–February 2002, p. 77.

38. Company website, "Establishment of Internal Audit Function," KPMG, www.kpmg.com, accessed April 6, 2019; J. Pett and D. Poritz, "A More Effective Approach for Internal Audit," *Journal of Accountancy,* March 1, 2018, www.journalofaccountancy.com.

39. M. Alic and B. Rusjan, "Contribution of the ISO 9001 Internal Audit to Business Performance," *International Journal of Quality and Reliability Management* 27 (2010), pp. 916–37.

40. L. A. Henry, T. Buyl, and R. J. G. Jansen, "Leading Corporate Sustainability: The Role of Top Management Team Composition for Triple Bottom Line Performance," *Business Strategy and the Environment* 28 (2019), pp. 173–84; Jan Tullberg, "Triple Bottom Line—a Vaulting Ambition?" *Business Ethics: A European Review* 21 no. 3 (June 2012), pp. 310–24; Grant Davis, "The Triple Bottom Line Goal of Sustainable Businesses," *Entrepreneur,* April 24, 2013, http://www.entrepreneur.com; Rebecca Coons, "Corporate Social Responsibility: Pursuing the Triple Bottom Line," *IHS Chemical Week,* May 27–June 3, 2013, pp. 21–23.

41. Company website, "Sustainable Business: Stepping Up on Healthcare and Sustainability," Novo Nordisk, accessed April 6, 2019.

42. D. C. Nowak and C. Linder, "Do You Know How Much Your Expatriate Costs? An Activity-Based Cost Analysis of Expatriation," *Journal of Global Mobility* 4 (2016), pp. 88–107.

43. Pam Schuneman, "Master the 'ABCs' of Activity-Based Costing," *Managed Care,* May 1997, http://www.managedcaremag.com; Ivana Drazic Lutilsky and Martina Dragija, "Activity Based Costing as a Means to Full Costing: Possibilities and Constraints for European Universities," *Management* 17 no. 1 (June 2012), pp. 33–57.

44. J. Farre-Mensa, "Managerial Myopia: Why Public Companies Underinvest in the Future," *Forbes,* February 3, 2013, http://www. forbes.com; K. Merchant, *Control in Business Organizations* (Boston: Pitman, 1985); C. W. Chow, Y. Kato, and K. A. Merchant, "The Use of Organizational Controls and Their Effects on Data Manipulation and Management Myopia," *Accounting, Organizations, and Society* 21, nos. 2/3 (February–April 1996), pp. 175–92.

45. E. E. Lawler III and J. Rhode, *Information and Control in Organizations* (Pacific Palisades, CA: Goodyear, 1976); A. Ferner, "The Underpinnings of 'Bureaucratic' Control Systems: HRM in European Multinationals," *Journal of Management Studies* 37, no. 4 (June 2000), pp. 521–39; M. S. Fenwick, "Cultural and Bureaucratic Control in MNEs: The Role of Expatriate Performance Management," *Management International Review* 39 (1999), pp. 107–25.

46. Hindo, "At 3M, a Struggle between Efficiency and Creativity, https://www.bloomberg.com/news/articles/2007-06-10/at-3m-a-struggle-between-efficiency-and-creativity." See also Jason J. Dahling, Samantha L. Chau, and Alison O'Malley, "Correlates and Consequences of Feedback Orientation in Organizations," *Journal of Management* 38 no. 2 (2012), pp. 531–46.

47. J. Veiga and J. Yanouzas, *The Dynamics of Organization Theory,* 2nd ed. (St. Paul, MN: West, 1984).

48. JPW, "Humanyze-ing the Workplace: Gathering and Analyzing Unique Data on Employee Interaction to Improve Productivity," *Harvard Business School Digital Initiative,* April 4, 2018, https://digit.hbs.org/ submission/humanyze-ing-the-workplace-gathering-and-analyzing-unique-data-on-employee-interaction-to-improve-productivity/.

49. Stephen Turban, Laura Freeman, and Ben Waber, "A Study Used Sensors to Show That Men and Women Are Treated Differently at Work," *Harvard Business Review,* October 26, 2017, https://hbr.org/ 2017/10/a-study-used-sensors-to-show-that-men-and-women-are-treated-differently-at-work.

50. Mark Feffer, "Should You Track the Social Media of Fired Employees?" Society for Human Resource Management, SHRM.org, January 30, 2017, https://www.shrm.org/resourcesandtools/hr-topics/employee-relations/pages/social-media-tracking.aspx.

51. L. Ryan, "I Got Ambushed at My Performance Review—And I Just Found Out Why," *Forbes,* May 21, 2018, www.forbes.com.

52. D. Vater, Y. Cho, and P. Sidebottom, "The Digital Challenge to Retail Banks," Bain & Company, 2012, http://www.bain.com.

53. E. E. Lawler III and J. Rhode, *Information and Control in Organizations* (Pacific Palisades, CA: Goodyear, 1976); J. A. Gowan Jr. and R. G. Mathieu, "Critical Factors in Information System Development for a Flexible Manufacturing System," *Computers in Industry* 28, no. 3 (June 1996), pp. 173–83.

54. Company website, "Our Promise," Ethicon, www.ethicon.com, accessed April 6, 2019; Adrienne Selko, "Ethicon: Employee Engagement Results in Zero Product Recalls," *IndustryWeek,* January 17, 2013, http://www.industryweek.com.

55. S. Islam, "A Practitioner's Guide to the Design of Strategy Map Frameworks," *Pacific Accounting Review* 30 (2018), pp. 334–51.

56. R. Massingham, P. R. Massingham, and J. Dumay. "Improving Integrated Reporting: A New Learning and Growth Perspective for the Balanced Scorecard," *Journal of Intellectual Capital* 20 (2019), pp. 60–82; R. S. Kaplan and D. P. Norton, *The Balanced Scorecard: Translating Strategy into Action* (Boston: Harvard Business School Press, 1996); Z. Hoque, "20 Years of Studies on the Balanced Scorecard: Trends, Accomplishments, Gaps and Opportunities for Future Research," *The British Accounting Review,* March 2014, pp. 33–59.

57. "National Marrow Donor Program (NMDP) Case Study," Balanced Scorecard Institute, http://www.theinstitutepress.com, accessed June 12, 2015; National Marrow Donor Program and Be The Match, "Key Messages, Facts & Figures," http://www.bethematch.org, accessed June 12, 2015.

58. K. Moores and J. Mula, "The Salience of Market, Bureaucratic, and Clan Controls in the Management of Family Firm Transitions: Some Tentative Australian Evidence," *Family Business Review* 13, no. 2 (June 2000),

pp. 91–106; A. Walker and R. Newcombe, "The Positive Use of Power on a Major Construction Project," *Construction Management and Economics* 18, no. 1 (January–February 2000), pp. 37–44.

59. A. Grandori, "Knowledge-Intensive Work and the (Re)Emergence of Democratic Governance," *Academy of Management Perspectives* 30 (2016), pp. 167–81.

60. P. H. Fuchs, K. E. Mifflin, D. Miller, and J. O. Whitney, "Strategic Integration: Competing in the Age of Capabilities," *California Management Review* 42, no. 3 (Spring 2000), pp. 118–47; M. A. Lando, "Making Compliance Part of Your Organization's Culture," *Healthcare Executive* 15, no. 5 (September–October 1999), pp. 18–22; K. A. Frank and K. Fahrbach, "Organization Culture as a Complex System: Balance and Information in Models of Influence and Selection," *Organization Science* 10, no. 3 (May–June 1999), pp. 253–77; Serge A. Rijsdijk and Jan van den Ende, "Control Combinations in New Product Development Projects," *Journal of Product Innovation Management* 28, no. 6 (November 2011), pp. 868–80.

61. Starbucks website, "Control," www.starbucks.com, accessed May 2, 2017.

62. "The Workplace of the Future Tracks Your Every Move, Whether You Like It or Not," DigitalTrends.com, February 15, 2017, http://www.digitaltrends.com/home/smart-sensors-in-the-workplace/.

63. Lee Michael Katz, "Monitoring Employee Productivity: Proceed with Caution," Society for Human Resource Management, SHRM.org, June 1, 2015, https://www.shrm.org/hr-today/news/hr-magazine/pages/0615-employee-monitoring.aspx.

64. Christopher Rowland, "With Fitness Trackers in the Workplace, Bosses Can Monitor Your Every Step—and Possibly More," *Washington Post,* February 16, 2019, https://www.washingtonpost.com/business/economy/with-fitness-trackers-in-the-workplace-bosses-can-monitor-your-every-step--and-possibly-more/2019/02/15/75ee0848-2a45-11e9-b011-d8500644dc98_story.html?utm_term=.fb77b439f658.

65. Stefanie Valentic, "More Employers Offer Health and Wellness Programs," *EHS Today,* January 12, 2018, https://www.ehstoday.com/health/more-employers-offer-health-and-wellness-programs-infographic.

CHAPTER 17
Managing Technology and Innovation

> Technology is mostly used as a force for good, but its adverse consequences are also spreading at the same time.
>
> —Tim Cook

sfam_photo/Shutterstock

learning objectives

After studying Chapter 17, you will be able to:

LO 17-1 List the types of processes that spur development of new technologies.

LO 17-2 Describe how technologies proceed through a life cycle.

LO 17-3 Discuss ways to manage technology for competitive advantage.

LO 17-4 Summarize how to assess technology needs.

LO 17-5 Identify alternative methods of pursuing technological innovation.

LO 17-6 Define key roles in managing technology.

LO 17-7 Describe the characteristics of innovative organizations.

LO 17-8 Describe the characteristics of successful development projects.

chapter outline

Technology and Innovation
   Technology Life Cycle
   Diffusion of Technological Innovations

Technology Leadership and Followership
   Technology Leadership   Technology Followership

Assessing Technology Needs
   Measuring Current   Assessing External
   Technologies   Technological Trends

Making Technology Decisions
   Anticipated Market   Anticipated Capability
   Receptiveness   Development
   Technological Feasibility   Organizational Suitability
   Economic Viability

Sourcing and Acquiring New Technologies
   Internal Development   Technology Trading
   Purchase   Research Partnerships
   Contracted Development   and Joint Ventures
   Licensing   Acquiring a Technology
               Owner

Technology and Managerial Roles

Organizing for Innovation
   Unleashing Creativity   Implementing Develop-
   Bureaucracy Busting   ment Projects
   Design Thinking   Technology, Job Design,
               and Human Resources

Management in Action

ELON MUSK: EMBRACING TECHNOLOGY'S POSSIBILITIES AND CHALLENGES

MANAGER'S BRIEF

PROGRESS REPORT

ONWARD

Elon Musk's passions are many and varied; many people believe that's the reason he is such a successful innovator and entrepreneur, launching multibillion-dollar ventures in fields as different as digital payment systems, solar panels, automobiles, and space travel. He is a co-founder of PayPal (later sold to eBay); founder and CEO of the commercial rocket company SpaceX; and chair and CEO of Tesla, the maker of electric and self-driving cars. These and other industry-changing ventures have made him one of the wealthiest and most influential people in the world.

Musk recently started a new firm, called the Boring Company, that is attempting to create new energy-efficient, high-speed transportation tunnels in densely populated urban areas. What he's calling the Hyperloop was recently unveiled in Los Angeles for initial testing.[1] When he's not exploring beneath Earth's crust, he's exploring ways to make human life sustainable beyond its orbit. His SpaceX company is trying to make Mars a habitable Earth-like planet by warming it with nuclear fusion. Musk envisions a human settlement there in the not-too-distant future. His goal is literally and truly to change the world.

But trying to change the world is not without its challenges, and Musk and his companies have experienced their fair share recently. Musk himself has come under increased scrutiny for erratic and questionable behavior. Internally, some managers and employees have cited temperamental behavior, with one former Tesla executive going so far as to say "everyone in Tesla is in an abusive relationship with Elon."[2] His more public problems have included controversial and insulting messages conveyed on social media, run-ins with the Securities and Exchange Commission, and a radio interview in which he was allegedly smoking pot.[3]

Robyn Beck-Pool/Getty Images

Similar to the discomforting news surrounding Musk himself, news about his various ventures have also been more negative than positive lately. Scalable production of the Hyperloop has been slow to develop, and cities that were expected to invest in the transportation system, such as Chicago and Washington, DC, are now beginning to get cold feet.[4] After delivering two quarters of strong profits in 2018, Tesla reported big losses at the start of 2019 and is struggling to deliver its latest car, the Model 3.[5]

Compounding these internal issues, competition is building in areas once exclusively dominated by Musk and his organizations. The markets for electric vehicles and space travel are particularly heating up. Does this mean all Musk has worked for is slipping away? Far from it. All bold visionaries face obstacles and require persistence and resilience to overcome. In this regard, Musk is not invincible.

Elon Musk is an innovative thinker who is attempting to translate his ideas into action. As you read this chapter, think about how technology and innovation present unlimited possibilities and also complex challenges.

Although some visionaries such as Tesla's Elon Musk seem fearless, technological innovation is daunting in its complexity and pace of change. But it is vital for a firm's competitive advantage—not to mention its survival.[6]

Not long ago, new products took years to plan and develop, were standardized and mass produced, and were pushed onto the market through extensive selling and marketing campaigns. Production and sales forecasts were projected over decades. That's all changed. Product development now is a race to become the first to launch innovative products that often live for months rather than years, as they are displaced by ever more technologically sophisticated products. For example, robotics technology used to apply only to repetitive, programmable tasks like those found in manufacturing. Now it is used in a variety of human–machine interface contexts, from health care to automotive and aviation.[7]

Today's organizations depend on effective technology management to remain competitive by cutting costs and continually offering new goods or services. In a marketplace where technology and rapid innovation are critical for success, managers must understand how technologies emerge, develop, and change the ways companies compete and people work. This chapter discusses how to integrate technology into competitive strategy, how to assess technological needs, and how to meet these needs.

Bottom Line

Innovation is critical for competitiveness.

Why does innovation matter for a service business?

Technology and Innovation

LO 17-1 List the types of processes that spur development of new technologies.

technology

The systematic application of scientific knowledge to a new product, process, or service.

innovation

The introduction of new goods and services; a change in method or technology; a positive, useful departure from previous ways of doing things.

We defined **technology** in Chapter 9 as the methods, processes, systems, and skills used to transform resources into products. It is not contradictory to add now that we can view technology as the commercialization of science: the systematic application of scientific knowledge to a new product, process, or service. In this sense, technology is embedded in every product, service, and procedure used or produced.[8]

When technology is used to create a new good or service, or a new way of working, it is a form of innovation. Innovation differs from invention, or turning new ideas into realities, which may or may not add value to an organization. In the context of management, **innovation** is any new way of working that creates value.

Innovations can be of these fundamental types:[9]

- *Product innovation* is a change in the outputs (goods or services) the organization produces. If BP's research into biofuels results in a new kind of fuel to sell, this would be an example of product innovation.
- *Process innovation* is a change in the way outputs (goods or services) are produced. If BP's research into biofuels resulted in a more efficient way to produce fuel from sugarcane, it's a process innovation. Other examples of process innovation are flexible manufacturing processes discussed in Chapter 9, including mass customization, just-in-time, and concurrent engineering.
- *Business model innovation* refers to a change in the way the organization creates and delivers value. The change may affect any component of a company's business model: its customer value proposition (the basic problem it solves, such as eco-friendly fuel for about the same cost as fossil fuels), its profit formula (the financial road map for its success), its key resources (people, technology, facilities, brand), and its key processes. Exhibit 17.1 has additional examples.

These categories cover many creative new ideas (see the nearby "Social Entrepreneurship" box), which in every business can include product offerings, brand, platforms or processes of product creation, solutions to customer problems, customers served, nature of the customer experience, ways of earning money, process efficiencies, organization structure, supply chain, physical or virtual points of customer interactions, and more.[10]

Product innovation	Process innovation	Business model innovation
• Drones that fly themselves and can follow people through forests and around bends. • Foldable phones and rollup TVs.	• Robotic and robotic-assisted surgery. • More natural and fluid voice-driven interactions with digital assistants.	• AI-powered chatbots serving customers. • Blockchain technology cutting transaction costs and risk.

EXHIBIT 17.1
Fundamental Types of Innovation

Technologies emerge, develop, and are replaced in predictable patterns. Critical forces converge to create new technologies, which then follow well-defined life-cycle patterns. We describe the technology life cycle after noting these driving forces of technological development:

1. *Need or demand.* Without a need or demand for the technology, there is no reason for technological innovation to occur.
2. *Feasibility.* Meeting the need must be theoretically possible, and basic science must contain the knowledge that makes it possible.
3. *Practicality.* We must be able to convert the scientific knowledge into practice in both engineering and economic terms. If we can theoretically do something but doing it is economically impractical, the technology cannot yet emerge.
4. *Resource availability.* The funding, skilled labor, time, space, and other resources needed to develop the technology must be available.
5. *Entrepreneurialism.* Entrepreneurial initiative is needed to identify and pull all the necessary elements together.

Technology Life Cycle

Technological innovations typically follow a predictable pattern called the **technology life cycle**, shown in Exhibit 17.2. Early progress can be slow as competitors continually experiment with product design and operational characteristics to meet consumer needs. This stage is where the rate of product innovation tends to be highest. For example, during the

technology life cycle

A predictable pattern followed by a technological innovation, from its inception and development to market saturation and replacement.

LO 17-2 Describe how technologies proceed through a life cycle.

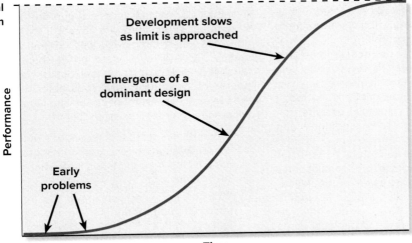

EXHIBIT 17.2
The Technology Life Cycle

early years of the auto industry, companies tried a wide range of machines, including electric and steam-driven cars, to determine which would be most effective. Eventually the internal combustion engine emerged as the dominant design, and the number of product innovations leveled off.

> Once early problems are resolved and a dominant design emerges, improvements come more from process innovations.

Once early problems are resolved and a dominant design emerges, improvements come more from process innovations to refine the technology. At this point managers gain advantage by finding process efficiencies and lower cost. In the auto example, as companies settled on a product standard, they began leveraging the benefits of mass production and vertical integration to improve productivity. These process innovations lowered production costs and brought automobile prices in line with consumer budgets.[11]

Eventually the new technology begins to reach the upper limits of both its performance capabilities and the spread of its use. Development slows and becomes increasingly costly, and the market becomes saturated (there are few new customers). The technology can remain in this mature stage for some time—as with autos—or can be replaced quickly by another technology offering superior performance or economic advantage.

Life cycles can take decades or even centuries, as with iron- and steel-making technologies. After making the world's first telephone call in 1876, Alexander Graham Bell created a new industry that would take many forms. Rotary phones appeared in the 1920s, and touchtone phones in the 1960s. The early 1970s brought the first cell phone call, by a Motorola employee. Text messaging began in the early 1990s. Apple introduced the iPhone in 2007, and a year later Google unveiled Android. Smartphones now, of course, are everywhere.[12]

Inclusiveness Works

Reducing Unconscious Biases with Tech

One set of challenges to creating diverse and inclusive workplaces are ways of behaving and thinking that we are unaware of. Referred to as *unconscious biases*, they can have a profound impact on organizations, from recruiting and hiring to team collaboration and productivity. Because everyone harbors unconscious biases, and because these biases are difficult to detect, companies have struggled to mitigate their influence. Increasingly, firms are turning to technology to help solve this problem.

AI programs can detect job descriptions that include language biased toward a certain race, religion, or gender.[13] Integrating objective AI analysis has a twofold benefit: (1) job descriptions that don't seem to favor one group (and thereby exclude others) draw a wider range of diverse candidates and (2) managers who are hiring can prevent or correct in future workplace practices and interactions.

Firms also take advantage of data analytics to better understand how employees develop relationships in organizations. One such system is Organizational Network Analysis (ONA),[14] which helps to better understand inclusion in the workplace. Firms can use internal surveys, employee communications on computers and mobile devices, and biometric sensors to create visualization maps of the relationship networks of each employee plus the strength of those relationships.[15] Companies can then compare relationship networks with one another to determine where biased behaviors are most common. For example, ONA visualizations found that those who self-identified as introverts formed stronger relationships when their desk was central to informal office activities like the water cooler than those who identified as introverts whose desks were on the periphery. Essentially, ONA was able to show that the physical placement of certain individuals directly influenced their feelings of inclusion.

- How effective do you think the use of technology can really be in better understanding and developing inclusive workplaces, and what other uses can you envision?

- What challenges do you see as technology is deployed to better understand and mitigate employee biases?

As the phone example shows, a technology life cycle can be made up of many individual product life cycles. Each product performs a similar task—delivering better quality and functionality—yet each is an improvement over its predecessors. Significant innovations, often entirely new technologies, are followed by many small, incremental innovations.

Ongoing development of a technology increases the benefits it provides, makes it easier to use, and generates new applications. In the process, the technology spreads to new adopters.

Diffusion of Technological Innovations

Like the technology life cycle, the adoption of new technology over time follows an S-shaped pattern (top line in Exhibit 17.3). The percentage of people using the technology is small in the beginning, but increases dramatically as the technology succeeds and spreads through the population. Eventually the number of users peaks and levels off when the market for the technology is saturated. This pattern, first observed in 1903, has been verified with many new technologies and ideas in a wide variety of industries and settings.[16]

The adopters of a new technology fall into five groups (see the bottom line in Exhibit 17.3). Each group presents different challenges and opportunities to managers who want to market a new innovation.

The first group, representing approximately 2.5 percent of adopters, is the *innovators.* Typically, innovators are adventurous and willing to take risks. They pay a premium for latest new technology or product and champion it if they like it. The enthusiasm of innovator-adopters is no guarantee of success—for example, the product may still be too expensive for the general market. But a lack of enthusiasm in this group often signals serious problems with the new technology, and a need for further development.

The next group to adopt a new technology are *early adopters.* This group is crucial and includes well-respected opinion leaders. Early adopters often are those whom others look to for leadership, up-to-date technological information, and suggestions.

Marketing managers often spend heavily in promotion to these first two adopter groups. For example, companies are increasingly using gamification to engage their customers and employees.

The next group is the *early* and *late majorities.* The members of the majority groups are more skeptical of technological change and approach innovation with great caution, often adopting only because of economic necessity or social pressure.

The final 16 percent are *laggards.* Often isolated and highly conservative, laggards are suspicious of innovation and change.

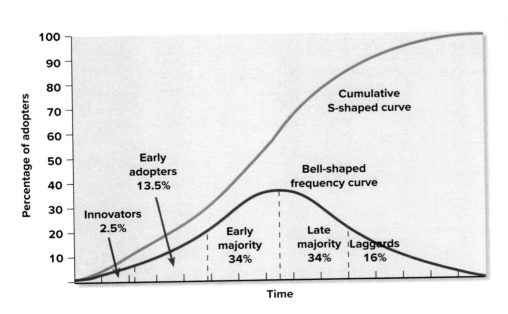

EXHIBIT 17.3

Technology Dissemination Pattern and Adopter Categories

Social Entrepreneurship

Providing Clean Water via "Water ATMs"

"Problems of poverty are, on most occasions, inextricably linked with those of water—its availability, its proximity, its quantity, and its quality."[17] So said the United Nations in its recent World Water Development Report. For example, many of India's more than 1.3 billion people rely on untreated water, and about 75 percent of all diseases in that country, some fatal, can be traced to these contaminated supplies.

Centralized water treatment plants are expensive, and pipelines can bring water only so far, meaning the country's remote populations still face the problem of carrying heavy containers over long distances to their homes. This time-consuming daily chore usually falls to women and girls.

Founded by Anand Shah in 2008, Piramal Sarvajal is a social enterprise dedicated to leveraging technology to help remedy this urgent health problem. The Sarvajal solution is to build local water treatment plants and then distribute the clean water through innovative, solar-powered vending machines, referred to as "water ATMs," available 24 hours a day. The organization currently serves nearly 600,000 consumers daily in 20 of India's 29 states via nearly 500 of these water ATMs.[18]

Using their mobile phones to buy prepaid, refillable cards, customers are allowed to purchase a specific amount of water and collect it in their own containers for the relatively short trip home. People who live below the national poverty line (about 30 percent of the population) receive water that is either free or subsidized by Sarvajal.

fotosunny/Shutterstock

With training in the purification technology and in maintenance and marketing, local franchisees own and operate the water ATMs and treatment systems. The franchise system ensures that clean water reaches street corners, stores, schools, and other gathering places even in remote villages. Not only is Piramal Sarvajal saving lives with the dispensing of millions of gallons of clean drinking water, but it generates an estimated $4 million annually to each local economy.[19]

- Into which technology type(s) mentioned in the text would you classify Sarvajal's water ATMs?
- Would you expect the technology that powers water ATMs to follow the typical S-shaped pattern of diffusion? Why or why not?

The speed with which an innovation spreads depends largely on certain attributes. An innovation will spread quickly if it

- Has a great advantage over its predecessor.
- Is compatible with existing systems, procedures, infrastructures, and ways of thinking.
- Has less rather than greater complexity.
- Can be tried or tested easily without significant cost or commitment.
- Can be observed and copied easily.

Designing products with these considerations in mind can make a huge contribution to their success.

Technology Leadership and Followership

LO 17-3 Discuss ways to manage technology for competitive advantage.

Discussions about technology life cycles and diffusion patterns can imply that technological change occurs naturally or automatically. But just the opposite is true: Change is neither easy nor natural (we discuss change more fully in our final chapter). Decisions about technology and innovation are highly strategic, and managers need to approach them systematically and thoughtfully.

In Chapter 4, we discussed two generic strategies a company can use to position itself in the market: low cost and differentiation. With low-cost leadership, the company maintains an advantage because it operates at lower cost than its competitors. With a differentiation strategy, the advantage comes from having a unique good or service for which customers are willing to pay a premium price.[20]

Technological innovations can support either of these strategies: They gain cost advantage through pioneering lower-cost product designs and creating low-cost ways to operate. And, they can support differentiation by pioneering unique goods or services that increase buyer value and thus command premium prices.

Clayton Christensen coined the term **disruptive innovation** to describe situations in which a new and unrefined technology swiftly takes over the market.[21] For example, MP3 file technology surprised many record companies that were heavily invested in CD technology. Cloud computing removed the need for companies to maintain internal servers. Airbnb disrupted the hotel industry by directly connecting home owners with travelers. And 5G networks, with speeds expected to be from 10 to 100 times over 4G, will revolutionize our digital experiences.[22]

A disruptive innovation creates a dilemma for managers: Should they continue with tried and true, functional technology and possibly lose the advantages of early adoption? Or, should managers invest in newer, unproven technology, possibly resulting in inferior products that may or may not succeed?

Sustaining technology relies on incremental improvements to an already established technology. Disruptive technology lacks refinement, often has performance problems because it is new, appeals to a limited audience, and may not yet have a proven practical application.

The usual tendency is to innovate to the point that goods or services become too sophisticated, inconvenient, or expensive for buyers' tastes, creating new opportunities for the next disruptive innovation. To be a disruptive innovator, focus on the users of a product and look for customers whose needs are being ignored—say, because they want something that costs less or is easier to use. For example, innovative food producers are disrupting the meat and protein substitutes market. Known as "meatless meats," producers like Impossible Foods, Beyond Meat, and Memphis Meats want to displace tofu and Quorn. Some praise these new protein alternatives as looking, smelling, and tasting like real meat.[23]

But industries do not transform overnight. Typically, signs of a new technology's impact are visible well in advance, leaving time for companies to respond. Almost every competitor in the telecommunications industry fully understood the value of cellular technology. Often the key issue is not whether to adopt a new technology, but when, plus how to integrate it with the organization's operating practices and strategies.

Technology Leadership

The saying "timing is everything" applies to many things, from financial investments to telling jokes. It applies also to developing and exploiting new technologies. Industry leaders such as Google, Toyota, Airbus, and DuPont built and maintain their competitive positions through early development and application of new technologies. However, technology leadership imposes costs and risks, and is not always the best approach (see Exhibit 17.4).[24] Apple is well known for its technology leadership, beginning with its Macintosh computer, which pioneered the mouse and graphical desktop icons instead of strings of typed computer commands. Not to mention a string of popular innovations ever since.[25]

> A key question is not whether to adopt a useful new technology, but when.

Advantages of Technology Leadership Technology leadership is attractive thanks to its potential for high profits and first-mover advantages. If technology leadership increases a firm's efficiency relative to competitors, it achieves a cost advantage. The advantage generates greater profits and can attract more customers through lower prices. And if a company is first to market, it might charge a premium price because it faces no competition. Higher prices and greater profits defray the costs of developing new technologies.

Bottom Line

Innovation can improve all bottom-line practices. *How can innovation support a differentiation strategy?*

disruptive innovation

A process by which a product, service, or business model takes root initially in simple applications at the bottom of a market and then moves "up market," eventually displacing established competitors.

EXHIBIT 17.4
Advantages and
Disadvantages of
Technology Leadership

Advantages	Disadvantages
First-mover advantage	Greater risks
Little or no competition	Cost of technology development
Greater efficiency	Costs of market development and customer education
Higher profit margins	Infrastructure costs
Sustainable advantage	Costs of learning and eliminating defects
Reputation for innovation	Possible cannibalization of existing products
Establishment of entry barriers	
Occupation of best market niches	
Opportunities to learn	

Top pharmaceutical companies depend on patents to allow them several years of selling new drugs without competition before cheaper generic versions of their drugs appear. They must develop new drugs in the meantime to sustain their success.

Jupiterimages/Thinkstock/Getty Images

The first mover can beat competitors to the best market niches.

This one-time advantage of being the technology leader can be turned into a sustainable advantage. Sustaining the lead depends on competitors' ability to duplicate the technology and the firm's ability to keep improving quickly enough to outpace competitors.

A firm can do this in several ways. The reputation for being an innovator can create an ongoing advantage and even spill over to the company's other products. For example, 3M's reputation for innovation and quality differentiates some of its standard products, such as adhesive tape, and allows them to command a premium price. A competitor may be able to copy the product but not the reputation. 3M's strong reputation stems partly from how it dedicates about 6 percent—nearly $1.8 billion in 2018—of its annual revenue to research and development.[26]

Patents and other institutional barriers can be used to block competitors and maintain leadership. The big players in the pharmaceutical industry invest heavily in research and development; they depend on patents to give them several years to sell their new drugs without competition before generic versions are permitted. For example, pharmaceutical company Roche is expected to lose patent protection on three of its blockbuster drugs: Rituxam, Herceptin, and Avastin.[27] The three drugs generated over $10 billion in revenue for the company in 2018.[28] As additional blockbuster drug patents expire, pharmaceutical companies face a tremendous challenge to develop the next new drugs.

The first mover also can preempt competitors by capturing the best market niches. If it can establish high switching costs (Chapter 2) for repeat customers, these positions can be difficult for competitors to capture.

Technology leadership can provide an important learning advantage. Competitors may copy or adopt a new technology, but new learning by the technology leader can generate minor improvements that are difficult to imitate. Many Japanese manufacturers use several small, incremental improvements generated with their *kaizen* programs (Chapter 9) to continually upgrade their process and product quality. Competitors cannot easily copy these many small improvements, which collectively provide significant advantage.[29]

Disadvantages of Technology Leadership

Being the first to develop or adopt a new technology does not always lead to immediate advantage and high profits. Such potential may exist, but technology leadership does impose high costs and risks that followers do not have to bear. Being the leader thus can be more costly than being the follower; there's good reason the forefront of technology is often called the "bleeding edge." Costs include educating buyers unfamiliar with the new technology, building an infrastructure to support it, and developing complementary products to help achieve its full potential.

When the personal computer was first developed in the 1970s, dozens of computer companies entered the market. Almost all of them failed, usually because they lacked the financial, marketing, and sales ability needed to attract and service customers. Also, many new products require regulatory approval. Developing a new drug, including testing and obtaining FDA approval, can take 10 years or more and cost an average of $2.6 billion or more. After that, developers enjoy a profitable period of patent protection until competitors move in with low-cost generics. Although these followers do not get the benefits of being first to market, they can copy the drug for a fraction of the cost once the original patents expire. This strategy can be highly profitable.[30]

Being a pioneer carries other risks. If raw materials and equipment are new or have unique specifications, a ready supply at a reasonable cost may not be available. Or the technology may not be fully developed, and presents unresolved problems. In addition, the unproven market creates uncertainty in demand. Finally, the new technology may have an adverse impact on existing business. It may cannibalize current products or make current investments obsolete.

Technology Followership

Not all organizations are equally prepared to be technology leaders, nor would leadership benefit each organization equally. In deciding whether to be a technology leader or follower, managers consider their company's competitive strategy, the benefits to be gained through the technology, and characteristics of their organization.[31]

Technology followership shares a feature with technology leadership: it too can be used to support both low-cost and differentiation strategies. If the follower learns from the leader's experience, it can avoid the costs and risks of leadership and thereby establish a low-cost position. Generic drugmakers use this strategy.

Followership also can support differentiation. By learning from the leader, followers can adapt the products or delivery systems to fit buyers' needs more closely.

Microsoft built great success on this type of followership. After technology leaders paved the way, the company launched many products, including music players, video game consoles, spreadsheet and word-processing software, and web browsers,. Likewise, Facebook came to dominate social networking only after Friendster and MySpace burned through money introducing the concept. Newer competitors, such as YouTube, Instagram, Snapchat, WhatsApp, and TikTok (China), continue to compete in the market hoping they can lure away users with services that improve on Facebook's.[32] But this follower strategy is more challenging once an industry leader has established widespread customer loyalty.

Management decisions about when to adopt new technologies depend also on their potential benefits plus their organization's technology skills. As described earlier, technologies do not emerge in their final state; rather, they develop continually. This eventually makes them easier to use and more adaptable to various strategies. For example, high-bandwidth communication networks enabled more companies to work with suppliers located abroad.

At the same time, complementary products and technologies can make the main technology more useful. For example, doctors and nurses now use a phone app to track eight vital signs, from heart and respiratory rates to body temperature.[33] The phone app works with a small biosensor patch applied to the skin of patients.[34] While this technology is not yet replacing traditional monitoring (such as heart rate tracking equipment and manual blood pressure testing), it holds great promise for improving the patient experience during hospital stays.

These complementary products and technologies combine with the gradual diffusion of the technology to form a shifting competitive impact. The best time to adopt a technological innovation is when the costs and risks of switching to the technology are outweighed by the benefits. This point will be different for each organization; some will benefit from a leadership (early adopter) role, and others from a followership role, depending on organizational characteristics and strategies.[35]

Assessing Technology Needs

LO 17-4 Summarize how to assess technology needs.

The biggest industry sector in the U.S. economy is health care services, where spending is soaring, much to the dismay of the insurers and patients paying the medical bills. One reason U.S. health care costs so much is that the industry has been slower than others to adopt technologies that can make day-to-day operations more efficient. An Accenture study found that the shift to virtual annual patient visits with primary care physicians, ongoing patient management, and self-care will save the U.S. health system approximately $10 billion over the next few years.[36]

Virtual health care is technology-enabled services that do not have to be performed in a doctor's office or medical facility, including videoconferences with physicians, remote biometric tracking, and mobile apps for managing health. About one in five Americans has tried this novel approach to annual health care checkups.[37]

Failure to correctly assess your organization's technology needs can fundamentally impair its effectiveness. A thorough assessment measures current technologies plus external trends affecting the industry.

Measuring Current Technologies

technology audit

Process of clarifying the key technologies on which an organization depends.

Before managers can devise strategies for developing and exploiting technological innovation, they must gain a clear understanding of their current technology base. A **technology audit** helps identify which technologies offer the most competitive value.

One technique for measuring competitive value uses four technology categories:[38]

- *Emerging technologies* are still under development and thus are unproved. They may, however, significantly alter the rules of competition in the future. Managers should monitor emerging technologies but might not invest in them until they are developed more fully.
- *Pacing technologies* have yet to prove their full value but have the potential to alter the rules of competition. When first installed, computer-aided manufacturing was a pacing technology. Its potential was not fully understood, but companies that used it effectively realized major speed and cost advantages.
- *Key technologies* have proved effective, and provide advantage because not everyone uses them. They continue to provide some first-mover advantages. A key technology for Intel is a powerful proprietary processing chip. Eventually, alternatives to key technologies can emerge. Until alternatives merge, key technologies provide a major competitive edge that prevents threats from new entrants.
- *Base technologies* are commonplace in the industry; everyone in the industry must have them. Thus they provide little or no advantage. Managers have to invest merely to ensure their organization's continued competence.

Technologies can evolve rapidly from one category to the next. Electronic word processing was an emerging technology in the late 1970s. By the early 1980s, it was a pacing technology. With continued improvements and more powerful computer chips, it quickly became a key technology. Costs dropped, usage spread, and it enhanced productivity demonstrably. By the late 1980s, electronic word processing was a base technology in most applications, the most routine of activities.

Assessing External Technological Trends

As with any planning, decisions about technology must balance internal capabilities (strengths and weaknesses) with external opportunities and threats. Managers can use several techniques to understand better how technologies are changing within industries.

Benchmarking   Technology benchmarking (Chapter 4) varies across industries. Competitors understandably are reluctant to share their secrets, but trading information for benchmarking purposes can prove highly valuable. For example, Harley-Davidson recovered its reputation for manufacturing quality motorcycles only after company executives toured Honda's plant and learned firsthand the relative weaknesses of Harley's manufacturing technologies and the vast potential for improvement.

Benchmarking against potential competitors in other countries can be useful. Companies may find key or pacing technologies overseas that they can import easily and to significant advantage. Overseas firms may be more willing to share their knowledge if they are not direct competitors and if they can receive beneficial information in exchange.

Scanning   Whereas benchmarking identifies current practices, scanning uncovers what is being developed. In other words, benchmarking examines key and perhaps some pacing technologies, whereas scanning seeks pacing and emerging technologies—those just being introduced or still under development.

Blockchain is likely a revolutionary, game-changing technology: a decentralized database that distributes online transactions (bank deposits, medical records, legal documents, and beyond) across millions of databases. Imagine the efficiencies compared with each organization managing its own centralized database. Moreover, it's very secure because it uses state-of-the-art encryption technology.[39]

Every other sector can potentially benefit from blockchain. It can provide students and institutions a fast and safe way to access transcripts and educational records and help government agencies reduce corruption and enhance the integrity of voting systems.[40]

Scanning requires companies to continually monitor potential sources of new technologies. Informed managers read cutting-edge research journals and blogs, and attend research conferences and seminars. Organizations that operate close to the cutting edge need forward-looking individuals who identify and embrace pacing and emerging technologies.

Bottom Line

Benchmarking can decrease costs and increase speed, quality, sustainability, and customer service.
What are some limits on benchmarking as a source of technology ideas?

By touring a Honda plant, Harley Davidson executives identified the weaknesses within their own company and use that knowledge to improve their products and boost their reputation.

Tofudevil/Shutterstock

Making Technology Decisions

Once managers have analyzed their organization's current technological position, they can decide how to develop or exploit emerging innovations. Decision making must balance the many interrelated factors discussed next.

LO 17-5 Identify alternative methods of pursuing technological innovation.

Anticipated Market Receptiveness

The first strategic consideration is market potential. Often innovations are stimulated by external demand for new goods and services. A Gartner study predicts that by 2022, many U.S. companies will be experimenting with immersive technologies for consumer and industrial use.[41] These technologies will meet growing demand for virtual and augmented reality applications in marketing, training and simulation, and design visualization. The goal is to provide users with a "multiexperience" that taps multiple senses.[42] Time will tell if the market is ready for these experiences.

In assessing market receptiveness, executives need to make two determinations:

1. In the short run, the new technology should have an immediate, valuable application.
2. In the long run, the technology must be able to satisfy future market needs.

franky242/Alamy Stock Photo

For example, many brick-and-mortar retailers are looking for innovative ways to increase sales by motivating their tech-friendly customers to visit and make purchases in their physical stores. This priority is especially important for retailers who want to avoid the fate of once-dominant brands like Sears that didn't adapt successfully to technology-enabled retail.

Retailers are attracting customer visits with "in-store" technology. At its flagship store in New York City, Macy's opened a floor called "One Below" featuring selfie walls and 3D printing for customizing accessories.[43] Neiman Marcus also installed interactive touchscreens in its fitting rooms to allow customers to adjust the lighting and request different sizes and colors of clothes they are trying on. Then, shoppers can check out from the dressing rooms.[44]

Technological Feasibility

In addition to market receptiveness, managers must consider an innovation's feasibility. Visions can stay unrealized for a long time. Technical obstacles block progress.

For example, security experts for years have wanted reliable facial recognition systems. Such systems, if they could accurately link a recorded face to an identity in a database, could help locate wanted criminals, reduce fraudulent use of driver's licenses and stolen credit cards, and streamline security checks. Innovative efforts continue, and accuracy of facial recognition keeps improving.[45]

In the oil industry, technological barriers prevent exploration and drilling in the deepest parts of the ocean. In medicine, scientists and doctors struggle mightily to find causes of and cures for deadly diseases. Makers of electronic devices are constantly challenged by how to keep their processors cool enough to function properly even as they get smaller and more powerful.

GE Global Research developed advanced cooling jets that are quieter and use less energy to keep electronic components from overheating. The jets can be scaled to cool smaller (a laptop) or larger (an aircraft engine) electronic applications.[46] But as time passes, manufacturers will surely be looking for something even smaller. Each of these innovations is slowed by the limits of currently available technologies.

Economic Viability

Technological feasibility relates closely to economic viability. Apart from whether a firm can pull off a technological innovation, executives must find enough financial incentive to try. Hydrogen-powered fuel cell technology for automobiles is almost feasible technically, but its costs are still too high. Even with lower costs, lack of supporting societal infrastructure—such as hydrogen refueling stations—remains a barrier to economic viability.

But if a company can find niche markets for a high-priced new technology, it often can advance the technology so that applications become more customized and affordable. Three-dimensional (3D) printers read plans and translate them into physical objects by spraying out extremely thin layers of plastic or other materials to create the physical object. A skilled designer can create a 3D model of a part in a matter of hours and then direct the printer to finish the job.

Technological feasibility and economic viability are closely related.

Automaker BMW uses 3D printing to assemble tools used to fit bumpers onto its vehicles with a printer, rather than machine aluminum. The part went from taking more than two weeks and $420 to make, to 26 hours at $176. That's a 92 percent reduction in time and a 58 percent drop in price.[47]

Less futuristic innovations, as well, require a careful assessment of economic viability. New technologies often represent an expensive and long-term commitment of resources.

Once an organization commits to an innovation, changing direction is costly and difficult. For these reasons, a careful, objective analysis of technology costs versus benefits is essential.

Of course, benefits as well as costs can be substantial. Spending on health care technology is helping people live longer.[48] While that is a positive, the cost of such life-extending technology is a major contributing factor to the rising costs of health care services and insurance.[49]

The exploding growth in piracy and fake products adds new barriers to economic viability.[50] Globalization has created a worldwide market for goods produced by low-cost counterfeiters and pirates, who incur no research and development expense. Furthermore, technology makes it easy to copy software and download movies and music without paying for it. Michael Kors, Nike, Ray Ban, Rolex, and LEGOs—all these and many more products are counterfeited or illegally copied and sold. According to the International Trademark Association, the worldwide cost of counterfeiting and piracy is projected to reach $2.3 trillion by 2022.[51]

Anticipated Capability Development

It bears repeating that organizations should (and do) build their strategies based on core capabilities. This advice applies as well to technology and innovation strategies. Merck, Apple, and Intel are prime examples of companies with core capabilities in research and development. But even in these cases, research capabilities are not always a good match with market opportunities. Merck and other firms found that new opportunities for fighting disease are in biotechnology, but their primary expertise was chemistry-based drugs. So they added new capabilities by acquiring or partnering with biotechnology start-ups.

Some innovations are competency enhancing—exploiting or strengthening a core capability—whereas others are competency destroying. Continuing the Merck example, most core capabilities in the industry are in chemistry-based drugs, which continue to play an important role in its success. Sales of the cancer-fighting drug Keytruda earned over $2 billion in the fourth quarter of 2018, a milestone for the blockbuster drug.[52] Ken Frazier, CEO of Merck, summarized the blended strategy this way: "The performance of Merck's broad and balanced portfolio allows us to remain committed to biomedical innovation that saves and improves lives and delivers long-term value to shareholders."[53]

A firm may not be technology oriented, but it still must pay attention to changing technology because it will need new capabilities to survive. When Amazon.com revolutionized retailing in the 1990s, traditional brick-and-mortar bookstores had to adapt quickly. To regain competitiveness, they had to dramatically overhaul their information technology capabilities.

The upshot: Although a new technology may have tremendous market potential, managers must have or develop the internal capabilities needed to execute the new strategy. Without proper implementation, the most promising technological advances can prove disastrous.

Organizational Suitability

Additional considerations in choosing technological innovations are your organization's culture, managers' interests, and stakeholders' expectations. Ranked in BCG's Most Innovative Companies 2019, Alphabet/Google and Amazon are proactive innovators with outward-looking, opportunistic cultures. Executives in such *prospector* firms tend to have bold visions of the future, and give considerable priority to developing and exploiting technology. In many cases, these executives are more concerned about the opportunity costs of not taking action than they are about the potential to fail.

In contrast, *defender* firms, such as utility companies and supermarkets, are generally more cautious regarding innovation. These firms operate in more stable environments, so their strategies employ complementary technologies that extend rather than replace their current ones. For example, public utilities are investing in digital meter technology that provides real-time electric and water usage data to customers' mobile devices.[54] To reduce

Bottom Line

Innovation requires financial feasibility.

Say an innovation is exciting but unprofitable. What are the pros and cons of pursuing it anyway?

EXHIBIT 17.5
Key Considerations in
Technology Decisions

Considerations	Sample Contexts
Market receptiveness—assess external demand for the technology (short/long run).	Digital voice assistants, wearable technology, water-conserving washers.
Technological feasibility—evaluate technical barriers to progress.	Deep-sea oil exploration and safe autonomous driving vehicles.
Economic viability—examine any cost considerations and forecast profitability.	Solar energy and in-home robotic technology.
Competence development—determine whether current capabilities are sufficient.	Information technology in health care and digital technology in cameras.
Organizational suitability—assess the fit with culture and managerial systems.	Steel companies focusing on creativity and innovation.

costs, some supermarkets are shifting to digital label technology that eliminates the need for paper labels on shelf edges that display prices, discounts, and nutritional information.[55]

As an *analyzer* firm, Samsung needs to stay technologically competitive but tends to allow others like Apple to demonstrate solid demand in new arenas before it responds. Analyzers adopt early follower strategies to grab dominant positions using their strengths in marketing and manufacturing more than through technological innovation.[56]

Early adopters of new technologies tend to be larger, more profitable, and more specialized—putting them in an economic position to absorb the risks. Managers who adopt early are comfortable dealing with uncertainty and have strong problem-solving capabilities. Thus early adopters manage the difficulties of less fully developed technologies.[57]

Another consideration is the impact the new technology will have on employees. Their cooperation (or lack thereof) often is a major factor in determining how difficult and costly the introduction of new technology will be. We discuss how to manage such change in our final chapter.

Exhibit 17.5 summarizes these considerations in making decisions about technology innovations. A shortage of just one can derail an otherwise promising project. For example, consider how these factors apply to Tesla Motors's introduction of a luxury electric car as you read "Management in Action: Progress Report."

Sourcing and Acquiring New Technologies

Developing new technology may conjure up visions of scientists and product developers working in famous research and development (R&D) laboratories like those of Thomas J. Watson Research Center and MIT Media Lab Research.[58] However, new technologies come from many other sources including suppliers, manufacturers, users, other industries, universities, the government, and overseas companies. Every source of innovation should be explored, but each industry usually has specific sources for most of its new technologies.

For example, farming innovations most often come from manufacturers, suppliers, and government extension services. Seed manufacturers develop and market superior hybrids, chemical producers improve pesticides and herbicides, and equipment manufacturers design improved farm equipment. Land grant universities develop new farming techniques, and extension agents spread their usage.

In many industries, however, the primary innovators are firms that improve upon the technologies they employ. For example, most scientific instrument innovations come from users who improve and then sell or license them to manufacturers or suppliers.[59]

The question of how to acquire a new technology is essentially a **make-or-buy decision**. Should the organization develop the technology itself, or acquire it from an outside source? This decision is not nearly as simple as it sounds; many options exist, and each has advantages and disadvantages as discussed next.

make-or-buy decision

The question an organization asks itself about whether to acquire new technology from an outside source or develop it itself.

Management in Action

RACING TO PRODUCE THE WORLD'S BEST ELECTRONIC VEHICLE

For Tesla to continue leading in what founder and CEO Elon Musk sees as the future of driving, it must produce and sell enough electric vehicles at scale to earn a sufficient profit. Initial orders for the Model S sedan arrived faster than Tesla could make them, and the company quickly ramped up production. The Model X sport-utility vehicle soon followed.

To broaden its customer base, Tesla has recently launched a mass-market vehicle, the Model 3. At $35,000, the Model 3 will have the lowest price point Tesla has ever offered. But the lower price brings back the question of profitability and scale. After a promising start with two quarters of strong profits in 2018, Tesla reported sizable losses in the first quarter of 2019.[60] Since its founding, Tesla has been unable to generate consistent profits, and the market is beginning to waver on whether Tesla can deliver on its promises.

Challenges for Tesla are nothing new. In fact, as a startup with an innovative product in an industry as mature and entrenched as the car industry, Tesla always had a steep hill to climb. Tesla needed a plan for getting cars and information to consumers. Instead of approaching auto dealerships, the company opened stores in upscale shopping centers. Each store displays a Tesla car surrounded by exhibits about its features. At touch screens, shoppers learn what they can save on gas, select options, and see an image of their car. It's more like an Apple store than a car dealership. But these display rooms are expensive to maintain and are increasing overhead costs, so Tesla has been shifting its emphasis back to online selling and closing down display rooms.[61]

Another roadblock for Tesla is the same for all electric vehicles: infrastructure, which is designed for the internal combustion engine, not electric batteries. Stations for recharging a car away from home have been few, and fully recharging can take hours. Tesla developed battery technology that takes a car farther—about 270 miles in the case of the Model 3. It also is building a network of Supercharger stations, where 30 minutes of charging provides up to 170 miles of range.

Time is running out, however, as Elon Musk is no longer the only person who sees electrical vehicles as the future of driving; the CEOs of pretty much every car manufacturer now see electric vehicles as the future as well. The problem for Tesla isn't so much the new competition; it's that traditional car companies like Chevrolet, BMW, Volkswagen, and Nissan are better equipped to bring their vehicles to scale—and they're doing so at an increasingly faster pace.

Both the Nissan Leaf and the Chevy Volt have price points at or below Tesla's lowest list price for the Model 3, with similar charge ranges. The Volt was listed in *U.S. News* as 2018's best electric car.[62] BMW and Volkswagen are both set to release new electric vehicles that have mileage ranges that exceed 300 miles a charge.[63]

Ultimately this increased competition is a positive development because more affordable and efficient electric vehicles mean fewer carbon emissions and a cleaner energy future. However, it's unclear whether Musk's vision of a world populated by electric vehicles will ultimately be realized by another firm.

- What are the advantages and disadvantages to Tesla Motors in being a technology leader?
- Check in with Tesla. How is Tesla Motors faring in comparison to its competitors? How well has it overcome its challenges?

Internal Development

Developing a new technology within the company has the great potential advantage of keeping it proprietary—exclusive to the organization. The disadvantage is that it usually requires staff and funding for an extended period. Even if the development succeeds, considerable time elapses before realizing the benefits. Managers must carefully weigh the potential benefits of proprietary technology against the cost of developing it.

Intel balances risks and benefits by operating research and development laboratories in several locations, including Oregon, Israel, India, and China. Engineers in the various labs come up with breakthrough ideas, and labs in offshore locations can avoid legal restrictions on imports, plus save money relative to the cost of hiring talent in the United States.[64]

Purchase

Most technology already in use is available openly for purchase. A bank that needs sophisticated information technology need not develop it itself. It can simply buy it from manufacturers or suppliers. Usually this is the simplest, easiest, and most cost-effective way to acquire new technology. However, the technology itself will not provide competitive advantage.

Contracted Development

If the technology is not available and a company lacks the resources or time to develop it internally, it can contract the development from outside sources. Possible contractors include other companies, independent research laboratories, and university and government institutions. Usually outside contracting involves an agreed-upon series of objectives and timetables, with payments made as each part of the project is tested and achieved.

charnsitr/Shutterstock

Licensing

Technologies that are not easily purchased can be licensed for a fee. Companies like EA Sports, maker of such online games as Madden NFL, FIFA, and NBA Live, allows others to license these and other video games. The artwork, characters, and music for a game may be unique, but the basic laws of physics apply to the action shown in today's sophisticated games, so there is no advantage to programming these aspects of each game. Licensing is more economical.[65]

Technology Trading

Another way to gain access to new technologies is with technology trading. Mary Jo Cartwright, a director of plant operations at Batesville Casket Company, adopted Toyota's manufacturing philosophy of lean production and continuous improvement. This decreased manufacturing costs by 25 percent and the number of hours to make a coffin by 40 percent. Prior to adopting the "Toyota way," 20 percent of manufactured coffins needed repair. That rate fell to 1 percent.[66]

Sometimes even rival companies trade technologies. Not all industries or companies are amenable, but technology trading is increasing because of the high cost of developing advanced technologies independently.[67]

Toyota, known for not sharing with competitors its manufacturing techniques, plans to sell complete powertrain modules (and share the technology) of Prius cars to rivals. This unprecedented decision is driven by the world's largest automaker's desire to defray its research and development costs.[68]

Research Partnerships and Joint Ventures

Organizations form research partnerships to jointly develop specific new technologies. Typically the members complement one another with different skills or resources. One common and effective combination is an established company and a start-up. Joint ventures are similar in most respects to research partnerships, but they tend to have greater permanence, and they result in entirely new companies.[69]

As we noted in Chapter 9, sometimes even powerful competitors collaborate on projects. Nestlé Health Sciences and Chi-Med, a health care group in China, established Nutrition Science Partners, a joint venture to develop and market "innovative nutritional and medicinal products derived from botanical plants." This venture brings together Nestlé's knowledge of marketing to global customers and Chi-Med's expertise in traditional Chinese medicine plus its collection of more than 50,000 extracts from 1,200 different herbal plants.[70]

> Sometimes even direct competitors collaborate on projects.

The Digital World

BYOD and BYOA Policies

Most employees view their mobile devices as indispensable tools for both fun and work activities. Today, many firms allow employees to use their personal smartphones and tablets for work-related activities. However, as with so many things, both advantages and disadvantages come from adopting a *bring your own device* (*BYOD*) policy:[71]

Employee attitudes toward security matter, too.[73] A recent study found that 70 percent of Millennials "admitted to bringing outside applications into the enterprise in violation of IT policies, compared to just 31 percent of Baby Boomers."[74]

Mobile devices and boundaryless work are here to stay. A major goal for managers will continue to

Advantages	Disadvantages
1. Reduces a company's equipment costs.	1. Increases risk of security breaches and data loss.
2. Reduces training time because employee knows device.	2. Increases cost of supporting various devices.
3. Improves employee job satisfaction and morale.	3. Shifts purchase cost of devices to employees.
4. Boosts innovation as new applications are used.	4. Enables non-work-related activities.

A related trend known as *bring your own app* (*BYOA*) is when employees use their own applications for work-related purposes. For example, employees may find that transferring large files via Dropbox is faster and easier than using their company e-mail accounts. Though good for employee morale and innovation, unsecured devices and applications are vulnerable to security threats like hacking, lost data, or theft of the device.[72]

be how to balance employee independence and innovation with effective security policies.

1. Do you think the advantages of BYOD policies outweigh the disadvantages? Why or why not?
2. As a manager, what are two rules you would place on employee personal device use? Explain your thinking.

Acquiring a Technology Owner

If a company lacks a needed technology but wants to acquire proprietary ownership, one option is to purchase the company that owns it. This transaction can take a number of forms, from outright purchase of the entire company to a minority interest sufficient to gain access to the technology. Over the past few years, Facebook has purchased several privately owned tech companies to fulfill its growth strategy.[75] Among these acquisitions were Oculus, Snapchat, and FacioMetrics. These moves gave Facebook instant ownership of virtual reality technology, a popular image messaging and multimedia mobile app, and facial recognition developer tools.

Choosing among these alternatives becomes easier by asking these basic questions:

1. Is it important (and possible) in terms of competitive advantage for the technology to remain proprietary?
2. Are the time, skills, and resources for internal development available?
3. Is the technology readily available outside the company?

As Exhibit 17.6 illustrates, the answers to these questions guide the manager to the most appropriate acquisition options.

If managers decide to acquire a company, they take additional steps to ensure that the acquisition will make sense for the long term. They try to make sure that key employees will remain with the firm instead of leaving and taking essential technical expertise with them. As with any large investment, managers carefully assess whether the financial benefits of the acquisition justify the purchase price.

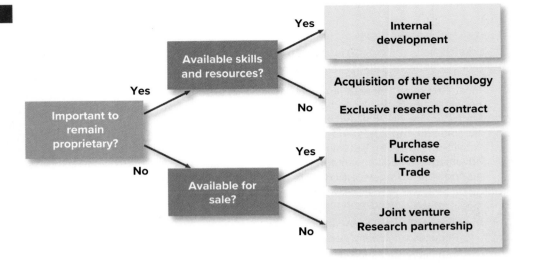

EXHIBIT 17.6
Technology Acquisition
Options

Technology and Managerial Roles

LO 17-6 Define key roles in managing technology.

chief information officer (CIO)

Executive in charge of information technology strategy and development.

Within organizations, technology traditionally was the responsibility of vice presidents for research and development. These executives are responsible for corporate and divisional R&D laboratories; typically their jobs have a functional orientation. But increasingly executives with technology responsibilities hold the prestigious position of **chief information officer (CIO)**, often called the chief technology officer (CTO).

The CIO is a senior position at the corporate level with broad, integrative responsibilities. CIOs help ensure adequate cybersecurity measures are in place; coordinate the technological efforts of the various business units; identify ways that technology can support the company's strategy; supervise new technology development; and assess the technological implications of major strategic initiatives such as acquisitions, new ventures, and strategic alliances. They also lead their organization's information technology (IT) group.[76]

Particularly when organizations highly value the agility resulting from continuous learning, this position is called *chief innovation officer,* another variation of the CIO or CTO. Whatever the C-level title, this officer ensures that technology advances in line with the company's strategy, and that ideas and knowledge flow freely between R&D, managers, and other employees.[77]

Without the CIO's integrative role, different departments could adopt different technology tools and standards, leading to much higher equipment and maintenance expense and difficulties in connecting the different parts of the organization. And because technologists often have very specialized expertise, managers without such expertise would find it difficult to supervise them effectively. A CIO can help managers ensure that the work technologists do is coordinated and aligned with their business goals.

Chief technology officers also perform an important boundary role: They work directly with outside organizations. For example, they work with universities funding research to stay abreast of technical developments, and with regulatory agencies to ensure compliance with regulations, identify trends, and influence the regulatory process.

Sophie Vandebroek, chief technology officer and president of the innovation group of Xerox, took on this role with the goal of making Xerox's systems simpler, speedier, smaller, smarter, more secure, and socially responsible—what she calls the "six S's."

nesquik007/Shutterstock

In addition to the entrepreneurs who invent new products or find new ways to deliver old products, other key technology roles are the technical innovator, product champion, and executive champion.[78]

Technical innovators develop the new technology or have the skills needed to install and operate it. They possess the requisite technical skills but not always the time or the managerial skills needed to push the idea forward and secure acceptance in the organization.

This is where the product champion gets involved, because introducing new technology requires someone to promote the idea. The **product champion**—sometimes at some professional risk—promotes the idea seeking support. The champion can be a high-level manager but often is not. If the champion lacks the needed power and financial resources to act independently, she or he must convince people who have such authority to support the innovation. In other words, product champions must get sponsorship.

Sponsorship comes from the **executive champion**, who has the status, authority, and financial resources to support the project and protect the product champion. Without this support and protection, the product champion, and thus the new technology, could fail.

technical innovator

A person who develops a new technology or has the key skills to install and operate the technology.

product champion

A person who promotes a new technology throughout the organization in an effort to obtain acceptance of and support for it.

executive champion

An executive who supports a new technology and protects the product champion.

Organizing for Innovation

Successful innovation is much more than a great idea. A Boston Consulting Group study found that lack of good ideas is hardly ever the obstacle to profitable innovation. Far more often, ideas fail to generate financial returns because the organization isn't set up to innovate.

One requirement for innovation is to find new developments from external sources that can bring lasting value. Another is overcoming internal resistance (a "not invented here" mindset) and reluctance to change (discussed in the final chapter) in order to apply the new technologies to complement or enhance internal processes.[79] Alternatively, Exhibit 17.7 shows that innovation has a chance to flourish when constructive values are in place, when

LO 17-7 Describe the characteristics of innovative organizations.

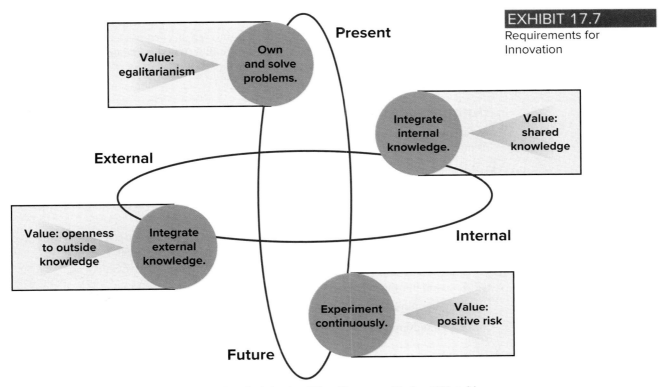

EXHIBIT 17.7

Requirements for Innovation

SOURCE: Leonard Barton, Dorothy, "The Factory as Learning Laboratory," *Sloan Management Review,* 1992, p. 34.

the organization integrates internal and external knowledge, and when people are encouraged to solve problems and to experiment continuously.

> Creative ideas can fail to generate financial returns because the organization isn't ready to innovate.

In Chapter 9 we described learning organizations—companies that excel at solving problems, seeking and finding new approaches, and sharing knowledge throughout the organization. Learning organizations are well positioned to develop useful innovations.

Recalling from Chapter 9, some innovations *exploit existing capabilities*—to improve production speed or product quality, for example. Other innovations *explore new knowledge,* seeking to develop new products or services.[80] Ambidexterity—engaging both innovation processes—is a very worthy aspiration. Innovative learning organizations use their strengths to improve their operations and thus their bottom lines, plus encourage people to explore new possibilities that will ensure their long-term competitiveness.

Unleashing Creativity

3M has a strong orientation toward intrapreneurship, and derives a substantial amount of its revenues from new products. 3M, Google, Apple, and IBM have proud histories of producing many great new technologies and products. What sets these and other continuous innovators apart? One thing they have in common is a culture that encourages innovation.[81]

Consider the 3M story from the early 1920s about inventor Francis G. Okie. Okie dreamed up the idea of using sandpaper instead of razor blades for shaving. The aim was to

> Failure, managed properly, spurs learning, growth, and future successes.

reduce the risk of nicks and avoid sharp instruments. The idea failed, but rather than being punished for the failure, Okie was encouraged to champion other ideas, which included 3M's first blockbuster success: waterproof sandpaper. That's just one example of a culture that permits well-intended efforts that "fail."

As counterintuitive as it may seem at first blush, celebrating good-faith flops can be vital to the innovation process.[82] Failure, managed properly, spurs learning, growth, and future successes. Innovative companies have many balls in the air at all times, with many people trying many new ideas. Most are strikeouts, but through this process a few home runs turn a company into an innovative star. This management perspective and approach fosters creative thinking and innovative efforts throughout the ranks. Exhibit 17.8 summarizes the most essential activities that enhance innovation.

Bureaucracy Busting

Bureaucracy is an enemy of innovation. Although it helps maintain orderliness and gain efficiencies, it also can work directly against innovation. Developing new technologies requires a fluid and flexible (organic) structure that does not restrict thought and action.

To balance innovation with other business goals, companies often can establish special temporary project structures that are isolated from the rest of the organization and allowed

Bottom Line
Bureaucracy busting encourages innovation. *Name three ways to bust bureaucracy.*

EXHIBIT 17.8
Elements Essential to Innovation

- **Experimenting** with new ideas and drawing on data to inform decisions.
- **Removing obstacles** throughout the company so innovation can occur.
- **Keeping up** with changing customer expectations and new technologies.
- **Collaborating** across boundaries to see challenges from multiple perspectives.
- **Implementing** by aligning vision and execution.

SOURCE: Schwab, K., "Ideo Studied Innovation in 100+ Companies—Here's What It Found," *Fast Codesign,* March 3, 2017, www.fastcodesign.com.

to operate under different rules. These units go by many names, including skunkworks (Chapter 7), greenhouses, and reserves. At General Motors, former chief talent officer Michael Arena launched Innovation Xchange Lab. The lab's goal was to "Connect employees and ideas across the business to amplify impact." The ultimate goal of these interactions was to inspire new innovations.[83]

To foster an innovative culture, software maker Intuit created Innovation Lab. The company encourages employees to spend 10 percent of their time working on activities they choose personally—developing creative new product ideas they feel passionate about, or simply devoting company time to learning about new technologies. Intuit also sponsors idea jams—one-day events, four times per year, when employees with an idea assemble their own development teams.[84] The excitement of Innovation Lab and idea jams motivates Intuit employees to pursue innovations such as the mobile version of QuickBooks Online, GoPayment, and ViewMyPaycheck.[85]

Design Thinking

Many organizations now use **design thinking**, a human-centered approach to innovation that integrates customer needs, the potential of technology, and the requirements for business success.[86] Championed by the Institute of Design at Stanford University, design thinking relies on "close, almost anthropological observation of people to gain insight into problems that may not be articulated yet."[87] Applying design thinking processes can help develop an organizational culture that is more customer-centric, collaborative, and open to uncertainty, risk, and experimentation.[88]

IDEO, the global design firm that uses design thinking with clients, views the process as a "system of overlapping spaces rather than a sequence of orderly steps."[89] The company defines the three interrelated spaces this way: (1) *inspiration* is the motivating problem or solution; (2) *ideation* is the process of generating, developing, and testing ideas; and (3) *implementation* is the path that leads from the project stage into customers' lives. The problem-solving process is not linear but rather moves iteratively, in and out of these spaces.

Traditionally, when a company wanted to redesign or create a new product, it would use customer focus groups to provide feedback on projects already under development.[90] Design thinking differs by starting with developing a thorough understanding (through direct observation) of current and potential customers. Design teams, consisting of people with diverse expertise (engineering, anthropology, design, marketing, and so forth), work together to identify "what people want and need in their lives and what they like or dislike about the way particular products are made, packaged, marketed, sold, and supported."[91] Experts like Jeanne Liedtka and Tim Ogilvie have developed prominent practical applications.[92]

Health care provider Kaiser Permanente used design thinking to improve the process by which nursing shifts change at its hospitals. A core project team, consisting of a strategist (former nurse), a technology expert, a process designer, designers from IDEO, and others, observed that nurses at four hospitals spent 45 minutes of each shift changeover discussing patient status. Depending on the hospital, nurses used different methods to exchange and record patient information. Some nurses, despite the time spent, missed or failed to relay important patient information.

The project team brainstormed and prototyped potential solutions for improving the changeover process. After evaluating the options, the team decided that (1) the arriving and departing nurses would exchange

design thinking

A human-centered approach to problem solving and solution finding that is based on nonlinear iterations of inspiration, ideation, and implementation.

James Leynse/Corbis/Getty Images

information in front of their patients (instead of at the nurses' station), and (2) new easy-to-use software would enable nurses to check notes from the previous shifts and enter new notes. This cut in half the average time between a nurse's arrival and first contact with patients, and increased nurses' job satisfaction. Kaiser introduced the new program in all of its health care facilities and established a new innovation center based on design thinking to continuously improve the quality of patient care.[93]

LO 17-8 Describe the characteristics of successful development projects.

---

development project

A focused organizational effort to create a new product or process via technological advances.

Implementing Development Projects

A powerful tool for managing technology and innovations is the **development project**:[94] a focused organizational effort to create a new product or process via technological advances.

Development projects typically feature a special cross-functional team working together on an overall concept or idea. The development teams interact frequently with suppliers and customers, complicating their work but strengthening the final product. Due to urgency and strategic importance, most development teams work under intense pressures.

Development projects have multiple benefits. They create new products and processes, plus cultivate skills and knowledge useful for future endeavors. Thus, the capabilities that companies gain from development projects frequently can be turned into a source of competitive advantage. When Ford launched a development project to design an air-conditioning compressor to outperform its Japanese rival, executives discovered new processes that Ford could use in the future. Their new capability in integrated design and manufacturing helped Ford reduce costs and lead times for other projects. Thus organizational learning is one criterion for evaluating project benefits.

To achieve their full potential benefit, development projects should build on core capabilities; have a guiding vision about what must be accomplished and why; have a committed team; strive for continuous improvement; and ensure integrated, coordinated efforts across all units.

Technology, Job Design, and Human Resources

Adopting a new technology may require changes in job design. Often job redesign forces people to fit into the demands of the technology to maximize operational efficiency. But this often backfires, because it neglects the human part of the productivity equation. Social relationships and the positive human aspects of work may suffer, reducing overall performance.

sociotechnical systems

An approach to job design that attempts to redesign tasks to optimize operation of a new technology while preserving employees' interpersonal relationships and other human aspects of the work.

The **sociotechnical systems** approach to work redesign addresses this problem directly. This approach redesigns tasks to jointly optimize the social and technical efficiencies of work. Beginning in 1949 with studies of new coal-mining technologies, the sociotechnical systems approach used small, self-regulating work groups.[95] Today's trends in bureaucracy bashing, lean and flat organizations, self-managed teams, and an empowered workforce are logical extensions of the sociotechnical philosophy.

Technology can limit employees' responsibilities and "de-skill" the workforce, thus turning people into servants of the technology. Alternatively, managers can select and train people to master the technology, achieve great things, and improve the quality of work lives. Technology, managed smartly,[96] can empower people as it improves a company's competitiveness.[97]

Taken as a whole, these considerations provide guidelines for managing the strategic and organizational issues associated with technology and innovation. The issues are relevant whether a company is simply automating an activity or, as in the case of Tesla Motors, entering a new high-tech business (see "Management in Action: Onward"). In our final chapter, we expand on these processes by discussing leading change, learning and adapting as we go, and shaping our futures.

Management in Action

COMPETITION AND INNOVATION IN THE RACE FOR SPACE

Have you ever wanted to see Mars up close? Elon Musk, the entrepreneur behind SpaceX, hopes to land a manned craft on Mars by 2024. His company reached a milestone of spacecraft reusability in 2017 with the first successful relaunch of an orbital-class rocket.

Musk founded SpaceX to design, manufacture, and launch rockets and spacecraft. Its mission is simple: to allow humans to live on other planets.[98] Musk sees humanity facing two alternate futures: to stay on Earth forever and face eventual extinction due to climate change or "to become a spacefaring civilization and a multi-planetary species." He's determined to make the latter goal achievable "in our lifetimes."

Despite some initial failures, including an unmanned rocket that exploded on the launchpad in 2016, SpaceX has won NASA's praise for undertaking the $12 billion effort to support "a sustainable human presence on Mars." The first ship planned for a Mars landing will carry 100 to 200 passengers and be nearly twice as long as a Boeing 747. It will refuel from other ships remaining in Earth's orbit, but it may be able to synthesize its own fuel for return journeys by transforming water and carbon dioxide on Mars. Reusability and self-fueling capabilities are important, not only for ensuring the sustainability of the craft but also to help reduce the price of passage.

Musk and SpaceX have been working on this project for nearly two decades now, in which time new technologies have emerged, many from other start-ups in the space exploration market. Relativity Space, for example, is organizing for innovation, attracting top talent from Amazon's Blue Origin, Waymo, and Musk's firms, Tesla and SpaceX.[99] Under the direction of co-founder and CEO Tim Ellis, Relativity Space makes rockets with 3D printing technology. Says Ellis, "Other companies, by our estimates, are 3D-printing less than 1% of their parts, and we're looking at achieving 95% by the end of 2020."[100]

Ellis started Relativity Space because, despite the ventures of SpaceX and other organizations, no one had "innovated on the fundamental manufacturing problems that the aerospace has dealt with."[101] Because 3D printing is so much cheaper and faster than traditional manufacturing, Relativity Space may be able eventually to make rockets in days instead of years.

- Is Relativity Space a prospector, a defender, or an analyzer firm? How did you draw your conclusion?
- Check in on Relativity Space. Is this a start-up that is continuing to make progress toward its innovative vision? Or have internal and external obstacles impeded its progress?

KEY TERMS

chief information officer (CIO), p. 542

design thinking, p. 545

development project, p. 546

disruptive innovation, p. 531

executive champion, p. 543

innovation, p. 526

make-or-buy decision, p. 538

product champion, p. 543

sociotechnical systems, p. 546

technical innovator, p. 543

technology, p. 526

technology audit, p. 534

technology life cycle, p. 527

RETAINING WHAT YOU LEARNED

In Chapter 17, you learned that different forces, like scientific knowledge and capital resources, encourage development of new technologies. New technologies follow a predictable life cycle. Companies adopt technology at different times. Some desire to be first movers while others prefer to be followers. Technology can be managed for competitive advantage and used to support a firm's low-cost or differentiation strategy. Selecting an appropriate technology strategy depends on the degree to which the technology supports the organization's competitive requirements. A company assesses its technology needs by benchmarking, or comparing, the technologies it employs with those of both competitors and noncompetitors. New technologies can be acquired through acquisition and other means, or developed internally. People play many roles in managing technology such as chief information officer, entrepreneur, technical innovator, product champion, and executive champion. Innovative organizations establish cultures that support creativity and intrapreneurship. Successful development projects share characteristics like building on core capabilities, having a guiding vision of what needs to be achieved, and having a committed team.

LO 17-1   List the types of processes that spur development of new technologies.

- Forces that compel the emergence of a new technology include (1) a need for the technology, (2) the requisite scientific knowledge, (3) the technical convertibility of this knowledge, (4) the resources to fund development, and (5) the entrepreneurial insight and initiative to pull the components together.

LO 17-2   Describe how technologies proceed through a life cycle.

- New technologies follow a predictable life cycle. First, a workable idea about how to meet a market need is developed into a product innovation. Early progress can be slow.
- Eventually a dominant design emerges as the market accepts the technology, and further refinements to the technology result from process innovations.
- As the technology begins to approach both the theoretical limits to its performance potential and market saturation, growth slows and the technology matures. At this point, the technology can remain stable or be replaced by new technology.

LO 17-3   Discuss ways to manage technology for competitive advantage.

- Adopters of new technologies are categorized according to the timing of their adoption: innovators, early adopters, the early majority, the late majority, and laggards.
- Technology leadership offers many first-mover advantages but also poses significant disadvantages. The same is true for followership.
- Technology that helps improve efficiency will support a low-cost strategy, whereas technologies that help make products more distinctive or unique support a differentiation strategy.
- Determining an appropriate technology strategy depends on the degree to which the technology supports the organization's competitive requirements. If a technology leadership strategy is preferred, management should consider the company's ability (skills, resources, and commitment) to deal with the risks and uncertainties of leadership.

LO 17-4   Summarize how to assess technology needs.

- Assessing a company's technology needs begins by benchmarking, or comparing, the technologies it employs with those of both competitors and noncompetitors. Benchmarking should be done on a global basis to understand practices used worldwide.
- Technology scanning helps identify emerging technologies and those still under development in an effort to project their eventual competitive impact.

LO 17-5   Identify alternative methods of pursuing technological innovation.

- New technologies can be acquired or developed. Options include internal development, purchase, contracted development, licensing, trading, research partnerships and joint ventures, and acquisition.
- The approach used depends on the existing availability of the technology; the skills, resources, and time available; and the importance of keeping the technology proprietary.

LO 17-6   Define key roles in managing technology.

- Many roles contribute to technology management. The chief information officer can go by other titles as well and has broad, integrative responsibility for technological innovation.
- The entrepreneur is the person who recognizes and pursues the competitive potential of the technology.
- Technical innovators develop or install and operate the technology.
- A product champion promotes the new idea(s) to gain support within the organization.
- The executive champion is the person providing authority and resources to support the project.

LO 17-7   Describe the characteristics of innovative organizations.

- Organizing for innovation involves unleashing the creative energies of employees while directing their efforts toward meeting market needs in a timely manner.
- Companies can unleash creativity by establishing a culture that encourages intrapreneurship, accepts failure as a sign of innovation, and reinforces innovation.
- The organization's structure should balance process controls with a flexibility that allows innovation to take place. Development projects provide an opportunity for cross-functional teamwork aimed at innovation.
- Job design should consider and attempt to optimize social relationships as well as technical efficiencies.

LO 17-8   Describe the characteristics of successful development projects.

- For development projects to achieve fullest benefit, they should (1) build on core capabilities; (2) have a guiding vision about what must be accomplished and why; (3) have a committed team; (4) instill a philosophy of continuous improvement; and (5) generate integrated, coordinated efforts across all relevant teams and units.

DISCUSSION QUESTIONS

1. According to Francis Bacon, "A wise man will make more opportunities than he finds." What does this have to do with technology and innovation? What does it have to do with competitive advantage?

2. What examples of technological innovation can you identify? What forces led to the commercialization of the science behind those technologies? Did the capability exist before the market demand, or was the demand there before the technology was available?

3. Thomas Edison once said that most innovations are 10 percent inspiration and 90 percent perspiration. How does this match what you know about technology life cycles?

4. Why would a company choose to follow rather than lead technological innovations? Is the potential advantage of technological leadership greater when innovations are occurring rapidly, or is it better in this case to follow?

5. If you were in the grocery business, whom would you benchmark for technological innovations? What could you possibly learn from companies outside the industry?

6. Think about the key roles in technology management. Which ones appeal to you most, and how can you learn the necessary skills?

7. Among those same roles, how and why might conflicts arise? And how would you deal with them?

8. Think about an employer you are familiar with, or your school. How would you describe it using the concepts in this chapter? Where and how could it become more effective?

EXPERIENTIAL EXERCISES

17.1   Technology Life Cycle

OBJECTIVES

To explore the different stages of the technology life cycle.

INSTRUCTIONS

Refer back to the technology life cycle in Exhibit 17.2. Review each product or technology listed below and indicate whether it is in the first, second, or third stage of the cycle.

STAGES

Stage 1: A new technology is created to address a need. Competitors experiment with operational designs and product characteristics. Progress is slow. The rate of product innovation is high.

Stage 2: As initial problems are resolved and a dominant design emerges, technology is refined through process innovations. Efficiencies and cost competitiveness are pursued.

Stage 3: The technology reaches the limit of its performance capabilities and usage. In this mature stage, development slows and production becomes increasingly costly.

Product or Technology	Stage 1	Stage 2	Stage 3
Apple Watch	_____	_____	_____
Twitter	_____	_____	_____
Microsoft Windows	_____	_____	_____
Google self-driving car	_____	_____	_____
McGraw-Hill eBook	_____	_____	_____

17.2   Innovation for the Future

OBJECTIVES

To look ahead into the future.

INSTRUCTIONS

Choose a partner. Together, develop an innovative product or service that will be popular in the year 2025. As you develop your product or service, ask yourselves the following questions:

1. What trends lead you to believe that this product or service will be successful?

2. What current technologies, services, or products will your idea replace?

Present your idea to the class for discussion.

Concluding Case

INNOVATING AT WORLDWIDE GAMES

Worldwide Games develops and markets gaming software and devices. Game enthusiasts are always on the lookout for game-playing experiences that are more intense and lifelike, so Worldwide is constantly looking to innovate. The company has developed several advances in screen resolution, processor speed, new kinds of controllers, creative story lines, and more. Its console division focuses on hardware technology, and its online division focuses on powerful new gaming software, often involving elaborate story lines played by subscribers around the world. Continuous innovation in both divisions keeps Worldwide on par with its major competitors.

In recent years, two related areas of technology have fueled the growth of Worldwide and its competitors: social networking and the ability of broadband Internet connections to deliver fast audio and video streams for playing elaborate games online. 5G will likely further accelerate this growth. Worldwide's console division has adopted technology by inviting purchasers of its latest console to join its Players Network. Those who join the Players Network can use their console to play online with other members anywhere in the network. In addition, Worldwide's online division continues to push the limits of online gaming.

Because a necessary component of any Worldwide game is for players to register and pay a fee or join the Players Network, Worldwide collects not only money from customers but also information about them. That system came under real risk when hackers recently broke into first the Players Network database and then the registration records of Worldwide Online's subscribers.

As soon as the company detected an intrusion into the Players Network, it shut down the network. When the company's security employees realized they couldn't immediately prevent intrusions within a day or two, Worldwide announced that hackers had obtained the names and possibly the credit card numbers of its tens of millions of network members. Until the problem was fixed, they would be able to play games from disks loaded into their consoles but would not be able to use the network.

Fixing the problem, which took about a month, included adding firewalls and encryption to the existing security measures. Afterward the company reopened the network, apologized to consumers, and offered a month of free access to paid services. Returning customers had to download upgraded security software before they could resume play. The entire incident cost the company hundreds of millions of dollars for the investigation, upgrades, and lost sales.

As operations returned to normal, Worldwide announced that it had hired a chief information security officer. This manager reports to the company's chief information officer, who reports to the chief transformation officer, who reports to the chief executive officer.

DISCUSSION QUESTIONS

1. Is Worldwide Games a technology leader or a technology follower? What are the risks and benefits of staking out this position?

2. What opportunities might Worldwide be missing by not having its chief information officer report directly to the CEO?

3. What makes innovation important for Worldwide? Following the hacking incident, how might bureaucracy be expected to interfere with innovation? How should Worldwide engage in bureaucracy busting without compromising security?

ENDNOTES

1. Ed Owald, "Here's Everything You Need to Know about the Boring Company," *Digital Trends,* February 26, 2019, https://www.digitaltrends.com/cool-tech/what-is-the-boring-company/.
2. Charles Duhigg, "Dr. Elon and Mr. Musk: Life Inside Tesla's Production Hell," *Wired,* December 13, 2018, https://www.wired.com/story/elon-musk-tesla-life-inside-gigafactory/.
3. Sean Czarnecki, "Timeline of a Crisis: Tesla and the Most Expensive Tweet Ever," *PR Week,* October 1, 2018, https://www.prweek.com/article/1494535/timeline-crisis-tesla-expensive-tweet-ever; Victor Reklaitis, "Elon Musk Appears to Smoke Marijuana during an Interview," *MarketWatch,* September 7, 2018, https://www.marketwatch.com/story/elon-musk-appears-to-smoke-marijuana-during-an-interview-2018-09-07-51033514.
4. Kelly Weill, "Elon Musk Hyperloop Dreams Slam into Cold Hard Reality," *Daily Beast,* March 29, 2019, https://www.thedailybeast.com/elon-musk-hyperloop-dreams-slam-into-cold-hard-reality.
5. Tim Higgins, "Tesla Reports Loss, as Elon Musk Talks of Raising Capital," *The Wall Street Journal,* April 24, 2019, https://www.wsj.com/articles/tesla-reports-loss-amid-stuggles-delivering-model-3-cars-11556141829?mod=hp_lead_pos4.
6. W. McKinley, S. Latham, and M. Braun, "Organizational Decline and Innovation: Turnarounds and Downward Spirals," *Academy of Management Review* 39 (2014), pp. 88–110.
7. D. Patel, "Human Machine Interface Example in Industry," *The Automization,* October 7, 2018, www.theautomization.com.
8. R. A. Burgelman, M. A. Maidique, and S. C. Wheelwright, *Strategic Management of Technology and Innovation* (New York: McGraw-Hill, 2000); Panagiotis Ganotakis and James H. Love, "The Innovation Value Chain in New Technology-Based Firms," *Journal of Product Innovation Management* 29, no. 5 (September 2012), pp. 839–60.
9. D. C. L. Prestwood and P. A. Schumann Jr., "Revitalize Your Organization," *Executive Excellence* 15, no. 2 (February 1998),

p . 16; C. Y. Baldwin and K. B. Clark, "Managing in an Age of Modularity," *Harvard Business Review* 75, no. 5 (September–October 1997), pp. 84–93; S. Gopalakrishnan, P. Bierly, and E. H. Kessler, "A Reexamination of Product and Process Innovations Using a Knowledge-Based View," *Journal of High Technology Management Research* 10, no. 1 (Spring 1999), pp. 147–66; J. Pullin, "Bombardier Commands Top Marks," *Professional Engineering* 13, no. 3 (July 5, 2000), pp. 40–46; M. Johnson, C. Christensen, and H. Kagermann, "Reinventing Your Business Model," *Harvard Business Review,* December 2008, pp. 50–59; C. M. Christensen, *The Innovator's Dilemma* (Boston: Harvard Business Publishing, 1997); C. M. Christensen, S. D. Anthony, and E. A. Roth, *Seeing What's Next* (Boston: Harvard Business Publishing, 2004).

10. M. Sawhney, R. C. Wolcott, and I. Arroniz, "The 12 Different Ways for Companies to Innovate," *MIT Sloan Management Review* 47, no. 3 (Spring 2006), pp. 75–81; Julian Birkinshaw, Gary Hamel, and Michael J. Mol, "Management Innovation," *Academy of Management Review* 33 (October 2008), pp. 825–45.

11. G. P. Pisano, *The Development Factory: Unlocking the Potential of Process Innovation* (Boston: Harvard Business School Press, 1996); R. Leifer, C. M. McDermott, G. C. O'Connor, L. S. Peters, M. Rice, and R. W. Veryzer, *Radical Innovation: How Mature Companies Can Outsmart Upstarts* (Cambridge MA: Harvard Business School Press, 2000).

12. A. Trowbridge, "Evolution of the Phone: From the First Call to the Next Frontier," *CBS News,* December 16, 2014, www.cbsnews.com.

13. Tom Loeffert, "Can Technology Remove Bias from the Workplace?" *Digitalist Magazine,* February 19, 2018, https://www.digitalistmag.com/future-of-work/2018/02/19/can-technology-remove-bias-from-workplace-05869340.

14. Hrvoje Bulat, "Organizational Network Analysis: The Missing Piece of Digital Transformation," *Digital HR Tech,* https://www.digitalhrtech.com/organizational-network-analysis-the-missing-piece-of-digital-transformation/, accessed April 29, 2019.

15. Mary Young, "More Than a Feeling: Measuring Workplace Inclusion," *Work Design Magazine,* March 28, 2019, https://workdesign.com/2019/03/more-than-a-feeling-measuring-workplace-inclusion/.

16. H. M. O'Neill, R. W. Pounder, and A. K. Buchholtz, "Patterns in the Diffusion of Strategies across Organizations: Insights from the Innovation, Diffusion Literature," *Academy of Management Review* 23, no. 1 (January 1998), pp. 98–114; E. M. Rogers, *Diffusion of Innovations* (New York: Free Press, 1995); B. Guilhon, ed., *Technology and Markets for Knowledge: Knowledge Creation, Diffusion and Exchange within a Growing Economy,* Economics of Science, Technology and Innovation 22 (Dordrecht, Netherlands: Kluwer Academic Publishing, 2000).

17. UNESCO website, "The UN World Water Development Report 2015, Water for a Sustainable World," http://www.unesco.org/new/en/natural-sciences/environment/water/wwap/wwdr/2015-water-for-a-sustainable-world/, accessed April 29, 2019.

18. Organization website, http://www.sarvajal.com, accessed April 29, 2019.

19. Organization website, http://www.sarvajal.com, accessed April 29, 2019.

20. M. E. Porter, *Competitive Strategy* (New York: Free Press, 1980).

21. C. M. Christensen, S. D. Anthony, and E. A. Roth, *Seeing What's Next* (Boston: Harvard Business Publishing, 2004); Clayton Christensen, "Key Concepts: Disruptive Innovation," http://www.claytonchristensen.com; Innosight, "Expertise: Driving New Growth through Disruptive Innovation," http://www.innosight.com; Matthew Yglesias, "Stop 'Disrupting' Everything," *Slate,* May 1, 2013, http://www.slate.com.

22. D. Newman, "5 Emerging Technologies That 5G Will Positively Disrupt," *Forbes,* August 14, 2018, www.forbes.com.

23. R. Prevett, "18 Disruptive Technology Trends for 2018," *Disruption Hub,* January 11, 2018, www.disruptionhub.com.

24. S. A. Zahra, S. Nash, and D. J. Bickford, "Transforming Technological Pioneering in Competitive Advantage," *Academy of Management Executive* 9, no. 1 (1995), pp. 17–31; M. Sadowski and A. Roth, "Technology Leadership Can Pay Off," *Research Technology Management* 42, no. 6 (November–December 1999), pp. 32–33.

25. L. Luk, "Apple Plans Force of Touch Technology for New iPhones," *The Wall Street Journal,* March 11, 2015, http://www.wsj.com.

26. Company website, "3M: 2018 Sustainability Report," www.3m.com, accessed April 23, 2019.

27. E. Sagonowsky, "Top 10 Drugs Losing Exclusivity in 2019," *Fierce Pharma,* March 4, 2019, www.fiercepharma.com.

28. E. Sagonowsky, "Top 10 Drugs Losing Exclusivity in 2019," *Fierce Pharma,* March 4, 2019, www.fiercepharma.com.

29. C. Trudell, Y. Hagiwara, and J. Ma, "Humans Replacing Robots Herald Toyota's Vision of Future," *Bloomberg Business,* April 7, 2014, http://www.bloomberg.com; M. Imai and G. Kaizen, *A Commonsense, Low-Cost Approach to Management* (New York: McGraw-Hill, 1997); M. Imai and G. Kaizen, *The Key to Japan's Competitive Success* (New York: McGraw-Hill, 1986).

30. Press release, "Tufts CSDD Assessment of Cost to Develop and Win Marketing Approval for a New Drug," Tufts Center for the Study of Drug Development, March 10, 2016, www.csdd.tufts.edu; "2015 Profile: Biopharmaceutical Research Industry," www.phrma-docs.org, accessed May 14, 2017; D. Lazarus, "An Insider's View of Generic-Drug Pricing," *Los Angeles Times,* March 25, 2013, http://www.latimes.com.

31. See Matthew Semadeni and Brian S. Anderson, "The Follower's Dilemma: Innovation and Imitation in the Professional Services Industry," *Academy of Management Journal* 53 (October 2010), pp. 1175–93.

32. S. Rodriguez, "Snap Adds TikTok, One of the Hottest Social Networking Apps, to Its List of Competitors," *CNBC,* February 6, 2019, www.cnbc.com.

33. Company website, "VitalPatch: Shattering the Paradigm of Patient Care," www.vitalconnect.com, accessed May 14, 2017.

34. Company website, Vital Connect, https://vitalconnect.com, accessed April 24, 2019.

35. P. A. Geroski, "Models of Technology Diffusion," *Research Policy* 29, no. 4/5 (April 2000), pp. 603–25; L. A. Thomas, "Adoption Order of New Technologies in Evolving Markets," *Journal of Economic Behavior & Organization* 38, no. 4 (April 1999), pp. 453–82.

36. K. Safavi and F. Dare, "Health Care Could Save the U.S. Billions Each Year," *Harvard Business Review,* April 3, 2018, www.hbr.org.

37. "78% of Americans Support This Revolutionary Healthcare Technology, but Only 21% Have Tried It," *Fox Business News,* March 2, 2017, www.foxbusiness.com.

38. R. E. Oligney and M. I. Economides, "Technology as an Asset," *Hart's Petroleum Engineer International* 71, no. 9 (September 1998), p . 27; C. MacKechnie, "What Are the Types of Business Technology?" *Chron,* http://smallbusiness.chron.com, accessed June 15, 2014; J. Manyika, M. Chul, J. Bughin, R. Dobbs, P. Bisson, and A. Marrs, "Disruptive Technologies: Advances That Will Transform Life, Business, and the Global Economy," *McKinsey & Company Report,* May 2013, http://www.mckinsey.com.

39. B. Marr, "Here Are 10 Industries Blockchain Is Likely to Disrupt," *Forbes,* July 18, 2018, www.forbes.com.

40. B. Marr, "Here Are 10 Industries Blockchain Is Likely to Disrupt," *Forbes,* July 18, 2018, www.forbes.com.

41. K. Panetta, "Gartner Top 10 Strategic Technology Trends for 2019," Gartner, October 15, 2018, www.gartner.com.

42. K. Panetta, "Gartner Top 10 Strategic Technology Trends for 2019," Gartner, October 15, 2018, www.gartner.com.

43. "These 5 Retail Innovations Could Actually Make You Want to Shop in a Store Again," *Entrepreneur,* May 23, 2016, www.entrepreneur.com.

44. Press release, "Neiman Marcus Opens a Multi Level Retail Experience at Hudson Yards in New York City," *PRNewswire,* March 12, 2019, www.prnewswire.com.

45. P. Grother, G. Quinn, and M. Ngan, "Face In Video Evaluation (FIVE) Face Recognition on Non-Cooperative Subjects," National Institute of Standards and Technology, March 2017, http://www.nist.gov.

46. General Electric, "GE's Dual Peizoelectric Cooling Jets (DCJ) Are Cool and Quiet," www.geglobalresearch.com, accessed May 15, 2017.

47. B. Nadell, "The Best Industrial 3D Printers Of 2019," *Business,* February 14, 2019, www.business.com.

48. A. Frakt, "Blame Technology, Not Longer Life Spans, for Health Spending Increases," *The New York Times,* January 23, 2017, www.nytimes.com.

49. A. Frakt, "Blame Technology, Not Longer Life Spans, for Health Spending Increases," *The New York Times,* January 23, 2017, www.nytimes.com.

50. "CBP, ICE HSI Report $1.2 Billion in Counterfeit Seizures in 2014," U.S. Customs and Border Protection, April 2, 2015, http://www.cbd.gov.

51. Press release, "Global Impact of Counterfeiting and Piracy Projected to Reach $2.3 Trillion by 2022," www.inta.org, accessed April 27, 2019.

52. "Merck's Keytruda Tops $2 Billion in Quarterly Sales, Shares Rise," *CNBC,* February 1, 2019, www.cnbc.com.

53. M. Baccardax, "Merck Posts In-Line Fourth-Quarter Earnings, Issues Cautious 2017 Sales Outlook," *The Street,* February 2, 2017, www.thestreet.com.

54. "Advanced Metering Infrastructure and Customer Systems," U.S. Department of Energy, September 2016, www.energy.gov.

55. L. Bondoim, "How Smart Shelf Technology Will Change Your Supermarket," *Forbes,* December 23, 2018, www.forbes.com.

56. J. Birkinshaw and K. Brewis, "Lessons from the World's Best-Known Fast-Follower: Samsung," London Business School, October 12, 2016, www.london.edu.

57. R. Reinhardt and S. Gurtner, "Differences between Early Adopters of Disruptive and Sustaining Innovations," *Journal of Business Research* 68 (2015), pp. 137–45; R. Dewan, B. Jing, and A. Seidmann, "Adoption of Internet-Based Product Customization and Pricing Strategies," *Journal of Management Information Systems* 17, no. 2 (Fall 2000), pp. 9–28; P. A. Geroski, "Models of Technology Diffusion," *Research Policy* 29, no. 4/5 (April 2000), pp. 603–25; E. M. Rogers, *Diffusion of Innovations* (New York: Free Press, 1995).

58. See the IBM Thomas J. Watson Research Center, www.ibm.com, and MIT Media Lab Research, https://www.media.mit.edu/research/?filter=groups, accessed April 27, 2019.

59. E. Von Hippel, *The Sources of Innovation* (Oxford, UK: Oxford University Press, 1994); D. Leonard, *Wellsprings of Knowledge: Building and Sustaining the Sources of Innovation* (Cambridge, MA: Harvard Business School Press, 1998); Melissa E. Graebner, Kathleen M. Eisenhardt, and Philip T. Roundy, "Success and Failure in Technology Acquisitions: Lessons for Buyers and Sellers," *Academy of Management Perspectives* 24, no. 3 (August 2010), pp. 73–92.

60. Tim Higgins, "Tesla Reports Loss, as Elon Musk Talks of Raising Capital," *The Wall Street Journal,* April 24, 2019, https://www.wsj.com/articles/tesla-reports-loss-amid-stuggles-delivering-model-3-cars-11556141829?mod=hp_lead_pos4.

61. Neal E. Boudette, "Tesla's Troubles Mount: Shuttered Showrooms and Sinking Shares," *The New York Times,* March 6, 2019, https://www.nytimes.com/2019/03/06/business/energy-environment/tesla-stock-strategy.html.

62. "Who Are Tesla's (TSLA) Main Competitors?" *Investopedia,* January 7, 2019, https://www.investopedia.com/ask/answers/120314/who-are-teslas-tsla-main-competitors.asp.

63. Mark Matousek, "10 Electric Cars That Will Challenge Tesla's Model 3," *Business Insider,* January 30, 2019, https://www.businessinsider.com/electric-cars-challenging-tesla-model-3-2018-1.

64. N. Clayton, "Israel at Center of Intel Empire," *The Wall Street Journal Tech Europe,* March 19, 2012, http://blogs.wsj.com; T. Krazit, "Intel R&D on Slow Boat to China," *CNet News,* April 16, 2007, http://news.com.

65. Company website, "EA Sports Games," EA Sports, www.easports.com, accessed April 27, 2019.

66. B. Austen, "Bringing the Coffin Industry Back from the Dead," *The Atlantic,* December 2010, www.theatlantic.com.

67. E. Von Hippel, *The Sources of Innovation* (Oxford, UK: Oxford University Press, 1995); D. Leonard, *Wellsprings of Knowledge: Building and Sustaining the Sources of Innovation* (Cambridge, MA: Harvard Business School Press, 1998).

68. N. Tajitsu and M. Shiraki, "Toyota Unlocks Its Engine Technology, Could Sell to Rivals," Reuters, December 15, 2016, www.reuters.com.

69. J. Hagedoorn, A. N. Link, and N. S. Vonortas, "Research Partnerships," *Research Policy* 29, no. 4/5 (April 2000), pp. 567–86; S.-S. Yi, "Entry, Licensing and Research Joint Ventures," *International Journal of Industrial Organization* 17, no. 1 (January 1999), pp. 1–24; Satish Nambisan and Mohanbir Sawhney, "Orchestration Processes in Network-Centric Innovation: Evidence from the Field," *Academy*

of Management Perspectives 25 (August 2011), pp. 40–57; Ulrich Lichtenthaler, "Open Innovation: Past Research, Current Debates, and Future Directions," *Academy of Management Perspectives* 25 (February 2011), pp. 75–93; Esteve Almirall and Ramon Casadesus-Masanell, "Open versus Closed Innovation: A Model of Discovery and Divergence," *Academy of Management Review* 35 (January 2010), pp. 27–47; Corey C. Phelps, "A Longitudinal Study of the Influence of Alliance Network Structure and Composition on Firm Exploratory Innovation," *Academy of Management Journal* 53 (August 2010), pp. 890–913.

70. Company website, "Key Investments," Nestlé Health Science, www.nestlehealthscience.com, accessed May 16, 2017; A. Ward and P. Waldmeir, "Chi-Med Draws on the Past for the Future," *Financial Times,* August 25, 2014, http://www.ft.com; Nestlé website, "New Partnership Gives Nestlé Health Science Access to One of the World's Leading Traditional Chinese Medicine Libraries," press release, November 28, 2012, http://www.nestle.com.

71. Elizabeth Wiese, "Bring Your Own Dilemmas: Dealing with BYOD and Security," *USA Today,* August 26, 2014, https://www.usatoday.com/story/tech/2014/08/26/byod-bring-your-own-device/14393635/.

72. Jeff Pochepan, "Employees Working on Their Personal Devices? Here's How You Can Protect Your Business Data," *Inc.,* https://www.inc.com/jeff-pochepan/employees-working-on-their-personal-devices-heres-how-you-can-protect-your-business-data.html, accessed April 29, 2019.

73. Omar Eiferman, "Millennials Don't Care about Mobile Security, and Here's What to Do about It," *Wired,* https://www.wired.com/insights/2014/09/millennials-mobile-security/, accessed April 20, 2019.

74. Angelique Kramer, "35 Cyber Security Statistics Every CIO Should Know in 2017," June 9, 2017, https://etsconnect.com/35-cyber-security-statistics-every-cio-know-2017/.

75. A. Heath, "Mark Zuckerberg Explains Facebook's Secrets for Acquiring Companies," *Business Insider,* January 18, 2017, www.businessinsider.com; K. Yeung, "Facebook Bought a Face-Tracking Startup to Help It Take on Snapchat," *Business Insider,* November 16, 2016, www.businessinsider.com.

76. C. Pellerin, "CIO Priorities Include Cybersecurity, Innovation, Retaining IT Workforce," U.S. Department of Defense, March 23, 2016, www.defense.gov; P. Arandjelovic, L. Bulin, and N. Khan, "Why CIOs Should Be Business-Strategy Partners," *McKinsey Insights and Publications,* February 2015, http://www.mckinsey.com.

77. "Information Resources: The Evolution of R&D," *Research-Technology Management,* May–June 2011, pp. 65–66; J. C. Spender and B. Strong, "Who Has Innovative Ideas? Employees," *The Wall Street Journal,* August 23, 2010, http://online.wsj.com.

78. D. L. Day, "Raising Radicals: Different Processes for Championing Innovative Corporate Ventures," *Organization Science* 5, no. 2 (May 1994), pp. 148–72; C. Siporin, "Want Speedy FDA Approval? Hire a 'Product Champion,'" *Medical Marketing & Media,* October 1993, pp. 22–28; C. Siporin, "How You Can Capitalize on Phase 3B," *Medical Marketing & Media,* October 1994, pp. 72–72; E. H. Kessler, "Tightening the Belt: Methods for Reducing Development Costs Associated with New Product Innovation," *Journal of Engineering and Technology Management* 17, no. 1 (March 2000), pp. 59–92.

79. M. Ringel, A. Taylor, and H. Zablit, "The Most Innovative Companies 2016," Boston Consulting Group, January 2017, www.bcg.com.

80. J. G. March, "Exploration and Exploitation in Organizational Learning," *Organization Science* 2, no. 1 (1991), pp. 71–87; S. C. Kang and S. A. Snell, "Intellectual Capital Architectures and Ambidextrous Learning: A Framework for Human Resource Management," *Journal of Management Studies* 46, no. 1 (2009), pp. 65–92.

81. Jeff DeGraff, "Why the 'Most Innovative Companies' Aren't," *Fortune,* March 13, 2013, http://management.fortune.com; Henry Chesbrough, "Why Bad Things Happen to Good Technology," *The Wall Street Journal,* June 19, 2012, http://online.wsj.com; Steven Levy, "Google's Larry Page on Why Moon Shots Matter," *Wired,* January 17, 2013, http://www.wired.com.

82. D. A. Fields, "How to Stop the Dumbing Down of Your Company," *Industry Week,* March 7, 2007, http://www.industryweek.com; L. K. Gundry, J. R. Kickul, and C. W. Prather, "Building the Creative Organization," *Organizational Dynamics* 22, no. 2 (Spring 1994), pp. 22–36; T. Kuczmarski, "Inspiring and Implementing the Innovation Mind-Set," *Planning Review,* September–October 1994, pp. 37–48.

83. Talent Management Exchange, "Speaker Information," http://www.talentmanagementexchange.com, accessed June 18, 2015.

84. "100 Best Companies to Work For 2012", *CNNMoney,* https://money.cnn.com/magazines/fortune/best-companies/2012/snapshots/19.html, accessed May 5, 2019.

85. See company website, "Innovation at Intuit," Intuit, www.intuit.com, accessed April 27, 2019.

86. T. Brown, "Design Thinking," *Harvard Business Review* 86, no. 6 (June 2008), pp. 84–92.

87. M. Korn and R. Silverman, "Business Education: Forget B-School, D-School Is Hot," *The Wall Street Journal*, June 7, 2012, http://www.wsj.com.

88. K. D. Elsbach and I. Stigliani, "Design Thinking and Organizational Culture: A Review and Framework for Future Research," *Journal of Management* 44 (2018), pp. 2274–2306.

89. IDEO website, "About Ideo," http://www.ideo.com, accessed July 5, 2015.

90. M. Korn and R. Silverman, "Business Education: Forget B-School, D-School Is Hot," *The Wall Street Journal*, June 7, 2012, http://www.wsj.com.

91. Source: T. Brown, "Design Thinking," *Harvard Business Review* 86, no. 6 (June 2008), pp. 84–92.

92. J. Liedtka and T. Ogilvie, *Designing for Growth: A Design Thinking Tool Kit for Managers* (New York: Columbia Business School Publishing, 2011).

93. T. Brown, "Design Thinking," *Harvard Business Review* 86, no. 6 (June 2008), pp. 84–92.

94. H. K. Bowen, K. B. Clark, C. A. Holloway, and S. C. Wheelwright, "Development Projects: The Engine of Renewal," *Harvard Business Review,* September–October 1994, pp. 110–20; C. Eden, T. Williams, and F. Ackermann, "Dismantling the Learning Curve: The Role of Disruptions on the Planning of Development Projects," *International Journal of Project Management* 16, no. 3 (June 1998), pp. 131–38; M. V. Tatikonda and S. R. Rosenthal, "Technology Novelty, Project Complexity, and Product Development Project Execution Success: A Deeper Look at Task Uncertainty in Product Innovation," *IEEE Transactions on Engineering Management* 47, no. 1 (February 2000), pp. 74–87.

95. E. Trist, "The Evolution of Sociotechnical Systems as a Conceptual Framework and as an Action Research Program," in *Perspectives on Organizational Design and Behavior,* ed. A. Van de Ven and W. F. Joyce (New York: Wiley, 1981), pp. 19–75; A. Molina, "Insights into the Nature of Technology Diffusion and Implementation: The Perspective of Sociotechnical Alignment," *Technovation* 17, nos. 11/12 (November–December 1997), pp. 601–26.

96. D. Stone, D. Deadrick, K. Lukaszewski, and R. Johnson, "The Influence of Technology on the Future of Human Resource Management," *Human Resource Management Review* 25 (2015), pp. 216–31.

97. Wayne F. Cascio and R. Montealegre, "How Technology Is Changing Work and Organizations," *Annual Review of Organizational Psychology and Organizational Behavior* 3 (2016), pp. 349–75; Lynda Aiman-Smith and Stephen G. Green, "Implementing NewManufacturing Technology: The Related Effects of Technology Characteristics and User Learning Activities," *Academy of Management Journal* 45 (April 2002), pp. 421–30; Terri L. Griffith, "Technology Features as Triggers for Sensemaking," *Academy of ManagementReview* 24 (July 1999), pp. 472–88.

98. SpaceX website, "About SpaceX," https://www.spacex.com/about, accessed April 25, 2019.

99. Michael Sheetz, "Rocket Start-Up Relativity Quadruples Resources in a Year, Adds Former SpaceX Leaders," *CNBC,* February 17, 2019, https://www.cnbc.com/2019/02/17/relativity-space-rocket-development-more-3d-printers-spacex-leaders.html.

100. Dave Mosher, "Defectors from SpaceX, Blue Origin, and Tesla Are Developing a Remarkable Technology Called 'Stargate' to Help Colonize Other Planets," *Business Insider,* October 22, 2018, https://www.businessinsider.com/relativity-space-3d-printed-rockets-mars-2018-10.

101. Dave Mosher, "Defectors from SpaceX, Blue Origin, and Tesla Are Developing a Remarkable Technology Called 'Stargate' to Help Colonize Other Planets," *Business Insider,* October 22, 2018, https://www.businessinsider.com/relativity-space-3d-printed-rockets-mars-2018-10.

CHAPTER 18
Creating and Leading Change

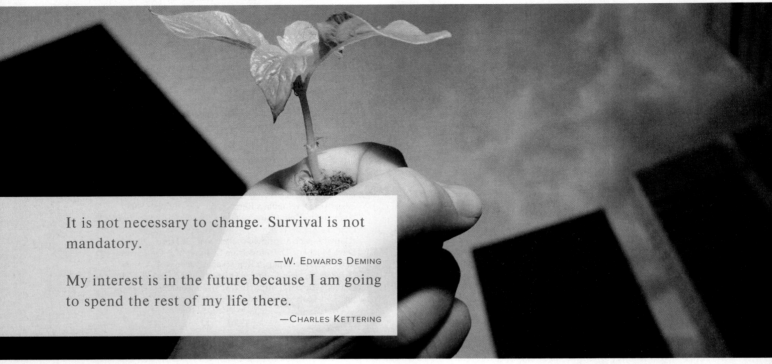

It is not necessary to change. Survival is not mandatory.

—W. Edwards Deming

My interest is in the future because I am going to spend the rest of my life there.

—Charles Kettering

Darren Greenwood/Design Pics

learning objectives

After studying Chapter 18, you will be able to:

LO 18-1 Discuss what it takes to be world class.

LO 18-2 Describe how to manage and lead change effectively.

LO 18-3 Describe strategies for creating a successful future.

chapter outline

Management in Action

SHELL OIL'S MANAGERS FACE OFF WITH INVESTORS OVER CLIMATE CHANGE

As the world grapples with global climate change, many in private industry are working to provide solutions. Because we live in an energy-dependent world and much of that energy comes from burning fossil fuels, the oil industry is under intense scrutiny. Many of the major oil companies, however, have been notoriously slow to acknowledge the existence of global climate change and even slower to mitigate carbon emissions. However, some positive changes are afoot.

Shell Oil Company, one of the world's largest oil companies, saw nearly 99 percent of its investors vote to support a motion that it report on whether its activities supported worldwide governments' goals to limit climate change. Shell responded to these and other concerns about its environmental impact by creating a New Energies Division to invest in renewable and sustainable power sources like wind, solar, and electric. New Energies's initial budget was $1.7 billion, less than 1 percent of the amount the company invested in oil and gas production, but Shell promised to grow the division. In 2019, it increased its investment in low-carbon energy to $4 billion annually and pledged to invest approximately $1.5 billion annually on renewable energy, a total that now comprises nearly 15 percent of Shell's budget.[1]

Shell isn't alone in supporting a clean energy future. More than a dozen of the world's largest oil companies formed the Oil and Gas Climate Initiative. This CEO-led voluntary initiative aims to harness the oil companies' "collective strength to lower carbon footprints of energy, industry, transportation value chains via engagements, policies, investments and deployment."[2] Thus far, the initiative has invested more than $1 billion in start-ups trying to find new ways to reduce methane leakage and to reduce and recycle carbon dioxide.[3]

ExxonMobil, perhaps the biggest climate change denier in the industry, was one of the last of the major oil companies to sign on to the initiative, in late 2018.[4] The committed dollar amount was pocket change for Exxon, and many still believe that it is merely "greenwashing." The firm's public acknowledgment of climate change as a reality that poses environmental and human risks is a reversal that came amid an avalanche of negative publicity about coverups.

> Changes like the ones demanded of fossil-fuel companies are not easy, do not happen automatically, and often require managers to reverse course and overcome serious obstacles. As you study this chapter, think about why the ability to change is both challenging and essential.

An ever-changing world is full of uncertainty and risk.[5] Now and in the foreseeable future, just a sampling of the many disruptive forces in play includes a fragile financial system, breakdowns in global trade, growing income inequality, political upheavals, environmental degradation, declining public health and education, and underperforming institutions.[6] These and other dynamic forces make it essential for organizations (and people) to cope, anticipate, adapt, and change.

Lest the preceding paragraph sound like gloom and doom, one useful perspective is to view problems as opportunities.[7] As but one example, manufacturing was presumed in recent years to be virtually dead in the United States, but global circumstances are changing, and leaders and entrepreneurs are attempting a manufacturing comeback.[8] A recent survey reported over 90 percent of American manufacturers are optimistic about the business climate.[9]

As you can imagine, now and forevermore, some organizations and people deal with change more effectively than others. The challenge for organizations is not just to produce successful new products, but to create a culture that is innovative and that builds a sustainable business. For individuals, the ability to cope with change affects their job performance, the rewards they receive,[10] their career success, and feelings they hold toward their employer.[11]

But coping with change isn't enough. Managers and their organizations need to create desired changes, and improve constantly, to achieve world-class excellence and competitive advantage into the future. For Shell and its leaders, a changing environment is something they must deal with by creating their own changes.

Becoming World Class

LO 18-1 Discuss what it takes to be world class.

Managers want, or *should* want, their organizations to perform at high levels, even to become world class.[12] Being world class requires applying the best and latest knowledge and ideas and having the ability to operate at the highest standards of any place anywhere.[13] Thus becoming world class does not mean merely improving. It means becoming one of the very best in the world at what you do.

Striving for world-class excellence might seem a lofty, unnecessary, impossible quest. But for every manager and organization, achieving excellence can serve as a stretch goal that helps one survive and succeed in a competitive world.

Becoming world class doesn't apply only to the private sector. People worry about globalization's negative effects on local communities as plants shut down and people lose their jobs. But local communities do have options—not easy ones, but doable.

World-class companies create high-value products and earn superior profits over the long run. They demolish the obsolete methods, systems, and cultures of the past that impeded their progress and apply more effective strategies, structures, technologies, and leadership processes. And as you know, companies are vehicles for accomplishing societal purposes.[14] Great leaders, collaborating with others, build enduring institutions that can compete successfully, and even serve society, on a global basis.[15]

Bottom Line

Aspire to become world class at every one of your competitive goals.
What does it mean to be world class at a goal such as quality or sustainability?

Sustainable, Great Futures

Two Stanford professors, James Collins and Jerry Porras, wrote a famous (in management circles) book titled *Built to Last* describing their studies of 18 corporations that had achieved and maintained greatness for half a century or more.[16] The companies included 3M, American Express, Disney, General Electric, Procter & Gamble, Sony, and Walmart. Over the years, these companies have been widely admired, been considered the premier institutions in their industries, and made a substantial impact on the world. Although every company goes through periodic downturns—and these are no exceptions over their long histories—these companies have consistently prevailed across the decades. They turn in extraordinary performance over the long run, rather than fleeting greatness.

The researchers sought to identify the essential characteristics of enduringly great companies. These companies have strong core values in which they believe deeply, and they communicate and live the values consistently. They are driven by stretch goals (Chapter 13), not just incremental improvements or business-as-usual goals. They change continuously, driving for progress via adaptability, experimentation, trial and error, entrepreneurial thinking, and fast action. And they do not focus on beating the competition; they focus primarily on beating themselves. They continually ask, "How can we improve ourselves to do better tomorrow than we did today?"

But underneath the action and the changes, the core values and vision remain steadfast and uncompromised. Exhibit 18.1 displays the core values of several companies that were built to last. Note that the values are not all the same. In fact, no set of common values consistently predicts success. Instead the critical factor is that great companies *have* core values, *know* what they are and what they mean, and *live* by them—year after year.

The Tyranny of the *Or*

Many companies, and individuals, are plagued by the **tyranny of the** *or*. This refers to binary thinking, the belief that things must be either A or B and cannot be both. The authors of *Built to Last* provide many common examples: beliefs that you must choose either change or stability; be conservative or bold; have control and consistency or creative freedom; do well in the short term or invest for the future; plan methodically or be opportunistic; create shareholder wealth or do good for the world; be pragmatic or idealistic.[17] Such beliefs, that only one goal but not another can be attained, often are invalid and certainly are constraining—unnecessarily so.

tyranny of the *or*

The belief that things must be either A or B and cannot be both; that only one goal and not another can be attained.

EXHIBIT 18.1
Core Ideologies in Built-to-Last Companies

3M	Innovation—"Thou shalt not kill a new product idea."
	Absolute integrity.
	Respect for individual initiative and personal growth.
	Tolerance for honest mistakes.
	Product quality and reliability.
	"Our real business is solving problems."
Sony	To experience the sheer joy that comes from the advancement, application, and innovation of technology that benefits the general public.
	To elevate the Japanese culture and national status.
	Being pioneers—not following others, but doing the impossible.
	Respecting and encouraging each individual's ability and creativity.
Walmart	"We exist to provide value to our customers"—to make their lives better via lower prices and greater selection; all else is secondary.
	Swim upstream, buck conventional wisdom.
	Be in partnership with employees.
	Work with passion, commitment, and enthusiasm.
	Run lean.
	Pursue ever-higher goals.
Disney	No cynicism allowed.
	Fanatical attention to consistency and detail.
	Continuous progress via creativity, dreams, and imagination.
	Fanatical control and preservation of Disney's "magic" image.
	"To bring happiness to millions" and to celebrate, nurture, and promulgate "wholesome American values."

SOURCE: Collins, James C. and Porras, Jerry I., *Built to Last*. New York: HarperCollins, 1997.

The Genius of the *And*

genius of the *and*

Ability to achieve multiple objectives simultaneously.

organizational ambidexterity

Ability to achieve multiple objectives simultaneously.

In contrast to the tyranny of the *or,* the **genius of the *and***—of which Chapter 9's **organizational ambidexterity** is an important example—refers to being able to achieve multiple objectives at the same time.[18] It develops via the actions of many individuals throughout the organization. We discussed earlier in the book the importance of delivering multiple competitive values to customers, performing all the management functions, reconciling hard-nosed business logic with ethics, leading and empowering, and others. Authors Collins and Porras have their own list:[19]

- Purpose beyond profit *and* pragmatic pursuit of profit.
- Relatively fixed core values *and* vigorous change and movement.
- Conservatism with the core values *and* bold business moves.
- Clear vision and direction *and* experimentation.
- Stretch goals *and* incremental progress.
- Control based on values *and* operational freedom.
- Long-term thinking and investment *and* demand for short-term results.
- Visionary, futuristic thinking *and* daily, nuts-and-bolts execution.

Your organization and its managers collectively should not lose sight of any of these tensions, or paradoxes[20]—in your thoughts or your actions. To achieve them all, ebbing and flowing over time, requires the continuous and effective management of change.

Achieving Sustained Greatness

A Harvard/McKinsey study of 200 management techniques employed by 160 companies over 10 years identified the specific management practices that lead to sustained, superior performance.[21] The authors boiled their findings down to four key factors:

1. *Strategy*—focused on customers, continually fine-tuned based on marketplace changes, and clearly communicated to employees.
2. *Execution*—good people, with decision-making authority on the front lines, doing quality work and cutting costs.
3. *Culture*—one that motivates, empowers people to innovate, rewards people appropriately (psychologically as well as economically), entails strong values, challenges people, and provides a satisfying work environment.
4. *Structure*—making the organization easy to work in and easy to work with, characterized by cooperation and the exchange of information and knowledge throughout the organization.

You have been learning about these concepts throughout this course. Now, looking to the future, it is important to know that companies and people must continue to change and better themselves.

Even companies that have performed well and had excellent reputations over many years can founder. Kodak dominated the photography industry for most of the 20th century. After inventing the digital camera in the mid-1970s, the company was unable to pivot away from its lucrative film development business to the digital camera space.[22]

> Becoming world class doesn't apply only to the private sector.

Becoming world class doesn't apply only to the private sector. People worry about globalization's negative effects on local communities as plants shut down and people lose their jobs. But local communities do have options—not easy ones, but doable.

A locality can strive to become a world-class center of *thinkers, makers,* or *traders.*[23] An analysis of 135 global cities found that New York was first for business activity. San Francisco was the leader in terms of innovation. Sydney ranked the highest in environmental performance. And Frankfurt earned top marks for its infrastructure.[24] The key to creating world-class local communities includes visionary leadership, a climate friendly to business, a commitment to training workers, and collaboration among businesses and between business and local government.[25]

Intervention	Goals
Strategic	Helping organizations conduct mergers and acquisitions, change their strategies, and develop alliances.
Techno-structural	Relating to organization structure and design, employee involvement, and work design.
Human process	Improving conflict resolution, team building, communication, and leadership.
Human resource management	Attracting good people, setting goals, and appraising and rewarding performance.

EXHIBIT 18.2
Basic Types of OD Interventions

SOURCE: Cummings, T. and Worley, C., *Organization Development and Change,* 10th ed. Stamford, CT: Cengage, 2015.

The city rankings shown above appeared in *Harvard Business Review* in 2003. Do you have any thoughts about how the defining characteristics of world-class communities have changed since then? More concretely, what cities and regions might have fallen and risen in the rankings?

Organization Development

How do organizations become more ambidextrous and move in the other positive directions described throughout this book? This chapter discusses a variety of approaches that—implemented thoughtfully—can create such positive changes. We begin here with an umbrella concept called organization development.

Probably the single most widely used approach to organizational change in the Western world, applied increasingly on a global scale,[26] is **organization development (OD)**. OD is a systemwide application of behavioral science knowledge to develop, improve, and reinforce the strategies, structures, and processes that lead to organization effectiveness.[27]

The systemwide component of the OD definition means that it is not a narrow improvement in technology or operations but a broader approach to changing people, teams, work units, and organizations. The behavioral science component means that OD does not *directly* emphasize economic, financial, or technical aspects of the organization—although those aspects should benefit through changes in people's behavior. The other key part of the definition—to develop, improve, and reinforce—refers to the actual process of changing for the better and for the long term.

Two additional features of organization development are important to note.[28] First, it aims to increase organizational effectiveness—improving the organization's ability to deal with customers, stockholders, governments, employees, and other stakeholders, which results in better-quality products, higher financial returns, and high quality of work life. Second, OD has an underlying value orientation: It supports human potential, development, and participation in addition to organizational performance and competitive advantage.

Many specific OD techniques fit under this philosophical umbrella (see Exhibit 18.2).[29] Much of what you have already learned in this course pertains, and this final chapter offers more yet on creating and leading change.

organization development (OD)

The systemwide application of behavioral science knowledge to develop, improve, and reinforce the strategies, structures, and processes that lead to organizational effectiveness.

Managing Change

People are the key to successful change.[30] For an organization to be great, or even just to survive, its people have to care about its fate and know how they can contribute. But typically leadership lies with only a few people at the top. Too few take on the burden of change; the number of people who care deeply, and who make innovative contributions, is too small. People throughout the organization need to take a greater interest and a more active role in

LO 18-2 Describe how to manage and lead change effectively.

helping the business as a whole. Ideally, people will identify with and commit to the entire organization, not just with their unit and close colleagues.

In other words, shared leadership is crucial to the success of most change efforts—people must be not just supporters of change but also implementers.[31]

This shared responsibility for change is not unusual in start-ups and very small organizations. But too often it is lost with growth and over time. In large, bureaucratic corporations, it is all too rare. Organizations need to rekindle individual responsibility and creativity. The essential task is to motivate people to keep adapting to new business challenges.

Motivating People to Change

If people are to change, they must be motivated to do so. But often they resist management's change initiatives. Managers tend to underestimate the amount of resistance they will encounter.[32]

Many people (and organizations) often settle for business-as-usual rather than aspire to excellence. When told by their managers, "We have to become world class," their reactions resemble the following statements:

- "Those world-class performance numbers are ridiculous! They're impossible to reach!"
- "Sure, maybe some companies achieve those numbers, but there's no hurry, we're doing all right. Sales were up 5 percent this year, costs were down 2 percent."
- "We can't afford to be world class like those big global companies; we don't have the capital or staff."
- "We don't need to expand internationally. One of our local competitors tried that a few years ago and failed miserably."
- "It's not a level playing field; the others have unfair advantages."

To deal with such reactions and successfully implement positive change, managers must understand why people often resist changing.

Why People Resist Change   Many factors explain people's resistance to, ambivalence toward, or readiness for change.[33] Exhibit 18.3 shows some common reasons for resistance, discussed next.[34]

- *Inertia.* Usually people don't want to disturb the status quo. The old ways of doing things are comfortable and easy, so people don't want to shake things up and try something new. For example, it is easier to keep living in the same apartment or house than to move to another.
- *Timing.* Maybe you would like to move to a different place to live, but do you want to move this week? If managers or employees are (as usual) busy or under stress, or if relations between management and workers are strained, the change will be difficult. Where possible, managers should introduce change when people are receptive.
- *Surprise.* If the change is sudden or extreme, resistance may be the initial reaction. Suppose your school announced an increase in tuition starting next term. Wouldn't you want more time to prepare? Managers or others initiating a change often forget that others haven't given the matter much thought; when possible the change leaders show allow time for people to prepare.

EXHIBIT 18.3

Reasons for Resistance to Change

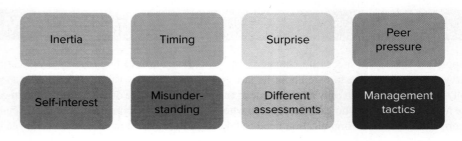

Inclusiveness Works

Changing for Religious Inclusion

Conversations about diversity and inclusion in the workplace often center on gender, race, sexual identity, or age. No less important but less discussed is formulating policies for religious inclusivity in the workplace. The past 15 years have brought a 50 percent increase in the number of religious discrimination suits in the United States.[35]

As the religious demographics of the country continue to change, firms need policies for religious tolerance and inclusion. In fact, except for firms bearing "undue hardship," being adaptable to an employee's religious rituals or ceremonies is protected by federal law.

These accommodations might include time off for a religious holiday and adjustments to a company's dress code due to a faith-based need to wear certain attire or maintain their appearance in a certain way.[36]

Truly inclusive organizations go beyond mere legal compliance. But how?

"Employers often think that religion needs to be treated differently than other facets of work-life accommodation," says Mark Fowler, an employee at Tanenbaum, a nondenominational secular organization dedicated to combatting religious prejudice of all kinds. "But in many instances the practices a company already has in place can be used to accommodate religious beliefs and practices too."[37]

EY, a multinational accounting firm, has "quiet rooms" in many of its North American offices for people to de-stress, quietly reflect, or pray. The rooms aren't designed exclusively for religion, but by taking into account the diversity and needs of its staff, the company accommodates a variety of religions.[38] Organizations also can provide appropriate foods and beverages at cafeterias, with descriptions of ingredients and how the food is prepared. Such practices aid not just those with specific dietary needs due to religion, but also those who may have allergies or diverse political beliefs.

Creating a tolerant and inclusive atmosphere for those of different religions can include mentioning on company calendars all religious holidays and observances. Such gestures can make employees of all religions feel understood and valued. Overall, the same best practices apply for fostering any productive and inclusive workplace: Be transparent, empathetic toward those who may differ from you, and proactive in fostering dialogue and open communication.

- Have the workplaces you've experienced done enough to promote an inclusive environment for all religions? Why or why not?
- Do you agree that most of the best practices for fostering an inclusive workplace environment are the same for religion in particular? Why or why not?

- *Peer pressure.* Even if individual members do not strongly oppose the suggested change, the team may band together in opposition. Peer pressure will cause individuals to resist even reasonable changes, especially if a group is highly cohesive and has anti-management norms (Chapter 14). But change leaders who invite—and listen to—ideas from team members may find that peer pressure becomes a positive force that helps drive the change's success.
- *Self-interest.* People resist change if they think it will cause them to lose something of value. At worst, they could lose their jobs, if management is considering closing a store or plant. A merger, reorganization, or technological change could create the same fear. Other fears include losing the feeling of being competent in a familiar job, expectations that the job will become more difficult or time-consuming, and concerns about the organization's future.
- *Misunderstanding.* People resist change when they do not understand it; perhaps they don't have much information, or see how it fits with the firm's strategy, or see its advantage over current practices.[39] One company tried to introduce flexible working hours, a system in which workers have some say regarding the hours they work. A false rumor circulated among employees that people would have to work evenings, weekends, or whenever their supervisors wanted. The initiative was dropped.
- *Different assessments.* Employees receive different—and usually less—information than management receives. Such discrepancies cause people to develop different opinions regarding the proposed change. Some may be aware that the benefits outweigh the costs, whereas others may see only the costs and not the benefits. This is a common

problem when management announces a change and doesn't explain to employees why it is needed. Management expects benefits, but workers may see the change as another arbitrary, ill-informed management rule that causes headaches for those who must carry it out.

- *Management tactics.* Management may attempt to force the change without addressing people's concerns. Or it may fail to provide the necessary resources, knowledge, or leadership to help the change succeed. Managers who overpromise what they, or the change, can deliver may discover that the next time they introduce a change, they have lost credibility, so employees resist.

Employees' assessments can be more accurate than management's; employees may know a change won't work even if management doesn't. In this case, resistance to change is a useful thing—if the bosses can learn some valid reasons. Thus, even though management typically views resistance as an obstacle that must be overcome, it actually may be an important signal that the proposed change requires further, more open-minded scrutiny.[40]

A General Model for Managing Resistance

Motivating people to change often requires the three basic stages shown in Exhibit 18.4: unfreezing, moving to institute the change, and refreezing.[41]

unfreezing

Realizing that current practices are inappropriate and that new behavior is necessary.

performance gap

The difference between actual performance and desired performance.

Unfreezing   In the **unfreezing** stage, management realizes that its current practices are no longer appropriate and the company must break out of (unfreeze) its present mold by doing things differently. People must come to recognize that some of the past ways of thinking and doing things are obsolete.[42] A direct and sometimes effective way to do this is to communicate the negative consequences of the old ways by comparing the organization's performance with that of its competitors. As discussed in Chapter 15, management can share with employees data about costs, quality, and profits.[43]

A gap typically but not always indicates a major performance issue.

Recognizing a performance gap is a gateway to the unfreezing process. A **performance gap** is the difference between actual performance and the performance that should or could exist.[44] As an impetus for change, a performance gap can apply to the organization as a whole; it also can apply to departments, groups, and individuals.

A gap typically implies poor performance; for example, sales, profits, stock price, or other financial indicators are down. This situation attracts management's attention, and management introduces changes to try to correct things.

But another, very important form of performance gap can exist. This type of gap occurs when performance is good but someone realizes that it could be better. Thus the gap is between what is and what could be. Important changes can and should be made even when performance is good.[45]

People are particularly motivated when a sense of urgency that comes from seeing a pressing problem combines with a sense of excitement that comes from spotting an opportunity. Furthermore, managers communicating a performance gap should remember that

Bottom Line

A useful tactic for innovating toward a positive future is to imagine the difference between what *is* and what *could be.*

EXHIBIT 18.4

Motivating People to Change

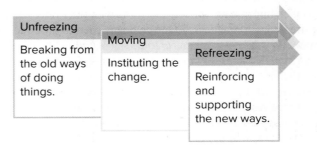

Unfreezing

Breaking from the old ways of doing things.

Moving

Instituting the change.

Refreezing

Reinforcing and supporting the new ways.

employees care about things other than market share and revenues. Employees want to know how a change can help them, plus how it might have a positive impact on their work group, customers, company, and community.

A financial services company met resistance when it tried to persuade employees that a change would enhance the company's competitive position. Employees got on board only after the change leaders started talking about how the change would help employees reduce errors, enable teams to avoid duplication of effort, make jobs more interesting, and help the organization fulfill its mission to deliver affordable housing.[46]

Moving   The example above includes part of the next step, **moving** to institute the change, started by establishing a vision of a better future. The desired future state can be achieved through strategic, structural, cultural, and individual change. But opposing forces cause conflict for people; some things make people want to change while other things—including the reasons discussed earlier—make them resist change.

One technique for managing the change process, **force-field analysis**, identifies the specific forces that keep people from changing plus the different forces that drive people toward change.[47] Eliminating the restraining forces helps people unfreeze, and increasing the driving forces helps and motivates people to move forward.

The great 20th-century social psychologist Kurt Lewin developed force-field analysis and the unfreezing/moving/refreezing model, which for decades served as a foundation for many change management models.[48] Lewin theorized that although driving forces can be easy to change, changing them may increase conflict and opposition, thereby creating new restraining forces. Therefore, to create change, it is crucial to remove restraining forces as well as add driving forces.

Refreezing   Finally, **refreezing** means strengthening the new behaviors that support the change. Refreezing involves implementing control systems that support the change (Chapter 16), applying corrective action when necessary, and reinforcing behaviors and performance (Chapter 13) that support the new agenda. Management should consistently support and reward evidence of movement in the right direction.[49]

Refreezing works when it permanently installs behaviors that focus on important business results and maintains essential core values. But it doesn't realize it's long-term potential if it creates and rewards new behaviors that are as rigid as the old ones. Refreezing should not create new rigidities that might become dysfunctional as the business environment continues to change.[50] Managers should refreeze behaviors that promote continued adaptability, flexibility, experimentation, assessment of results, and continuous improvement—in other words, lock in key values, capabilities, and strategic mission but not necessarily specific practices and procedures.

Enlisting Cooperation

You can try to command people to change, but the key to long-term success is to use other approaches.[51] Developing true support is better than simply driving a program forward.[52] How, more specifically, can managers motivate people to change?

Most managers underestimate the variety of influence strategies available for motivating people during a period of change.[53] Exhibit 18.5 shows effective useful options for managing resisting and enlisting cooperation.

Education and Communication   Management should educate people about upcoming changes before they occur. It should communicate not only the nature of the change, but its logic. This process can include one-on-one discussions, presentations to groups, and reports. And as we discussed in Chapter 15, effective communication includes feedback

moving

Instituting the change.

force-field analysis

An approach to implementing the unfreezing/moving/ refreezing model by identifying the forces that prevent people from changing and those that will drive people toward change.

refreezing

Strengthening the new behaviors that support the change.

Larry Ellison, board chair and chief technology officer of Oracle, knows what it takes to convey a vision for successful change. Oracle often acquires other companies, creating change that challenges its people and the company.

Justin Sullivan/Getty Images

EXHIBIT 18.5   Methods for Managing Resistance to Change

Approach	Commonly Used in Situations	Advantage	Drawbacks
Education and communication	When there is a lack of information or inaccurate information and analysis.	Once persuaded, people will often help with the implementation of the change.	Can be very time-consuming if lots of people are involved.
Participation and involvement	When the initiators do not have all the information they need to design the change and when others have considerable power to resist.	People who participate will be committed to implementing change, and any relevant information they have will be integrated into the change plan.	Can be very time-consuming if participators design an inappropriate change.
Facilitation and support	When people are resisting because of adjustment problems.	No other approach works as well with adjustment problems.	Can be time-consuming and expensive and still fail.
Negotiation and rewards	When someone or some group will clearly lose out in a change and when that group has considerable power to resist.	Sometimes it is a relatively easy way to avoid major resistance.	Can be too expensive in many cases if it alerts others to negotiate for compliance.
Manipulation and cooptation	When other tactics will not work or are too expensive.	It can be a relatively quick and inexpensive solution to resistance problems.	Can lead to future problems if people feel manipulated.
Explicit and implicit coercion	When speed is essential, and the change initiators possess considerable power.	It is speedy and can overcome any kind of resistance.	Can be risky if it leaves people angry at the initiators.

SOURCE: Kotter, John P. and Schlesinger, Leonard A., "Choosing Strategies for Change," *Harvard Business Review,* March–April 1979.

and listening. That provides an environment in which management can not just explain the rationale for the change, but improve it.

Participation and Involvement   The people who are affected by the change should be involved in its design and implementation. For major, organizationwide change, participation in the process can extend from the highest to the lowest levels.[54] When feasible, management should use the input of people throughout the organization. This may sound time-consuming and impractical, but most managers err on the side of too little participation, when in fact the time taken usually returns a strong payoff.

As you learned in Chapter 3, people who are involved in decisions understand them more fully and are more committed to them. These are vital ingredients in successful change implementation. Participation also provides an excellent opportunity for education and communication.

Facilitation and Support   Management should make the change as easy as possible for employees and support their efforts. Facilitation involves providing the training and other resources people need to carry out the change and perform their jobs under the new circumstances. This step often includes decentralizing authority to appropriate levels and empowering people—giving them the power to make the decisions and changes needed to improve.

Offering support involves listening patiently to problems, being understanding if performance drops temporarily or the change is not perfected immediately, and generally being on the employees' side and showing consideration during a difficult period.

Negotiation and Rewards   When necessary and appropriate, management can offer concrete incentives for cooperation with the change. Perhaps job enrichment is acceptable only with a higher wage rate, or a work rule change is resisted until management agrees to a concession on some other rule (say, regarding taking breaks). Even among higher-level managers, one executive might agree to another's idea for a policy change only in return for support on some other issue of more personal importance. Rewards such as bonuses, wages and salaries, recognition, job assignments, and perks can be examined and perhaps restructured to reinforce the direction of the change.[55]

When people trust one another, change is easier. But change is further facilitated by demonstrating its benefits to people.[56] Describing benefits can take place in the context of negotiation or collaborating to find mutually acceptable ways to implement the change.

Envision provides services to adults and children with developmental disabilities to enhance their quality of life, and depends on employees' commitment to its mission.[57] Former executive director Mary Lu Walton set up a team of employees to figure out how to cut costs, and she encouraged them to focus on eliminating the tasks employees dislike. The team members restructured work, sparing 7 or the 10 jobs originally targeted for layoffs. Within a few months, Envision was a leaner organization with employees fully committed to the change.[58] Today, the nonprofit continues its mission and enlists the support of many volunteers and sponsors.

Manipulation and Cooptation   Sometimes managers use subtler, more covert tactics to implement change. One form is cooptation, which involves giving a resisting individual a desirable role in the change process. For example, management might invite a union leader to become a member of an executive committee or ask a member of a useful outside organization to join the company's board of directors. As a person becomes involved in the change, he or she becomes more familiar with and sometimes even committed to the actions of the coopting group or organization.

Explicit and Implicit Coercion   Some managers apply punishment or the threat of punishment to those who resist change. In other words, they force people to comply with their wishes, perhaps by threatening them with job loss, denial of a promotion, or an undesirable work assignment. Sometimes managers rely too heavily on coercion, but sometimes you just have to be firm and tell it like it is.

Each approach to managing resistance has advantages and drawbacks, and each is useful in different situations. Look back at Exhibit 18.5, which summarizes the advantages, drawbacks, and appropriate circumstances for these various strategies. As the exhibit implies, managers should not rely on just one or two approaches, regardless of circumstances. Effective change managers are familiar with the various approaches and know how to apply them all, according to the situation.

Throughout the process, change leaders need to build in some stability. Recall that built-to-last companies have essential core characteristics that they refuse to abandon. In the midst of change, turmoil, and uncertainty, people need anchors onto which they can latch.[59] Making an organization's values and mission constant and visible can serve this stabilizing function.

Staying mindful of the company's history[60] and applying strategic principles can provide important anchors during change.[61] Maintaining the visibility of key people, continuing key assignments and projects, and making announcements about what will *not* change can serve as anchors that reduce anxiety and help overcome resistance.

Harmonizing Multiple Changes

No single approach exists to always result in successful change. Usually many issues need simultaneous attention, and any single, small change will be absorbed by the prevailing culture and disappear.

Management in Action

BALANCING THE ENERGY NEEDS OF TODAY AND TOMORROW

Even as fossil-fuel companies begin to pivot to address consumers' and investors' concerns about climate change, they have not abandoned the fossil-fuel business. In 2018, for example, the world's largest oil companies spent on average just 1 percent of their 2018 budgets on clean energy.[62] ExxonMobil is in fact planning on producing 25 percent more oil and gas in 2025 than it did 10 years prior to keep up with growing demand.[63]

Still, there's a general acknowledgment that the world's sources of energy can and will change. The question that each oil company has to answer is, how fast will change come? In contrast to their American counterparts, European energy firms, due in no small part to more rigorous public pressure and government regulations, are betting change will come more quickly. Not surprisingly, European-based firms, such as Shell and Total, are investing more heavily in clean, renewable energy.

Shell has been looking more concertedly in the power sector, investing in electric utilities, solar companies, and car-charging businesses.[64] More recently, Shell bought Sonnen, one of Tesla's major competitors for home batteries. It's clear Shell believes the future is electric. As Maarten Wetselaar, director of Shell's New Energies division, says, "It's mostly driven by the . . . irreversible choice the world has made to decarbonize, to address climate change, and to go to [a] net-zero energy system. And by far, the easiest form of energy consumption that can be carbon-free is electricity."[65]

Total, a French oil company, is also making investments in electric and solar. It now owns more than half of American-based solar panel manufacturer SunPower, has invested over a billion dollars in an energy storage firm, and is investing heavily in synthetic biotechnology for renewable fuels. It's making these investments for change, while also making a big shift to cleaner-burning liquefied natural gas.[66]

For all of these oil majors, it's a balancing act. Each is trying to manage the inevitable changes occurring in the energy industry, as well as the world around us due to climate change. The companies that manage these changes more successfully will be the ones that own the future of the energy sector.

1. If you were the CEO of a major oil firm, how would you respond to pressures to become a more environmentally friendly company?
2. Do you agree with Shell's director of New Energies that the future is a net-zero energy system? Explain.

---

large group interventions for total organization change

Introducing and sustaining multiple policies, practices, and procedures across multiple units and levels.

Large group interventions[67]—those attempting **total organization change**—involve introducing, coordinating, and sustaining multiple policies, practices, and procedures across multiple units and levels.[68] Such change affects the thinking and behavior of everyone in the organization, can enhance the organization's culture and success, and can be sustained over time.

But commonly it's more like John Kotter reported in his groundbreaking book *Leading Change:* only about one in three change initiatives succeed.[69] A subsequent study of nearly 3,200 executives found similar lackluster results.[70] Other studies reveal remarkably similar findings.[71] The problem is, these efforts usually are simultaneous but not coordinated. As a result, changes get muddled; people lose focus.[72] People suffer from confusion, frustration, low morale, and low motivation.

Because companies introduce new changes constantly, many people complain about their companies' approach to change. That is, employees often see many change efforts as the company just jumping on the latest bandwagon or fad. The more these change fads come and go, the more cynical people become, and the more difficult it is to get them committed to making the change a success.[73]

> Many people complain about their companies' "flavor of the month" approach to change.

So an important question is, Which change efforts are really worth undertaking? Here are some specific questions to ask before embarking on a change project:[74]

- What is the evidence that the approach really can produce positive results?
- Is the approach relevant to your company's strategies and priorities?

- Can you assess the costs and potential benefits?
- Does it really help people add value through their work?
- Does it help the company focus better on customers and the things they value?
- Can you go through the decision-making process described in Chapter 3, understand what you're facing, and feel that you are taking the right approach?

Management also needs to connect the dots—that is, integrate the various efforts into a coherent picture that people can see, understand, and get behind.[75] You connect the dots by understanding each change program and its goals, by identifying similarities among the programs and their differences, and by dropping programs that don't meet priority goals or demonstrate clear results.

Most important, you do it by communicating to everyone concerned the common themes among the various programs: their common rationales, objectives, and methods. You show them how the various parts fit the strategic big picture and how the changes will make things better for the company and its people. You should communicate these benefits thoroughly, honestly, and frequently.[76]

Leading Change

Successful change requires managers to lead it actively. The essential activities of leading change are summarized in Exhibit 18.6.

The companies that lead change most effectively *establish a sense of urgency.*[77] To do this, managers can examine current realities and pressures in the marketplace and the competitive arena, identify both crises and opportunities, and be frank and honest about them. In this sense, urgency is a reality-based sense of determination, not just fear-based busyness. The immediacy of the need for change is an important component, in part because so many large companies grow complacent.

EXHIBIT 18.6
Leading Change

1. Establishing a sense of urgency
2. Creating the guiding coalition
3. Developing a vision and strategy
4. Communicating the change vision
5. Empowering broad-based action
6. Generating short-term wins
7. Consolidating gains and producing more change
8. Anchoring new approaches in the culture

SOURCE: Kotter, John P., *Leading Change.* Boston: Harvard Business School Publishing, 1996.

EXHIBIT 18.7
Sources of Complacency

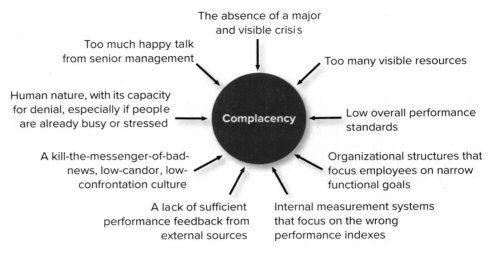

The absence of a major
and visible crisis

Too much happy talk
from senior management

Too many visible resources

Human nature, with its capacity
for denial, especially if people
are already busy or stressed

Complacency

Low overall performance
standards

A kill-the-messenger-of-bad-
news, low-candor, low-
confrontation culture

Organizational structures that
focus employees on narrow
functional goals

A lack of sufficient
performance feedback from
external sources

Internal measurement systems
that focus on the wrong
performance indexes

SOURCE: John P. Kotter, *Leading Change* (Boston: Harvard Business School Publishing, 1996).

Exhibit 18.7 shows some common reasons for complacency. To stop complacency and create urgency, a manager can talk candidly about the organization's weaknesses compared with competitors, backing statements with data. Other tactics include setting stretch goals, putting employees in direct contact with unhappy customers and shareholders, distributing worrisome information to all employees instead of merely engaging in management happy talk, eliminating excessive perks, and highlighting to everyone opportunities that the organization so far has failed to pursue.

Ultimately, urgency is driven by time pressure along with compelling business reasons to change. Survival, competition, and winning in the marketplace are compelling; they provide a sense of direction and energy around change. Change becomes not a hobby, a luxury, or something nice to do, but a business necessity.[78]

To *create a guiding coalition* means putting together a group with enough power to lead the change. Change efforts fail without a sufficiently powerful coalition.[79] Major organization change requires leadership from top management, working as a team. But over time, the support must gradually expand downward and outward throughout the organization. Middle managers and supervisors are essential. Groups at all levels are the glue that can hold change efforts together, the medium for communicating about the changes, and the means for supporting new behaviors.[80]

Developing a vision and strategy, as discussed in earlier chapters, directs the change effort. This process involves determining the idealized, expected state of affairs after the change is implemented. Because confusion is common during major organizational change, the clearest possible image of the future state must be developed and conveyed to everyone.[81] This image, or vision, is a target or guideline that can clarify expectations, dispel rumors, and mobilize people's energies.

The portrait of the future also should communicate how the transition will occur, why the change is being implemented, and how people will be affected by the change. The power of a compelling vision is one of the most important aspects of change and should not be underestimated or underused.

Communicating the change vision requires using every possible channel and opportunity to talk up and reinforce the vision and required new behaviors. It is said that aspiring change leaders undercommunicate the vision by a factor of 10, or even 100 or 1,000, seriously undermining the chances of success.[82] In delivering more messages, however, do not forget that communication is a two-way street.

Empowering broad-based action means getting rid of obstacles to success, including systems and structures that constrain rather than facilitate. Encourage risk taking and experimentation and empower people by providing information, training, authority, and rewards, as described in Chapter 13.

Generate short-term wins. Don't wait for the ultimate grand realization of the vision. You need to show some early progress. As small victories accumulate, you make the transition from an isolated initiative to an integral part of the business.[83] Plan for and create small victories that indicate to everyone that progress is being made. Recognize and reward the people who made the wins possible, doing it visibly so that people notice and the positive message permeates the organization.

Make sure you *consolidate gains and produce more change.* With the well-earned credibility of previous successes, keep changing things in ways that support the vision. Hire, promote, and develop people who will further the vision. Reinvigorate the organization and your change efforts with new projects and change agents.

Finally, *anchor new approaches in the culture.*[84] Highlight positive results, communicate the connections between the new behaviors and the improved results, and keep developing new change agents and leaders. Continually increase the number of people joining you in taking responsibility for change.[85]

Shaping the Future

Most change is reactive. A better approach is to be proactive. **Reactive change** means responding to pressure after a problem has arisen. It also implies being a follower. **Proactive change** means anticipating and preparing for an uncertain future. It implies being a leader and creating the future you want.

The road to the future includes drivers, passengers, and road kill. Put another way: On the road to the future, who will be the windshield, and who will be the bug?[86] Needless to say, it's best to be a driver.[87]

How do you become a driver? By being proactive more than merely reactive, by really thinking about the future, and by *creating* desired futures.

LO 18-3 Describe strategies for creating a successful future.

reactive change

A response that occurs under pressure; problem-driven change.

proactive change

A response that is initiated before a performance gap has occurred.

Thinking about the Future

If you think only about the present or simply wallow in the uncertainties of the future, your future is just a roll of the dice. It is far better to exercise foresight, set an agenda for the future, and pursue it with everything you've got.

Before the 20th century, people lived without antibiotics, automobiles, airplanes, tractors, and air conditioning. Imagine how this combination of inventions has revolutionized where and how well people live.

> On the road to the future, who will be the windshield, and who will be the bug?

And in recent years, we have seen the invention and spread of smartphones, 3D printing, artificial intelligence, machine learning, robotics, reusable rocket technology, and the mapping of the human genome. These innovations are still shaping how we learn, communicate, and treat disease.

When recently asked to identify inventions that will change the world for the better, Bill Gates provided the following examples of innovative technology:[88]

- Improved robot dexterity that will do things that only humans currently do.
- New-wave nuclear power that combines fission and fusion technologies.
- Small, swallowable devices to capture detailed images of the stomach without anesthesia.
- Practical and affordable ways to capture carbon dioxide to reduce greenhouse-gas emissions.
- Energy-efficient toilets that can function without a sewer system and treat waste on the spot.

The potential for innovation and growth is unprecedented in areas such as artificial intelligence, smart cities, interplanetary space travel, and renewable energy technologies.[89]

The Digital World

Tech-Savvy Gen Z Enters the Workforce

Move over Millennials, a new generation is entering the workforce. Generation Z (aka, Gen Z, Centennials, or iGen) refers to people born in the mid-1990s or later. While much has been written about the Millennial generation, less is known about this younger generation and how its members view technology and work.

Gen Zers were the first truly digital natives who grew up with smartphones. According to Jason Dorsey, co-founder of the Center for Generational Kinetics: "When you come from an age never remembering a time before smartphones, which is true for all Gen Zers in the U.S., it fundamentally changes your learning, communication, and workplace expectations."[90] This immersion into smartphone technology has enabled Gen Zers to become extremely web- and app-savvy.

In contrast to Millennials, this younger generation is more weary of posting personal information on platforms that store it. Gen Zers shun e-mail and Facebook for more personal and immediate social media platforms like Snapchat and Instagram that don't "leave a trail."[91]

When Gen Zers want to learn something new, check the news, or connect with friends, they turn to their phones. According to Dorsey: "as Gen Z enters the workforce, they expect everything to be mobile first, from communication and collaboration to training, retention, and engagement strategies."[92] To attract members of the Gen Z generation, experts report that companies should look to invest in the latest tech for employee collaboration, communication, and productivity.[93]

1. In what other ways do you think members of Gen Z may differ from members of other generations based on their technological savvy?
2. In what other ways do you think employers will need to adapt to attract Gen Z workers?

Deep-neural networks, an emerging branch of the artificial intelligence field, are expected to become invisible parts of every organization. Programmers will embed learning algorithms into images, video, and text. Machines learn from these online interactions and will replace many human tasks.[94]

Companies like IBM, Microsoft, and Cisco are using big data and the Internet of Things to help cities around the world become smarter.[95] Spending on "smarter city" technologies is expected to reach $135 billion by 2021.[96] More than half of the world's population lives in urban environments, and city leaders want to improve their citizens' quality of life. Urban dwellers benefit from omnipresent free Wi-Fi spots, sophisticated data hubs, buildings that react to weather, drone deliveries, and autonomous vehicles.[97]

Renewable energies like wind and solar power continue to grow. Most electricity in the United States now comes from renewables.[98] Worldwide, digital technologies and the Internet of Things improve wind farm efficiency and drive more solar panel use.[99] Development and use of renewable energy sources will accelerate into the foreseeable future.

Just as technologies change, so do other trends rise and fall, recently including a (temporary, most likely) damper on globalization, rising distrust of business, a growing role of government, strains on natural resources, and changing patterns of global consumption.[100] Vast new markets will exist, new kinds of companies will appear, and new business models will emerge.[101] All offer prime opportunity to those who create the future.

Creating the Future

Companies can try different strategic postures in preparing to compete in an uncertain future. **Adapters** take the current industry structure and its future evolution as givens, conduct standard strategic analyses, and then choose where to compete. In contrast, **shapers** try to change the structure of industries, creating future competitive landscapes of their own design.[102]

Shapers can be high-tech industry disruptors or innovators in any industry.[103] Purple is changing the mattress industry by selling its products online, directly to customers; by

adapters

Companies that take the current industry structure and its evolution as givens, and choose where to compete.

shapers

Companies that try to change the structure of their industries, creating a future competitive landscape of their own design.

Social Entrepreneurship

Leveraging AI to Build a Better Future

The ultimate goal of any social enterprise is to do good—for people, the environment, perhaps even the world. But as technology and especially artificial intelligence become an integral part of our lives, social entrepreneurs need to be mindful of how to deploy AI in ways that advance social justice and equality while mitigating its potential pitfalls.

A recent report by McKinsey spotlights the dangers that AI poses to individuals, organizations, and society, such as "privacy violations, discrimination, accidents, and manipulation of political systems."[104] The risks to misusing AI, either intentionally or unintentionally, are real, and entrepreneurs need to be vigilant in accounting for how they integrate it into their social enterprises. Fortunately, the skills that will be integral to work in the digital age are those that many social entrepreneurs already possess: creativity, command of technology, analytic thinking, sound judgment and leadership skills, as well as a willingness to embrace change, among others.[105]

Many social entrepreneurs are already integrating AI in their enterprises in ways that are benefiting their mission and society. One example is Lemonade, a start-up insurance company that charges a low flat fee for renters and homeowners' insurance. The firm uses AI and chatbots to deliver and handle insurance claims. Using AI accelerates the claims process for those in need and keeps rates low. AI enhances Lemonade's mission to transform insurance from a necessary evil into a social good.[106]

- What's your take on AI? A useful tool for the future of social enterprises? A risky, corrupting effect on social entrepreneurs?

- Take another look at the example of Lemonade insurance. If you were the founder of this start-up, what risks would you need to manage as you grow the enterprise?

cutting out distributors and retailers, it sells at lower prices. Sourcify saves entrepreneurs search time and lowers their risk by using algorithms to match them with trustworthy manufacturers.[107] Financial service firms are investing aggressively in start-up firms like Circle Internet Financial, Coinbase, and Ripple that use blockchain technology (the distributed ledger technology behind bitcoin).[108] Blockchain technology is expected to disrupt the financial services industry (among others) by increasing the efficiency, transparency, and security of financial transactions.[109]

Not every company can create an idea that is so revolutionary that it disrupts an industry. However, a strategy that focuses primarily on delivering the same services or products to current customers will not thrive. An ever-growing field of competitors, advancing technology, and changing customer preferences require companies to continuously offer new goods and services that meet or exceed the needs of current and future customers.

Exhibit 18.8 shows four quadrants depicting growth opportunities based on customers' needs. Companies that follow a business-as-usual philosophy meet customers' needs with current product offerings, in the lower left quadrant. An example is a municipal utility serving city residents by purchasing and distributing power from coal-fired power plants.

Forward-looking utilities purchase more from natural gas plants and renewable energies like water, wind, and solar.[110] These strategies occupy the lower right quadrant, offering new goods and services to existing customers. Or a company can use new products to attract new customers, thus operating in the upper right quadrant.

For example, because research showed that the hardest problem facing small businesses was "finding the right people to hire," Facebook started allowing companies to post job ads on its news feeds. With job seekers applying for more positions more efficiently via Facebook, future business customers will use the new service in recruiting. Meanwhile, in the upper left quadrant, Facebook keeps using current products to attract future customers—for instance, with its e-commerce platform Delivery.com, where business sells directly to customers.[111]

EXHIBIT 18.8

Opportunity Is Finding
Ways to Meet Customers'
Needs

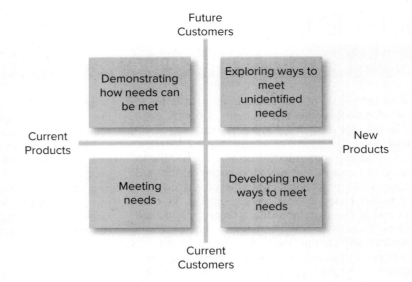

World-class companies are typically the most proactive and can operate successfully in all four quadrants. They meet their current customers' needs by continually updating existing products or launching new goods and services. They try to shape their future by prospecting for new and future customers. They show how current products can solve the needs of new customers, while searching continuously for unidentified needs to address. For example, developed and fast-developing nations present problems in the strain they put on the planet's resources, but proactive firms see opportunities to serve new customers with new products that are made more sustainably or enable consumers to live more sustainable lifestyles.[112]

Other companies hope to meet unidentified needs by developing cutting-edge technologies. The nanometer, one billionth of a meter, is the building block of an emerging industry, nanotechnology. The nanometer is so important because matter at this scale behaves differently—speeding electrons through circuits faster, conducting heat better, or offering qualities such as greater strength.[113] Current applications include diagnosing medical problems at earlier stages; making personal body armor stronger; enhancing the efficiency of fuel production; improving the durability of eyeglass lenses; and decreasing the weight of cars, trucks, and airplanes to reduce fuel costs.[114]

Is nanotech—for that matter, are most industries of the future—overhyped? Products using nanotech materials surpassed $1 trillion in global sales.[115] In 2018, important breakthroughs in nanotechnology included using solar energy to purify water and testing a nanoparticle flu vaccine in the 2018–2019 flu season.[116] Both applications hold great promise.

However, nanotechnology may be risky.[117] The particles are so small that they can pass through most manufactured filters and cell walls, and reactions at the atomic level could have negative chemical and biological consequences. Thus the industry must apply this exciting new technology while protecting workers and customers against risks that aren't yet known.[118]

Whatever your industry, all things considered, which of the following should you and your firm do?

- Preserve old advantages or create new advantages?
- Lock in old markets or create new markets?
- Take the path of greatest familiarity or the path of greatest opportunity?
- Be only a benchmarker or a pathbreaker?
- Place priority on short-term financial returns or on making a real, long-term impact?
- Do only what seems doable or what is difficult and worthwhile?
- Change what is or create what isn't?
- Look to the past or live for the future?[119]

Shaping Your Own Future

If you are a manager and your employer operates in traditional ways, perhaps you can help start a revolution, genetically reengineering your company before it becomes a dinosaur of the modern era.[120]

But maybe you are not going to lead a revolution. Maybe you just want a good career and a good life. You still must be able to choose and pursue long-term goals[121] and deal with an economic environment that is highly competitive and fast-moving.[122]

Creating the future you want for yourself requires setting high personal standards. Don't settle for mediocrity; don't assume that good is necessarily good enough—for yourself or for your employer. Think about how not just to meet expectations but to exceed them; not merely to live with apparent constraints but break free of the unimportant, arbitrary, or imagined ones; and to seize opportunities instead of letting them pass by.[123]

> Look for positions that stretch you and for managers who could be mentors.

The most successful individuals take charge of their own development the way an entrepreneur takes charge of a business.[124] More specific advice from the leading authors on career management:[125] Consciously and actively manage your own career. Develop marketable skills, as depicted in Exhibit 18.9, and keep developing more. Make career choices based on personal growth, development, and learning opportunities. Look for positions that stretch you and for bosses who develop their protégés. Seek environments that provide training and the opportunity to experiment and innovate. And know yourself; assess your strengths and weaknesses, your true interests, and ethical standards. If you are not already thinking in these terms and taking commensurate action, you can start now.

Additionally, become indispensable to your organization. Be enthusiastic in your job and committed to doing great work, but don't be blindly loyal to one company. Be prepared to leave if necessary. View your job as an opportunity to prove what you can do and increase what you can do, not as a comfortable niche for the long term.[126] Go out on your own if it meets your skills and temperament to do so.

This points out the need to maintain your options. More and more, contemporary careers can involve leaving behind a large organization and going entrepreneurial, becoming self-employed in the postcorporate world.[127] In such a career, independent individuals are free to make their own choices. They can flexibly and quickly respond to demands and opportunities. Developing start-up ventures, consulting, accepting temporary employment, doing project work for one organization and then another, working in professional partnerships, being a constant deal maker—these can be the elements of a successful career. Ideally, this self-employed model contributes to work–life balance.

This go-it-alone approach can sound ideal, but it also has downsides. Independence can be frightening, the future unpredictable. It can isolate road warriors who are always on the go, working from their cars and airports, and can interfere with social and family life.[128] Effective self-management is essential to keep career and family obligations in perspective and under control.

Coping with uncertainty and change is easier if you develop resilience. To become more resilient, practice thinking of the world as complex but full of opportunities; expect change, but view it as interesting and potentially rewarding, even if difficult. Keep a sense

Creativity	Emotional intelligence
Analytical (critical) thinking	Active learning with a growth mindset
Judgment and decision making	Interpersonal communication skills
Leadership skills	Diversity and cultural intelligence
Technology skills	Embracing change

EXHIBIT 18.9
Critical Skills You'll Need for the Future

SOURCE: Marr, B., "The 10 Vital Skills You Will Need for the Future of Work," *Forbes*, April 29, 2019, www.forbes.com.

Don't think taking risks and being fearless is only for companies; think of your own quest for personal advantage in the same way. Ultimately, where you go, what you do, and who you become are up to you.

Burdun Iliya/Shutterstock

of purpose, set priorities for your time, be flexible when facing uncertainty or a need to change, and take an active role rather than waiting for change to happen to you.[129]

Learning and Leading: Leaning into the Future

Continuous learning is a vital route to renewable competitive advantage.[130] People in your organization—and you, personally—should constantly explore, discover, and take action, as illustrated in Exhibit 18.10. With this approach, you can learn what is effective and what is not, and adjust and improve accordingly. The philosophy of continuous learning helps your company achieve lower cost, higher quality, better service, superior innovation, greater sustainability, and greater speed—and helps you grow and develop on a personal level.

Commit to lifelong learning, which includes moving outside your comfort zone (forgive the cliché; it's true). Lifelong learning requires occasionally taking risks, honestly assessing the reasons behind your successes and failures, asking for and listening to other people's information and opinions, and being open to new ideas.[131]

Practice lifelong learning.

In a career, a person inhabits and can move through the hierarchy of stages in Exhibit 18.11 from Jim Collins's book *Good to Great*. The descriptions in the hierarchy suggest not only that you might do these things, but that you should do them well. Your first job may not include managerial responsibilities, but it will require you to be an individual contributor and probably to be part of a team. Level 3 is where managerial capabilities are required, whereas Level 4 distinguishes true leadership from competent management. Level 5 represents a leadership style that you read about briefly in Chapter 12, combining personal humility with strong will and determination. Level 5 leadership represents a peak achievement, the ultimate contribution of a leader who can turn a good company into a great one.[132]

You might ask yourself, What is my level now (or where will I be after graduation)? What do I aspire to? What have I learned to this point that can help me progress, and what do I need to learn to develop myself further?

A leader—and this can include you—should be able to create an environment in which "others are willing to learn and change so their organizations can adapt and innovate [and]

Bottom Line

Continuous learning provides a competitive advantage by helping you and your organization achieve difficult goals.
What are the three phases in the process of continuous learning?

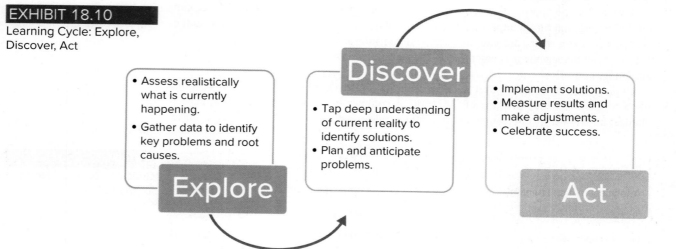

EXHIBIT 18.10

Learning Cycle: Explore, Discover, Act

Explore
- Assess realistically what is currently happening.
- Gather data to identify key problems and root causes.

Discover
- Tap deep understanding of current reality to identify solutions.
- Plan and anticipate problems.

Act
- Implement solutions.
- Measure results and make adjustments.
- Celebrate success.

SOURCE: Adapted from Binney, George and Williams, Collin, *Leaning into the Future: Changing the Way People Change Organizations*. Boston: Nicholas Brealey Publishing, 1997.

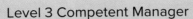

| **Level 5 Executive** |
| Builds enduring greatness through a paradoxical blend of personal humility and professional will. |

| **Level 4 Effective Leader** |
| Catalyzes commitment to and vigorous pursuit of a clear and compelling vision, stimulating higher performance standards. |

| **Level 3 Competent Manager** |
| Organizes people and resources toward the effective and efficient pursuit of predetermined objectives. |

| **Level 2 Contributing Team Member** |
| Contributes individual capabilities to the achievement of group objectives and works effectively with others in a group setting. |

| **Level 1 Highly Capable Individual** |
| Makes productive contributions through talent, knowledge, skills, and good work habits. |

EXHIBIT 18.11
Level 5 Hierarchy

SOURCE: Collins, Jim, *Good to Great*. New York: HarperCollins, 2001.

inspire diverse others to embark on a collective journey of continual learning and leading."[133] Learning leaders exchange knowledge freely; commit to their own continuous learning as well as to others'; examine their own behaviors and defensiveness that may inhibit their learning; devote time to their colleagues, suspending their own beliefs while they listen thoughtfully; and develop a broad perspective, recognizing that organizations are an integrated system of human relationships.[134]

Long-term success derives from adapting to the world *and* shaping the future; being responsive to others' perspectives *and* being clear about what you want to change; encouraging others to change *while* recognizing what you need to change about yourself; understanding current realities *and* passionately pursuing your vision for the future; learning *and* leading.

Remember the importance of ambidexterity, and the genius of the *and*.

A Collaborative, Sustainable Future?

As you lead and learn into the future, we urge you to (1) think long term, along with handling the immediate demands you must face; and (2) consider collaboration as a key to sustained success. You've learned about many of today's big challenges. The good news is that new business models and new forms of collaboration are taking root, and others are waiting to be created.[135] Entrepreneurs with societal goals are driving new approaches to commerce. The private sector is tackling social and environmental issues, the public sector is enacting market-based approaches to delivering services, and nonprofits pursue sustainable business models.

Business and tomorrow's leaders in every sector help determine the world's future. It would be naïve to think that long-term considerations will guide our behavior more than do the short-term pressures for immediate results. And the controversy persists over what the obligations of business really are. But only a long-term perspective, balanced with prudent near-term considerations, will sustain your purpose enduringly over time.

Management in Action

DEVELOPING ENVIRONMENTALLY FRIENDLY POLICIES *AND* ACHIEVING ECONOMIC GROWTH?

Climate change in conjunction with other social and political forces is forcing disruptive change within Shell, Exxon, and the rest of the fossil-fuel industry. But firms in a wide array of industries are being forced to adapt to the economic and environmental realities of our time. Many are trying to maintain profitability in their respective markets while also helping to generate solutions to challenges we face. Siemens, a global technology leader, is an example of a firm that is trying to reinvent itself in order to reinvent the future.

Siemens is a multinational firm that originated in Germany over 170 years ago as a manufacturer of equipment for the telegraph. While it's since been instrumental in innovating in a wide range of industries, from aerospace to mining to food and beverage services, such huge global conglomerates have struggled in recent decades, as the pace of business increases with digitization and markets have become more integrated and fluid. Siemens CEO Joe Kaeser made the bold decision to adapt to the quickly changing 21st-century landscape by restructuring and streamlining Siemens's 18 divisions to just three.[136]

By 2020, Siemens will be comprised of three operating companies: Gas and Power, Smart Infrastructure, and Digital Industries. Kaeser feels these three branches will provide more entrepreneurial freedom to innovate and are best suited to tackle the challenges of climate change.[137] Says Kaeser: "[E]lectrifying the world's commercial and industrial infrastructure is the critical next step to de-carbonization."[138]

As Siemens has restructured to better meet the needs of the 21st century, it has also begun reevaluating its internal processes and place in the supply chain. It has pledged to go carbon neutral by 2030, an ambitious goal for any firm, let alone one the size and scope of Siemens. At a recent conference, Siemens CEO USA, Barbara Humpton, conceded that achieving carbon neutrality by then would be very difficult but that Siemens was willing to accept the short-term costs for the long-term gains.[139]

Perhaps because of such bold clean energy goals, Siemens topped *Fortune*'s World's Most Admired Companies in 2019—for the fourth year in a row.[140]

- Like any organization, Siemens has to manage change by taking into account short-term versus long-term goals, as well as its internal and external stakeholders. Assess Siemens's plan for the future. Do you think it is moving too fast? Not fast enough? Explain.
- Kaeser has staked the future of Siemens on his belief that electrifying the industrial infrastructure is critical to de-carbonization. Check in on how Siemens is doing, as well as global energy trends. Is his vision proving correct, or does he seem to have been off somehow?

Collaboration will not replace competition. Competition has upsides and downsides, and although new competitors continually appear, former competitors become collaborators when they realize the potential advantages.[141] Certainly at local levels and sometimes at regional and global levels, multisector clusters of businesses, schools, universities, nonprofits, and governments are collaborating in mutually beneficial and effective ways. People are learning how to work more effectively together—not just within but across organizational, industry, and sector boundaries—to produce new models for action that revitalize commerce and will indeed create the future.[142]

KEY TERMS

adapters, p. 570

force-field analysis, p. 563

genius of the *and*, p. 558

large group interventions, p. 566

moving, p. 563

organization development (OD), p. 559

organizational ambidexterity, p. 558

performance gap, p. 562

proactive change, p. 569

reactive change, p. 569

refreezing, p. 563

shapers, p. 570

total organization change, p. 566

tyranny of the *or*, p. 557

unfreezing, p. 562

RETAINING WHAT YOU LEARNED

In Chapter 18, you learned what it takes to achieve world-class excellence. Sustaining greatness requires having strong core values and striving for continuous improvement, among other things. It is crucial to believe that multiple important goals can be achieved simultaneously and synergistically. Effective change management occurs when organizations move from their current state to a desired future state. General reasons that people resist change include inertia, poor timing, surprise, self-interest, and others. Motivating people to change requires a general process of unfreezing, moving, and refreezing. More specific strategies include education and communication, participation and involvement, facilitation and support, negotiation and rewards, manipulation and cooptation, and coercion. Each approach has strengths, weaknesses, and appropriate uses, and multiple approaches can be used. Effective change requires active leadership, including creating a sense of urgency, forming a guiding coalition, developing a vision and strategy, and taking further actions. You can proactively forge the future by being a shaper more than an adapter, creating new competitive advantages, actively managing your career and your personal development, and becoming an active leader and a lifelong learner.

LO 18-1   Discuss what it takes to be world class.

- You should strive for world-class excellence, which means using the very best and latest knowledge and ideas to operate at the highest standards of any place anywhere.
- Sustainable greatness comes from, among other things, having strong core values, living those values constantly, striving for continuous improvement, experimenting, and always trying to do better tomorrow than today.
- It is essential not to fall prey to the tyranny of the *or*—that is, the belief that one important goal can be attained only at the expense of another. The genius of the *and* is that multiple important goals can be achieved simultaneously and synergistically.

LO 18-2   Describe how to manage and lead change effectively.

- Effective change management occurs when the organization moves from its current state to a desired future state without excessive cost to the organization or its people.
- People resist change for a variety of reasons, including inertia, poor timing, surprise, peer pressure, self-interest, misunderstanding, different information about (and assessments of) the change, and management's tactics.
- Motivating people to change requires a general process of unfreezing, moving, and refreezing, with the caveat that appropriate and not inappropriate behaviors be refrozen.
- More specific techniques to motivate people to change include education and communication, participation and involvement, facilitation and support, negotiation and rewards, manipulation and cooptation, and coercion. Each approach has strengths, weaknesses, and appropriate uses, and multiple approaches can be used. It is important to harmonize the multiple changes that are occurring throughout the organization.
- Effective change requires active leadership, including creating a sense of urgency, forming a guiding coalition, developing a vision and strategy, communicating the change vision, empowering broad-based action, generating short-term wins, consolidating gains and producing more change, and anchoring the new approaches in the culture.

LO 18-3   Describe strategies for creating a successful future.

- Preparing for an uncertain future requires a proactive approach.
- You can proactively forge the future by being a shaper more than an adapter, creating new competitive advantages, actively managing your career and your personal development, and becoming an active leader and a lifelong learner.

DISCUSSION QUESTIONS

1. Why do some people resist the goal of becoming world class? How can this resistance be overcome?

2. Generate specific examples of world-class business that you have seen as a consumer. Also, generate examples of poor business practice. Why and how do some companies inspire world-class practices while others do not?

3. How might blogging and other social forms of communication via social media affect the process of managing change? What are the professional and career implications of blogging for you?

4. Generate and discuss examples of problems and opportunities that have inspired change, both in businesses and in you personally.

5. Review the methods for dealing with resistance to change. Generate specific examples of each that you have seen and analyze why they worked or failed to work.

6. Choose some specific types of changes you would like to see happen in groups or organizations with which you are familiar. Imagine that you were to try to bring about these changes. What sources of resistance should you anticipate? How would you manage the resistance?

7. Develop a specific plan for becoming a continuous learner.

8. In your own words, what does the idea of creating the future mean to you? How can you put this concept to good use? Again, generate some specific ideas that you can really use.

9. In what ways do you think the manager's job will be different in 20 years from what it is today? How can you prepare for that future?

EXPERIENTIAL EXERCISES

18.1   Overcoming Resistance to Change

OBJECTIVE

To learn how to overcome resistance to change.

INSTRUCTIONS

Refer back to Exhibit 18.5 and the different ways to manage resistance to change. Next, think about the last time you tried to introduce a new idea or way of doing things at work, school, or some other organization. Describe the new idea and which approach(es) you used to overcome others' resistance to trying out the new idea.

Resistance to Change Worksheet

Describe a new idea you tried to introduce at work, school, or some other organization:

_____

_____

_____

_____

Which (if any) of the following approaches to overcoming resistance to change did you use? (Please check all that apply)

_____Education and communication   _____Negotiation and rewards

_____Participation and involvement   _____Manipulation and cooptation

_____Facilitation and support   _____Explicit and implicit coercion

What was the outcome? To what degree were you successful in overcoming the resistance to change? Explain.

_____

_____

_____

If you could go back in time, would you use a different approach to overcome the resistance to your new idea? Why or why not?

_____

_____

_____

SOURCE: de Janasz, Suzanne C., O'Dowd, Karen and Schneider, Beth Z., *Interpersonal Skills in Organizations*. New York: McGraw-Hill/Irwin, 2002, p. 212.

18.2   Networking Scenarios

1. Working on your own, develop a networking strategy for the following three scenarios. (10 min.)

2. Working with your partner or small group, collaborate on identifying the best strategy for dealing with each of the three scenarios. Each group should develop one best strategy for each scenario. (20 min.)

3. Each group reports, sharing its best strategies for each of the three scenarios (or at least one if not enough time is available). (2–3 min. per group per strategy)

4. The large group or class engages in discussion, using the questions at the end. (10 min.)

SCENARIOS

I. You are running for student government president. What steps would you take to make your candidacy a success?

1. _____
2. _____
3. _____
4. _____
5. _____
6. _____

II. You are in an internship and are interested in becoming a permanent full-time employee at the organization. What people would you approach and what steps could you take to obtain an offer?

1. _____
2. _____
3. _____
4. _____
5. _____
6. _____

III. You just moved to a new community, and your company's business growth relies heavily on referrals. How do you make contacts in a place where you don't know anyone? How can you build a client base?

1. _____
2. _____
3. _____
4. _____
5. _____
6. _____

QUESTIONS

1. What was difficult about this exercise?
2. What creative means were devised to build networks of contacts in these scenarios?
3. Which of these ideas would be easy to implement? Which would be difficult? What makes some strategies easier to do than others?
4. What personal qualities are needed actually to use these strategies?
5. How can someone who is shy about approaching new people use (some or all of) these strategies successfully?
6. What did you learn about yourself and others from this exercise?

SOURCE: de Janasz, Suzanne C., O'Dowd, Karen and Schneider, Beth Z., *Interpersonal Skills in Organizations*. New York: McGraw-Hill/Irwin. 2002, p. 212.

Concluding Case

EATWELL TECHNOLOGIES

Cristina Muñoz and Rashid Prakash started EatWell Technologies as a result of conversations they had while graduate students in bioengineering. Both were interested in how to develop crops offering superior nutrition in developing countries, and both believed that business innovation could and should drive social change. They focused their research on a genetically modified strain of rice that is drought tolerant and high in vitamin A and iron.

Upon completing their studies, they wrote a business plan and formed EatWell Technologies to commercialize their rice. Their aim was to sell first in Africa, where nutrition is an urgent problem and the potential for economic development presents huge opportunities for business. They selected Nigeria as their first target market.

Working through the government and with nongovernmental development organizations and local farmers, Cristina and Rashid established a reputation for integrity and reliability. As farmers began purchasing their rice, the two owners hired research assistants, office staff, and sales representatives. They began to enjoy modest profits and started paying themselves a monthly salary—far from what they could earn as scientists in a large corporation but enough to live on. They began discussing what products to offer next. Cristina suggested they develop leafy greens to provide variety in local diets; Rashid was inclined to add new strains of rice, their area of greatest knowledge.

Cristina and Rashid also realized that as their venture grew, it needed management expertise. They interviewed Victoria Jensen, a retired vice president of a community bank. Victoria was impressed with the company's mission and thought an interesting project would be to help EatWell become financially stronger. Rashid, Cristina, and Victoria reached an agreement by which Victoria would become a third partner in exchange for investing $450,000. The partners met daily, and Victoria helped Cristina and Rashid track cash flow, choose suppliers, and meet experts who could help the business expand into new markets.

At one of their meetings, Rashid and Cristina agreed it was time to settle on the direction for product development: Would EatWell be a rice company or should it diversify into vegetables? Victoria pointed out that rice and leafy greens are commodities, and EatWell will never get much of a return from investing in commodities. Instead, she pointed out the value of the rice as a brand. She explained her entire vision. "Imagine where EatWell could go by incorporating the rice into other products, such as energy bars and breakfast cereal. We could go beyond farming into the cities and sell to Africa's rapidly growing middle class, who could pay a premium. We could even start paying ourselves salaries in line with our expertise and the risks we took by forming the company."

Rashid and Cristina were shocked. From their viewpoint, Victoria had lost sight of the company's purpose.

DISCUSSION QUESTIONS

1. Why do you think Rashid and Cristina feel that Victoria's vision is not aligned with the founding principals of the company? Do you think they are correct in their assessment? Why or why not?

2. In this case, where do you see resistance to change? What could Victoria say, if anything, to persuade Rashid and Cristina to change their minds?

3. What advice would you give Cristina and Rashid about shaping their future?

ENDNOTES

1. Energy Reporters, "Shell Set to Double Renewable Budget," *Energy Reporters,* December 27, 2018, https://www.energy-reporters.com/environment/shell-set-to-double-renewable-budget/.
2. OGSI website, https://oilandgasclimateinitiative.com/, accessed April 29, 2019.
3. OGSI website, https://oilandgasclimateinitiative.com/climate-investments/#our-agenda, accessed April 29, 2019.
4. Adam Vaughn, "ExxonMobil Agrees to Join Oil and Gas Climate Change Alliance," *The Guardian,* September 20, 2018, https://www.theguardian.com/business/2018/sep/20/exxonmobil-joins-oil-gas-climate-change-alliance-global-warming.
5. V. Bruno and H. Shin, "Globalization of Corporate Risk Taking," *Journal of International Business Studies* 45 (2014), pp. 800–20; M. Reeves and M. Deimler, "Adaptability: The New Competitive Advantage," *Harvard Business Review,* July–August 2011, pp. 135–41.
6. J. Bower, H. Leonard, and L. Paine, "Global Capitalism at Risk: What Are You Doing about It?" *Harvard Business Review,* September 2011, pp. 105–12.
7. J. Bower, H. Leonard, and L. Paine, "Global Capitalism at Risk: What Are You Doing about It?" *Harvard Business Review,* September 2011, pp. 105–12.
8. T. Schooley, "Manufacturing Leader Optimistic for Industry's Future," *Business Times,* February 28, 2017, www.bizjournals.com.
9. "2019 1st Quarter Manufacturers' Outlook Survey," National Manufacturers Association, www.nam.org, accessed April 30, 2019.
10. T. A. Judge, C. J. Thoresen, V. Pucik, and T. M. Welbourne, "Managerial Coping with Organizational Change: A Dispositional Perspective," *Journal of Applied Psychology* 84 (1999), pp. 107–22.
11. M. Fugate, A. Kinicki, and G. Prussia, "Employee Coping with Organizational Change: An Examination of Alternative Theoretical Perspectives and Models," *Personnel Psychology* 61 (2008), pp. 1–36.
12. C. Giffi, A. Roth, and G. Seal, *Competing in World-Class Manufacturing: America's 21st Century Challenge* (Homewood, IL: Business One Irwin, 1990).
13. R. M. Kanter, *World Class: Thriving Locally in the Global Economy* (New York: Touchstone, 1995).
14. R. M. Kanter, "How Great Companies Think Differently," *Harvard Business Review,* November 2011, pp. 66–78; U. Stephan, M.

Patterson, C. Kelly, and J. Mair, "Organizations Driving Positive Social Change: A Review and an Integrative Framework of Change Processes," *Journal of Management* 42 (2016), pp. 1250–81.
15. C. Giffi, A. Roth, and G. Seal, *Competing in World-Class Manufacturing: America's 21st Century Challenge* (Homewood, IL: Business One Irwin, 1990).
16. J. Collins and J. Porras, *Built to Last* (London: Century, 1996).
17. J. Collins and J. Porras, *Built to Last* (London: Century, 1996).
18. Ming-Jer Chen, "Becoming Ambicultural: A Personal Quest, and Aspiration for Organizations" *Academy of Management Review* 39 (2014), pp. 119–37; D. Waldman and D. Bowen, "Learning to Be a Paradox-Savvy Leader" *Academy of Management Perspectives* 30 (2016), pp. 316–27; P. Junni, R. Sarala, V. Taras, and S. Tarba, "Organizational Ambidexterity and Performance: A Meta-Analysis," *Academy of Management Perspectives* 27, no. 4 (2013), pp. 299–312; C. Gibson and J. Birkinshaw, "The Antecedents, Consequences, and Mediating Role of Organizational Ambidexterity," *Academy of Management Journal* 47 (2004), pp. 209–26.
19. J. Collins and J. Porras, *Built to Last* (London: Century, 1996).
20. D. A. Waldman and D. E. Bowen, "Learning to Be a Paradox-Savvy Leader," *Academy of Management Perspectives* 30 (2016), pp. 316–27; E. Miron-Spektor, A. Ingram, J. Keller, et al., "Microfoundations of Organiztional Paradox: The Problem Is How We Think about the Problem," *Academy of Management Journal* 61 (2018), pp. 26–45.
21. N. Nohria, W. Joyce, and B. Roberson, "What Really Works," *Harvard Business Review,* July 2003, pp. 42–52.
22. G. Satell, "How Blockbuster, Kodak and Xerox Really Failed (It's Not What You Think)," *Inc.,* July 7, 2018, www.inc.com.
23. R. M. Kanter, "Thriving Locally in the Global Economy," *Harvard Business Review,* August 2003, pp. 119–27.
24. E. Peterson, M. Hales, A. Peña, and N. Dessibourg-Freer, "2018 Global Cities Report," A.T. Kearney, www.atkearney.com, accessed April 30, 2019.
25. R. M. Kanter, "Thriving Locally in the Global Economy," *Harvard Business Review,* August 2003, pp. 119–27; R. M. Kanter, "How Great Companies Think Differently," *Harvard Business Review,* November 2011, pp. 66–78.

26. B. Burnes and B. Cooke, "The Past, Present and Future of Organization Development: Taking the Long View," *Human Relations* 65 (2012), pp. 1395-1429.

27. T. Cummings and C. Worley, *Organization Development and Change,* 8th ed. (Mason, OH: Thomson/South-Western, 2005); J. Bartunek, J. Balogun, and B. Do, "Considering Planned Change Anew: Stretching Large Group Interventions Strategically, Emotionally, and Meaningfully," *Academy of Management Annals* 5 (2011), pp. 1-52.

28. T. Cummings and C. Worley, *Organization Development and Change,* 8th ed. (Mason, OH: Thomson/South-Western, 2005); J. Bartunek, J. Balogun, and B. Do, "Considering Planned Change Anew: Stretching Large Group Interventions Strategically, Emotionally, and Meaningfully," *Academy of Management Annals* 5 (2011), pp. 1-52.

29. T. Cummings and C. Worley, *Organization Development and Change,* 8th ed. (Mason, OH: Thomson/South-Western, 2005).

30. J. Fairest, "Leading Employees through Major Organizational Change," *Ivey Business Journal Online* 1 (July-August 2014); D. R. Conner, *Managing at the Speed of Change* (New York: Random House, 2006); R. Teerlink, "Harley's Leadership U-Turn," *Harvard Business Review,* July-August 2000, pp. 43-48.

31. E. E. Lawler III, *Treat People Right!* (San Francisco: Jossey-Bass, 2003).

32. P. Zigarmi and J. Hoekstra, "Leadership Strategies for Making Change Stick," *Perspectives* (Ken Blanchard Companies, 2008), http://www.kenblanchard.com; D. Erwin and Garman, "Resistance to Organizational Change: Linking Research and Practice," *Leadership & Organization Development Journal* 31 (2010), pp. 39-56.

33. B. Shimoni, "What Is Resistance to Change? A Habitus-Oriented Approach," *Academy of Management Perspectives* 31 (2017), pp. 257-70.

34. B. Shimoni, "What Is Resistance to Change? A Habitus-Oriented Approach," *Academy of Management Perspectives* 31 (2017), pp. 257-70; J. D. Ford and L. W. Ford, "Decoding Resistance to Change," *Harvard Business Review,* April 2009, pp. 99-103; J. P. Kotter and L. A. Schlesinger, "Choosing Strategies for Change," *Harvard Business Review,* March-April 1979, pp. 106-14; P. Zigarmi and J. Hoekstra, "Leadership Strategies for Making Change Stick," *Perspectives* (Ken Blanchard Companies, 2008), http://www.kenblanchard.com.

35. Dina Gerdeman, "Religion in the Workplace: What Managers Need to Know," Harvard Business School, September 27, 2018, https://hbswk.hbs.edu/item/religion-in-the-workplace-what-managers-need-to-know.

36. Justin Walker, "Understanding Religion in the Workplace," *Business.com,* March 5, 2018, https://www.business.com/articles/religion-in-the-workplace/.

37. Alison Moodie, "Are US Businesses Doing Enough to Support Religious Diversity in the Workplace?" *The Guardian,* January 28, 2016, https://www.theguardian.com/sustainable-business/2016/jan/28/religious-diversity-us-business-muslim-hijab-discrimination-equal-employment-eeoc.

38. Alison Moodie, "Are US Businesses Doing Enough to Support Religious Diversity in the Workplace?" *The Guardian,* January 28, 2016, https://www.theguardian.com/sustainable-business/2016/jan/28/religious-diversity-us-business-muslim-hijab-discrimination-equal-employment-eeoc.

39. "HR Best Practices during Organizational Change," American Management Association, June 19, 2014, http://www.amanet.org; D. Zell, "Overcoming Barriers to Work Innovations: Lessons Learned at Hewlett-Packard," *Organizational Dynamics,* Summer 2001, pp. 77-85.

40. E. B. Dent and S. Galloway Goldberg, "Challenging Resistance to Change," *Journal of Applied Behavioral Science,* March 1999, pp. 25-41; J. D. Ford and L. W. Ford, "Decoding Resistance to Change," *Harvard Business Review,* April 2009, pp. 99-103; P. Zigarmi and J. Hoekstra, "Leadership Strategies for Making Change Stick," *Perspectives* (Ken Blanchard Companies, 2008), http://www.kenblanchard.com; J. Ford, L. Ford, and A. D'Amelio, "Resistance to Change: The Rest of the Story," *Academy of Management Review* 33 (2008), pp. 362-77.

41. S. Cummings, T. Bridgman, and K. Brown, "Unfreezing Change as Three Steps: Rethinking Kurt Lewin's Legacy for Change Management," *Human Relations* 69 (2016), pp. 33-60; G. Johnson, *Strategic Change and the Management Process* (New York: Basil Blackwell, 1987); K. Lewin, "Frontiers in Group Dynamics," *Human Relations* 1 (1947), pp. 5-41.

42. E. H. Schein, "Organizational Culture: What It Is and How to Change It," in *Human Resource Management in International Firms,* ed. P. Evans, Y. Doz, and A. Laurent (New York: St. Martin's Press, 1990).

43. M. Beer, R. Eisenstat, and B. Spector, *The Critical Path to Corporate Renewal* (Cambridge, MA: Harvard Business School Press, 1990).

44. D. Hellriegel and J. W. Slocum Jr., *Management,* 4th ed. (Reading, MA: Addison-Wesley, 1986).

45. F. Vermeulen, P. Puranam, and R. Gulate, "Change for Change's Sake," *Harvard Business Review* 88 (June 2010),pp. 70-76.

46. C. Aiken and S. Keller, "The Irrational Side of Change Management," *McKinsey Quarterly,* April 2009, http://www.mckinseyquarterly.com.

47. K. Lewin, "Frontiers in Group Dynamics," *Human Relations* 1 (1947), pp. 5-41.

48. S. Cummings, T. Bridgman, and K. Brown, "Unfreezing Change as Three Steps: Rethinking Kurt Lewin's Legacy for Change Management," *Human Relations* 69 (2016), pp. 33-60.

49. E. H. Schein, "Organizational Culture: What It Is and How to Change It," in *Human Resource Management in International Firms,* ed. P. Evans, Y. Doz, and A. Laurent (New York: St. Martin's Press, 1990).

50. E. E. Lawler III, *From the Ground Up* (San Francisco: Jossey-Bass, 1995).

51. Q. Nguyen Huy, "Time, Temporal Capability, and Planned Change," *Academy of Management Review* 26 (2001), pp. 601-23.

52. J. Shin, M. Taylor, and M. Seo, "Resources for Change: The Relationships of Organizational Inducements and Psychological Resilience to Employees' Attitudes and Behaviors Toward Organizational Change," *Academy of Management Journal* 55 (2012), pp. 727-48; B. Sugarman, "A Learning-Based Approach to Organizational Change: Some Results and Guidelines," *Organizational Dynamics,* Summer 2001, pp. 62-75.

53. J. P. Kotter and L. A. Schlesinger, "Choosing Strategies for Change," *Harvard Business Review,* March-April 1979, pp. 106-14.

54. R. H. Miles, "Beyond the Age of Dilbert: Accelerating Corporate Transformations by Rapidly Engaging all Employees," *Organizational Dynamics,* Spring 2001, pp. 313-21; D. Aguirre and M. Alpern, "10 Principles of Leading Change Management," *Strategy1Business,* June 26, 2014, http://www.strategy-business.com.

55. D. A. Nadler, "Managing Organizational Change: An Integrative Approach," *Journal of Applied Behavioral Science* 17 (1981), pp. 191-211; T. Laffoley, "Making Change Work," UNC Executive Development 2013, http://www.kenan-flagler.unc.edu.

56. D. Rousseau and S. A. Tijoriwala, "What's a Good Reason to Change? Motivated Reasoning and Social Accounts in Promoting Organizational Change," *Journal of Applied Psychology* 84 (1999), pp. 514-28.

57. "About Us," Envision, www.envisionco.org, accessed May 8, 2017.

58. Dori Meinert, "Wings of Change," *HR Magazine,* November 2012, Business Insights: Global, http://bi.galegroup.com.

59. C. F. Leana and B. Barry, "Stability and Change as Simultaneous Experiences in Organizational Life," *Academy of Management Review* 25 (2000), pp. 753-59; A. Muller and R. Kräussl, "The Value of Corporate Philanthropy during Times of Crisis: The Sensegiving Effect of Employee Involvement," *Journal of Business Ethics* 103 (2011), pp. 203-20.

60. R. Suddaby and W. Foster, "History and Organizational Change," *Journal of Management* 43 (2017), pp. 19-38.

61. O. Gadiesh and J. Gilbert, "Transforming Corner-Office Strategy into Frontline Action," *Harvard Business Review,* May 2001, pp. 72-79.

62. Ron Bousso, "Big Oil Spent 1 Percent on Green Energy in 2018," Reuters, November 11, 2018, https://www.reuters.com/article/us-oil-renewables/big-oil-spent-1-percent-on-green-energy-in-2018-idUSKCN1NH004.

63. "The Truth about Big Oil and Climate Change," *The Economist,* February 9, 2019, https://www.economist.com/leaders/2019/02/09/the-truth-about-big-oil-and-climate-change?cid1=cust/ednew/n/bl/n/2019/02/7n/owned/n/n/nwl/n/n/NA/199141/n.

64. Sarah Kent, "Oil Giant Shell Wants to Sell You Electricity," *The Wall Street Journal,* March 29, 2018, https://www.wsj.com/articles/oil-giant-shell-wants-to-sell-you-electricity-1522315801.

65. Julia Pyper, "Shell New Energies Director on Investing in Clean Energy: 'It's about Survival,'" *Green Tech Media,* April 1, 2019, https://www.greentechmedia.com/articles/read/shell-new-energies-director-on-investing-in-clean-energy#gs.8qzjff.

66. Maxx Chatsko, "3 Oil Companies Getting Serious about Renewable Energy—and 2 That Aren't," *Motley Fool,* June 29, 2018, https://www.fool.com/investing/2018/06/29/3-oil-companies-getting-serious-about-renewable-en.aspx.

67. J. Bartunek, J. Balogun, and B. Do, "Considering Planned Change Anew: Stretching Large Group Interventions Strategically, Emotionally, and Meaningfully," *Academy of Management Annals* 5 (2011), pp. 1-52.

68. B. Schneider, A. Brief, and R. Guzzo, "Creating a Climate and Culture for Sustainable Organizational Change," *Organizational Dynamics,* Spring 1996, pp. 7-19.

69. J. Kotter, *Leading Change* (Boston: Harvard Business School Press, 1996).

70. "Creating Organizational Transformations," *McKinsey Quarterly,* July 2008, www.mckinsey.com.

71. C. Dewar and S. Kellar, "The Irrational Side of Change Management, *McKinsey Quarterly,* April 2009, www.mckinsey.com.

72. M. Beer and N. Nohria, "Cracking the Code of Change," *Harvard Business Review,* May–June 2000, pp. 133-41; A. Spaulding, L. Gamm, J. Kim, and T. Menser, "Multiproject Interdependencies in Health Systems Management: A Longitudinal Qualitative Study," *Health Care Management Review* 39 (2014), p. 31.

73. N. Nohria and J. Berkley, "Whatever Happened to the Take-Charge Manager?" *Harvard Business Review,* January–February 1994, pp. 128-37.

74. D. Miller, J. Hartwick, and I. Le Breton-Miller, "How to Detect a Management Fad—and Distinguish It from a Classic," *Business Horizons,* July–August 2004, pp. 7-16.

75. Price Waterhouse Change Integration Team, *Better Change: Best Practices for Transforming Your Organization* (Burr Ridge, IL: Irwin, 1995).

76. Price Waterhouse Change Integration Team, *Better Change: Best Practices for Transforming Your Organization* (Burr Ridge, IL: Irwin, 1995).

77. J. P. Kotter, "Accelerate!" *Harvard Business Review,* November 2012, pp. 46-58; Kotter International, "Our Principles: Urgency," http://www.kotterinternational.com.

78. E. E. Lawler III, *From the Ground Up* (San Francisco: Jossey-Bass, 1995).

79. J. Kotter, *Leading Change* (Boston: Harvard Business School Press, 1996).

80. B. Schneider, A. Brief, and R. Guzzo, "Creating a Climate and Culture for Sustainable Organizational Change," *Organizational Dynamics,* Spring 1996, pp. 7-19.

81. R. Beckhard and R. Harris, *Organizational Transitions* (Reading, MA: Addison-Wesley, 1977); A. Carton, C. Murphy, and J. Clark, "A (Blurry) Vision of the Future: How Leader Rhetoric about Ultimate Goals Influences Performance," *Academy of Management Journal* 57 (2014), pp. 1544-70.

82. J. Kotter, *Leading Change* (Boston: Harvard Business School Press, 1996).

83. G. Hamel, "Waking Up IBM," *Harvard Business Review,* July–August 2000, pp. 137-46; A. Deutschman (2009), *Change or Die.* Boston: HarperCollins.

84. J. Kotter, *Leading Change* (Boston: Harvard Business School Press, 1996).

85. D. Smith, *Taking Charge of Change* (Reading, MA: Addison-Wesley, 1996).

86. G. Hamel, "Killer Strategies That Make Shareholders Rich," *Fortune,* June 23, 1997, pp. 22-34.

87. G. Hamel and C. K. Prahalad, *Competing for the Future* (Boston: Harvard Business School Press, 1994).

88. B. Gates, "10 Breakthrough Technologies 2019," *MIT Technology Review,* February 27, 2019, www.technologyreview.com.

89. "How Artificial Intelligence Is Shaping the Future of Energy," *Open Energi,* February 9, 2017, www.openenergi.com.

90. Aliah Wright, "Generation Z's Tech Habits May Surprise HR," Society for Human Resource Management, February 29, 2016, www.shrm.org.

91. "Gen Z and Millennials Collide at Work," Randstad USA, www.randstad.com, accessed May 17, 2017.

92. Aliah Wright, "Generation Z's Tech Habits May Surprise HR," Society for Human Resource Management, February 29, 2016, www.shrm.org.

93. M. Ward, "Gen Z Is about to Hit the Workforce—Here's What They Want in a Job," *CNBC,* August 30, 2016, www.cnbc.com.

94. T. Reddy, "Have You Seen the Future? Top 5 Predictions from the 2017 Tech Trends Report," IBM, January 23, 2017, www.ibm.com.

95. U. Saiidi, "How Smart Cities Are Building the Future," *CNBC,* February 9, 2017, www.cnbc.com.

96. S. Russo and B. Baron, "Do You Know the Price of Poor Infrastructure?" IBM, April 24, 2019, www.ibm.com.

97. J. Macomber, "The Smart Way to Build Smart Cities," *Forbes,* April 4, 2018, www.forbes.com.

98. "Smart Cities to Ease Traffic Congestion, Saving 4.2 Billion Man-Hours per Year by 2021," Juniper Research, June 27, 2016, www.juniperresearch.com.

99. G. Bell, "2017: Industrial IOT to Accelerate a Bright Future for Renewables," *Renewable Energy World,* February 16, 2017, www.renewableenergyworld.com.

100. E. Beinhocker, I. Davis, and L. Mendenca, "The 10 Trends You Have to Watch," *Harvard Business Review* 87 (July–August 2009), pp. 5-60.

101. S. Zuboff and J. Maxim, *The Support Economy* (New York: Penguin, 2004); R. M. Kanter, "How Great Companies Think Differently," *Harvard Business Review,* November 2011, pp. 66-78.

102. H. Courtney, J. Kirkland, and P. Viguerie, "Strategy under Uncertainty," *Harvard Business Review,* November–December 1997, pp. 66-79.

103. H. Courtney, J. Kirkland, and P. Viguerie, "Strategy under Uncertainty," *Harvard Business Review,* November–December 1997, pp. 66-79.

104. Benjamin Cheatham, Kia Javanmardian, and Hamid Samandari, "Confronting the Risks of Artificial Intelligence," *McKinsey Quarterly,* April 2019, https://www.mckinsey.com/business-functions/mckinsey-analytics/our-insights/Confronting-the-risks-of-artificial-intelligence?cid=other-eml-alt-mcq-mck&hlkid=81 3ae614ab12424f83d3e83d486cb782&hctky=9616900&hdpid=4c9baef0-8a99-4bb9-bdff-0327ade1db12.

105. Bernard Marr, "The 10 Vital Skills You Will Need for the Future of Work," *Forbes,* April 29, 2019, https://www.forbes.com/sites/bernardmarr/2019/04/29/the-10-vital-skills-you-will-need-for-the-future-of-work/#48d8b56c3f5b.

106. Lemonade website, https://www.lemonade.com/giveback, accessed April 30, 2019.

107. N. Resnick, "How One Company Is Disrupting the $600 Billion Dollar Manufacturing Industry," *Huffington Post,* June 20, 2016, www.huffpost.com.

108. "The March of Financial Services Giants into Bitcoin and Blockchain Startups in One Chart," *CBInsights,* February 19, 2017, www.cbinsights.com.

109. "Seven Industries That Blockchain Will Disrupt in 2017," *Bitcoin Magazine,* January 17, 2017, www.nasdaq.com.

110. C. Krauss, and D. Cardwell, "Policy Shift Helps Coal, but Other Forces May Limit Effect," *The New York Times,* March 28, 2017, www.nytimes.com; C. Sweet, "Despite Trump Move on Climate Change, Utilities' Shift from Coal Is Set to Continue," *The Wall Street Journal,* March 28, 2017, www.wsj.com.

111. S. Condon, "Facebook Ramps Up Ecommerce Offerings," *ZDNet,* October 19, 2016, www.zdnet.com.

112. D. Brodwin, "Unsustainable America: Consumers in India and China Are Ready to Live Sustainably," *U.S. News & World Reports,* March 23, 2015, www.usnews.com; A. Scott, "Sustainability: Building Better Practices," *Chemical Week,* October 11, 2010, pp. 24-27.

113. "Proof That Materials Behave Differently at the Nanoscale," *Nanowerk* (University of Cambridge), September 30, 2016, www.nonowerk.com; "Nanotechnology: The Promises and Pitfalls of Science at the Nanoscale," American Chemical Society, 2016, www.acs.org.

114. "Nanotechnology and You: Benefits and Applications," National Nanotechnology Initiative, www.nano.gov, accessed May 11, 2017; "Global Nanotechnology Market Outlook 2016-2024 Featuring Altair, Nanophase Tech & Nanosys," Research and Markets press release, March 1, 2017, www.researchandmarkets.com.

115. National Science Foundation, "Market Report on Emerging Nanotechnology Now Available," Media Advisory 14-004, February 25, 2014, http://www.nsf.gov.

116. "What Was the Most Important Breakthrough in Nanotechnology in 2018?" *Forbes,* January 3, 2019, www.forbes.com.

117. "Continuing to Protect the Nanotechnology Workforce: NIOSH Nanotechnology Research Plan for 2018-2025,"Centers for Disease Control and Prevention, January 2019, www.cdc.gov.

118. "Nanotechnology," Centers for Disease Control and Prevention, January 5, 2017, www.cdc.gov; L. Walter (2013), "Sizing Up Nanotechnology Safety" April 18; "News in Nanotechnology," *EHS Today,* December 2012, p . 20, https://www.ehstoday.com/safety/assp-releases-revised-z10-standard.

119. G. Hamel and C. K. Prahalad, *Competing for the Future* (Boston: Harvard Business School Press, 1994).

120. J. Kotter, *The New Rules: How to Succeed in Today's Post-Corporate World* (New York: Free Press, 1995).

121. T. Bateman and B. Barry, "Masters of the Long Haul: Pursuing Long-Term Work Goals," *Journal of Organizational Behavior,* 2012.

122. J. Kotter, *The New Rules: How to Succeed in Today's Post-Corporate World* (New York: Free Press, 1995).

123. T. Bateman and C. Porath, "Transcendent Behavior," in *Positive Organizational Scholarship,* ed. K. Cameron, J. Dutton, and R. Quinn (San Francisco: Barrett-Koehler, 2003).

124. L. A. Hill, "New Manager Development for the 21st Century," *Academy of Management Executive,* August 2004, pp. 121-26; D. A. Ready, J. A. Conger, and L. A. Hill, "Are You a High Potential?" *Harvard Business Review* 88 (June 2010), pp. 78-84.

125. E. E. Lawler III, *From the Ground Up* (San Francisco: Jossey-Bass, 1995); J. Kotter, *The New Rules: How to Succeed in Today's Post-Corporate World* (New York: Free Press, 1995).

126. E. E. Lawler III, *Treat People Right!* (San Francisco: Jossey-Bass, 2003).

127. M. Peiperl and Y. Baruck, "Back to Square Zero: The Post-Corporate Career," *Organizational Dynamics,* Spring 1997, pp. 7-22.

128. M. Peiperl and Y. Baruck, "Back to Square Zero: The Post-Corporate Career," *Organizational Dynamics,* Spring 1997, pp. 7-22.

129. D. R. Conner, *Managing at the Speed of Change* (New York: Random House, 2006), pp. 235-45.

130. J. W. Slocum Jr., M. McGill, and D. Lei, "The New Learning Strategy Anytime, Anything, Anywhere," *Organizational Dynamics,* Autumn 1994, pp. 33-37.

131. J. Kotter, *The New Rules: How to Succeed in Today's Post-Corporate World* (New York: Free Press, 1995).

132. J. Collins, *From Good to Great* (New York: HarperBusiness, 2001).

133. L. A. Hill, "New Manager Development for the 21st Century," *Academy of Management Executive,* August 2004, p . 125.

134. J. A. Raelin, "Don't Bother Putting Leadership into People," *Academy of Management Executive,* August 2004, pp. 131-35.

135. P. Omidyar, "How Great Companies Think Differently: eBay's Founder on Innovating the Business Model of Social Change," *Harvard Business Review,* September 2011, pp. 41-44; M. Porter and M. Kramer, "Creating Shared Value," *Harvard Business Review,* January-February 2011, pp. 62-77; H. Sabeti, "The For-Benefit Enterprise," *Harvard Business Review,* November 2011, pp. 99-104.

136. O. Sachgau and C. Reiter, "The Dismantling of Germany Inc.," *Bloomberg,* July 23, 2018, https://www.bloomberg.com/news/articles/2018-07-22/the-dismantling-of-germany-inc.

137. John Revill, "Siemens Lifts Profit Goals under New Vision 2020+ Strategy," Reuters, August 1, 2018, https://www.reuters.com/article/us-siemens-strategy/siemens-lifts-profit-goals-under-new-vision-2020-strategy-idUSKBN1KM5Y2.

138. Joe Kaeser, "To Beat Climate Change, Digitalize the Electrical World," *Time,* December 1, 2016, http://time.com/4587228/joe-kaeser-climate-change-energy/.

139. David Wemer, "Siemens USA CEO Advocates Using Technological Change for Good," Atlantic Council, December 13, 2018, https://www.atlanticcouncil.org/blogs/new-atlanticist/siemens-usa-ceo-advocates-using-technological-change-for-good.

140. "World's Most Admired Companies," *Fortune,* http://fortune.com/worlds-most-admired-companies/list/filtered?industry=Industrial%20Machinery&sortBy=industry-rank, accessed April 30, 2019.

141. P. Adler, "Alternative Economic Futures: A Research Agenda for Progressive Management Scholarship," *Academy of Management Perspectives* 30 (2016), pp. 123-38; R. Gulati, F. Wohlgezogen, and P. Zhelyazkov "The Two Facets of Collaboration: Cooperation and Coordination in Strategic Alliances," *Academy of Management Annals* 6 (2012), pp. 531-83.

142. P. Adler, "Alternative Economic Futures: A Research Agenda for Progressive Management Scholarship," *Academy of Management Perspectives* 30 (2016), pp. 123-38; R. Gulati, F. Wohlgezogen, and P. Zhelyazkov "The Two Facets of Collaboration: Cooperation and Coordination in Strategic Alliances," *Academy of Management Annals* 6 (2012), pp. 531-83.

PART FIVE   SUPPORTING CASE

Technology Helps Dollar General Remain Competitive

More and more consumers determined to save money are winding up at deep-discount retailers popularly known as dollar stores. These relatively small stores—including Dollar General, Family Dollar, and Dollar Tree—offer food, clothing, and household items at deep discounts. Discounters such as Target and Walmart offer a wider selection, but more consumers are trading down to find the best possible prices.

Competing with Walmart on price is hardly an easy strategy. When Kathleen Guion took charge of store operations and store development for Dollar General, she got to work initiating a whole host of changes. Many of these were aimed at controlling costs and helping the stores run more efficiently, and many of the changes involved improving the technology used by store employees, bringing it more in line with industry standards.

Guion found that Dollar General used some truly low-tech approaches to activities involved in running the stores. When trucks pulled up with deliveries, for example, store employees pulled cartons out of the truck one by one and carried them into the store for stocking the shelves. And whenever items languished on shelves too long, the same employees would repack them in boxes and carry them into the back room for storage. Not only were these methods slow, but employees hated lugging the boxes around. Calling her change program EZ Store, Guion simplified those jobs. She bought large wheeled bins called rolltainers, which employees use to move products from the trucks to back rooms to the sales floor. And when products don't sell as expected, the EZ Store plan calls for marking down the price low enough that the products do get sold. Not only does EZ Store make working for Dollar General more enjoyable by eliminating undesirable chores, but the greater efficiency gives employees more time to serve customers.

Under Guion's direction, Dollar General also upgraded its computer systems to deliver better information faster. The company introduced handheld scanners connected to an inventory management system so employees can quickly and accurately see which items need to be replenished and when. Computers linked to headquarters have been installed in the back rooms of all the stores. (Surprising as it may sound, until 2009, headquarters sent messages to stores via postal mail.) The company introduced computer-based training programs to improve employees' skills, as well as software for screening job candidates to identify which of them have qualities associated with success. And to reduce thefts in the stores, the company installed closed-circuit television systems.

Managers also have been given better technology. Dollar General bought district managers personal computers with software that monitors performance and flags exceptions to standards. It also gave them BlackBerry handheld devices so they can keep in touch with their people and keep up to date on store performance while they travel. The technology has enabled Dollar General to widen the district managers' span of control because fewer managers can keep up with more stores. More efficient management, in turn, has supported the company's program of rapidly opening new stores. (It now has more than 12,000 in 43 states.)

These efficiency improvements are essential for remaining successful in the changing deep-discount retailing industry. Dollar General's competitor Dollar Tree surprised industry observers by announcing that it would be purchasing Family Dollar for nearly $9 billion. This new entity (it'll keep both brands) will be larger than Dollar General in both sales and number of stores. In response to the move, former Dollar General CEO Richard Dreiling postponed his retirement to help the retailer adjust to the new competitive landscape. As Dollar General tries to maintain profitability, it will keep looking for ways to change how it does business, and technology will continue to play a role in the solutions. So far, it's a strategy that has fueled tremendous growth at Dollar General even as other retailers are struggling to maintain sales volume.

QUESTIONS

1. What types of control are important at Dollar General? Why are these important?

2. What technological innovations did Kathleen Guion introduce at Dollar General? How did these innovations support the company's strategy?

3. What challenges would you have expected Guion to face in introducing these changes? What principles of managing change would you have suggested she apply?

SOURCES: Based on company website, "Dollar General Opens 12,000th Store," May 30, 2015, http://www.dollargeneral.com; Ziobro, P., "Dollar Tree Wins the Battle for Family Dollar," *The Wall Street Journal*, January 22, 2015, http://www.wsj.com; Townsend, M., "Family Dollar Holders Accept $8.81 Billion Dollar Tree Bid," *Bloomberg Business*, January 22, 2015, http://www.bloomberg.com; "Operational Improvements Benefit Employees, Customers," *MMR*, May 17, 2010, Business & Company Resource Center, http://galenet.galegroup.com; Jannarone, J., "Will Dollar General Lead Retailers into Battle?" *The Wall Street Journal*, June 6, 2011, http://online.wsj.com; Zimmerman, A., "Dollar Stores Find Splurges Drying Up," *The Wall Street Journal*, July 11, 2011, http://online.wsj.com; Burritt, C., "Dollar Stores: More Brands, More Customers," *Bloomberg Businessweek*, July 29, 2010, http://www.businessweek.com; Jarzemsky, M., "Dollar General's Earnings Gain 15%," *The Wall Street Journal*, June 1, 2011, http://online.wsj.com; Dollar General, "About Us," http://dollargeneral.com; Dollar General, "Dollar General Announces Kathleen Guion, Division President of Store Operations and Store Development, Will Transition to Retirement," news release, July 25, 2011, http://newscenter.dollargeneral.com.

Budget and reward system, 113
Budgetary control, 503–505

Budgeting The process of investigating what is being done and comparing the results with the corresponding budget data to verify accomplishments or remedy differences; also called budgetary controlling, **503**

Budget types, 504

Buffering Creating supplies of excess resources in case of unpredictable needs, **61**–62

Building information model (BIM), 287
Built to Last (Collins/Porras), 556–557

Bureaucracy A classical management approach emphasizing a structured, formal network of relationships among specialized positions in the organization, **36**, 38

> in evolution of management thought, 32, 36–38, 61
> and technological innovation, 544–545

Bureaucratic control The use of rules, regulations, and authority to guide performance, **494**. *See also* Managerial control, bureaucratic control systems

Bureau of Labor Statistics, 233, 341
Burt's Bees, 158
Business
> geography of, 177
>> Africa and Middle East, 176
>> Americas, 175–176
>> China and India, 174–175
>> key aspects of global environment, 174
>> Western Europe, 173–174
> leader knowledge of, 373–374

Business accelerator Organization that provides support and advice to help young businesses grow, **211**

Business ethics The moral principles and standards that guide behavior in the world of business, **142**, 144–145. *See also* Ethics

Business Gateway site, of Business.gov, 234

Business incubators Protected environments for new, small businesses, **211**

Business model innovation, 526–527

Business plan A formal planning step that focuses on the entire venture and describes all the elements involved in starting it, **214**–215

Business practice, 64
Business Roundtable, 60

Business strategy The major actions by which a business competes in a particular industry or market, **128**–129

Business-to-business (B2B) e-commerce, 451
Business-to-business (B2B) model, 206
Business-to-business (B2B) selling, 54
Buyers, 44, 68
BYOA. *See* Bring your own app (BYOA)
BYOD. *See* Bring your own device (BYOD) policy

C

Cadillac, 59, 175

Cafeteria benefit program An employee benefit program in which employees choose from a menu of options to create a benefit package tailored to their needs, **318**

CAFTA-DR. *See* Central America-Dominican Republic Free Trade Agreement (CAFTA-DR)
Calamities, 204
Cambridge Analytica, 97, 140
Campfire, 64
Canada, 176
Canadian North, 213
Capability development, and technology, 537–538
Capital budget, 504
Capitalism, 154
Capital requirement, 52
Capterra, 81–82, 84–85
Carbon emissions, 158

Carbon footprint The output of carbon dioxide and other greenhouse gases, **157**

CareerBuilder, 303
Career development
> being accountable, 22–23
> be self-reliance, 20
> connecting with people, 20–21
> continuous learning, 574
> critical skills, 573–574
> emotional intelligence, 19
> expert advice, 20
> generalist, 19
> learning and leading, 574–575
> learning cycle, 574
> Level 5 hierarchy, 574–575
> lifelong learning, 574–575
> and promotions, 352
> relationship with organization, 21
> specialist, 19
Career path, 246
Career Solvers, 473
Carlo's Bake Shop, 123
Carnival Corporation, 339
Cases
> Best Trust Bank, 485
> Big Bison Resorts, 426–427
> DIY Stores, 291–292
> Invincibility Systems, 327–328
> Niche Hotel Group (NHG), 357–358
> Oré Earth Skin Care, 163–164
> Quadra Drilling Systems, 455–456
> Soaring Eagle Skate Company, 102–103

Soft Scroll, 227
Stanley Lynch Investment Group, 264
Tata Motors, 71–72
Treasure Cup, 194
Wish You Wood Toy Store, 135
Worldwide Games, 550
Cash budget, 504
Cash cow, in BCG matrix, 127–128
Caterpillar, 179, 251, 349

Caux Principles A regenerative, collaborative economic system that contrasts with the linear economy described earlier by minimizing input, waste, emissions, and energy leakage, **143**

Cement companies, 239
Centennials, 570
Center for Generational Kinetics, 570
Central America-Dominican Republic Free Trade Agreement (CAFTA-DR), 176
Centralization, 35

Centralized organization An organization in which high-level executives make most decisions and pass them down to lower levels for implementation, **245**

CEO pay, as ethical issue, 145
CEO. *See* Chief executive officer (CEO)
Ceremony, 65

Certainty The state that exists when decision makers have accurate and comprehensive information, **78**

Challenge, 388
Change and change management
> achieving sustained greatness, 558–559
> anchor new approaches in culture, 569
> becoming world class, 556–559
> consolidate gains and produce more, 569
> creating and leading, 1
> education and communication, 563–564
> enlisting cooperation, 563–565
> explicit and implicit coercion, 564–565
> facilitation and support, 564–565
> genius of the *and*, 558
> harmonizing multiple changes, 565–567
> leading, 559–560, 567–569
> managing resistance, 560–565
> manipulation and cooptation, 564–565
> motivating people, 560–562
> moving, 563
> negotiation and rewards, 564–565
> organizational development, 559
> participation and involvement, 564
> refreezing, 563
> sustainable, great futures, 556–557
> tyranny of the *or,* 557
> unfreezing, 562–563
> *See also* Shaping the future
Change vision, communication, 568
ChanZuckerberg Initiative, 22

Charismatic leader A person who is dominant, self-confident, convinced of the moral righteousness of his or her beliefs, and able to arouse a sense of excitement and adventure in followers, **383**

Chatbot, 6
Chevrolet, 539
Chevron, 187
Chevy, 53
Chick-fil-A, 53, 123, 401
Chief executive officer (CEO), 16, 119, 241–242, 247

Chief information officer (CIO)   Executive in charge of information technology strategy and development, 16, 242, **542**

Chief innovation officer, 542
Chief operating officer (COO), 16
Chief technology officer (CTO), 542
Child labor provisions, 318
Chile, 176
Chi-Med, 540
China, 274
    charismatic leaders from, 383
    companies outsourcing jobs to, 172
    disaster-resilient homes in, 386
    Disney theme park in, 131
    doing business via joint ventures, 184
    environmental problems in, 157
    feedback to employees in, 310
    Foxconn as employer in, 232
    and inexpensive labor force, 51
    and international licensing, 183
    and international management, 174–175
    lack of qualified executives, 185
    pressures for local responsiveness, 178–179
    problems with counterfeits, 191
    Quadra Drilling Systems in, 455
    socializing with boss, 465
    substitutes for leadership, 382
    tech-savvy shoppers in, 169
    top global firms in, 171
    trade war with, 4
    transnational model, 181
China National Petroleum (China), 4, 171
Chipotle, 53, 283, 498
Chipotle Mexican Grill, 116
Chrysler, 489
Church & Dwight Company, 126
Cigna Group, 59
CIM. *See* Computer-integrated manufacturing (CIM)
CIO. *See* Chief information (or technology, or knowledge) officer (CIO)
Circle Internet Financial, 571

Circular economy   A regenerative, collaborative economic system that contrasts with the linear economy described earlier by minimizing input, waste, emissions, and energy leakage, **159**

Cisco, 434, 443, 466, 570
Cisco Foundation, 277
Cisco WebEx, 46
Citibank, 152
Citigroup, 306
Civil aspiration, 154
Civil Rights Act (1964), 334–335, 338
Civil Rights Act (1991), 308

Civil Rights Act (1964), Title VII of, 308
Clairol, 126

Clan control   Control based on the norms, values, shared goals, and trust among group members, **494**–495

Classical approaches, to management, 32–33
CliftonStrengths assessment, 20
Climate, 44, 68
    company responsibility of impact on, 145
    organizational, 65–66
Climate change, 49, 61, 158, 204, 555
Clinton Global Initiative, 177
Closeness of supervision, 375
Cloud computing, 531
CM. *See* Crisis management (CM)

Coaching   Dialogue with a goal of helping another be more effective and achieve his or her full potential on the job, 310, **476**

Coalition, 60–61, 568

Coalition model   Model of organizational decision making in which groups with differing preferences use power and negotiation to influence decisions, **96**

Coal mining, 319
Coal-mining technologies, 546
Coca-Cola, 5, 49, 51–52, 54, 152, 155, 187, 207, 273
Cocheco Company, 33
Coercion, for managing resistance to change, 564–565
Coercive power, 372
Cognitive ability test, 305

Cognitive conflict   Issue-based differences in perspectives or judgments, **93**

Cohesiveness   The degree to which a group is attractive to its members, members are motivated to remain in the group, and members influence one another, **445**–448, 451–452

Coinbase, 571
Cold Stone Creamery, 183, 309
Colgate, 186
Colgate-Palmolive, 158

Collaboration   A style of dealing with conflict emphasizing both cooperation and assertiveness to maximize both parties' satisfaction, 7–8, 240, **450**, 452, 545, 575–576

Collective bargaining, 320–321
Collectivism. *See* Individualism/collectivism
Colombia, 176
Comcast NBCUniversal, 336, 366
Communicating, 1
    encouraging open, 511
    general model of, 462
    improving skills, 469–475
    interpersonal, 462–469
    for managing resistance to change, 563–564

media richness, 468
one-way *versus* two-way, 462–463
oral and written channels, 464
organizational, 475–480
pitfalls of, 463–464
SoundCloud, 461
See also entries for specific types of communication

Communication   The transmission of information and meaning from one party to another through the use of shared symbols, **462**

Communitarian entrepreneurial identity, 208

Comparable worth   Principle of equal pay for different jobs of equal worth, **318**

Compassion, 190
Compensation and benefits, legal issues in, 316, 318
Competence skills of workforce, 117

Competing   A style of dealing with conflict involving strong focus on one's own goals and little or no concern for the other person's goals, **450**

Competition, 217, 446
Competitive action, 62
Competitive advantage, 62
Competitive aggression, 59–60, 221

Competitive environment   The immediate environment surrounding a firm; includes suppliers, customers, rivals, and the like, **44**

    competitors, 51–52, 68
    customers, 54–55, 68
    new entrants, 52, 68
    opportunities and threats in, 124–125
    substitutes and complements, 52–53, 68
    suppliers, 53–54, 68

Competitive intelligence   Information that helps managers determine how to compete better, **57**

Competitive landscape
    collaboration across boundaries, 7–8
    globalization, 4–5
    knowledge management, 6–7
    technological change, 5–6
Competitive pacification, 59
Competitor analysis, 121
Competitors (rival firms), 50–52, 57, 68
Complement, 52–53

Compliance-based ethics program   Company mechanisms typically designed by corporate counsel to prevent, detect, and punish legal violations, **149**

Compromise   A style of dealing with conflict involving moderate attention to both parties' concerns, **449**

Computer-aided design, 284
Computer-aided manufacturing, 284
Computer chip, 534

Computer-integrated manufacturing (CIM) The use of computer-aided design and computer-aided manufacturing to sequence and optimize a number of production processes, **284**

Concentration A strategy an organization uses to operate a single business and compete in a single industry, **126**–127

Concentric diversification A strategy used to add new businesses that produce related products or are involved in related markets and activities, **127**

Conceptual and decision skill Skill pertaining to abilities that help to identify and resolve problems for the benefit of the organization and its members, **18**

Concern for people, 375, 377
Concern for production, 375, 377

Concurrent control The control process used while plans are being carried out, including directing, monitoring, and fine-tuning activities as they are performed, **499**–500

Concurrent engineering A design approach in which all relevant functions cooperate jointly and continually in a maximum effort aimed at producing high-quality products that meet customers' needs, **287**

Conference Board, 58

Conflict Opposing pressures from different sources, occurring on the level of psychological conflict or conflict between individuals or groups, **80**

    constructive, in decision making, 92–93
    and culture, 449
    management strategies for, 449–451
    managing, 449–451
Conflict style, 449–451

Conglomerate diversification A strategy used to add new businesses that produce unrelated products or are involved in unrelated markets and activities, **127**–128

Congressional testimony, 3
Consequences, 404
Consideration, 375–376
Constructive conflict, 92–93
Constructive conflict management, 448
Consulting firms, 234
Consumer Expenditure Survey, 233
Container Store, 280
Contemporary approaches, to management, 32, 37
Content validity, 306

Contingencies Factors that determine the appropriateness of managerial actions, **38**

Contingency perspective An approach to the study of management proposing that the managerial strategies, structures, and processes that result in high performance depend on the characteristics, or important contingencies, of the situation in which they are applied, 32, **37**–38

Contingency plans Alternative courses of action that can be implemented based on how the future unfolds, **83,** 111–112

Contingency theory, 32, 37–38
Contingent worker, 62
Continuous improvement, 9

Continuous process A process that is highly automated and has a continuous production flow, **283**

Contracted development, of technology, 540
Contraction, 60–62

Control Any process that directs the activities of individuals toward the achievement of organizational goals, **494**

Control culture, 71
Control cycle, 495–499

Controlling The management function of monitoring performance and making needed changes, 1, 12, **14**–15

Control systems, designing effective, 510–513
Conventional stage, 144
Cooperation, 449–450
Cooperation, enlisting, 563–565

Cooperative strategies Strategies used by firms who want to reach their objectives in cooperation with other firms through alliances and partnerships rather than by competing with them, **60**–61

Coopetition Simultaneous competition and cooperation among companies with the intent of creating value, **8**

Cooptation, 60–61, 564–565

Coordination The procedures that link the various parts of an organization for the purpose of achieving the organization's overall mission, **239,** 240

Coordination and communication, 258–259

Coordination by mutual adjustment Units interact with one another to make accommodations to achieve flexible coordination, **257**–258

Coordination by plan Interdependent units are required to meet deadlines and objectives that contribute to a common goal, **256**

Coordination by standardization, 256
COO. *See* Chief operating officer (COO)
CopyShark.net, 212

Core capability (competence) A unique skill and/or knowledge an organization possesses that gives it an edge over competitors, **123**–124, 272

Corning, 124
Corporate citizenship, 117

Corporate diplomacy An umbrella term for attempting to influence external stakeholders through a variety of strategic activities, **60**

Corporate entrepreneurship
    building intrapreneurship, 220
    management challenges, 220–221
    orientation, 221
    support for idea, 219–220
Corporate ethical standards, 147

Corporate governance The role of a corporation's executive staff and board of directors in ensuring that the firm's activities meet the goals of the firm's stakeholders, **242**

Corporate Knights, 11
Corporate mission statement, 64
Corporate responsibility, 1
    contrasting views, 154–155
    corporate social responsibility (CSR), 153
    philanthropic responsibilities, 154
    pyramid of global corporate social responsibility and performance, 153
    reconciliation, 155
    stewardship, 152
    transcendent education, 154

Corporate social responsibility (CSR) Obligation toward society assumed by business, **153,** 207
See also Ethics

Corporate strategy The set of businesses, markets, or industries in which an organization competes and the distribution of resources among those entities, **126,** 127–128

Costa Rica, 176
Cost budget, 504
Costco, 117, 169

Cost competitiveness Keeping costs low to achieve profits and be able to offer prices that are attractive to consumers, **11**–12

Costs
    and ethics, 150
    of technology, 533–534
Counterfeits, 191
County business patterns, 233
Courage, 150–151, 386–387
Cowork Café, 443
Co-working, 443
CPO Commerce, 477
Cradle-to-cradle approach, 158
Creativity, 573
    actions, 94
    brainstorming, 94–95

Digital communication, social media and, 465–468
Digital entrepreneur, 206
Digital wallet payment, 206
Digital World boxes
artificial intelligence (AI), 351, 388
BYOD and BYOA policies, 541
chatbot, 6
crowdfunding, 212
digital monitoring and ethics, 147
employee performance reviews, 497
global mail etiquette, 190
global virtual teamwork, 440
Gmail, 468
online networks replace traditional hierarchies, 257
organization culture, 64
predictive analytics, 89
"social listening," 280
social media profiles, 304
technological advances, 122
technology to motivate, 420
tech-savvy Gen Z enters workforce, 570
D&I initiatives, 436, 501
Dillard's, 286
Direct contact (mutual adjustment), 259
Directive leadership, 375, 381
Disabilities, including people with, 336, 340–341
Disaster, contingency plan for, 112
Disaster-resilient homes, engineering, 386
Discipline, 35

Discounting the future (also **Discount the future**) A bias weighting short-term costs and benefits more heavily than longer-term costs and benefits, **87**

Discover learning cycle, 574
Discrimination, 152, 335
See also Diversity
D&I. See Diversity and inclusion (D&I) initiative (D&I)
Disney, 203, 556–557
Disney Plus, 131

Disruptive innovation A process by which a product, service, or business model takes root initially in simple applications at the bottom of a market and then moves "up market," eventually displacing established competitors, **531**

Disseminator, 17
Distribution channel, 127
Disturbance, 17
Diverse supplier, 336
Diverse team, 92

Diverse workforce One in which there are both similarities and differences among employees in terms of age, cultural background, physical abilities and disabilities, race, religion, sex, and sexual orientation, **334**

Diversification A firm's investment in a different product, business, or geographic area, **59, 128**

Diversity Bringing in multiple distinctive categories of people sharing human commonalities; a broad term used to refer to all kinds of differences. These differences include education, political belief, religion, and income in addition to gender, race, ethnicity, and nationality, **335, 342, 348–349**

accountability, 352
advantages of, in workforce, 1, 48
advantages through, and inclusion, 343
age, 341
assumptions and implications, 348
attracting, 349
awareness building among, 350–351
and brand marketing, 126
career development and promotions, 35
changing workforce, 335–341
company diversity initiatives, examples of, 336
components of diversified workforce, 335–336
and cultural intelligence, 573
educational, 446
education levels, 341
gender issues, 336
history, 334–335
and inclusion, 342–347
management, 448
mental and physical disabilities, 340–341
mentoring, 352
minorities and immigrants, 339–340
multicultural organizations, 347–348
national, 446
and pay inequities, 152
retaining, 351–352
skill building, 351
start-ups and, 217
in teams, 92
training, 350–351
women, top companies for, 338
See also entries for specific types of diversity; Inclusion; Recruitment
Diversity and inclusion (D&I) initiative (D&I), 416
Diversity council, sponsoring, 336
Diversity management, 448

Diversity training Programs that focus on identifying and reducing hidden biases against people with differences and developing the skills needed to manage a diversified workforce, **310**

Divestiture A firm selling one or more businesses, **59**

Divisional organization Departmentalization that groups units around products, customers, or geographic regions, **249–251**

Division of labor The assignment of different tasks to different people or groups, **238**

Division of work, 35
DIY Stores, 291–292

Dogs, in BCG matrix, 127–128

Domain selection Entering a new market or industry using an existing expertise, **58**

Dominican Republic, 176
Domino's, 498
Donor Alliance, 281
Dow Chemical, 158, 186
Dow Jones, 233
Dow Jones Industrial Average, 45

Downsizing The planned elimination of positions or jobs, **278,** 306

Downward communication Information that flows from higher to lower levels in the organization's hierarchy, **475**

coaching, 476
in difficult times, 476–477
information loss in, 475–476
open-book management, 477
DPMO. *See* Defects per million opportunities (DPMO)
Drive, leader, 373–374
Dropbox, 53, 440
Dr Pepper Snapple, 63, 273
Drug-Free Workplace Act of 1988, 305
Drug testing, 305
Dual-career couple, 186
DuPont, 531

Dynamic capabilities Higher-level strategic capabilities (compared with ordinary capabilities) that aid rapid adaptation, **272**

Dynamic network Temporary arrangements among partners that can be assembled and reassembled to adapt to the environment, **254**

Dynamic organization, building, 14

E
Early adopter, 529, 534, 538. *See also* Technology
EA Sports, 540
Eastman Kodak, 184
eBay, 49, 82, 207, 525
EBSCOhost, 233
Ecomagination, 157
E-commerce, 205–206
Economic dislocation, 204
Economic environment, 174, 211
Economic programs (data by sector), 233

Economic responsibilities To produce goods and services that society wants at a price that perpetuates the business and satisfies its obligations to investors, **153**

Economic strike, 321
Economic viability, 536–538

Economies of scale Reductions in the average cost of a unit of production as the total volume produced increases, **32**, 39, 276, 280

Economies of scope Economies in which materials and processes employed in one product can be used to make other, related products, 275–**276**

Economist's Global Forecasting Service, 58
Economy, 44–46, 68
　global, 170–173
　government influence over, 45
EDGAR database, 233
Edmunds.com, 82
Edom Nutritional Solutions, 208
Education
　diversity and levels of, 341
　diversity in, 446
　for managing resistance to change, 563
　of workforce, 48
EEOC. *See* Equal Employment Opportunity Commission (EEOC)
Effective, 12
Effects, 404
Efficient, 12
Effort-to-performance link, 406–407
Egalitarianism, 543

Egoism An ethical system defining acceptable behavior as that which maximizes consequences for the individual, **143**

Electrical grid, 97
Electronic word processing, 534
El Salvador, 176
Email, 465–468. *See also* Digital communication
Email etiquette, 190
Emerging technologies, 534

Emotional intelligence (EQ) Skills of understanding yourself, managing yourself, and dealing effectively with others, **19,** 573

Empathy, 154, 436
Employee benefits, 317–318

Employee engagement When employees invest their physical, mental, and emotional energy into performing their jobs, including working hard and producing, taking initiative, and contributing additional citizenship behaviors, **415**

Employee feedback, 314
Employee monitoring, future trends in, 516
Employee Polygraph Protection Act
　(EPPA), 305
Employee Retirement Income Security Act
　(ERISA), 318
Employee satisfaction and well-being, 419–422
Employee tracking, 509

Employment-at-will The legal concept that an employer can terminate an employee for any reason, **307**

Empowering, 444

Empowerment The process of sharing power with employees, thereby enhancing

their confidence in their ability to perform their jobs and their belief that they are influential contributors to the organization, **61, 415**–416

Energy efficiency, 204
Energy needs, managing, 566
Engineering, 122
Entrance, 446

Entrepreneur Individual who establishes a new organization without the benefit of corporate sponsorship, 17, **201**

Entrepreneur.com and magazine, 233

Entrepreneurial orientation The tendency of an organization to identify and capitalize successfully on opportunities to launch new ventures by entering new or established markets with new or existing goods or services, **221**

Entrepreneurial personality, 208–210

Entrepreneurial venture A new business having growth and high profitability as primary objectives, **200**

Entrepreneur magazine, 205

Entrepreneurship The pursuit of lucrative opportunities by enterprising individuals, 1, **200**

　corporate, 219–221
　e-commerce, 205–206
　entrepreneurial personality, 208–210
　franchises, 204–205
　idea, 203
　increasing chances of success, 214–219
　information/resources, 233–234
　innovation, 209–210
　Latina entrepreneurs, 207
　making good choices, 209–210
　management challenges, 211–214
　myths about, 200–201
　next frontiers for, 205
　nonfinancial resources, 218–219
　opportunity, 203–204
　risk, 209–210
　role of economic environment, 211
　social, 206–208
　Starbucks, 199–200, 210, 222
　start-ups and diversity, 217
　strategy matrix, 209–210
　success and failure, 210–211
　successful entrepreneurs, 201–202
　what it takes to succeed, 203
　who is an entrepreneur, 203, 224
　why become an entrepreneur, 22
Entry mode
　exporting, 182–183
　franchising, 182–183
　joint ventures, 182, 184
　licensing, 182–183
　wholly owned subsidiaries, 182, 184
Environmental agenda, 158–159
Environmental analysis, 55–58, 120–121
　attractive and unattractive environments, 57
　benchmarking, 58
　forecasting, 58

　scanning, 57
　scenario development, 57
　uncertainty, 56
Environmental complexity, 56
Environmental degradation, 157
Environmental dynamism, 56
Environmental risk, 157

Environmental scanning Searching for and sorting through information about the environment, **57**

Environmental uncertainty When managers do not have enough information about the environment to understand or predict the future, **56**

Environment context, 217
EPPA. *See* Employee Polygraph Protection Act (EPPA)
EQ. *See* Emotional intelligence (EQ)
Equal Employment Opportunity Commission (EEOC), 308
Equal employment laws, U.S., 308–309
Equal Employment Opportunity Commission (EEOC), 47, 338
Equal pay, 152
Equal Pay Act (1963), 308, 318
Equal-pay-for-equal-work, 318
Equifax, 155
Equity, 35, 417–418

Equity theory A theory stating that people assess how fairly they have been treated according to two key factors: outcomes and inputs, **416**–418

ERF theory, Alderfer's, 409
ERISA. *See* Employee Retirement Income Security Act (ERISA)
Ernst & Young. *See* EY (formerly Ernst & Young)
ESPN, 131
Esprit de corps, 35
Esteem or ego needs, 409–410

Ethical climate In an organization, the processes by which decisions are evaluated and made on the basis of right and wrong, **146**

Ethical issue Situation, problem, or opportunity in which an individual must choose among several actions that must be evaluated as morally right or wrong, **142**

Ethical leader One who is both a moral person and a moral manager influencing others to behave ethically, **147**

Ethical responsibilities Meeting other social expectations, not written as law, **153**

Ethics The system of rules that governs the ordering of values, 1, **140**

　astroturfing, 142
　business, 144–145
　codes, 147–148
　corporate standards, 147

costs and, 150
courage, 150–151
cross-selling, 140
danger signs of unethical behavior, 146
in decision making, 149–150
economic responsibilities, 153
egoism, 143
ethical responsibilities, 153
fictional blogs, 142
issues in international management, 190–191
issues of, in business, 145
legal responsibilities, 153
lying/truth-telling, 141
programs, 148
relativism, 143–144, 149
scandals, 140
systems, 142–144
triple bottom line, 153
universalism, 142–143, 149
utilitarianism, 143
virtue, 143–144
Ethics codes, 147–148
Ethics of Management, The (Hosmer), 150
Ethics Resource Center, 148
Ethnic diversity, 48
Ethnic News Watch, 233

Ethnocentrism The tendency to judge others by the standards of one's own group or culture, which are seen as superior, **187**, 348

Etsy, 299, 349
Euro, 173–174
Euromonitor, 233
European Union (EU)
  and Brexit, 79
  and international management, 173–174
  and ISO 9001, 282
  pressures for local responsiveness, 178–179
  uncertainty and risk, 70
Eurozone, 38
EU. *See* European Union (EU)
Evaluating, and human resources, 299–302, 323
Evernote, 53
Everyone-else-does-it self-defense, 147
Ewing Marion Kauffman Foundation, 233
Executive, international, 186

Executive champion An executive who supports a new technology and protects the product champion, **543**

Executive Orders 11246 and 11375 (1965), 308
Executive pay, 317
Existence needs, 410

Expatriates Parent-company nationals who are sent to work at a foreign subsidiary, **185**, 186

Expectancy Employees' perception of the likelihood that their efforts will enable them to attain their performance goals, **406**–407

Expectancy theory A theory proposing that people will behave based on their perceived likelihood that their effort will

lead to a certain outcome and on how highly they value that outcome, **406**–407

Experimenting, and innovation, 544
Expert power, 372–373
Explicit and implicit coercion, for managing resistance to change, 564
Exploitation, 270, 544
Exploration, 270, 544
Explore learning cycle, 574
Exporting, 182–183
Express Scripts Holding Co., 59
Extended enterprise, 54

External audit An evaluation conducted by one organization, such as a CPA firm, on another, **502**

External environment All relevant forces outside a firm's boundaries, such as competitors, customers, the government, and the economy, 1, 38, **44**, 68

  acquisition, 59
  actively managing, 58–62
  adapting to, 61–62
  changing, 58–59
  changing organization, 61–62
  choosing approach, 62
  cooperative action, 60–61
  diversification, 59
  domain selection, 58–59
  influencing, 59–60
  merger, 59
  strategic maneuvering, 58
External locus of control, 381
External opportunities and threats, in management process, 118–121
External recruiting, 303
External technological trends, 534–535

Extinction Withdrawing or failing to provide a reinforcing consequence, **404**

Extrinsic reward Reward given to a person by the boss, the company, or some other person, **411**

ExxonMobil, 171, 305, 555, 566
EY (formerly Ernst & Young), 233, 301, 336, 340, 352, 561

F

Facebook, 3–4, 6, 10, 15, 97, 142, 242, 303, 305, 337, 341, 465, 533, 541, 570–571
Facebook–Cambridge Analytica data breach, 140
Face-to-face communication, 468
Facilitation and support, for managing resistance to change, 564–565
FacioMetrics, 541
Factiva, 233
Fail-safing, 287
Failure, of entrepreneur, 212–213

Failure rate The number of expatriate managers of an overseas operation who come home early, **186**

Fair Labor Standards Act (1938), 308, 318

Fairness, 190
  assessing equity, 417–418
  equity theory, 416–418
  procedural justice, 418–419
  restoring equity, 418
Family, accommodating work needs and, 350
Family and Medical Leave Act (1991), 308
Family-friendly benefit, 337
Farming innovations, 538
Fast Company, 233
Fast-food companies, 239
FCA. *See* Fiat-Chrysler Automobiles (FCA)
FDA. *See* Food & Drug Administration (FDA)
FDI. *See* Foreign direct investment (FDI)
Federal Express Corporation, 444
Federal Interagency Reentry Council, 350
Federal Reserve, 45
Federal Reserve Board, 146
Federal Reserve Bulletin, 233
FedEx, 54, 340
Feedback, 415
  providing, 405–406
  and younger employees, 273

Feedback control Control that focuses on the use of information about previous results to correct deviations from the acceptable standard, **499**, 500

Feedforward control The control process used before operations begin, including policies, procedures, and rules designed to ensure that planned activities are carried out properly, **499**, 500

Femininity. *See* Masculinity/femininity
Fiat-Chrysler Automobiles (FCA), 8
Fictional blog, 142
Fidelity Investments, 337

Fiedler's contingency's model of leadership effectiveness A situational approach to leadership postulating that effectiveness depends on the personal style of the leader and the degree to which the situation gives the leader power, control, and influence over the situation, **379**–380

Fifth Amendment, 147
Figurehead, 17

Filtering The process of withholding, ignoring, or distorting information, **463**

Final consumer A customer who purchases products in their finished form, **54**

Financial analysis, 122
Financial control
  balance sheet, 505–506
  financial ratios, 507–508
  profit and loss statement, 507
Financial goal, 117
First Data Corp., 366
FirstSearch, 233
Fitbit, 212
500 Startups, 211

Flexible benefit programs Benefit programs in which employees are given credits to spend on benefits that fit their unique needs, **318**

Flexible factory   Manufacturing plant that has short production runs, is organized around products, and uses decentralized scheduling, 62, **284**

Flexible manufacturing, 283–285

Flexible processes   Methods for adapting the technical core to changes in the environment, **62**

Flexible work arrangement, 273
Flipkart, 206, 274
Followership, 371, 533–534
Food & Drug Administration (FDA), 52, 498
Food poisoning, 116
Food safety violations, 116
Foolproofing, 287
Footprint, **157**

Force-field analysis   An approach to implementing the unfreezing/moving/refreezing model by identifying the forces that prevent people from changing and those that will drive people toward change, **563**

Ford Motor Company, 18, 72, 113, 184, 313, 386–387, 489, 546

Forecast (or forecasting)   Method for predicting how variables will change the future, **58**

Foreign Corrupt Practices Act, 146
Foreign direct investment (FDI), 170
Forever 21, 339

Formalization   The presence of rules and regulations governing how people in the organization interact, **256**

Formal position authority, 240
Formal structure, of organization, 270–271
Formulation, in management process, 118–119, 124–129
401(k) plan, 318
40K Plus Education, 208
Foxconn, 232
Fox studio, 131

Framing effect   A decision bias influenced by the way in which a problem or decision alternative is phrased or presented, **87**

Franchise, 204–205
Franchise Chat, 205

Franchising   An entrepreneurial alliance between a franchisor (an innovator who has created at least one successful store and wants to grow) and a franchisee (a partner who manages a new store of the same type in a new location), 182–183, **204**

Freenome, 204
Friendster, 533

Frontline manager   Lower-level manager who supervises the operational activities of the organization, **16**–17, 114, 116

Functional manager, 253

Functional organization   Departmentalization around specialized activities such as production, marketing, and human resources, **247,** 248–249

Functional strategy   Strategy implemented by each functional area of the organization to support the organization's business strategy, **129**

Functions of the Executives, The (Barnard), 35
Fundamental budgetary considerations, 503–504
FundersClub, 215
Fundly, 212

G

GAAP. *See* Generally accepted accounting principles (GAAP)
Gale Group, 233
Gallup, 20
Gambling, 86
Gap Inc., 49, 169, 302, 310, 463, 497

Garbage can model   Model of organizational decision making depicting a chaotic process and seemingly random decisions, **96**

Gatekeeper   A team member who keeps abreast of current developments and provides the team with relevant information, **447**

Gatorade GX, 9
GDP. *See* Gross domestic product (GDP)
GE Capital, 128
Geert Hofstede, 188–189
GE Global Research, 536
Gender diversity, 48, 335–339. *See also* Diversity
General Dynamics, 337
General Electric Corporation, 127–128, 156–157, 275–276, 281, 349–350, 480, 497, 556–557
Generalist, 19
Generality, 154
Generally accepted accounting principles (GAAP), 504
General Mills, 49, 338
General model for managing resistance, 562–563
General Motors (GM), 59, 110–111, 113, 124, 150, 175, 237–238, 246, 250–251, 260, 275–276, 283, 337, 384, 489, 504, 545
Generation X (Gen X), 7
Generation Z (Gen Z), 7, 570
Generic drug maker, 533
Generic value chain, 279

genius of the *and*   Ability to achieve multiple objectives simultaneously, **558**

Geographic division, 250
Ghana, 80, 206

Glass ceiling   An invisible barrier that makes it difficult for women and minorities to move beyond a certain hierarchical level, **337**

Glassdoor.com, 316
GlaxoSmithKline, 241
Global business. *See* Business, geography of
Global Business Institute (Indiana University), 5
Global economy. *See* Economy
Global Environment Fund, 159
Global expansion, 182
Global Fund, 59
Global Insight (formerly DRI-WEFA), 233
Global integration, 177–178
Globalization
    and competitive landscape, 4–5, 8
    ethical issues in business, 145, 558
    ethnocentrism and, 187, 189, 191
    inclusiveness, 352
    international management, 174

Global model   An organizational model consisting of a company's overseas subsidiaries and characterized by centralized decision making and tight control by the parent company over most aspects of worldwide operations; typically adopted by organizations that base their global competitive strategy on cost considerations, 178, **180**

Global Reporting Initiative (GRI), 157
Global strategy
    choosing, 179–182
    and global integration, 177–178
    global model, 180
    international model, 179
    and local responsiveness, 178–179
    multinational model, 179–180
    transnational model, 180–182
Global virtual teamwork, 440
GM, 184
GMail, 220, 468

Goal   A target or end that management desires to reach, **111**–112

Goal displacement   A decision-making group loses sight of its original goal and a new, less important goal emerges, 90–**91**

Goal setting
    limitations of, 402–403
    setting own, 403
    stretch goals, 402

Goal-setting theory   A motivation theory stating that people have conscious goals that energize them and direct their thoughts and behaviors toward a particular end, **401**

GoFundMe, 212
Goldman Sachs, 147
Good to Great (Collins), 574–575
Goodwill, 408
Google, 8, 53*l*, 87, 217, 220, 274, 297, 310, 322, 337, 468, 528, 544, 549
Google Docs, 440

Illusion of control People's belief that they can influence events even when they have no control over what will happen, **86**

Immersive technology, 535
Immigrants and immigration, 339–340
    effect on U.S. population and labor force, 48
    and managing diversity, 334
    See also Diversity
Impact Value Chain (IVC), 496
Implementation, 545
    barriers to, 130
    in management process, 118–119, 129–130
    of plan, 112–113
    of planning strategy, 129–130
    strategic, 118–119
    See also Development project
Implicit coercion, for managing resistance to change, 564–565
Impossible Foods, 531
Inbound logistics, 279
Inc., 233
Incentive systems, 316–317

Inclusion Offering to a diverse workforce a fair opportunity to participate and contribute fully, support to be authentically themselves, and reasonable access to decision-making processes, 334, **343**

    at Accenture North America, 333
    advantage through, 343
    affirmative action, 342
    age discrimination, 342
    alternative work arrangements, 350
    attracting employees, 349–350
    cohesiveness, 345
    communication problems, 345
    as company top priority, 347
    cultivating, 348–353
    diversity and, 342–347
    leadership and commitment, 348–349
    leveraging employee differences, 346
    managing diversity and, 343–347
    mistrust and tension, 345
    organizational assessment, 349
    retaining employees, 351–352
    social entrepreneurship, 344
    stereotyping, 345–346
    training employees, 350–351
    unexamined assumptions, 345
Inclusiveness Works boxes
    age discrimination, 342
    bridging cultural divides, 188
    changing for religious inclusion, 560
    changing workforce, 7
    communication in storytelling, 463
    D&I initiatives, 501
    D&I initiatives with intrinsic motivation, 416
    diverse teams, 92
    empathy in teams, 436
    employee feedback strategy, 310
    hierarchical structure, 255
    LGBTQ community, 367
    making diversity and inclusion the brand, 126
    pay without discrimination, 152
    start-ups and diversity, 217

unconscious biases with tech, 528
    women in leadership, 48
    See also Diversity
Incogneato, 465

Incremental model Model of organizational decision making in which major solutions arise through a series of smaller decisions, **96**

Independent action, 221

Independent strategies Strategies that an organization acting on its own uses to change some aspect of its current environment, **59,** 60–61

India
    AppIt Ventures in, 171
    Barefoot College in, 156, 175, 185
    charismatic leadership in, 383
    Flipkart online retailer in, 274
    IBM employees in, 5
    international management, 174–175
    lack of local, qualified management talent, 185
    offshoring and jobs, 172
    Quadera Drilling System in, 455
Indiana University Health Center, 493
Indiegogo, 212, 215
inDinero, 202
Individualism/collectivism, 188
Individual pay decisions, 315–316
Individual performance goal, 402–403
Individual retirement account, 318
Industrial-age system, 155
Industrial pollution, 157
Industry analysis, 121
Inequity, 417
Inertia, and resistance to, 560
Inflation rate, 45
Informal authority, 240
Informal communication, 479
Informal structure, of organization, 270–271
Information processing, 258–259
Information technology, 258
    See also Technology
Information technology (IT) group, 542

Informing A team strategy that entails making decisions with the team and then informing outsiders of its intentions, 447

InfoTech Trends, 233
InfoTrac, from Gale Group, 233

Initial public offering (IPO) Sale to the public, for the first time, of federally registered and underwritten shares of stock in the company, 3–4, 211, **214**–215

Initiating structure, 375–376
Initiative, 35

Innovation The introduction of new goods and services; a change in method or technology; a positive, useful departure from previous ways of doing things, 1, **8**–10, 12, 117, 156, 221, **526**

    and bureaucracy, 544–545
    design thinking and, 545–*546*
    disruptive, 531

elements essential to, 544–545
    organizing for, 543–546
    requirements for, 543
    technology, job design, and human resources, 546
    types of, 526–527
Innovation Lab, 545
InnovationXchange Lab, 545
Innovator, 529

Inpatriate A foreign national brought in to work at the parent company, **189**

Inputs Goods and services organizations take in and use to create products or services, **44**

Inshoring Moving work from other countries back to the headquarters country. Work may be done by a domestic provider or in-house, **172**

Inside director, 240–241
Insider trading, 144

Insourcing Producing in-house one or more of an organization's goods or services, **173**

Inspiration, 545
Instagram, 15, 202, 341, 533, 570
"In-store" technology, 536

Instrumentality The perceived likelihood that performance will be followed by a particular outcome, **407**

Integrated Project Management Company Inc., 281, 477

Integration The degree to which differentiated work units work together and coordinate their efforts, **238**–240

    coordination and communication, 258–259
    coordination by mutual adjustment, 257–258
    coordination by plan, 256
    coordination by standardization, 256
Integrity, leader, 373–374

Integrity-based ethics programs Company mechanisms designed to instill in people a personal responsibility for ethical behavior, **149**

Integrity test, 305–306
Intel, 49, 152, 206, 217, 338, 534, 537, 540
Intellectual property protection report, 191
Interest, 45

Intergroup leader A leader who leads collaborative performance between groups or organizations, **385**

Intermediate consumer A customer who purchases raw materials or wholesale products before selling them to final customers, **54**

Internal audit A periodic assessment of a company's own planning, organizing, leading, and controlling processes, **502**

Labor-Management Relations Act, 319
Labor-Management Reporting and Disclosure
    Act, 320
Labor market, 301

Labor relations The system of relations
between workers and management, **319**

    collective bargaining, 320–321
    future of, 321–322
    laws, 319–320
    unionization, 320
Labor supply forecast, 300–301
Laggard, 529

Laissez-faire A leadership philosophy
characterized by an absence of managerial
decision making, **376**

Landrum-Griffin Act (1959), 320
Language, 471–472. *See also* Communication

Large batch Technologies that produce
goods and services in high volume, **283**

**Large group interventions for total
organization change** Introducing and
sustaining multiple policies, practices,
and procedures across multiple units and
levels, **566**

Late majority, 529

Lateral leadership Style in which
colleagues at the same hierarchical level
are invited to collaborate and facilitate joint
problem solving, **385**

Lateral relationships
    being mediator, 450–451
    conflict, 449–451
    lateral role relationships, 447–448
    managing, 447–451
    outward, 447
    virtual and e-conflict, 451
Latina entrepreneur, 207
Latin America
    empowering Latina entrepreneurs, 207
    ethical issues, 190
    international management, 185
Latino immigrants, 319
Latinos, 335. *See also* Diversity

Law of effect A law formulated by
Edward Thorndike in 1911 stating that
behavior that is followed by positive
consequences will likely be repeated, **403**

Laws and regulations, 44, 68. *See also entries
    for specific laws*
Layoff, 306
LCA. *See* Life-cycle analysis (LCA)
Leader, 17

**Leader–member exchange (LMX)
theory** Highlights the importance of
leader behaviors not just toward the group
as a whole but toward individuals on a
personal basis, **376**

Leadership, 1, 213
    and artificial intelligence, 388
    behavioral approach, 374–376

behaviors of, 374–376
business knowledge, 373–374
contemporary perspectives on, 383–387
and courage, 386–387
defined, 366
developing skills, 387–389
drive, 373–374
effectiveness of, 373–374
effect of behaviors of, 376–378
follower behaviors, 371
at General Motors (GM), 237–238
in group decision making, 92
Hersey and Blanchard's situational
    theory, 380
integrity of, 373–374
leader traits, 373–374
leading and following, 370–371
leading and managing, 370–371
motivation of, 373–374
opportunities, 385
power and, 371–373
self-confidence of, 373–374
situational approaches to, 378–382
technology, 530–534
traditional approaches to understanding,
    373–382
traits of, 373–382
vision, 367–369
Vroom model of, 378–379
women in, 48
See also Change and change management
Leadership Grid (Blake/Mouton), 377
Leadership skills, 573
Leadership style, 91–93

Leading The management function that
involves the manager's efforts to stimulate
high performance by employees, 1, 12,
14–15

Leading Change (Kotter), 567–568
Leaning into the Future (Binney/Collins), 574

Lean manufacturing An operation
that strives to achieve the highest possible
productivity and total quality, cost-
effectively, by eliminating unnecessary
steps in the production process and
continually striving for improvement,
281, **285**

Lean six sigma, 281
Lean Startup, The, (Ries), 10
Learning and growth goal, 117
Learning cycles, 574–575
Least-preferred co-worker (LPC), 380
Legal action, 59–60
Legal department, 249
Legal issues, and equal employment
    opportunity, 308–309
Legal/regulatory environment, 174

Legal responsibilities To obey local,
state, federal, and relevant international
laws, **153**

Legendary Entertainment Group, 170
Legg Mason, 47

Legitimacy People's judgment of a
company's acceptance, appropriateness,

and desirability, generally stemming from
company goals and methods that are
consistent with societal values, **218**–219

Legitimate power, 371
LEGO, 49, 54–55, 537
Lenovo, 54
Lesbian, gay, bisexual, or transgender (LGBT),
    338–339, 367

Level 5 leadership A combination of
strong professional will (determination)
and humility that builds enduring
greatness, **384**

Leverage ratio, 508
Levi Strauss & Co., 158
LEXIS/NEXIS, 233
LGBT. *See* Lesbian, gay, bisexual, or
    transgender (LGBT)
LGBT employee, 336

Liabilities The amounts a corporation
owes to various creditors, **505**

Liaison, 17, 259
Liaison relationships, 448
Licensing, 182–183, 540, 542

Life-cycle analysis (LCA) A process of
analyzing all inputs and outputs, through
the entire "cradle-to-grave" life of a
product, to determine total environmental
impact, **157**

Life-cycle theory of leadership, 380. *See also*
    Hersey and Blanchard's situational theory
Lifestyle and taste changes, 204
LifeStyle Market Analyst, 233

Line department Unit that deals
directly with the organization's primary
goods and services, **246**

Line manager, 246
LinkedIn, 21, 55, 303, 305, 341, 463, 465
Liquidity ratio, 507
Listening, 472–474
Little Gym, The, 183
Living Goods, 277
Lockheed Martin, 337, 340, 438
Locos of control, 381

Logistics The movement of the right
goods in the right amount to the right place
at the right time, **286**

L'Oréal, 158

Low-cost strategy A strategy an
organization uses to build competitive
advantage by being efficient and offering a
standard no-frills project, **128**

Lower-level manager, 116
Lowe's, 339
Low-growth, strong-competitive-position
    business, 127–128
Low-growth, weak-competitive-position
    business, 127–128
Loyalty program, 129
LPC. *See* Least-preferred co-worker (LPC)

information to regulate activities within organizations, **494**–495

at business unit level, 514
at corporate level, 514
examples of, 513
at individual level, 514–515
Marketing and sales, 279
Marketing audit, 122
Marketing Management: Analysis, Planning, Implementation and Control (Kotler), 55
Market receptiveness, 535–536, 538
MarketResearch.com, 233
Market research firms, 234
Marriott, 127, 158
Marriott International, 179, 338, 387
Marriott Starwood Hotels, 97
Mars, 49
Marvel Studios, 114
Mary Kay Cosmetics, 411
Masculinity/femininity, 188
Maslow, Abraham, 36

Maslow's need hierarchy   A conception of human needs organizing needs into a hierarchy of five major types, **409**–410

Mass customization   The production of varied, individually customized products at the low cost of standardized, mass-produced products, 62, **283**–284

Massey Energy Company's Upper Big Branch Mine, 319
Master budget, 504
Mastercard, 152, 339
Matrix diamond, 253

Matrix organization   An organization composed of dual reporting relationships in which some employees report to two superiors—a functional manager and a divisional manager, **251**, 259

matrix form today, 253–254
operating in, 251–252
pros and cons of, 252–253
survival skills, 253
unity-of-command principle, 252–253
Mattel, 187

Maximizing   A decision realizing the best possible outcome, **84**, 86

Maximum hour, 318
Mazda, 489
MBWA. *See* Management by wandering around (MBWA)
McClelland's needs, 411
McCormick, 11
McDonald's, 153, 183, 306, 319
McGraw-Hill Education, 549
McKinsey, 8, 95
McKinsey & Company, 48

Mechanistic organization   A form of organization that seeks to maximize internal efficiency, **270**

Media Networks, 114

Media richness   The degree to which a communication channel conveys information, **468**

Mediator   A third party who intervenes to help others manage their conflict, **450**

Melting pot myth, 348
Melwood, 350
Member commitment, 441
Member satisfaction, 441
Memorial Hospital and Health Care Center, 281
Memphis Meats, 531
Men, and career-family balance, 338
Menlo Innovations, 405
Mental disability, 340–341
Mentoring, 336, 352

Mentors   Higher-level managers who help ensure that high-potential people are introduced to top management and socialized into the norms and values of the organization, **352**

Mercedes-Benz, 1216
Merck & Co., 339, 365, 369, 537
Mercosur, 176

Merger   One or more companies combining with another, **59**, 63–65, 128

Mexico, 175–176
Michael Kors, 537
Microcomputer, 204
Microsoft, 46, 49, 78, 129, 158, 169, 206, 222, 232, 301, 339–340, 465, 533, 549, 570
MidAmerican Energy Co., 158
Middle East
corporate social responsibility, 155
globalization, 5
IKEA's "War Child" initiative, 152
international management, 176, 190
sale of motorcycles in, 170

Middle-level managers   Managers located in the middle layers of the organizational hierarchy, reporting to top-level executives, **16**

and planning, 114
Midvale Steel Company, 33–34
Millennial generation, 7, 257, 541
Mine Safety and Health Administration, 319
Minimum wage, 318
Ministry of Supply, 213
Minority, 339–340

Mission   An organization's basic purpose and scope of operations, 118, **119**, 120

Missionary entrepreneurial identity, 208
Mission statement, corporate, 64
Mistakes, managing, 405
Misunderstanding, and resistance to change, 560–561
MIT Media Lab Research, 538
Modern slavery, 144
Modular (or virtual) corporation, 254
Module, 283
Mondelez International, 144
Monitor, 17

Monolithic organization   An organization that has a low degree of structural integration—employing few women, minorities, or other groups that differ from the majority—and thus has a highly homogeneous employee population, **347**

Monsanto, 49, 186
Monster, 303
Moral awareness, 149
Moral character, 149
Moral judgment, 149

Moral philosophy   Principles, rules, and values people use in deciding what is right or wrong, **142**

Moringa School, 206
Moscow State University, 184
Motivating for change, 560–562
Motivating jobs
empowerment and employee engagement, 415–416
extrinsic reward, 411–413
Hackman and Oldham model, 413–415
Herzberg two-factor theory, 413
intrinsic reward, 411–413

Motivation   Forces that energize, direct, and sustain a person's efforts, **400**

impact on, 407
of leadership, 373–374
technology for, 420

Motivators   Factors that make a job more motivating, such as additional job responsibilities, opportunities for personal growth and recognition, and feelings of achievement, **413**

Motorola, 187, 281, 528
Motorola Mobility, 170

Moving   Instituting the change, 562–**563**

MP3, 531

Multicultural organization   An organization that values cultural diversity and seeks to utilize and encourage it, 347, **348**

Multiexperience, 535

Multinational model (multidomestic)   An organizational model that consists of the subsidiaries in each country in which a company does business, and provides a great deal of discretion to those subsidiaries to respond to local conditions, **179**–180

Multitasking, 404
Must-have management skills, 18
Mutuality, 154
MyFitnessPal, 97
MySpace, 533

N

NAACP. *See* National Association for the Advancement of Colored People (NAACP)
Nabisco, 143–144

NAFTA. *See* North American Free Trade Agreement (NAFTA)
NanoHealth, 177
Nanometer, 572
Nanotechnology, 204, 572
Narcissism, 374
NASA. *See* National Aeronautics and Space Administration (NASA)
NASDAQ Composite, 45
National Aeronautics and Space Administration (NASA), 119, 205, 251, 547
National Association for the Advancement of Colored People (NAACP), 335
National Counterterrorism Center, 257
National diversity, 446. *See also* Diversity
National Industries for the Blind (NIB), 340
Nationality, 335. *See also* Diversity
National Labor Relations Act, 319
National Labor Relations Board (NLRB), 47, 319–320
National Marrow Donor Program (NMDP), 512–513
National Restaurant Association, 338
National Retail Federation, 338
National Venture Capital Association, 214
Natural disaster, 112, 204
Natural environment, 44, 68, 174
    and sustainability, 155–159
    sustainability and, 50
NBA, 131
NBCUniversal, 128

Needs assessment An analysis identifying the jobs, people, and departments for which training is necessary, **309**

Negative reinforcement Removing or withholding an undesirable consequence, **403**–404

Negotiation and rewards, for managing resistance to change, 564–565
Negotiator, 17
Neiman Marcus, 536
Nestlé, 4, 245, 434, 540
Netflix, 8, 49, 52, 55, 89, 131, 170, 183, 242, 384
Network for Good, 277

Network organization A collection of independent, mostly single-function firms that collaborate on a good or service, **254**–255

Networks, 21, 219
New Belgium Brewing Company, 316, 401
New entrants, 44, 50, 52, 68
New Strategist Publications, 233
New York Life, 338
New York Times, The, 233
Next Day Flyers, 125
NFL, 131
NHG. *See* Niche Hotel Group (NHG)
NIB. *See* National Industries for the Blind (NIB)
Nicaragua, 176
Niche Hotel Group (NHG), 357–358
"Nightmare Traits," 374
NIH. *See* Not Invented Here (NIH) syndrome

Nike, 9, 49, 126, 179, 280, 537
Nintendo, 232
Nissan, 8, 539
NLRB. *See* National Labor Relations Board (NLRB)
NMPD. *See* National Marrow Donor Program (NMDP)
Non-cohesiveness group, 445–446
Nonmonetary rewards, 405

Nonprogrammed decisions New, novel, complex decisions having no proven answers, **78**

Nonverbal skills, 472
Nordstrom, 129

Norms Shared beliefs about how people should think and behave, 144, **443**, 445–446

North American Free Trade Agreement (NAFTA) An economic pact that combined the economies of the United States, Canada, and Mexico into one of the world's largest trading blocs, 4, **175**–176

Not Invented Here (NIH) syndrome A negative attitude toward knowledge (ideas, technologies) derived from an external source, **124**

Not Mass Produced, 208
Novo Nordisk, 113, 503
Nuclear fusion, 525
Nurturing role, 255
Nutrition Science Partners, 540
Nvidia, 146

O
Oberlo, 206
Obesity, as ethical issue in business, 145
Objectives-strategies-tactics (OST) system, 131
OB mod. *See* Organizational behavior modification (OB mod)
Observing, 474–475
Occupational Safety and Health Administration (OSHA), 47, 318
Oculus, 541
OFCCP. *See* Office of Federal Contract Compliance Programs (OFCCP)
Office of Federal Contract Compliance Programs (OFCCP), 47, 308

Offshoring Moving work to other countries, **172**

Ohio State studies, 377
Oil and Gas Climate Initiative, 555
Oil industry, 536
Omnica, 435
ONA. *See* Organizational Network Analysis (ONA)
One-best-way myth, 348

One-way communication A process in which information flows in only one direction—from the sender to the receiver, with no feedback loop, **462**–463

Online network, 257
Online privacy, as ethical issue in business, 145
Only-one-way myth, 348
Opel, 124

Open-book management Practice of sharing with employees at all levels of the organization vital information previously meant for management's eyes only, **477**

Open communication, 511. *See also* Communication
Openness to outside knowledge, 543

Open system An organization that isn't affected by, and that affects, its environment, **44**

Open-system perspective, 37–38
Operational excellence, 117
Operational improvements, 117

Operational planning The process of identifying the specific procedures and processes required at lower levels of the organization, 115, **116,** 117–118

Operations, 279
Operations analysis, 122
Operations and processes, 284
OppenheimerFunds, 463
Opportunity, 217

Opportunity analysis A description of the good or service, an assessment of the opportunity, an assessment of the entrepreneur, specification of activities and resources needed to translate your idea into a viable business, and your source(s) of capital, **214**–215

Optimizing Achieving the best possible balance among several goals, **84**

Oracle, 337, 563
Order, 35

Ordinary capabilities Capabilities pertaining to basic administrative and operational functions, **272**

Oré Earth Skin Care, 163–164

Organic structure An organizational form that emphasizes flexibility, 61, **270**

Organizational agility, 1
    concurrent engineering, 287
    core capabilities, 272
    customer relationship management (CRM), 278–280
    customers and responsive organization, 278–282
    flexible manufacturing, 283–285
    high-involvement organization, 285
    quality initiatives, 280–282
    responsive organization, 270–271
    size and, 275–278
    strategic alliances, 272–275
    strategy and, 271–275
    technology and, 282–287
    technology configurations, 282–283
    time-based competition, 286–287

Organizational ambidexterity Ability to achieve multiple objectives simultaneously, **558**

Organizational assessment, 349

Organizational behavior A contemporary management approach that studies and identifies management activities that promote employee effectiveness by examining the complex and dynamic nature of individual, group, and organizational processes, 32, **37**, 39

Organizational Behavior (Krietner/Kinicki), 39
Organizational Behavior (McShane/Von Gilnow), 70
Organizational Behavior, Structure, Processes (Gibson/Ivancevich/Donnelly/ Konopaske), 79

Organizational behavior modification (OB mod) The application of reinforcement theory in organizational settings, **403**

Organizational climate The patterns of attitudes and behavior that shape people's experience of an organization, **65**–66

Organizational communication
    downward communication, 475–477
    horizontal communication, 478–479
    informal communication, 479
    transparency, 479–480
    upward communication, 477–478
Organizational decision making. *See* Decision making
Organizational Network Analysis (ONA), 528
Organizational politics, 96
Organizational suitability, 537–538
    and technology, 537–538

Organization chart The reporting structure and division of labor in an organization, **238**–239

Organization culture The set of important assumptions about the organization and its goals and practices that members of the company share, **63**

Organization development (OD) The systemwide application of behavioral science knowledge to develop, improve, and reinforce the strategies, structures, and processes that lead to organizational effectiveness, **559**

Organization Development and Change (Cummings/Worley), 559
Organization structure, 1, 284
    at General Motors (GM), 237–238, 260
    horizontal
        departmentalization, 246–247
        divisional organization, 249–251
        functional organization, 247–249
        line departments, 246
        line managers, 246

        matrix organization, 251–254
        network organization, 254–255
        staff departments, 246
    integration
        coordination and communication, 258–259
        coordination by mutual adjustment, 257–258
        coordination by plan, 256
        coordination by standardization, 256
        defined, 238
    looking ahead, 259–260
    organizing fundamentals
        differentiation, 238–239
        integration, 239–240
    vertical
        authority in organizations, 240–242
        decentralization, 245–246
        delegation, 242–245
        hierarchical levels, 242
        span of control, 242–243

Organizing The management function of assembling and coordinating human, financial, physical, informational, and other resources needed to achieve goals, 1, 12–14, **13**

Orientation training Training designed to introduce new employees to the company and familiarize them with policies, procedures, culture, and the like, **310**

OSHA. *See* Occupational Safety and Health Administration (OSHA)
OshKosh, 147
OST. *See* Objectives-strategies-tactics (OST) system
Otto, 206
Outbound logistics, 279

Outcome A consequence a person receives for his or her performance, **407**

Outplacement The process of helping people who have been dismissed from the company regain employment elsewhere, **306**

Outputs The products and services organizations create, **44**

Outsourcing Contracting with an outside provider to produce one or more of an organization's goods or services, **172**

OWN, 384

P

P2P Credit, 215
Pacing technologies, 534
Packaging, 158
Pakistan, 189, 206
Palo Alto Networks, 302
Panama, 176
Panasonic, 181–182
Panera Bread, 54, 112, 204–205, 283
Papa & Barkley, 434
Paper and Occidental Chemicals, 283

Parading A team strategy that entails simultaneously emphasizing internal team building and achieving external visibility, **447**

Paralee Boyd, 285

Parallel teams Teams that operate separately from the regular work structure and are temporary, **435**

Paris Agreement, 49
Parochialism, 348
Participation and involvement, for managing resistance to change, 564

Participation in decision making Leader behaviors that managers perform in involving their employees in making decisions, **376**

Participation leader, 446
Participation rate, 45
Participative leadership, 381
Partner, and entrepreneurship, 219
PartPic, 202
PA. *See* Performance appraisal (PA)
Patagonia, 11, 49, 157
Patent and Trademark Office, 234

Path–goal theory A theory that concerns how leaders influence subordinates' perceptions of their work goals and the paths they follow toward attainment of those goals, **380**–382

Patient Protection and Affordable Care Act, 318
Paychex, 387
Pay decisions, 315–316
Pay level, 315
PayPal, 174, 525
Pay structure, 315–316
Peer pressure, and resistance to change, 560–561
Peer-to-peer loan, 215
Penguin Random House, 313
Pension plan, 317–318
People analytics, 509
People skills, 18
PepsiCo, 5, 49, 51–54, 59, 62, 210, 273, 352, 384

Perception The process of receiving and interpreting information, **463**

Performance
    delivering all types of, 11–12
    employee satisfaction and well-being, 419
    fairness, 416–419
    leader behavior, 376–378
    Maslow's needs, 409–411
    motivating for, 1, 400–401
    past, current, and future, 81
    reinforcing, 403–406

Performance appraisal (PA) Assessment of an employee's job performance, **311**

    categories of, 312
    employee feedback, 314–315
    interview format for underperforming employees, 314–315
    reasons for, 312–313

Psychological contract A set of perceptions of what employees owe their employers, and what their employers owe them, **420–421**

Psychological maturity An employee's self-confidence and self-respect, **380**

Psychological safety When employees feel they can speak up honestly and freely without fear, 439–**440**

Psychopathy, 374
Public filings, 234
Publicly held company, 46
Public relations, 59–60

Punishment Administering an aversive consequence, **403–405**

Purchase, technology, 540
Purchasing, 122
Purple, 570–571
PwC, 366

Q

Quadra Drilling Systems, 455–456
Quaker, 51, 53
Qualcomm, 60

Quality The excellence of your product (goods or services), **9**, 12

Quality initiative, 280–282
Quality management, 284

Quality of work life (QWL) programs Programs designed to create a workplace that enhances employee well-being, **419**–420

Quantitative management A contemporary management approach that emphasizes the application of quantitative analysis to managerial decisions and problems, 32, **37**, 39

Quest Diagnostics, 305
Question mark, in BCG matrix, 127–128
QuickBooks, 276, 545
Quicken Loans, 10–11
Quid pro quo harassment, 338
Quorn, 531
QWL. *See* Quality of work life (QWL) programs, 419–420

R

Race discrimination, 335. *See also* Diversity
Racial segregation, 334
Radio frequency identification (RFID) tag, 286
Rainmaker Thinking, 341
Rakuten, 274
Ramesh Tainwala, 304
Randstad US, 387
Ray Ban, 537
Razorfish, 475
RCA, 180
RCA Corporation, 183

RDS Business Reference Suite, 233

Reactive change A response that occurs under pressure; problem-driven change, **569**

Reading, 474
Read-write-execute, 6

Ready-made solutions Ideas that have been seen or tried before, **81**

Receiver skills, 472–475
Reconciliation, and corporate responsibility, 155
Recruit, 446

Recruitment The development of a pool of applicants for jobs in an organization, **302,** 303, 349–350

RED, 123
Red Hat, 139
Red Stripe, 180
Reference check, 304
Referent power, 372

Reflection Process by which a person states what he or she believes the other person says or means, **473**

Refreezing Strengthening the new behaviors that support the change, 562–**563**

Regulations. *See* Laws and regulation
Regulator, 47

Reinforcer Positive consequence that motivates behavior, **403,** 405, 411

Relatedness needs, 410
Relating, 444
Relationship culture, 71

Relationship-motivated leadership Style in which leader focuses on interpersonal relationships for measuring performance, **380**

Relativism Philosophy that bases ethical behavior on the opinions and behaviors of relevant other people, 143–**144,** 149

Relativity Space, 547

Reliability The consistency of test scores over time and across alternative measurements, **306**

Religion, 335. *See also* Diversity
Religious inclusion, 561
Reluctance to change, 543
Remuneration, 35
Renewable energy, 204
Research and development, 122, 279
Research partnership, for technology development, 540
Resistance
   to change, 560–565
   to control, 510

Resource Input to a system that can enhance performance, **123**–124

Resource allocator, 17

Resource director, 17
Respect, 190

Responsibility The assignment of a task that an employee is supposed to carry out, 190, **243,** 244

Responsible leadership Style in which leader focuses on decision-making processes and choices that support corporate social responsibility, **385**

Responsive culture, 71
Responsive organization
   ambidextrous, 270
   customer relationship management (CRM), 278–280
   formal and informal, 270–271
   mechanistic, 270
   organic, 270
   quality initiatives, 280–282
Restaurant, 249
Results appraisal, 312
Résumé, job, 303
Retail, agile, 288
Retail Consulting, 241
Retail industry, and technology, 536

Return on investment (ROI) A ratio of profit to capital used, or a rate of return from capital, 62, **508**

Reuters, 233
Revenue growth, 117
Reward power, 372
Rewards, 437
   managing, 404–405
   motivating jobs, 411–416
   to team performance, 446
Reward system, 113, 405
   designing, 315–319
   employee benefits, 317–318
   executive pay and stock options, 317
   health and safety, 318–319
   incentive systems and variable pay, 316–317
   legal issues in compensation and benefits, 318
   pay decisions, 315–316
RFID. *See* Radio frequency identification (RFID) tag
Rice Inc., 177

Right-to-work Legislation that allows employees to work without having to join a union, **321**

Ripple, 571

Risk The state that exists when the probability of success is less than 100 percent and losses may occur, **79,** 217

Risk society, 157
Risk taker, 220
Rite, 65
Rituxam, 532
Ritz-Carlton, 385
Rival firm. *See* Competitive environment
Rivals, 44
Robotics, 204
Roche, 532

Small business A business having fewer than 500 employees, independently owned and operated, not dominant in its field, and not characterized by many innovative practices, **200**

Small Business Administration, 200, 205, 214, 227
Small business grant, 212
Small Business Learning Center, 214
SMART, 403
Smart Compose, 468
"Smarter city" technologies, 570
Smarter Planet, 176
Smart goals, 401–402
Smartphones, popularity of, 3
Smithfield Foods, 153–154

Smoothing Leveling normal fluctuations at the boundaries of the environment, **62**

SMRC. See Student Movement for Real Change (SMRC)
Snagajob, 303
Snapchat, 202, 533, 541, 570
SnapChat, 15
Snap Inc., 248
Soaring Eagle Skate Company, 102–103
Social analysis, 121

Social capital Goodwill stemming from your social relationships; a competitive advantage in the form of relationships with other people and the image other people have of you, **21, 219**

Social CRM, 280. See also Customer relationship management (CRM)

Social enterprise Organization that applies business models and leverages resources in ways that address social problems, **206,** 207–208

Social Enterprise Alliance, 473

Social entrepreneurship Leveraging resources to address social problems, **206**–207

Social Entrepreneurship boxes, 13
    artificial intelligence, 571
    climate change, 49
    communicating success, 473
    co-working, 443
    engineering disaster-resilient homes, 386
    growth as goal, 300
    Kiva, 248
    learning-by-doing training programs, 156
    measuring social impact, 496
    nonprofit or for-profit, 80
    Novo Nordisk, 113
    scaling social enterprises, 277
    student social entrepreneurs, 177
    Team Rubicon, 412–413
    water ATMs, 520

Social facilitation effect Working harder when in a group than when working alone, **442**

Social impact, measuring, 496
Social issues, 44, 49, 68, 174

Socialization, 446
Socialization standards, 446
Socialized power, 411
"Social listening," 280

Social loafing Working less hard and being less productive when in a group, 90–91, **442**

Social media
    digital communication and, 465
    as ethical issue in business, 145
    profiles prospective employees, 304
Social networking, 5–6
Social or belongingness needs, 409–410
Social relationships, 21
Social responsibility, 154, 163. See also Corporate social responsibility (CSR)
Social Security Act of 1935, 317–318
Social Security verification, 304–305

Sociotechnical systems An approach to job design that attempts to redesign tasks to optimize operation of a new technology while preserving employees' interpersonal relationships and other human aspects of the work, 546, **546**

SodaStream, 49
SOE. See State-owned enterprise (SOE)
Soft Scroll, 227
Solidarium, 208
Solutionary, 450
Sonnen, 566
Sony, 172, 180, 203, 232, 556–557
Sony Electronics, 338
SoundCloud, 461, 469, 480
Sourcify, 571
South Africa, 176
South America, 176
South Asia, 206
Southwest Airlines, 37, 59, 65, 385
SpaceX, 120, 367, 525, 547
Spacious, 443

Span of control The number of subordinates who report directly to an executive or supervisor, **242**–243

Spanx, 203
Specialist, 19

Specialization A process in which different individuals and units perform different tasks, **238**

Speech recognition tools, 6

Speed Fast and timely execution, response, and delivery of products, **10**–12, 286–287

Speed trap. See Time pressure
Spirit Airlines, 11
Spokesperson, 17
Sport Clips, 219
Spotify, 202, 480
Sprint, 466
Stability and tenure of personnel, 35
Stabilization relationships, 448

Staff departments Units that support line departments, **246**

Staffing
    at Google, 311
    recruitment, 302–303
    selection, 303–306
    workforce reductions, 306–309

Stakeholders Groups and individuals who affect and are affected by the achievement of the organization's mission, goals, and strategies, **120**

Standard Expected performance for a given goal: a target that establishes a desired performance level, motivates performance, and serves as a benchmark against which actual performance is assessed, **496**

Standardization Establishing common routines and procedures that apply uniformly to everyone, **256**

Standard and Poor's 500, 45
Stanford University, 545
Stanley Lynch Investment Group, 264
Staples, 49
Starbucks, 9, 49, 60, 152, 169, 175, 199–200, 274, 277, 401, 515
Stars, in BCG matrix, 127–128
Start-up, 216–217. See also Entrepreneurship
State Farm Insurance, 414
State Grid (China), 4, 171
State-owned enterprise (SOE), 184
Statistical Abstract of the United States, 233
Statistical Analysis Software (SAS), 399–400
Stat-USA, 233
Status symbol, 65

Stewardship Contributing to the long-term welfare of others, **152**

Stockholders' equity The amount accruing to the corporation's owners, **505**

Stock market, 45
Stock options, 317
Stonewalling, 147
Stonyfield's, 158
Stories, 15
Stories Ads, 15

Strategic alliance A formal relationship created among independent organizations with the purpose of joint pursuit of mutual goals, 272, **273,** 274–276

Strategic control, 118–119, 131

Strategic control system A system designed to support managers in evaluating the organization's progress regarding its strategy and, when discrepancies exist, taking corrective action, **130**

Strategic goals Major targets or end results relating to the organization's long-term survival, value, and growth, **114**

Strategic intervention, 559

Strategic leadership Behavior that gives purpose and meaning to organizations, envisioning and creating a positive future, **370**

Strategic management A process that involves managers from all parts of the organization in the formulation and implementation of strategic goals and strategies, 1, **118,** 119

Strategic manager, 16

Strategic maneuvering An organization's conscious efforts to change the boundaries of its task environment, **58**

Strategic planning A set of procedures for making decisions about the organization's long-term goals and strategies, **114,** 116–118

See also Planning
Strategic triangle, 278

Strategic vision The long-term direction and strategic intent of a company, **119**

Strategy A pattern of actions and resource allocations designed to achieve the organization's goals, **115,** 568

Strategy implementation, 129–130

Strategy map A depiction of how an organization plans to convert its various assets into desired outcomes, 117, **511**–512

Strengths, weaknesses, opportunities, and threats. *See* SWOT analysis

Stretch goals Targets that are particularly demanding, sometimes even thought to be impossible, **402**

Structured interview Selection technique that involves asking all applicants the same questions and comparing their responses to a standardized set of answers, **303**–304

Student Movement for Real Change (SMRC), 80
Student social entrepreneurs, 177
Subordination of individual interest to general interest, 35
Substitutes and complements, 44, 50, 52–53, 57, 68

Substitutes for leadership Factors in the workplace that can exert the same influence on employees as leaders would provide, **382**

Subunit Subdivisions of an organization, **242**

Subway, 204
Sunday Riley, 142
Sun Microsystems, 340
SunPower, 566

Superordinate goals Higher-level goals taking priority over specific individual or group goals, **450**

Superstorm Sandy, 97
Supervisor, 16

Supervisory leadership Behavior that provides guidance, support, and corrective feedback for day-to-day activities, **370**

Suppliers
    in competitive environment, 44, 50, 57, 68
    and switching costs, 53–54
    as unattractive and attractive environmental factors, 57
Supply and demand, reconciling, 301–302
Supply chain, 127

Supply chain management The managing of the network of facilities and people that obtain materials from outside the organization, transform them into products, and distribute them to customers, **54**

Support, 388
Support groups, 351
Supporting Case boxes
    Apple, 232
    Foxconn, 232
    Zappos, 361–362
Supportive leadership, 375, 381
Surprise, and resistance to change, 560
Survey of Current Business, 233
Sustainability audit, 502–503

Sustainability Minimizing the use of resources, especially those that are polluting and nonrenewable, 1, **11**–12

    and natural environment, 50
    natural environment and, 155–159
Sustainable Development Goals (SDGs), 159

Sustainable growth Economic growth and development that meets present needs without harming the needs of future generations, **157**

Sustainable Ocean Alliance, 206
Sustainable practices, 61
Suuchi Inc., 284
SVP. *See* Senior vice president (SVP)
Sweatshop, 144

Switching costs Fixed costs buyers face when they change suppliers, **53**–54

SWOT analysis A comparison of strengths, weaknesses, opportunities, and threats that helps executives formulate strategy, 118–119, **124,** 125–129, 151

Symbol, status, 65
Sympathy, 154

System 1 information processing A type of decision-making process that is reflexive and done quickly without careful thought, **86**

System 2 information processing A type of decision-making process that is reflective and done slowly with deliberative thought, **86**

Systematic management A classical management approach that attempted to build into operations the specific procedures and processes that would ensure coordination of effort to achieve established goals and plans, 32, **33**–34, 39

Systems accommodations, 352

Systems theory A theory stating that an organization is a managed system that changes inputs into outputs, 32, **37,** 39

T

Taco Bell, 60, 178, 204
Tactical behavior, 509–510

Tactical planning A set of procedures for translating broad strategic goals and plans into specific goals and plans that are relevant to a distinct portion of the organization, such as a functional area like marketing, 115–118, **116**

Taft-Hartley Act (1947), 319
Taiwan, 175, 189
Take-make-waste production model, 158
Tannenbaum, 561
Tarang Amin, 434
Target, 59, 64, 152, 169, 181
Tariff, 179
Task force, 259
Task identity, 414

Task-motivated leadership Leadership that places primary emphasis on completing a task, **380**

Task performance behavior Actions taken to ensure that the work group or organization reaches its goals, **375,** 382

Task significance, 414

Task specialist role An individual who has more advanced job-related skills and abilities than other group members possess, **444**

Tata Motors, 71–72
TBC. *See* Time-based competition (TBC)
TBL. *See* Triple bottom line (TBL) strategy
TD Bank, 511

Team A small number of people with complementary skills who are committed to a common purpose, set of performance goals, and approach for which they hold themselves mutually accountable, **438**

Teaming A strategy of teamwork on the fly, creating many temporary, changing teams, **435**

Team leader, 16, 436

Team maintenance role Individual who develops and maintains team harmony, **444**

Team productivity, 441
Team Rubicon, 412
Teams and teamwork, 1
  building effective teams, 441–446
  challenges, 439
  cohesiveness, 445–446
  contributions, 434
  critical periods, 439
  diverse, 92
  empowering, 441
  failure of, 440–441
  group processes, 438–439
  inclusiveness, 436
  lateral relationships, 447–451
  members contributions, 443
  motivating, 442
  norms, 443–444
  performance focus, 441–442
  roles, 444
  types of, 434–438
  virtual, and e-conflict, 451
  work, 434
  See also Decision making, in groups

Team training Training that provides employees with the skills and perspectives they need to collaborate with others, **310**

Tecate, 180

Technical innovator A person who develops a new technology or has the key skills to install and operate the technology, **543**

Technical skill The ability to perform a specialized task involving a particular method or process, **18**

  See also Career development
Technological analysis, 121
Technological change, 5–6
Technological development, 527
Technological discovery, 204
Technological environment, 174
Technological feasibility, 536, 538
Technological innovation, 529–530
Technological leadership, 532–533
Technological risk, 157
Technological trends, 534–535

Technology The systematic application of scientific knowledge to a new product, process, or service, 1, 44, 68, **282, 526**

  acquisition options, 542
  adopters, 529–530, 533–534
  anticipated market receptiveness, 535–536
  decisions regarding, 535–538
  dissemination pattern and adopter categories, 529
  effective systems, 117
  and innovation, 526–530
  large batch, 283
  leadership and followership, 530–534

and macroenvironment, 46
and managerial roles, 542–543
managing impact of, 122
and measuring competitive value, 534
measuring current, 534
and organizational agility, 282–287
small batch, 282–283
sourcing and acquiring, 538–542
vulnerability of, in crisis, 97
See also Innovation

Technology audit Process of clarifying the key technologies on which an organization depends, **534**

Technology benchmarking, 534
Technology configuration, 282–283
Technology followership, 533–534
Technology leadership, 530-534

Technology life cycle A predictable pattern followed by a technological innovation, from its inception and development to market saturation and replacement, **527**–529

Technology owner, acquiring, 541–542
Technology skills, 573
Technology training, 540
Techno-structural intervention, 559
TechStars, 211
Teco Energy, 494
Teenage employee, 338
Telecommunication industry, 531
Teledyne, 217
Termination, 307, 309

Termination interview A discussion between a manager and an employee about the employee's dismissal, **307**

Tesco, 313
Tesla Motors, 306, 367, 465, 525–526, 538–539, 546–547, 566
Texas Instruments, 251
Theory X, 37
Theory Y, 37
ThinkImpact, 80

Third-country nationals Natives of a country other than the home country or the host country of an overseas subsidiary, **185**

Thomas J. Watson Research Center, 538
ThomsonResearch, 233
Thomson Reuters Diversity and Inclusion Index, 333
Thomson Venture Economics, 233
Threat of entry, 57
3D printing, 46, 122, 128, 536
3M, 123, 147, 368, 434, 508, 532, 544, 556–557

360-degree appraisal Process of using multiple sources of appraisal to gain a comprehensive perspective on one's performance, **313**–314

Tiger, 180
TikTok, 533
Timberland, 158

Time-based competition (TBC) Strategies aimed at reducing the total time needed to deliver a good or service, **286**–287

Time pressure, 87–89
Time Warner, 493
Timing, and resistance to change, 560
Titles, elimination of, 106–107
Title VII of Civil Rights Act (1964), 308
Tivity Health, 204
T-Mobile, 123, 465
TNGA. *See* Toyota New Global Architecture (TNGA)
Tom's of Maine, 158

Top-level manager Senior executive responsible for the overall management and effectiveness of the organization, **16**

  C-suite, 241–242
  in matrix diamond, 253
  and planning, 114
Top management, 219
Toshiba, 123, 232
Total, 566

Total organization change Introducing and sustaining multiple policies, practices, and procedures across multiple units and levels, **566**

Total quality management (TQM) An integrative approach to management that supports the attainment of customer satisfaction through a wide variety of tools and techniques that result in high-quality goods and services, **280**

Touchstone Pictures, 114
Toyota, 4, 8, 124, 158, 171–172, 179–180, 187, 238, 283, 343, 489, 502, 531
Toyota New Global Architecture (TNGA), 180
Toys 'R' Us, 269
Trade Associations, 234
Trade policy, U.S., 178
Trader Joe's, 126

Training Teaching lower-level employees how to perform their present jobs, **309**

  inclusiveness, 350–351
  processes, 311
  types of, 310–311

Trait approach A leadership perspective that attempts to determine the personal characteristics that great leaders share, **373**, 374

Trait scale, 312

Transactional leader Leader who manages through transactions, using legitimate, reward, and coercive powers to give commands and exchange rewards for services rendered, **383**

Transcendent education An education with five higher goals that balance self-interest with responsibility to others, **154**

Transfer price Price charged by one unit for a good or service provided to another unit within the organization, **514**

Transformational leader A leader who motivates people to transcend their personal interests for the good of the group, **383**, 384–385, 404, 448

Transgender community, 435

Transnational model An organizational model characterized by centralizing certain functions in locations that best achieve cost economies; basing other functions in the company's national subsidiaries to facilitate greater local responsiveness; and fostering communication among subsidiaries to permit transfer of technological expertise and skills, 178, **180**, 181–182

Transnational teams Teams composed of multinational members whose activities span multiple countries. Such teams differ from other work teams by being multicultural and by often being geographically dispersed, being psychologically distant, and working on highly complex projects having considerable impact on company objectives, **435**

Transparency People's beliefs that the information their employer and others send them is of high quality, as defined by accuracy, timeliness, and full disclosure of relevant information, **479**, 480

Treasure Cup, 194
TripAdvisor, 8

Triple bottom line (TBL) Economic, social, and environmental performance, 113, **153, 502–503**

Tropicana, 53
Truth telling, 141. *See also* Ethics
TRW, 251
TTEC, 254
TurboTax, 276
20 Percent Rule, 220
20th Century Fox, 114
Twitter, 8, 303, 305, 341, 465, 549
"Two-boss" manager/employee, 253

Two-factor theory Herzberg's theory describing two factors affecting people's work motivation and satisfaction, **413**

Two-way communication A process in which information flows in two directions—the receiver provides feedback, and the sender is receptive to the feedback, **462**, 463

Tyranny of the *or* The belief that things must be either A or B and cannot be both; that only one goal and not another can be attained, **557**

U

Uber, 4, 88, 98
Uber Technologies, 77

Uncertainty The state that exists when decision makers have insufficient information, **79**

Uncertainty avoidance, 188
Unconscious bias, 528
Unemployment insurance, 317–318
Unemployment rate, 45
Unethical behavior, 402

Unfreezing Realizing that current practices are inappropriate and that new behavior is necessary, **562,** 563

Unilever, 123, 158, 168
Union contract, 307
Unionization, 320
Union membership, decline in, 321–322

Union shop An organization with a union and a union security clause specifying that workers must join the union after a set period of time, **321**

Union voting behavior, 320
Unisys, 466
United Nations, 159
United States
    affirmative action, 341
    age diversity, 341
    Chinese company expansion in, 169
    and climate change, 49
    competitive environment, 51, 62
    and conflict management styles, 449
    cross-cultural differences, 376
    dependence on foreign old, 176
    diverse workflow in, 334
    and diversity, 152
    e-commerce in, 205
    education levels in, 341
    employment of people with disabilities, 340
    entrepreneurship in, 205
    environmental problems, 157
    ethics, 143–145, 147
    executive pay and stock options, 317
    feedback to employees in, 310
    generational shift in organization structure and functions, 257
    and globalization, 5
    goal setting, 401
    innovation in, 9
    and inpatriates, 189
    inshoring jobs to, 172
    international licensing, 183
    labor and supply forecasts, 300–301
    labor relations, 319–321
    languages varied by culture, 471
    Latina population in, 207
    laws and regulations, 47
    literacy in, 474
    manufacturing in, 278
    minorities and immigrants, 336, 339
    mortality and succession in family businesses, 215
    motivating employees, 411, 413
    and need for achievement, 411

North American Free Trade Agreement (NAFTA), 175–176
    offshoring jobs from, 172
    recognizing cultural differences, 437
    right-to-work states, 321
    small businesses in, 200
    Student Movement for Real Change (SMRC), 80
    sustainability, 11
    top global companies in, 171
    and world trade, 170–171, 174–175
United Steel Workers of America, 33
United Technologies, 47

Unity-of-command principle A structure in which each worker reports to one boss, who in turn reports to one boss, 35, **252**, 253

Unity of direction, 35

Universalism The ethical system stating that all people should uphold certain values that society needs to function, **142,** 149

Unstructured interview, 304
UPS, 206, 385, 504

Upward communication Information that flows from lower to higher levels in the organization's hierarchy, **477**, 478

USA Hospital Supply, 27–28
U.S. Army, 46
U.S. Bureau of Labor Statistics, 319
U.S. Bureau of the Census, 233
U.S. Chamber of Commerce, 60
U.S. Department of Agriculture, 155
U.S. Department of State, 5
U.S. Equal Employment Opportunity Commission (EEOC), 98
U.S. Small Business Administration, 234

Utilitarianism An ethical system stating that the greatest good for the greatest number should be the overriding concern of decision makers, **143,** 144

V

Valence The value an outcome holds for the person contemplating it, **407**, 408

Validity The degree to which a selection test predicts or correlates with job performance, **306**

Value The monetary amount associated with how well a job, task, good, or service meets users' needs, **13,** 44, 68, 117

Value-added manufacturing, 287

Value chain The sequence of activities that flow from raw materials to the delivery of a good or service, with additional value created at each step, **279,** 280

Value Line Investment Survey, 233

Value proposition, 115
Vans, 59
Variable pay, 316–317
Vegetarian Butcher, The, 158
Veil of ignorance, 149
Venezuela, 176, 189
Venture capitalist, 212
Verizon, 87

Vertical integration   The acquisition or development of new businesses that produce parts or components of the organization's product, **126,** 127

Veteran, employing, 336
Veterans United Home Loans, 498
Videoconference, 46
ViewMyPaycheck, 545

Vigilance   A process in which a decision maker carefully executes all stages of decision making, **86**

Vioxx scandal, 365
Virgin Group, 61, 367
Virginia Mason Medical Center, 500

Virtual office   A mobile office in which people can work anywhere, as long as they have the tools to communicate with customers and colleagues, **467**

Virtual teams   Teams that are physically dispersed and communicate electronically more than face-to-face, **435,** 440

Virtual teamwork, 440

Virtue ethics   Perspective that what is moral comes from what a mature person with "good" moral character would deem right, 143–**144**

Vision   A mental image of a possible and desirable future state of the organization, 367, **368,** 369, 568

Vocational Rehabilitation Act (1973), 308

Voice   When people speak up with good intentions about work-related issues, rather than remaining silent, **478**

Voice mail, 465. *See also* Digital communication
Volcker Rule, 146
Volkswagen, 72, 168, 171, 238, 248, 489, 539
Voluntary action, 59–60
Voting, 320, 334

Vroom model   A situational model that focuses on the participative dimension of leadership, **378,** 379

VUCA (volatility, uncertainty, complexity, and ambiguity), 271–272

W

Wages, 144, 145
Wagner Act, 319
Wall Street Journal, The, 233
Walmart, 4, 11, 60, 112, 117, 153, 171, 203, 206, 208, 241, 269–270, 274–276, 286, 288, 316, 401, 556–557
Walmart Stores, 128, 275
Walt Disney Company, 63, 123, 131, 152
Walt Disney Studios, 109–110, 114
Warby Parker, 63
Water ATM, 530
Water-Less initiative, 158
Waymo, 547
Web 2.0, 5–6
Web 3.0, 6
Wegmans Food Markets, 410
Wells Fargo, 11, 140
Western Electric Company, 35
Western Europe, 173–174
Westin Hotels, 94
Weyerhaeuser, 87
WhatsApp, 533
Whistleblowing, 150–151
White House Equal Pay Pledge, 152
Whole Foods Market, 43, 64, 116, 433–434, 437, 452
Wholly owned subsidiaries, 182, 184
Wildcat strikes, 321
Wipro, 124
Wish You Wood Toy Store, 135
W. L. Gore, 410, 434
Women, 156, 335
  career development programs and, 352
  and family-friendly benefits, 337
  glass ceiling, 337
  harassment, 338
  in leadership, 48
  top companies for, 338
  top executives, 337
  See also Diversity
Women's Network, 349
Women's rights movement, 334
Workers' compensation, 317–318
Workflow relationship, 448
Workforce

changing, 7, 335–341
developing, 309–311
reductions in, 306–309
See also Staffing
Workforce management, 284
WorkForce Software, 241
Working group, 438
Working leaders, with broad responsibilities, 17–18
Working overseas, 185
  cultural issues, 187–189
  ethical issues, 190–191
  failed, 186–187

Work team   Team that makes or does things like manufacture, assemble, sell, or provide service, **434**

World Development Indicators—World Bank, 233
World Social Enterprise Forum, 300
World Trade Organization (WTO), 173, 183
Worldwide Games, 550
World Wildlife Fund, 155
Worn Wear program, 11
Worst-case scenario, 57
Writing skills, 471
WTO. *See* World Trade Organization (WTO)

X

Xerox, 179, 340, 542
XFactor Ventures, 202

Y

Yahoo!, 87, 277
Yammer, 440
Y Combinator, 211
Yelp, 8
YouEarnedIt, 408
YouTube, 465, 533
Yum! Brands, 5

Z

Zappos, 106–107, 201, 217, 361–362
Zenith, 180
Zero defects, achieving, 9
Zero Waste Solutions, 202
Zip code business patterns, 233
Zoom, 46
Zytiga, 52

Davila, A., 520
Davis, Edward W., 73
Davis, Grant, 521
Davis, I., 582
Davis, K., 489
Davis, S., 103, 266
Davison, R., 459
Davison, S., 456
Day, D. L., 552
Day, G. S., 265
Deadrick, D., 327, 553
Dean, J., 293
Dean, J. W., Jr., 74, 104–105
Deane, B. R., 359
De Castro, Al., 429
DeChurch, L. A., 458, 486
Deci, E., 429
Decker, C. D., 487
De Cremer, D., 429
De Dreu, C., 104
De George, R. T., 165
DeGraff, Jeff, 552
Dehaze, Alain, 62
Deimler, M., 580
de Janasz, Suzanne, 26
de Jong, M., 105
DeJoy, D. M., 429
Dekas, K., 29
Delaney, Hollie, 361
De Lea, B., 195
Delmas, M., 166
DeMers, J., 487
Deming, W. Edwards, 9, 29, 280–281, 554
Denisi, A., 327, 488
Denison, D. R., 74
Denning, S., 107
Dent, E. B., 581
DeRue, D. S., 293, 397, 457–458
Dess, G. G., 231
Dessibourg-Freer, N., 580
Dessler, A., 74
DeStobbeleir, K., 105
DeSue, Tedra, 28
Devers, C., 330
De Vries, T., 459
Dewan, R., 552
Dewar, C., 582
de Weerd Nederhof, P. C., 266
de Wit, F. R. C., 459
Dewnarain, S., 293
Dhanani, L., 359
Dhillon, K., 195
Dhiraj, Amarendra Bhushan, 31
Diamond, Justin, 392–393
Diaz-Uda, A., 359
Dickson, M., 486
Diener, E., 430
Dienhart, J., 165
Difonzo, N., 489
Dimitratos, P., 231
Dimock, M., 29
Dinlersoz, E., 228
D'Innocenzo, L., 396
Dionne, S., 395
Dlouhy, J., 105
Do, B., 581–582
Dobbin, Frank, 429
Dobbs, R., 328, 551

Doerr, E., 293
Doiron, K., 30
Donahue, L., 456
Donahue, Mark, 430
Donahue, R., 457
Donald, Arnold, 339
Donnelly, J., Jr., 79
Donovan, A., 520
Dooley, R., 104
Doppelt, B., 29, 167
Dorfman, P., 395
Dormehl, L., 195
Dorsey, Jason, 570
Dou, E., 232
Douma, B., 427
Dowd, Karen O., 26
Doyle, A., 359
Doz, Y., 581
Drach-Zahavy, A., 456
Dragija, Martina, 521
Drake, N., 136
Drayton, Bill, 29–30
Dreiling, Richard, 583
Driver, M., 229
Driver, Saige, 328
Drnovsek, M., 229
Droge, C., 265
Drouin, M., 486
Drucker, P. F., 230
Drucker, Peter, 31, 42, 214
Druskat, V. U., 458, 521
Duffy, M., 458–459
Dulebohn, J., 327–328, 396, 456
Dumay, J., 522
Dunfee, T., 164
Dunn, Catherine, 397
Durham, C., 458
Durson, Laura E., 393
Dutton, J., 30, 105, 583
Dwertmann, D., 395
Dwilson, Stephanie, 393
Dyer, L., 292

E

Earley, P. C., 427, 456, 487
Eastman, L. J., 293
Ebben, P., 487
Eckes, G., 522
Economides, M. I., 551
Economy, P., 487
Edinger, S., 457
Edison, Thomas, 94
Edmans, A., 430
Edmondson, A. C., 456–457
Edwards, M., 329
Egan, M., 74, 164, 195
Eiferman, Omar, 552
Einstein, Albert, 94
Eisenberg, B., 358
Eisenhardt, K., 105, 456
Eisenhardt, Kathleen M., 552
Eisenstat, R., 581
Eisenstat, R. A., 130, 137
Eisenstein, P., 167
Ek, Daniel, 202, 383
Ekegren, G., 427
Elahi, A., 328

Elias, Jennifer, 196
Elliott-McCrea, Kellan, 360
Elliott-Miller, P., 265
Ellis, A. P. J., 458
Ellis, K. M., 265
Ellis, Tim, 547
Ellison, Lawrence, 563
Ellison, Marvin, 339
Ellram, L., 195
Ellwardt, L., 488
Elsbach, K. D., 553
Elsesser, Kim, 429, 456
Ely, R. J., 360
Emerson, Ralph Waldo, 398
Engel, A., 29
Engelen, A. A., 231
Epitropaki, O., 396
Erdogan, B., 104, 430
Erez, A., 395
Erez, M., 458
Erickson, T., 456
Ericsson, A., 30
Eriksson, D., 195
Erlanger, S., 195
Ernst, H., 459
Erskine, R., 486
Ertug, G., 30
Erwin, D., 581
Esenhardt, K. M.
Essens, P., 459
Esty, D., 167
Etternson, R., 167
Ettkin, L. P., 294
Ettlie, J. E., 294
Etzion, D., 166
Eure, J., 521
Eva, N., 396, 457
Evans, J. R., 294
Evans, P., 73, 581
Evans, R., 103–104
Evanschitzky, Heiner, 429
Ewen, A. J., 329

F

Fahrbach, K., 522
Fainshmidt, S., 457
Fairesrt, 581
Fairlie, R., 228
Falbe, C., 394
Faleye, O., 264
Falkenberg-Hull, E., 196
Fallon, N., 487
Fallon, Nicole, 486
Fanelli, A., 395, 429
Fang, M., 329, 428
Farh, J. L., 457, 459
Farmer, S., 105
Farnen, Karen, 197
Farnham, A., 486
Farr, Christina, 31, 520
Farrell, C., 293
Farrell, D., 103
Farre-Mensa, J., 521
Fauchart, E., 229
Fay, C., 330
Fayol, Henri, 35
Feffer, M., 522

Globe, D., 360
Glover, S., 165
Glover, S. L., 141
Glueck, William F., 26–27
Glunk, U., 30
Glynn, M., 74
Gnyawali, D. R., 74, 293
Godrey, P., 166
Goel, V., 28
Goldberg, E., 196
Goldberg, S. Galloway, 581
Goldman, D., 360
Goldman, J., 265
Goleman, D., 394
Gonzalez, Oscar, 266
González-Navarro, P., 486
Goodheim, L., 395
Goodman, Tim, 72
Goodney, Chris, 299
Goodnight, James, 399, 408, 421
Goodson, E., 488
Goomas, David T., 521
Gopalakrishnan, S., 551
Gordon, Judith R., 27, 102
Gordon, S., 74
Gore, W. L., 410, 428
Gorman, C., 73
Gorscurth, C., 74
Goshal, S., 30
Goudreau, J., 396, 486
Gowan, J. A., Jr., 522
Gradwhol Smith, W., 395
Graebner, Melissa E., 552
Grafton, L., 457
Graham, Cat, 266
Graham, G., 488
Graham, Jefferson, 105
Grandori, A., 522
Grant, A., 394, 458
Grant, A. M., 395
Grant, B., 330
Grant, S., 458
Gratton, L., 456
Gratton, Lynda, 457
Green, D., 29
Green, S., 28
Green, Stephen G., 553
Greenbaum, R., 396
Greenberg, E., 428, 430
Greenfield, A., 29
Greenfield, R., 105, 328, 362
Greening, D., 166
Greenleaf, Robert K., 385, 396
Greer, L., 459
Greer, Lindred, 104
Griffith, Terri L., 553
Grimaldi, E., 394
Grimes, M., 229
Groening, Christopher, 429
Gross, A., 72–73
Gross, S., 329
Grosser, T., 488
Grote, D., 329
Grote, G., 430
Grothaus, M., 195
Grother, P., 551
Grover, S. L., 164
Gruber, M., 229

Grunberg, L., 430
Gryta, T., 427
Guarraia, P., 294
Guerci, M., 359
Guest, D., 430
Guilhon, B., 551
Guion, Kathleen, 583–584
Gulate, R., 581
Gulati, R., 293, 583
Guler, I., 428
Gundry, L. K., 552
Gunther, M., 167
Guo, C., 30
Gupta, A., 293
Gupta, K., 30
Gupta, V., 231
Gurchiek, K., 362
Gurtner, S., 552
Gustafson, K., 29
Gutknecht, J., 488
Gutman, M., 488
Guy, M. E., 164
Guynn, Jessica, 137
Guzzo, R., 582
Gwin, M., 521

H

Ha, A., 104
Haanaes, K., 167
Hackman, J. R., 428, 430, 456–458
Hackman, J. Richard, 413–415
Hagan, C., 329
Hage, J., 293
Hagedoorn, J., 552
Hagen, A. F., 73
Hagiwara, Y., 551
Haidt, J., 430
Hakonen, M., 456
Hale, J., 165
Hales, M., 580
Hall, D. T., 30, 488
Hallen, B., 230
Hall-Merenda, K. E., 395
Hallowel, E., 487
Halverson, K. C., 395
Hambrick, D., 456
Hambrick, D. C., 136
Hamel, G., 292, 582–583
Hamel, Gary, 551
Hamilton, A., 164
Hamilton, Isobel Asher, 74
Hamilton, J., 165
Hamilton, Lynn, 470
Hammond, M., 396
Handmaker, David, 125
Handrick, L., 458
Handy, C., 165–166
Haney, W. V., 486
Hannah, S., 165
Hansen, Morten T., 29
Hanson, F., 396
Hao, Karen, 31
Hara, K., 265
Harbert, T., 488
Hardy, K., 136
Harkins, S., 104
Harlow, Poppy, 228

Harmon, S., 458
Harper, Stephen C., 521
Harrington, B., 487
Harrington, R., 393
Harris, E., 394
Harris, R., 582
Harris, Russell, 135
Harris, Vanessa, 135
Harrison, D., 165
Harrison, D. A., 265, 360
Harrison, David A., 358
Harrison, J. Kline, 396
Harrison, J. S., 136
Harrison, Scott, 206
Hart, S. L., 29, 167
Harter, J., 252, 429
Harter, J. K., 430
Hartley, D. E., 328
Hartman, N. S., 397
Hartung, A., 104
Hartwick, J., 582
Harvey, S., 105
Harwell, Drew, 30
Harzing, A. W., 196
Hassan, F., 28
Hasson, R., 458
Hastings, Reed, 384
Hathaway, I., 229
Hauenstein, N. M. A., 394
Hausler, Elizabeth, 385
Hayek, M., 293
Hayes, T., 429
Haynes, K. T., 330
Heaphy, E., 30
Heath, A., 202, 552
Heathfield, S., 429
Heaton, S., 292
Hedlund, Marc, 349
Heggeness, M., 358
Heidrich, 471
Heijltjes, M., 30
Heine, C., 29
Helfat, C., 292
Helletofth, P., 195
Hellofs, L. L., 293
Helms, M. M., 294
Hembree, D., 330
Hempel, Jessi, 137
Henderson, A., 396
Hendricks, Ken, 211
Heneman, H. G., III, 328
Henne, D., 429
Henning, E., 137
Henning, P., 72
Henry, L. A., 521
Henshaw, Todd, 521
Heogl, M., 459
Hernandez, E., 486
Hernandez, M., 166
Herrmann, Pol, 196
Herron, M., 428
Hersey, P., 395
Herzberg, F., 428
Herzberg, Frederick, 413
Hesketh, B., 328
Hess, A., 30
Hessels, J., 228
Hewson, Marillyn, 337

Laval, Zac, 230
Lavoie, Johanne, 397
Lawler, E. E., III, 265–266, 293, 393, 427–430,
    456–458, 521–522, 581–583
Lawrence, P., 238–239, 264, 266
Layton, Hunt D., 265
Lazarova, Mila, 196
Lazarus, D., 551
Lazenby, J., 428
Leaf, Clifton, 394
Leana, C. F., 581
Leavitt, K., 164
LeBreton, J., 394
Le Breton-Miller, I., 582
Lechner, C., 105
Ledford, G. E., 293
Lee, April, 358
Lee, Bo Young, 98
Lee, C., 459
Lee, H. L., 73, 293
Lee, M., 265
Lee, M. D., 360
Lee, Peter, 456
Lee, T., 429
Legere, John, 465
Lei, D., 74, 583
Leifer, R., 551
Lencioni, P., 459
Lengel, R., 487
Lengnick-Hall, C., 29
Lengnick-Hall, M., 29
Lengnick-Hall, M. L., 360
Leonard, D., 552
Leonard, H., 580
Leon-Perez, J., 459
Lepak, D., 30
Lepine, J., 488
LePine, M. A., 395
Leskin, P., 105
Lesser, E., 488
Leswing, K., 164
Leung, T. Y., 359
Levin, D., 488
Levine, J. M., 458
Levinson, Marc, 72
Levinthal, D., 265
Levitin, D., 427
Levy, Steven, 552
Lewin, D., 330
Lewin, Kurt, 581
Li, C., 74
Li, D., 228
Li, Ming, 197
Liak, T., 167
Liakopoulos, Andrew, 521
Liang, Lim Yan, 197
Liao, B., 456
Liao, C., 396
Lichtenhaler, Ulrich, 552
Liden, R., 104, 396
Liden, R. C., 429
Liedtka, J., 553
Liedtka, Jeanne, 545
Lifei, Z., 232
Light, J., 328
Liker, J. K., 294
Likert, R., 394
Lilius, J., 105

Linder, C., 521
Lindorff, D., 486
Lindsay, W. M., 294
Ling, Y., 231, 395
Link, A. N., 552
Lippitt, R., 394
Litchfield, R. C., 427
Liu, D., 429
Liu, Y., 360
Ljung, Alexander, 461
Llopis, G., 103, 393
Lloyd, S., 265
Llvne-Tarandach, R., 30
Locke, E., 394, 427, 429, 458
Locke, E. A., 30, 229, 393
Lockwood, C., 74
Loeffert, Tom, 551
Loftus, P., 521
Loftus, Peter, 393
Logan, Gordon, 219
Logue, C. M., 474, 487
Lohr, S., 427
Lohr, Steve, 164
Lombardo, M., 487
Longenecker, C. O., 459
Lopez, Nina, 194
Lopez-Kidwell, V., 488
Lord, R. G., 395
Lorinkova, N., 429, 457
Lorsch, J., 238–239, 264
Lott, A., 458
Lott, B., 458
Loughry, M., 312, 329
Lovallo, D., 105
Loveday, S., 196
Low, M., 229
Lowe, K., 197, 394
Lu, D. J., 293
Lu, Y., 428
Lubatkin, M., 230–231, 395
Lublin, J. S., 196
Lublin, Joann S., 104
Lucas, A., 73
Luccock, Halford, E., 432
Ludgate, Kristen, 147
Ludwig, Timothy D., 521
Luk, L., 551
Lukas, B. A., 196
Lukaszewski, K., 553
Lumpkin, G., 229
Lumpkin, G. T., 231
Luo, X. R., 29
Luo, Y., 197
Lussier, R., 209
Luthans, F., 396, 427
Lutilsky, Ivana Drazic, 521
Lynch, J., 165

M

Ma, J., 551
Ma, Jack, 169, 181
Maak, Thomas, 197
Macadam, S., 488
MacDermid, S. M., 360
Macdonell, Robby, 487
Mace, M., 456
Macey, W., 429

MacKechnie, C., 551
Mackey, A., 396
Mackey, John, 433, 452
MacLean, T., 457
Macomber, J., 582
Macy, B., 457
Maddux, William W., 487
Madison, Adam, 427
Madjar, N., 428
Magasin, M., 103
Mahoney, J. D., 186, 196
Maidique, M. A., 550
Maier, N. R. F., 104
Maignan, I., 196
Mainwaring, Simon, 73
Mair, J., 229, 580
Maishe, A., 458
Majchrzak, A., 436
Makhani, Sanya, 396
Makridakis, S., 73
Maldegen, R., 328
Malhotra, A., 436
Malone, Post, 480
Malone, T., 264
Malouf, A., 74
Mandel, E., 73
Mandela, Nelson, 373
Mann, Jennifer, 421
Mann, L., 104
Mann, T., 137
Manning, T., 394
Mannix, E., 458
Mannucci, P. V., 105
Manyika, J., 195, 328, 487, 551
Manz, C., 394
March, J., 103
March, J. G., 266, 552
Marchington, M., 293, 328, 428
Marcus, A., 165–166
Marcus, Bonnie, 359
Marcus, J., 72–73
Marie, Carley, 489
Markman, G. D., 230
Marks, M., 28, 457
Marler, J., 327
Marlow, S., 486
Marquis, C., 28–29
Marr, B., 551, 573
Marr, Bernard, 582
Marriott, Bill, 478
Marriott, J. Willard, 203
Marriott, William, 127
Marrone, J., 396, 458
Marrone, J. A., 459
Marrs, A., 551
Marston, N., 105
Marte, J., 330
Marti, I., 229
Martin, A., 265
Martin, C., 167
Martin, C. F., 127
Martin, J., 292, 456
Martin, K., 164
Martin, R., 167, 394
Martin, Roger, 115, 136
Martineau, Paris, 230

Martinez-Moreno, E., 486
Marx, G., 166
Mas, A., 458
Mascia, K., 487
Maslow, Abraham, 409, 428
Mason, A., 29
Massey, A., 459
Massingham, P. R., 522
Massingham, R., 522
Matear, M., 229
Mathias, B., 228
Mathies, D., 103
Mathieson, R., 195
Mathieu, J., 396, 429, 457
Mathieu, R. G., 522
Mathur, A., 328
Matlett, T., 429
Matousek, M., 395
Matousek, Mark, 552
Matson, E., 394
Matten, D., 166
Matthews, G., 265
Mattioli, D., 393
Matusak, L. R., 393, 396
Mauborgne, R., 429
Mavondo, F., 293
Maxim, J., 582
May, D., 165
May, M., 428
Mayer, D. M., 396
Mayer, Marissa, 87
Maynard, M. T., 429, 457
Mayo, Elton, 35-36
Mayrhofer, W., 327
Mays, K., 195
McBride, S., 456
McCall, M., 103, 105, 397, 487
McCall, M. W., 186, 196
McCanse, Anne Adams, 377
McCaskey, M. B., 487
McCauley, C. D., 397
McClelland, D., 428
McClendon, J. A., 330
McClesky, J., 30
McCollum, J. K., 266
McCormack, M., 486
McCracken, M., 521
McCracken, Mike, 501
McCullen, P., 294
McDermott, C. M., 551
McDonald, J., 195
McDonough, Megan, 167
McDowell, T., 265, 456
McFarland, Matt, 72
McGee, J. E., 74
McGeever, J., 195
McGill, M., 583
McGinnis, L. F., 294
McGirt, Ellen, 329
McGranahan, D., 327
McGraw, Madison, 105
McGreal, C., 74
McGregor, J., 28
McGregor, Jena, 166
McIntosh, T., 166
McIntyre, Hugh, 486
McIntyre, K. Kung, 105
McIver, D., 29

McKee, A., 30
McKinley, W., 550
McKnight, William, 415
McLarnon, M., 459
McLernon, N., 195
McMillan-Capehart, A., 359
McMillion, Doug, 274-275
McMullen, J., 229
McPherson, S., 456
McShane, Steven L., 70
McWilliams, A., 167
Medina, F., 459
Megginson, L., 228
Megginson, W., 228
Mehler, M., 328
Mehrabian, A., 487
Meiland, D., 28
Meinert, Dori, 581
Meister, J., 487
Mellahi, K., 74
Mena, S., 166
Mendenca, L., 582
Mendoca, J., 195
Menser, T., 582
Menz, M., 30
Menza, Justin, 266
Meola, A., 28
Merchant, K., 521
Merchant, K. A., 520-521
Mesmer-Magnus, J. R., 458, 486
Messick, D., 103-104
Meuser, J., 396
Meyer, C., 428, 458
Meyer, E., 104, 197
Meyer, Erin, 329
Meyer, K., 294
Meyer, P., 265
Meyerhoff, Robin, 328, 359
Meyers, G., 97, 105
Meznar, M. B., 74
Michael, D., 167
Michaels, Daniel, 104
Mifflin, K. E., 522
Mikel, Betsy, 330
Miles, R. E., 266
Miles, R. H., 73, 581
Miles, Raymond E., 254
Miles, S., 488
Miliard, Mike, 428
Milkovich G., 329
Mille, D., 456
Miller, B., 520-521
Miller, C., 195
Miller, D., 265, 486, 522, 582
Miller, T., 229
Milliken, D., 103
Milliken, F. J., 458
Mills, M., 394
Milner, C., 396
Milstein, M. B., 167
Miniti, Huang, M., 229
Minniti, M., 229
Mintz, H. K., 487
Mintzberg, H., 2, 30
Miremadi, M., 195
Miron-Spektor, E., 580
Misangyi, V., 429
Misangyi, V. F., 395

Mishra, A. K., 293
Misumi, J., 375, 394-395
Misumi, K., 394
Mitchell, T., 427
Mitroff, I. I., 105
Mitsuhashi, H., 292
Mittal, Vikas, 429
Mittendorg, B., 265
Mobley, William H., 197
Model, J., 229
Moed, J., 195
Moeller, Sara B., 521
Mohammed, S., 486
Mohrman, S. A., 266, 293
Mol, Michael J., 551
Molina, A., 553
Molinski, Andy, 329
Mom, T., 292
Montealegre, R., 553
Montgomery, C. A., 73, 136
Montoya-Weiss, M., 459
Moodie, Alison, 581
Moon, C. H., 196
Moon, J., 166
Moore, C., 165
Moore, S., 105, 430
Moores, K., 522
Moran, G., 394, 487
Moran, P., 430
Moran, Tyler, 72
Moregeson, F. P., 328
Moretti, E., 458
Morgan, E., 230-231
Morgan, J. M., 294
Morgan, N., 487
Morgeson, F., 457
Morris, C., 195
Morris, S., 266
Morris, S. M., 196
Morris, Shad S., 196
Morrison, A., 487
Morrison, E. W., 30
Mortensen, R., 196
Mosakowski, E., 229, 487
Mosher, Dave, 553
Moss, Angelique, 230
Moss, S., 428
Moss, T., 229
Mote, J., 293
Mount, I., 230
Mouton, J., 394
Moxley, R., 397
Moyer, J., 167
Muczyk, J., 394
Muethel, M., 457
Mukherjee, Ajoy
Mukherjee, D., 457
Mula, J., 522
Mulally, Alan, 386-387
Mule, Ann C., 397
Mullainathan, S., 359
Mullen, B., 458
Muller, A., 581
Mullins, L., 456
Munduate, L., 459
Muñoz, Cristina, 579
Murnieks, C., 229
Murnighan, K., 165

Roth, E. A., 551
Roth, K., 167
Roth, P., 328
Rotondo, D. M., 329
Rottig, D., 457
Roundy, Philip T., 552
Rouse, E. D., 230
Rousseau, D., 430, 581
Roussin, C., 457
Rowland, Christopher, 522
Roy, Sanjit Bunker, 156
Roy, U., 294
Rubin, B.
Rubin, C., 328
Ruch, W. V., 488
Ruddy, T., 457
Rudolph, J., 457
Ruef, M., 228, 230
Ruff, Kate, 520
Ruhe, G., 104
Rui, O., 359
Ruiz, Gisel, 339
Rupp, D., 429
Rusjan, B., 521
Russo, S., 582
Ruthrsdotter, M., 358
Ryan, A. M., 429-430
Ryan, Chris, 304
Ryan, Katherine, 360
Ryan, L., 522
Rynes, S., 166, 360

S

Sabeti, H., 229, 583
Sachgau, O., 583
Sadler-Smith, E., 104
Sadowski, M., 551
Safani, Barbara, 473
Safavi, K., 551
Safferstone, T., 394
Safian, R., 73
Sagonwsky, E., 551
Sahin, F., 285, 294
Sahlman, W. A., 230
Saiidi, U., 582
Sakano, T., 293
Salas, E., 456, 486
Salvador, R., 396
Samandari, Hamid, 582
Sambamurthy, V., 265
Sampson, R. C., 293
Sanborn, G., 428
Sanchez, D., 327, 359
Sanchez, Daniel, 489
Sanchez, J., 185, 428
Sanchez, Raul, 197
Sanchez-Burks, J., 30
Sandberg, J., 196
Sandberg, Sheryl, 10, 15, 337
Sanders, Lorraine, 20
Sandino, T., 520
Santamaria, J. A., 458
Sapienza, H. J., 231
Saprrowe, R. T., 429
Sarala, R., 30, 457, 580
Saridakis, G., 327

Sarker, S., 457
Sarooghi, H., 228
Sashittal, H., 458
Sashkin, M., 429
Satell, G., 29, 396, 580
Sauer, P. J., 228
Sawers, P., 195
Sawhney, M., 551
Sawhney, Mohanbir, 552
Saxton, M. J., 74
Sayles, L., 459
Sayles, Leonard, 249
Schaeffer, B. S., 429
Schaffer, B. S., 429
Schaub, Michael, 72
Schaubroeck, J., 456, 486
Scheer, S., 73
Schein, E. H., 74, 581
Schere, R., 393
Schermerhorn, Jr, J., 165
Schillebeeckx, S., 167
Schippers, M., 458
Schisgall, O., 36
Schlangenstein, M., 29, 74
Schleicher, A., 329
Schlesinger, L. A., 581
Schlesinger, Leonard A., 564
Schmann P. A., Jr., 550
Schmid, T., 136
Schmidt, Eric, 322
Schmidt, F., 166, 429
Schmidt, F. L., 329, 430
Schmidt, W., 394-395
Schmulen, M., 486
Schnackenberg, A., 489
Schnatterly, K., 164
Schneider, B., 429, 582
Schneider, Beth Z., 26
Schneider, Michael, 237
Schoemaker, P., 292
Schoemaker, P. J. H., 73
Schoenberger, Chana R., 457
Schooley, T., 580
Schouten, M., 456
Schrempf-Stirling, J., 166
Schroeder, R., 457
Schuler, D., 166
Schuler, R., 327
Schuler, R. S., 329
Schultz, Howard, 199-200, 210, 222
Schultz, P., 394
Schulze, W., 230
Schuman, Frank, 426
Schuneman, Pam, 505, 521
Schwab, K., 544
Schwartz, E., 395
Schwartz, J., 73
Schwarz, J. L., 359
Schwarz, N., 430
Schweiger, D., 488
Schweitzer, M., 427
Schwenk, C., 104
Scipioni, J., 29, 329
Scott, A., 582
Scott, J., 328
Scott, K., 458-459
Scott, S. R., Jr., 228
Scroxton, A., 28

Scullion, H., 327
Seal, G., 580
Seals, A., 360
Seashore, S. E., 458
Sebastian, P., 292
Sedgwick, D., 489
Segaar, P., 135
Segal, J. A., 329
Seggerman, T. K., 230-231
Seibert, J., 293
Seibert, S., 457
Seidmann, A., 552
Seijts, G., 427
Sekerka, L., 165
Seligman, M. E. P., 30
Seligson, H., 488
Selingo, J., 328
Semadeni, Matthew, 551
Sendjaya, S., 396
Senge, P. M., 167
Sengul, M., 229
Seo, M., 581
Serpa, R., 74
Seseri, Rudina, 360
Shafer, Scott M., 521
Shaffer, Margaret A., 196
Shah, Anand, 530
Shah, P. P., 329
Shalley, C., 427, 457
Shamir, B., 395
Shane, D., 328
Shane, S., 228
Shao, R., 429
Shapiro, D., 457
Shapiro, E. C., 393
Sharf, S., 29
Sharfman, M., 104-105
Sharifi, S., 264
Sharma, P. N., 457
Sharma, V., 196
Sharp, A., 427
Sharp, Rachel, 266
Sharpe, M. E., 330
Shaw, G. B., 460
Shaw, J., 458-459
Shaw, K. N., 402
Shead, S., 229
Sheetz, Michael, 553
Shehadi, R., 457
Shemla, Meir, 104
Shen, J., 196
Shen, L., 30
Sheng, Ellen, 197
Shephard, M., 74
Shepherd, D., 228-229
Shergill, P., 359
Sheridan, K., 328
Sheridan, R., 428
Sheridan, Richard, 405
Sherman, A., 316
Sherman, A. W., Jr., 330
Sherman, Alex, 164
Sherman, M., 486
Shih, H. A., 459
Shimoni, B., 581
Shin, H., 580
Shin, J., 581
Shin, Shung J., 358